Objective General English

OBJECTIVE GENERAL ENGLISH

10,000 Plus Questions

An ideal book for

* Bank PO, SBI-PO, RBI Exam.
* MBA, Hotel Management.
* Railway Recruitment Exam.
* NDA, CDS.
* IES, LIC-AAO, GIC-AAO.
* Income Tax and Central Excise.
* Sub-Inspectors of Police Exam.
* Asstt. Grade, Section Officers, UDC.

Dr. R.S. Aggarwal
M.Sc., Ph.D.
Vikas Aggarwal

S. CHAND PUBLISHING
empowering minds

S. CHAND & COMPANY PVT. LTD.
(AN ISO 9001: 2008 COMPANY)
RAM NAGAR, NEW DELHI-110 055

S. CHAND
PUBLISHING
empowering minds

S. CHAND & COMPANY PVT. LTD.

(An ISO 9001 : 2008 Company)
Head Office: 7361, RAM NAGAR, NEW DELHI - 110 055
Phone: 23672080-81-82, 9899107446, 9911310888 Fax: 91-11-23677446
www.schandpublishing.com; e-mail: helpdesk@schandpublishing.com

Branches

Ahmedabad	:	Ph: 27541965, 27542369, ahmedabad@schandpublishing.com
Bengaluru	:	Ph: 22268048, 22354008, bangalore@schandpublishing.com
Bhopal	:	Ph: 4274723, 4209587, bhopal@schandpublishing.com
Chandigarh	:	Ph: 2725443, 2725446, chandigarh@schandpublishing.com
Chennai	:	Ph. 28410027, 28410058, chennai@schandpublishing.com
Coimbatore	:	Ph: 2323620, 4217136, coimbatore@schandpublishing.com (Marketing Office)
Cuttack	:	Ph: 2332580; 2332581, cuttack@schandpublishing.com
Dehradun	:	Ph: 2711101, 2710861, dehradun@schandpublishing.com
Guwahati	:	Ph: 2738811, 2735640, guwahati@schandpublishing.com
Hyderabad	:	Ph: 27550194, 27550195, hyderabad@schandpublishing.com
Jaipur	:	Ph: 2219175, 2219176, jaipur@schandpublishing.com
Jalandhar	:	Ph: 2401630, 5000630, jalandhar@schandpublishing.com
Kochi	:	Ph: 2378740, 2378207-08, cochin@schandpublishing.com
Kolkata	:	Ph: 22367459, 22373914, kolkata@schandpublishing.com
Lucknow	:	Ph: 4026791, 4065646 lucknow@schandpublishing.com
Mumbai	:	Ph: 22690881, 22610885, mumbai@schandpublishing.com
Nagpur	:	Ph: 6451311, 2720523, 2777666, nagpur@schandpublishing.com
Patna	:	Ph: 2300489, 2302100, patna@schandpublishing.com
Pune	:	Ph: 64017298, pune@schandpublishing.com
Raipur	:	Ph: 2443142, raipur@schandpublishing.com (Marketing Office)
Ranchi	:	Ph: 2361178, ranchi@schandpublishing.com
Siliguri	:	Ph: 2520750, siliguri@schandpublishing.com (Marketing Office)
Visakhapatnam	:	Ph: 2782609 visakhapatnam@schandpublishing.com (Marketing Office)

First Edition 1997;
Reprints 1998 Twice), 99, 2000, 2001, 2002, 2003, 2004 (Twice), 2005, 2006 (Twice), 2007 (Twice), 2009 (Twice), 2010 (Thrice), 2011 (Twice), 2012, 2013 (Twice), 2014 (Twice), Reprint 2015
Reprint 2016

ISBN : 978-81-219-1531-1 **Code :** 1006D 082

This book is for Sale in India & other SAARC Countries only.

PRINTED IN INDIA

By Nirja Publishers & Printers Pvt. Ltd., 54/3/2, Jindal Paddy Compound, Kashipur Road, Rudrapur-263153, Uttarakhand and published by S. Chand & Company Pvt. Ltd., 7361, Ram Nagar, New Delhi -110 055.

PREFACE

Encouraged and enthused by the popularity of our books among the candidates appearing in various competitive examinations, and a continuous demand from them for bringing out a book of similar nature on **Objective General English,** prompted us to take up this project.

The subject matter in this book is comprehensive, rigorous and yet very simple. Even an average student will find no difficulty in understanding the various concepts.

The book has been divided into six units, namely :

I. *Vocabulary Usage*
II. *Comprehension Ability*
III. *Selecting Phrases / words*
IV. *Error Detection*
V. *Rearrangement*
VI. *General Usage*

The salient features of the book are :

(*i*) Its coverage of all types of questions asked in various entrance examinations.

(*ii*) Huge collection of practisable questions (over 10,000).

(*iii*) References given on memory basis shall help to know the types of questions being asked in various competitive examinations.

The requirements of the candidates has been a major factor kept in mind during the compilation of this book. We are sure that the book will serve the purpose of leading the readers to success.

For taking all pains and interest in the publication of this book, we are thankful to Shri Ravindra Kumar Gupta (Director) & Shri T.N. Goel (Manager), S. Chand & Company Ltd., New Delhi. For good type-setting we are thankful to Mr. Amit Maheshwari, Director of *Brilliant Computers, Meerut.*

One of the authors Monika Aggarwal conveys her gratitude to husband ***Devendra*** and son ***Kunal*** for their kind co-operation during the project.

Dr. Aggarwal conveys his sincere thanks to his son Vikas Aggarwal for working day and night with him to complete the project.

–AUTHORS

CONTENTS

UNIT I
VOCABULARY USAGE

1. SYNONYMS

What are Synonyms ?

Words with nearly the same meaning but used differently, are called **Synonyms**.

Example : Abstain and Refrain are two words that seem very nearly the same. But, we abstain from a thing and refrain from a habit or an action.

The following sentences make it clear.

(i) We should **abstain** from wine.

(ii) We should **refrain** from drinking.

TYPE 1 : CHOOSING THE CORRECT SYNONYM OF THE GIVEN WORD

In this type of questions, generally a word is given, followed by four or five alternatives. The candidate is required to choose the word which is nearest in meaning to the given word.

Example 1 : ***Choose the correct synonym of the given word :***

IMPLICATE

(*a*) Include (*b*) Entreat (*c*) Suggest (*d*) Imply

Solution : The word 'Implicate' may be used in a sentence as :

The man ***implicated*** him falsely in the case.

Clearly, the word means 'involve' or 'include'.

Hence, the answer is (*a*).

Example 2 : ***Choose the word which best expresses the meaning of the given word :***

DILIGENT

(*a*) Intelligent (*b*) Difficult (*c*) Laborious (*d*) Quick

Solution : 'Diligent' means 'hard-working' So, another word for it could be 'Laborious'. Hence, the answer is (*c*).

PRACTICE SET 1

Directions : ***In each of the following questions, out of the given alternatives, choose the one which best expresses the meaning of the given word.***

1. EAGER **(Stenographers' Exam, 1994)**
(*a*) Clever (*b*) Enthusiastic
(*c*) Curious (*d*) Devoted

2. PLACID
(*a*) Clear (*b*) Calm
(*c*) Enjoyable (*d*) Dull

3. COMMEMORATE
(*a*) Boast (*b*) Remember
(*c*) Manipulate (*d*) Harmonise

4. DEIFY **(C.B.I. 1995)**
(*a*) Face (*b*) Worship
(*c*) Flatter (*d*) Challenge

5. AMENITIES
(*a*) Pageantries (*b*) Privileges
(*c*) Facilities (*d*) Courtesies

6. DISPARITY
(*a*) Injustice (*b*) Unlikeness
(*c*) Partiality (*d*) Distortion

7. BARBARIAN
(*a*) Arrogant (*b*) Impolite
(*c*) Uncivilised (*d*) Unkind

8. LETHAL **(Hotel Management, 1992)**
(*a*) Unlawful (*b*) Deadly
(*c*) Sluggish (*d*) Smooth

9. SERENE
(*a*) Solemn (*b*) Meak
(*c*) Delicate (*d*) Calm

10. GRUESOME
(*a*) Hateful (*b*) Painful
(*c*) Tragic (*d*) Frightful

11. SECURE
(*a*) Secret (*b*) Comfortable
(*c*) Safe (*d*) Independent

12. TYRANNY **(Railways, 1991)**
(*a*) Misrule (*b*) Power
(*c*) Madness (*d*) Cruelty

13. OBLIGATORY
(*a*) Useful (*b*) Required
(*c*) Stubborn (*d*) Agreeable

14. CONNOISSEUR **(Railways, 1996)**
(*a*) Ignorant (*b*) Interpreter
(*c*) Delinquent (*d*) Lover of art

15. IMPETUOUS
(*a*) Violent (*b*) Resourceful
(*c*) Pleasing (*d*) Rash

16. NEBULOUS
(a) Tiny (b) Vague
(c) Insignificant (d) Inadequate

17. WRATH **(Assistant Grade, 1995)**
(a) Jealousy (b) Hatred
(c) Anger (d) Violence

18. ABANDON
(a) Abscond (b) Discontinue
(c) Neglect (d) Condense

19. BASHFUL
(a) Vigilant (b) Confident
(c) Shy (d) Hopeful

20. GARNER
(a) Distribute (b) Decorate
(c) Preserve (d) Collect

21. LETHARGY
(a) Laxity (b) Impassivity
(c) Serenity (d) Listlessness

22. VERATE
(a) Scold (b) Judge
(c) Downgrade (d) Deny

23. MORIBUND
(a) Stagnant (b) Gloomy
(c) Dying (d) Superfluous

24. REBATE **(S.S.C. 1991)**
(a) Loss (b) Refund
(c) Compensation (d) Discount

25. BEMOAN
(a) Lament (b) Soothe
(c) Denounce (d) Loathe

26. SPITE
(a) Concern (b) Admiration
(c) Malice (d) Indifference

27. PROLIFIC **(NABARD, 1987)**
(a) Plenty (b) Competent
(c) Fertile (d) Predominant

28. DEBILITATE
(a) Weaken (b) Attack
(c) Surmount (d) Destroy

29. OSTENTATIOUS
(a) Pretty (b) Modest
(c) Showy (d) Flagrant

30. AFFABLE **(C.B.I. 1994)**
(a) Friendly (b) Cheerful
(c) Helpful (d) Neutral

31. DEFLECT
(a) Frustrate (b) Cheat
(c) Pervert (d) Depress

32. DAWDLE
(a) Assess (b) Evaluate
(c) Fickle (d) Loiter

33. EXORBITANT **(Railways, 1995)**
(a) Odd (b) Ridiculous
(c) Excessive (d) Threatening

34. PIVOTAL
(a) Movable (b) Crucial
(c) Internal (d) Mechanical

35. VULGAR
(a) Thoughtless (b) Unkind
(c) Coarse (d) Illiterate

36. OBVERSE
(a) Bitter (b) Reverse
(c) Opposite (d) Adverse

37. MIRTH
(a) Sorrow (b) Enthusiasm
(c) Adventure (d) Merriment

38. TERRIFIC **(U.D.C. 1994)**
(a) Big (b) Excellent
(c) Tragic (d) Terrible

39. DILIGENT
(a) Intelligent (b) Energetic
(c) Modest (d) Industrious

40. ABRIDGE
(a) Abort (b) Span
(c) Shorten (d) Cross

41. WHIM
(a) Fancy (b) Clumsy
(c) Desire (d) Strange behaviour

42. DISSOLUTE
(a) Distant (b) Repulsive
(c) Honest (d) Immoral

43. FALSE **(Clerks' Grade, 1993)**
(a) Defective (b) Untrue
(c) Incorrect (d) Inaccurate

44. ANATHEMA
(a) Religious chant (b) Pun
(c) Musical subject (d) Curse

45. NIGGARD
(a) Miser (b) Loyal
(c) Divine (d) Shrewd

46. PLACATE
(a) Pity (b) Embroil
(c) Appease (d) Amuse

47. ABNEGATION **(C.B.I. 1990)**
(a) Self-denial (b) Self-sacrifice
(c) Self-praise (d) Self-criticism

48. SUPERVENE
(a) Ensue (b) Interfere
(c) Displace (d) Precede

49. ABRADE
(a) Scold (b) Attach
(c) Wear off (d) Twist

50. SANGUINE
(a) Clever (b) Proud
(c) Hopeful (d) Modest

ANSWERS

1. (*c*)	**2.** (*b*)	**3.** (*b*)	**4.** (*b*)	**5.** (*b*)	**6.** (*b*)	**7.** (*c*)	**8.** (*b*)	**9.** (*d*)	**10.** (*d*)
11. (*c*)	**12.** (*d*)	**13.** (*b*)	**14.** (*b*)	**15.** (*d*)	**16.** (*b*)	**17.** (*c*)	**18.** (*b*)	**19.** (*c*)	**20.** (*d*)
21. (*a*)	**22.** (*a*)	**23.** (*c*)	**24.** (*d*)	**25.** (*a*)	**26.** (*c*)	**27.** (*c*)	**28.** (*a*)	**29.** (*c*)	**30.** (*a*)
31. (*c*)	**32.** (*d*)	**33.** (*c*)	**34.** (*b*)	**35.** (*c*)	**36.** (*c*)	**37.** (*d*)	**38.** (*d*)	**39.** (*d*)	**40.** (*c*)
41. (*a*)	**42.** (*d*)	**43.** (*b*)	**44.** (*d*)	**45.** (*a*)	**46.** (*c*)	**47.** (*a*)	**48.** (*b*)	**49.** (*c*)	**50.** (*c*)

PRACTICE SET 2

Directions : *Pick up the correct synonyms for each of the following words.*

1. AFFLUENT **(Railways, 1993)**
(*a*) Prosperous (*b*) Poor
(*c*) Talkative (*d*) Close

2. LIMP
(*a*) Kneel (*b*) Bend
(*c*) Falter (*d*) Stoop

3. INFREQUENT **(Railways, 1996)**
(*a*) Never (*b*) Usual
(*c*) Rare (*d*) Sometimes

4. MASSACRE **(Section Officers, 1993)**
(*a*) Stab (*b*) Slaughter
(*c*) Murder (*d*) Assassinate

5. BELITTLE
(*a*) Diminish (*b*) Mock
(*c*) Disparage (*d*) Scoff

6. REVISE
(*a*) Edit (*b*) Alter
(*c*) Correct (*d*) Reconsider

7. DISTINGUISH
(*a*) Darken (*b*) Abolish
(*c*) Differentiate (*d*) Confuse

(Stenographers' Exam, 1993)

8. ACCUSE
(*a*) Absolve (*b*) Exonerate
(*c*) Vindicate (*d*) Impeach

9. RECOVER
(*a*) Recoup (*b*) Revive
(*c*) Heal (*d*) Return

10. ADMONISH
(*a*) Threaten (*b*) Praise
(*c*) Appeal (*d*) Support

11. GRATIFY **(U.D.C.1995)**
(*a*) Frank (*b*) Appreciate
(*c*) Pacify (*d*) Indulge

12. PENCHANT
(*a*) Like (*b*) Eagerness
(*c*) Disability (*d*) Dislike

13. BARTER
(*a*) Deal (*b*) Return
(*c*) Lend (*d*) Exchange

14. UNCONSCIONABLE
(*a*) Distasteful (*b*) Unmanageable
(*c*) Excessive (*d*) Unmindful

15. TERMINATE **(Central Excise,1994)**
(*a*) Suspend (*b*) Dismiss
(*c*) End (*d*) Interrupt

16. DANK
(*a*) Dangerous (*b*) Ugly
(*c*) Plunder (*d*) Damp

17. BOUNTY
(*a*) Donation (*b*) Gift
(*c*) Pleasure (*d*) Reward

18. DIVVY
(*a*) Selfless (*b*) Foolish
(*c*) Follower (*d*) Pioneer

19. OBJECT **(Stenographers' Exam,1995)**
(*a*) Disobey (*b*) Challenge
(*c*) Deny (*d*) Disapprove

20. RANGE
(*a*) Level (*b*) Expanse
(*c*) Grade (*d*) Standing

21. BASH
(*a*) Strike (*b*) Neglect
(*c*) Ignore (*d*) Embrace

22. HAGGLE
(*a*) Postpone (*b*) Accept
(*c*) Bargain (*d*) Reject

23. ABSTRUSE
(*a*) Awful (*b*) Irrelevant
(*c*) Shallow (*d*) Profound

24. YOB
(*a*) Annoyed (*b*) Intelligent
(*c*) Humble (*d*) Aggressive

25. APOGEE
(*a*) Climax (*b*) Beginning
(*c*) Middle (*d*) Bottom

26. MOROSE
(*a*) Gloomy (*b*) Diseased
(*c*) Calm (*d*) Disappointed

27. ADVERSITY **(Steno. Exam, 1994)**
(*a*) Crisis (*b*) Misfortune
(*c*) Failure (*d*) Helplessness

28. CANDID
(a) Rude (b) Impertinent
(c) Blunt (d) Frank

29. EPHEMERAL
(a) Unreal (b) Mythical
(c) Short-living (d) Artificial

30. STUBBORN **(R.R.B.1991)**
(a) Easy (b) Obstinate
(c) Willing (d) Pliable

31. PROGNOSIS
(a) Indentification (b) Preface
(c) Forecast (d) Scheme

32. ENGENDER
(a) Confound (b) Suffer
(c) Sacrifice (d) Beget

33. GLIB
(a) Smooth (b) Indifferent
(c) Gainful (d) Rough

34. TACITURNITY **(Asstt. Grade,1996)**
(a) Reserve (b) Hesitation
(c) Changeableness (d) Dumbness

35. APPAREL
(a) Appearance (b) Clothing
(c) Confidence (d) Manner

36. DOLEFUL
(a) Colourful (b) Jovial
(c) Bright (d) Mournful

37. EFFACE
(a) Wipe out (b) Weaken
(c) Insult (d) Repair

38. BLITHE **(Railways,1991)**
(a) Graceful (b) Joyous
(c) Giddy (d) Other worldly

39. ERRAND
(a) Foolishness (b) Mission
(c) Misadventure (d) Error

40. RIBALD
(a) Vulgar (b) Attractive
(c) Refined (d) Indifferent

41. PERTINACIOUS
(a) Defensive (b) Humble
(c) Determined (d) Delicate

42. ADMIT **(B.S.R.B.1992)**
(a) Decide (b) Realise
(c) Accept (d) Commit

43. STAID
(a) Depressive (b) Sedate
(c) Backward (d) Dull

44. PERILOUS
(a) Uncertain (b) Agreeable
(c) Talkative (d) Dangerous

45. LAVISH
(a) Profuse (b) Showy
(c) Gay (d) Carefree

46. ELICIT **(Central Excise, 1992)**
(a) Induce (b) Extract
(c) Divulge (d) Instil

47. GRAVE
(a) Formidable (b) Bitter
(c) Pregnant (d) Solemn

48. DUD
(a) Failure (b) Foolishness
(c) Sickness (d) Negligence

49. PORTRAY **(Stenographers' Exam,1995)**
(a) Communicate (b) Paint
(c) Express (d) Draw

50. INVIDIOUS
(a) Weak (b) Unpopular
(c) Flourishing (d) Starving

ANSWERS

1. (a)	2. (c)	3. (d)	4. (b)	5. (c)	6. (b)	7. (c)	8. (d)	9. (a)	10. (a)
11. (c)	12. (a)	13. (d)	14. (c)	15. (c)	16. (d)	17. (b)	18. (d)	19. (d)	20. (b)
21. (a)	22. (c)	23. (d)	24. (d)	25. (a)	26. (a)	27. (b)	28. (d)	29. (c)	30. (b)
31. (c)	32. (d)	33. (a)	34. (a)	35. (b)	36. (d)	37. (a)	38. (b)	39. (b)	40. (a)
41. (c)	42. (c)	43. (b)	44. (d)	45. (a)	46. (b)	47. (d)	48. (a)	49. (d)	50. (b)

PRACTICE SET 3

Directions: ***In each of the following questions, out of the given alternatives, choose the one which best expresses the meaning of the given word.***

1. ALERT **(S.S.C.1994)**
(a) Smart (b) Active
(c) Watchful (d) Live

2. MAJESTIC
(a) Attractive (b) Extraordinary
(c) Grand (d) Interesting

3. FAITH
(a) Proof (b) Belief
(c) Repose (d) Trust

4. TARNISH
(a) Ornate (b) Blemish
(c) Destroy (d) Scrub

5. ARTIFACT **(Railways,1995)**
(*a*) Synthetic (*b*) Man-made
(*c*) Natural (*d*) Exact copy

6. VESTIGE
(*a*) Invention (*b*) Example
(*c*) Evidence (*d*) Experiment

7. AMPLE
(*a*) Sufficient (*b*) Swift
(*c*) Detailed (*d*) Huge

8. OGLE
(*a*) Complain (*b*) Mix
(*c*) Separate (*d*) Stare

9. PILFER **(Asstt. Grade, 1991)**
(*a*) Destroy (*b*) Damage
(*c*) Steal (*d*) Snatch

10. TRIUMPH
(*a*) Joy (*b*) Excitement
(*c*) Gain (*d*) Victory

11. DEPLETE
(*a*) Destroy (*b*) Finish
(*c*) Exhaust (*d*) Vanish

12. APPORTIONMENT
(*a*) Allotment (*b*) Bestowal
(*c*) Delivery (*d*) Presentation

13. DEAR **(Clerks' Grade, 1993)**
(*a*) Due (*b*) Close
(*c*) Costly (*d*) Young

14. PREDICT
(*a*) Explain (*b*) Foretell
(*c*) Assert (*d*) Observe

15. LUDICROUS
(*a*) Absurd (*b*) Clear
(*c*) Simple (*d*) Dismal

16. NEMESIS
(*a*) Victory (*b*) Adventure
(*c*) Reward (*d*) Punishment

17. LETHAL **(Central Excise, 1990)**
(*a*) Dreary (*b*) Dreadful
(*c*) Deadly (*d*) Strange

18. GAMBIT
(*a*) Expression (*b*) Trick
(*c*) Explanation (*d*) Appeal

19. FAD
(*a*) Charity (*b*) Weakness
(*c*) Fashion (*d*) Folly

20. BOWDLERISE
(*a*) Dictate (*b*) Persuade
(*c*) Confuse (*d*) Censor

21. INFINITE **(C.B.I. 1991)**
(*a*) Strange (*b*) Endless
(*c*) Indefinite (*d*) Vague

22. FADE
(*a*) Suffer (*b*) Fall
(*c*) Wither (*d*) Lose

23. BAULK
(*a*) Identify (*b*) Prevent
(*c*) Encourage (*d*) Verify

24. FERRY
(*a*) Bargain (*b*) Celebrate
(*c*) Transport (*d*) Drown

25. LOQUACIOUS
(*a*) Sad (*b*) Secretive
(*c*) Quiet (*d*) Talkative

26. TEDIOUS **(S.S.C. 1991)**
(*a*) Painful (*b*) Troublesome
(*c*) Lengthy (*d*) Tiresome

27. CELIBATE
(*a*) Saint (*b*) Widower
(*c*) Bachelor (*d*) Teetotaller

28. DEARTH
(*a*) Decrease (*b*) Loss
(*c*) Reduction (*d*) Scarcity

29. EXPOSE
(*a*) Open (*b*) Reveal
(*c*) Declare (*d*) Conceal

30. OBSCENE **(C.B.I. 1994)**
(*a*) Objectionable (*b*) Indecent
(*c*) Displeasing (*d*) Condemnable

31. DELETERIOUS
(*a*) Morose (*b*) Devious
(*c*) Harmful (*d*) Remorseful

32. ELUDE
(*a*) Confuse (*b*) Dodge
(*c*) Despair (*d*) Mislead

33. AUTHENTIC
(*a*) Apparent (*b*) Intricate
(*c*) Stable (*d*) Factual

34. UNIFORMITY **(U.D.C. 1994)**
(*a*) Routine (*b*) Continuity
(*c*) Stability (*d*) Consistency

35. DOCILE
(*a*) Stubborn (*b*) Stupid
(*c*) Gentle (*d*) Vague

36. PAROCHIAL
(*a*) Reluctant (*b*) Narrow-minded
(*c*) Troublesome (*d*) Gloomy

37. KID
(*a*) Regulate (*b*) Divert
(*c*) Entertain (*d*) Cheat

38. MYSTIQUE **(Railways, 1991)**
(*a*) Fame (*b*) Reputation
(*c*) Admirable quality (*d*) Popularity

39. GENRE
(*a*) Nature (*b*) Kind
(*c*) Story (*d*) Gender

40. RESILIENT
(*a*) Flexible (*b*) Proud
(*c*) Separable (*d*) Rigid

41. DUBIOUS
(*a*) Straight (*b*) Sincere
(*c*) Zig zag (*d*) Doubtful

42. CAVIL
(*a*) Appreciate (*b*) Amuse
(*c*) Quibble (*d*) Munch

43. INFERNAL (Central Excise, 1989)
(*a*) Hateful (*b*) Exciting
(*c*) Devilish (*d*) Damaging

44. EQUIVOCAL
(*a*) Quarrelsome (*b*) Feasible
(*c*) Ambiguous (*d*) Reasonable

45. OBFUSCATE
(*a*) Compete (*b*) Confuse
(*c*) Remove (*d*) Push

46. REPRISAL (C.B.I. 1990)
(*a*) Appreciation (*b*) Retaliation
(*c*) Assessment (*d*) Compensation

47. FESTAL
(*a*) Serious (*b*) Sad
(*c*) Merry (*d*) Noisy

48. ASPERITY
(*a*) Harshness (*b*) Hope
(*c*) Slander (*d*) Trouble

49. CONCISE (Stenographers' Exam, 1995)
(*a*) Strong (*b*) Solid
(*c*) Brief (*d*) Small

50. TRADUCE
(*a*) Harden (*b*) Force
(*c*) Build (*d*) Betray

ANSWERS

1. (*c*)	**2.** (*c*)	**3.** (*d*)	**4.** (*b*)	**5.** (*b*)	**6.** (*c*)	**7.** (*a*)	**8.** (*d*)	**9.** (*c*)	**10.** (*d*)
11. (*c*)	**12.** (*a*)	**13.** (*c*)	**14.** (*b*)	**15.** (*a*)	**16.** (*d*)	**17.** (*c*)	**18.** (*b*)	**19.** (*c*)	**20.** (*d*)
21. (*b*)	**22.** (*c*)	**23.** (*b*)	**24.** (*c*)	**25.** (*d*)	**26.** (*d*)	**27.** (*c*)	**28.** (*d*)	**29.** (*b*)	**30.** (*b*)
31. (*c*)	**32.** (*b*)	**33.** (*d*)	**34.** (*d*)	**35.** (*c*)	**36.** (*b*)	**37.** (*d*)	**38.** (*c*)	**39.** (*b*)	**40.** (*a*)
41. (*d*)	**42.** (*c*)	**43.** (*c*)	**44.** (*c*)	**45.** (*b*)	**46.** (*b*)	**47.** (*c*)	**48.** (*a*)	**49.** (*c*)	**50.** (*d*)

PRACTICE SET 4

Directions : ***In each of the following questions, out of the given alternatives, choose the one which best expresses the meaning of the given word.***

1. ADEPT (Asstt. Grade, 1995)
(*a*) Intelligent (*b*) Sufficient
(*c*) Proficient (*d*) Professional

2. LURID
(*a*) Happy (*b*) Abundant
(*c*) Bright (*d*) Shocking

3. BUFF
(*a*) Slave (*b*) Enthusiast
(*c*) Clown (*d*) Simpleton

4. BLUSTER
(*a*) Abuse (*b*) Tolerate
(*c*) Suffer (*d*) Threat

5. PREEN
(*a*) Redeem (*b*) Groom
(*c*) Ponder (*d*) Prick

6. BRASH
(*a*) Slow (*b*) Cultured
(*c*) Aggressive (*d*) Humble

7. ADMONITION (R.R.B. 1995)
(*a*) Warning (*b*) Pardon
(*c*) Amazement (*d*) Award

8. ONEROUS
(*a*) Difficult (*b*) Awesome
(*c*) Burdensome (*d*) Dutiful

9. APPLAUD
(*a*) Flatter (*b*) Pray
(*c*) Praise (*d*) Request

10. IDENTIFY
(*a*) Picture (*b*) Envision
(*c*) Notice (*d*) Recognise

11. RETICENCE
(*a*) Reserve (*b*) Sincerity
(*c*) Frankness (*d*) Generosity

12. CONCEAL (B.S.R.B. 1992)
(*a*) Steal (*b*) Hide
(*c*) Avoid (*d*) Keep

13. RECTIFY
(*a*) Connect (*b*) Mend
(*c*) Resolve (*d*) Solve

14. IMPINGE
(*a*) Soak (*b*) Ridicule
(*c*) Argue (*d*) Strike

15. TENTATIVE (I. Tax, 1990)
(*a*) Unreliable (*b*) Current
(*c*) Provisional (*d*) Final

16. OBTUSE
(*a*) Distant (*b*) Blunt
(*c*) Excessive (*d*) Vague

17. RENEGADE
(*a*) Rebel (*b*) Substitute
(*c*) Informer (*d*) Reformer

18. RECOLLECT (S.S.C. 1995)
(*a*) Remember (*b*) Revive
(*c*) Memorise (*d*) Recover

19. THRIFT
(*a*) Wickedness (*b*) Miserliness
(*c*) Economy (*d*) Extravagance

20. TEEMING
(*a*) Encroaching (*b*) Abounding with
(*c*) Surrounding (*d*) Working together

21. STRINGENT **(Railways, 1996)**
(*a*) Tense (*b*) Stringy
(*c*) Strict (*d*) Causing to shrink

22. PREVENT
(*a*) Restrict (*b*) Stop
(*c*) Interrupt (*d*) Obstruct

23. GORGEOUS
(*a*) Refined (*b*) Tasteful
(*c*) Elegant (*d*) Dazzling

24. HUMBUG
(*a*) Deceit (*b*) Desire
(*c*) Craving (*d*) Illusion

25. IMPROVEMENT
(*a*) Promotion (*b*) Advancement
(*c*) Betterment (*d*) Preference

26. RESTITUTE
(*a*) Help (*b*) Avenge
(*c*) Revenge (*d*) Repair

27. ENTANGLE
(*a*) Confuse (*b*) Trap
(*c*) Perplex (*d*) Submerge

28. RETRIBUTION **(C.B.I. 1994)**
(*a*) Contempt (*b*) Revenge
(*c*) Punishment (*d*) Discount

29. INTRINSIC
(*a*) Introvert (*b*) Intricate
(*c*) Complicated (*d*) Secret

30. APPRAISAL
(*a*) Estimation (*b*) Praise
(*c*) Approval (*d*) Investigation

31. LUMINARY
(*a*) Bright (*b*) Lightning
(*c*) Famous (*d*) Dashing

32. STRINGENT **(U.D.C. 1995)**
(*a*) Shrill (*b*) Rigorous
(*c*) Dry (*d*) Strained

33. EXOTIC
(*a*) Beautiful (*b*) Colourful
(*c*) Excellent (*d*) Unusual

34. ESTRANGE
(*a*) Puzzling (*b*) Endanger
(*c*) Alienate (*d*) Miscalculate

35. JEREMAID
(*a*) Friction (*b*) Incident
(*c*) Trouble (*d*) Accident

36. WHIMPER
(*a*) Prevent (*b*) Cry
(*c*) Instigate (*d*) Pacify

37. HARASS **(I. Tax, 1994)**
(*a*) Grieve (*b*) Injure
(*c*) Excite (*d*) Annoy

38. GADFLY
(*a*) Horror (*b*) Nuisance
(*c*) Gain (*d*) Blessing

39. HYBRID
(*a*) Unusual (*b*) Hackneyed
(*c*) Pedigreed (*d*) Crossbred

40. MAIM
(*a*) Disfigure (*b*) Slit
(*c*) Severe (*d*) Slash

41. MINIMUM **(Clerks' Grade, 1993)**
(*a*) Little (*b*) Lowest
(*c*) Minimal (*d*) Meagre

42. EXCRUCIATE
(*a*) Refine (*b*) Torture
(*c*) Extract (*d*) Imprison

43. OUTRE
(*a*) Fair (*b*) Traditional
(*c*) Real (*d*) Eccentric

44. TEDIOUS
(*a*) Tiresome (*b*) Painful
(*c*) Troublesome (*d*) Lengthy

45. ASSIMILATE **(Central Excise, 1992)**
(*a*) Absorb (*b*) Arrange
(*c*) Receive (*d*) Assemble

46. COTERIE
(*a*) Mob (*b*) Group
(*c*) Family (*d*) Institution

47. OBEISANCE
(*a*) Insult (*b*) Obedience
(*c*) Indifference (*d*) Disrespect

48. FATIGUE **(Stenographers' Exam, 1995)**
(*a*) Weariness (*b*) Sweating
(*c*) Tension (*d*) Drowsiness

49. PERFIDY
(*a*) Debauchery (*b*) Deceit
(*c*) Treachery (*d*) Conceit

50. MASTICATE
(*a*) Devour (*b*) Drink
(*c*) Chew (*d*) Swallow

ANSWERS

1. (*c*)	**2.** (*d*)	**3.** (*b*)	**4.** (*d*)	**5.** (*b*)	**6.** (*c*)	**7.** (*a*)	**8.** (*c*)	**9.** (*c*)	**10.** (*d*)
11. (*a*)	**12.** (*b*)	**13.** (*b*)	**14.** (*d*)	**15.** (*c*)	**16.** (*b*)	**17.** (*a*)	**18.** (*a*)	**19.** (*c*)	**20.** (*b*)
21. (*c*)	**22.** (*b*)	**23.** (*d*)	**24.** (*a*)	**25.** (*c*)	**26.** (*d*)	**27.** (*b*)	**28.** (*c*)	**29.** (*a*)	**30.** (*a*)
31. (*c*)	**32.** (*b*)	**33.** (*d*)	**34.** (*c*)	**35.** (*c*)	**36.** (*b*)	**37.** (*d*)	**38.** (*b*)	**39.** (*d*)	**40.** (*d*)
41. (*c*)	**42.** (*b*)	**43.** (*d*)	**44.** (*a*)	**45.** (*a*)	**46.** (*b*)	**47.** (*b*)	**48.** (*a*)	**49.** (*c*)	**50.** (*c*)

PRACTICE SET 5

Directions : *In each of the following questions, out of the given alternatives, choose the one which is the nearest in meaning to the given word.*

1. INDICT **(C.B.I. 1995)**
(*a*) Accuse (*b*) Condemn
(*c*) Allege (*d*) Reprimand
2. SUPERANNUATED
(*a*) Accepted (*b*) Senile
(*c*) Retired (*d*) Experienced
3. ENDORSEMENT
(*a*) Reprimand (*b*) Censure
(*c*) Commendation (*d*) Reproach
4. STAMINA **(S.S.C. 1994)**
(*a*) Endurance (*b*) Intensity
(*c*) Eagerness (*d*) Energy
5. BRASH
(*a*) Invective (*b*) Rude
(*c*) Abusive (*d*) Superficial
6. DECRY
(*a*) Deviate (*b*) Despoil
(*c*) Demure (*d*) Disparage
7. MOLLIFY
(*a*) Chastise (*b*) Testify
(*c*) Rebuke (*d*) Appease
8. RECALL **(Railways, 1991)**
(*a*) Speak (*b*) Receive
(*c*) Face (*d*) Remember
9. JEOPARDY
(*a*) Magic (*b*) Adventure
(*c*) Enmity (*d*) Danger
10. ECONOMISE
(*a*) Accumulate (*b*) Minimise
(*c*) Save (*d*) Reduce
11. JUVENILE
(*a*) Hidden (*b*) Young
(*c*) Humorous (*d*) Tedious
12. VENTURE
(*a*) Entrust (*b*) Risk
(*c*) Travel (*d*) Adventure
13. IMPERTINENT **(R.R.B. 1995)**
(*a*) Impudent (*b*) Sceptical
(*c*) Thoughtless (*d*) Irritable
14. IMPEDIMENT
(*a*) Passage (*b*) Obstruction
(*c*) Fateful (*d*) Destruction
15. LURID
(*a*) Sensational (*b*) Old
(*c*) Obscene (*d*) Pale
16. MASTERPIECE
(*a*) Sample (*b*) Wonder
(*c*) Miracle (*d*) Model
17. ALERT **(Stenographers' Exam, 1995)**
(*a*) Watchful (*b*) Intelligent
(*c*) Observant (*d*) Energetic
18. ARTICULATE
(*a*) Distinct (*b*) Aggressive
(*c*) Wayward (*d*) Confused
19. VEER
(*a*) Shift (*b*) Dominate
(*c*) Delegate (*d*) Concentrate
20. SUPERCILIOUS **(C.B.I. 1990)**
(*a*) Indifferent (*b*) Annoyed
(*c*) Haughty (*d*) Angry
21. DEMIT
(*a*) Promote (*b*) Judge
(*c*) Appoint (*d*) Resign
22. BERSERK
(*a*) Clever (*b*) Morose
(*c*) Cheerful (*d*) Wild
23. GROTESQUE
(*a*) Fantastic (*b*) Exaggerated
(*c*) Colourful (*d*) Pompous
24. COUNSEL **(Railways, 1993)**
(*a*) Correct (*b*) Publish
(*c*) Oppose (*d*) Advise
25. SUCCULENT
(*a*) Fluid (*b*) Sucking
(*c*) Juicy (*d*) Sweet
26. TESTIFY
(*a*) Witness (*b*) Describe
(*c*) Recognise (*d*) Appreciate
27. ASCEND **(Section Officers, 1993)**
(*a*) Leap (*b*) Mount
(*c*) Deviate (*d*) Grow
28. OSTRACIZE
(*a*) Cut off (*b*) Expedite
(*c*) Welcome (*d*) Include
29. FORLORN
(*a*) Uncared (*b*) Funny
(*c*) Fearful (*d*) Fortunate
30. RILE
(*a*) Drag (*b*) Agree
(*c*) Please (*d*) Annoy
31. LAZE
(*a*) Abdicate (*b*) Rest
(*c*) Waste (*d*) Wander
32. UGLY **(Clerks' Grade, 1993)**
(*a*) Fearful (*b*) Hateful
(*c*) Evilsome (*d*) Repulsive
33. EFFETE
(*a*) Affected (*b*) Injured
(*c*) Feeble (*d*) Sick
34. SLOPPY
(*a*) Drunk (*b*) Careless
(*c*) Tired (*d*) Untrustworthy
35. HARBINGER **(Asstt. Grade, 1996)**
(*a*) Pilot (*b*) Forerunner
(*c*) Steward (*d*) Messenger

36. INDOLENCE
(*a*) Leniency (*b*) Relaxation
(*c*) Laziness (*d*) Stagnation

37. ACCENTUATED **(Bank P.O. 1996)**
(*a*) Projected (*b*) Exhibited
(*c*) Sharpened (*d*) Mitigated

38. DISRUPT
(*a*) Deny (*b*) Refuse
(*c*) Break (*d*) Join

39. SUMPTUOUS **(C.B.I. 1991)**
(*a*) Lavish (*b*) Fancy
(*c*) Meagre (*d*) Irritable

40. LATENT
(*a*) Prompt (*b*) Lethargic
(*c*) Apparent (*d*) Concealed

41. NUMINOUS
(*a*) Dull (*b*) Awful
(*c*) Bright (*d*) Dark

42. STUPID **(S.S.C. 1995)**
(*a*) Silly (*b*) Disobedient
(*c*) Insane (*d*) Incapable

43. BUCOLIC
(*a*) Helpless (*b*) Intoxicated
(*c*) Shameless (*d*) Rustic

44. GROGGY
(*a*) Unsteady (*b*) Sensible
(*c*) Sensitive (*d*) Pensive

45. VIE
(*a*) Hesitate (*b*) Compete
(*c*) Refuse (*d*) Shirk

46. CONSOLE **(Central Excise, 1994)**
(*a*) Sympathise (*b*) Share
(*c*) Pacify (*d*) Assist

47. GENESIS
(*a*) Relevant (*b*) Beginning
(*c*) Style (*d*) Movement

48. SULTRY
(*a*) Unpleasant (*b*) Ill-smelling
(*c*) Impure (*d*) Hot & oppressive

49. HEDGE
(*a*) Curse (*b*) Injure
(*c*) Evade (*d*) Harm

50. WAN
(*a*) Tired (*b*) Strong
(*c*) Cheerful (*d*) Unhappy

ANSWERS

1. (*a*)	**2.** (*c*)	**3.** (*c*)	**4.** (*d*)	**5.** (*b*)	**6.** (*d*)	**7.** (*d*)	**8.** (*d*)	**9.** (*d*)	**10.** (*c*)
11. (*b*)	**12.** (*b*)	**13.** (*a*)	**14.** (*b*)	**15.** (*a*)	**16.** (*d*)	**17.** (*a*)	**18.** (*a*)	**19.** (*a*)	**20.** (*c*)
21. (*d*)	**22.** (*d*)	**23.** (*a*)	**24.** (*d*)	**25.** (*c*)	**26.** (*a*)	**27.** (*b*)	**28.** (*a*)	**29.** (*a*)	**30.** (*d*)
31. (*b*)	**32.** (*d*)	**33.** (*c*)	**34.** (*b*)	**35.** (*d*)	**36.** (*c*)	**37.** (*c*)	**38.** (*c*)	**39.** (*a*)	**40.** (*d*)
41. (*b*)	**42.** (*a*)	**43.** (*d*)	**44.** (*a*)	**45.** (*b*)	**46.** (*c*)	**47.** (*a*)	**48.** (*d*)	**49.** (*c*)	**50.** (*a*)

PRACTICE SET 6

Directions ; *In each of the following questions, out of the given alternatives, choose the one which best expresses the meaning of the given word.*

1. INGENUOUS
(*a*) Cunning (*b*) Frank
(*c*) Courteous (*d*) Clever

2. CONSEQUENCE
(*a*) Manner (*b*) Result
(*c*) Cause (*d*) Order
(Stenographers' Exam, 1994)

3. EROTIC
(*a*) Sexual (*b*) Sensuous
(*c*) Beautiful (*d*) Attractive

4. CRUEL
(*a*) Hateful (*b*) Dreadful
(*c*) Indifferent (*d*) Merciless

5. DODGE
(*a*) Confuse (*b*) Avoid
(*c*) Thwart (*d*) Frustrate

6. INEXPLICABLE **(U.D.C. 1995)**
(*a*) Unconnected (*b*) Chaotic
(*c*) Unaccountable (*d*) Confusing

7. OBSTREPEROUS
(*a*) Obstinate (*b*) Calm
(*c*) Noisy (*d*) Cheerful

8. CHIMERICAL
(*a*) Erratic (*b*) Imaginary
(*c*) Uncertain (*d*) Short-lived

9. CONUNDRUM
(*a*) Question (*b*) Discussion
(*c*) Explanation (*d*) Solution

10. IRK **(Asstt. Grade, 1991)**
(*a*) Bore (*b*) Insult
(*c*) Urge (*d*) Annoy

11. MUFFLE
(*a*) Wrap (*b*) Soften
(*c*) Hasten (*d*) Disturb

12. SUSTAIN
(a) Support (b) Revive
(c) Believe (d) Allow

13. SCOUR
(a) Search (b) Flow
(c) Raise (d) Push

14. INDUSTRIOUS **(Clerks' Grade, 1993)**
(a) Intelligent (b) Hard working
(c) Clever (d) Reserved

15. LACHRYMOSE
(a) Unimpressive (b) Mournful
(c) Moist (d) Impious

16. FORAGE
(a) Search (b) Research
(c) Fly (d) Travel

17. ULTERIOR
(a) Revealed (b) Implied
(a) Extreme (b) Decisive

18. WARY **(I. Tax & Central Excise, 1990)**
(a) Cautious (b) Accurate
(c) Quick (d) Practical

19. WELTER
(a) Sacrifice (b) Clarity
(c) Height (d) Confusion

20. RETRIEVE
(a) Repeat (b) Repose
(c) Retort (d) Recover

21. GARNISH
(a) Decorate (b) Compose
(c) Impress (d) Impose

22. ALLOW **(S.S.C. 1995)**
(a) Accept (b) Seek
(c) Permit (d) Wish

23. CAVEAT
(a) Dispute (b) Challenge
(c) Advice (d) Warning

24. LIABILITY
(a) Debt (b) Debit
(c) Asset (d) Credit

25. AMALGAMATE
(a) Try (b) Collect
(c) Mix (d) Hate

26. CONDEMN **(Stenographers' Exam, 1993)**
(a) Blame (b) Underrate
(c) Hate (d) Avoid

27. FICKLE
(a) Constant (b) Nervous
(c) Changeable (d) Poor

28. CONGREGATION
(a) Combination (b) Meeting
(c) Assembly (d) Collection

29. HASSLE
(a) Greed (b) Jealousy
(c) Gossip (d) Wrangle

30. ROTUND
(a) Flat (b) Fat
(c) Foolish (d) Weak

31. DELIRIOUS
(a) Content (b) Happy
(c) Insane (d) Amused

32. EXTRAVAGANZA **(Railways, 1995)**
(a) Profligacy (b) Spectacular show
(c) Over reaching (d) Falsification

33. DETECT
(a) Discover (b) Invent
(c) Determine (d) Fix

34. COUNTERVAIL
(a) Recreate (b) Demolish
(c) Equalise (d) Contradict

35. LANGUOR
(a) Excitement (b) Irritation
(c) Weariness (d) Agitation

36. FIDDLE
(a) Examine (b) Trifle
(c) Discard (d) Frown

37. BENEFACTOR **(U.D.C, 1994)**
(a) Guardian (b) Saint
(c) Do-gooder (d) Friend

38. AMICABLE
(a) Interesting (b) Loving
(c) Affectionate (d) Friendly

39. ENTHUSE
(a) Pester (b) Provoke
(c) Excite (d) Annoy

40. GRUBBY **(I. Tax & Central Excise, 1989)**
(a) Wet (b) Muddy
(c) New (d) Unwashed

41. AROMATIC
(a) Stinking (b) Sentimental
(c) Fragrant (d) Crippled

42. AMBIT
(a) Eviction (b) Scope
(c) Restriction (d) Barrier

43. ENTHUSIASTIC **(Central Excise, 1992)**
(a) Angry (b) Excited
(c) Noisy (d) Violent

44. QUELL
(a) Postpone (b) Avoid
(c) Complain (d) Suppress

45. OMINOUS
(a) Poisonous (b) Foregone
(c) Foreboding (d) Bad

46. MISFORTUNE
(a) Misery (b) Poverty
(c) Ill-luck (d) Sadness

(Stenographers' Exam, 1995)

47. INDOMITABLE
(a) Inactive (b) Authoritative
(c) Rebellious (d) Unconquerable

48. LUG
(a) Drag (b) Denounce
(c) Decline (d) Degrade

49. LEVITATE
(a) Float (b) Dance
(c) Waver (d) Harass

50. RANCOUR **(Investigators' Exam, 1988)**
(*a*) Prejudice (*b*) Enmity (*c*) Disappointment (*d*) Hatred

ANSWERS

1. (*b*)	**2.** (*b*)	**3.** (*a*)	**4.** (*d*)	**5.** (*b*)	**6.** (*c*)	**7.** (*c*)	**8.** (*b*)	**9.** (*a*)	**10.** (*d*)
11. (*b*)	**12.** (*a*)	**13.** (*a*)	**14.** (*b*)	**15.** (*b*)	**16.** (*a*)	**17.** (*b*)	**18.** (*a*)	**19.** (*d*)	**20.** (*d*)
21. (*a*)	**22.** (*c*)	**23.** (*d*)	**24.** (*a*)	**25.** (*c*)	**26.** (*a*)	**27.** (*c*)	**28.** (*c*)	**29.** (*d*)	**30.** (*b*)
31. (*c*)	**32.** (*b*)	**33.** (*a*)	**34.** (*c*)	**35.** (*c*)	**36.** (*b*)	**37.** (*c*)	**38.** (*d*)	**39.** (*c*)	**40.** (*d*)
41. (*c*)	**42.** (*b*)	**43.** (*b*)	**44.** (*d*)	**45.** (*c*)	**46.** (*c*)	**47.** (*d*)	**48.** (*a*)	**49.** (*a*)	**50.** (*d*)

PRACTICE SET 7

Directions : ***In each of the following questions, choose one alternative which best expresses the meaning of the given word.***

1. COMBAT **(Section Officers, 1993)**
(*a*) Quarrel (*b*) Fight
(*c*) Conflict (*d*) Feud

2. SUBSIDE
(*a*) Submit (*b*) Oppress
(*c*) Subdue (*d*) Surrender

3. ABSCOND
(*a*) Turn (*b*) Flee
(*c*) Manage (*d*) Avoid

4. GAINSAY
(*a*) Advantage (*b*) Proposal
(*c*) Contradict (*d*) Suggestion

5. PROFOUND **(Assistant Grade, 1995)**
(*a*) Profuse (*b*) Boundless
(*c*) Deep (*d*) Fathomless

6. SOPORIFIC
(*a*) Lethargic (*b*) Merry
(*c*) Soothing (*d*) Impressive

7. ANNEAL
(*a*) Commence (*b*) Forget
(*c*) Patch (*d*) Temper

8. ABOMINATION
(*a*) Revulsion (*b*) Disgust
(*c*) Criticism (*d*) Attack

9. BURLESQUE
(*a*) Insult (*b*) Irritate
(*c*) Mock (*d*) Annoy

10. FOSTER **(Central Excise, 1994)**
(*a*) Encourage (*b*) Fabricate
(*c*) Foment (*d*) Nurture

11. ENIGMA
(*a*) Elusive (*b*) Clear
(*c*) Puzzle (*d*) Praise

12. FILTHY
(*a*) Healthy (*b*) Ugly
(*c*) Dirty (*d*) Angry

13. NOSTALGIC
(*a*) Soothing (*b*) Homesick
(*c*) Diseased (*d*) Indolent

14. OVERSEE **(B.S.R.B. 1992)**
(*a*) Supervise (*b*) Glance
(*c*) Contest (*d*) Look

15. DECIEVE
(*a*) Mislead (*b*) Challenge
(*c*) Harm (*d*) Defeat

16. COMPUNCTION
(*a*) Anger (*b*) Appreciate
(*c*) Regret (*d*) Wonder

17. PREROGATIVE **(C.B.I. 1990)**
(*a*) Privilege (*b*) Request
(*c*) Desire (*d*) Command

18. AFICIONADO
(*a*) Rival (*b*) Enthusiast
(*c*) Critic (*d*) Indifferent

19. SOLICIT
(*a*) Beseech (*b*) Demand
(*c*) Claim (*d*) Require

20. RADIANT **(Stenographers' Exam, 1995)**
(*a*) Bright (*b*) Beautiful
(*c*) Light (*d*) Influential

21. PRUNE
(*a*) Lend (*b*) Reduce
(*c*) Expand (*d*) Prolong

22. DILETTANTE
(*a*) Opponent (*b*) Specialist
(*c*) Amateur (*d*) Expert

23. FLAK
(*a*) Adventure (*b*) Advice
(*c*) Criticism (*d*) Praise

24. HOODLUM
(*a*) Pioneer (*b*) Criminal
(*c*) Devotee (*d*) Scholar

25. SPASMODIC
(*a*) Continuous (*b*) Gradual
(*c*) Intermittent (*d*) Spontaneous

26. PARAMOUR
(*a*) Lover (*b*) Companion
(*c*) Friend (*d*) Rival

27. REFECTORY **(C.B.I. 1995)**
(*a*) Dining Room (*b*) Parlour
(*c*) Living Room (*d*) Restaurant

28. ASSENT
(*a*) Compromise (*b*) Judgement
(*c*) Agreement (*d*) Expression

29. BAFFLE
(*a*) Tease (*b*) Trick
(*c*) Puzzle (*d*) Hoodwink

30. CONFIDENTIAL **(S.S.C. 1994)**
(*a*) Hidden (*b*) Private
(*c*) Trusted (*d*) Secret

31. LOATHE
(*a*) Abuse (*b*) Hurt
(*c*) Repel (*d*) Detest

32. VENDETTA
(*a*) Proposal (*b*) Feud
(*c*) Revenge (*d*) Compromise

33. PRESSED **(Railways, 1991)**
(*a*) Stressed (*b*) Urged
(*c*) Demanded (*d*) Emphasised

34. TACITURNITY
(*a*) Violence (*b*) Insolence
(*c*) Prudence (*d*) Silence

35. INGENUOUS
(*a*) Active (*b*) Frank
(*c*) Skilful (*d*) Smart

36. PROMULGATE **(I. Tax, 1992)**
(*a*) Proclaim (*b*) Inform
(*c*) Promote (*d*) Enforce

37. INSIDIOUS
(*a*) Slow (*b*) Treacherous
(*c*) Pessimistic (*d*) Unfortunate

38. UBIQUITOUS
(*a*) Inescapable (*b*) Crowded
(*c*) Solitary (*d*) Defensive

39. WILT
(*a*) Collapse (*b*) Strike
(*c*) Challenge (*d*) Warn

40. HANDSOME **(Clerks' Grade. 1995)**
(*a*) Noble (*b*) Gentle
(*c*) Good-looking (*d*) Polite

41. NINCOMPOOP
(*a*) Joker (*b*) Trader
(*c*) Magician (*d*) Fool

42. CONVENED
(*a*) Summoned (*b*) Collected
(*c*) Associated (*d*) Ended

43. ADDLE
(*a*) Soar (*b*) Strike
(*c*) Stop (*d*) Confuse

44. EXPLICIT **(Central Excise, 1994)**
(*a*) Clear (*b*) Exciting
(*c*) Precise (*d*) Refined

45. ANIMOSITY
(*a*) Vanity (*b*) Empathy
(*c*) Indifference (*d*) Treason

46. BEFUDDLED
(*a*) Wounded (*b*) Crowded
(*c*) Enlightened (*d*) Stupid

47. VENT **(M.B.A. 1994)**
(*a*) Stodge (*b*) Opening
(*c*) End (*d*) Past tense of 'go'

48. TEETER
(*a*) Hesitate (*b*) Descend
(*c*) Pretend (*d*) Climb

49. YANK
(*a*) Excuse (*b*) Swear
(*c*) Pull (*d*) Drag

50. CAVORT
(*a*) Suppress (*b*) Jump
(*c*) Annoy (*d*) Entertain

ANSWERS

1. (*b*)	**2.** (*c*)	**3.** (*b*)	**4.** (*c*)	**5.** (*c*)	**6.** (*c*)	**7.** (*d*)	**8.** (*b*)	**9.** (*c*)	**10.** (*d*)
11 (*c*)	**12.** (*c*)	**13.** (*b*)	**14.** (*a*)	**15.** (*a*)	**16.** (*c*)	**17.** (*a*)	**18.** (*b*)	**19.** (*a*)	**20.** (*a*)
21. (*b*)	**22.** (*c*)	**23.** (*d*)	**24.** (*b*)	**25.** (*c*)	**26.** (a)	**27.** (a)	**28.** (*c*)	**29.** (*c*)	**30.** (*d*)
31. (*d*)	**32.** (*c*)	**33.** (*b*)	**34.** (*d*)	**35.** (*b*)	**36.** (a)	**37.** (*b*)	**38.** (a)	**39.** (*a*)	**40.** (*c*)
41. (*d*)	**42.** (*a*)	**43.** (*d*)	**44.** (*a*)	**45.** (*c*)	**46.** (*d*)	**47.** (*b*)	**48.** (*a*)	**49.** (*c*)	**50.** (*b*)

PRACTICE SET 8

Directions : *In each of the following questions, choose the meaning of the given word from the given alternatives.*

1. IRRUPTION **(Railways, 1995)**
(*a*) Hate (*b*) Bursting in
(*c*) Interference (*d*) Altercation
2. ECHELON
(*a*) Rank (*b*) Opponent
(*c*) Follower (*d*) Identity
3. PREVARICATE
(*a*) Anticipate (*b*) Lie
(*c*) Delay (*d*) Authenticate
4. EXUDE
(*a*) Ooze (*b*) Wither
(*c*) Overflow (*d*) Evaporate
5. PRECARIOUS **(Asstt. Grade, 1996)**
(*a*) Brittle (*b*) Perilous
(*c*) Critical (*d*) Cautious
6. MALAISE
(*a*) Stagnation (*b*) Spite
(*c*) Curse (*d*) Sickness
7. VOGUE
(*a*) Fashion (*b*) Rejection
(*c*) Order (*d*) Satisfaction
8. IMPREGNATE
(*a*) Conceal (*b*) Suffer
(*c*) Affect (*d*) Conclude
9. DELEGATE **(S.S.C. 1993)**
(*a*) Officer (*b*) Participant
(*c*) Member (*d*) Representative
10. ABANDON
(*a*) Admit (*b*) Refrain
(*c*) Abstain (*d*) Forsake
11. AVER
(*a*) Assert (*b*) Confess
(*c*) Impress (*d*) Trust
12. YAW
(*a*) Dedicate (*b*) Soar
(*c*) Arouse (*d*) Drift
13. DELECTABLE **(I. Tax & Excise, 1990)**
(*a*) Attractive (*b*) Delightful
(*c*) Desirable (*d*) Delicate
14. HINDER
(*a*) Obstruct (*b*) Challenge
(*c*) Damage (*d*) Ruin
15. REITERATE
(*a*) Reassess (*b*) Rewrite
(*c*) Repeat (*d*) Stutter
16. FEIGN **(C.B.I. 1991)**
(*a*) Pretend (*b*) Attend
(*c*) Condemn (*d*) Condone
17. VITUPERATE
(*a*) Appreciate (*b*) Abuse
(*c*) Appraise (*d*) Encourage
18. NAUSEATE
(*a*) Tempt (*b*) Sicken
(*c*) Despise (*d*) Detest
19. INIQUITOUS
(*a*) Unequal (*b*) Curious
(*c*) Biased (*d*) Wicked
20. ECSTATIC **(Railways, 1996)**
(*a*) Animated (*b*) Enraptured
(*c*) Bewildered (*d*) Fitful
21. REPLENISH
(*a*) Fill (*b*) Supply
(*c*) Provide (*d*) Restore
22. WALLOW
(*a*) Luxuriate (*b*) Suffer
(*c*) Sacrifice (*d*) Prosper
23. INNATE **(M.B.A. 1991)**
(*a*) Unique (*b*) Important
(*c*) Inborn (*d*) Essential
24. FURTIVE
(*a*) Baffling (*b*) Fleeing
(*c*) Hasty (*d*) Stealthy
25. ACCOLADE
(*a*) Welcome (*b*) Award
(*c*) Affection (*d*) Arrival
26. INDIGENCE
(*a*) Poverty (*b*) Prosperity
(*c*) Suffering (*d*) Scarcity
27. DISTINCTION
(*a*) Degree (*b*) Difference
(*c*) Diffusion (*d*) Disagreement
(Stenographers' Exam, 1994)
28. STALEMATE
(*a*) Deadly (*b*) Dead-end
(*c*) Deadlock (*d*) Dead-drunk
29. REQUITE **(Assistant Grade, 1991)**
(*a*) Repay (*b*) Demand
(*c*) Refuse (*d*) Requisition
30. COMPENDIUM
(*a*) Glossary (*b*) Reference
(*c*) Index (*d*) Summary
31. VAPID
(*a*) Virtuous (*b*) Priceless
(*c*) Dull (*d*) Vital
32. CONTROL
(*a*) Restrain (*b*) Influence
(*c*) Regulate (*d*) Dominate
33. OVERSTRUNG **(I. Tax & Excise, 1989)**
(*a*) Active (*b*) Energetic
(*c*) Concerned (*d*) Too sensitive
34. FRATERNISE
(*a*) Associate (*b*) Organise
(*c*) Expel (*d*) Cheat

35. NUGATORY
(a) Worthless (b) Cheerful
(c) Negative (d) Migratory

36. AID (S.S.C. 1995)
(a) Supervision (b) Co-operation
(c) Assistance (d) Disease

37. DERIDE
(a) Mock (b) Confuse
(c) Shout (d) Snarl

38. SAVVY
(a) Deform (b) Understand
(c) Destroy (d) Taste

39. COMMISERATE
(a) Sympathise (b) Placate
(c) Commemorate (d) Consecrate
(Translators' Exam, 1994)

40. REIN
(a) Overcome (b) Fling
(c) Control (d) Pour

41. GOOEY
(a) Evasive (b) Sentimental
(c) Ideal (d) Realistic

42. FORAY
(a) Indulgence (b) Raid
(c) Repentance (d) Pilgrimage

43. ABSOLUTE (M.B.A. 1989)
(a) Reasonable (b) Narrow
(c) Limitless (d) Reliable

44. GLITZY
(a) Glamorous (b) Boring
(c) Interesting (d) Serious

45. VENALITY
(a) Hope (b) Sacrifice
(c) Respect (d) Corruption

46. WARY (M.B.A. 1994)
(a) Tired (b) Distorted
(c) Vigilant (d) Sad

47. PIQUE
(a) Subdue (b) Irritate
(c) Repent (d) Request

48. ICON
(a) Monument (b) Memorial
(c) Painting (d) Statue

49. HANKER
(a) Denounce (b) Debar
(c) Renounce (d) Desire

50. CONDONE
(a) Bring together (b) Pardon
(c) Surround (d) Contribute

ANSWERS

1. (b)	2. (a)	3. (b)	4. (a)	5. (c)	6. (d)	7. (a)	8. (c)	9. (d)	10. (d)
11. (a)	12. (d)	13. (b)	14. (a)	15. (c)	16. (a)	17. (b)	18. (b)	19. (d)	20. (b)
21. (d)	22. (a)	23. (c)	24. (d)	25. (b)	26. (a)	27. (b)	28. (c)	29. (a)	30. (b)
31. (c)	32. (a)	33. (d)	34. (a)	35. (a)	36. (c)	37. (a)	38. (b)	39. (a)	40. (c)
41. (b)	42. (b)	43. (c)	44. (a)	45. (d)	46. (c)	47. (b)	48. (c)	49. (d)	50. (b)

PRACTICE SET 9

Directions ***In each of the following questions, out of the given alternatives, choose the one which best expresses the meaning of the given word.***

1. CITE (R.R.B. 1993) (S.S.C. 1991)
(a) Illustrate (b) Reveal
(c) Recollect (d) Quote

2. BESIEGE
(a) Acquire (b) Attack
(c) Sieze (d) Surround

3. BANDIT
(a) Convict (b) Robber
(c) Thief (d) Cut-throat

4. MELEE (Hotel Management, 1992)
(a) Primitive dance (b) Kindness
(c) Simple song (d) Brawl

5. MARVELLOUS
(a) Wonderful (b) Attractive
(c) Pleasing (d) Charming

6. MORBID
(a) Diseased (b) Dying
(c) Irritated (d) Angry

7. INSOLVENT (U.D.C. 1995)
(a) Poor (b) Bankrupt
(c) Broke (d) Penniless

8. PARADIGM
(a) Theme (b) Example
(c) Proof (d) Paragone

9. AUGUR
(a) Heal (b) Hurt
(c) Signify (d) Reform

10. MAUNDER
(a) Warn (b) Capture
(c) Concentrate (d) Wander

11. JINK
(*a*) Inherit (*b*) Refrain
(*c*) Dodge (*d*) Travel

12. RELUCTANT **(Clerks' Grade, 1993)**
(*a*) Ready (*b*) Willing
(*c*) Hesitating (*d*) Inclined

13. ADMIT
(*a*) Adjourn (*b*) Confess
(*c*) Relate (*d*) Commit

14. DOWDY
(*a*) Unstylish (*b*) Elegant
(*c*) Rakish (*d*) Corpulent

15. ASSUAGE
(*a*) Rub (*b*) Prohibit
(*c*) Ease (*d*) Enlarge

16. RECKLESS **(Stenographers' Exam, 1995)**
(*a*) Daring (*b*) Bold
(*c*) Rash (*d*) Courageous

17. CATAPULT
(*a*) Restrain (*b*) Control
(*c*) Contain (*d*) Shoot

18. MUTATION
(*a*) Variation (*b*) Display
(*c*) Severance (*d*) Silence

19. CONTEMPLATIVE **(I. Tax, 1994)**
(*a*) Morbid (*b*) Serious
(*c*) Calm (*d*) Thoughtful

20. BROOK
(*a*) Indulge (*b*) Serve
(*c*) Tolerate (*d*) Taste

21. DEFERENCE
(*a*) Obligation (*b*) Respect
(*c*) Postponement (*d*) Pride

22. NEPOTISM **(Investigators' Exam, 1988)**
(*a*) Favouritism (*b*) Carelessness
(*c*) Inefficiency (*d*) Corruption

23. BIFURCATED
(*a*) Reduced (*b*) Stabbed
(*c*) Ploughed (*d*) Forked

24. LIBERAL **(Stenographers' Exam, 1993)**
(*a*) Progressive (*b*) Tolerant
(*c*) Generous (*d*) Educated

25. INTERIM
(*a*) Temporary (*b*) Internal
(*c*) Interval (*d*) Timely

26. HOOD-WINK
(*a*) Deceive (*b*) Stab
(*c*) Prefer (*d*) Collide

27. IMPRECATION
(*a*) Abuse (*b*) Blessing
(*c*) Bliss (*d*) Oath

28. JAUNTY
(*a*) Readiness (*b*) Hesitation
(*c*) Reluctance (*d*) Cheerfulness

29. LEEWAY **(Railways, 1995)**
(*a*) Flexibility (*b*) Leisure
(*c*) Permissiveness (*d*) Course

30. SOZZLED
(*a*) Burnt (*b*) Cultured
(*c*) Drunk (*d*) Moderate

31. AFFILIATE
(*a*) Control (*b*) Associate
(*c*) Copy (*d*) Discriminate

32. GAWK
(*a*) Sweeten (*b*) Stare
(*c*) Perspire (*d*) Swallow

33. BENEVOLENT **(I. Tax, 1992)**
(*a*) Charitable (*b*) Sympathetic
(*c*) Liberal (*d*) Beneficial

34. HEGEMONY
(*a*) Domination (*b*) Materialism
(*c*) Subordination (*d*) Booty

35. ENCUMBRANCE
(*a*) Disturbance (*b*) Burden
(*c*) Distraction (*d*) Hindrance

36. SURREPTITIOUS **(C.B.I. 1990)**
(*a*) Mysterious (*b*) Abstract
(*c*) Secretive (*d*) Secret

37. CAPITULATE
(*a*) Surrender (*b*) Withdraw
(*c*) Execute (*d*) Summarize

38. HOCK
(*a*) Repent (*b*) Pledge
(*c*) Promise (*d*) Punish

39. DYNAMIC **(S.S.C. 1995)**
(*a*) Vigorous (*b*) Forceful
(*c*) Robust (*d*) Active

40. HERETICAL
(*a*) Fiery (*b*) Corrupt
(*c*) Impious (*d*) Disputable

41. OBDURATE
(*a*) Adamant (*b*) Helpful
(*c*) Simple (*d*) Flexible

42. IRONIC **(Railways, 1996)**
(*a*) Good natured (*b*) Inflexible
(*c*) Disguisedly sarcastic (*d*) Bitter

43. LIBERTY
(*a*) Obligation (*b*) Rights
(*c*) Freedom (*d*) Democracy

44. VIRILE
(*a*) Boastful (*b*) Manly
(*c*) Pompous (*d*) Athletic

45. LEGITIMATE
(*a*) Rightful (*b*) Valid
(*c*) Illicit (*d*) Correct

46. AMBITION **(M.B.A. 1989)**
(*a*) Expectation (*b*) Desire
(*c*) Aspiration (*d*) Goal

47. FRACTIOUS
(*a*) Disheartening (*b*) Irritable
(*c*) Comic (*d*) Pleasing

48. FLABBY
(*a*) Obese (*b*) Fatty
(*c*) Chubby (*d*) Loose

49. DEMISE
(*a*) Decline (*b*) Decay
(*c*) Dormant (*d*) End

50. PRISTINE
(*a*) Traditional (*b*) Expensive
(*c*) Original (*d*) Meritorious

ANSWERS

1. (*d*)	**2.** (*d*)	**3.** (*b*)	**4.** (*d*)	**5.** (*a*)	**6.** (*a*)	**7.** (*b*)	**8.** (*b*)	**9.** (*c*)	**10.** (*d*)
11. (*c*)	**12.** (*c*)	**13.** (*b*)	**14.** (*a*)	**15.** (*c*)	**16.** (*c*)	**17.** (*d*)	**18.** (*a*)	**19.** (*d*)	**20.** (*c*)
21. (*b*)	**22.** (*a*)	**23.** (*d*)	**24.** (*c*)	**25.** (*a*)	**26.** (*a*)	**27.** (*d*)	**28.** (*d*)	**29.** (*d*)	**30.** (*c*)
31. (*b*)	**32.** (*b*)	**33.** (*a*)	**34.** (*a*)	**35.** (*b*)	**36.** (*d*)	**37.** (*a*)	**38.** (*b*)	**39.** (*d*)	**40.** (*c*)
41. (a)	**42.** (c)	**43.** (c)	**44.** (b)	**45.** (d)	**46.** (b)	**47.** (b)	**48.** (d)	**49.** (d)	**50.** (c)

PRACTICE SET 10

Directions : ***In each of the following questions, out of the given alternatives, choose the one which is nearest in meaning to the given word.***

1. TURN UP **(C.B.I. 1995)**
(*a*) Show up (*b*) Come up
(*c*) Land up (*d*) Crop up

2. EDIFY
(*a*) Consume (*b*) Satisfy
(*c*) Instruct (*d*) Amuse

3. ROTUND
(*a*) Stout (*b*) Round
(*c*) Resonant (*d*) Gilded

4. APOLOGUE
(*a*) Moral fable (*b*) After thought
(*c*) Ancient legend (*d*) Explanation

5. OPTIMISTIC **(Asstt. Grade, 1995)**
(*a*) Optician (*b*) Favourable
(*c*) Wishful (*d*) Hopeful

6. CANDID
(*a*) Sincere (*b*) Polite
(*c*) Plain-spoken (*d*) Rude

7. INCENSED
(*a*) Inspired (*b*) Encouraged
(*c*) Incited (*d*) Affected

8. INCONTINENT
(*a*) Unrestrained (*b*) Restless
(*c*) Inconstant (*d*) Uncertain

9. RECIPROCATE **(U.D.C. 1994)**
(*a*) Grant (*b*) Interchange
(*c*) Receive (*d*) Deliver

10. ABSTAIN
(*a*) Resist (*b*) Refrain
(*c*) Assist (*d*) Attain

11. NIMBLE
(*a*) Agile (*b*) Clean
(*c*) Soft (*d*) Delicate

12. OFFAL
(*a*) Tendency (*b*) Sacrifice
(*c*) Refuse (*d*) Poison

13. COLOSSUS **(S.S.C. 1993)**
(*a*) Towering (*b*) Tall
(*c*) Lofty (*d*) Huge

14. HELM
(*a*) Corner (*b*) Handle
(*c*) Head (*d*) Edge

15. OCCULT
(*a*) Mysterious (*b*) Harmless
(*c*) Dreadful (*d*) Amazing

16. REPURCUSSION
(*a*) Remuneration (*b*) Consequence
(*c*) Reaction (*d*) Recollection

17. CIVIL **(Clerks' Grade, 1995)**
(*a*) Sophisticated (*b*) Social
(*c*) Formal (*d*) Polite

18. ADJURE
(*a*) Provoke (*b*) Adjust
(*c*) Entreat (*d*) Enjoy.

19. PANDER
(*a*) Encourage (*b*) With-hold
(*c*) Recommend (*d*) Withdraw

20. RANCOUS
(*a*) Noisy (*b*) Harmful
(*c*) Pleasant (*d*) Harsh

21. BROWSE **(M.B.A. 1994)**
(*a*) Strike (*b*) Examine
(*c*) Deceive (*d*) Heal

22. PRIVY
(*a*) Secret (*b*) Dispossessed
(*c*) Open (*d*) Deprived

23. ACERB
(*a*) Unwilling (*b*) Harsh
(*c*) Dangerous (*d*) Foreign

24. INANITION
(*a*) Silliness (*b*) Passivity
(*c*) Emptiness (*d*) Strictness

25. SPECTATORS
(*a*) Listeners (*b*) Audience
(*c*) Onlookers (*d*) Participants
(Stenographers' Exam, 1994)

26. ENTICE
(*a*) Tease (*b*) Tempt
(*c*) Charm (*d*) Attract

27. SEVERE
(*a*) Rigid (*b*) Aggressive
(*c*) Offensive (*d*) Sickening

28. RESTORATION **(C.B.I. 1994)**
(*a*) Renovation (*b*) Renewal
(*c*) Reinstatement (*d*) Recreation

29. MODISH
(*a*) Adorned (*b*) Sentimental
(*c*) Stylish (*d*) Vacillating

30. IMPECCABLE
(*a*) Precise (*b*) Faultless
(*c*) Fussy (*d*) Having integrity

31. INTERNECINE
(*a*) Deadly (*b*) Foolhardy
(*c*) Stealthy (*d*) International

32. UMBRAGE
(*a*) Debate (*b*) Battle
(*c*) Offence (*d*) Quarrel

33. PARAMOUNT **(Central Excise, 1994)**
(*a*) Prestigious (*b*) Supreme
(*c*) Valuable (*d*) Urgent

34. LICENTIOUS
(*a*) Immoral (*b*) Hungry
(*c*) Gay (*d*) Generous

35. COVETOUS
(*a*) Thrifty (*b*) Grasping
(*c*) Hidden (*d*) Sheltered

36. SIMON-PURE
(*a*) False (*b*) Genuine
(*c*) Holy (*d*) Artificial

37. VILIFY **(Asstt. Grade, 1991)**
(*a*) Desert (*b*) Deprive
(*c*) Defame (*d*) Deceive

38. YAMMER
(*a*) Lament (*b*) Shiver
(*c*) Strike (*d*) Whimper

39. STRIDENCY
(*a*) Harshness (*b*) Flippancy
(*c*) Stress (*d*) Consistency

40. DROWSY **(Stenographers' Exam, 1995)**
(*a*) Soothing (*b*) Lazy
(*c*) Exhausted (*d*) Sleepy

41. LISSOME
(*a*) Deceptive (*b*) Dull
(*c*) Graceful (*d*) Slow

42. GAFFE
(*a*) Competition (*b*) Blunder
(*c*) Compulsion (*d*) Virtue

43. INTIMIDATE **(Railways, 1996)**
(*a*) Harass (*b*) Bluff
(*c*) Frighten (*d*) Hint

44. DENOUNCE
(*a*) Lower in quality (*b*) Influence easily
(*c*) Talk insincerely
(*d*) Talk publicly against

45. RAP
(*a*) Transfer (*b*) Criticise
(*c*) Advise (*d*) Participate

46. ABSTEMIOUS
(*a*) Moderate (*b*) Proud
(*c*) Excessive (*d*) Rustic

47. EXCLUSIVE **(Investigators' Exam, 1988)**
(*a*) Extensive (*b*) Sole
(*c*) External (*d*) Excessive

48. SPECIOUS
(*a*) Insincere (*b*) Sharp
(*c*) Straight (*d*) Frank

49. MELLIFLUOUS
(*a*) Stupid (*b*) Stale
(*c*) Sweet (*d*) Tasteful

50. BLITHE
(*a*) Other worldly (*b*) Giddy
(*c*) Graceful (*d*) Joyous

ANSWERS

1. (*b*)	**2.** (*c*)	**3.** (*b*)	**4.** (*a*)	**5.** (*d*)	**6.** (*c*)	**7.** (*c*)	**8.** (*a*)	**9.** (*b*)	**10.** (*a*)
11. (*a*)	**12.** (*c*)	**13.** (*a*)	**14.** (*c*)	**15.** (*a*)	**16.** (*c*)	**17.** (*d*)	**18.** (*c*)	**19.** (*a*)	**20.** (*d*)
21. (*b*)	**22.** (*a*)	**23.** (*b*)	**24.** (*b*)	**25.** (*c*)	**26.** (*b*)	**27.** (*a*)	**28.** (*a*)	**29.** (*c*)	**30.** (*b*)
31. (*a*)	**32.** (*c*)	**33.** (*b*)	**34.** (*a*)	**35.** (*b*)	**36.** (*b*)	**37.** (*c*)	**38.** (*a*)	**39.** (*a*)	**40.** (*d*)
41. (*c*)	**42.** (*b*)	**43.** (*c*)	**44.** (*d*)	**45.** (*b*)	**46.** (*a*)	**47.** (*b*)	**48.** (*a*)	**49.** (*c*)	**50.** (*d*)

PRACTICE SET 11

Directions : *In each of the following questions, out of the given alternatives, choose the one which best expresses the meaning of the given word.*

1. CANTANKEROUS **(Asstt. Grade, 1996)**
(*a*) Disrespectful (*b*) Noisy
(*c*) Quarrelsome (*d*) Rash
2. MALIGN
(*a*) Assign (*b*) Deviate
(*c*) Depriciate (*d*) Harmful
3. TENEBROUS
(*a*) Obstinate (*b*) Gloomy
(*c*) Fragile (*d*) Overhanging
4. OBLOQUY
(*a*) Forgetfulness (*b*) Prejudice
(*c*) Conference (*d*) Defamation
5. SORDID **(I. Tax & Central Excise, 1990)**
(*a*) Harmful (*b*) Dirty
(*c*) Splendid (*d*) Dangerous
6. ABASH
(*a*) Refuse (*b*) Amaze
(*c*) Embarrass (*d*) Squash
7. NUMINOUS
(*a*) Amazing (*b*) Ugly
(*c*) Inspiring (*d*) Heavy
8. CONTUMACY
(*a*) Divorce (*b*) Relation
(*c*) Resistance (*d*) Cooperation
9. INSIPID **(C.B.I. 1991)**
(*a*) Lucid (*b*) Wily
(*c*) Witty (*d*) Flat
10. KNAVERY
(*a*) Heroism (*b*) Cowardice
(*c*) Dishonesty (*d*) Stupidity
11. TRUNCATE
(*a*) Cancel (*b*) Act cruelly
(*c*) Cut off (*d*) End swiftly
12. GRAPHIC **(S.S.C. 1995)**
(*a*) Squarish (*b*) Geometrical
(*c*) Pictorial (*d*) Mathematical
13. INTREPID
(*a*) Coward (*b*) Fearless
(*c*) Selfish (*d*) Ugly
14. LAMENTABLE
(*a*) Deplorable (*b*) Contemptible
(*c*) Remorseful (*d*) Scornful
15. DEFT **(Stenographers' Exam, 1995)**
(*a*) Skilful (*b*) Vigorous
(*c*) Swift (*d*) Deceitful
16. HOARD
(*a*) Destroy (*b*) Hide
(*c*) Store (*d*) Divide
17. WAFT
(*a*) Climb (*b*) Float
(*c*) Sink (*d*) Drown
18. QUIBBLE
(*a*) Argue (*b*) Depress
(*c*) Express (*d*) Quarrel
19. MELD **(M.B.A. 1994)**
(*a*) Glisten (*b*) Purchase
(*c*) Merge (*d*) Soothe
20. DIVULGE
(*a*) Reveal (*b*) Explore
(*c*) Conceal (*d*) Strip
21. SCUTTLE
(*a*) Pollute (*b*) Sabotage
(*c*) Shout (*d*) Succeed
22. INDIGENOUS
(*a*) Normal (*b*) Internal
(*c*) Natural (*d*) Native
(Transmission Executives, 1994)
23. OPULENT
(*a*) Greedy (*b*) Hungry
(*c*) Heavy (*d*) Wealthy
24. SABULOUS
(*a*) Splotched (*b*) Itching
(*c*) Sandy (*d*) Furry
25. MERE **(Clerks' Grade, 1991)**
(*a*) Some (*b*) Empty
(*c*) Only (*d*) Complete
26. IMMANENT
(*a*) Inherent (*b*) Soon
(*c*) Impending (*d*) Urgent
27. SURFEIT
(*a*) Satiate (*b*) Pass
(*c*) Confiscate (*d*) Drop
28. DESTITUTION **(Section Offiers, 1993)**
(*a*) Beggary (*b*) Poverty
(*c*) Humility (*d*) Moderation
29. MOOT
(*a*) Invisible (*b*) Obsequious
(*c*) Unexpected (*d*) Controversial
30. PREDILECTION
(*a*) Repulsion (*b*) Hastiness
(*c*) Preference (*d*) Hesitation
31. COMPETENCE **(M.B.A. 1989)**
(*a*) Efficiency (*b*) Competition
(*c*) Ability (*d*) Compensation
32. ADJUNCT
(*a*) Adaptation (*b*) Addition
(*c*) Decree (*d*) Oath
33. WHITTLE
(*a*) Decrease (*b*) Avoid
(*c*) Renounce (*d*) Conceal
34. MORONIC
(*a*) Sharp (*b*) Invective
(*c*) Imbecile (*d*) Abusive

35. SYNTHETIC (C.B.I. 1990)
(*a*) Scientific (*b*) Fake
(*c*) Artificial (*d*) Superficial

36. JUVENILE
(*a*) Childish (*b*) Tedious
(*c*) Humorous (*d*) Pious

37. ERSATZ
(*a*) Inferior (*b*) Imitation
(*c*) Genuine (*d*) Original

38. MAGNANIMOUS (I. Tax, 1994)
(*a*) Loyal (*b*) Generous
(*c*) Kind (*d*) Loving

39. JOVIAL
(*a*) Merry (*b*) Funny
(*c*) Smart (*d*) Triumphant

40. EXCERPT
(*a*) Extract (*b*) Invitation
(*c*) Debate (*d*) Speech

41. ERADICATE
(*a*) Complicate (*b*) Indicate
(*c*) Dedicate (*d*) Eliminate

(Stenographers' Exam, 1991)

42. OSTENTATIOUS
(*a*) Noisy (*b*) Talkative
(*c*) Showy (*d*) Wealthy

43. ENERVATE
(*a*) Energise (*b*) Lure
(*c*) Weaken (*d*) Calm

44. CONTRITE
(*a*) Repentant (*b*) Shy
(*c*) Uncertain (*d*) Serious

45. TIMID (Railways, 1988)
(*a*) Cowardly (*b*) Plucky
(*c*) Veteran (*d*) Fearful

46. TUTELAGE
(*a*) Perfection (*b*) Dejection
(*c*) Rejection (*d*) Protection

47. BOTCH
(*a*) Borrow (*b*) Promote
(*c*) Collect (*d*) Bungle

48. CONVIVIAL
(*a*) Jovial (*b*) Solitary
(*c*) Aloof (*d*) Crowded

49. ACUITY
(*a*) Sullen (*b*) Dullness
(*c*) Sordid (*d*) Sharpness

50. CELERITY
(*a*) Insincerity (*b*) Quickness
(*c*) Illusion (*d*) Innocence

ANSWERS

1. (*c*)	**2.** (*d*)	**3.** (*b*)	**4.** (*d*)	**5.** (*b*)	**6.** (*c*)	**7.** (*c*)	**8.** (*c*)	**9.** (*d*)	**10.** (*c*)
11. (*c*)	**12.** (*c*)	**13.** (*b*)	**14.** (*a*)	**15.** (*a*)	**16.** (*c*)	**17.** (*b*)	**18.** (*a*)	**19.** (*c*)	**20.** (*a*)
21. (*b*)	**22.** (*d*)	**23.** (*d*)	**24.** (*c*)	**25.** (*c*)	**26.** (*a*)	**27.** (*a*)	**28.** (*b*)	**29.** (*d*)	**30.** (*c*)
31. (*c*)	**32.** (*b*)	**33.** (*a*)	**34.** (*c*)	**35.** (*c*)	**36.** (*a*)	**37.** (*b*)	**38.** (*b*)	**39.** (*a*)	**40.** (*a*)
41. (*d*)	**42.** (*c*)	**43.** (*c*)	**44.** (*a*)	**45.** (*a*)	**46.** (*d*)	**47.** (*d*)	**48.** (*a*)	**49.** (*d*)	**50.** (*b*)

PRACTICE SET 12

Directions : ***In each of the following questions, out of the given alternatives, choose the one which is nearest in meaning to the given word.***

1. ERROR (Stenographers' Exam, 1994)
(*a*) Blunder (*b*) Misadventure
(*c*) Ambiguity (*d*) Misgiving

2. EBULLIENT
(*a*) Gilted (*b*) Enthusiastic
(*c*) Luscious (*d*) Arrogant

3. ACRID
(*a*) Dirty (*b*) Pungent
(*c*) Unripe (*d*) Bitter

4. POW-WOW
(*a*) Gossip (*b*) Meeting
(*c*) Elite (*d*) Discussion

5. BADGER
(*a*) Attempt (*b*) Convince
(*c*) Pester (*d*) Persuade

6. CAUTIOUSLY (S.S.C. 1993)
(*a*) Genuinely (*b*) Carefully
(*c*) Secretly (*d*) Somewhat

7. TRUCULENT
(*a*) Servile (*b*) Trashy
(*c*) Ferocious (*d*) Juicy

8. REQUITE
(*a*) Spare (*b*) Repay
(*c*) Favour (*d*) Punish

9. SUPERNAL
(*a*) Haughty (*b*) Official
(*c*) Heavenly (*d*) Needless

10. PLUSH (I. Tax & Central Excise, 1989)
(*a*) Comforting (*b*) Tasty
(*c*) Luxurious (*d*) Delicious

11. SPORADIC
(*a*) Genuine (*b*) Accidental
(*c*) Irregular (*d*) Instinctive

12. LARGESSE
(*a*) Splendid (*b*) Liberal
(*c*) Bribe (*d*) Extravagant

13. DECIMATE **(Translators' Exam, 1994)**
(*a*) Disseminate (*b*) Dissipate
(*c*) Disfigure (*d*) Destroy

14. BELLIGERENT
(*a*) Reasonable (*b*) Aggressive
(*c*) Generous (*d*) Pacifist

15. BATTLE
(*a*) Check (*b*) Quibble
(*c*) Quarrel (*d*) Fight

16. REBATE **(M.B.A. 1989)**
(*a*) Commission (*b*) Interest
(*c*) Discount (*d*) Gift

17. VERNAL
(*a*) Dirty (*b*) Luxuriant
(*c*) Spring like (*d*) Prone

18. ESCULENT
(*a*) Edible (*b*) Hungry
(*c*) Thick (*d*) Lovable

19. MOROSE
(*a*) Gloomy (*b*) Stupid
(*c*) Serious (*d*) Stern

20. WHOLESOME
(*a*) Special (*b*) Complete
(*c*) Healthy (*d*) Handsome

21. ENNUI
(*a*) Weariness (*b*) Conviction
(*c*) Comedy (*d*) Expulsion

22. DESULTORY
(*a*) Obedient (*b*) Punctual
(*c*) Regular (*d*) Aimless

23. STYMIE
(*a*) Express (*b*) Hinder
(*c*) Flourish (*d*) Stagnate

24. ETHNIC
(*a*) Racial (*b*) Legal
(*c*) Moral (*d*) Foreign

25. AUDACIOUS **(Railways, 1993)**
(*a*) Obvious (*b*) Daring
(*c*) Manifest (*d*) Venture

26. INFERNAL
(*a*) Exacting (*b*) Hateful
(*c*) Devilish (*d*) Damaging

27. MAGNANIMOUS
(*a*) Splendid (*b*) Marvellous
(*c*) Gentle (*d*) Benevolent

28. MYOPIC **(G.I.C.A.A.O. 1990)**
(*a*) Blind (*b*) Short-sighted
(*c*) Astigmatic (*d*) Cross-eyed

29. MOTLEY
(*a*) Variegated (*b*) Active
(*c*) Disguised (*d*) Somber

30. WALLOW
(*a*) Awaken (*b*) Urge
(*c*) Dislike (*d*) Delight

31. CONJURE
(*a*) Damage (*b*) Destroy
(*c*) Revoke (*d*) Invoke

32. ACOLYTE
(*a*) Helper (*b*) Assistant
(*c*) Inferior (*d*) Servant

33. UNTIE **(Stenographers' Exam, 1995)**
(*a*) Unfold (*b*) Unchain
(*c*) Undo (*d*) Unhinge

34. WRY
(*a*) Twisted (*b*) Undeserved
(*c*) Sad (*d*) Smiling

35. ESCHEW
(*a*) Adapt (*b*) Oppress
(*c*) Avoid (*d*) Encourage

36. KNUCKLE
(*a*) Resign (*b*) Surrender
(*c*) Face (*d*) Struggle

37. RIVAL **(Clerks' Grade, 1995)**
(*a*) Enemy (*b*) Claimant
(*c*) Competitor (*d*) Partner

38. PROWESS
(*a*) Bravery (*b*) Eagerness
(*c*) Keenness (*d*) Understanding

39. VULPINE
(*a*) Crafty (*b*) Wolfish
(*c*) Hoggish (*d*) Ravenous

40. IMBROGLIO
(*a*) Callous (*b*) Coercion
(*c*) Confusion (*d*) Compulsion

41. IMPASSE **(Central Excise, 1994)**
(*a*) Stalemate (*b*) Impossibility
(*c*) Difficulty (*d*) Confrontation

42. FIASCO
(*a*) Hope (*b*) Failure
(*c*) Success (*d*) Strength

43. PERKY
(*a*) Pretty (*b*) Clear
(*c*) Comic (*d*) Buoyant

44. RANT **(M.B.A. 1994)**
(*a*) Treat with screen (*b*) Preach noisily
(*c*) Formalize (*d*) Praise inordinately

45. COZEN
(*a*) Ridicule (*b*) Cheat
(*c*) Convince (*d*) Flatter

46. SCHISM
(*a*) Split (*b*) Conspiracy
(*c*) Revolt (*d*) Ritualism

47. DISINTER
(*a*) Bury (*b*) Befool
(*c*) Unearth (*d*) Disguise

48. TERSE **(Railways, 1988)**
(*a*) Local (*b*) Shrewd
(*c*) Holy (*d*) Compact

49. BRACE
(*a*) Waste (*b*) Support
(*c*) Define (*d*) Confine

50. BAFFLE
(*a*) Insult (*b*) Frustrate
(*c*) Defame (*d*) Antagonise

ANSWERS

(*a*)	**2.** (*b*)	**3.** (*d*)	**4.** (*b*)	**5.** (*c*)	**6.** (*b*)	**7.** (*c*)	**8.** (*b*)	**9.** (*c*)	**10.** (*c*)
11. (*c*)	**12.** (*b*)	**13.** (*d*)	**14.** (*b*)	**15.** (*d*)	**16.** (*c*)	**17.** (*c*)	**18.** (*a*)	**19.** (*a*)	**20.** (*c*)
21. (*a*)	**22.** (*d*)	**23.** (*b*)	**24.** (*a*)	**25.** (*b*)	**26.** (*c*)	**27.** (*d*)	**28.** (*b*)	**29.** (*a*)	**30.** (*d*)
31. (*d*)	**32.** (*b*)	**33.** (*c*)	**34.** (*a*)	**35.** (*c*)	**36.** (*b*)	**37.** (*c*)	**38.** (*a*)	**39.** (*a*)	**40.** (*c*)
41. (*a*)	**42.** (*b*)	**43.** (*d*)	**44.** (*b*)	**45.** (*b*)	**46.** (*a*)	**47.** (*c*)	**48.** (*d*)	**49.** (*b*)	**50.** (*b*)

PRACTICE SET 13

Directions : ***In each of the following questions, out of the given alternatives, choose the one which best expresses the meaning of the given word.***

1. HALLOWED **(Assistant Grade, 1991)**
(*a*) Decayed (*b*) Sacred
(*c*) Historical (*d*) Ancient

2. CREDENCE
(*a*) Preference (*b*) Credit
(*c*) Assurance (*d*) Belief

3. VILIFY
(*a*) Defame (*b*) Perform
(*c*) Commend (*d*) Communicate

4. EMPIRICAL
(*a*) Spiritual (*b*) Royal
(*c*) Practical (*d*) Theoretical

5. MOLLIFY **(C.B.I. 1990)**
(*a*) Flatter (*b*) Appease
(*c*) Sympathise (*d*) Avenge

6. PASTIME
(*a*) Tardiness (*b*) Recreation
(*c*) Memory (*d*) Antiquity

7. CHARTER
(*a*) Announcement (*b*) Article
(*c*) Declaration (*d*) Document

8. THWARTED
(*a*) Accepted (*b*) Opposed
(*c*) Diverted (*d*) Advocated

9. VOCATION **(Clerks' Grade, 1995)**
(*a*) Hobby (*b*) Occupation
(*c*) Post (*d*) Employment

10. PRATTLE
(*a*) Construct (*b*) Loiter
(*c*) Chatter (*d*) Meditate

11. FLOUNDER
(*a*) Run (*b*) Fluctuate
(*c*) Jump (*d*) Stumble

12. COY **(Stenographers' Exam, 1995)**
(*a*) Beautiful (*b*) Sweet
(*c*) Talented (*d*) Shy

13. ERUDITE
(*a*) Strong (*b*) Precious
(*c*) Learned (*d*) Courteous

14. GRIPE
(*a*) Complaint (*b*) Journey
(*c*) Resentment (*d*) Satisfaction

15. EXTRANEOUS **(Translators' Exam, 1994)**
(*a*) Shallow (*b*) Superficial
(*c*) Irrelevant (*d*) Nonsensical

16. PROCURE
(*a*) Obtain (*b*) Endanger
(*c*) Incur (*d*) Rescue

17. MAVERICK
(*a*) Reformer (*b*) Unorthodox
(*c*) Novice (*d*) Conservative

18. COMMENSURATE **(Railways, 1996)**
(*a*) Appropriate (*b*) Beginning
(*c*) Proportionate (*d*) Measurable

19. ADAGE
(*a*) Mystery (*b*) Request
(*c*) Order (*d*) Proverb

20. DAUNT
(*a*) Detain (*b*) Annoy
(*c*) Abuse (*d*) Intimidate

21. IMPASSIONED
(*a*) Ardent (*b*) Impressive
(*c*) Sympathetic (*d*) Irresponsible
(Investigators' Exam, 1988)

22. IMMACULATE
(*a*) Spotless (*b*) Dirty
(*c*) Shining (*d*) Clean

23. LUGUBRIOUS
(*a*) Consolatory (*b*) Deceitful
(*c*) Sleek (*d*) Mournful

24. DISPARAGE
(*a*) Belittle (*b*) Compare
(*c*) Discourage (*d*) Separate

25. HEDIOUS
(*a*) Secret (*b*) Loathsome

(*c*) Disliked (*d*) Hidden

26. PROLIFERATE
(*a*) Assist (*b*) Proclaim
(*c*) Generate (*d*) Support

27. IMPEDE
(*a*) Hinder (*b*) Reverse
(*c*) Impose (*d*) Expedite

28. MUNDANE
(*a*) Global (*b*) Worldly
(*c*) Luxurious (*d*) Spiritual

29. EXTRICATE **(U.D.C. 1995)**
(*a*) Pull (*b*) Free
(*c*) Tie (*d*) Complicate

30. GRAPHIC
(*a*) Vague (*b*) Distinct
(*c*) Vivid (*d*) Conspicuous

31. DEPRECATE
(*a*) Accept (*b*) Attack
(*c*) Praise (*d*) Condemn

32. INTERROGATE **(M.B.A. 1989)**
(*a*) To interfere (*b*) To question
(*c*) To stop (*d*) To enter the gate

33. WRANGLE
(*a*) Competition (*b*) Race
(*c*) Dispute (*d*) Wrestling

34. QUIP
(*a*) Comment (*b*) Injury
(*c*) Blow (*d*) Joke

35. KNAVE
(*a*) Rogue (*b*) Ignorant
(*c*) Innocent (*d*) Simple

36. JEOPARDY **(Stenographers' Exam, 1991)**
(*a*) Enmity (*b*) Danger
(*c*) Adventure (*d*) Magic

37. REPUGNANCE
(*a*) Approval (*b*) Affection
(*c*) Like (*d*) Disinclination

38. PETTIFOGGING
(*a*) Lenient (*b*) Unimportant
(*c*) Stable (*d*) Strong

39. TROTH **(Railways, 1988)**
(*a*) Ego (*b*) Faithful
(*c*) Colourist (*d*) Disloyal

40. PERSPICACITY
(*a*) Bad (*b*) Shrewd
(*c*) Hazy (*d*) Clear

41. ENTHRAL
(*a*) Persuade (*b*) Glorify
(*c*) Annoy (*d*) Charm

42. BEWAIL
(*a*) Envy (*b*) Accuse
(*c*) Tear apart (*d*) Lament

43. EPISTLE
(*a*) Practice (*b*) Sermon
(*c*) Note (*d*) Letter

44. ABSOLVE
(*a*) Exonerate (*b*) Consume
(*c*) Maltreat (*d*) Engage

45. KEN **(M.B.A. 1994)**
(*a*) Knowledge (*b*) Trial
(*c*) Witness (*d*) Ignorance

46. CONSTRUE
(*a*) Interpret (*b*) Scatter
(*c*) Confuse (*d*) Unite

47. KIBITZ
(*a*) Evade (*b*) Befriend
(*c*) Avoid (*d*) Interfere

48. INORDINATE
(*a*) Extraordinary (*b*) Inanimate
(*c*) Subordinate (*d*) Excessive
(Transmission Executives, 1994)

49. BALMY
(*a*) Fruitful (*b*) Tempestuous
(*c*) Soothing (*d*) Modest

50. SIMULATE
(*a*) Presume (*b*) Warn
(*c*) Imitate (*d*) Take

ANSWERS

1. (*b*) **2.** (*b*) **3.** (*a*) **4.** (*c*) **5.** (*b*) **6.** (*b*) **7.** (*d*) **8.** (*b*) **9.** (*b*) **10.** (*c*)
11. (*d*) **12.** (*d*) **13.** (*c*) **14.** (*a*) **15.** (*c*) **16.** (*a*) **17.** (*b*) **18.** (*c*) **19.** (*d*) **20.** (*d*)
21. (*a*) **22.** (*a*) **23.** (*d*) **24.** (*a*) **25.** (*b*) **26.** (*c*) **27.** (*a*) **28.** (*b*) **29.** (*b*) **30.** (*c*)
31. (*d*) **32.** (*b*) **33.** (*c*) **34.** (*d*) **35.** (*a*) **36.** (*b*) **37.** (*d*) **38.** (*b*) **39.** (*b*) **40.** (*b*)
41. (*d*) **42.** (*d*) **43.** (*d*) **44.** (*a*) **45.** (*a*) **46.** (*a*) **47.** (*d*) **48.** (*d*) **49.** (*c*) **50.** (*c*)

PRACTICE SET 14

Directions : ***In each of the following questions, out of the given alternatives, choose the one which best expresses the meaning of the given word.***

1. INSOLENT **(Stenographers' Exam, 1993)**
(*a*) Nervous (*b*) Rude
(*c*) Proud (*d*) Assertive

2. INSPIRE
(*a*) Compel (*b*) Persuade
(*c*) Infuse (*d*) Encourage

3. EXTRAVAGANT
(*a*) Proud (*b*) Expensive
(*c*) Wasteful (*d*) Reckless

4. INEBRIATE **(Asstt. Grade, 1996)**
(*a*) Drunken (*b*) Unsteady
(*c*) Stupefied (*d*) Dreamy

5. PROSCRIBE
(*a*) Recommend (*b*) Allow
(*c*) Advance (*d*) Banish

6. EGREGIOUS
(*a*) Progressive (*b*) Superficial
(*c*) Exceptional (*d*) Cowardly

7. ABBREVIATE
(*a*) Shorten (*b*) Enlarge
(*c*) Decrease (*d*) Change

8. ABOMINABLE
(*a*) Weird (*b*) Awful
(*c*) Odd (*d*) Fine

9. PLACID **(Central Excise, 1989)**
(*a*) Clear (*b*) Calm
(*c*) Enjoyable (*d*) Dull

10. PREDICT
(*a*) Determine (*b*) Analyse
(*c*) Foretell (*d*) Describe

11. MULL
(*a*) Recommend (*b*) Think
(*c*) Punish (*d*) Provoke

12. WHIRL
(*a*) Reap (*b*) Turn
(*c*) Agitate (*d*) Weep

13. VINDICTIVE **(C.B.I. 1991)**
(*a*) Strategic (*b*) Triumphant
(*c*) Revengeful (*d*) Demonstrative

14. ALACRITY
(*a*) Suspicion (*b*) Unwillingly
(*c*) Unhesitatingly (*d*) Eagerly

15. PROEM
(*a*) Proclamation (*b*) Narrative
(*c*) Conclusion (*d*) Preface

16. FEROCIOUS
(*a*) Predatory (*b*) Fertile
(*c*) Overpowering (*d*) Fierce

17. MEDIOCRE **(Translators' Exam, 1994)**
(*a*) Mild (*b*) Indifferent
(*c*) Stupid (*d*) Average

18. SURFEIT
(*a*) Satiate (*b*) Pass
(*c*) Confiscate (*d*) Delegate

19. DOGMA
(*a*) Possibility (*b*) Feeling
(*c*) Tenet (*d*) Doubt

20. ZANY **(M.B.A. 1994)**
(*a*) Magician (*b*) Pet
(*c*) Thief (*d*) Clown

21. LANGUISH
(*a*) Condemn (*b*) Condone
(*c*) Console (*d*) Decline

22. RAKISH
(*a*) Frivolous (*b*) Immoral
(*c*) Aggressive (*d*) Childish

23. DILIGENT **(Stenographers' Exam, 1991)**
(*a*) Industrious (*b*) Intelligent
(*c*) Modest (*d*) Energetic

24. RICOCHET
(*a*) Spare (*b*) Turn down
(*c*) Ride (*d*) Rebound

25. SCINTILLATING **(C.B.I. 1995)**
(*a*) Warming (*b*) Touching
(*c*) Glittering (*d*) Smouldering

26. MUSTY
(*a*) Stale (*b*) Irritable
(*c*) Hungry (*d*) Ugly

27. REGALE
(*a*) Harass (*b*) Entertain
(*c*) Express (*d*) Suppress

28. LASCIVIOUS
(*a*) Lustful (*b*) Foul
(*c*) Fragrant (*d*) Naughty

29. EMPHASISE **(Asstt. Grade, 1995)**
(*a*) Suggest (*b*) Plead
(*c*) Stress (*d*) Force

30. OBLIGATORY
(*a*) Required (*b*) Stubborn
(*c*) Agreeable (*d*) Useful

31. SLAKE
(*a*) Erase (*b*) Quench
(*c*) Rub (*d*) Sharpen

32. BARGE
(*a*) Interpret (*b*) Shout
(*c*) Restrain (*d*) Enter

33. APPURTENANCE
(*a*) Privilege (*b*) Journey
(*c*) Concept (*d*) Necessity

34. SYCOPHANT **(U.D.C. 1994)**
(*a*) Suppliant (*b*) Follower
(*c*) Flatterer (*d*) Admirer

35. DODGE
(*a*) Avoid (*b*) Break up
(*c*) Drag (*d*) Push forward

36. RECEPTIVE
(*a*) Pretentious (*b*) Observant
(*c*) Gracious (*d*) Generous

37. WELSH
(*a*) Perspire (*b*) Inspire
(*c*) Encourage (*d*) Default

38. VINDICATE **(Central Excise, 1994)**
(*a*) Judge (*b*) Justify
(*c*) Argue (*d*) Explain

39. OVERTURES
(*a*) Observations (*b*) Offers
(*c*) Agreements (*d*) Promises

40. CRASS
(*a*) Wicked (*b*) Zig zag
(*c*) Spiritless (*d*) Insensitive

41. BESIEGED **(Stenographers' Exam, 1995)**
(*a*) Encircled (*b*) Skirted
(*c*) Troubled (*d*) Destroyed

42. STERNUTATION
(*a*) Sneezing (*b*) Trepidation
(*c*) Reversal (*d*) Hardening

43. JINGOISTIC
(*a*) Victorious (*b*) Compromise
(*c*) Cooperative (*d*) Dashing

44. YOKEL
(*a*) Illiterate (*b*) Simple-minded
(*c*) Canny (*d*) Crafty

45. GERMANE
(*a*) Cruel (*b*) Relevant
(*c*) Obstinate (*d*) Smart
(Transmission Executives, 1994)

46. COUNTERMAND
(*a*) Criticise (*b*) Cancel
(*c*) Devastate (*d*) Intrigue

47. APLOMB
(*a*) Agitation (*b*) Noise
(*c*) Sacrifice (*d*) Self-control

48. ABROGATION
(*a*) Abridgement (*b*) Deprivation
(*c*) Annulation (*d*) Dismissal

49. PLACID
(*a*) Clear (*b*) Calm
(*c*) Enjoyable (*d*) Dull

50. MAGNILOQUENT
(*a*) Amusing (*b*) Boastful
(*c*) Humorous (*d*) Tactful

ANSWERS

1. (*b*)	**2.** (*d*)	**3.** (*c*)	**4.** (*a*)	**5.** (*d*)	**6.** (*c*)	**7.** (*a*)	**8.** (*b*)	**9.** (*b*)	**10.** (*c*)
11. (*b*)	**12.** (*b*)	**13.** (*c*)	**14.** (*d*)	**15.** (*d*)	**16.** (*d*)	**17.** (*d*)	**18.** (*a*)	**19.** (*c*)	**20.** (*c*)
21. (*d*)	**22.** (*b*)	**23.** (*a*)	**24.** (*d*)	**25.** (*c*)	**26.** (*a*)	**27.** (*b*)	**28.** (*a*)	**29.** (*c*)	**30.** (*a*)
31. (*b*)	**32.** (*d*)	**33.** (*a*)	**34.** (*c*)	**35.** (*a*)	**36.** (*b*)	**37.** (*d*)	**38.** (*b*)	**39.** (*b*)	**40.** (*d*)
41. (*a*)	**42.** (*a*)	**43.** (*d*)	**44.** (*b*)	**45.** (*b*)	**46.** (*b*)	**47.** (*d*)	**48.** (*c*)	**49.** (*b*)	**50.** (*b*)

PRACTICE SET 15

Directions : *In each of the following questions, out of the given alternatives, choose the one which best expresses the meaning of the given word.*

1. CATALOGUE
(*a*) Menu (*b*) Record
(*c*) List (*d*) Pamphlet
(Stenographers' Exam, 1994)
2. OVERSTRUNG
(*a*) Concerned (*b*) Active
(*c*) Sensitive (*d*) Energetic
3. GREGARIOUS
(*a*) Sociable (*b*) Turbulent
(*c*) Pugnacious (*d*) Clumsy
4. ACCOST
(*a*) Hesitate (*b*) Speculate
(*c*) Insult (*d*) Address
5. DEFUNCT
(*a*) Active (*b*) Clever
(*c*) Alive (*d*) Extinct
6. SAGACITY **(Translators' Exam, 1994)**
(*a*) Morality (*b*) Wisdom
(*c*) Sanity (*d*) Uprightness
7. ANGST
(*a*) Anxiety (*b*) Pride
(*c*) Modesty (*d*) Simplicity
8. KULAK
(*a*) Fortress (*b*) Priest
(*c*) Insane (*d*) Farmer
9. SALACITY **(M.B.A. 1994)**
(*a*) Recession (*b*) Indecency
(*c*) Depression (*d*) Bliss
10. VULGAR
(*a*) Enthusiastic (*b*) Wild
(*c*) Coarse (*d*) Noisy
11. UMBRAGE
(*a*) Sensitive (*b*) Shabbiness
(*c*) Premature (*d*) Resentment
12. EMULATE **(Stenographers' Exam, 1991)**
(*a*) Trying to do as well (*b*) Enable
(*c*) Likely to be late (*d*) Inspite to win
13. AMNESTY
(*a*) Revolt (*b*) Privilege
(*c*) Farewell (*d*) Pardon
14. HIATUS
(*a*) Gap (*b*) Contempt
(*c*) Tight (*d*) Narrow
15. KITTY
(*a*) Romantic (*b*) Cheap
(*c*) Pooled fund (*d*) Drowsy
16. FRAGMENT **(S.B.I.P.O. 1989)**
(*a*) Dissection (*b*) Cut
(*c*) Crumble (*d*) Scrap
17. CADGE
(*a*) Beg (*b*) Hide
(*c*) Bicker (*d*) Imprison
18. EXORCISE
(*a*) Expel (*b*) Expose
(*c*) Explain (*d*) Mock
19. AMBITION **(Railways, 1992)**
(*a*) Plan (*b*) Proclamation
(*c*) Desire (*d*) Decision
20. TAINT
(*a*) Soil (*b*) Stain
(*c*) Dirty (*d*) Corrupt
21. PROMISCUOUS
(*a*) Casual (*b*) Selective
(*c*) Discriminate (*d*) Pure
22. KEMP
(*a*) Professional (*b*) Parasite
(*c*) Tent (*d*) Champion
23. UNCANNY
(*a*) Unmistaken (*b*) Strange
(*c*) Fearful (*d*) Internal
24. UNDULATE
(*a*) Retard (*b*) Decrease
(*c*) Wave (*d*) Flood
25. VORACIOUS **(Section Officers, 1993)**
(*a*) Quick (*b*) Angry
(*c*) Hungry (*d*) Wild
26. PESTER
(*a*) Console (*b*) Disturb
(*c*) Gratify (*d*) Torture
27. REDUNDANT
(*a*) Rude (*b*) Brutish
(*c*) Superfluous (*d*) Coarse
28. INEVITABLE **(C.B.I. 1994)**
(*a*) Unavoidable (*b*) Probable
(*c*) Expected (*d*) Fixed
29. VENDETTA
(*a*) Feud (*b*) Friendship
(*c*) Mortal (*d*) Threat
30. SMEAR
(*a*) Encourage (*b*) Quarrel
(*c*) Avoid (*d*) Mark
31. CALUMNIATE
(*a*) Approve (*b*) Slander
(*c*) Warn (*d*) Delay
32. PARVENU
(*a*) Pretender (*b*) Privileged
(*c*) Royal (*d*) Intelligent
33. GRAND **(Clerks' Grade, 1993)**
(*a*) Noble (*b*) Aristocratic
(*c*) Great (*d*) Splendid
34. ATTRITION
(*a*) Friction (*b*) Decline
(*c*) Suffering (*d*) Attraction
35. MURKY
(*a*) Ugly (*b*) Dishonest

(c) Dull (d) Lazy

36. LAPIDARY
(a) High-sounding (b) Abusive
(c) Dignified (d) Harmful
(Stenographers' Exam, 1995)

37. MOVING
(a) Turning (b) Shifting
(c) Toying (d) Taking

38. MORDANT
(a) Mild (b) Sarcastic
(c) Festering (d) Depressed

39. FOMENT
(a) Incite (b) Restrict
(c) Rectify (d) Pacify

40. DAUB
(a) Publish (b) Advertise
(c) Paint (d) Propagate

41. CONSOLIDATE
(a) Contrive (b) Connive
(c) Unite (d) Conspire
(Transmission Executives, 1994)

42. BAWDY
(a) Crude (b) Vulgar
(c) Proud (d) Arrogant

43. JEER
(a) Inspire (b) Enjoy
(c) Encourage (d) Ridicule

44. COGNOSCENTE **(M.B.A. 1995)**
(a) Speculator (b) Teacher
(c) Critic (d) Preacher

45. BUFF
(a) Polish (b) Insult
(c) Injure (d) Sweep

46. FANCIFUL
(a) Unreal (b) Faithful
(c) Glorious (d) Eccentric

47. AVARICIOUS **(Bank P.O. 1989)**
(a) Abundant (b) Envious
(c) Greedy (d) Unwilling

48. BIZARRE
(a) Happy (b) Grotesque
(c) Refined (d) Boisterous

49. DEMURE
(a) Intentional (b) Retiring
(c) Unreserved (d) Blunt

50. KOWTOW
(a) Respect (b) Illuminate
(c) Practise (d) Blockhead

ANSWERS

1. (c)	**2.** (c)	**3.** (a)	**4.** (d)	**5.** (d)	**6.** (b)	**7.** (a)	**8.** (d)	**9.** (b)	**10.** (c)
11. (d)	**12.** (a)	**13.** (d)	**14.** (a)	**15.** (c)	**16.** (d)	**17.** (a)	**18.** (a)	**19.** (c)	**20.** (d)
21. (a)	**22.** (d)	**23.** (b)	**24.** (c)	**25.** (c)	**26.** (b)	**27.** (c)	**28.** (a)	**29.** (a)	**30.** (d)
31. (b)	**32.** (a)	**33.** (d)	**34.** (a)	**35.** (a)	**36.** (c)	**37.** (b)	**38.** (b)	**39.** (a)	**40.** (c)
41. (c)	**42.** (b)	**43.** (d)	**44.** (c)	**45.** (a)	**46.** (a)	**47.** (c)	**48.** (b)	**49.** (b)	**50.** (a)

TYPE 2 : CHOOSING THE SYNONYM OF A WORD AS USED IN A SENTENCE

In this type of questions, you are given a sentence in which a word has been italicised. Some alternatives are suggested below it. The candidate is required to choose that word which can substitute the italicised word in the sentence without changing the meaning of the sentence.

Example : *Choose the word which best expresses the meaning of the word printed in italics bold in the sentence.*

He gave an ***expeditious*** reply. **(N.D.A. 1996)**

(a) prompt (b) slow (c) elaborate (d) exact

Solution : In the above example, the word 'prompt' is nearest in meaning to 'expeditious'. Hence, the answer is (a).

PRACTICE SET 16

Directions : *In each of the following questions, out of the given alternatives, choose the one which best expresses the meaning of the italicised bold part of the sentence.*

1. Deepak has a ***penchant*** for fine poetry.
(a) desire (b) bias
(c) liking (d) training

2. The defendant was grateful for the judge's ***clemency***. **(N.D.A. 1994)**
(a) patience (b) mercy

(*c*) relaxed attitude (*d*) politeness

3. He ***hardly*** works.
(*a*) strenuously (*b*) scarcely
(*c*) mostly (*d*) arduously

4. This machine was ***fabricated*** in our own workshop.
(*a*) operated (*b*) constructed
(*c*) installed (*d*) designed

5. The number of ***aboriginal*** inhabitants in Australia is considerable. **(C.D.S. 1994)**
(*a*) primitive (*b*) ancient
(*c*) unoriginal (*d*) irrational

6. The quiz game ***comprises*** three rounds.
(*a*) involves (*b*) incorporates
(*c*) retains (*d*) consists of

7. Harish ***ran*** the marathon race in less than two hours.
(*a*) succeeded (*b*) rushed
(*c*) completed (*d*) scored

8. Since he promised to do so, I ***presume*** he will come.
(*a*) think (*b*) guess
(*c*) suppose (*d*) believe

9. The inspector was a ***vigilant*** young man. **(Railways, 1994)**
(*a*) smart (*b*) watchful
(*c*) ambitious (*d*) intelligent

10. The American policy did much to ***escalate*** the conflict.
(*a*) to spread in a wider area
(*b*) to scale up
(*b*) to reduce in intensity
(*d*) to put an end to

11. Ashish did not ***admit*** his mistake in the beginning.
(*a*) commit (*b*) apologize
(*c*) accept (*d*) realise

12. Man has to ***encounter*** many hardships in life. **(I.E.S. 1993)**
(*a*) solve (*b*) face
(*c*) bear (*d*) overcome

13. His wife ***enjoined*** him to change his ways.
(*a*) asked (*b*) pleaded
(*c*) urged (*d*) threatened

14. He would have been successful, but for his lack of ***temerity***.
(*a*) audacity (*b*) sincerity
(*c*) confidence (*d*) strength

15. That was the time when there was a ***hunger*** for foreign knowledge and foreign thought.
(*a*) wish (*b*) appetite
(*c*) desire (*d*) greed

16. I could achieve success through ***conscious efforts.*** **(Bank P.O. 1992)**
(*a*) efforts done after gaining consciousness
(*b*) efforts made with critical awareness
(*c*) efforts done without any desire
(*d*) tremendous efforts

17. He is quite ***meticulous*** in his dealings with others.
(*a*) reserved (*b*) haughty
(*c*) indifferent (*d*) very careful

18. Sanjay is going to ***foot*** the bill for the repairs.
(*a*) own (*b*) pay
(*c*) bear (*d*) stand

19. He used to ***regale*** us with anecdotes.
(*a*) bore (*b*) flatter
(*c*) entertain (*d*) tire **(C.D.S. 1992)**

20. Different races follow different ***modes*** of living.
(*a*) ways (*b*) standards
(*c*) customs (*d*) attitudes

21. The operator was commended for his ***dexterity.***
(*a*) cooperation (*b*) courtesy
(*c*) punctuality (*d*) skill

22. Millionaires become ***eccentric*** in their old age. **(N.D.A. 1993)**
(*a*) irritable (*b*) peculiar
(*c*) dull (*d*) miserly

23. She would take a deep sigh and ***lapse*** into silence.
(*a*) pass (*b*) revert
(*c*) turn (*d*) get

24. His ***judicious*** handling of the matter saved the situation from going out of control. **(N.D.A. 1996)**
(*a*) nervous (*b*) helpful
(*c*) sensible (*d*) cautious

25. The prisoners of war were subjected to bestial ***atrocities.***
(*a*) hardships (*b*) punishments
(*c*) cruelties (*d*) jobs

26. We didn't believe in his statement, but ***subsequent*** events proved that he was right. **(Bank P.O. 1993)**
(*a*) later (*b*) earlier (*c*) many
(*d*) few (*e*) conclusive

27. The ***lurid*** details of the murder in broad day light sent chilling sensations down the spine of everybody.
(*a*) realistic (*b*) vivid
(*c*) bleak (*d*) ghastly

28. The sight moved him to pity and ***compunction***.
(*a*) confusion (*b*) wonder
(*c*) regret (*d*) anger

29. Few teachers have been spared the problem of an ***obstreperous*** pupil in the class. **(I.E.S. 1994)**
(*a*) awkward (*b*) lazy
(*c*) unruly (*d*) sullen

30. Radhey Shyam does ***unpaid*** work for the charity school.
(*a*) honourable (*b*) honorary
(*c*) honest (*d*) honorific

31. The host looked quite ***jaded*** by the time the party was over.
(*a*) miserable (*b*) cheerful
(*c*) inspiring (*d*) exhausted

32. Many people buy charms and ***talismans*** because they think they will bring them luck.
(*a*) amulets (*b*) tokens
(*c*) lucky cards (*d*) stones

33. How beautiful ! This is really something to ***ponder*** over. **(Clerk's Grade, 1992)**
(*a*) sing (*b*) dance
(*c*) think (*d*) wonder

34. Too many drugs are apt to cause ***distress.***
(*a*) misery (*b*) depression
(*c*) suffering (*d*) melancholy

35. Drinking is a ***vice*** which ultimately ruins a person.
(*a*) habit (*b*) crime
(*c*) sin (*d*) evil

36. Ritu asked Rashmi not to ***meddle*** in her affairs. **(Railways, 1995)**
(*a*) intercede (*b*) impose
(*c*) cross (*d*) interfere

37. His speech was full of ***affectation.***
(*a*) boasting (*b*) pretence
(*c*) pedantry (*d*) euphemism

38. Cross-examination could not ***elicit*** any reason for his being absent.
(*a*) prove (*b*) find fault with
(*c*) produce (*d*) draw out

39. Many people feel ***queasy*** while travelling on a bus on hilly roads.
(*a*) uneasy (*b*) mobile
(*c*) drowsy (*d*) dynamic

40. I wrote to him as ***lately*** as last week.
(*a*) late (*b*) recently
(*c*) early (*d*) immediately
(C.D.S. 1993)

41. He listened to my request with ***indifference.***
(*a*) caution (*b*) displeasure
(*c*) concern (*d*) disinterest

42. The patient began to ***rave*** incoherently in a fit of high fever.
(*a*) talk wildly (*b*) express anger
(*c*) pray meekly (*d*) deny forcefully

43. His grand parents had grown ***feeble*** and helpless.
(*a*) weak (*b*) incapacitated
(*c*) timid (*d*) humiliated

44. ***Incensed*** by his rude behaviour, the manager suspended the worker.
(*a*) Enthused (*b*) Enraged
(*c*) Inflamed (*d*) Excited
(Hotel Management, 1993)

45. ***Foolhardiness*** is the result of constant strains.
(*a*) Exhaustion (*b*) Obstinacy
(*c*) Sickness (*d*) Foolishness

46. Physical courage ***urges*** a man to risk injury or death.
(*a*) compels (*b*) forces
(*c*) persuades (*d*) forbids

47. Even the loss of her jewels did not disturb the lady's ***equanimity.***
(*a*) temper (*b*) composure
(*c*) affability (*d*) humour
(C.D.S. 1992)

48. Many cities were ***incinerated*** during the war.
(*a*) destroyed (*b*) shaken
(*c*) bombed (*d*) burnt

49. The Japanese have introduced a ***nippy*** little car for joy riders.
(*a*) funny (*b*) cheap
(*c*) quick (*d*) expensive

50. The data ***compiled*** by the organisation was very useful. **(N.D.A. 1991)**
(*a*) analysed (*b*) enclosed
(*c*) collected (*d*) published

ANSWERS

1. (*c*)	**2.** (*b*)	**3.** (*b*)	**4.** (*d*)	**5.** (*a*)	**6.** (*d*)	**7.** (*c*)	**8.** (*c*)	**9.** (*b*)	**10.** (*b*)
11. (*c*)	**12.** (*b*)	**13.** (*c*)	**14.** (*a*)	**15.** (*c*)	**16.** (*b*)	**17.** (*d*)	**18.** (*b*)	**19.** (*c*)	**20.** (*a*)
21. (*d*)	**22.** (*b*)	**23.** (*a*)	**24.** (*c*)	**25.** (*c*)	**26.** (*a*)	**27.** (*d*)	**28.** (*c*)	**29.** (*c*)	**30.** (*b*)
31. (*d*)	**32.** (*a*)	**33.** (*c*)	**34.** (*b*)	**35.** (*d*)	**36.** (*d*)	**37.** (*b*)	**38.** (*d*)	**39.** (*a*)	**40.** (*b*)
41. (*d*)	**42.** (*a*)	**43.** (*a*)	**44.** (*b*)	**45.** (*d*)	**46.** (*c*)	**47.** (*b*)	**48.** (*d*)	**49.** (*c*)	**50.** (*c*)

PRACTICE SET 17

Directions : *In each of the following questions, out of the given alternatives, choose the one which best expresses the meaning of the italicised bold part of the sentence.*

1. ***Sporadic*** rise in his temperature has caused us much worry. **(C.D.S. 1994)**
(*a*) Frequent (*b*) Irksome
(*c*) Irregular (*d*) Scattered

2. Ant is believed to be the most ***industrious*** creature.
(*a*) sensible (*b*) diligent
(*c*) successful (*d*) punctual

3. The tour was cancelled on account of ***incessant*** rain.
(*a*) constant (*b*) heavy
(*c*) intermittent (*d*) unexpected

4. I ***disdain*** those who tell lies.
(*a*) condemn (*b*) scorn
(*c*) hate (*d*) despise

5. The ***benevolence*** of the God of Rain has seen a very successful monsoon this year too. **(M.B.A. 1994)**
(*a*) vision (*b*) morbidity
(*c*) kindness (*d*) ill-will

6. The country's resources should be ***judiciously*** used.
(*a*) sparingly (*b*) reasonably
(*c*) adequately (*d*) immensely

7. Everyone tries to avoid his company because he is in the habit of using too many ***jibes.***
(*a*) jokes (*b*) abuses
(*c*) criticism (*d*) taunts

8. The story is too fantastic to be ***credible.***
(*a*) praiseworthy (*b*) readable
(*c*) believable (*d*) false
(C.D.S. 1995)

9. A government rocked by frequent scandals is an ***effete*** set of people with no credibility.
(*a*) innocent (*b*) stupid
(*c*) excited (*d*) exhausted

10. She does not get her work done punctually and properly because she is always ***dawdling.***
(*a*) confused (*b*) playing
(*c*) loitering (*d*) chit-chatting

11. The little ***coy*** bride was admired by everyone.
(*a*) beautiful (*b*) shy
(*c*) talented (*d*) sweet

12. The small boy was able to give a ***graphic*** description of the thief.
(*a*) vague (*b*) broad (*c*) vivid
(*d*) drawing (*e*) picture **(Bank P.O. 1994)**

13. He was ***dismissed*** from service because they found him dishonest.
(*a*) prevented (*b*) removed
(*c*) retired (*d*) stopped

14. If you ***waver*** at the last minute, you shall face failure.
(*a*) resolve (*b*) decide
(*c*) settle (*d*) hesitate

15. Reading of poetry is not ***congenial*** to his taste. **(N.D.A. 1992)**
(*a*) suited (*b*) beneficial
(*c*) helpful (*d*) preferable

16. Gandhiji always advocated the cause of ***indigenous*** industries.
(*a*) foreign (*b*) big
(*c*) cottage (*d*) native

17. Kamini could not ***recollect*** the incident that had happened in her childhood.
(*a*) remind (*b*) recall
(*c*) memorise (*d*) assemble

18. He was warned at the ***outset*** of his career. **(Railways, 1994)**
(*a*) end (*b*) beginning
(*c*) middle (*d*) entrance

19. The ***bounties*** of nature are being exploited by man.
(*a*) gifts (*b*) products
(*c*) rules (*d*) ecological balances

20. There is no ***efficacious*** remedy to unemployment problem in a country which has no ideological convictions.
(*a*) suitable (*b*) possible
(*c*) effective (*d*) proper

21. A bone got stuck in his ***gullet.***
(*a*) stomach (*b*) molars
(*c*) chest (*d*) throat
(N.D.A. 1993)

22. India is still a ***virgin*** land exploring its tourism potential.
(*a*) undone (*b*) unexplored
(*c*) uncouth (*d*) unexploited

23. The need of the hour is to initiate the ***renaissance*** of moral conscience and halt the rampant corruption, for it could even hasten the end of our civilisation.
(*a*) rise (*b*) introduction
(*c*) revival (*d*) significance

24. I have told him ***many*** times not to do that. **(Bank P.O. 1993)**
(*a*) several (*b*) unlimited (*c*) endless
(*d*) numberless (*e*) infinite

25. Methods of spreading the family planning message have been as ***fecund*** as they have been abortive.
(*a*) fruitful (*b*) failing
(*c*) peculiar (*d*) false

26. After his graduation, he had to pass through a period of ***privation.***
(*a*) hardship (*b*) uncertainty
(*c*) prosperity (*d*) privacy

27. Now the ***fury*** of the demonstrators turned against the machines.
(*a*) asperity (*b*) passion
(*c*) rage (*d*) acrimony
(N.D.A. 1995)

28. His commands were so ***peremptory*** that we felt humiliated.
(*a*) specious (*b*) poignant
(*c*) dictatorial (*d*) rough

29. He would have been his close ***associate*** had he not been disloyal.
(*a*) employee (*b*) competitor
(*c*) colleague (*d*) executive

30. Every body laughed at the ***puerility*** of his statement. **(C.D.S. 1994)**
(*a*) inaccuracy (*b*) childishness
(*c*) insincerity (*d*) falsehood

31. All the streets looked ***just*** the same.
(*a*) decisively (*b*) normally
(*c*) exactly (*d*) simply

32. At the Hardy house there was great ***consternation*** when Aunt Gertrude saw Joe helping Frank up the stairs.
(*a*) surprise (*b*) panic
(*c*) gaity (*d*) anxiety

33. He is a ***candid*** politician. **(N.D.A. 1991)**
(*a*) frank (*b*) faithful
(*c*) fearless (*d*) soft spoken

34. The purpose of his speech was to ***lampoon*** the leading politicians of the day.
(*a*) praise (*b*) expose
(*c*) ridicule (*d*) defame

35. ***Sagacity*** increases with age.
(*a*) Wisdom (*b*) Love
(*c*) Maturity (*d*) Efficiency

36. She has an ***insatiable*** love for music.
(*a*) undesirable (*b*) irreconcilable
(*c*) unchanging (*d*) unsatisfiable
(C.D.S. 1993)

37. I was shocked to see my friend lying at the ***edge*** of the road.
(*a*) side (*b*) bank
(*c*) corner (*d*) border

38. He is very ***discreet*** while deciding such matters.
(*a*) obstinate (*b*) cunning
(*c*) prudent (*d*) trustworthy

39. Science has ***revealed*** the mysteries of nature to man.
(*a*) released (*b*) disclosed
(*c*) opened (*d*) cleared

40. It is a ***scandal*** that the murderer was declared innocent.
(*a*) rumour (*b*) silly notion
(*c*) talk (*d*) disgraceful action
(Hotel Management, 1993)

41. Ever since the death of his mother, my friend is utterly ***forlorn*** and wretched.
(*a*) frustrated (*b*) lonely
(*c*) fearful (*d*) gloomy

42. The ***rancous*** shouts of the audience forced the management to call off the show.
(*a*) unpleasant (*b*) loud
(*c*) harsh (*d*) harmful

43. He was ***admonished*** for the delay.
(*a*) dismissed (*b*) admired
(*c*) censured (*d*) advised
(C.D.S. 1992)

44. What is the ***ultimate*** goal of life?
(*a*) fixed (*b*) final
(*c*) desired (*d*) immediate

45. Everyone who has worked for him ***hammers*** home that point because they feel that it is widely unappreciated.
(*a*) hints (*b*) stresses
(*c*) strikes (*d*) directs

46. We must ***eradicate*** corruption.
(*a*) minimise (*b*) control
(*c*) condemn (*d*) uproot
(Railways, 1995)

47. During his stay in Canada, he had quite a few ***frustrating*** experiences.
(*a*) disappointing (*b*) disenchanting
(*c*) humiliating (*d*) repulsive

48. I tried to persuade him to change his mind, but he remained ***adamant.***
(*a*) foolish (*b*) aggressive
(*c*) stubborn (*d*) defensive

49. The weavers have to do ***monotonous*** work. **(N.D.A. 1995)**
(*a*) repititive (*b*) exhausting
(*c*) irksome (*d*) autonomous

50. There was always an ***imminent*** danger of the falling of that damaged roof.
(*a*) constant (*b*) impending
(*c*) remote (*d*) favourable

ANSWERS

1. (*c*)	**2.** (*b*)	**3.** (*a*)	**4.** (*c*)	**5.** (*c*)	**6.** (*b*)	**7.** (*d*)	**8.** (*c*)	**9.** (*d*)	**10.** (*c*)
11. (*b*)	**12.** (*c*)	**13.** (*b*)	**14.** (*d*)	**15.** (*a*)	**16.** (*d*)	**17.** (*b*)	**18.** (*b*)	**19.** (*a*)	**20.** (*c*)
21. (*d*)	**22.** (*b*)	**23.** (*c*)	**24.** (*a*)	**25.** (*a*)	**26.** (*a*)	**27.** (*c*)	**28.** (*c*)	**29.** (*c*)	**30.** (*b*)
31. (*c*)	**32.** (*a*)	**33.** (*a*)	**34.** (*c*)	**35.** (*a*)	**36.** (*d*)	**37.** (*a*)	**38.** (*c*)	**39.** (*b*)	**40.** (*d*)
41. (*b*)	**42.** (*c*)	**43.** (*c*)	**44.** (*b*)	**45.** (*b*)	**46.** (*d*)	**47.** (*a*)	**48.** (*c*)	**49.** (*a*)	**50.** (*b*)

PRACTICE SET 18

Directions : *In each of the following questions, out of the given alternatives, choose the one which can replace the word printed in bold in the sentence without changing the meaning of the sentence.*

1. She is really a ***fantastic*** girl. **(I.E.S. 1993)**
(*a*) wonderful (*b*) charming
(*c*) beautiful (*d*) intelligent

2. In present day society, money plays the only dominant role in almost all ***transactions.***
(*a*) jobs (*b*) negotiations
(*c*) business (*d*) proceedings

3. The old man was fond of giving ***homilies*** whenever we went to him with a problem.
(*a*) alternatives (*b*) advice
(*c*) suggestions (*d*) sermon

4. He enjoyed the ***salubrious*** climate of the place.
(*a*) cold (*b*) temperate
(*c*) warm (*d*) healthful

5. The soldier displayed ***exceptional*** courage and saved the Major from the enemy's hand. **(Bank P.O. 1994)**
(*a*) new (*b*) strange (*c*) abnormal
(*d*) unusual (*e*) avoidable

6. The house cannot ***accomodate*** more people.
(*a*) hold (*b*) allow
(*c*) hide (*d*) associate

7. If you want the quality of your writings to improve, then avoid ***redundant*** words.
(*a*) unwilling (*b*) mistaken
(*c*) wrong (*d*) repititive

8. Catching snakes can be ***hazardous*** for people untrained in the art. **(C.D.S. 1995)**
(*a*) dangerous (*b*) difficult
(*c*) harmful (*d*) tricky

9. In order to tarnish the public image of his opponent, he has got a ***mendacious*** story planted in the local newspaper.
(*a*) false (*b*) fabricated
(*c*) imaginary (*d*) horrible

10. The sentiments expressed by him in the speech were ***odious.***
(*a*) significant (*b*) hateful
(*c*) admirable (*d*) common

11. A civilised Roman ***banquet*** was a thing of great richness, style and decorum.
(*a*) palace (*b*) feast
(*c*) ornament (*d*) table
(N.D.A. 1995)

12. The troops were ***mobilised*** to take control of the tensed situation.
(*a*) organised into platoons
(*b*) summoned to headquarters
(*c*) prepared for active service
(*d*) collected hurriedly

13. He listened to her mellifluous music under the ***genial*** influence of wine.
(*a*) heavy (*b*) stressing
(*c*) drowsy (*d*) sympathetic

14. His ***lascivious*** habits brought him nothing but bad name. **(C.D.S. 1994)**
(*a*) treacherous (*b*) erotic
(*c*) lustful (*d*) vicious

15. The fishing boat pulled away from the ***wharf*** and chugged smoothly down the bay.
(*a*) harbour (*b*) shore
(*c*) quay (*d*) anchor

16. The people attending the ***carnival*** looked gay and happy.
(*a*) occasion (*b*) fair
(*c*) function (*d*) revelry

17. The ***aberration*** in the Indian economy can be attributed to short-sightedness of its political masters. **(M.B.A. 1994)**
(*a*) deviation (*b*) steadfastness
(*c*) privilege (*d*) procrastination

18. Feeling ***drowsy*** may be a side effect of too many antibiotics.
(*a*) dizzy (*b*) energetic
(*c*) irritable (*d*) sluggish

19. India has too often to ***fulminate*** against Pakistan's role in aiding and abetting acts of militancy on her soil.
(*a*) think (*b*) consider
(*c*) conspire (*d*) protest

20. Everyone was listening to the news of earthquake with mounting ***anxiety.***
(*a*) interest (*b*) eagerness
(*c*) uneasiness (*d*) grief
(*e*) curiosity **(Bank P.O. 1993)**

21. The accident occurred due to his ***lapse.***
(*a*) haste (*b*) error
(*c*) ignorance (*d*) carelessness

22. ***Courtesy*** does not cost one anything.
(*a*) Gentility (*b*) Civility
(*c*) Amiability (*d*) Urbanity

23. It was ***incumbent*** on him to report the matter at once.
(*a*) pointless (*b*) depending
(*c*) pressing (*d*) optional

24. The intruders ***strangled*** the lady to death.
(*a*) thrashed (*b*) forced
(*c*) compressed (*d*) throttled

25. Only my neighbour ***succoured*** me during my illness. **(Central Excise, 1991)**
(*a*) nourished (*b*) treated
(*c*) aided (*d*) attended

26. That case is not ***amenable*** to ordinary rules.
(*a*) applicable (*b*) interpreted
(*c*) contradictory (*d*) dealt with

27. As they whispered, I felt ***awkward*** in their company.
(*a*) inconvenient (*b*) clumsy
(*c*) ashamed (*d*) embarrassed

28. Lost in his own revery, he forgot that ***vicissitudes*** can change the course of man's life.
(*a*) difficulties (*b*) changes of fortune
(*c*) impediments (*d*) good fortunes

29. He tried to ***cajole*** her, but it was in vain.
(*a*) enjoin (*b*) coax
(*c*) rejoice (*d*) inspire
(N.D.A. 1992)

30. Pakistan has been vigorously pursuing a ***clandestine*** nuclear weapons programme.
(*a*) nefarious (*b*) progressive
(*c*) systematic (*d*) secretive

31. He was annoyed at his ***flippant*** remark.
(*a*) discourteous (*b*) bitter
(*c*) humorous (*d*) casual

32. Some people are extremely ***fastidious*** in their choice of dress. **(C.D.S. 1994)**
(*a*) pompous (*b*) fussy
(*c*) discriminating (*d*) careless

33. The magazine was ***embellished*** with amusing articles.
(*a*) filled (*b*) replete
(*c*) adorned (*d*) sprinkled

34. His views on children and their upbringing are indeed ***outlandish.***
(*a*) realistic (*b*) funny
(*c*) strange (*d*) offensive

35. Sumit ***neglected*** to remit the fees in time and therefore had to pay a fine.
(*a*) exempted (*b*) refused (*c*) failed
(*d*) promised (*e*) obstructed
(Bank P.O. 1993)

36. His ***credulous*** nature often landed him in trouble.
(*a*) dreamy (*b*) naughty (*c*) innocent
(*d*) willing to believe easily

37. 'To be or not to be' was the ***dilemma*** of Hamlet.
(*a*) question (*b*) obsession
(*c*) problem (*d*) helplessness
(*e*) confusion

38. You should have watched that ***glint*** in her eyes when speaking of her husband.
(*a*) disgust (*b*) sparkle
(*c*) anger (*d*) sadness

39. War always has a ***baneful*** effect on the people of a nation.
(*a*) unpleasant (*b*) foul
(*c*) pernicious (*d*) harmful
(C.D.S. 1995)

40. People refuse to pay ***obeisance*** to people whom they do not accept as their leaders.
(*a*) attention (*b*) respect
(*c*) obedience (*d*) command

41. His endeavours proved ***fruitful.***
(*a*) justified (*b*) futile
(*c*) efficient (*d*) productive

42. The newly found drug on the epidemic was not at all ***deleterious.***
(*a*) effective (*b*) intoxicating
(*c*) noxious (*d*) successful

43. The boy was ***chided*** for his impertinence.
(*a*) praised (*b*) beaten
(*c*) applauded (*d*) rebuked

44. People of different ***persuasions*** have met on the same platform. **(C.D.S. 1992)**
(*a*) personalities (*b*) tastes
(*c*) qualifications (*d*) convictions

45. The problem is ***tedious*** to tackle.
(*a*) easy (*b*) difficult
(*c*) tiring (*d*) troublesome

46. We were ***touched*** by the honesty of the beggar.
(*a*) impressed (*b*) moved
(*c*) surprised (*d*) horrified

47. The time I spent in the library was the most ***rewarding*** one. **(Railways, 1994)**
(*a*) precious (*b*) serviceable
(*c*) profitable (*d*) paying

48. The food we had to eat was ***incompatible*** to our needs.
(*a*) harmonising (*b*) according
(*c*) corresponding (*d*) unsuitable

49. The kingdom suffered a constant threat from certain ***predatory*** tribes.
(*a*) wild (*b*) violent
(*c*) rebellious (*d*) plundering

50. He decided to ***accost*** a big financier for his new scheme.
(*a*) employ (*b*) consult (*c*) hire
(*d*) deceive (*e*) approach

ANSWERS

1. (*a*)	**2.** (*d*)	**3.** (*d*)	**4.** (*d*)	**5.** (*d*)	**6.** (*a*)	**7.** (*d*)	**8.** (*a*)	**9.** (*a*)	**10.** (*b*)
11. (*b*)	**12.** (*d*)	**13.** (*b*)	**14.** (*c*)	**15.** (*c*)	**16.** (*d*)	**17.** (*a*)	**18.** (*d*)	**19.** (*d*)	**20.** (*c*)
21. (*b*)	**22.** (*b*)	**23.** (*c*)	**24.** (*d*)	**25.** (*c*)	**26.** (*a*)	**27.** (*d*)	**28.** (*b*)	**29.** (*b*)	**30.** (*d*)
31. (*a*)	**32.** (*b*)	**33.** (*c*)	**34.** (*c*)	**35.** (*c*)	**36.** (*d*)	**37.** (*e*)	**38.** (*b*)	**39.** (*c*)	**40.** (*c*)
41. (*d*)	**42.** (*c*)	**43.** (*d*)	**44.** (*d*)	**45.** (*c*)	**46.** (*a*)	**47.** (*c*)	**48.** (*d*)	**49.** (*d*)	**50.** (*e*)

PRACTICE SET 19

Directions : ***In each of the following questions, out of the given alternatives, choose the one which can best replace the italicised word in the sentence without changing the meaning of the sentence.***

1. Many species of animals have become ***extinct*** during the last hundred years.
(*a*) feeble (*b*) aggressive
(*c*) scattered (*d*) non-existent
(C.D.S. 1995)

2. Fifty years after independence there can be no ***alibi*** for not providing basic amenities to every citizen.
(*a*) cause (*b*) plea
(*c*) factor (*d*) reason

3. The community is ***agog*** with speculation about the fate of the money collected.
(*a*) excited (*b*) worried
(*c*) depressed (*d*) annoyed

4. The President of the party ***deprecated*** the move of the Government to introduce electoral reforms in a haste.
(*a*) extricated (*b*) humiliated (*c*) denied
(*d*) protested (*e*) welcomed
(Bank P.O. 1994)

5. He was drawn to the ***vortex*** of politics at a very early age.
(*a*) whirlpool (*b*) field
(*c*) arena (*d*) hell

6. Quite often parents have to cut a sorry figure when their children display ***fractious*** reaction over trifles.
(*a*) pleasing (*b*) absurd (*c*) comic
(*d*) irritable (*e*) disheartening

7. He enjoys ***vicarious*** authority.
(*a*) tenuous (*b*) limited
(*c*) delegated (*d*) wide

8. He has ***propensity*** for getting into debt.
(*a*) characteristic (*b*) quality
(*c*) natural tendency (*c*) aptitude
(Hotel Management, 1993)

9. If you lack in ***magnanimity***, all your wealth and luxury is useless.
(*a*) planning (*b*) purposiveness
(*c*) management (*d*) generosity

10. Seeds need sufficient water and air to ***germinate.***
(*a*) grow (*b*) reproduce
(*c*) breed (*d*) sprout

11. They tolerated him though they disliked his ***craven*** behaviour.
(*a*) silly (*b*) cowardly
(*c*) indecent (*d*) mean

12. For quick promotion, he hit on a plan to ***propitiate*** the Manager.
(*a*) evict (*b*) incite
(*c*) praise (*d*) conciliate
(Bank P.O. 1992)

13. The ***antidote*** to these problems is hard to find. **(C.D.S. 1994)**
(*a*) remedy for (*b*) consequence of
(*c*) cause for (*d*) result of

14. Poets and writers are ***sensuous*** by nature.
(*a*) sensible (*c*) sentimental
(*c*) sensual (*d*) sensitive

15. I am quite ***content*** to stay here.
(*a*) eager (*b*) happy
(*c*) frightened (*d*) determined

16. The petals of the flowers are usually ***conspicuous*** to attract birds for pollination.
(*a*) prominent (*b*) beautifully shaped
(*c*) colourful (*d*) scented

17. The man ***vehemently*** denied all the charges of corruption that were levelled against him. **(Railways, 1995)**
(*a*) devoutly (*b*) hysterically
(*c*) forcefully (*d*) serenely

18. The artists worked with tremendous ***felicity*** in expressive poetic language.
(*a*) zeal (*b*) excitement
(*c*) happiness (*d*) expertise

19. Those who ***man*** government-run shops also have their palm greased.
(*a*) control (*b*) operate
(*c*) administer (*d*) rule

20. The cyclone had blown some of the cars on to ***funny*** places. **(Bank P.O. 1993)**
(*a*) humorous (*b*) cranky (*c*) irregular
(*d*) odd (*e*) unconventional

21. Despite his pompous style and gestures, the audience failed to ***evince*** any interest in his lecture.
(*a*) display (*b*) hide
(*c*) develop (*d*) take

22. I have worked in this organization for five years trying to check the ***erosion*** of ethical values.
(*a*) decay (*b*) corrosion
(*c*) misuse (*d*) expansion

23. When he returned he was accompanied by a ***sprightly*** young girl. **(C.D.S. 1993)**
(*a*) sportive (*b*) intelligent
(*c*) lively (*d*) beautiful

24. The story which Gaurav ***narrated*** was very exciting.
(*a*) disclosed (*b*) told
(*c*) revealed (*d*) explained

25. It was ***presumptuous*** of him to make a remark in the assembly.
(*a*) ridiculous (*b*) unthoughtful
(*c*) self-confident (*d*) ambiguous

26. The earth from here is a grand ***oasis*** in the vastness of space.
(*a*) greenland (*b*) landscape
(*c*) waterhole (*d*) wetland

27. It is quite ***unseemly*** that person should so behave with his elders.
(*a*) childish (*b*) ugly
(*c*) discourteous (*d*) improper

28. The police need ***tangible*** proof of his guilt before they can act against him.
(*a*) convincing (*b*) strong
(*c*) emphatic (*d*) clear and certain
(N.D.A. 1994)

29. It is a popular ***fallacy*** that all man-eaters are old and mangy.
(*a*) observation (*b*) belief
(*c*) fact (*d*) illusion

30. Her new glasses make her look rather ***owlish.***
(*a*) foolish (*b*) solemn
(*c*) silly (*d*) stupid

31. ***Malice*** is a feeling that we should always avoid. **(C.D.S. 1992)**
(*a*) Envy (*b*) Cruelty
(*c*) Spite (*d*) Hatred

32. He spent his whole life caught up in ***mundane*** matters.
(*a*) foolish (*b*) worldly
(*c*) inconsequential (*d*) criminal

33. He deserved the ***accolade*** he received.
(*a*) comment (*b*) honour
(*c*) appreciation (*d*) blame

34. He was given a ***severe*** warning for coming late.
(*a*) rigorous (*b*) stern
(*c*) harsh (*d*) strict

35. The notice said that the meeting would begin ***precisely*** at 9.00 a.m.
(*a*) concisely (*b*) approximately
(*c*) exactly (*d*) accurately
(Railways, 1994)

36. All incoming and outgoing mail is ***censored*** by the Government during the times of war.
(*a*) distributed (*b*) confiscated
(*c*) checked (*d*) supervised

37. The ***ascending*** temperature in many parts of the world confirms global warming which is an environmental hazard. **(N.D.A. 1993)**
(*a*) rising (*b*) falling
(*c*) shooting (*d*) mounting

38. It is ***risky*** to go beyond this barricade.
(*a*) stupid (*b*) adventurous
(*c*) hazardous (*d*) inadvisable

39. He was ***sentenced*** to four year's imprisonment.
(*a*) punished (*b*) acquitted
(*c*) assigned (*d*) convicted

40. The art movie I watched this evening has put me in a ***pensive*** mood.
(*a*) cheerful (*b*) reflective
(*c*) confused (*d*) depressed
(C.D.S. 1993)

41. He died as an ***impecunious*** man in a charitable hospital.
(a) innocent (b) ignorant
(c) faultless (d) having no money

42. He was punished for ***shirking*** his official work. **(S.S.C. 1992)**
(a) slowing (b) postponing
(c) avoiding (d) delegating

43. The British ***levied*** unusally high taxes on export of Indian goods.
(a) implemented (b) stipulated
(c) imposed (d) enacted

44. The one who is rich possesses many ***superfluous*** things.
(a) needless (b) superior
(c) essential (d) expensive

45. Many of his acquaintances avoid him because he is so ***garrulous***. **(C.D.S. 1994)**
(a) proud (b) unreasonable
(c) talkative (d) quarrelsome

46. He had been living his life according to set ***pattern***.
(a) design (b) model
(c) conduct (d) behaviour

47. Your explanation that your social ***commitments*** tie you down, does not convince me.
(a) duties (b) responsibilities
(c) restrictions (d) obligations

48. Absolute silence reigned in the whole ***necropolis***. **(C.D.S. 1992)**
(a) cemetery (b) hell
(c) cenotaph (d) churchyard

49. Her today's story was merely an ***exaggeration*** of what happened before my eyes.
(a) overstatement (b) reproduction
(c) falsehood (d) understatement

50. When kept in water, grapes become ***turgid***.
(a) bloated (b) swollen (c) rotten
(d) fomented (e) fermented

ANSWERS

1. (d)	**2.** (b)	**3.** (a)	**4.** (d)	**5.** (a)	**6.** (d)	**7.** (c)	**8.** (c)	**9.** (d)	**10.** (d)
11. (b)	**12.** (d)	**13.** (a)	**14.** (d)	**15.** (b)	**16.** (a)	**17.** (c)	**18.** (c)	**19.** (b)	**20.** (d)
21. (a)	**22.** (b)	**23.** (c)	**24.** (b)	**25.** (c)	**26.** (c)	**27.** (d)	**28.** (d)	**29.** (b)	**30.** (b)
31. (c)	**32.** (b)	**33.** (c)	**34.** (b)	**35.** (c)	**36.** (d)	**37.** (a)	**38.** (c)	**39.** (a)	**40.** (b)
41. (d)	**42.** (c)	**43.** (c)	**44.** (a)	**45.** (c)	**46.** (b)	**47.** (d)	**48.** (a)	**49.** (a)	**50.** (a)

PRACTICE SET 20

Directions : ***In each of the following questions, out of the given alternatives, choose the one which is nearest in meaning to the italicised word in the sentence.***

1. The ***facade*** of our school building got a face-lift recently. **(C.D.S. 1992)**
(a) basement (b) floor
(c) top (d) front

2. The stratospheric ozone layer plays an important protective role for life on earth and its disruption is obviously ***fraught*** with dangerous consequences.
(a) involving (b) concerned
(c) followed (d) caused

3. There is not a single word that is ***redundant*** in the report. **(N.D.A. 1995)**
(a) bombastic (b) unimportant
(c) flowery (d) not needed

4. In the company of smart and crafty fellows, a ***gaby*** finds himself out of place.
(a) simpleton (b) innocent
(c) honest (d) cunning

5. Being a member of this club, he has certain ***rights***.
(a) virtues (b) facilities
(c) gains (d) privileges

6. How I ***envy*** the man who can always produce his reading glasses at a moment's notice. **(ACC, 1991)**
(a) begrudge (b) desire
(c) crave (d) covet

7. The ***munificence*** of the businessman was great.
(a) generosity (b) stinginess
(c) misery (d) tactfulness

8. The next day she ***pacified*** the teacher explaining her the reason for the previous day's leave.
(a) quietened (b) silenced
(c) pleased (d) flattered

9. He could not suppress his ***resentment*** against that decision.
(*a*) excitement (*b*) irritation
(*c*) displeasure (*d*) indignation

10. We did not expect such a ***judicious*** remark from him. **(C.D.S. 1995)**
(*a*) legal (*b*) shrewd
(*c*) rational (*d*) sagacious

11. Despite a full one hour meeting, they could not arrive at any ***consensus***.
(*a*) settlement (*b*) unity (*c*) harmony
(*d*) agreement (*e*) consent

12. During his meeting with the owners of the company he made a number of ***overtures.***
(*a*) observations (*b*) offers
(*c*) agreements (*d*) promises

13. You cannot befool your mother by these ***pretences.***
(*a*) accusations (*b*) excuses
(*c*) statements (*d*) promises

14. The eyewitness testimony was ***incontrovertible.*** **(N.D.A. 1994)**
(*a*) unquestionable (*b*) disputable
(*c*) unacceptable (*d*) debatable

15. I realised they wanted to be alone together, so I felt very ***awkward.***
(*a*) ashamed (*b*) inconvenient
(*c*) embarrassed (*d*) clumsy

16. He was punished to rigorous imprisonment for ***larceny.***
(*a*) murder (*b*) forgery
(*c*) stealing (*d*) dacoity

17. The drugs were ***innocuous*** and had no side effect.
(*a*) effective (*b*) harmless
(*c*) imported (*d*) newly discovered

18. He is being treated for his ***somnolence.***
(*a*) weakness
(*b*) severe pain in the joints
(*c*) intoxication (*d*) sleepiness
(C.D.S. 1994)

19. The pupil was asked to ***rectify*** the mistake.
(*a*) correct (*b*) condone
(*c*) clarify (*d*) repeat

20. I used to skate quite well but I have lost the ***knack*** now.
(*a*) agility (*b*) strength
(*c*) skill (*d*) stamina

21. The ***criterion*** of judgement would be fixed soon.
(*a*) result (*b*) decision (*c*) standard
(*d*) consideration (*e*) approach

22. He did not hesitate to ***pester*** the sleeping mother when he wanted money.
(*a*) shake (*b*) wake (*c*) trouble
(*d*) disturb (*e*) annoy

23. Inspite of their efforts, the team of scientists could not make much ***headway*** to solve the problem.
(*a*) results (*b*) start (*c*) efforts
(*d*) progress (*e*) thinking **(Bank P.O. 1994)**

24. The speech he made on the occasion was quite ***exhilarating.***
(*a*) irrelevant (*b*) boring
(*c*) lively (*d*) learned

25. After that tiresome long journey, he felt ***drowsy.***
(*a*) sluggish (*b*) irritable
(*c*) energetic (*d*) dizzy

26. The ***terminus*** of his progress would be reached when he accomplishes that honour.
(*a*) beginning (*b*) highest stage
(*c*) last point (*d*) result

27. Several ***ancillary*** units were patronized by that large store.
(*a*) small (*b*) temporary
(*c*) standing (*d*) subordinate

28. I don't see why he should be so ***obsequious*** to his brother just because the latter is rich. **(C.D.S. 1994)**
(*a*) unusually kind (*b*) unfriendly
(*c*) excessively respectful (*d*) offensive

29. An issue of the highest sensitivity, which required the greatest ***finesse*** and delicacy, was handled in the most slapdash manner.
(*a*) carefulness (*b*) attention
(*c*) tact (*d*) action

30. Corruption ***stalks*** every sphere of national life. **(C.D.S. 1992)**
(*a*) pervades (*b*) penetrates
(*c*) pollutes (*d*) poisons

31. The militant was ***nabbed*** at the airport.
(*a*) caught (*b*) pursued
(*c*) arrested (*d*) beaten

32. I am afraid I cannot ***relate*** the details now.
(*a*) describe (*b*) recount
(*c*) recollect (*d*) tell

33. Both young ***sleuths*** felt sure there was a link between the two.
(*a*) travellers (*b*) boys
(*c*) convicts (d) detectives

34. He did not succeed in his ***endeavour***.
(*a*) enterprise (*b*) effort
(*c*) trick (*d*) plan
(I.E.S. 1993)

35. Five year plans have been put into operation to ***mitigate*** the sufferings of the poor.
(*a*) lessen (*b*) remove
(*c*) reduce (*d*) cut

36. These recent developments seem to be quite ***adverse*** to our interests.
(*a*) favourable (*b*) indifferent
(*c*) unfortunate (*d*) opposed

37. He gave such a ***vivid*** description of the house we wanted to rent that we did not have to look at it. **(N.D.A. 1995)**
(*a*) simple (*b*) detailed
(*c*) clear (*d*) confused

38. If you don't care for the ***blemishes*** of his style, you will find that the writer has a powerful message to convey.
(*a*) excellences (*b*) qualities
(*c*) accusations (*d*) faults

39. He gave an ***expeditious*** reply.
(*a*) exact (*b*) slow
(*c*) elaborate (*d*) prompt

40. He does not know how to ***husband*** his resources.
(*a*) manage (*b*) govern
(*c*) rule (*d*) watch

41. ***Brevity*** pays in debate.
(*a*) Conciseness (*b*) Sharpness
(*c*) Quickness (*d*) Confidence

42. The Border Security Force ***intercepted*** yesterday a truck carrying arms and ammunition. **(S.S.C. 1992)**
(*a*) found (*b*) stopped
(*c*) met (*d*) interrupted

43. His style is quite ***transparent.***
(*a*) witty (*b*) lucid
(*c*) involved (*d*) verbose

44. Your present statement has ***allayed*** my fears.
(*a*) relieved (*b*) obliterated
(*c*) aroused (*d*) eradicated

45. Because of a family ***feud***, he never spoke to his wife's parents. **(N.D.A. 1993)**
(*a*) problem (*b*) quarrel
(*c*) crisis (*d*) trouble

46. The speaker drew examples ***copiously*** from various books.
(*a*) largely (*b*) continuously
(*c*) plentifully (*d*) completely

47. The attitude of the Western countries towards the Third World countries is rather ***callous*** to say the least.
(*a*) unfeeling (*b*) cursed
(*c*) unkind (*d*) passive
(C.D.S. 1995)

48. Hearing the news, the workers were in a state of ***euphoria.***
(*a*) pleasant excitement
(*b*) intense indignation
(*c*) utter depression
(*d*) great disorder

49. He ***kindled*** the spirit of revenge in him and used it to his advantage.
(*a*) contrived (*b*) provoked
(*c*) dolted (*d*) burnt

50. He was the only ***reckless*** worker in the entire staff.
(*a*) bold (*b*) rash
(*c*) courageous (*d*) daring

ANSWERS

1. (*d*)	**2.** (*a*)	**3.** (*d*)	**4.** (*a*)	**5.** (*d*)	**6.** (*a*)	**7.** (*a*)	**8.** (*a*)	**9.** (*c*)	**10.** (*d*)
11. (*d*)	**12.** (*b*)	**13.** (*b*)	**14.** (*a*)	**15.** (*c*)	**16.** (*c*)	**17.** (*b*)	**18.** (*d*)	**19.** (*a*)	**20.** (*c*)
21. (*c*)	**22.** (*d*)	**23.** (*d*)	**24.** (*c*)	**25.** (*a*)	**26.** (*c*)	**27.** (*d*)	**28.** (*c*)	**29.** (*c*)	**30.** (*a*)
31. (*a*)	**32.** (*b*)	**33.** (*d*)	**34.** (*b*)	**35.** (*a*)	**36.** (*d*)	**37.** (*c*)	**38.** (*d*)	**39.** (*d*)	**40.** (*a*)
41. (*a*)	**42.** (*b*)	**43.** (*b*)	**44.** (*a*)	**45.** (*b*)	**46.** (*c*)	**47.** (*a*)	**48.** (*a*)	**49.** (*b*)	**50.** (*b*)

PRACTICE SET 21

Directions : ***In each of the following questions, out of the given alternatives, choose the one which best expresses the meaning of the italicised bold part of the sentence.***

1. He had the ***nerve*** to suggest that I was cheating. **(C.D.S. 1992)**
(*a*) courage (*b*) audacity
(*c*) capacity (*d*) strength

2. Your ***despicable*** remarks call for no reply.
(*a*) sarcastic (*b*) contemp uous
(*c*) critical (*d*) contemptible

3. He earns enough to satisfy his ***wants***.
(*a*) desires (*b*) aims
(*c*) pleasures (*d*) needs

4. The merchant was ***renowned*** for his simple way of living.
(*a*) notorious (*b*) famous
(*c*) noted (*d*) notable

5. "I have learnt a great deal working in factories, and for a time I've been a weaver. Here are my ***testimonials***, Mr.Davis." **(Railways, 1994)**
(*a*) credentials (*b*) tokens
(*c*) testaments (*d*) witnesses

6. The Director leaves on Tuesday on ***tour*** of the overseas branches of the company.
(*a*) round up (*b*) private visit
(*c*) journey (*d*) official visit

7. He is ***gregarious***, he is loner, he loves argument, he cannot bear to lose one.
(*a*) silent (*b*) talkative
(*c*) greedy (*d*) sociable

8. The base of Indian politicians is the group of ***sycophants*** around them who earn bad name for their leaders.
(*a*) critics (*b*) flatterers
(*c*) foppish (*d*) jarnor
(M.B.A. 1994)

9 Twenty people were killed as the boat ***fondered*** in the storm.
(*a*) drowned (*b*) capsized
(*c*) lost (*d*) disintegrated

10. The ***oppressive*** weather made the work difficult for them.
(*a*) turbulent (*b*) disappointing
(*c*) unbearable (*d*) cold

11. The Opposition made a ***stident*** demand for putting the bill to vote. **(C.D.S. 1992)**
(*a*) courageous (*b*) brave
(*c*) vociferous (*d*) powerful

12. It was his ***practice*** to go for a walk every morning.
(*a*) convention (*b*) habit
(*c*) fashion (*d*) rule

13 She was not the one who committed the crime, but she was ***culpable*** too.
(*a*) guilty (*b*) involved
(*c*) affected (*d*) sentenced

14. He adopted quite a ***diffident*** stand when it was a matter of son's career.
(*a*) confident (*b*) bold
(*c*) forward (*d*) unassuming

15. ***Eventually*** vision is affected and the patient is only able to see if light is present. **(N.D.A. 1992)**
(*a*) Initially (*b*) Primarily
(*c*) Ultimately (*d*) Gradually

16. He has saved money because his wife is ***frugal.***
(*a*) strict (*b*) economic
(*c*) economical (*d*) miserly

17. His ***craven*** behaviour makes him an object of mockery.
(*a*) indecent (*b*) cowardly
(*c*) mean (*d*) silly

18. Before finalising this transaction, I had to sign ***an indemnity bond.***
(*a*) a compensation bond
(*b*) a security bond
(*c*) a partnership bond
(*c*) a reparation bond **(C.D.S. 1994)**

19. Feeling humiliated and frustrated, he could no longer ***brook*** the indifferent attitude of the government.
(*a*) suffer (*b*) support
(*c*) condone (*d*) tolerate

20. The incident was a grim ***reflection*** of the bizarre things that go on in the village.
(*a*) summary (*b*) picture
(*c*) comment (*d*) portrait

21. The District Collector made it clear that the Government cannot ***sustain*** for long the support for such schemes.
(*a*) pay (*b*) succeed (*c*) manage
(*d*) continue (*e*) subsidise
(Bank P.O. 1993)

22. The most common type of colour blindness involves inability to ***tell*** red from green.
(*a*) prove (*b*) detect
(*c*) distinguish (*d*) extract

23. The collection of poems, in a slim volume, is ***gleaned*** from several anthologies of ancient Indian poetry.
(*a*) gathered (*b*) extracted
(*c*) compiled (*d*) copied

24. Even today many people are guided by ***abstruse*** moral values. **(C.D.S. 1993)**
(*a*) irrational (*b*) obscure
(*c*) impracticable (*d*) dangerous

25. As the jockey tried to ride the horse, it suddenly ***went berserk.***
(*a*) broke the carriage
(*b*) on a galloping speed
(*c*) became uncontrollably wild
(*d*) began to kick back

26. His visit to foreign countries brought about a ***sea change*** in his outlook and his attitude to the people.
(*a*) favourable change
(*b*) complete change
(*c*) unfavourable change
(*d*) partial change **(I.E.S. 1994)**

27. The cordial talks between the two foreign ministers cover the entire ***gamut*** of their relations.
(*a*) range (*b*) scope
(*c*) sphere (*d*) territory

28. He could not tolerate his friend rejoicing in his ***ignominy.***
(*a*) defeat (*b*) dishonour
(*c*) misery (*d*) victory

29. It is difficult to ***authenticate*** these old manuscripts. **(C.D.S. 1994)**
(*a*) illustrate (*b*) edit properly
(*c*) elucidate
(*d*) establish the genuineness of

30. The teacher felt ***nettled*** at the rowdiness of the boys.
(*a*) displeased (*b*) annoyed
(*c*) disgusted (*d*) perplexed

31. He is a ***disinterested*** investigator.
(*a*) uninterested (*b*) bored
(*c*) unbiased (*d*) reluctant

32. The ***indiscriminate*** demand for mass consumption goods is deplorable.
(*a*) discreet (*b*) undifferentiated
(*c*) desperate (*d*) insensitive

33. The boy was ***fired*** for continually coming late to school.
(*a*) beaten (*b*) scolded
(*c*) abused (*d*) dismissed

34. They ***venerated*** the old teacher.
(*a*) humiliated (*b*) teased
(*c*) respected (*d*) let go

35. Nobody has yet seen the ***peregrination*** of heavenly beings on earth.
(*a*) visit (*b*) arrival
(*c*) travelling (*d*) casting glance on

36. The prisoner has been ***languishing*** in the jail for the last many years.
(*a*) enjoying (*b*) avoiding
(*c*) suffering (*d*) convicted
(*e*) attempting **(Bank P.O. 1994)**

37. Some people adopt excellent manners only to ***camouflage*** their real character.
(*a*) project (*b*) hide
(*c*) misrepresent (*d*) reveal

38. The new scheme was aimed at prohibiting all people from ***imbibing*** alcoholic drinks.
(*a*) offering (*b*) smuggling
(*c*) preparing (*d*) drinking

39. The guests were offended by his ***uncouth*** manners. **(N.D.A. 1995)**
(*a*) wasteful (*b*) dirty
(*c*) undesirable (*c*) ungracious

40. Persons with ***abstemious*** habits can adjust themselves in any social set up.
(*a*) rustic (*b*) lavish
(*c*) moderate (*d*) lucrative

41. He did not make any attempt to ***placate*** her.
(*a*) please (*b*) pacify
(*c*) serve (*d*) satisfy

42. The actor with many ***graces*** leaves the stage and becomes only a memory in a world of happy memories.
(*a*) delicacies (*b*) tacts
(*c*) charms (*d*) gestures

43. An enquiry was ordered to ***ascertain*** the actual cause of the accident.
(*a*) determine (*b*) investigate
(*c*) discover (*d*) prove

44. Whatever the ***verdict*** of history may be, Chaplin will occupy a unique place in its pages. **(C.D.S. 1995)**
(*a*) prediction (*b*) outcome
(*c*) judgement (*d*) voice

45. Miss Universe ***pageant*** was really worth seeing.
(*a*) contest (*b*) show
(*c*) function (*d*) carnival

46. Shobha painted some ***delightful*** pictures of children.
(*a*) funny (*b*) colourful
(*c*) charming (*d*) happy

47. During negotiations, the Managing director remained ***obdurate.***
(*a*) adamant (*b*) tough
(*c*) co-operative (*d*) flexible

48. He kept his eyes peeled and his ears pricked for some important ***clue.***
(*a*) hint (*b*) inkling
(*c*) intimation (*d*) signal
(N.D.A. 1994)

49. He was ***reasonable*** enough to behave according to the circumstances.
(*a*) peaceful (*b*) attentive
(*c*) sensitive (*d*) determined

50. She ***overruled*** her son's demand of a motorbike.
(*a*) neglected (*b*) disallowed
(*c*) ignored (*d*) fulfilled

ANSWERS

1. (*b*)	**2.** (*d*)	**3.** (*d*)	**4.** (*c*)	**5.** (*a*)	**6.** (*d*)	**7.** (*d*)	**8.** (*b*)	**9.** (*b*)	**10.** (*c*)
11. (*c*)	**12.** (*b*)	**13.** (*a*)	**14.** (*d*)	**15.** (*c*)	**16.** (*c*)	**17.** (*b*)	**18.** (*b*)	**19.** (*d*)	**20.** (*b*)
21. (*d*)	**22.** (*c*)	**23.** (*a*)	**24.** (*b*)	**25.** (*c*)	**26.** (*b*)	**27.** (*a*)	**28.** (*b*)	**29.** (*d*)	**30.** (*b*)
31. (*c*)	**32.** (*c*)	**33.** (*d*)	**34.** (*c*)	**35.** (*c*)	**36.** (*c*)	**37.** (*b*)	**38.** (*d*)	**39.** (*d*)	**40.** (*c*)
41. (*b*)	**42.** (*c*)	**43.** (*a*)	**44.** (*c*)	**45.** (*b*)	**46.** (*c*)	**47.** (*a*)	**48.** (*a*)	**49.** (*c*)	**50.** (*b*)

PRACTICE SET 22

Directions : ***In each of the following questions, out of the given alternatives, choose the one which would not change the meaning of the original sentence, if it were substituted for the italicised word in the sentence.***

1. The claims of students look hollow when they ***attribute*** their poor performance to difficulty of examination. **(M.B.A. 1994)**
(*a*) inundate (*b*) inhere
(*c*) impute (*d*) infer

2. He is known for his ***compliant*** nature.
(*a*) livid (*b*) complaining
(*c*) adamant (*d*) yielding

3. I found his crude manners ***abominable.***
(*a*) flattering (*b*) sloppy
(*c*) detestable (*d*) attractive

4. Most of the politicians these days have a large number of ***toadies*** around them.
(*a*) followers
(*b*) professional assistants
(*c*) servants (*d*) sycophants
(N.D.A. 1995)

5. Social reformers and thinkers ***abominate*** every type of discrimination and injustice practised anywhere in the world.
(*a*) eradicate (*b*) detest
(*c*) condemn (*d*) violate

6. He was a very ***docile*** person and thus a favourite of his neighbours.
(*a*) easily irritated (*b*) easily managed
(*c*) easily disturbed (*d*) easily fooled

7. We ***cherish*** the tradition of bravery.
(*a*) revive (*b*) learn
(*c*) hold dear (*d*) imitate

8. On scrutiny the police officer found out that the documents provided by the landlord were totally ***fabricated***.
(*a*) historical (*b*) genuine
(*c*) forged (*d*) prepared
(*e*) constructed **(Bank P.O. 1994)**

9. The man did not ***relish*** his nearness to the tigress.
(*a*) enjoy (*b*) like
(*c*) guess (*d*) risk

10. Nearly half of India's population is still living in ***abject*** poverty.
(*a*) wretched (*b*) solid
(*c*) grave (*d*) enough

11. The ***fetid*** mound of waste near the town was a major cause of the epidemic.
(*a*) doomed (*b*) dangerous (*c*) stinking
(*d*) stagnant (*e*) disease-breeding

12. They are ***cautiously*** optimistic about the effects of the new medicine.
(*a*) carefully (*b*) genuinely
(*c*) secretly (*d*) curiously

13. His ***trite*** remarks failed to cut any ice with the audience. **(C.D.S. 1994)**
(*a*) illogical (*b*) hackneyed
(*c*) bitter (*d*) sharp

14. In the meeting the minister ***floated*** a couple of new ideas.
(*a*) gave (*b*) presented
(*c*) advised (*d*) offered

15. Some army units were ***decimated*** during the surprise attack.
(*a*) denounced (*b*) captured
(*c*) defeated (*d*) destroyed

16. Everybody in the Assembly shouted and there was a ***pandemonium*** in the hall.
(*a*) crowd (*b*) noise
(*c*) disorderly scene (*d*) laughter
(C.D.S. 1989)

17. Please ***sound*** the Principal about the reaction of the students.
(*a*) support (*b*) discuss
(*c*) tell (*d*) caution

18. People who hold very unorthodox views, are sometimes ***ostracized.***
(*a*) hated (*b*) shut out from society
(*c*) criticised (*d*) applauded

19. Indian economy has always shown enough ***resilience*** in crisis.
(*a*) strength (*b*) adjustment
(*c*) elasticity (*d*) diversity

20. ***Defection*** is quite common in our present day political life. **(I. Tax, 1991)**
(*a*) Desertion (*b*) Disobedience
(*c*) Disloyalty (*d*) Indiscipline

21. Speaking in a ***tremulous*** tone, he took everybody to task.
(*a*) confident (*b*) angry
(*c*) feeble (*d*) trembling

22. His ***judicious*** handling of the matter saved the situation from going out of control. **(N. D. A. 1996)**
(*a*) sensible (*b*) nervous
(*c*) cautious (*d*) helpful

23. The prince fell in love with a ***comely*** young maiden. **(Railways, 1994)**
(*a*) elegant (*b*) homely
(*c*) pretty (*d*) delightful

24. The bedroom is at the ***rear*** side of this house.
(*a*) front (*b*) back
(*c*) upper (*d*) different

25. The boy was ***incorrigible*** and a constant source of trouble to his mother.

(*a*) truant (*b*) bad beyond correction
(*c*) rash (*d*) dishonest

26. Dr.S.Radhakrishnan has written an ***erudite*** commentary on the Bhagwad Gita. **(C.D.S. 1995)**
(*a*) scholarly (*b*) inspiring
(*c*) effective (*d*) perfect

27. The river level was rising ***drastically*** after that heavy rain.
(*a*) slightly (*b*) suddenly
(*c*) greatly (*d*) unexpectedly

28. It was very ***perspicacious*** of the judicial investigation officer to find the cause of the problem so quickly.
(*a*) discerning (*b*) mysterious
(*c*) clever (*d*) quick

29. The parade route was down the main ***boulevard.*** **(N.D.A. 1994)**
(*a*) alley (*b*) highway
(*c*) avenue (*d*) driveway

30. He gave me a detailed ***account*** of the meeting.
(*a*) report (*b*) summary
(*c*) explanation (*d*) precis

31. The only way to ***subvert*** the money power and let truth triumph is by enhancing the perks or income of the individuals.
(*a*) reduce (*b*) abolish
(*c*) overthrow (*d*) subdue

32. A ***conscientious*** worker is always admired by his employers. **(I.E.S. 1993)**
(*a*) obedient (*b*) sincere
(*c*) skillful (*d*) careful

33. The employee was ***ousted*** from the office.
(*a*) pushed (*b*) dismissed
(*c*) forced (*d*) expelled

34. A factory manufacturing ***illicit*** liquor was unearthed by the police yesterday.
(*a*) poisonous (*b*) unlawful
(*c*) intoxicating (*d*) cheap

35. A pervading sense of ***ennui*** grips Gaurav. **(C.D.S. 1992)**
(*a*) anger (*b*) anxiety
(*c*) weariness (*d*) melancholy

36. The demand for an ***autonomous*** state is responsible for insurgence of terrorism in Punjab.
(*a*) separate (*b*) independent
(*c*) secluded (*d*) self-governed

37. He could not suppress his ***resentment*** against that decision.
(*a*) indignation (*b*) irritation
(*c*) displeasure (*d*) excitement

38. It is so ***gratifying*** to know that there are not many small-pox cases these days.
(*a*) pleasing (*b*) surprising
(*c*) satisfying (*d*) happy
(N.D.A. 1995)

39. Without science and the scientific spirit, we shall just ***drift*** along.
(*a*) move gently (*b*) move aimlessly
(*c*) move cautiously (*d*) live peacefully

40. He was given to ***fanaticism*** in his political beliefs.
(*a*) limitations
(*b*) unreasoning enthusiasm
(*c*) falsehood (*a*) having no grounds

41. No civilised society can allow the ***subversion*** of its institutions by extremists.
(*a*) domination (*b*) subservience
(*c*) destruction (*d*) subordination
(*e*) absorption

42. It is the Prime Minister's ***prerogative*** to appoint or dismiss a Minister.
(*a*) function (*b*) monopoly
(*c*) authority (*d*) privilege

43. He cast a ***cursory*** glance over the papers before signing them.
(*a*) short (*b*) eager
(*c*) inquisitive (*d*) hurried

44. He had to ***curtail*** his leave as a lot of work was pending in his office.
(*a*) cancel (*b*) extend
(*c*) shorten (*d*) postpone
(Clerk's Grade, 1992)

45. In the absence of the Chief Guest, the host himself acted as his ***surrogate*** and presided over the function.
(*a*) counterpart (*b*) alliance
(*c*) assistant (*d*) substitute

46. The incident ***affected*** him so much that he could not forget it for several days.
(*a*) upset (*b*) changed
(*c*) influenced (*d*) controlled

47. The traditional methods of doing things have now become ***obsolescent.***
(*a*) harmful (*b*) out of date
(*c*) unrewarding (*d*) unpopular

48. This was his ***maiden*** performance on the stage and he did very well.
(*a*) primary (*b*) first
(*c*) opening (*d*) girlish
(N.D.A. 1993)

49. It is the ***inherent*** quality of matter to expand on being heated.
(*a*) eternal (*b*) hidden
(*c*) internal (*d*) natural

50. The isolated and dilapidated palace has become a ***rendezvous*** for the unsocial elements.
(*a*) resort (*b*) hiding place
(*c*) public place (*d*) meeting place

ANSWERS

1. (*c*)	**2.** (*d*)	**3.** (*c*)	**4.** (*d*)	**5.** (*b*)	**6.** (*b*)	**7.** (*c*)	**8.** (*c*)	**9.** (*a*)	**10.** (*a*)
11. (*c*)	**12.** (*a*)	**13.** (*b*)	**14.** (*b*)	**15.** (*d*)	**16.** (*c*)	**17.** (*d*)	**18.** (*b*)	**19.** (*c*)	**20.** (*a*)
21. (*d*)	**22.** (*c*)	**23.** (*c*)	**24.** (*b*)	**25.** (*b*)	**26.** (*a*)	**27.** (*c*)	**28.** (*a*)	**29.** (*c*)	**30.** (*a*)
31. (*c*)	**32.** (*b*)	**33.** (*d*)	**34.** (*b*)	**35.** (*c*)	**36.** (*d*)	**37.** (*c*)	**38.** (*c*)	**39.** (*b*)	**40.** (*b*)
41. (*c*)	**42.** (*d*)	**43.** (*d*)	**44.** (*c*)	**45.** (*d*)	**46.** (*c*)	**47.** (*b*)	**48.** (*b*)	**49.** (*d*)	**50.** (*d*)

PRACTICE SET 23

Directions : ***In each of the following questions, out of the given alternatives, choose the one which is closest in meaning to the italicised word in the sentence.***

1. The poem is written in a very ***lucid*** style. **(Railways, 1994)**
(*a*) intricate (*b*) noble
(*c*) elaborate (*d*) clear

2. It goes against my ***grain*** to be running around the courts for justice.
(*a*) character (*b*) nature
(*c*) training (*d*) personality

3. The man lived in a ***dilapidated*** house made of mud and bricks.
(*a*) crumbling (*b*) old
(*c*) thatched (*d*) crashing

4. Whatever opinion he gives is ***sane.***
(*a*) arrogant (*b*) wild
(*c*) obscure (*d*) rational
(C.D.S. 1995)

5. The workers struck work asking for ***interim*** relief.
(*a*) immediate (*b*) extra
(*c*) urgent (*d*) provisional

6. He is ***urbane*** in his manners.
(*a*) urban (*b*) genteel
(*c*) civil (*d*) sane

7. He has won great admiration amongst his students because of his ***verdant*** outlook.
(*a*) wide (*b*) optimistic
(*c*) fresh (*d*) logical

8. The great dancer impressed the appreciative crowd by his ***nimble*** movements. **(Bank P.O. 1994)**
(*a*) subtle (*b*) clear (*c*) quickening
(*d*) lively (*e*) unrythmic

9. Wisdom seems to have got lost in a ***welter*** of knowledge.
(*a*) confusion (*b*) height
(*c*) clarity (*d*) sacrifice

10. The story began in an ***eerie*** situation.
(*a*) dangerous (*b*) thrilling
(*c*) wonderful (*d*) strange
(*e*) dismaying

11. He was a ***vulpine*** person and so avoided by his neighbours.
(*a*) indolent (*b*) miserly
(*c*) haughty (*d*) crafty

12. The prisoner made an ***abortive*** attempt to escape from the jail. **(C.D.S. 1995)**
(*a*) courageous (*b*) futile
(*c*) illegal (*d*) furtive

13. A ***reliable*** friend is the gift of God.
(*a*) helpful (*b*) dependable
(*c*) honest (*d*) true

14. War was not the only ***inevitable*** means to decide that dispute.
(*a*) indefinite (*b*) imminent
(*c*) unavoidable (*d*) improbable

15. The tinned food that we bought in the way was all ***tained*** and spoiled.
(*a*) contaminated (*b*) rotten
(*c*) adulterated (*d*) noxious

16. We must not take his ***facetious*** remarks very seriously. **(C.D.S. 1994)**
(*a*) amusing (*b*) critical
(*c*) casual (*d*) flippantly humorous

17. My uncle was so ***chagrined*** that he avoided mentioning the incident.
(*a*) frustrated (*b*) annoyed
(*c*) disappointed (*d*) tired

18. He was ***ingenious*** enough to know how to get out of the clutches of law.
(*a*) clever (*b*) intelligent
(*c*) alert (*d*) cunning

19. The recent acts of ***vandalism*** in the country cannot be ignored.
(*a*) disturbance (*b*) ravage
(*c*) provocation (*d*) violence
(Railways, 1995)

20. Hearing to the complaints of the villagers, the father would come and box his ears, and ***cuff*** him.

(*a*) lock (*b*) abuse
(*c*) scold (*d*) slap

21. Everyone in the bazaar turned to stare at the visitor and his ***preposterous*** dress.
(*a*) pompous (*b*) vague
(*c*) absurd (*d*) strange

22. Vishal had got ***an indication*** from his friend about the changes in the export market. **(Bank P.O. 1993)**
(*a*) a feeling (*b*) a hint (*c*) a guess
(*d*) a signal (*e*) an ultimatum

23. Those who acquire quick money are impatient to ***flaunt*** their wealth and material possessions.
(*a*) waste (*b*) squander
(*c*) hide (*d*) show off

24. India's attitude towards China has all along been ***pusillanimous.***
(*a*) generous (*b*) cowardly
(*c*) subversive (*d*) restrained

25. Parents should ***cultivate*** in their children the habit of helping others.
(*a*) propagate (*b*) sprout
(*c*) create (*d*) foster

26. A person unrestrained by the rules of morality or tradition is called a ***licentious*** person. **(C.D.S. 1993)**
(*a*) freelance (*b*) criminal
(*c*) loafer-type (*d*) libertine

27. The Principal's advice will prove ***salutary*** for the students.
(*a*) encouraging (*b*) remarkable
(*c*) beneficial (*d*) harmful

28. The child ***merits*** serious attention at this age.
(*a*) demands (*b*) deserves
(*c*) suits (*d*) invites

29. His ***sententious*** reply impressed the visitor.
(*a*) sharp (*b*) quick
(*c*) insipid (*d*) meaningful

30. She looked ***gorgeous*** in her new dress.
(*a*) great (*b*) fantastic
(*c*) silly (*d*) splendid

31. Scientific knowledge is an intoxicating ***draught,*** and it may be one in which the human race is unable to sustain.
(*a*) drink (*b*) product
(*c*) disease (*d*) process
(N.D.A. 1992)

32. He is ***deluding*** himself with false hopes.
(*a*) satisfying (*b*) entertaining
(*c*) misleading (*d*) assuring

33. There has been considerable ***furore*** both within Parliament and without about the proposed hike in tele-communication tariff.
(*a*) opposition (*b*) criticism
(*c*) uproar (*d*) disagreement

34. The obstacles seem to be ***insurmountable***, but no one should doubt what this fearless woman can accomplish. **(C.D.S. 1994)**
(*a*) too easy to achieve
(*b*) too difficult to overcome
(*c*) too tall and too high
(*d*) too trivial to attract attention

35. Article 26 of the Constitution is ,in fact, a ***corollary*** to Article 25.
(*a*) proof (*b*) summary
(*c*) synopsis (*d*) deduction

36. The father advised his errant son not to ***maunder*** about but do something worthwhile.
(*a*) trouble (*b*) wander
(*c*) run (*d*) play

37. The scheme failed for want of ***adequate*** funds.
(*a*) necessary (*b*) recommended
(*c*) required (*d*) sufficient

38. No one will invite her to a tea for she is so ***garrulous.*** **(Hotel Management, 1993)**
(*a*) repeats gossip (*b*) talks a lot
(*c*) giggles all the time (*c*) laughs a lot

39. The meeting was called to ***ruminate*** on recent events in the subcontinent.
(*a*) ponder (*b*) examine
(*c*) argue (*d*) discuss

40. Slangs in a language are usually ***ephemeral*** in nature.
(*a*) transient (*b*) customary
(*c*) necessary (*d*) obvious

41. On the stage of this world, the drama of life is ***transitory*** as well as traumatic.
(*a*) transitional (*b*) dull
(*c*) fleeting (*d*) painful

42. He has always been an ***elusive*** customer.
(*a*) clever (*b*) unreliable
(*c*) deceitful (*d*) quarrelsome

43. The new government decided to ***rescind*** most of the decisions of its predecessor.
(*a*) rectify (*b*) modify
(*c*) revoke (*d*) reconsider
(C.D.S. 1992)

44. The man ***succumbed*** to his injuries the day following the day of accident.
(*a*) surrendered (*b*) yielded
(*c*) fell down (*d*) died

45. The ***slump*** in business made Ratanlal bankrupt.
(*a*) loss (*b*) extortion
(*c*) fall (*d*) failure

46. They feel that we should be fully aware of our own ***environment.***
(*a*) heredity (*b*) family

(c) nationality (d) nature
(e) surroundings **(Bank P.O. 1993)**

47. The two brothers should not ***vie*** with each other but work in co-operation.
(a) fight (b) conspire
(c) compete (d) envy

48. The rebels returned home under an ***amnesty.***
(a) general pardon
(b) financial assistance
(c) police security (d) judicial trial

49. The ship was caught in the ***tempest*** and all but the captain were drowned.
(a) bad weather (b) violent storm
(c) typhoon (c) whirlpool

50. He is just ***dabbling*** in politics to promote his business interests.
(a) including (b) participating
(c) helping (d) interfering

ANSWERS

1. (d)	**2.** (b)	**3.** (a)	**4.** (d)	**5.** (d)	**6.** (c)	**7.** (c)	**8.** (c)	**9.** (a)	**10.** (d)
11. (d)	**12.** (b)	**13.** (b)	**14.** (c)	**15.** (a)	**16.** (d)	**17.** (c)	**18.** (a)	**19.** (d)	**20.** (d)
21. (c)	**22.** (b)	**23.** (d)	**24.** (b)	**25.** (d)	**26.** (d)	**27.** (c)	**28.** (b)	**29.** (d)	**30.** (d)
31. (a)	**32.** (c)	**33.** (c)	**34.** (b)	**35.** (d)	**36.** (b)	**37.** (d)	**38.** (b)	**39.** (a)	**40.** (a)
41. (c)	**42.** (a)	**43.** (c)	**44.** (b)	**45.** (c)	**46.** (e)	**47.** (c)	**48.** (a)	**49.** (b)	**50.** (b)

PRACTICE SET 24

Directions : *In each of the following questions, out of the given alternatives, choose the one which is nearest in meaning to the italicised bold part of the sentence.*

1. My philosophy lecturer is unfailingly ***bombastic***. **(C.D.S. 1989)**
(a) pompous (b) impressive
(c) impressionistic
(d) sensitive in the use of words

2. Work that does not engage a person will never seem rewarding, no matter how ***lucrative*** it becomes.
(a) promising (b) easy
(c) comfortable (d) profitable

3. The scheme failed for want of ***adequate***. funds. **(N.D.A. 1996)**
(a) required (b) recommended
(c) sufficient (d) necessary

4. The leader's ***charisma*** attracted many followers. **(I.E.S. 1993)**
(a) humility (b) power
(c) magnetic appeal (d) candour

5. The growth in agriculture has a very ***salutary*** effect because we also offer food aid to the less fortunate masses in Asia and Africa.
(a) advantageous (b) good
(c) far-reaching (d) respectable

6. The lovers met in a ***sylvan*** setting.
(a) silent (b) natural
(c) wooden (d) romantic

7. He took a ***momentous*** decision in this case.
(a) transient (b) important
(c) wrong (d) hopeless

8. The young leader was ***reluctant*** to shoulder the responsibilities of the ministerial office.
(a) eager (b) anxious
(c) unwilling (d) wanting

9. He ***corroborated*** the statement of his brother. **(C.D.S. 1995)**
(a) condemned (b) confirmed
(c) seconded (d) disproved

10. He is ***averse*** to the idea of holding elections now.
(a) convinced (b) angry
(c) opposed (d) indifferent

11. To the mother's surprise, the soup had gone completely ***mouldy***.
(a) finished (b) cold
(c) stale (d) sour

12. Tired and ***weary*** he returned home late that night.
(a) exhausted (b) frustrated (c) lithe
(d) emancipated (e) wretched

13. He was adjudged as the best ***orator*** of the college.
(a) critic (b) debater
(c) singer (d) speaker

14. His ***forthright*** behaviour shows that he is honest but he seems rude to some people. **(N.D.A. 1994)**
(*a*) courteous (*b*) correct
(*c*) straightforward (*d*) tactful

15. Prashant likes his friend, Rishabh inspite of his little ***frailties***.
(*a*) weaknesses (*b*) oddities
(*c*) timidness (*d*) failures

16. Ramlal is quite ***parsimonious*** by nature.
(*a*) cruel (*b*) miserly
(*c*) prodigal (*d*) haughty

17. The device which ***measures*** earthquakes is called the Richter scale. **(C.D.S. 1992)**
(*a*) prevents (*b*) weighs
(*c*) gauges (*d*) calculates

18. He did not continue for long with his ***murky*** intentions.
(*a*) dishonest (*b*) dull
(*c*) lazy (*d*) ominous

19. Success is achieved by the degree to which society is prepared to ***police*** itself.
(*a*) oppress (*b*) perform
(*c*) control (*d*) suppress

20. The Government must do something about the ***runaway*** increase in prices.
(*a*) unpardonable (*b*) uncontrollable
(*c*) unreasonable (*d*) inflationary

21. He tried to ***mollify*** my hurt fellings.
(*a*) arouse (*b*) ignore
(*c*) soften (*d*) suppress
(I. Tax, 1991)

22 All his friends marvelled at his power of ***ratiocination***.
(*a*) ruminating (*b*) speculation
(*c*) imagination (*d*) reasoning

23. His singing ***enthralled*** the entire audience.
(*a*) disappointed (*b*) captivated
(*c*) entertained (*d*) surprised

24. A ***rupture*** in the relationship of the two brothers is quite apparent.
(*a*) gap (*b*) damage
(*c*) break (*d*) breach
(Railways, 1994)

25. The Pandavas led an ***austere*** life in the mountains.
(*a*) harsh (*b*) religious
(*c*) lacking (*d*) insteady

26. At the yesterday's meeting, he adopted a ***recalcitrant*** attitude.
(*a*) conciliatory (*b*) obstinate
(*c*) sympathetic (*d*) courteous

27. The committee did not find him ***fit*** for the job. **(B.S.R.B. 1993)**
(*a*) genuine (*b*) correct
(*c*) suitable (*d*) selected

28. After a dynamic speech by the Prime Minister, one often hears ***repurcussions*** abroad.
(*a*) recriminations
(*b*) far-reaching effects
(*c*) interpretations (*d*) gesticulations

29. The army has laid out an entire web of agents to detect the ***surreptitious*** activities of the enemy.
(*a*) hostile (*b*) secret
(*c*) intriguing (*d*) foppish

30. The value of some shares has ***appreciated*** considerably after the last budget.
(*a*) changed (*b*) increased
(*c*) decreased (*d*) crashed
(S.S.C. 1992)

31. The Court had to ***reprieve*** the hanging of the condemned prisoner.
(*a*) pardon (*b*) forgive
(*c*) forego (*d*) delay

32. Fed up of social atrocities, she finally decided to lead a ***sequestered*** life.
(*a*) virtuous (*b*) bold
(*c*) enlivened (*d*) secluded

33. After the ***dismal*** performance of the team in the series concluded yesterday, the captain offered his resignation to the President of the Club. **(Bank P.O. 1994)**
(*a*) poor (*b*) miserly
(*c*) short (*d*) sorrowful

34. Some people enjoy ***hobnobbing*** with the rich and famous.
(*a*) associating (*b*) chatting
(*c*) conspiring (*d*) living

35. He is in the habit of talking ***superfluously***.
(*a*) continuously (*b*) needlessly
(*c*) fluently (*d*) authoritatively

36. Quite ***unabashed***, he began his scholarly lecture on what was obvious to everyone. **(C.D.S. 1992)**
(*a*) unashamed (*b*) unimpressed
(*c*) unnerved (*d*) unchecked

37. When the editor refused to publish my first article, I was totally ***disheartened***.
(*a*) displeased (*b*) discouraged
(*c*) dissatisfied (*d*) disturbed

38. He was a ***contemplative*** person.
(*a*) thoughtful (*b*) careless
(*c*) over-zealous (*d*) mischievous

39. The ***intrepid*** mountaineers who scaled the peak in winter should be specially congratulated. **(C.D.S. 1995)**
(*a*) bold (*b*) courageous
(*c*) vigorous (*d*) brave

40. The ***ubiquity*** of God cannot be questioned.
(*a*) greatness (*b*) mystery

(c) omnipresence (d) existence

41. Our ***posterity*** shall hold us responsible for the devastation caused by cutting of trees.
(a) predecessors (b) successors
(c) offsprings (d) followers

42. He whirled round in ***a trice***, with a revolver in his hand. **(C.D.S. 1994)**
(a) a circle (b) a trifle
(c) an instant (d) hurry

43. The pick pocket was ***brandishing*** a knife.
(a) using (b) pointing
(c) showing (d) waving

44. The manager was not present at the ***inception*** of the programme.
(a) beginning (b) conclusion
(c) demonstration (d) rejection

45. The old man shows no sign of ***infirmity*** even though he is eighty years old.
(a) indolence (b) fickleness
(c) feebleness (d) lack of firmness
(N.D.A. 1995)

46. Ambition is ***subdued*** by poverty.
(a) modified (b) challenged
(c) affected (d) diluted

47. Her ***hazel*** eyes are really attractive.
(a) blue (b) greenish blue
(c) green (d) reddish brown

48. He is considered by every one as a man of ***integrity***.
(a) power (b) character
(c) wealth (d) influence

49. The man had transformed the courtyard into a junkyard, all he ever planted in it was ***trash***.
(a) ugly (b) baseless
(c) splendid (d) nonsense

50. We should abstain from ***casting aspersions*** on the character of our colleagues
(a) cracking silly jokes
(b) passing slanderous remarks
(c) passing critical remarks
(d) paying left-handed compliments
(C.D.S. 1994)

ANSWERS

1. (a)	**2.** (d)	**3.** (c)	**4.** (c)	**5.** (b)	**6.** (c)	**7.** (b)	**8.** (c)	**9.** (b)	**10.** (c)
11. (c)	**12.** (a)	**13.** (d)	**14.** (c)	**15.** (a)	**16.** (b)	**17.** (c)	**18.** (a)	**19.** (c)	**20.** (b)
21. (c)	**22.** (d)	**23.** (b)	**24.** (c)	**25.** (a)	**26.** (b)	**27.** (c)	**28.** (b)	**29.** (b)	**30.** (b)
31. (d)	**32.** (d)	**33.** (a)	**34.** (a)	**35.** (b)	**36.** (a)	**37.** (b)	**38.** (a)	**39.** (a)	**40.** (c)
41. (b)	**42.** (c)	**43.** (d)	**44.** (a)	**45.** (c)	**46.** (d)	**47.** (d)	**48.** (b)	**49.** (d)	**50.** (b)

PRACTICE SET 25

Directions : ***Pick out the word(s) which can correctly replace the word(s) printed in italic bold in the sentence without changing the meaning of it.***

1. Ramnath is such a ***sham*** that it is difficult to get along with him.
(a) pretender (b) unnatural (c) blunt
(d) farcical (e) unfair
(Bank P.O. 1993)

2. Of all the ***indignities*** man has suffered at the hands of man, slavery is perhaps the most degrading.
(a) insult (b) atrocities
(c) evils (d) dangers

3. For want of adequate funds, non-plan expenditure has been further ***pruned*** in this year's budget.
(a) prolonged (b) expanded
(c) reduced (d) included

4. The school took us on a three days' ***excursion*** to Goa.
(a) trip (b) picnic
(c) visit (d) tournament

5. One who ***despises*** his colleagues can never be successful.
(a) accuses (b) ignores
(c) hates (d) discourages

6. Lack of occupation is not necessarily revealed by ***manifest*** idleness.
(a) easily acquired (b) easily deflected
(c) easily perceived (d) easily infected
(C.D.S. 1993)

7. He did his job with ***scrupulous*** care.
(a) exact (b) marvellous (c) great
(d) inattentive (e) superfluous

8. It was on the ***behest*** of the officer that he made those improvements.
(a) suggestion (b) orders
(c) recommendation (d) request

9. Your master will like you if you are ***diligent.*** **(N.D.A. 1996)**
(*a*) conscientious (*b*) obedient
(*c*) meticulous (*d*) hard - working

10. One of the most ***tenacious*** and dangerous legends about the shark is that he has poor eyesight.
(*a*) brave (*b*) strong
(*c*) heroic (*d*) foolish

11. The poetic art of Keats reached ***consummation*** at the end of his poetic career.
(*a*) failure (*b*) deterioration
(*c*) completion (*d*) frivolty

12. ***Adverse*** remarks against the leader provoked his followers.
(*a*) Dangerous (*b*) Unnecessary
(*c*) Severe (*d*) Unfavourable

13. Gandhiji had ***proposed*** the path of non-violence.
(*a*) followed (*b*) suggested
(*c*) adopted (*d*) accepted

14. What India ***hankers*** for most at this moment is security and stability.
(*a*) dreams (*b*) plans
(*c*) desires (*d*) aims

15. Before I could ***expostulate*** he had spoken again. **(N.D.A. 1993)**
(*a*) postulate (*b*) protest
(*c*) explain (*d*) disclose

16. The wail of the call to prayer ***floated*** over the darkened streets.
(*a*) jumped (*b*) drifted
(*c*) hovered (*d*) soaked

17. The police arrested the thief but his ***accomplice*** escaped.
(*a*) friend (*b*) colleague
(*c*) companion (*d*) partner

18. We should always try to maintain and promote communal ***amity*** . **(C.D.S. 1995)**
(*a*) understanding (*b*) bondage
(*c*) friendship (*d*) contention

19. The meeting was ***adjourned*** after discussing on the matter for about two hours.
(*a*) postponed (*b*) stopped
(*c*) begun (*d*) reviewed

20. The old man asserted that the whole art of medicine lay in ***judicious*** poisoning.
(*a*) discreet (*b*) clever
(*c*) cautious (*d*) careful

21. It was a ***fabulous*** idea.
(*a*) handsome (*b*) fruitful
(*c*) legendry (*d*) precious

22. Some of the Asian countries have been ***enmeshed*** in an inescapable debt trap.
(*a*) entangled (*b*) struck (*c*) hit
(*d*) arrested (*e*) ensured

23. The thieves left her tied up with rope but she ***wriggled*** herself free.
(*a*) shook (*b*) escaped
(*c*) made (*d*) allowed

24. You will have to arrange for a ***provisional*** licence.
(*a*) transient (*b*) restricted
(*c*) routine (*d*) temporary

25. His project was merely meant to ***stall*** the road construction in the village.
(*a*) ignore (*b*) begin
(*c*) obstruct (*d*) evade

26. Plants that grow and exist in deserts have highly specialized means of adapting themselves to the ***arid*** environment. **(N.D.A. 1993)**
(*a*) unproductive (*b*) useless
(*c*) withering (*d*) dry

27. The king's palace was really a ***magnificent*** one.
(*a*) popular (*b*) splendid
(*c*) decorative (*d*) illuminated

28. Ganpat finds it difficult to ***rear*** his family with the present income.
(*a*) support (*b*) live (*c*) control
(*d*) supply (*e*) entertain

29. The ***agility*** of the body of the athlete was very much appreciated by the spectators. **(C.D.S. 1995)**
(*a*) briskness (*b*) suppleness
(*c*) alertness (*d*) sprightliness

30. Babur's ***memoirs*** are contained in 'Tuzuk-i-Baburi'.
(*a*) life (*b*) speech
(*c*) memory (*d*) events

31. He is in the habit of ***thriving*** on others' money.
(*a*) reviving (*b*) surviving
(*c*) prospering (*d*) entertaining

32. All the characters in the novel are ***fictitious.*** **(Railways, 1995)**
(*a*) unreliable (*b*) unbelievable
(*c*) unreal (*d*) imaginative

33. He has travelled all over the continent by ***hitchhiking*** most of the time.
(*a*) flying from city to city
(*b*) driving his own car
(*c*) working at different places
(*d*) getting free rides on request

34. After the ***acrimonious*** debate in the Lok Sabha, some members walked out.
(*a*) bitter (*b*) lively
(*c*) disgusting (*d*) short

35. A stray dog kept ***whimpering*** all night.
(*a*) barking (*b*) crying
(*c*) whining (*d*) sobbing

36. Our talks with the foreign delegation were really ***productive.*** **(B.S.R.B. 1993)**

(*a*) growing (*b*) efficient
(*c*) fruitful (*d*) lengthy

37. Miss Margaret is a ***genteel*** lady.
(*a*) well-bred (*b*) delicate
(*c*) attractive (*d*) beautiful

38. ISI marked goods are always ***pure***.
(*a*) clear (*b*) fresh
(*c*) unmixed (*d*) clean

39. I don't mean to be ***flippant*** but there is no nice way to kill somebody in a war.
(*a*) frivolous (*b*) mean
(*c*) desperate (*d*) naughty

40. The arguments of the lowyer of the accused were so ***persuasive*** that the judge acquitted him.
(*a*) clever (*b*) logical
(*c*) eloquent (*d*) convincing
(N.D.A. 1996)

41. He had a strange ***quirk*** of hitting his sister every now and then.
(*a*) fondness (*b*) aversion
(*c*) habit (*d*) diversion

42. I found myself ***befogged*** in that situation.
(*a*) panicky (*b*) puzzled
(*c*) surprised (*d*) happy

43. He ***declined*** to speak about the problem when I asked him.
(*a*) agreed (*b*) promised
(*c*) refused (*d*) permitted

44. The arguments of the lawyer of the accused were so ***persuasive*** that the judge acquitted him. **(N.D.A. 1996)**
(*a*) convincing (*b*) clever
(*c*) eloquent (*d*) logical

45. The appointments were made quite ***judiciously***.
(*a*) legally (*b*) reasonably (*c*) lawfully
(*d*) justifiably (*e*) impartially

46. Nowadays, pollution is ***rampant*** in all major urban centres.
(*a*) fashionable (*b*) chronic
(*c*) deep-rooted (*d*) excessive

47. That young man is quite ***sanguine*** about the result of his competitive examination. **(Railways, 1994)**
(*a*) optimistic (*b*) anxious
(*c*) depressed (*d*) pessimistic

48. One could see the magnitude of tragedy in the ***limpid*** eyes of the earthquake victims.
(*a*) ugly (*b*) crying
(*c*) wet (*d*) transluscent

49. The ***affluence*** of most visiting Arabs is astonishing.
(*a*) ostentation (*b*) wealth
(*c*) influence (*d*) endeavour

50. He has ***implicated*** them in the conspiracy.
(*a*) interested (*b*) involved
(*c*) affected (*d*) influenced

ANSWERS

1. (*a*)	**2.** (*a*)	**3.** (*c*)	**4.** (*a*)	**5.** (*c*)	**6.** (*c*)	**7.** (*b*)	**8.** (*b*)	**9.** (*d*)	**10.** (*b*)
11. (*c*)	**12.** (*d*)	**13.** (*b*)	**14.** (*c*)	**15.** (*b*)	**16.** (*c*)	**17.** (*d*)	**18.** (*c*)	**19.** (*a*)	**20.** (*a*)
21. (*a*)	**22.** (*a*)	**23.** (*a*)	**24.** (*d*)	**25.** (*c*)	**26.** (*d*)	**27.** (*b*)	**28.** (*a*)	**29.** (*a*)	**30.** (*a*)
31. (*c*)	**32.** (*d*)	**33.** (*d*)	**34.** (*a*)	**35.** (*c*)	**36.** (*c*)	**37.** (*a*)	**38.** (*c*)	**39.** (*a*)	**40.** (*d*)
41. (*c*)	**42.** (*b*)	**43.** (*c*)	**44.** (*a*)	**45.** (*e*)	**46.** (*d*)	**47.** (*a*)	**48.** (*d*)	**49.** (*b*)	**50.** (*b*)

PRACTICE SET 26

Directions : ***In each of the following questions, choose the alternative which can replace the word printed in italic bold without changing the meaning of the sentence.***

1. Even though Akshay does not study hard, he always ***comes*** first in his class.
(*a*) scores (*b*) stands
(*c*) arrives (*d*) completes
(B.S.R.B. 1993)

2. The minister tried to ***assure*** the people regarding their safety.
(*a*) convince (*b*) warn
(*c*) provide (*d*) protect

3. He had a ***catastrophic*** defeat.
(*a*) improbable (*b*) disastrous
(*c*) revolutionary (*d*) pessimistic

4. The international community may begin to doubt the ***credentials*** of the largest democracy in the world. **(C.D.S. 1993)**
(*a*) dependability (*b*) trustworthiness

(*c*) principles
(*d*) capacity to return loans

5. He failed to ***savvy*** the full implications of the agreement that he had signed.
(*a*) remember (*b*) memorise
(*c*) understand (*d*) taste

6. Nathuram's desire to help the villagers is ***genuine***.
(*a*) accurate (*b*) good (*c*) real
(*d*) sincere (*e*) correct

7. The election campaign brings out the reality of the country in its most ***articulate*** form.
(*a*) confused (*b*) aggressive
(*c*) distinct (*d*) wayward

8. ***Weird*** noises came from the haunted houses. **(N.D.A. 1994)**
(*a*) Beastly (*b*) Unpleasant
(*c*) Frightening (*d*) Unnatural

9. The country has a ***potential*** to exploit more mineral resources.
(*a*) fortune (*b*) hidden possibility
(*c*) capacity (*d*) good luck

10. I tried to persuade him to change his mind, but he remained ***adamant***.
(*a*) fixed (*b*) stubborn
(*c*) aggressive (*d*) defensive

11. Grandfather has been getting ***feeble*** of late. **(N.D.A. 1992)**
(*a*) tall (*b*) weak
(*c*) diseased (*d*) small

12. A feeling of brotherhood should be ***nurtured*** in the masses.
(*a*) brought out (*b*) brought up
(*c*) admired (*d*) encouraged

13. Seeing the room in a disorderly state, Ravi concluded that someone had ***ransacked*** the place.
(*a*) upset (*b*) destroyed
(*c*) searched (*d*) attacked

14. The courage shown by the soldiers at this moment of crisis is ***exemplary***.
(*a*) admirable (*b*) clear
(*c*) elementary (*d*) suitable
(Railways, 1994)

15. The dispute between India and Pakistan can only be settled through ***negotiations***.
(*a*) peace treaties (*b*) mutual discussions
(*c*) nuclear wars
(*d*) imposing certain conditions

16. His style is quite ***transparent***.
(*a*) vivid (*b*) witty
(*c*) verbose (*d*) lucid

17. Elsie is seventy years old and a ***fanatical*** gardener. **(C.D.S. 1995)**
(*a*) crazy (*b*) fantastic
(*c*) excessively enthusiastic
(*d*) obsessed

18. He murdered the man without any ***qualms*** of conscience.
(*a*) hesitation (*b*) pang
(*c*) excitement (*d*) curiosity

19. The novel was so interesting that I was ***oblivious*** of my surroundings.
(*a*) indifferent (*b*) watchful (*c*) aware
(*d*) unmindful (*e*) precarious
(Bank P.O. 1994)

20. Her extraordinary stage performance should not be attributed to sheer ***fluke*** only.
(*a*) event (*b*) accidence
(*c*) stroke (*d*) meeting

21. It is not for ***lay*** readers to evaluate a great poet.
(*a*) learned (*b*) ordinary
(*c*) idle (*d*) expert

22. The examination is going to ***commence*** on the 10th of this month.
(*a*) finish (*b*) begin
(*c*) cancel (*d*) continue

23. The invasion force had no artillery and was completely ***annihilated***.
(*a*) reduced (*b*) destroyed
(*c*) dismembered (*d*) split
(Hotel Management, 1993)

24. Tax evasion amounts to ***larcenous*** accumulation of public money by some unscrupulous individuals.
(*a*) miserly (*b*) extravagant
(*c*) theft (*d*) shrewd

25. It was a ***facetious*** remark which totally failed to make any impression.
(*a*) irrelevant to the situation
(*b*) witty joking
(*c*) reconciliatory (*d*) meaningless

26. The eyewitness testimony was ***incontrovertible***. **(N.D.A. 1994)**
(*a*) debatable (*b*) unquestionable
(*c*) unacceptable (*d*) disputable

27. The tendency to act becomes ***ingrained*** in us only in proportion to the frequency with which such actions actually occur.
(*a*) fixed (*b*) marked
(*c*) destined (*d*) desired

28. Jawaharlal Nehru was an ***outstanding*** personality.
(*a*) interesting (*b*) notorious
(*c*) admirable (*d*) prominent

29. When youngsters do not have good role-models to ***emulate*** they start searching for them among sportsmen or filmstars. **(M.B.A. 1994)**
(*a*) inhabit (*b*) imitate
(*c*) mollify (*d*) modify

30. This group is quite ***heterogeneous*** some are very rich while some are very poor.
(*a*) contradictory (*b*) uniform
(*c*) confusing (*d*) varied

31. There was nothing ***casual*** about my father's interests.
(*a*) ordinary (*b*) incidental
(*c*) funny (*d*) accidental

32. I was shocked at his ***crass*** behaviour
(*a*) indifferent (*b*) rigid
(*c*) stupid (*d*) difficult

33. The state finds itself in a ***bind*** in this matter as on many other issues.
(*a*) conflict (*b*) nuisance
(*c*) problem (*d*) depression

34. John Milton wrote 'Paradise Lost' to ***vindicate*** the ways of God to man.
(*a*) explain (*b*) support
(*c*) justify (*d*) criticise
(C.D.S. 1995)

35. The man looked at the poor boy with ***contempt***.
(*a*) disrespect (*b*) pity
(*c*) jealousy (*d*) concern

36. He couldn't ***comprehend*** the details of the document.
(*a*) emphasise (*b*) grasp
(*c*) condense (*d*) implement

37. True religion does not require one to ***proselytise*** through guile or force.
(*a*) convert (*b*) attack
(*c*) hypnotise (*d*) translate
(C.D.S. 1995)

38. The press man's question provokes the minister and the latter reaches ***apoplexy*** in his reaction.
(*a*) loss of feeling (*b*) heights
(*c*) loss of insight (*d*) the end

39. I had a terrible dream last night and I was very much ***scared***.
(*a*) frightened (*b*) excited
(*c*) injured (*d*) unhappy

40. Due to the long ***lapse*** of time, I could not recognise my old friend. **(B.S.R.B. 1992)**
(*a*) delay (*b*) passage
(*c*) duration (*d*) movement

41. Power went to her head and she could not ***stand*** even minor criticism.
(*a*) appreciate (*b*) digest
(*c*) accept (*d*) bear

42. He was ***enticed*** into entering into this deal.
(*a*) tempted (*b*) attracted
(*c*) teased (*d*) rebuked

43. We don't know how we are to ***recompense*** you for the trouble you have taken. **(C.D.S. 1992)**
(*a*) reward (*b*) help
(*c*) praise (*d*) thank

44. The book shows in poor light the ***execrable*** regime of corruption, falsehood and destruction of institutions by the ruler.
(*a*) exhaustive (*b*) deplorable
(*c*) abominable (*d*) continuous

45. He was not able to ***unearth*** his secret to the last.
(*a*) suppress (*b*) discover
(*c*) disclose (*d*) decode

46. The growing ***disparity*** between the rich and the poor has been a cause of global concern.
(*a*) difference (*b*) diversity
(*c*) segregation (*d*) inequality

47. Peace keeping for the United Nations is, at best of times an ***arduous*** task.
(*a*) laborious (*b*) inconvenient
(*c*) difficult (*d*) delicate
(C.D.S. 1995)

48. I had to ***disclose*** the information due to some reasons.
(*a*) discuss (*b*) review
(*c*) suppress (*d*) expose

49. Before my work on the writer appeared there were many vague ideas ***afloat*** about him.
(*a*) circulating (*b*) prevalent
(*c*) stagnant (*d*) primitive

50. The teacher felt that the student lacked ***discrimination*** in the study of his data.
(*a*) imagination (*b*) good taste
(*c*) objectivity (*d*) good judgement
(N.D.A. 1996)

ANSWERS

1. (*b*)	**2.** (*a*)	**3.** (*b*)	**4.** (*b*)	**5.** (*c*)	**6.** (*c*)	**7.** (*c*)	**8.** (*d*)	**9.** (*b*)	**10.** (*b*)
11. (*b*)	**12.** (*b*)	**13.** (*c*)	**14.** (*a*)	**15.** (*b*)	**16.** (*d*)	**17.** (*c*)	**18.** (*b*)	**19.** (*d*)	**20.** (*c*)
21. (*b*)	**22.** (*b*)	**23.** (*b*)	**24.** (*c*)	**25.** (*b*)	**26.** (*b*)	**27.** (*a*)	**28.** (*d*)	**29.** (*b*)	**30.** (*d*)
31. (*a*)	**32.** (*c*)	**33.** (*b*)	**34.** (*c*)	**35.** (*a*)	**36.** (*b*)	**37.** (*a*)	**38.** (*a*)	**39.** (*a*)	**40.** (*c*)
41. (*d*)	**42.** (*a*)	**43.** (*a*)	**44.** (*c*)	**45.** (*b*)	**46.** (*d*)	**47.** (*c*)	**48.** (*d*)	**49.** (*a*)	**50.** (*d*)

PRACTICE SET 27

Directions : ***In each of the following questions, choose the alternative which best expresses the meaning of the word printed in italic bold in the sentence.***

1. He was sad that his seniority had been ***overlooked***. **(S.C.R.A. 1993)**
(*a*) rejected (*b*) neglected
(*c*) confused (*d*) sidestepped

2. Vanity is often ***noticeable*** in a great leader.
(*a*) desirable (*b*) admirable
(*c*) remarkable (*d*) visible

3. In his lust for wealth, he had reached the ***zenith*** of criminal activity.
(*a*) acme (*b*) nadir
(*c*) culmination (*d*) end

4. It was pure fabrication with an ***eye*** for a sensation. **(M.B.A. 1990)**
(*a*) observation (*b*) wish
(*c*) desire (*d*) aim

5. A ***reliable*** friend is the gift of God.
(*a*) dependable (*b*) true
(*c*) helpful (*d*) honest

6. Public opinion will ***pillory*** these agents of crime.
(*a*) scorn (*b*) subserve
(*c*) recall (*d*) declare

7. All his colleagues bore an innate reverence for his ***immaculate*** character.
(*a*) refined (*b*) pure
(*c*) faithful (*d*) splendid

8. His ***adulatory*** remarks surprised us.
(*a*) discreet (*b*) insulting
(*c*) appreciate (*d*) funny
(R.R.B. 1993)

9. For New Delhi, it is time to re-examine its Pakistan policy and reduce the suspicion that it is trying to ***torpedo*** the talks.
(*a*) attack (*b*) quiet down
(*c*) weaken (*d*) refute

10. The ***rapacious*** plunderers did not spare even the people living in the slums.
(*a*) warlike (*b*) barbarous
(*c*) avaricious (*d*) nomadic

11. To avoid future complications, the boundary between neighbours should be properly ***defined***.
(*a*) limited (*b*) demarcated
(*c*) explained (*d*) interpreted

12. Indian economy has always shown enough ***resilience*** in crisis. **(M.B.A. 1992)**
(*a*) diversity (*b*) strength
(*c*) elasticity (*d*) adjustment

13. His physician has ***proscribed*** non-vegetarian diet.
(*a*) recommended (*b*) allowed
(*c*) increased (*d*) forbidden

14. Long illness has ***mascerated*** his body so much so that he is reduced to flesh and bones.
(*a*) affected (*b*) eaten into
(*c*) devastated (*d*) wasted away

15. He ***remonstrated*** with his father about his decision of donating the entire property to the society for the disabled.
(*a*) agreed (*b*) felt pleased
(*c*) protested (*d*) apologized

16. We walked down a ***precipitous*** slope.
(*a*) precarious (*b*) steep
(*c*) precise (*d*) gradual
(Railways, 1993)

17. This is ***blatant*** injustice done to him.
(*a*) conceited (*b*) contorted
(*c*) openly hostile (*d*) too obvious

18. Some of the members of the Board indulged in highly ***scurrilous*** talk at the meeting.
(*a*) irrelevant (*b*) superfluous
(*c*) abusive (*d*) objectionable

19. It is ***compulsory*** for all the students to join this tour. **(S.B.I.P.O. 1991)**
(*a*) regular (*b*) necessary
(*c*) dutiful (*d*) obligatory

20. Decay is an ***immutable*** factor of human life.
(*a*) important (*b*) unique
(*c*) unchangeable (*d*) awful

21. Some of the discoveries of modern science are simply ***marvellous***.
(*a*) praiseworthy (*b*) commendable
(*c*) amazing (*d*) admirable
(S.C.R.A. 1993)

22. The cordial talks between the two foreign ministers cover the entire ***gamut*** of their relations.
(*a*) territory (*b*) range
(*c*) sphere (*d*) scope

23. AIDS is a ***chronic*** disease.
(*a*) incurable (*b*) infectious
(*c*) contagious (*d*) deep-rooted

24. We heard him ***asseverate*** his good intentions but his actions belied his words.
(*a*) affirm (*b*) incite
(*c*) defy (*d*) cancel

25. His unscrupulous act would only ***tantamount*** to ravage and destruction.
(*a*) cause (*b*) result
(*c*) equal (*d*) repetitious

26. The medicine was ***aperient***.
(*a*) bitter (*b*) sweet
(*c*) giddy (*d*) laxative

27. It was an ***ignominous*** defeat for the team.
(*a*) shameful (*b*) unexpected
(*c*) unaccountable (*d*) humiliating

28. There must be lively discussion of Indian authors if we are to ***foster*** our national literature. **(M.B.A. 1991)**
(*a*) promote (*b*) cherish
(*c*) nourish (*d*) nurture

29. His ***conjecture*** was better than mine.
(*a*) guess (*b*) knowledge
(*c*) intuition (*d*) experience

30. The problem of unemployment is ***emasculating*** our youth from making concrete innovations.
(*a*) hindering (*b*) pressurizing
(*c*) encouraging (*d*) making weak

31. Forgetting their old enmity, they joined hands with a spirit of ***camaraderie***.
(*a*) animosity (*b*) love
(*c*) friendliness (*d*) trust

32. She leaned back, feeling ***enervated***.
(*a*) disheartened (*b*) confused
(*c*) saddened (*d*) weakened
(R.R.B. 1993)

33. All his documents were ***confiscated***.
(*a*) cancelled (*b*) seized
(*c*) forfeited (*d*) destroyed

34. The speech was filled with ***rigmarole***.
(*a*) nonsense (*b*) details
(*c*) quotes (*d*) examples

35. Deepak employed my friend only when I agreed to ***avouch*** for his honesty.
(*a*) vow (*b*) affirm
(*c*) pay (*d*) guarantee

36. The boy gave a ***vivid*** description of all that happened. **(Bank P.O. 1992)**
(*a*) brilliant (*b*) fresh
(*c*) explanatory (*d*) picturesque

37. We ***cherish*** the tradition of bravery.
(*a*) imitate (*b*) hold dear
(*c*) learn (*d*) revive

38. He was the most ***disputatious*** student I ever had.
(*a*) scandalous (*b*) argumentative
(*c*) uncertain (*d*) opinionated

39. The relics of the Roman rule are still ***extant*** in England.
(*a*) hidden (*b*) scattered
(*c*) existent (*d*) spread

40. Most of the staff is ***restive*** under the new manager's rule. **(M.B.A. 1995)**
(*a*) relaxed (*b*) friendly (*c*) uneasy
(*d*) obstinate (*e*) discontented

41. Instead of being ***arraigned*** in public, the child should be quietly interviewed in public.
(*a*) punished severely
(*b*) openly declared (*c*) scolded
(*d*) called upon to answer a charge

42. They knew by his ***sophomoric*** remarks that he was still knave in the field.
(*a*) casual (*b*) unpalatable
(*c*) immature (*d*) ignorant

43. Last fortnight the rains came to the parched soils of India after the merciless drought had already ***sapped*** the vitality and livelihood of millions of peasants.
(*a*) decreased (*b*) demolished
(*c*) destroyed (*d*) drained away
(Railways, 1993)

44. His impertinence and his ***salacious*** remarks spoke voliably of his degradation.
(*a*) rude (*b*) indecent
(*c*) distraught (*d*) poor

45. Buoyed by these visions of the future of his son, the artist ***soldiered*** on.
(*a*) continued bravely (*b*) stopped further
(*c*) struggled hard (*d*) fought on
(M.B.A. 1990)

46. They all shunned him because he was a ***lecherous*** man always looking for an opportunity to cheat others.
(*a*) cunning (*b*) deceptive
(*c*) lustful (*d*) dishonest

47. A million cinemas a year bring the same stale ***bladerdash***. **(S.C.R.A. 1993)**
(*a*) adventure (*b*) nonsense
(*c*) thriller (*d*) romance

48. After the severe riots, the police continued the curfew lest there was no ***recrudescence*** of disorder.
(*a*) new outburst (*b*) spread
(*c*) exaggeration (*d*) aggravation

49. Whenever I go by that shop, the diamond necklace in the window ***tantalises*** me.
(*a*) humiliates (*b*) excites
(*c*) teases (*d*) amplifies

50. The army has laid out an entire web of secret agents to detect the ***surreptitious*** activities of the enemy.
(*a*) hostile (*b*) secret
(*c*) intriguing (*d*) foppish

ANSWERS

1. (*b*)	**2.** (*d*)	**3.** (*a*)	**4.** (*d*)	**5.** (*a*)	**6.** (*a*)	**7.** (*b*)	**8.** (*c*)	**9.** (*a*)	**10** (*c*)
11. (*b*)	**12.** (*c*)	**13.** (*d*)	**14.** (*b*)	**15.** (*c*)	**16.** (*b*)	**17.** (*c*)	**18.** (*c*)	**19.** (*d*)	**20.** (*c*)
21. (*c*)	**22.** (*b*)	**23.** (*d*)	**24.** (*a*)	**25.** (*c*)	**26.** (*d*)	**27.** (*a*)	**28.** (*a*)	**29.** (*a*)	**30.** (*d*)
31. (*c*)	**32.** (*d*)	**33.** (*b*)	**34.** (*a*)	**35.** (*b*)	**36.** (*d*)	**37.** (*b*)	**38.** (*b*)	**39.** (*c*)	**40.** (*d*)
41. (*d*)	**42.** (*c*)	**43.** (*d*)	**44.** (*b*)	**45.** (*a*)	**46.** (*c*)	**47.** (*b*)	**48.** (*a*)	**49.** (*c*)	**50.** (*b*)

PRACTICE SET 28

Directions : ***In each of the following passages, there are some words in bold italics and numbered. These numbers are printed below the passage and against each, some words/group of words are suggested. Select the word which has most nearly the same meaning as the original phrase/word.***

Passage 1 **(Railways, 1995)**

Glowing in the heart of the Thar, the burnished sandstone, toda is an ***intricately*** (1) moulded wonderland. Once, what was ***formidable (2)*** desert land, toda is a place of ***gilded (3)*** magic. The sunset has a ***peculiar (4)*** glow here. As the night ***descends (5)*** slowly the sky goes up in flames, which then ***fades (6)*** leaving a few ***embers (7)*** till it becomes coal black. The sun and the sky together create a new ***monument (8)*** here everyday, leaving behind an ***exhilaration (9).*** Here the blazing sun creates ***illusions (10)*** of shimmering lakes on the wide expanse.

1. (*a*) difficult (*b*) magic (*c*) unbelievable (*d*) confused

2. (*a*) formations (*b*) untrue (*c*) difficult (*d*) great, causing fear

3. (*a*) guiding (*b*) covered with gold (*c*) gliding (*d*) pleasant

4. (*a*) untrue (*b*) rare (*c*) strange (*d*) spectacular

5. (*a*) imagination (*b*) go down (*c*) falls (*d*) gives way

6. (*a*) colours (*b*) nature (*c*) lose strength (*d*) hushes

7. (*a*) stains (*b*) colours (*c*) hot piece of wood (*d*) streaks

8. (*a*) fort (*b*) building (*c*) residence (*d*) built to keep alive

9. (*a*) joyful (*b*) pity (*c*) excess breathing (*d*) enjoyable

10. (*a*) sun rays (*b*) sand dunes (*c*) not true (*d*) mirage

Passage 2 **(Bank P.O. 1991)**

During the last year, the business ***ran into (11) unanticipated (12)*** difficulties and this had an ***adverse (13)*** effect on the trading position. As a result, the profit for that year was less than ***forecast (14).*** But the business ***picked up (15)*** this year.

11. (*a*) moved into (*b*) came across (*c*) reached (*d*) fell into (*e*) encountered

12. (*a*) unusual (*b*) unimagined (*c*) unforeseen (*d*) undesirable (*e*) unfavourable

13. (*a*) negative (*b*) hostile (*c*) opposite (*d*) unlucky (*e*) counteractive

14. (*a*) predicated (*b*) prospective (*c*) prepared for (*d*) expected (*e*) looked forward

15. (*a*) developed (*b*) increased (*c*) gathered (*d*) selected (*e*) consolidated

ANSWERS

1. (*a*)	**2.** (*d*)	**3.** (*b*)	**4.** (*c*)	**5.** (*c*)	**6.** (*c*)	**7.** (*c*)	**8.** (*b*)	**9.** (*a*)	**10.** (*c*)
11. (*e*)	**12.** (*c*)	**13.** (*a*)	**14.** (*d*)	**15.** (*b*)					

2. ANTONYMS

What are Antonyms ?

A word which is opposite in meaning to the given word is called its **Antonym.**

Example : The word **'Autonomy'** means *'Independence'*.
So, its antonym would be 'Dependence'.

TYPE 1 : CHOOSING THE CORRECT ANTONYM OF THE GIVEN WORD

In this type of questions, generally a word is given, followed by four or five alternatives. The candidate is required to choose the word which is nearest to the opposite in meaning of the given word.

Example : *Choose the correct antonym of the given word :*

OBSCURE
(*a*) Pedantic (*b*) Implicit (*c*) Explicit (*d*) Obnoxious

Solution: *'Obscure'* means *'secret'*. So, the antonym would be 'Explicit.'
Hence, the answer is (*c*)

PRACTICE SET 1

Directions : *In each of the following questions, choose the word opposite in meaning to the given word.*

1. AUTONOMY **(Assistant Grade, 1996)**
(*a*) Submissiveness (*b*) Dependence
(*c*) Subordination (*d*) Slavery

2. RECEDE
(*a*) Rush (*b*) Advance
(*c*) Approach (*d*) Forward

3. TRAGEDY
(*a*) Humorous (*b*) Comedy
(*c*) Romance (*d*) Calamity

4. KINDLE
(*a*) Ignite (*b*) Encourage
(*c*) Ignore (*d*) Extinguish

5. SHALLOW **(Stenographers' Exam, 1993)**
(*a*) High (*b*) Hidden
(*c*) Deep (*d*) Hollow

6. LENIENT
(*a*) Obstinate (*b*) Annoyed
(*c*) Rude (*d*) Harsh

7. ASSERT
(*a*) Agree (*b*) Acquiesce
(*c*) Abjure (*d*) Abdicate

8. OVERT **(R.R.B. 1995)**
(*a*) Deep (*b*) Shallow
(*c*) Secret (*d*) unwritten

9. ACCORD **(Railways, 1991)**
(*a*) Solution (*b*) Act
(*c*) Dissent (*d*) Concord

10. START
(*a*) Close (*b*) Shut
(*c*) End (*d*) Finish

11. UNIVERSAL
(*a*) Narrow (*b*) Regional
(*c*) Miniature (*d*) Subsidiary

12. ALIVE **(S.S.C. 1991)**
(*a*) Passive (*b*) Dead
(*c*) Asleep (*d*) Drowsy

13. ANCESTORS
(*a*) Supporters (*b*) Disciples
(*c*) Followers (*d*) Descendants

14. ENDOW
(*a*) Borrow (*b*) Steal
(*c*) Snatch (*d*) Extort

15. SYNTHETIC **(M.B.A. 1994)**
(*a*) Cosmetic (*b*) Plastic
(*c*) Affable (*d*) Natural

16. BLISS
(*a*) Anguish (*b*) Sorrow
(*c*) Agony (*d*) Suffering

17. SPREAD
(*a*) Subdue (*b*) Repress
(*c*) Suppress (*d*) Contract

18. PRECARIOUS **(S.S.C. 1992)**
(*a*) Dangerous (*b*) Safe
(*c*) Cautious (*d*) Easy

19. PROFANE
(*a*) Arrogant (*b*) Benign
(*c*) Respectful (*d*) Pious

20. MISERLY
(*a*) Hospitable (*b*) Generous
(*c*) Extravagant (*d*) Philanthropic

21. DEEP **(I. Tax, 1994)**
(*a*) Elementary (*b*) Superficial
(*c*) Shallow (*d*) Perfunctory

22. OBSTINATE
(*a*) Inflexible (*b*) Prominent
(*c*) Pliable (*d*) Fashionable

23. UNSTABLE
(*a*) Changing (*b*) Constant
(*c*) Stagnant (*d*) Steady (*e*) Confined

24. VALIDATE
(*a*) Legalise (*b*) Spurious
(*c*) Authenticate (*d*) Disprove

25. LEND **(Section Officers' 1993)**
(*a*) Hire (*b*) Pawn
(*c*) Cheat (*d*) Borrow

26. JUDICIOUS
(*a*) Unequal (*b*) Unlawful
(*c*) Impure (*d*) Indiscreet

27. JUXTAPOSITION
(*a*) Difference (*b*) Opposition
(*c*) Separation (*d*) Appropriateness

28. PAUCITY **(Bank P.O. 1991)**
(*a*) Surplus (*b*) Scarcity
(*c*) Presence (*d*) Richness
(*e*) Want

29. OFFER
(*a*) Beg (*b*) Borrow
(*c*) Snatch (*d*) Request

30. BURY
(*a*) Examine (*b*) Open
(*c*) Disinter (*d*) Dig

31. MINOR **(Stenographers' Exam, 1994)**
(*a*) Heavy (*b*) Tall
(*c*) Major (*d*) Big

32. LUSCIOUS
(*a*) Dry (*b*) Sour
(*c*) Ugly (*d*) Stale

33. AMELIORATE
(*a*) Lessen (*b*) Hasten
(*c*) Expedite (*d*) Worsen

34. GORGEOUS
(*a*) Desperate (*b*) Plain
(*c*) Fashionable (*d*) Sumptuous

35. FORMER
(*a*) Subsequent (*b*) Later
(*c*) Resultant (*d*) Latter

36. IMPERVIOUS
(*a*) Penetrable (*b*) Hidden
(*c*) Tolerable (*d*) Gentle

37. APPROPRIATE **(Assistant Grade, 1995)**
(*a*) Unskilled (*b*) Unsuitable
(*c*) Unqualified (*d*) Unable

38. RETRIEVE
(*a*) Respond (*b*) Dismiss
(*c*) Foil (*d*) Abandon

39. RABID
(*a*) Decent (*b*) Fair
(*c*) Rational (*d*) Pure

40. OPAQUE **(Clerks' Grade, 1993)**
(*a*) Misty (*b*) Covered
(*c*) Clear (*d*) Transparent

41. FRATERNITY
(*a*) Hospitabilty (*b*) Hostility
(*c*) Brotherhood (*d*) Enmity

42. PRETENTIOUS
(*a*) Deranged (*b*) Small
(*c*) Depressing (*d*) Humble

43. MAWKISH
(*a*) Sentimental (*b*) Intelligent
(*c*) Certain (*d*) Carefree

44. RUTHLESS **(Central Excise, 1990)**
(*a*) Mindful (*b*) Compassionate
(*c*) Majestice (*d*) Merciful

45. ABDICATE
(*a*) Claim (*b*) Snatch
(*c*) Plunder (*d*) Seize

46. DECEIT
(*a*) Reality (*b*) Trust
(*c*) Truthfulness (*d*) Fact

47. VIOLENT **(U.D.C. 1995)**
(*a*) Tame (*b*) Humble
(*c*) Gentle (*d*) Harmless

48. ABHORRENCE
(*a*) Aversion (*b*) Liking
(*c*) Appreciation (*d*) Fear

49. PARSIMONIOUS
(*a*) Generous (*b*) Frugal
(*c*) Crude (*d*) Stingy

50. DEARTH **(C.B.I. 1990)**
(*a*) Extravagance (*b*) Scarcity
(*c*) Abundance (*d*) Sufficiency

ANSWERS

1. (*b*)	**2.** (*b*)	**3.** (*b*)	**4.** (*d*)	**5.** (*c*)	**6.** (*d*)	**7.** (*b*)	**8.** (*c*)	**9.** (*c*)	**10.** (*d*)
11. (*b*)	**12.** (*b*)	**13.** (*d*)	**14.** (*a*)	**15.** (*d*)	**16.** (*b*)	**17.** (*d*)	**18.** (*b*)	**19.** (*d*)	**20.** (*c*)
21. (*c*)	**22.** (*c*)	**23.** (*d*)	**24.** (*d*)	**25.** (*d*)	**26.** (*d*)	**27.** (*c*)	**28.** (*a*)	**29.** (*d*)	**30.** (*c*)
31. (*c*)	**32.** (*b*)	**33.** (*d*)	**34.** (*b*)	**35.** (*d*)	**36.** (*a*)	**37.** (*b*)	**38.** (*d*)	**39.** (*c*)	**40.** (*d*)
41. (*b*)	**42.** (*d*)	**43.** (*b*)	**44.** (*d*)	**45.** (*a*)	**46.** (*c*)	**47.** (*c*)	**48.** (*b*)	**49.** (*a*)	**50.** (*c*)

PRACTICE SET 2

Directions : ***In each of the following questions, choose the word opposite in meaning to the given word.***

1. TRANSPARENT **(I. Tax, 1993)**
(*a*) Coloured (*b*) Childlike
(*c*) Opaque (*d*) Imminent
2. PRIDE
(*a*) Humility (*b*) Shame
(*c*) Humbleness (*d*) Debasement
3. ACQUISITIVE
(*a*) Miserly (*b*) Frugal
(*c*) Simple (*d*) Austere
4. URBAN
(*a*) Country-made (*b*) Pastoral
(*c*) Provincial (*d*) Rural
5. BLATANT
(*a*) Noisy (*b*) Quiet
(*c*) Barren (*d*) Slow
6. PRIM
(*a*) Rash (*b*) Extravagant
(*c*) Foul (*d*) Shameful
7. EXHIBIT **(Clerks' Grade, 1994)**
(*a*) Conceal (*b*) Prevent
(*c*) Withdraw (*d*) Concede
8. SALVAGE
(*a*) Outfit (*b*) Lose
(*c*) Burn (*d*) Remove
9. KEEN
(*a*) Dull (*b*) Rogue
(*c*) Ardent (*d*) Shrewd
10. HAUGHTY **(S.S.C. 1991)**
(*a*) Pitiable (*b*) Scared
(*c*) Humble (*d*) Cowardly
11. UNDERTAKING
(*a*) Resignation (*b*) Trial
(*c*) Refusal (*d*) Denial
12. AUDACIOUS
(*a*) Timid (*b*) Vulgar
(*c*) Low (*d*) Unpractised
13. ENOUGH
(*a*) Inadequate (*b*) Scarce
(*c*) Deficit (*d*) Less
14. VIRTUE **(Stenographers' Exam, 1993)**
(*a*) Vice (*b*) Fraud
(*c*) Wickedness (*d*) Crime
15. ZEAL
(*a*) Hostility (*b*) Diffidence
(*c*) Apathy (*d*) Contempt
16. SYMPATHY
(*a*) Enmity (*b*) Cruelty
(*c*) Abhorrence (*d*) Apathy
17. ERUDITE **(Assistant Grade, 1991)**
(*a*) Professional (*b*) Immature
(*c*) Unimaginative (*d*) Ignorant
18. HAPLESS
(*a*) Lucky (*b*) Kind
(*c*) Helpful (*d*) Futile
19. HAPPINESS
(*a*) Contentment (*b*) Grief
(*c*) Renunciation (*d*) Beatitude
20. ACQUITTED **(M.B.A. 1994)**
(*a*) Entrusted (*b*) Convicted
(*c*) Burdened (*d*) Freed
21. VULGAR
(*a*) Refined (*b*) Cheerful
(*c*) Jolly (*d*) Relevant
22. THRIFT
(*a*) Purchase (*b*) Destroy
(*c*) Waste (*d*) Invest
23. LACONIC **(Central Excise, 1993)**
(*a*) Prolix (*b*) Profligate
(*c*) Prolific (*d*) Bucolic
24. QUERULOUS
(*a*) Bright (*b*) Splendid
(*c*) Smart (*d*) Happy
25. ABSOLUTE **(Stenographers' Exam, 1995)**
(*a*) Scarce (*b*) Limited
(*c*) Faulty (*d*) Deficient
26. TRUMPERY
(*a*) Defeat (*b*) Wastage
(*c*) Treasure (*d*) Vague
27. MAGNIFY **(M.B.A. 1989)**
(*a*) Induce (*b*) Diminish
(*c*) Destroy (*d*) Shrink
28. DISSENT
(*a*) Agreement (*b*) Dispute
(*c*) Disunity (*d*) Controversy
29. CELIBACY
(*a*) Chastity (*b*) Misogyny
(*c*) Matrimony (*d*) Divorce
30. BOOST **(Railways, 1993)**
(*a*) Hinder (*b*) Obstruct
(*c*) Discourage (*d*) Rebuke
31. IMPROPRIETY
(*a*) Decorum (*b*) Purity
(*c*) Ideal (*d*) Conformity
32. UNSULLIED
(*a*) Visible (*b*) Foul
(*c*) Stainless (*d*) Strong
33. SMOOTH **(U.D.C. 1994)**
(*a*) Ugly (*b*) Awkward
(*c*) Hard (*d*) Rough
34. NERVOUS
(*a*) Bold (*b*) Doubtful
(*c*) Timid (*d*) Shrewish
35. ACUTE
(*a*) Sharp (*b*) Critical
(*c*) Dull (*d*) Sensitive

36. BASE **(Central Excise, 1992)**
(*a*) Roof (*b*) Height
(*c*) Top (*d*) Climax

37. DISSUADE
(*a*) Incite (*b*) Persuade
(*c*) Advise (*d*) Instigate

38. NAIVE
(*a*) Cunning (*b*) Wealthy
(*c*) Sophisticated (*d*) Complicated

39. MOIST **(Clerks' Grade, 1993)**
(*a*) Parched (*b*) Dry
(*c*) Hard (*d*) Crisp

40. ANATHEMATISE
(*a*) Radiate (*b*) Regulate
(*c*) Deceive (*d*) Bless

41. FECUND
(*a*) Barren (*b*) Solid
(*c*) Unploughed (*d*) Hard

42. DEMON **(Railways, 1995)**
(*a*) Charitable (*b*) Kind-hearted
(*c*) Angel (*d*) Fair-minded

43. VANQUISH
(*a*) Surrender (*b*) Debase
(*c*) Destroy (*d*) Ruin

44. BELIE
(*a*) Argue (*b*) Justify
(*c*) Admire (*d*) Approve

45. DELETE **(C.B.I. 1990)**
(*a*) Impound (*b*) Insert
(*c*) Inspire (*d*) Injure

46. DESPONDENCY
(*a*) Humility (*b*) Pleasure
(*c*) Cheerfulness (*d*) Excitement

47. MISERLY
(*a*) Liberal (*b*) Spendthrift
(*c*) Charitable (*d*) Generous

48. DISCOUNT
(*a*) Interest (*b*) Premium
(*c*) Profit (*d*) Concession

49. VOLUNTARY
(*a*) Ordered (*b*) Alternative
(*c*) Compulsory (*d*) Essential

50. ONEROUS **(Central Excise, 1989)**
(*a*) Straight-forward (*b*) Easy
(*c*) Complex (*d*) Plain

ANSWERS

1. (*c*)	**2.** (*a*)	**3.** (*d*)	**4.** (*d*)	**5.** (*b*)	**6.** (*a*)	**7.** (*a*)	**8.** (*b*)	**9.** (*a*)	**10.** (*c*)
11. (*c*)	**12.** (*a*)	**13.** (*a*)	**14.** (*a*)	**15.** (*c*)	**16.** (*d*)	**17.** (*d*)	**18.** (*a*)	**19.** (*b*)	**20.** (*b*)
21. (*a*)	**22.** (*c*)	**23.** (*a*)	**24.** (*d*)	**25.** (*b*)	**26.** (*c*)	**27.** (*b*)	**28.** (*a*)	**29.** (*c*)	**30.** (*a*)
31. (*a*)	**32.** (*b*)	**33.** (*d*)	**34.** (*a*)	**35.** (*c*)	**36.** (*c*)	**37.** (*b*)	**38.** (*c*)	**39.** (*b*)	**40.** (*d*)
41. (*a*)	**42.** (*c*)	**43.** (*a*)	**44.** (*b*)	**45.** (*b*)	**46.** (*c*)	**47.** (*d*)	**48.** (*b*)	**49.** (*c*)	**50.** (*b*)

PRACTICE SET 3

Directions : ***In each of the following questions, choose one alternative which is opposite in meaning to the given word.***

1. COMIC **(Section Officers' 1993)**
(*a*) Painful (*b*) Fearful
(*c*) Tragic (*d*) Emotional

2. COMMUNICATIVE
(*a*) Primitive (*b*) Passive
(*c*) Dumb (*d*) Reticent

3. RETAIN
(*a*) Reject (*b*) Renounce
(*c*) Spare (*d*) Eject

4 ESCALATE
(*a*) Lessen (*b*) Subside
(*c*) Reduce (*d*) Heal

5. TERRIBLE **(Clerks'Grade 1994)**
(*a*) Horrible (*b*) Awesome
(*c*) Delightful (*d*) Hideous

6. INTRUDE
(*a*) Withhold (*b*) Withdraw
(*c*) Accept (*d*) Surrender

7. FACSIMILE
(*a*) Reproduction (*b*) Sincere
(*c*) Original (*d*) Engineered

8. BAGGY
(*a*) Strict (*b*) Compact
(*c*) Firm (*d*) Tight

9. ADDITION **(Stenographers' Exam, 1994)**
(*a*) Multiplication (*b*) Subtraction
(*c*) Enumeration (*d*) Division

10. LOYAL
(*a*) Rebellious (*b*) Courageous
(*c*) Faithful (*d*) Friendly

11. SUBJUGATE
(*a*) Liberate (*b*) Enslave
(*c*) Enrich (*d*) Identify

12. EVACUATE **(C.B.I. 1991)**
(*a*) Admit (*b*) Emerge
(*a*) Abandon (*b*) Invade

13. OUTMODED
(*a*) Polished (*b*) Practicable
(*c*) Stylish (*d*) Fashionable

14. CONDENSE
(*a*) Lengthen (*b*) Expand
(*c*) Distribute (*d*) Interpret

(S.S.C. 1992)

15. BRIDGE
(*a*) Divide (*b*) Bind
(*c*) Release (*d*) Open

16. TRANQUIL
(*a*) Impatient (*b*) Agitated
(*c*) Vociferous (*d*) Noisy

17. INDULGE
(*a*) Avoid (*b*) Abstain
(*c*) Forego (*d*) Neglect

(Central Excise, 1994)

18. ATTRACT
(*a*) Repulse (*b*) Reject
(*c*) Repel (*d*) Distract

19. RESPITE
(*a*) Tension (*b*) Exertion
(*c*) Regularity (*d*) Delay

20. BACCHANAL
(*a*) Cautious (*b*) Grave
(*c*) Cunning (*d*) Sober

(I.Tax, 1992)

21. GRATUITY
(*a*) Annuity (*b*) Stipend
(*c*) Discount (*d*) Wages

22. ECLIPSE
(*a*) Shine (*b*) Enlarge
(*c*) Goggle (*d*) Gleam

23. MALFORMED
(*a*) Fetid (*b*) Sketchy
(*c*) Curvaceous (*d*) Shapely

(Clerks' Grade,1995)

24. KNOWLEDGE
(*a*) Ignorance (*b*) Illiteracy
(*c*) Foolishness (*d*) Backwardness

25. DEGENERATE
(*a*) Create (*b*) Progress
(*c*) Restore (*d*) Reproduce

(Assistant Grade, 1996)

26. NADIR
(*a*) Progress (*b*) Liberty
(*c*) Zenith (*d*) Modernity

27. WRECK
(*a*) Make (*b*) Build
(*c*) Restore (*d*) Relieve

28. DELIBERATE
(*a*) Premeditated (*b*) Sparking
(*c*) Methodical (*d*) Impulsive

29. FLACCID
(*a*) Upright (*b*) Taut
(*c*) Uneven (*d*) Tough

(Steno. 1993)

30. FOREIGNER
(*a*) National (*b*) Stranger
(*c*) Native (*d*) Alien

31. AVOIDANCE
(*a*) Possession (*b*) Passion
(*c*) Pursuit (*d*) Power

32. IMPOUND
(*a*) Generate (*b*) Strengthen
(*c*) Stimulate (*d*) Release

(Railways, 1991)

33. LANGUID
(*a*) Smart (*b*) Energetic
(*c*) Fast (*d*) Ferocious

34. COMPLY
(*a*) Refuse (*b*) Agree
(*c*) Disagree (*d*) Deny

35. BAULK
(*a*) Admire (*b*) Strengthen
(*c*) Clamour (*d*) Encourage

(M.B.A. 1994)

36. STRINGENT
(*a*) Magnanimous (*b*) Lenient
(*c*) Vehement (*d*) General

37. IGNORE
(*a*) Support (*b*) Favour
(*c*) Redress (*d*) Accept

38. DEBAUCHEE
(*a*) Moralist (*b*) Thinker
(*c*) Schemer (*d*) Dreamer

39. ALLEVIATION
(*a*) Exaggeration (*b*) Exasperation
(*c*) Magnification (*d*) Intensification

40. MITIGATE
(*a*) Stagnate (*b*) Suffer
(*c*) Aggravate (*d*) Instigate

41. MINION
(*a*) Master (*b*) Quorum
(*c*) Majority (*d*) Host

42. GOBLIN
(*a*) Angel (*b*) Hermit
(*c*) Traveller (*d*) Pilot

43. ALIENATE
(*a*) Gather (*b*) Identify
(*c*) Assemble (*d*) Unite

(I. Tax & Central Excise, 1990)

44. HAMPER
(*a*) Open (*b*) Release
(*c*) Hold (*d*) Hasten

45. EVANESCENT
(*a*) Blooming (*b*) Growing
(*c*) Twinkling (*d*) Teasing

(U.D.C. 1995)

46. MALICIOUS
(*a*) Boastful (*b*) Indifferent
(*c*) Kind (*d*) Generous

47. OFFICIAL
(*a*) Domestic (*b*) General
(*c*) Public (*d*) Private

48. HOLY
(*a*) Offensive (*b*) Orthodox
(*c*) Profane (*d*) Obnoxious

(C.B.I. 1990)

49. SPURIOUS
(*a*) False (*b*) Genuine
(*c*) Simple (*d*) Systematic

50. LISSOME
(*a*) Ungainly (*b*) Huge
(*c*) Pungent (*d*) Crude

ANSWERS

1. (*c*)	**2.** (*d*)	**3.** (*c*)	**4.** (*b*)	**5.** (*c*)	**6.** (*b*)	**7.** (*c*)	**8.** (*d*)	**9.** (*b*)	**10.** (*a*)
11. (*a*)	**12.** (*a*)	**13.** (*d*)	**14.** (*b*)	**15.** (*d*)	**16.** (*b*)	**17.** (*b*)	**18.** (*c*)	**19.** (*b*)	**20.** (*d*)
21. (*d*)	**22.** (*a*)	**23.** (*d*)	**24.** (*a*)	**25.** (*b*)	**26.** (*c*)	**27.** (*c*)	**28.** (*d*)	**29.** (*b*)	**30.** (*c*)
31. (*c*)	**32.** (*d*)	**33.** (*b*)	**34.** (*a*)	**35.** (*d*)	**36.** (*b*)	**37.** (*c*)	**38.** (*a*)	**39.** (*b*)	**40.** (*c*)
41. (*a*)	**42.** (*a*)	**43.** (*b*)	**44.** (*d*)	**45.** (*a*)	**46.** (*d*)	**47.** (*d*)	**48.** (*c*)	**49.** (*b*)	**50.** (*a*)

PRACTICE SET 4

Directions : ***In each of the following questions, choose the word opposite in meaning to the given word.***

1. HINDRANCE
(*a*) Agreeement (*b*) Cooperation
(*c*) Persuasion (*d*) Aid
(Stenographers' Exam, 1995)
2. JEER
(*a*) Mourn (*b*) Praise
(*c*) Mock (*d*) Sneer
3. BEAUTIFUL
(*a*) Ugly (*b*) Dark
(*c*) Rough (*d*) Dirty
4. ADEQUATE
(*a*) Profuse (*b*) Abounding
(*c*) Scanty (*d*) Abundant
5. PLACATE
(*a*) Embroil (*b*) Antangonize
(*c*) Amuse (*d*) Pacify
6. FRAILTY
(*a*) Emaciation (*b*) Strength
(*c*) Health (*d*) Boldness
7. PROHIBIT **(C.B.I. 1994)**
(*a*) Accept (*b*) Permit
(*c*) Agree (*d*) Grant
8. EMBRACE
(*a*) Suspect (*b*) Harm
(*c*) Reject (*d*) Hurt
9. BASHFUL
(*a*) Daring (*b*) Boastful
(*c*) Upright (*d*) Confident
10. ROUGHLY **(Clerks' Grade, 1994)**
(*a*) Exactly (*b*) Completely
(*c*) Pointedly (*d*) Largely
11. EXONERATE
(*a*) Compel (*b*) Accuse
(*c*) Imprison (*d*) Boldness
12. LIBERALISM
(*a*) Humanism (*b*) Dynamism
(*c*) Sectarianism (*d*) Totalitarianism
13. MISERLY **(S.S.C. 1991)**
(*a*) Generous (*b*) Liberal
(*c*) Spend thrift (*d*) Charitable
14. WONDER
(*a*) Stock (*b*) Amusement
(*c*) Expectation (*d*) Surprise
15. MALICE
(*a*) Honour (*b*) Ecstasy
(*c*) Goodwill (*d*) Happiness
16. DENSITY **(Central Excise, 1992)**
(*a*) Brightness (*b*) Clarity
(*c*) Intelligence (*d*) Rarity
17. COMMODIOUS
(*a*) Limited (*b*) Expensive
(*c*) Numerous (*d*) Leisurely
18. APPOINTMENT
(*a*) Disappointment (*b*) Suspension
(*c*) Dismissal (*d*) Discharge
19. CONTENTED **(Railways, 1995)**
(*a*) Rash (*b*) Narrow-minded
(*c*) Gloomy (*d*) Disappointed
20. MAMMOTH
(*a*) Dull (*b*) Weak
(*c*) Tiny (*d*) Bright
21. CONCEAL **(Stenographers' Exam, 1995)**
(*a*) Unfold (*b*) Reveal
(*c*) Open (*d*) Discover
22. EXTENSION
(*a*) Condensation (*b*) Subtraction
(*c*) Deletion (*d*) Weakening
(*e*) Diminution
23. KILL
(*a*) Azure (*b*) Relief
(*c*) Execute (*d*) Animate
24. SELDOM **(I. Tax, 1993)**
(*a*) Rarely (*b*) Daily
(*c*) Often (*d*) Never
25. PERTINENT
(*a*) Indifferent (*b*) Detached
(*c*) Determined (*d*) Irrelevant
26. AMALGAMATE
(*a*) Generate (*b*) Repair
(*c*) Materialise (*d*) Separate

27. GUILTY (M.B.A. 1989)
(*a*) Innocent (*b*) Pure
(*c*) Virtuous (*d*) Argelic

28. DREARY
(*a*) Plenty (*b*) Monotonous
(*c*) Unhappy (*d*) Cheerful

29. BESEECH
(*a*) Bully (*b*) Solicit
(*c*) Demand (*d*) Dismiss

30. SEETHE
(*a*) Plumb (*b*) Cool
(*c*) Freeze (*d*) Chill

31. HUMBLE (Assistant Grade, 1995)
(*a*) Dominant (*b*) Proud
(*c*) Despotic (*d*) Pompous

32. EXECRABLE
(*a*) Importable (*b*) Acceptable
(*c*) Desirable (*d*) Irritable

33. STRIDENT
(*a*) Stable (*b*) Pleasant
(*c*) Musical (*d*) Melodious

34. REAR (U.D.C. 1994)
(*a*) Front (*b*) Foreground
(*c*) Forehead (*d*) Forward

35. BATTY
(*a*) Prudent (*b*) Sane
(*c*) Cunning (*d*) Cautious

36. MILITANT
(*a*) Religious (*b*) Combative
(*c*) Spiritual (*d*) Pacifist

37. PACIFY (I. Tax, 1989)
(*a*) Insult (*b*) Injure
(*c*) Offend (*d*) Aggravate

38. SUBLIME
(*a*) Strange (*b*) Low
(*c*) Ridiculous (*d*) Mean

39. GRADUALLY
(*a*) Hastily (*b*) Suddenly
(*c*) Thoughtlessly (*d*) Impulsively

40. SAGE (Clerks' Grade, 1993)
(*a*) Rogue (*b*) Fool
(*c*) Egoist (*d*) Snob

41. ACCLAMATION
(*a*) Denunciation (*b*) Suppression
(*c*) Termination (*d*) Applause

42. AMBIGUOUS
(*a*) Obscure (*b*) Secular
(*c*) Explicit (*d*) Equivocate

43. ANTIPATHY (C.B.I. 1990)
(*a*) Obedience (*b*) Admiration
(*c*) Agreement (*d*) Fondness

44. BLISS
(*a*) Paradise (*b*) Heaven
(*c*) Misery (*d*) Happiness

45. EUPHONIOUS
(*a*) Strident (*b*) Lethargic
(*c*) Literary (*d*) Musical

46. EXTERIOR (S.S.C. 1995)
(*a*) Internal (*b*) Inner
(*c*) Interior (*d*) Inward

47. IMPOUND
(*a*) Release (*b*) Strengthen
(*c*) Generate (*d*) Stimulate

48. COMPACT
(*a*) Shattered (*b*) Enlarged
(*c*) Spread (*d*) Diffused

49. HOST (Stenographers' Exan, 1995)
(*a*) Accomplice (*b*) Enlarged
(*c*) Spread (*d*) Diffused

50. VIGOUR
(*a*) Failure (*b*) Negligence
(*c*) Frailty (*d*) Health

ANSWERS

1. (*d*)	**2.** (*b*)	**3.** (*a*)	**4.** (*c*)	**5.** (*b*)	**6.** (*b*)	**7.** (*b*)	**8.** (*c*)	**9.** (*d*)	**10.** (*a*)
11. (*b*)	**12.** (*d*)	**13.** (*a*)	**14.** (*c*)	**15.** (*c*)	**16.** (*d*)	**17.** (*a*)	**18.** (*c*)	**19.** (*d*)	**20.** (*c*)
21. (*b*)	**22.** (*a*)	**23.** (*d*)	**24.** (*c*)	**25.** (*d*)	**26.** (*d*)	**27.** (*a*)	**28.** (*d*)	**29.** (*c*)	**30.** (*b*)
31. (*b*)	**32.** (*c*)	**33.** (*b*)	**34.** (*a*)	**35.** (*b*)	**36.** (*d*)	**37.** (*c*)	**38.** (*b*)	**39.** (*b*)	**40.** (*a*)
41. (*a*)	**42.** (*c*)	**43.** (*b*)	**44.** (*c*)	**45.** (*a*)	**46.** (*c*)	**47.** (*a*)	**48.** (*b*)	**49.** (*d*)	**50.** (*c*)

PRACTICE SET 5

Directions : *In each of the following questions, choose the word opposite in meaning to the given word.*

1. UNREALISTIC (Bank P.O. 1991)
(*a*) Natural (*b*) Visionary
(*c*) Reasonable (*d*) Actual
(*e*) Intelligent

2. DEPRAVED
(*a*) Great (*b*) Enhanced
(*c*) Moral (*d*) Prosperous

3. METICULOUS (M.B.A. 1994)
(*a*) Slovenly (*b*) Meretricious

(*c*) Shaggy (*d*) Mutual

4. AMICABLE
(*a*) Cunning (*b*) Shy
(*c*) Hostile (*d*) Crazy

5. CLARITY **(Clerks' Grade, 1992)**
(*a*) Exaggeration (*b*) Candour
(*c*) Confusion (*d*) Reserve

6. OPULENT
(*a*) Wealthy (*b*) Poor
(*c*) Sumptuous (*d*) Drooping

7. SANCTIFY
(*a*) Dedicate (*b*) Patronise
(*c*) Venerate (*d*) Pollute

8. CHALLENGE **(Central Excise, 1994)**
(*a*) Admire (*b*) Accept
(*c*) Favour (*d*) Praise

9. TEDIOUS
(*a*) Pleasant (*b*) Lovely
(*c*) Lively (*d*) Gay

10. COMMEND
(*a*) Censure (*b*) Condemn
(*c*) Defy (*d*) Defame

11. SUPERFICIAL **(S.S.C. 1993)**
(*a*) Artificial (*b*) Deep
(*c*) Shallow (*d*) Real

12. EFFETE
(*a*) Adamant (*b*) Strong
(*c*) Courageous (*d*) Bold

13. COMMEND **(I. Tax & Excise, 1990)**
(*a*) Suspend (*b*) Admonish
(*c*) Hate (*d*) Dislike

14. SERENE
(*a*) Jovial (*b*) Moving
(*c*) Agitated (*d*) Nervous

15. ANTIPATHY
(*a*) Fondness (*b*) Obedience
(*c*) Agreement (*d*) Admiration

16. DAUNTLESS **(C.B.I. 1990)**
(*a*) Cautious (*b*) Thoughtful
(*c*) Weak (*d*) Adventurous

17. CHAFFING
(*a*) Expensive (*b*) Achieving
(*c*) Capitalistic (*d*) Serious

18. TRAGIC **(S.S.C. 1995)**
(*a*) Funny (*b*) Comic
(*c*) Light (*d*) Humorous

19. EXODUS **(Assistant Grade, 1996)**
(*a*) Restoration (*b*) Return
(*c*) Home-coming (*d*) Influx

20. PREVENT
(*a*) Excite (*b*) Support
(*c*) Invite (*d*) Incite

21. RUGGED
(*a*) Delicate (*b*) Coarse
(*c*) Tough (*d*) Timid

22. EDIFICATION
(*a*) Lamentation (*b*) Annotation
(*c*) Corruption (*d*) Segregation

23. INNOCENT **(Stenographers' Exam, 1993)**
(*a*) Sinful (*b*) Guilty
(*c*) Deadly (*d*) Corruption

24. PACIFY
(*a*) Quarrel (*b*) Challenge
(*c*) Threaten (*d*) Darken

25. FURTIVE
(*a*) Straight (*b*) Obvious
(*c*) Unambiguous (*d*) Open

26. SECULAR
(*a*) Righteous (*b*) Religious
(*c*) Spiritual (*d*) Moral

27. DEAR **(Section Officers' 1993)**
(*a*) Cheap (*b*) Worthless
(*c*) Free (*d*) Priceless

28. ASCETICISM
(*a*) Bliss (*b*) Pleasure
(*c*) Joy (*d*) Trance

29. PREDILECTION
(*a*) Denial (*b*) Concealment
(*c*) Aversion (*d*) Attraction

30. APPOSITE **(Asstt. Grade, 1991)**
(*a*) Inappropriate (*b*) Intemperate
(*c*) Inconsistent (*d*) Irregular

31. JETTISON
(*a*) Rejoice (*b*) Surrender
(*c*) Accept (*d*) Defend

32. PERSISTENT
(*a*) Wavering (*b*) Obstinate
(*c*) Enduring (*d*) Steady

33. SCOLD
(*a*) Enamour (*b*) Rebuke
(*c*) Criticise (*d*) Praise

34. PODGY **(S.S.C. 1991)**
(*a*) Short (*b*) Thin
(*c*) Weak (*d*) Slim

35. SEGREGATION
(*a*) Appreciation (*b*) Cohesion
(*c*) Integration (*d*) Union

36. JITTERY
(*a*) Profuse (*b*) Tense
(*c*) Bold (*d*) Shaky

37. VIRTUOUS **(Stenographers' Exam, 1994)**
(*a*) Scandalous (*b*) Vicious
(*c*) Wicked (*d*) Corrupt

38. EXASPERATE
(*a*) Belittle (*b*) Annoy
(*c*) Please (*d*) Tarnish

39. SORDID
(*a*) Steady (*b*) Enthusiastic
(*c*) Generous (*d*) Splendid

40. GRIM **(C.B.I. 1991)**
(*a*) Serious (*b*) Satisfying
(*c*) Delightful (*d*) Painful

41. DEPLETE
(*a*) Refund (*b*) Replenish
(*c*) Fulfil (*d*) Recover

42. CAJOLE
(*a*) Dissuade (*b*) Detract
(*c*) Disclose (*d*) Confide

43. PATERNITY **(I. Tax & Excise, 1993)**
(*a*) Posterity (*b*) Successors
(*c*) Offspring (*d*) Ancestors

44. BOORISH
(*a*) Handsome (*b*) Happy
(*c*) Quite (*d*) Genteel

45. BENIGN
(*a*) Gracious (*b*) Sinister
(*c*) Novel (*d*) Humane

46. DEVIATE
(*a*) Follow (*b*) Locate
(*c*) Break (*d*) Concentrate

47. AMPLIFY
(*a*) Mummify (*b*) Shock
(*c*) Curtail (*d*) Embalm

48. SPARSE
(*a*) Expensive (*b*) Heavy
(*c*) Scattered (*d*) Lavish

49. EXOTIC
(*a*) Poor (*b*) Inexpensive
(*c*) Ugly (*d*) Conventional

50. AMNESTY
(*a*) Hostility (*b*) Punishment
(*c*) Immunity (*d*) Acquittal

ANSWERS

1. (*c*)	2. (*c*)	3. (*a*)	4. (*c*)	5. (*c*)	6. (*b*)	7. (*d*)	8. (*b*)	9. (*c*)	10. (*a*)
11. (*b*)	12. (*b*)	13. (*d*)	14. (*c*)	15. (*a*)	16. (*d*)	17. (*d*)	18. (*b*)	19. (*d*)	20. (*b*)
21. (*a*)	22. (*c*)	23. (*b*)	24. (*a*)	25. (*d*)	26. (*b*)	27. (*a*)	28. (*b*)	29. (*c*)	30. (*a*)
31. (*c*)	32. (*a*)	33. (*d*)	34. (*b*)	35. (*c*)	36. (*c*)	37. (*b*)	38. (*c*)	39. (*c*)	40. (*c*)
41. (*b*)	42. (*a*)	43. (*c*)	44. (*d*)	45. (*b*)	46. (*a*)	47. (*c*)	48. (*d*)	49. (*d*)	50. (*b*)

PRACTICE SET 6

Directions : ***Pick out the word that is most nearly the opposite in meaning of the word given in capitals.***

1. ACUMEN **(Railways, 1991)**
(*a*) Intelligence (*b*) Imbecility
(*c*) Potentiality (*d*) Unfamiliarity

2. EXPLICIT
(*a*) Inspiring (*b*) Plain
(*c*) Invigorating (*d*) Implied

3. VIRULENT
(*a*) Harmless (*b*) Malignant
(*c*) Hostile (*d*) Vicious

4. DEFICIT **(M.B.A. 1989)**
(*a*) Superfluous (*b*) Surplus
(*c*) Explicit (*d*) Implicit

5. FRANTIC
(*a*) Calm (*b*) Hopeful
(*c*) Active (*d*) Bitter

6. REDOLENT
(*a*) Pesticised (*b*) Sticky
(*c*) Yellowish (*d*) Stinking

7. TURBULENT
(*a*) Turbid (*b*) Violent
(*c*) Steady (*d*) Critical

8. ADVERSITY
(*a*) Enmity (*b*) Severity
(*c*) Prosperity (*d*) Calamity

9. MUSTY
(*a*) Fresh (*b*) Expensive
(*c*) Clean (*d*) Fine

10. PROPEL
(*a*) Hide (*b*) Shove
(*c*) Hesitate (*d*) Check

11. PATCHY **(Central Excise, 1992)**
(*a*) Clear (*b*) Simple
(*c*) Uniform (*d*) Attractive

12. VANITY
(*a*) Modesty (*b*) Kindness
(*c*) Compassion (*d*) Moderation

13. STRENUOUS
(*a*) Unfaltering (*b*) Irresolute
(*c*) Unwavering (*d*) Lazy
(*e*) Unenterprising

14. WANE
(*a*) Swell (*b*) Prosper
(*c*) Fatten (*d*) Widen

15. ILLEGIBLE **(C.B.I. 1994)**
(*a*) Clear (*b*) Imitable
(*c*) Clean (*d*) Readable

16. ROBUST
(*a*) Thin (*b*) Emaciated
(*c*) Light (*d*) Strong

17. CARNAL
(*a*) Sensuous (*b*) Spiritual
(*c*) Visionary (*d*) Imaginary

18. FLEXIBLE **(S.S.C. 1994)**
(*a*) Brittle (*b*) Rigid
(*c*) Hard (*d*) Solid

19. DEVOUT
(*a*) Irreverent (*b*) Sincere
(*c*) Homely (*d*) Magnificent

20. RELINQUISH
(*a*) Withdraw (*b*) Attack
(*c*) Assume (*d*) Conquer

21. CONSPICUOUS **(I. Tax, 1992)**
(*a*) Indifferent (*b*) Harmless
(*c*) Insignificant (*d*) Unknown

22. LEVITY
(*a*) Stupidity (*b*) Gravity
(*c*) Lofty (*d*) Absurdity

23. GLUT
(*a*) Dearth (*b*) Limit
(*c*) Drain (*d*) Supply

24. AROMATIC
(*a*) Tart (*b*) Disagreeable
(*c*) Sour (*d*) Odorous
(*e*) Oppressive

25. VIVACIOUS
(*a*) Quarrelsome (*b*) Sober
(*c*) Notorious (*d*) Drunken

26. CONFESS **(Stenographers' Exam, 1995)**
(*a*) Deny (*b*) Refuse
(*c*) Contest (*d*) Contend

27. INFALLIBLE
(*a*) Erring (*b*) Untrustworthy
(*c*) Dubious (*d*) Unreliable

28. GATHER
(*a*) Separate (*b*) Suspend
(*c*) Scatter (*d*) Spend

29. EXALT
(*a*) Depreciate (*b*) Ennoble
(*c*) Glorify (*d*) Simplify

30. HOARD **(I. Tax, 1993)**
(*a*) Deposit (*b*) Supply
(*c*) Satisfy (*d*) Accumulate

31. DISINGENOUS
(*a*) Industrious (*b*) Cumbersome
(*c*) Slothful (*d*) Naive

32. EFFETE
(*a*) Strong (*b*) Adamant
(*c*) Bold (*d*) Courageous

33. PROVOCATION **(M.B.A. 1994)**
(*a*) Destruction (*b*) Peace
(*c*) Pacification (*d*) Vocation

34. SUCCUMB
(*a*) Curb (*b*) Resist
(*c*) Injure (*d*) Shoot

35. JOCOSE
(*a*) Dull (*b*) Humorous
(*c*) Playful (*d*) Diseased

36. FACT **(Railways, 1993)**
(*a*) Fable (*b*) Story
(*c*) Illusion (*d*) Fiction

37. GAINSAY
(*a*) Affirm (*b*) Reject
(*c*) Appreciate (*d*) Lose

38. CRYPTIC
(*a*) Superficial (*b*) Secret
(*c*) Artificial (*d*) Candid

39. NATIVE **(U.D.C. 1994)**
(*a*) Alien (*b*) Foreigner
(*c*) Newcomer (*d*) Stranger

40. AFFECTATION
(*a*) Love (*b*) Good
(*c*) Likable (*d*) Natural

41. RADICAL
(*a*) Uncompromising (*b*) Basic
(*c*) Thorough (*d*) Superficial

42. MODICUM **(I. Tax & Excise, 1989)**
(*a*) Simplicity (*b*) A large amount
(*c*) Brazenness (*d*) Immodesty

43. SLUR
(*a*) Promise (*b*) Hope
(*c*) Credit (*d*) Virtue

44. DEBILITATING
(*a*) Strengthening (*b*) Enfeebling
(*c*) Occupying (*d*) Inhabiting

45. MASK **(Clerks' Grade, 1993)**
(*a*) Deface (*b*) Injure
(*c*) Expose (*d*) Hit

46. FICKLE
(*a*) Diseased (*b*) Fast
(*c*) Constant (*d*) Quick

47. PASSIONATE
(*a*) Calm (*b*) Arrogant
(*c*) Sure (*d*) Fervent

48. CHOICE **(Railways, 1995)**
(*a*) Refusal (*b*) Dilemma
(*c*) Harm (*d*) Approval

49. DAINTY
(*a*) Splendid (*b*) Aggressive
(*c*) Vigorous (*d*) Towering

50. NIMBLE
(*a*) Giant (*b*) Clumsy
(*c*) Quick (*d*) Frank

ANSWERS

1. (*b*)	**2.** (*d*)	**3.** (*a*)	**4.** (*b*)	**5.** (*a*)	**6.** (*d*)	**7.** (*c*)	**8.** (*c*)	**9.** (*a*)	**10.** (*d*
11. (*c*)	**12.** (*a*)	**13.** (*d*)	**14.** (*b*)	**15.** (*d*)	**16.** (*b*)	**17.** (*b*)	**18.** (*b*)	**19.** (*a*)	**20.** (*c*)
21. (*c*)	**22.** (*b*)	**23.** (*a*)	**24.** (*d*)	**25.** (*c*)	**26.** (*a*)	**27.** (*a*)	**28.** (*c*)	**29.** (*a*)	**30.** (*b*)
31. (*d*)	**32.** (*a*)	**33.** (*c*)	**34.** (*b*)	**35.** (*a*)	**36.** (*d*)	**37.** (*a*)	**38.** (*d*)	**39.** (*a*)	**40.** (*d*)
41. (*d*)	**42.** (*b*)	**43.** (*c*)	**44.** (*a*)	**45.** (*c*)	**46.** (*c*)	**47.** (*a*)	**48.** (*b*)	**49.** (*c*)	**50.** (*b*

PRACTICE SET 7

Directions : ***In each of the following questions, choose the word opposite in meaning to the given word.***

1. RESERVED **(Stenographers' Exam, 1993)**
(*a*) Likeable (*b*) Talkative
(*c*) Popular (*b*) Companionable
2. SUB ROSA
(*a*) Fresh (*b*) Intoxicating
(*c*) Open (*d*) Repulsive
3. CULPRIT
(*a*) Jury (*b*) Witness
(*c*) Accused (*d*) Victim
4. INVETERATE **(Asstt. Grade, 1991)**
(*a*) Stupid (*b*) Uneducated
(*c*) Ignorant (*d*) Inexperienced
5. ZANY
(*a*) Cautious (*b*) Calculating
(*c*) Cunning (*d*) Sane
6. DISDAIN
(*a*) Depreciate (*b*) Admiration
(*c*) Penitence (*d*) Contempt
7. OBSOLETE **(C.B.I. 1991)**
(*a*) Conducive (*b*) Rare
(*c*) Useless (*d*) Recent
8. HAWK
(*a*) Conciliation (*b*) Dove
(*c*) Pacifist (*d*) Pigeon
9. INFRUCTUOUS
(*a*) Devious (*b*) Straight
(*c*) Remote (*d*) Attractive
10. INSANITY **(Clerks' Grade, 1993)**
(*a*) Sanity (*b*) Normality
(*c*) Lucidity (*d*) Sobriety
11. IMMEDIATE
(*a*) Delayed (*b*) Gradual
(*c*) Leisurely (*d*) Slow
12. QUIESCENT
(*a*) Troublesome (*b*) Weak
(*c*) Indifferent (*d*) Unconcerned
13. CHURLISH **(I. Tax & Excise, 1990)**
(*a*) Accomodating (*b*) Polite
(*c*) Helpful (*d*) Happy
14. HARMONY
(*a*) Hatred (*b*) Friction
(*c*) Discord (*d*) Enmity
15. GROTESQUE
(*a*) Imaginary (*b*) Familiar
(*c*) Hateful (*d*) Natural
16. ARTIFICIAL **(U.D.C. 1995)**
(*a*) Solid (*b*) Truthful
(*c*) Authentic (*d*) Natural
17. DEBACLE
(*a*) Regain (*b*) Progress
(*c*) Rise (*d*) Movement
18. ARCHAIC
(*a*) Modern (*b*) Broken
(*a*) Old (*b*) Dilapidated
19. CAPITULATE
(*a*) Conquer (*b*) Venerate
(*c*) Destroy (*d*) Surrender
20. MUNDANE **(I. Tax, 1993)**
(*a*) Extraordinary (*b*) Superb
(*c*) Heavenly (*d*) Excellent
21. INDOLENT
(*a*) Desirable (*b*) Adequate
(*c*) Energetic (*d*) Consistent
22. COSSET
(*a*) Neglect (*b*) Divert
(*c*) Pamper (*d*) Pinch
23. DOLEFUL
(*a*) Poor (*b*) Happy
(*c*) Rich (*d*) Steady
24. MORTAL **(Section Officiers', 1993)**
(*a*) Eternal (*b*) Spiritual
(*c*) Immortal (*d*) Divine
25. MASTICATE
(*a*) Gobble (*b*) Conceal
(*c*) Chew (*d*) Review
26. UNDERHAND
(*a*) Cruel (*b*) Quiet
(*c*) Secret (*d*) Open
27. NEAT
(*a*) Sloppy (*b*) Fragrant
(*c*) Spruce (*d*) Prodigal
28. TERSE **(Clerks' Grade, 1991)**
(*a*) Concise (*b*) Detailed
(*c*) Expressive (*d*) Descriptive
29. ILLUSTRIOUS
(*a*) Uneducated (*b*) Uncivilised
(*c*) Unintelligent (*d*) Unknown
30. PASTEL
(*a*) Urban (*b*) Delicate
(c) Bright (*d*) Sweet
31. LETHAL
(*a*) Safe (*b*) Playful
(*c*) Virulent (*d*) Forgiving
32. ENCOURAGE
(*a*) Warn (*b*) Discourage
(*c*) Dampen (*d*) Disapprove
(Stenographers' Exam, 1994)
33. INNOCENCE
(*a*) Crime (*b*) Mischief
(*c*) Guilt (*d*) Sin
34. DIABOLIC
(*a*) Patient (*b*) Generous
(*c*) Kind (*d*) Simple
35. FRUGAL **(S.S.C. 1992)**
(*a*) Gaudy (*b*) Generous
(*c*) Extravagant (*d*) Charitable

36. JUSTIFY
(*a*) Accuse (*b*) Infuriate
(*c*) Absolve (*d*) Vindicate

37. ERRATIC
(*a*) Regular (*b*) Right
(*c*) Punctual (*d*) Free

38. CRITICISE **(Central Excise, 1994)**
(*a*) Judge (*b*) Appreciate
(*c*) Flatter (*d*) Analyse

39. MONOLOGUE
(*a*) Dialogue (*b*) Prologue
(*c*) Epilogue (*d*) Catalogue

40. CATHOLIC
(*a*) Rigid (*b*) Orthodox
(*c*) Strict (*d*) Narrow-minded

41. CHIDE **(C.B.I. 1990)**
(*a*) Praise (*b*) Fear
(*c*) Criticise (*d*) Flatter

42. UNCOUTH
(*a*) Crude (*b*) Awkward
(*c*) Courteous (*d*) Refined

43. BLEMISH
(*a*) Preserve (*b*) Purify
(*c*) Defect (*d*) Tarnish

44. RELIGIOUS **(Clerks' Grade, 1995)**
(*a*) Atheistic (*b*) Immoral
(*c*) Secular (*d*) Sinful

45. REPRISAL
(*a*) Relief (*b*) Forgiveness
(*c*) Exemption (*d*) Relaxation

46. DISCREPANCY
(*a*) Variance (*b*) Inappropriate
(*c*) Consistency (*d*) Inconsistency

47. FRIEND **(Stenographers' Exam, 1995)**
(*a*) Rival (*b*) Acquaintance
(*c*) Foe (*d*) Competitor

48. DIVERGE
(*a*) Repulse (*b*) Converge
(*c*) Resurge (*d*) Constrict

49. ALLURE
(*a*) Repulse (*b*) Develop
(*c*) Entice (*d*) Decoy

50. CRASS
(*a*) Gross (*b*) Refined
(*c*) Coarse (*d*) Dense

ANSWERS

1. (*b*)	**2.** (*c*)	**3.** (*d*)	**4.** (*d*)	**5.** (*d*)	**6.** (*b*)	**7.** (*d*)	**8.** (*b*)	**9.** (*b*)	**10.** (*a*)
11. (*d*)	**12.** (*a*)	**13.** (*b*)	**14.** (*c*)	**15.** (*d*)	**16.** (*d*)	**17.** (*c*)	**18.** (*a*)	**19.** (*a*)	**20.** (*c*)
21. (*c*)	**22.** (*a*)	**23.** (*b*)	**24.** (*c*)	**25.** (*a*)	**26.** (*d*)	**27.** (*a*)	**28.** (*b*)	**29.** (*d*)	**30.** (*c*)
31. (*a*)	**32.** (*b*)	**33.** (*c*)	**34.** (*c*)	**35.** (*c*)	**36.** (*a*)	**37.** (*a*)	**38.** (*b*)	**39.** (*a*)	**40.** (*d*)
41. (*a*)	**42.** (*c*)	**43.** (*b*)	**44.** (*c*)	**45.** (*b*)	**46.** (*c*)	**47.** (*c*)	**48.** (*b*)	**49.** (*a*)	**50.** (*b*)

PRACTICE SET 8

Directions : *In each of the following questions, choose the word opposite in meaning to the given word.*

1. CULPABLE **(Assistant Grade, 1996)**
(*a*) Irresponsible (*b*) Careless
(*c*) Blameless (*d*) Defendable

2. VENERATE
(*a*) Accuse (*b*) Defame
(*c*) Criticise (*d*) Abuse

3. DENOUNCE
(*a*) Defend (*b*) Gather
(*c*) Fight (*d*) Rally

4. HESITATE **(I. Tax, 1993)**
(*a*) Proud (*b*) Confident
(*c*) Certain (*d*) Reluctant

5. TACIT
(*a*) Order (*b*) Written
(*c*) Oral (*d*) Understanding

6. DOUR
(*a*) Radical (*b*) Active
(*c*) Young (*d*) Cheerful

7. WRATH
(*a*) Solace (*b*) Peace
(*c*) Delight (*d*) Choler

8. VITAL **(Bank P.O. 1991)**
(*a*) Peripheral (*b*) Dead
(*c*) Unimportant (*d*) Outer

9. COVERT
(*a*) Clandestine (*b*) Open
(*c*) Virtuous (*d*) Wide

10. VILIFY
(*a*) Commend (*b*) Pray
(*c*) Admonish (*d*) Worship

11. CAPACIOUS **(M.B.A. 1994)**
(*a*) Changeable (*b*) Foolish
(*c*) Caring (*d*) Limited

12. HATE
(*a*) Admire (*b*) Abhor
(*c*) Concern (*d*) Loathe

13. VINDICATE
(*a*) Exonerate (*b*) Condemn
(*c*) Defend (*d*) Excuse

14. ADMONISH **(Clerks' Grade, 1991)**
(*a*) Commend (*b*) Tolerate
(*c*) Flatter (*d*) Approve

15. GLIB
(*a*) Unwilling (*b*) Dumb
(*c*) Modest (*d*) Halting

16. POMPOUS
(*a*) Feeble (*b*) Normal
(*c*) Humble (*d*) Mild

17. LEAP **(U.D.C. 1994)**
(*a*) Plunge (*b*) Sink
(*c*) Immerse (*d*) Fall

18. INSIPID
(*a*) Nervous (*b*) Pungent
(*c*) Saucy (*d*) Sour

19. POLEMIC
(*a*) Cooperation (*b*) Amity
(*c*) Friendship (*d*) Agreement

20. BIZARRE **(Central Excise, 1989)**
(*a*) Soft (*b*) Usual
(*c*) Gentle (*d*) Same

21. EDACIOUS
(*a*) Smart (*b*) Gluttonous
(*c*) Fasting (*d*) Even

22. MORBID
(*a*) Healthy (*b*) Clever
(*c*) Upright (*d*) Sickly

23. ADVANCE **(S.S.C. 1995)**
(*a*) Retreat (*b*) Restrain
(*c*) Withhold (*d*) Defend

24. CONSIDERATE
(*a*) Harsh (*b*) Infuriated
(*c*) Opposed (*d*) Indifferent

25. ALIEN **(Stenographers' Exam, 1995)**
(*a*) Resident (*b*) Natural
(*c*) Domiciled (*d*) Native

26. HAGGARD
(*a*) Healthy (*b*) Animated
(*c*) Robust (*d*) Hearty

27. NUGATORY
(*a*) Voluptuous (*b*) Slender
(*c*) Valuable (*d*) Worthless

28. BOISTEROUS **(C.B.I. 1994)**
(*a*) Calm (*b*) Comfortable
(*c*) Good (*d*) Happy

29. EVIDENT
(*a*) Suspected (*b*) Disagreed
(*c*) Doubtful (*d*) Unimportant

30. DESTROY
(*a*) Invent (*b*) Make
(*c*) Produce (*d*) Create

31. ESTABLISH **(Clerks' Grade, 1994)**
(*a*) Disrupt (*b*) Uproot
(*c*) Corrode (*d*) Negate

32. ACCELERATE
(*a*) Creep (*b*) Drag
(*c*) Lag (*b*) Move slowly

33. COARSE
(*a*) Beautiful (*b*) Soft
(*c*) Fine (*d*) Attractive

34. DEFIANCE **(Central Excise, 1993)**
(*a*) Dismay (*b*) Suspicion
(*c*) Obedience (*d*) Anxiety

35. EVOLVING
(*a*) Retreating (*b*) Stifling
(*c*) Stagnating (*d*) Suffering

36. OVERWEENING
(*a*) Humble (*b*) Sedate
(*c*) Miserly (*d*) Clever

37. PRESUMPTION **(I. Tax, 1992)**
(*a*) Resumption (*b*) Proposition
(*c*) Humility (*d*) Assumption

38. REDOLENT
(*a*) Stinking (*b*) Sickly
(*c*) Yellowish (*d*) Gloomy

39. KOOK
(*a*) Illiterate (*b*) Sane
(*c*) Peculiar (*d*) Foolish

40. CALLOUS **(S.S.C. 1993)**
(*a*) Confident (*b*) Sentimental
(*c*) Sensitive (*d*) Capable

41. SUBJUGATE
(*a*) Enrich (*b*) Liberate
(*c*) Enslave (*d*) Free

42. DEBONAIR
(*a*) Worried (*b*) Pensive
(*c*) Grim (*d*) Serious

43. CONCEALMENT **(Railways, 1995)**
(*a*) Identification (*b*) Broadness
(*c*) Evidence (*d*) Indication

44. IMMERSE
(*a*) Disinter (*b*) Douse
(*c*) Engross (*d*) Disappear

45. ARROGANT
(*a*) Proud (*b*) Meek
(*c*) Insolent (*d*) Rude

46. ASTUTE **(C.B.I. 1990)**
(*a*) Cowardly (*b*) Foolish
(*c*) Wicked (*d*) Impolite

47. PANIC
(*a*) Alarm (*b*) Indifference
(*c*) Serenity (*d*) Cautiousness

48. LEGATO
(*a*) Uneven (*b*) Brief
(*c*) Silent (*d*) Smooth

49. CO-OPERATION
(*a*) Rebellion (*b*) Resistance
(*c*) Hindrance (*d*) Opposition

50. BRILLIANT
(*a*) Dusty (*b*) Dull
(*c*) Dumb (*d*) Dud
(Stenographers' Exam, 1994)

ANSWERS

1. (*d*)	**2.** (*b*)	**3.** (*a*)	**4.** (*c*)	**5.** (*b*)	**6.** (*d*)	**7.** (*c*)	**8.** (*c*)	**9.** (*b*)	**10.** (*a*)
11. (*d*)	**12.** (*a*)	**13.** (*b*)	**14.** (*a*)	**15.** (*b*)	**16.** (*c*)	**17.** (*d*)	**18.** (*b*)	**19.** (*d*)	**20.** (*b*)
21. (*c*)	**22.** (*a*)	**23.** (*a*)	**24.** (*d*)	**25.** (*d*)	**26.** (*b*)	**27.** (*c*)	**28.** (*a*)	**29.** (*c*)	**30.** (*d*)
31. (*b*)	**32.** (*d*)	**33.** (*c*)	**34.** (*c*)	**35.** (*c*)	**36.** (*a*)	**37.** (*c*)	**38.** (*a*)	**39.** (*b*)	**40.** (*c*)
41. (*b*)	**42.** (*d*)	**43.** (*d*)	**44.** (*a*)	**45.** (*b*)	**46.** (*b*)	**47.** (*c*)	**48.** (*a*)	**49.** (*d*)	**50.** (*b*)

PRACTICE SET 9

Directions : *In each of the following questions, choose the word opposite in meaning to the given word.*

1. TENTATIVE **(S.S.C. 1991)**
(*a*) Immediate (*b*) Urgent
(*c*) Developed (*d*) Final

2. PARALLEL
(*a*) Divergent (*b*) Curved
(*c*) Random (*d*) Wavy

3. STUBBORN
(*a*) Willing (*b*) Consenting
(*c*) Pliable (*d*) Easy

4. NOVEL
(*a*) Formal (*b*) Ancient
(*c*) Customary (*d*) Traditional

5. LIABILITY **(Stenographers' Exam, 1994)**
(*a*) Treasure (*b*) Debt
(*c*) Assets (*d*) Property

6. MANAGE
(*a*) Direct (*b*) Avail
(*c*) Bungle (*d*) Wild

7. ILLUSORY
(*a*) Deceptive (*b*) Real
(*c*) Imaginary (*d*) Certain

8. ARID **(Assistant Grade, 1995)**
(*a*) Plentiful (*b*) Productive
(*c*) Humid (*d*) Agreeable

9. DISPERSE
(*a*) Collect (*b*) Assemble
(*c*) Hoard (*d*) Save

10. IMPULSIVE
(*a*) Cautious (*b*) Considerate
(*c*) Clever (*d*) Cunning

11. AUSPICIOUS **(Clerks' Grade, 1992)**
(*a*) Spicy (*b*) Unfavourable
(*c*) Conspicuous (*d*) Condemnatory

12. ENGULFED
(*a*) Encircled (*b*) Groped
(*c*) Disfigured (*d*) Detached

13. CONVEX
(*a*) Flat (*b*) Protuberant
(*c*) Full (*d*) Indented

14. LUXURIANT
(*a*) Barren (*b*) Small
(*c*) Ghastly (*d*) Decaying

15. GLIB **(I. Tax & Central Excise, 1990)**
(*a*) Unwilling (*b*) Hesitant
(*c*) Dumb (*d*) Modest

16. ZEST
(*a*) Restive (*b*) Callous
(*c*) Indifference (*d*) Distate

17. BAROQUE
(*a*) Direct (*b*) Straight
(*c*) Plain (*d*) Strong

18. REPEL **(U.D.C. 1995)**
(*a*) Attract (*b*) Concentrate
(*c*) Attend (*d*) Continue

19. CAPRICIOUS
(*a*) Satisfied (*b*) Scattered
(*c*) Steadfast (*d*) Insured

20. FACTITIOUS
(*a*) Ridiculous (*b*) Genuine
(*c*) Engineered (*d*) Magnificent

21. SAGACIOUS **(C.B.I. 1990)**
(*a*) Casual (*b*) Cunning
(*c*) Foolish (*d*) False

22. EPILOGUE
(*a*) Conversation (*b*) Dialogue
(*c*) Dramatic (*d*) Prologue

23. PERSUASIVE
(*a*) Demoralizing (*b*) False
(*c*) Discouraging (*d*) Unconvincing

24. BANISH
(*a*) Abandon (*b*) Harbour
(*c*) Intrude (*d*) Drop

25. REWARD **(Stenographers' Exam, 1993)**
(*a*) Demotion (*b*) Forfeiture
(*c*) Penalty (*d*) Retribution

26. REJECT
(*a*) Agree (*b*) Accept
(*c*) Embrace (*d*) Adopt

27. FOSTER
(*a*) Repress (*b*) Curb
(*c*) Check (*d*) Control

28. WITHIN
(a) Without (b) Past
(c) Over (d) Beyond

29. BRAZEN **(Railways, 1991)**
(a) Respectful (b) Innocent
(c) Delicious (d) Helpful

30. ADVERSITY
(a) Diversity (b) Affliction
(c) Prosperity (d) Catastrophe

31. PALTRY
(a) Strong (b) Worthwhile
(c) Mean (d) Bitter

32. DORSAL **(M.B.A. 1994)**
(a) Inactive (b) Ventral
(c) Peripheral (d) Central

33. VAGUE
(a) Known (b) Published
(c) Popular (d) Definite

34. SUPERVISE
(a) Overlook (b) Misdirect
(c) Neglect (d) Forget

35. MAGNANIMOUS **(C.B.I. 1991)**
(a) Selfish (b) Naive
(c) Generous (d) Small

36. CULMINATE
(a) Frustrate (b) Fail
(c) Abort (d) Defeat

37. AMENABLE
(a) Stubborn (b) Docile
(c) Obedient (d) Offensive

38. ACQUIT **(I. Tax, 1994)**
(a) Confirm (b) Blame
(c) Punish (d) Indict

39. FORBIDDEN
(a) Allowed (b) Prohibited
(c) Agreed (d) Foresaken

40. DISSIPATE
(a) Sustain (b) Conserve
(c) Preserve (d) Maintain

41. CONFIDENT **(S.S.C. 1995)**
(a) Diffident (b) Timid
(c) Reserved (d) Shy

42. FILTHY
(a) Stainless (b) Shining
(c) Sterilized (d) Clean

43. CROWDED
(a) Deserted (b) Lonely
(c) Empty (d) Barren

44. DIM **(Stenographers' Exam, 1994)**
(a) Bright (b) Understandable
(c) Loud (d) Clear

45. CONFORM
(a) Disappoint (b) Reform
(c) Deform (d) Dissent

46. ABORIGINAL
(a) Modern (b) Popular
(c) Current (d) Contemporary

47. INDIGENOUS
(a) Native (b) Cheap
(c) Foreign (d) Inferior

48. FRAIL
(a) Vigorous (b) Sturdy
(c) Hardy (d) Strong

49. ACCOMPLICE **(Central Excise, 1993,**
(a) Friend (b) Accessory
(c) Escort (d) Opponent

50. CONVENE
(a) Cancel (b) Adjourn
(c) Dissolve (d) Postpone

ANSWERS

1. (d)	2. (a)	3. (c)	4. (d)	5. (c)	6. (c)	7. (b)	8. (c)	9. (b)	10. (a)
11. (b)	12. (d)	13. (d)	14. (a)	15. (c)	16. (d)	17. (c)	18. (a)	19. (c)	20. (b)
21. (c)	22. (d)	23. (d)	24. (b)	25. (c)	26. (b)	27. (a)	28. (d)	29. (a)	30. (c)
31. (b)	32. (b)	33. (d)	34. (b)	35. (a)	36. (c)	37. (a)	38. (d)	39. (a)	40. (b)
41. (a)	42. (d)	43. (a)	44. (a)	45. (d)	46. (a)	47. (c)	48. (d)	49. (d)	50. (a)

PRACTICE SET 10

Directions : *In each of the following questions, choose the word opposite in meaning to the given word.*

1. VALUABLE **(Stenographer's Exam, 1995)**
(a) Inferior (b) Invaluable
(c) Lowly (d) Worthless

2. INTRANSIGENT
(a) Ever-ready (b) Faithful
(c) Flexible (d) Obedient

3. ENGULFED
(a) Detached (b) Dislocated
(c) Devastated (d) Disfigured

4. COMPETITION
(a) Rivalry (b) Compromise
(c) Monopoly (d) Contest

5. THEORY
(*a*) Imagination (*b*) Fact
(*c*) Chance (*d*) Thought

6. INIMICAL **(Section Officers' 1993)**
(*a*) Friendly (*b*) Cheerful
(*c*) Neutral (*d*) Emotional

7. PROSCRIBE
(*a*) Interdict (*b*) Allow
(*c*) Extend (*d*) Betray

8. INTRICATE
(*a*) Foolish (*b*) Simple
(*c*) Straight forward (*d*) Easy

9. MEAGRE **(U.D.C. 1994)**
(*a*) Average (*b*) Plentiful
(*c*) Extravagant (*d*) Excessive

10. DORMANT
(*a*) Active (*b*) Modern
(*c*) Permanent (*d*) Transient

11. ADHERENT
(*a*) Rival (*b*) Alien
(*c*) Detractor (*d*) Enemy

12. EQUANIMITY **(I. Tax, 1992)**
(*a*) Excitement (*b*) Duplicity
(*c*) Dubiousness (*d*) Resentment

13. TURBID
(*a*) Easy (*b*) Hazy
(*c*) Clear (*d*) Distinct

14. OBFUSCATE
(*a*) Simplify (*b*) Explain
(*c*) Describe (*d*) Clarify

15. BEGUILE **(S.S.C. 1993)**
(*a*) Persuade (*b*) Cheat
(*c*) Flatter (*d*) Smile

16. HAMSTRING
(*a*) Strengthen (*b*) Enlarge
(*c*) Stimulate (*d*) Awaken

17. SCEPTICAL
(*a*) Inquisitive (*b*) Hopeful
(*c*) Indictive (*d*) Intuitive

18. DESTINY **(Railways, 1995)**
(*a*) Vulnerability (*b*) Chance
(*c*) Self-dependence (*d*) Fate

19. PERDITION
(*a*) Excitement (*b*) Reward
(*c*) Inspiration (*d*) Salvation

20. SHAME
(*a*) Glorify (*b*) Exalt
(*c*) Dignify (*d*) Enshrine

21. RESCUE
(*a*) Extricate (*b*) Waver
(*c*) Bind (*d*) Desert

22. AGONY **(Central Excise, 1993)**
(*a*) Pleasure (*b*) Bliss
(*c*) Ecstasy (*d*) Fear

23. REQUISITE
(*a*) Dispensable (*b*) Random
(*c*) Inappropriate (*d*) Chaotic

24. VIE
(*a*) Guard (*b*) Maintain
(*c*) Discover (*d*) Yield

25. FLURRY
(*a*) Disclose (*b*) Soothe
(*c*) Pelt (*d*) Achieve

26. SUBSERVIENT **(Assistant Grade, 1996)**
(*a*) Aggressive (*b*) Dignified
(*c*) Straight forward (*d*) Supercilious

27. JUBILANT
(*a*) Scared (*b*) Disturbed
(*c*) Gloomy (*d*) Quiet

28. LUXURY
(*a*) Sadness (*b*) Treachery
(*c*) Duplicity (*d*) Austerity

29. FORBID **(Central Excise, 1993)**
(*a*) Provoke (*b*) Appreciate
(*c*) Celebrate (*d*) Permit

30. DEFECTION
(*a*) Resignation (*b*) Invitation
(*c*) Joining (*d*) Co-operation

31. DUSKY
(*a*) Visible (*b*) Fair
(*c*) Obscure (*d*) Shadowy

32. PUNCTILIOUS **(Asstt. Grade, 1991)**
(*a*) Irregular (*b*) Fussy
(*c*) Careless (*d*) Curious

33. CAPRICIOUS
(*a*) Fixed (*b*) Solid
(*c*) Firm (*d*) Reliable

34. SHAMEFUL
(*a*) Naked (*b*) Brazen
(*c*) Wanton (*d*) Unblushing

35. FLAGITIOUS **(M.B.A. 1994)**
(*a*) Frivolous (*b*) Ignorant
(*c*) Vapid (*d*) Innocent

36. BENEVOLENCE
(*a*) Contempt (*b*) Malevolence
(*c*) Hatred (*d*) Derision

37. KNACK
(*a*) Dullness (*b*) Balance
(*c*) Talent (*d*) Dexterity

38. CELIBATE **(C.B.I. 1994)**
(*a*) Profligate (*b*) Reprobate
(*c*) Extravagant (*d*) Prodigal

39. DITHER
(*a*) Cry (*b*) Refer
(*c*) Decide (*d*) Defer

40. CONSOLIDATE
(*a*) Isolate (*b*) Weaken
(*c*) Divide (*d*) Identify

41. INSOLENT **(Clerks' Grade, 1994)**
(*a*) Agreeable (*b*) Coward
(*c*) Polite (*d*) Considerate

42. LIABILITY
(*a*) Assumption (*b*) Exemption
(*c*) Consumption (*d*) Presumption

43. PUTRID
(*a*) Fresh (*b*) Fragrant
(*c*) Sweet (*d*) Agreeable

44. OVERWROUGHT **(I. Tax, 1989)**
(*a*) Alert (*b*) Alive
(*c*) Excited (*d*) Calm

45. DEROGATORY
(*a*) Immediate (*b*) Praising
(*c*) Opinionated (*d*) Roguish

46. BALMY
(*a*) Hard (*b*) Genuine
(*c*) Mild (*d*) Fragrant

47. OSTENTATIOUS **(Central Excise, 1992)**
(*a*) Awkward (*b*) Bankrupt
(*c*) Ignorant (*d*) Unpretentious

48. PROBLEM
(*a*) Reply (*b*) Solution
(*c*) Answer (*d*) Resolution

49. EXECRATE
(*c*) Care (*d*) Praise
(*c*) Love (*d*) Bless

50. MODERATE
(*c*) Radical (*d*) Revolutionary
(*c*) Nihilist (*d*) Anarchist

ANSWERS

1. (*d*)	**2.** (*c*)	**3.** (*a*)	**4.** (*c*)	**5.** (*b*)	**6.** (*a*)	**7.** (*b*)	**8.** (*c*)	**9.** (*b*)	**10.** (*a*)
11. (*c*)	**12.** (*a*)	**13.** (*c*)	**14.** (*d*)	**15.** (*a*)	**16.** (*a*)	**17.** (*b*)	**18.** (*c*)	**19.** (*d*)	**20.** (*b*)
21. (*d*)	**22.** (*c*)	**23.** (*a*)	**24.** (*d*)	**25.** (*b*)	**26.** (*b*)	**27.** (*c*)	**28.** (*d*)	**29.** (*d*)	**30.** (*c*)
31. (*b*)	**32.** (*c*)	**33.** (*d*)	**34.** (*b*)	**35.** (*d*)	**36.** (*b*)	**37.** (*a*)	**38.** (*b*)	**39.** (*c*)	**40.** (*b*)
41. (*c*)	**42.** (*b*)	**43.** (*a*)	**44.** (*d*)	**45.** (*b*)	**46.** (*a*)	**47.** (*d*)	**48.** (*b*)	**49.** (*d*)	**50.** (*c*)

TYPE 2 : CHOOSING THE ANTONYM OF A WORD USED IN A SENTENCE

In this type of questions, you are given a sentence in which a word has been italicised. Some alternatives are suggested below it. The candidate is required to choose that word which is opposite in meaning to the italicised word.

Example : ***Choose the word which is most opposite in meaning to the word bold italicised in the sentence :***

Mahatma Gandhi led a very ***austere*** life.
(*a*) exciting (*b*) boisterous (*c*) luxurious (*d*) eventful (*e*) adventurous

Solution : 'Austere' here means 'simple'. So the opposite of 'austere' is luxurious'
Hence, the answer is (c).

PRACTICE SET 11

Directions : ***Each of the following questions consists of a word or phrase which is italicised bold in the sentence given. It is followed by certain words or phrases. Select the word or phrase which is closest to the opposite in meaning of the italicised bold word or phrase.***

1. He is a very ***timid*** person. **(N.D.A. 1992)**
(*a*) dashing (*b*) outgoing
(*c*) bold (*d*) chivalrous

2. Raju ***often*** walks to school.
(*a*) rarely (*b*) never
(*c*) always (*d*) sometimes

3. One can ***acquire*** fame only by being truthful, honest and faithful.
(*a*) lose (*b*) deprive
(*c*) forsake (*d*) surrender

4. The treaty was ***ratified*** by the heads of states. **(C.D.S. 1994)**
(*a*) set aside (*b*) unsettled
(*c*) destroyed (*d*) annulled

5. Always ***avoid*** late-night jobs.
(*a*) inspire (*b*) compel
(*c*) pursue (*d*) take

6. Mother Teresa devoted her life to the service of the poor and the ***destitute***.
(*a*) greedy (*b*) noble
(*c*) rich (*d*) extraordinary

7. Many people try to ***resist*** reforms in the society. **(I.E.S. 1994)**
(*a*) repel (*b*) welcome
(*c*) accept (*d*) fight

8. He was always prepared to ***refute*** the idea.
(*a*) agree (*b*) subscribe
(*c*) recommend (*d*) endorse

9. There was a marked ***deterioration*** in his condition.
(*a*) reformation (*b*) amendment
(*c*) improvement (*d*) revision

10. We should not ***belittle*** others' achievements. **(Central Excise 1991)**
(*a*) recommend (*b*) praise
(*c*) encourage (*d*) inspire

11. He has a ***delicate*** constitution.
(*a*) fit (*b*) ungainly
(*c*) strong (*d*) rugged

12. The palace was indeed ***grotesque***.
(*a*) good (*b*) decent
(*c*) filthy (*d*) congruous

13. She is ***slender*** in figure. **(C.D.S. 1990)**
(*a*) strong (*b*) well-built
(*c*) stout (*d*) slim

14. He seems to have a ***propensity*** to fight.
(*a*) scepticism (*b*) penchant
(*c*) aversion (*d*) proclivity

15. The man's actions made it ***obvious*** that he had a wicked plan in mind.
(*a*) false (*b*) obscure
(*c*) uncertain (*d*) difficult

16. The Commission took two years to go through the ***massive*** collection of files and documents before preparing its report. **(Bank P.O. 1994)**
(*a*) ugly (*b*) short (*c*) light
(*d*) heavy (*e*) meagre

17. Religion teaches us not to run after the ***transient*** pleasures of the world.
(*a*) permanent (*b*) sinful
(*c*) unnatural (*d*) joyful

18. He is ***adamant*** on going.
(*a*) confused (*b*) lenient (*c*) stressing
(*d*) indecisive (*e*) yielding.

19. The two friends were ***distinct*** in every thing; dress, manners, hair-style and food habits. **(N.D.A. 1994)**
(*a*) similar (*b*) uniform
(*c*) opposite (*d*) different

20. The climbers found the ***ascent*** nerve breaking.
(*a*) slide (*b*) decline
(*c*) fall (*d*) descent

21. His ***appointment*** was confirmed last month.
(*a*) disappointment (*b*) discharge
(*c*) suspension (*d*) dismissal

22. The Ganga is as ***deep*** in midstream as at the banks.
(*a*) wide (*b*) narrow
(*c*) hollow (*d*) shallow

23. Unsettled conditions in the land led to the ***exodus*** of hundreds of its citizens.
(*a*) expulsion (*b*) invasion
(*c*) immigration (*d*) entry

24. With the advent of Green Revolution, India now produces ***sufficient*** quantity of foodgrains every year.
(*a*) short (*b*) inadequate
(*c*) small (*d*) more

25. All his neighbours are aware of his ***acrimonious*** nature.
(*a*) informal (*b*) sympathetic
(*c*) cooperative (*d*) charitable

26. Such a scene ***attracts*** the onlookers.
(*a*) instigates (*b*) annoys
(*c*) repels (*d*) revolts
(Railways,1993)

27. This window-pane is ***transparent***.
(*a*) opaque (*b*) transluscent
(*c*) solid (*d*) fragile

28. ***Ambiguity*** of thoughts can prove disastrous.
(*a*) Rigidity (*b*) Clarity
(*c*) Certainty (*d*) Rationality

29. Professors are generally ***serious*** about what they say. **(Clerks' Grade, 1988)**
(*a*) jolly (*b*) thoughtful
(*c*) smug (*d*) insincere

30. He ***urges*** to learn everything.
(*a*) desires (*b*) denies
(*c*) dislikes (*d*) recommends

31. He was found ***guilty***.
(*a*) true (*b*) right
(*c*) innocent (*d*) correct

32. ***Honesty*** is the best policy.
(*a*) Sobriety (*b*) Deceit
(*c*) Uprightness (*d*) Rectitude

33. The Chairman ***initiated*** the proceedings with a brief speech. **(Railways, 1994)**
(*a*) complicated (*b*) started
(*c*) closed (*d*) confused

34. William Wordsworth is ***celebrated*** for his lucid style.
(*a*) notorious (*b*) unpopular
(*c*) unknown (*d*) renowned
(*e*) undistinguished

35. The king ***consolidated*** the empire into a powerful nation.
(*a*) divided (*b*) isolated
(*c*) fragmented (*d*) weakened

36. It used to be said that travel ***broadens*** one's outlook. **(C.D.S. 1992)**
(*a*) restricts (*b*) contracts
(*c*) shrinks (*d*) narrows

37. He has enrolled himself to an ***elementary*** course in computer.
(*a*) secondary (*b*) tough
(*c*) advanced (*d*) simple

38. ***Abrupt*** decisions are often wrong.
(*a*) Gradual (*b*) Rough
(*c*) Sharp (*d*) Hurried

39. He climbed up a ***stationary*** wagon.

39. He climbed up a ***stationary*** wagon.
(*a*) moving (*b*) speeding
(*c*) shunting (*d*) standing
(N.D.A. 1995)

40. He is in the habit of taking a ***casual*** leave quite often.
(*a*) futile (*b*) regular
(*c*) formal (*d*) systematic

41. A ***serene*** mind can never be the pioneer of a great revolution.
(*a*) nervous (*b*) jocular
(*c*) earnest (*d*) agitated

42. Of all the companions of our joyous ***ascent***, there were only the two of us left. **(C.D.S. 1989)**
(*a*) decent (*b*) descent
(*c*) descant (*d*) descendant

43. He returned home much ***inspired***, no wonder the plan had worked.
(*a*) overwhelmed (*b*) dispirited
(*c*) disillusioned (*d*) sceptical

44. You must ***quote*** examples to support your statement.
(*a*) reveal (*b*) restrain
(*c*) contradict (*d*) adduce

45. Only an ***agile*** person can be a successful sportsman.
(*a*) brisk (*b*) emaciated
(*c*) feeble (*d*) sluggish

46. Such ***lofty*** dreams can never come true.
(*a*) puny (*b*) humble
(*c*) insignificant (*d*) casual

47. The decision to stop firing across the border was a ***unilateral*** one.
(*a*) collective (*b*) bilateral
(*c*) multilateral (*d*) multiple

48. We were advised not to ***extinguish*** our hopes for the time being.
(*a*) aggravate (*b*) intensify (*c*) inflate
(*d*) promote (*e*) expand

49. You can't work out this project with ***nebulous*** plans in mind.
(*a*) useful (*b*) practical
(*c*) clear (*d*) fundamental

50. He ***abandoned*** his family. **(C.D.S. 1995)**
(*a*) saved (*b*) supported
(*c*) pleased (*d*) encouraged

ANSWERS

1. (*c*)	**2.** (*a*)	**3.** (*a*)	**4.** (*d*)	**5.** (*c*)	**6.** (*c*)	**7.** (*b*)	**8.** (*d*)	**9.** (*c*)	**10.** (*b*)
11. (*c*)	**12.** (*d*)	**13.** (*c*)	**14.** (*c*)	**15.** (*b*)	**16.** (*e*)	**17.** (*a*)	**18.** (*e*)	**19.** (*a*)	**20.** (*d*)
21. (*d*)	**22.** (*d*)	**23.** (*d*)	**24.** (*b*)	**25.** (*c*)	**26.** (*c*)	**27.** (*a*)	**28.** (*b*)	**29.** (*d*)	**30.** (*d*)
31. (*c*)	**32.** (*b*)	**33.** (*c*)	**34.** (*c*)	**35.** (*d*)	**36.** (*d*)	**37.** (*c*)	**38.** (*a*)	**39.** (*a*)	**40.** (*c*)
41. (*d*)	**42.** (*b*)	**43.** (*b*)	**44.** (*c*)	**45.** (*d*)	**46.** (*b*)	**47.** (*b*)	**48.** (*d*)	**49.** (*c*)	**50.** (*b*)

PRACTICE SET 12

Directions : ***In each of the following sentences, a word has been printed in italics bold. Out of the given alternatives, choose the one which is closest to the opposite in meaning of the italicised word.***

1. I thought about her a lot during the ***following*** months. **(Railways, 1994)**
(*a*) receding (*b*) preceding
(*c*) proceeding (*d*) succeeding

2. This is the ***cardinal*** point of the issue.
(*a*) minor (*b*) vital
(*c*) debatable (*d*) insignificant
(*e*) avoidable

3. She is indeed ***human***.
(*a*) universal (*b*) devilish
(*c*) terrestrial (*d*) divine

4. It was universally characterised as a ***progressive*** measure. **(C.D.S. 1994)**
(*a*) abhorrent (*b*) retrograde
(*c*) obstructive (*d*) regressive

5. Geetanjali is loved by all for her ***meekness***.
(*a*) harshness (*b*) pride
(*c*) anger (*d*) passion

6. It was a ***voluntary*** gesture.
(*a*) compulsory (*b*) violent
(*c*) deliberate (*d*) valuable

7. There has always been a feeling of ***rancour*** between the two families.
(*a*) rivalry (*b*) competition
(*c*) friendliness (*d*) suspicion
(I. Tax & Central Excise, 1988)

8. The government is taking measures to ***augment*** the country's food supply.
(*a*) prohibit (*b*) decrease
(*c*) surpass (*d*) compensate

9. People know him for his ***vanity***.
(*a*) humanity (*b*) honesty
(*c*) courtesy (*d*) modesty
10. Let us not ***aggravate*** the sufferings of the poor. **(N.D.A. 1993)**
(*a*) abbreviate (*b*) alleviate
(*c*) advocate (*d*) appreciate
11. It was a mystery as to where the young girl had acquired such a ***cynical*** attitude.
(*a*) mature (*b*) naive
(*c*) eccentric (*d*) crazy
12. Avogadro's ***hypothesis*** has proved significant till the present day.
(*a*) fact (*b*) theory
(*c*) conclusion (*d*) experiment
13. He stood gazing at the ***serene*** expanse of the sea. **(N.D.A. 1996)**
(*a*) scenic (*b*) clear
(*c*) tranquil (*d*) ruffled
14. The authorities inflicted harsh ***penalty*** on him for indulging in forgery.
(*a*) commendation (*b*) default
(*c*) concession (*d*) reward
15. He is always ***hungry*** for wealth.
(*a*) ravenous (*b*) famished
(*c*) satiated (*d*) greedy
16. Machine-civilisation has made human life ***artificial.*** **(N.D.A. 1992)**
(*a*) genuine (*b*) natural
(*c*) true (*d*) authentic
17. This shop keeps only ***genuine*** articles.
(*a*) imported (*b*) spurious
(*c*) antique (*d*) duplicate
18. He has been ***commended*** for all that he did.
(*a*) dismissed (*b*) condemned
(*c*) censured (*d*) rejected
19. The drug will have ***pernicious*** effect on your health. **(C.D.S. 1994)**
(*a*) beneficial (*b*) prolonged
(*c*) ruinous (*d*) pornographic
20. It was a ***unanimous*** decision.
(*a*) uncertain (*b*) partial
(*c*) discordant (*d*) divergent
21. Phoolan Devi had to ***surrender*** under the most pressing circumstances.
(*a*) release (*b*) claim
(*c*) plunder (*d*) attack
22. The students ***assembled*** in the meeting hall. **(B.S.R.B. 1992)**
(*a*) removed (*b*) diffused
(*c*) dispersed (*d*) eliminated
23. His ***boorish*** ways amused everyone.
(*a*) refined (*b*) funny
(*c*) eccentric (*d*) friendly
24. How can you cut an apple with this ***blunt*** knife?
(*a*) pointed (*b*) sharpened
(*c*) polished (*d*) filed
25. He has suspended his secretary on a ***flimsy*** ground. **(C.D.S. 1995)**
(*a*) vigorous (*b*) strong
(*c*) sound (*d*) salutory
26. A faithful officer is always ***vigilant*** towards his duties.
(*a*) innocent (*b*) ignorant
(*c*) irresponsible (*d*) careless
27. The ***gross*** domestic product (GDP) is an essential component of economy.
(*a*) rough (*b*) coarse
(*c*) refined (*d*) estimated
28. It was really a ***gracious*** occasion for me.
(*a*) benign (*b*) infructuous
(*c*) churlish (*d*) wasteful
29. The man at the gate had a ***forbidding*** appearance. **(N.D.A. 1994)**
(*a*) lenient (*b*) handsome
(*c*) tranquil (*d*) mild
30. Terrorism is a serious ***hazard*** to the country.
(*a*) chance (*b*) peril
(*c*) safety (*d*) problem
31. ***Nourishing*** food is a necessity both for a pregnant mother and a baby.
(*a*) Unhygienic (*b*) Poor
(*c*) Undercooked (*d*) Heavy
32. There is a ***dearth*** of milk in Delhi nowadays.
(*a*) extravagance (*b*) scarcity
(*c*) abundance (*d*) sufficiency
33. Gandhi did not welcome the idea of being a mute spectator to the ***atrocious*** behaviour of the whites towards the non-whites in Africa.
(*a*) gracious (*b*) noble
(*c*) civilised (*d*) pleasing
34. A ***friendly*** dog met us at the farmgate.
(*a*) hostile (*b*) quiet
(*c*) understanding (*d*) helpful **(C.D.S. 1995)**
35. The scene was indeed ***captivating***.
(*a*) hateful (*b*) disgusting
(*c*) repulsive (*d*) obscene
36. That police officer is known to be ***humane*** in his approach.
(*a*) unsympathetic (*b*) uncultured
(*c*) uncompromising (*d*) uncivilised
37. A crowd ***gathered*** quickly when the police came. **(N.D.A. 1995)**
(*a*) collected (*b*) dispersed
(*c*) spread (*d*) disappeared
38. Matter ***expands*** on heating.
(*a*) shrinks (*b*) reduces
(*c*) diminishes (*d*) contracts

39. Hydra is biologically believed to be ***immortal***.
(*a*) undying (*b*) perishable
(*c*) ancient (*d*) eternal

40. ***Crestfallen*** he returned as he had never faced such humiliation in the whole of his life. **(C.D.S. 1993)**
(*a*) Disturbed (*b*) Vainglorious
(*c*) Triumphant (*d*) Indignant

41. A feeling of brotherhood should be ***propagated*** amongst the masses.
(*a*) disseminated (*b*) suppressed
(*c*) dissipated (*d*) crushed
(*e*) countered

42. She is beautiful as well as ***frivolous***.
(*a*) indecent (*b*) serious
(*c*) insane (*d*) rude
(Railways, 1993)

43. The problem of dowry in our country has assumed ***gargantuan*** proportions.
(*a*) negligible (*b*) bearable
(*c*) minute (*d*) minimal

44. The boy found himself in a ***pathetic*** situation.
(*a*) comical (*b*) marvellous
(*c*) common (*d*) surprising

45. We must realise the ***futility*** of wars.
(*a*) urgency (*b*) usefulness
(*c*) value (*d*) importance
(N.D.A. 1993)

46. The scheme proved harmful for the people, the middle income group in ***particular***.
(*a*) common (*b*) usual
(*c*) specific (*d*) general

47. His punctuality and regularity ***propitiates*** everyone with whom he deals.
(*a*) depresses (*b*) excites
(*c*) enrages (*d*) appeases

48. Most surfaces are made ***glossy*** by polishing.
(*a*) rough (*b*) crude
(*c*) dull (*d*) ugly

49. It is ***obligatory*** for a common citizen to follow the rules. **(C.D.S. 1992)**
(*a*) optional (*b*) superfluous
(*c*) necessary (*d*) advisable

50. Every detail of the painting is ***prominent*** enough to be seen.
(*a*) negligible (*b*) insignificant
(*c*) trifling (*d*) inconspicuous

ANSWERS

1. (*b*)	**2.** (*d*)	**3.** (*d*)	**4.** (*d*)	**5.** (*b*)	**6.** (*a*)	**7.** (*c*)	**8.** (*b*)	**9.** (*d*)	**10.** (*b*)
11. (*b*)	**12.** (*a*)	**13.** (*d*)	**14.** (*d*)	**15.** (*d*)	**16.** (*b*)	**17.** (*b*)	**18.** (*c*)	**19.** (*a*)	**20.** (*c*)
21. (*b*)	**22.** (*c*)	**23.** (*a*)	**24.** (*b*)	**25.** (*d*)	**26.** (*d*)	**27.** (*d*)	**28.** (*c*)	**29.** (*b*)	**30.** (*c*)
31. (*a*)	**32.** (*c*)	**33.** (*b*)	**34.** (*a*)	**35.** (*c*)	**36.** (*a*)	**37.** (*b*)	**38.** (*d*)	**39.** (*b*)	**40.** (*c*)
41. (*b*)	**42.** (*b*)	**43.** (*c*)	**44.** (*a*)	**45.** (*b*)	**46.** (*d*)	**47.** (*c*)	**48.** (*c*)	**49.** (*a*)	**50.** (*d*)

PRACTICE SET 13

Directions : ***Each question below consists of a word or a phrase which is italicised in the sentence given. It is followed by some words or phrases. Select the word or phrase which is closest to the opposite in meaning of the italicised word or phrase.***

1. He is extremely ***intelligent*** but proud.
(*a*) simple (*b*) ignorant
(*c*) weak (*d*) dull
(C.D.S. 1995)

2. She looked ***gorgeous*** in her new dress.
(*a*) ugly (*b*) beautiful
(*c*) ordinary (*d*) shabby

3. We all heard her but it was a ***superficial*** talk.
(*a*) profound (*b*) difficult
(*c*) secretive (*d*) mystical

4. In ancient days, a ***fragile*** glass jar was considered to be more valuable than a human slave. **(N.D.A 1994)**
(*a*) broad (*b*) tall
(*c*) strong (*d*) heavy

5. The Gupta rulers ***patronised*** all cultural activities and thus the Gupta era came to be known as 'the Golden Era' of Indian history.
(*a*) criticised (*b*) rejected
(*c*) opposed (*d*) spurned

6. Last month tomatoes were quite ***cheap***.
(*a*) inexpensive (*b*) costly

(*c*) insufficient (*d*) less **(S.S.C. 1993)**

7. His move was a ***calculated*** one.
(*a*) idiotic (*b*) simple
(*c*) thoughtless (*d*) artless

8. I ***accept*** your plan.
(*a*) deny (*b*) dismiss
(*c*) reject (*d*) decline

9. Sherlock Holmes is a ***fictitious*** character. **(C.D.S. 1990)**
(*a*) real (*b*) imaginative
(*c*) fancy (*d*) foreign

10. It was really a ***sinister*** move on his part.
(*a*) malevolent (*b*) sinful
(*c*) auspicious (*d*) right

11. Politicians today are ***robbing*** the nation of its wealth.
(*a*) strengthening (*b*) protecting
(*c*) helping (*d*) enriching
(*e*) advancing

12. That man is known for his ***elegance***.
(*a*) awkwardness (*b*) indelicacy
(*c*) clumsiness (*d*) savagery

13. It is a ***Herculean*** task for me.
(*a*) indecent (*b*) puny
(*c*) ponderous (*d*) big **(M.B.A. 1992)**

14. The man was ***liberated*** from the charge.
(*a*) emancipated (*b*) enclosed
(*c*) concealed (*d*) imprisoned

15. ***Genuine*** drugs are available in most of the medical shops. **(N.D.A. 1992)**
(*a*) harmful (*b*) wrong
(*c*) dubious (*d*) spurious

16. For the first time I saw him speaking so ***rudely*** to Ranjeet.
(*a*) softly (*b*) gently
(*c*) politely (*d*) slowly

17. The new government has ***abolished*** the Gold Control Act.
(*a*) approved (*b*) passed
(*c*) restored (*d*) removed

18. He was asked to ***accelerate*** the pace of work. **(Railways, 1994)**
(*a*) check (*b*) control
(*c*) slacken (*d*) supervise

19. He looked ***elated*** on hearing the news.
(*a*) exasperated (*b*) depressed
(*c*) desperate (*d*) anxious

20. Gandhiji always advocated the use of ***indigenous*** goods.
(*a*) cheap (*b*) native
(*c*) silly (*d*) foreign

21. His ***timidity*** proved to be costly.
(*a*) boldness (*b*) arrogance
(*c*) self-assertion (*d*) self-confidence **(C.D.S. 1994)**

22. In all places, and at all times, there is a ***profusion*** of talents.
(*a*) plenty (*b*) generosity
(*c*) aversion (*d*) scarcity

23. He is a man of ***mellow*** temper.
(*a*) excitable (*b*) hot
(*c*) irrational (*d*) fickle

24. The actor is well known both for his ***humility*** and courage. **(I.E.S. 1994)**
(*a*) gentleness (*b*) honesty
(*c*) determination (*d*) pride

25. He was in a ***dejected*** mood.
(*a*) irritable (*b*) romantic
(*c*) jubilant (*d*) rejected

26. Ashish has an ***innate*** sense of humour.
(*a*) natural (*b*) inborn
(*c*) unusual (*d*) acquired

27. He could not ***confirm*** that he had made any such statement.
(*a*) reject (*b*) avoid
(*c*) deny (*d*) refuse **(I. Tax & Central Excise, 1991)**

28. Rajesh's ***rustic*** behaviour astonished the teacher.
(*a*) impolite (*b*) genuine
(*c*) sophisticated (*d*) awkward

29. This piece of land is the most ***fertile*** and yields a good harvest each year.
(*a*) startling (*b*) sterile
(*c*) worthless (*d*) futile

30. Always be ***impartial*** in your dealings.
(*a*) discourteous (*b*) impudent
(*c*) disrespectful (*d*) unfair

31. The General Manager is quite ***tactful*** and handles the workers' union very effectively. **(Bank P.O. 1994)**
(*a*) relaxed (*b*) strict
(*c*) naive (*d*) disciplined (*e*) loose

32. ***Repression*** in China has deepened during the past few months.
(*a*) Regeneration (*b*) Liberation
(*c*) Agitation (*d*) Expression

33. Dhanik Lal is a ***deceitful*** man and cannot be relied upon.
(*a*) honest (*b*) sincere
(*c*) gentle (*d*) simple

34. We should not ***belittle*** the value of small things. **(C.D.S. 1992)**
(*a*) expand (*b*) inflate
(*c*) praise (*d*) extol

35. My parents were ***confident*** of my success in the examination.
(*a*) worried (*b*) pessimistic
(*c*) diffident (*d*) depressed

36. Rajesh is a ***shrewd*** person.
(*a*) boisterous (*b*) aggressive
(*c*) foolish (*d*) intelligent

37. Nothing has been organised properly and confusion seems ***inevitable***. **(C.D.S. 1994)**
(*a*) uncertain (*b*) ineligible
(*c*) inevident (*d*) inefficient

38. He ***denied*** the accusation.
(*a*) justified (*b*) spoke
(*c*) publicised (*d*) affirmed

39. Everyone could see that it was a ***prejudiced*** decision.
(*a*) unbiased (*b*) candid
(*c*) helpful (*d*) logical

40. I think this would be a ***quixotic*** project for me.
(*a*) wasteful (*b*) profitable
(*c*) fantastic (*d*) practical

41. The geologists declared that the fossil was ***authentic***. **(N.D.A. 1995)**
(*a*) old (*b*) fake
(*c*) new (*d*) beautiful

42. He found it hard to ***withstand*** the stress of circumstances.
(*a*) endure (*b*) resist
(*c*) tolerate (*d*) yield

43. Never adopt a ***callous*** attitude towards your duties.
(*a*) cooperative (*b*) cautious
(*c*) considerate (*d*) courteous

44. He ***frequently*** visits his old uncle in his native village. **(Railways, 1993)**
(*a*) temporarily (*b*) rarely
(*c*) irregularly (*d*) secretly

45. Hearing the news, he jumped up in ***ecstasy***.
(*a*) misery (*b*) beatitude
(*c*) exaltation (*d*) rapture

46. Such comparisons in poetry are now ***obsolete***.
(*a*) permanent (*b*) ancient
(*c*) renovated (*d*) recent

47. Only an ***inquisitive*** person can gain proper knowledge.
(*a*) careless (*b*) indolent
(*c*) dull (*d*) uninterested

48. In the interest of one's own reputation one should avoid ***ostentation*** while entertaining friends. **(C.D.S. 1993)**
(*a*) innocence (*b*) purity
(*c*) simplicity (*d*) miserliness

49. India is a land of ***abundant*** resources.
(*a*) enough (*b*) poor
(*c*) deficient (*d*) limited

50. Ours is undoubtedly a ***morbid*** society.
(*a*) healthy (*b*) virtuous
(*c*) liberal (*d*) progressive

ANSWERS

1. (*d*)	**2.** (*d*)	**3.** (*a*)	**4.** (*c*)	**5.** (*c*)	**6.** (*b*)	**7.** (*c*)	**8.** (*c*)	**9.** (*a*)	**10.** (*c*)
11. (*d*)	**12.** (*c*)	**13.** (*b*)	**14.** (*d*)	**15.** (*d*)	**16.** (*c*)	**17.** (*b*)	**18.** (*c*)	**19.** (*b*)	**20.** (*d*)
21. (*a*)	**22.** (*d*)	**23.** (*b*)	**24.** (*d*)	**25.** (*c*)	**26.** (*d*)	**27.** (*c*)	**28.** (*c*)	**29.** (*b*)	**30.** (*d*)
31. (*c*)	**32.** (*b*)	**33.** (*b*)	**34.** (*d*)	**35.** (*c*)	**36.** (*c*)	**37.** (*c*)	**38.** (*d*)	**39.** (*a*)	**40.** (*d*)
41. (*b*)	**42.** (*d*)	**43.** (*c*)	**44.** (*b*)	**45.** (*a*)	**46.** (*d*)	**47.** (*d*)	**48.** (*c*)	**49.** (*d*)	**50.** (*a*)

PRACTICE SET 14

Directions : ***In each of the following sentences, a word or phrase is italicised and it is followed by some words marked (a), (b), (c), (d) and/or (e). Choose from these words the one which is most nearly opposite in meaning to the italicised word and indicate your choice by the corresponding letter (a), (b), (c), (d) or (e).***

1. The criminal was ***detained*** by the police. **(C.D.S. 1992)**
(*a*) protected (*b*) dismissed
(*c*) released (*d*) deterred

2. The long sickness has turned the boy ***flimsy***.
(*a*) healthy (*b*) strong
(*c*) agile (*d*) wholesome

3. His ***depressing*** attitude became a cause of trouble for us all.
(*a*) horrifying (*b*) uplifting
(*c*) bewildering (*d*) digressing

4. He failed to ***perceive*** that his bad habit was having an adverse effect on his son too.
(*a*) ignore (*b*) apprehend
(*c*) conceive (*d*) create

5. What he tells me ***confirms*** my ideas.
(*a*) verifies (*b*) contradicts
(*c*) opposes (*d*) strengthens
(Railways, 1994)

6. He is very ***meticulous*** in keeping accounts.
(*a*) clumsy (*b*) irregular
(*c*) careless (*d*) irresponsible

7. Discipline is being ***demoted*** in most of the present day institutions.
(*a*) uplifted (*b*) regained
(*c*) nurtured (*d*) projected

8. We had a ***delectable*** meal yesterday
(*a*) nice (*b*) tasty
(*c*) unsavoury (*d*) heavy
(C.D.S. 1994)

9. He is known for his ***uncouth*** manners.
(*a*) courteous (*b*) usual
(*c*) petty (*d*) mean

10. Ranjeet is suffering from ***benign*** tumor.
(*a*) contagious (*b*) infectious
(*c*) spreading (*d*) malignant

11. The patient looks a little more ***cheerful*** this morning. **(N.D.A. 1995)**
(*a*) depressed (*b*) dull
(*c*) energetic (*d*) stupid

12. His logic seemed ***absurd***.
(*a*) fictional (*b*) rational
(*c*) proportional (*d*) useless

13. I can say for sure that this document is ***authentic***.
(*a*) fictitious (*b*) duplicate
(*c*) fallacious (*d*) erroneous

14. Don't ***scold*** the boy over such trifles.
(*a*) pacify (*b*) console
(*c*) praise (*d*) vituperate

15. History ***abounds*** in instances of courge.
(*a*) fails (*b*) suffices
(*c*) lacks (*d*) shines
(C.D.S.1995)

16. Democracy is a government by ***conciliation***.
(*a*) non-cooperation (*b*) dispute
(*c*) confrontation (*d*) irritation

17. It was ***evident*** that he was happy.
(*a*) doubtful (*b*) clear
(*c*) unimportant (*d*) understood

18. ***Feasibility*** of the project is under study.
(*a*) Unsuitability (*b*) Impracticability
(*c*) Impropriety (*d*) Cheapness
(I.E.S. 1994)

19. To ***purge*** all social evils is really a difficult job.
(*a*) promote (*b*) increase
(*c*) rehabilitate (*d*) encourage

20. Mrs. Higgins is a ***humble*** lady.
(*a*) whimsical (*b*) youthful
(*c*) vain (*d*) unassuming

21. Those whose views are ***progressive*** often meet with formidable impediments when they begin to act. **(C.D.S. 1993)**
(*a*) outmoded (*b*) brave
(*c*) revolutionary (*d*) retrograde

22. Very rich fathers generally have ***stingy*** sons.
(*a*) reckless (*b*) careless
(*c*) spendthrift (*d*) miserly

23. The teacher gave a ***vivid*** description of the next day's programme.
(*a*) obscure (*b*) inanimate
(*c*) hazy (*d*) unintelligible

24. The ***indignation*** of the retreating troops resulted in large scale killings.
(*a*) displeasure (*b*) happiness
(*c*) orderliness (*d*) anger
(N.D.A. 1993)

25. He has bought ***genuine*** pearls.
(*a*) inexpensive (*b*) unattractive
(*c*) spurious (*d*) extraneous

26. The stuffed toy bore a ***glossy*** look.
(*a*) obscene (*b*) dull
(*c*) sleek (*d*) ventilating

27. This area is well known for ***plentiful*** rain.
(*a*) poor (*b*) impoverished
(*c*) scarce (*d*) miserly
(Railways, 1993)

28. It was a ***horrible*** sight.
(*a*) pleasing (*b*) veracious
(*c*) repulsive (*d*) attractive

29. The idea of uniting the two Germanys was ***seductive***.
(*a*) foolish (*b*) depressive
(*c*) unacceptable (*d*) repulsive

30. The covalent compounds consist of ***discrete*** molecules.
(*a*) concrete (*b*) grouped
(*c*) separate (*d*) convoluted

31. The ***mammoth*** structure overlooked the building.
(*a*) affluent (*b*) tiny
(*c*) huge (*d*) narrow

32. He felt tired with the ***monotony*** of his daily routine.
(*a*) peacefulness (*b*) variety
(*c*) excitement (*d*) range

33. Earthquakes are ***frequent*** in Japan.
(*a*) extinct (*b*) unusual
(*c*) few (*d*) rare
(N.D.A. 1992)

34. He was given in to much ***fanaticism***.
(*a*) reason (*b*) kindness
(*c*) passivity (*d*) violence

35. I cannot bear with that ***niggard*** fellow any more.
(*a*) miserly (*b*) generous
(*c*) extravagant (*d*) avaricious

36. Never consider your ***opponent*** to be weaker than you.
(*a*) friend (*b*) rival
(*c*) antagonist (*d*) ally

37. She handled the machine with ***deft*** fingers. **(C.D.S. 1994)**
(*a*) clumsy (*b*) sturdy
(*c*) delicate (*d*) quick

38. The teacher instructed the students to draw the ***marginal*** lines.
(*a*) central (*b*) fractional
(*c*) global (*d*) angular

39. It was a ***sagacious*** decision on his part.
(*a*) casual (*b*) cunning
(*c*) foolish (*d*) false

40. The children are playing in the ***nearby*** park. **(B.S.R.B. 1992)**
(*a*) different (*b*) close
(*c*) separate (*d*) distant

41. She sat all alone in the party bearing that ***sulky*** face.
(*a*) kind (*b*) loving
(*c*) mild (*d*) cheerful

42. The passing of the Bill was followed by a large scale ***retaliation*** by the citizens.
(*a*) procreation (*b*) reconciliation
(*c*) conciliation (*d*) redressal

43. The members of the opposition party made ***derogatory*** remarks about the policies of the government.
(*a*) praiseworthy (*b*) laudatory
(*c*) respectable (*d*) admirable
(C.D.S. 1995)

44. The lady shouted with a loud, ***shrill*** voice.
(*a*) feeble (*b*) blunt
(*c*) muffled (*d*) inaudible

45. Merit need not be ***swamped*** while filling vacancies through a quota system.
(*a*) considered (*b*) raised
(*c*) remembered (*d*) heeded

46. On the face of it Poirot's glance conveyed ***humorous*** impatience. **(N.D.A.1993)**
(*a*) disappointed (*b*) dejected
(*c*) pathetic (*d*) dismayed

47. The intricate carvings on the panels are ***notable***.
(*a*) hateful (*b*) uncommon
(*c*) ordinary (*d*) absurd

48. ***Ostentation*** is now the life style of big cities.
(*a*) Ugliness (*b*) Poverty
(*c*) Frugality (*d*) Modesty

49. Lucy is a ***smart*** girl.
(*a*) casual (*b*) indecent
(*c*) active (*d*) lazy

50. Mr. Arun Lal is a ***noted*** personality in the town.
(*a*) condemned (*b*) ostracised
(*c*) notorious (*d*) obscure

ANSWERS

1. (*c*)	**2.** (*b*)	**3.** (*b*)	**4.** (*a*)	**5.** (*b*)	**6.** (*c*)	**7.** (*c*)	**8.** (*c*)	**9.** (*a*)	**10.** (*a*)
11. (*a*)	**12.** (*b*)	**13.** (*d*)	**14.** (*c*)	**15.** (*c*)	**16.** (*c*)	**17.** (*a*)	**18.** (*b*)	**19.** (*c*)	**20.** (*c*)
21. (*d*)	**22.** (*c*)	**23.** (*a*)	**24.** (*b*)	**25.** (*c*)	**26.** (*b*)	**27.** (*c*)	**28.** (*a*)	**29.** (*b*)	**30.** (*b*)
31. (*b*)	**32.** (*b*)	**33.** (*d*)	**34.** (*a*)	**35.** (*b*)	**36.** (*d*)	**37.** (*a*)	**38.** (*a*)	**39.** (*c*)	**40.** (*d*)
41. (*d*)	**42.** (*b*)	**43.** (*b*)	**44.** (*c*)	**45.** (*b*)	**46.** (*c*)	**47.** (*c*)	**48.** (*d*)	**49.** (*d*)	**50.** (*d*)

PRACTICE SET 15

Directions : *In each of the following questions, out of the given alternatives, choose the one which is most nearly opposite in meaning to the italicised word.*

1. We have no doubt about the ***veracity*** of the statement. **(C.D.S. 1994)**
(*a*) morality (*b*) falsity
(*c*) propriety (*d*) truthfulness

2. Good actions cannot ***camouflage*** one's bad qualities.
(*a*) exhibit (*b*) demonstrate
(*c*) reveal (*d*) parade

3. His family has ***accumulated*** wealth over the years.
(*a*) drained (*b*) squandered
(*c*) amassed (*d*) dispersed

4. There was a ***marginal*** increase in his pay.
(*a*) unforeseen (*b*) negligible
(*c*) significant (*d*) peripheral
(N.D.A. 1995)

5. This tonic serves to ***vitalise*** your hairs.
(*a*) shorten (*b*) enfeeble
(*c*) repress (*d*) clamour

6. I liked the poem for its ***literal*** meaning.
(*a*) complex (*b*) figurative

(c) deep (d) fictitious

7. The leader was ***pragmatic*** in his approach to the problems facing the country. **(C.D.S. 1993)**
(a) optimistic (b) idealistic
(c) indefinite (d) vague

8. He is really an ***obstinate*** man.
(a) considerate (b) friendly
(c) understanding (d) compliant

9. His ***diabolical*** ways made him unpopular.
(a) mischievous (b) lavish
(c) seraphic (d) azure

10. Under the circumstances, such ***pejorative*** comments should have been avoided. **(I.E.S. 1993)**
(a) soothing (b) sporting
(c) appreciative (d) critical

11. The property of ***contraction*** of matter on cooling is put to several practical uses.
(a) improvement (b) growth
(c) expansion (d) dimunition

12. He is a man with a ***jovial*** nature.
(a) talkative (b) morose
(c) monotonous (d) quiet

13. It was a very ***dreary*** day. **(N.D.A. 1994)**
(a) drab (b) dangerous
(c) beautiful (d) bright

14. The flight was ***delayed*** because of bad weather.
(a) quickened (b) released
(c) expedited (d) triggered

15. The beautiful girl looked so ***morose***.
(a) healthy (b) gloomy
(c) haggard (d) cheerful

16. The error in the newspaper article is ***accidental***. **(Railways, 1994)**
(a) permissible (b) usual
(c) conventional (d) intentional

17. The General ordered the troops to ***advance*** to the fort.
(a) retire (b) return
(c) escape (d) retreat (e) abscond

18. She bought a ***gaudy*** shawl as a wedding gift for her sister.
(a) fatuous (b) sober
(c) garnish (d) ornate

19. His friends liked everything about him except his ***frugality***. **(C.D.S. 1994)**
(a) short temper (b) extravagance
(c) shabbiness (d) punctuality

20. Our knowledge of the past is still largely a matter of informed ***conjecture***.
(a) guess (b) position
(c) certainty (d) form

21. The teacher told the student to ***abridge*** the essay he had written.
(a) amplify (b) shorten
(c) increase (d) modify

22. The minister was accused of indulging in ***nepotism***. **(Central Excise, 1991)**
(a) impartiality (b) hatred
(c) condemnation (d) indifference

23. His living style and his conduct showed him ***opulent***.
(a) sumptuous (b) drooping
(c) wealthy (d) poor

24. Joys and tensions are ***ephemeral*** aspects of life.
(a) stable (b) permanent
(c) spiritual (d) ethical

25. The thief ***confessed*** at the police station that he had stolen my watch.
(a) concealed (b) disproved
(c) denied (d) admitted
(Clerks' Grade, 1993)

26. Do not ***follow*** others.
(a) emulate (b) praise
(c) oppose (d) criticise

27. The complete eradication of poverty from our country is really ***an illusion***.
(a) a truth (b) a fact
(c) a reality (d) an actuality

28. The revised pay scale is ***uniform***.
(a) equal (b) different
(c) opposite (d) varied
(C.D.S. 1990)

29. Sarita did not heed the ***disdain*** she had to bear at the hands of her step-mother.
(a) penitence (b) humility
(c) love (d) admiration

30. I was shocked to hear the ***scurrilous*** talks of the members of the Board.
(a) decent (b) relevant
(c) accurate (d) useful

31. Much to the ***chagrin*** of his parents, Ajit married a very poor girl.
(a) satisfaction (b) relief
(c) pleasure (d) excitement

32. His attitude is very ***hostile***. **(N.D.A. 1992)**
(a) friendly (b) kind
(c) humane (d) helpful

33. ***Tolerance*** is the essence of religion.
(a) Impatience (b) Cruelty
(c) Bigotry (d) Indifference

34. He made an ***exhaustive*** list of the items his secretary should attend to.
(a) meticulous (b) short
(c) interesting (d) incomplete

35. His ***urbane*** attitude won him many friends. **(C.D.S. 1992)**
(a) rude (b) rustic
(c) violent (d) indifferent

36. The wife fainted away, ***lamenting*** the death of her husband.

(*a*) smiling (*b*) ridiculing
(*c*) enjoying (*d*) rejoicing

37. I can't understand him; he is really a ***queer*** fellow.
(*a*) strange (*b*) careless
(*c*) ordinary (*d*) unusual

38. His books are well known for their ***progressive*** ideas. **(Railways, 1993)**
(*a*) useless (*b*) old-fashioned
(*c*) complex (*d*) reactionary

39. His ***disposition*** towards labour made him endearing to the Manager.
(*a*) inclination (*b*) unwillingness
(*c*) temperament (*d*) watchfulness

40. He does every job with great ***zeal*** and vigour.
(*a*) indifference (*b*) constraint
(*c*) passion (*d*) difficulty

41. Their meeting was rather ***boisterous***.
(*a*) quiet (*b*) business like
(*c*) noisy (*d*) calm
(C.D.S. 1995)

42. The minister was punished with ***defection*** for his anti-party activities.
(*a*) resignation (*b*) co-operation
(*c*) invitation (*d*) joining

43. You should ***quote*** this example as an evidence.
(*a*) reveal (*b*) adduce
(*c*) restrain (*d*) contradict

44. There is an ***obscure*** cave on the other side of the hill. **(N.D.A. 1996)**
(*a*) admired (*b*) notorious
(*c*) infamous (*d*) well-known

45. Mr. Lal was a ***reserved*** man.
(*a*) talkative (*b*) defamed
(*c*) popular (*d*) companionable

46. She ***detests*** government jobs.
(*a*) approves of (*b*) is fond of
(*c*) adores (*d*) is interested in
(C.D.S. 1990)

47. The officer incharge was quite ***humane*** in his approach.
(*a*) uncultured (*b*) unsympathetic
(*c*) uncivilised (*d*) uncompromising

48. The habit of ***squandering*** money should not be encouraged. **(C.D.S. 1995)**
(*a*) saving (*b*) collecting
(*c*) hoarding (*d*) discarding

49. Moments of solitude and silence helped the poet to ***concentrate*** on his poetic combination.
(*a*) confound (*b*) disturb
(*c*) contradict (*d*) distract

50. All these measures will ***augment*** employment opportunities.
(*a*) constrain (*b*) restrain
(*c*) diminish (*d*) circumscribe
(N.D.A. 1994)

ANSWERS

1. (*b*)	**2.** (*c*)	**3.** (*b*)	**4.** (*c*)	**5.** (*b*)	**6.** (*b*)	**7.** (*b*)	**8.** (*d*)	**9.** (*c*)	**10.** (*c*)
11. (*c*)	**12.** (*b*)	**13.** (*d*)	**14.** (*c*)	**15.** (*d*)	**16.** (*d*)	**17.** (*d*)	**18.** (*b*)	**19.** (*b*)	**20.** (*c*)
21. (*a*)	**22.** (*a*)	**23.** (*d*)	**24.** (*b*)	**25.** (*c*)	**26.** (*c*)	**27.** (*c*)	**28.** (*d*)	**29.** (*d*)	**30.** (*a*)
31. (c)	**32.** (a)	**33.** (c)	**34.** (d)	**35.** (b)	**36.** (d)	**37.** (c)	**38.** (d)	**39.** (b)	**40.** (a)
41. (a)	**42.** (d)	**43.** (d)	**44.** (d)	**45.** (a)	**46.** (c)	**47.** (b)	**48.** (a)	**49.** (d)	**50.** (c)

PRACTICE SET 16

Directions : ***In each of the following questions, pick up the choice which is most opposite in meaning of the word italicised bold in the sentence.***

1. The chairman ***rebuked*** the accounts officer for not supervising the work of his coordinates. **(Bank P.O. 1994)**
(*a*) praised (*b*) received
(*c*) awarded (*d*) invited
(*e*) strengthened

2. The incident ***cemented*** their relations.
(*a*) destroyed (*b*) wasted
(*c*) corroded (*d*) disintegrated

3. Many of the propositions he put up at the conference were ***ludicrous***.
(*a*) obnoxious (*b*) humorous
(*c*) praiseworthy (*d*) impractical

4. We received a ***cordial*** welcome from our host. **(C.D.S. 1992)**
(*a*) official (*b*) cold
(*c*) distrustful (*d*) indifferent

Everyone ***admired*** his ideas on this issue.
(*a*) disappointed (*b*) discarded
(*c*) neglected (*d*) disapproved

6. Every move I make seems to affect him ***adversely***. **(N.D.A. 1996)**
(*a*) deeply (*b*) favourably
(*c*) badly (*d*) internally

7. The director had a ***derisive*** attitude towards some of the members of the committee. **(Railways, 1993)**
(*a*) enthusiastic (*b*) respectful
(*c*) deprecatory (*d*) encouraging

8. I think this article ought to have been put in a ***compact*** from.
(*a*) expanded (*b*) enlarged
(*c*) diffused (*d*) broken

9. Some people indulge in loud ***vulgar*** talk.
(*a*) simple (*b*) restrained
(*c*) graceful (*d*) refined

10 He was the most ***eccentric*** and difficult patron. **(C.D.S. 1990)**
(*a*) normal (*b*) sober
(*c*) genial (*d*) sociable

11. Everyone wanted to be the ***harbinger*** of the good news to the king.
(*a*) precursor (*b*) tender
(*c*) opponent (*d*) follower

12. The two girls are always together. There is a great ***affinity*** between them.
(*a*) apathy (*b*) empathy
(*c*) antipathy (*d*) sympathy
(A.A.O. 1995)

13. He ***confessed*** having done a mistake.
(*a*) granted (*b*) conceded
(*c*) acknowledged (*d*) concealed

14. Pradeep is always ***jeered*** at by his companions.
(*a*) praised (*b*) scorned
(*c*) mocked (*d*) mourned

15. There are reports that many poor people ***abandon*** female children. **(N.D.A. 1992)**
(*a*) like (*b*) reject
(*c*) keep (*d*) help

16. ***Unity*** of thought and action has been the basis of India's strength and stability.
(*a*) Bias (*b*) Diversity
(*c*) Division (*d*) Weakness
(*e*) Din

17. Their team bore ***delinquent***, participants.
(*a*) reverent (*b*) uncivil
(*c*) quarrelsome (*d*) law abiding

18. In ancient India, scholars had no interest in political power or ***material*** growth.
(*a*) celestial (*b*) psychic
(*c*) spiritual (*d*) internal
(C.D.S. 1995)

19. It's a rule of the company to ***endow*** the Manager with all essential perks.
(*a*) rob (*b*) dispossess
(*c*) divest (*d*) snatch

20. The story was set up in an ***eerie*** atmosphere.
(*a*) delightful (*b*) weird
(*c*) warm (*d*) canny

21. There are four chapters that are ***extraneous*** to the structure of the book.
(*a*) relevant (*b*) integral
(*c*) important (*d*) needful
(Central Excise, 1988)

22. He makes ***occasional*** visits to Delhi.
(*a*) accidental (*b*) strange
(*c*) regular (*d*) frivolous

23. They have not been eating ***nourishing*** food.
(*a*) heavy (*b*) undercooked
(*c*) unhygienic (*d*) poor

24. The plantation workers were on a ***collision*** course before the labour officer intervened. **(C.D.S. 1993)**
(*a*) circuitous (*b*) retaliatory
(*c*) conciliatory (*d*) perfunctory

25. The new officer is a ***brash*** young man.
(*a*) polite (*b*) arrogant
(*c*) kind (*d*) handsome

26. She decided to finish the work before it became ***onerous***.
(*a*) unfamiliar (*b*) light
(*c*) burdensome (*d*) unique

27. His ***unscrupulous*** pursuit of wealth finally landed him in prison.
(*a*) superfluous (*b*) single minded
(*c*) dedicated (*d*) conscientious

28. The sudden appearance of the stranger in the cottage despite all doors being closed is ***questionable***.
(*a*) casual (*b*) surprising
(*c*) dubious (*d*) certain

29. Mr. Khanna is held in high ***esteem*** by the residents of the colony.
(*a*) revere (*b*) hatred
(*c*) disdain (*d*) notoriety

30. The inhabitants of the island were ***barbarians***. **(Railways, 1994)**
(*a*) bad (*b*) uncivilised
(*c*) cruel (*d*) civilised

31. Old people are usually more ***conservative*** than young people.
(*a*) reproachful (*b*) liberal
(*c*) dynamic (*d*) modern

32. His was a ***sulky*** disposition. **(C.D.S. 1994)**
(*a*) mild (*b*) cheerful
(*c*) loving (*d*) kind

33. I know you would have to ***prolong*** your tour; but still I advise you to complete this job also.
(*a*) obstruct (*b*) curtail

(c) hinder (d) restrain

34. He found an ***ancient*** statue in the village.
(a) fresh (b) new
(c) recent (d) modern
(e) refreshed

35. This is a ***trivial*** matter. **(N.D.A. 1995)**
(a) difficult (b) easy
(c) small (d) important

36. Elephants, when they go ***wild***, ought to be killed.
(a) tame (b) meek
(c) mild (d) domestic

37. Her coming to this place tomorrow is ***definite***.
(a) doubtful (b) regrettable
(c) questionable (d) unpredictable

38. His knowledge of the subject is quite ***extensive***. **(Clerks' Grade, 1988)**
(a) ordinary (b) little
(c) limited (d) restricted

39. He ***abdicated*** his post of his own accord.
(a) acquired (b) inherited
(c) seized (d) usurped

40. They invited him to ***sumptuous*** lunch.
(a) cheap (b) meagre
(c) poor (d) nutritious

41. Life in the villages is very ***dull***.
(a) serious (b) wasteful
(c) bluffing (d) pleasant
(B.S.R.B. 1992)

42. We must ***abolish*** evil customs.
(a) eradicate (b) restore
(c) revive (d) encourage

43. The boy was ***accused*** of theft.
(a) liberated (b) impeached
(c) exonerated (d) sentenced

44. This is not ideology but ***pragmatic*** language teaching. **(N.D.A. 1992)**
(a) impractical (b) improper
(c) imperfect (d) impossible

45. The incident ***frustrated*** all his ambitions.
(a) satiated (b) appeased
(c) cloyed (d) satisfied

46. When asked whether he was an atheist, he simply ***quibbled***.
(a) frowned (b) wavered
(c) affirmed (d) denied

47. Everybody was astonished when he used such a ***profane*** langage. **(C.D.S. 1994)**
(a) sacred (b) pure
(c) profound (d) high

48. My uncle is very wealthy, but rather ***parsimonious*** in his habits.
(a) extravagant (b) generous
(c) careless (d) strict
(Central Excise, 1988)

49. I am somewhat ***sceptical*** about his claim.
(a) optimistic (b) convinced
(c) credulous (d) hopeful

50. His writings have been much ***eulogised*** by Indian scholars. **(C.D.S. 1995)**
(a) condemned (b) flouted
(c) disapproved (d) disparaged

ANSWERS

1. (a)	**2.** (d)	**3.** (c)	**4.** (b)	**5.** (d)	**6.** (b)	**7.** (b)	**8.** (c)	**9.** (d)	**10.** (a)
11. (d)	**12.** (c)	**13.** (d)	**14.** (a)	**15.** (c)	**16.** (b)	**17.** (d)	**18.** (c)	**19.** (c)	**20.** (d)
21. (b)	**22.** (c)	**23.** (c)	**24.** (c)	**25.** (a)	**26.** (b)	**27.** (d)	**28.** (d)	**29.** (c)	**30.** (d)
31. (b)	**32.** (b)	**33.** (b)	**34.** (d)	**35.** (d)	**36.** (a)	**37.** (a)	**38.** (c)	**39** (d)	**40.** (b)
41. (d)	**42.** (c)	**43.** (c)	**44.** (a)	**45.** (d)	**46.** (c)	**47.** (a)	**48.** (a)	**49.** (b)	**50.** (a)

PRACTICE SET 17

Directions : ***In each of the following questions, choose the alternative which is closest to the opposite in meaning of the italicised word or phrase in the sentence.***

1. She was ***sceptical*** about the safety of the new drug. **(C.D.S. 1994)**
(a) sanguine (b) hopeful
(c) certain (d) doubtful

2. The members of the Board were impressed by the candidates ***urbane*** behaviour.
(a) rural (b) indifferent
(c) rude (d) negative

3. ***Infringement*** of law has to be prevented in order to maintain peace and order in the country.
(a) Review (b) Revision
(c) Relaxation (d) Obedience

4. He puts on airs and claims himself to be ***omniscient***.
(*a*) ignorant (*b*) uneducated
(*c*) unqualified (*d*) backward
(I. Tax & Central Excise, 1993)

5. It was ***altercation*** throughout and there was no discussion.
(*a*) resonance (*b*) alternative
(*c*) consonance (*d*) inconsistency

6. Anarchy ***emerges*** out of the wars of succession.
(*a*) disappears (*b*) sinks
(*c*) falls (*d*) drowns
(*e*) extinguishes

7. Unlike in Bihar Board, English is an ***optional*** subject in the U.P. Board.
(*a*) elementary (*b*) compulsory
(*c*) voluntary (*d*) necessary
(Clerks' Grade, 1993)

8. He was really ***delighted*** to see me.
(*a*) scared (*b*) disturbed
(*c*) surprised (*d*) displeased

9. This offer has come as a great ***boon*** to me.
(*a*) misfortune (*b*) blemish
(*c*) curse (*d*) trouble

10. The committee set about making ***provisional*** arrangements for the annual conference. **(N.D.A. 1995)**
(*a*) unconditional (*b*) abiding
(*c*) permanent (*d*) lasting

11. This painting is full of ***radiant*** colours.
(*a*) delicate (*b*) dull
(*c*) bright (*d*) rare

12. She began to ***babel*** in front of the guests.
(*a*) quiet (*b*) din
(*c*) mourn (*d*) cry

13. She used to ***disparage*** her neighbour every now and then. **(C.D.S. 1993)**
(*a*) denigrate (*b*) belittle
(*c*) praise (*d*) please

14. Soon the boys realised his ***peevish*** ways and began to avoid him.
(*a*) amiable (*b*) unpleasant
(*c*) snappish (*d*) authoritative

15. The priest would not allow anyone to ***desecrate*** the sanctity of the temple.
(*a*) desist (*b*) integrate
(*c*) intensify (*d*) consecrate

16. His ***vindictive*** nature often came up for comment among his friends.
(*a*) timid (*b*) obedient
(*c*) forgiving (*d*) forgetful
(Railways, 1994)

17. It's not fair to leave dogs ***loose.***
(*a*) closed (*b*) chained
(*c*) tight (*d*) locked

18. She was born rich and had a ***sophisticated*** taste.
(*a*) vigorous (*b*) simple
(*c*) artificial (*d*) superficial

19. His ***servility*** makes him detestable.
(*a*) bravery (*b*) prudence
(*c*) insolence (*d*) slavery
(C.D.S. 1994)

20. ***Recession*** causes unemployment
(*a*) Poverty (*b*) Computerisation
(*c*) Education (*d*) Inflation
(A.A.O. 1995)

21. I think it would be better if this paragraph is ***eliminated***.
(*a*) added (*b*) improved
(*c*) deleted (*d*) shortened

22. It was an ***arduous*** task for me.
(*a*) easy (*b*) time consuming
(*c*) quick (*d*) difficult

24. Under conditions of anxiety, the blood vessels ***dilate***.
(*a*) squeeze (*b*) swell
(*c*) constrict (*d*) shorten

25. He is quite ***industrious***. **(C.D.S. 1990)**
(*a*) hard working (*b*) indifferent
(*c*) lazy (*d*) indisposed

26. The luxurious hotel is a paradise for ***hedonists***.
(*a*) stoics (*b*) ascetics
(*c*) adventurers (*d*) saints

27. By murdering that woman, he has committed a ***hideous*** crime.
(*a*) normal (*b*) generous
(*c*) handsome (*d*) fair
(*e*) logical

28. The last show of the concert at the Ritz Theatre was a ***fiasco***. **(C.D.S. 1995)**
(*a*) triumph (*b*) victory
(*c*) fruitful (*d*) success

29. From his acts of hunting, it can be inferred that he is a ***wicked*** man.
(*a*) innocent (*b*) decent
(*c*) pious (*d*) peaceful

30. She was in a state of ***anxiety*** when I met her.
(*a*) pleasure (*b*) happiness
(*c*) relief (*d*) laughter

31. Tuberculosis is ***endemic*** in this area now a days.
(*a*) concentrated (*b*) scattered
(*c*) limited (*d*) sporadic

32. I think you should ***undertake*** this job; it would really be a profitable venture for you.
(*a*) refrain (*b*) leave
(*c*) conceal (*d*) retrieve

33. That was a ***dauntless*** action!
(*a*) devious (*b*) subtle
(*c*) secret (*d*) cowardly
(N.D.A. 1992)

34. The duty of a true citizen is to ***thwart*** social evils as untouchability, dowry system etc.
(*a*) favour (*b*) sustain
(*c*) promote (*d*)frustrate

35. Sunil spent most of his time in ***recreation***.
(*a*) work (*b*) boredom
(*c*) leisure (*d*) diversion

36. ***Adversity*** teaches man to be humble and self- reliant. **(C.D.S. 1995)**
(*a*) Prosperity (*b*) Curiosity
(*c*) Animosity (*d*) Sincerity

37. He appears to be a ***phony*** person.
(*a*) ugly (*b*) genuine
(*c*) unreal (*d*) beautiful

38. There is ***scarcity*** of milk in Delhi.
(*a*) shortage (*b*) abundance
(*c*) excess (*d*) sufficiency

39. Why do you ***disparage*** him all the time?
(*a*) abuse (*b*) criticise
(*c*) encourage (*d*) glorify
(Railways, 1993)

40. Political differences introduced a note of ***discord*** into their relationship.
(*a*) tranquility (*b*) familiarity
(*c*) concord (*d*) benevolence

41. The guard was given ***explicit*** orders about whom to admit.
(*a*) wrong (*b*) inadequate
(*c*) no (*d*) ambiguous

42. Her ***modesty*** prevented her from making her feelings known to him.
(*a*) vanity (*b*) superiority
(*c*) hypocrisy (*d*) arrogance

43. Double-decker buses are still ***extant*** in some cities of India.
(*a*) unheeded (*b*) forgotten
(*c*) destroyed (*d*) extinguished

44. People understand speech in the context of their ***accumulated*** experience.
(*a*) scattered (*b*) dissipated
(*c*) partial (*d*)

45. Even for the citizens of the East Bloc's most ***prosperous*** nation, the lure of capitalism is irresistible. **(N.D.A. 1996)**
(*a*) exploited (*b*) under-developed
(*c*) impoverished (*d*) destitute

46. Many snakes are ***innocuous.*** **(A.A.O. 95)**
(*a*) poisonous (*b*) harmful
(*c*) deadly (*d*) ferocious

47. Never be ***impulsive*** in taking decisions.
(*a*) considerable (*b*) cunning
(*c*) clever (*d*) cautious

48. The primary duty of our countrymen at present should be to ***curb*** such social evils as casteism and untouchability.
(*a*) recommend (*b*) restore
(*c*) encourage (*d*) reinstate

49. The Government empowered itself to ***attach*** the assets of all the scam suspects. **(C.D.S. 1992)**
(*a*) detach (*b*) donate
(*c*) return (*d*) release

50. The ***comely*** young girl proved to be a good receptionist.
(*a*) inexperienced (*b*) unattractive
(*c*) gloomy (*d*) depressed

ANSWERS

1. (*c*)	**2.** (*c*)	**3.** (*d*)	**4.** (*a*)	**5.** (*c*)	**6.** (*a*)	**7.** (*b*)	**8.** (*d*)	**9.** (*c*)	**10.** (*c*)
11. (*b*)	**12.** (*a*)	**13.** (*c*)	**14.** (*a*)	**15.** (*a*)	**16.** (*c*)	**17.** (*b*)	**18.** (*b*)	**19.** (*c*)	**20.** (*d*)
21. (*a*)	**22.** (*a*)	**23.** (*a*)	**24.** (*c*)	**25.** (*c*)	**26.** (*b*)	**27.** (*c*)	**28.** (*d*)	**29.** (*c*)	**30.** (*c*)
31. (*d*)	**32.** (*b*)	**33.** (*b*)	**34.** (*c*)	**35.** (*b*)	**36.** (*a*)	**37.** (*b*)	**38.** (*b*)	**39.** (*d*)	**40.** (*c*)
41. (*d*)	**42.** (*a*)	**43.** (*c*)	**44.** (*b*)	**45.** (*c*)	**46.** (*b*)	**47.** (*d*)	**48.** (*c*)	**49.** (*c*)	**50.** (*b*)

PRACTICE SET 18

Directions : ***Each of the following questions consists of a sentence in which one word is italicised. It is followed by some words. Select the word which is closest to the opposite in meaning to the italised word.***

1. His interpretation of the poem is ***superficial***. **(I.E.S. 1994)**
(*a*) mystical (*b*) profound
(*c*) difficult (*d*) mysterious

2. Should I ***communicate*** the date of the meeting to all the members?
(*a*) yield (*b*) conceal
(*c*) refrain (*d*) withhold

3. He has a ***superficial*** knowldege of the subject. **(N.D.A. 1996)**
(*a*) wide (*b*) profound
(*c*) sufficient (*d*) excessive

4. His style of writing is quite ***verbose***.
(*a*) lucid (*b*) succinct
(*c*) unusual (*d*) comical

5. His ***smooth*** manners endeared him to everyone.
(*a*) hard (*b*) rough
(*c*) gruff (*d*) tough

6. Everybody called it a ***lavish*** party.
(*a*) expensive (*b*) frugal
(*c*) wasteful (*d*) big
(N.D.A. 1995)

7. This is only the most ***tenuous*** evidence for it.
(*a*) abundant (*b*) enough
(*c*) reasonable (*d*) less

8. The dinner set she presented to me was ***durable*** enough.
(*a*) worn out (*b*) fragile
(*c*) light (*d*) delicate

9. His ***meanness*** is proverbial. **(S.S.C. 1988)**
(*a*) generosity (*b*) pragmatism
(*c*) timidity (*d*) kindness

10. Vigour and excitement are the prime characteristus of ***youth***.
(*a*) adolescence (*b*) teenage
(*c*) childhood (*d*) senility

11. I ***worship*** him as my ideal.
(*a*) deify (*b*) despise
(*c*) abuse (*d*) neglect

12. The influence of political broadcasts on elections is ***considerable***. **(C.D.S. 1995)**
(*a*) inadequate (*b*) uninfluential
(*c*) negligible (*d*) insignificant

13. There was not a single ***bibulous*** adventurer in our expedition.
(*a*) fearful (*b*) cowardly
(*c*) sober (*d*) unenergetic

14. Ranjeet drove to the place by a ***circuitous*** route.
(*a*) short (*b*) roundabout
(*c*) direct (*d*) obvious

15. The minister gave a public speech on the controversial subject to ***precipitate*** the matter. **(Bank P.O. 1994)**
(*a*) pull (*b*) push
(*c*) defer (*d*) create
(*e*) aggravate

16. Only ***egalitarianism*** can lay the foundations of a strong nation.
(*a*) dictatorship (*b*) domination
(*c*) imperialism (*d*) elitism

17. The stranger who stayed with us was a ***ruthless*** fellow.
(*a*) candid (*b*) sympathetic
(*c*) cordial (*d*) courteous

18. The club meets on the Last Thursday of every month in a ***dilapidated*** palace.
(*a*) furnished (*b*) renovated
(*c*) neglected (*d*) regenerated
(Railways, 1994)

19. People who are actually running the system often take a ***myopic*** view of the situation.
(*a*) blind (*b*) visionary
(*c*) glassy (*d*) farsighted

20 His ***arrogant*** behaviour made him successful in his trade.
(*a*) flattering (*b*) humble
(*c*) polite (*d*) pleasant

21. The Principal hardly managed to give the papers a ***cursory*** glance. **(C.D.S. 1992)**
(*a*) superficial (*b*) through
(*c*) thorough (*d*) curious

22. He exhibited a ***comprehensive*** approach towards the matter in hand.
(*a*) slipshod (*b*) sketchy
(*c*) exhaustive (*d* superficial

23. Giving alms to the poor is considered ***holy***.
(*a*) horrible (*b*) obnoxious
(*c*) profane (*d*) offensive

24. Mohini was often teased as ***corpulent*** by her friends. **(C.D.S. 1993)**
(*a*) belligerent (*b*) gaunt
(*c*) garrulous (*d*) fat

25. He received a flattering ***compliment*** from Sunita immediately after the speech.
(*a*) disparagement (*b*) eulogy
(*c*) contempt (*d*) notoriety

26. The gatekeeper ought to be more ***vigilant*** these days.
(*a*) irresponsible (*b*) ignorant
(*c*) careless (*d*) innocent

27. The police tried to find out the ***rightful*** owner of the ornaments left in the train.
(*a*) indefinite (*b*) mistaken
(*c*) unlawful (*d*) claimant
(B.S.R.B. 1992)

28. He nurtured in him a strong craving for ***revenge*** from those criminals
(*a*) mercy (*b*) pardon
(*c*) pity (*d*) forgiveness

29. He was often sent to ***foreign*** tours by the company.
(*a*) native (*b*) inland
(*c*) homely (*d*) local

30. The Minister is ***optimistic*** about the new project just launched. **(N.D.A. 1992)**
(*a*) stoical (*b*) dubious
(*c*) pessimistic (*d*) cynical

31. Though several meetings have been held, yet the members of the Board have not been able to arrive at a ***consensus***.
(*a*) conflict (*b*) confusion
(*c*) crisis (*d*) disagreement

32. One should never be ***reckless*** in his dealings with others.
(*a*) indifferent (*b*) careful
(*c*) imprudent (*d*) lenient

33. His short put pointed speech was ***applauded*** by all sections of the audience. **(C.D.S. 1995)**
(*a*) welcomed (*b*) praised
(*c*) misunderstood (*d*) disapproved

34. The doctor advised us to give him ***wholesome*** nutrition.
(*a*) sickly (*b*) stupendous
(*c*) depressing (*d*) fragmentary

35. He is a good fellow ; but what I dislike is his ***reckless*** handling of things.
(*a*) intelligent (*b*) cautious
(*c*) dilligent (*d*) brilliant

36. Her ***vivacity*** attracted everybody.
(*a*) beauty (*b*) humour
(*c*) apathy (*d*) truthfulness
(N.D.A. 1993)

37. ***Vanity*** never pays in the long run.
(*a*) Profanity (*b*) Conceit
(*c*) Pretence (*d*) Humility

38. Unlike his brother, he is fat and ***flabby***.
(*a*) healthy (*b*) tall
(*c*) skinny (*d*) thin

39. James had the habit of ***running down*** his colleagues. **(Railways, 1993)**
(*a*) deriding (*b*) pushing down
(*c*) praising (*d*) supporting

40. After meeting the holy man, his nagging mood of ***diffidence*** suddenly changed.
(*a*) confusion (*b*) self-assurance
(*c*) contentment (*d*) consternation
(A.A.O. 1995)

41. The room was filled with a ***delicious*** odour.
(*a*) bitter (*b*) repulsive
(*c*) strange (*d*) unpalatable

42. I suppose you should ***authorise*** him to do so.
(*a*) pulverize (*b*) prescribe
(*c*) detach (*d*) proscribe

43. Mahatma Gandhi said that ***compassion*** is more important than truth.
(*a*) violence (*b*) uncivility
(*c*) callousness (*d*) hardihood

44. The British policy was not one of ***domination*** but that of suppression.
(*a*) licence (*b*) liberty
(*c*) freedom (*d*) charity

45. She was surprised by his ***amiability***.
(*a*) pessimism (*b*) prudence
(*c*) sincerity (*d*) petulance
(C.D.S. 1994)

46. A ***terrestrial*** being can never be immortal.
(*a*) abnormal (*b*) marvellous
(*c*) amphibious (*d*) celestial

47. He was ***dejected*** when he heard the news. **(N.D.A. 1995)**
(*a*) elated (*b*) impressed
(*c*) hilarious (*d*) gleeful

48. You cannot blame him because all his dealings are ***above board***.
(*a*) under board (*b*) boring
(*c*) underhand (*d*) beneath

49. Overeating can often be ***detrimental*** to health.
(*a*) beneficial (*b*) injurious
(*c*) useful (*d*) destructive
(N.D.A. 1996)

50. His partners felt that it was a ***viable*** business proposition. **(N.D.A. 1996)**
(*a*) impracticable (*b*) inviolable
(*c*) unavailable (*d*) enviable

ANSWERS

1. (*b*)	**2.** (*d*)	**3.** (*b*)	**4.** (*b*)	**5.** (*c*)	**6.** (*b*)	**7.** (*a*)	**8.** (*b*)	**9.** (*a*)	**10.** (*d*)
1. (*b*)	**12.** (*c*)	**13.** (*c*)	**14.** (*c*)	**15.** (*c*)	**16.** (*d*)	**17.** (*b*)	**18.** (*b*)	**19.** (*d*)	**20.** (*b*)
21. (*c*)	**22.** (*d*)	**23.** (*c*)	**24.** (*b*)	**25.** (*a*)	**26.** (*c*)	**27.** (*c*)	**28.** (*d*)	**29.** (*b*)	**30.** (*c*)
31. (*d*)	**32.** (*b*)	**33.** (*d*)	**34.** (*a*)	**35.** (*b*)	**36.** (*c*)	**37.** (*d*)	**38.** (*c*)	**39.** (*c*)	**40.** (*b*)
41. (*d*)	**42.** (*d*)	**43.** (*c*)	**44.** (*c*)	**45.** (*d*)	**46.** (*d*)	**47.** (*a*)	**48.** (*c*)	**49.** (*a*)	**50.** (*a*)

PRACTICE SET 19

Directions : ***In each of the following questions, pick up the choice which is most opposite in meaning of the word italicised bold in the sentence.***

1. Like poverty, ***affluence*** can sometimes create its own problems. **(C.D.S. 1995)**
(*a*) sorrow (*b*) indigence
(*c*) exuberance (*d*) opulence

2. On hearing the news he was in a state of ***ecstasy***.
(*a*) depression (*b*) pain
(*c*) disappointment (*d*) trance

3. Many reactions take place in the blast furnace ***simultaneously***.
(*a*) invariably (*b*) contemporarily
(*c*) separately (*d*) momentarily

4. This author has ***perspicuity*** in his style.
(*a*) frankness (*b*) bluntness
(*c*) obtuseness (*d*) vivacity
(Railways, 1993)

5. The food served at the official dinner was very ***bland***.
(*a*) inedible (*b*) spicy
(*c*) nutritious (*d*) tasty

6. An artisan well is dug upto an ***impervious*** layer of rocks.
(*a*) hidden (*b*) penetrable
(*c*) hard (*d*) dry

7. ***Miscellaneous*** items were discussed at the meeting. **(I.E.S. 1993)**
(*a*) Minor (*b*) Unrelated
(*c*) Mixed (*d*) Classified

8. He felt ***gratified*** to the old man for his help.
(*a*) depressed (*b*) discouraged
(*c*) distressed (*d*) frustrated

9. He tried to ***conceal*** the secret that they were already married. **(C.D.S. 1990)**
(*a*) state (*b*) declare
(*c*) reveal (*d*) announce

10. As long as he remained in that office, he maintained his ***hegemony***.
(*a*) predominance (*b*) poverty
(*c*) subordination (*d*) chaos

11. That was an ***exquisite*** piece of art which won the admiration of one and all.
(*a*) ugly (*b*) cheap
(*c*) old (*d*) expensive

12. Silence in this place is ***mandatory***.
(*a*) optional (*b*) compulsory
(*c*) imperative (*d*) irritating
(N.D.A. 1994)

13. ***Expediency*** is the guiding factor in politics.
(*a*) Novelty (*b*) Short-sightedness
(*c*) Unsuitability (*d*) Inconvenience

14. He holds ***extreme*** views on education.
(*a*) ordinary (*b*) casual
(*c*) timid (*d*) moderate

15. His ***frivolous*** remarks provoked no comments. **(C.D.S. 1994)**
(*a*) serious (*b*) momentous
(*c*) frantic (*d*) fanciful

16. By warning him prior to action, he has landed himself in a ***precarious*** situation.
(*a*) carefree (*b*) safe
(*c*) easy (*d*) cautious
(*e*) harmless

17. The key words in planning for an unpredictable future are focus and ***flexibility***. **(N.D.A. 1996)**
(*a*) complexity (*b*) tensity
(*c*) pliability (*d*) rigidity

18. He proved utterly ***capricious*** in his dealings with his friends.
(*a*) helpful (*b*) steadfast
(*c*) understanding (*d*) obstinate
(Central Excise, 1991)

19. Rohit is a very ***courageous*** boy.
(*a*) frightened (*b*) naughty
(*c*) cowardly (*d*) happy

20. He was ***exonerated*** of the charge of theft when the woman gave an evidence in his favour.
(*a*) imprisoned (*b*) complained
(*c*) expelled (*d*) accused

21. Her ***impetuous*** behaviour was attributed to her upbringing.
(*a*) poised (*b*) rash
(*c*) quiet and gentle (*d*) sluggish
(N.D.A. 1994)

22. His book has a short but useful ***introduction***.
(*a*) deduction (*b*) end
(*c*) termination (*d*) conclusion

23. He has been ***acquitted*** of the charge of theft.
(*a*) punished (*b*) convicted
(*c*) released (*d*) exonerated

24. Her new hair style looks very ***attractive***.
(*a*) unblooming (*b*) grand
(*c*) unbecoming (*d*) fascinating

25. Everything about him, especially his talkative nature, proclaims his ***effeminacy***. **(C.D.S. 1993)**
(*a*) boorishness (*b*) manliness
(*c*) aggressiveness (*d*) attractiveness

26. He harvested a rich crop from that ***fecund*** land.
(*a*) fertile (*b*) obsolete
(*c*) barren (*d*) fruitless

27. He said it would be ***convenient*** for him to meet me there.
(*a*) inadvisable (*b*) objectionable
(*c*) troublesome (*d*) desirable

28. His ***tardy*** manners were a great impediment in the path of his success.
(*a*) quick (*b*) enthusiastic
(*c*) sluggish (*d*) progressive

29. The usual ***adulation*** of the officers must end. **(N.D.A. 1996)**
(*a*) back-biting (*b*) flattery
(*c*) condemnation (*d*) praise

30. He harboured a feeling of ***malice*** towards his younger brother.
(*a*) love (*b*) rancour
(*c*) spite (*d*) goodwill

31. They had an ***insipid*** conversation.
(*a*) curious (*b*) loud
(*c*) argumentative (*d*) lively
(Railways, 1994)

33. Self-reliance has been ***adopted*** as an important objective of economic planning in modern India.
(*a*) discarded (*b*) denied
(*c*) forsaken (*d*) refused

33. I found my views to be ***congruous*** to those of my father.
(*a*) irregular (*b*) mismatch
(*c*) inconsistent (*d*) disagreeing

34. The leader might have had some ***covert*** reason for the change of his political affiliations. **(C.D.S. 1992)**
(*a*) flimsy (*b*) inexplicable
(*c*) obvious (*d*) unjustifiable

35. The fifteenth century witnessed an era of ***Renaissance*** in Europe.
(*a*) pestilence (*b*) decadence
(*c*) immorality (*d*) prehistory

36. The Chief Minister was given a warm welcome at the ***onset*** of the function.
(*a*) hindrance (*b*) commencement
(*c*) finale (*d*) conclusion

37. It is surprising to find her ***condoning*** such an act. **(N.D.A. 1995)**
(*a*) disparaging (*b*) condemning
(*c*) disliking (*d*) forbidding

38. His conduct on the stage was ***applauded*** unanimously.
(*a*) booed (*b*) silenced
(*c*) hated (*d*) disturbed

39. Worldly-wise people find it prudent to adopt a morally ***flexible*** attitude towards current behaviour patterns.
(*a*) weak (*b*) uncompromising
(*c*) hostile (*d*) neutral

40. At least some students are in the habit of doing their exercises in a ***slovenly*** manner. **(C.D.S. 1995)**
(*a*) neat (*b*) proper
(*c*) decent (*d*) correct

41. The heroine's ***infidelity*** finds no mention in this biography.
(*a*) loyalty (*b*) innocence
(*c*) intelligence (*d*) charity

42. If you read the novel carefully, you will realise that her character is ***irreproachable***.
(*a*) flawed (*b*) blemished
(*c*) defective (*d*) deformed

43. Sanjay's point of view was correct but his behaviour with his father was quite ***impertinent***. **(Bank P.O. 1994)**
(*a*) impressive (*b*) smooth
(*c*) healthy (*d*) respectful
(*e*) inadequate

44. The deliberate ***suavity*** of Dev's behaviour made the emotions of the audience volatile. **(A.A.O. 1995)**
(*a*) politeness (*b*) impetuosity
(*c*) stupidity (*d*) pleasant

45. The attack on the freedom of the press is a ***retrograde*** step.
(*a*) aggressive (*b*) progressive
(*c*) punitive (*d*) stubborn

46. The momentum of the movement ***slackened*** in course of time.
(*a*) recovered (*b*) multiplied
(*c*) quickened (*d*) stopped
(N.D.A. 1992)

47. Her ***debonair*** manners were noticed by everyone present in the city.
(*a*) stiff (*b*) cheerless
(*c*) courteous (*d*) pleasant

48. ***Misogynists*** are not applauded in society. **(N.D.A. 1993)**
(*a*) Philanderers (*b*) Philologists
(*c*) Philanthropists (*d*) Philogynists

49. There was no ***altruistic*** motive that prompted him to help her. **(C.D.S. 1994)**
(*a*) wicked (*b*) brutal
(*c*) inhuman (*d*) selfish

50. According to a great philosopher ***magnamity*** in a man implies many other qualities.
(*a*) poverty (*b*) jealousy
(*c*) meanness (*d*) enmity

ANSWERS

1. (*b*)	**2.** (*a*)	**3.** (*c*)	**4.** (*c*)	**5.** (*d*)	**6.** (*b*)	**7.** (*a*)	**8.** (*d*)	**9.** (*c*)	**10.** (*c*)
11. (*a*)	**12.** (*a*)	**13.** (*c*)	**14.** (*d*)	**15.** (*a*)	**16.** (*b*)	**17.** (*d*)	**18.** (*b*)	**19.** (*c*)	**20.** (*d*)
21. (*c*)	**22.** (*d*)	**23.** (*b*)	**24.** (*c*)	**25.** (*b*)	**26.** (*c*)	**27.** (*c*)	**28.** (*a*)	**29.** (*c*)	**30.** (*d*)
31. (*d*)	**32.** (*c*)	**33.** (*c*)	**34.** (*c*)	**35.** (*b*)	**36.** (*c*)	**37.** (*b*)	**38.** (*a*)	**39.** (*b*)	**40.** (*d*)
41. (*a*)	**42.** (*c*)	**43.** (*d*)	**44.** (*b*)	**45.** (*b*)	**46.** (*c*)	**47.** (*b*)	**48.** (*d*)	**49.** (*d*)	**50.** (*c*)

TYPE 3 : FILLING THE BLANKS WITH THE ANTONYM OF THE ITALICISED WORD

In this type of questions, a sentence is given, in which a word is italicised. The candidate is required to choose one word out of the given alternatives which is opposite in meaning to the italicised word and can fill in the blank provided in the sentence,to make it meaningfully complete.

Example : Gandhiji believed that a (an) .... life can never be as fruitful as a ***sober*** one.
(*a*) excited (*b*) abstemious (*c*) tipsy (*d*) immoderate

Solution : 'Sober' means 'decent'. Clearly, the opposite of it is 'abstemious.'
Hence, the answer is (*b*).

PRACTICE SET 20

Directions : ***In each of the following sentences, choose the word opposite in meaning to the italicised word to fill in the blanks.***

1. Wood is ***opaque*** but glass is ....
(*a*) hard (*b*) smooth
(*c*) soft (*d*) transparent

2. My plans may sound rather ***nebulous*** to you, but they are very .... to me.
(*a*) clear (*b*) concrete
(*c*) prominent (*d*) conspicuous
(C.B.I. 1988)

3. Take these ***stale*** buns away and bring the ....ones.
(*a*) new (*b*) fresh
(*c*) good (*d*) sweet

4. Though they expected a ***surplus,*** the annual accounts showed a .... of several thousand rupees.
(*a*) reduction (*b*) shortness
(*c*) loss (*d*) deficit

5. People often prefer ***ambiguity*** to ....
(*a*) clarity (*b*) perversity
(*c*) rationality (*d*) certainty
(I.E.S. 1994)

6. You can't ***tackle*** him, so just .... him.
(*a*) oppose (*b*) overlook
(*c*) avoid (*d*) appease

7. Never ***neglect*** the ideals of elders, rather always .... them.
(*a*) follow (*b*) cherish
(*c*) praise (*d*) grasp

8. I had always thought that Manick was ***candid*** in his dealings, but he turned out to be ....
(*a*) rude (*b*) cunning
(*c*) vague (*d*) deceptive

9. Never ***dissipate*** energy resources, but always .... them.
(*a*) utilise (*b*) organise
(*c*) mobilise (*d*) conserve

10. What one considers .... may be ***vice*** to another. **(C.B.I. 1987)**
(*a*) courtesy (*b*) kindness
(*c*) virtue (*d*) goodness

11. ***Saviour*** is always better than the ....
(*a*) torturer (*b*) redeemer
(*c*) executioner (*d*) destroyer

12. The Mayor was a ***miser*** while his son was a ....
(*a*) wreck (*b*) generous person
(*c*) spendthrift (*d*) liberal person

13. Just ***incorporate*** the necessary details and .... the rest.
(*a*) dissect (*b*) differentiate
(*c*) disjoin (*d*) exclude

14. History has seen more .... wars than ***civil*** wars.
(*a*) political (*b*) urban
(*c*) military (*d*) rural

15. A ***sedentary*** worker requires more calories than a .... one.
(*a*) laborious (*b*) stationary
(*c*) mobile (*d*) efficient

16. If your knife has become ***blunt***, you should get it ....
(*a*) filed (*b*) polished
(*c*) pointed (*d*) sharpened

17. I ***never*** drive to work, I .... walk.
(*a*) seldom (*b*) often
(*c*) always (*d*) sometimes
(C.B.I. 1988)

18. You shouldn't ***taunt*** him, rather .... his talents.
(*a*) praise (*b*) publicise
(*c*) boost (*d*) encourage

19. Nature teaches us not to ***destroy***, but to ....
(*a*) invest (*b*) produce
(*c*) create (*d*) make

20. He is always ***casual*** and never .... with his friends.
(*a*) harsh (*b*) systematic
(*c*) formal (*d*) regular

21. Pleasure is .... and not ***eternal.***
(*a*) immaterial (*b*) divine
(*c*) spiritual (*d*) transient

22. A ***bold*** man can live life better than a .... one.
(*a*) gentle (*b*) weak
(*c*) meek (*d*) ineffective

23. .... youths disturb the ***tranquil*** atmosphere by indulging in anti-social activities.
(*a*) Frustrated (*b*) Anxious
(*c*) Agitated (*d*) Quarrelsome

24. He holds ***extreme*** views on taxation, but there are others whose views are ....
(*a*) refined (*b*) moderate
(*c*) plain (*d*) ordinary
(C.B.I. 1987)

25. He was ***dismissed*** from the office, but when all the charges against him proved to be false, he was ....
(*a*) accepted (*b*) employed
(*c*) recalled (*d*) reinstated

26. I had left the room in an ***orderly*** state, but on returning I found it in a state of ....
(*a*) confusion (*b*) awkwardness
(*c*) turmoil (*d*) rummage

27. Shalini has a ***slender*** figure, while her husband is ....
(*a*) brave (*b*) frail
(*c*) healthy (*d*) stout

28. .... always helps man succeed, but ***lethargy*** makes him suffer in life.
(*a*) Intelligence (*b*) Activity
(*c*) Sharpness (*d*) Quickness

29. All her life she has been ***insulated from*** the harsh realities of the world but now she is .... all kinds of hardship.
(*a*) exposed to (*b*) troubled by
(*c*) used to (*d*) worried about
(C.B.I. 1987)

30. You must ***avenge*** your father's death, and not .... the culprit.
(*a*) exempt (*b*) reward
(*c*) forgive (*d*) save

31. Such talks are ***absurd***; you should indulge in .... talks.
(*a*) correct (*b*) fictional
(*c*) proportional (*d*) rational

32. I feel ***at home*** in the hostel but .... in my house.
(*a*) unwelcome (*b*) unhappy
(*c*) unpleasant (*d*) ill at ease

33. You shouldn't be ***proud***, but be .... your conduct.
(C.B.I. 1987)
(*a*) unsure of (*b*) worried about
(*c*) ashamed of (*d*) concerned about

34. Mohan is a ***diligent*** worker, while his brother Kishen is a .... one.
(*a*) sedulous (*b*) lazy
(*c*) sedentary (*d*) attentive

35. Ram Lal, through his hard labour, converted the .... land into a ***fertile*** one.
(*a*) unproductive (*b*) dry
(*c*) barren (*d*) deserted

36. ***Elevation*** and .... are important features of geographical study.
(*a*) Reduction (*b*) Compression
(*c*) Retardation (*d*) Depression

37. Sherlock Holmes is a ***fictitious*** character and not a .... one.
(*a*) authentic (*b*) concrete
(*c*) proven (*d*) real

38. All what he said was ***pertinent*** to the topic, and nothing was ....
(*a*) different (*b*) detached
(*c*) obsolete (*d*) irrelevant

39. This book seems rather ***complicated***, I think this matter should be .... and categorised.
(*a*) smooth (*b*) simple
(*c*) fragmented (*d*) straight

40. She has an ***attractive*** figure, but her temper is most .... **(C.B.I. 1987)**
(*a*) complex (*b*) unpredictable
(*c*) distracting (*d*) repulsive

41. We should ***condemn*** social evils, and .... those who did a lot to eradicate them.
(*a*) praise (*b*) prefer
(*c*) accept (*d*) enamour

42. I would advise you to ***pacify*** your father, and not .... him by arguing.
(*a*) insult (*b*) offend
(*c*) aggravate (*d*) injure

43. In these days of rising prices, you must be ***economical*** in your habits, don't be so ....
(*a*) cheap (*b*) extravagant
(*c*) miserly (*d*) expensive

44. I felt ***tired*** here, but the holiday in Ooty made me feel ....
(*a*) healthy (*b*) recovered
(*c*) rested (*d*) refreshed

45. Generally she is ***cautious***, but you can't predict when she is .... **(C.B.I. 1987)**
(*a*) kind (*b*) fast
(*c*) rash (*d*) hurtful

46. .... and not ***hesitation*** works in business.
(*a*) Optimism (*b*) Firmness
(*c*) Decision (*d*) Strength

47. These ***spurious*** documents can never substitute the .... ones.
(*a*) obvious (*b*) authentic
(*c*) fictitious (*d*) genuine

48. During our long freedom struggle, the non-violent movements received huge ***acclamation*** while those involving violence and bloody massacres faced ....
(*a*) denunciation (*b*) suppression
(*c*) termination (*d*) applause

49. ***Absolute*** control of the firm is what he wanted, but he ended up with .... powers. **(C.B.I. 1987)**
(*a*) little (*b*) few
(*c*) complex (*d*) limited

50. ISI marked goods are always ***pure*** and never ....
(*a*) dirty (*b*) mixed
(*c*) adulterated (*d*) stained

ANSWERS

1. (*d*)	**2.** (*a*)	**3.** (*b*)	**4.** (*d*)	**5.** (*a*)	**6.** (*c*)	**7.** (*b*)	**8.** (*d*)	**9.** (*d*)	**10.** (*c*)
11. (*d*)	**12.** (*c*)	**13.** (*d*)	**14.** (*c*)	**15.** (*c*)	**16.** (*d*)	**17.** (*c*)	**18.** (*a*)	**19.** (*c*)	**20.** (*c*)
21. (*d*)	**22.** (*c*)	**23.** (*c*)	**24.** (*b*)	**25.** (*d*)	**26.** (*c*)	**27.** (*d*)	**28.** (*b*)	**29.** (*a*)	**30.** (*c*)
31. (*d*)	**32.** (*d*)	**33.** (*c*)	**34.** (*b*)	**35.** (*c*)	**36.** (*d*)	**37.** (*d*)	**38.** (*d*)	**39.** (*c*)	**40.** (*d*)
41. (*a*)	**42.** (*c*)	**43.** (*b*)	**44.** (*d*)	**45.** (*c*)	**46.** (*b*)	**47.** (*d*)	**48.** (*a*)	**49.** (*d*)	**50.** (*c*)

3. VOCABULARY TEST

This section deals with questions on general vocabulary. In this type of questions, a word is given, followed by some alternatives. The candidate is required to choose either the synonym or the antonym, whichever is present, for the given word from among the alternatives provided.

Directions : ***Pick out the word that is either most nearly the same in meaning or opposite of the word printed in capitals.***

Ex. 1. EXHORT

(*a*) Condemn (*b*) Urge (*c*) Prevent (*d*) Waste

Sol. Clearly, 'urge' is a synonym of 'exhort'.

Hence, the answer is (*b*).

Ex. 2. ERUDITE

(*a*) Unfamiliar (*b*) Illiterate (*c*) Unknown (*d*) Ignorant

Sol. 'Erudite' means 'Knowledgeable'.

So, its antonym is 'ignorant'.

Hence, the answer is (*d*).

PRACTICE SET 1

Directions : In each question below, a word is given in capitals. Against this word there are some alternatives, one of which is either same in meaning (synonym) or opposite in meaning (antonym) of the word printed in BOLD TYPE. Find out which of the given alternatives is either a synonym or an antonym of the word printed in capitals.

1. CONSEQUENCE **(S.B.I.P.O. 1991)**
(*a*) Indifference (*b*) Affect
(*c*) Serial (*d*) Outcome
(*e*) Divergence

2. ENIGMATIC
(*a*) Short-sighted (*b*) Learned
(*c*) Puzzling (*d*) Displeased

3. VIRTUOUS
(*a*) Vulgar (*b*) Insincere
(*c*) Vicious (*d*) Miserly

4. IMPETUOUS
(*a*) Pleasing (*b*) Rash
(*c*) Violent (*d*) Resourceful

5. INTERIM
(*a*) Interval (*b*) Temporary
(*c*) Timely (*d*) Internal

6. EXPURGATE
(*a*) Admit (*b*) Renew
(*c*) Stain (*d*) Entertain

7. ABATE **(Bank P.O. 1996)**
(*a*) Tighten (*b*) Increase
(*c*) Abandon (*d*) Diminish
(*e*) Postpone

8. TEMPERAMENTAL
(*a*) Satisfied (*b*) Contented
(*c*) Unruffled (*d*) Pleased

9. SLOTHFUL
(*a*) Ignorant (*b*) Lazy
(*c*) Stubborn (*d*) Fat

10. EULOGISTIC
(*a*) Critical (*b*) Stern
(*c*) Brief (*d*) Free

11. DEVIATE
(*a*) Locate (*b*) Obliviate
(*c*) Concentrate (*d*) Follow

12. SOPORIFIC
(*a*) Soothing (*b*) Lethargic
(*c*) Merry (*d*) Impressive

13. CANDID
(*a*) Shallow (*b*) Vague
(*c*) Secretive (*d*) Anxious

14. GRANDIOSE
(*a*) Proud (*b*) Heavy
(*c*) Clumsy (*d*) Simple

15. BUCOLIC
(*a*) Healthy (*b*) Rustic
(*c*) Intoxicated (*d*) Sick

16. LIBERAL **(S.B.I.P.O. 1991)**
(*a*) Unreliable (*b*) Strong
(*c*) Intolerant (*d*) Responsible
(*e*) Independent

17. PROGNOSIS
(*a*) Identification (*b*) Prefaee
(*c*) Scheme (*d*) Forecast

18. UNRULY
(*a*) Indifferent (*b*) Obedient
(*c*) Intelligent (*d*) Curious

19. AMALGAMATE
(*a*) Frustrate (*b*) Astonish
(*c*) Gather (*d*) Unite

20. STRIDENT
(*a*) Melodious (*b*) Stable
(*c*) Musical (*d*) Pleasant

21. INQUISITIVE
(*a*) Careful (*b*) Indolent
(*c*) Uninterested (*d*) Dull

22. RUMINATE **(Bank P.O. 1996)**
(*a*) Anticipate (*b*) Concentrate
(*c*) Ponder (*d*) Abscond
(*e*) Terminate

23. PEREMPTORY
(*a*) Dictatorial (*b*) Unexpected
(*c*) Military (*d*) Unreasonable

24. LACHRYMOSE
(*a*) Impious (*b*) Mournful
(*c*) Unimpressive (*d*) Moist

25. INHIBIT
(*a*) Surrender (*b*) Refrain
(*c*) Discard (*d*) Activate

26. FURTIVE
(*a*) Straight (*b*) Obvious
(*c*) Unambiguous (*d*) Open

27. TACIT **(Bank P.O. 1995)**
(*a*) Trivial (*b*) Spoken
(*c*) Lengthy (*d*) Neutral
(*e*) Inconspicuous

28. EMULATE
(*a*) Discuss (*b*) Question
(*c*) Deny (*d*) Imitate

29. INCENTIVE
(*a*) Beginning (*b*) Objective
(*c*) Goad (*d*) Stimulation

30. FESTAL
(*a*) Merry (*b*) Serious
(*c*) Noisy (*d*) Sad

31. PUISSANT
(*a*) Weak (*b*) Intelligent
(*c*) Careful (*d*) Indifferent

32. EXONERATE
(*a*) Admit (*b*) Accuse
(*c*) Contract (*d*) Reject

33. VEHEMENTLY **(S.B.I.P.O. 1991)**
(*a*) Openly (*b*) Widely
(*c*) Abruptly (*d*) Forcefully
(*e*) Spontaneously

34. STINGY
(*a*) Cheerful (*b*) Extravagant
(*c*) Rich (*d*) Generous

35. VINDICTIVE
(*a*) Revengeful (*b*) Petty
(*c*) Prejudiced (*d*) Unpopular

36. RECEDE
(*a*) Increase (*b*) Bloom
(*c*) Advance (*d*) Diminish

37. PROWESS
(*a*) Bravery (*b*) Eagerness
(*c*) Keenness (*d*) Understanding

38. PRECIPITOUS
(*a*) Steep (*b*) Absurd
(*c*) Exact (*d*) Uncertain

39. ANATHEMATISE
(*a*) Radiate (*b*) Bless
(*c*) Deceive (*d*) Locate

40. BOISTEROUS
(*a*) Adolescent (*b*) Conflicting
(*c*) Grateful (*d*) Vociferous

41. INSTIL
(*a*) Express (*b*) Extract
(*c*) Expand (*d*) Eradicate

42. PROFANE **(Bank P.O. 1996)**
(*a*) Respectful (*b*) Arrogant
(*c*) Impious (*d*) Intelligent
(*e*) Praiseworthy

43. COMPENDIUM
(*a*) Glossary (*b*) Reference
(*c*) Index (*d*) Summary

44. OBSCENE
(*a*) Unwanted (*b*) Dirty
(*c*) Unhealthy (*d*) Indecent

45. EXTANT
(*a*) Unheeded (*b*) Forgotten
(*c*) Extinguished (*d*) Destroyed

46. TURGID
(*a*) Detailed (*b*) Bright
(*c*) Clean (*d*) Smooth

47. PUNITIVE **(Bank P.O. 1995)**
(*a*) Inconsistent (*b*) Rewarding
(*c*) Cognisable (*d*) Punctual
(*e*) Escalating

48. REPRIMAND
(*a*) Release (*b*) Encourage
(*c*) Praise (*d*) Recommend

49. CAJOLE
(*a*) Persuade (*b*) Scold
(*c*) Threaten (*d*) Intimidate

50. REITERATE
(*a*) Deny (*b*) Frustrate
(*c*) Repeat (*d*) Illustrate

ANSWERS

The alphabets 'S' and 'A' given along with each of the followng answers indicates whether the alternative chosen is a synonym or antonym of the given word.

1. (*d*) : S **2.** (*c*) : S **3.** (*c*) : A **4.** (*b*) : S **5.** (*b*) : S **6.** (*a*) : A **7.** (*b*) : A
8. (*c*) : A **9.** (*b*) : S **10.** (*a*) : A **11.** (*d*) : A **12.** (*a*) : S **13.** (*c*) : A **14.** (*d*) : A

15. (*b*) : S **16.** (*c*) : A **17.** (*a*) : S **18.** (*b*) : A **19.** (*d*) : S **20.** (*d*) : A **21** (*c*) : A
22. (*c*) : S **23.** (*a*) : S **24.** (*b*) : S **25.** (*d*) : A **26.** (*a*) : A **27.** (*b*) : S **28.** (*d*) : S
29. (*d*) : S **30.** (*a*) : S **31.** (*a*) : A **32.** (*b*) : A **33.** (*d*) : S **34.** (*d*) : A **35.** (*a*) : S
36. (*c*) : A **37.** (*a*) : S **38.** (*a*) : S **39.** (*b*) : A **40.** (*d*) : S **41.** (*b*) : A **42.** (*c*) : A
43. (*b*) : S **44.** (*d*) : S **45.** (*d*) : S **46.** (*c*) : A **47.** (*b*) : A **48.** (*c*) : A **49.** (*a*) : A
50. (*c*) : S

PRACTICE SET 2

Directions : *Pick out the word that is either most nearly the same in meaning or opposite of the word printed in capitals.*

1. VIRILE
(*a*) Pompous (*b*) Boastful
(*c*) Athletic (*d*) Manly

2. SLAKE
(*a*) Erase (*b*) Quench
(*c*) Rub (*d*) Sharpen

3. CHIMERICAL
(*a*) Wonderful (*b*) Unnatural
(*c*) Realistic (*d*) Economical

4. IMPECCABLE
(*a*) Faulty (*b*) Repulsive
(*c*) Practical (*d*) Reasonable

(S.B.I.P.O. 1991)

5. RECOLLECT
(*a*) Forget (*b*) Memory
(*c*) Distribute (*d*) Assemble
(*e*) Rearrange

6. GENUINE
(*a*) Impure (*b*) Unsound
(*c*) Bogus (*d*) Rotten

7. CHURLISH
(*a*) Coarse (*b*) Modest
(*c*) Niggardly (*d*) Courteous

8. BELLICOSE
(*a*) Amusing (*b*) War-Like
(*c*) Errant (*d*) Naval

(Bank P.O. 1995)

9. PARITY
(*a*) Vicinity (*b*) Similarity
(*c*) Equivocal (*d*) Originality
(*e*) Versatility

10. RECTIFY
(*a*) Build (*b*) Command
(*c*) Correct (*d*) Destroy

11. INSPIRED
(*a*) Dispirited (*b*) Sceptical
(*c*) Overwhelmed (*d*) Disillusioned

12. DISSOLUTE
(*a*) Repulsive (*b*) Distant
(*c*) Honest (*d*) Immoral

(Bank P.O. 1996)

13. SALUBRIOUS
(*a*) Essential (*b*) Tarnished
(*c*) Benign (*d*) Unhealthy
(*e*) Resourceful

14. LETHARGY
(*a*) Listlessness (*b*) Serenity
(*c*) Laxity (*d*) Impassivity

15. GLOSSY
(*a*) Dull (*b*) Ventilating
(*c*) Sleek (*d*) Obscene

16. INCOMPATIBLE
(*a*) Contradictory (*b*) Capable
(*c*) Indifferent (*d*) Faulty

17. ARCANE
(*a*) Old fashioned (*b*) Modern
(*c*) Common place (*d*) Secret

18. ATTRITION
(*a*) Suffering (*b*) Friction
(*c*) Attraction (*d*) Decline

19. MALAISE
(*a*) Stagnation (*b*) Spite
(*c*) Sickness (*d*) Curse

20. EUPHONIOUS
(*a*) Strident (*b*) Lethargic
(*c*) Distasteful (*d*) Significant

21. BOUNTIFUL
(*a*) Shameful (*b*) Pretty
(*c*) Spiritual (*d*) Generous

22. FRUGAL
(*a*) Gaudy (*b*) Extravagant
(*c*) Charitable (*d*) Generous

(S.B.I.P.O. 1991)

23. INACCESSIBLE
(*a*) Irrepairable (*b*) Vulnerable
(*c*) Uncountable (*d*) Measurable
(*e*) Unapproachable

24. PRIVY
(*a*) Secretive (*b*) Dishonest
(*c*) Quiet (*d*) Cautious

25. DAINTY
(*a*) Delectable (*b*) Coarse
(*c*) Obedient (*d*) Graceful

26. NOISOME
(*a*) Dirty (*b*) Sleepy
(*c*) Clean (*d*) Pleasant

27. BRAZEN
(*a*) Modest (*b*) Shameless
(*c*) Quick (*d*) Pleasant

28. VIVACIOUS
(*a*) Bright (*b*) Strong
(*c*) Languid (*d*) Open

29. ENDOW
(*a*) Divest (*b*) Snatch
(*c*) Rob (*d*) Dispossess

30. VINDICTIVE **(Bank P.O. 1995)**
(*a*) Apologetic (*b*) Uncompromising
(*c*) Revengeful (*d*) Fearful
(*e*) Unpardonable

31. KNACK
(*a*) Disharmony (*b*) Skill
(*c*) Clumsiness (*d*) Inferiority

32. OSTENTATIOUS
(*a*) Showy (*b*) Talkative
(*c*) Noisy (*d*) Wealthy

33. INGENUITY
(*a*) Certainty (*b*) Sentimental
(*c*) Dullness (*d*) Skilfulness

34. LABYRINTHINE
(*a*) Obscure (*b*) Clear
(*c*) Straight (*d*) Opaque

35. QUELL
(*a*) Contract (*b*) Incite
(*c*) Recommend (*d*) Praise

36. GERMANE **(Bank P.O. 1996)**
(*a*) Impossible (*b*) Illogical
(*c*) Irrelevant (*d*) Irresponsible
(*e*) Irrepressible

37. NOSTALGIC
(*a*) Soothing (*b*) Homesick
(*c*) Diseased (*d*) Indolent

38. EXHUME
(*a*) Enter (*b*) Decipher
(*c*) Admit (*d*) Integrate

39. EXACERBATE
(*a*) Throw up (*b*) Aggravate
(*c*) Wear away (*d*) Bring out

40. OBLITERATE
(*a*) Decline (*b*) Block up
(*c*) Slow down (*d*) Blot out

41. BENIGN
(*a*) Gentle (*b*) Favourable
(*c*) Peaceful (*d*) Wavering

42. DILETTANTE
(*a*) Professional (*b*) Tidy
(*c*) Stupid (*d*) Rapid

43. INCARCERATE
(*a*) Liberate (*b*) Impress
(*c*) Impersonate (*d*) Mobilise

44. ESOTERIC
(*a*) Pleasant (*b*) Native
(*c*) Familiar (*d*) External

45. SERENE
(*a*) Complicated (*b*) Showy
(*c*) Impure (*d*) Agitated

46. RECUPERATE **(Bank P.O. 1995)**
(*a*) Resolve (*b*) Avenge
(*c*) Cooperate (*d*) Recover
(*e*) Rectify

47. RAVISH
(*a*) Misuse (*b*) Uphold
(*c*) Preserve (*d*) Accumulate

48. BALEFUL
(*a*) Virtuous (*b*) Deadly
(*c*) Virtual (*d*) Doubtful

49. ABJURE
(*a*) Project (*b*) Perjure
(*c*) Discuss (*d*) Renounce

50. MEDDLE
(*a*) Interfere (*b*) Overlook
(*c*) Disregard (*d*) Free

ANSWERS

The alphabets 'S' and 'A' given along with each of the following answers indicates whether the alternative chosen is a synonym or antonym of the given word.

1. (*d*) : S **2.** (*b*) : S **3.** (*c*) : A **4.** (*a*) : A **5.** (*a*) : A **6.** (*c*) : A **7.** (*d*) : A
8. (*b*) : S **9.** (*b*) : S **10.** (*c*) : S **11.** (*a*) : A **12.** (*d*) : S **13.** (*d*) : S **14.** (*c*) : S
15. (*a*) : A **16.** (*a*) : S **17.** (*d*) : S **18.** (*b*) : S **19.** (*c*) : S **20.** (*a*) : A **21.** (*d*) : S
22. (*b*) : A **23.** (*e*) : S **24.** (*a*) : S **25.** (*b*) : A **26.** (*d*) : A **27.** (*b*) : S **28.** (*c*) : A
29. (*d*) : A **30.** (*c*) : S **31.** (*b*) : A **32.** (*a*) : S **33.** (*c*) : A **34.** (*c*) : A **35.** (*b*) : A
36. (*c*) : A **37.** (*b*) : S **38.** (*a*) : A **39.** (*b*) : S **40.** (*d*) : S **41.** (*a*) : S **42.** (*c*) : A
43. (*a*) : A **44.** (*c*) : A **45.** (*d*) : A **46.** (*d*) : S **47.** (*a*) : S **48.** (*b*) : S **49.** (*d*) : S
50. (*a*) : S

4. DOUBLE SYNONYMS

WHAT ARE DOUBLE SYNONYMS?

These are words which may be used to express the meanings of two or more words used in different sentences.

Example : ***Choose from the given words below the two sentences I and II, that word which can substitute the italicised words in both the sentences.***

I. The Commissioner has issued strict orders to ***arrest*** the anti-social elements responsible for recent cases of burglary and chain snatching in the area.

II. I ***fear*** you won't be able to rise to the occasion at this critical hour.

(*a*) check (*b*) presume (*c*) suspect (*d*) apprehend (*e*) round up

Solution : Clearly, 'apprehend' may be used to express both the meanings—'to arrest' and 'to think with fear'.

Hence, the answer is (*d*).

PRACTICE SET

Directions : ***In each of the following questions, choose from the given words below the two sentences, that word which has the same meaning and can be used in the same context as the part given in italics in both the sentences.***

1. I. The organisation was established at the ***beginning*** of this century.

II. The little boy could not ***twist*** the cap off the bottle. **(NABARD, 1994)**

(*a*) break (*b*) turn (*c*) swing (*d*) crack (*e*) dawn

2. I. The story is so dramatic that one cannot guess the ***ultimate result***.

II. I could not understand the ***purpose*** of his visit.

(*a*) motive (*b*) end (*c*) consequence (*d*) lot

3. I. The truck was coming and its light was falling ***straight*** in my eyes.

II. After the death of the manager, there was no one to properly ***guide*** the company.

(*a*) correct (*b*) head (*c*) direct (*d*) hook (*e*) line

4. I. Ashok has got a ***friendly*** disposition.

II. The ***warm*** sunshine in the morning filled my heart with joy.

(*a*) joyous (*b*) pleasing (*c*) genial (*d*) happy (*e*) congenial

(Bank P.O. 1991)

5. I. I cannot ***endure*** such a loud noise any more.

II. He preferred to consider the other ***view***.

(*a*) bear (*b*) support (*c*) stand (*d*) opinion (*e*) position

6. I. He had a very ***difficult*** period during his sickness.

II. Kanti's father advised him that IAS was a career worth ***attempting***. **(Bank P.O. 1990)**

(*a*) competing (*b*) trying (*c*) intending (*d*) contending (*e*) experimenting

7. I. The document was declared ***void*** by the Court.

II. I felt pity for the ***sickly person*** lying on the pavement.

(*a*) useless (*b*) defective (*c*) invalid (*d*) destitute (*e*) feeble

8. I. Some of the edible oils ***have*** a high cholestrol level.

II. The forest authorities have failed to ***control*** poaching in that area.

(*a*) comprise (*b*) possess (*c*) restrain (*d*) contain (*e*) suppress

(NABARD, 1994)

9. I. Just leave a ***small line*** to be filled in by the requisite word.

II. I expected you to ***rush*** to the place as soon as you heard the news.

(*a*) dash (*b*) blank (*c*) void (*d*) bustle (*e*) intervene

10. I. He failed to produce any ***reason*** for his having behaved the way he did.

II. Man must live, struggle and die for a ***mission***.

(*a*) target (*b*) goal (*c*) cause (*d*) purpose (*e*) explanation

11. I. His ***understanding*** of the subject was really good.

II. Vijay had to ***hold on*** to the handle of the door with all his strength.

(a) make (b) power (c) pull
(d) seizure (e) grasp **(R.B.I. 1991)**

12. I. These ***trees*** yield commercially valuable varieties of wood.
II. The man who ***desires*** for many things at a time gets none.
(a) barks (b) pines
(c) trunks (d) yearns

13. I. The government decided to ***start*** a new series of lectures called the 'Honour Lecture Series'.
II. The decision to ***set up*** a new University in that town was welcomed by the people.
(a) manage (b) organise (c) institute
(d) build (e) plan **(S.B.I.P.O. 1992)**

14. I. The issue was finally ***settled,*** though with great difficulty.
II. Working women are given ***definite*** advantages over the men in our office.
(a) destined (b) fixed (c) installed
(d) negotiated (e) decided

15. I. Priya spends her ***leisure*** time reading novels.
II. Kamal had a ***lean*** body and could manage to squeeze into the little space available. **(Bank P.O. 1990)**
(a) spare (b) relaxed (c) free
(d) thin (e) disjointed

16. I. I found it difficult to find the man for I was not ***acquainted*** to the place.
II. The two articles had something ***common*** between them.
(a) similar (b) known (c) familiar
(d) resembling (e) same

17. I. The morning was clear and warm and not a single ***flake*** of snow was noticed.
II. Santosh Yadav was the first Indian woman to ***ascend*** the Mt. Everest.
(a) climb (b) scale (c) level
(d) step (e) pare

18. I. Mrs. Menon ***put*** all her jewellery in one box carelessly.
II. The equipment had to be ***stored*** in this ware house at short notice.
(a) stacked (b) dumped (c) stocked
(d) stowed (e) treasured **(R.B.I. 1991)**

19. I. His was the only ***remark*** which was pertinent to the topic.
II. To check the insurgence of anti-social elements into the country, several ***vigilance*** posts were set up along the border.
(a) view (b) inspection (c) notice
(d) assertion (e) observation

20. I. He is ***frank*** in his dealings with others.
II. The offer for the job is still ***available***. **(Bank P.O. 1991)**
(a) due (b) open (c) honest
(d) plain (e) operating

21. I. Mr. Roy soon earned great ***admiration*** from his fellow workers for his fair and frank dealings.
II. There was a substantial ***rise*** in the value of money with the sharp de-escalation of prices.
(a) acclamation (b) resilience
(c) assessment (d) appreciation
(e) encouragement

22. I. The stadium is so big that it can ***seat*** more than one lakh spectators.
II. Deepak is willing to ***adjust*** his itinerary with mine.
(a) hold (b) arrange (c) view
(d) participate (e) accomodate
(NABARD, 1994)

23. I. Huge crowds ***flung*** into the hall as soon as the doors were opened.
II. As the dam broke, the water of the river ***flowed*** into the village and destroyed all crops.
(a) drained (b) poured (c) gushed
(d) threw (e) rained

24. I. Avinash was the ***first*** suspect in that case.
II. The driver decided to ***tune*** the engine before going to sleep that day. **(S.B.I.P.O. 1992)**
(a) major (b) suffer (c) counter
(d) prime (e) complete

25. I. The Government pleaded the terrorists to ***release*** the abducted ambassador.
II. Don't be so ***lavish*** in your habits.
(a) liberalise (b) liberate (c) free
(d) squander (e) discharge

26. I. Saurabh was ***going*** to the library when he met me.
II. The newspapers carried the news about the murder with a large ***caption***. **(R.B.I. 1991)**
(a) starting (b) venturing (c) heading

(*d*) prefixing (*e*) beginning

27. I. I couldn't ***refuse*** to accept his proposal.

II. Our country is witnessing a steady ***fall*** in the moral standards of political leaders.

(*a*) retrograde (*b*) refute (*c*) droop
(*d*) decline (*e*) neglect

28. I. The tree was ***leaning*** towards the building.

II. I was ***willing*** to accept the first offer made by the shopkeeper.

(*a*) sloped (*b*) disposed (*c*) bent
(*d*) forced (*e*) inclined

(Bank P.O. 1990)

29. I. The constables decided to ***separate*** at the corner and approach the house from the two sides.

II. Shaloo was not willing to give her friend even a small ***portion*** of the cake she had.

(*a*) split (*b*) part (*c*) cut
(*d*) break (*e*) divide

30. I. Stars ***emit*** light.

II. The poor farmer lived in a ***small hut***.

(*a*) shred (*b*) shade (*c*) cote
(*d*) shed (*e*) dwell

31. I. I saw your photograph with that ***fat*** fellow.

II. I cannot do this work, was my ***instantaneous*** reply.

(*a*) plump (*b*) stout (*c*) bulky
(*d*) curt (*e*) prompt **(Bank P.O. 1991)**

32. I. Literature is an imperishable and veritable ***arsenal*** where all weapons of wit and irony are stored.

II. The youth are the ***store-house*** of all that is vital and strength-giving in life.

(*a*) collection (*b*) godown
(*c*) depository (*d*) heap

33. I. Sam's ***ready*** wit often got him out of tight spots.

II. The task they did was so different that the difference was ***apparent***.

(*a*) sharp (*b*) clear (*c*) intelligible
(*d*) visible (*e*) transparent

(S.B.I.P.O. 1992)

34. I. The ***aviator*** was responsible for the fatal crash.

II. The ship was bound to sink but the captain continually attempted to ***steer*** the vessel out of danger.

(*a*) driver (*b*) guide (*c*) pilot
(*d*) navigate (*e*) voyage

35. I. The commander gave order to ***aim*** the guns at enemy positions.

II. It was interesting to see the ***line*** of ducklings following the man.

(*a*) retinue (*b*) array (*c*) target
(*d*) turn (*e*) train **(NABARD, 1994)**

36. I. Every ***confession*** must be made in the name of God.

II. The concept of not allowing ***entry*** into the public places or temples, merely owing to caste barriers, is against humanity.

(*a*) appearance (*b*) disclosure
(*c*) permission (*d*) admission
(*e*) expression

37. I. I feel scared when I look at ***towering*** buildings.

II. Because of his ***arrogant*** behaviour, many people are offended with him. **(Bank P.O. 1991)**

(*a*) proud (*b*) lofty (*c*) haughty
(*d*) high (*e*) exalted

38. I. Be calm and ***composed*** in every situation.

II. The ***invalid*** must be given desired attention.

(*a*) patient (*b*) mute
(*c*) sick (*d*) concerned

39. I. The distance from Amman to Bombay is too ***far*** to be covered by the A 320 planes.

II. Ashish waited at the door for his father with a ***sad*** face. **(R.B.I. 1991)**

(*a*) bad (*b*) heavy (*c*) long
(*d*) unlucky (*e*) heavy

40. I. The waiter ***pulled*** the teapoy towards the chair.

II. The advocate ***wrote*** up an agreement for the partners.

(*a*) dragged (*b*) hauled (*c*) made
(*d*) drew (*e*) arranged

(S.B.I.P.O. 1992)

41. I. She was sitting under the **shadow** of the tree.

II. The customer wanted another ***colour*** of the paint on the kitchen wall of his house.

(*a*) fade (*b*) tint (*c*) cloud
(*d*) shade (*e*) reflection

42. I. His ***aloof*** behviour is an indication of his arrogance.

II. During our field visits we visited ***remote*** parts of Rajasthan.

(*a*) inner (*b*) distant (*c*) far-off
(*d*) introvert (*e*) depressed

(Bank P.O. 1991)

43. I. I think this particular ***book*** gives you all the desired knowledge on this topic.

II. For packaging one needs to have an idea of the desired ***dimensions*** of the box in which a set of items is to be contained.

(*a*) text (*b*) volume (*c*) matter
(*d*) edition (*e*) composition

44. I. Students started ***picking up*** their books when the bell rang.

II. There was a huge ***crowd*** at the Airport waiting for the President.

(*a*) arraying (*b*) collection
(*c*) swarming (*d*) gathering
(*e*) numbering **(Bank P.O. 1990)**

45. I. I entreated before him several times but without any ***result***.

II. The Minister asked the officers to put the scheme into ***operation***.

(*a*) influence (*b*) expression (*c*) effect
(*d*) consequence (*e*) conduct

46. I. People are ***worried*** about the growing corruption in our society.

II. Inspite of all the provocations, he ***maintained*** utmost patientce.

(*a*) restrained (*b*) exercised
(*c*) sustained (*d*) inflicted
(*e*) aggrieved **(NABARD, 1994)**

47. I. The place of ***joining*** of three rivers—Ganga, Yamuna & Saraswati is considered a sacred place.

II. Marriage provides a happy ***bond*** between souls.

(*a*) connection (*b*) union (*c*) linkage
(*d*) conjunction (*e*) coordination

48. I. The message was written on a ***piece*** of paper.

II. Gautam got into a ***fight*** with his classmate. **(S.B.I.P.O. 1992)**

(*a*) grab (*b*) box (*c*) scrap
(*d*) brush (*e*) fist

49. I. The officer lost his sense of integrity and managed to ***embezzle*** a large amount of money from the public funds.

II. The remarks he made in the presence of members of the Board were really not ***opportune***.

(*a*) defalcate (*b*) opine (*c*) proper
(*d*) divest (*e*) appropriate

50. I. Sachin managed to ***hold*** the ball even though he had to run a long distance.

II. Anshul said that the plan was not as simple as I was making it out and there was some ***trap*** in it.

(*a*) take (*b*) catch (*c*) grab
(*d*) bring (*e*) clutch **(R.B.I. 1991)**

51. I. The Management did not find her ***suitable*** for the job of a receptionist.

II. Kanak failed to ***arrange*** the parts of the machine properly.

(*a*) fit (*b*) harbour (*c*) adjust
(*d*) deploy (*e*) harness

52. I. Marriage is not only a meeting of two individuals in the physical and social sense, but a spiritual ***union*** between two souls.

II. They have executed a ***deed*** to transfer their property rights in favour of the organisation of which they have been dedicated members for years.

(*a*) harmony (*b*) unison (*c*) bond
(*d*) treaty (*e*) agreement

ANSWERS

1. (*b*)	**2.** (*b*)	**3.** (*c*)	**4.** (*b*)	**5.** (*c*)	**6.** (*b*)	**7.** (*c*)	**8.** (*d*)	**9.** (*a*)	**10.** (*c*)
11. (*e*)	**12.** (*b*)	**13.** (*c*)	**14.** (*e*)	**15.** (*a*)	**16.** (*c*)	**17.** (*b*)	**18.** (*b*)	**19.** (*e*)	**20.** (*b*)
21. (*d*)	**22.** (*e*)	**23.** (*b*)	**24.** (*d*)	**25.** (*c*)	**26.** (*c*)	**27.** (*d*)	**28.** (*e*)	**29.** (*b*)	**30.** (*d*)
31. (*b*)	**32.** (*c*)	**33.** (*a*)	**34.** (*c*)	**35.** (*e*)	**36.** (*d*)	**37.** (*b*)	**38.** (*a*)	**39.** (*c*)	**40.** (*d*)
41. (*d*)	**42.** (*b*)	**43.** (*b*)	**44.** (*d*)	**45.** (*c*)	**46.** (*b*)	**47.** (*b*)	**48.** (*c*)	**49.** (*e*)	**50.** (*b*)
51. (*a*)	**52.** (*c*)								

---

5. HOMONYMS

Homonyms are words that have the same or almost the same pronounciation but are different in meaning.

Example : *'Aught'* and *'ought'* sound similar. But *'aught'* means 'anything' and *'ought'* means 'should' as is clear from the sentences below.

Tell me frankly, if you have *aught* to say.

We *ought* to obey our parents.

PRACTICE SET

Directions : ***In each question below are given two sentences numbered I and II. In these sentences, two homonyms are given in italics type, which may be either mis-spelt or inappropriate in the context of the sentences. Read both the sentences carefully and decide on their correctness on the basis of the italicised words.***

Give answer

(*a*), ***if only sentence I is correct;***

(*b*), ***if only sentence II is correct;***

(*c*), ***if both the sentences I and II are correct;***

(*d*), ***if I as well as II are incorrect, but both could be made correct by interchanging the italicised words;***

(*e*), ***if neither I nor II is correct and the sentence could not be made correct by interchanging the italicised words.***

1. I. *Cannons* are used in war.
II. The Geeta deals with high *canons* of morality and religion.

2. I. An *ordnance* declaring President's rule in the state has been issued today.
II. The *ordinance* depot is situated far away from this city. **(NABARD, 1994)**

3. I. A painter is an *artiste.*
II. Raj Kapoor is a skilled *artist.*

4. I. You should not interfere in one's *personal* affairs.
II. The *personel* of ICS were proud of their positions during the British rule in India.

5. I. It is on account of his extensive social service that people *deify* him everywhere.
II. We should not *defy* the authority of the Government.

6. I. The Government plans to take some *sanitory* measures in the state.
II. The *sanitary* condition of the town is not good.

7. I. You should talk to your boss in a *revrent* manner
II. Our *revrend* Principal is coming.

8. I. This drawer is the *depositary* of my private letters.
II. Now a days it it not wise to be *depository* of other's valuables.

9. I. He was being laughed at for his *antic* gesture.
II. *Anticue* articles are priced much these days.

10. I. This is the best *stationary* shop in our locality.
II. I saw a *stationery* van there.

11. I. The tragic tale narrated by the old man *affected* all the children.
II. The humane attitude of the new manager *efected* a profound change in labour relations. **(NABARD, 1994)**

12. I. Ghosts are not *corporeal* beings.
II. Saints care little for *corporal* affairs.

13. I. A volcanic *erruption* engulfed the entire city.
II. Alexander's *iruption* is a memorable event in Indian history.

14. I. He is respected for his *peity.*
II. Have *pity* on the poor.

15. I. He is *wrapt* up in pleasurable contemplation.
II. I listened to her song with *rapt* attention.

16. I. I think this electric *metre* is faulty.
II. I require two *meters* of cloth for this purpose. **(Bank P.O. 1995)**

17. I. *Plane* living and high thinking should be our motto.
II. Men in the *plains* are generally less hardy then the hillmen.

18. I. His manners are *urban.*
II. People of *urbane* area are civil in manners.

19. I. Quinine is an efficacious *physic* for the cure of malaria.

II. He is a man of strong *physicue.*

20. I. Living organisms tend to have an inbuilt system to *adopt* themselves to changing environment.
II. He is an *adapt* criminal.

21. I. Mr. Khanna died in a railway *collision.*
II. Some gentlemen act in *collusion* with robbers.

22. I. He won the election only because of the support he got from his *zealous* party workers.
II. Savita's friends were *jaelous* of her success in the prestigious competition. **(NABARD, 1994)**

23. I. His views are *opposite* to mine.
II. The speech was *aposite* to the occasion.

24. I. It is a *knaughty* problem.
II. Suresh is a *naughty* boy.

25. I. He *practices* what he preaches.
II. The *practise* of closing shops on Sundays is quite common.

26. I. I saw a *hord* of nomads.
II. Ali Baba found out the *hoard* of robbers' gold and jewels.

27. I. During the *riegn* of Gupta rulers, India made tremendous advancements in art and culture.
II. He has taken over the *riens* of the new government.

28. I. He outght to have *persecuted* his studies.
II. Trespassers will be *prosecuted.*

29. I. I *loathe* flattery.
II. He was *loth* to go with Rahul.

30. I. Some of the African *immigrants* indulge in smuggling in our country.
II. Many *emmigrants* from India have settled in America. **(Bank P.O. 1995)**

31. I. He did not *acceed* to may request.
II. Don't *exceed* the limits.

32. I. Order for ten *bails* of cotton.
II. He was released on *bale.*

33. I. He broke my cycle *carier* yesterday.
II. A slight carelessness on your part can spoil your *career.*

34. I. The *tenur* of his speech was not clear.
II. His *teneur* of office is drawing to a close.

35. I. Archana bought the expensive costume to *complement* her wardrobe for the beauty contest.
II. When James remarked that she looked gorgeous, Jane thanked him for the *compliment.*

36. I. Don't *merge* your hand in hot water.
II. A dolphin *emerged* out of the ocean.

37. I. He *waived* his sword in the air.
II. I *wave* my claim in your favour.

38. I. This dress does not *suit* you.
II. He filed a civil *suite* against Mr. Arora.

39. I. The white colour in our National Flag is a *symbol* of purity of thought.
II. The folk singers sang to the accompaniment of the *cymbol.*

40. I. He drank a *draut* of wine.
II. Crops failed due to *drout.*
(Bank P.O. 1995)

41. I. Raju is an *ingenious* worker.
II. He made an *ingenuous* confession of his fault.

42. I. An over-*doze* of this medicine might be harmful for you.
II. You are not allowed to *dose* in the class.

43. I. A vote of *censur* was passed against the President.
II. Before release, every film is sent to the *censor* office for recommendation.

44. I. Despite all our efforts, success remainded *elusive.*
II. His manners are *ilusive.*

45. I. His dismissal is a *foregone* conclusion.
II. I cannot *forgo* my claim.

46. I. Deepak did not get involved in the scandal on account of his friend's wise *councel.*
II. Some of the members of the *counsil* walked out in protest during the session. **(NABARD, 1994)**

47. I. There is a great *affection* between the two brothers.
II. Her modesty is mere *affectation.*

48. I. We look for the date and day in a *calandar.*
II. Sheet rubber is made by passing rubber through *calenders.*

49. I. Sudden *lightening* and the rumble of thunder frightened the baby.
II. Mercury lamps are used for *lightning* the roads.

50. I. Painting is done on *canvass.*
II. He was *canvasing* for votes.

ANSWERS

[Along with answers, the meanings of each pair of homonyms are given in brackets for better understanding.]

1. (*c*) : [Cannon = military tank,
Canon = rule of conduct]

2. (*d*) : [Ordinance = enactment;
Ordnance = military stores]

3. (*d*) : [Artist = a person skilled in fine arts, such as drawing, poetry etc.;
Artiste = a person skilled in theatrical arts such as singing, dancing, acting.]

4. (*a*) : The correct word in II should be *'personnel'*.
[Personal = private;
Personnel = body of persons employed in a dapartment.]

5. (*c*) : [Deify = to worship as God;
Defy = to challenge]

6. (*b*) : The correct word in I should be *sanatory.*
[Sanatory = promoting health,
Sanitary = hygienic]

7. (*e*) : The correct word in I is *'reverent'* and that in II is *'reverend'*.
[Reverent = respectful;
Reverend = respectable]

8. (*d*) : Depository = place where anything is deposited
Depositary = one with whom a thing is deposited]

9. (*a*) : The correct word in II should be *'Antique'*.
[Antic = odd, Antique = old]

10. (*d*) : [Stationery = a shop selling writing materials,
Stationary = immobile]

11. (*a*) : The correct word in II should be *'effected'*.
[effect = result, affect = to influence]

12. (*a*) : The correct word in II should also be *'corporeal'*.
[Corporal = bodily;
Corporeal = having body or material]
e.g. Corporal punishment is not justified.

13. (*e*) : The correct word in I should be *'eruption'* and that in II should be *'irruption'*.
[Eruption = sudden outbreak,
irruption = invasion]

14. (*b*) : The correct word in I should be *'piety'*.
[Pity = compassion; piety = piousness]

15. (*c*) : [Wrapt = lost in something,
Rapt = enraptured]

16. (*d*) : [Meter = a measuring apparatus,
Metre = unit of length]

17. (*b*) : The correct word in I should be *'Plain'*.
[Plain = clear, level;
Plane = level surface]
e.g. Only one circle can be drawn through three points on the same plane.

18. (*d*) : [Urbane = courteous;
Urban = pertaining to city]

19. (*a*) : The correct word in II should be *'physique'*.
[Physic = medicine;
Physique = bodily structure]

20. (*e*) : The correct word in I should be *'adapt'* and that in II should be *'adept'*.
[Adapt = change accordingly;
adept = skilled;
adopt = to take recourse to]
e.g. Do not adopt foul means to earn money.

21. (*c*) : [Collision = violent clash;
Collusion = secret agreement to act unlawfully]

22. (*a*) : The correct word in II should be *'jealous'*.
[Zealous = full of zeal;
Jealous = envious]

23. (*a*) : The correct word in II should be *'apposite'*.
[Opposite = contrary;
Apposite = suitable]

24. (*b*) : The correct word in I should be *'knotty.'*
[Naughty = wicked,
Knotty = difficult to solve]

25. (*d*) : [Practice = a noun;
Practise = verb of 'practice']

26. (*b*) : The correct word in I should be *'horde'*.

27. (*e*) : The correct word in I should be *'reign'* and that in II should be *'rein'*.
[Reign = rule; Rein = rigid control]

28. (*c*) : [Persecute = to pursue,
Prosecute = treat cruelly]

29. (*c*) : [Loathe = dislike,
Loth/Loath = unwilling]

30. (*a*) : The correct word in II should be '*migrants*'.
[Emigrant = one who leaves his country to settle in any other country;
Immigrant = one who enters a country to settle there]

31. (*b*) : The correct word in I should be '*accede*'.
[Accede = agree; Exceed = surpass]

32. (*d*) : [Bale = bundle; Bail = security]

33. (*b*) : The correct word in I should be '*carrier*'.
[Carrier = that which carries,
Career = progress through life]

34. (*e*) : The correct word in I should be 'tenor' and that in II should be 'tenure'.
[Tenor = general meaning,
Tenure = duration of holding office]

35. (*c*) : [Complement = that which completes,
Compliment = greetings]

36. (*b*) : The correct word in I should be '*immerge*'.
[Immerge/Immerse = to dip into;
Emerge = to come out]

37. (*d*) : The correct word in I should be '*waved*' and that in II should be '*waive*'.
[wave = brandish; waive = give up]

38. (*a*) : The correct word in II should be '*suit*'.
[Suit = case, to fit;
Suite = attendants or followers of a person]
e.g. The prince and his *suite* took shelter in a cave.

39. (*a*) : The correct word in II should be '*cymbal*'.
[Symbol = sign;
Cymbal = musical instrument]

40. (*e*) : The correct word in I should be '*draught*' and that in II should be '*drought*'.
[Draught = act of swallowing without taking breath,
Drought = want of rain]

41. (*c*) : [Ingenious = skilful,
Ingenuous = frank]

42. (*d*) : The correct word in I should be '*dose*' and that in II should be '*doze*'.
[Dose = quantity of medicine to be taken at a time,
Doze = to slumber for short periods]

43. (*b*) : The correct word in I should be '*censure*'.
[Censure = no-confidence;
Censor = official who examines plays, films, books etc.]

44. (*a*) : The correct word in II should be '*illusive*'.
[Elusive = difficult to grasp,
Illusive = deceptive]

45. (*c*) : [Forego = to precede,
Forgo = to give up]

46. (*e*) : The correct word in I should be '*counsel*' and that in II should be '*council*'.
[Counsel = opinion;
Council = assembly]

47. (*c*) : [Affection = love;
Affectation = pretence]

48. (*b*) : The correct word in I should be '*calendar*'.
[Calender = a roller-machine]

49. (*e*) : The correct word in I should be '*lightning*' and that in II should be '*lighting*'.
[Lightning = electric discharge from clouds
Lighting = providing light,
Lightening = making less heavy]

50. (*d*) : [Canvas = a tough cloth,
Canvass = to propagate]

6. ONE WORD SUBSTITUTION

This chapter deals with two types of questions :

(*i*) Selecting a single word for a given phrase or sentence

(*b*) Selecting a single word for a group of words used in a sentence.

PRACTICE SET 1

Directions : ***In each of the following questions, out of the four alternatives, choose the one which can be substituted for the given words/sentence.***

1. To examine one's own thoughts and feelings **(C.B.I. 1993)**
(*a*) Meditation (*b*) Retrospection
(*c*) Reflection (*d*) Introspection

2. A short, usually amusing, story about some real person or event
(*a*) Anecdote (*b*) Antidote
(*c*) Tale (*d*) Allegory

3. Woman who offers the use of her body for sexual intercourse to any one who will pay for this
(*a*) Voluptuary (*b*) Cuckold
(*c*) Prostitute (*d*) Concubine

4. Life history of a person written by another
(*a*) Autobiography (*b*) Biography
(*c*) Bibliography (*d*) Memoir

5. Custom of having many wives
(*a*) Monogamy (*b*) Bigamy
(*c*) Polygamy (*d*) Matrimony **(M.B.A. 1989)**

6. A person who does not believe in any religion
(*a*) Philatelist (*b*) Rationalist
(*c*) Atheist (*d*) Pagan

7. Bringing about gentle and painless death from incurable disease
(*a*) Suicide (*b*) Euphoria
(*c*) Gallows (*d*) Euthanasia

8. A man of lax moral
(*a*) Ruffian (*b*) Licentious
(*c*) Pirate (*d*) Vagabond

9. A small enclosure for cattle, sheep, poultry etc.
(*a*) Cellar (*b*) Sty
(*c*) Pen (*d*) Lair

10. To cause troops etc. to spread out in readiness for battle **(U.D.C. 1995)**
(*a*) Align (*b*) Collocate
(*c*) Deploy (*d*) Disperse

11. One who forcibly seizes control of a bus or an aircraft
(*a*) Pirate (*b*) Swindler
(*c*) Hijacker (*d*) Pilferer

12. The act of killing one's wife
(*a*) Genocide (*b*) Uxoricide
(*c*) Canicide (*d*) Avicide

13. Music sung or played at night below a person's window
(*a*) Serenade (*b*) Sonnet
(*c*) Lyric (*d*) Primo

14. A government by the nobles
(*a*) Democracy (*b*) Bureaucracy
(*c*) Autocracy (*d*) Aristocracy

15. Anything written in a letter after it is signed **(S.B.I. P.O. 1991)**
(*a*) Posterity (*b*) Postdiction
(*c*) Postscript (*d*) Corrigendum

16. Strong and settled dislike between two persons
(*a*) Apathy (*b*) Hatred
(*c*) Antipathy (*d*) Animosity

17. A person who has no money to pay off his debts
(*a*) Debtor (*b*) Pauper
(*c*) Beggar (*d*) Insolvent

18. An entertainer who performs difficult physical actions
(*a*) Clown (*b*) Gymnast
(*c*) Magician (*d*) Acrobat

19. A small house with all rooms on one floor
(*a*) Bungalow (*b*) Cottage
(*c*) Flat (*d*) Castle

20. A song embodying religious and sacred emotions
(*a*) Lyric (*b*) Ode
(*c*) Hymn (*d*) Ballad

21. The policy of extending a country's empire and influence
(*a*) Imperialism (*b*) Capitalism
(*c*) Internationalism (*d*) Communism **(Assistant Grade, 1994)**

22. Government by a single person
(*a*) Monarchy (*b*) Autocracy
(*c*) Plutocracy (*d*) Aristocracy

23. Practice of a married woman having extra marital relationship
(*a*) Polygamy (*b*) Puberty
(*c*) Lechery (*d*) Adultery

24. A workman who fits and repairs pipes
(*a*) Mechanic (*b*) Blacksmith
(*c*) Plumber (*d*) Technocrat

25. Part of a church in which bells hang
(*a*) Minaret (*b*) Chapel
(*c*) Belfry (*d*) Spire

26. Mania for balking
(*a*) Logomania (*b*) Pyromania
(*c*) Biblomania (*d*) Kleptomania

27. The custom of having more than one husband at the same time
(*a*) Polygamy (*b*) Polyandry
(*c*) Debauchery (*d*) Bigamy
(Section Officer's Exam, 1993)

28. An extremely deep crack or opening in the ground
(*a*) Chasm (*b*) Aperture
(*c*) Ditch (*d*) Pit

29. The study of ancient societies
(*a*) History (*b*) Anthropology
(*c*) Ethnology (*d*) Archaeology

30. The foolish belief that one is God
(*a*) Blasphemy (*b*) Theocracy
(*c*) Paranoia (*d*) Theomania

31. List of headings of the business to be transacted at a meeting
(*a*) Schedule (*b*) Agenda
(*c*) Proceedings (*d*) Excerpts
(Assistant Grade, 1991)

32. A process involving too much official formality
(*a*) Nepotism (*b*) Diplomacy
(*c*) Red-tapism (*d*) Bureaucracy

33. Person who brings an action at law
(*a*) Plaintiff (*b*) Litigant
(*c*) Deponent (*d*) Defendant

34. The short remaining end of a cigarette
(*a*) Stump (*b*) Stub
(*c*) Rag (*d*) Scrap

35. The place where public, government or historical records are kept
(*a*) Coffer (*b*) Pantry
(*c*) Scullery (*d*) Archives

36. A post without remuneration
(*a*) Voluntary (*b*) Sinecure
(*c*) Honorary (*d*) Involuntary
(Central Excise, 1994)

37. Large scale departure of people
(*a*) Migration (*b*) Emigration
(*c*) Immigration (*d*) Exodus

38. Lottery in which an article is assigned by lot to one of those buying tickets
(*a*) Auction (*b*) Raffle
(*c*) Audit (*d*) Transit

39. To send an unwanted person out of the country **(B.Ed. Entrance, 1993)**
(*a*) Exclude (*b*) Ostracise
(*c*) Deport (*d*) Expatriate

40 Voluntarily giving up throne by king in favour of his son
(*a*) Abdication (*b*) Resurrection
(*c*) Accession (*d*) Renunciation

41. Child bereaved of one or both the parents
(*a*) Desolate (*b*) Destitute
(*c*) Orphan (*d*) Lout

42. Gift left by will
(*a*) Alimony (*b*) Parimony
(*c*) Legacy (*d*) Property

43. A government run by a dictator
(*a*) Democracy (*b*) Autocracy
(*c*) Oligarchy (*d*) Theocracy
(C.B.I. 1994)

44. One who always runs away from danger
(*a*) Escapist (*b*) Timid
(*c*) Coward (*d*) Shirker

45. A poem written on the death of someone loved and lost
(*a*) Ode (*b*) Epic
(*c*) Sonnet (*d*) Elegy

46. One who despises persons of lower social position
(*a*) Prim (*b*) Snob
(*c*) Prig (*d*) Aristocrat

47. Gradual recovery from illness
(*a*) Hysteria (*b*) Amnesia
(*c*) Superannuation (*d*) Convalescence

48. One who is determined to exact full vengeance for wrongs done to him
(*a*) Vindicator (*b*) Usurer
(*c*) Vindictive (*d*) Virulent
(Assistant Grade, 1994)

49. A person who believes that pleasure is the chief good
(*a*) Stoic (*b*) Hedonist
(*c*) Epicure (*d*) Sensual

50. Commencement of words with the same letter
(*a*) Rhyme (*b*) Alliteration
(*c*) Pun (*d*) Oxymoron

ANSWERS

1. (*d*)	**2.** (*a*)	**3.** (*c*)	**4.** (*b*)	**5.** (*c*)	**6.** (*d*)	**7.** (*d*)	**8.** (*b*)	**9.** (*c*)	**10.** (*c*)
11. (*c*)	**12.** (*b*)	**13.** (*a*)	**14.** (*d*)	**15.** (*c*)	**16.** (*c*)	**17.** (*d*)	**18.** (*d*)	**19.** (*a*)	**20.** (*c*)
21. (*a*)	**22.** (*b*)	**23.** (*d*)	**24.** (*c*)	**25.** (*c*)	**26.** (*a*)	**27.** (*b*)	**28.** (*a*)	**29.** (*d*)	**30.** (*d*)
31. (*b*)	**32.** (*c*)	**33.** (*a*)	**34.** (*b*)	**35.** (*d*)	**36.** (*c*)	**37.** (*d*)	**38.** (*b*)	**39.** (*c*)	**40.** (*a*)
41. (*c*)	**42.** (*c*)	**43.** (*b*)	**44.** (*b*)	**45.** (*d*)	**46.** (*b*)	**47.** (*d*)	**48.** (*c*)	**49.** (*b*)	**50.** (*b*)

PRACTICE SET 2

Directions : ***In each of the following questions, choose the most suitable "one word" for the given expressions.***

1. An office or post with no work but high pay **(Railways, 1991)**
(a) Honorary (b) Sinecure
(c) Gratis (d) Ex-officio
2. One who is well-versed in any subject; a critical judge of any art, particularly fine arts
(a) Veteran (b) Philistine
(c) Dilettante (d) Connoisseur
3. Person who is indifferent to both pleasure and pain
(a) Saint (b) Ascetic
(c) Stoic (d) Hermit
4. A person who is against the standards of ordinary society especially in dressing
(a) Joker (b) Hippy
(c) Scapegoat (d) Butt
5. Murder of a brother
(a) Patricide (b) Regicide
(c) Homicide (d) Fratricide
(Stenographer's Exam, 1993)
6. Mania for stealing articles
(a) Logomania (b) Nymphomania
(c) Kleptomania (d) Hypomania
7. Mental weariness for want of occupation
(a) Fatigue (b) Ennui
(c) Languor (d) Debility
8. One who loves all and sundry
(a) Optimist (b) Humanist
(c) Altruist (d) Philanthropist
9. Mania for travel
(a) Dromomania (b) Pyromania
(c) Biblomania (d) Logomania
10. A person living permanently in a certain place **(B.Ed. Entrance, 1992)**
(a) Native (b) Resident
(c) Domicile (d) Subject
11. Paying back injury with injury
(a) Vendetta (b) Repression
(c) Subjugation (d) Reprisal
12. Acutely affected by external impressions
(a) Ingenious (b) Impressionable
(c) Credulous (d) Sensitive
13. To slap with a flat object
(a) Hew (b) Swat
(c) Chop (d) Gnaw
(Central Excise, 1995)
14. An assembly of hearers
(a) Audience (b) Crowd
(c) Congregation (d) Assemblage
15. An associate in an office or institution
(a) Companion (b) Ally
(c) Colleague (d) Accomplice
16. One who is unrelenting and cannot be moved by entreaties
(a) Inexorable (b) Infallible
(c) Impregnable (d) Inexplicable
17. Regard for others as a principle of action
(a) Cynicism (b) Nepotism
(c) Philanthropy (d) Altruism
(Assistant Grade, 1991)
18. Person who claims to have great love for and understanding of what is beautiful in nature, art etc.
(a) Critic (b) Aesthete
(c) Connoisseur (d) Artist
19. A disease which spreads by contact
(a) Infectious (b) Contagious
(c) Contiguous (d) Contextual
20. An animal story with a moral
(a) Fable (b) Tale
(c) Anecdote (d) Parable
21. To change shape, nature or substance of
(a) Modulate (b) Substitute
(c) Remodel (d) Transmute
22. Person who believes that God is every thing and everything is God
(a) Agnostic (b) Theist
(c) Pantheist (d) Pantecnnicon
(B.S.R.B. 1995)
23. Person who pilots or travels in a balloon, airship or other aircraft
(a) Aeronaut (b) Astronaut
(c) Aerobat (d) Acrobat
24. Witty, clever retort
(a) Sarcasm (b) Repartee
(c) Platitude (d) Invective
25. Words different in meaning but similar in sound
(a) Homonym (b) Synonym
(c) Acronym (d) Antonym
26. Simplest and smallest form of plant life, present in air, water and soil; essential to life but may cause disease **(U.D.C. 1993)**
(a) Virus (b) Amoeba
(c) Bacteria (d) Toxin
27. A girl or woman who flirts, that is, tries to attract people and make advances in love simply to satisfy her vanity
(a) Prostitute (b) Coquette
(c) Spinster (d) Concubine
28. A person who regards the whole world as his country
(a) Patriot (b) Nationalist

(*c*) Cosmopolitan (*d*) Metropolitan

29. Relationship by blood or birth
(*a*) Parentage (*b*) Affiliation
(*c*) Consanguinity (*d*) Nepotism
(Translators' Exam., 1994)

30. A story in which ideas are symbolised as people
(*a*) Allegory (*b*) Fable
(*c*) Legend (*d*) Parable

31. The cessation of warfare before a treaty is signed
(*a*) Affidavit (*b*) Agreement
(*c*) Armistice (*d*) Amnesty

32. A person who makes love without serious intentions
(*a*) Consort (*b*) Philanderer
(*c*) Romeo (*d*) Goon

33. Opposed to great or sudden change
(*a*) Static (*b*) Revolutionary
(*c*) Conservative (*d*) Evolutionary
(S.B.I.P.O. 1991)

34. Having no beginning or end to its existence
(*a*) Eternal (*b*) Obscure
(*c*) Universal (*d*) Immeasurable

35. The art of cutting trees and bushes into ornamental shapes
(*a*) Horticulture (*b*) Bonsai
(*c*) Pruning (*d*) Topiary

36. Walking in sleep
(*a*) Somniloquism (*b*) Somnambulism
(*c*) Obsession (*d*) Hallucination

37. One who cannot die **(U.D.C. 1994)**
(*a*) Stable (*b*) Immortal
(*c*) Perpetual (*d*) Perennial

38. A formal written charge against a person for some crime or offence
(*a*) Accusation (*b*) Indictment
(*c*) Allegation (*d*) Acrimony

39. Language difficult to understand because of bad form
(*a*) Rhetoric (*b*) Jargon
(*c*) Pedantic (*d*) Verbatim

40. Belief or opinion contrary to what is generally accepted **(Central Excise, 1994)**
(*a*) Unbelief (*b*) Superstition
(*c*) Non conformity (*d*) Heresy

41. A person obsessed with exclusively one idea or subject
(*a*) Crazy (*b*) Kleptomaniac
(*c*) Monomaniac (*d*) Nymphomaniac

42. A child of unusual or remarkable talent
(*a*) Scholar (*b*) Diligent
(*c*) Freak (*d*) Prodigy

43. A disease which ends in death
(*a*) Contagious (*b*) Lethal
(*c*) Fatal (*d*) Deadly

44. A person who kills somebody especially for political reasons
(*a*) Criminal (*b*) Murderer
(*c*) Assassin (*d*) Hangman

45. One who loves mankind **(C.B.I. 1993)**
(*a*) Anthropologist (*b*) Philanthropist
(*c*) Seismologist (*d*) Optometrist

46. A small piece of potato
(*a*) Chunk (*b*) Chip
(*c*) Scrap (*d*) Bit

47. A child who stays away from school without any good reason
(*a*) Vagabond (*b*) Delinquent
(*c*) Schizophrenic (*d*) Truant

48. A common place remark
(*a*) Dialogue (*b*) Platitude
(*c*) Epigram (*d*) Statement

49. Line at which the earth or sea and sky seem to meet
(*a*) Horizon (*b*) Zenith
(*c*) Fringe (*d*) Plinth

50. A person who rules without consulting the opinion of others **(Asstt. Grade, 1995)**
(*a*) Democrat (*b*) Bureaucrat
(*c*) Autocrat (*d*) Fanatic

ANSWERS

1. (*b*)	**2.** (*d*)	**3.** (*c*)	**4.** (*b*)	**5.** (*d*)	**6.** (*c*)	**7.** (*b*)	**8.** (*d*)	**9.** (*a*)	**10.** (*c*)
11. (*d*)	**12.** (*d*)	**13.** (*b*)	**14.** (*a*)	**15.** (*c*)	**16.** (*a*)	**17.** (*d*)	**18.** (*b*)	**19.** (*b*)	**20.** (*a*)
21. (*d*)	**22.** (*c*)	**23.** (*a*)	**24.** (*b*)	**25.** (*a*)	**26.** (*c*)	**27.** (*b*)	**28.** (*c*)	**29.** (*c*)	**30.** (*a*)
31. (*c*)	**32.** (*b*)	**33.** (*c*)	**34.** (*a*)	**35.** (*d*)	**36.** (*b*)	**37.** (*b*)	**38.** (*b*)	**39.** (*b*)	**40.** (*d*)
41. (*c*)	**42.** (*d*)	**43.** (*c*)	**44.** (*c*)	**45.** (*b*)	**46.** (*b*)	**47.** (*d*)	**48.** (*b*)	**49.** (*a*)	**50.** (*c*)

PRACTICE SET 3

Directions : *In each question below, a phrase is given below which some alternatives are given. One of these is the most appropriate word i.e. it best conveys the meaning of the phrase. Find out the most appropriate word in each case.*

1. Study of mankind **(Asstt. Grade, 1991)**
(*a*) Pathology (*b*) Physiology
(*c*) Philology (*d*) Anthropology
2. Intentional destruction of racial groups
(*a*) Homicide (*b*) Genocide
(*c*) Fratricide (*d*) Regicide
3. One who is interested in the welfare of women
(*a*) Feminine (*b*) Feminist
(*c*) Effeminate (*d*) Flamboyant
4. Study of statistics of births, deaths, diseases to show the state of community
(*a*) Geography (*b*) Anthropology
(*c*) Topography (*d*) Demography
5. Through which light cannot pass
(*a*) Dull (*b*) Dark
(*c*) Obscure (*d*) Opaque
(Stenographer's Exam, 1993)
6. A sudden rush of wind
(*a*) Gale (*b*) Typhoon
(*c*) Gust (*d*) Storm
7. One who takes delight in excessive cruelty
(*a*) Anarchist (*b*) Sophist
(*c*) Sadist (*d*) Nihilist
8. An unexpected stroke of good luck
(*a*) Fortune (*b*) Windfall
(*c*) Boon (*d*) Breakthrough
9. A person who helps you break the law
(*a*) Spy (*b*) Collaborator
(*c*) Ally (*d*) Accomplice
10. Not conforming to ordinary rules of behaviour
(*a*) Lunatic (*b*) Absurd
(*c*) Eccentric (*d*) Maniacal
11. Stealing from the writings of others
(*a*) Copying (*b*) Reframing
(*c*) Reproducing (*d*) Plagiarism
(Central Excise, 1994)
12. Short descriptive poem of picturesque scene or incident
(*a*) Malady (*b*) Sonnet
(*c*) Idyll (*d*) Charade
13. A man who starves body for the good of soul
(*a*) Monk (*b*) Ascetic
(*c*) Saint (*d*) Spiritualist
14. A person who is reserved in talks
(*a*) Reticent (*b*) Silent
(*c*) Mendicant (*d*) Garrulous
15. A short stay at a place
(*a*) Halt (*b*) Interlude
(*c*) Intermission (*d*) Sojourn
(Translator's Exam, 1994)
16. A raised place on which offerings to a god are made
(*a*) Mound (*b*) Chapel
(*c*) Altar (*d*) Archives
17. To talk much without coming to the point
(*a*) Verbosity (*b*) Garrulousness
(*c*) Loquacity (*d*) Circumlocution
18. Constant effort to achieve something
(*a*) Perseverance (*b*) Attempt
(*c*) Enthusiasm (*d*) Vigour
(S.B.I. P.O. 1991)
19. A place where a wild animal lives
(*a*) Forest (*b*) Stable
(*c*) Lair (*d*) Sanctuary
20. A person who looks on the bright side of things
(*a*) Sycophant (*b*) Optimist
(*c*) Cynic (*d*) Pessimist
21. One who lends money at high rate of interest
(*a*) Solvent (*b*) Uxorious
(*c*) Usurer (*d*) Shylock
22. One who cuts precious stones
(*a*) Philatelist (*b*) Drover
(*c*) Lapidist (*d*) Oculist
23. Government by the Gods
(*a*) Plutocracy (*b*) Theocracy
(*c*) Thearchy (*d*) Pantisocracy
24. A person not sure of the existence of God
(*a*) Theist (*b*) Atheist
(*c*) Agnostic (*d*) Cynic
(Assistant Grade, 1994)
25. One who comp le dictionary
(*a*) Calligrapher (*b*) Editor
(*c*) Lexicographer (*d*) Compiler
26. Which can be easily believed
(*a*) Credulous (*b*) Creditable
(*c*) Trustworthy (*d*) Credible
27. Woman trained to help other women in child birth
(*a*) Virgin (*b*) Midwife
(*c*) Matron (*d*) Nurse
28. A person with full discretionary powers to act on behalf of a country
(*a*) Ambassador (*b*) Emissary
(*c*) Plenipotentiary (*d*) Envoy

29. Design made by putting together coloured pieces of glass or stones
(*a*) Oleograph (*b*) Mosaic
(*c*) Tracery (*d*) Relief
(C.B.I. 1995)

30. To deprive a thing of its holy character
(*a*) Sacrilege (*b*) Blasphemy
(*c*) Consecrate (*d*) Desecrate

31. A man with prejudiced views against religion
(*a*) Orthodox (*b*) Bigot
(*c*) Fanatic (*d*) Profane

32. The school or college in which one has been educated
(*a*) Matinee (*b*) Alumni
(*c*) Alma mater (*d*) Calvin

33. One who deserts his religion
(*a*) Deserter (*b*) Turn-coat
(*c*) Fanatic (*d*) Apostate
(Railways, 1991)

34. Medicine which lessens pain
(*a*) Balm (*b*) Panacea
(*c*) Anodyne (*d*) Antibiotic

35. A woman whose husband is dead
(*a*) Virgin (*b*) Spinster
(*c*) Wedlock (*d*) Widow

36. To take one to task
(*a*) Disgrace (*b*) Handle
(*c*) Entreat (*d*) Rebuke

37. One who uses fear as a weapon of power
(*a*) Terrorist (*b*) Militant
(*c*) Extremist (*d*) Anarchist
(Stenographer's Exam, 1993)

38. A small piece of wood
(*a*) Splinter (*b*) Crumb
(*c*) Scrap (*d*) Chip

39. Mania for setting fires
(*a*) Pyromania (*b*) Kleptomania
(*c*) Logomania (*d*) Nymphomania

40. A pioneer of a reform movement
(*a*) Renegade (*b*) Apostle
(*c*) Apotheosis (*d*) Apothecary

41. Wicked to a high degree
(*a*) Cruel (*b*) Hateful
(*c*) Heinous (*d*) Abominable

42. The original inhabitants of a country
(*a*) Aborigines (*b*) Citizens
(*c*) Natives (*d*) Primitive
(Bank P.O. 1990)

43. Dungeon entered by trapdoor
(*a*) Cellar (*b*) Ditch
(*c*) Vault (*d*) Oubliette

44. One desirous of of getting money
(*a*) Avaracious (*b*) Voracious
(*c*) Garrulous (*d*) Greedy

45. Place where birds are kept **(C.B.I. 1994)**
(*a*) Zoo (*b*) Apiary
(*c*) Armoury (*d*) Aviary

46. A person with a beautiful and elegant handwriting
(*a*) Calligrapher (*b*) Collier
(*c*) Choreographer (*d*) Cartographer

47. A person who is always dissatisfied
(*a*) Heretic (*b*) Felon
(*c*) Malcontent (*d*) Surrogate

48. Loss of power to move in any or every part of the body
(*a*) Rheumatism (*b*) Paralysis
(*c*) Eczema (*d*) Leprosy

49. One who does not care for literature or art **(Asstt. Grade, 1994)**
(*a*) Barbarian (*b*) Philistine
(*c*) Illiterate (*d*) Primitive

50. A group of three novels or plays, each complete in itself
(*a*) Triplet (*b*) Triumvir
(*c*) Trilogy (*d*) Trivet

ANSWERS

1. (*d*)	**2.** (*b*)	**3.** (*b*)	**4.** (*d*)	**5.** (*d*)	**6.** (*c*)	**7.** (*c*)	**8.** (*b*)	**9.** (*d*)	**10.** (*c*)
11. (*d*)	**12.** (*c*)	**13.** (*b*)	**14.** (*a*)	**15.** (*d*)	**16.** (*c*)	**17.** (*d*)	**18.** (*b*)	**19.** (*c*)	**20.** (*b*)
21. (*c*)	**22.** (*c*)	**23.** (*c*)	**24.** (*c*)	**25.** (*c*)	**26.** (*d*)	**27.** (*b*)	**28.** (*c*)	**29.** (*b*)	**30.** (*d*)
31. (*b*)	**32.** (*c*)	**33.** (*d*)	**34.** (*c*)	**35.** (*d*)	**36.** (*d*)	**37.** (*a*)	**38.** (*d*)	**39.** (*a*)	**40.** (*b*)
41. (*c*)	**42.** (*a*)	**43.** (*d*)	**44.** (*a*)	**45.** (*d*)	**46.** (*a*)	**47.** (*c*)	**48.** (*b*)	**49.** (*b*)	**50.** (*c*)

PRACTICE SET 4

Directions : ***In each of the following questions, out of the given alternatives, choose the one which can be substituted for the given words/sentence.***

1. A person who speaks for or supports an idea
(*a*) Pioneer (*b*) Adviser
(*c*) Advocate (*d*) Ideologist
2. A man of odd habits
(*a*) Eccentric (*b*) Cynical
(*c*) Introvert (*d*) Moody
(Stenographers' Exam, 1993)
3. A thing or person behind time
(*a*) Lazy (*b*) Sluggish
(*c*) Indolent (*d*) Antiquated
4. One whose attitude is: 'eat, drink and be merry'
(*a*) Epicurean (*b*) Cynic
(*c*) Materialistic (*d*) Stoic
5. Science of printing
(*a*) Calligraphy (*b*) Typography
(*c*) Topography (*d*) Cryptography
6. Man whose wife has been unfaithful to him
(*a*) Dandy (*b*) Bastard
(*c*) Concubine (*d*) Cuckold
7. Deriving pleasure from inflicting pain on others **(Section Officers' Exam, 1993)**
(*a*) Sadism (*b*) Malevolence
(*c*) Bigotry (*d*) Masochism
8. One who robs smuggler of his smuggled goods after the border has been crossed
(*a*) Pirate (*b*) Malefactor
(*c*) Hijacker (*d*) Philanderer
9. Course for chariot races
(*a*) Sanatorium (*b*) Hangar
(*c*) Hippodrome (*d*) Arena
10. One who pretends illness to escape duty
(*a*) Truant (*b*) Malingerer
(*c*) Hypocrite (*d*) Concubine
11. The power of reading the thoughts of others **(B.Ed. Entrance, 1992)**
(*a*) Psychopathy
(*b*) Telecommunication
(*c*) Psychology (*d*) Telepathy
12. Use of more words than are needed to express the meaning
(*a*) Circumlocution (*b*) Verbatim
(*c*) Ventriloquism (*d*) Pleonasm
13. The science of judging a person's character, capabilities, etc. from an examination of the shape of his skull
(*a*) Physiology (*b*) Anthropology
(*c*) Phrenology (*d*) Morphology
14. One filled with excessive and mistaken enthusiasm in cause **(Asstt. Grade, 1991)**
(*a*) Martyr (*b*) Pedant
(*c*) Fanatic (*d*) Patriot
15. A person who rarely speaks the truth
(*a*) Scoundrel (*b*) Liar
(*c*) Crook (*d*) Hypocrite
16. Time after twilight and before night
(*a*) Evening (*b*) Dawn
(*c*) Dusk (*d*) Eclipse
17. Custom of having many wives
(*a*) Polyandry (*b*) Polygygny
(*c*) Matrimony (*d*) Celibacy
18. To bring peace, and end violence
(*a*) Soothe (*b*) Harmonise
(*c*) Pacify (*d*) Tranquilize
19. Animals living on land and in water
(*a*) Ambiguous (*b*) Amphibian
(*c*) Amorphous (*d*) Ambivalent
(Bank P.O. 1990)
20. One who plays a game for pleasure and not professionally
(*a*) Veteran (*b*) Player
(*c*) Connoisseur (*d*) Amateur
21. That which can be interpreted in any way
(*a*) Ambient (*b*) Ambivalent
(*c*) Amphibious (*d*) Ambiguous
22. A political leader who tries to stir up people
(*a*) Demagogue (*b*) Dictator
(*c*) Statesman (*d*) Martinet
23. A light sailing boat built especially for racing **(I. Tax & Central Excise, 1995)**
(*a*) Dinghy (*b*) Canoe
(*c*) Yacht (*d*) Frigate
24. Person who has long experience
(*a*) Stalwart (*b*) Pedantic
(*c*) Itinerant (*d*) Veteran
25. Atonement for one's sins
(*a*) Redemption (*b*) Repentance
(*c*) Salvation (*d*) Expiation
26. An instrument for viewing objects at a distance
(*a*) Microscope (*b*) Telescope
(*c*) Periscope (*d*) Kaleidoscope
27. Be the embodiment or perfect example of
(*a*) Signify (*b*) Characterise
(*c*) Personify (*d*) Masquerade
(Bank P.O. 1995)
28. A general pardon of political offenders
(*a*) Parole (*b*) Forgiveness
(*c*) Clemency (*d*) Amnesty
29. A man who operates on sick people
(*a*) Physician (*b*) Operator
(*c*) Surgeon (*d*) Physiotherapist

30. A person who maliciously destroys by fire
(*a*) Antagonist (*b*) Activist
(*c*) Terrorist (*d*) Incendiary

31. A house for storing grains **(C.B.I. 1994)**
(*a*) Cellar (*b*) Store
(*c*) Godown (*d*) Granary

32. A person very hard to please
(*a*) Obstinate (*b*) Unconquerable
(*c*) Fastidious (*d*) Invincible

33. A person claiming to be superior in culture and intellect to others
(*a*) Intellectual (*b*) Aristocrat
(*c*) Elite (*d*) Highbrow

34. One who totally abstains from alcoholic drinks
(*a*) Puritan (*b*) Samaritan
(*c*) Pedant (*d*) Teetotaller

35. A name adopted by an author in his writings **(Asstt. Grade, 1994)**
(*a*) Title (*b*) Nomenclature
(*c*) Nickname (*d*) Pseudonym

36. The line which a plough cuts in the ground
(*a*) Vale (*b*) Trench
(*c*) Furrow (*d*) Trough

37. A man who pays too much attention to his clothes and personal appearance
(*a*) Snob (*b*) Duffer
(*c*) Dandy (*d*) Licentious

38. A person who forsakes religion
(*a*) Charlatan (*b*) Apostle
(*c*) Renegade (*d*) Apotheosis

39. Of unknown and unadmitted authorship
(*a*) Gullible (*b*) Anonymous
(*c*) Unanimous (*d*) Vexation
(Railways, 1991)

40. Contempt of God
(*a*) Athesim (*b*) Nihilism
(*c*) Blasphemy (*d*) Agnosticism

41. Person holding a scholarship at a university
(*a*) Intellectual (*b*) Pedant
(*c*) Scholar (*d*) Bursar

42. A person concerned with practical results and values
(*a*) Plagiarist (*b*) Realist
(*c*) Pragmatist (*d*) Fundamentalist

43. Member of a band of robbers **(B.Ed. 1993)**
(*a*) Dacoit (*b*) Brigand
(*c*) Thief (*d*) Pirate

44. A person without manners or polish
(*a*) Rustic (*b*) Naive
(*c*) Boorish (*d*) Barbarian

45. A speech by an actor at the end of a play
(*a*) Epilogue (*b*) Monologue
(*c*) Duologue (*d*) Prologue

46. Responsible according to law
(*a*) Liable (*b*) Eligible
(*c*) Legalised (*d*) Legitimate

47. A funny imitation of a poem
(*a*) Counterfeit (*b*) Sonnet
(*c*) Caricature (*d*) Parody

48. Decision made upon a political question by the votes of all qualified persons
(*a*) Veto (*b*) Suffrage
(*c*) Plebiscite (*d*) Franchise

49. Wistful longing for something one has known in the past
(*a*) Hysteria (*b*) Megalomania
(*c*) Nostalgia (*d*) Logomania

50. A person who is made to bear the blame due to others **(Translator's Exam, 1994)**
(*a*) Innocent (*b*) Scapegoat
(*c*) Ignoramus (*d*) Nincompoop

ANSWERS

1. (*c*)	**2.** (*a*)	**3.** (*d*)	**4.** (*a*)	**5.** (*b*)	**6.** (*d*)	**7.** (*a*)	**8.** (*c*)	**9.** (*c*)	**10.** (*b*)
11. (*d*)	**12.** (*d*)	**13.** (*c*)	**14.** (*c*)	**15.** (*b*)	**16.** (*c*)	**17.** (*b*)	**18.** (*c*)	**19.** (*b*)	**20.** (*d*)
21. (*d*)	**22.** (*a*)	**23.** (*c*)	**24.** (*d*)	**25.** (*b*)	**26.** (*b*)	**27.** (*c*)	**28.** (*d*)	**29.** (*c*)	**30.** (*d*)
31. (*d*)	**32.** (*c*)	**33.** (*d*)	**34.** (*d*)	**35.** (*d*)	**36.** (*c*)	**37.** (*c*)	**38.** (*c*)	**39.** (*b*)	**40.** (*c*)
41. (*d*)	**42.** (*c*)	**43.** (*b*)	**44.** (*a*)	**45.** (*a*)	**46.** (*d*)	**47.** (*d*)	**48.** (*c*)	**49.** (*c*)	**50.** (*b*)

PRACTICE SET 5

Directions : *Choose the most suitable 'one word' for the following phrases/expressions.*

1. Act of taking one's life
(*a*) Suicide (*b*) Slaughter
(*c*) Homicide (*d*) Immolation

2. A person who brings goods illegally into the country **(Asstt. Grade, 1994)**
(*a*) Exporter (*b*) Importer

(*c*) Smuggler (*d*) Imposter

3. A man who dances to the tunes of his wife
(*a*) Effeminate (*b*) Slave
(*c*) Henpecked (*d*) Chum

4. A place of ideal peace and happiness
(*a*) Asylum (*b*) Utopia
(*c*) El Dorado (*d*) Elysium

5. One who stirs people for personal politics or profit
(*a*) Pedagogue (*b*) Demagogue
(*c*) Dictator (*d*) Hypocrite

6. One who is honourably discharged from service
(*a*) Emeritus (*b*) Honorary
(*c*) Sinecure (*d*) Retired

7. Shining, brilliant and magnificent
(*a*) Luminous (*b*) Gleaming
(*c*) Resplendent (*d*) Polished

8. Cutting for stone in the bladder
(*a*) Dichotomy (*b*) Tubectomy
(*c*) Vasectomy (*d*) Lithotomy
(Bank P.O. 1990)

9. A heavy unnatural slumber
(*a*) Nap (*b*) Insomnia
(*c*) Coma (*d*) Stupor

10. Changing one's mind too quickly
(*a*) Adaptability (*b*) Instability
(*c*) Versatility (*d*) Vacillation

11. A person who travels to a sacred place as an act of religious devotion
(*a*) Hermit (*b*) Pilgrim
(*c*) Saint (*d*) Mendicant
(B.Ed. Entrance, 1993)

12. To do away with a rule
(*a*) Cancel (*b*) Repeal
(*c*) Obliterate (*d*) Abrogate

13. One who talks very little
(*a*) Reserved (*b*) Mute
(*c*) Phlegmatic (*d*) Stoic

14. A person sharing responsibility for a political party's discipline and tactics
(*a*) Statesman (*b*) Diplomat
(*c*) Whip (*d*) Defector

15. Food which agrees with one's taste
(*a*) Pungent (*b*) Palatable
(*c*) Sensuous (*d*) Edible
(Transmission Executives, 1994)

16. Government by the representatives of the people
(*a*) Diplomacy (*b*) Democracy
(*c*) Socialism (*d*) Autocracy

17. Informal business communication with a personal signature
(*a*) Agendum (*b*) Corrigendum
(*c*) Plagiarism (*d*) Memorandum

18. One who loves books **(C.B.I. 1993)**
(*a*) Bibliophobe (*b*) Bibliographer
(*c*) Bibliophile (*d*) Bibliophagist

19. One knowing everything
(*a*) Learned (*b*) Omnipresent
(*c*) Omnipotent (*d*) Omniscient

20. A story in verse
(*a*) Elegy (*b*) Hymn
(*c*) Sonnet (*d*) Ballad

21. Plain or self-evident truth
(*a*) Proverb (*b*) Precept
(*c*) Truism (*d*) Formula

22. The list of courses at a meal or of dishes that can be served in a restaurant
(*a*) Agenda (*b*) Menu
(*c*) Biodata (*d*) Catalogue

23. Parts of a country behind the coast or a river's banks **(U.D.C. 1995)**
(*a*) Swamps (*b*) Archipelago
(*c*) Hinterland (*d*) Isthmus

24. Printed notice of somebody's death
(*a*) Condolence (*b*) Calumny
(*c*) Obituary (*d*) Ouija

25. A room leading into a large room or hall
(*a*) Anteroom (*b*) Lounge
(*c*) Lobby (*d*) Pantry

26. Just punishement for wrong doing
(*a*) Nemesis (*b*) Purgation
(*c*) Wrath (*d*) Catharsis

27. A person who has just started learning
(*a*) Foreman (*b*) Accomplice
(*c*) Novice (*d*) Apprentice

28. A low-area storm with high winds rotating about a centre of low atmospheric pressure
(*a*) Cyclone (*b*) Tornado
(*c*) Typhoon (*d*) Hurricane
(Assistant Grade, 1993)

29. To break off proceedings of a meeting for a time
(*a*) Convene (*b*) Terminate
(*c*) Adjourn (*d*) Procrastinate

30. A fault that may be forgiven
(*a*) Mercenary (*b*) Venial
(*c*) Pardonable (*d*) Excusable

31. One who promotes the idea of absence of government of any kind, when every man should be a law unto himself
(a) Anarchist (b) Belligerent
(c) Iconoclast (d) Agnostic
(B.Ed. 1994)

32. One who is likeable
(*a*) Amicable (*b*) Amiable
(*c*) Effusive (*d*) Ebullient

33. Person who gives himself upto luxury and sexual pleasures
(*a*) Masochist (*b*) Voluptuary
(*c*) Debauch (*d*) Epicure

34. A field or a part of a garden where fruit trees grow
(*a*) Park (*b*) Nursery
(*c*) Yard (*d*) Orchard

35. Something which is not thorough or profound **(Stenographer's Exam, 1993)**
(*a*) Superficial (*b*) Superstitious
(*c*) Superfluous (*d*) Supernatural

36. A woman of lax moral
(*a*) Prostitute (*b*) Harlot
(*c*) Concubine (*d*) Hostess

37. A slow-witted and incompetent person
(*a*) Nigger (*b*) Dud
(*c*) Snotty (*d*) Duffer

38. Using of new words
(*a*) Coinage (*b*) Vocabulary
(*c*) Neologism (*d*) Malapropism

39. Indifference to pleasure or pain
(*a*) Docility (*b*) Stoicism
(*c*) Patience (*d*) Reticence
(Translator's Exam, 1994)

40. One who is neither intelligent nor dull
(*a*) Tolerable (*b*) Commoner
(*c*) Mediocre (*d*) Diligent

41. Equal in rank, merit or quality
(*a*) Chum (*b*) Contemporary
(*c*) Peer (*d*) Colleague

42. Person who gives written testimony for use in a law court
(*a*) Deponent (*b*) Appellant
(*c*) Withness (*d*) Litigant

43. Present opposing arguments or evidence
(*a*) Rebut (*b*) Criticise
(*c*) Rebuff (*d*) Reprimand
(Bank P.O. 1995)

44. Books, pictures etc. intended to arouse sexual desire
(*a*) Lewd (*b*) Licentious
(*c*) Pornography (*d*) Erotica

45. A person who makes and sells ladies' hats, etc.
(*a*) Draper (*b*) Tinker
(*c*) Milliner (*d*) Farrier

46. Careful in performing duties
(*a*) Punctual (*b*) Punctilious
(*c*) Sincere (*d*) Pugnacious

47. To mediate between two parties in a dispute **(Central Excise, 1994)**
(*a*) Interfere (*b*) Interact
(*c*) Interrupt (*d*) Intercede

48. A thing liable to be easily broken
(*a*) Breakable (*b*) Ductile
(*c*) Brittle (*d*) Delicate

49. The place where bricks are baked
(*a*) Foundry (*b*) Mint
(*c*) Cemetery (*d*) Kiln

50. The branch of medical science which deals with the problems of the old
(*a*) Oncology (*b*) Geriatrics
(*c*) Obstetrics (*d*) Endocrinology
(Section Officer's Exam, 1993)

ANSWERS

1. (*a*)	**2.** (*c*)	**3.** (*c*)	**4.** (*d*)	**5.** (*b*)	**6.** (*a*)	**7.** (*c*)	**8.** (*d*)	**9.** (*d*)	**10.** (*d*)
11. (*b*)	**12.** (*d*)	**13.** (*a*)	**14.** (*c*)	**15.** (*b*)	**16.** (*b*)	**17.** (*d*)	**18.** (*c*)	**19.** (*d*)	**20.** (*d*)
21. (*c*)	**22.** (*b*)	**23.** (*c*)	**24.** (*c*)	**25.** (*a*)	**26.** (*a*)	**27.** (*d*)	**28.** (*a*)	**29.** (*c*)	**30.** (*b*)
31. (*a*)	**32.** (*b*)	**33.** (*b*)	**34.** (*d*)	**35.** (*a*)	**36.** (*d*)	**37.** (*d*)	**38.** (*c*)	**39.** (*b*)	**40.** (*c*)
41. (*c*)	**42.** (*a*)	**43.** (*a*)	**44.** (*c*)	**45.** (*c*)	**46.** (*b*)	**47.** (*d*)	**48.** (*c*)	**49.** (*d*)	**50.** (*b*)

PRACTICE SET 6

Directions : *In each of the following questions, choose the word which can be substituted for the given phrase/sentence.*

1. One who specialises in the study of birds
(*a*) Biologist (*b*) Naturalist
(*c*) Zoologist (*d*) Ornithologist
(C.B.I. 1994)

2. Property inherited from one's father or ancestors
(*a*) Alimony (*b*) Patrimony
(*c*) Legacy (*d*) Inheritance

3. Connoisseur of choice food
(*a*) Greedy (*b*) Glutton
(*c*) Gourmet (*d*) Gourmand

4. Person who makes love for amusement without serious intentions

(*a*) Concubine (*b*) Philanderer
(*c*) Dandy (*d*) Flirt

5. A person pretending to be somebody he is not **(Asstt. Grade, 1994)**
(*a*) Imposter (*b*) Liar
(*c*) Rogue (*d*) Magician

6. One who eats human flesh
(*a*) Beast (*b*) Savage
(*c*) Cannibal (*d*) Carnivorous

7. Allowance due to a wife from her husband on separation
(*a*) Bail (*b*) Alimony
(*c*) Dole (*d*) Compensation

8. Fear of going to bed
(*a*) Clinophobia (*b*) Ballistophobia
(*c*) Xenophobia (*d*) Stenophobia

9. Official incharge of a museum
(*a*) Dean (*b*) Warden
(*c*) Curator (*d*) Supervisor

10. The doctrine that human souls pass from one body to another at the time of death
(*a*) Metamorphosis (*b*) Transition
(*c*) Transmigration (*d*) Extrapolation
(B.Ed. Entrance, 1992)

11. People at a lecture or concert
(*a*) Congregation (*b*) Audience
(*c*) Mob (*d*) Spectators

12. A person's first speech
(*a*) Preface (*b*) Maiden
(*c*) Opener (*d*) Extempore

13. To come as a settler into another country
(*a*) Alienate (*b*) Emigrate
(*c*) Migrate (*d*) Immigrate

14. A drawing on transparent paper
(*a*) Red print (*b*) Blue print
(*c*) Negative (*d*) Transparency
(I. Tax, 1996)

15. Giving undue favours to one's own kith and kin **(Stenographers' Exam, 1993)**
(*a*) Favouritism (*b*) Nepotism
(*c*) Corruption (*d*) Worldliness

16. A person who is very fond of sensuous enjoyments
(*a*) Epicure (*b*) Stoic
(*c*) Lusty (*d*) Hedonist

17. A person who pretends to have more knowledge or skill than he really has
(*a*) Renegade (*b*) Apostle
(*c*) Charlatan (*d*) Apotheosis

18. The act of violating the sanctity of church
(*a*) Heresy (*b*) Desecration
(*c*) Sacrilege (*d*) Blasphemy

19. One who sacrifices his life for a cause
(*a*) Soldier (*b*) Revolutionary
(*c*) Martyr (*d*) Patriot
(Assistant Grade, 1994)

20. Bring to an end
(*a*) Hurl (*b*) Hustle
(*c*) Final (*d*) Finish

21. An old unmarried woman
(*a*) Virgin (*b*) Bachelor
(*c*) Spinster (*d*) Matron

22. A style in which a writer makes a display of his knowledge **(Central Excise, 1995)**
(*a*) Pedantic (*b*) Ornate
(*c*) Verbose (*d*) Pompous

23. A person guilty of malicious setting on fire of property etc.
(*a*) Plagiarist (*b*) Anarchist
(*c*) Arsonist (*d*) Incendiarist

24. One who thinks that human nature is essentially evil **(Translators' Exam, 1994)**
(*a*) Agnostic (*b*) Cynic
(*c*) Sceptic (*d*) Misogynist

25. Science of bodily structure
(*a*) Anthropology (*b*) Neurology
(*c*) Hygiene (*d*) Anatomy

26. That which makes it difficult to recognise the presence of real nature of somebody or something **(C.B.I. 1993)**
(*a*) Cover (*b*) Mask
(*c*) Pretence (*d*) Camouflage

27. A person who lives by himself
(*a*) Venerable (*b*) Sage
(*c*) Quietus (*d*) Recluse

28. A written declaration made on oath in the presence of a magistrate
(*a*) Voucher (*b*) Dossier
(*c*) Affidavit (*d*) Document

29. A physician who delivers babies
(*a*) Paediatrician (*b*) Obstetrician
(*c*) Gynaecologist (*d*) Psychiatrist

30. The loop of rope with a running knot used to hang a person
(*a*) Noose (*b*) Cable
(*c*) Cord (*d*) Chord

31. Yearly celebration of a date or an event
(*a*) Centenary (*b*) Jubilee
(*c*) Anniversary (*d*) Birthday
(Assistant Grade, 1994)

32. Public building where weapons and ammunition are made or stored
(*a*) Godown (*b*) Cellar
(*c*) Armoury (*d*) Arsenal

33. The caretaker of a public building
(*a*) Dean (*b*) Curator
(*c*) Custodian (*d*) Warden

34. Interested mainly in a small group, country etc.
(*a*) Fanatic (*b*) Patriotic
(*c*) Insular (*d*) Usurer

35. One who cannot be corrected **(I. Tax, 1991)**
(*a*) Invulnerable (*b*) Hardened

(*c*) Incurable (*d*) Incorrigible

36. A person who enters without any invitation
(*a*) Burglar (*b*) Intruder
(*c*) Thief (*d*) Vandal

37. The period between two reigns
(*a*) Lapse (*b*) Interregnum (*c*) Stasis
(*d*) Anachronism (*e*) Intermission

38. Poem in short stanzas narrating a popular story
(*a*) Ballet (*b*) Epic
(*c*) Ballad (*d*) Sonnet

39. Lack of enough blood
(*a*) Amnesia (*b*) Insomnia
(*c*) Anaemia (*d*) Allergy

40. A man who is having the qualities of woman
(*a*) Loquacious (*b*) Celibate
(*c*) Effeminate (*d*) Epicurean

41. A word no longer in use **(C.B.I. 1994)**
(*a*) Exotic (*b*) Primitive
(*c*) Obsolete (*d*) Ancient

42. One who does not know how to save money
(*a*) Reckless (*b*) Lavish
(*c*) Careless (*d*) Spendthrift

43. A person 70 to 79 years old
(*a*) Nonagenarian (*b*) Centenarian
(*c*) Octogenarian (*d*) Septuagenarian

44. A person who sneaks into a country
(*a*) Infiltrater (*b*) Sniper
(*c*) Invader (*d*) Aggressor

45. A short journey made by a group of persons together **(B.Ed. Entrance, 1992)**
(*a*) Hike (*b*) Excursion
(*c*) Picnic (*d*) Stroll

46. People in a rowdy scene
(*a*) Mob (*b*) Crowd
(*c*) Rabble (*d*) Congregation

47. Creature having both male and female organs
(*a*) Sodomite (*b*) Homosexual
(*c*) Masochist (*d*) Hermaphrodite

48. One who has suddenly gained new wealth, power or prestige **(C.B.I. 1995)**
(*a*) Aristocrat (*b*) Affluent
(*c*) Maverick (*d*) Parvenu

49. A person working in the same place with another
(*a*) Comrade (*b*) Colleague
(*c*) Assistant (*d*) Contemporary

50. Interval between two events or two periods of time of different character
(*a*) Intermission (*b*) Interlude
(*c*) Interpolation (*d*) Appendix

ANSWERS

1. (*d*)	**2.** (*b*)	**3.** (*c*)	**4.** (*b*)	**5.** (*a*)	**6.** (*c*)	**7.** (*b*)	**8.** (*a*)	**9.** (*c*)	**10.** (*c*)
11. (*b*)	**12.** (*b*)	**13.** (*d*)	**14.** (*d*)	**15.** (*b*)	**16.** (*a*)	**17.** (*c*)	**18.** (*c*)	**19.** (*c*)	**20.** (*d*)
21. (*c*)	**22.** (*a*)	**23.** (*c*)	**24.** (*b*)	**25.** (*d*)	**26.** (*d*)	**27.** (*d*)	**28.** (*c*)	**29.** (*b*)	**30.** (*a*)
31. (*c*)	**32.** (*d*)	**33.** (*c*)	**34.** (*c*)	**35.** (*d*)	**36.** (*b*)	**37.** (*b*)	**38.** (*c*)	**39.** (*c*)	**40.** (*c*)
41. (*c*)	**42.** (*d*)	**43.** (*d*)	**44.** (*a*)	**45.** (*b*)	**46.** (*c*)	**47.** (*d*)	**48.** (*d*)	**49.** (*b*)	**50.** (*b*)

PRACTICE SET 7

Directions : *In each of the following questions, choose the most suitable 'one word' for the given expression.*

1. One who comes from a country area and is often considered to be stupid
(*a*) Villager (*b*) Rustic
(*c*) Bumpkin (*d*) Philanderer

2. Murder of a new-born child **(M.B.A. 1992)**
(*a*) Homicide (*b*) Regicide
(*c*) Fratricide (*d*) Infanticide

3. Walk in a vain, self-important way
(*a*) Jog (*b*) Trek
(*c*) Trudge (*d*) Strut

4. Place which provides both board and lodging
(*a*) Cafe (*b*) Inn
(*c*) Restaurant (*d*) Motel

5. Clumsy or ill-bred fellow
(*a*) Boor (*b*) Oaf
(*c*) Lout (*d*) Yokel

6. A small shop that sells fashionable clothes, cosmetics etc.
(*a*) Booth (*b*) Stall
(*c*) Boutique (*d*) Store

7. Thing that can be felt or touched
(*a*) Pandemic (*b*) Palpable
(*c*) Paltry (*d*) Panchromatic
(B.S.R.B. 1995)

8. A person who readily believes others
(*a*) Credible (*b*) Credulous
(*c*) Sensible (*d*) Sensitive

9. A book containing summarised information on all branches of knowledge
(*a*) Dictionary (*b*) Anthology
(*c*) Encyclopaedia (*d*) Directory

10. The normal abode of any animal or plant
(*a*) Environment (*b*) Habitat
(*c*) Settlement (*d*) Niche

11. Extreme old age when a man behaves like a fool **(Asstt. Grade, 1996)**
(*a*) Dotage (*b*) Imbecility
(*c*) Senility (*d*) Superannuation

12. A violent and bad-tempered woman
(*a*) Prostitute (*b*) Concubine
(*c*) Virago (*d*) Amazon

13. One who talks continuously
(*a*) Impecunious (*b*) Loquacious
(*c*) Voracious (*d*) Avaricious

14. A person who is skilled in horsemanship
(*a*) Cavalier (*b*) Equestrian
(*c*) Jockey (*d*) Cavalryman
(U.D.C. 1994)

15. To atone for one's sins
(*a*) Apologise (*b*) Ingratiate
(*c*) Expiate (*d*) Propitiate

16. The rule of a person who is tyrant
(*a*) Despotism (*b*) Anarchy
(*c*) Tyranny (*d*) Dictatorship

17. A paper written in one's own handwriting **(C.B.I. 1993)**
(*a*) Manuscript (*b*) Scroll
(*c*) Parchment (*d*) Transcript

18. To congratulate someone in a formal manner
(*a*) Wish (*b*) Solemnize
(*c*) Celebrate (*d*) Felicitate

19. Interested in and clever at many things
(*a*) Manicure (*b*) Manifest
(*c*) Intelligent (*d*) Versatile

20. Code of diplomatic etiquette and precedence **(Asstt. Grade, 1996)**
(*a*) Formalism (*b*) Statesmanship
(*c*) Protocol (*d*) Hierarchy

21. People in a riot
(*a*) Crowd (*b*) Rabble
(*c*) Mob (*d*) Congregation

22. That which can be carried
(*a*) Handy (*b*) Portable
(*c*) Potable (*d*) Bearable

23. Of outstanding significance
(*a*) Meaningful (*b*) Ominous
(*c*) Evident (*d*) Monumental
(*e*) Rational **(Bank P.O. 1995)**

24 A small, named group of fixed stars
(*a*) Galaxy (*b*) Cluster
(*c*) Constellation (*d*) Congregation

25. Run away from home with lover
(*a*) Ostracize (*b*) Vanquish
(*c*) Abscond (*d*) Elope

26. A place of good climate for invalids
(*a*) Asylum (*b*) Hospital
(*c*) Cemetery (*d*) Sanatorium
(Stenographers' Exam, 1991)

27. A tumour which is not likely to spread
(*a*) Benign (*b*) Localised
(*c*) Dead (*d*) Malignant

28. Place where bankers exchange cheques and adjust balances
(*a*) Exchequer (*b*) Clearing house
(*c*) Bank (*d*) Commerce house

29. One who promotes the idea of absence of government of any kind, when every man should be a law into himself
(Assistant Grade, 1991)
(*a*) Anarchist (*b*) Belligerent
(*c*) Iconoclast (*d*) Agnostic

30. To remove the skin of a potato or an orange
(*a*) Rinse (*b*) Peel
(*c*) Scrub (*d*) Remove

31. Irrational fear of crowds
(*a*) Ochlophobia (*b*) Claustrophobia
(*c*) Sitophobia (*d*) Astrophobia

32. One appointment by two parties to settle a dispute
(*a*) Arbiter (*b*) Mediator
(*c*) Negotiator (*d*) Middleman

33. A list of explanation of words, especially unusual ones at the end of a book
(*a*) Appendix (*b*) Index
(*c*) Glossary (*d*) Bibliography

34. One who can use either of his hands with ease **(Railways, 1991)**
(*a*) Amateur (*b*) Expert
(*c*) Ambidextrous (*d*) Gluttonous

35. A statement which cannot be understood
(*a*) Infallible (*b*) Illegible
(*c*) Inexplicable (*d*) Incomprehensible

36. The plants and vegetation of a region
(*a*) Flora (*b*) Fauna
(*c*) Landscape (*d*) Environment

37. A person who is talkative
(*a*) Garrulous (*b*) Speaker
(*c*) Orator (*d*) Laxative

38. Medical study of the skin and its diseases **(C.B.I. 1995)**
(*a*) Dermatology (*b*) Orthopaedics
(*c*) Venereology (*d*) Homeopathy

39. Room with toilet facilities
(*a*) Suite (*b*) Deluxe
(*c*) Lavatory (*d*) Cabin

40. One who speaks or understands many languages
(*a*) Scholar (*b*) Grammarian
(*c*) Linguist (*d*) Polyglot

41. To talk without respect of something sacred or holy
(*a*) Blasphemy (*b*) Obscenity
(*c*) Rudeness (*d*) Vulgarity
(Stenographers' Exam, 1993)

42. A person who lives alone and avoids other people
(*a*) Ascetic (*b*) Recluse
(*c*) Unsocial (*d*) Agnostic

43. Explicit undertaking to do something
(*a*) Agreement (*b*) Decision
(*c*) Settlement (*d*) Promise

44. Murder of a king **(Bank P.O. 1995)**
(*a*) Matricide (*b*) Genocide
(*c*) Regicide (*d*) Homicide

45. To surround with armed forces
(*a*) Seize (*b*) Attack
(*c*) Cease (*d*) Besiege

46. A person who wishes to throw over all establishments
(*a*) Rebel (*b*) Anarchist
(*c*) Terrorist (*d*) Hooligan

47. A dramatic performance
(*a*) Mask (*b*) Mosque
(*c*) Masque (*d*) Mascot
(Central Excise, 1996)

48. Seat on elephant's back
(*a*) Saddle (*b*) Howdah
(*c*) Lounge (*d*) Hoof

49. An expression of mild disapproval
(*a*) Reproof (*b*) Impertinence
(*c*) Warning (*d*) Denigration
(Stenographers' Exam, 1995)

50. Forcing out (blood, etc.) from its vessel
(*a*) Extrapolate (*b*) Extravasate
(*c*) Exuberate (*d*) Extricate

ANSWERS

1. (*c*)	**2.** (*d*)	**3.** (*d*)	**4.** (*b*)	**5.** (*a*)	**6.** (*c*)	**7.** (*b*)	**8.** (*b*)	**9.** (*c*)	**10.** (*b*)
11. (*a*)	**12.** (*c*)	**13.** (*b*)	**14.** (*b*)	**15.** (*c*)	**16.** (*a*)	**17.** (*a*)	**18.** (*d*)	**19.** (*d*)	**20.** (*c*)
21. (*c*)	**22.** (*b*)	**23.** (*d*)	**24.** (*c*)	**25.** (*d*)	**26.** (*d*)	**27.** (*a*)	**28.** (*b*)	**29.** (*a*)	**30.** (*b*)
31. (*a*)	**32.** (*a*)	**33.** (*c*)	**34.** (*c*)	**35.** (*d*)	**36.** (*a*)	**37.** (*a*)	**38.** (*a*)	**39.** (*c*)	**40.** (*d*)
41. (*a*)	**42.** (*b*)	**43.** (*d*)	**44.** (*c*)	**45.** (*d*)	**46.** (*b*)	**47.** (*c*)	**48.** (*b*)	**49.** (*a*)	**50.** (*b*)

PRACTICE SET 8

Directions : *In each of the following questions, out of the given alternatives, choose the one which can be substituted for the given words/sentence.*

1. Incapable of being explained or accounted for
(*a*) Incredible (*b*) Inexplicable
(*c*) Inexplicit (*d*) Inexpressible

2. A person interested in reading books and nothing else **(Assistant Grade, 1994)**
(*a*) Student (*b*) Book worm
(*c*) Scholar (*d*) Book-keeper

3. A book or picture produced merely to bring in money
(*a*) Money-spinner (*b*) Pot-hook
(*c*) Pot-boiler (*d*) Blue-bird

4. Deviation or departure from common rule or standard
(*a*) Heterogeneity (*b*) Anomaly
(*c*) Unanimity (*d*) Anonymity

5. A person who hates women
(*a*) Misanthropist (*b*) Masochist
(*c*) Misogynist (*d*) Misogamist

6. Elderly woman in charge of a girl on social occasions
(*a*) Spinster (*b*) Matron
(*c*) Chaperon (*d*) Chandler

7. Land so surrounded by water as to be almost an island **(Bank P.O. 1990)**
(*a*) Archipelago (*b*) Isthmus
(*c*) Peninsula (*d*) Lagoon

8. A place adjoining kitchen, for washing dishes etc.
(*a*) Cellar (*b*) Wardrobe
(*c*) Scullery (*d*) Pantry

9. Incapable of being wounded
(*a*) Invulnerable (*b*) Invincible
(*c*) Infallible (*d*) Impregnable

10. A fixed orbit in space in relation to earth
(*a*) Geological (*b*) Geo-synchronous

(*c*) Geocentric (*d*) Geo-stationary

(Central Excise, 1995)

11. Part-song for several voices without instrumental accompaniment
(*a*) Ballad (*b*) Madrigal
(*c*) Panegyric (*d*) Limerick

12. A person who is the property of another and bound to serve him
(*a*) Bondsman (*b*) Slave
(*c*) Servant (*d*) Subordinate

13. A perception without objective reality
(*a*) Allusion (*b*) Illusion
(*c*) Dyspepsia (*d*) Hallucination

14. One who possesses many talents.
(*a*) Versatile (*b*) Gifted
(*c*) Exceptional (*d*) Nubile

(Asstt. Grade, 1996)

15. A person who studies the formation of the earth
(*a*) Meteorologist (*b*) Anthropologist
(*c*) Geologist (*d*) Seismologist

16. A tube filled at one end with mirrors and pieces of coloured glass which shows many coloured patterns when turned
(*a*) Kaleidoscope (*b*) Periscope
(*c*) Microscope (*d*) Gyroscope

17. Word for word reproduction
(*a*) Copying (*b*) Mugging
(*c*) Verbatim (*d*) Photostat

(Stenographer's Exam, 1993)

18. A person who collects coins
(*a*) Philatelist (*b*) Numismatist
(*c*) Narcissist (*d*) Fatalist

19. Open rebellion of soldiers and sailors against lawful authority
(*a*) Revolt (*b*) Revolution
(*c*) Mutiny (*d*) Anarchy

20. A school for infants and young children
(*a*) School (*b*) Nursery
(*c*) Infantile (*d*) Kindergarten

21. Policy of a political party
(*a*) Manifesto (*b*) Agenda
(*c*) Report (*d*) Circular

22. Story told to illustrate a moral or spiritual truth **(B.S.R.B. 1995)**
(*a*) Didactic (*b*) Parable
(*c*) Paragon (*d*) Paradigm

23. One who believes that everything is pre-destined
(*a*) Pessimist (*b*) Fatalist
(*c*) Palmist (*d*) Astrologer

24. A person who betrays a friend
(*a*) Traitor (*b*) Cheat
(*c*) Hypocrite (*d*) Disloyal

25. A verse letter
(*a*) Epistle (*b*) Epitaph
(*c*) Pantomime (*d*) Lay

26. One who eats everything **(Bank P.O. 1995)**
(*a*) Omnipotent (*b*) Insolvent
(*c*) Omniscient (*d*) Omnivorous

27. Joint sovereignty exercised over a country by two or more countries
(*a*) Colonialism (*b*) Entente
(*c*) Pandemonium (*d*) Condominium

28. Stage between boyhood and youth
(*a*) Puberty (*b*) Adolescence
(*c*) Infancy (*d*) Maturity

29. To move along with quick, short twistings
(*a*) Swagger (*b*) Stumble
(*c*) Wriggle (*d*) Crawl

(Transmission Executives, 1994)

30. That which cannot be done without
(*a*) Irrevocable (*b*) Impracticable
(*c*) Indispensable (*d*) Impossible

(S.B.I.P.O. 1991)

31. That which cannot be rectified or made good
(*a*) Irreparable (*b*) Irrevocable
(*c*) Irreconcilable (*d*) Irreplaceable

32. A ride on someone else's back or shoulders
(*a*) Hunchback (*b*) Piggyback
(*c*) Kickback (*d*) Cuddle

33. A cure for all diseases
(*a*) Excorcism (*b*) Incantation
(*c*) Panacea (*d*) Antibiotic

(Bank P.O. 1995)

34. Unreasoning enthusiasm for the glorification of one's country
(*a*) Communism (*b*) Imperialism
(*c*) Patriotism (*d*) Chauvinism

35. The form of madness which gives a person the idea that his importance is very great
(*a*) Paroxysm (*b*) Megalomania
(*c*) Insanity (*d*) Braggart

36. One who travels from place to place
(*a*) Itinerant (*b*) Mendicant
(*c*) Journeyman (*d*) Tramp

(C.B.I.1995)

37. That which is perceptible by touch
(*a*) Tangible (*b*) Tenacious
(*c*) Contagious (*d*) Contingent

38. A person who is bad in spelling
(*a*) Calligraphist (*b*) Pedant
(*c*) Cacographist (*d*) Linguist

39. A short walk for pleasure or exercise
(*a*) Jog (*b*) Stroll
(*c*) Gallop (*d*) Promenade

(I. Tax, 1994)

40. That which cannot be understood
(*a*) Illegible (*b*) Unintelligible
(*c*) Unknown (*d*) Undecipherable

(Section Officers' Exam, 1993)

41. A person who is more interested in himself rather than anything that is going on around him
(*a*) Egoist (*b*) Extrovert
(*c*) Introvert (*d*) Eccentric

42. A story that can hardly be believed
(*a*) Fictitious (*b*) Imaginary
(*c*) Concocted (*d*) Incredible

43. Something which can be taken for granted
(*a*) Doctrine (*b*) Maxim
(*c*) Tenet (*d*) Postulate

44. A sea abounding in islands **(C.B.I. 1993)**
(*a*) Strait (*b*) Archipelago
(*c*) Ocean (*d*) Gulf

45. One who resides in a country of which he is not a citizen
(*a*) Alien (*b*) Native
(*c*) Foreigner (*d*) Prodigal

46. One who draws maps and charts
(*a*) Lexicographer (*b*) Mappier
(*c*) Cartographer (*d*) Graphologist

47. Anything which destroys the effect of poison
(*a*) Serum (*b*) Antiseptic
(*c*) Seramycin (*d*) Antidote

48. A song sung at a burial
(*a*) Elegy (*b*) Ode
(*c*) Dirge (*d*) Ballad

49. Words used in ancient times but no longer in general use now
(*a*) Extinct (*b*) Antiquated
(*c*) Ancient (*d*) Archaic
(Section Officers' Exam, 1993)

50. Ridiculous use of words
(*a*) Onomatopoeia (*b*) Malapropism
(*c*) Neologism (*d*) Pun

ANSWERS

1. (*b*)	**2.** (*b*)	**3.** (*c*)	**4.** (*b*)	**5.** (*c*)	**6.** (*c*)	**7.** (*c*)	**8.** (*c*)	**9.** (*a*)	**10.** (*d*)
11. (*b*)	**12.** (*b*)	**13.** (*d*)	**14.** (*a*)	**15.** (*c*)	**16.** (*a*)	**17.** (*c*)	**18.** (*b*)	**19.** (*c*)	**20.** (*d*)
21. (*a*)	**22.** (*b*)	**23.** (*b*)	**24.** (*a*)	**25.** (*a*)	**26.** (*d*)	**27.** (*d*)	**28.** (*b*)	**29.** (*c*)	**30.** (*c*)
31. (*a*)	**32.** (*b*)	**33.** (*c*)	**34.** (*d*)	**35.** (*b*)	**36.** (*a*)	**37.** (*a*)	**38.** (*c*)	**39.** (*b*)	**40.** (*b*)
41. (*c*)	**42.** (*d*)	**43.** (*d*)	**44.** (*b*)	**45.** (*a*)	**46.** (*c*)	**47.** (*d*)	**48.** (*c*)	**49.** (*d*)	**50.** (*b*)

PRACTICE SET 9

Directions : ***In each of the following questions, find out which one of the words given below the sentence can most appropriately replace the group of words italicised in the sentence.***

1. He spent a long time *cutting* all the waste paper *into pieces.* **(R.B.I. 1990)**
(*a*) slashing (*b*) ripping
(*c*) shredding (*d*) disposing

2. The *stableman at the inn* was the only witness to the murder.
(*a*) butler (*b*) ostler
(*c*) imposter (*d*) jockey

3. A *nation engaged in war* cannot attain high levels of excellence in cultural fields.
(*a*) bellicose (*b*) belligerent
(*c*) imperialist

4. Sunil was buying tickets at the counter when suddenly he noticed a *lady's purse* lying on the floor.
(*a*) raticule (*b*) parasol
(*c*) vestibule (*d*) veil

5. The man's nervousness depicted that it was the *first speech delivered by him.*
(*a*) matin (*b*) peroration
(*c*) maiden (*d*) platitude

6. Nowdays, we often come across cases of admission to institutions through *counterfeit certificates and documents.*
(*a*) stoicism (*b*) pugnacity
(*c*) epitaph (*d*) forgery

7. He is very *careful and particular* about everything he does.
(*a*) precise (*b*) scrupulous
(*c*) meticulous (*d*) conscientious

8. A *soldier who fights for sake of money* cannot be branded as courageous and patriotic.
(*a*) sinecure (*b*) honorary
(*c*) mercenary (*d*) equestrian

9. *Government by all* cannot ensure order.
(*a*) democracy (*b*) bureaucracy
(*c*) plutocracy (*d*) pantisocracy

10. The most comon local means of transport in British times was a *two-wheeled cab for two to ride inside with driver mounted up behind*.
(*a*) carriage (*b*) wagon
(*c*) locomotive (*d*) hansom

11. We are *looking forward to* a good winter this year. **(Bank P.O. 1992)**
(*a*) encouraging (*b*) getting (*c*) hoping
(*d*) predicting (*e*) visualising

12. The automobile has tended to *destroy without any trace* the difference between rural and urban life.
(*a*) cancel (*b*) negate
(*c*) obliterate (*d*) nullify

13. Virus is a *biological entity which lives on another organism*.
(*a*) dependant (*b*) parasite
(*c*) symbiotic (*d*) plebiscite

14. The discovery of the *instrument with lenses for making very small objects appear larger* widened our scope of knowledge.
(*a*) telescope (*b*) binoculars
(*c*) microscope (*d*) bioscope

15. We should always be grateful to *one who has suffered for a great cause*.
(*a*) fanatic (*b*) martyr
(*c*) devotee (*d*) patriot

16. *Study of environment* is a newly evolving branch of science.
(*a*) Geography (*b*) Ethnology
(*c*) Geology (*d*) Ecology

17. Rajesh was a *hater of learning and knowledge*. **(M.B.A. 1994)**
(*a*) misogynist (*b*) misologist
(*c*) misanthropist (*d*) bibliophile

18. He is *working in return for being taught the trade*.
(*a*) disciple (*b*) pupil
(*c*) apprentice (*d*) sobriquet

19. Submarines operate *below the surface* of the seas.
(*a*) superfluous (*b*) surreptitious
(*c*) perspicacious (*d*) subterranean

20. Tuberculosis is *a disease which spreads by contact*.
(*a*) infectious (*b*) contiguous
(*c*) fatal (*d*) contagious

21. Ravi impressed everyone with his *persuasive and fluent speech*. **(R.B.I. 1990)**
(*a*) discourse (*b*) expression
(*c*) eloquence (*d*) lecture

22. *A loud talk or speech* is never impressive.
(*a*) Magniloquence (*b*) Harangue
(*c*) Erudition (*d*) Malevolence

23. No theorem can be proved without using the *statements which are taken for granted*.
(*a*) maxims (*b*) tenets
(*c*) postulates (*d*) stipulation

24. The bus has to *go back and forth* every six hours. **(R.B.I. 1990)**
(*a*) travel (*b*) run (*c*) cross
(*d*) shuttle (*e*) commute

25. The Committee insisted on a total check on all social evils and he was the *one who heralded the revolution*.
(*a*) harbinger (*b*) apostate
(*c*) renegade (*d*) apostle

26. During the Sultanate rule in India, men were not allowed to enter the *women's part of dwelling*.
(*a*) wardrobe (*b*) pantry
(*c*) harem (*d*) anteroom

27. You are requested to send a *list of goods sent, with their prices* along with the parcel so that the payment can be done immediately.
(*a*) agenda (*b*) invoice
(*c*) catalogue (*d*) inventory

28. It is a custom of Christianity to sing *morning prayer in the church* regularly
(*a*) epilogue (*b*) matin
(*c*) epitaph (*d*) vesper

29. Not many people were impressed by a *speech delivered without previous preparation*.
(*a*) epilogue (*b*) prologue
(*c*) soliloquy (*d*) extempore

30. A man can be sentenced to death for *killing another human being*.
(*a*) fratricide (*b*) regicide
(*c*) homicide (*d*) genocide
(N.D.A. 1988)

31. The complete eradication of poverty is an *unreal and visionary* ideal.
(*a*) meditative (*b*) fantastic
(*c*) chimerical (*d*) contemplative

32. *The caretaker of a public building* needs to a vigilant and an honest person.
(*a*) custodian (*b*) curator
(*c*) watchman (*d*) dean

33. *A careful preservation and protection* of wildlife is the need of the hour.
(*a*) Embarkment (*b*) Promotion
(*c*) Conservation (*d*) Management
(*e*) Enhancement **(Bank P.O. 1992)**

34. Both Buddha and Mahavira *lived at the same time*.
(*a*) simultaneous (*b*) contemporary
(*c*) coincident (*d*) synchronised

35. This process is a long one as it involves *too much official formality*.
(*a*) diplomacy (*b*) bureaucracy
(*c*) nepotism (*d*) red-tapism

36. *Those who pass through this gate without permission* will be prosecuted.
(*a*) Bypassers (*b*) Culprits
(*c*) Absconders (*d*) Thoroughfares
(*e*) Trespassers

37. The officer was *not willing to take a definite stand* on that point. **(R.B.I. 1990)**
(*a*) vague (*b*) evasive
(*c*) ambiguous (*d*) complex

38. The *shelter for cow* ought to be clean and well ventilated.
(*a*) hutch (*b*) byre (*c*) hangar
(*d*) kennel (*e*) barracks

39. The servant had not even left the place when a *sudden rush of wind* blew away the clothes which he had just dried.
(*a*) breeze (*b*) storm (*c*) gale
(*d*) typhoon (*e*) gust

40. I find that your views are *not to my liking*.
(*a*) abhorrent (*b*) irritating
(*c*) painful (*d*) revolting

41. His father is a *doctor who treats children and infants*.
(*a*) dermatologist (*b*) gynaecologist
(*c*) podiatrist (*d*) paediatrician

42. The fashion of bell-bottomed trousers has become *out of date*.
(*a*) preposterous (*b*) debilitating
(*c*) obsolescent (*d*) obstreperous

43. Rajiv Gandhi was awarded 'Bharat Ratna' *after his death*
(*a*) ephemeral (*b*) posthumous
(*c*) extempore (*d*) maiden

44. He does *unpaid work* for the Red Cross.
(*a*) honorific (*b*) honest
(*c*) honorary (*d*) honourable
(C.D.S. 1989)

45. The education in primitive gurukuls comprised mainly of telling the *stories of old time gods or heroes*.
(*a*) ode (*b*) epic
(*c*) allegory (*d*) legend

46. The conclusions derived from experiments showed *deviation from the common rule*.
(*a*) heterogeneity (*b*) anomaly
(*c*) anonymity (*d*) strange

47. In the olden days, the king was considered *all powerful*.
(*a*) veteran (*b*) omnipotent
(*c*) omnivorous (*d*) omniscient

48. Despite being in the career of singing for the last ten years, he has not been able to earn fame on account of his *practice of borrowing ideas and words from others and using them as his own*.
(*a*) adaptation (*b*) pantomime
(*c*) imitation (*d*) plagiarism

49. Every person is not allowed to enter *the place where public, government or historical records are kept*.
(*a*) scullery (*b*) pantry
(*c*) archives (*d*) coffer

50. The advertisement assured the public that the medicine would *give back* to the users, *their youthful vigour and appearance*. **(R.B.I. 1990)**
(*a*) rejuvenate (*b*) restore
(*c*) replenish (*d*) render

ANSWERS

1. (*c*)	**2.** (*b*)	**3.** (*b*)	**4.** (*a*)	**5.** (*c*)	**6.** (*d*)	**7.** (*c*)	**8.** (*c*)	**9.** (*d*)	**10.** (*d*)
11. (*c*)	**12.** (*c*)	**13.** (*b*)	**14.** (*c*)	**15.** (*b*)	**16.** (*d*)	**17.** (*b*)	**18.** (*c*)	**19.** (*d*)	**20.** (*d*)
21. (*c*)	**22.** (*b*)	**23.** (*c*)	**24.** (*d*)	**25.** (*a*)	**26.** (*c*)	**27.** (*b*)	**28.** (*b*)	**29.** (*d*)	**30.** (*c*)
31. (*c*)	**32.** (*a*)	**33.** (*c*)	**34.** (*b*)	**35.** (*d*)	**36.** (*e*)	**37.** (*b*)	**38.** (*b*)	**39.** (*e*)	**40.** (*b*)
41. (*d*)	**42.** (*c*)	**43.** (*b*)	**44.** (*c*)	**45.** (*d*)	**46.** (*b*)	**47.** (*b*)	**48.** (*d*)	**49.** (*c*)	**50.** (*a*)

UNIT II

COMPREHENSION ABILITY

7. COMPREHENSION—I
(Long Passages)

To **comprehend** means 'to understand and grasp'. A comprehension exercise is, therefore, meant to test a candidate's ability to understand and retain the contents of a given passage.

Trend of Questions :

In this type of questions, generally a long passage consisting of certain paragraphs is given, followed by 10—15 questions based on it. The questions may be based on :

(i) Theme of the passage

(ii) Choosing the correct or wrong statement on the basis of the given passage

(iii) View of the author regarding the main point discussed in the passage

(iv) Synonyms or Antonyms of some selected words in the passage

Technique of Solving :

1. Read the passage carefully once and detect its theme.
2. Note what the questions are about.
3. Answer the questions.

*In questions on Synonyms & Antonyms, what is to be remembered is that the answer is to be given according to the sense in which the word has been used in the passage, not just on the basis of its literal meaning.

Example : ***Read the following passage and answer the questions that follow :***

Nature is like business. Business sense dictates that we guard our capital and live from the interest. Nature's capital is the enormous diversity of living things. Without it, we cannot feed ourselves, cure ourselves of illness or provide industry with the raw materials of wealth creation. Professor Edward Wilson, of Harvard University says, "The folly our descendants are least likely to forgive us is the ongoing loss of genetic and species diversity. This will take millions of years to correct."

Only 150 plant species have ever been widely cultivated. Yet over 75,000 edible plants are known in the wild. In a hungry world, with a population growing by 90 million each year, so much *wasted* potential is tragic. Medicines from the wild are *worth* around 40 billion dollars a year. Over 5000 species are known to yield chemical with cancer fighting potential Scientists currently estimate that the total number of species in the world is between 10–30 million with only around 1.4 million identified.

The web of life is torn when mankind exploits natural resources in short-sighted ways. The trade in tropical hardwoods can destroy whole forests to extract just a few commercially attractive specimens. Bad agricultural practice *triaggers* 24 billion tonnes of top soil erosion a year losing the equivalent of 9 million tonnes of grain output. *Cutting* this kind of unsuitable exploitation and instituting "sustainable utilisation" will help turn the environmental crisis around.

1. Why does the author compare 'nature' to business?
(*a*) Because of the capital depletion in nature and business
(*b*) Because of the similarity with which one should use both
(*c*) Because of the same interest level yield
(*d*) Because of the diversity of the various capital inputs

2. "The folly our descendants are least likely to forgive us." What is the business equivalent of the folly the author is referring to?
(*a*) Reducing the profit margin
(*b*) Not pumping some money out of profits into the business.
(*c*) Eroding the capital lease of the business
(*d*) Putting interest on capital back into the business

3. Which of the following statements is false in context of the given passage?
(*a*) The diversity of plant life is essential for human existence.
(*b*) Scientists know the usefulness of most plant species.
(*c*) Chemicals for cancer treatment are available from plants.

(*d*) There are around ten times the plant species undiscovered as compared to the discovered ones.

4. Which of the following correctly reflects the opinion of the author to take care of hunger in the world?

(*a*) Increase the number of edible plants being cultivates.

(*b*) Increase cultivation of the 150 species presently under cultivation.

(*c*) Increase the cultivation of medical plants.

(*d*) Increase the potential of the uncultivated edible plants?

5. Which of the following is mentioned as the immediate cause for the destruction of plant species?

(*a*) Soil Erosion (*b*) Destruction of habitat

(*c*) Cultivation (*d*) Agricultural practices

Directions : *Choose the word which is nearly same in meaning to the given word as used in the passage.*

6. WASTED

(*a*) Consumed (*b*) Squandered

(*c*) Unutilised (*d*) Unprofitable

7. TRIGGERS

(*a*) Starts (*b*) Makes

(*c*) Results (*d*) Causes

8. WORTH

(*a*) Cost (*b*) Purchase

(*c*) Deserving (*d*) Sell

Directions : *Choose the word which is nearly opposite in meaning to the given word as used in the passage.*

9. CUTTING

(*a*) Uniting (*b*) Increasing

(*c*) Joining (*d*) Combining

10. GUARD

(*a*) Demolish (*b*) Relieve

(*c*) Consume (*d*) Release

Solution :

1. (*b*) : According to the author, just as in business, capital is kept safe and its interest is utilised, similarly man should increase the potential of available diversity for his benefit and not destroy the bounties of nature.

2. (*c*) : Same clue as Q. 1.

3. (*b*) : The author's statement that some plant varieties are edible, some have medicinal uses, some varieties yield cancer fighting drugs, uses, some varieties yield cancer fighting drugs etc. Confirms (*a*).
The author's statement that over 5000 species are known to yield chemical with cancer fighting potential verifies (*c*).
According to the passage, the total number of plant species is 10–30 million and that of those identified is 1.4 million. Thus, (d) is correct.

4. (*d*) : The author says that out of 75,000 edible plant species, only 150 are cultivated. So, to take care of hunger in the world, the potential of uncultivated edible species should be increased.

5. (*b*) : The last paragraph of the passage gives us the answer

6. (*c*) : The author talks about cultivating only 150 species out of 75,000 as 'wasted potential'. Thus, 'wasted' means 'untilised'.

7. (*d*) : 'Triggers' as used in third paragraph means 'causes'.

8. (*c*) : 'worth' as used in second paragraph means 'deserving'.

9. (*b*) : 'Cutting' as used in last sentence means 'reducing'. So, opposite of it is 'increasing'.

10. (*a*) : 'Guard' as used in first paragraph means 'protect'. So, opposite of it is 'demolish'.

PRACTICE SET

Directions : *Read the following passage carefully and answer the questions given below it. Certain words/phrases in the passage are printed in italics to help you to locate them while answering some of the questions.*

Passage 1 **(S.B.I.P.O. 1994)**

Today the import duty on a complete machine is 35% for all practical purposes, whereas the import duty on the raw materials and components ranges from 40% to 85%. The story does not end here. After paying such high import duties on components, once a machine is made, it suffers excise duty from 5% to 10% (including on the customs duty already paid). At the time of sale, the machine tools suffer further taxation,i.e., central sales tax or state sales taxes which range from 4% to 16%. This much for the tax angle. Another factor which pushes the cost of manufacture of machine tools is the very high rate of interest payable to banks ranging upto 22%, as against 4%-7% prevailing in advanced countries.

The production of machine tools in India being not of the same *scale* as it is in other countries, the price which India's machine tools builders have to pay for components is more or less based on pattern of high pricing applicable to the prices of spares. The above represents only a few of the extraneous reasons for the high cost of Indian machines.

The machine tool industry in India has an *enviable* record of very quick technology absorption, assimilation and development. There are a number of success stories about how machine tool builders were of help at the most critical times. It will be a pity, in fact a tragedy, if we allow this industry to die and disappear from the scene.

It is to be noted that India is at least 6000 km away from any *dependable* source of supply of machine tools. The Government of India has always given a great deal of importance to the development of small scale and medium scale industries. This industry has also performed pretty well. Today, they are in need of help from India's machine tool industry to enable them to produce quality components at reduced costs. Is it anybody's case that the needs of this fragile sector (which needs tender care) will be met from 6000 km away?

Then, what is it that the industry requests from the Government? *It wants level playing field.* In fact, all of us must have a deep introspection and recognise the fact that the machine tool industry has a very special place in the country from the point of strategic and vital *interests* of the nation. Most important, it requests for the Govt's consideration and understanding.

1. According to the passage, assembling imported components into machines proves ultimately
(*a*) cheaper than importing complete machine
(*b*) costlier than importing machine
(*c*) more cost effective than importing machine
(*d*) on par with the cost of imported machine
(*e*) a very stupendous and unmanageable task

2. According to the passage, all the following factors are responsible for high cost of Indian machines except
(*a*) higher import duty on spares
(*b*) excise duty
(*c*) bank's rate of interest on loans for manufacture
(*d*) high profit margin expected by manufacturers
(*e*) sales tax

3. If the bank's rate of interest in India is made on par with that in advanced countries, the cost of manufacture of machine tools
(*a*) may go up by about 4 to 7%
(*b*) may increase by about 22%
(*c*) may decrease by about 4 to 7%
(*d*) may decrease by about 15 to 18%
(*e*) will remain the same due to import duty

4. The availability of Indian machine tool industries' help to small scale industry is most likely to result into

(*a*) increase in the demand of imported machine tools
(*b*) deterioration in the quality of components manufactured by them
(*c*) further increase in the customs duty on imported machines
(*d*) enhancement in the quality and quantity of their production at a cheaper cost
(*e*) severe competition among the small and medium scale industries

5. Which of the following is true in the context of the passage?
(*a*) India's machine tool industry has a praise-worthy record of performance.
(*b*) In critical times, the machine tool builders allowed the industry to perish.
(*c*) In the case of machines, the excise duty is levied only on the cost price.
(*d*) India's quantum of production of machine tools is more than that of other advanced countries.
(*e*) None of these

6. The disparity in the quantum of machine production in India and that in other countries leads to
(*a*) the development of small scale and medium scale industries
(*b*) lethargy in the process of absorption and assimilation of new technology
(*c*) a need to pay higher for components and spares
(*d*) overproduction of machines as compared to the actual need.
(*e*) the necessity to export the machine from India to other countries

7. Which of the following statements is definitely true in the context of the passage?
A. The vital role of India's machine tool industry has not been duly recognised by the Government.
B. Small scale industries' performance can be further improved with the help from Indian machine tool industry.
C. The author of the passage has not discussed all the factors which are responsible for high cost of Indian machines.
(*a*) A & B (*b*) A & C (*c*) B & C
(*d*) All of these (*e*) None of these

8. Which of the following best explains the sentence 'It wants a level playing field' as used in the passage? The machine tool industry in India
(*a*) wants to adopt novel marketing strategies for sale promotion
(*b*) seeks to have small scale industry as its patron
(*c*) needs freedom to import the desired components at a low cost
(*d*) needs land for opening more factories
(*e*) None of these

9. Why do small and medium scale industries look for help from India's machine tool industry?
(*a*) To produce low cost components without dilution in quality
(*b*) To produce cheaper components notwithstanding the poor quality
(*c*) To remain in Governments' focus of attention
(*d*) To improve their poor financial status
(*e*) None of these

10. Which of the following inferences can be drawn from the content of the passage?
(*a*) The Govt. of India has duly recognised the role of machine tool industry.
(*b*) Levying heavy custom duty is absolutely necessary.
(*c*) The Govt. of India was not considerate to the difficulties faced by machine tool industry.
(*d*) India should not waste its precious resources on the production of machine tools.
(*e*) Banks in other countries are running in loss owing to a low interest rate.

11. Which of the following is the principal focus of the content of the passage?
(*a*) Reduction in rate of interest on loans to machine tool industry
(*b*) Indian machine tool industry and its vital role in country's development
(*c*) Encouragement to small and middle scale industries
(*d*) Unrealistic strategy of development of technology
(*e*) Exhorbitant sales tax

Passage 2

Motivations for ruralism in under developed countries are understandably different from those in developed countries. There, it is a sheer physical necessity for the very act of man's survival. In the Third

World countries, which are *predominantly* rural, the only *lever* that can lift human life above its present subhuman level, is rural development. Rural life in such countries has been stagnating for countries on end. Nothing worthwhile has been done to *ameliorate* the conditions of the rural population which is only slightly different from that of their quadruped counterparts. Ignorance, ill health and poverty have become synonyms of rural life in the undeveloped and underdeveloped countries. But the worst tragedy is that the concerned human populations have taken this state of affairs for granted, as something unalterable, something for which there is no remedy. Every ray of hope has gone out of their lives. In such countries, Rural Development is the inevitable condition of any material or non-material advancement. As such, *enlightened sections* of all such countries have been taking ever growing interest in the question of Rural Development.

This was also part of the legacy of their freedom struggle. In countries like India, it is well-known that attempts at Rural Development were an inseparable part of the Independence movement. Leaders like Gandhiji realised quite well that Real India lived in her stagnating villages. Cities, which were mostly the products of Western colonialism, were just artificial showpieces. Even there, there were two worlds. The posh areas, where the affluent few, mostly the products and custodians of imperial interest lived, were little islands *engulfed* by the vast ocean of dirt, represented by the vast majority of people.

Cities were by no means unknown to India, but in ancient India, they were integral parts, organically related to the rest of the country and society. But, modern cities are exotic centres of commercial and industrial exploitation. Cities in ancient India were the flowers of cultural and artistic excellence of the nation, modern cities are just parasites, preying on and *debilitating* the country.

Hence, Gandhiji started the 'Go to Village Movement' which alone, according to him, could bring freedom to India and sustain it. Rural Development had the pride of place in his strategy for the nation's freedom. Thus, it had its origin in the freedom struggle.

1. People are taking growing interest in Rural Development because
   (*a*) nothing worthwhile can be done in the near future.
   (*b*) they have now become optimistic about it.
   (*c*) they have realised the indispensability of it.
   (*d*) they have been suffering from severe health problems.
2. Which of the following is the 'lever' according to the passage?
   (*a*) Upliftment of the rural masses
   (*b*) Enlightenment of certain sections of the society
   (*c*) Non-material advancement
   (*d*) Stagnation of rural life
3. Which of the following is the worst tragedy according to the author?
   (*a*) Lack of realisation of the importance of rural development
   (*b*) Exploitation of the rural people by the city-dwellers
   (*c*) The subhuman condition of the people
   (*d*) The pessimism of the rural people about their own conditions.
4. Which of the following statements is not true in the context of the passage?
   (*a*) Most of the rich people dwelling in modern cities are genuinely concerned about rural development.
   (*b*) Rural development is a pre-requisite of any other advancement and progress.
   (*c*) The rural folk in the Third World countries feel that their subhuman condition cannot be improved.
   (*d*) Only rural development can raise the standard of living of people in the Third World countries.
5. Rural Development was considered as a part of India's freedom movement because
   (*a*) Gandhiji was against the Western colonialism.
   (*b*) real India was then under the British rule.
   (*c*) imperial interest lived only in villages.
   (*d*) the country comprised of mainly villages.
6. The standard of living of human beings in the Third World countries is

(a) subhuman despite best efforts for improvement
(b) not far better than that of animals
(c) improving very rapidly
(d) immune to any improvement

7. In which of the following aspects were the ancient Indian cities *different* from the modern ones?
(a) Wealth (b) Growing population
(c) Trade and Commerce
(d) Oneness with the society
(e) Posh localities

8. Which of the following best describes the two divergent worlds of the modern cities?
(a) Commercial and industrial exploitation
(b) Patrons of western products and custodians of imperial interests
(c) A few rich people and many poor people
(d) Posh area and affluent people

9. Which of the following statements is true in the context of the passage?
(a) The rural folk are very optimistic about improvement in their condition.
(b) In the present context, ignorance, poverty and ill health are inseparable parts of rural life.
(c) Most of the Third World countries are undergoing fast urbanisation.
(d) India's struggle for freedom has been considered as a part of rural development.

Directions *(Questions 10-12)* : ***Choose the word which is most nearly the same in meaning as the given word as used in the passage.***

10. PREDOMINANTLY
(a) extra-ordinarily (b) mostly
(c) forcefully (d) undoubtedly

11. ENLIGHTENED
(a) clearly visible (b) shining brightly
(c) economically privileged
(d) fully awakened

12. SECTIONS
(a) groups of people
(b) combination of units
(c) collection of thoughts
(d) assembly of spectators

Directions *(Questions 13-15)* : ***Choose the word which is opposite in meaning to the given word as used in the passage.***

13. AMELIORATE
(a) Expedite (b) Hasten
(c) Worsen (d) Lessen

14. ENGULFED
(a) Disfigured (b) Dislocated
(c) Different (d) Detached

15. DEBILITATING
(a) Inhabiting (b) Strengthening
(c) Enfeebling (d) Occupying

Passage 3 **(Bank P.O. 1994)**

Although cynics may like to see the government's policy for women in terms of the party's internal power struggles, it will nevertheless be churlish to deny that it represents a pioneering effort aimed at bringing about *sweeping* social reforms. In its language, scope and strategies, the policy document displays a degree of understanding of women's needs that is uncommon in government pronouncements. This is due in large part to the participatory process that marked its formulation, seeking the active involvement right from the start of women's groups, academic institutions and non-government organisations with grass roots experience. The result is not just a *lofty* declaration of principles but a blueprint for a practical programme of action. The policy *delineates* a series of concrete measures to accord women a decision-making role in the political domain and greater control over their economic status. Of especially far-reaching impact are the *devolution* of control of economic infrastructure to women, notably at the gram panchayat level, and the amendments proposed in the Hindu Succession Act of 1956 to give women coparcenary rights.

An enlightened aspect of the policy is its recognition that actual change in the status of women can not be brought about by the mere enactment of socially progressive legislation. Accordingly, it focusses on reorienting development programmes and sensitising administrations to address specific situations as, for instance, the growing number of households headed by women, which is a consequence of rural-urban migration. The proposal to create an equal-opportunity police force and give women greater control of police stations is an acknowledgement of the biases and *callousness* displayed by the generally all-male law-enforcement authorities in cases of dowry and domestic violence. While the mere *enunciation* of such a policy has the salutary effect of sensitising the administration as a whole, it does not make the task of its implementation any easier. This is because the changes it envisages in the political and economic status of women strike at the root of power structures in society and the basis of man-woman relationships. There is also the danger that reservation for women in public life, while necessary for their greater visibility, could lapse into tokenism or become a tool in the hands of vote seeking politicians. Much will depend on the dissemination of the policy and the ability of elected representatives and government agencies to reorder their priorities.

1. Which of the following can be inferred from the passage?
   (*a*) Most of the government's policies are formulated through participatory process.
   (*b*) There is need for stricter legislation.
   (*c*) The policy recommends reservation for women.
   (*d*) Domestic violence is on the rise.
   (*e*) Women already had coparcenary rights.
2. Which of the following is true about the policy?
   (*a*) This is another pronouncement by the government.
   (*b*) It is a pioneering effort.
   (*c*) It is not based on the understanding of woman's needs.
   (*d*) It has made many big declarations.
   (*e*) In its formulation, participatory approach was not followed.
3. According to the passage, which of the following is a consequence of rural-urban migration?
   (*a*) Legislation is not enforced properly.
   (*b*) Many women migrate to urban areas leaving their family in the rural areas.
   (*c*) Industries do not get sufficient manpower in rural areas.
   (*d*) Development programmes are not effective.
   (*e*) None of the above
4. Which of the following is one of the far-reaching impacts of the policy?
   (*a*) Give women coparcenary rights
   (*b*) Reservation for women
   (*c*) Creating an equal-opportunity police force
   (*d*) Accord women a decision making role in political sphere
   (*e*) None of the above
5. According to the passage which of the following is not true?
   (*a*) The policy gives a blue print for programme of action.
   (*b*) The women should be given greater control of police stations.
   (*c*) There is no law-enforcement bias in cases of dowry.
   (*d*) For effective implementation, the government agencies will have to reorder their priorities.
   (*e*) The policy is based on the understanding of the needs of women.
6. Which of the following has the danger of becoming a token?
   (*a*) Socially progressive legislation
   (*b*) Policy for women
   (*c*) Coparcenary rights to women
   (*d*) Man-woman relationships
   (*e*) Reservation for women
7. Which of the following is opposite in meaning to *'lofty'* as used in the passage?
   (*a*) Sublimated (*b*) Humble
   (*c*) Inferior (*d*) Exalted
   (*e*) Undignified
8. Which of the following words is the most opposite in meaning to *'sweeping'* as used in the passage?
   (*a*) Limited (*b*) Half-hearted
   (*c*) Acceptable (*d*) Incomplete
   (*e*) Inconclusive
9. Which of the following is nearly the same in meaning as the word *'devolution'* as used in the passage?
   (*a*) Relegation (*b*) Succession
   (*c*) Deployment (*d*) Decentralisation
   (*e*) Revolution
10. Which of the following words is most nearly the same in meaning as the word *'enunciation'* as used in the passage?
    (*a*) Suggestion (*b*) Formulation
    (*c*) Recommendation (*d*) Proclamation
    (*e*) Recognition
11. According to the passage, which of the following aspects has been identified as, it alone would not bring change in the status of women?
    (*a*) Coparcenary rights to women
    (*b*) Decision making role in political area
    (*c*) Greater control over economic status
    (*d*) Creating equal-opportunity police force

(*e*) Enactment of socially progressive legislation

12. Which of the following is the most nearly the same in meaning to *'callousness'* as used in the passage?
(*a*) Prejudice (*b*) Insensitivity
(*c*) Obliquities (*d*) Casual
(*e*) Superiority

13. Which of the following is nearly the same in meaning to the word *'delineates'* as used in the passage?
(*a*) Discusses (*b*) Demarcates
(*c*) Suggests (*d*) Outlines
(*e*) Propagates

14. At which stage were the grass-root level organisations involved for the policy?
(*a*) After the interim report
(*b*) From the start
(*c*) At the final stages
(*d*) Not mentioned in the passage
(*e*) None of these

15. According to the passage, which of the following is the basic block in the effective implementation of the policy?
(*a*) Prevalent power structure in society
(*b*) Inadequate legislation
(*c*) Insensitive administration
(*d*) Lack of political will
(*e*) Male dominated law-enforcing authorities.

Passage 4

A great deal of discussion continues as to the real extent of global environmental degradation and its implications. What few people challenge however, is that the renewable natural resources of developing countries are today subject to stresses of unprecedented magnitude. These pressures are brought about, in part, by increased population and the quest for an ever expanding food supply. Because the health, nutrition and general well- being of the poor majority are directly dependent on the integrity and productivity of their natural resources, the capability of governments to manage them effectively over the long term becomes of paramount importance.

Developing countries are becoming more aware of the ways in which present and future economic development must build upon a sound and sustainable natural resource base. Some are looking at our long tradition in environmental protection and are receptive to US assistance which recognises the uniqueness of the social and ecological systems in these tropical countries. Developing countries recognise the need to improve their capability to analyse issues and their own natural resource management. In February 1981, for example AID funded a National Academy of Sciences panel to advise Nepal on their severe natural resource degradation problems. Some countries such as Senegal, India, Indonesia and Thailand, are now including conservation concerns in their economic development planning process.

Because so many governments of developing nations have recognised the importance of these issues, the need today is not merely one of raising additional consciousness, but for carefully designed and sharply focussed activities aimed at the establishment of effective resource management regimes that are essential to the achievement of sustained development.

1. Some of the developing countries of Asia and Africa have
(*a*) formulated very ambitious plans of protecting habitat in the region
(*b*) laid a great stress on the conservation of natural resources in their educational endeavour
(*c*) carefully dovetailed environmental conservation with the overall strategy of planned economic development
(*d*) sought the help of US experts in solving the problem of environmental degradation

2. Technical know-how developed in the USA
(*a*) cannot be easily assimilated by the technocrats of the developing countries
(*b*) can be properly utilised on the basis of developing countries being able to launch an in-depth study of their specific problems
(*c*) can be easily borrowed by the developing countries to solve the problem of environmental degradation
(*d*) can be very effective in solving the problem of resource management in tropical countries

3. There has been a pronounced deterioration of habitat all over the globe because of

(a) rigorous operation of the Malthusian principle
(b) unprecedented urbanisation and dislocation of self contained rural communities
(c) optimum degree of industrialisation in the developing countries
(d) large scale deforestation and desertification

4. The poor people of the developing world can lead a happy and contented life if
(a) there is a North-South dialogue and aid flows freely to the developing world.
(b) industries based on agriculture are widely developed.
(c) economic development takes place within the ambit of conservation of natural resources.
(d) there is an assured supply of food and medical care.

5. How much environmental pollution has taken place in the developing and the developed world?
(a) There has been a marginal pollution of environment in the developed world and extensive damage in the developing world.
(b) There has been a considerable pollution of environment all over the globe.
(c) There has been an extensive environmental degradation both in the developed and the developing world.
(d) The environmental pollution that has taken place all over the globe continues to be a matter of speculation and enquiry.

Passage 5 **(Bank P.O. 1994)**

A leading Indian industrialist in a recent article on ways to strengthen India's economy has drawn attention to the problems of inflation and industrial sickness among other things. One of the main reasons for industrial sickness in our country has been the fact that business and industrial managers, have not been able to look beyond the *immediate* future. They have been too preoccupied with their attempts to report favourable results for the current year- higher profits and larger dividends to the share holders. The planning horizon has hardly ever exceeded five years. Investments have been inadequate for new plants and towards diversification and expansions. Modernisation and asset creation has seriously lagged behind. In business, growth is needed for survival; one has to grow if one does not want to be *wiped out*. This is particularly true today with liberalisation of imports and increasing competition. More over, growth and higher productivity create employment and higher employment creates larger markets both for industrial and consumer products. It was Henry Ford who brought home the need for the creation of a larger and a more stable middle class, that is, a larger number of people who can afford more and more of goods and services. Even after forty years of independence our industrialists have not been able to *shed* the petty shopkeeper's mentality and our highly educated management has tagged along merrily and without concern. **(Bank P.O. 1994)**

1. Which of the following short comings of Indian industrialists has been highlighted by the author?
(a) They invest unreasonably high amount on diversification and expansion.
(b) They are more concerned for immediate net gains than for developmental activities.
(c) They are reluctant to maintain the shopkeeper mentality.
(d) They are less concerned for payment of dividends to shareholders.
(e) None of the above

2. The leading industrialist attributes industrial sickness mainly to
(a) lacunae in five-year plans
(b) preoccupations of managers with matters unrelated to business
(c) higher profits and larger dividends to shareholders
(d) lack of foresight among managers
(e) inflation and other economic problems

3. According to the passage, growth and increasing productivity lead to
(a) imposition of restrictions on imports
(b) employment and thus provide an outlet to industrial and consumer products
(c) encouragement to export of excess consumer goods
(d) disproportionate surplus of commodities

(*e*) None of the above

4. Why did Henry Ford stress the need for a more stable middle class?
   (*a*) They are mostly service oriented.
   (*b*) They do not have shopkeeper mentality.
   (*c*) They can afford to buy more and more expensive goods.
   (*d*) They are most unstable.
   (*e*) None of these
5. 'The planning horizon has hardly ever exceeded five years' implies
   (*a*) Planning should not be for a period of less than five years.
   (*b*) The planning process is very time consuming.
   (*c*) The planners are not inclined to think of future.
   (*d*) Planning should take care of all probable ups and downs in the next five-year period.
   (*e*) Five-year period is too short for successful implementation of plans.
6. According to the passage, the net gains pursued by managers are at the cost of
   (*a*) Diversification, modernisation and asset creation
   (*b*) Availability of markets for industrial and consumer products
   (*c*) Inflation and industrial sickness
   (*d*) Liberalisation of imports and increasing competition
   (*e*) Higher profits and larger dividends to shareholders
7. In order to improve the condition of Indian industries, the industrialist should do all of the following except
   (*a*) giving up the narrow mentality which very small shopkeepers generally have
   (*b*) striving to earn long term profits
   (*c*) encouraging competition from industrialists within the country and from abroad
   (*d*) resorting to long-term planning for industrial growth and expansion in diverse fields
   (*e*) adopting strategies for diversification and modernisation

Passage 6

The public distribution system, which provides food at low prices, is a subject of vital concern. There is a growing realisation that though India has enough food to feed its masses two *square* meals a day, the monster of starvation and food insecurity continues to haunt the poor in our country.

Increasing the purchasing *power* of the poor through providing productive employment leading to rising income, and thus good standard of living is the ultimate objective of public policy. However, till then, there is a need to provide assured supply of food through a restructured, more efficient and decentralised public distribution system (PDS).

Although the PDS is extensive—it is one of the largest such *systems* in the world—it has yet to reach the rural poor and the far off places. It remains an urban phenomenon, with the majority of the rural poor still out of its reach due to lack of economic and physical access. The poorest in the cities and the migrants are left out, for they generally do not possess ration cards. The allocation of PDS supplies in big cities is larger than in rural areas. In view of such deficiencies in the system, the PDS urgently needs to be streamlined. Also, considering the large foodgrains production combined with food subsidy on one hand and the continuing slow starvation and dismal poverty of the rural population on the other, there is a strong case for making PDS target group oriented.

The growing salaried class is provided job security, regular income, and social security. It enjoys almost hundred percent insulation against inflation. These gains of development have not percolated down to the vast majority of our working population. If one compares only dearness allowance to the employees in public and private sector and looks at its growth in the past few years, the rising food subsidy is insignificant to the *point* of inequity. The food subsidy is a kind of D.A. to the poor, the self-employed and those in the unorganised sector of the economy. However, what is most unfortunate is that out of the large budget of the so called food subsidy, the major part of it is administrative cost and wastages. A small portion of the above budget goes to the real consumer and an even lesser portion to the poor who are in real need.

It is true that subsidies should not become a permanent feature, except for the destitute, disabled widows and the old. It is also true that subsidies often create a psychology of dependence and hence is habit-forming, killing the general initiative of the people. By making PDS target group oriented, not only the poorest and neediest would be reached without additional cost, but it will actually *cut* overall costs incurred on large cities and for better off localities. When the food and food subsidy are limited, the rural and urban poor should have the priority in the PDS supplies. The PDS should be closely linked with programmes of employment generation and nutrition improvement.

1. Which of the following is the main reason for insufficient supply of enough food to the poorest?
   (*a*) Mismanagement of foodstocks
   (*b*) Absence of proper public distribution system
   (*c*) Production of food is less than the demand
   (*d*) Government's apathy towards the poor
   (*e*) None of these
2. What, according to the passage, is the main purpose of public policy in the long run?
   (*a*) Reducing the cost of living index by increasing supplies
   (*b*) Providing enough food to all the citizens
   (*c*) Good standard of living through productive employment
   (*d*) Equalising per capita income across different strata of society
   (*e*) None of these
3. Which of the following is true of public distribution system?
   (*a*) It has improved its effectiveness over the years.
   (*b*) It has remained effective only in the cities.
   (*c*) It is the unique in the world because of its effectiveness.
   (*d*) It has reached the remotest corner of the country.
   (*e*) None of these
4. The word 'square' as used in the passage means
   (*a*) rich (*b*) sumptuous
   (*c*) sufficient (*d*) quality
   (*e*) None of these
5. Which of the following words is the same in meaning as 'power' as used in the passage?
   (*a*) vigour (*b*) energy
   (*c*) influence (*d*) capacity
6. What, according to the passage, is the main concern about the PDS?
   (*a*) It has not been able to develop confidence in the people at large.
   (*b*) It has not been able to utilise the entire foodgrains stock available.
   (*c*) It has effectively channelized the foodgrains to all sectors.
   (*d*) It has not been able to provide sufficient food to the poorer section of the society.
   (*e*) None of these
7. What should be an appropriate step to make the PDS effective?
   (*a*) To make it target group oriented
   (*b*) To increase the amount of food grains per ration card
   (*c*) To decrease the allotment of foodgrains to urban sector
   (*d*) To reduce administrative cost
   (*e*) To increase the amount of foodgrains available for distribution
8. Which of the following, according to the passage, is compared with dearness allowance?
   (*a*) Food for work programme
   (*b*) Unemployment allowance
   (*c*) Food subsidy
   (*d*) Procurement price of food grains
   (*e*) Poverty Alleviation Programme
9. Food subsidy leads to which of the following?
   (*a*) Sense of insecurity
   (*b*) Increased dependence
   (*c*) Shortage of foodgrains
   (*d*) Decrease in foodgrains production
   (*e*) None of these
10. What, according to the passage, would be the outcome of making the PDS target group oriented?
    (*a*) It will abolish the imbalance of urban and rural sector.
    (*b*) It will remove poverty.
    (*c*) It will give food to the poorest without additional cost.
    (*d*) It will motivate the target group population to work more.
11. Which is the same in meaning as 'system' as used in the passage?
    (*a*) routine (*b*) mechanism
    (*c*) machine (*d*) procedure
    (*e*) collection
12. Which, according to the passage, consumes the major part of the allocated food subsidy?
    A. Urban population
    B. High administrative cost
    C. Wastage
    (*a*) A only (*b*) A & B (*c*) B & C

(*d*) B or C (*e*) A & C

13. What does 'cut', as used in the passage, mean?

(*a*) damage (*b*) cease
(*c*) destroy (*d*) reduce
(*e*) none of these

14. Which is the same in meaning as the word 'point'?

(*a*) extent (*b*) direct
(*c*) tip (*d*) position
(*e*) none of these

15. The author's writing style is

(*a*) simplistic (*b*) argumentative
(*c*) verbose (*d*) descriptive
(*e*) analytic

Passage 7 **(Bank P.O. 1995)**

Amnesty International's charge that 'tens of thousands' of political prisoners, including prisoners of conscience, are languishing in Indian jails and that prisoners are routinely tortured in this country has to be seen in a much wider context than the organisation's annual report cares to do. In its overall appraisal of 151 countries, Amnesty has accused 112 of torturing prisoners, 63 of harbouring prisoners of conscience, 61 of resorting to political killings and 53 of detaining people without a trial. Of these apparently *overlapping* categories, India seems to have been excluded from the list of the 61 which undertake political killings. The report has however, pointed out that scores of people in India die of torture in police and military custody and that many also simply disappear. Clearly, only a thin line separates the 61 charged with political murder from the rest. Before coming to such conclusions, however, it may also be necessary to classify the various countries according to their political systems. Torture by the security forces and killings at the behest of the government make no difference to the victims whether they are in a democratic country or a totalitarian one. It is also nobody's case that a democratic country is less *culpable* than a dictatorship in the event of human rights violations. But the point perhaps still needs to be made that torture or 'disappearances' represent a failure of the system in a democracy in contrast to being an integral part of state policy in a country ruled by an autocrat who is answerable to no one.

India may be guilty of keeping 'tens of thousands' behind bars and of the other human rights abuses mentioned by Amnesty, but it still remains a qualitatively different place from a totalitarian country. It is in this respect that Amnesty has been less than fair. It has chosen to ignore the distinctions between the good, the bad and the ugly. The openness of Indian society will be evident to anyone who spends half an hour in one of its chaotic market-places or visits the law courts or watches a political rally or reads a newspaper or *strikes up* a conversation with any person on the roads. There is no sense of fear in India, as in a dictatorship. There is also scope for securing relief from the heavy-handed behaviour of the authorities, even if the human rights commission has not yet lived up to expectations. Unless such points are recognised, Amnesty's assessment will seem to be a dry recital of statistics which may *pillory* India simply because of its larger population. Mercifully, Amnesty nowadays at least notes that the terrorists also indulge in human rights violations and that India has to cope with several insurgencies *fomented* by a country where the military does not always seem to be under the control of the elected government. True, there is much that is wrong in India's prison system and with the way the terrorist challenge is sometimes met, but the stress should be on activating the self-correcting mechanism within a democracy and not merely on painting a grim, even biased, picture.

1. In the report, India has been excluded from which of the following categories of violating human rights?

(*a*) Torturing prisoners
(*b*) Detaining without trial
(*c*) Political killings
(*d*) Harbouring prisoners of conscience
(*e*) None of these

2. Which of the following is not true in the context of the passage?

(*a*) India is guilty of some human rights abuses.
(*b*) Amnesty International appraised all the democratic countries.
(*c*) There is overlapping of cases in the categories of human rights abuses.
(*d*) India was one of the countries appraised by Amnesty International.

(*e*) The report notes that the terrorists also violate human rights.

3. According to the passage, through which media or forum Amnesty International has hurled the charges?
(*a*) Seminar on Human rights
(*b*) Its Regional Meet
(*c*) Its Annual Report
(*d*) Its International Meet
(*e*) None of these

4. The author of the passage
(*a*) agrees with the report
(*b*) disagrees with the report
(*c*) disagrees that conditions of prisons in India is bad
(*d*) supports the totalitarian approach
(*e*) disagrees with report on terrorists

5. The Amnesty International's report is based on the information of how many countries?
(*a*) 63 (*b*) 112 (*c*) 131
(*d*) 115 (*e*) None of these

6. The author suggests classification of various countries on one additional dimension. Which of the following is that dimension?
(*a*) Economic progress
(*b*) Human Rights
(*c*) Industrial progress
(*d*) Political systems
(*c*) None of these

7. According to the passage, what does political murder in a democratic country signify?
(*a*) Failure of system
(*b*) Policy of the country
(*c*) Need for autocratic rule
(*d*) Openness of society
(*e*) Heavy-handed behaviour of the authorities

8. Which of the following human rights violation is most prevalent among the countries?
(*a*) Killing with political motive
(*b*) Detaining without trial
(*c*) Torturing prisoners
(*d*) Harbouring prisoners of conscience
(*e*) None of these

9. Which of the following is the meaning of the phrase 'strike up' as used in the passage?
(*a*) hit sharply (*b*) initiate
(*c*) discussion (*d*) protest
(*e*) undertake

10. Which of the following seems to be the main purpose of writing this passage?
(*a*) To highlight the sufferings of prisoners
(*b*) To condemn political killings
(*c*) To highlight the role of Amnesty International
(*d*) To further the cause of human rights
(*e*) None of these

11. According to the author, among the good, the bad and the ugly, what at worst is the situation in India?
(*a*) Good (*b*) Bad
(*c*) Ugly (*d*) Good or ugly
(*e*) Bad or Ugly

12. Which of the following is true according to the passage?
(*a*) There is a need to check political killings in India.
(*b*) The Human Rights Commission has done commendable service.
(*c*) There is a need to improve India's prison system.
(*d*) India is not at all guilty of human rights violation.
(*e*) None of these

Directions (Q. 13-16) : *Choose the word which is most nearly the same in meaning as the given word as used in the passage.*

13. SCORE
(*a*) many (*b*) majority
(*c*) a few (*d*) grudge
(*e*) variety

14. FOMENTED
(*a*) suppressed (*b*) instigated
(*c*) faced (*d*) disturbed
(*e*) formed

15. CULPABLE
(*a*) cynical (*b*) troublesome
(*c*) capable (*d*) imputable
(*e*) adulatory

16. LANGUISH
(*a*) hold grudge (*b*) become sick
(*c*) torture (*d*) remain neglected
(*e*) terrorize

Directions (Q. 17-18) : *Choose the word which is most nearly the opposite in meaning of the given word as used in the passage.*

17. OVERLAPPING
(*a*) different (*b*) override
(*c*) dependent (*d*) coincidental
(*e*) independent

18. PILLORY
(*a*) penalise (*b*) damage
(*c*) appreciate (*d*) exclude
(*e*) include

Passage 8

Ironically enough, the very 'Success' of Operation Flood which is to make the cities flush with milk, has proved its undoing. Farmers in Maharashtra, Gujarat, Karnataka, Tamil Nadu and Kerala are now faced with a surplus of supplies for which there are no takers. Indeed, some experts in the Union agricultural ministry are even going so far as to suggest that the country should export to neighbouring countries—Bangladesh, for example, which imports milk and dairy products. Does this mean that the needs of consumers at home are met? Far from it. The fact that a dairy technology mission was created to improve the nutritional status of the rural poor speaks for itself. The *protagonists* of Operation Flood argue that the per capita consumption of milk has gone up from 108 gm in 1967 to 158 gm in 1987 and an expected 196 gm in 1995, when the third phase of the programme comes to an end. But it is clear that consumption has been limited to the cities and that too to the relatively better off households. Four out of every ten citizens in larger cities, officially estimated to be living in slums, are unable to afford sufficient milk for all their needs. What the much-vaunted 'surplus' thus amounts to therefore is a saturation of the market comprising the other half. Even in Bombay, the most affluent metropolis, housewives find it difficult to meet their milk bills because it is priced the highest in the country.

The inadequate offtake of milk is thus related to its price. The anomaly should be sufficient to prompt a thorough revaluation of Operation Flood, which is based on improving technology in the dairy industry to increase yields though at higher costs. Somewhat like the Green Revolution in cereals, the 'White revolution' has its share of critics who argue that instead of concentrating on increasing the supply of milk in a few pockets (though the co-operatives are inherently preferable to private suppliers), the authorities ought to spread the benefits of improved dairying throughout the countryside. Like the Green Revolution which demands capital-intensive inputs and energy, Operation Flood requires genetically superior cattle which in turn have to be provided with fodder, now in extremely short supply all over the country. What is more, schemes such as Operation Flood only *sharpen* the urban-rural *divide*, instead of narrowing it, which should surely be the objective of any development scheme.

1. Which of the following has the same meaning as the word 'protagonist' as used in the passage?
   (*a*) opponent (*b*) intellectual
   (*c*) supporter (*d*) preserver
   (*e*) practitioner
2. Which of the following is true according to the passage?
   (*a*) Certain states in India have excess production of milk.
   (*b*) Operation Flood does not operate in Karnataka.
   (*c*) Gujarat cities have less milk than cities in Maharashtra.
   (*d*) Certain states are producing excess raw material for milk production.
   (*e*) None of these
3. Which of the following, as can be inferred from the passage, is not an outcome of 'Operation Flood'?
   (*a*) The urban areas are benefitted by improved milk supply.
   (*b*) Nutritional standard of rural poor has gone down.
   (*c*) It has hiked up the price of milk.
   (*d*) Milk output has increased in the country.
   (*e*) It has improved the per capita milk intake.
4. Which of the following is true regarding the price of milk?
   (*a*) It is high because of middlemen.
   (*b*) It is high because cost of production is high.
   (*c*) It is low because of establishment of co-operatives.
   (*d*) It is high only in metropolitan areas.
   (*e*) None of these
5. What is the charge being levelled against Operation Flood by its critics?
   (*a*) It is benefitting only in certain areas.
   (*b*) Milk is being sold at high prices.
   (*c*) It is not increasing the milk production.
   (*d*) Milk products have limited export market and hence it is useless.
6. Which of the following has the same meaning as 'divide' as used in the passage?
   (*a*) partition (*b*) cut off
   (*c*) disagreement (*d*) difference
   (*e*) separate
7. Which of the following is true according to the passage? That people living in slums
   (*a*) get half their requirement only

(*b*) get sufficient milk
(*c*) buy some milk
(*d*) do not buy milk at all
(*e*) are not affected by milk prices

8. Which of the following, according to the author, should be the main objective of schemes like Operation Flood?
(*a*) To increase the availability of milk products in urban areas
(*b*) To make use of surplus inputs available in plenty in the country
(*c*) To increase the production of milk in rural areas
(*d*) To decrease the poverty in rural areas and bring down differences
(*e*) None of these

9. The word 'sharpen' as used in the passage means
(*a*) prepare (*b*) provide (*c*) force
(*d*) widen (*e*) surmount

10. Which of the following can be inferred from the passage?
(*a*) Milk needs of the urban group are being met.
(*b*) Six out of ten people in urban areas buy milk.
(*c*) Milk needs of only the affluent people in urban areas are being met.
(*d*) Milk needs of the entire country are being met.
(*e*) None of these

Passage 9 **(Section Officers, 1993)**

Democratic societies from the earliest times have expected their governments to protect the weak against the strong. No 'era of good feeling' can justify discharging the police force or giving up the idea of public control over concentrated private wealth. On the other hand, it is obvious that a spirit of self-denial and moderation on the part of those who hold economic power will greatly soften the demand for absolute equality. Men are more interested in freedom and security than in an equal distribution of wealth. The extent to which Government must interfere with business, therefore, is not exactly measured by the extent to which economic power is concentrated into a few hands. The required degree of government interference depends mainly on whether economic powers are oppressively used, and on the necessity of keeping economic factors in a tolerable state of balance.

But with the necessity of meeting all these dangers and threats to liberty, the powers of government are unavoidably increased, whichever political party may be in office. The growth of government is a necessary result of the growth of technology and of the problems that go with the use of machines and science. Since the government in our nation, must take on more powers to meet its problems, there is no way to preserve freedom except by making democracy more powerful.

1. The advent of science and technology has increased the
(*a*) freedom of people
(*b*) tyranny of the political parties
(*c*) powers of the government
(*d*) chances of economic inequality

2. A spirit of moderation on the economically sound people would make the less privileged
(*a*) unhappy with the rich people
(*b*) more interested in freedom and security
(*c*) unhappy with their lot
(*d*) clamour less for absolute equality

3. The growth of government is necessitated to
(*a*) make the rich and the poor happy
(*b*) curb the accumulation of wealth in a few hands
(*c*) monitor science and technology
(*d*) deploy the police force wisely

4. 'Era of good feeling' in sentence 2 refers to
(*a*) time of prosperity
(*b*) time of adversity
(*c*) time without government
(*d*) time of police atrocities

5. 'Tolerable state of balance' in the last sentence may mean
(*a*) an adequate level of police force
(*b*) a reasonable level of economic equality
(*c*) a reasonable amount of government interference
(*d*) a reasonable check on economic power

Passage 10

Educational planning should aim at *meeting* the educational needs of the entire population of all age groups. While the traditional structure of education as a three layer hierarchy from the primary stage to the university represents the core, we should not overlook the periphery which is equally important. Under modern conditions, workers need to rewind, or renew their enthusiasm, or strike out in a new direction, or improve their skills as much as any university professor. The retired and the aged have their needs as well. Educational planning, in their words, should take care of the needs of everyone.

Our structures of education have been built up on the assumption that there is a terminal point to education. This basic defect has become all the more harmful today. A UNESCO report entitled 'Learning to Be' prepared by Edgar Faure and others in 1973 asserts that the education of children must prepare the future adult for various forms of self-learning. A viable education system of the future should consist of modules with different kinds of functions serving a diversity of constituents. And performance, not the period of study, should be the basis for credentials. The writing is already on the wall.

In view of the fact that the significance of a commitment of lifelong learning and lifetime education is being discussed only in recent years even in educationally advanced countries, the possibility of the idea becoming an *integral* part of educational thinking seems to be *a far cry*. For, to move in that direction means much more than some simple *rearrangement* of the *present* organisation of education. But a good beginning can be made by developing open university programmes for older learners of different categories and introducing extension services in the conventional colleges and schools. Also these institutions should learn to cooperate with the numerous community organisations such as libraries, museums, municipal recreational programmes, health services etc.

1. What is the main thrust of the author ?
(*a*) Traditional systems should be strengthened.
(*b*) Formal education is more important than non-formal.
(*c*) One should never cease to learn.
(*d*) It is impossible to meet the needs of everyone.
(*e*) There is no substitute for the extant system of education.

2. Which of the following best describes the purpose of the author?
(*a*) To criticise the present educational system
(*b*) To strengthen the present educational practices
(*c*) To support non-conventional educational organisations
(*d*) To present a pragmatic point of view
(*e*) None of these

3. According to the passage, the present education structures assume which of the following?
(*a*) All people can be educated as per their needs.
(*b*) Present educational planning is very much practical.
(*c*) Education is a one time process.
(*d*) Simple rearrangement of the present educational system is a must.
(*e*) Discussions on lifelong learning should continue for some more time.

4. What should be the major characteristic of the future educational system?
(*a*) Different modules with same function
(*b*) Same module for different groups
(*c*) No modules but standard compulsory programme for all
(*d*) Rearrangement of various course contents
(*e*) None of these

5. According to the author, educational plan should attempt to
(*a*) train the people at the core
(*b*) encourage conventional schools and colleges
(*c*) decide a terminal point to education
(*d*) overlook the people on the periphery
(*e*) fulfil the educational needs of everyone

6. According to the author, what measures should open university adopt to meet modern conditions?
(*a*) Develop various programmes for adult learners.
(*b*) Open more colleges on traditional lines.
(*c*) Cater to the needs of those who represent 'core'.
(*d*) Primary education should be under the control of open universities.
(*e*) De-recognition of various community organisations.

7. According to the author, what should be the basis for awarding credentials?
(*a*) Duration of the course
(*b*) Competence of the course teachers
(*c*) Diversity of the topics covered

(*d*) Real grasp of matter or skill
(*e*) Participation in community activities

8. Which of the following is not true in context of the given passage?
(*a*) Lifelong learning is a recent concept.
(*b*) Workers' knowledge and skills also need to be updated constantly.
(*c*) 'Learning to Be' defends that there is a terminal point to education.
(*d*) Schools and colleges should open extension services.
(*e*) Needs of aged and retired should also be considered.

9. According to the author, the concept of 'lifetime education' is
(*a*) as old as traditional education
(*b*) still in formative stages
(*c*) in vogue in advanced countries
(*d*) not practical
(*e*) not desirable

10. Integrating the concepts of lifelong learning with the educational structure would imply
(*a*) closing down conventional schools and colleges
(*b*) longer durations for all formal courses
(*c*) simple rearrangement of present educational organisations
(*d*) more weightage for actual performance than real understanding
(*e*) None of these

11. In the context of the passage, what is the meaning of the sentence 'The writing is already on the wall'?
(*a*) Everything is uncertain now-a-days.
(*b*) Changes have already taken place.
(*c*) The signs of change are already visible.
(*d*) You cannot change the future.
(*e*) It is a mysterious process.

12. Which of the following is most nearly the same in meaning as the word 'meeting' as used in the passage?
(*a*) approaching (*b*) contacting
(*c*) introducing (*d*) representing
(*e*) satisfying

13. Which of the following is most opposite in meaning to the word 'integral' as used in the passage?
(*a*) essential (*b*) independent
(*c*) major (*d*) minor
(*e*) unwilling

14. Which of the following is most opposite in meaning to the phrase 'a far cry' as used in the passage?
(*a*) A reality
(*b* A theoretical suggestion
(*c*) Very funny
(*d*) Next to impossible
(*e*) None of these

Passage 11 **(R.B.I. 1990)**

Recent advances in science and technology have made it possible for geneticists to find out abnormalities in the unborn foetus and take remedial action to rectify some defects which would otherwise prove to be fatal to the child. Though genetic engineering is still at its infancy, scientists can now predict with greater accuracy a genetic disorder. It is not yet an exact science since they are not in a position to predict when exactly a genetic disorder will set in. While they have not yet been able to change the genetic order of the gene in germs, they are optimistic and are *holding out* that in the near future they might be successful in achieving this *feat*. They have, however, acquired the ability in manipulating tissue cells. However, genetic mis-information can sometimes be damaging for it may adversely affect people psychologically. Genetic information may lead to a tendency to brand some people as inferiors. Genetic information can therefore be *abused* and its application in deciding the sex of the foetus and its subsequent abortion is now hotly debated on ethical lines. But on this issue geneticists cannot be *squarely* blamed though this *charge* has often been levelled at them. It is mainly a societal problem. At present genetic engineering is a costly process of detecting disorders but scientists hope to reduce the costs when technology becomes more advanced. This is why much progress in this area has been possible in scientifically advanced and rich countries like the U.S.A., U.K. and Japan. It remains to be seen if in the future this science will lead to the development of a race of supermen or will be able to *obliterate* disease from this world.

1. Which of the following is the same in meaning as the phrase 'holding out' as used in the passage?
(*a*) catching (*b*) expounding
(*c*) sustaining (*d*) restraining
(*e*) controlling

2. According to the passage, the question of abortion is
(*a*) ignored (*b*) hotly debated
(*c*) unanswered

(*d*) left to the scientists to decide
(*e*) already settled

3. Which of the following is true regarding the reasons for progress in genetic engineering?
(*a*) It has become popular to abort female foetuses.
(*b*) Human beings are extremely interested in heredity.
(*c*) Economically sound and scientifically advanced countries can provide the infrastructure for such research.
(*d*) Poor countries desperately need genetic information.

4. Which of the following is the same in meaning as the word 'obliterate' as used in the passage?
(*a*) wipe off (*b*) eradicate
(*c*) give birth to (*d*) wipe out
(*e*) very literate

5. Which of the following is the opposite in meaning to the word 'charged' as used in the passage?
(*a*) calm (*b*) disturbed
(*c*) discharged (*d*) settled
(*e*) peaceful

6. Which of the following is not true of the genetic engineering movement?
(*a*) Possibility of abuse
(*b*) It is confronted by ethical problems.
(*c*) Increased tendency to manipulate gene cells
(*d*) Acquired ability to detect genetic disorders in unborn babies
(*e*) Acquired ability to manipulate tissue cells

7. Which of the following is the same in meaning as the word 'feat' as used in the passage?
(*a*) process (*b*) focus (*c*) fact
(*d*) possibility (*e*) goal

8. Why, according to the author, is genetic misinformation severely damaging?
A. The cost involved is very high.
B. Some people are unjustly branded as inferior.
(*a*) A only (*b*) B only
(*c*) Both A and B (*d*) Neither A nor B
(*e*) Either A or B

9. In the passage, 'abused' means
(*a*) insulted (*b*) talked about
(*c*) killed (*d*) misused
(*e*) changed

10. At present genetic engineering can rectify all genetic disorders. Is it?
(*a*) Yes (*b*) No
(*c*) It can do so only in some cases

11. Which of the following, according to the author, are the short-comings of genetics in becoming an exact science?
A. Technicians will not be able to determine the time when genetic disorder will set in.
B. Technicians have not been able to manipulate germ cells.
(*a*) A only (*b*) B only
(*c*) Both A and B (*d*) Either A or B
(*e*) Neither A nor B

12. Which of the following is the same in meaning as the word 'squarely' as used in the passage?
(*a*) rigidly (*b*) firmly
(*c*) directly (*d*) at right angle
(*e*) straight

13. Which of the following is not true, according to the passage?
(*a*) Society is not affected by the research in genetic engineering.
(*b*) Genetic engineers are not able to say some things with certainty.
(*c*) If genetic information is not properly handled, it will create problems.
(*d*) Manipulation of genes is presently done only in tissue cell.
(*e*) Scientists recognise the possibilities of abuse of information related to genetics.

14. According to the author, the present state of knowledge about heredity has made geneticists
(*a*) introspective (*b*) accusative
(*c*) arrogant (*d*) optimistic
(*e*) reckless

15. What is the tone of the author in the last sentence of the passage?
(*a*) resignation (*b*) cautious
(*c*) relief (*d*) concern
(*e*) unconcern

Passage 12

Political education may be defined as the preparation of a citizen to take well informed, responsible and sustained action for participation in the national struggle for the realization of the socio-economic objectives of the country. The overriding socio-economic objectives in India are the abolition of poverty and the creation of a modern democratic, secular and socialist society in place of the present traditional, feudal, hierarchical and inegalitarian one.

Under the British rule, the Congress leaders argued that political education was an important part of education and refused to accept the official view that education and politics should not be mixed with one another. But when they came to power in 1947 they almost adopted the British policy and began to talk of education being defiled by politics. 'Hands off education' was the call to political parties. But inspite of it, political infiltra- tion into the educational system has greatly increased in the sense that different political parties vie with each other to capture the minds of teachers and students. The wise academicians wanted political support, without political interfer- ence. What we have actually received is infinite political interference with little genuine political support. This interference with the educational system by political parties for their own ulterior motives is no political education at all; and with the all round growth of elitism, it is hardly a matter for surprise that real political education within the school system (which really means the creation of a commitment to social transformation) has been even weaker than in the pre-independence period.

At the same time, the freedom struggle came to an end and the major non-formal agency of political education disappeared. The press could and did provide some political education. But it did not utilise the opportunity to the full and the strangle hold of vested interests continued to dominate it. The same can be said of political parties as well as of other institutions and agencies outside the school system which can be expected to provide political education. All things considered, it appears that we have made no progress in genuine political education in the post-independence period and have even slided back in some respects. For instance, the education system has become even more elite-oriented. Patriotism has become the first casualty. Gandhiji gave us the courage to oppose government when it was wrong, in a disciplined fashion and on basic principles. (he believed the means to be as important as the ends) and taught us to work among the poor people for mobilizing and organizing them. Today, we have even lost the courage to fight on basic issues in a disciplined manner because agitational and anarchic politics for individual, group or party aggrandisement has become common. The education system of today continues to support domination of the privileged groups and domestication of the under-privileged ones. The situation will not change unless we take vigorous steps to provide genuine political education on an adequate scale. This is one of the major educational reforms we need; and if it is not carried out, mere linear expansion of the existing system of formal education will only support the status quo and hamper radical social transformation.

1. Which is the major pitfall of the present education system?

(*a*) It is mainly represented by the downtrodden masses.

(*b*) It perpetuates the domination of the privileged few.

(*c*) It is based on the British model of education.

(*d*) It is highly hierarchical and inegalitarian in nature.

(*e*) It does not inculcate values among the students.

2. Which of the following is true in the context of the passage?

(*a*) British rulers wanted Indian education system to be influenced by politics.

(*b*) Academic institutions receive genuine political support.

(*c*) Real political education should aim at creating an elitist society.

(*d*) The Indian press has been under the influence of privileged groups.

(*e*) Our education system caters to the needs of the masses.

3. Which word is nearly same in meaning as 'defile' as used in the passage?

(*a*) disparage (*b*) tarnish

(*c*) degenerate (*d*) criticise

(*e*) contaminate

4. What should be the ultimate objective of political education?

(*a*) To foster all round growth of elitism

(*b*) To bring quantitative change in the entire education system

(*c*) To create an egalitarian society

(*d*) To prepare students with high intellectual acumen

(*e*) To provide genuine support to educational institutions

5. According to the passage, what is the main contribution of Mahatma Gandhi to the field of political education?

(*a*) He spread 'political literacy' among the people through non-formal political education.
(*b*) He emphasized the need of keeping education free from political interference.
(*c*) He taught us agitational and anarchic politics in a disciplined manner.
(*d*) He made us believe that our political end should be compatible with the means.

6. What was the policy of the ruling party regarding political education immediately after independence?
(*a*) Education should keep itself clean of politics.
(*b*) Political education should be imparted through formal means.
(*c*) Press should take up the responsibility of imparting political education.
(*d*) Political education should not be devoid of socio-economic realities.
(*e*) Political parties should impart political education through formal means.

7. Which of the following statements is not true?
(*a*) The spirit of patriotism is on the verge of extinction.
(*b*) Political parties provide proper political education.
(*c*) We do not have courage to fight on basic issues.
(*d*) Freedom struggle helped educate people politically.
(*e*) Political education is necessary for bringing about social change.

8. How has politics been related to educational institutions after independence?
(*a*) They got political support devoid of political interference.
(*b*) They got almost no political support as well as political interference.
(*c*) They got political support at the cost of political interference.
(*d*) There was substantial interference without political support.
(*e*) None of these

9. According to the passage, political education in the real sense should
(*a*) impede the process of creating an ideal society
(*b*) develop people who will be committed to bring social change
(*c*) make political parties aware of the need of major educational reforms
(*d*) strengthen the traditional and feudal elements of the society
(*e*) develop patriotism among people of the privileged class

10. Which is the most opposite in meaning to the word 'hamper' as used in the passage?
(*a*) expedite (*b*) enhance (*c*) foster
(*d*) oppose (*e*) initiate

Passage 13 **(Bank P.O. 1994)**

In terms of the total energy consumed by different sectors, the largest consumer is understandably the industrial sector, which accounts for nearly half the total energy used in the country today. This is followed by the transport sector which consumes about 25%, the household sector (about 14%) and the agricultural sector (about 9%). This last sector has shown considerable increase in energy use over the last four decades. Among the primary fuels, the relative proportion of coal has dropped from nearly 80% to 40% and that of oil has gone up from 17% to 44% over the same period.

Total energy consumption in India today is equivalent to 291 million tons of oil of which 26% comes from wood. On a per capita basis it works out to about one litre of oil per day, which is extremely low by international standards. The future energy demand depends upon the level of development envisaged and also on the sections of people to be affected by it.

The energy disparity between the urban and the rural population is at present *as wide as* between nations on a *worldwide scale*. There is apparently a greater need to provide energy in the rural areas and to improve the efficiency of energy use than merely to increase the national figures for energy consumption limiting its use to those who are getting the bulk share already.

With the projected rate of population growth, improving upon the per capita energy consumption is a Herculean task as our coal reserves and the capacity to import oil cannot be increased beyond a point. *There is clearly no escape* from the utilisation of renewable energy sources in a big way if the gap between the desired levels of energy supply and available resources has to be kept at the minimum.

1. Which of the following styles has been adopted by the author?
(*a*) Unsubstantiated arguments and views
(*b*) Data-based, but coloured by socialism
(*c*) Highly subjective with bias for rural people
(*d*) Objective, descriptive, lacking clarity
(*e*) Data-based, objective, positive, solution oriented

2. The author is laying greater emphasis on which of the following?
A. Efficient use of energy
B. Increasing national indices for energy consumption
C. Controlling population growth
(*a*) Only A (*b*) Only B
(*c*) Only C (*d*) All the three
(*e*) Both B & C

3. Which of the following shows correctly the different sectors consuming energy arranged in ascending order?
I. Agriculture II. Household
III. Industrial IV. Transport
(*a*) I, IV, II, III (*b*) I, II, IV, III
(*c*) III, IV, II, I (*d*) III, II, I, IV
(*e*) None of these

4. According to the passage, the energy requirement of the future will be decided on the basis of which of the following?
A. Total energy already consumed by us in the past
B. Level of development of oil industry
C. Profile of the affected people
(*a*) Only A (*b*) Only B
(*c*) Only C (*d*) Both A & B
(*e*) Both B & C

5. 'There is clearly no escape' means
(*a*) there is also no solution to this.
(*b*) there is a way out, but it is ambiguous.
(*c*) there is a problem, but not without solution.
(*d*) there is hardly any alternative except
(*e*) there is more than one way.

6. The author feels that increasing per capita use of energy is
(*a*) not at all desirable
(*b*) a matter of great difficulty
(*c*) a routine matter
(*d*) rather difficult, but not impossible
(*e*) not easy but certainly achievable

7. Which of the following statements is true?
(*a*) Industrial sector uses 50% of total energy used in India.
(*b*) Energy consumption in India is 26% of world consumption.
(*c*) The household sector has shown considerable increase in energy use.
(*d*) Use of oil has increased from 40% to 80%.
(*e*) Import of oil to the extent required is quite possible.

8. 'The energy disparity ... as wide as ... worldwide scale', the first sentence of third paragraph means
(*a*) disparity in urban and rural is observed in all nations.
(*b*) in no other nation such disparity is observed.
(*c*) developed countries consume more energy than developing countries.
(*d*) worldwide scale is different for rural and urban areas.
(*e*) None of these

9. Which of the following has been suggested by the author as the best possible solution to overcome energy crisis?
(*a*) Exploration of oil reserves
(*b*) Maximisation of renewable sources
(*c*) Importing large quantities of coal
(*d*) Reducing share of bulk users
(*e*) Reducing the energy disparity between urban and rural areas

10. Which of the following has been mentioned as a major hurdle in enhancing per capita consumption of energy in India?
(*a*) Present level of development in India
(*b*) International norm of 1 litre of oil per day per person
(*c*) Disparity in use of energy in rural and urban areas
(*d*) Increased use of energy in Agricultural sector
(*e*) None of these

Passage 14

It is common knowledge that the root cause of our backwardness in most *fields* is illiteracy. Campaigns for the *eradication* of this drawback *gathered momentum* in the past four decades after independence. The results are, as expected, dramatic. However, while the percentage of literacy in India is going up, the number of illiterates has also been increasing, which is really incredible. Thus according to the 1991 census figures, there were 503 million illiterates in the country, 30 million more than in 1981. During the same period, the percentage of literacy went up from 34 to 39 percent. There is no need of any sophisticated technique to explain the cause of this paradox, as it is obviously the result of the rapid growth of population. The rapid growth of population has *outpaced* whatever little progress had been achieved in literacy. For instance, from 1971 to 1981, literacy increased at an annual average rate of 0.7 percent, while the country's population grew by 2.15 per cent every year. In the following decade the average rate of annual increase in literacy was 0.95 percent, whereas the population grew by almost 2.85 percent every year during that decade. But population explosion is not entirely responsible for the growing number of illiterates. The apathy of most states in failing to tackle the problem of adult illiteracy is also partly to blame. Till now, they have shown little awareness of the magnitude of the problem. Moreover, follow-up measures to prevent *neo-literates* from relapsing into illiteracy are just as important as the initial adult literacy campaigns. In this case too, the State Education authorities are negligent. Not sufficient provision has been made for 'continued education'. This can be done by setting up more rural libraries, adult schools and correspondence courses.

1. Which of the following appears unbelievable, according to the passage?
   (*a*) Growing illiteracy is owing to non-availability of reading facilities to rural masses.
   (*b*) Sufficient provision for continued education has not been made.
   (*c*) The increase in literacy percentage and also the increase in number of illiterates
   (*d*) Population explosion is the only reason for increase in the number of illiterates.
2. The term 'Neo-literate' as used in the passage refers to a person who
   (*a*) is not literate
   (*b*) has newly become literate
   (*c*) is a little literate
   (*d*) is a literate with no school education
   (*e*) is illiterate but capable of becoming literate with formal training
3. In the passage, the rapid growth of population has been attributed to
   (*a*) illiteracy
   (*b*) apathy of government officials
   (*c*) want of continued education
   (*d*) None of these
4. Which of the following statements is not true in the context of the passage?
   A. An effective check on population growth is the only solution for attainment of full literacy.
   B. The cause of the paradox mentioned in the passage can be explained by using sophisticated techniques.
   C. Adequate number of libraries and adult schools are not available in our country.
   (*a*) Only A (*b*) Only B (*c*) Only C
   (*d*) A & B (*e*) A & C
5. Which of the following is the same in meaning as the word 'outpaced' as used in the passage?
   (*a*) surpassed (*b*) nullified
   (*c*) ruled out (*d*) spoiled
6. Which of the following has been referred to as a paradox?
   (*a*) The literacy percentage increases and the number of illiterates decreases.
   (*b*) The literacy percentage increases in proportion to the rate of increase in population.
   (*c*) The government is sensitive to the problem only at the planning stage but not at the implementation stage.
   (*d*) The literacy percentage and the number of illiterates are both increasing.
7. According to the passage, the problem could have been tackled by which one or more of the following measures?
   A. Checking the growth of population
   B. Making the adult literacy campaign more effective
   C. Providing continued education to neo-literates
   (*a*) A & C (*b*) A & B
   (*c*) B & C (*d*) All of these
   (*e*) None of these
8. Which of the following is as important as the literacy campaign?
   (*a*) Checking the rapid growth of population
   (*b*) Starting correspondence courses and providing reading facilities
   (*c*) Awareness of the magnitude of the problem of illiteracy
   (*d*) Making sufficient provision for continued education

9. 'Eradication', as used in the passage means
(*a*) removal (*b*) destruction
(*c*) starvation (*d*) evaporation

10. Which of the following is true in the context of the passage?
(*a*) Continued education programmes are now adequately funded.
(*b*) All the State governments have now fully realised the problem of illiteracy.
(*c*) Literacy campaigns in the pre-independence period were more fruitful than the later ones.
(*d*) Literacy campaign achieved desired results in the post-independence period.

Passage 15

Economists, ethicists and business sages *persuade* us that honesty is the best policy, but their evidence is weak. We hoped to find data that would support their theories and thus, perhaps encourage higher standards of business behaviour. To our surprise, our pet theories failed to *stand up*. Treachery, we found, can pay. There is no compelling economic reason to tell the truth or keep one's word punishment for the treacherous in the real world is neither swift nor sure.

Honesty is, in fact, primarily a moral choice. Business people do tell themselves that, in the long run, they will do well by doing good. But there is little factual or logical basis for this conviction. Without values, without a basic preference for right over wrong, trust based on such self-delusion would crumble in the face of temptation. Most of us choose virtue because we want to believe in ourselves and have others' respect and belief in us.

And for this, we should be happy. We can be proud of a system in which people are honest because they want to be, not because they have to be. Materially, too, trust based on morality provides great advantages. It allows us to join in great and exciting enterprises that we could never undertake if we relied on economic incentives alone.

Economists tell us that trust is enforced in the market place through retaliation of reputation. If you violate a trust your victim is apt to seek revenge and others are likely to stop doing business with you, at least under favourable terms. A man or woman with a reputation for fair dealing will prosper. Therefore, profit maximizers are honest. This sounds plausible enough until you look for concrete examples. Cases that apparently demonstrate the awful consequences of trust turns out to be few and weak, while evidence that treachery can pay seems *compelling*.

1. What did the author find out about the theory that honesty is the best policy?
(*a*) It is a useless theory.
(*b*) It is correct on many occasions.
(*c*) It is correct for all businessmen.
(*d*) It is correct only occasionally.

2. Why does the author say that one can be proud of the present situation? Because people are
(*a*) respect seekers
(*b*) honest without compulsion
(*c*) unselfish (*d*) self respecting

3. What do economists and ethicists want us to believe?
(*a*) Businessmen are honest only at times.
(*b*) Businessmen should be honest at all times.
(*c*) Businessmen cannot be honest at all times.
(*d*) Businessmen turn dishonest at times.

4. Which is the material advantage which the author sees in being honest? It permits one to
(*a*) undertake activities which may not be economically attractive
(*b*) be honest for the sake of honesty alone
(*c*) make a lot of profit in various areas
(*d*) None of these

5. Which of the following is the same in meaning as 'persuade' as used in the passage?
(*a*) try to convince (*b*) cheat
(*c*) motivate (*d*) give assurance
(*e*) give opinion

6. Which of the following is false according to the passage?
(*a*) People are generally honest because it pays in the long run.
(*b*) Virtuous behaviour earns the self respect of others.
(*c*) Economists believe that all businessmen are dishonest.
(*d*) Generally people are honest to earn self-respect.

7. Why do businessmen, according to economists, remain honest? Because dishonest businessmen
(*a*) are flogged in the market place
(*b*) are always prosecuted
(*c*) can make more money
(*d*) cannot stay in business for long

8. The phrase 'stand up' as used in the passage means
(*a*) hold up (*b*) get up
(*c*) supported (*d*) get established

9. Which is the same in meaning as the word 'compelling' as used in the passage?
(*a*) coercive (*b*) binding
(*c*) forceful (*d*) mandatory

10. Which of the following best describes what the author is trying to point out through the last sentence of the passage 'Cases that .... compelling'?
(*a*) Economists predict correctly
(*b*) The consequences of dishonesty
(*c*) The contradictions in the real world
(*d*) Theories do not seem to be true

Passage 16 **(Bank P.O. 1995)**

Two principles are involved in the controversy about the presence of foreign-controlled media in the country; the free flow of ideas and images across national borders and the need to safeguard the national interest and preserve cultural autonomy. Both are valid but both are *at loggerheads* because each has been used to promote less lofty goals. The first principle conforms to a moral imperative; freedom of expression cannot *rhyme* with restrictions imposed by any government. But the free flow *rhetoric* also clouds the fact that the powerful Western, and especially American, media can and often do present, subtly or brazenly, news in a manner which promotes Western political, ideological and strategic interests. Besides, Western entertainment programmes present lifestyles and values cherished by traditional societies. All this explains why so many Indian newspapers, magazines and news agencies have sought protection from the courts to prevent foreign publications and news agencies from operating in the country. Their arguments are weak on two counts. As the bitter debate on a new world information and communication order demonstrated in the late seventies and early eighties, many of those who resent Western 'invasion' in the information and cultural fields are no great friends of democracy. Secondly, the threat of such an 'invasion' has been aired by those media groups in the developing countries who fear that their business interests will be harmed if Western groups, equipped with large financial and technological resources and superior management skills, are allowed to operate in the country *without let*.

The fear is valid but it goes against the gain of the economic reform programme. The presence of foreign newspapers and television channels will increase competition which, in course of time, can only lead to the upgradation of dynamic Indian newspapers and television channels even while they drive the rest out of the market. One way to strike a balance between the two *antagonistic* principles would be to allow foreign media entry into the country, provided the Indian state treats them on par with the domestic media on all fronts. On the import of technology, for instance, foreign media cannot be allowed duty concessions denied to their Indian counterparts. Foreign media will also have to face the legal consequences should they run foul of Indian laws. Why, for example, should the BBC, or Time magazine or The Economist get away with showing a map of Kashmir which is *at variance* with the office Indian map? Why should they go scot-free when they allow secessionists and terrorists to air their views without giving the government the right of reply? Or when they depict sexually explicit scenes which would otherwise not be cleared by the Censor Board? Since the government can do precious little in the matter, especially about satellite broadcasts, what if it should consider attaching the properties of the offending parties? Demands of this kind are bound to be voiced unless New Delhi makes it clear to the foreign media that they will have to respect Indian *susceptibilities* especially where it concerns the country's integrity and its culture. It may be able to derive some inspiration from France's successful attempts in the recent GATT to protect its cinematographic industry.

1. Which of the following is one of the points weakening the argument to prevent entry of foreign media?

(*a*) The foreign media may not be treated on par with the domestic media.
(*b*) Such entry would be against traditional culture.
(*c*) The arguments being put forth are at loggerheads.
(*d*) The threat being voiced by those whose business will be harmed by such an entry.
(*e*) None of these.

2. Which of the following has been the major recommendation regarding the entry of foreign media?
(*a*) Allow entry provided they do not ask for duty concessions on import of technology.
(*b*) Allow entry treating them on par with domestic media.
(*c*) It should be welcomed without putting any restrictions.
(*d*) It should not be allowed.
(*e*) None of these.

3. Which of the following means 'without let'?
(*a*) without confinement
(*b*) without restrictions
(*c*) with no difficulty
(*d*) with strings
(*e*) conducive environment

4. Which of the following means 'at loggerheads' as used in the passage?
(*a*) opposite to each other
(*b*) unsuited to each other
(*c*) in league with
(*d*) unimportant
(*e*) out of place

5. Why should the entry of foreign media harm local interests?
(*a*) Different sets of laws and rules were made applicable for foreign media.
(*b*) Economic reform programmes will get a setback.
(*c*) The cultural heritage will be lost.
(*d*) They are better equipped— managerially and technologically.
(*e*) None of these

6. In the controversy involving two principles regarding allowing foreign media, which of the following is against its entry?
(*a*) Governmental restrictions
(*b*) Preserve culture
(*c*) Security across national borders
(*d*) Western ideology
(*e*) Free flow of ideas

7. Which of the following will be the impact of increasing competition?
(*a*) It will improve Indian newspapers and television.
(*b*) The domestic media will not be able to withstand it.
(*c*) The Indian news agencies will seek protection from the court.
(*d*) The foreign media will not be allowed duty concessions on import of technology.
(*e*) None of these

8. Which of the following means 'at variance' as used in the passage?
(*a*) at large (*b*) in conformity
(*c*) variable (*d*) discrepancy
(*e*) differing

9. A country has been cited as having succeeded in protecting which of the following?
(*a*) News Agencies (*b*) Television
(*c*) GATT (*d*) Cultural relations
(*e*) None of these

10. According to the passage, which media in particular promotes Western interests?
(*a*) Western (*b*) Foreign (*c*) American
(*d*) French (*e*) None of these

11. Which of the following seems to be the most likely purpose of writing this passage?
(*a*) To highlight the exploitation by developed nations
(*b*) To make the public aware of the technological and managerial superiority of western media
(*c*) To criticise foreign media
(*d*) To highlight the steps and caution to be taken about the entry of foreign media
(*e*) To prevent foreign media from entering our country

Passage 17 **(Bank P.O. 1995)**

The recent passage of the Bill, on the transplantation of human organs, by Parliament, is a long-overdue measure aimed at curbing widespread trafficking in organs, especially kidneys. As the only country where kidneys can be transplanted from donors unrelated to the patient, India, and notably Bombay, has gained international notoriety as the capital of the organ trade. Wealthy patients from India and abroad, unscrupulous doctors and rapacious brokers have made this a multi-crore racket in which the only loser is the impoverished donor *parting with* an organ for small money. The legislation strikes at such exploitative transactions by stipulating that blood relations and spouses are the only live donors from whom kidneys can be transplanted, and making the buying and selling of human organs a cognisable offence. By allowing the transport of cadaver organs, the Act not only opens new avenues in the treatment of renal failure, where the availability of donor kidneys falls far short of demand, but paves the way for liver transplants for which expertise exists in India. The statutory recognition of brain stem death, which is accepted medical practice the world over, widens the scope of cadaver transplants by making 'beating heart' cadavers another source for donor organs.

True, the mere enactment of such legislation cannot put an end to an entrenched practice that *thrives on patronage* from sections of the medical community, and political and public apathy. The delay of nearly two years between the introduction of the Bill and its passage and the attempts of people with vested interests to introduce certain dubious 'amendments' are an indication of what the law is up against. The effectiveness of the law will depend, therefore, on the state's determination to implement it through vigilant monitoring. The provisions for cadaveric transplants will remain on paper in the absence of public education to encourage the voluntary donation of bodies and organs overcoming religious taboos, and the setting up of institutional facilities for organ retrieval and storage. Most of all, the law *rests on* the realisation by medical professionals that ethical and humane values must *prevail over* other considerations. The removal of organs from unrelated donors is almost invariably a transfer of health from the poor and weak to the rich. It cannot be defended on any ground.

1. Which of the following means 'thrives on patronage'?
   (*a*) supports the practice
   (*b*) confusion by the patron
   (*c*) prospers on support
   (*d*) fails in spite of support
   (*e*) disintegrates
2. Which of the following is the meaning of the phrase 'parting with' as used in the passage?
   (*a*) sacrificing (*b*) fall in line
   (*c*) coming together (*d*) partition into two
   (*e*) dining with
3. Which of the following is the reason for Bombay gaining international notoriety?
   (*a*) Human organs like kidney are smuggled here.
   (*b*) There is no legislation against kidney transplantation.
   (*c*) There are international underworld gangs operating.
   (*d*) Even patients from other countries come here for kidney transplantation donated by poor people.
   (*e*) None of these
4. Which of the following is one of the features of the Bill?
   (*a*) It allows for transplant of only cadaver organs.
   (*b*) Hefty sum is to be paid to the donors.
   (*c*) Total ban on kidney transplantation
   (*d*) Only blood relations and spouses can be the live donors.
   (*e*) None of these
5. Which of the following would be an impediment in getting donation of cadaver organs?
   (*a*) Storage problems
   (*b*) Religious taboos
   (*c*) Absence of adequate legislation
   (*d*) Effective implementation of law
   (*e*) None of these
6. How much time was spent in drafting the Bill before its introduction?
   (*a*) 2 years (*b*) 3 years
   (*c*) 4 years (*d*) Not specified
   (*e*) None of these
7. Which of the following is not true in the context of the passage?
   (*a*) There is a widespread organ trafficking of livers.
   (*b*) India does not have expertise for liver transplantation.
   (*c*) The problems of transplantation of human organs have been unnecessarily highlighted.
   (*d*) The Bill on human organs transplantation was needed much earlier.
   (*e*) The final Bill has not been passed so far.
8. Which of the following means 'prevail over' as used in the passage?
   (*a*) spread along (*b*) predominate
   (*c*) triumph (*d*) insist upon
   (*e*) convince
9. Which of the following means 'rests on' as used in the passage?
   (*a*) based on (*b*) depends on

(*c*) lingers along (*d*) puts an end to
(*e*) support

10. Which of the following can be correctly inferred from the passage about kidney transplantation in other countries?
(*a*) There is no legislation against kidney transplantation in some other countries.
(*b*) There is a ban on kidney transplantation in some of the countries.
(*c*) In other countries, kidney is transplanted only if it is donated by the patient's relative.
(*d*) There are unscrupulous doctors in other countries also.
(*e*) None of these

Passage 18

The political system always dominates the entire social scene; and hence those who wield political power are generally able to control all the different social sub-systems and manipulate them to their own advantage. The social groups in power, therefore, have always manipulated the education systems, especially when these happen to depend upon the State for their very existence, to strengthen and perceptuate their own privileged position. But herein lies a contradiction. For the very realization of their selfish ends, the social groups in power are compelled to extend the benefits of these educational systems to the under-privileged groups also. The inevitable task is generally performed with three precautions abundantly taken care of :

A. the privileged groups continue to be the principal beneficiaries of the educational system, dominate the higher stages of education or the hard core of prestigious and quality institutions or the most useful of courses, so as to safeguard their dominant position of leadership in all walks of life;

B. the system is so operated that under-privileged groups can utilize it only marginally in real terms and the bulk of them become either drop-outs or push-outs and get reconciled to their own interior status in society; and

C. the few from the weaker sections that survive and succeed in spite of all the handicaps are generally co-opted within the system to prevent dissatisfaction. But education is essentially a liberating force so that, as time passes some under-privileged groups do manage to become aware of the reality, the number of the educated persons soon becomes too large to be fully co-opted, and many able individuals among them strive to organize, and liberate the weak and the under-privileged. The resultant awareness of the people, combined with suitable organization necessary leads to adjustment in the social structure and to an increase in vertical mobility so that new groups begin to share power. Eventually, other social changes also follow and the traditional, inegalitarian and hierarchical social structure tends to be replaced by another which is more modern, less hierarchical and more egalitarian. The educational system, therefore, is never politically neutral, and it always performs three functions simultaneously viz, it helps the privileged to dominate, domesticates the underprivileged to their own status in society, and also tends to liberate the oppressed. Which of these functions shall dominate and to what extent, depends mostly on one crucial factor, viz, the quality and quantity of the political education which the system provides or upon its 'political content'.

The developments in Indian society, polity and education during the past 175 years should be viewed against the back ground of this broad philosophy. From very ancient times, the Indian society has always been elitist and power, wealth and education were mostly confined to the upper castes of the society. What is important to note is that the system has an infinite capacity to adjust or to absorb and, for that very reason, it is extremely resistant to any radical transformation. The social system continued to exist almost unchanged till the British administrators began to lay the foundation of the modern system of education.

1. Which of the following statements is not true in the context of the passage?
(*a*) The privileged groups try to deprive the 'have nots' of the real benefits of education.
(*b*) The education system is never politically biased.

(*c*) Educational system tends to enlighten the minds of the under privileged.
(*d*) The privileged class depends upon the Government for their survival.
(*e*) Credit for bringing modern system of education goes to Britishers.

2. According to the passage, the Indian society has always been
(*a*) politically neutral
(*b*) insensitive to the needs of elite groups
(*c*) conscious about the sufferings of the underprivileged
(*d*) less hierarchical
(*e*) None of these

3. Which of the following is the most opposite in meaning to the word 'radical' as used in the passage?
(*a*) superficial (*b*) simple
(*c*) slow (*d*) narrow

4. How does education work for ameliorating the lot of the under privileged classes?
(*a*) It encourages them to domesticate the privileged people.
(*b*) It helps the underprivileged people to dominate others.
(*c*) Some educated persons from this class organise and liberate the weak people.
(*d*) It helps them to achieve higher goals in life.

5. In the context of the passage, which of the following statements is true regarding those who control political power?
(*a*) They facilitate the upward mobility of the underprivileged classes.
(*b*) They try to establish a just social order.
(*c*) They facilitate the upward mobility of the privileged classes.
(*d*) They try to control all the different social sub systems.

6. Sharing of power by new groups is an outcome of
(*a*) increase in the vertical mobility of the underprivileged groups
(*b*) a liberal democratic approach of the privileged class
(*c*) the total replacement of the traditional social structure by a modern one
(*d*) a politically neutral educational system

7. According to the passage, why do the majority of underprivileged groups become drop-outs?
(*a*) They constantly suffer from the feeling of inferiority.
(*b*) The system is so manipulated that they cannot utilize it meaningfully.
(*c*) They do not possess the required intellectual potential to survive in the educational system.
(*d*) The privileged class continues to be the major beneficiary of the system.

8. According to the passage, the social groups in power have manipulated the educational system because
(*a*) they wanted to make it politically neutral.
(*b*) they wanted to give maximum benefits to the underprivileged.
(*c*) they wanted to introduce social changes through the educational system.
(*d*) they wanted to preserve their special status.
(*e*) None of these

9. The Indian social system is resistant to the major changes because
(*a*) it is basically elitist.
(*b*) it can absorb social changes without changing its basic frame-work.
(*c*) it is extremely traditional and conservative.
(*d*) power, wealth and education are mostly confined to the upper classes.

10. According to the passage, social groups in power extend the benefits of education to the under-privileged groups because
(*a*) they want to achieve their selfish objectives.
(*b*) they want to create an egalitarian society.
(*c*) they have realized that the growth of a nation depends upon the spread of education.
(*d*) they want to abdicate their dominant position of leadership in all walks of life.

Passage 19 **(NABARD, 1994)**

Though the U.S. prides itself on being a leader in the world community, a recent report shows that it lags far behind other industrialised countries in meeting the needs of its youngest and most *vulnerable* citizens. The U.S. has a higher infant mortality rate, a higher proportion of low birthweight babies, a smaller proportion of babies immunised against childhood diseases and a much higher rate of adolescent pregnancies. These findings, described as a "quiet crisis" requiring immediate and far-reaching action, appeared in a report prepared by a task force of educators, doctors, politicians and business people. According to the report , a fourth of the nation's 12 million infants and toddlers live in poverty. As many as half *confront* risk factors that could harm their ability to develop intellectually, physically and socially. Child immunisations are too low, more children are born into poverty, more are in *substandard* care while their parents work and more are being raised by single parents. When taken together, these and other risk factors can lead to educational and health problems that are much harder and more costly to reverse.

The crisis begins in the womb with unplanned parenthood. Women with unplanned pregnancies are less likely to seek pre-natal care. In the U.S. 80% of teenage pregnancies and 56% of all pregnancies are unplanned. The problems continue after birth where unplanned pregnancies and *unstable* partnerships often go hand in hand. Since 1950, the number of single parent families has nearly tripled. More than 25 percent of all births today are to unmarried mothers. As the number of single parent families grows and more women enter the work force, infants and toddlers are increasingly in the care of people other than their parents.

Most disturbingly, recent statistics show that American parents are increasingly neglecting or *abusing* their children. In only four years from 1987-1991 the number of children in foster care increased by over 50 percent. Babies under the age of one are the fastest growing category of children entering foster care. The crisis affects children under the age of three most *severely*, the report says. Yet, it is this period-from infancy through preschool years-that sets the stage for a child's future.

1. The main focus of the passage is on the plight of
(*a*) orphaned children
(*b*) teenage mothers
(*c*) low birth weight babies
(*d*) unwed mothers
(*e*) None of these

2. Children falling in which age group are most severely affected by the 'quiet crisis'?
(*a*) Below 1 year (*b*) Below 3 years
(*c*) Between 2 & 3 years
(*d*) Between 1 & 3 years
(*e*) None of these

3. Which of the following does not constitute the 'quiet crisis' in the U.S. as per the task force report?
(*a*) Lower proportion of new born babies with normal weight
(*b*) Higher incidence of adolescent girls becoming mothers
(*c*) Lower rate of babies surviving childhood diseases
(*d*) Larger proportion of babies who are deprived of immunisation
(*e*) Increasing cases of teenage couples getting divorced

4. Which of the following statements is not true in the context of the passage?
(*a*) The number of single-parent families today is approximately three times that four decades ago.
(*b*) The number of children in the U.S. entering foster care has decreased after 1991.
(*c*) In the U.S., the number of infants living in poverty is about 3 million.
(*d*) Only 20 percent of all the pregnancies in the U.S. are planned.
(*e*) About 6 million infants in the U.S. are likely to develop educational and health problems.

5. The number of children born to married mothers in the U.S. is approximately how many times the number of children born to unwed mothers?
(*a*) 1.5 times (*b*) 2 times
(*c*) 3 times (*d*) 3.5 times
(*e*) Not mentioned in the passage

6. Children born out of unplanned pregnancies are highly vulnerable because
(*a*) they are raised by single parents.
(*b*) their parents are mostly poor.
(*c*) they are mostly malnourished.
(*d*) they are less likely to receive prenatal care.
(*e*) their parents are emotionally immature.

7. Decide which of the following factors is/are responsible for the physical, intellectual and social under-development of infants in the U.S.?

A. Illiteracy of parents
B. Lack of parental care
C. Poverty
(*a*) Only A (*b*) Only B
(*c*) Only C (*d*) Both A & C
(*e*) Both B& C

8. An increasing number of infants in the U.S. are in foster care on account of
(*a*) an increasing number of single parent families with the female member working
(*b*) an increasing number of women maintaining the status of unwed motherhood and becoming economically independent
(*c*) an increasing number of employed couples who are required to stay apart
(*d*) an increasing number of women getting divorced and abandoning their babies
(*e*) an increasing number of parents who lack awareness about baby-care

9. The task force report seems to be based on the data pertaining to the period
(*a*) 1987-91
(*b*) 1950 onwards till date
(*c*) 1987 onwards till date
(*d*) 1950-91 (*e*) 1991 onwards till date

Directions (Q 10-12) : *Choose the word which is most nearly the same in meaning as the given word as used in the passage.*

10. CONFRONT
(*a*) Face (*b*) Tolerate
(*c*) Succumb (*d*) Eliminate
(*e*) Oppose

11. VULNERABLE
(*a*) Insecure (*b*) Indispensable
(*c*) Risky (*d*) Promising
(*e*) Delicate

12. ABUSING
(*a*) Cursing (*b*) Beating
(*c*) Ill treating (*d*) Accusing
(*e*) Oppressing

Directions (Q. 13-15) : *Choose the word which is most opposite in meaning to the given word as used in the passage.*

13. SEVERELY
(*a*) Drastically (*b*) Intensely
(*c*) Minutely (*d*) Normally
(*e*) Slightly

14. UNSTABLE
(*a*) Changing (*b*) Steady
(*c*) Stagnant (*d*) Confined
(*e*) Constant

15. SUBSTANDARD
(*a*) Impoverished (*b*) Compassionate
(*c*) Excellent (*e*) Valuable
(*d*) Beneficial

Passage 20

The history of literature really began long before man learned to write. Dancing was the earliest of the arts. Man danced for joy round his primitive camp fire after the defeat and slaughter of his enemy. He yelled and shouted as he danced and gradually the yells and shouts became coherent and caught the measure of the dance and thus the first war song was sung. As the idea of God developed prayers were framed. The songs and prayers became traditional and were repeated from one generation to another, each generation adding something of its own.

As man slowly grew more civilised, he was compelled to invent some method of writing by three urgent necessities. There were certain things that it was dangerous to forget and which, therefore, had to be recorded. It was often necessary to communicate with persons who were some distance away and it was necessary to protect one's property by making tools, cattle and so on, in some distinctive manner. So man taught himself to write and having learned to write purely for utilitarian reasons he used this new method for preserving his war songs and his prayers. Of course, among these ancient peoples, there were only a very few individuals who learned to write, and only a few could read what was written.

1. Before man invented writing
(*a*) literature was passed on by word of mouth.
(*b*) prayers were considered literature.
(*c*) literature was just singing and dancing.
(*d*) there was no literature.

2. As for the war songs and prayers each generation
(*a*) added something of its own to the stock
(*b*) blindly repeated the songs and prayers
(*c*) composed its own songs and prayers.
(*d*) repeated what has handed down to it

3. The first war-song
(*a*) was inspired by God
(*b*) developed spontaneously

(*c*) was a song traditionally handed down
(*d*) was composed by leading dancers

4. The war song evolved out of
(*a*) creative inspiration
(*b*) there was no literature
(*c*) artistic urge
(*d*) yelling and shouting

5. Man invented writing because he wanted
(*a*) to be artistic
(*b*) to write war song
(*c*) to write literature
(*d*) to record and communicate

6. The word 'measure' in the context of the passage means
(*a*) weight (*b*) rhythm
(*c*) size (*d*) quantity

Passage 21 **(I. Tax & Central Excise, 1994)**

The stock-taking done at the first national convention on consumer protection served to highlight the areas that called for special attention to sustain the momentum of the movement as genuine forum for safeguarding the people's interests. Spreading awareness about the rights of the consumers and the relief open to them in case they did not get their money's worth of goods and services has rightly been identified as the first priority. While this may not be a difficult task in urban areas, where the movement is concentrated at present, taking it to the vast rural hinterland calls for a multi-media approach in which radio and television have a crucial role to play. The involvement of the 500-odd consumer organisations in the country in publicising the concept of fair trade practices and the remedies available against their violation will prove rewarding, if the message is conveyed through village bodies.

Government efforts remain confined at best to setting up the infrastructure after the formal launch of the movement with the enactment of the Consumer Protection Act. The mounting backlog of cases in consumer courts, points to the need for toning up the district level redressal machinery.

The main objective of the movement is the creation of a culture that denies place in the market for products that are not consumer friendly. This is possible only if consumer bodies take over the watchdog role performed by the Government till now and exercise social control over the market to see that the benefits of liberalisation are not reaped by traders alone. But the plea to industry to exercise self-regulation and maintain minimum standards of quality and devise appropriate pricing is bound to go unheeded unless strict measures are taken to ensure compliance. **(I. Tax, 1994)**

1. The first national convention on Consumer Protection has
(*a*) highlighted the areas for special attention
(*b*) spread awareness about consumer rights
(*c*) specified in relief open to the consumer
(*d*) given it a momentum

2. Consumer Protection Act proposes to give the consumer protection against
(*a*) highly priced substandard goods
(*b*) cheating by selling substandard goods
(*c*) not getting his money's worth
(*d*) denial of relief if the product is not upto the mark

3. Government contributed to the Consumer Protection Movement by
(*a*) toning up a district level redressal machinery
(*b*) clearing the backlog cases in the consumer court
(*c*) setting by infrastructure
(*d*) enactment of the Consumer Protection Act

4. Spreading Consumer Protection Movement to the rural areas needs
(*a*) official patronage
(*b*) a multi-media approach
(*c*) consumer organisation to canvass this
(*d*) message to be conveyed by village bodies

5. Role of consumer bodies is
(*a*) To maintain minimum standards of quality
(*b*) To function as a watchdog
(*c*) To make a plea to industry to exercise self control
(*d*) To exercise social control over the market

Passage 22

Power and possession have been *central* pursuits of modern civilisation for a long time. They blocked out or distorted other features of the western renaissance (revival) which promised so much for humanity. What people have been and are still being taught to prize are money, success, control over the lives of others, acquisition of more and more objects. Modern social, political, and economic systems, whether capitalist, fascist or communist, reject in their working the basic principle that the free and creative unfoldment of every man, woman and child is the true measure of the worth of any society. Such infoldment requires understanding and imagination, integrity and compassion, cooperation among people and harmony between the human species and the *rest* of nature. Acquisitiveness and the pursuit of power have made the modern man an aggressor against everything that is non-human, an exploiter and appressor of those who are poor, meek and unorganised, a pathological type which hates and distrusts the world and suffers from both acute loneliness and false pride.

The need for a new renaissance is *deeply* felt by those sensitive and conscientious men and women who not only perceive the dimensions of the crisis of our age but who also realise that only through conscious and cooperative human effort may this crisis be *met* and probably even overcome.

1. The author appears to be advocating which of the following approaches to be adopted by the society?
(*a*) Capitalistic (*b*) Communist
(*c*) Humanistic (*d*) Authoritarian
(*e*) Socialist

2. Which of the following best describes the behaviour of modern man?
(*a*) Imaginative and sympathetic
(*b*) Cruel and greedy
(*c*) Conscientious and cooperative
(*d*) Perceptive and creative
(*e*) Seeker of truth and non-violence

3. According to the passage, why has modern man turned out as an enemy of everything that is non-human?
(*a*) He hates and distrusts other human beings.
(*b*) Non-human have refused cooperation to human beings.
(*c*) He has been dominated by drives of acquisitiveness and power.
(*d*) He consciously practises spirit of cooperation.
(*e*) None of these

4. Which of the following statements is not true in context of the given passage?
(*a*) Power and possession go hand in hand.
(*b*) There is a need for a new renaissance.
(*c*) Poor and weak people are oppressed by the modern man.
(*d*) The modern man is not individualist.
(*e*) Western renaissance had held so much promise for the mankind.

5. The real attainment of any society can be adjudged by which of the following?
(*a*) The encouragement for acquisitive tendencies
(*b*) Total victimisation of conscientious persons
(*c*) The degree of freedom for pursuing more and more power
(*d*) Strict adherence to authoritarian structure
(*e*) None of these

6. Which of the following is one of the requirements bringing out the best in man?
(*a*) Money (*b*) Success
(*c*) Power (*d*) Understanding
(*e*) Acquisitiveness

7. The western renaissance could not make total impact on today's humanity because
(*a*) it was conceptually weak.
(*b*) it was against basic principle.
(*c*) conscientious men opposed it.
(*d*) old civilisation was based on acquisitiveness and control over others.
(*e*) None of these

8. The author hopes that the present crisis can be solved by
(*a*) devoted individual efforts
(*b*) different political systems
(*c*) purpose and collective human efforts
(*d*) spiritually developed individuals
(*e*) powerful elite human beings

9. The modern value systems encourage the importance of which one of the following?
(*a*) Craving for power and possession
(*b*) Basic respect for all individuals
(*c*) Spiritual development of all individuals
(*d*) Spirit of inquiry and knowledge
(*e*) Recognition of freedom and equality

10. Which of the following is most opposite in meaning to the word 'central' as used in the passage?
(*a*) Lateral (*b*) Inadequate
(*c*) Peripheral (*d*) Major
(*e*) Insignificant

11. Which of the following is most nearly the same in meaning as the word 'rest' as used in the passage?
(*a*) Partial (*b*) Remaining

(*c*) Relax (*d*) All
(*e*) Everything

12. Which of the following is most opposite in meaning to the word 'deeply' as used in the passage?
(*a*) Widely (*b*) Superficially
(*c*) Wrongly (*d*) Openly
(*e*) Intensely

13. Which of the following is most nearly the same in meaning as the word 'met' as used in the passage?
(*a*) Introduced (*b*) Found
(*c*) Dealt with (*d*) Discovered
(*e*) Satisfied with

Passage 23 **(Bank P.O. 1994)**

What is the future which awaits our children? The underlying assumption of the question that Indian children have a common future is itself dubious. It can legitimately be asked whether a student who is well-fed, attending a boarding school in the salubrious climate of the hills, and learning to use computers has any future in common with a malnourished child who goes to a school with no black boards, if indeed he does go to school. The latter may have no worthwhile future at all. And it might be worthwhile to analyse the significance of this marginalisation of more than 75 per cent of the children of this country.

The failure to provide an infrastructure for primary education in the villages of India more than 40 years after Independence is in sharp contrast with the sophisticated institutions, for technical institutes of higher education are funded by government, which essentially means that the money to support them comes from taxes. And since indirect taxation forms a substantial part of the taxes collected by the government, the financial burden is borne by all the people. L.K. Jha put it graphically when he observed that 25 paise of every rupee spent on educating an IIT student comes from the pockets of men and women whose children may never enter a proper classroom.

1. The author is trying to highlight which of the following?
(*a*) The greatness of L.K. Jha
(*b*) Need to have common future for Indian children
(*c*) Need of sophisticated education for rural poor
(*d*) Faulty system of direct taxes
(*e*) None of these

2. What seems to be the likely answer of the author to the question posed by him in the first sentence of the passage?
A. There is no common future for the Indian children.
B. The future is worthwhile for majority of Indian children.
C. The majority may never enter a proper classroom.
(*a*) Only A (*b*) Only B
(*c*) Only C (*d*) Both A and B
(*e*) Both B and C

3. Which of the following pairs have been termed as 'sharp contrast' by the author?
I. Infrastructure for technical education
II. Lack of infrastructure for rural primary schools
III. 25 paise of every rupee earned by Government is spent on education.
IV. The financial burden of higher technical education is borne by all people.
V. 75% of children have limited opportunities.
(*a*) II & IV (*b*) II & III
(*c*) III & IV (*d*) I & II
(*e*) IV & V

4. According to the author, who among the following does not have a hopeful and a prosperous future?
A. All students from technical institutes
B. All students financially supported by the Government
(*a*) Only A (*b*) Only B
(*c*) Both A and B (*d*) Neither A nor B
(*e*) Not mentioned in the passage

5. Which of the following statements is not true?
A. The author welcomes Govt's initiative on primary education.
B. 75% of the children have a bright future.
C. 25% cost of educating a technocrat comes from poor people.
(*a*) Only A (*b*) Only B
(*c*) Only C (*d*) Only A & B
(*e*) Only A & C

Passage 24

The past decade has upset many preconceptions above development and this, more than anything else, makes it difficult to be overly definite about what the next decade has in store. But there are a few things that one can assert with some confidence. First, education, health and productive employment are crucial both for growth and for equity. We have tended to assume that all of these are the consequences of rapid economic growth and that only growth can generate the resources required for these purposes. But, increasingly, it appears that these are better seen as the causes rather than as consequences of development. Virtually every case of successful development involves a prior improvement in literacy, technical skills, health status and access to productive work.

Second, technological competence is the most important resource endowment and it explains a far larger proportion of growth in output and trade than more conventional factors like natural resources or capital accumulation. The competence required is not just in research. In fact technological dynamism in the factory and the farm is more important than the presence of large research establishment.

Third, the environmental imperative can no longer be ignored. Today, as an international issue, it is second only to disarmament. Nationally, the developmental consequences of environmental neglect are increasingly obvious.

In the Indian context there are atleast two further factors which *reinforce* the above propositions. The first is population growth. Given the pace of expansion of the population and the work force, human resource development acquires an added urgency. Population growth is also one, but not necessarily the most important factor, which underlines environmental stress in rural and urban areas. The second factor is that as a large country we cannot *carve* out an independent position in the global system without building up a substantial capacity for self- reliant growth. The acquisition of technical competence is crucial for this purpose.

Until now we have tended to *treat* human resource development, technology issues and environment as subsidiary to the main task of planning. The thrust has been on: Quantitative expansion of infrastructure and production with a focus on production targets like tonnes of steel, kWh of electricity etc., capacity targets like road length, rail kilometerage; and coverage targets like number of schools and students, number of villages electrified etcetra, *catching up* with known technologies —Fuller, use of natural resources —Maximum mobilisaton of financial resources.

1. What seems to be the purpose of the author in writing this passage?
   (*a*) To appreciate the steps taken by our Government in the past and doubts about future
   (*b*) To show how the policy makers have failed
   (*c*) A review of world affairs with special emphasis on developed countries
   (*d*) Review of the past with a view to evolve positive directions for future
   (*e*) To prove how his predictions have turned out to be correct
2. According to the passage, we have so far placed more emphasis on which of the following?
   (*a*) Optimum use of available natural resources
   (*b*) Increased number of basic facilities and meeting number targets
   (*c*) Maximum utilisation of available finances
   (*d*) Following known technologies
   (*e*) All of these
3. According to the author, which of the following factors support and strengthen his point of view?
   A. Necessity for carrying out growth on the basis of our own strength
   B. Increased emphasis on production and coverage targets
   (*a*) Only A (*b*) Only B
   (*c*) Either A or B (*d*) Both A and B
   (*e*) Not mentioned in the passage
4. According to the author, which of the following is a less important factor resulting in environmental stress in rural and urban areas?
   (*a*) Increase in capital accumulation
   (*b*) Rapid economic growth
   (*c*) Rate of growth of population
   (*d*) Availability of productive employment
   (*e*) Continued environmental neglect
5. According to the author, at the national level, with passage of time, the effects of which of the following are being felt?
   (*a*) Expansion of work force of high quality

(*b*) Lack of attention and action for protecting environmental wealth
(*c*) Reduction in growth rate of population
(*d*) Progressive degradation of technological competence in urban areas
(*e*) Emphasis on slow rate of disarmament as compared to other nations

6. Which of the following statements is not true in the context of the passage?
(*a*) Optimum self reliance is the need of the day.
(*b*) We will have bright future by only catching up known technologies.
(*c*) We have to now emphasise aspects of human resource development.
(*d*) Technological competence has to be given due priority over more conventional factors.
(*e*) We cannot afford to ignore the importance of environment.

7. According to the author, which of the following cannot be viewed as cause of development?
(*a*) Betterment in health services
(*b*) Increase in underemployment
(*c*) Speedy economic growth
(*d*) Enhancement in technical skills
(*e*) Improvement in literacy

8. What seems to be the approach of the author regarding present status of research?
A. He desires that more research establishments should come up.
B. Application of new technologies in factories and field is more vital than setting-up of research laboratories.
(*a*) Only A (*b*) Only B
(*c*) Neither A nor B (*d*) Both A and B
(*e*) Not mentioned in the passage

Directions (Q. 9-12) : *Choose the word which is most nearly the same in meaning as the given word as used in the passage.*

9. PURPOSE
(*a*) effect (*b*) ability (*c*) outcome
(*d*) reason (*e*) use

10. CARVE
(*a*) drive (*b*) cover (*c*) forget
(*d*) decide (*e*) acquire

11. LARGE
(*a*) long (*b*) free (*c*) uncontrolled
(*d*) big (*e*) diverse

12. CATCHING UP
(*a*) coming down (*b*) lifting up
(*c*) drawing level with (*d*) leading from
(*e*) throwing up

Directions (Q 13-15) : *Choose the word which is opposite in meaning to the given word as used in the passage.*

13. TREAT
(*a*) consider (*b*) disregard
(*c*) dislike (*d*) misbehave
(*e*) unwind

14. REINFORCE
(*a*) strengthen (*b*) remove
(*c*) weaken (*d*) delink
(*e*) simplify

15. OVERLY
(*a*) casually (*b*) certainly
(*c*) insignificantly (*d*) minutely
(*e*) inwardly

ANSWERS

Passage 1

1. (*a*) **2.** (*d*) **3.** (*d*) **4.** (*d*) **5.** (*a*) **6.** (*c*) **7.** (*a*) **8.** (*c*) **9.** (*a*) **10.** (*d*)
11. (*b*)

Passage 2

1. (*c*) **2.** (*a*) **3.** (*d*) **4.** (*a*) **5.** (*d*) **6.** (*b*) **7.** (*d*) **8.** (*c*) **9.** (*b*) **10.** (*b*)
11. (*d*) **12.** (*a*) **13.** (*c*) **14.** (*d*) **15.** (*b*)

Passage 3

1. (*c*) **2.** (*b*) **3.** (*e*) **4.** (*a*) **5.** (*c*) **6.** (*e*) **7.** (*e*) **8.** (*a*) **9.** (*d*) **10.** (*d*)
11. (*e*) **12.** (*b*) **13.** (*d*) **14.** (*b*) **15.** (*a*)

Passage 4

1. (*c*) **2.** (*b*) **3.** (*a*) **4.** (*c*) **5.** (*d*)

Passage 5

1. (*b*) **2.** (*d*) **3.** (*b*) **4.** (*c*) **5.** (*e*) **6.** (*a*) **7.** (*b*)

Passage 6

1. (*b*) **2.** (*c*) **3.** (*b*) **4.** (*c*) **5.** (*d*) **6.** (*d*) **7.** (*a*) **8.** (*c*) **9.** (*b*) **10.** (*c*)
11. (*b*) **12.** (*c*) **13.** (*d*) **14.** (*a*) **15.** (*b*)

Passage 7

1. (*c*) **2.** (*b*) **3.** (*c*) **4.** (*b*) **5.** (*e*) **6.** (*b*) **7.** (*a*) **8.** (*c*) **9.** (*b*) **10.** (*a*)
11. (*d*) **12.** (*c*) **13.** (*c*) **14.** (*b*) **15.** (*d*) **16.** (*b*) **17.** (*a*) **18.** (*a*)

Passage 8

1. (*c*) **2.** (*a*) **3.** (*c*) **4.** (*b*) **5.** (*a*) **6.** (*d*) **7.** (*c*) **8.** (*d*) **9.** (*d*) **10.** (*a*)

Passage 9

1. (*c*) **2.** (*d*) **3.** (*a*) **4.** (*a*) **5.** (*c*)

Passage 10

1. (*c*) **2.** (*d*) **3.** (*c*) **4.** (*e*) **5.** (*e*) **6.** (*a*) **7.** (*d*) **8.** (*c*) **9.** (*d*) **10.** (*c*)
11. (*c*) **12.** (*e*) **13.** (*b*) **14.** (*a*)

Passage 11

1. (*b*) **2.** (*b*) **3.** (*c*) **4.** (*b*) **5.** (*d*) **6.** (*c*) **7.** (*e*) **8.** (*b*) **9.** (*d*) **10.** (*c*)
11. (*c*) **12.** (*c*) **13.** (*a*) **14.** (*d*) **15.** (*b*)

Passage 12

1. (*b*) **2.** (*d*) **3.** (*e*) **4.** (*c*) **5.** (*d*) **6.** (*a*) **7.** (*b*) **8.** (*d*) **9.** (*b*) **10.** (*a*)

Passage 13

1. (*e*) **2.** (*a*) **3.** (*b*) **4.** (*e*) **5.** (*d*) **6.** (*b*) **7.** (*a*) **8.** (*c*) **9.** (*b*) **10.** (*e*)

Passage 14

1. (*c*) **2.** (*b*) **3.** (*d*) **4.** (*d*) **5.** (*a*) **6.** (*d*) **7.** (*c*) **8.** (*b*) **9.** (*a*) **10.** (*d*)

Passage 15

1. (*d*) **2.** (*b*) **3.** (*b*) **4.** (*a*) **5.** (*a*) **6.** (*c*) **7.** (*d*) **8.** (*d*) **9.** (*c*) **10.** (*d*)

Passage 16

1. (*d*) **2.** (*b*) **3.** (*b*) **4.** (*a*) **5.** (*d*) **6.** (*b*) **7.** (*a*) **8.** (*e*) **9.** (*e*) **10.** (*c*)
11. (*d*)

Passage 17

1. (*c*) **2.** (*a*) **3.** (*d*) **4.** (*d*) **5.** (*b*) **6.** (*d*) **7.** (*e*) **8.** (*b*) **9.** (*b*) **10.** (*c*)

Passage 18

1. (*b*) **2.** (*e*) **3.** (*a*) **4.** (*c*) **5.** (*d*) **6.** (*a*) **7.** (*b*) **8.** (*d*) **9.** (*b*) **10.** (*a*)

Passage 19

1. (*c*) **2.** (*b*) **3.** (*e*) **4.** (*b*) **5.** (*c*) **6.** (*d*) **7.** (*e*) **8.** (*a*) **9.** (*d*) **10.** (*a*)
11. (*e*) **12.** (*c*) **13.** (*e*) **14.** (*b*) **15.** (*d*)

Passage 20

1. (*c*) **2.** (*a*) **3.** (*b*) **4.** (*d*) **5.** (*d*) **6.** (*b*)

Passage 21

1. (*a*) **2.** (*b*) **3.** (*c*) **4.** (*b*) **5.** (*d*)

Passage 22

1. (*c*) **2.** (*b*) **3.** (*c*) **4.** (*d*) **5.** (*e*) **6.** (*d*) **7.** (*e*) **8.** (*c*) **9.** (*a*) **10.** (*c*)
11. (*b*) **12.** (*c*) **13.** (*e*)

Passage 23

1. (*b*) **2.** (*a*) **3.** (*a*) **4.** (*a*) **5.** (*d*) **6.** (*a*)

Passage 24

1. (*b*) **2.** (*b*) **3.** (*a*) **4.** (*c*) **5.** (*b*) **6.** (*b*) **7.** (*b*) **8.** (*b*) **9.** (*c*) **10.** (*e*)
11. (*d*) **12.** (*c*) **13.** (*b*) **14.** (*c*) **15.** (*a*)

---

8. COMPREHENSION–II (Brief Passages)

This section comprises of questions based upon a brief passage usually consisting of one or two paragraphs. The candidate is required to analyse the contents of the passage and then answer the questions that follow.

ILLUSTRATIVE EXAMPLES

Example 1 : ***Read the following passage carefully and answer the questions that follow.***

Many poor farmers had been compelled to take up indigo cultivation when the British settlers were given the right to purchase and cultivate land in India. Many whites, therefore, either acquired land or advanced loans to poor farmers and pressured them to forsake the farming of foodgrains and other cash crops for indigo cultivation. Indigo export to Europe was lucrative for the British settlers who held a monopoly of this business. Within a few years, most of the fertile lands had undergone forcible indigo cultivation, resulting in a famine situation in Bengal. When the farmers declined to cultivate indigo, they were tortured, jailed and even killed. **(N.D.A. 1996)**

1. The poor farmers in Bengal took up indigo cultivation because

(*a*) the government gave them subsidies for this purpose.

(*b*) it was a money earning crop.

(*c*) they were forced to do so.

(*d*) this was the only crop that would grow in this region.

2. British settlers bought land in Bengal in order to

(*a*) cultivate indigo (*b*) grow crops for the poor farmers

(*c*) own agricultural property (*d*) settle down in India

3. Indigo export was profitable for the British settlers because

(*a*) labour was cheap. (*b*) they had no competitiors.

(*c*) the land was fertile. (*d*) they could oppress the farmers.

Solution :

1. (*c*) : The statement that 'Many poor farmers had been compelled to take up indigo cultivation' gives the answer.

2. (*a*) : Clearly, the fact is evident from the statement 'Many whites .... cultivation.'

3. (*b*) : It is mentioned in the passage that the British held a monopoly of indigo business and this indicates that they had no competitors.

Example 2 : ***Read the following passage carefully and answer the questions based on it.***

The Rajputs occupy an honoured place in the history of India. They were a war-like, people, proud and patriotic. They were jealous of their honour, and would lay down their lives to uphold it. They loved their homes and fought bravely to defend the honour of their women-folk. Nothing would tame their spirits. Perils only called forth their courage and poverty only increased their power of resistance. None could fight like them. Their motto was 'Better death than dishonour.'

1. Which of the following represents the central theme of the passage?

(*a*) The pride of the Rajputs

(*b*) Rajputs and their sacrifices

(*c*) The rise and fall of the Rajputs

(*d*) Rajputs - the spirited heroes of Indian history

2. Which of the following is opposite in meaning to the word 'proud' in the passage ?
   (*a*) humble (*b*) kind (*c*) courteous (*d*) cowardly
3. The expression 'tame their spirits' in the passage means
   (*a*) suppress their ambitions (*b*) arouse their enthusiasm
   (*c*) develop their courage (*d*) curb their enthusiasm
4. Which of the following statements is not true in the context of the passage ?
   (*a*) The Rajputs achieved eminence in history due to their great bravery.
   (*b*) They were homely people and would fight for upholding women's honour.
   (*c*) In moments of danger they would exhibit great courage.
   (*d*) They could not, however, face the challenge of poverty.
5. According to the writer, the Rajputs occupy an honoured place in history, becuase
   (*a*) they were fond of wars.
   (*b*) they were proud of their war.
   (*c*) they were jealous of people's honour.
   (*d*) they lived and died upholding their self respect.

Solution :

1. (*d*) : The passage talks about the qualities of the Rajputs which gave them an honourable place in history.

2. (*a*) : The opposite of 'proud' is 'humble'.

3. (*d*) : 'tame' means 'domesticate' or 'curb' and 'spirits' stands for 'enthusiasm'.

4. (*d*) : The first sentence of the passage verifies (*a*).
The sentence 'They loved .... folk' in the passage proves (*b*) to be correct.
The sentence 'Perils ...... courage' in the passage verifies the truth of (*c*).
The sentence '........ and poverty .... resistance' in the passage indicates that Rajputs were not afraid of poverty. Hence, (*d*) is not true.

5. (*d*) : The statement (*d*) is clearly implied from the passage.

Example 3 : *Read the following passage carefully and answer the questions that follow :* **(N.D.A. 1996)**

In the past thirty years, drugs have been discovered that prevent and cure physical disease and reverse the disturbances that occur in some mental illness. Excitement over what drugs can do has led people to believe that any ailment, infective or psychic, can be relieved by taking a pill. At the first sign of nervousness, they try pep pills. Medical journals now advertise tranquillizers, and other mood-altering drugs; doctors prescribe them; and the public expects miracles from them. In such an atmosphere, it is not surprising that drug abuse has spread.

1. According to the author, in recent years there has been
   (*a*) a misplaced trust in drugs (*b*) a distrust of drugs
   (*c*) recognition of the ill-effects of medicine (*d*) None of the above
2. According to the passage, the medicines that have been discovered in recent times
   (*a*) can cure mental illnesses
   (*b*) can help treat some symptoms of mental illnesses
   (*c*) can reduce mental illnesses
   (*d*) cannot cure mental illnesses
3. People often believe that
   (*a*) medicines cannot cure all the diseases.

(*b*) doctors can cure all the diseases.

(*c*) medicines can cure all the diseases.

(*d*) doctors cannot cure all the diseases.

Solution :

1. (a) : The author talks of the immense trust of people in drugs followed by the statement '....... drug abuse has spread'. This indicates a misplaced trust in drugs.

2. (b) : The statement 'drugs .... reverse the disturbancesthat occur in some mental illness' give the answer.

3. (c) : The sentence 'Excitement ...... pill' gives us the answer.

Example 4 : ***Read the following two letters carefully and answer the questions given below them.***

Dear Shri Chhatre,

The umbrella, which you have forgotten during your visit to our departmental store day before yesterday, is still here. It gives a very obnoxious look, besides emitting some foul smell. Will you please take the trouble to collect it as early as possible? Tomorrow it being our weekly off, our store is closed. You may collect your 'precious' umbrella day after tomorrow i.e. on Sunday.

Yours sincerely.
C.F. Francis

Dear Shri Francis,

Thank you for your letter. The time that I must spend to visit your store is much more important than my precious umbrella. Also, you have now known the worth of my umbrella. I, therefore, would like to donate it generously to a friend like you. You may keep it on display in your big store as a historical monument. Thanking you once again for your kindness to remind me of my lost property.

Yours sincerely,
Akash Chhatre

1. Mr. Francis wrote to Chhatre because

(*a*) Chhatre was his close friend.

(*b*) Chhatre was a very busy man.

(*c*) the umbrella was really very precious.

(*d*) he was concerned about Chhatre's love for the umbrella.

(*e*) Chhatre's umbrella was a nuisance to his store.

2. Shri Chhatre had visited the departmental store on which of the following days?

(*a*) Monday (*b*) Wednesday (*c*) Thursday

(*d*) Friday (*e*) None of these

3. Which of the following is true about the umbrella, as mentioned by Mr. Francis?

(*a*) The umbrella was a problem to the customers' eyes only.

(*b*) The umbrella was a problem to the customers' noses only.

(*c*) The umbrella was a problem to the customers' nose and eyes.

(*d*) The umbrella was a very expensive item.

(*e*) The umbrella was like a historical monument.

4. Chhatre's act of donating the umbrella to Francis reveals that

(*a*) Chhatre is a very generous person.

(*b*) Francis needed the umbrella very much.

(*c*) he had a lot of sympathy for Francis' store.

(*d*) he could not afford to spend money to collect it.

(*e*) None of these

5. On the basis of these two letters, which of the following can be inferred to be definitely true?

(*a*) Francis and Chhatre do not have good relations with each other.

(*b*) Chhatre's umbrella was very expensive.

(*c*) The departmental store is closed on Saturday.

(*d*) Francis' store would benefit by preserving the umbrella.

(*e*) None of these

Solution :

1. (*e*) : The sentence 'It gives .... foul smell' in Francis' letter gives the answer.

2. (*b*) : According to Francis, day after 'tomorrow' is Sunday i.e. he writes the letter on Friday. Chhatre visited the store day before 'yesterday' i.e. Wednesday.

3. (*c*) : The expressions 'obnoxious look' and 'foul smell' indicate that the umbrella was a problem to the customers' noses and eyes.

4. (*e*) : Chhatre donated the umbrella because it was totally worn out and of no use to him.

5. (*c*) : Francis says that day after 'tomorrow' is Sunday and tomorrow the store is closed. Thus the store remains closed on Saturday.

PRACTICE SET 1

Passage 1 **(S.S.C.1995)**

Primitive man was probably more concerned with fire as a source of warmth and as a means of cooking food than as a source of light. Before he discovered less laborious ways of making fire, he had to preserve it, and whenever he went on a journey he carried a firebrand with him. His discovery that the firebrand, from which the torch may very well have developed, could be used for illumination was probably incidental to the primary purpose of preserving a flame.

Lamps, too, probably developed by accident. Early man may have had his first conception of a lamp while watching a twig or fibre burning in the molten fat dropped from a roasting carcass. All he had to do was to fashion a vessel to contain fat and float a lighted reed in it. Such lamps, which were made of hollowed stones or sea shells, have persisted in identical form up to quite recent times.

1. Primitive man's most important use for fire was
(*a*) to provide warmth (*b*) to cook food
(*c*) to provide light (*d*) Both (*a*) and (*b*)

2. The firebrand was used to
(*a*) prevent accidents (*b*) provide light
(*c*) scare animals (*d*) save labour

3. By 'primary' the author means
(*a*) primitive (*b*) fundamental
(*c*) elemental (*d*) essential

4. Lamps probably developed through mere
(*a*) hazard (*b*) fate
(*c*) chance (*d*) planning

5. Early lamps were made by
(*a*) using a reed as a wick in the fat
(*b*) letting a reed soak the fat
(*c*) putting the fat in a shell and lighting it
(*d*) floating a reed in the sea-shell

Passage 2

The crowd surged forward through the narrow streets of Paris. There was a clatter of shutters being closed hastily by trembling hands—the citizens of Paris knew that once the fury of the people was excited there was no telling what they might do. They came to an old house which had a workshop on the ground floor. A head popped out of the door to see what it was all about. 'Get him! Get Thimonier! Smash his devilish machines!', yelled the crowd.

They found the workshop without its owner. M.Thimonier had escaped by the back door. Now the fury of the demonstrators turned against the machines that were standing in the shop, ready to be delivered to buyers. They were systematically broken up and destroyed -dozens of them. Only when the last wheel and spindle had been trampled under foot did the infuriated crowd recover their senses.

'That is the end of M' sieur Thimonier and his sewing machines', they said to one another, and went home satisfied. Perhaps now they would find work, for they were all unemployed tailors and seamstresses who believed that their livelihood was threatened by that new invention.

6. The passage throws light on
   (*a*) why inventions should be avoided altogether.
   (*b*) how a well-meant invention can be misunderstood.
   (*c*) what mischief an inventor can do to ordinary people.
   (*d*) how dangerous an invention can prove to be.
7. The crowd was protesting against
   (*a*) the closing of workshops
   (*b*) the misdoings of Thimonier
   (*c*) the newly invented sewing machine
   (*d*) Thimonier keeping the invention a secret
8. The aim of the crowd was to
   (*a*) kill Thimonier
   (*b*) drive Thimonier away
   (*c*) bring discredit to Thimonier
   (*d*) destroy the sewing machines
9. The people thought that
   (*a*) their lives were in danger.
   (*b*) Thimonier was mad.
   (*c*) the sewing machine was dangerous.
   (*d*) Thimonier was depriving them of their livelihood.
10. Shutters were being closed hastily because the shopkeepers
   (*a*) wanted to attack the crowd
   (*b*) wanted to protect Thimonier
   (*c*) feared their shops would be invaded
   (*d*) wanted to show their solidarity with the crowd

Passage 3 **(I.E.S. 1993)**

The last half of my life has been lived in one of those painful epochs of human history during which the world is getting worse, and past victories which had seemed to be definitive have turned out to be only temporary. When I was young, Victorian optimism was taken for granted. It was thought that freedom and prosperity would speed gradually throughout the world by an orderly process, and it was hoped that cruelty, tyranny, and injustice would continually diminish. Hardly anyone was haunted by the fear of great wars. Hardly anyone thought of the nineteenth century as a brief interlude between past and future barbarism.

11. The author feels sad about the later part of his life because
   (*a*) the world had not become prosperous.
   (*b*) he was nostalgic about his childhood.
   (*c*) the world was painfully disturbed during that period of time.
   (*d*) the author had not won any further victories.
12. The victories of the past
   (*a*) filled men with a sense of pessimism
   (*b*) proved to be temporary events
   (*c*) ended cruelty, tyranny, and injustice
   (*d*) brought permanent peace and security
13. The world 'definitive' as used in the passage means
   (*a*) incomplete (*b*) defined
   (*c*) temporary (*d*) final
14. During the Victorian age people believed that
   (*a*) there would be unlimited freedom.
   (*b*) strife would increase.
   (*c*) peace would prevail and happiness would engulf the whole world.
   (*d*) wars would be fought on a bigger scale.
15. 'A brief interlude between past and future barbarism' can be interpreted as
   (*a*) a dramatic performance during wars
   (*b*) an interval between cruel wars
   (*c*) a short space of time between two great events
   (*d*) a short period of time between past and future acts of savagery

Passage 4

Patience is better than wisdom : An ounce of patience is worth a pound of brains. All men praise patience, but few can practise it. It is medicine which is good for all diseases, but it is not every garden that grows the herbs to make it with. Many people are born crying, live complaining and die disappointed. They think every other person's burden to be light and their own feathers to be heavy as lead, and yet if the truth were known, it is their fancy rather than their fate that makes things go so hard with them. Many would be well off they could but think so.

16. Which of the following is the most suitable explanation to the author's remark that 'an ounce of patience is worth a pound of brains'?
(*a*) Intelligence and wisdom can be attained only by practising patience.
(*b*) Patience comes first, intelligence next.
(*c*) Patience is essential for every achievement in life.
(*d*) Without patience intelligence cannot be used properly.

17. Which one is the most likely explanation, among the following, of the author's metaphorical statement that 'it is not every garden that grows the herbs to make it with'?
(*a*) Patience is a must for solving all our problems in life.
(*b*) Patience is a rare herb that cures all diseases.
(*c*) Patience is quite difficult to practise.
(*d*) It is only a small number of people that are found observing patience in life.

18. The writer's remark "They think every person's burden to be light and their own feathers to be heavy as lead" is very significant. It means
(*a*) they are always worried and dejected.
(*b*) they consider their own problem to be difficult to solve as compared with problems of other people.
(*c*) they feel that they alone face serious problems while others have a nice time.
(*d*) they remain very much worried about their own problem.

19. The writer's remark "It is their fancy rather than their fate" means
(*a*) they are unhappy because they think that way and not because it is their destiny.
(*b*) they are fatalists rather than imaginative.
(*c*) they have a wrong approach to life.
(*d*) they are very much absorbed in their own problems.

Passage 5 **(U.D.C.1995)**

It is difficult to reconcile the ideas of different schools of thought on the question of education Some people maintain that pupils at school should concentrate on a narrow range of subjects which will benefit them directly in their subsequent careers. Others contend that they should study a wide range of subjects so that they have not only the specialised knowledge necessary for their chosen careers but also sound general knowledge about the world they will have to work and live in. Supporters of the first theory state that the greatest contributions to civilisation are made by those who are most expert in their trade or profession. Those on the other side say that, unless they have a broad general education, the experts will be too narrow in their outlook to have sympathy with their follows or a proper sense of responsibility towards humanity as a whole.

20. 'Schools of thought' can be explained as
(*a*) groups of people whose job is to think
(*b*) groups of people who are schooled to think
(*c*) groups of people who study in a particular school thoughtfully
(*d*) groups of people having the same ideas but with different perception on a particular subject

21. Broad general knowledge is necessary because
(*a*) specialisation is incomplete without it.
(*b*) without it no one would get a job.
(*c*) it teaches us about different things.
(*d*) it broadens one's outlook.

22. The idea of the first school of thought in the passage is that
(*a*) students should concentrate on studies.
(*b*) students should not undertake any specialised work.
(*c*) students should study all the subjects they want to.
(*d*) students should study a few subjects that will help them in their profession.

23. Supporters of the first theory say that
(*a*) experts have contributed most to progress in the modern world.
(*b*) people with general knowledge have contributed to civilisation.
(*c*) experts have done nothing to help mankind.
(*d*) people with general knowledge are more useful than experts.

24. According to the second school of thought, education will not be very effective if pupils

(a) have indequate knowledge of their own work
(b) do not have a wide general education
(c) ignore the study of fine arts
(d) have nothing but general knowledge

ANSWERS

1. (d)	**2.** (b)	**3.** (d)	**4.** (c)	**5.** (a)	**6.** (b)	**7.** (c)	**8.** (a)	**9.** (d)	**10.** (c)
11. (c)	**12.** (b)	**13.** (d)	**14.** (c)	**15.** (d)	**16.** (b)	**17.** (d)	**18.** (c)	**19.** (a)	**20.** (d)
21. (d)	**22.** (d)	**23.** (a)	**24.** (b)						

PRACTICE SET 2

Passage 1 **(C.D.S.1995)**

Culture is the cultivation of a plant or garden, not the eradication of its roots, it is an understanding of the roots and seeds, their patient care and instructed nourishment. Culture is not knowledge, nor is it art, still less is its acquaintance with literature and art. By culture I mean first of all what the anthropologists mean; the way of life of a particular people living together in one place. That culture is made visible in their arts, in their social system, in their habits and customs, in their religion. It is an aggregate of customs, institutions, manners, standards, tastes, morals and beliefs. Now these are transmitted rather by the family than by the school, hence when family life fails to play its part, we must expect our culture to deteriorate. It is a delusion to think that the maladies of the modern world can be put right by a system of instruction. On the contrary, universal education, by lowering standards, morals and tastes to a common denominator, and by sharpening the wits rather than disciplining character, tends to break down existing checks and balances. Education should be the drawing forth of potential values, it should not be the destruction of the safeguards that tradition places around young egos naturally inclined to willful and precarious flights.

1. The writer uses the term 'culture' to refer to
(a) the cultivation of a plant or garden by a community
(b) one's acquaintance with literature and art
(c) one's acquisition of knowledge
(d) the way of life of a particular people living together in one place

2. The passage suggests that universal education
(a) is,in fact, aggravating the existing problems of the modern world
(b) is the solution to the problems in the modern world
(c) would prevent us from transmitting culture to the future generation
(d) would help retain the cultural values

3. The culture of a community is said to deteriorate when
(a) there is a fall in its educational standards.
(b) the family life fails to play its part.
(c) there is universal education.
(d) it adopts the modern system of instruction.

4. The culture of a community is transmitted
(a) more by school than the familly
(b) more by the family than school
(c) equally by both
(d) by the peer group

5. According to the passage, education is
(a) the sharpening of wits
(b) tapping and encouraging the inherent values in man
(c) the substitution of old traditions with new ones
(d) the development of moral standards

Passage 2

There are some men who seem to be always on the lookout for trouble and, to tell the truth, they are seldom disappointed. Listening to such men one would think that this world is one of the stormiest and most disagreeable places. Yet, after all it is not such a bad place and the difficulty is often in the man who is too thin- skinned. On the other hand, the man who goes out expecting people to be like himself, kind and brotherly, will be surprised at the kindness he meets even in the most unlike quarters. A smile is apt to be met with a responsive smile while the sneer is just as apt to provoke a snarl.Men living in the same neighbourhood may live vastly different lives. But it is not the neighbourhood which is quarrelsome, but the man within us. And we have it in our power to change our neighbourhood into a pleasant one by simply changing our own ways.

6. The passage is about
(*a*) our disagreeable and hostile world
(*b*) a kindly and pleasant world
(*c*) our indifferent and unresponsive world
(*d*) the world and what one makes of it

7. "....... they are seldom disappointed". The statement denotes that such men
(*a*) welcome difficulties as a morale booster
(*b*) do not have to face any trouble
(*c*) manage to keep unruffled in the face of discomforts
(*d*) generally do not fail to come across troubles

8. The author's own view of the world is that it is
(*a*) one of the loveliest and quietest places
(*b*) an unpleasant and turbulent place
(*c*) one's own excessive sensitivity that makes it a bad place
(*d*) a sordid place for those who suffer in life

9. Which of the following is opposite in meaning to the expression 'thin-skinned' as used in the passage?
(*a*) Insensitive (*b*) Intelligent
(*c*) Awkward (*d*) Obstinate

10. "On the other hand ..... unlikely quarters". The statement shows that people's reaction to our attitude is
(*a*) generally indifferent
(*b*) surprisingly responsive
(*c*) often adverse
(*d*) mainly favourable.

Passage 3 **(N.D.A. 1996)**

Among the earliest memories of my childhood are the stories from these epics told to me by my mother or the older ladies of the house, just as a child in Europe or America might listen to fairy tales or stories of adventure. There was for me both the adventure and the fairy tale element in them. And then I used to be taken every year to the popular open-air performances where the Ramayana story was enacted.

11. The author of this passage is in
(*a*) a reflective mood
(*b*) a reminiscent mood
(*c*) a critical mood
(*d*) an introspective mood

12. 'Epics' are
(*a*) long historical stories
(*b*) poetic works of excellence
(*c*) long narrative poems of the adventures of mythical heroes
(*d*) popular versions of national histories

13. The second sentence shows that the writer
(*a*) tolerated the old stories and open-air performances
(*b*) analysed old stories for their value
(*c*) enjoyed them
(*d*) dismissed them as untrue and silly

Passage 4

Newspapers sell because of news and editorial coverage but it gets more revenue from advertisements . News costs money, while advertisements fetch money. The economics of modern newspapers is such that it cannot run by just selling news; it has to depend on advertisements. The economics of newspaper publishing requires both subscribers who can afford to buy newspapers and businessmen who can afford to advertise in it . The growth of the press depends on both. Therefore, in newspaper management neither aspect can be neglected.

Co-ordination among the various departments - editorial, circulation, advertising and production - is very essential for effective and better management. The head of various departments must be part of the management of a newspaper. They must be aware of the goals set, policies and future plans of the management. They cannot afford to remain cut off from the mainstream of management function. In addition, each department should keep the other department managers informed of those of its activities that will be useful to them. This is a vital aspect of newspaper management.

14. The growth of a newspaper depends on
(*a*) the editorial and news coverage
(*b*) large scale subscribers
(*c*) advertisers
(*d*) subscribers and advertisers

15. The main idea of the first paragraph of the passage is
(*a*) The growth of the press
(*b*) News and editorial coverage
(*c*) The economics of newspaper publishing
(*d*) The importance of advertisements .

16. The main idea of the second paragraph of the passage is
(*a*) The future of newspapers
(*b*) How to sell newspapers
(*c*) Effective newspaper management
(*d*) The role of the heads of departments

17. The word 'goal' in the passage means
(*a*) aim (*b*) conclusion
(*c*) result (*d*) benefit

18. The word 'vital' as used in the context means
(*a*) primary (*b*) important
(*c*) healthy (*d*) lively

Passage 5 **(Hotel Management, 1996)**

The strength of the electronics industry in Japan is the Japanese ability to organise production and marketing rather than their achievements in original research. The British are generally recognised as a far more inventive collection of individuals, but never seem able to exploit what they invent. There are many examples, from the TSR Z hovercraft, high speed train and Sinclair scooter to the Triumph, BSA and Norton motorcycle which all prove this sad rule. The Japanese were able to exploit their strengths in marketing and development many years ago, and their success was at first either not understood in the West or was dismissed as something which could have been produced only at their low price. They were sold because they were cheap copies of other peoples' ideas churned out of a workhouse which was dedicated to hard grind above all else.

19. The main theme of this passage is
(*a*) electronics industry in Japan
(*b*) industrial comparison between Japan and Britain
(*c*) the importance of original research in industry
(*d*) the role of marketing efficiency in industrial prosperity

20. The TSR Z hovercraft, high speed train, Sinclair Scooter, etc are the symbols of
(*a*) Japanese failure
(*b*) Japanese success
(*c*) British failure
(*d*) British success

21. The sad rule mentioned in this passage refers to
(*a*) the lack of variety in Japanese inventions
(*b*) the inability of the Japanese to be inventive like the British
(*c*) the poorer marketing ability of the British
(*d*) the inability of the British to be industrious like the Japanese

22. According to the passage, prosperity in industry depends upon
(*a*) marketing ability
(*b*) productivity
(*c*) official patronage
(*d*) inventiveness

23. It is evident from this passage that the strength of a country's industry depends upon
(*a*) electronic development
(*b*) dedicated work force
(*c*) original research
(*d*) international cooperation

Directions : *Read the following letter carefully and answer the questions given below it. Certain words in the letter have been printed in italics to help you locate them easily for answering some of the questions.* **(B.S.R.B. 1996)**

Dear Mrs. Kapdawalla,

We certainly agree with you that it is inconvenient to run a home without a washing machine. For that reason, we have lost no time in investigating the *source* of the trouble in your machine.

The report from our repair department indicates that your washing machine has a burned-out bearing which was caused by the fact that it has not been oiled. Although we guarantee our washing machines for three years against all defects in workmanship or materials, we cannot assume responsibility for repairs *necessitated* by improper care. We, therefore, cannot *grant your request* to repair your machine without charges.

We shall, however, be glad to put your washing machine in brand new condition at the actual cost of the parts i.e. Rs. 325/-. When your machine is returned to you, it will be completely oiled and ready to operate. Then, if you follow the directions for oiling, which are given on page 3 of your instruction book, you will get years of trouble - free service from your washing machine.

Just mail the enclosed postcard today, authorising us to proceed with the repairs. We return your machine on Saturday.

Yours sincerely,

Mr. M.N. Laundrywalla

24. This letter seems to be a reply to
(*a*) a customer's letter requesting the dealer to pay compensation for defective machine
(*b*) a letter for replacement of an old washing machine with a brand new one
(*c*) a request to a dealer to send his mechanic for repairing a washing machine
(*d*) a letter requesting the dealer for free repair of a washing machine
(*e*) an inquiry about the probable defects in a washing machine

25. The washing machine needed repair due to
(*a*) faulty material (*b*) overloading
(*c*) improper care (*d*) over use
(*e*) defective workmanship

26. From the letter, it can be inferred that Mrs. Kapdawalla
(*a*) had been very careful in maintaining the washing machine
(*b*) had been running her home without a washing machine for the past three years
(*c*) had purchased the washing machine during the past three years
(*d*) was put to a lot of inconvenience due to the dealer's fault
(*e*) had paid Rs. 325/- to the dealer for the repairs done by him

27. "Your request" (2nd para, last sentence) refers to
(*a*) Mr. Laundrywalla's request for return of the authorisation card
(*b*) Mrs. Kapdawalla's request for a brand new washing machine
(*c*) a customer's request to a trader for free repair of a washing machine
(*d*) Mrs. Kapdawalla's request for increasing the guarantee period
(*e*) None of these

28. Mr. Laundrywalla rejected Mrs. Kapdawalla's request because
(*a*) she had not purchased the washing machine from his shop.
(*b*) the guarantee period of the washing machine was over.
(*c*) the defect in the washing machine was due to faulty material provided.
(*d*) the defect occurred due to careless maintenance by his repair department.
(*e*) the machine had gone out of order due to improper care.

29. It appears that when the above letter was written, the washing machine was
(*a*) at Mrs. Kapdawalla's residence
(*b*) at Mr. Laundrywalla's repairs shop
(*c*) yet to be examined to find out the defect
(*d*) already repaired by Mr. Laundrywalla's mechanics
(*e*) sent back to Mrs. Kapdawalla's residence

Directions : *Choose the word which is most nearly the same in meaning as the given word as used in the passage.*

30. SOURCE
(*a*) Gravity (*b*) Origin (*c*) Effect
(*d*) Remedy (*e*) Maintenance

31. NECESSITATED
(*a*) Permitted (*b*) Imposed
(*c*) Demanded (*d*) Enforced
(*e*) Warranted

Directions : *Choose the word which is most opposite in meaning of the word given in capitals as used in the passage.*

32. INCONVENIENT
(*a*) Possible (*b*) Easily
(*c*) Desirable (*d*) Troublesome
(*e*) Comfortable

33. GRANT
(*a*) Reject (*b*) Stop (*c*) Send
(*d*) Accept (*e*) Suppose

ANSWERS

1. (*d*)	**2.** (*c*)	**3.** (*b*)	**4.** (*b*)	**5.** (*a*)	**6.** (*d*)	**7.** (*d*)	**8.** (*c*)	**9.** (*a*)	**10.** (*b*)
11. (*b*)	**12.** (*c*)	**13.** (*c*)	**14.** (*d*)	**15.** (*c*)	**16.** (*d*)	**17.** (*a*)	**18.** (*b*)	**19.** (*d*)	**20.** (*c*)
21. (*c*)	**22.** (*a*)	**23.** (*b*)	**24.** (*d*)	**25.** (*c*)	**26.** (*c*)	**27.** (*c*)	**28.** (*e*)	**29.** (*b*)	**30.** (*b*)
31. (*d*)	**32.** (*e*)	**33.** (*a*)							

PRACTICE SET 3

Passage 1 **(I. Tax & Central Excise,1993)**

It will be a mistake to think that he was given only 'bouquets',he also received many 'brickbats'.The Christian missionaries took alarm at his popularity. They used to raise funds by preaching that India was a land of heathens waiting to be saved by Christianity. The American press now began to say that it was a shame that any body should try to teach India religion, rather the world should sit at her feet to learn it. Vivekananda also said that India did not need religion but material support. The missionaries found that the subscriptions they had so long been receiving from the people were steadily declining. They blamed it on Swamiji. They now started denigrating him in all manner of ways. They even began to spread scandals against his personal character. Strangely enough, even some of his own countrymen joined them in this for reasons of their own. But 'Truth alone prevails', as Swamiji always preached. He did not try to defend himself, but others stood up for him and vehemently protested. Finally, all such mean attempts failed and his reputation only rose higher and higher.

1. The passage teaches us
(*a*) not to believe in religions other than our own
(*b*) not to get involved in scandals
(*c*) not to visit foreign lands
(*d*) not to deviate from the path of truth

2. Vivekananda was criticised by missionaries in America because
(*a*) he was a bad student of Western theology.
(*b*) he opposed the tenets of Christianity.
(*c*) Americans had become very fond of him.
(*d*) he did not allow them to raise funds in India.

3. Swami Vivekananda told the American people that India
(*a*) did not approve of the Catholic Church
(*b*) would teach religion to those who sit at her feet
(*c*) required religious and material help
(*d*) was self sufficient in religion though poor

4. Vivekananda's rapport with the American people
(*a*) helped India get substantial aid
(*b*) made his friends desert him
(*c*) annoyed the American Government
(*d*) caused a drop in Church's collections

5. Vivekananda did not defend himself because
(*a*) he believed in the ultimate triumph of truth.
(*b*) he was in a foreign land.
(*c*) some of his countrymen were opposing him.
(*d*) he had brought many friends along to fight for him.

Passage 2

A book is written, not to multiply the voice merely, not to carry it merely but to perpetuate it . The author has something to say which he perceives to be true and useful or helpfully beautiful. So far he knows no one has said it , so far as he knows no one else can say it. He is bound to say it clearly and melodiously if he may; clearly at all events. In the sum of his life, he finds this to be the thing or group of things, manifest him; this, the piece of true knowledge, or sight, which his share of sunshine and earth has permitted him to seize. That is a book.

6. The opening sentence of the passage implies that the aim of writing a book is to
(*a*) repeat the message it contains
(*b*) enable the author to express his ideas in writing
(*c*) preserve from extinction the message it contains
(*d*) propagate the ideology of the author

7. Which of the following would be the most suitable title for the passage ?
(*a*) Contribution of an author
(*b*) Aim of writing a book
(*c*) Book- the source of true knowledge
(*d*) Writers and their books

8. According to the writer, a person is impelled to write a book, because
(*a*) he wishes to satisfy his ego.
(*b*) he has something nice and pleasing to say.
(*c*) he is capable of expressing whatever he wants to say.
(*d*) he has discovered something unique, true and good which he must convey distinctly and musically.

9. Which of the following is not implied in the passage ?

(*a*) A writer is motivated to write a book if he discerns a great truth.

(*b*) An author of a book generally gathers some common truths and gives them a popular and pleasing expression.

(*c*) A great writer is convinced that whatever he says is not an echo or imitation of what others have said.

(*d*) An eminent writer's message is conveyed through plain unambiguous language.

10. Which of the following is opposite in meaning to the word 'manifest' given in the passage ?

(*a*) unclear (*b*) dark

(*c*) pure (*d*) hard

Passage 3 **(C.B.I.1995)**

When we are suddenly confronted with any terrible danger, the change of nature we undergo is equally great. In some cases fear paralyses us. Like animals, we stand still, powerless to move a step in fright or to lift a hand in defence of our lives, and sometimes we are seized with panic, and again, act more like the inferior animals than rational beings. On the other hand, frequently in cases of sudden extreme peril, which cannot be escaped by flight, and must be instantly faced, even the most timid men at once as if by miracle, become possessed of the necessary courage, sharp quick apprehen- sion, and swift decision. This is a miracle very common in nature. Man and the inferior animals alike, when confronted with almost certain death 'gather resolution from despair' but there can really be no trace of so debilitating a feeling in the person fighting, or prepared to fight for dear life. At such times the mind is clearer than it has ever been; the nerves are steel, there is nothing felt but a wonderful strength and daring. Looking back at certain perilous moments in my own life, I remember them with a kind of joy, not that there was any joyful excitement then; but because they brought me a new experience- a new nature, as it were- and lifted me for a time above myself.

11. An appropriate title for the above passage would be

(*a*) The Will to Fight

(*b*) The Miracle of Confronting Danger

(*c*) The Change of Nature

(*d*) Courage and Panic

12. The author names three different ways in which a man may react to sudden danger. What are they ?

(*a*) He may flee in panic, or fight back or stand still.

(*b*) He may be paralysed with fear, seized with panic or act like an inferior animal.

(*c*) He may be paralysed with fear, or seized with panic, or as if by miracle, become possessed of the necessary courage, and face the danger.

(*d*) He may be paralysed with fear, run away or fight.

13 The distinction between 'inferior animals' and 'rational beings' is that

(*a*) the former are incapable of fighting.

(*b*) the latter are clever.

(*c*) the latter are stronger.

(*d*) the latter are capable of reasoning things out whereas the former cannot do so.

14. Explain the phrase 'gather resolution from danger'.

(*a*) Find hope and courage

(*b*) A state of utter hopelessness steels one to fight out the danger

(*c*) Not to lose hope, but fight

(*d*) Find courage to face the danger

15. The author feels happy in the recollection of dangers faced and overcome because

(*a*) they brought him a new experience.

(*b*) they brought him a new experience, and lifted him above himself for a time.

(*c*) he survived his ordeal.

(*d*) he was lucky to be alive.

Passage 4 **(C.D.S.1994)**

The artificial ways of inducing sleep are legion, and are only alike in their ineffectuality. In *Lavengro* there is an impossible character, a victim of insomnia, who finds that a volume of Wordsworth's poems is the only sure soporific, but that was Borrow's Malice. The famous old plan of counting sheep jumping over a stile has never served a turn. I have herded imaginary sheep until they insisted on turning themselves into white bears or blue pigs, and I defy any reasonable man to fall asleep while mustering a herd of stupid swine.

16. The author points out that

(*a*) sleep can easily be induced.

(*b*) the artificial means of inducing sleep are not good.

(*c*) artificial ways of inducing sleep are ineffective.
(*d*) artificial ways of inducing sleep are expensive.

17. According to the author the character in *Lavengro*
(*a*) resorts to external aids to get some sleep
(*b*) is an admirer of Wordsworth
(*c*) spends sleepless nights reading Wordsworth
(*d*) is an avid reader of poetry

18. The author uses "impossible" for the character of *Lavengro* in the sense of
(*a*) funny (*b*) unrealistic
(*c*) queer (*d*) imaginary

19. Borrow's malice is most probably directed at
(*a*) sleeplessness
(*b*) the artificial ways of inducing sleep
(*c*) Wordsworth's poetry
(*d*) poetry in general

20. In order to cure his insomnia, the writer
(*a*) does a lot of reading
(*b*) vainly tries to concentrate on imaginary situations
(*c*) keeps a flock of sheep
(*d*) counts sheep jumping over a stile

Passage 5

Experiments with the Sulphonamides have made clear a fact about germs which is gaining increasing importance in fighting them. Germs, it seems, have the same ability as all the other living things gradually to change themselves to suit new conditions. But, as the generation of germs lasts only twenty, twenty five or thirty minutes, before all the germs divide to form new ones, changes that would take many years in animals can be achieved by germs in a few hours. Perhaps, then, you give the attacking germ a dose of Sulphonamides which upsets them somewhat but is not strong enough to prevent them from multiplying; if so, they very rapidly develop new powers which enable them to resist the effects of the drug. After this has happened, even the strongest dose will fail to disturb them.

21. Experiments with Sulphonamides have led to the important discovery that
(*a*) germs are living things, and can change themselves to suit new conditions.
(*b*) one generation of germs lasts only twenty, twenty five or thirty minutes.
(*c*) germs can adjust themselves to live and multiply in new conditions.
(*d*) germs are not disturbed even by the strongest possible dose of Sulphonamides.

22. Like all other living things, germs can change themselves to suit new conditions. This adjustment is possible because the germs have
(*a*) the power of fluctuation
(*b*) the power of compliance
(*c*) the power of adoptability
(*d*) the power of adaptability

23. Since germs can change themselves to suit new conditions, the task of fighting them has become
(*a*) absolutely impossible
(*b*) much easier
(*c*) much more difficult
(*d*) increasingly important

24. Germs which are not disturbed even by the strongest possible dose of the Sulphonamides are said to have become
(*a*) immortal (*b*) immune
(*c*) improvised (*d*) immobile

25. One generation of germs expires, bringing into existence the next generation
(*a*) in twenty minutes
(b) in twenty five minutes
(*c*) in not more than half an hour
(*d*) in a few hours

ANSWERS

1. (*d*)	**2.** (*c*)	**3.** (*d*)	**4.** (*d*)	**5.** (*a*)	**6.** (*d*)	**7.** (*c*)	**8.** (*d*)	**9.** (*b*)	**10.** (*a*)
11. (*b*)	**12.** (*c*)	**13.** (*d*)	**14.** (*b*)	**15.** (*b*)	**16.** (*c*)	**17.** (*d*)	**18.** (*b*)	**19.** (*c*)	**20.** (*b*)
21. (*a*)	**22.** (*d*)	**23.** (*c*)	**24.** (*b*)	**25.** (*c*)					

PRACTICE SET 4

Passage 1 **(I.E.S.1994)**

Religion is the greatest instrument for so raising us. It is amazing that a person not intellectually bright, perhaps not even educated, is capable of grasping and living by something so advanced as the principles of Christianity. Yet, there is a common phenomenon. It is not, however, in my province to talk about religion, but rather to stress the power which great literature and the great personalities whom we meet in it and in history have to open and enlarge over minds, and to show us what is first rate in human personality and human character by showing us goodness and greatness.

1. In the passage, the author's ultimate intention is to talk about
(*a*) religion (*b*) history
(*c*) education (*d*) character

2. The phrase "so raising us" means
(*a*) giving us a sense of spiritual superiority
(*b*) making us feel that we are more important than we really are
(*c*) improving our mental abilities
(*d*) making us realise that we all are children of God

3. What surprises the author is that
(*a*) even uneducated people are attracted towards Christianity.
(*b*) Christianity is practised by a large number of people.
(*c*) despite being difficult and complex, the principles of Christianity are practised by so many people.
(*d*) even very intelligent people cannot understand the principles of Christianity.

4. The author hesitates to talk about religion because
(*a*) he does not feel himself competent to talk about it.
(*b*) nobody around him likes to talk about it.
(*c*) he does not believe in any religion.
(*d*) he does not fully understand its importance.

5. According to the author, we come across examples of greatness and nobility in
(*a*) great works of literature
(*b*) literary and historical works
(*c*) historical records
(*d*) books on Christianity

Passage 2

It is strange that, according to his position in life, an extravagant man is admired or despised. A successful business man does nothing to increase his popularity by being careful with his money. He is expected to display his success, to have a smart car, an expensive life,and to be lavish with his hospitality. If he is not so, he is considered mean, and his reputation in business may even suffer in consequence. The paradox remains that if he had not been careful with his money in the first place, he would never have achieved his present wealth.

Among the low income group, a different set of values exists. The young clerk, who makes his wife a present of a new dress when he hasn't paid his house rent, is condemned as extravagant. Carefulness with money to the point of meanness is applauded as a virtue. Nothing in his life is considered more worthy than paying his bills. The ideal wife for such a man separates her housekeeping money into joyless little piles- so much for rent, for food, for the children's shoes; she is able to face the milkman with equanimity every month, satisfied with her economising ways, and never knows the guilt of buying something she can't really afford.

As for myself, I fall into neither of these categories. If I have money to spare, I can be extravagant, but when, as is usually the case, I am hard up, then I am the meanest man imaginable.

6. Which of the following would be the most suitable title for the passage ?
(*a*) Extravagance is always condemnable
(*b*) Extravagance leads to poverty
(*c*) Extravagance in the life of the rich and the poor
(*d*) Miserly habits of the poor

7 In the opinion of the writer, a successful businessman
(*a*) should not bother about popularity
(*b*) is expected to have expensive tastes
(*c*) is more popular if he appears to be doing nothing
(*d*) must be extravagant before achieving success

8. The phrase 'lavish with his hospitality' in the third sentence of the first paragraph, signifies
(*a*) considerateness in spending on guests and strangers
(*b*) indifference in treating his friends and relatives
(*c*) miserliness in dealing with his friends
(*d*) extravagance in entertaining guests

9. The word 'paradox' in the last sentence of the first paragraph means
(*a*) statement based on the popular opinion
(*b*) that which is contrary to received opinion
(*c*) statement based on facts
(*d*) that which brings out the inner meaning

10. It seems that low paid people should
(*a*) feel guilty if they overspend
(*b*) borrow money to meet their essential needs
(*c*) not keep their creditors waiting
(*d*) not pay their bills promptly

11. How does the housewife, described by the writer, feel when she saves money ? She .....
(*a*) wishes she could sometimes be extravagant
(*b*) is still troubled by a sense of guilt
(*c*) wishes life were less burdensome
(*d*) is content to be so thrifty

12. The statement "she is able to face the milkman with equanimity" implies that
(*a*) she is not upset as she has been paying the milkman his dues regularly.
(*b*) she loses her nerve at the sight of the milkman who always demands his dues.
(*c*) she manages to keep cool as she has to pay the milkman only a month's dues.
(*d*) she remains composed and confident as she knows that she can handle the milkman tactfully.

13. Which of the following is opposite in meaning to the word 'applauded' in the passage ?
(*a*) suppressed (*b*) cherished
(*c*) decried (*d*) humiliated

14. We understand from the passage that
(*a*) thrift may lead to success.
(*b*) wealthy people are invariably successful.
(*c*) all mean people are wealthy.
(*d*) carefulness generally leads to failure.

15. As far as money is concerned, we get the impression that the writer
(*a*) doesn't often have any money to save
(*b*) would like to be considered extravagant
(*c*) is never inclined to be extravagant
(*d*) is incapable of saving anything.

Passage 3 **(Bank P.O.1995)**

The recent rapid growth of industry has, in some cases, been so excessive that too much manufacturing capacity has been developed in some fields of production, which forces companies to sell their surplus products in world markets at prices lower than normal. This will make it almost impossible to develop local industries producing the same items because consumers will prefer to buy the cheaper imported product.

16. Why is it necessary for companies to sell products at cheaper prices ?
(*a*) The cost of production has been considerably low.
(*b*) The local industries also manufacture the same product.
(*c*) There is a heavy demand for these products.
(*d*) The demand has been lowered significantly.
(*e*) None of these

17. According to the passage, the situation resulting from the rapid industrial growth is
(*a*) favourable to the manufacturers
(*b*) disastrous to the exporters
(*c*) conducive to the growth of local industries
(*d*) unfavourable to the consumers
(*e*) None of these

18. 'This will make ....'— in this sentence, 'This' refers most closely and directly to
(*a*) development of local industries
(*b*) the recent rapid growth of industry
(*c*) selling products of excessively higher prices
(*d*) companies manufacturing surplus products
(*e*) companies selling their production at cheaper prices

19. Which of the following is/are most likely to hamper the development of local industries ?
A. Availability of imported product at cheaper rates
B. Consumer's tendency to refrain from using imported products

C. Excessive production capacity and low production cost

(*a*) Only A (*b*) Only B
(*c*) Only C (*d*) A and B
(*e*) A and C

20. 'Imported product' as used in the last product refers to
(*a*) product manufactured locally but of export quality
(*b*) product sold to such other country which can't locally manufacture it
(*c*) product of a foreign country available at a below normal price
(*d*) surplus product manufactured by foreign country and sold at a normal price

Passage 4

Gandhiji had to travel by train from Durban to Pretoria in connection with his job. Once while travelling by train, he was asked by the white passengers to leave the first class compartment and shift to the van compartment. He refused to do so. Thereafter he was pushed forcibly out of the compartment and his luggage was thrown on the platform. It was winter and he kept shivering all night. He did not go to the waiting room because the white men sleeping there might insult him further. This event was a turning point in the life of Gandhiji and he decided to stay back in South Africa and fight against this blatant injustice.

21. The White people asked Gandhiji to abandon the first class compartment because
(*a*) they wanted to annoy him.
(*b*) they wanted to avenge themselves on Gandhiji.
(*c*) they treated Indians as inferior to them.
(*d*) they were looking for a chance to talk to him.

22. Why was he thrown out of the compartment? Because......
(*a*) he misbehaved with the Whites.
(*b*) they wanted him to spend the night in the waiting room.
(*c*) they wanted to insult him.
(*d*) he refused to shift to the van compartment.

23. Why did he not go to the waiting room to spend the night?
(*a*) The room was unclean.
(*b*) He wanted to sleep in the open.
(*c*) He was badly hurt and so couldn't move to the room.
(*d*) He feared that the White men there might insult him further.

24. 'This event was a turning point in the life of Gandhiji'. The event being talked about here is
(*a*) Gandhiji' being ill treated by the Whites
(*b*) Gandhiji's spending night on the platform
(*c*) Gandhiji's travel by a train
(*d*) Gandhiji's staying back in Africa

25. Gandhiji stayed back in South Africa
(*a*) to avenge himself on the Whites who had insulted him
(*b*) because his work was still not complete
(*c*) to fight against racial discrimination in Africa
(*d*) to build up an army and fight against the White people

ANSWERS

1. (*c*)	**2.** (*d*)	**3.** (*c*)	**4.** (*a*)	**5.** (*b*)	**6.** (*c*)	**7.** (*b*)	**8.** (*d*)	**9.** (*b*)	**10.** (*a*)
11. (*d*)	**12.** (*a*)	**13.** (*c*)	**14.** (*b*)	**15.** (*a*)	**16.** (*e*)	**17.** (*e*)	**18.** (*b*)	**19.** (*e*)	**20.** (*c*)
21. (*c*)	**22.** (*d*)	**23.** (*d*)	**24.** (*a*)	**25.** (*c*)					

PRACTICE SET 5

Passage 1 **(Assistant Grade, 1995)**

Nationalism, of course, is a curious phenomenon which at a certain stage in a country's history gives life, growth and unity but, at the same time, it has a tendency to limit one, because one thinks of one's country as something different from the rest of the world. One's perspective changes and one is continuously thinking of one's own struggles and virtues and failing to the exclusion of other thoughts. The result is that the same nationalism which is the symbol of growth for a people becomes a symbol of the cessation of that growth in the mind. Nationalism, when it becomes successful, sometimes goes on spreading in an aggressive way and becomes a danger internationally. Whatever line of thought you follow, you arrive at the conclusion that some kind of balance must be found. Otherwise something that was good can turn into evil. Culture, which is essentially good becomes not only static but aggressive and something that breeds conflict and hatred when looked at from a wrong point of view. How are you to find a balance, I don't know. Apart from the political and economic problems of the age, perhaps that is the greatest problem today because behind it there is a tremendous search for something which it cannot find. We turn to economic theories because they have an undoubted importance. It is folly to talk of culture or even of God when human beings starve and die. Before one can talk about anything else one must provide the normal essentials of life to human beings. That is where economics comes in. Human beings today are not in the mood to tolerate this suffering and starvation and inequality when they see that the burden is not equally shared. Others profit while they only bear the burden.

1. The most suitable title for the above passage would be
   (*a*) Nationalism- a road to world unity
   (*b*) Nationalism breeds unity
   (*c*) Nationalism and national problems
   (*d*) Nationalism is not enough
2. Aggressive nationalism
   (*a*) isolates a country
   (*b*) endangers national unity
   (*c*) leads to stunted growth
   (*d*) breeds threat to international relations
3. Negative national feeling can make a nation
   (*a*) dangerous (*b*) indifferent
   (*c*) self-centred (*d*) selfish
4. 'The greatest problem' in the middle of the passage refers to the question
   (*a*) how to curb international hatred
   (*b*) how to share the economic burden equally
   (*c*) how to contain the dangers of aggressive nationalism
   (*d*) how to mitigate hardship to human beings
5. 'Others' in the last sentence refers to
   (*a*) other neighbours (*b*) other nations
   (*c*) other communities (*d*) other people

Passage 2

Culture is not merely learning. It is discrimination, understanding of life. Liberal education aims at producing moral gifts as well as intellectual, sweetness of temper as much as sanity of outlook. Into the art of living, the cultured man carries a certain grace,a certain refinement, a certain distinction which redeems him from the sterile futility of aimless struggle. Culture is not a pose of intellect or a code of convention, but an attitude of life which finds nothing human, alien, common or unclean. An education that brings up a young man in entire indifference to the misery and poverty surrounding him, to the general stringency of life, to the dumb pangs of tortured bodies and the lives submerged in the shadows, is essentially a failure. If we do not realise the solidarity of the human community, nor have human relations with those whom the world passes by as the lowly and the lost, we are not cultured.

6. Which of the following statements best expresses the theme of the passage?
   (*a*) Culture lends grace and sanity to man.
   (*b*) Culture and education are complementary to each other.
   (*c*) Liberal education makes man cultured.
   (*d*) Education brings man closer to life.
7. According to the writer,the function of liberal education is to
   (*a*) change the outlook of a person
   (*b*) increase intellectual powers
   (*c*) improve a person morally
   (*d*) develop sensitivity to human dignity
8. Consider the following :
   1. Brotherhood of man
   2. Understanding of pain and suffering
   3. Better human relations
   4. Sweetness of temper
   Which of the above expressions describes proper education?
   (*a*) 1 and 3 (*b*) 2 and 4
   (*c*) 2,3 and 4 (*d*) All the four
9. Culture redeems a person from the sterile futility of aimless struggle because
   (*a*) it makes man learned.
   (*b*) it makes man more intelligent.
   (*c*) it brings about a better understanding of life.
   (*d*) it prepares man for struggle.

10. Education is sometimes a failure. Which one of the following is the most likely reason for this?

(*a*) It improves the intellect only.

(*b*) It does not prepare man for struggle.

(*c*) It does not make man refined.

(*d*) It carries a man away from life around him.

Passage 3 **(U.D.C.1993)**

The supervisor would have to change his attitude towards people first. The staff under him must be perceived as human beings with feelings and needs. They are not automations within a complex work machinery. One of the greatest needs of today's worker is to have a feeling that he is in control of his work place and not vice versa.The best way is to satisfy this need as far as possible. He must feel firstly,that his work is meaningful. To do this the supervisor must delegate responsibility and limited authority for the man to execute his job well. The subordinate must be properly trained to assume responsibility and authority. Once he is ready to assume these he can be made accountable for his job. Very often supervisors assume all responsibility and accountability for fear of losing control of the workplace. This makes workers under him pawns in a vast chessboard. Delegating accountability gives the worker a purpose in life and the need to do a job well. Most important is to sit with each worker and chalk out common objectives and agreed norms to achieve them. This gives workers a security as to what is expected of them. When he has met his objectives he certainly has a feeling of achievement. This feeling of achievement is the greatest motivator.

11. A humane attitude on the part of the supervisor towards his staff is necessary to

(*a*) get them to work

(*b*) keep them happy

(*c*) have a congenial atmosphere at workplace

(*d*) get the best out of them

12. Responsibility and accountability make a worker

(*a*) shirk his duties

(*b*) do his job properly

(*c*) tense and frightened

(*d*) vulnerable before his supervisors

13. Supervisors do not delegate responsibility and authority to their subordinates because

(*a*) subordinates are not capable enough.

(*b*) they can't trust their subordinates.

(*c*) they are apprehensive of losing their hold on the place of work.

(*d*) final responsibility is theirs.

14. Orientation of subordinates of common objectives and how to achieve them is

(*a*) not very important (*b*) a must

(*c*) not at all necessary (*d*) optional

15. The greatest motivator is

(*a*) a good supervisor

(*b*) a good environment

(*c*) a sense of security

(*d*) fulfilment of purpose

Passage 4

The greatest enemy of mankind, as people have discovered is not science, but war. Science merely reflects the social forces by which it is surrounded. It is found that when there is peace, science is constructive, when there is war, science is perverted to destructive ends. The weapons which science gives us do not necessarily create war,these make war increasingly more terrible. Until now, it has brought us to the doorstep of doom. Our main problem, therefore, is not to curb science, but to stop war- to substitute law for force, and international government for anarchy in the relations of one nation with another. That is a job in which everybody must participate, including the scientists. But the bomb of Hiroshima suddenly woke us up to the fact that we have very little time. The hour is late and our work has scarcely begun. Now we are face to face with this urgent question : "Can education and tolerance, understanding and creative intelligence run fast enough to keep us abreast with our own mounting capacity to destroy?" That is the question which we shall have to answer one way or the other in this generation. Science must help us in the answer, but the main decision lies within ourselves.

16. An appropriate title for the passage would be

(*a*) Science and the new generation

(*b*) Science and social forces

(*c*) Science and the horrors of war

(*d*) Science and world peace

17. According to the author, the real enemy of mankind is not science but war, because
(*a*) science during wars is so destructive.
(*b*) science merely invents the weapons with which war is fought.
(*c*) the weapons that science invents necessarily lead to war.
(*d*) the weapons invented by science do not cause war, though these make it more destructive.
18. War can be stopped, if
(*a*) weapons invented by science are not used to launch a war.
(*b*) science is restricted to be utilised only during war time.
(*c*) science is not allowed to lead us to utter destruction.
(*d*) we replace force and lawlessness by law and international government.
19. According to the writer, the main problem we are faced with, is to
(*a*) prevent scientists from participating in destructive activities
(*b*) abolish war
(*c*) stop scientific activities everywhere
(*d*) stop science from reflecting social forces
20. Our mounting capacity to destroy can be kept under control by
(*a*) encouraging social forces
(*b*) education and broadmindedness
(*c*) insight and constructive thinking
(*d*) Both (*b*) and (*c*) together
21. The expression "bring to the doorstep of doom" means
(*a*) lead to the threshold of a new destiny
(*b*) introduce to an unpredictable destiny
(*c*) carry close to death and destruction
(*d*) induct in a ruinous activity
22. Which of the following is opposite in meaning to the word 'anarchy' as used in the passage?
(*a*) Law and order
(*b*) Economic prosperity
(*c*) Political dominance
(*d*) Communal harmony
23. The phrase 'our work has scarcely begun' implies that our work
(*a*) has not yet begun
(*b*) has begun but not yet completed
(*c*) has only just begun
(*d*) has been half through
24. The expression 'keep us abreast' in the passage means
(*a*) prevent from escaping
(*b*) hold out a challenge
(*c*) keep at a side
(*d*) keep side by side
25. Which of the following statements is not implied in the passage?
(*a*) Science is misused for destructive purposes.
(*b*) Neither science nor the weapons it invents add to the horrors of war.
(*c*) People needlessly blame science for war.
(*d*) The role of science in ensuring world peace is subsidiary to that of man.

ANSWERS

1. (*d*)	**2.** (*a*)	**3.** (*c*)	**4.** (*c*)	**5.** (*d*)	**6.** (*a*)	**7.** (*d*)	**8.** (*d*)	**9.** (*c*)	**10.** (*d*)
11. (*d*)	**12.** (*b*)	**13.** (*c*)	**14.** (*b*)	**15.** (*d*)	**16.** (*c*)	**17.** (*d*)	**18.** (*d*)	**19.** (*b*)	**20.** (*d*)
21. (*c*)	**22.** (*a*)	**23.** (*c*)	**24.** (*d*)	**25.** (*b*)					

PRACTICE SET 6

Passage 1 **(I.E.S. 1994)**

Some prophets of doom assert that we shall soon exhaust the Earth's resources or pollute ourselves to death. Optimists assert that Earth's systems are robust and that improved technologies will ease all the pressures on the planet. Others see the main concerns as political, with environmental issues carrying the seeds of inequality and war.

Scientific understanding is too limited to say where the truth lies. If the care of the planet is a management task, our species is in the position of a child who has to fly a jet plane without knowing what all the switches and levers do.

1. The blame for the environmental crisis facing the Earth lies with
(*a*) pressures of over population
(*b*) rapid technological growth

(*c*) inadequate management of Earth's resources

(*d*) man's greed and selfishness

2. Which of the following statements is true according to the passage ?

(*a*) People will feel exhausted owing to the green house effect.

(*b*) Sometimes political motives influence people's concern for the planet.

(*c*) Men should feel responsible towards society.

(*d*) Wars will cause greater pollution on Earth.

3. According to the passage, nobody knows the truth because

(*a*) objective analyses are not thorough or exhaustive.

(*b*) there are very few scientists capable of research in this area.

(*c*) scientists often are used by politicians.

(*d*) people do not think of what the future holds for them.

4. What does the comparison in the last sentence of the passage convey?

(*a*) We are as ignorant as infants.

(*b*) Our efforts to save the planet are childish.

(*c*) Most of the people do not know how to fly an aeroplane.

(*d*) We, on Earth, are inexperienced in managing Earth's resources.

Passage 2

It is a commonly held belief that quality and productivity are a function of technology or a set of new equipment. No doubt these are essential, but they alone are not sufficient for bringing about improvements in productivity or quality. It is the men and women behind the machines and the people who manage the technology who are critical in bringing about these improvements. It has been a strange paradox of India's economic development that even though people are our most abundant resource, they have so far either been neglected or treated as liabilities rather than as assets. Part of the reason for this has been outdated labour laws which have been a deterrent for industrialists and employers, leading them to establish capital-intensive rather than labour-intensive operations. The other reason has been a confrontationist attitude, both on the part of labour as well as managements. A change must come about in both these factors, outside representation and leadership of unions etc need to change. At the same time, the attitude of confrontation must change to one of cooperation and active collaboration.

5. Which of the following arguments has been emphasized in the paragraph?

(*a*) Only technology or a new set of equipment can improve quality and productivity.

(*b*) Only management behind any type of machines can improve quality and productivity.

(*c*) By managing the new technology, labour can bring about improvements in quality and productivity.

(*d*) Indian labour and management is neither quality nor productivity conscious.

6. The word 'critical' in the passage means

(*a*) crucial (*b*) judicial

(*c*) analytical (*d*) judicious

7. India's strange contradiction of development is

(*a*) people are resourceful but, new equipment is not given to them.

(*b*) people are resourceful but they are neglected.

(*c*) labour is not earnest and therefore it is no longer a liability.

(*d*) labour is inefficient but still it is pampered.

8. Capital-intensive operations can lead to

(*a*) strict labour laws

(*b*) new labour laws

(*c*) too many labour laws

(*d*) irrelevant labour laws

9. The opposite of 'deterrent' as used in the passage is

(*a*) help (*b*) non-interference

(*c*) influence (*d*) patronage

10. Labour-intensive operations can lead to

(*a*) better relations between labour and management

(*b*) fear of unemployment

(*c*) industrial process needing to employ many people

(*d*) None of these

11. Which of the following statements on confrontation between labour and management is false?

(*a*) Too much governmental interference between labour and management

(*b*) Conflicting attitude of labour and management

(*c*) Establishment of capital-intensive industries

(*d*) Neglect of labour-intensive operations

Passage 3 **(C.D.S. 1995)**

It is generally acknowledged that children learn a lot from their parents. It is not so commonly admitted that parents learn a great deal from their children. As adults, it is easy to assume that we are always right, but the laugh was on me one beautiful day.

My daughter Kashmira knew how much I loved flowers. One day when she was of nine years, she picked some branches from our neighbour's blossoming fruit tree. Realising she intended to please me, I didn't scold her, but chose a different approach.

"These are lovely, dear, but do you realise that if you had left them on the tree, each of these blossoms would have become a cherry?"

"No, they wouldn't have", she said firmly.

"Oh, yes, they would have. Each of these blossoms would have grown into a cherry."

"Well okay, mother, if you insist", she finally conceded, "but they were plums last year".

12. What is not commonly acknowledged is that
(*a*) children learn a lot from their parents.
(*b*) parents teach their children a great deal.
(*c*) parents learn a great deal from their children.
(*d*) children learn a great deal inspite of their parents.

13. "The laugh was on me" means that
(*a*) the mother was caught in the wrong.
(*b*) the daughter was wrong.
(*c*) people laughed at the mother.
(*d*) the mother laughed at herself.

14. What the daughter picked from the neighbour's garden were
(*a*) some branches (*b*) some flowers
(*c*) some branches with blossoms
(*d*) some branches with fruit

15. The mother did not scold the daughter because
(*a*) she loved flowers.
(*b*) she liked cherry blossoms.
(*c*) she did not understand why her daughter had done so.
(*d*) she decided to indirectly make her daughter realise her mistake.

16. The mother was caught in the wrong because the daughter
(*a*) proved that she had not picked the branch with the blossom
(*b*) reminded her that she loved flowers.
(*c*) reminded her that the branch with blossoms was from a plum tree.
(*d*) proved that those blossoms would not yield any fruit.

Passage 4

S.N. Bose's experimental skill was not confined to physics alone. His energy had been channelised in several directions. One direction in which his energy flowed more consistently than in any other was the popularisation of science. In a newly independent country like India, determined to develop her industries as quickly as possible, there was every danger of leadership in scientific research falling into the hands of those whom C.P. Snow has called 'slide-rule' scientists. As a safeguard against this, even before independence, Bose found a scientific journal in Bengali, *Bijnan Parichaya*, to spread scientific knowledge among the common people.

17. Bose could allow his energy to flow successfully in several directions. Bose was, thus,
(*a*) a vivacious man
(*b*) an energetic man
(*c*) a versatile man
(*d*) a virulent man

18. S.N. Bose made a major contribution to the spread of scientific knowledge among common people
(*a*) by channelising his energies in several directions
(*b*) by consistently working for the popularisation of science
(*c*) by becoming a 'slide-rule' scientist
(*d*) by founding a scientific journal in Bengali

19. It is learnt from the passage that India, immediately after becoming independent, sought to progress
(*a*) by means of industrialisation
(*b*) by means of popularisation of science
(*c*) by encouraging scientists like S.N. Bose
(*d*) by offering the leadership of scientific research to slide-rule scientists

20. A 'slide-rule' scientist is likely to be interested in
(*a*) spreading scientific knowledge among common people
(*b*) diverting his energy in several channels

(*c*) depriving common people of scientific knowledge
(*d*) carrying on scientific research on stereotyped ideas

21. S.N. Bose's scientific journal *Bijnan Parichaya* must have come out
(*a*) before 1947 (*b*) after 1947
(*c*) between 1947 and 1957 (*d*) after 1957

Passage 5 **(N.D.A. 1993)**

The avowed purpose of the exact sciences is to establish complete intellectual control over experience in terms of precise rules which can be formally set out and empirically tested. Could that ideal be fully achieved, all truth and all error could henceforth be ascribed to an exact theory of the universe, while we who accept this theory would be relieved of any occasion for exercising our personal judgement. We should only have to follow the rules faithfully. Classical mechanics approaches this ideal so closely that is often thought to have achieved it. But this leaves out of account the element of personal judgement involved in applying the formulae of mechanics to the facts of experience.

22. In exact sciences,
(*a*) one does not find answers to all questions and problems.
(*b*) one interprets the universe according to one's wish.
(*c*) personal judgements are set aside in favour of a mechanical theory.
(*d*) one reposes faith in actual experience.

23. The purpose of the exact sciences is to
(*a*) formulate principles which will help us to exercise our personal judgement
(*b*) make formal and testable rules which can help verify experience
(*c*) form opinions about our experience
(*d*) assert our intellectual superiority

24. An exact theory of the universe is
(*a*) not desirable (*b*) improbable
(*c*) yet to be made (*d*) possible

25. Classical mechanics
(*a*) has gained intellectual control over the world
(*b*) just falls short of achieving intellectual control over experience
(*c*) has formulated precise rules
(*d*) has formulated an exact theory of the universe

ANSWERS

1. (*d*)	**2.** (*b*)	**3.** (*a*)	**4.** (*d*)	**5.** (*c*)	**6.** (*a*)	**7.** (*b*)	**8.** (*d*)	**9.** (*a*)	**10.** (*c*)
11. (*a*)	**12.** (*c*)	**13.** (*a*)	**14.** (*c*)	**15.** (*d*)	**16.** (*c*)	**17.** (*c*)	**18.** (*b*)	**19.** (*a*)	**20.** (*d*)
21. (*a*)	**22.** (*c*)	**23.** (*b*)	**24.** (*b*)	**25.** (*b*)					

PRACTICE SET 7

Passage 1

Teaching, more even than most other professions, has been transformed during the last hundred years from a small, highly skilled profession concerned with a minority of the population, to a large and important branch of the public service. The profession has a great and honourable tradition, extending from the dawn of history until recent times, but any teacher in the modern world who allows himself to be inspired by the ideals of his predecessors is likely to be made sharply aware that it is not his function to teach what he thinks, but to instil such beliefs and prejudices as are thought useful by his employers.

1. In ancient times the teaching profession was
(*a*) reserved for the upper class
(*b*) reserved for a privileged few
(*c*) open to all
(*d*) limited to a highly skilled minority

2. What has transformed teaching into an important branch of public service is
(*a*) teaching skills
(*b*) technical developments
(*c*) utilitarian philosophy
(*d*) the demand of the employing industry

3. According to this passage, in modern times a successful teacher is primarily supposed to
(*a*) impart knowledge
(*b*) impart new and the latest skills

(c) toe the lines preferred by those in authority
(d) instil values he cherishes the most

4. The modern teacher is not able to follow the ideals of his predecessors because
(a) of tremendous advancements in professional skills
(b) of social and financial constraints
(c) the students are not serious about studies.
(d) the modern teacher has more interest in politics than in academic activity.

5. The author seems to
(a) be against the current trend in the teaching profession
(b) approve the recent developments in the mode of teaching
(c) be a traditionalist in his views
(d) consider education as a part of public service

Passage 2

How long I remained in the room with the cobra I cannot say. My servant said later that it was only half an hour, and no sound has ever been more welcome to me than the sounds I heard as my servant laid the table for dinner. I called him to the bathroom door, and told him of my predicament and instructed him to fetch a lantern and a ladder. After another long wait, I heard the babel of voices, followed by the scraping of the ladder against the outer wall of the house. When the lantern had been lifted to the window, ten feet above the ground, it did not illuminate the room, so I told the man who was holding it to break a pane of glass and pass the lantern through the opening. The opening was too small for the lantern to be passed in upright. However, after it had been relit three times, it was finally inserted into the room and, feeling that the cobra was behind me, I turned my head and saw it lying at the bottom of the bedroom door two feet away. Leaning forward very slowly, I picked up the heavy bath-mat, raised it high and let it fall as the cobra was sliding over the floor towards me. Fortunately I judged my aim accurately and the bath-mat crashed down on the cobra's neck six inches from its head. As it bit at the wood and lashed about with its tail, I took a hasty stride to the verandah door and in a moment was outside among a crowd of men, armed with sticks and carrying lanterns, for word had got round to the railway quarters that I was having a life-and-death struggle with a big snake in a locked room.

6. The incident narrated in the passage is
(a) humorous (b) tragic
(c) dramatic (d) thrilling

7. The room in which the writer is locked in with the cobra is his
(a) drawing room (b) bath-room
(c) toilet (d) bed-room

8. "It did not illuminate the room". Here 'illuminate' can be replaced by
(a) light up brightly (b) make colourful
(c) throw faint light (d) enlighten

9. A large crowd had gathered outside the writer's room, presumably to
(a) catch the snake
(b) kill the snake if it came out
(c) watch the writer's struggle with the cobra
(d) break open the door of the room

Passage 3 **(N.D.A. 1993)**

It is not luck but labour that makes men. Luck, says an American writer, is ever waiting for something to turn up; labour with keen eyes and strong will always turns up something. Luck lies in bed and wishes the postman would bring him news of a legacy; labour turns out at six and with busy pen and ringing hammer lays the foundation of competence. Luck whines, labour watches. Luck relies on chance, labour on character. Luck slips downwards to self-indulgence; labour strides upwards and aspires to independence. The conviction, therefore, is extending that diligence is the mother of good luck; in other words, that a man's success in life will be proportionate to his efforts, to his industry, to his attention to small things.

10. Which of the following statements sums up the meaning of the passage?
(a) Luck often ends in defeat but labour produces luck.
(b) Luck is self-indulgent but labour is selfless.
(c) Luck waits and complains without working while labour achieves success although it complains.
(d) Luck waits without exertion but labour exerts without waiting.

11. "........labour turns out at six and with busy pen and ringing hammer lays the foundation of competence".
This statement means

(*a*) the labourer lays the foundation of the building.
(*b*) there is no worker who works so hard as the labourer who begins his day at six in the morning.
(*c*) hard work of all kinds makes people efficient.
(*d*) the writer and the labourer are the true eyes of the society.

12. Which of the following words in the passage indicate that the writer does not ultimately reject the element of luck?
(*a*) "luck .... is ever waiting"
(*b*) "luck .... the postman would bring him news"
(*c*) "luck whines"
(*d*) "diligence is the mother of good luck"

13. Which of the following statements is true about the passage?
(*a*) Success depends only on hard work.
(*b*) Success is exactly proportionate to hard work.
(*c*) Luck is necessary for success.
(*d*) Expectation of good luck always meets with disappointment.

Passage 4

With the coming of the television, the radio no longer holds the same attraction for people as it did once. Yet somehow I have not quite reconciled myself to the idea of sitting in front of the TV, viewing it. I prefer the radio set, the good old box by your bedside. And here, again, the older and the larger the radio set the better for me. I do not like these new-fangled transistors. May be, I am old-fashioned.

14. "........I have not quite reconciled myself to ...." implies that the person has not fully
(*a*) applied (*b*) admitted
(*c*) accepted (*d*) understood

15. The word 'new-fangled' suggests
(*a*) very complex
(*b*) recently assembled
(*c*) colourfully decorated
(*d*) newly come into fashion

16. The passage implies that the author
(*a*) has a liking for television
(*b*) dislikes radio sets
(*c*) prefers transistors to radio sets
(*d*) prefers radio sets to transistors and the television

Passage 5 **(Bank P.O. 1995)**

Although a smiling face often disguises the mind and heart of villain, an indiscriminate generalisation of this phenomenon will do injustice to the innocent children whose faces bloom like flowers.

17. Which of the following is most nearly the same in meaning as the word 'disguises' as used in the sentecne?
(*a*) proves (*b*) hides (*c*) reflects
(*d*) conceals (*e*) reveals

18. The intention of the author seems to be
(*a*) to create a favourable opinion about people with smiling faces
(*b*) to forcefully defend the kind acts of villains
(*c*) to point out to an exception to the general rule
(*d*) to give justice to the generous actions of everyone
(*e*) to argue in favour of children who are sometimes guilty

19. The author of the sentence accepts the fact that
(*a*) the faces of the villains are never smiling.
(*b*) the faces of innocent children are as pleasing as the flowers in bloom.
(*c*) the faces of innocent children disguise ill acts.
(*d*) all the things that appear most beautiful are the ugliest within.
(*e*) an indiscriminate generalisation is justifiable in this case.

20. Which of the following is most opposite of the word 'indiscriminate' as used in the sentence?
(*a*) selective (*b*) broad
(*c*) conspicuous (*d*) promiscuous
(*e*) undistinguished

21. The author feels that an indiscriminate generalisation of the phenomenon
(*a*) should be done in all cases except children and flower
(*b*) would prevent villains from committing ill acts
(*c*) may lead good people to involve in ill actions
(*d*) would do justice to the children who are guilty
(*e*) would brand all people with smiling faces as villain

Passage 6

Do not study too long at once. So long as the mind works with ease, it may be allowed to continue working but if we find it moves slowly and extra trouble is needed to keep the attention fixed, it is far better to break off and take a walk or have some other recreation, than to go on plodding until one feels wholly exhausted. To continue to force the mind to work is likely to lead to injurious result and may end in a nervous breakdown from which recovery is slow and troublesome.

22. While making the observation "Do not study too long", the author suggests that
(*a*) excess of everything is bad.
(*b*) reading continuously for long hours is tiring.
(*c*) mind is delicate and it should not be taxed too much.
(*d*) doing mental work beyond a certain limit may cause serious injury to the man.

23. The underlying tone of the passage is that
(*a*) man should work within limits.
(*b*) man is delicate and should be handled carefully.
(*c*) an injury to the mind is more difficult to cure than an injury to any other part of the body.
(*d*) mind controls the entire physical system and should be kept in a perfect state.

24. A man feels that he is exhausted when
(*a*) he finds his mind working slowly
(*b*) he has a headache
(*c*) his thought process is clouded
(*d*) he finds it difficult to concentrate

25. The writer suggests that the main cause of nervous breakdown is
(*a*) a life of anxiety and worry
(*b*) too much work and little diversion
(*c*) exeessive mental work leading to exhaustion
(*d*) a strenuous life

ANSWERS

1. (*d*)	**2.** (*c*)	**3.** (*c*)	**4.** (*a*)	**5.** (*a*)	**6.** (*c*)	**7.** (*b*)	**8.** (*a*)	**9.** (*b*)	**10.** (*a*)
11. (*c*)	**12.** (*d*)	**13.** (*b*)	**14.** (*c*)	**15.** (*d*)	**16.** (*d*)	**17.** (*d*)	**18.** (*e*)	**19.** (*b*)	**20.** (*a*)
21. (*a*)	**22.** (*d*)	**23.** (*c*)	**24.** (*d*)	**25.** (*c*)					

PRACTICE SET 8

Passage 1 **(C.D.S. 1993)**

Mahatma Gandhi believed that industrialisation was no answer to the problems that plague the mass of India's poor and that villagers should be taught to be self-sufficient in food, weave their own cloth from cotton and eschew the glittering prizes that the twentieth century so temptingly offers. Such an idyllic and rural paradise did not appear to those who inherited the reins of political power.

1. Mahatma Gandhi's views opposed industrialisation of villages because
(*a*) it would take away the skill of the villagers.
(*b*) it would undermine self-sufficiency and destroy the beauty of life of the villager.
(*c*) it would help the poor and not the rich.
(*d*) it would affect the culture of the Indians.

2. The meaning of 'the glittering prizes that the twentieth century so temptingly offers' is
(*a*) replacement of rural by urban interests
(*b*) absence of violence and corruption
(*c*) pursuit of a commercialized material culture
(*d*) complete removal of poverty

3. The basis of 'an idyllic and rural paradise' is
(*a*) self-sufficiency in food and clothes and simplicity of life style
(*b*) supporting those holding powerful political positions
(*c*) rapid industrialisation of villages
(*d*) bringing to the villages the glittering prizes of the twentieth century

4. Which of the following best illustrates the relationship between the phrases :
(i) 'eschew the glittering prizes'; and
(ii) 'idyllic and rural paradise' ?
(*a*) the meaning of (i) is directly opposite to (ii).
(*b*) (i) and (ii) are identical in meaning.
(*c*) first of all you must have (ii) in order to do (i).
(*d*) unless you do (i), you cannot have (ii).

Passage 2

We are tempted to assume that technological progress is real progress and that material success is the criterion of civilisation. If the Eastern people become fascinated by machines and techniques and use them, as western nations do, to build huge industrial organisations and large military establishments, they will get involved in power politics and drift into the danger of death. Scientific and technological civilisation brings great opportunities and great rewards but also great risks and temptations. Science and technology are neither good nor bad. They are not to be tabooed but tamed and assigned their proper place. They become dangerous only if they become idols.

5. Science and technology will bring benefits to
(*a*) nobody
(*b*) only Western nations
(*c*) only Eastern countries
(*d*) all, if tamed properly

6. From the passage, one gathers that the Eastern people must
(*a*) build huge industrial organisations
(*b*) avoid being controlled by machines and techniques
(*c*) be fascinated by machines
(*d*) appreciate scientific achievements

7. According to the author, science and technology should be
(*a*) tabooed and eliminated from life
(*b*) used in a controlled and careful manner
(*c*) encouraged and liberally used
(*d*) extensively exploited for industrial production

8. According to the author, people think that real progress lies in
(*a*) working on the same lines as the Western nations
(*b*) taking risks and facing temptations
(*c*) material success and technological growth
(*d*) having large industries and political power

Passage 3 **(Translators' Exam, 1994)**

In this work of incessant and feverish activity, men have little time to think, much less to consider ideals and objectives. Yet how are we to act, even in the present, unless we know which way we are going and what our objectives are? It is only in the peaceful atmosphere of a university that these basic problems can be adequately considered. It is only when the young men and women, who are in the university today and on whom the burden of life's problems will fall tomorrow, learn to have clear objectives and standards of values that there is hope for the next generation. The past generation produced some great men but as a generation it led the world repeatedly to disaster. Two world wars are the price that has been paid for the lack of wisdom on man's part in this generation.

I think that there is always a close and intimate relationship between the end we aim at and the means adopted to attain it. Even if the end is right but the means are wrong, it will vitiate the end or divert us in a wrong direction. Means and ends are thus intimately and inextricably connected and cannot be separated. That, indeed, has been the lesson of old taught us by many great men in the past, but unfortunately it seldom remembered.

9. People have little time to consider ideals and objectives because
(*a*) they consider these ideals meaningless.
(*b*) they do not want to burden themselves with such ideas.
(*c*) they have no inclination for such things.
(*d*) they are excessively engaged in their routine activities.

10. 'The burden of life's problems' in the fourth sentence refers to
(*a*) the incessant and feverish activities
(*b*) the burden of family responsibilities
(*c*) the onerous duties of life
(*d*) the sorrows and sufferings

11. The two world wars are the price that man paid due to
(*a*) the absence of wisdom and sagacity
(*b*) his not caring to consider the life's problems
(*c*) his ignoring the ideals and objectives of life
(*d*) his excessive involvement in feverish activities

12. According to the writer the adoption of wrong means even for the right end would
(*a*) not let us attain our goal
(*b*) bring us dishonour
(*c*) impede our progress
(*d*) deflect us from the right path

13. The word 'vitiate' used in the second paragraph means

(a) negate (b) debase
(c) tarnish (d) destroy

Passage 4

If non-Hindi speaking people fought for one of their own languages to be declared as the official language, it should not have been so great matter of surprise, as it is when one finds these brave patriotic people fighting tooth and nail to retain English as the lingua franca which is as best as foreign language. Mahatma Gandhi never gave the problem of the necessity of a national language any lesser degree of importance than the problem of a national independence. He was strongly opposed to those blind protagonists of English who failed to realise the worth of a national language. He held it a crime against the children to educate them through the medium of foreign language.

14. Which of the following is the first step towards the progress of a nation?
(a) Promotion of national language
(b) Achievement of independence
(c) Educating the children through the medium of national language
(d) Having a foreign language as the official language

15. 'To fight tooth and nail' means
(a) to oppose
(b) to do a work with all possible ideas
(c) to fight with every possible effort
(d) to retain English as the official language

16. Which of the following represents Gandhiji's views on the education of children through foreign language?
(a) Nothing could be done as there was no national language.
(b) It was necessary for the moral development of the nation.
(c) It was a necessary step to develop relations with other countries.
(d) It was not the right act.

17. Which of the following is true in context of the given passage?
(a) English should be made the national language.
(b) Non-Hindi speaking people should fight for one of their own languages to be declared as the official language.
(c) Gandhiji laid more stress on having a national language than on achieving independence.
(d) Gandhiji was of the opinion that children should be educated through the medium of national language.

Passage 5 **(N.D.A. 1995)**

But I did not want to shoot the elephant. I watched him beating his bunch of grass against his knees, with that preoccupied grandmotherly air that elephants have. It seemed to me that it would be murder to shoot him. I had never shot an elephant and never wanted to. (Somehow it always seems worse to kill a large animal). Besides, there was the beast's owner to be considered. But I had got to act quickly. I turned to some experienced looking Burmans who had been tnere when we arrived, and asked them how the elephant had been behaving. They all said the same thing : he took no notice of you if you left him alone, but he might charge if you went close to him.

18. From the passage it appears that the author was
(a) a worried man
(b) possessed with fear
(c) kind and considerate
(d) an inexperienced hunter

19. The phrase 'preoccupied grandmotherly air' signifies
(a) calm, dignified and affectionate disposition
(b) a very superior attitude
(c) pretending to be very busy
(d) being totally unconcerned

20. The author did not want to shoot the elephant because he
(a) did not find the elephant to be ferocious
(b) was afraid of it
(c) did not wish to kill an animal which was not doing anybody any harm
(d) did not have the experience of shooting big animals

Passage 6 **(C.D.S. 1995)**

After submitting his resignation, Albert came out and took the long narrow road leading to the railway station which was one of the busiest roads in the city. Sad and depressed and worried about looking for a new job, Albert looked around for a cigarette shop. He walked up to the end of the road but found no tobacconist. It was odd that such a busy thoroughfare with thousands of people passing through did not even have a single cigarette shop. He suddenly felt that it was no longer necessary for him to hunt for a job. He decided to open a tobacco shop himself. It was bound to be profitable, he felt.

21. After submitting his resignation, Albert came out worried about
(a) a shelter (b) cigarettes
(c) a job (d) the next available train

22. Albert was sad and depressed because
(a) he had no money for the train journey.
(b) he had had to walk on a long road.
(c) he was not able to buy cigarettes.
(d) he was worried about finding a job.

23. There was no cigarette shop on that road because
(a) smoking is banned in that area.
(b) just by chance nobody had opened one on that road.
(c) it was a very narrow road.
(d) cigarette-shop owners do not make any profit.

24. Albert decided not to look for a new job because
(a) the thought of having to look for a job greatly distressed him.
(b) he did not want to work at all.
(c) there was no hope of finding a job.
(d) he saw the possibility of self-employment.

25. A cigarette shop on a busy road was bound to be profitable because
(a) cigarette shops are known to make a great deal of profit.
(b) any shop on a busy street would attract a large number of customers.
(c) cigarettes are inexpensive items and people buy them willingly.
(d) a cigarette shop on a busy road would attract a large number of customers.

ANSWERS

1. (b)	2. (c)	3. (a)	4. (d)	5. (d)	6. (b)	7. (b)	8. (c)	9. (d)	10. (c)
11. (a)	12. (d)	13. (b)	14. (b)	15. (c)	16. (d)	17. (d)	18. (c)	19. (a)	20. (d)
21. (c)	22. (d)	23. (b)	24. (d)	25. (d)					

PRACTICE SET 9

Passage 1 **(N.D.A. 1994)**

Most employees decide their own working hours, set production quotas, improving product and processes, are responsible for their own quality and for approval of leadership appointments. Every one votes on major corporate decisions and on how to split the profits.

As confidence in its novel approach has grown, Semco has happily abolished a lot more of the conventions by which businesses are usually run. No secretaries, receptionists or personal assistants. Reserved parking spaces and dining rooms, dress codes and almost all rules have gone, including those for travel and expenses.

1. From the passage it is clear that the novel approach referred to is
(a) Aristocratic (b) Autocratic
(c) Democratic (d) Bureaucratic

2. The employees referred to are
(a) Employees of a public sector undertaking
(b) Employees of a private company
(c) Employees of essential services
(d) Government Employees

3. In the given passage, 'Semco' is the name of
(a) A business establishment
(b) A brand of the product
(c) A novel approach to things and affairs
(d) The leader of secretaries, receptionists and personal assistants

4. The term 'leadership appointments' has been used in this passage to signify
(a) appointing officers-in-charge of various units/sections
(b) selecting political leaders
(c) selecting Company Directors
(d) choosing trade union leaders

Passage 2

It was clear that to climb Annapurna the right men had to be sufficiently high up on the mountain tc make their attempt on the peak while still fresh and strong. To ensure that, a chain of high camps must be established and the greater part of the work done by the Sherpas, so that the mountaineers would not tire themselves before they were in a position to attack the peak. Like all other expeditions to the Himalayas, the Frenchmen were to realise the value of the hardy mountain people, without whom they would soon find themselves too helpless to achieve their goal.

5. Annapurna must be the name of
(*a*) a mountain scape
(*b*) a mountain chain
(*c*) a mountain summit
(*d*) a mountain pass

6. To make the final attempt to climb Annapurna, the work that was to be done first was
(*a*) to have a station built on a high position of the mountain
(*b*) to have the greater part of the work done by the Sherpas
(*c*) to realise the nature of the hardy mountain people
(*d*) to remain fresh and strong

7. The work of establishing a chain of high camps had to be mainly done by the Sherpas because
(*a*) the Sherpas were particularly skilled.
(*b*) the Sherpas were particularly hardy.
(*c*) the mountaineers had to preserve their energy.
(*d*) the mountaineers had to maintain their superior status.

8. In the given context the expression 'to attack the peak' means
(*a*) to begin to climb the peak desperately
(*b*) to begin the final phase of climbing the peak with all vigours
(*c*) to rush upon the peak
(*d*) to use all force to climb the peak

9. The author is of the opinion that the French expedition would fail
(*a*) if the mountaineers did not establish a chain of high camps
(*b*) if the mountaineers failed to realise the nature of the Sherpas
(*c*) if the mountaineers did not remain fresh and strong
(*d*) if the mountaineers were deserted by the Sherpas

Passage 3 **(Bank P.O. 1994)**

The goals of our present system of primary and secondary schooling is to prepare students for the examination system which will take them to the best technical institutions in the country. While the teaching of science and mathematics has over the years been upgraded, the teaching of the humanities and social sciences continues to be straightjacketed in grotesque ways. Those areas of the Indian reality which ought to form the proper subject like caste, poverty and environmental degradation, if we are to create a responsible and aware body of citizens, form no part of the syllabus.

The capacity to think independently and critically about problems that plague modern Indian society, which ought really to be a prominent part of a humanities curriculum, is perceived to be intractable from the point of view of the examiner. Lest the evaluation become subjective, every effort is made to reduce both history and economics to a series of facts; a one-to-one correlation between facts ensures proper systems of grading.

10. What seems to be the purpose of the author in writing this passage?
(*a*) To appreciate the present educational system
(*b*) To reduce importance of science and mathematics in our system of education
(*c*) To critically look into the methods of teaching of science and mathematics
(*d*) To point out the deficiencies in the curriculum and examination system
(*e*) To put up a case for proper objective system of grading

11. According to the author, the present educational system ultimately helps the students in which of the following?
1. Understanding the real problems of the people
2. Acquiring various techniques to face the challenges of the future
3. Getting admission to renowned technical institutions

(*a*) Only 1 (*b*) Only 2 (*c*) Only 3
(*d*) Only 1 and 2 (*e*) 1,2 and 3

12. According to the author which of the following is the main reason leading to upgradation of teaching of science and mathematics?
(*a*) It inculcates proper values for becoming an ideal citizen.
(*b*) The syllabus of science and mathematics have been modified from time to time.
(*c*) Science and mathematics can solve our problems.
(*d*) The evaluation of these subjects is objective and critical.
(*e*) Not mentioned in the passage

13. According to the author, the teaching of science and mathematics develops capacity of the students in which of the following?

1. Considering pros and cons of each decision
2. Examining the problem minutely with proper analysis

(*a*) Only 1 (*b*) Only 2
(*c*) Both 1 and 2 (*d*) Either 1 or 2
(*e*) Not mentioned in the passage

14. The author seems to believe in which of the following?

1. Proper education can help a person to become a responsible and responsive citizen.
2. Objective evaluation is necessary for social sciences.
3. The capacity to think can be developed by a properly designed curriculum of humanities and social sciences.

(*a*) Only 1 (*b*) Only 2
(*c*) Only 3 (*d*) Both 1 and 3
(*e*) 1, 2 and 3

15. What problems does the author see in the improvement of the teaching of humanities and social sciences?

1. The present system of evaluation
2. The present syllabus of these subjects
3. The difficulties of the examiners

(*a*) Only 1 (*b*) Only 2
(*c*) Only 3 (*d*) 1, 2 and 3
(*e*) Not mentioned in the passage

Passage 4

Journalism combines writing with news gathering and interpretation. While the journalist's work obviously varies from newspaper to newspaper and from magazine to magazine, all journalists are as much research workers, as they are writers. They cannot write their news or feature stories, unless they locate it and research them first. They must be able to read the in-between lines of the main source-news and interpret that. A great many stories hunt the journalist, who rejects most of them. He carefully sorts and sifts those, taking only a relatively very small proportion of news, may be, coming from an unexpected source. A successful journalist may gather news to the tune of 100 percent but he can use them for his profession only 3-5 percent. He must be able to see or forecast to himself, the news of tomorrow or the day after, from the news of today; because newspapers want advance news or advance warning to give a good, exclusive and exhaustive coverage to anything of interest. But a real 'scoop' is a very rare event. And bogus scoops also bring disrepute to the newspaper.

16. According to the passage, a journalist's work includes

(*a*) writing
(*b*) news gathering
(*c*) sorting out the news
(*d*) all of the above

17. What, according to the passage, is the common characteristic of all journalists?

(*a*) They all write for the newspapers.
(*b*) They all have to first probe into the news they gather.
(*c*) They all make an adventure to find a worthy news.
(*d*) They all can forecast future news.

18. What is most important for a journalist?

(*a*) He must be able to interpret the news correctly.
(*b*) He must know how to sort out the news.
(*c*) He must be able to write effectively.
(*d*) He must know how to gather the right news.

19. What does the passage say about successful journalists?

(*a*) They reject a major portion of the gathered news.
(*b*) They can use a relatively small portion of the news.
(*c*) Their news come from unexpected sources.
(*d*) They present advance news.

20. What is the basic requisite for exclusive and exhaustive coverage of newspapers?

(*a*) Forecast of tomorrow's news from today's news
(*b*) Collecting the news of a 'real scoop'
(*c*) Selection of a small portion of the gathered news
(*d*) Effective style of writing

Passage 5

He had never thought much about the origin of wealth nor about the inequity of human conditions. He firmly believed that if this world was evil, the next could not but be good, and this faith upheld him. He was not like the clever fellows who sell their souls to the devil; he never took the name of God in vain; he lived the life of an honest man, and though he had no wife of his own, he did not covet his neighbour's, for woman is the enemy of strong men, as he learnt by the story of Samson which is written in the scriptures.

21. The passage indicates that the person the writer is talking about was
(*a*) not well-educated
(*b*) a deeply religious person
(*c*) an eccentric
(*d*) a scholar of the scriptures

22. The person described in the passage believed that
(*a*) one must remain a bachelor if one wanted to be happy.
(*b*) one must lead an honest life.
(*c*) if this world is not good, the next would certainly bring him happiness.
(*d*) repeating the name of God would give him peace of mind.

23. In this passage, the expression "he did not covet his neighbour's" means
(*a*) he never showed any anxiety to possess his neighbour's wealth.
(*b*) as he had no wife of his own he eagerly desired to have a woman in his life.
(*c*) though he had no wife of his own he never showed any interest in the wife of his neighbour.
(*d*) he did not find his neighbour's wife attractive.

24. The person mentioned in the passage presumed that woman was the enemy of a strong man because
(*a*) he firmly believed that woman was evil.
(*b*) he had read the story of Samson.
(*c*) surrendering to woman meant for him selling his soul to the devil.
(*d*) woman might spoil his chances in the next world.

25. "To sell one's soul to the devil" means to
(*a*) sell oneself to make both ends meet
(*b*) suppress the voice of one's conscience and take to an immoral life
(*c*) sell one's honesty for the sake of monetary benefits
(*d*) buy evil by mortgaging goodness

ANSWERS

1. (*c*)	**2.** (*b*)	**3.** (*d*)	**4.** (*d*)	**5.** (*c*)	**6.** (*d*)	**7.** (*c*)	**8.** (*b*)	**9.** (*b*)	**10.** (*d*)
11. (*c*)	**12.** (*d*)	**13.** (*e*)	**14.** (*d*)	**15.** (*d*)	**16.** (*d*)	**17.** (*b*)	**18.** (*a*)	**19.** (*b*)	**20.** (*a*)
21. (*c*)	**22.** (*b*)	**23.** (*c*)	**24.** (*b*)	**25.** (*c*)					

PRACTICE SET 10

Passage 1 **(Stenographer's Exam, 1995)**

Mountaineering is now looked upon as the king of sports. But men have lived amongst the mountains since pre-historic times and in some parts of the world, as in the Andes and Himalayas, difficult mountain journeys have inevitably been part of their everyday life. However, some of the peaks were easily accessible from most of the cities of Europe. It is quite interesting that while modern mountaineers prefer difficult routes for the greater enjoyment of sport, the early climbers looked for the easiest ones, for the summit was the prize they all set their eyes on. Popular interest in mountaineering increased considerably after the ascent of the Alpine peak of Matterhorn in 1865 and Edward Whymper's dramatic account of the climb and fatal accident which occurred during the descent.

In the risky sport of mountaineering the element of competition between either individuals or teams is totally absent. Rather one can say that the competition is between the team and the peaks themselves. The individuals making up a party must climb together as a team, for they depend upon one another for their safety. Mountaineering can be dangerous unless reasonable precautions are taken. However, the majority of fatal accidents happen to parties which are inexperienced or not properly equipped. Since many accidents are caused by bad weather, the safe climber is the man who knows when it is time to turn back, however tempting it may be to press on and try to reach the summit.

1. Mountaineering is different from other sports because
(*a*) it can be fatal.
(*b*) it is risky and dangerous.
(*c*) there is no competition between individuals.
(*d*) it is most thrilling and exciting.

2. People living in the Andes and the Himalayas made mountain journeys because
(a) they lived in pre-historic times.
(b) of the challenge offered by the difficult journey
(c) it was a kind of sport.
(d) they had to undertake them in their day-to-day life.

3. Mountaineers climb as a team because
(a) there is no competition among them.
(b) the competition is between the team and the peak.
(c) the height is too much for one individual.
(d) they have to rely on each other for safety.

4. "........ the summit was the prize they all set their eyes on". In the context of the passage this means
(a) they kept their eyes steadily on reaching the peak.
(b) reaching the top was their exclusive concern.
(c) they chose a route from which they could see the summit clearly.
(d) they cared for nothing but the prize of reaching the summit.

5. "to press on" in the last sentence means
(a) to force upon others
(b) to struggle in a forceful manner
(c) to continue in a determined manner
(d) to work fearlessly

Passage 2

India has always been an utmost inspiration for the world at large for her fabulous wealth, both material and economic prosperity as well as her spiritual excellence. It brought here both traders and invaders along with preachers and seekers in search of truth and salvation. All of them came through land routes by undertaking long and hazardous journeys which put a lot of stress and strain on their physique and nerves. Thus, the troops of Alexander mutinied and refused to march beyond Beas because of their weariness and fatigue in fighting and homesickness. They had, therefore, to be perforce despatched back. Many invading tribes like Kushans, Huns and Sakas in the ancient era and the Turks and Mughals during the medieval age, however, chose to make this land their own home and absorbed themselves in the stream of her life. They attempted their best to bring more and more lustre to her glory and enriched her culture, heritage and tradition.

6. The passage speaks voliably of
(a) India's past glory
(b) invaders who attacked India
(c) India's fabulous wealth
(d) India as a home for foreigners

7. What in India attracted traders, invaders and preachers?
(a) Its material and economic prosperity
(b) Its material and spiritual wealth
(c) The knowledge of truth and salvation
(d) Its fabulous wealth and glory

8. What exerted the foreigners who came to India?
(a) India's immense riches
(b) India's land routes
(c) Tiresome and risky jouneys to India
(d) Fighting with natives

9. What forced Alexander to move back to his country?
(a) The resistance of the natives
(b) The revolt of his armymen
(c) Sickness in his troops
(d) Lack of fighting spirit in his people

10. What good did Mughals bring to this country?
(a) They absorbed themselves into the stream of her life.
(b) They made India their homeland.
(c) They enriched its glory.
(d) They increased its wealth.

Passage 3 **(C.D.S. 1993)**

In most Western countries, it is required that every young man, when his education is complete, shall give three, four or five years to military service. He goes into barracks, is regimented and drilled, makes a unit in the standing army and passes out usually when his term is ended, an efficient soldier, to remain for the rest of his life ready at any moment to join in the armed defence of his country.

11. In the passage, the author opines that
(a) military training is more important than general education.
(b) military training should precede college education since it builds up one's mental and physical abilities.
(c) military training is as important as general training.
(d) military training must be included in the curricula of schools and colleges

12. Military training is as important as mental training because
(a) otherwise young men are useless.

(*b*) it is good that every scholar should also be an efficient soldier and be available for the country's defence.
(*c*) one gets a chance to live in barracks.
(*d*) war has become a daily affair.

13. Every young man has to undergo military training because he can
(*a*) get a job after such training
(*b*) supplement his general education according to his wish
(*c*) join the army whenever his country needs to be defended in war
(*d*) learn and practise discipline

14. In Eastern countries like India, military training of students should be made compulsory
(*a*) to fight the anti-social elements in every village or town
(*b*) to make youth serve the nation during times of war and peace
(*c*) as it can solve the unemployment problem by providing more jobs
(*d*) to repress communal riots

15. The author, writing in the early part of twentieth century, does not seem to talk about the need of military training for women because
(*a*) women's education was a new thing then.
(*b*) she thinks women are not physically strong enough to undergo military training.
(*c*) women taking part in military service is only a recent phenomenon.
(*d*) according to her, women should remain indoors.

Passage 4

The greatest thing this age can be proud of is the birth of Man in the consciousness of men. In his drunken orgies of power and national pride man may flout and jeer at it. When organised national selfishness, racial antipathy and commercial self-seeking begin to display their ugly deformities in all their nakedness, then comes the time for man to know that his salvation is not in political organisations and extended trade relations, not in any mechanical re-arrangement of social system but in a deeper transformation of life, in the liberation of consciousness in love, in the realisation of God in man.

16. In the phrase 'the birth of Man in the consciousness of men', Man stands for
(*a*) noble human qualities
(*b*) power and arrogance
(*c*) an idealistic notion of the human self
(*d*) egocentricity

17. People jeer at the 'birth of Man' in the human consciousness when they
(*a*) restructure the social system
(*b*) become power hungry
(*c*) begin to think of themselves as God
(*d*) become mentally deranged

18. In this passage, the phrase 'God in man' implies
(*a*) God having assumed the shape of man
(*b*) neither fully godly nor fully human
(*c*) man being transformed into God
(*d*) the divine qualities in man

19. According to the author, 'salvation' of human beings lies in the
(*a*) orgy of national pride
(*b*) extended trade relations
(*c*) spiritual transformation of life
(*d*) whole-hearted participation in political organisations

20. The author uses the expression 'ugly deformities' to show his indignation at
(*a*) the liberation of human consciousness
(*b*) selfishness and materialism of the people
(*c*) the drunken orgies of power
(*d*) political organisations

Passage 5 **(S.S.C. 1995)**

The ancient Azects, Chinese, Greeks and Romans played games in which a ball was kicked. A game called "futballe" was so popular in merry old England that King Henry II (1154-1189) became alarmed because he feared his soldiers would neglect practising archery. He, therefore, threatened to imprison any player and any one on whose land the game was played. The game was against the law in England for 400 years. It was made legal during the sixteenth century. By that time archery wasn't needed because firearms were used in warfare. King James I gave the sport his blessing, praising it as a clean, honourable and manly sport.

In 1863, many British football clubs formed an association and agreed to call the game association football. It is also called soccer, a word that comes from the *soc* in association. In most parts of the world the game is called football. At least ten different forms of football are played in the world today.

21. The writer implies that
(*a*) English kings were interested in sports.
(*b*) football became popular in 19th century England.
(*c*) modern football originated in England.
(*d*) football is an ancient game.

22. 'Futballe' was banned in England in the 12th century because
(*a*) players were using other people's land.
(*b*) King Henry was scared of sports.
(*c*) very few people wanted to join the army.
(*d*) soldiers were neglecting archery practice.

23. King Henry's law said that
(*a*) people playing the game would be imprisoned.
(*b*) spectators would be imprisoned.
(*c*) owners of football fields would be imprisoned.
(*d*) Both (*a*) and (*c*)

24. King James allowed people to play football because
(*a*) he was kinder than Henry II.
(*b*) he did not force people to practice archery for warfare.
(*c*) he liked the game very much.
(*d*) firearms were used in war instead of bows & arrows.

25. Football is a popular sport because
(*a*) it is an ancient sport.
(*b*) it is played in England.
(*c*) it is played all over the world.
(*d*) there are ten different forms of the sport.

ANSWERS

1. (*a*)	**2.** (*d*)	**3.** (*d*)	**4.** (*b*)	**5.** (*c*)	**6.** (*a*)	**7.** (*b*)	**8.** (*c*)	**9.** (*b*)	**10.** (*c*)
11. (*d*)	**12.** (*b*)	**13.** (*c*)	**14.** (*b*)	**15.** (*c*)	**16.** (*c*)	**17.** (*b*)	**18.** (*d*)	**19.** (*c*)	**20.** (*b*)
21. (*d*)	**22.** (*d*)	**23.** (*d*)	**24.** (*d*)	**25.** (*c*)					

PRACTICE SET 11

Passage 1 **(Hotel Management, 1993)**

The village has customarily been very conservative in his attitude and approach. He is reluctant to change his traditional way of thinking and doing things. His attitude, in many respects, is : 'home-made is best'. For instance, most cattle-farmers in the villages, prefer to feed their cows and buffaloes with a home-mix comprising of local oil-cakes like mustard or cottonseed, pulses, jaggery, salt etc. It takes numerous visits, hard-convincing, daily trials and experiments to convince the rural cattle farmer that compound feeds, scientifically formulated, improve the yields of milk, without any incremental costs.

The age-old values and attitudes towards caste, creed, women, time and money take time to change. The villager, has traditionally been a believer in the philosophy of 'Karma' or fate. He has found it more convenient to blame his economic destitution, poor living conditions, and straitened social status on 'bhagya', 'Karma' or 'fate'. The security that the villagers find in the 'status quo', acts as a discentive to change and experiment, in the short run. Many of these antiquated attitudes, value-system and outlooks are changing, due to improved levels of awareness and education. However, the rate of change is sluggish. Attitudes that have fossilised over the centuries, do take time to change.

1. When will you call a person conservative in his attitude and approach?
(*a*) When he would like to try out every new idea before accepting it
(*b*) When he sticks to old ways of thinking and doing
(*c*) When he solves his problems through tried out methods
(*d*) When he imputes motives to change-agents

2. What does the phrase "home-made is best" imply?
(*a*) Whatever is being practised is better than what is new.
(*b*) The best should not be discarded.
(*c*) Change for the sake of change is not good.
(*d*) People should go in for Swadeshi because it is home-made.

3. What is the best method to convince the average Indian villager about the superiority of a new cattle-feed?
(a) Home-visits (b) Field demonstration
(c) Discussion
(d) Distribution of related literature

4. Which of the following is not the usual reason offered by an average Indian villager for his poverty?
(a) It is his destiny.
(b) It is because of his resistance to new ideas.
(c) It is God's will.
(d) It is a result of some of his bad deeds committed in this or the previous birth.

5. Why does a villager feel secure in maintaining 'status quo'?
(a) Because change is seldom for the better
(b) Because of the imagined risk involved in trying a new approach
(c) Because whatever is known should be the best
(d) Because too many people go without advising him

Passage 2

Something is radically wrong with the entire structure of human relationships that makes man delight in killing man, whether it be in the name of civilisation or religion or anything else. Two wrongs do not make a right, hatred must beget hatred. It is this fundamental truth that women have got to bring home to the people in their respective countries. No peace treaties can avail that have revenge as their basis and self righteous arrogance and hypocrisy in the so called victors. But women are the natural preservers of life.

6. Which of the following expresses most accurately the idea contained in the opening sentence of the passage?
(a) Man destroying another man is a painful practice.
(b) A social structure that permits people to kill each other for religion is inherently rotten.
(c) It is strange that one religion encourages its followers to kill the followers of another religion.
(d) It is wrong on man's part to derive pleasure out of killing others for any motive whatsoever.

7. The expression 'Two wrongs do not make a right' means that
(a) a wrong action in retaliation does not mend matters.
(b) hatred destroys the person who perpetrates it.
(c) a tit for tat policy aggravates hatred.
(d) even repeated assertions of a wrong statement do not make it right.

8. Which of the following statements is not implied in the passage?
(a) It is human tendency to kill others professing different religion.
(b) It is the duty of women to foster peace and harmony amongst their countrymen.
(c) Peace treaties among nations tend to establish peace in the world.
(d) If you hate someone, he is bound to respond with the same feeling.

9. Which word is opposite in meaning to '*preserver*' as used in the passage?
(a) enemy (b) destroyer
(c) rival (d) belligerent

10. Which of the following would sum up most suitably the central idea of the passage?
(a) The role of women in the world of hatred and violence
(b) Man's instinct of destroying others
(c) Hatred leads to further hatred
(d) The significance of peace treaties

Passage 3 **(S.S.C. 1992)**

Bansilal's train was late and it reached Bombay a little after midnight. It was his first visit to the city, and he didn't know where to go. He thought he would go to a choultry where he would not have to pay rent, but he did not know how to find one at that hour. He asked a porter to get him a cheap room. The porter said that if Bansilal gave him three rupees, he would take him to one. But Bansilal waved him away and walked out of the station. He wandered through the streets and asked a number of people, but could not find a room cheap enough for him. He sat down on a park bench to think what he should do next. He was very tired and fell asleep on the bench. He woke up the next morning stiff in every limb-but he smiled when he realised that it was the cheapest night's lodging that he had ever had.

11. In the passage, the word 'choultry' should mean
(a) a highway motel
(b) an expensive hotel
(c) a free resting place
(d) a roadside eating shop

12. The porter refused to help Bansilal because
(*a*) he refused to pay the porter any tips.
(*b*) he spoke a language which the porter could not understand.
(*c*) he had no previous acquaintance with the porter.
(*d*) he was rude to the porter.

13. Bansilal could not get any accommodation for the night because
(*a*) he wanted to spend the night in the open.
(*b*) all the hotels in the city were closed.
(*c*) all the hotel rooms were booked.
(*d*) the hotels were too expensive for him to afford.

14. The night long in the open
(*a*) did not affect him at all
(*b*) made his limbs stronger
(*c*) gave him aches all over his body
(*d*) refreshed Bansilal

15. From the passage, Bansilal emerges as
(*a*) a fun-loving person
(*b*) an adventure-seeking person
(*c*) an extravagant spender
(*d*) a thrifty person

Passage 4

If the census tells us that India has two or three hundred languages, it also tells us, I believe, that Germany has about fifty or sixty languages. I do not remember anyone pointing out this fact in proof of the disunity or disparity of Germany. As a matter of fact, a census mentions all manner of petty languages, sometimes spoken by a few thousand persons only; and often dialects are classed for scientific purposes as different languages. India seems to me to have surprisingly few languages, considering its area. Compared to the same area in Europe, it is far more closely allied in regard to language, but because of widespread illiteracy, common standards have not developed and dialects have formed. The principal languages of India are Hindustani (of the two varieties, Hindi and Urdu), Bengali, Gujarati, Marathi, Tamil, Telugu, Malayalam and Kannada. If Assamese, Oriya, Sindhi, Kashmiri, Pushtu and Punjabi are added, the whole country is covered except for some hill and forest tribes. Of these, the Indo-Aryan languages, which cover the whole north, centre and west of India, are closely allied; and the southern Dravidian languages, though different, have been greatly influenced by Sanskrit, and are full of Sanskrit words.

16. In the passage the author
(*a*) compares India with Germany
(*b*) defends the multilingual situation of India
(*c*) criticises the illiteracy in India
(*d*) classifies the Indian languages

17. One of the reasons why there are many dialects in India is
(*a*) vast area (*b*) population
(*c*) more communities (*d*) illiteracy

18. The Dravidian languages have been greatly influenced by Sanskrit. This
(*a*) makes them inferior to the Indo-Aryan languages
(*b*) makes them superior to the Indo-Aryan languages
(*c*) brings them close to the Indo-Aryan languages
(*d*) makes them very different from the other Indian languages

19. Which of the following statements is true according to the given passage?
(*a*) India has far too many languages.
(*b*) India is a vast country with not too many languages.
(*c*) India has as many languages as Europe does.
(*d*) Indian languages are not as well developed as those of Europe.

Passage 5 (C.D.S. 1995)

At this stage of the civilisation, when many nations are brought into close and vital contact for good and evil, it is essential, as never before, that their gross ignorance of one another should be diminished, that they should begin to understand a little of one another's historical experience and resulting mentality. It is a fault of the English to expect the people of other countries to react as they do, to political and international situations. Our genuine goodwill and good intentions are often brought to nothing, because we expect other people to be like us. This would becorrected if we knew the history, not necessarily in detail but in broad outlines, of the social and political conditions which have given to each nation its present character.

20. The need for a greater understanding between nations
(*a*) will always be there
(*b*) is more today than ever before
(*c*) was always there

(*d*) is no longer there

21. According to the author the 'mentality' of a nation is mainly a product of its
(*a*) present character (*b*) politics
(*c*) international position (*d*) history

22. Englishmen like others to react to political situations like
(*a*) each other (*b*) others
(*c*) themselves (*d*) us

23. According to the author his countrymen should
(*a*) have vital contacts with other nations
(*b*) not react to other nations
(*c*) have a better understanding of other nations
(*d*) read the history of other nations

24. The character of a nation is the result of its
(*a*) socio-political conditions
(*b*) gross ignorance
(*c*) cultural heritage (*d*) mentality

ANSWERS

1. (*b*)	**2.** (*a*)	**3.** (*b*)	**4.** (*d*)	**5.** (*c*)	**6.** (*d*)	**7.** (*a*)	**8.** (*c*)	**9.** (*b*)	**10.** (*a*)
11. (*c*)	**12.** (*a*)	**13.** (*d*)	**14.** (*c*)	**15.** (*d*)	**16.** (*b*)	**17.** (*d*)	**18.** (*c*)	**19.** (*b*)	**20.** (*b*)
21. (*d*)	**22.** (*c*)	**23.** (*c*)	**24.** (*a*)						

PRACTICE SET 12

Passage 1 **(S.S.C. 1994)**

Education, as Mahatma Gandhi described it, "is the tool for the development of consciousness and reconstitution of society". Since Independence, India has stressed reforming and restructuring the educational system as part of state intervention. The National Policy on Education (NPE), 1986, which is hailed as a landmark in the Indian educational system, provided a comprehensive framework to guide the development of education in the country. The NPE and its Programme of Action was again updated in 1992 through similar consensual process involving all the State governments, resource organisations and educationists.

What has been worrying the critics and educationists alike is the non-fulfilment of one of the NPE objectives: education of girl. It has been stated in the NPE that the 'Education For All' meet should have a strong gender focus as Education For All by definition is gender inclusive.

1. According to Mahatma Gandhi, education is
(*a*) a medium through which people are taught to become sensitive to the realities around them
(*b*) a tool to develop their conscience and constitution
(*c*) a tool to develop their understanding of the constitution of society
(*d*) an instrument to develop their society consciously

2. The National Policy on Education provided
(*a*) guidelines for the comprehension of education in the country
(*b*) guidance material to develop education in the country
(*c*) a comprehensive plan for the development of education in the country
(*d*) comprehensive development of education in the country

3. According to the passage, critics and educationists are worried that
(*a*) the education of girls is one of the objectives of NPE.
(*b*) the objectives of NPE have not been fulfilled.
(*c*) non-fulfilment of NPE leads to the education of girls.
(*d*) one of the objectives of NPE has not been fulfilled.

4. According to the passage, 'a strong gender focus' means
(*a*) a focus on the strength of gender
(*b*) a focus on strong gender
(*c*) a strong focus on gender bias
(*d*) a focus on male-female ratio

5. In the passage, the author makes a plea for
(*a*) free education
(*b*) universal education
(*c*) the education of men
(*d*) the education of women

Passage 2 **(C.D.S. 1993)**

Modern economics does not differentiate between renewable and non-renewable materials, as its method is to measure everything by means of a money price. Thus, taking various alternative fuels, like coal, oil, wood or water power: the only difference between them recognised by modern economics is relative cost per equivalent unit. The cheapest is automatically the one to be preferred, as to do otherwise would be irrational and 'uneconomic.' From a Buddhist point of view, of course, this will not do, the essential difference between non-renewable fuels like coal and oil on the one hand and renewable fuels like wood and water–power on the other cannot be simply overlooked. Non-renewable goods must be used only if they are indispensable, and then only with the greatest care and the highest concern for conservation. To use them carelessly or extravagantly is an act of violence, and while complete non-violence may not be possible on this earth, it is none the less the duty of man to aim at the ideal of non-violence in all he does.

6. In this passage, the author is trying to
(*a*) differentiate between two economic philosophies
(*b*) underline the need for conserving natural resources
(*c*) show that the modern economist is concerned only with costs
(*d*) differentiate between renewable and non-renewable materials

7. According to the passage, Buddhist economists are not in favour of
(*a*) using non-renewable sources
(*b*) measuring everything in terms of money
(*c*) applying non-violence to every sphere of life
(*d*) economic development

8. The Buddhist economist's attitude implies that fuels like coal and oil must be used only if
(*a*) there is no alternative fuel available.
(*b*) the relative cost of each is lower than that of wood and water.
(*c*) wood and water power can be dispensed with.
(*d*) there is a plentiful supply.

9. Which of the following statements may be assumed to be false from information in the passage?

1. The writer finds the attitude of modern economists towards natural resources to be uneconomic.
2. Buddhist economists are indifferent to the cost of fuels.
3. To use oil on non-essentials is contrary to the Buddhist economic philosophy.
4. To fell a tree is an act of violence not permitted by Buddhist economists.

Of the above statements, the correct ones are
(*a*) 1 and 2 (*b*) 1,2 and 4
(*c*) 3 and 4 (*d*) 1,2,3 and 4

10. Fill in the blanks with the appropriate pair of phrases:
The passage suggests that while a modern economist considers it uneconomic to use .... form of fuel, a Buddhist economist considers it uneconomic to use .... form of fuel.
(*a*) a rational - an unessential
(*b*) an expensive - an unrenewable
(*c*) an irrational - an essential
(*d*) a cheap - a renewable

Passage 3 **(C.D.S. 1993)**

Over all the countryside, wherever one goes, indications of technique are visible to the seeing eye. By technique is meant an exercise of skill acquired by practice and directed to a well- foreseen end. It is the name for the action of any of our powers after they have been so improved by training as to perform that action with certainty and success.

11. The italicised phrase in the sentence "Over all the countryside, wherever one goes, indications of technique are visible to *the seeing eye*" implies
(*a*) seeing the particular characteristics of things
(*b*) seeing with a clear eyesight
(*c*) perception caused by understanding
(*d*) application of some special device for the analysis of the things seen

12. The most important aspect of 'technique', as defined in the passage, is the use of skill
(*a*) for handling tools and machines
(*b*) for an understanding of the functions of tools and machinery
(*c*) for observation and analysis
(*d*) for a definite purpose

13. 'Skill' in this passage means
(*a*) 'any of our powers'
(*b*) the ability to do things well by hand

(*c*) the ability to master techniques
(*d*) the ability that has been tested by experience which makes success sure

14. The definition of the word 'technique' as given in the passage, does not overemphasize
(*a*) scientific methods (*b*) results
(*c*) theoretical knowledge
(*d*) practice and performance

15. The implied intention of the writer is to
(*a*) widen the scope of the term 'technique'
(*b*) mock at the modern craze for gadgets
(*c*) reject the popular meaning of the term 'technique'
(*d*) uphold the superiority of traditional techniques

Passage 4

We stand poised precariously and challengingly on the razor's edge of destiny. We are now at the mercy of atom bombs and the like which would destroy us completely if we fail to control them wisely. And wisdom in this crisis means sensitiveness to the basic values of life; it means a vivid realisation that we are literally living in one world where we must either swim together or sink together. We cannot afford to tamper with man's single minded loyalty to peace and international understanding. Anyone who does it is a traitor not only to man's past and present, but also to his future, because he is mortgaging the destiny of unborn generations.

16. From the tone and style of the passage it appears that the writer is
(*a*) a prose writer with a fascination for images and metaphors
(*b*) a humanist with a clear foresight
(*c*) a traitor who wishes to mortgage the destiny of future generations
(*d*) unaware of the global power situation

17. The best way to escape complete annihilation in an atomic war is to
(*a*) work for international understanding and harmony
(*b*) invent more powerful weapons
(*c*) turn to religion
(*d*) ban nuclear weapons

18. The phrase 'razor's edge of destiny' means a/an
(*a*) enigma that cuts through the pattern of life like the edge of a razor
(*b*) a critical situation that foreordains the future
(*c*) a sharp line of division that marks the alternative courses of action in the future
(*d*) destiny having sharp edges

19. According to the writer, 'wisdom' in the present crisis means
(*a*) awareness that we stand poised precariously on the razor's edge of destiny
(*b*) determination to ban nuclear weapons
(*c*) responsibility to the 'unborn generations'
(*d*) awareness of the basic values of life

20. The author is so concerned about the threat of nuclear weapons because he feels that
(*a*) a nuclear war will destroy human civilisation.
(*b*) all countries are interlinked and one cannot escape the consequences of what happens to another country.
(*c*) the world is on the brink of disaster.
(*d*) his country is threatened by a nuclear war.

Passage 5 **(I.E.S. 1993)**

Until very recently, it was universally believed that men are congenitally more intelligent than women; even so enlightened a man as Spinoza decided against votes for women on this ground. Among white men, it is held that white men are by nature superior to men of other colours, and especially to black men; in Japan, on the contrary, it is thought that yellow is the best colour. In Haiti, when they make statues of Christ and Satan, they make Christ black and Satan white. Aristotle and Plato considered Greeks so innately superior to barbarians that slavery was justified so long as the master was Greek and the slave barbarian.

21. 'Congenitally' means
(*a*) falsely (*b*) fantastically
(*c*) innately (*d*) certainly

22. Spinoza decided against votes for women because according to him
(*a*) they did not deserve to have votes.
(*b*) they were less educated than men.
(*c*) they were generally unintelligent.

(*d*) they were naturally less gifted with intelligence.

23. In Haiti, Christ's statue is black and Satan's white because the people there believe that
(*a*) black was good
(*b*) all white men are evil
(*c*) Christ was evil (*d*) Satan was good

24. Aristotle and Plato supported slavery because they thought
(*a*) slaves to be inferior
(*b*) that the barbarians belonged to Greece
(*c*) the Greeks to be superior to barbarians
(*d*) the barbarians to be superior to Greeks

25. The author believes that
(*a*) colours vary from country to country.
(*b*) some colours are superior to other colours.
(*c*) some colours are inferior to other colours
(*d*) colours have no relevance to superiority

ANSWERS

1. (*d*)	**2.** (*c*)	**3.** (*d*)	**4.** (*c*)	**5.** (*d*)	**6.** (*c*)	**7.** (*b*)	**8.** (*a*)	**9.** (*c*)	**10.** (*b*)
11. (*c*)	**12.** (*d*)	**13.** (*d*)	**14.** (*a*)	**15.** (*a*)	**16.** (*b*)	**17.** (*a*)	**18.** (*c*)	**19.** (*d*)	**20.** (*a*)
21. (*c*)	**22.** (*d*)	**23.** (*b*)	**24.** (*c*)	**25.** (*d*)					

PRACTICE SET 13

Passage 1 **(N.D.A. 1993)**

Books are, by far, the most lasting product of human effort. Temples crumble into ruin, pictures and statues decay, but books survive. Time does not destroy the great thoughts which are as fresh today as when they first passed through their author's mind. These thoughts speak to us through the printed page. The only effect of time has been to throw out of currency the bad products. Nothing in literature which is not good can live for long. Good books have always helped man in various spheres of life. No wonder that the world keeps its books with great care.

1. Of the products of human effort, books are the most
(*a*) enjoyable (*b*) useful
(*c*) permanent (*d*) important

2. Time does not destroy books because they contain
(*a*) high ideals (*b*) great ideas
(*c*) useful material
(*d*) subject-matter for education

3. "To throw out of currency" means
(*a*) extinguish (*b*) forget
(*c*) destroy (*d*) put out of use

4. The world keeps its books with care because
(*a*) they make us successful.
(*b*) they help us in various spheres of life.
(*c*) they bring great ideas to us.
(*d*) they educate us.

Passage 2

Democracy, so long as it is what it is, imperfectly educated, throws a great responsibility on the leaders. The average voter even in educated England has no opinion of his own on many questions. He chooses his party by tradition or by his agreement with its central aims in those matters on which he has strong views. On other questions he takes his opinions from the leaders. His conscience is clear when the party is chosen and for the rest the leaders decide and the voters obey. In a complex social machine, it is difficult for the units to exercise thought. It is more easy to be obedient automata. It does not even pay to think. Perhaps thought may prove costly. If the leaders want to create public opinion, the machinery of the press and the wireless makes it most easy. Modern conditions afford propagandists vastly increased opportunities of promoting collective excitement and setting the world in a conflagration. A few clever and adventurous leaders can excite people's passions and suppress intellectual freedom. In these circumstances, truth does not win as there is no attempt to find out truth.

5. The most suitable title for the given passage would be
(*a*) Democracy and public opinion
(*b*) Democracy and intellectual freedom
(*c*) The role of leaders in a democracy
(*d*) The role of voters in a democracy

6. The opening sentence of the passage implies that
(*a*) the responsibility of educating a democracy lies with its leaders.
(*b*) leaders in democracy with imperfectly educated voters have to shoulder great responsibility.
(*c*) a well educated democracy is based on responsible leadership.
(*d*) in a democracy with uneducated masses the leaders are highly duty conscious.

7. From the third sentence "He chooses his party by tradition ....", we gather that
(*a*) an English voter selects a party which strongly stands for traditional and popular beliefs.
(*b*) the average voter in England votes for a party because of tradition irrespective of his agreement or disagreement with its basic policies.
(*c*) in England an average voter supports a party either as a practice or because of his agreement with its broad policies.
(*d*) in a democracy one votes for a party with whose objectives and policies he agrees on all matters.

8. "In a complex social machine .... "— the statement implies that
(*a*) it is difficult for an individual to challenge a complicated social machinery.
(*b*) in a society which works like a machine an individual cannot be permitted to have his own political ambitions.
(*c*) in a mechanical age a person cannot have individual aspirations.
(*d*) an individual finds it hard to formulate his own opinion in a complicated social structure.

9. The statement: "it does not even pay to think" means that
(*a*) thinking is actually discouraged.
(*b*) thoughtful persons are condemned.
(*c*) thinking brings no advantage.
(*d*) thinking is not allowed.

10. According to the author, it is most convenient for a leader to "create public opinion" because
(*a*) he has been chosen by the public whom he represents.
(*b*) the modern means of mass communi cation are readily available to him.
(*c*) even an educated voter takes his opinion from the leader.
(*d*) the average voter has no opinion of his own.

11. The word 'conflagration' in the passage signifies
(*a*) confusion (*b*) widespread fire
(*c*) conflict (*d*) unforeseen calamity

12. Which of the following has the opposite meaning to the word 'suppress' as used in the passage?
(*a*) encourage (*b*) tolerate
(*c*) dominate (*d*) describe

13. Which of the following statements expresses most accurately the idea contained in the last sentence of the paragraph?
(*a*) Some adventurous leaders encourage people's free thinking in an effort to get down to the true state of things.
(*b*) An overambitious leader infuriates the mob and thus spreads falsehoods to serve his own ends.
(*c*) At a time when clever leaders fan public feelings, nobody wants to know the truth which thus gets lost.
(*d*) When public fury is aroused by cunning leaders some people are fed on lies.

14. Which one of the following statements is not implied in the passage?
(*a*) In democracy an average voter is generally led by the leader.
(*b*) An individual in a democracy finds it easier to obey his leader than to do his own thinking.
(*c*) A propagandist leader in a democracy can excite mob hysteria so as to cloud the truth.
(*d*) A clever leader in a democracy arouses strong public frenzy in an effort to find out the truth

Passage 3 **(I.E.S. 1994)**

The low unit of gas is a real temptation to anyone choosing between gas and electrical processes. But gas-fired processes are often less efficient, require more floor space, take longer and produce more variable product quality. The drawbacks negate the savings many businesses believe they make.

By contrast, electricity harnesses a unique range of technologies unavailable with gas. And many electric processes are well over 90 percent efficient, so far less energy is wasted with benefits in terms of products quality and overall cleanliness, it can so often be the better and cheaper choice. Isn't that tempting?

15. The passage can be described as
(*a*) an account of the growth of technology
(*b*) an appeal not to use gas
(*c*) an advertisement for electricity and its efficiency
(*d*) an extract from a science journal

16. What does the writer mean by 'variable quality'?
(*a*) The kind of products vary from time to time.
(*b*) The quality of the products is not uniform.
(*c*) The quality of the products cannot be assessed.
(*d*) Products from gas-fired processes are inefficient.

17. "Electricity harnesses a unique range of technologies"— What does the writer mean?
Electricity
(*a*) depends on new kinds of technology
(*b*) makes use of several technologies
(*c*) has developed new technologies
(*d*) ensures power for electricity and its efficiency

Passage 4

There are certain people, however, with whom one has a right to be bored-people who are so self-centred that they cannot listen to anyone else talking, people who engage in long conversations with their cats when visitors are present, people who engage endless reminiscences of their old school when in the company of a man who was at a different school. Such people are boring because they make one feel for the time being an outsider.

18. Boring persons are generally
(*a*) talkative (*b*) quiet
(*c*) indifferent (*d*) tedious

19. The most pleasing type of company is where people
(*a*) chit-chat with you in a patronising mood
(*b*) listen to you with awe and respect
(*c*) make you feel that they appreciate your conversation
(*d*) shower on you a lot of flattering remarks

20. The expression 'endless reminiscences' stands for
(*a*) a boring and lengthy talk
(*b*) a very long conversation
(*c*) a long chain of events
(*d*) an unending recollection of past experiences

21. A person feels an outsider in a company when
(*a*) everybody wants to know the details about him.
(*b*) he finds that people are talking of things which do not concern him.
(*c*) he does not know anybody.
(*d*) he finds that everyone present there is more intelligent than he is.

Passage 5 **(Railways, 1993)**

Gandhiji recognised that while all men should have equal opportunity, all did not have the same capacity. Some had the ability to earn more than others. But he believed that those who had talent would be performing the work of society if they used their talent wisely and well. Gandhiji said that he would allow a man of intellect to earn more and not suppress his talent. But it was his view that the bulk of his larger earnings should go to the common fund. Those with talent and opportunity would find their fulfillment as trustees. Gandhiji extended this concept of trusteeship to cover all fields of life.

22. The title of the passage should be
(*a*) Gandhiji's philosophy
(*b*) Gandhiji's services
(*c*) Gandhiji's views
(*d*) Gandhiji's character

23. According to Gandhiji, one can serve the society
(*a*) if he worked honestly
(*b*) if he earned well
(*c*) if he is talented
(*d*) if he used his talent wisely

24. Gandhiji never believed in
(*a*) political equality
(*b*) social equality
(*c*) equality of opportunities
(*d*) complete equality in all respects

25. The meaning of 'Trustee' is
(*a*) person having confidence
(*b*) person who has charge of property in trust
(*c*) a number of trusts
(*d*) state official who executes wills and trusts

ANSWERS

1. (c) 2. (b) 3. (d) 4. (b) 5. (c) 6. (b) 7. (c) 8. (d) 9. (c) 10. (b)
11. (a) 12. (a) 13. (c) 14. (d) 15. (d) 16. (b) 17. (b) 18. (a) 19. (c) 20. (d)
21. (b) 22. (c) 23. (d) 24. (d) 25. (b)

PRACTICE SET 14

Passage 1 **(C.B.I. 1995)**

There was a marked difference of quality between the personages who haunted the near bridge of brick and the personages who haunted the far one of stone. Those of lowest character preferred the former, adjoining the town; they did not mind the glare of the public eye. They had been of no account during their successes; and though they might feel dispirited, they had no sense of shame in their ruin. Instead of sighing at their adversaries they spat, and instead of saying the iron had entered into their souls they said they were down on their luck. The miserables who would pause on the remoter bridge were of a politer stamp—persons who did not know how to get rid of the weary time. The eyes of this species were mostly directed over the parapet upon the running water below. While one on the townward bridge did not mind who saw him so, and kept his back to the parapet to survey the passer-by, one on this never faced the road, never turned his head at coming foot-steps, but, sensitive to his own condition, watched the current whenever a stranger approached, as if some strange fish interested him, though every finned thing had been poached out of the river years before.

1. The two bridges were known
   (a) for being haunted places
   (b) for their similar design
   (c) for attracting dejected people to them
   (d) for being equi-distant from town
2. People belonging to the lower strata, in their moments of distress
   (a) visited the brick-made bridge
   (b) remembered their days of glory
   (c) felt ashamed of their failures
   (d) dressed shabbily to earn sympathy
3. The bridge of stone was frequented by
   (a) those fond of fishing
   (b) the sophisticated but luckless
   (c) all the sections of society
   (d) None of the above
4. The attitude of the lowly and genteel towards strangers was
   (a) entirely different
   (b) virtually the same
   (c) virulently hostile
   (d) completely indifferent
5. In this passage, the author is trying to
   (a) explain the difference between the construction of two bridges
   (b) describe the way different sections of people like to dress
   (c) explain the variety of ways in which strangers can be treated
   (d) describe how people of different classes behaved when unhappy

Passage 2 **(N.D.A. 1995)**

The last twenty years have witnessed an explosion of growth opportunities for women in industry, especially at the decision-making level. Today more and more young women have a chance to walk the competitive edge and prove that their abilities are at par with, if not better than, those of their male colleagues.

However, as they are beginning to storm the traditionally male bastions of management they are finding out that the roads to success are paved with difficulties. They discover very early in their career that the battle for supremacy in corporate organisations calls into play not only the forces of power, control and dominance, but issues of gender, attitude and acceptance of women.

6. The first sentence of the passage implies that job opportunities
   (a) in industry have increased
   (b) for women have increased
   (c) in the corporate sector have increased
   (d) for women at the managerial level have increased

7. According to the passage, women in high positions also have
   (*a*) no problems at all
   (*b*) some problems
   (*c*) problems related to roles of women in society
   (*d*) problems related to power and control
8. Which of the following phrases best reflects the meaning of 'male bastions'?
   (*a*) Management areas dominated by males
   (*b*) Management abilities of males
   (*c*) Management styles of males
   (*d*) Careers for males

Passage 3 **(N.D.A. 1994)**

As far as industrial pollution is concerned, while a commendable job has been done by the department of environment in making environmental impact assessment studies and ensuring that new big industries have built-in systems for pollution abatement and control, the problem of controlling pollution caused by small new units and existing plants has so far eluded solution.

The 1986 Act has undoubtedly given greater legal powers to State Pollution Boards and other concerned authorities to penalise offenders. However, it must be recognised that punitive action alone will not suffice. If we are really serious about controlling industrial pollution, the carrot must be used along with the stick.

9. The problem of controlling industrial pollution remains unsolved because
   (*a*) offenders are not punished.
   (*b*) State Pollution Boards and other concerned authorities haven't got sufficient legal powers to deal with the offenders.
   (*c*) the problem has not been dealt with in a comprehensive manner.
   (*d*) the industrialists are not cooperating with the government.
10. In order to control industrial pollution
    (*a*) existing plants without pollution abatement and control systems should be closed down.
    (*b*) no new small units should be allowed to come up.
    (*c*) no new big industries should be allowed to come up.
    (*d*) only such new big industries should be allowed to come up that have built-in-systems for pollution control.
11. Industrial pollution can be controlled only when
    (*a*) State Pollution Boards and other concerned authorities are given more legal powers to deal with the offenders.
    (*b*) the policy of reward and punishment is introduced.
    (*c*) no small units are allowed to come.
    (*d*) existing plants without pollution abatements and control systems are closed down.
12. The author feels that the 1986 Act
    (*a*) is of immense help in controlling industrial pollution
    (*b*) deters offenders
    (*c*) is not of much help in controlling industrial pollution
    (*d*) gives more legal powers to State Pollution Boards and other concerned authorities.

Passage 4

Even an ordinary everyday activity may lead to an insight into human nature.

A picnic had been arranged by the department. Everyone was supposed to join it. I, being older than a good many, was ill at ease at the thought of joining a bunch of callow youngsters dreaming of some soft and sweet company on the way to the hill resort.

But the morning of the adventure found the boy in me climbing the first ascent-rather steep and hard, to the applause of all Adams and Eves in the troop.

Half way through we started finding snow all around us, but, the boy in me by then was once again lost into oblivion. I found myself lagging behind and often falling down on the soft snow due to soft foam rubber soles of my shoes.

A laughing stock I was. But, soon I found strong healthy arms supporting me. I pleaded, "Let me go, I'll not be able to make it", but they would not let me.

They were the arms of two hill folks who as people, had been described as withdrawn, selfish and aloof by my friends from the plains.

13. The narrator in this passage felt ill at ease at the thought of joining the picnic party because there was an age gap between him and the rest of the party. Which one of the following do you think is right?
    (*a*) He would feel insulted because of the youngsters treating him as their equal

(*b*) He felt he would not be able to stand to the nonsense of the youth.
(*c*) He would be embarrassed at lagging behind the youngsters while climbing the mountain.
(*d*) He would suffer psychologically in the company of the youth indulging in romantic approaches and conversations.

14. The writer climbed the first ascent rather fast because
(*a*) the sight of so many youngsters infused a spirit in him which made him feel like a young man.
(*b*) he suddenly felt that he was still young.
(*c*) he became competitive in the company of young boys and girls.
(*d*) the sight of so many youngsters reminded him of his younger days.

15. The writer got tired soon because
(*a*) his age prevented him from exerting himself for a long time inspite of his best spirit.
(*b*) climbing a steep and hard rock was strenuous.
(*c*) he had difficulty in walking on the snow.
(*d*) falling behind the young climbers dampened his spirit and depressed him.

16. The hill folk did not let him go because
(*a*) they had seen that others did not help him.
(*b*) they had seen others laughing at him and wanted to add to their joy by supporting him in this way.
(*c*) they realised the difficulty of a man from the plains in climbing up the hills which they could do very easily.
(*d*) they had seen that he was a weakling and needed support.

Passage 5 (C.D.S. 1995)

Speech is a great blessing but it can also be a great curse, for while it helps us to make our intentions and desires known to our fellows, it can also, if we use it carelessly, make our attitude completely misunderstood. A slip of the tongue, the use of an unusual word, or of an ambiguous word, and so on, may create an enemy where we had hoped to win a friend. Again, different classes of people use different vocabularies, and the ordinary speech of an educated man may strike an uneducated listener as pompous. Unwittingly, we may use a word which bears a different meaning to our listener from what it does to men of our own class. Thus speech is not a gift to use lightly without thought, but one which demands careful handling. Only a fool will express himself alike to all kinds and conditions of men.

17. Speech can be a curse, because it can
(*a*) reveal our intentions
(*b*) lead to carelessness
(*c*) hurt others
(*d*) create misunderstanding

18. A 'slip of the tongue' means something said
(*a*) unintentionally
(*b*) wrongly by chance
(*c*) without giving proper thought
(*d*) to hurt another person

19. The best way to win a friend is to avoid .... in speech.
(*a*) ambiguity (*b*) verbosity
(*c*) prompposity (*d*) irony

20. While talking to an uneducated person, we should use
(*a*) polite language (*b*) ordinary speech
(*c*) his vocabulary (*d*) simple words

21. If one used the same style of language with everyone, one would sound
(*a*) democratic (*b*) foolish
(*c*) boring (*d*) flat

Passage 6 (N.D.A. 1994)

The Nobel Committee, in fact, a notoriously conservative body which among other things had a marked antipathy to pure sciences, especially to Mathematical Physics. Restrained by a clause in Alfred Nobel's will that the prize should go to the person whose 'discovery or invention' shall have conferred the greatest benefit to mankind, the committee initially ignored the great theoretical advances in Physics. Wrecked, no doubt, by guilt that he had become a merchant of death through his invention of dynamite and smokeless powder and plagued by sadistic fantasies of destruction, the Swedish chemist, engineer and aspiring poet, Alfred Nobel, who has been described as Europe's richest vagabond, left his colossal fortune to the cause of progress in human knowledge. Five prizes were installed, one each for literature ('to the person who shall have produced in the field of literature, the most outstanding work of an idealistic tendency'), Physics, Chemistry, medicine and peace ('to the person who shall have done the most or the best work for fraternity among nations for abolition or reduction of armies, and for holding or promotion of peace').

22. The Nobel Committee has been called a conservative body because
(*a*) it is conservative in choice of subjects.
(*b*) its members believe in a conservative ideology.
(*c*) its members are old fashioned.
(*d*) it awards prizes only to those people who adopt a conservative approach.

23. In the beginning, the Nobel Committee gnored the great advances in theoretica physics because
(*a*) they were different from other branches of physics.
(*b*) they were concerned with theory and did not suggest its application.
(*c*) the Committee felt that the discovery and invention in the field did not contribute to the benefit of mankind.
(*d*) they proved to be merchants of death and hence dangerous to mankind.

24. Nobel prize would not be given to
(*a*) a diplomat who negotiated a peace settlement
(*b*) a doctor who discovered a vaccine
(*c*) a composer who composed a symphony
(*d*) an author who wrote a novel

25. Alfred Nobel left his colossal fortune to the cause of progress in human knowledge because he
(*a*) was 'Europe's richest vagabond'
(*b*) was a chemist, engineer and an aspiring poet
(*c*) felt guilty for having invented highly destructive things
(*d*) felt guilty for having earned so much money

ANSWERS

1. (*c*)	**2.** (*b*)	**3.** (*d*)	**4.** (*a*)	**5.** (*d*)	**6.** (*d*)	**7.** (*c*)	**8.** (*a*)	**9.** (*c*)	**10.** (*d*)
11. (*b*)	**12.** (*d*)	**13.** (*d*)	**14.** (*b*)	**15.** (*c*)	**16.** (*c*)	**17.** (*d*)	**18.** (*c*)	**19.** (*a*)	**20.** (*c*)
21. (*b*)	**22.** (*a*)	**23.** (*c*)	**24.** (*c*)	**25.** (*c*)					

PRACTICE SET 15

Passage 1

Ernest Rutherford was the son of a Scot emigrant to New Zealand. His parents had 12 children, of whom Ernest was the fourth. His education was in a state primary school from which children at the age of 13 could get grants of scholarships to secondary schools and to the universities. Rutherford had no intention of following an academic career. He was no book-worm. He was good in any rough-and-tumble and a keen football player. But he was good at Latin and he had a passion for music and a mechanical bent of mind. At Nelson College, a state boarding school, he was an outstanding pupil, he sat for a scholarship to Canterbury College and this was because his masters expected it of him, and he won it. There, Rutherford as a student was fascinated by Hertz's work on radio waves and he began to conduct his own experiments in the clock room of the college, where the students, hung their gowns.

1. Rutherford was his parent's ...... child.
(*a*) last (*b*) only
(*c*) fourth (*d*) second

2. Nelson College was a
(*a*) state boarding school in New Zealand
(*b*) college in England
(*c*) school in Scotland
(*d*) school in the United States

3. Rutherford sat for a scholarship test because
(*a*) he was an outstanding student.
(*b*) he was a bookworm.
(*c*) he thought of following an academic career.
(*d*) his masters wanted him to do that.

4. Rutherford carried out his own private experiments in
(*a*) some corner of the cloakroom of Nelson College
(*b*) some corner of the cloakroom of Canterbury College
(*c*) a corner of the room allotted to him in the boarding house
(*d*) in the laboratory of Nelson College

5. The phrase 'mechanical bent' suggests that Rutherford
(*a*) was quite mechanical
(*b*) was devoid of human warmth, emotion, feeling, intelligence etc.
(*c*) did things and lived as thoughtlessly as a machine
(*d*) had an aptitude for the science of machinery

Passage 2 **(Hotel Management, 1995)**

It is to progress in the human sciences that we must look to undo the evils which have resulted from a knowledge of the physical world hastily and superficially acquired by populations unconscious of the changes in themselves that the new knowledge has made imperative. The road to a happier world than any known in the past lies open before us if atavistic destructive passions can be kept in leash while the necessary adaptations are made. Fears are inevitable in our time, but hopes are equally rational and far more likely to bear good fruit. We must learn to think rather less of the dangers to be avoided than of the good that will lie within our grasp if we can believe in it and let it dominate our thoughts. Science, whatever unpleasant consequences it may have by the way, is in its very nature a liberator, a liberator of bondage to physical nature and in to come, a liberator from the weight of destructive passions. We are on the threshold of utter disaster or unprecedentedly glorious achievement. No previous age has been fraught with problems so momentous; and it is to science that we must look to for a happy future.

6. What does science liberate us from? It liberates us from
(*a*) bondage to physical nature
(*b*) fears and destructive passions
(*c*) idealistic hopes of a glorious future
(*d*) slavery to physical nature and fron. passions

7. To carve out a bright future a man should
(*a*) try to avoid dangers
(*b*) overcome fears and dangers
(*c*) cultivate a positive outlook
(*d*) analyse dangers that lie ahead

8. If man's bestial yearning is controlled
(*a*) the present will be brighter than the future.
(*b*) the present will become tolerant.
(*c*) the future will be brighter than the present.
(*d*) the future will be tolerant.

9. Fears and hopes, according to the author
(*a*) can yield good results
(*b*) can bear fruit
(*c*) are irrational
(*d*) are closely linked with the life of modern man

10. Should human sciences be developed because they will
(*a*) eliminate the destruction caused by a superficial knowledge of the physical world
(*b*) make us conscious of the changes in ourselves
(*c*) make us conscious of the changing world
(*d*) provide more knowledge of the physical world

Passage 3 **(Translator's Exam, 1994)**

That artificial intelligence quotient should seek to replace the time-tested I.Q. as a measure of mental ability is perfectly in consonance with the present day standards in a plastic society. However, the battle over grey cells, whether in human or mechanical minds, whose latest round has found Uncle Sam shedding crocodile tears over Japan's failure to deliver on its promise to produce a fifth generation computer, may find the Asian Tiger Cubs—The under–35 Japanese researchers—having the last laugh. For, though all the boastful Tokyo talk a decade ago to build 1,000 processor computers to process knowledge — and not merely numbers which is all the Silicon Valley Chips supposedly do — has remained just talk, the 180 young scientists in the 10-year venture have nevertheless made the big brains at Silicon Valley look rather silly with their product which has a yen for logical programming. The jubilation in the Valley may turn to depression when the inexorable logic of this development pulls down Washington from its pedestal of supercomputer supremacy.

11. Asian Tiger Cubs are
(*a*) young Japanese researchers
(*b*) mechanical minds
(*c*) the big brains at Silicon Valley
(*d*) fifth generation computers

12. Uncle Sam reacts to their failure with
(*a*) sorrow (*b*) depression
(*c*) jubilation (*d*) insincere sorrow

13. What have the cubs failed to produce?
(*a*) Numbers processing computer
(*b*) Grey cells
(*c*) The fifth generation computer
(*d*) A plastic society

14. What have they succeeded in producing?
(*a*) Grey cells
(*b*) A fifth generation computer
(*c*) A knowledge processing computer
(*d*) A product which has a yen for logical programming.

15. How is their success likely to affect Washington's supremacy?
(*a*) It is likely to make it look silly.
(*b*) It is likely to dislodge it.
(*c*) It is likely to have the last laugh.
(*d*) It is likely to produce jubilation in the Valley.

Passage 4 **(C.D.S. 1994)**

Corduroy is fast establishing itself as this year's fabric. While the ribbed cotton itself provides utilitarian tenacity, texture and warmth, it is the fabric's long-held associations that may provide a hint to its current revival as a fabric for all seasons.

It is Corduroy's link with good breeding and country living that made it an essential ingredient in the gentleman's wardrobe along with Wellington boots and a decent wolly. It combines the comfortable no-nonsense appeal of cotton with the perfectly correct luxury finish of velvet. Corduroy has the ability to appear either supremely sophisticated or rough and ready.

16. According to the author, the special quality of Corduroy is that
(*a*) it combines the virtues of both cotton and velvet.
(*b*) both the rich and the not-so-rich can afford to buy it.
(*c*) it contains the correct mixture of cotton and velvet.
(*d*) it needs no ironing.

17. Corduroy is essential in a gentleman's wardrobe because
(*a*) it goes with Wellington boots.
(*b*) it can be an idea alternative to woollen clothes.
(*c*) its current revival gives a taste of the latest fashion.
(*d*) it has its associations with good upbringing and a conservative life style.

18. Corduroy is a fabric for all seasons because
(*a*) of its peculiar texture and warmth
(*b*) it is made popular by catchy advertisements.
(*c*) it can be worn not only in winter but also in summer.
(*d*) gentlemen can wear it on both formal and informal occasions.

19. When the writer refers to Corduroy's 'utilitarian tenacity' he means that
(*a*) it does not need frequent washing.
(*b*) though expensive, it is economic in the long run.
(*c*) it has remained fashionable over several years.
(*d*) it is useful because it is durable.

20. Which one of the following best describes the passage?
(*a*) It tells us about the usefulness of Corduroy.
(*b*) It talks about the virtues of Corduroy.
(*c*) It pursuades us to buy Corduroy.
(*d*) It makes us understand the everlasting appeal of Corduroy to the young.

Passage 5

Man is not destined to vanish. He can be killed, but he cannot be destroyed, because his soul is deathless and his spirit is irrepressible. Therefore, though the situation seems dark in the context of the confrontation between the super powers, the silver lining is provided by the amazing phenomenon that the very nations which have spent incalculable resources and energy for the production of deadly weapons are desperately trying to find out how they might never be used. They threaten each other, intimidate each other and go to the brink, but before the fatal hour arrives they withdraw from the brink.

21. Which of the following correctly expresses the author's view?
(*a*) Huge stockpiles of destructive weapons have so far saved mankind from a catastrophe.
(*b*) Mankind is heading towards complete destruction.
(*c*) Nations in possession of huge stock piles of lethal weapons are trying hard to avoid actual conflict.
(*d*) Super powers have at least realised the need for abandoning the production of lethal weapons.

22. 'Irrepressible' in the second sentence means
(*a*) unrestrainable (*b*) oppressive
(*c*) strong (*d*) incompatible

23. The phrase 'go to the brink' in the passage means
(*a*) declare war on each other
(*b*) negotiate for peace
(*c*) retreating from extreme danger
(*d*) advancing to the stage of war but not engaging in it

24. The author's main point is that
(*a*) man's destiny is not fully clear or visible.
(*b*) man's safety is assured by the delicate balance of power in terms of nuclear weapons.
(*c*) human society will survive despite the serious threat of total annihilation.
(*d*) man's soul and spirit cannot be destroyed even by the super powers.

25. Which of the following best expresses the theme of the above passage?
(*a*) Mounting cost of modern weapons
(*b*) Man's desire to survive inhibits use of deadly weapons.
(*c*) Threats and intimidation between super powers.
(*d*) Destruction of mankind is inevitable.

Directions : ***Read the following two letters and answer the questions given below them :*** **(B.S.R.B. 1996)**

Dear Shri Phutke,

Our earlier letter received no response from you.

What will your neighbours think if we have to send our truck out to your house to repossess that furniture on which you have so far not paid your last as many as six instalments out of the ten?

Sincerely yours,
Feroz Lakdawala

Dear Shri Lakdawala,

I have discussed the matter you wrote about with all my neighbours and every one of them thinks it would be a mean act by a big and prestigious firm like yours.

Yours truly,
M.T. Phutke

26. It appears that Shri Lakdawala's main purpose of writing the letter is to
(*a*) inform Shri Phutke's neighbours about the kind of furniture he sells
(*b*) recover the unpaid balance amount from Shri Phutke
(*c*) refund the amount of furniture sold by him
(*d*) pay the last six unpaid instalments immediately
(*e*) send his truck to Shri Phutke to shift his luggage

27. Which of the following made Lakdawala write a letter to Shri Phutke?
(*a*) Discussions with Phutke's neighbours
(*b*) Delay in recovery of the furniture
(*c*) Prompt payment of six instalments
(*d*) Purchase of furniture
(*e*) None of these

28. How many instalments had Shri Lakdawala received from Shri Phutke?
(*a*) Four (*b*) Six (*c*) Ten
(*d*) Cannot be determined
(*e*) None of these

29. Shri Phutke responded to Shri Lakdawala's letter by
(*a*) paying the unpaid dues
(*b*) returning the furniture
(*c*) asking the neighbours for help
(*d*) writing a humorous reply
(*e*) permitting Lakdawala to take away his furniture

30. Which of the following can be definitely inferred from the above correspondence?
(*a*) Lakdawala has so far refrained from writing any letter to Phutke.
(*b*) Phutke's neighbours purchase furniture items from Lakdawala.
(*c*) Phutke would not like Lakdawala to repossess the furniture.
(*d*) Shri Phutke is no longer in need of the furniture he bought from Lakdawala.
(*e*) Shri Phutke doesn't intend to withhold the payment any further.

ANSWERS

1. (*c*)	**2.** (*a*)	**3.** (*d*)	**4.** (*b*)	**5.** (*d*)	**6.** (*d*)	**7.** (*c*)	**8.** (*c*)	**9.** (*d*)	**10.** (*a*)
11. (*a*)	**12.** (*d*)	**13.** (*c*)	**14.** (*d*)	**15.** (*b*)	**16.** (*b*)	**17.** (*d*)	**18.** (*c*)	**19.** (*d*)	**20.** (*b*)
21. (*c*)	**22.** (*a*)	**23.** (*d*)	**24.** (*c*)	**25.** (*b*)	**26.** (*b*)	**27.** (*e*)	**28.** (*a*)	**29.** (*d*)	**30.** (*c*)

9. THEME DETECTION

In this type of questions, a paragraph is given followed by certain statements which may or may no be inferred from the passage. The candidate is required to choose that statement which contains the jist or the theme of the passage i.e. the idea that it conveys.

Example : Through advertising, manufacturing exercises a high degree of control over consumer's desires. However, the manufacturer assumes enormous risks in attempting to predict what consumers will want and in producing goods in quantity and distributing them in advance of final selection by the consumers.

The paragraph best supports the statement that manufacturers— **(S.B.I.P.O. 1995)**

(*a*) distribute goods directly to the consumers

(*b*) can eliminate the risk of overproduction by advertising

(*c*) always take moderate and calculated risk

(*d*) can predict with great accuracy the success of any product they put on the market

(*e*) must depend upon the final consumers for the success of their undertakings

Solution : According to the passage, it is very difficult for the manufacturer to predict the consumers' response to his products. But by advertising, he can stimulate the consumers to buy his product. So, the theme of the paragraph is best mentioned in (*b*). Hence (*b*) is the answer.

(*a*) is incorrect because it is mentioned in the paragraph that manufacturers distribute goods in advance of their demands and not directly to the consumers.

(*c*) is wrong because according to the passage, manufacturers take 'enormous' and not 'moderate' risks.

(*d*) is wrong because it is mentioned in the passage that manufacturers take great risk in predicting what the consumers want.

(*e*) is a true statement but it does not depict the complete theme of the passage.

PRACTICE SET

Directions : ***Each of the following questions contains a small paragraph followed by a question on it. Read each paragraph carefully and answer the question given below it :***

1. The virtue of art does not allow the work to be interfered with or immediately ruled by anything other than itself. It insists that it alone shall touch the work in order to bring it into being. Art requires that nothing shall attain the work except through art itself. **(Bank P.O. 1996)**

This passage best supports the statement that

(*a*) art is governed by external rules and conditions.

(*b*) art is for the sake of art and life.

(*c*) art is for the sake of art alone.

(*d*) artist realizes his dreams through his artistic creation.

(*e*) artist should use his art for the sake of society.

2. Though the waste of time or the expenditure on fashions is very large, yet fashions have come to stay. They will not go, come what may. However, what is now required is that strong efforts should be made to displace the excessive craze for fashion from the minds of these youngsters.

The passage best supports the statement that :

(*a*) fashion is the need of the day.

(*b*) the excessive craze for fashion is detrimental to one's personality.

(*c*) the hoard for fashion should be done away with so as not to let down the constructive development.

(*d*) work and other activities should be valued more than the outward appearance.

3. Due to enormous profits involved in smuggling, hundreds of persons have been attracted towards this anti-national activity. Some of them became millionaires overnight. India has a vast coast line both on the Eastern and Western Coast. It has been a heaven for smugglers who have been carrying on their activities with great impunity. There is no doubt, that from time to time certain seizures were made by the enforcement authorities, during raids and ambush but even allowing these losses the smugglers made huge profits.

The passage best supports the statement that :

(*a*) smuggling hampers the economic development of a nation.
(*b*) smuggling ought to be curbed.
(*c*) authorities are taking strict measures to curb smuggling.
(*d*) smuggling is fast increasing in our country owing to the quick profit it entails.

4. The only true education comes through the stimulation of the child's powers by the demands of the social situations in which he finds himself. Through these demands he is stimulated to act as a member of a unity, to emerge from his original narrowness of action and feeling, and to conceive himself from the stand point of the welfare of the group to which he belongs. **(Bank P.O. 1996)**

The passage best supports the statement that real education—

(*a*) will take place if the children imbibe action and feeling
(*b*) will take place if the children are physically strong
(*c*) is not provided in our schools today
(*d*) comes through the interaction with social situations
(*e*) comes from the self-centred approach of the students

5. Emerson said that the poet was landlord, sealord, airlord. The flight of imagination made the poet master of land, sea and air. But a poet's dream of yesterday becomes today an actual achievement and a reality for all men. Even those who invented, improved and perfected the aeroplane could hardly have dreamt of the possibility of flight into outer space.

The passage best supports the statement that

(*a*) seemingly impossible imaginations make one a good poet.
(*b*) all imaginations become a reality some day
(*c*) what man imagined has never been impossible; he has always turned it a reality through his conception of ideas and sheer hard labour
(*d*) man has reached the climax of technological development with his exploration into outer space.

6. The prevention of accidents makes it necessary not only that safety devices be used to guard exposed machinery but also that mechanics be instructed in safety rules which they must follow for their own protection, and that lighting in the plant be adequate. **(S.B.I.P.O. 1995)**

The passage best supports the statement that industrial accidents—

(*a*) are always avoidable
(*b*) may be due to ignorance
(*c*) cannot be entirely overcome
(*d*) can be eliminated with the help of safety rules
(*e*) usually result from inadequate machinery

7. It is upto our government and planners to devise ways and means for the mobilisation of about ten crore workers whose families total up about forty crore men, women and children. Our agriculture is over-manned. A lesser number of agriculturists would mean more purchasing or spending power to every agriculturist. This will result in the shortage of man-power for many commodities to be produced for which there will be a new demand from a prosperous agrarian class. This shortage will be removed by surplus man-power released from agriculture as suggested above.

The passage best supports the statement that—

(*a*) employment in production is more fruitful than the employment in agriculture.
(*b*) Indian economy is in a poor shape basically due to improper mobilisation of man-power.
(*c*) a shift of labour from agricultural sector to the industrial sector would uplift the living standard.
(*d*) the industrial sector is labour-deficient while the agricultural sector is over-manned in our country.

8. To forgive an injury is often considered to be a sign of weakness; it is really a sign of strength. It is easy to allow oneself to be carried away by resentment and hate into an act of vengeance; but it takes a strong character to restrain those natural passions. The man who forgives an injury proves himself to be the superior of the man who wronged himself and puts the wrong-doer to shame. **(Bank P.O. 1996)**

The passage best supports the statement that :

(*a*) the sufferer alone knows the intensity of his sufferings.

(*b*) people tend to forgive the things happened in the past.

(*c*) natural passions are difficult to suppress.

(*d*) mercy is the noblest form of revenge.

(*e*) a person with calm and composed nature has depth of thought and vision.

9. Exports and imports, a swelling favourable balance of trade, investments and bank-balances, are not an index or a balance sheet of national prosperity. Till the beginning of the Second World War, English exports were noticeably greater than what they are today. And yet England has greater national prosperity today than it ever had. Because the income of average Englishmen, working as field and factory labourers, clerks, policemen, petty shopkeepers and shop assistants, domestic workers and other low-paid workers, has gone up.

The passage best supports the statement that :

(*a*) a country's economic standard can be best adjudged by the per capita income.

(*b*) a country's balance of trade is the main criteria of determining its economic prosperity.

(*c*) a nation's economy strengthens with the increase in exports.

(*d*) English trade has continually increased since the Second World War.

10. Throughout the ages the businessman has helped build civilisation's great cities, provided people with luxuries and artists with patronage, and lift his fellow citizens to understand the standard of living. In the last few centuries the businessman has seeded the Industrial Revolution around the world.

(S.B.I.P.O. 1995)

The passage best supports the statement that the businessman

(*a*) is accountable to the society

(*b*) lives luxurious and comfortable life

(*c*) is the beneficiary of the Industrial Revolution

(*d*) is capable of raising his standard of living

(e) has contributed to the growth of civilisation

11. Industrial exhibitions play a major role in a country's economy. Such exhibitions, now regularly held in Delhi, enable us to measure the extent of our own less advanced industrial progress and the mighty industrial power and progress of countries like the U.K., U.S.A. and Russia whose pavilions are the centres of the greatest attention and attractions.

The passage best supports the statement that the industrial exhibitions—

(*a*) greatly tax the poor economies

(*b*) are more useful for the developed countries like U.S.A. whose products stand out superior to those of the developing countries

(*c*) are not of much use to the countries who are industrially backward

(*d*) boost up production qualitatively and quantitatively by analytical comparison of a country's products with those of the developed countries

12. Satisfaction with co-workers, promotion opportunities, the nature of work, and pay goes with high performance among those with strong growth needs. Among those with weak growth needs, no such relationship is present — and, in fact, satisfaction with promotion opportunities goes with low performance.

This passage best supports the statement that :

(*a*) satisfaction is an inevitable organisational variable.

(*b*) job satisfaction and performance are directly and closely related.

(*c*) relationship between job satisfaction and performance is moderated by growth need.

(*d*) every organisation has few employees having weak growth need.

(*e*) high performance is essential for organisational effectiveness.

13. The attainment of individual and organisational goals is mutually interdependent and linked by a common denominator — employee work motivation. Organisational members are motivated to satisfy their personal goals, and they contribute their efforts to the attainment of organisational objectives as means of achieving these personal goals. **(S.B.I.P.O. 1995)**

The passage best supports the statement that motivation

(*a*) encourages an individual to give priority to personal goals over organisational goals
(*b*) is crucial for the survival of an individual and organisation
(*c*) is the product of an individual's physical and mental energy
(*d*) is the external force which induces an individual to contribute his efforts
(*e*) makes organisation and society inseparable

14. The consumption of harmful drugs by the people can be prevented not only by banning their sale in the market but also by instructing users about their dangerous effects which they must understand for their safety. Also the drug addicts may be provided with proper medical facilities for their rehabilitation. This will help in scaling down the use of drugs. **(Bank P.O. 1996)**

The passage best supports the statement that consumption of harmful drugs—

(*a*) are on increase in the society.
(*b*) can always be reduced.
(*c*) are due to lack of medical facilities.
(*d*) can be eliminated with the help of banning their sale.
(*e*) may be channelised through proper system

15. The future of women in India is quite bright and let us hope that they will justify their abilities by rising to the occasion. Napolean was right when he declared that by educating the women we can educate the whole nation. Because a country can never rise without the contribution of 50% of their population.

The passage best supports the statement that

(*a*) India is striving hard for the emancipation of women.
(*b*) all women should be well educated.
(*c*) a nation can progress only when women are given equal rights and opportunities as men.
(*d*) women ought to be imparted full freedom to prove their worth and contribute to the progress of the nation.

16. The school has always been the most important means of transferring the wealth of tradition from one generation to the next. This applies today in an even higher degree than in former times for, through the modern development of economy, the family as bearer of tradition and education has become weakened.

This passage best supports the statement that for transferring the wealth of tradition from one generation to the next—

(*a*) there are means other than the school
(*b*) several different sources must be tried
(*c*) economic development plays a crucial role
(*d*) modern technology must be put to use
(*e*) family, as ever, is the most potent means **(S.B.I.P.O. 1995)**

17. One of the important humanitarian by-products of technology is the greater dignity and value that it imparts to human labour. In a highly industrialized society, there is no essential difference between Brahmin and Dalit, Muslim and Hindu; they are equally useful and hence equally valuable, for in the industrial society individual productivity fixes the size of the pay cheque and this fixes social status. **(Bank P.O. 1996)**

The passage best supports the statement that :

(*a*) technology decides individual's social status.
(*b*) castes and religions are man made.
(*c*) human labour has dignity and value.
(*d*) all individuals, irrespective of caste and creed, are born equal.
(*e*) industrial society is a great leveller of men.

18. The paragraph above also supports the statement that:

(*a*) there are individual differences in industrial productivity.
(*b*) there are numerous side-effects of technology.
(*c*) size of the pay and social status contradict each other.

(*d*) labour force is treated well in modern day industries.

(*e*) division of labour based on caste was justified.

19. The Press should not be afraid of upholding and supporting a just and righteous cause. It should not be afraid of criticising the government in a healthy manner. The Press has to be eternally vigilant to protect the rights of the workers, backward and suppressed sections of the society. It should also give a balanced view of the things so that people can be helped in the formation of a healthy public opinion.

The passage best supports the statement that—

(*a*) press has a great role to play in a democracy.

(*b*) the press is the only means to project to the masses the policies of the government.

(*c*) the freedom of press is essential for the proper functioning of democracy.

(*d*) the press can be used by the governments as an effective media for the upliftment of the backward sections of society.

(*e*) all the information given by the press should be well- articulated so as to gain a good opinion towards the ruling party.

20. There is a shift in our economy from a manufacturing to a service orientation. The increase in service-sector will require the managers to work more with people rather than with objects and things from the assembly line.

(Bank P.O. 1996)

This passage best supports the statement that—

(*a*) managers should have a balanced mind.

(*b*) assembly line will exist in serve organisations.

(*c*) interpersonal skills will become more important in the future work place.

(*d*) manufacturing organisations ignore importance of people.

(*e*) service organisations will not deal with objects and things.

ANSWERS

1. (*c*)	**2.** (*c*)	**3.** (*d*)	**4.** (*d*)	**5.** (*c*)	**6.** (*d*)	**7.** (*b*)	**8.** (*d*)	**9.** (*a*)	**10.** (*e*)
11. (*d*)	**12.** (*c*)	**13.** (*a*)	**14.** (*d*)	**15.** (*d*)	**16.** (*c*)	**17.** (*c*)	**18.** (*a*)	**19.** (*c*)	**20.** (*c*)

10. DERIVING CONCLUSIONS FROM PASSAGES

Directions : ***Each of the passages given below is followed by some questions. Each question comprises three statements (A), (B) and (C). In the context of the passage, decide which one, two, three or none of the statements is/are true.***

Passage 1 (Qs. 1 to 5) (S.B.I.P.O. 1995)

"In the Pandit's complaint he asks why entries could not be made in the savings bank pass book on the strength of the counterfoil of the pay-in-slip. This would save the customer from waiting until the actual voucher passed through various desks/books. The use of the voucher is, in fact the correct procedure. The delay experienced by Mr. Pandit on that day could have been avoided. On our instructions the branch manager concerned has met the complaint and explained the matter. He has also emphasised the great risk to the customer and the bank if entries are made on the basis of the counterfoils."

1. (A) The writer of this paragraph is another dissatisfied customer.
(B) The paragraph emphasises that counterfoils should not be used instead of vouchers.
(C) Use of counterfoils alone may not lead to any risk.
(*a*) Only A (*b*) Only B
(*c*) Only C (*d*) Only A and B
(*e*) Only B and C

2. (A) Mr. Pandit complains about a delay in some transaction at his bank.
(B) Mr. Pandit wants banks to make book entries on the basis of counterfoils.
(C) Entries made on the basis of vouchers do not involve risk.
(*a*) A and B (*b*) B and C
(*c*) A and C (*d*) A, B and C
(*e*) None is true

3. (A) In following the correct procedure, unreasonable delays are always inevitable.
(B) Mr. Pandit's complaint was based on full knowledge of the banking procedure.
(C) Mr. Pandit's suggestion was appreciated by the bank authorities.
(*a*) Only A (*b*) Only B
(*c*) Only C (*d*) A and B
(*e*) None is true

4. (A) The delay experienced by Mr. Pandit was caused by some temporary problem.
(B) The entries relating to Mr. Pandit's case were not done according to proper procedure.
(C) Mr. Pandit was already aware of the proper procedure.
(*a*) Only A (*b*) Only B
(*c*) Only C (*d*) A and B
(*e*) B and C

5. (A) Using counterfoils instead of vouchers is risky not only to the customers but also to the bank.
(B) The bank authorities were not insensitive to Mr. Pandit's complaint.
(C) The branch manager paid no heed to the authorities' instructions.
(*a*) Only A (*b*) Only B
(*c*) Only C (*d*) A and B
(*e*) A and C

Passage 2

There are two ways of avoiding fear-one is by persuading ourselves that we are immune from disaster, and the other is by the practice of sheer courage. The latter is difficult, and to everybody becomes impossible at a certain point. The former has, therefore, always been more popular. Primitive magic has the purpose of sucuring safety, either by injuring enemies, or by protecting oneself by talismans, spells or incantations. Without any essential change, belief in such ways of avoiding danger survived throughout the many centuries of Babylonian civilization, spread from Babylon throughout the Empire of Alexander, and was acquired by the Romans in the course of their absorption of Hellenistic culture. From the Romans it descended to medieval Christendom and Islam. Science has low lessened the belief in magic, but many people place more faith in mascots than they are willing to avow, and sorcery, while condemned by the Church, is still officially a possible sin.

1. (A) Superstitious beliefs can help man avoid fear.
(B) The medieval civilisations were also characterised by superstitious beliefs.

(C) Avoiding fear is difficult for a common man.
(*a*) Only A (*b*) Only B
(*c*) Only C (*d*) Only A and B
(*e*) Only A and C

2. (A) The ancient method of avoiding fear has survived the test of time.
(B) Belief in charms and amulets was a salient feature of ancient civilisations.
(C) Science has eradicated man's belief in magic altogether.
(*a*) A and B (*b*) B and C
(*c*) A and C (*d*) A, B and C
(*e*) None is true

Passage 3 **(Bank P.O. 1995)**

Amar Steels, an existing profit-making company enters the capital market with a public issue of 80 lakh shares of Rs. 10/- each on 1st December. The company is engaged in ship breaking at ports in Vishakhapatnam and Madras. It operates a steel-rolling mill in Vishakhapatnam which utilises the scrap from ships. The company is expanding its ship-breaking capacity. Its entitlement to break foreign ships has just been extended to cover Indian flagships.

1. (A) Amar Steels had so far not entered the capital market because of its profit-making status.
(B) Amar Steels had so far not entered the capital market because it had no expansion plans.
(C) Amar Steels expects to get Indian ships also for ship-breaking.
(*a*) Only A and B (*b*) Only B and C
(*c*) Only A and C (*d*) A, B and C
(*e*) None is true

2. (A) The public can purchase shares from Amar Steels before 1st December.
(B) Amar Steels is expected to start making profits after the expansion programme is carried out
(C) Amar Steels gets scrap from other companies for its steel-rolling mills.
(*a*) Only A (*b*) Only B
(*c*) Only C (*d*) A and B
(*e*) None is true

3. (A) Amar Steels so far could not break Indian flagships
(B) The Vishakhapatnam plant of the company will not be allowed to utilise scrap from foreign ships
(C) The company needs money for its expansion activities
(*a*) Only A (*b*) Only B
(*c*) Only C (*d*) Only A and B
(*e*) Only B and C

Passage 4 **(Bank P.O. 1995)**

The newly introduced non-stop city buses are a good new service, though they are really useful only during the morning and evening rush hours. During most of the day these buses carry few passengers. I request the State Transport Corporation to run these buses as limited-stop services during the non-rush periods of the day.

1. (A) The non-stop buses are small ones that carry only a limited number of passengers.
(B) Non-Stop buses are now available at all times.
(C) The competent authority to govern these buses is the State Transport Corporation.
(*a*) Only A (*b*) Only B
(*c*) Only C (*d*) Only A and B
(*e*) Only B and C

2. (A) The writer says that when there is no rush, limited-stop buses will be more useful.
(B) The writer wants all the non-stop buses to be changed to limited-stop buses.
(C) There are not many commuters except during the morning and the evening.
(*a*) Only A and B (*b*) Only A and C
(*c*) A, B and C (*d*) None is true
(*e*) Only A

ANSWERS

Passage 1 :	**1.** (*b*)	**2.** (*d*)	**3.** (*d*)	**4.** (*c*)	**5.** (*d*)
Passage 2 :	**1.** (*b*)	**2.** (*a*)			
Passage 3 :	**1.** (*c*)	**2.** (*d*)	**3.** (*a*)		
Passage 4 :	**1.** (*e*)	**2.** (*b*)			

TEST YOUSELF

Directions : In each of the following questions, choose the word which can be substituted for the given phrase/sentence.

1. A man who has not been married
(*a*) Solitary (*b*) Widower
(*c*) Bachelor (*d*) Spinster

2. Something that cures any evil or trouble
(*a*) Panacea (*b*) Manna
(*c*) Potion (*d*) Elixer

3. Person who doubts the truth of a particular claim
(*a*) Nihilist (*b*) Cynic
(*c*) Sceptic (*d*) Pugnacious

4. One who knows many arts and sciences
(*a*) Polyglot (*b*) Plagiarist
(*c*) Polymath (*d*) Sophist

5. Continuing fight between parties, families, clans etc
(*a*) Enmity (*b*) Feud
(*c*) Quarrel (*d*) Skirmish

6. One who breaks into a house at night in order to steal
(*a*) Dacoit (*b*) Thief
(*c*) Burglar (*d*) Pilferer

7. Remarks which have no order or connection
(*a*) Incognito (*b*) Irrelevant
(*c*) Incoherent (*d*) Puissant

8. Not to the point
(*a*) Exaggerated (*b*) Incorrect
(*c*) Inadequate (*d*) Irrelevant

9. A man devoid of kindly feeling and sympathy
(*a*) Callous (*b*) Cruel
(*c*) Brute (*d*) Egoist

10. One who is easily led
(*a*) Tenable (*b*) Usurious
(*c*) Tractable (*d*) Subservient

11. Person who practices unnatural sexual intercourse, especially between male persons
(*a*) Voluptuary (*b*) Sodomite
(*c*) Prostitute (*d*) Masochist

12. To issue a thunderous verbal attack
(*a*) Animate (*b*) Invigorate
(*c*) Fulminate (*d*) Languish

13. A man who asks many questions
(*a*) Vociferous (*b*) Frugal
(*c*) Prodigious (*d*) Inquisitive

14. One who prescribes corrective lenses
(*a*) Optician (*b*) Optometrist
(*c*) Oculist (*d*) Ophthalmologist

15. The firing of a number of guns together as a salute
(*a*) Jingoism (*b*) Reception
(*c*) Salvo (*d*) Gun Salute

16. Internal telephonic system
(*a*) Interim (*b*) Interlocutor
(*c*) Intercourse (*d*) Intercom

17. List and explanations of several words
(*a*) Agendum (*b*) Appendix
(*c*) Addendum (*d*) Glossary

18. One who is very exact in forms of behaviour
(*a*) Punctilious (*b*) Corpulent
(*c*) Puerile (*d*) Connubila

19. Mental disorder marked by fixed delusions
(*a*) Monomania (*b*) Hypermania
(*c*) Paranoia (*d*) Nostalgia

20. A person who introduces the performers, speakers etc.
(*a*) Host (*b*) Compere
(*c*) Impostor (*d*) Presentor

21. Something that relates to everyone in the world
(*a*) Usual (*b*) General
(*c*) Universal (*d*) Common

22. An expert who calculates rates of insurance
(*a*) Account ant (*b*) Statistician
(*c*) Actuary (*d*) Calculator

23. A person who attacks first
(*a*) Invader (*b*) Aggressor
(*c*) Initiater (*d*) Offender

24. A man who attempts to pass for more than he is worth
(*a*) Senile (*b*) Pretentious
(*c*) Extenuating (*d*) Retentive

25. Figure of speech in which term is transferred to something it does not literally apply to
(*a*) Metaphor (*b*) Simile
(*c*) Epitome (*d*) Epithet

26. A medicine that induces sleep
(*a*) Narcotic (*b*) Psychotherapeutic
(*c*) Panacea (*d*) Anodyne

27. An animal with four complete digestive cavities or stomachs
(*a*) Carnivore (*b*) Ruminant
(*c*) Candelabra (*d*) Proboscis
(*e*) Matador

ANSWERS

1. (*c*) **2.** (*a*) **3.** (*c*) **4.** (*c*) **5.** (*b*) **6.** (*c*) **7.** (*c*) **8.** (*d*) **9.** (*a*) **10.** (*c*)
11. (*b*) **12.** (*c*) **13.** (*d*) **14.** (*b*) **15.** (*c*) **16.** (*d*) **17.** (*d*) **18.** (*a*) **19.** (*c*) **20.** (*b*)
21. (*c*) **22.** (*c*) **23.** (*b*) **24.** (*b*) **25.** (*a*) **26.** (*a*) **27.** (*b*)

UNIT III
SELECTING WORDS / PHRASES

AN
ADVANCED APPROACH
TO
DATA INTERPRETATION

R.S. Aggarwal

For Bank P.O., S.B.I.P.O., R.B.I., M.B.A., Hotel Management, Railways, I. Tax and Central Excise, I.A.S. (Prelims & Mains), C.B.I., Asstt. Grade, U.D.C., L.I.C., G.I.C.A.A.O. etc.

* A whole lot of questions on Bar Graphs, Line Graphs, Pie-Charts and Tabulation, fully solved.
* Illustrative examples with techniques to solve all types of problems.
* Previous years' questions included.

11. SENTENCE COMPLETION

I. VOCABULARY USAGE

TYPE 1 : Selecting the appropriate word from five alternatives provided

PRACTICE SET 1

Directions : ***Pick out the most effective word from the given words to fill in the blank to make the sentence meaningfully complete.***

1. These essays are intellectually .... and represent various levels of complexity.
(*a*) revealing (*b*) modern
(*c*) superior (*d*) demanding
(*e*) persistent **(Bank P.O. 1995)**

2. It was almost impossible for him to put out of his mind the .... words which he heard from his clever father-in-law.
(*a*) inspiring (*b*) witty
(*c*) sarcastic (*d*) soothing
(*e*) exhortative

3. Integrity of character, honesty, dependability and discipline .... with a genuine interest in your work will go a long way in the achievement of success in your professional life.
(*a*) coupled (*b*) adjoined (*c*) fixed
(*d*) attached (*e*) joined

4. The soldiers were instructed to .... restraint and handle the situation peacefully. **(Bank P.O. 1993)**
(*a*) exercise (*b*) control (*c*) prevent
(*d*) enforce (*e*) remain

5. Ishwar Chandra Vidyasagar was one of the chief .... of women's rights.
(*a*) promoters (*b*) facilitators
(*c*) instigators (*d*) organisers
(*e*) protagonists

6. The two sisters look so .... that it is difficult to tell one from the other.
(*a*) same (*b*) similar (*c*) identical
(*d*) alike (*e*) resembling

7. Since one cannot read every book, one should be content with making a .... selection. **(Bank P.O. 1991)**
(*a*) normal (*b*) standard (*c*) sample
(*d*) moderate (*e*) judicious

8. Success comes to those who are vigilant not to permit .... from the chosen path.
(*a*) diversion (*b*) deviation
(*c*) obstruction (*d*) alienation
(*e*) distraction

9. His actions had .... pain and suffering on thousands of people.
(*a*) deplored (*b*) eliminated
(*c*) affected (*d*) inflicted
(*e*) imposed

10. He has good .... over the famous world languages.
(*a*) authority (*b*) expertise (*c*) hold
(*d*) command (*e*) knowledge

11. Everyday, in the school, one period is .... to games, sports and physical exercise.
(*a*) entrusted (*b*) dedicated
(*c*) conceded (*d*) devoted
(*e*) conferred

12. What frustrates the opposition's effort of unity is the absence of a .... long term strategy.
(*a*) credible (*b*) contestable
(*c*) creditable (*d*) compatible
(*e*) conceivable

13. Some people .... themselves into believing that they are indispensable to the organisation they work for.
(*a*) keep (*b*) fool (*c*) force
(*d*) denigrate (*e*) delude
(S.B.I.P.O. 1994)

14. The Government sought to set at .... speculation that there may be a shift in our nuclear policy.
(*a*) pace (*b*) rest (*c*) peace
(*d*) fire (*e*) right

15. How do you expect that country to progress when her government is corrupt, ... and still largely feudal?
(*a*) devalued (*b*) dwindling
(*c*) despotic (*d*) demeaning
(*e*) demobilised **(Bank P.O. 1993)**

16. The petition before the Court prayed for .... the appointment orders issued by the management.
(*a*) removing (*b*) granting
(*c*) posting (*d*) quashing
(*e*) dismissing

17. I have a profound respect for his political ....
(*a*) personality (*b*) ambition
(*c*) temperament (*d*) sagacity
(*e*) involvement

18. The truck was .... the traffic and the policeman asked the driver to move off.
(*a*) failing (*b*) obstructing
(*c*) obviating (*d*) hiding

(*e*) disturbing **(Bank P.O. 1993)**

19. The paternalistic attitude is so ingrained in the managements that they will have to .... try to change it.
(*a*) casually (*b*) slowly
(*c*) subtly (*d*) inadvertently
(*e*) conscientiously

20. For a few seconds, Madan was .... blinded by the powerful lights of the oncoming car.
(*a*) heavily (*b*) largely (*c*) greatly
(*d*) powerfully (*e*) totally

21. His interest in the study of human behaviour is indeed very ....
(*a*) strong (*b*) large (*c*) broad
(*d*) vast (*e*) deep **(L.I.C. 1995)**

22. The police have .... a complaint against four persons.
(*a*) entered (*b*) lodged
(*c*) registered (*d*) noted
(*e*) received

23. The improvement made by changes in the system was .... and did not warrant the large expenses. **(R.B.I. 1991)**
(*a*) large (*b*) small (*c*) minute
(*d*) marginal (*e*) uncertain

24. The man who is .... hesitating which of the two things he will do first, will do neither.
(*a*) persistently (*b*) constantly
(*c*) insistently (*d*) consistently
(*e*) perpetually

25. He is too .... to be deceived easily.
(*a*) strong (*b*) modern (*c*) kind
(*d*) honest (*e*) intelligent
(B.S.R.B. 1992)

26. In .... of the recommendations the Board has established a counter to entertain the complaints from consumers.
(*a*) adherence (*b*) relation
(*c*) pursuance (*d*) accordance
(*e*) relevance

27. There has been a .... lack of efficiency in all the crucial areas of the working of Public Sector Undertakings.
(*a*) positive (*b*) surprising
(*c*) conspicuous (*d*) stimulative
(*e*) insignificant **(Bank P.O. 1994)**

28. The propeller driven fighter planes of the Second World War have long been completely ....
(*a*) old (*b*) aged (*c*) ancient
(*d*) obsolete (*e*) decayed

29. Unlike most rulers in that .... age, Akbar believed in religious tolerance.
(*a*) ancient (*b*) historical
(*c*) feudal (*d*) bigoted
(*e*) aristocratic

30. He is so .... of his own idea that he will not entertain any suggestion from others.
(*a*) hopeful (*b*) enchanted
(*c*) enamoured (*d*) jealous
(*e*) possessed

31. Undoubtedly, English is the most .... spoken language in the world today.
(*a*) broadly (*b*) widely
(*c*) greatly (*d*) beautifully
(*e*) elaborately

32. I will be leaving for Delhi tonight and .... to return by this week end.
(*a*) waiting (*b*) plan (*c*) going
(*d*) likely (*e*) making **(B.S.R.B. 1995)**

33. The vacancy .... by the dismissal of the superintendent is expected to be filled up by the promotion of a U.D.C.
(*a*) made (*b*) created (*c*) caused
(*d*) generated (*e*) procured

34. Stone age research was always on a low .... in India.
(*a*) key (*b*) scale (*c*) profile
(*d*) point (*e*) ebb

35. Ravi's behaviour is worthy of .... by all the youngsters. **(S.B.I.P.O. 1992)**
(*a*) trial (*b*) emulation
(*c*) following (*d*) exploration
(*e*) experiment

36. The Minister called upon the people to .... their religious differences and strengthen secularism in the country.
(*a*) condemn (*b*) abolish (*c*) sink
(*d*) exhort (*e*) weaken

37. Nothing can be achieved without .... a certain amount of discomfort while making an effort.
(*a*) getting (*b*) sacrificing
(*c*) enduring (*d*) imbibing
(*e*) internalizing

38. When Mr. Kant heard the news of his son's selection to the college team, he felt ....
(*a*) enamoured (*b*) elated
(*c*) exasperated (*d*) embittered
(*e*) effervescent

39. Even at the risk of economic loss, he .... refused to take the beaten track.
(*a*) repeatedly (*b*) often
(*c*) regularly (*d*) continuously
(*e*) steadfastly **(R.B.I. 1990)**

40. The only way to .... the country from the evils of communalism is to enforce the rule of law.
(*a*) eradicate (*b*) mobilise

(*c*) extricate (*d*) purge
(*e*) strengthen

41. On his sudden demise, my emotions were so complicated that it was .... how I felt. **(Bank P.O. 1991)**
(*a*) unreasonable (*b*) impossible
(*c*) intolerable (*d*) unimaginable
(*e*) inexplicable

42. A solution may not yet be in sight, but the important thing was to get a .... between them started.
(*a*) conflict (*b*) debate
(*c*) dialogue (*d*) conversation
(*e*) discussion

43. After consulting a .... of doctors he eventually thought of consulting a specialist.
(*a*) chain (*b*) string (*c*) mass
(*d*) series (*e*) majority

44. The presence of their teacher .... the chit-chat of the girls in the restaurant.
(*a*) limited (*b*) interrupted
(*c*) inhibited (*d*) obstructed
(*e*) prohibited

45. The man was about to move his bike into the compound of his apartment when a passer by .... down the motorbike.
(*a*) forced (*b*) fell (*c*) turned
(*d*) climbed (*e*) knocked

46. Sarita could have .... in the examination inspite of her efforts had the examination been more difficult.
(*a*) managed (*b*) failed (*c*) competed
(*d*) tried (*e*) passed

47. The .... with which he is able to wield the paint brush is really remarkable.
(*a*) ease (*b*) sweep (*c*) skill
(*d*) majesty (*e*) practice

48. Two of the fugitives managed to remain free by adeptly avoiding the .... of the police. **(S.B.I.P.O. 1992)**
(*a*) torture (*b*) pursuit
(*c*) discovery (*d*) following
(*e*) repression

49. The accused .... to the judge for mercy.
(*a*) asked (*b*) applied
(*c*) demanded (*d*) appealed
(*e*) requested

50. Experts fail to understand the .... behind the decision to move coal by road when there is enough rail capacity in this sector.
(*a*) ideology (*b*) judgement
(*c*) rationale (*d*) politics
(*e*) logistics

ANSWERS

1. (*c*)	**2.** (*b*)	**3.** (*a*)	**4.** (*a*)	**5.** (*e*)	**6.** (*d*)	**7.** (*e*)	**8.** (*b*)	**9.** (*d*)	**10.** (*d*)
11. (*d*)	**12.** (*a*)	**13.** (*e*)	**14.** (*b*)	**15.** (*c*)	**16.** (*d*)	**17.** (*d*)	**18.** (*b*)	**19.** (*c*)	**20.** (*e*)
21. (*e*)	**22.** (*c*)	**23.** (*d*)	**24.** (*a*)	**25.** (*e*)	**26.** (*c*)	**27.** (*c*)	**28.** (*d*)	**29.** (*b*)	**30.** (*c*)
31. (*b*)	**32.** (*b*)	**33.** (*c*)	**34.** (*a*)	**35.** (*b*)	**36.** (*c*)	**37.** (*c*)	**38.** (*b*)	**39.** (*e*)	**40.** (*d*)
41. (*c*)	**42.** (*c*)	**43.** (*b*)	**44.** (*c*)	**45.** (*e*)	**46.** (*b*)	**47.** (*a*)	**48.** (*b*)	**49.** (*d*)	**50.** (*c*)

PRACTICE SET 2

Directions : ***Pick out the most effective word from the given words to fill in the blanks to make the sentence meaningfully complete.***

1. Macbeth is a tragedy of a man who was .... with great qualities.
(*a*) possessed (*b*) empowered
(*c*) privileged (*d*) endowed
(*e*) obsessed

2. Mounting unemployment is the most serious and .... problem faced by India today. **(Bank P.O. 1995)**
(*a*) dubious (*b*) profound
(*c*) unpopular (*d*) intractable
(*e*) unattainable

3. Democracy .... some values which are fundamental to the realisation of the dignity of man.
(*a*) cherishes (*b*) nourishes
(*c*) espouses (*d*) nurtures
(*e*) harbours

4. Successful people are genuinely very efficient in .... their tasks.
(*a*) making (*b*) attaining
(*c*) achieving (*d*) completing
(*e*) accomplishing

5. Automobile manufacturers are reviving up to launch a campaign designed to increase consumer .... about the new emmission control. **(Bank P.O. 1990)**
(*a*) production (*b*) education
(*c*) capacity (*d*) knowledge
(*e*) awareness

6. To break the stalemate over the controversial issue, the Prime Minister held discussions today with four other leaders to .... a consensus.
(*a*) evolve (*b*) win (*c*) capture
(*d*) emerge (*e*) develop

7. Forests on the whole are less .... than farms to flood damage.
(*a*) exposed (*b*) affected
(*c*) destroyed (*d*) vulnerable
(*e*) destructible

8. His logic .... everyone, including the experts. **(R.B.I. 1990)**
(*a*) teased (*b*) defied
(*c*) surprised (*d*) confounded
(*e*) overwhelmed

9. The factory went into a state of suspended .... today with all its workers on strike.
(*a*) symbiosis (*b*) animation
(*c*) ways (*d*) condition
(*e*) mortification

10. It is not fair to cast .... on honest and innocent persons. **(S.B.I.P.O. 1987)**
(*a*) aspiration (*b*) aspersions
(*c*) inspiration (*d*) adulation

11. The code of Manu from the theological aspect is regarded as .... from God.
(*a*) originating (*b*) issuing
(*c*) generating (*d*) emanating
(*e*) coming forth

12. This book is about a man who .... his family and went to live in the Himalayas.
(*a*) exiled (*b*) deserted
(*c*) banished (*d*) expelled
(*e*) admonished

13. You must .... your career with all seriousness. **(B.S.R.B. 1992)**
(*a*) direct (*b*) complete (*c*) follow
(*d*) manage (*e*) pursue

14. The affluent life styles of contemporary politicians are in sharp contrast to the .... ways of living of the freedom fighters.
(*a*) austere (*b*) agnostic
(*c*) stingy (*d*) extravagant
(*e*) disciplined

15. The villagers .... the death of their leader by keeping all the shops closed.
(*a*) announced (*b*) protested
(*c*) mourned (*d*) consoled
(*e*) avenged **(Bank P.O. 1993)**

16. Everyone of us should endeavour to .... the miseries of the poor.
(*a*) diffuse (*b*) mitigate (*c*) condemn
(*d*) suppress (*e*) acknowledge

17. The government will .... all resources to fight poverty.
(*a*) move (*b*) collect (*c*) harness
(*d*) exploit (*e*) muster

18. These medicines are .... for curing cold.
(*a*) proper (*b*) real (*c*) effective
(*d*) capable (*e*) powerful **(B.S.R.B. 1991)**

19. It is easy to .... but impossible to replace English medium education.
(*a*) deny (*b*) approve
(*c*) propagate (*d*) castigate
(*e*) eliminate

20. Since she is a teacher of language, one would not expect her to be guilty of a ....
(*a*) aberration (*b*) solecism
(*c*) schism (*d*) bombast
(*e*) stanchion

21. The poor ones continue to .... out a living inspite of economic liberalisation in that country. **(Bank P.O. 1994)**
(*a*) find (*b*) go (*c*) eke
(*d*) bring (*e*) manage

22. I will write a letter to you tentatively .... the dates of the programme.
(*a*) involving (*b*) urging (*c*) guiding
(*d*) indicating (*e*) propagating
(B.S.R.B. 1996)

23. He should be dismissed for his .... remarks about his superiors.
(*a*) critical (*b*) depreciatory
(*c*) scurrilous (*d*) laudatory
(*e*) impeccable

24. Contemporary economic development differs .... from the Industrial Revolution of the 19th century.
(*a*) naturally (*b*) usually
(*c*) literally (*d*) specially
(*e*) markedly **(Bank P.O. 1995)**

25. After discussing the matter for about an hour, the committee .... without having reached any decision.
(*a*) dispersed (*b*) dissolved
(*c*) postponed (*d*) withdrew
(*e*) adjourned

26. The word gharana points to the .... concepts of stylistic individuality and handing down of tradition within family confines.
(*a*) joint (*b*) conflicting (*c*) dual
(*d*) contradictory (*e*) extraordinary

27. The Government is certain to .... the publication of any details of this fraudulent research.
(*a*) retain (*b*) restrict (*c*) delay
(*d*) prohibit (*e*) conceal

28. It was the help he got from his friends which .... him through the tragedy.
(*a*) helped (*b*) boosted (*c*) perked
(*d*) supported (*e*) sustained
(R.B.I. 1990)

29. The security for the Ministers has been .... up following the attack at a public meeting last evening.
(*a*) steered (*b*) geared (*c*) speeded
(*d*) bloated (*e*) beefed

30. The criminals managed to escape from the prison even though two armed policemen were .... vigil over them.
(*a*) taking (*b*) putting (*c*) guarding
(*d*) keeping (*e*) looking **(Bank P.O. 1993)**

31. General awareness and education facilitate the .... of specific skills.
(*a*) creation (*b*) requirement
(*c*) acquisition (*d*) procurement
(*e*) organisation

32. The speaker did not properly use the time as he went on .... on one point alone. **(Bank P.O. 1992)**
(*a*) dilating (*b*) devoting
(*c*) deliberating (*d*) diluting
(*e*) distributing

33. A number of advances in medicine would have been .... sooner if free enquiry had been common and orthodox thinking habits had been rare.
(*a*) persisted (*b*) inducted
(*c*) secured (*d*) achieved
(*e*) propagated

34. The final electoral rolls have been intensively revised through house to house ....
(*a*) investigation (*b*) enunciation
(*c*) enumeration (*d*) documentation
(*e*) categorization

35. Ravi had to drop his plan of going to picnic as he had certain .... to meet during that period. **(S.B.I.P.O. 1994)**
(*a*) preparations (*b*) observations
(*c*) urgencies (*d*) transactions
(*e*) commitments

36. The unruly behaviour of the students .... their teacher.
(*a*) tempered (*b*) incensed
(*c*) aggrieved (*d*) clashed
(*e*) impeached

37. Although it is two years since this book was first published, its Indian edition has just been ....
(*a*) sold (*b*) started (*c*) published
(*d*) launched (*e*) marketed

38. Even in today's modern society, people .... god to bring rains. **(Bank P.O. 1993)**
(*a*) provoke (*b*) evoke (*c*) appeal
(*d*) propitiate (*e*) superimpose

39. The Union leader assured the workers that their grievances could be .... through negotiations.
(*a*) attended (*b*) heard (*c*) settled
(*d*) answered (*e*) satisfied

40. The good is often .... with their bones.
(*a*) buried (*b*) covered (*c*) exhumed
(*d*) interred (*e*) fleshed **(Railways, 1991)**

41. If this interpretation is held valid, then the states are .... of power to plan, implement and monitor their schemes.
(*a*) awarded (*b*) invested (*c*) relieved
(*d*) delegated (*e*) divested

42. He knew that social evils were only .... of deeper maladies.
(*a*) cause (*b*) indications (*c*) part
(*d*) consequences (*e*) manifestations

43. Eight scientists have .... the national awards for outstanding contribution and dedication to the profession.
(*a*) bestowed (*b*) picked
(*c*) bagged (*d*) conferred
(*e*) discovered **(Bank P.O. 1994)**

44. The judge complimented the young witness for standing upto the .... cross examination.
(*a*) terrible (*b*) tedious (*c*) arduous
(*d*) lengthy (*e*) gruelling

45. Defection is an unprincipled practice which can do .... damage to the democratic process.
(*a*) incalculable (*b*) inalienable
(*c*) intolerable (*d*) infallible
(*e*) indispensable

46. With the growing .... in the country the Government is gearing itself to quell the rebellion.
(*a*) disturbances (*b*) tension
(*c*) unrest (*d*) insurgency
(*e*) coup

47. It was .... hot that day and the cable suffered the brunt of the heat.
(*a*) treacherously (*b*) acceptably
(*c*) unfailingly (*d*) unbelievably
(*e*) uncompromisingly **(S.B.I P.O. 1992)**

48. Sachin was to reach that afternoon but was .... up at Delhi for some personal work.
(*a*) kept (*b*) held (*c*) delayed

(*d*) stayed (*e*) detained

49. I do not think the evidence you have heard .... your opinion.
(*a*) promotes (*b*) accuses
(*c*) commits (*d*) warrants
(*e*) convinces

50. He .... his shoes till they shone.
(*a*) brushed (*b*) scrubbed
(*c*) shined (*d*) polished
(*e*) wiped

ANSWERS

1. (*d*)	**2.** (*d*)	**3.** (*a*)	**4.** (*e*)	**5.** (*e*)	**6.** (*a*)	**7.** (*d*)	**8.** (*c*)	**9.** (*b*)	**10.** (*b*)
11. (*d*)	**12.** (*b*)	**13.** (*e*)	**14.** (*a*)	**15.** (*c*)	**16.** (*b*)	**17.** (*e*)	**18.** (*c*)	**19.** (*d*)	**20.** (*b*)
21. (*c*)	**22.** (*d*)	**23.** (*c*)	**24.** (*e*)	**25.** (*e*)	**26.** (*c*)	**27.** (*d*)	**28.** (*e*)	**29.** (*e*)	**30.** (*d*)
31. (*c*)	**32.** (*c*)	**33.** (*d*)	**34.** (*c*)	**35.** (*e*)	**36.** (*b*)	**37.** (*d*)	**38.** (*b*)	**39.** (*c*)	**40.** (*d*)
41. (*e*)	**42.** (*e*)	**43.** (*c*)	**44.** (*e*)	**45.** (*a*)	**46.** (*c*)	**47.** (*d*)	**48.** (*b*)	**49.** (*d*)	**50.** (*d*)

PRACTICE SET 3

Directions : *In each of the following questions, pick out the most effective word from the given words to fill in the blank to make the sentence meaningfully complete.*

1. His companions prevailed upon him not to .... to violence.
(*a*) refer (*b*) resort (*c*) prone
(*d*) provoke (*e*) pertain

2. No country can .... to practice a constant, rigid foreign policy in view of the world power dynamics.
(*a*) obliviate (*b*) anticipate
(*c*) afford (*d*) envisage
(*e*) visualise **(S.B.I.P.O. 1994)**

3. If the President does not grant .... in his case, he will be hanged shortly.
(*a*) parole (*b*) release (*c*) freedom
(*d*) gratitude (*e*) clemency

4. The cancer patients are .... into their mode of life for research purposes.
(*a*) diagnosed (*b*) checked
(*c*) probed (*d*) examined
(*e*) investigated

5. I request you to .... your crime.
(*a*) apologise (*b*) agree (*c*) confess
(*d*) pardon (*e*) submit **(B.S.R.B. 1992)**

6. The payment was .... delayed this time because some of the supporting documents for the claim were missing.
(*a*) unduly (*b*) unjustifiably
(*c*) unforeseenly (*d*) undeservedly
(*e*) unquestionably

7. The prisoner was released on .... for good behaviour. **(Railways, 1991)**
(*a*) probation (*b*) bail (*c*) parole
(*d*) grounds (*e*) guarantee

8. Although religion does not inhibit acquisition of wealth, the tenor of its teaching is to induce an attitude of .... to worldly things.
(*a*) indifference (*b*) hostility
(*c*) affinity (*d*) immunity
(*e*) attachment

9. .... eye witnesses, the news reporter gave a graphic description of how the fire broke. **(Bank P.O. 1994)**
(*a*) Reporting (*b*) Observing
(*c*) Seeing (*d*) Quoting
(*e*) Examining

10. The library expects you to return each and every book that you have ....
(*a*) demanded (*b*) taken (*c*) lent
(*d*) handed (*e*) given **(B.S.R.B. 1994)**

11. .... between labour and management is inevitable in any industrial society.
(*a*) Controversy (*b*) Friction
(*c*) Association (*d*) Competition
(*e*) Coordination

12. This article tries to .... us with problems of poor nations so that we help them more effectively. **(Bank P.O. 1995)**
(*a*) allow (*b*) enable (*c*) convince
(*d*) project (*e*) acquaint

13. One should develop a .... habit of going through a newspaper, some selected magazines and general literature.
(*a*) continuous (*b*) constant
(*c*) regular (*d*) persistent
(*e*) recurring

14. The current .... in global negotiations over the ban on nuclear test does not augur well for the future.

(*a*) moratorium (*b*) controversy
(*c*) insight (*d*) stalemate
(*e*) reapproachment

15. Improvement in efficiency and productivity has to be the key .... of policy in respect of both the public and the private sectors in the Five Year Plans.
(*a*) ingredient (*b*) purpose (*c*) role
(*d*) platform (*e*) criterion

16. The skill and ease with which he repaired the machine proved that he is a/an .... mechanic. **(R.B.I. 1990)**
(*a*) able (*b*) handy (*c*) nimble
(*d*) maladroit (*e*) competent

17. The chemical warfare capability of Iraq is a .... to aggression even by the Super powers.
(*a*) pretext (*b*) deterrent
(*c*) constraint (*d*) detriment
(*e*) precaution

18. Though the issue of bonus provision was not on the agenda of the meeting, the Chairman was sure that this would .... up.
(*a*) bring (*b*) shoot (*c*) trickle
(*d*) crop (*e*) heat

19. They have decided to meet the Prime Minister in order to have their .... heard. **(Bank P.O. 1993)**
(*a*) agony (*b*) apathy (*c*) woes
(*d*) sorrow (*e*) sufferings

20. The foundation of all civilisations and societies is the ability of humans to .... with each other.
(*a*) bear (*b*) dispense (*c*) unite
(*d*) collaborate (*e*) exchange

21. The children .... crackers to celebrate the victory of their team.
(*a*) burst (*b*) fired (*c*) shot
(*d*) broke (*e*) released

22. The .... the council has passed against the magazine for their irresponsibility in reporting are justified.
(*a*) laws (*b*) ban (*c*) penalty
(*d*) codes (*e*) strictures

23. After a recent mild paralytic attack, his movements are .... restricted, otherwise he is still very active.
(*a*) entirely (*b*) nowhere (*c*) not
(*d*) slightly (*e*) frequently
(B.S.R.B. 1994)

24. His .... of the topic was so good that students had few doubts to raise at the end.
(*a*) handling (*b*) clarity
(*c*) exposure (*d*) exposition
(*e*) picturisation

25. The purpose of education must be to .... attitudes as well as to impart knowledge and skills.
(*a*) manage (*b*) rationalise
(*c*) adjust (*d*) internalize
(*e*) channelise

26. Freedom and equality are the .... rights of every human being.
(*a*) inalienable (*b*) inscrutable
(*c*) incalculable (*d*) institutional
(*e*) insufferable **(Bank P.O. 1993)**

27. The teacher .... upon the students the importance of studying science.
(*a*) taught (*b*) encouraged
(*c*) inflicted (*d*) appealed
(*e*) impressed

28. The older generation is .... in its outlook and hence cannot tolerate independent ideas of the youngsters.
(*a*) paradox (*b*) progressive
(*c*) liberal (*d*) orthodox
(*e*) restricted

29. Vinayak is the .... head of the family and commands a lot of respect from the family members.
(*a*) solely (*b*) strongest
(*c*) undisputed (*d*) full
(*e*) controversial

30. The audience .... at the end of the drama.
(*a*) appreciated (*b*) praised
(*c*) appraised (*d*) exploded
(*e*) applauded

31. He has not yet attained the age of 21. He has, therefore, no .... to vote in this election.
(*a*) claim (*b*) authority (*c*) power
(*d*) right (*e*) permission

32. A candidate in an election needs to conduct an .... campaign so as to become known as quickly as possible to the electorate.
(*a*) extensive (*b*) energetic
(*c*) elaborate (*d*) orderly
(*e*) intensive

33. The new industrial policy is a result of the confidence the government has in the .... of the Indian industry.
(*a*) opinion (*b*) existence
(*c*) status (*d*) maturity
(*e*) profitability **(S.B.I.P.O. 1991)**

34. The most obvious reason for his lack of popularity was his .... to find fault with others.
(*a*) propensity (*b*) reluctance
(*c*) notoriety (*d*) ability
(*e*) premonition

35. Modern public sector managers have become quite .... in shifting their loyalties. **(Bank P.O. 1990)**
(*a*) overt (*b*) inept (*c*) learned
(*d*) adept (*e*) ignorant

36. The conference was successful, your style of presentation was ....; everyone liked it. **(B.S.R.B. 1996)**
(*a*) valuable (*b*) difficult (*c*) conducive
(*d*) wonderful (*e*) trustworthy

37. A large crowd used to .... to listen to his speech. **(B.S.R.B. 1992)**
(*a*) follow (*b*) gather (*c*) deliver
(*d*) collect (*e*) attract

38. The peasant's produce was .... in lieu of his previous year's rent.
(*a*) quelled (*b*) mobbed
(*c*) vanquished (*d*) captured
(*e*) confiscated

39. Most of the issues discussed in the meeting were trivial and only a few were .... **(Bank P.O. 1993)**
(*a*) practical (*b*) complex
(*c*) interesting (*d*) irrelevant
(*e*) significant

40. Many times newspapers .... the news to make it sensational.
(*a*) disturb (*b*) devalue (*c*) distort
(*d*) divulge (*e*) disfigure

41. There is an urgent need for .... and rejuvenation of our old values.
(*a*) retention (*b*) projection
(*c*) relocation (*d*) establishment
(*e*) reaffirmation

42. Rajeev is too .... as far as his food habits are concerned. **(Bank P.O. 1994)**
(*a*) enjoyable (*b*) fastidious (*c*) curious
(*d*) involved (*e*) interesting

43. Even though Manoj is usually calm, he appeared .... and was walking up and down.
(*a*) disagreed (*b*) displeased
(*c*) disgraced (*d*) discontented
(*e*) disconcerted

44. I am .... forward to our picnic scheduled in the next month.
(*a*) seeing (*b*) going (*c*) looking
(*d*) planning (*e*) organising **(B.S.R.B. 1994)**

45. They decided to .... down their original plans for the bigger house and make it smaller.
(*a*) rule (*b*) turn (*c*) change
(*d*) scale (*e*) play

46. My father keeps all his .... papers in a lock and key. **(B.S.R.B. 1992)**
(*a*) required (*b*) necessary
(*c*) useful (*d*) confidential
(*e*) enclosed

47. Everyone knows that he is not .... to hard work.
(*a*) trained (*b*) accustomed
(*c*) willing (*d*) suitable
(*e*) addicted

48. The Supreme Court had recently .... the government from implementing the Finance Commission Report in view of adverse economic situation in the country.
(*a*) abstained (*b*) avoided
(*c*) directed (*d*) withheld
(*e*) restrained

49. He made a slight .... of judgement for which he had to repent later.
(*a*) error (*b*) slip (*c*) mistake
(*d*) blunder (*e*) inexactness

50. Freedom is not a .... but our birth right. **(B.S.R.B. 1992)**
(*a*) sin (*b*) gift (*c*) farce
(*d*) illusion (*e*) presentation

ANSWERS

1. (*b*)	**2.** (*c*)	**3.** (*e*)	**4.** (*e*)	**5.** (*c*)	**6.** (*a*)	**7.** (*c*)	**8.** (*a*)	**9.** (*d*)	**10.** (*b*)
11. (*b*)	**12.** (*e*)	**13.** (*c*)	**14.** (*d*)	**15.** (*c*)	**16.** (*e*)	**17.** (*b*)	**18.** (*d*)	**19.** (*e*)	**20.** (*d*)
21. (*a*)	**22.** (*e*)	**23.** (*d*)	**24.** (*d*)	**25.** (*b*)	**26.** (*a*)	**27.** (*e*)	**28.** (*d*)	**29.** (*c*)	**30.** (*e*)
31. (*d*)	**32.** (*a*)	**33.** (*d*)	**34.** (*a*)	**35.** (*d*)	**36.** (*d*)	**37.** (*d*)	**38.** (*e*)	**39.** (*e*)	**40.** (*c*)
41. (*e*)	**42.** (*b*)	**43.** (*e*)	**44.** (*c*)	**45.** (*d*)	**46.** (*d*)	**47.** (*b*)	**48.** (*e*)	**49.** (*a*)	**50.** (*b*)

PRACTICE SET 4

Directions : *Fill in the blanks in the following sentences by selecting the most appropriate alternative from amongst the five choices given under each sentence.*

1. Rajeev failed in the examination because none of her answers were .... to the questions asked.
(*a*) allusive (*b*) revealing
(*c*) pertinent (*d*) referential
(*e*) impeccable

2. There are .... views on the issue of giving bonus to the employees.
(*a*) independent (*b*) divergent
(*c*) modest (*d*) adverse
(*e*) valuable **(B.S.R.B. 1992)**

3. Man who has committed such an .... crime must get the most severe punishment.
(*a*) injurious (*b*) uncharitable
(*c*) unworthy (*d*) abominable
(*e*) irreproachable

4. He has .... people visiting him at his house because he fears it will cause discomfort to neighbours.
(*a*) curtailed (*b*) requested
(*c*) stopped (*d*) warned
(*e*) forbidden **(B.S.R.B. 1995)**

5. Although he never learnt to read, his exceptional memory and enquiring mind eventually made him a very .... man.
(*a*) dedicated (*b*) erudite
(*c*) pragmatic (*d*) benevolent
(*e*) charismatic

6. Traffic problems in Bombay are as serious as in any other city in India; and they are complicated by digging of roads by corporations on this or that ....
(*a*) reason (*b*) instance (*c*) aspect
(*d*) intention (*e*) pretext

7. The defending champion justified his top .... by clinching the title.
(*a*) skill (*b*) form (*c*) technique
(*d*) supremacy (*e*) billing
(Bank P.O. 1991)

8. We must .... our students on subjects like health and sanitation besides the usual subjects.
(*a*) learn (*b*) teach (*c*) insist
(*d*) educate (*e*) impart

9. The judge used his .... power and let him off with a reprimand
(*a*) residuary (*b*) official (*c*) legal
(*d*) absolute (*e*) discretionary

10. He applied for and was .... legal aid by the Labour Ministry. **(B.S.R.B. 1990)**
(*a*) offered (*b*) granted (*c*) allowed
(*d*) awarded (*e*) implemented

11. The President called upon politicians not to .... themselves with communal and parochial forces.
(*a*) counter (*b*) favour (*c*) cope
(*d*) align (*e*) confront

12. A glue produced by bees to .... their hives appears to contain antibiotic substances. **(Bank P.O. 1990)**
(*a*) collect (*b*) design (*c*) build
(*d*) decorate (*e*) structure

13. The authorities are .... through the records of criminals to make arrangements for making security arrests.
(*a*) wading (*b*) waxing (*c*) studying
(*d*) scratching (*e*) analysing

14. He very successfully .... all the allegations levelled against him.
(*a*) extricated (*b*) eradicated
(*c*) retaliated (*d*) rebutted
(*e*) protected **(Bank P.O. 1993)**

15. I want to have a .... of flats on rental basis.
(*a*) block (*b*) pack (*c*) set
(*d*) conclave (*e*) suite

16. The passengers and crew members of the aeroplane had a .... escape when it was taking off from the runway.
(*a*) narrow (*b*) large (*c*) little
(*d*) brief (*e*) better **(Bank P.O. 1994)**

17. He has already made up his mind on this issue. Now it is .... to argue with him.
(*a*) vague (*b*) futile (*c*) coherent
(*d*) contradictory (*e*) useless

18. .... by people's perception it seems that democracy has succeeded in India.
(*a*) Following (*b*) Going (*c*) Making
(*d*) Planned (*e*) Liked **(B.S.R.B. 1995)**

19. Deepak put on a very .... face when he said something silly and the contrast made everyone laugh.
(*a*) funny (*b*) comic (*c*) serious
(*d*) great (*e*) humorous

20. The President asked people not to .... language for political or religious purposes.
(*a*) use (*b*) handle (*c*) employ
(*d*) exploit (*e*) utilize

21. I am given to .... that you are going abroad. **(B.S.R.B. 1990)**
(*a*) learn (*b*) think (*c*) predict
(*d*) understand (*e*) apprehend

22. The police had to .... to force when the terrorists refused to surrender.
(*a*) confine (*b*) adhere (*c*) resort
(*d*) adapt (*e*) respond

23. Man power is the .... means of converting other resources to mankind's use and benefit. **(Bank P.O. 1995)**
(*a*) insuperable (*b*) inimitable
(*c*) indivisible (*d*) indispensable
(*e*) inequitable

24. Rights .... automatically to him who duly performs his duties.
(*a*) belong (*b*) transfer (*c*) issue
(*d*) accrue (*d*) acquire

25. Raghu was so good at Algebra that his friends considered him to be a ....
(*a*) prodigy (*b*) prolocutor
(*c*) profligate (*d*) primeval
(*e*) prodigal

26. The petition before the Court prayed for .... the appointment orders issued by the management. **(C.B.I. 1989)**
(*a*) granting (*b*) removing
(*c*) posting (*d*) quashing
(*e*) dismissing

27. The sale of the cassette .... to an astonishing figure of 20 lakh.
(*a*) jumped up (*b*) soared up
(*c*) shot up (*d*) went up
(*e*) rose up

28. In the departmental inquiry, it was denied that the police had committed any .... on people under their custody.
(*a*) injuries (*b*) crime (*c*) blunder
(*d*) beatings (*e*) excesses
(Bank P.O. 1991)

29. Pradeep's face spoke .... of the happiness he was feeling
(*a*) elegantly (*b*) tons (*c*) much
(*d*) volumes (*e*) forever

30. Only those who have completed eighteen years are .... to apply for this post.
(*a*) elected (*b*) legible (*c*) selected
(*d*) forced (*e*) eligible

31. How much did it .... to reach Bombay by car? **(S.S.C. 1991)**
(*a*) charge (*b*) price (*c*) cost
(*d*) estimate (*e*) pay

32. Every one should .... himself against illness since medical care has now become expensive. **(L.I.C. 1994)**
(*a*) vaccinate (*b*) insure (*c*) brace
(*d*) ensure (*e*) innoculate

33. Since Rohit stays far away from our place, we do not meet each other ....
(*a*) timely (*b*) rarely (*c*) shortly
(*d*) momentarily (*e*) frequently

34. The crooks did not .... any resistance.
(*a*) put (*b*) show (*c*) offer
(*d*) exert (*e*) exercise

35. The explorers' path was .... with dangers.
(*a*) beset (*b*) replete (*c*) bestowed
(*d*) exhausted (*e*) afflicted

36. Changes in the socio-economic environment have generated a sense of .... crisis among the people.
(*a*) fearful (*b*) profound
(*c*) damaging (*d*) deliberate
(*e*) questionable

37. The unity and integrity of our country is not .... at any cost and cannot be a party issue.
(*a*) indispensable (*b*) debatable
(*c*) negotiable (*d*) questionable
(*e*) susceptible

38. Research has also .... the illusion that childhood dreams are pure innocence.
(*a*) accepted (*b*) observed
(*c*) dispelled (*d*) discovered
(*e*) established **(Bank P.O. 1990)**

39. Of the several issues that were discussed in the meeting, only a few were pertinent and most of them were ....
(*a*) futile (*b*) detached
(*c*) contrasting (*d*) irrelevant
(*e*) independent

40. The .... weather also affected the road transportation.
(*a*) non-relenting (*b*) inclement
(*c*) disrupted (*d*) iconoclast
(*e*) unbridled

41. Dowry is no longer permitted by law even in .... marriage. **(Railways, 1991)**
(*a*) love (*b*) conventional
(*c*) natural (*d*) bigamous
(*e*) polygamous

42. His speech was disappointing; it .... all the major issues.
(*a*) projected (*b*) revealed
(*c*) skirted (*d*) analysed
(*e*) encompassed

43. After reaching New York, Ramakant will have to .... himself to the new surroundings. **(B.S.R.B. 1995)**
(*a*) mix (*b*) develop (*c*) submit
(*d*) adapt (*e*) acquaint

44. To say that a rectangle will never be a square because it is a rectangle is simply to .... the very thing you profess to prove.
(*a*) assume (*b*) insure (*c*) ensure
(*d*) subsume (*e*) contradict

45. Belying his mother's worries, Rajesh's behaviour throughout the function was .... **(R.B.I. 1991)**
(*a*) immodest (*b*) impeccable
(*c*) imaginable (*d*) imperial
(*e*) impervious

46. Even if the most lenient and charitable view is taken, Mandeep cannot be completely .... of the blame.
(*a*) saved (*b*) stripped (*c*) absolved
(*d*) devoid (*e*) dissolved

47. There is no doubt that one has to keep .... with the changing times.
(*a*) aside (*b*) oneself
(*c*) pace (*d*) himself
(*e*) tuning **(Bank P.O. 1994)**

48. Kamal's friends had nothing to offer him other than .... in his grief.
(*a*) friendship (*b*) kindness
(*c*) solution (*d*) consolation
(*e*) happiness **(S.B.I.P.O. 1992)**

49. The party failed to .... enough volunteers to bring its traditional voters to the polling booths.
(*a*) manage (*b*) collect (*c*) mobilise
(*d*) assemble (*e*) accumulate

50. Robbers often act in .... with the police.
(*a*) connection (*b*) conformity
(*c*) collusion (*d*) co-ordination
(*e*) co-operation

ANSWERS

1. (*c*)	**2.** (*b*)	**3.** (*d*)	**4.** (*c*)	**5.** (*b*)	**6.** (*e*)	**7.** (*e*)	**8.** (*d*)	**9.** (*e*)	**10.** (*b*)
11. (*d*)	**12.** (*c*)	**13.** (*a*)	**14.** (*d*)	**15.** (*c*)	**16.** (*a*)	**17.** (*b*)	**18.** (*b*)	**19.** (*c*)	**20.** (*d*)
21. (*d*)	**22.** (*c*)	**23.** (*d*)	**24.** (*d*)	**25.** (*a*)	**26.** (*d*)	**27.** (*c*)	**28.** (*e*)	**29.** (*d*)	**30.** (*e*)
31. (*c*)	**32.** (*b*)	**33.** (*e*)	**34.** (*c*)	**35.** (*a*)	**36.** (*b*)	**37.** (*c*)	**38.** (*c*)	**39.** (*d*)	**40.** (*b*)
41. (*a*)	**42.** (*c*)	**43.** (*d*)	**44.** (*d*)	**45.** (*b*)	**46.** (*c*)	**47.** (*c*)	**48.** (*d*)	**49.** (*c*)	**50.** (*c*)

TYPE 2 : Selecting the appropriate word from the four alternatives provided

PRACTICE SET 5

Directions : ***In each of the following questions, a sentence is given with a blank to be filled in with an appropriate word. Four alternatives are suggested for each question. Choose the correct alternative.***

1. If a universal language really existed, people like tourists and businessmen would find it easier to .... with foreigners. **(I. Tax, 1994)**
(*a*) transact (*b*) communicate
(*c*) deal (*d*) exchange

2. On account of his humiliating defeat in the recent elections, he appeared unusually .... when I called on him the other day.
(*a*) oppressed (*b*) repressed
(*c*) depressed (*d*) suppressed

3. You need .... shoes for walking in the hills. **(Asstt. Grade, 1995)**
(*a*) good (*b*) comfortable
(*c*) satisfactory (*d*) sturdy

4. Amongst the two brothers, Sameer being worthier often .... the younger Deepak.
(*a*) dominates (*b*) eclipses
(*c*) subdues (*d*) overshadows

5. It was difficult to see through the .... of the head lights of the cars.
(*a*) shine (*b*) glare
(*c*) dazzle (*d*) brilliance

6. The teacher ordered Kamal to leave the room and .... him to return.
(*a*) stopped (*b*) refused
(*c*) forbade (*d*) challenged
(Clerks' Grade, 1992)

7. I hope you must have .... by now that failures are the stepping stones to success.
(*a*) known (*b*) felt
(*c*) decided (*d*) realised

8. The tyrant .... anyone whom he regarded as a rival.
(*a*) massacred (*b*) killed
(*c*) exterminated (*d*) slaughtered

9. In a little publicised deal, Pepsi Cola has .... the entire soft drink market in Afghanistan. **(M.B.A. 1994)**
(*a*) conquered (*b*) swallowed
(*c*) captured (*d*) occupied

10. Inspite of some ...., Ashish is a good sportsman.
(*a*) felonies (*b*) mistakes
(*c*) offences (*d*) misdemeanours

11. Anita .... me of a girl I used to know.
(*a*) remembers (*b*) recalls
(*c*) recollects (*d*) reminds
(C.D.S. 1994)

12. The steam engine was .... by James Watt.
(*a*) discovered (*b*) manufactured
(*c*) created (*d*) invented

13. His most striking .... is the enthusiasm which he brings to everything he does.
(*a*) character (*b*) factor
(*c*) characteristic (*d*) attitude
(C.B.I. 1991)

14. Cholera is mainly .... through contaminated food and drinks.
(*a*) conducted (*b*) transferred
(*c*) circulated (*d*) transmitted

15. Authority .... when it is not supported by the moral purity of its user.
(*a*) waits (*b*) crumbles
(*c*) empowers (*d*) prevails
(R.R.B. 1995)

16. When the courtier had advanced to the highest position attainable, his friends felt jealous about his having reached the ....
(*a*) vigil (*b*) precipice
(*c*) threshold (*d*) pinnacle

17. The bill in the Parliament was .... by fifty five votes.
(*a*) accepted (*b*) voted
(*c*) carried (*d*) opposed

18. The principal and staff have made .... efforts to enable the students to attend college on the days of the bus strike.
(*a*) integrated (*b*) deliberate
(*c*) concerted (*d*) systematic
(C.D.S. 1992)

19. We .... the family members after expressing our grief at the tragedy.
(*a*) condoled (*b*) satisfied
(*c*) mourned (*d*) consoled

20. The defending champion .... to victory in just 30 minutes.
(*a*) led (*b*) rushed
(*c*) reached (*d*) cruised

21. Inspite of our best efforts, we failed to .... any new facts from him.
(*a*) elicit (*b*) evoke
(*c*) eject (*d*) enlist
(Translator's Exam, 1994)

22. A number of advances in medicine would have been .... sooner if free enquiry had been common.
(*a*) secured (*b*) persisted
(*c*) achieved (*d*) propagated

23. His fired speeches .... the people to cry for justice and achieve it by their united efforts.
(*a*) prompted (*b*) inflamed
(*c*) instigated (*d*) inspired

24. This book is a useful .... to our library.
(*a*) arrival (*b*) discovery
(*c*) asset (*d*) addition
(Stenographers' Exam, 1994)

25. The interior of the concert hall is .... to the eye.
(*a*) delicious (*b*) veritable
(*c*) visual (*d*) hopeless

26. No one likes to be forced into .... situations.
(*a*) humble (*b*) insulting
(*c*) humiliating (*d*) infuriating

27. He admired precision in everything, but it never hampered his quick ....
(*a*) finalisation (*b*) dealing
(*c*) action (*d*) decision
(Stenographers' Exam, 1995)

28. He was not willing to accept the ....
(*a*) wrong (*b*) blame
(*c*) fault (*d*) sorry

29. The Government's economic policy includes certain projects for .... the living conditions of the poor.
(*a*) bettering (*b*) harmonising
(*c*) manipulating (*d*) doing away with
(C.D.S. 1989)

30. The reward is a .... of her service to mankind.
(*a*) momento (*b*) memorial
(*c*) recognition (*d*) witness

31. They have .... up the deficit.
(*a*) covered (*b*) filled
(*c*) made (*d*) pulled

32. A restaurant that presents spick and span look will naturally .... more customers. **(S.S.C. 1995)**
(*a*) accomodate (*b*) invite
(*c*) avoid (*d*) attract

33. Though they did not speak to each other much, there was a .... understanding between them. **(C.D.S. 1995)**
(*a*) placid (*b*) contractual
(*c*) tacit (*d*) verbal

34. My friend took his first pay to the bank to .... it in his account. **(C.B.I. 1993)**
(*a*) deposit (*b*) deficit
(*c*) debit (*d*) demote

35. When Satish .... that he was guilty, he was pardoned.
(*a*) claimed (*b*) boasted
(*c*) confessed (*d*) confided

36. Family planning is essential for curbing the rapid .... in population.
(*a*) spread (*b*) increase
(*c*) spurt (*d*) augment
(LI.C.A.A.O. 1993)

37. Ajay was .... on meeting his boss yesterday only.
(*a*) keen (*b*) determined
(*c*) sure (*d*) decided

38. We must .... the tickets for the movie in advance. **(Central Excise, 1989)**
(*a*) draw (*b*) buy
(*c*) remove (*d*) take

39. The State Transport Corporation has .... a loss of Rs. 5 crore this year.
(*a*) obtained (*b*) derived
(*c*) incurred (*d*) formulated

40. One .... and you know who among them is the culprit. **(U.D.C. 1994)**
(*a*) look (*b*) peep
(*c*) sight (*d*) gaze

41. When Aditya returned he gave his friends a short .... of his holiday.
(*a*) story (*b*) account
(*c*) tale (*d*) history

42. The ties that bind a family together are so .... that they can hardly withstand any strain. **(Railways, 1993)**
(*a*) tenacious (*b*) twisted
(*c*) tenuous (*d*) tentative

43. The stenographer is very efficient. He is ..... to his firm. **(Hotel Management, 1993)**
(*a*) a credit (*b*) a blessing
(*c*) an asset (*d*) a boon

44. His death is a great blow, most terrible to ....
(*a*) bear (*b*) imagine
(*c*) accept (*d*) sustain

45. The music for Asiad was .... by Pandit Ravi Shankar.
(*a*) displayed (*b*) composed
(*c*) demonstrated (*d*) made
(Stenographers' Exam, 1995)

46. The little girl .... for the light switch in the dark.
(*a*) groped (*b*) grappled
(*c*) gripped (*d*) grovelled

47. The summit meeting provided him the much .... shot in the arm.
(*a*) required (*b*) desired
(*c*) needed (*d*) urgent

48. If you drink too much, it will .... your judgement
(*a*) obstruct (*b*) impede
(*c*) impair (*d*) hinder

49. The government should provide attractive tax .... to create the market for quality goods. **(C.D.S. 1995)**
(*a*) controls (*b*) incentives
(*c*) revenues (*d*) structures

50. Each cause conditions a .... effect and there can be no cause without effect
(*a*) specific (*b*) relevant
(*c*) requisite (*d*) proper

ANSWERS

1. (*b*)	**2.** (*c*)	**3.** (*b*)	**4.** (*d*)	**5.** (*c*)	**6.** (*c*)	**7.** (*d*)	**8.** (*c*)	**9.** (*c*)	**10.** (*d*)
11. (*d*)	**12.** (*d*)	**13.** (*c*)	**14.** (*d*)	**15.** (*b*)	**16.** (*d*)	**17.** (*c*)	**18.** (*c*)	**19.** (*d*)	**20.** (*d*)
21. (*a*)	**22.** (*c*)	**23.** (*d*)	**24.** (*d*)	**25.** (*b*)	**26.** (*c*)	**27.** (*d*)	**28.** (*b*)	**29.** (*a*)	**30.** (*c*)
31. (*c*)	**32.** (*d*)	**33.** (*c*)	**34.** (*a*)	**35.** (*c*)	**36.** (*b*)	**37.** (*a*)	**38.** (*b*)	**39.** (*c*)	**40.** (*a*)
41. (*b*)	**42.** (*c*)	**43.** (*c*)	**44.** (*a*)	**45.** (*b*)	**46.** (*a*)	**47.** (*c*)	**48.** (*c*)	**49.** (*b*)	**50.** (*a*)

PRACTICE SET 6

Directions : *Each of the following sentences has a blank space and four words are given after the sentence. Select whichever word you consider most appropriate for the blank space and indicate your choice.*

1. The young man lost his way in the forest and found that he had become a/an .... to the dacoits. **(Assistant Grade, 1993)**
(*a*) enemy (*b*) adversary
(*c*) decoy (*d*) quarry

2. The firm .... its workers well.
(*a*) treated (*b*) regarded
(*c*) behaved (*d*) cared

3. Barring last minute surprise he is .... to become the President of the Committee.
(*a*) designed (*b*) poised
(*c*) elected (*d*) endorsed

4. He sold his property because he was under a lot of ....
(*a*) account (*b*) debt

(*c*) loan (*d*) credit

(Stenographers' Exam, 1993)

5. My boss .... my request to increase my allowance.
(*a*) refused (*b*) denied
(*c*) resisted (*d*) withheld

6. The accused .... having made any statement.
(*a*) declined (*b*) refused
(*c*) denied (*d*) rejected

7. The problems suggested by style as a sign and index of personality may be .... from many points of view.
(*a*) approached (*b*) encountered
(*c*) confronted (*d*) upheld

(C.D.S. 1991)

8. The Committee's .... to establish a 'Home For The Destitute' has been rejected.
(*a*) argument (*b*) decision
(*c*) view (*d*) proposal

9. Some people in Punjab .... from voting at the last elections.
(*a*) refused (*b*) refrained
(*c*) denied (*d*) abstained

10. He is a person of sound character and .... disposition. **(Section Officers' 1993)**
(*a*) amicable (*b*) amiable
(*c*) morous (*d*) beneficent

11. To break the stalemate over the controversial issue, the Prime Minister held discussions today with four other leaders to .... a consensus.
(*a*) emerge (*b*) win
(*c*) evolve (*d*) capture

12. Waking at three o'clock, I heard the .... of thunder. **(C.B.I. 1995)**
(*a*) clank (*b*) crackle
(*c*) rumble (*d*) ripple

13. Pratibha had a cold and couldn't go to the party, so I bought her a cake to make up for her ....
(*a*) disillusion (*b*) disappointment
(*c*) disgust (*d*) depression

14. If negotiations are to prove fruitful, there must not only be sincerity on each side, but there must also be .... in the sincerity of the other side. **(C.D.S. 1993)**
(*a*) certainty (*b*) substance
(*c*) faith (*d*) belief

15. Jail officials .... that the plot for the escape may have been hatched by local criminals.
(*a*) doubt (*b*) suspect
(*c*) hold (*d*) believe

16. Known as devout and serious person, she also has a .... sense of humour.
(*a*) good (*b*) better
(*c*) quick (*d*) beautiful

17. Judicial decrees may not change the heart, but they can .... the heartless.
(*a*) subdue (*b*) regulate
(*c*) transform (*d*) disarm

(C.D.S. 1993)

18. Untouchability is still in vogue and atrocities are being .... against poor people.
(*a*) perpetuated (*b*) transmitted
(*c*) executed (*d*) perpetrated

19. The .... is working on wood.
(*a*) artefact (*b*) artiste
(*c*) artist (*d*) artisan

(Hotel Management, 1992)

20. The .... arts are those that pertain to writing or drawing.
(*a*) cartographic (*b*) graphic
(*c*) elocutionery (*d*) theatrical

21. I tried to give him some good advice but he .... to listen. **(Assistant Grade, 1993)**
(*a*) prevented (*b*) avoided
(*c*) refused (*d*) denied

22. Due to stringent financial conditions of the firm, several workers have been declared ....
(*a*) extra (*b*) abundant
(*c*) redundant (*d*) superfluous

23. One of the time-tested ways of remembering a series of items is known as a .... device.
(*a*) intellectual (*b*) schematic
(*c*) mnemonic (*d*) ingenious

24. When the bus was at full speed, its brakes failed and an accident was ....
(*a*) inevitable (*b*) infallible
(*c*) essential (*d*) undeniable

(C.D.S. 1994)

25. He .... all his energies to bear upon the task.
(*a*) brought (*b*) devoted
(*c*) put (*d*) organised

26. A cup of water was enough to .... his thirst.
(*a*) satisfy (*b*) appease
(*c*) quench (*d*) extinguish

27. The .... of the Minister's statement cannot be verified by people who have no access to official records.
(*a*) validity (*b*) veracity
(*c*) ambiguity (*d*) verbosity

(Assistant Grade, 1996)

28. The lost child was .... to his parents.
(*a*) restored (*b*) sent
(*c*) dispatched (*d*) returned

29. If something is beyond the .... of human knowledge man can know nothing about it. **(I. Tax, 1995)**

(a) edge (b) view
(c) end (d) boundary

30. The liquid seems .... but I am sure that it will prove poisonous.
(a) innocuous (b) insane
(c) incongruent (d) inflammable

31. There is a .... possibility of an understanding between India and Pakistan on the nuclear issue.
(a) high (b) distinct
(c) sound (d) clear

32. The higher class students should be careful as regards discipline as the youngsters tend to .... them.
(a) mimic (b) ape
(c) simulate (d) emulate

33. The prolonged illness left him totally .... **(C.B.I. 1994)**
(a) enervated (b) invalid
(c) indisposed (d) healthy

34. The .... arguments put forth for not disclosing the facts did not impress anybody.
(a) convincing (b) specious
(c) intemperate (d) spurious

35. The boy made good .... in his studies.
(a) progress (b) development
(c) growth (d) advancement

36. It was .... that a mind so pure and searching could miss the truth.
(a) likely (b) unlikely
(c) possibly (d) scarcely
(Railways, 1992)

37. The punch made the boxer .... with pain.
(a) grumble (b) gape
(c) wince (d) fumble

38. He tried to .... himself against a horde of ruffians. **(U.D.C. 1995)**
(a) save (b) collect
(c) defend (d) support

39. It is equally important to .... one's goal, as it is to set one.
(a) obtain (b) realise
(c) establish (d) prove

40. The poor fellow can't even afford daily food, ... alone buying a house.
(a) cast (b) forget
(c) let (d) leave
(C.B.I. 1990)

41. It is a rugged, restless and uncertain existence that the ..... lead.
(a) travellers (b) nomads
(c) sailors (d) tourists
(Central Excise, 1995)

42. Handle with care, it is ....
(a) agile (b) volatile
(c) ductile (d) fragile

43. The annual ... ... of industrial products has risen enormously in recent years.
(a) outlay (b) outcome
(c) output (d) outbreak

44. Prospective candidates have to prove that they have sufficient money to cover their .... and tuition.
(a) boarding (b) lodging
(c) sustenance (d) maintenance
(Stenographers' Exam, 1994)

45. We had a .... of warm weather in March.
(a) period (b) phase
(c) time (d) spell

46. Tension is likely to .... in the Kashmir valley now.
(a) decline (b) drop
(c) ease (d) fall

47. The degrees were awarded in the annual ....
(a) conference (b) convention
(c) convolution (d) convocation

48. What's so special about it is that the author has tried to .... all the worth while information in this book into a few pages.
(a) compact (b) abstract
(c) contract (d) condense

49. He is .... dancer.
(a) a skilled (b) an adept
(c) an adapt (d) an adopt
(Hotel Management, 1991)

50. Her parents will never give their .... to such an unsuitable match.
(a) willingness (b) agreement
(c) consent (d) acquiescence

ANSWERS

1. (d)	**2.** (a)	**3.** (b)	**4.** (b)	**5.** (a)	**6.** (c)	**7.** (a)	**8.** (d)	**9.** (b)	**10.** (b)
11. (c)	**12.** (c)	**13.** (b)	**14.** (c)	**15.** (b)	**16.** (a)	**17.** (a)	**18.** (d)	**19.** (d)	**20.** (b)
21. (c)	**22.** (c)	**23.** (c)	**24.** (a)	**25.** (a)	**26.** (c)	**27.** (b)	**28.** (a)	**29.** (d)	**30.** (a)
31. (b)	**32.** (d)	**33.** (a)	**34.** (b)	**35.** (a)	**36.** (b)	**37.** (c)	**38.** (c)	**39.** (b)	**40.** (d)
41. (b)	**42.** (d)	**43.** (c)	**44.** (a)	**45.** (d)	**46.** (c)	**47.** (d)	**48.** (d)	**49.** (a)	**50.** (c)

PRACTICE SET 7

Directions : ***Fill in the blanks in the following sentences by selecting the most appropriate alternative from amongst the four choices given under each sentence.***

1. Through perseverance and hard work we can keep the .... of liberty burning even during dark and trying times.
(*a*) flame (*b*) lamp
(*c*) goal (*d*) light
(Stenographers' Exam, 1995)

2. If arms race goes on between the super powers, chances for world peace will be ....
(*a*) hindered (*b*) elapsed
(*c*) nipped (*d*) jeopardized

3. Planets move in elliptical .... round the sun. **(C.D.S. 1995)**
(*a*) figures (*b*) orbits
(*c*) shapes (*d*) circles

4. Election .... by both the rival contestants was in full swing.
(*a*) propaganda (*b*) canvassing
(*c*) campaigning (*d*) publicity

5. Since the road was closed for repairs he took the .... **(S.S.C. 1995)**
(*a*) deviation (*b*) digression
(*c*) diversion (*d*) divergence

6. The helpful onlooker was badly injured when he tried to .... to end the quarrel.
(*a*) intrude (*b*) intervene
(*c*) interfere (*d*) intimidate

7. Take possession of the records immediately lest they are .... with.
(*a*) tampered (*b*) destroyed
(*c*) mishandled (*d*) malhandled
(L.I.C.A.A.O. 1989)

8. We should always make a .... selection of books.
(*a*) just (*b*) judicial
(*c*) judicious (*d*) justified

9. He was an .... who was fond of weird pets. **(S.C.R.A. 1993)**
(*a*) ambitious (*b*) amiable
(*c*) eccentric (*d*) emotional

10. He is .... for his evil deeds.
(*a*) notorious (*b*) famous
(*c*) celebrated (*d*) noted

11. The table drawer was .... and could not be opened.
(*a*) barred (*b*) fastened
(*c*) bound (*d*) jammed

12. Once you suspect a person of double dealing, you ought to keep him at arm's .... **(Stenographers' Exam, 1994)**
(*a*) width (*b*) length
(*c*) distance (*d*) aim

13. The children were eagerly waiting to eat a .... cake. **(M.B.A. 1990)**
(*a*) delicate (*b*) dainty
(*c*) appetising (*d*) delicious

14. And why did the police suspect you? It just does not make any .... to me.
(*a*) truth (*b*) reason
(*c*) point (*d*) sense
(Railways, 1989)

15. She is .... for the final round of the competition.
(*a*) declared (*b*) decided
(*c*) qualified (*d*) superior

16. Have you heard the .... news?
(*a*) late (*b*) later
(*c*) latest (*d*) latter
(Stenographers' Exam, 1991)

17. A relief team was sent to .... food and medicine among the refugees.
(*a*) sanction (*b*) distribute
(*c*) contribute (*d*) separate
(R.R.B. 1992)

18. Some of our external problems have completely .... our national leaders.
(*a*) beguiled (*b*) belaboured
(*c*) baffled (*d*) blustered

19. He was one of the .... spirits behind the 'Quit India' Movement. **(B.S.R.B. 1991)**
(*a*) strong (*b*) rising
(*c*) amazing (*d*) moving

20. Burglary is a ....
(*a*) evil (*b*) sin
(*c*) vice (*d*) crime

21. Ajay was .... with a serious crime.
(*a*) convicted (*b*) accused
(*c*) condemned (*d*) charged
(Stenographers' Exam, 1995)

22. It was a .... moment for Ravi when he finally gathered up his courage and told Aruna that he loved her.
(*a*) trying (*b*) poignant
(*c*) complicated (*d*) distressing

23. I .... missed the train this morning as I got up late. **(C.B.I. 1987)**
(*a*) quite (*b*) scarcely
(*c*) narrowly (*d*) hardly

24. A speedy response is one that is made with ....
(*a*) surmise (*b*) grimaces
(*c*) alacrity (*d*) fear

25. Parliamentary democracy demands a discipline and .... to the rules.
(*a*) adherence (*b*) obligation

(*c*) subjection (*d*) liability **(C.D.S. 1995)**

26. The increasing .... of the oceanic water because of dumping of nuclear waste is posing a serious challenge to the survival of the marine life.
(*a*) depletion (*b*) degeneration
(*c*) density (*d*) contamination

27. Macbeth was .... by his wife to commit the murder of Duncan.
(*a*) forced (*b*) excited
(*c*) instigated (*d*) incited

28. He bought new shoes last month but they are already .... out. **(U.D.C. 1993)**
(*a*) given (*b*) gone
(*c*) knocked (*d*) worn

29. Make the most of a bad ....
(*a*) bargain (*b*) job
(*c*) business (*d*) work

30. His .... for his brother's son knew no bounds.
(*a*) reverie (*b*) melange
(*c*) ill-will (*d*) malignity

31. The lovers were meeting each other secretly, but their .... affair was soon known to everyone. **(Railways, 1994)**
(*a*) clandestine (*b*) candid
(*c*) unknown (*d*) covert

32. Inflation will never be brought under control while prices continue to ....
(*a*) mount (*b*) fly
(*c*) ascend (*d*) soar

33. They were awaiting official .... of the news they had heard from a friend.
(*a*) ratification (*b*) confirmation
(*c*) sanction (*d*) recommendation **(C.D.S. 1994)**

34. They offered a .... of incentives to attract qualified people for the post.
(*a*) bundle (*b*) assurance
(*c*) package (*d*) gift

35. Those who have .... the transition from villages to cities have been able to secure good jobs.
(*a*) tried (*b*) arranged
(*c*) planned (*d*) managed

36. Success gives only .... pleasure.
(*a*) mordant (*b*) momentary
(*c*) monotonous (*d*) momentous **(I. Tax & Central Excise, 1991)**

37. The striking transport operators have decided to .... their agitation.
(*a*) intensify (*b*) prolong
(*c*) worsen (*d*) aggravate

38. The speaker .... the scope of his paper on 'Work- ethic' at the outset.
(*a*) declined (*b*) ascribed
(*c*) defined (*d*) delineated

39. The point you are raising is not .... to the subject.
(*a*) proper (*b*) fit
(*c*) required (*d*) pertinent

40. You cannot devise a method which .... all possibility of error.
(*a*) ignores (*b*) avoids
(*c*) excludes (*d*) includes **(Assistant Grade, 1994)**

41. He .... in wearing the old fashioned coat inspite of his wife's disapproval.
(*a*) resists (*b*) desists
(*c*) persists (*d*) insists **(C.D.S. 1995)**

42. The .... of nuclear power feel that it is one of the most dangerous developments in modern civilisation.
(*a*) activists (*b*) antagonists
(*c*) victims (*d*) opponents

43. The house is in a terrible state; the paint on the doors is .... badly.
(*a*) flaking (*b*) rotting
(*c*) eroding (*d*) decaying

44. A man who is well-bred and honourable invariably shows .... for the feelings of other people. **(Translators' Exam, 1994)**
(*a*) complacence (*b*) concern
(*c*) consideration (*d*) contempt

45. The Board called on a meeting to .... the financial situation of the Company.
(*a*) revise (*b*) cover
(*c*) review (*d*) support

46. To promote trade, it is necessary for the government to .... restrictions on exports.
(*a*) reduce (*b*) relax
(*c*) break (*d*) modify

47. We had a .... of warm weather in February. **(Stenographers' Exam, 1994)**
(*a*) phase (*b*) length
(*c*) spell (*d*) time

48. The landlord has threatened to .... me, if I do not vacate the house by next month.
(*a*) charge (*b*) sue
(*c*) suspend (*d*) accuse

49. The Spanish regarded him as an .... and called him a villain.
(*a*) imposter (*b*) apostle
(*c*) informer (*d*) archer

50. This item will not figure in the .... for today's meeting. **(Assistant Grade, 1993)**
(*a*) list (*b*) schedule
(*c*) programme (*d*) agenda

ANSWERS

1. (*a*)	**2.** (*d*)	**3.** (*b*)	**4.** (*c*)	**5.** (*c*)	**6.** (*b*)	**7.** (*a*)	**8.** (*c*)	**9.** (*c*)	**10.** (*a*)
11. (*d*)	**12.** (*b*)	**13.** (*d*)	**14.** (*d*)	**15.** (*c*)	**16.** (*c*)	**17.** (*b*)	**18.** (*c*)	**19.** (*d*)	**20.** (*d*)
21. (*d*)	**22.** (*b*)	**23.** (*c*)	**24.** (*c*)	**25.** (*a*)	**26.** (*d*)	**27.** (*d*)	**28.** (*d*)	**29.** (*a*)	**30.** (*d*)
31. (*a*)	**32.** (*d*)	**33.** (*b*)	**34.** (*c*)	**35.** (*d*)	**36.** (*d*)	**37.** (*a*)	**38.** (*d*)	**39.** (*d*)	**40.** (*c*)
41. (*c*)	**42.** (*c*)	**43.** (*a*)	**44.** (*c*)	**45.** (*c*)	**46.** (*b*)	**47.** (*c*)	**48.** (*b*)	**49.** (*a*)	**50.** (*d*)

PRACTICE SET 8

Directions : *Of the four alternatives given under each sentence, find the one that best fits into the blank space.*

1. It is impossible for an ordinary mortal to .... all these figures to memory.
(*a*) keep (*b*) commit
(*c*) retain (*d*) hoard
(U.D.C. 1993)

2. Experts fail to understand the .... behind the decision.
(*a*) ideology (*b*) judgement
(*c*) politics (*d*) rationale

3. Many of the advances of civilisation have been conceived by young people just on the .... of adulthood. **(C.D.S. 1995)**
(*a*) horizon (*b*) boundary
(*c*) peak (*d*) threshold

4. The servant obeyed the master's orders in .... manner.
(*a*) candid (*b*) plaintive
(*c*) obsequious (*d*) complaisant

5. The ship was .... from its course by bad weather.
(*a*) drawn (*b*) diverted
(*c*) distracted (*d*) pushed

6. Can anything .... a mother's love for her child?
(*a*) exchange (*b*) replace
(*c*) compensate (*d*) displace

7. The accused .... that he had met the deceased before. **(Assistant Grade, 1995)**
(*a*) remarked (*b*) refused
(*c*) exclaimed (*d*) denied

8. Pandit Nehru's life .... some of the greatest events of the century.
(*a*) overcame (*b*) spanned
(*c*) included (*d*) encompassed

9. His father-in-law .... him up in business. **(Stenographers' Exam, 1994)**
(*a*) made (*b*) put
(*c*) built (*d*) set

10. There was an .... silence after the announcement.
(*a*) awkward (*b*) uneasy
(*c*) eternal (*d*) eerie

11. This was the first time Roshan had been found guilty. He had no .... convictions.
(*a*) past (*b*) earlier
(*c*) previous (*d*) former
(C.D.S. 1992)

12. There was no .... of projects to be posed for aid.
(*a*) want (*b*) paucity
(*c*) dearth (*d*) scarcity

13. The .... to distinguish differences is the basis of science and art. **(I. Tax 1994)**
(*a*) power (*b*) tact
(*c*) strength (*d*) wisdom

14. The firm is .... heavy losses due to wrong policies.
(*a*) making (*b*) maintaining
(*c*) incurring (*d*) reporting

15. The basic issue is that the system of education has got .... within.
(*a*) oppressed (*b*) exhausted
(*c*) corroded (*d*) deteriorated

16. The Defence Minister said today that the Government was determined to .... the accord and fulfil the legitimate aspirations of the people.
(*a*) perform (*b*) practise
(*c*) implement (*d*) entertain

17. Speeding and blocking are traffic offences which lead to .... accidents.
(*a*) winsome (*b*) urban
(*c*) gruesome (*d*) minor
(Railways, 1995)

18. He did not make a single .... to any controversial matter in his speech.
(*a*) illusion (*b*) allusion
(*c*) elision (*d*) elucidation

19. The strike in the paper mill has resulted in a .... loss.
(*a*) commendable (*b*) voluminous
(*c*) colossal (*d*) comprehensive

20. However, the group's long term strategy is to .... on core sector businesses connected with infrastructure and energy. **(M.B.A. 1994)**
(*a*) depend (*b*) breed
(*c*) develop (*d*) concentrate

21. He begged leave of the king on the .... that he had to attend his ill wife.
(*a*) offer (*b*) excuse
(*c*) pardon (*d*) pretext

22. Finding that there was no use moving any further, the officer ordered the army's ....
(*a*) withdrawal (*b*) retreat
(*c*) restoration (*d*) revival

23. Kavita .... a sum of Rs. 200 out of the bank every Monday.
(*a*) extracts (*b*) draws
(*c*) obtains (*d*) pulls
(Stenographers' Exam, 1994)

24. We offered a .... of incentives to attract a new banker.
(*a*) bundle (*b*) assurance
(*c*) gift (*d*) package

25. These facts had been .... into them.
(*a*) digested (*b*) dictated
(*c*) drummed (*d*) spoken

26. Every individual wishes to lead a .... life. **(Assistant Grade, 1993)**
(*a*) respected (*b*) respectful
(*c*) respectable (*d*) respective

27. I have lost my purse. Can I .... some money from you?
(*a*) borrow (*b*) hire
(*c*) demand (*d*) loan

28. The more your action and thought are allied and ...., the happier you grow.
(*a*) invincible (*b*) divergent
(*c*) integrated (*d*) unravelled
(C.D.S. 1995)

29. You must .... facts and not run away from the truth.
(*a*) realise (*b*) notice
(*c*) face (*d*) know

30. Some students are .... and want to take only the courses for which they see immediate value.
(*a*) indolent (*b*) foolish
(*c*) pragmatic (*d*) theoretical

31. A cheerful man .... all difficulties and hardships with a smile on his face.
(*a*) challenges (*b*) embraces
(*c*) resists (*d*) endures
(Clerks' Grade, 1992)

32. Such .... clothes did not appeal to her nor did they suit her.
(*a*) simple (*b*) gaudy
(*c*) ornate (*d*) fatuous

33. He requested all his office .... to join him at the party.
(*a*) comrades (*b*) companions
(*c*) colleagues (*d*) collaborators

34. He knew what he was doing was right and so their catcalls did not .... him.
(*a*) worry (*b*) threaten
(*c*) faze (*d*) disconcert

35. I listened, but I had no idea what he was .... about. **(Railways, 1994)**
(*a*) saying (*b*) telling
(*c*) talking (*d*) discussing

36. The doctor was overcome with .... when he came to know that the patient had died due to negligence on his part.
(*a*) conscience (*b*) remorse
(*c*) humiliation (*d*) emotion

37. Although I have been interested in photography, yet I am only a/an ....
(*a*) novice (*b*) amateur
(*c*) apprentice (*d*) unprofessional

38. You will have to face some practical problems when you start .... this plan.
(*a*) prosecuting (*b*) projecting
(*c*) prescribing (*d*) proscribing
(Translators' Exam, 1994)

39. There are various hobbies for us to .... in our leisure hours.
(*a*) pursue (*b*) follow
(*c*) absorb (*d*) contribute

40. Every Shakespearean hero has an internal .... in his character.
(*a*) fault (*b*) defect
(*c*) flaw (*d*) weakness
(C.D.S. 1994)

41. Statistics are .... as a means of determining public opinion.
(*a*) unreliable (*b*) dubious
(*c*) uncertain (*d*) phoney

42. He was able to .... his small income by working in a hotel at night. **(C.B.I. 1991)**
(*a*) amplify (*b*) supplement
(*c*) expand (*d*) multiply

43. The solution to the problem .... me.
(*a*) outgrew (*b*) outraged
(*c*) evaded (*d*) undermined

44. This test .... no previous knowledge of the subject : any graduate is expected to complete it successfully. **(C.D.S. 1992)**
(*a*) concerns (*b*) presupposes
(*c*) assumes (*d*) necessitates

45. The clever politician .... his way to the ministerial position in a short time.
(*a*) faked (*b*) wangled
(*c*) scaled (*d*) moved

46. The rain water that does not flow to the rivers, ... beneath the soil to form underground water.

(*a*) flows (*b*) penetrates
(*c*) seeps (*d*) percolates

47. The river overflowed its .... and flooded the area. **(Stenographers' Exam, 1994)**
(*a*) banks (*b*) limits
(*c*) edges (*d*) fronts

48. Questions will be answered by a .... of experts.
(*a*) group (*b*) staff
(*c*) band (*d*) panel

49. Being well qualified, he has good .... in the profession.
(*a*) prospectus (*b*) perspectives
(*c*) prospects (*d*) prospectives

50. The .... animal was on the look out for food. **(Stenographers' Exam, 1995)**
(*a*) uncivilized (*b*) wild
(*c*) primitive (*d*) savage

ANSWERS

1. (*b*)	**2.** (*d*)	**3.** (*d*)	**4.** (*d*)	**5.** (*c*)	**6.** (*b*)	**7.** (*d*)	**8.** (*b*)	**9.** (*d*)	**10.** (*b*)
11. (*b*)	**12.** (*c*)	**13.** (*d*)	**14.** (*c*)	**15.** (*c*)	**16.** (*c*)	**17.** (*c*)	**18.** (*b*)	**19.** (*c*)	**20.** (*d*)
21. (*d*)	**22.** (*b*)	**23.** (*b*)	**24.** (*d*)	**25.** (*c*)	**26.** (*c*)	**27.** (*a*)	**28.** (*c*)	**29.** (*c*)	**30.** (*c*)
31. (*d*)	**32.** (*b*)	**33.** (*c*)	**34.** (*c*)	**35.** (*c*)	**36.** (*b*)	**37.** (*a*)	**38.** (*b*)	**39.** (*a*)	**40.** (*c*)
41. (*a*)	**42.** (*b*)	**43.** (*c*)	**44.** (*c*)	**45.** (*b*)	**46.** (*d*)	**47.** (*a*)	**48.** (*d*)	**49.** (*c*)	**50.** (*b*)

PRACTICE SET 9

Directions : ***Each of the following sentences has a blank space and four words given after the sentence. Select whichever word you consider most appropriate for the blank space and indicate your choice.***

1. The brilliant students will be .... scholarships. **(Railways, 1995)**
(*a*) honoured (*b*) awarded
(*c*) rewarded (*d*) forwarded

2. The dictionary of a language .... usage.
(*a*) prescribes (*b*) describes
(*c*) decides (*d*) imbibes

3. "Mind your own business", he said ....
(*a*) meekly (*b*) heavily
(*c*) sharply (*d*) clumsily

4. He had incurred such heavy debts that nothing short of a .... could save him from bankruptcy.
(*a*) loan (*b*) windfall
(*c*) lottery (*d*) miracle

5. According to corporate circles, Datta is pushing through the merger to create a financially .... company in the processed foods business, the group's thrust area for the 1990s. **(M.B.A. 1994)**
(*a*) straight (*b*) powerful
(*c*) leading (*d*) acceptable

6. One of the most .... events in the history of India was the attainment of its freedom.
(*a*) efferminate (*b*) epochal
(*c*) enterprising (*d*) greatest

7. The glib .... of the sales girl helped her a lot in her profession.
(*a*) patter (*b*) chatter
(*c*) tapping (*d*) jabber

8. A stone that goes on rolling .... no moss. **(Stenographer's Exam, 1994)**
(*a*) gets (*b*) accumulates
(*c*) collects (*d*) gathers

9. Even after a long discussion, the committee could not reach a .... decision.
(*a*) cordial (*b*) joint
(*c*) unanimous (*d*) common

10. The British are generally .... as a far more inventive collection of individuals.
(*a*) consigned (*b*) characterised
(*c*) expected (*d*) recognised

11. The doctor gave the woman a .... to calm her down. **(Central Excise, 1991)**
(*a*) tonic (*b*) sedative
(*c*) antiseptic (*d*) antidote

12. He was extremely ....; he would believe anything you told him.
(*a*) believable (*b*) gullible
(*c*) affable (*d*) reliable

13. Several of our players were injured, so our losing the match was almost ....
(*a*) necessary (*b*) indispensable
(*c*) inevitable (*d*) inexcusable
(C.B.I. 1991)

14. The naked human eye cannot .... minute flaws in complicated mechanisms.
(*a*) understand (*b*) detect
(*c*) comprehend (*d*) visualize

15. There could have been a war on it, but in the end reason ....
(*a*) persisted (*b*) counted
(*c*) prevailed (*d*) survived

16. My friend says that he drinks tea because it is the best .... in the world.
(*a*) fluid (*b*) drink
(*c*) beverage (*d*) liquid
(Asstt. Grade, 1995)

17. Every human being in the developed country .... over five pounds of solid wastes per day in various forms.
(*a*) contributes (*b*) fosters
(*c*) produces (*d*) develops

18. By sheer hard work, Sushil has .... out a niche for himself in the field of journalism.
(*a*) carved (*b*) worked
(*c*) derived (*d*) accomplished

19. The President of the Students' Union played into the hands of some political leaders and .... the students to go on a strike. **(Translators' Exam, 1994)**
(*a*) invited (*b*) ignited
(*c*) instigated (*d*) inspired

20. We should not mix with those men who have an .... reputation.
(*a*) unsafe (*b*) unsavoury
(*c*) unsteady (*d*) unsanctified

21. They are refugees in need of ....
(*a*) renovation (*b*) recapitulation
(*c*) restoration (*d*) rehabilitation
(C.D.S. 1994)

22. The teacher promised to .... a prize to the boy who stood first in the class.
(*a*) reward (*b*) award
(*c*) promote (*d*) secure

23. If our friends are not able to take us in their car, we must make .... arrangements to go to the airport.
(*a*) possible (*b*) alternate
(*c*) another (*d*) alternative

24. Please do not .... the offer made by the Chairman. **(I. Tax, 1989)**
(*a*) refrain (*b*) refute
(*c*) refuse (*d*) refuge

25. It is generally believed that the rats are the first to leave a .... ship.
(*a*) moving (*b*) anchored
(*c*) sinking (*d*) drowning

26. My mother upset the kettle of boiling water and .... her right hand badly.
(*a*) wounded (*b*) sizzled
(*c*) scorched (*d*) scalded
(U.D.C. 1993)

27. Legislation was passed to punish brokers who .... their clients' funds.
(*a*) devour (*b*) defalcate
(*c*) devastate (*d*) embezzle

28. The figures were barely .... in the dim light.
(*a*) obvious (*b*) perceived
(*c*) perceptive (*d*) susceptible

29. It is my considered opinion that English education in the manner it has been given has .... the English educated Indians.
(*a*) emasculated (*b*) exocommunicated
(*c*) castrated (*d*) intimidated

30. .... learning does not help the mental growth of a student. **(Railways, 1995)**
(*a*) Guided (*b*) Rote
(*c*) Assisted (*d*) Fast

31. The new Ambassador presented his .... to the President at a formal ceremony.
(*a*) documents (*b*) credentials
(*c*) papers (*d*) testimonials

32. The accused denied having committed the crime but could advance no sound arguments to .... the charges.
(*a*) refuse (*b*) repress
(*c*) refute (*d*) reproof
(Translators' Exam, 1994)

33. My mother always kept .... cash for day-to-day expenses in the drawer.
(*a*) small (*b*) little
(*c*) running (*d*) petty

34. The outlines of the figure were barely .... in the darkness.
(*a*) susceptible (*b*) obvious
(*c*) perceptive (*d*) perceived

35. Manuring in agricultural fields increases .... **(C.D.S. 1992)**
(*a*) income (*b*) fertility
(*c*) profitability (*d*) productivity

36. We did not have the .... idea of the problems involved in the work.
(*a*) closest (*b*) feeblest
(*c*) weakest (*d*) faintest

37. The whole lot of us .... a sigh of relief when he finally emigrated to Canada.
(*a*) showed (*b*) breathed
(*c*) heaved (*d*) expressed

38. Life is to death as pleasure is to ....
(*a*) suffering (*b*) pain
(*c*) poverty (*d*) anguish
(C.D.S. 1995)

39. A bad workman .... with his tools.
(*a*) plays (*b*) works
(*c*) quarrels (*d*) fights

40. Orchestral players are .... behind screens, and at no time do the judges bear their names.
(*a*) confined (*b*) conditioned
(*c*) visualised (*d*) auditioned

41. Giving to his sons the key to success, he slept a (an) .... sleep.
(*a*) perennial (*b*) amiable
(*c*) ephemeral (*d*) eternal

42. At one point, it looked as if an area of agreement would ...., specially over the issue of productivity linked wages.
(*a*) emerge (*b*) grow
(*c*) develop (*d*) come out
(Railways, 1994)

43. Reason is the highest faculty .... on man by his creator.
(*a*) entrusted (*b*) endowed
(*c*) bestowed (*d*) conferred

44. A speedy response is one that is made with ....
(*a*) surmise (*b*) alacrity
(*c*) grimaces (*d*) fear

45. Man must .... now to stop pollution.
(*a*) act (*b*) operate
(*c*) behave (*d*) perform
(Stenographers' Exam, 1994)

46. The principal was .... through some papers when I went there to meet him.
(*a*) shearing (*b*) sheafing
(*c*) shuffling (*d*) shelving

47. Laser is a (an) .... of Light Amplification by Stimulated Emission of Radiation.
(*a*) homonym (*b*) acronym
(*c*) malaprop (*d*) collocation

48. The annual .... of industrial products has risen enormously in recent years.
(*a*) outbreak (*b*) output
(*c*) outcome (*d*) outlay
(Central Excise, 1989)

49. The young man was quickly promoted when his Managing Director saw how .... he was.
(*a*) assiduous (*b*) cursory
(*c*) indigent (*d*) lethargic

50. The bank clerk tried to .... money from his friend's account.
(*a*) empower (*b*) embellish
(*c*) embroil (*d*) embezzle
(Stenographers' Exam, 1995)

ANSWERS

1. (*b*)	**2.** (*b*)	**3.** (*c*)	**4.** (*d*)	**5.** (*b*)	**6.** (*b*)	**7.** (*a*)	**8.** (*d*)	**9.** (*c*)	**10.** (*d*)
11. (*b*)	**12.** (*b*)	**13.** (*c*)	**14.** (*b*)	**15.** (*c*)	**16.** (*c*)	**17.** (*c*)	**18.** (*a*)	**19.** (*c*)	**20.** (*b*)
21. (*d*)	**22.** (*b*)	**23.** (*d*)	**24.** (*c*)	**25.** (*c*)	**26.** (*d*)	**27.** (*b*)	**28.** (*c*)	**29.** (*a*)	**30.** (*b*)
31. (*b*)	**32.** (*c*)	**33.** (*d*)	**34.** (*c*)	**35.** (*d*)	**36.** (*d*)	**37.** (*c*)	**38.** (*b*)	**39.** (*c*)	**40.** (*d*)
41. (*d*)	**42.** (*a*)	**43.** (*c*)	**44.** (*b*)	**45.** (*a*)	**46.** (*c*)	**47.** (*b*)	**48.** (*b*)	**49.** (*a*)	**50.** (*d*)

PRACTICE SET 10

Directions : ***Of the four alternatives given under each sentence, find the one that best fits into the blank space.***

1. He knew everything better than anybody else, and it was an affront to his .... vanity that you should disagree with him. **(C.D.S. 1993)**
(*a*) overwrought (*b*) overwhelming
(*c*) overweening (*d*) overstrung

2. She .... people who are good at sports.
(*a*) supports (*b*) admires
(*c*) attracts (*d*) appeals

3. From the shape of the present circumstances, he still cannot .... what's going to happen next.
(*a*) declare (*b*) foresee
(*c*) prognosticate (*d*) prodigy

4. He wanted to help .... poverty.
(*a*) diminish (*b*) reduce
(*c*) dwindle (*d*) deplete
(S.S.C. 1994)

5. He married many times, yet happiness .... him and he remained miserable as before.
(*a*) eluded (*b*) disappointed
(*c*) escaped (*d*) absconded

6. A .... thief was caught by the police last night.
(*a*) famous (*b*) popular
(*c*) renowned (*d*) notorious

7. The Government is confident that the standard of living will begin to .... again soon. **(I. Tax, 1993)**
(*a*) revive (*b*) lift
(*c*) fluorish (*d*) rise

8. India believes in tolerance, not in ...., acceptance or rejection.
(*a*) alienation (*b*) bigotry
(*c*) prejudice (*d*) aggression

9. All the employees of the firm are .... to a fortnight's holiday. **(C.D.S. 1991)**
(*a*) allowed (*b*) entitled
(*c*) required (*d*) able

10. The court of conscience .... all other courts.
(*a*) surpasses (*b*) excels
(*c*) supercedes (*d*) trespasses

11. The plant has been growing steadily, but of late its growth has ....
(*a*) shortened (*b*) thwarted
(*c*) retarded (*d*) hastened

12. Ambition is one of those .... which are never satisfied. **(C.B.I. 1995)**
(*a*) needs (*b*) ideas
(*c*) passions (*d*) fancies

13. The prisoner was .... to answering any of my questions. **(Asstt. Grade, 1993)**
(*a*) inverse (*b*) adverse
(*c*) reverse (*d*) averse

14. Dying is a very ...., dreary affair.
(*a*) boring (*b*) dull
(*c*) monotonous (*d*) drab

15. The new industrial policy is a result of the confidence the government has in the .... of the Indian industry.
(*a*) status (*b*) profitability
(*c*) existence (*d*) maturity

16. The senior officials of the Ministry charged the secretary with gross .... of duty and so suspended him. **(C.D.S. 1993)**
(*a*) disregard (*b*) negligence
(*c*) laxity (*d*) dishonesty

17. The resulting of his probing was .... evidence all pointing to a serious treachery.
(*a*) incriminating (*b*) dangerous
(*c*) frivolous (*d*) intimidatory

18. His parents did not pay .... attention to his studies. **(Stenographers' Exam, 1993)**
(*a*) suitable (*b*) just
(*c*) remarkable (*d*) proper

19. The top ranking student .... his success in his studies to his Headmaster's guidance.
(*a*) accounts (*b*) refers
(*c*) attributes (*d*) claims

20. I do not .... with the views expressed in your newspaper.
(*a*) confirm (*b*) coincide
(*c*) compromise (*d*) concur

21. The communalist represents the .... of everything noble that we have inherited from our culture and history.
(*a*) antagonism (*b*) immorality
(*c*) antidote (*d*) antithesis
(Section Officers' Exam, 1993)

22. Despite her pleas, the mistress did not .... to her request.
(*a*) accede (*b*) convince
(*c*) favour (*d*) approve

23. He could not stay here longer because he was not .... to such environment.
(*a*) adept (*b*) addicted
(*c*) accustomed (*d*) conducive

24. He is greatly admired for his .... behaviour. **(C.D.S. 1994)**
(*a*) decrepit (*b*) decorative
(*c*) decadent (*d*) decorous

25. His moral decadence was marked by his .... from the ways of integrity and honesty.
(*a*) declivity (*b*) departure
(*c*) obsession (*d*) opprobrium

26. Nobody can say what .... him to commit this crime.
(*a*) excited (*b*) attracted
(*c*) prompted (*d*) roused
(Assistant Grade, 1993)

27. A public figure loves to be the .... of a cartoonist.
(*a*) favourite (*b*) subject
(*c*) butt (*d*) model

28. The meeting .... with a vote of thanks.
(*c*) closed (*d*) finished
(*c*) stopped (*d*) concluded

29. The country needs a .... government to tackle the challenges it faces today.
(*a*) sustained (*b*) stable
(*c*) stationary (*d*) stagnant
(Clerks' Grade, 1991)

30. The enviroment was .... to his work and that's why he succeeded.
(*a*) suitable (*b*) confirming
(*c*) conducive (*d*) adequate

31. His .... income does not allow him to buy a new scooter.
(*a*) small (*b*) meagre
(*c*) spare (*d*) scarce

32. It is difficult to believe what he tells us because his account of any event is always full of .... of all sorts.
(*a*) discrepancies (*b*) differences
(*c*) discretions (*d*) distinctions
(C.D.S. 1991)

33. The poor women of the village could only afford ...., not costly ornaments.
(*a*) anklets (*b*) danglers
(*c*) baubles (*d*) adornments

34. As the waves rose and the ship tossed, many of the passengers felt ....
(*a*) lethargic (*b*) tremulous
(*c*) subdued (*d*) queasy

35. To explain his design to his visitor, the architect .... a simple plan on the blackboard. **(C.D.S. 1994)**
(*a*) constructed (*b*) made
(*c*) sketched (*d*) built

36. The government should crush with a heavy hand all the gangs of terrorists and foil their .... design against the integrity of our nation.
(*a*) foolish (*b*) nefarious
(*c*) ugly (*d*) undesirable

37. One .... and you know who among them is the culprit. **(U.D.C. 1994)**
(*a*) gaze (*b*) peep
(*c*) look (*d*) sight

38. The speaker .... the scope of his paper on 'Work ethic' at the outset.
(*a*) defined (*b*) delineated
(*c*) ascribed (*d*) declined

39. The criminal seems to have acted in .... with three others. **(C.D.S. 1993)**
(*a*) collision (*b*) collusion
(*c*) cohesion (*d*) coalition

40. He .... a lot over the pros and cons of the issue but could arrive at no fruitful result.
(*a*) envisioned (*b*) contemplated
(*c*) embodied (*d*) envisaged

41. If an indelible ink is used, this will not be .... **(Hotel Management, 1992)**
(*a*) observed (*b*) obligated
(*c*) obliterated (*d*) obviated

42. The custom officers .... gold worth Rs. 1 crore from the smugglers.
(*a*) snatched (*b*) captured
(*c*) mobbed (*d*) confiscated

43. The accused .... to answer any questions in the absence of his lawyer.
(*a*) declined (*b*) denied
(*c*) denounced (*d*) detested

44. On account of the dearth of grass on the arid plains the cattle became ....
(*a*) jubilant (*b*) emaciated
(*c*) flippant (*d*) agitated
(C.B.I. 1995)

45. The new Science teacher .... a great respect from his students.
(*a*) observed (*b*) acquired
(*c*) attained (*d*) commanded

46. His .... helped him rise so high in life.
(*a*) cleverness (*b*) wisdom
(*c*) cunningness (*d*) genius

47. The sound of the running water of the stream had a pleasantly .... effect on me. **(C.D.S. 1994)**
(*a*) sonorous (*b*) amusing
(*c*) loud (*d*) somnolent

48. The speaker painted a .... picture of hunger in parts of India.
(*a*) poignant (*b*) passionate
(*c*) parsimonious (*d*) chimirical

49. The .... statues resembled ludicrous figures found in ancient monuments.
(*a*) grotesque (*b*) impressive
(*c*) gregarious (*d*) magnificent

50. Some regions of our country still remain .... to the average man.
(*a*) impenetrable (*b*) impermeable
(*c*) inaccessible (*d*) impossible
(Assistant Grade, 1996)

ANSWERS

1. (*d*)	**2.** (*b*)	**3.** (*c*)	**4.** (*b*)	**5.** (*b*)	**6.** (*d*)	**7.** (*d*)	**8.** (*b*)	**9.** (*b*)	**10.** (*c*)
11. (*c*)	**12.** (*c*)	**13.** (*d*)	**14.** (*b*)	**15.** (*d*)	**16.** (*b*)	**17.** (*a*)	**18.** (*d*)	**19.** (*c*)	**20.** (*d*)
21. (*d*)	**22.** (*a*)	**23.** (*c*)	**24.** (*d*)	**25.** (*b*)	**26.** (*c*)	**27.** (*c*)	**28.** (*d*)	**29.** (*b*)	**30.** (*c*)
31. (*b*)	**32.** (*a*)	**33.** (*c*)	**34.** (*d*)	**35.** (*c*)	**36.** (*b*)	**37.** (*c*)	**38.** (*b*)	**39.** (*b*)	**40.** (*b*)
41. (*c*)	**42.** (*d*)	**43.** (*a*)	**44.** (*b*)	**45.** (*d*)	**46.** (*d*)	**47.** (*a*)	**48.** (*a*)	**49.** (*a*)	**50.** (*c*)

PRACTICE SET 11

Directions : ***In each of the following sentences, a blank has been given which can be filled correctly by one of the four alternatives given under it. That is your answer.***

1. If the downward trend in revenues is not ...., the shortfall at the end of the year may be most astonishing.
(*a*) eliminated (*b*) controlled
(*c*) reversed (*d*) suppressed

2. All too often journalists fail to .... personal privacy.
(*a*) consider (*b*) regard
(*c*) respect (*d*) admire
(Assistant Grade, 1995)

3. Mr. Roy was .... the Man of the Year by the Lion's Club Society.
(*a*) accounted (*b*) defined
(*c*) announced (*d*) designated
4. It .... to me that she was incurable.
(*a*) suggested (*b*) flashed
(*c*) happened (*d*) occurred
(C.D.S. 1994)
5. The controversy is likely to .... bad blood between the two communities.
(*a*) involve (*b*) improve
(*c*) infuse (*d*) create
6. I became alert because I .... trouble around me.
(*a*) comprehended (*b*) sensed
(*c*) transcended (*d*) saw
7. The police had to be called to control a .... between two political groups.
(*a*) brawl (*b*) confusion
(*c*) riot (*d*) disturbance
8. He is in the habit of .... his head whenever anything goes wrong.
(*a*) hiding (*b*) losing
(*c*) protecting (*d*) loosing
(Railways, 1995)
9. I am feeling .... better today.
(*a*) too (*b*) rather
(*c*) very (*d*) fairly
10. The driver suddenly applied the brakes when he saw a .... truck ahead of him.
(*a*) static (*b*) solitary
(*c*) stationary (*d*) immobile
(C.D.S. 1992)
11. When you were sick, it was your mother who .... you back to health.
(*a*) aroused (*b*) urged
(*c*) assured (*d*) nursed
12. The British were able to establish an empire in India, largely because the ruling Indian princes were ....
(*a*) disunited (*b*) disintegrated
(*c*) disjointed (*d*) disoriented
(Asstt. Grade, 1993)
13. ....an accident, the train will arrive in time. **(U.D.C. 1993)**
(*a*) Besides (*b*) Accepting
(*c*) Despite (*d*) Barring
14. Knowing that the news was a good one, he decided to be the ....
(*a*) messenger (*b*) harbinger
(*c*) informer (*d*) instructor
15. It was .... of him to act so in the company of his friends.
(*a*) ridiculous (*b*) funny
(*c*) amusing (*d*) mocking
16. But the introductory fee does not stop after the initial handshake; brokers have to .... it up after each transaction.
(*a*) bring (*b*) give
(*c*) boost (*d*) cough
(M.B.A. 1994)
17. As a witness of the court, you have to be .... in your statement.
(*a*) short (*b*) accurate
(*c*) pointed (*d*) prompt
18. The organisers of the conference have .... the allegations made against them.
(*a*) retorted (*b*) repulsed
(*c*) rebuked (*d*) repudiated
19. Hamlet wanted to .... the death of his father who was treacherously killed by his mother's lover.
(*a*) revenge (*b*) avenge
(*c*) forgive (*d*) vindicate
(Translators' Exam, 1994)
20. .... work is more enjoyable than compulsory work.
(*a*) Temporary (*b*) Voluntary
(*c*) Slavish (*d*) Mechanical
21. He has shown both by his hard work and by his conduct that he .... a special award.
(*a*) aspires (*b*) needs
(*c*) merits (*d*) dislikes
22. The old 'Nature Versus ....' debate regarding crime continues even today.
(*a*) Culture (*b*) Man
(*c*) Nurture (*d*) Universe
(C.D.S. 1995)
23. They .... a new plan to throw him out of that office.
(*a*) conspired (*b*) conceived
(*c*) connived (*d*) contrived
24. The sun .... at six this morning.
(*a*) arose (*b*) rose
(*c*) aroused (*d*) raised
(Stenographers' Exam, 1994)
25. The visit to my home town .... many happy memories of my own childhood.
(*a*) revived (*b*) recollected
(*c*) retained (*d*) reminded
26. Flood has .... the misery of the people already hit by the cyclone.
(*a*) worsened (*b*) intensified
(*c*) repeated (*d*) compounded
27. It has now been .... that 52 people died in the crash. **(C.B.I. 1991)**
(*a*) assured (*b*) confirmed
(*c*) counted (*d*) ensured
28. The prisoner was ordered to be released when it was discovered that there had been a .... of justice.
(*a*) mischance (*b*) miscarriage
(*c*) mishap (*d*) misdemeanour
29 My father was too .... to push open the heavy door. **(C.D.S. 1994)**

(*a*) timid (*b*) faint
(*c*) feeble (*d*) faltering

30. It was his .... that saved him from the coming danger.
(*a*) foresight (*b*) prediction
(*c*) presage (*d*) detection

31. Animals are such .... friends; they ask no questions and pass no criticism.
(*a*) useful (*b*) social
(*c*) humane (*d*) agreeable

32. The bureaucrat was .... for his role in the scam. **(C.B.I. 1993)**
(*a*) reinstated (*b*) criticised
(*c*) indicted (*d*) indited

33. Modern architecture has discarded the .... trimming on buildings and emphasizes simplicity of line..
(*a*) gaudy (*b*) flagrant
(*c*) gaunt (*d*) flamboyant

34. It is becoming more and more .... that the principal is losing the confidence of his staff. **(C.D.S. 1992)**
(*a*) prominent (*b*) conspicuous
(*c*) manifest (*d*) apparent

35. The presence of their professor in the very next table .... the conversation of the boys in the restaurant.
(*a*) obstructed (*b*) limited
(*c*) inhibited (*d*) interrupted

36. Health is too important to be ....
(*a*) neglected (*b*) detested
(*c*) despised (*d*) discarded
(Asstt. Grade, 1994)

37. The matter would have become serious if .... action had not been taken.
(*a*) deliberate (*b*) fast
(*c*) hasty (*d*) timely

38. As soon as the news of the Director's death reached the Board, the meeting was ....
(*a*) impounded (*b*) suspended
(*c*) banned (*d*) adjourned

39. He was in trouble because he did not .... the instructions.
(*a*) follow (*b*) observe
(*c*) confirm (*d*) chase
(Stenographers' Exam, 1993)

40. It is strange that he should be as .... as his brother is generous. **(U.D.C. 1993)**
(*a*) liberal (*b*) spendthrift
(*c*) reckless (*d*) stingy

41. Peace committees were formed and police vigilance intensified to prevent .... of further communal violence.
(*a*) emergence (*b*) occurrence
(*c*) recurrence (*d*) recrudescence

42. The labour leader .... the Government in the Assembly today of not protecting the interests of textile workers.
(*a*) assaulted (*b*) accused
(*c*) attacked (*d*) instigated

43. He finds it difficult to .... between blue and green as he is colour blind.
(*a*) distinguish (*b*) study
(*c*) recognise (*d*) see
(Stenographers' Exam, 1995)

44. He is not only kind but also .... in his dealings with the poor.
(*a*) courteous (*b*) churlish
(*c*) malicious (*d*) boorish

45. Owing to their unruly behaviour, some members of the cricket team were .... from taking part in the matches.
(*a*) banned (*b*) exempted
(*c*) excluded (*d*) outlawed

46. As the news of the natural .... spread offers of relief poured in.
(*a*) misery (*b*) misfortune
(*c*) calamity (*d*) collapse
(Asstt. Grade, 1995)

47. The committee met to .... the team for the tournament.
(*a*) appoint (*b*) select
(*c*) elect (*d*) nominate

48. People who have an .... reputation are often avoided by the rest.
(*a*) unsteady (*b*) unsavoury
(*c*) unsafe (*d*) unsanctified

49. On a final consideration, Mr. Abererombie's book strikes us as singular .... of thought. **(C.D.S. 1991)**
(*a*) attributive (*b*) significative
(*c*) symptomatic (*d*) evocative

50. The lions in the Gir forest are protected as they come under .... species.
(*a*) dangerous (*b*) engendered
(*c*) enamoured (*d*) endangered
(Translator's Exam, 1994)

ANSWERS

1. (*c*)	**2.** (*c*)	**3.** (*d*)	**4.** (*d*)	**5.** (*d*)	**6.** (*b*)	**7.** (*d*)	**8.** (*b*)	**9.** (*d*)	**10.** (*c*)
11. (*d*)	**12.** (*a*)	**13.** (*d*)	**14.** (*b*)	**15.** (*a*)	**16.** (*a*)	**17.** (*b*)	**18.** (*d*)	**19.** (*b*)	**20.** (*b*)
21. (*c*)	**22.** (*b*)	**23.** (*d*)	**24.** (*b*)	**25.** (*a*)	**26.** (*d*)	**27.** (*b*)	**28.** (*d*)	**29.** (*c*)	**30.** (*a*)
31. (*d*)	**32.** (*c*)	**33.** (*d*)	**34.** (*d*)	**35.** (*c*)	**36.** (*a*)	**37.** (*d*)	**38.** (*b*)	**39.** (*a*)	**40.** (*d*)
41. (*d*)	**42.** (*b*)	**43.** (*a*)	**44.** (*a*)	**45.** (*a*)	**46.** (*c*)	**47.** (*b*)	**48.** (*b*)	**49.** (*d*)	**50.** (*d*)

PRACTICE SET 12

Directions : *Pick out the most effective word from the given words to fill in the blanks to make the sentence meaningfully complete.*

1. 'Please' and 'Thank you' are the little courtesies by which we keep the .... of life oiled and running smoothly.
(*a*) river (*b*) garden
(*c*) path (*d*) machine
(C.D.S. 1995)

2. The bright colour of this shirt has .... away. **(Stenographers' Exam, 1995)**
(*a*) gone (*b*) disappeared
(*c*) faded (*d*) paled

3. By dint of his labour, he .... all that he had lost.
(*a*) replenished (*b*) restored
(*c*) refurbished (*d*) restounded

4. Their differences were amicably settled by a/an ....
(*a*) agent (*b*) arbiter
(*c*) mediator (*d*) arbitrator

5. One major .... between the Election Commission and the Union Government is related to the powers of the former in respect of the deployment of central police forces at places where an election is held. **(M.B.A. 1994)**
(*a*) conflict (*b*) pain
(*c*) irritant (*d*) culprit

6. Violent and sudden fluctuation in prices and total earnings of exports have a serious .... impact on the overall growth of the Third World Countries.
(*a*) unusual (*b*) opposite
(*c*) contrary (*d*) adverse

7. Even a .... glance will reveal the mystery. **(Hotel Management, 1992)**
(*a*) crude (*b*) cursory
(*c*) critical (*d*) curious

8. His standard of living has .... since his son joined service. **(U.D.C. 1993)**
(*a*) lifted (*b*) increased
(*c*) risen (*d*) heightened

9. If someone deliberately damages your property, he is .... to pay for the cost of repairs.
(*a*) compelled (*b*) forced
(*c*) liable (*d*) requested

10. The passengers were afraid but the captain .... them that there was no danger. **(C.D.S. 1994)**
(*a*) instructed (*b*) advised
(*c*) promised (*d*) assured

11. Parliamentary Democracy postulated a discipline and .... to the rules.
(*a*) liability (*b*) commitment
(*c*) obligation (*d*) subjection

12. His first failure did not .... him from making another attempt. **(C.B.I. 1991)**
(*a*) interfere (*b*) forbid
(*c*) frighten (*d*) deter

13. The lorry driver was arrested for rash driving and his licence was .... by the police.
(*a*) penalised (*b*) suspended
(*c*) impounded (*d*) banned

14. No one will .... you for having been rude to your teacher. **(Railways, 1995)**
(*a*) exclaim (*b*) admire
(*c*) advise (*d*) recommend

15. He married many times, yet happiness .... him and he remained miserable as before.
(*a*) absconded (*b*) escaped
(*c*) disappointed (*d*) eluded

16. Some people .... from voting at the last elections.
(*a*) denied (*b*) refused
(*c*) abstained (*d*) declined

17. The doctor .... the patient from taking certain medicines. **(Asstt. Grade, 1995)**
(*a*) banned (*b*) prohibited
(*c*) prescribed (*d*) proscribed

18. Sociologists believe that an element of violence is .... in all societies.
(*a*) passive (*b*) invisible
(*c*) active (*d*) latent

19. The missile launched by the US space station slowly .... towards the target.
(*a*) went (*b*) ascended
(*c*) raised (*d*) gravitated

20. I .... a car to be absolutely necessary these days. **(Stenographers' Exam, 1994)**
(*a*) think (*b*) regard
(*c*) consider (*d*) agree

21. A wife who is in the habit of .... at her husband over trifles, can never make a happy home.
(*a*) chastising (*b*) ranting
(*c*) scolding (*d*) thrashing

22. India would not be .... from its research and development programmes.
(*a*) stopped (*b*) forced
(*c*) debarred (*d*) deterred

23. Since life is a great ...., he couldn't see why death cannot be.
(*a*) marvel (*b*) mystery
(*c*) wonder (*d*) surprise

24. He didn t have the .... idea of the villager's problems.
(*a*) smallest (*b*) finest
(*c*) faintest (*d*) feeblest
(Translators' Exam, 1994)

25. The .... conclusion is that people will have to live with rising prices.
(*a*) final (*b*) ultimate
(*c*) inescapable (*d*) hopeless

26. On her sixteenth birthday, Ashish had gifted her a bottle of ....
(*a*) cologne (*b*) fragrance
(*c*) essence (*d*) perfume

27. This is a .... translation of the speech.
(*a*) verbatim (*b*) verbal
(*c*) literal (*d*) literary
(Stenographers' Exam, 1995)

28. As a last .... the students have appealed to the Principal.
(*a*) course (*b*) method
(*c*) chance (*d*) resort

29. He .... the policeman to help him catch the thief, but the policeman pretended not to hear.
(*a*) requested (*b*) asked
(*c*) importuned (*d*) pleaded

30. He has .... a wrong inference.
(*a*) inferred (*b*) derived
(*c*) drawn (*d*) concluded

31. The news of the secret deal soon .... despite official silence. **(S.S.C. 1995)**
(*a*) discovered (*b*) disclosed
(*c*) leaked out (*d*) divulged

32. No man had a more .... love for literature, or a higher respect for it, than Dr. Samuel Johnson. **(C.D.S. 1995)**
(*a*) arduous (*b*) ardent
(*c*) animated (*d*) adroit

33. He .... it as the kind cruelty of the doctor's knife.
(*a*) agreed (*b*) accepted
(*c*) believed (*d*) perceived

34. I have often .... why he went to live abroad. **(Railways, 1989)**
(*a*) puzzled (*b*) wondered
(*c*) thought (*d*) surprised

35. India, for the present, is deeply .... in political uncertainties.
(*a*) mired (*b*) engrossed
(*c*) absorbed (*d*) troubled

36. He lives near a lonely .... of countryside. **(Stenographers' Exam, 1994)**
(*a*) piece (*b*) length
(*c*) stretch (*d*) section

37. Rahul had .... pain in his stomach.
(*a*) high (*b*) strong
(*c*) deep (*d*) severe

38. As a .... of respect to the departed leader, members stood in silence for two minutes.
(*a*) mark (*b*) symbol
(*c*) sign (*d*) token

39. When their examinations were over, the children gleefully .... the books they had been reading.
(*a*) despised (*b*) neglected
(*c*) shelve (*d*) overthrew
(Assistant Grade, 1994)

40. Reena .... a taste for poetry in the company of her cousin.
(*a*) learnt (*b*) fostered
(*c*) cultivated (*d*) imbibed

41. Not only did she condemn vice, she almost equally despised the .... acceptance of an advantage.
(*a*) commendable (*b*) tacit
(*c*) unholy (*d*) furtive
(S.C.R.A. 1993)

42. He failed to get the job though he was .... for the interview.
(*a*) chosen (*b*) invited
(*c*) called (*d*) summoned

43. We must .... help to the people hit by cyclone.
(*a*) contribute (*b*) summon
(*c*) render (*d*) impart

44. To nobody else did the story seem ....
(*a*) contingent (*b*) credible
(*c*) credulous (*d*) creditable
(Stenographers' Exam, 1991)

45. The transfer of territories could not take place because one state .... the findings of the Commission. **(M.B.A. 1993)**
(*a*) objected (*b*) questioned
(*c*) rejected (*d*) disputed

46. His book was marked by many .... remarks which made us forget its main theme.
(*a*) foolish (*b*) idiotic
(*c*) digressive (*d*) humorous

47. These documents are of .... historical importance as they throw a lot of light on men and matters.
(*a*) major (*b*) immense
(*c*) terrific (*d*) high

48. Anticipating renewed rioting, the authorities erected .... to block off the streets. **(C.D.S. 1995)**
(*a*) dykes (*b*) barrages
(*c*) barricades (*d*) barracks

49. The charm of an Austrian gentleman, the brutality of a gangster, the ranting of a demagogue, the assurance of a diplomat .... one another in a kaleidoscope of performance. **(M.B.A. 1990)**

(*a*) succeeded (*b*) struck
(*c*) touched (*d*) joined

50. Let us take him upon his word. I see no room for any .... in the matter.
(*a*) deviation (*b*) duplicity
(*c*) difference (*d*) cynicism

ANSWERS

1. (*d*)	**2.** (*c*)	**3.** (*b*)	**4.** (*d*)	**5.** (*a*)	**6.** (*d*)	**7.** (*b*)	**8.** (*c*)	**9.** (*c*)	**10.** (*d*)
11. (*b*)	**12.** (*d*)	**13.** (*c*)	**14.** (*b*)	**15.** (*d*)	**16.** (*c*)	**17.** (*b*)	**18.** (*d*)	**19.** (*d*)	**20.** (*c*)
21. (*b*)	**22.** (*d*)	**23.** (*d*)	**24.** (*c*)	**25.** (*c*)	**26.** (*d*)	**27.** (*c*)	**28.** (*d*)	**29.** (*c*)	**30.** (*c*)
31. (*c*)	**32.** (*b*)	**33.** (*d*)	**34.** (*b*)	**35.** (*a*)	**36.** (*c*)	**37.** (*d*)	**38.** (*a*)	**39.** (*b*)	**40.** (*c*)
41. (*b*)	**42.** (*c*)	**43.** (*c*)	**44.** (*b*)	**45.** (*d*)	**46.** (*c*)	**47.** (*b*)	**48.** (*c*)	**49.** (*a*)	**50.** (*b*)

PRACTICE SET 13

Directions : ***In each of the following sentences, a blank has been given which can be filled correctly by one of the four alternatives given under it. That is your answer.***

1. Soft minded individuals are .... to embrace all kinds of superstitions.
(*a*) eager (*b*) prone
(*c*) disposed (*d*) reluctant
(C.D.S. 1993)

2. It is difficult at this stage to forecast the .... of results of the ongoing research on cancer.
(*a*) consequence (*b*) importance
(*c*) measure (*d*) magnitude

3. He was not happy because none of his children rose in life quite to his ....
(*a*) expectations (*b*) excellence
(*c*) elegance (*d*) enterprise

4. There was no .... in the railway compartment for additional passengers.
(*a*) space (*b*) place
(*c*) seat (*d*) room
(Stenographers' Exam, 1993)

5. The medicine gave him a short .... from the suffering.
(*a*) escape (*b*) relief
(*c*) respite (*d*) release

6. There was a look of .... on his face during the interrogation.
(*a*) disfavour (*b*) disguise
(*c*) dejection (*d*) disgrace

7. Like any other country India has its .... share of superstitions. **(C.B.I. 1995)**
(*a*) peculiar (*b*) fair
(*c*) proper (*d*) abundant

8. The serious .... with her is that she does not know typing.
(*a*) disadvantage (*b*) inconvenience
(*c*) handicap (*d*) obstacle

9. A standing army is necessary for each nation to save itself from the danger of foreign ....
(*a*) raids (*b*) incursions
(*c*) interference (*d*) insertion

10. Hindus believe that .... from the cycle of birth and rebirth can be attained only by good deeds. **(C.D.S. 1994)**
(*a*) bondage (*b*) deliverance
(*c*) delivery (*d*) retirement

11. I was astounded at his .... lack of knowledge about the continent of Africa.
(*a*) great (*b*) huge
(*c*) colossal (*d*) abundant
(Asstt. Grade, 1996)

12. With God not having a ...., nobody could complain to Him.
(*a*) telephone (*b*) wireless
(*c*) hotline (*d*) None of these

13. We were certain that the snowstorm was .... **(C.B.I. 1993)**
(*a*) immutable (*b*) imminent
(*c*) unavoidable (*d*) inherent

14. There was so much .... material in the essay that it was difficult to get the author's message.
(*a*) exemplary (*b*) extraneous
(*c*) variegated (*d*) superficial

15. The Marxists, following a theory of dialectical materialism, contend that man is merely a producing animal who supplies his own needs and whose life is largely .... by economic forces.

(*a*) determined (*b*) subordinated
(*c*) moulded (*d*) subjugated
(C.D.S. 1993)

16. He was virtually .... by the villagers for absconding with the girl.
(*a*) driven (*b*) banished
(*c*) ostracised (*d*) exploited

17. As soon as she saw him, she unleashed a .... of fond, praise and appreciation.
(*a*) rain (*b*) torrent
(*c*) chain (*d*) series

18. There are many .... to Greek mythology in English poetry.
(*a*) elusives (*b*) allusions
(*c*) illusions (*d*) delusions
(Hotel Management, 1992)

19. I .... he has been caught up in a traffic jam.
(*a*) suspect (*b*) suppose
(*c*) imagine (*d*) speculate

20. Gandhiji was a humble man known for his .... **(Clerks' Grade, 1991)**
(*a*) pleasantness (*b*) sweetness
(*c*) modesty (*d*) kindness

21. Mr. Shekhar .... the letter by return of post.
(*a*) replied (*b*) reciprocated
(*c*) answered (*d*) questioned

22. He was .... at the response from the audience.
(*a*) gratified (*b*) thanked
(*c*) paused (*d*) pleased

23. It being an .... issue, it is not correct to introduce questions of morality into the debate. **(Section Officers' 1993)**
(*a*) immoral (*b*) irrelevant
(*c*) moral (*d*) amoral

24. Sachin Tendulkar .... a century in that match.
(*a*) bowled (*b*) hit
(*c*) played (*d*) scored

25. Drinking too much .... one's judgement.
(*a*) imposes (*b*) impels
(*c*) impairs (*d*) impedes

26. There was a huge .... at the airport for the Prime Minister.
(*a*) mob (*b*) gathering
(*c*) rush (*d*) collection

27. Being guilty, my daughter was afraid to .... me in the eye. **(C.B.I. 1993)**
(*a*) look (*b*) confront
(*c*) encounter (*d*) meet

28. The Company demanded a certificate that I was a .... student of the university.
(*a*) benevolent (*b*) bonefide
(*c*) genuine (*d*) truthful

29. The new government wants to .... the life of a common man.
(*a*) replenish (*b*) ameliorate
(*c*) refurbish (*d*) revive

30. It is .... that we realise our duties to our motherland; if we fail to do so, our freedom will be in jeopardy.
(*a*) vicious (*b*) vile
(*c*) vital (*d*) virtuous
(Railways, 1995)

31. Will you please .... from interfering in my personal affairs?
(*a*) avoid (*b*) desist
(*c*) prohibit (*d*) abstain

32. During Diwali the shops are .... of people. **(U.D.C. 1995)**
(*a*) busy (*b*) crowded
(*c*) full (*d*) bubbling

33. The oil crisis highlighted the need to develop new .... of energy and to conserve those which are already in use.
(*a*) methods (*b*) sources
(*c*) means (*d*) preserves
(Stenographers' Exam, 1995)

34. The miser gazed .... at the pile of gold coins in front of him. **(C.B.I. 1995)**
(*a*) earnestly (*b*) thoughtfully
(*c*) avidly (*d*) admiringly

35. Despite everyone trying to convince him of the truth, he still sticks to his .... stand.
(*a*) haughty (*b*) obstinate
(*c*) arrogant (*d*) contumacious

36. Because of diesel .... many garages are introducing rationing. **(C.D.S. 1995)**
(*a*) deficit (*b*) lack
(*c*) shortage (*d*) scarce

37. The world is so constructed that if you wish to enjoy its pleasures you must also .... its pains. **(C.D.S. 1994)**
(*a*) deny (*b*) ignore
(*c*) endure (*d*) neglect

38. A man who commits a wrong, may be required to .... his property as a penalty.
(*a*) eschew (*b*) assess
(*c*) confiscate (*d*) forfeit

39. I think they allow their children too much .... **(C.D.S. 1993)**
(*a*) levity (*b*) lassitude
(*c*) latitude (*d*) liberality

40. A little sincerity is a dangerous thing, and a great of it is .... fatal.
(*a*) absolutely (*b*) entirely
(*c*) completely (*d*) thoroughly

41. The scheme failed due to the .... of funds.
(*a*) problem (*b*) scarcity

(c) paucity (d) reduction

42. It is not possible to .... the suffering.
(a) mitigate (b) masticate
(c) instigate (d) propitiate
(Hotel Management, 1992)

43. Knowledge of the local language .... the assimilation of the culture of the place.
(a) hastens (b) promotes
(c) facilitates (d) strengthens

44. Man does not live by .... alone.
(a) diet (b) food
(c) meals (d) bread
(Section Officers' 1993)

45. Vallabh Bhai Patel's life .... some of the greatest events of the century.
(a) spanned (b) included
(c) encompassed (d) overcame

46. Would you mind .... to the Principal how the trouble started? **(C.D.S. 1994)**
(a) talking (b) remarking
(c) telling (d) explaining

47. Please do not .... the offer made by the Chairman.
(a) refrain (b) refuse
(c) refute (d) refuge

48. No matter what .... come our way, we should not lose our temper. **(C.B.I. 1993)**
(a) provocations (b) distractions
(c) persons (d) temptations

49. It .... to me that she was incurable.
(a) happened (b) occurred
(c) flashed (d) suggested

50. In high school many of us never realised the importance that grammar would .... in later life. **(Assistant Grade, 1996)**
(a) exercise (b) figure
(c) portray (d) play

ANSWERS

1. (b)	**2.** (d)	**3.** (a)	**4.** (d)	**5.** (c)	**6.** (c)	**7.** (b)	**8.** (a)	**9.** (b)	**10.** (b)
11. (c)	**12.** (c)	**13.** (b)	**14.** (d)	**15.** (c)	**16.** (c)	**17.** (b)	**18.** (b)	**19.** (b)	**20.** (c)
21. (c)	**22.** (d)	**23.** (b)	**24.** (d)	**25.** (c)	**26.** (b)	**27.** (a)	**28.** (b)	**29.** (b)	**30.** (c)
31. (d)	**32.** (c)	**33.** (b)	**34.** (c)	**35.** (d)	**36.** (c)	**37.** (c)	**38.** (a)	**39.** (c)	**40.** (a)
41. (c)	**42.** (a)	**43.** (c)	**44.** (d)	**45.** (a)	**46.** (d)	**47.** (b)	**48.** (a)	**49.** (b)	**50.** (d)

PRACTICE SET 14

Directions : ***Of the four alternatives given under each sentence, find the one that best fits into the blank space.***

1. His life consists of .... of drinking punctuated by periods of drunken sleep.
(a) barrels (b) bouts
(c) bowls (d) pints
(Central Excise, 1995)

2. The fact is so .... that no one ever succeeded even in defining it.
(a) elusive (b) slanderous
(c) morbid (d) fragmentary

3. Important information was given by the convict while .... before the court.
(a) addressing (b) explaining
(c) deposing (d) expressing

4. Vishakha .... two minutes and thirty seconds to take the first place in the women's 800 m race. **(C.B.I. 1994)**
(a) ran (b) used
(c) timed (d) clocked

5. This is the .... chosen for the shopping complex to be built next year.
(a) area (b) locality
(c) site (d) sight

6. The Chairman treated the employees to a .... lunch at an expensive hotel.
(a) precious (b) sumptuous
(c) thriving (d) stupendous

7. Find the .... that accompany these cartoons. **(U.D.C. 1995)**
(a) captions (b) topics
(c) headlines (d) titles

8. The police .... the mob.
(a) disbanded (b) dispersed
(c) drove (d) scattered

9. The whole plot was .... well managed.
(a) perfectly (b) nicely
(c) exquisitely (d) exceedingly

10. When the morning .... the murder was discovered. **(Assistant Grade, 1994)**
(a) occurred (b) came
(c) arrived (d) happened

11. Students who have secured more than ninety percent marks are .... for this scholarship.
(a) worthy (b) legible

(*c*) eligible (*d*) permitted

12. Mr. Shyam Lal has gone to his native village with the .... of starting an adult school.
(*a*) suggestion (*b*) presumption
(*c*) opinion (*d*) intention

13. The twins are so alike that I cannot .... one from the other. **(I. Tax, 1995)**
(*a*) discern (*b*) tell
(*c*) say (*d*) notice

14. We must .... to authority.
(*a*) bend (*b*) surrender
(*c*) subdue (*d*) submit

15. Unscrupulous operators are running a .... racket in illegal international telephone calls.
(*a*) fruitful (*b*) prosperous
(*c*) rich (*d*) fluorishing

16. The chief guest's speech was so .... that I was all ears. **(C.B.I. 1994)**
(*a*) intricate (*b*) interminable
(*c*) interesting (*d*) indeterminate

17. The General said that the position must be .... at all costs.
(*a*) possessed (*b*) captured
(*c*) caught (*d*) arrested

18. Just like the nature we all have to follow .... routine. **(Railways, 1992)**
(*a*) timely (*b*) regular
(*c*) fixed (*d*) some

19. The .... of the discussion is still not known.
(*a*) effect (*b*) output
(*c*) product (*d*) outcome

20. The park was .... with bits of paper after the children had left. **(C.D.S. 1995)**
(*a*) cluttered (*b*) littered
(*c*) filled (*d*) scattered

21. A person's personality is said to be .... by a combination of inheritance, environment and upbringing.
(*a*) decided (*b*) shaped
(*c*) formed (*d*) moulded

22. There was a serious .... between the two brothers. **(Hotel Management, 1991)**
(*a*) aliteration (*b*) alteraction
(*c*) alteration (*d*) aberration

23. He never takes sides but always remains ....
(*a*) unbiased (*b*) prejudiced
(*c*) neutral (*d*) impartial

24. I hope I can .... my friend to lend his car for the weekend.
(*a*) order (*b*) authorise
(*c*) compel (*d*) persuade

25. The overthrow of a totalitarian regime by the people is truly the triumph of........ .
(*a*) imperialism (*b*) democracy
(*c*) dictatorship (*d*) communism
(Assistant Grade, 1993)

26. The country's major industrial houses have a .... in the political parties which they have always liberally funded.
(*a*) say (*b*) power
(*c*) stake (*d*) notion

27. A person who constantly calls attention to his trials and sufferings is in danger of developing a martyr complex and impressing others that he is .... seeking sympathy. **(C.D.S. 1993)**
(*a*) purposefully (*b*) emphatically
(*c*) consciously (*d*) willingly

28. Sachin doesn't need comics anymore, he has .... them.
(*a*) overcome (*b*) surpassed
(*c*) disowned (*d*) outgrown

29. Error can claim no ....
(*a*) ignorance (*b*) excuse
(*c*) exemption (*d*) concession

30. He is working under such .... conditions that it is difficult to maintain his self-respect. **(C.D.S. 1994)**
(*a*) low (*b*) difficult
(*c*) inimical (*d*) humiliating

31. The Hubble Space Telescope will search for planets around other stars, a key to the .... for extra terrestrial life, and examine interstellar dust and gases out of which stars are born. **(C.D.S. 1993)**
(*a*) discovery (*b*) perception
(*c*) quest (*d*) enquiry

32. He said that there was no going back because his decision was........ .
(*a*) palatable (*b*) parsimonious
(*c*) premeditated (*d*) peromptory

33. As an organisation changes from one system to another .... problems would no doubt arise.
(*a*) transient (*b*) temporary
(*c*) transitory (*d*) intervening

34. The manner in which bombs exploded in five trains within a short span of time suggests that it is a part of a ....
(*a*) game (*b*) villainy
(*c*) conspiracy (*d*) sabotage
(Assistant Grade, 1996)

35. Subject to the .... of the Court, at the hearing of an appeal not more than two advocates shall be heard on one side.
(*a*) requests (*b*) commands
(*c*) directions (*d*) requirements

36. He lives in the world of ....
(*a*) allusions (*b*) illusions
(*c*) conclusions (*d*) delusions
(Hotel Management, 1991)

37. He did not register his .... to the proposal. **(C.B.I. 1993)**
(*a*) deviation (*b*) divergence
(*c*) disfavour (*d*) dissent

38. For quite a long time he bore the burden but finally he had to ....
(*a*) yield (*b*) reconcile
(*c*) succumb (*d*) leave

39. The .... beauty of this land captivates our mind and makes us happy.
(*a*) grand (*b*) ideal
(*c*) scenic (*d*) great

40. He .... that he could speak five languages. **(Stenographers' Exam, 1992)**
(*a*) challenged (*b*) boasted
(*c*) submitted (*d*) suggested

41. The nude dance, it seems, was intended to arouse .... among the spectators.
(*a*) appetite (*b*) lust
(*c*) greed (*d*) lustre

42. Though Bonsai, a well-known art form, originated in China, it was .... by the Japanese. **(C.D.S. 1994)**
(*a*) finished (*b*) borrowed
(*c*) cultivated (*d*) perfected

43. The Manager gave her his .... that the complaint would be investigated.
(*a*) assurance (*b*) suggestion
(*c*) avowal (*d*) support

44. Will you, like the .... gentleman and solider you are, leave at once before he finds you here? **(C.D.S. 1991)**
(*a*) barbarous (*b*) ostentatious
(*c*) chivalrous (*d*) luminous

45. He .... the necessity of acting promptly.
(*a*) appreciated (*b*) admired
(*c*) praised (*d*) eulogised

46. It is not proper to .... a stranger in your house.
(*a*) accommodate (*b*) keep
(*c*) shelter (*d*) dwell

47. A crescendo of metallic thuds arose from the market, where the iron-smiths were .... the pieces of metals. **(C.B.I. 1995)**
(*a*) hammering (*b*) flattening
(*c*) thrashing (*d*) striking

48. I am feeling .... better today.
(*a*) rather (*b*) too
(*c*) fairly (*d*) very

49. The child's earliest words deal with concrete objects, only later he is able to grapple with ....
(*a*) abstractions (*b*) maxims
(*c*) opinions (*d*) decisions
(Stenographers' Exam, 1994)

50. He requested all his class .... to attend his birthday party.
(*a*) comrades (*b*) companions
(*c*) fellows (*d*) friends

ANSWERS

1. (*b*)	**2.** (*a*)	**3.** (*c*)	**4.** (*d*)	**5.** (*c*)	**6.** (*b*)	**7.** (*a*)	**8.** (*b*)	**9.** (*d*)	**10.** (*b*)
11. (*c*)	**12.** (*d*)	**13.** (*b*)	**14.** (*d*)	**15.** (*d*)	**16.** (*c*)	**17.** (*b*)	**18.** (*d*)	**19.** (*d*)	**20.** (*b*)
21. (*c*)	**22.** (*b*)	**23.** (*d*)	**24.** (*d*)	**25.** (*b*)	**26.** (*c*)	**27.** (*c*)	**28.** (*d*)	**29.** (*c*)	**30.** (*d*)
31. (*c*)	**32.** (*d*)	**33.** (*d*)	**34.** (*c*)	**35.** (*c*)	**36.** (*b*)	**37.** (*d*)	**38.** (*c*)	**39.** (*c*)	**40.** (*b*)
41. (*b*)	**42.** (*d*)	**43.** (*a*)	**44.** (*c*)	**45.** (*a*)	**46.** (*c*)	**47.** (*b*)	**48.** (*c*)	**49.** (*a*)	**50.** (*c*)

PRACTICE SET 15

Directions : *Fill in the blanks in the following sentences by selecting the most appropriate alternative from amongst the four choices given under each sentence.*

1. She practised very hard so that she could .... the trophy.
(*a*) replace (*b*) repeat
(*c*) restore (*d*) regain

2. He lost the match easily because he had played a .... five set match in the earlier round. **(S.C.R.A. 1993)**
(*a*) sensational (*b*) gruelling
(*c*) wonderful (*d*) controversial

3. It was impossible for the over-worked mother to .... with so many yelling children.
(*a*) cope (*b*) deal
(*c*) live (*d*) continue

4. In these days of inflation, the cost of consumer goods is .... **(C.D.S. 1995)**
(*a*) ascending (*b*) soaring
(*c*) climbing (*d*) raising

5. Ajay is not well .... with the culture of this state.

(*a*) conducive (*b*) accustomed
(*c*) acquainted (*d*) addicted

6. The most important task of the Air Force is to .... the country against an air attack by an enemy.
(*a*) protect (*b*) save
(*c*) defend (*d*) secure
(Stenographers' Exam, 1995)

7. The curfew in the riot ridden area was .... for a couple of hours.
(*a*) lifted (*b*) released
(*c*) removed (*d*) relaxed

8. The firm has enjoyed steady .... in the last ten years. **(S.S.C. 1995)**
(*a*) enhancement (*b*) expansion
(*c*) enlargement (*d*) extension

9. He was too .... to make a statement before the Principal.
(*a*) shy (*b*) timid
(*c*) audacious (*d*) coward

10. Prolongation of the worker's strike will have .... effect on the production.
(*a*) opposite (*b*) reverse
(*c*) negative (*d*) adverse

11. The man is so ill that he can .... walk.
(*a*) hardly (*b*) nearly
(*c*) quite (*d*) rarely
(C.B.I. 1987)

12. He .... his matriculation examination in 1992.
(*a*) obtained (*b*) performed
(*c*) passed (*d*) completed

13. Your case is so unique that I am not getting any .... to support it.
(*a*) help (*b*) precedent
(*c*) reason (*d*) happening
(L.I.C.A.A.O. 1989)

14. He .... all his energies to bear upon the task.
(*a*) put (*b*) organised
(*c*) brought (*d*) devoted

15. Usually the ascent of a mountain face is much easier than the ....
(*a*) descend (*b*) fall
(*c*) descent (*d*) decent
(Stenographers' Exam, 1995)

16. Ravi .... his head against the wall.
(*a*) forced (*b*) struck
(*c*) sounded (*d*) injured

17. If a speech is full of pompous words, it is .... **(M.B.A. 1990)**
(*a*) verbose (*b*) bombastic
(*c*) grandiose (*d*) grandiloquent

18. I can .... on him when I have some problem.
(*a*) bear (*b*) trust
(*c*) count (*d*) believe

19. I keep my .... opinions to myself.
(*a*) special (*b*) private
(*c*) particular (*d*) especial
(S.S.C. 1995)

20. Sushil .... the accident by sharply steering the car to the left leaving the road for the oncoming lorry.
(*a*) avoided (*b*) reverted
(*c*) diverted (*d*) averted

21. We had to pay the taxi more because he brought us by a .... route.
(*a*) longer (*b*) circumscribed
(*c*) circular (*d*) circuitous

22. The .... sounded lame to her and she did not want to give in. **(C.D.S. 1995)**
(*a*) excuses (*b*) statements
(*c*) promises (*d*) observations

23. She requested the student to .... a little water in a vessel.
(*a*) procure (*b*) collect
(*c*) fetch (*d*) bring

24. The movement of the train was so .... that all the passengers slept very well.
(*a*) distracting (*b*) noisy
(*c*) soothing (*d*) fast
(Stenographers' Exam, 1995)

25. The suspect was taken to the police, but the .... revealed nothing.
(*a*) inquiry (*b*) interrogation
(*c*) probe (*d*) investigation

26. The .... arguments put forth for not disclosing the facts did not impress anybody. **(L.I.C.A.A.O. 1989)**
(*a*) convincing (*b*) specious
(*c*) spurious (*d*) intemperate

27. We don't know what .... him to commit this crime. **(U.D.C. 1993)**
(*a*) excited (*b*) roused
(*c*) prompted (*d*) attracted

28. The teacher was .... by the student's performance and offered him further help.
(*a*) impressed (*b*) enchanted
(*c*) enthused (*d*) infatuated

29. He was in a .... what to do and what not to do.
(*a*) startle (*b*) fix
(*c*) trouble (*d*) confusion

30. In hot weather I like lying in the .... of a tree. **(Stenographers' Exam, 1994)**
(*a*) shadow (*b*) shelter
(*c*) protection (*d*) shade

31. Inspite of her other ...., Kamla still managed to find time for her hobbies.
(*a*) preoccupations (*b*) occupations
(*c*) business (*d*) predilections

32. The Committee's appeal to the people for money .... little response. **(C.D.S. 1993)**
(*a*) evoked (*b*) provoked

(*c*) gained (*d*) provided

33. My neighbour, Mr. Keshav Lal comes home at the .... of the month.
(*a*) conclusion (*b*) expiry
(*c*) completion (*d*) close

34. Rabindranath Tagore was a .... writer of his times.
(*a*) true (*b*) fantastic
(*c*) profound (*d*) prolific

35. The manager tried hard to .... his men to return to work before declaring a lockout. **(C.D.S. 1992)**
(*a*) motivate (*b*) persuade
(*c*) encourage (*d*) permit

36. There was so much .... material in the speech that it was difficult to know what the speaker wanted to stay.
(*a*) banal (*b*) extraneous
(*c*) superficial (*d*) variegated

37. Our flight was .... from Jaipur to Agra airport. **(Central Excise, 1991)**
(*a*) deflected (*b*) shifted
(*c*) diverted (*d*) reverted

38. His .... handling resulted in all that destruction and damage.
(*a*) inept (*b*) skilful
(*c*) sophisticated (*d*) uncouth

39. Once I forgot the piece of paper on which the name of the hotel was written, I was as .... as lost.
(*a*) much (*b*) sure
(*c*) good (*d*) bad
(I. Tax & Central Excise, 1994)

40. Infant mortality rate in China has .... from 200 per thousand to 14 per thousand.
(*a*) retarded (*b*) declined
(*c*) contracted (*d*) minimised

41. Time once lost cannot be ....
(*a*) gained (*b*) recalled
(*c*) renumerated (*d*) recovered

42. He is very .... on meeting foreigners and befriending them.
(*a*) anxious (*b*) fond
(*c*) insistent (*d*) keen
(Clerks' Grade, 1992)

43. Laser is a (an) .... of Light Amplification by Stimulated Emission of Radiation.
(*a*) homonym (*b*) acronym
(*c*) malaprop (*d*) collocation

44. The exhibition was a curious .... of the old and the new.
(*a*) melange (*b*) fervour
(*c*) mixture (*d*) blend

45. The Hubble Space Telescope will search for planets around other stars, a key to the .... for extra terrestrial life.
(*a*) discovery (*b*) quest
(*c*) perception (*d*) enquiry

46. Colgate has also set an ambitious aim of .... an eight per cent value share of the tooth paste market by the end of the first year. **(M.B.A. 1994)**
(*a*) keeping (*b*) distributing
(*c*) cornering (*d*) soliciting

47. Marie Curie was excited when she knew that she was on the .... of a new discovery.
(*a*) outskirts (*b*) frontier
(*c*) threshold (*d*) gateway

48. Many women in developing countries experience a cycle of poor health that .... before they are born and persists through adulthood passing from generation to generation. **(C.D.S. 1994)**
(*a*) derives (*b*) establishes
(*c*) begins (*d*) originates

49. I have .... for one month's leave.
(*a*) demanded (*b*) requested
(*c*) wanted (*d*) asked

50. A man remains narrow-minded, self complacent and ignorant unless he visits other people and .... from them.
(*a*) hears (*b*) earns
(*c*) learns (*d*) borrows
(Assistant Grade, 1994)

ANSWERS

1. (*d*)	**2.** (*b*)	**3.** (*a*)	**4.** (*b*)	**5.** (*c*)	**6.** (*c*)	**7.** (*d*)	**8.** (*b*)	**9.** (*b*)	**10.** (*d*)
11. (*a*)	**12.** (*c*)	**13.** (*b*)	**14.** (*c*)	**15.** (*c*)	**16.** (*b*)	**17.** (*d*)	**18.** (*c*)	**19.** (*b*)	**20.** (*d*)
21. (*d*)	**22.** (*a*)	**23.** (*c*)	**24.** (*c*)	**25.** (*b*)	**26.** (*b*)	**27.** (*c*)	**28.** (*a*)	**29.** (*b*)	**30.** (*d*)
31. (*b*)	**32.** (*a*)	**33.** (*d*)	**34.** (*c*)	**35.** (*b*)	**36.** (*c*)	**37.** (*c*)	**38.** (*a*)	**39.** (*c*)	**40.** (*b*)
41. (*b*)	**42.** (*d*)	**43.** (*b*)	**44.** (*a*)	**45.** (*b*)	**46.** (*c*)	**47.** (*c*)	**48.** (*d*)	**49.** (*d*)	**50.** (*c*)

TYPE 3 : Selecting the appropriate pair of words to fill in two blanks in a sentence

PRACTICE SET 16

Directions : ***In each sentence below, there are two blank spaces. Below each sentence some pairs of words are given which are numbered (a), (b), (c), (d) and (e). Pick out the most appropriate pair to fill in the blanks in the same order, to make the sentence meaningfully complete.***

1. Cholestrol has long been identified as a silent killer because the patient has no .... of the danger freely .... his system.
(*a*) idea, infecting
(*b*) thought, attacking
(*c*) notion, ravishing
(*d*) inkling, traversing
(*e*) information, invading

2. Only when .... failed, the police resorted to .... **(Bank P.O. 1993)**
(*a*) efforts, power
(*b*) arrests, imprisonment
(*c*) persuasions, force
(*d*) power, punishment
(*e*) manipulations, arrests

3. I have just the memory of my father to .... now, but my faith in him has never been ....
(*a*) recall, missing (*b*) store, forgotten
(*c*) love, shaken (*d*) worship, mistaken

4. Insurance companies are perfectly .... of the greed some people show in .... illnesses in order to get big settlements in the courts.
(*a*) conscious, serious
(*b*) known, ailing
(*c*) informed, false (*d*) aware, faking
(*e*) acquainted, perfect

5. The .... imposed for non-payment was too .... for it to bring in improvement in collection. **(S.B.I.P.O. 1992)**
(*a*) fine, severe (*b*) toll, simple
(*c*) penalty, low (*d*) damage, cruel
(*e*) punishment, harsh

6. Unfortunately, trade unions and organisations of various denominations have failed to realise that .... understanding, positive attitude and constructive approach are basic requirements tc make unions work on .... lines.
(*a*) common, ture (*b*) cooperative, better
(*c*) mutual, sound (*d*) general, desired

7. The practice of painting slogans on rock faces, once a thriving industry in Britain has fallen into .... but there has recently been a (an) .... in Country Antrim.
(*a*) oblivion, demand
(*b*) disfavour, upheavel
(*c*) disuse, recrudescence
(*d*) mediocrity, renascence

8. He shifted to his late parents' house not because of the .... it provided but for purely........ reasons.
(*a*) convenience, sentimental
(*b*) grace, aesthetic
(*c*) value, monetary
(*d*) comforts, personal
(*e*) benefit, extraneous **(Bank P.O. 1995)**

9. The Prime Minister said that the .... to increase employment will be .... on the efforts to raise productivity in the economy.
(*a*) scheme, complementary
(*b*) policy, dependent
(*c*) strategy, contingent
(*d*) determination, reliant
(*e*) programme, supplementary

10. India's .... armoury needs replacement despite its long-term indigenisation plans and leading international arms industries are eager to sell their latest .... to the Indian Armed Forces.
(*a*) exhausted, innovation
(*b*) old, equipment
(*c*) exorbitant, instruments
(*d*) fake, production
(*e*) ageing, gadgetry

11. He gave me an additional .... of Rs. 200 a month by .... of the Commissioner.
(*a*) allowance, permission
(*b*) pay, allowance
(*c*) salary, admittance
(*d*) payment, agreement
(Assistant Grade, 1991)

12. The impact of Western culture on India was the impact of a .... society, of a modern consciousness on a .... society wedded to medieval habits of thought.
(*a*) dynamic, static
(*b*) major, minor
(*c*) educated, illiterate
(*d*) active, passive
(*e*) progressive, regressive

13. Many of us who .... rational - emotive therapy are .... tense, angry or depressed.
(*a*) seek, often (*b*) follow, scarcely
(*c*) perform, usually
(*d*) implement, seldom
(*e*) practice, frequently

14. The speech .... with subtle threats has resulted in .... tension in the sensitive areas of the city.
(*a*) started, reduced
(*b*) replete, increased
(*c*) full, escalating (*d*) forced, dissolving
(*e*) followed, continuous **(Bank P.O. 1994)**

15. It is .... superstition to suppose that knowledge can be .... only by going to schools and colleges
(*a*) huge, accomplished
(*b*) hollow, garnered
(*c*) gross, obtained (*d*) great, achieved
(*e*) tremendous, attained

16. I am not .... to sell you my house unless you offer a more .... price.
(*a*) conform, true
(*b*) prepared, realistic
(*c*) ready, correct (*d*) having, actual

17. With the realisation, we have found ourselves left with .... moral values and little ethical ....
(*a*) fundamental, scruples
(*b*) stereotyped, perspective
(*c*) extreme, judgement
(*d*) incidental, standards
(*e*) obsolete, direction

18. If we do not take .... care in our industry, we will have to .... a grave problem. **(Bank P.O. 1995)**
(*a*) normal, experience
(*b*) proper, face
(*c*) adequate, catch
(*d*) intensive, aggravate
(*e*) preventive, solve

19. Education is .... to the economic and social fabric of the nation, but .... that few political parties have made it an election issue.
(*a*) eminent, barring
(*b*) concomitent, instead of
(*c*) basic, despite
(*d*) rudimentary, besides

20. Despite their strong resentment the tribals .... the new laws as long as the Government officials did not .... them too strenuously.
(*a*) welcomed, observe
(*b*) tolerated, enforce
(*c*) amended, follow
(*d*) laid, punish

21. Since we .... read every book, we .... only the famous ones. **(B.S.R.B. 1996)**
(*a*) have, sold (*b*) should, buy
(*c*) must, ignore (*d*) can, purchase
(*e*) cannot, select

22. Suddenly out of the .... of weariness an old lady .... unexpectedly.
(*a*) mosaic, raised (*b*) context, appeared
(*c*) texture, rose (*d*) fabric, awakened

23. We have to .... in our young men and women sense of discipline, which is a .... for progress and happiness.
(*a*) generate, concomitent
(*b*) instil, need
(*c*) produce, necessity
(*d*) inculcate, pre-requisite
(*e*) induce, requirement

24. .... of crops was due to continuous ....
(*a*) Destruction, draught
(*b*) Ruin, draft
(*c*) Failure, drought
(*d*) Depreciation, drift
(Assistant Grade, 1991)

25. Disarmament and development in our time are .... interrelated but .... development will depend on a change in the world's political thinking.
(*a*) inevitably, substantial
(*b*) closely, real
(*c*) essentially, true
(*d*) universally, ultimate
(*e*) naturally, final

26. How many of the books published each year in India make a .... contribution towards improving men's .... with each other?
(*a*) sensational, reservations
(*b*) referential, behaviour
(*c*) significant, relationship
(*d*) incorporated, obligation

27. Due to .... rainfall this year, they had to .... cut in water supply.
(*a*) scanty, lift (*b*) heavy, regulate
(*c*) regular, clamp (*d*) sufficient, enforce
(*e*) inadequate, impose **(B.S.R.B. 1996)**

28. The .... man treated everyone in a .... manner.
(*a*) defiant, belligerent
(*b*) corrupt, ubiquitous
(*c*) superficial, thorough
(*d*) suspicious, ingenuous
(*e*) supercilious, depreciatory

29. Mr. Johnson .... a boat and .... into the bay.
(*a*) hired, rowed (*b*) rented, swam
(*c*) boarded, went (*d*) borrowed, intruded

30. Those suffering from glaucoma find that their .... vision is .... and that they

can no longer see objects not directly in front of them. **(M.B.A. 1990)**
(*a*) optical, distorted
(*b*) peripheral, impaired
(*c*) prephrastic, demurred
(*d*) peripatetic, diminished

31. When it comes to back stabbing, a quill .... be .... than a dagger.
(*a*) must, better (*b*) should, keen
(*c*) can, deadlier (*d*) may, sharper
(*e*) will, superior

32. He was too .... to .... that he had been wrong.
(*a*) docile, accept (*b*) polite, agree
(*c*) nervous, rejoice (*d*) obstinate, admit
(*e*) determined, promise

33. The Education Minister emphasised the need to discover and .... each student's .... talents. **(S.B.I.P.O. 1995)**
(*a*) enlarge, dormant
(*b*) belittle, concealed
(*c*) suppress, potential
(*d*) flourish, hidden
(*e*) develop, intrinsic

34. In a free and democratic country each and every person has rights as well as duties and it is of .... importance that everything is .... in the right perspective.
(*a*) great, done
(*b*) significant, examined
(*c*) utmost, viewed
(*d*) overwhelming, taken
(*e*) absolute, understood

35. He is usually ...., but today he appears rather .... **(R.B.I. 1995)**
(*a*) strict, unwell (*b*) tense, restless
(*c*) quiet, calm (*d*) happy, humorous
(*e*) calm, disturbed

36. A dramatic .... on cinema of the life of Phoolan Devi is .... protests from some people.
(*a*) depiction, triggering
(*b*) show, generating
(*c*) portrayal, arousing
(*d*) delineation, provoking
(*e*) demonstration, eliciting

37. Class .... between capital and labour is .... for building a prosperous country.
(*a*) affinity, indispensable
(*b*) agreement, necessary
(*c*) control, important
(*d*) coordination, inevitable
(*e*) collaboration, essential

38. Knowing that Renu had a good vocabulary, the teacher .... her to .... an essay for the inter school competition.
(*a*) notified, do
(*b*) commissioned, draft
(*c*) entrusted, write
(*d*) demanded, prepare

39. It is now a proven fact that .... of child mortality is the best .... for family planning in developing countries.
(*a*) checking, method
(*b*) prevention, incentive
(*c*) control, formula
(*d*) elimination, inspiration
(*e*) decrease, encouragement

40. The war .... immediately after the cease-fire proposal was .... bilaterally.
(*a*) receded, exchanged
(*b*) started, prepared
(*c*) began, thwarted
(*d*) extended, mitigated
(*e*) ended, accepted **(S.B.I.P.O. 1991)**

41. It appears that in those drought stricken areas hunger had .... hundreds of persons to mere ....
(*a*) converted, phantoms
(*b*) transformed, shadows
(*c*) reduced, skeletons
(*d*) changed, spirits
(*e*) turned, ghosts

42. Sachin .... another feather .... his cap by his wonderful performance in the one day match. **(Bank P.O. 1994)**
(*a*) kept, by (*b*) captured, from
(*c*) took, in (*d*) created, for
(*e*) added, to

43. Some people have the .... for learning foreign languages but they have no .... in speaking any.
(*a*) mania, urge (*b*) aptitude, interest
(*c*) stamina, fondness
(*d*) capacity, ability
(*e*) compulsion, inclination

44. Any system is likely to .... for .... of support from the public. **(Bank P.O. 1993)**
(*a*) survive, lack (*b*) succeed, reason
(*c*) fail, want (*d*) finish, failure
(*e*) launch, paucity

45. What .... one is the total absence of a coherent programme either on the part of the ruling or the opposition party to give a .... to the poverty-stricken people that something will be really done to improve their condition.
(*a*) humiliates, promise
(*b*) frightens, hint
(*c*) astounds, feeling
(*d*) shakes, notion
(*e*) embarrasses, apprehension

46. He is bound to succeed because his .... nature will not permit him to ....
(*a*) persistent, subsist

(*b*) devoted, shirk
(*c*) imperious, follow
(*d*) pertinacious, quit
(*e*) determined, abandon

47. The partners broke off as they found each other .... of .... breach of promise. **(I. Tax & Central Excise, 1990)**
(*a*) faulty, severe
(*b*) responsible, serious
(*c*) guilty, flagrant
(*d*) accused, rigid

48. The factory workers .... threatened to launch an indefinite strike from next month to .... their demands.
(*a*) did, get (*b*) nearly, fulfil
(*c*) were, meet (*d*) have, press

49. The region is likely to witness a ....– up as competition for its precious resources ....
(*a*) rise, increases (*b*) soar, progresses
(*c*) hover, strengthens
(*d*) flare, intensifies

50. Weather ...., I shall .... the office.
(*a*) favourable, visit (*b*) allowing, reach
(*c*) permitting, attend
(*d*) granting, manage

ANSWERS

1. (*e*)	**2.** (*c*)	**3.** (*c*)	**4.** (*d*)	**5.** (*c*)	**6.** (*c*)	**7.** (*c*)	**8.** (*a*)	**9.** (*c*)	**10.** (*e*)
11. (*a*)	**12.** (*a*)	**13.** (*e*)	**14.** (*b*)	**15.** (*c*)	**16.** (*b*)	**17.** (*c*)	**18.** (*b*)	**19.** (*d*)	**20.** (*b*)
21. (*e*)	**22.** (*c*)	**23.** (*d*)	**24.** (*c*)	**25.** (*b*)	**26.** (*c*)	**27.** (*e*)	**28.** (*e*)	**29.** (*a*)	**30.** (*b*)
31. (*c*)	**32.** (*d*)	**33.** (*e*)	**34.** (*c*)	**35.** (*e*)	**36.** (*c*)	**37.** (*e*)	**38.** (*c*)	**39.** (*c*)	**40.** (*e*)
41. (*c*)	**42.** (*e*)	**43.** (*b*)	**44.** (*c*)	**45.** (*c*)	**46.** (*d*)	**47.** (*c*)	**48.** (*d*)	**49.** (*d*)	**50.** (*c*)

PRACTICE SET 17

Directions : ***In each sentence below, there are two blank spaces. Below each sentence some pairs of words are given which are numbered (a), (b), (c), (d) and (e). Pick out the most appropriate pair to fill in the blanks in same order, to complete the sentence meaningfully.***

1. We must prevent endangered wild animal species from becoming .... in order that our future generation may .... the great diversity of animal life.
(*a*) rare, escape (*b*) outdated, know
(*c*) volatile, notice (*d*) powerful, protect
(*e*) extinct, enjoy **(Bank P.O. 1995)**

2. India's immense physical size, as also the fact of its .... society .... any attempt towards a neat capsuled presentation on any subject.
(*a*) cultured, demonstrates
(*b*) pluralistic, defies
(*c*) multi-religious, fails
(*d*) amorphous, challenges
(*e*) variegated, frustrates

3. The man who is impatient to become rich can easily be .... to the race track or the gaming table, where a lucky .... might make him rich.
(*a*) enticed, chance (*b*) evoked, streak
(*c*) pushed, moment (*d*) lured, break
(*e*) pursued, challenge

4. The secretary .... the society's funds, ... he was dismissed.
(*a*) misplaced, soon (*b*) robbed, thus
(*c*) pirated, therefore
(*d*) misappropriated, so **(Asstt. Grade, 1991)**

5. There are attempts being made to try to .... languages through specific ...., but the result is that some tongues become conserved as if they were a museum piece.
(*a*) save, ways (*b*) conserve, factors
(*c*) preserve, measures (*d*) protect, tricks

6. They wanted to .... all these books, but they could not find .... time to do so.
(*a*) cover, almost (*b*) peruse, necessary
(*c*) dispose, some (*d*) read, sufficient
(*e*) buy, some **(B.S.R.B.1996)**

The boy felt .... when he knew that he had been ....
(*a*) joyful, lured (*b*) horrified, forced
(*c*) disgraced, wronged
(*d*) humiliated, cheated
(*e*) worried, tempted

8. It is .... for every tax-payer to .... the tax returns to the Income Tax Department. **(R.B.I.1995)**
(*a*) necessary, lodge (*b*) binding, pay

(*c*) obligatory, submit (*d*) possible, remit
(*e*) worthwhile, evade

9. It is useless to attempt to .... from every danger, some .... must be taken.
(*a*) escape, chances (*b*) free, challenges
(*c*) protect, decisions (*d*) flee, risks
(*e*) dissociate, opportunities

10. Fiction approximates to science, first in accepting the obligation of being .... to life as it is, and secondly, in asserting the right to ....
(*a*) faithful, explain (*b*) true, theorise
(*c*) close, describe (*d*) realistic, portray
(*e*) committed, narrate

11. The mill workers were not .... with their low wages and non-payment of wages for last three months .... fuel to the flames. **(Bank P.O. 1994)**
(*a*) good, put (*b*) satisfied, added
(*c*) joyful, poured (*d*) pleased, directed
(*e*) unhappy, meant

12. The educational .... of our people is far below what is necessary for effective individual living or for the .... of society.
(*a*) procurement, upliftment
(*b*) advancement, upkeep
(*c*) attainment, maintenance
(*d*) achievement, advancement
(*e*) accomplishment, regeneration

13. Santosh looked very happy and .... when he heard that his proposed scheme was .... by the committee.
(*a*) energetic, rejected
(*b*) elated, accepted
(*c*) satisfied, stalled
(*d*) disconsolate, approved
(*e*) overwhelming, received
(S.B.I.P.O. 1994)

14. The security forces fired at the .... who was armed to the ....
(*a*) criminal, toe (*b*) thief, head
(*c*) culprit, nail (*d*) dacoit, teeth

15. .... the broker had warned him that the stock was a .... investment, he insisted on buying a thousand shares.
(*a*) Because, prudent
(*b*) Since, negligible
(*c*) Because,speculative
(*d*) As, vulnerable
(*e*) Although, precarious
(S.B.I.P.O. 1995)

16. In Buddhism, it is impossible to keep ethics and psychology .... from one another, because they .... at so many points.
(*a*) apart, meet (*b*) aloof, merge
(*c*) separate, overlap (*d*) away, coexist
(*e*) disjoint, converge

17. I don't .... I shall be .... to go.
(*a*) know, wanting
(*b*) consider, desirous
(*c*) think, able
(*d*) believe, liking
(*e*) feel, available **(Bank P.O. 1993)**

18. Restlessness among the students of colleges and universities has .... from their deep rooted feeling that their views and aspirations are .... by their elders.
(*a*) arisen, humiliated
(*b*) followed, disregarded
(*c*) stemmed, ignored
(*d*) started, neglected
(e) percolated, pooh-poohed

19. Shalini was not .... by the criticism and paid no .... even when her best friend talked against her. **(S.B.I.P.O. 1992)**
(*a*) bothered, attention
(*b*) troubled, mind
(*c*) threatened, warning
(*d*) deterred, heed
(*e*) shaken, indication

20. There is no glory in war .... the blood it ....
(*a*) thinking, demands
(*b*) considering, sheds
(*c*) worth, costs
(*d*) comparing, spills

21. Hitler cast a .... and .... shadow upon world history.
(*a*) colossal, frightful
(*b*) Herculean, gloomy
(*c*) gigantic, horrifying
(*d*) huge, vast

22. Somesh .... me coming to his table, he smiled and .... me a chair.
(*a*) found, signalled (*b*) met, sat
(*c*) looked, gave (*d*) saw, offered
(*e*) welcomed, took **(Bank P.O. 1994)**

23. Although the leader's life was both .... and painful, it was not without .... for he had accomplished many of his goals.
(*a*) magnificent, success
(*b*) happy, frustration
(*c*) thrilling, ambition
(*d*) purposeful, danger
(*e*) arduous, satisfaction

24. Wars usually result from .... among the parties involved and a failure to .... them peacefully.
(*a*) doubts, dispel (*b*) hostilities. debate
(*c*) frustrations, understand
(*d*) disagreements, resolve

25. Though he is reputed for his technical ...., his books were sadly ....

of the work of others as he lacked originality.
(*a*) advice, unconscious
(*b*) skill, independent
(*c*) knowledge, ignorant
(*d*) expertise, derivative
(*e*) dependence, indicative
(Bank P.O. 1995)

26. Bandung .... the .... of a new and powerful body of opinion which could not be ignored by the great writers.
(*a*) started, formation
(*b*) reflected, onset
(*c*) signalled, emergence
(*d*) induced, debut
(*e*) initiated, appearance

27. It is .... that those who expect .... from others are seldom merciful themselves.
(*a*) stupid, sympathy
(*b*) repulsive, compassion
(*c*) strange, sincerity
(*d*) unpardonable, kindness
(*e*) paradoxical, clemency

28. He was .... of playing .... and loose with the sentiments of his dearest friends. **(I. Tax & Central Excise, 1990)**
(*a*) complained, thick (*b*) accused, tight
(*c*) innocent, false (*d*) guilty, fast

29. The new Principal .... stress on routine administration .... than on academic matters and examination reforms.
(*a*) released, only (*b*) began, even
(*c*) started, further (*d*) laid, rather
(*e*) gave, better

30. Nothing is so .... to a nation as an extreme of self partiality, and the total want of .... of what others will naturally hope or fear.
(*a*) detrimental, concern
(*b*) repugnant, sense
(*c*) unethical, discretion
(*d*) fatal, consideration
(*e*) delusionary, methodly

31. To .... yourself from .... wear warm clothes. **(B.S.R.B. 1996)**
(*a*) prohibit, heat (*b*) protect, cold
(*c*) save, heat (*d*) suffer, cold
(*e*) prevent, ice

32. Every nation has a certain .... of hostility that seeks a socially acceptable ....
(*a*) stock, display
(*b*) concept, expression
(*c*) reservoir, outlet
(*d*) ideology, demonstration
(*e*) experience, explanation

33. She found .... with me, that I was wanting in ....
(*a*) crime, wisdom (*b*) fault, intelligence
(*c*) sin, ration (*d*) vice, knowledge

34. Let us .... with due .... that ancient India was more civilised than modern India with its satellites in space.
(*a*) admit, humility (*b*) adopt, certainty
(*c*) suppose, timidness
(*d*) presume, meekness
(*e*) agree, reluctance

35. The .... words of the mother comforted the .... child. **(S.B.I.P.O. 1991)**
(*a*) harsh, naughty (*b*) sweet, happy
(*c*) soft, energetic (*d*) melodious, playful
(*e*) soothing, disappointed

36. Our socialism is .... because we maintain a huge public sector without any public sector ....
(*a*) sham, economy
(*b*) fraudulent, pursuit
(*c*) idealistic, theory
(*d*) counterfeit, phase
(*e*) phoney, philosophy

37. I would like to .... your attention to the second paragraph of my letter .... to the terms of sale of the machinery.
(*a*) invite, according
(*b*) withdraw, regarding
(*c*) react, mainly
(*d*) draw, pertaining
(*e*) focus, connecting **(Bank P.O. 1995)**

38. An .... facet of the Soviet perestroika is the search for a sweeping .... programme in foreign policy.
(*a*) essential, humanitarian
(*b*) interesting, moral
(*c*) important, economic
(*d*) immediate, social

39. Synthetic milk .... real milk in all .... except taste and nutritional qualities.
(*a*) resembles, factors
(*b*) exemplifies, respects
(*c*) copies, manners (*d*) marks, qualities
(*e*) mimics, aspects

40. We cannot .... such a/an .... act of violence. **(S.B.I.P.O. 1995)**
(*a*) tolerate, insipid
(*b*) consider, important
(*c*) commit, magnificent
(*d*) pardon, egregious
(*e*) neglect, insignificant

41. Civilisation, in the real sense of the term consists not in the .... but in the deliberate and voluntary .... of wants.
(*a*) multiplication, reduction
(*b*) increase, decrease
(*c*) hoarding, dehoarding

(*d*) overgrowth, diminishing

42. Public sector units running at a loss should be given the option to be .... to the highest bidder with a golden handshake for employees or to be converted into workers' cooperatives with workers holding .... ownership.
(*a*) sold, entire (*b*) credited, financial
(*c*) attributed, just
(*d*) handed, reasonable
(*e*) auctioned, equity

43. Ravi .... a bit .... he was not invited by his friend to attend the party.
(*a*) took, before (*b*) angered, since
(*c*) expressed, than (*d*) grumbled, when
(*e*) surprised, about **(Bank P.O. 1995)**

44. In architecture, much more than in any of the other arts, there is a marked time lag between the .... of ideas and their .... in the shape of completed buildings.
(*a*) dawn, practicability
(*b*) settlement, fruition
(*c*) emergence, application
(*d*) burgeoning, welcoming

45. The great scientist .... himself with ability and moderation all .... the conference. **(Bank P.O. 1994)**
(*a*) felt, about (*b*) displayed, in
(*c*) disclosed, besides
(*d*) conducted, through
(*e*) presented, though

46. In a world .... by men for so many years, women are only thought .... for jobs like typists, receptionists and teachers.
(*a*) created, suitable
(*b*) governed, qualified
(*c*) controlled, eligible
(*d*) dominated, competent
(*e*) ruled, fit

47. Hence the word sophistry has an unfavourable .... and means arguing deceitfully, attempting to turn a poor case into a good one by means of clever but .... reasoning.
(*a*) impact, cogent
(*b*) denotation, ingenuous
(*c*) significance, vague
(*d*) connotation, specious

48. This partly explains how the Mehta family has been able to .... its lavish lifestyle in recent times, despite the fact that all its assets have been ....
(*a*) keep up, destroyed
(*b*) develop, liquidated
(*c*) afford, attached
(*d*) keep, removed **(M.B.A. 1994)**

49. Kautilya was a great political thinker and his strong .... personality is .... throughout the thoughts and expressions in the Arthashastra.
(*a*) virile, observed (*b*) vigorous, noticed
(*c*) vivacious, reflected
(*d*) dynamic, detected
(*e*) defiant, discerned

50. The Minister felt that the .... made by the Committee was .... even though similar schemes had worked earlier.
(*a*) decision, gainful (*b*) choice, profitable
(*c*) acceptance, approved
(*d*) election, acceptable
(*e*) recommendation, infeasible
(S.B.I.P.O. 1992)

ANSWERS

1. (*e*)	**2.** (*b*)	**3.** (*d*)	**4.** (*d*)	**5.** (*c*)	**6.** (*d*)	**7.** (*e*)	**8.** (*c*)	**9.** (*d*)	**10.** (*b*)
11. (*b*)	**12.** (*c*)	**13.** (*b*)	**14.** (*a*)	**15.** (*e*)	**16.** (*c*)	**17.** (*c*)	**18.** (*c*)	**19.** (*d*)	**20.** (*b*)
21. (*c*)	**22.** (*d*)	**23.** (*e*)	**24.** (*d*)	**25.** (*d*)	**26.** (*c*)	**27.** (*e*)	**28.** (*b*)	**29.** (*d*)	**30.** (*d*)
31. (*b*)	**32.** (*c*)	**33.** (*b*)	**34.** (*a*)	**35.** (*e*)	**36.** (*e*)	**37.** (*d*)	**38.** (*a*)	**39.** (*e*)	**40.** (*d*)
41. (*a*)	**42.** (*e*)	**43.** (*d*)	**44.** (*c*)	**45.** (*d*)	**46.** (*d*)	**47.** (*d*)	**48.** (*a*)	**49.** (*a*)	**50.** (*e*)

PRACTICE SET 18

Directions : ***In each sentence below, there are two blank spaces. Below each sentence some pairs of words are given which are numbered (a), (b), (c), (d) and (e). Pick out the most appropriate pair to fill in the blanks in the same order, to complete the sentence meaningfully.***

1. The police .... any attempt of arson by .... at the trouble spot quite in time.
(*a*) squashed, surrounding
(*b*) made, encircling

(*c*) predisposed, visiting
(*d*) thwarted, presenting
(*e*) pre-empted, arriving **(R.B.I. 1995)**

2. Our youth and others have .... to drugs not only because their friends .... social pressures but also because escape with drugs is so complete and swift.
(*a*) clung, put (*b*) turned, enforce
(*c*) given, exhibit (*d*) moved, exert
(*e*) resorted, apply

3. Moreover, a fact-finding mission .... by BSN to India in January this year strongly recommended that the French group should go it alone, and not hand over .... to an Indian partner.
(*a*) constituted, authority
(*b*) organised, papers
(*c*) dispatched, control
(*d*) sponsored, power **(M.B.A. 1994)**

4. Though this is undoubtedly the greatest dictionary ever ...., it is designed for scholars and research workers rather than for the .... dictionary user.
(*a*) assembled, assiduous
(*b*) compiled, casual
(*c*) published, professional
(*d*) projected, omniscient

5. .... persons are inclined to ....
(*a*) Domineering, temperance
(*b*) Obese, corpulence
(*c*) Cowering, effrontery
(*d*) Vacillating, determination

6. He had managed to .... several times, but was finally .... by the police.
(*a*) deceive, cheated (*b*) defend, acquitted
(*c*) escape, arrested (*d*) cheat, robbed
(*e*) abscond, kidnapped **(S.B.I.P.O. 1994)**

7. Among the younger people there are complaints that the sight of ex-Nazis fluorishing recommends .... to youth, that it instills, instead of needed moral values, the dubious precept that .... is the best policy.
(*a*) emulation, honesty
(*b*) desperation, dishonesty
(*c*) selfishness, intolerance
(*d*) cynicism, expediency

8. The people of China who have .... their right to be free and frank, only to have it brutally ...., may also have the courage to manifest it in other ways.
(*a*) revived, crushed
(*b*) invoked, snatched
(*c*) claimed, denied
(*d*) asserted, suppressed
(*e*) manifested, repressed

9. Children are more .... than adults, it is .... their quickness in learning a new language. **(Bank P.O. 1995)**
(*a*) intelligent, disproved by
(*b*) adaptable, reflected in
(*c*) conservative, seen in
(*d*) susceptible, demonstrated in
(*e*) resourceful, proportionate to

10. The Government has .... a working group to .... technological gaps in selected industries in the small scale sector.
(*a*) organised, spot out (*b*) formed, locate
(*c*) constituted, identify
(*d*) planned, pin-point
(*e*) appointed, take stock of

11. Fear is one of those .... which frequently .... us to inaction.
(*a*) sentiments, lead (*b*) values, put
(*c*) feelings, take (*d*) emotions, root

12. She was .... because all her plans had gone .... **(Assistant Grade, 1991)**
(*a*) elated, wild (*b*) dejected, splendidly
(*c*) distraught, awry
(*d*) frustrated, magnificently

13. The educational systems of Japan and South Korea have long, tough work .... for students and it is no .... that both these countries are doing well.
(*a*) periods, accident
(*b*) schedules, coincidence
(*c*) routines, synchronisation
(*d*) moments, surprise

14. Very few of us are capable of seeing human .... the robes of a million aire and the rags of a beggar.
(*a*) status, through (*b*) nature, beneath
(*c*) dignity, in (*d*) condition, by
(*e*) glory, without

15. The candidates' .... at the polls was .... as he won with a striking margin.
(*a*) claim, unrealistic
(*b*) victory, overwhelming
(*c*) image, real
(*d*) strategy, unsuccessful
(*e*) candidature, inappropriate **(S.B.I.P.O. 1991)**

16. He is so .... that everyone is always .... to help him in his work. **(R.B.I. 1995)**
(*a*) helpful, reluctant
(*b*) aloof, cooperative
(*c*) adamant, enthusiastic
(*d*) miserly, ignorant
(*e*) magnanimous, eager

17. Democracy, as a way of life and not as a mere political arrangement, requires of its .... a regard not only for their own

rights but equally for the .... rights of others.
(*a*) exponents, identical
(*b*) votaries, related
(*c*) protagonists, same
(*d*) adherents, similar
(*e*) proponents, such

18. Conditions in the country have grown so .... that many refugees have risked death to ....
(*a*) worse, safety
(*b*) comfortable, survival
(*c*) different, life (*d*) bad, save
(*e*) severe, escape

19. The activities of the association have .... from the .... objectives set for it in the initial years. **(S.B.I.P.O. 1992)**
(*a*) grown, simple (*b*) deviated, original
(*c*) details, grand (*d*) emerged, total
(*e*) increased, perverse

20. He warned the workers against supporting these anti-social policies, which he declared would .... rather than .... the plight of the common people.
(*a*) impair, improving
(*b*) rescue, destroy
(*c*) protract, inhibit
(*d*) aggravate, alleviate

21. The police feel that the .... shown by the judges to first offenders unfortunately .... many youngsters to commit more and more crimes.
(*a*) clemency, encourages
(*b*) pity, predisposes
(*c*) leniency, prevents
(*d*) mercy, prohibits
(*e*) harshness, leads

22. Gandhiji was not enamoured .... the economic progress made by the modern West and did not .... the Western nations to be more civilised.
(*a*) at, believe (*b*) off, think
(*c*) of, consider (*d*) with, hold

23. The leaders were .... needed by those to .... they were addressed.
(*a*) angrily, who (*b*) readily, which
(*c*) scarcely, whom (*d*) rarely, where
(*e*) joyfully, when **(Bank P.O. 1994)**

24. The domestic and foreign policies of a nation state with a long .... and continuous historical tradition like India have a certain .... about them.
(*a*) relevant, mystery
(*b*) glorious, uncertainty
(*c*) coherent, inevitability
(*d*) splendid, certainty
(*e*) eventful, unintelligibility

25. Instead of ...., prove your worth by .... something.
(*a*) begging, demanding
(*b*) talking, doing
(*c*) worrying, paying
(*d*) writing, reading
(*e*) donating, demanding **(Bank P.O. 1993)**

26. It is the primary duty of any party elected to rule to .... stability and defence of the country and protect it both from internal and external ....
(*a*) ensure, subversions
(*b*) strengthen, aggressions
(*c*) protect, trauma
(*d*) assure, aspersions
(*e*) insure, submissions

27. Due to .... rainfall this year, there will be .... cut in water supply.
(*a*) enough, substantial
(*b*) meagre, least
(*c*) sufficient, no (*d*) surplus, abundant
(*e*) abundant, considerable
(B.S.R.B. 1996)

28. Foreign multinationals may be .... in implementing the infrastructural plan on condition of introducing labour intensive techniques which generate a minimum .... level of rural employment.
(*a*) deployed, prescribed
(*b*) debarred, ordained
(*c*) deplored, scheduled
(*d*) defamed, limited

29. We must explore .... sources of energy as our supply of fossil fuel has been ....
(*a*) alternate, depleted
(*b*) guaranteed, over
(*c*) natural, exhausted
(*d*) sufficient, increased
(*e*) innovative, augmented
(Bank P.O. 1995)

30. Many tourists to India visit the beautiful .... of Kashmir .... in spring and summer.
(*a*) town, frequently (*b*) valley, especially
(*c*) scenery, generally (*d*) lakes, rarely

31. We can .... to travel by air, but we .... train journey. **(S.B.I.P.O. 1991)**
(*a*) plan, enjoy (*b*) aspire, commute
(*c*) afford, prefer (*d*) decide, undertook
(*e*) decline, accepted

32. Because the inspector gave the plant a .... examination, he .... many defects.
(*a*) casual, missed
(*b*) meticulous, mentioned
(*c*) cursory, by passed
(*d*) peremptory, ignored
(*e*) perfunctory, overlooked

33. The .... of glory lead but to the ....
(*a*) acts, prosperity
(*b*) achievements, suffering
(*c*) paths, grave
(*d*) ways, happiness **(Asstt. Grade, 1991)**

34. We do not .... our dreams because they do not .... with our perceptions of waking life.
(*a*) admit, coincide (*b*) accept, mix
(*c*) value, match (*d*) believe, agree
(*e*) appreciate, corroborate

35. He granted the request because he was .... to .... his friend. **(S.B.I.P.O. 1994)**
(*a*) bound, hurt
(*b*) destined, agonise
(*c*) sure, displease (*d*) unwilling, please
(*e*) reluctant, disappoint

36. Mr. Rajesh ....his wife that he would take .... action to set right his erring son.
(*a*) called, strict (*b*) assured, stringent
(*c*) reitrated, strictly
(*d*) informed, constructive
(*e*) instructed, preventive

37. The charges made in the system were so .... that they didn't require any ....
(*a*) big, time (*b*) genuine, intelligence
(*c*) marginal, expenses
(*d*) certain, expertise
(*e*) obvious, modifications **(R.B.I. 1995)**

38. I shall .... him if he .... to me for his misconduct.
(*a*) pardon, commits
(*b*) forgive, apologises
(*c*) reprimand, commands
(*d*) punish, abuses

39. In .... of International matters, there is always an element of risk in .... one might do. **(Bank P.O. 1994)**
(*a*) view, whichever (*b*) many, doing
(*c*) defence, wrong (*d*) case, whatever
(*e*) spite, whatever

40. We have criticized our university students for preferring the security of political silence and the safety of .... to the excitement of social .... and humanitarian action.
(*a*) college, adventure
(*b*) concealment, revolution
(*c*) acquiescence, dissent
(*d*) tolerance, antagonism

41. .... is a criminal .... in England and covers cases where offensive descriptions of Christianity are published.
(*a*) Heathenism, act
(*b*) Sacrilege, violence
(*c*) Blasphemy, offence
(*d*) Obscenity, deviation
(*e*) Impiety, transgression **(M.B.A. 1995)**

42. The teacher told Kailash, "You should .... this paragraph to make the essay more ...."
(*a*) expunge, witty (*b*) enlarge, poignant
(*c*) delete, succinct (*d*) excise, expansive
(*e*) revise, abstruse

43. The hot tropical climate created a climate of .... and encouraged ....
(*a*) sweltering, agility
(*b*) enervation, activity
(*c*) listlessness, enphoria
(*d*) lassitude, drowsiness

44. We are .... to have him .... here to make this function a great success.
(*a*) proud, leave (*b*) happy, arrive
(*c*) sure, come (*d*) pleased, over
(*e*) wonderful, again **(Bank P.O. 1994)**

45. Babe Didrikson was a fantastic athlete who was .... outstanding in every athletic .... she undertook.
(*a*) seemingly, feat (*b*) truly, testimonial
(*c*) skilfully, play (*d*) basically, skill
(*e*) apparently, endeavour

46. He was so convinced that people were driven by .... motives that he believed there was no such thing as a purely .... act.
(*a*) personal, anti-social
(*b*) personal, eternal
(*c*) altruistic, praiseworthy
(*d*) ulterior, selfless
(*e*) sentimental, divine **(S.B.I.P.O. 1995)**

47. An administrator must .... evaluate his own views because his influence can be .... if he has personal prejudices.
(*a*) sincerely, significant
(*b*) regularly, acrimonious
(*c*) constantly, deleterious
(*d*) frequently, rash
(*e*) occasionally, undesirable

48. We .... him with many promises, but nothing would .... him **(Bank P.O. 1993)**
(*a*) tempted, influence
(*b*) provoked, dessicate
(*c*) attracted, fascinate
(*d*) gave, deprive (*e*) negotiated, please

49. Oddly enough .... the prestige of USA in countries like Britain, France and Italy is considered important here, Congress has been .... about supplying funds to the US Information Agency in these countries.
(*a*) when, generous
(*b*) since, dilatory
(*c*) whereas, wasteful
(*d*) although, niggardly

50. The counter clerk was very busy and .... not pay .... to Sameer's request.
(*a*) can, help (*b*) could, respect
(*c*) had, cash (*d*) did, attention
(*e*) certainly, acceptance **(Bank P.O. 1994)**

ANSWERS

1. (*e*)	**2.** (*e*)	**3.** (*c*)	**4.** (*b*)	**5.** (*b*)	**6.** (*c*)	**7.** (*d*)	**8.** (*b*)	**9.** (*b*)	**10.** (*c*)
11. (*d*)	**12.** (*c*)	**13.** (*b*)	**14.** (*c*)	**15.** (*b*)	**16.** (*e*)	**17.** (*d*)	**18.** (*e*)	**19.** (*b*)	**20.** (*d*)
21. (*a*)	**22.** (*c*)	**23.** (*c*)	**24.** (*c*)	**25.** (*b*)	**26.** (*a*)	**27.** (*c*)	**28.** (*a*)	**29.** (*c*)	**30.** (*b*)
31. (*c*)	**32.** (*e*)	**33.** (*c*)	**34.** (*d*)	**35.** (*e*)	**36.** (*b*)	**37.** (*e*)	**38.** (*b*)	**39.** (*d*)	**40.** (*c*)
41. (*c*)	**42.** (*c*)	**43.** (*d*)	**44.** (*d*)	**45.** (*e*)	**46.** (*d*)	**47.** (*c*)	**48.** (*a*)	**49.** (*d*)	**50.** (*d*)

PRACTICE SET 19

Directions : *In each sentence below, there are two blank spaces. Below each sentence some pairs of words are given. Pick out the most appropriate pair to fill in the blanks in the same order, to make the sentence meaningfully complete.*

1. Shailendra .... to a .... love for drugs.
(*a*) considered, reveal
(*b*) admitted, correct
(*c*) accepted, open (*d*) confessed, secret
(*e*) supposed, sacred

2. The admiration some leaders earn is ...., by their .... instinct for hitting the frontlines in newspapers.
(*a*) evolved, aggressive
(*b*) generated, feeble
(*c*) conceded, provocative
(*d*) engendered, unerring
(*e*) developed, uncanny

3. Irrigation from the canal is .... settlers for cultivation, which is .... eating into the wildlife habitat.
(*a*) attracting, gradually
(*b*) luring, steadily
(*c*) enticing, rapidly
(*d*) persuading, regularly
(*e*) ensnaring, stealthily

4. The construction of the hall has been .... because of the .... of cement in the market. **(Bank P.O. 1995)**
(*a*) held, non-availability
(*b*) denied, restrictions
(*c*) hampered, shortage
(*d*) prevented, supply
(*e*) completed, disappearance

5. The prince did not know what these omens might .... and he asked his soothsayers to .... them.
(*a*) implicate, clarify
(*b*) imply, illustrate
(*c*) portend, interpret
(*d*) propound, explain
(*e*) hold, dilate on

6. The bandit .... the traveller of his purse of gold and .... him grievously.
(*a*) snatched, hurt
(*b*) stole, injured
(*c*) demanded, beat
(*d*) robbed, wounded **(B.S.R.B. 1992)**

7. Only .... people are .... after death.
(*a*) virulent, glorified
(*b*) vicious, condemned
(*c*) virile, forgotten
(*d*) virtuous, remembered

8. He preaches liberal views but in practice, he is not .... and is .... narrow minded than almost any other person.
(*a*) hard, openly
(*b*) tolerant, more
(*c*) ambitious, hardly
(*d*) acceptable, genuinely
(*e*) approachable, less **(Bank P.O. 1994)**

9. The ancient Indian princes and rulers .... most of their time, energy and resources in .... warfare.
(*a*) squandered, common
(*b*) wasted, reciprocal
(*c*) exhausted, expensive
(*d*) dessicated, unnecessary
(*e*) dissipated, mutual

10. He is .... to .... any kind of work with due sincerity. **(B.S.R.B. 1996)**
(*a*) fond, perform
(*b*) reluctant, entrust
(*c*) determined, undertake
(*d*) eager, avoid
(*e*) willing, ignore

11. He was initially .... at the suggestion but was soon .... it himself.
(*a*) frowning, rejecting

(*b*) shocked, advocating
(*c*) impressed, negating
(*d*) thrilled, propagating
(*e*) suspicious, trusting

(S.B.I.P.O. 1992)

12. A whole generation of infants is at risk of .... diseases due to drinking poisonous milk being pumped into the market by .... traders.
(*a*) countering, false
(*b*) embibing, vivacious
(*c*) generating, unconscious
(*d*) encountering, dishonest
(*e*) developing, unscrupulous

13. Let us keep in mind the Buddha's .... that the only true victory is that in which there are no ....
(*a*) presumption, devastations
(*b*) precept, provocations
(*c*) proposition, malice
(*d*) admonition, vanquished
(*e*) premonition, casualties

14. It is not .... to come across a man who can take ups and downs without losing ....
(*a*) feasible, equipoise
(*b*) usual, patience
(*c*) common, equilibrium
(*d*) possible, self-control
(*e*) easy, equanimity

15. The increasing revival of dramatic classics is, to one critic, ...; it seems to him a sign of the .... of the modern theatre. **(M.B.A. 1995)**
(*a*) auspicious, resurgence
(*b*) deplorable, anaemia
(*c*) incomprehensible, paradox
(*d*) astounding, vitality

16. Fate is an ...., and in order that it may play an active part in human drama, it must be .... in some particular incarnation.
(*a*) idea, represented
(*b*) ideology, realised
(*c*) attitude, symbolised
(*d*) imagination, illustrated
(*e*) abstraction, personified

17. Prabha's .... in athletics yielded rich .... as she got a scholarship.
(*a*) performance, money
(*b*) defeat, results
(*c*) behaviour, appreciation
(*d*) excellence, dividends
(*e*) failure, disappointment

(S.B.I.P.O. 1994)

18. In a changing and .... unstructured business environment, creativity and innovation are being .... demanded of executives. **(M.B.A. 1994)**
(*a*) excessively, rapidly
(*b*) highly, extremely
(*c*) increasingly, moderately
(*d*) progressively, increasingly

19. If it were true that enduring lessons are learned from .... errors, Broadway would be the repository of .... theatrical wisdom.
(*a*) dubious, profound
(*b*) egregious, sublime
(*c*) dramatic, lasting
(*d*) stupid, tenuous

20. It is indeed ...., that 40 years after independence, we have failed to .... a suitable education or examination system. **(G.I.C.A.A.O. 1992)**
(*a*) bad, produce
(*b*) improper, create
(*c*) sad, evolve
(*d*) objectionable, present

21. The admiration Raja Rammohan Roy earned was .... by his .... concern for the welfare of Indian women.
(*a*) aroused, proverbial
(*b*) belied, prudent
(*c*) transcended, haughty
(*d*) developed, real
(*e*) engendered, sincere

22. .... by long queues and bad weather the voters .... their way to polling stations any way they could.
(*a*) Going, dropped
(*b*) Satisfied, turned
(*c*) Worried, lost
(*d*) Undaunted, made
(*e*) Encouraged, prepare

23. In his ...., he followed the .... course.
(*a*) agony, funny
(*b*) ignorance, wrong
(*c*) hurry, diversified
(*d*) predicament, proper
(*e*) bewilderment, appropriate

(S.B.I.P.O. 1994)

24. The Deputy Manager ....,to resign because all his proposals were .... down by his superiors.
(*a*) offered, thrown (*b*) gave, held
(*c*) began, kept (*d*) willing, knocked
(*e*) threatened, turned **(Bank P.O. 1994)**

25. Success in great ventures calls for .... concentration and strong personal ....
(*a*) hectic, interest
(*b*) unflagging, involvement
(*c*) continued, apathy
(*d*) standing, participation

ANSWERS

1. (d)	2. (e)	3. (b)	4. (c)	5. (c)	6. (d)	7. (d)	8. (b)	9. (e)	10. (c)
11. (b)	12. (e)	13. (d)	14. (b)	15. (b)	16. (e)	17. (d)	18. (d)	19. (b)	20. (c)
21. (e)	22. (d)	23. (b)	24. (e)	25. (b)					

II. GRAMMAR USAGE

PRACTICE SET 20

1. Priya is not .... for this kind of a job.
(*a*) cut in (*b*) cut up
(*c*) cut through (*d*) cut out
(Central Excise, 1995)

2. He left the book .... the telephone.
(*a*) around (*b*) beside
(*c*) besides (*d*) at

3. The waiter took the plates .... after we had finished eating.
(*a*) up (*b*) off (*c*) away (*d*) out

4. It is fourteen years since I .... him.
(*a*) saw (*b*) have seen
(*c*) did see (*d*) had seen
(C.D.S. 1993)

5. I have done my muddled but .... honest best.
(*a*) never the less (*b*) rather
(*c*) none the less

6. It is mainly due to their lethargy that the plan fell ....
(*a*) over (*b*) out
(*c*) through (*d*) off

7. She had just .... down when the telephone rang. **(N.D.A. 1993)**
(*a*) laid (*b*) lain (*c*) lay

8. Thinking that the other candidate was more deserving for the post, I .... in his favour.
(*a*) stood down (*b*) stood out
(*c*) stood over (*d*) stood off

9. This building comprises .... sixty rooms. **(Stenographers' Exam, 1993)**
(*a*) off (*b*) to (*c*) with (*d*) of

10. She always runs short .... money.
(*a*) of (*b*) by (*c*) in (*d*) to

11. Sunita decided to set .... some time every day for prayers. **(B.S.R.B. 1995)**
(*a*) up (*b*) in (*c*) on (*d*) aside

12. The Government agreed to pay compensation .... damaged crops, land and cattle.
(*a*) of (*b*) for (*c*) to (*d*) through

13. The boy you met yesterday is in class .... **(S.S.C. 1992)**
(*a*) ninth (*b*) the ninth
(*c*) nine (*d*) the nine

14. There was some confusion .... the agreement.
(*a*) on (*b*) in (*c*) around (*d*) over

15. Speak loudly as he is slow .... hearing.
(*a*) in (*b*) about (*c*) at (*d*) of

16. Will you .... my dog while I am on tour?
(*a*) look out (*b*) look up
(*c*) look on (*d*) look after
(Hotel Management, 1996)

17. Savita is disgusted .... the habits of her husband.
(*a*) of (*b*) from (*c*) with (*d*) at

18. Every man craves .... recognition.
(*a*) for (*b*) about (*c*) at (*d*) after

19. .... you meet my son in the market, ask him to come home at once.
(*a*) Will (*b*) While
(*c*) Should (*d*) Would
(Stenographers' Exam, 1995)

20. Sanjay was sure .... getting a first class in the examination
(*a*) at (*b*) of (*c*) on (*d*) about

21. She seems offended .... my remarks.
(*a*) with (*b*) for (*c*) upon (*d*) at

22. The mounting pressure was so overwhelming that he ultimately .... to her wish. **(N.D.A. 1993)**
(*a*) agreed in (*b*) cowed in
(*c*) gave in (*d*) yielded in

23. He has no objection .... my proposal.
(*a*) to (*b*) for (*c*) in (*d*) towards

24. Wash your hands .... water.
(*a*) from (*b*) with (*c*) by (*d*) in

25. It is no use .... to come now. He is very busy. **(S.S.C. 1993)**
(*a*) to ask him (*b*) asking him
(*c*) that you ask him (*d*) if you asked him

26. They are very grateful .... your kindness.

(*a*) towards (*b*) to
(*c*) with (*d*) for

27. He preferred cricket .... any other sport.
(*a*) against (*b*) to
(*c*) over (*d*) than

28. There is a disturbing nexus .... politics and sports in India. **(C.B.I. 1993)**
(*a*) between (*b*) with
(*c*) among (*d*) by

29. Don't loiter .... the street.
(*a*) in (*b*) about (*c*) on (*d*) into

30. The terms given to you are not acceptable .... me.
(*a*) for (*b*) by (*c*) with (*d*) to

31. You have played a great role, for .... your help I possibly would have landed myself into a problem. **(B.S.R.B. 1994)**
(*a*) after (*b*) despite (*c*) unless
(*d*) although (*e*) without

32. Fate smiled .... him in all his ventures.
(*a*) upon (*b*) on (*c*) at (*d*) over

33. I saw him resting .... the shade of a tree.
(*a*) below (*b*) into
(*c*) under (*d*) in

34. Besides other provisions, that shopkeeper deals .... cosmetics too.
(*a*) for (*b*) at (*c*) in (*d*) with
(Stenographers' Exam, 1995)

35. I will be .... a loss in this deal.
(*a*) to (*b*) on (*c*) at (*d*) for

36. We shall fail .... we are industrious.
(*a*) though (*b*) until (*c*) even
(*d*) whether (*e*) unless
(B.S.R.B. 1996)

37. It is time you .... home.
(*a*) go (*b*) have gone
(*c*) went (*d*) are going

38. I have been ill .... last sunday.
(*a*) for (*b*) since
(*c*) from (*d*) by
(M.B.A. 1989)

39. These days transport .... cheaper than ever before.
(*a*) becomes (*b*) would become
(*c*) is becoming (*d*) has become

40. The lawyer was threatened .... dire consequences. **(S.S.C. 1995)**
(*a*) from (*b*) by (*c*) with (*d*) of

41. I will have to dispense .... his services.
(*a*) off (*b*) of (*c*) at (*d*) with

42. It has been raining .... morning.
(*a*) for (*b*) from (*c*) till (*d*) since
(Railways, 1993)

43. .... all intents and purposes, the manager is the master of the firm.
(*a*) With (*b*) In (*c*) Upon (*d*) To
(C.B.I. 1995)

44. She has not recovered fully .... the shock.
(*a*) against (*b*) of
(*c*) from (*d*) off

45. One should not be indifferent .... the sufferings of others.
(*a*) about (*b*) to (*c*) of (*d*) at
(Central Excise, 1991)

46. Why don't you sit .... me?
(*a*) close (*b*) beside
(*c*) along (*d*) next

47. His conduct is bad, and his honesty is not .... suspicion.
(*a*) in (*b*) beyond
(*c*) under (*d*) above
(Hotel Management, 1993)

48. Father shall return .... an hour.
(*a*) during (*b*) after
(*c*) within (*d*) in

49. The car ran .... the railings.
(*a*) to (*b*) in (*c*) at (*d*) into

50. Everywhere elegant old buildings are being .... and mediocre modern structures are being put up.
(*a*) pulled off (*b*) pulled down
(*c*) pulled up (*d*) pulled through
(C.D.S. 1991)

ANSWERS

1. (*d*)	**2.** (*b*)	**3.** (*c*)	**4.** (*a*)	**5.** (*c*)	**6.** (*c*)	**7.** (*b*)	**8.** (*a*)	**9.** (*d*)	**10.** (*a*)
11. (*d*)	**12.** (*b*)	**13.** (*c*)	**14.** (*d*)	**15.** (*c*)	**16.** (*d*)	**17.** (*c*)	**18.** (*d*)	**19.** (*c*)	**20.** (*b*)
21. (*d*)	**22.** (*c*)	**23.** (*a*)	**24.** (*b*)	**25.** (*b*)	**26.** (*d*)	**27.** (*b*)	**28.** (*a*)	**29.** (*b*)	**30.** (*d*)
31. (*e*)	**32.** (*b*)	**33.** (*c*)	**34.** (*c*)	**35.** (*c*)	**36.** (*e*)	**37.** (*c*)	**38.** (*b*)	**39.** (*d*)	**40.** (*c*)
41. (*d*)	**42.** (*d*)	**43.** (*d*)	**44.** (*c*)	**45.** (*b*)	**46.** (*b*)	**47.** (*d*)	**48.** (*c*)	**49.** (*d*)	**50.** (*b*)

PRACTICE SET 21

1. .... being hardworking he is thoroughly honest. **(Stenographers' Exam, 1995)**
(*a*) Although (*b*) Over and above
(*c*) Betimes (*d*) Along with

2. Let us begin .... a new chapter.
(*a*) by (*b*) with (*c*) from (*d*) on

3. She has great affection .... me.
(*a*) for (*b*) in (*c*) with (*d*) to

4. The Press .... serve the profession better if it were objective in its reporting.
(*a*) would (*b*) may
(*c*) can (*d*) will
(U.D.C. 1994)

5. A committee was formed to look .... the building.
(*a*) after (*b*) at (*c*) upto (*d*) for

6. Reena is .... polite that everyone likes her.
(*a*) as (*b*) much (*c*) very (*d*) so

7. Kanak is endowed .... many great qualities. **(B.S.R.B. 1993)**
(*a*) in (*b*) with (*c*) of (*d*) by

8. The inspector must enquire .... the complaint.
(*a*) about (*b*) in (*c*) of
(*d*) into (*e*) to

9. One should remain aloof .... bad habit.
(*a*) from (*b*) to (*c*) against (*d*) of

10. A great change has come .... the world since the war. **(Central Excise, 1993)**
(*a*) about (*b*) over (*c*) into (*d*) in

11. .... duty calls, we must obey.
(*a*) As (*b*) While (*c*) If (*d*) When

12. Would anybody .... a mother have risked his or her life for the baby?
(*a*) rather (*b*) but
(*c*) however (*d*) than
(B.S.R.B. 1992)

13. Our country is committed .... a policy of peaceful co-existence.
(*a*) with (*b*) for (*c*) to (*d*) by

14. He has retired .... private life.
(*a*) into (*b*) from (*c*) for (*d*) by

15. We thought that she .... the job.
(*a*) gets (*b*) is getting
(*c*) will get (*d*) would get
(Stenographers' Exam, 1994)

16. I cannot agree .... your proposal.
(*a*) of (*b*) to (*c*) with (*d*) by

17. Life is a tale told by .... idiot.
(*a*) an (*b*) a
(*c*) the (*d*) None of these

18. Get me a glass of water, ...
(*a*) shall you? (*b*) won't you?
(*c*) will you? (*d*) wouldn't you?

19. He stumbled at the stone and fell .... a ditch. **(L.I.C. 1992)**
(*a*) on (*b*) into (*c*) in (*d*) within

20. She is tired .... making appeals to her in-laws.
(*a*) with (*b*) from (*c*) of (*d*) about

21. After the rain the weather .... and the sun came out.
(*a*) cleared off (*b*) cleared out
(*c*) cleared up (*d*) cleared away
(Stenographers' Exam, 1994)

22. This book is mine and that is ....
(*a*) of you (*b*) your
(*c*) your's (*d*) yours

23. Just try .... it.
(a) do (*b*) doing
(*c*) to do (*d*) and do

24. This brand of TV is quite inferior .... that one. **(Assistant Grade, 1994)**
(*a*) over (*b*) with (*c*) to (*d*) than

25. Rajesh has come up .... a problem.
(*a*) to (*b*) for
(*c*) against (*d*) into

26. He used to pray everyday, believing that as long as he .... so, he would be safe.
(*a*) is doing (*b*) does
(*c*) did (*d*) will do
(C.B.I. 1994)

27. He has shown utter neglect .... duty.
(*a*) for (*b*) of (*c*) to (*d*) in

28. I am fed up .... this type of behaviour.
(*a*) at (*b*) of (*c*) with (*d*) by

29. If they want to succeed, they .... have to work very hard. **(B.S.R.B. 1993)**
(*a*) will (*b*) ought
(*c*) must (*d*) should

30. Because of the bad weather we had to stay .... home.
(*a*) off (*b*) in (*c*) of (*d*) at

31. He succeeded in getting possession .... his land after a long court case.
(*a*) for (*b*) to (*c*) of
(*d*) with (*e*) against **(L.I.C. 1994)**

32. Now a days Rajani is .... busy to take care of her health.
(*a*) very (*b*) too
(*c*) so (*d*) extremely

33. Had the police not reached there in time the bandits .... him.
(*a*) did have killed (*b*) will have killed
(*c*) would kill (*d*) would have killed
(Hotel Management, 1995)

34. I cannot approve .... her conduct.
(*a*) of (*b*) with (*c*) by (*d*) to

35. I always like to eat .... of food.
(*a*) this kind (*b*) these kinds

(*c*) those kinds (*d*) this kinds

36. .... the rain stopped, the play had to be suspended. **(Central Excise, 1992)**
(*a*) Since (*b*) When
(*c*) Until (*d*) While

37. A man who connives .... the faults of his children is their worst enemy.
(*a*) with (*b*) at (*c*) of (*d*) on

38. Some people revel .... gossip.
(*a*) at (*b*) with (*c*) by (*d*) in

39. The officer warned me .... the office until five o' clock. **(S.S.C. 1993)**
(*a*) don't leave (*b*) to leave
(*c*) to not leave (*d*) not to leave

40. Even if it rains all day I will not be able to .... my journey.
(*a*) put by (*b*) put out
(*c*) put off (*d*) put away

41. Help yourself .... whatever you can use without wasting.
(*a*) with (*b*) to (*c*) by (*d*) on

42. There is an exception .... every rule.
(*a*) on (*b*) to (*c*) in (*d*) for
(Assistant Grade, 1995)

43. The storehouse was infested .... rats.
(*a*) by (*b*) of (*c*) with (*d*) in

44. Please distribute these sweets .... the children. **(Stenographers' Exam, 1991)**
(*a*) in (*b*) between
(*c*) amid (*d*) among

45. This custom seems to have originated .... an East European country.
(*a*) in (*b*) from (*c*) by (*d*) with

46. Madan .... the first prize in this competition.
(*a*) bore up (*b*) bore with
(*c*) bore out (*d*) bore away

47. In large cities people are cut .... from nature. **(Stenographers' Exam, 1994)**
(*a*) down (*b*) out (*c*) off (*d*) away

48. Your friend died .... over work.
(*a*) of (*b*) from
(*c*) due to (*d*) with

49. It is not easy to beat .... a swarm of wasps if they attack you.
(*a*) out (*b*) up (*c*) down (*d*) off

50. What a sensation it would cause if it .... now discovered that such a man had left behind a diary. **(M.B.A. 1990)**
(*a*) is (*b*) be (*c*) was (*d*) were

ANSWERS

1. (*d*)	**2.** (*b*)	**3.** (*a*)	**4.** (*c*)	**5.** (*a*)	**6.** (*d*)	**7.** (*b*)	**8.** (*d*)	**9.** (*a*)	**10.** (*b*)
11. (*d*)	**12.** (*b*)	**13.** (*c*)	**14.** (*a*)	**15.** (*d*)	**16.** (*b*)	**17.** (*a*)	**18.** (*c*)	**19.** (*b*)	**20.** (*c*)
21. (*c*)	**22.** (*d*)	**23.** (*c*)	**24.** (*c*)	**25.** (*c*)	**26.** (*c*)	**27.** (*b*)	**28.** (*c*)	**29.** (*a*)	**30.** (*d*)
31. (*c*)	**32.** (*b*)	**33.** (*d*)	**34.** (*a*)	**35.** (*a*)	**36.** (*c*)	**37.** (*b*)	**38.** (*d*)	**39.** (*d*)	**40.** (*c*)
41. (*b*)	**42.** (*b*)	**43.** (*c*)	**44.** (*d*)	**45.** (*a*)	**46.** (*d*)	**47.** (*c*)	**48.** (*a*)	**49.** (*d*)	**50.** (*d*)

PRACTICE SET 22

1. The passengers were very happy .... the friendly and warm treatment given to them. **(B.S.R.B. 1995)**
(*a*) by (*b*) about (*c*) from (*d*) to

2. The treatment given by him .... his subordinates was mean.
(*a*) of (*b*) for (*c*) towards
(*d*) to (*e*) about

3. He had developed prejudice .... the English.
(*a*) for (*b*) to
(*c*) against (*d*) towards

4. The higher you go, the more difficult it .... to breathe. **(S.S.C. 1993)**
(*a*) has become (*b*) becomes
(*c*) is becoming (*d*) became

5. He was sworn .... as the Chief Minister of the State yesterday.
(*a*) off (*b*) at (*c*) out (*d*) in

6. She yelled .... him and he hastily retreated.
(*a*) towards (*b*) at (*c*) to (*d*) on

7. The children were disappointed because they had hoped .... with us.
(*a*) to have gone (*b*) to go
(*c*) would have gone **(N.D.A. 1992)**

8. You must adapt yourself .... your new surroundings.
(*a*) towards (*b*) in (*c*) with (*d*) to

9. The city was plunged .... darkness due to a sudden power failure.
(*a*) through (*b*) to
(*c*) into (*d*) under

10. She stood .... Amit, but could not utter a single word for quite some time.
(*a*) for (*b*) to (*c*) about

(*d*) before (*e*) towards (B.S.R.B. 1994)

11. The Rajputs always fought .... the last man.
(*a*) to (*b*) till (*c*) until (*d*) upto

12. He is the friend .... I trust most.
(*a*) him (*b*) whom
(*c*) which (*d*) who
(Stenographers' Exam, 1992)

13. We should abide .... the rules of the institution.
(*a*) with (*b*) to (*c*) on (*d*) by

14. You must dispense .... his service.
(*a*) in (*b*) at (*c*) with (*d*) of
(Railways, 1993)

15. We waited at the bus stop .... the bus came.
(*a*) till (*b*) while
(*c*) until (*d*) unless

16. The telephone .... several times before I answered it. **(C.B.I. 1995)**
(*a*) would ring (*b*) had rung
(*c*) has rung (*d*) was ringing

17. I shall not desert him .... all the world.
(*a*) with (*b*) from (*c*) by (*d*) for
(Stenographers' Exam, 1995)

18. There .... both the challenge and the secret of success.
(*a*) lie (*b*) lay (*c*) lied (*d*) laid

19. We shall finish the work before he .... back.
(*a*) would come (*b*) comes
(*c*) will come (*d*) shall come

20. I bought a new car last year, but I .... my old car yet, so at present I have two cars. **(C.D.S. 1990)**
(*a*) could not sell (*b*) have not sold
(*c*) have sold (*d*) did not sell

21. He insists .... leaving immediately.
(*a*) over (*b*) at (*c*) for (*d*) on

22. No sooner did he go in .... he came out.
(*a*) then (*b*) when
(*c*) than (*d*) and
(Hotel Management, 1996)

23. Due to emergency conditions, the army was asked to ....
(*a*) stand out (*b*) stand up
(*c*) stand by (*d*) stand in

24. He is so bad-tempered that he has .... friends. **(S.S.C. 1995)**
(*a*) lot of (*b*) a lot of
(*c*) few (*d*) a few

25. Kamal walks as if he .... lame.
(*a*) is (*b*) had been
(*c*) was (*d*) were

26. It does not rest .... the collector to order his release.
(*a*) on (*b*) with (*c*) over (*d*) upon

27. Reena's marriage .... Rajesh was tumultous. **(C.B.I. 1993)**
(*a*) of (*b*) with
(*c*) between (*d*) to

28. If you live in a corrupt society, you cannot easily rise .... the prevailing corruption.
(*a*) beyond (*b*) upon
(*c*) above (*d*) over

29. I am glad .... the movie. **(N.D.A. 1993)**
(*a*) to have seen (*b*) to see
(*c*) had seen

30. The story developed .... a thrilling climax.
(*a*) out (*b*) up (*c*) over (*d*) into

31. That rule is applicable .... everyone.
(*a*) with (*b*) for (*c*) to (*d*) on
(Stenographers' Exam, 1995)

32. Everyone of us will have to atone .... his misdeeds.
(*a*) for (*b*) by (*c*) with (*d*) about

33. Never boast .... your wealth.
(*a*) for (*b*) about (*c*) in (*d*) of

34. Do you think you .... me somewhere before?
(*a*) saw (*b*) have seen
(*c*) were seeing (*d*) had seen

35. The examinee could guess .... the answer correctly. **(I. Tax, 1994)**
(*a*) with (*b*) of (*c*) about (*d*) at

36. We should always try to live .... the difficulties that we come across.
(*a*) over (*b*) through
(*c*) by (*d*) upon

37. He was reared up .... the foothills of Mussoorie.
(*a*) in (*b*) amidst (*c*) at (*d*) on

38. The stole away even though the guard was on a constant ....
(*a*) look for (*b*) look out
(*c*) look on (*d*) look after

39. My uncle decided to take .... and my sister to the market. **(U.D.C. 1995)**
(*a*) I (*b*) mine
(*c*) me (*d*) myself

40. A private secretary cannot have authority .... his boss.
(*a*) over (*b*) upon (*c*) on (*d*) for

41. Jayant plays football .... an experienced person.
(*a*) as (*b*) as though
(*c*) as of (*d*) as if
(Stenographers' Exam, 1994)

42. The rainy season has set ....
(*a*) on (*b*) off (*c*) out (*d*) in

43. He is being accused .... theft.
(*a*) to (*b*) for (*c*) of (*d*) about
(M.B.A. 1989)

44. Let's make .... our quarrel and be friends again.
(*a*) up (*b*) off (*c*) out (*d*) with

45. He has resigned himself .... fate.
(*a*) in (*b*) into (*c*) for (*d*) to
(R.R.B. 1993)

46. The ADM decided to resign when he was .... for promotion to DM.
(*a*) passed off (*b*) passed out
(*c*) passed over (*d*) passed by

47. He persisted .... saying so.
(*a*) on (*b*) in (*c*) with (*d*) over

48. A woman came in with a baby who, she said, ... a safety pin. **(C.B.I. 1995)**
(*a*) swallowed
(*b*) just swallowed
(*c*) had just swallowed
(*d*) was just swallowing

49. Cigarette smoking is injurious .... health.
(*a*) towards (*b*) for
(*c*) against (*d*) to

50. You must remember this lesson word .... word.
(*a*) by (*b*) to (*c*) on (*d*) for

ANSWERS

1. (*a*)	**2.** (*d*)	**3.** (*c*)	**4.** (*b*)	**5.** (*d*)	**6.** (*b*)	**7.** (*b*)	**8.** (*d*)	**9.** (*c*)	**10.** (*d*)
11. (*b*)	**12.** (*b*)	**13.** (*d*)	**14.** (*c*)	**15.** (*c*)	**16.** (*b*)	**17.** (*d*)	**18.** (*b*)	**19.** (*b*)	**20.** (*b*)
21. (*d*)	**22.** (*c*)	**23.** (*c*)	**24.** (*c*)	**25.** (*d*)	**26.** (*b*)	**27.** (*b*)	**28.** (*c*)	**29.** (*a*)	**30.** (*d*)
31. (*c*)	**32.** (*a*)	**33.** (*d*)	**34.** (*b*)	**35.** (*d*)	**36.** (*b*)	**37.** (*a*)	**38.** (*b*)	**39.** (*c*)	**40.** (*a*)
41. (*a*)	**42.** (*d*)	**43.** (*c*)	**44.** (*a*)	**45.** (*d*)	**46.** (*c*)	**47.** (*b*)	**48.** (*b*)	**49.** (*d*)	**50.** (*a*)

PRACTICE SET 23

1. The judge acquitted the prisoner .... the charge of murder.
(*a*) of (*b*) with (*c*) about (*d*) from
(Stenographers' Exam, 1995)

2 The habit of taking drugs has been growing .... the urban youth.
(*a*) within (*b*) in (*c*) from (*d*) upon

3. The horses stampeded and tore .... the street.
(*a*) off (*b*) out (*c*) up (*d*) down

4. An argument .... between the two friends. **(C.B.I. 1994)**
(*a*) sprang up (*b*) rose up
(*c*) broke out (*d*) broke in

5. They want to expel him for his anti-party activities .... the recent by-elections in the State.
(*a*) inside (*b*) during
(*c*) through (*d*) while

6. He has invited some of his friends .... tea.
(*a*) for (*b*) on (*c*) at (*d*) to

7. When I was a child, I .... to school everyday instead of going by cycle.
(*a*) walked (*b*) have been walking
(*c*) had walked (*d*) have walked
(S.C.R.A. 1994)

8. Geeta said that she had never .... a book she liked so much.
(*a*) saw into (*b*) come across
(*c*) held upon (*d*) viewed on

9. The examination will commence .... Monday.
(*a*) on (*b*) from (*c*) with (*d*) since

10. Nobody has come to see us .... we bought these fierce dogs. **(U.D.C. 1994)**
(*a*) when (*b*) till (*c*) since (*d*) for

11. He is busy .... his work.
(*a*) about (*b*) with (*c*) in (*d*) on

12. I .... for you all day long.
(*a*) had waited (*b*) have waited
(*c*) was waiting (*d*) have been waiting

13. He ran .... **(S.S.C. 1993)**
(*a*) quick (*b*) so quick
(*c*) quickly (*d*) so quickly

14. Indigenous products are now comparable .... imported goods in quality.
(*a*) with (*b*) than
(*c*) against (*d*) to

15. Kavita has no paper to write ....
(*a*) on (*b*) upon (*c*) at (*d*) over

16. In Bush, Saddam was up .... more than his match. **(Stenographers' Exam, 1994)**
(*a*) to (*b*) against
(*c*) into (*d*) for

17. Wickedness will draw .... punishment from a righteous God.
(*a*) in (*b*) out (*c*) down (*d*) near

18. I shall not come .... you need me.
(*a*) if not (*b*) without
(*c*) except (*d*) unless

19. The doctor advised him to go .... several medical tests. **(B.S.R.B. 1993)**
(*a*) under (*b*) about
(*c*) through (*d*) into

20. She is .... mother of two daughters.
(*a*) a (*b*) the
(*c*) an (*d*) None of these

21. If you persist in telling lies to me I shall sue you .... slander.
(*a*) with (*b*) to (*c*) for (*d*) on
(Section Officers' 1993)

22. Don't waste your time and energy in being jealous .... your rival's success.
(*a*) with (*b*) for (*c*) against (*d*) of

23. The waiter hasn't bought the coffee .... I've been here an hour already.
(*a*) still (*b*) yet (*c*) up (*d*) till
(Assistant Grade, 1994)

24. Infatuation .... wealth ruins a person.
(*a*) for (*b*) about
(*c*) towards (*d*) to

25. Your bad habits will .... your ruin.
(*a*) bring up (*b*) bring in
(*c*) bring about (*d*) bring forth

26. After a lot of argument I brought her .... my point of view.
(*a*) around (*b*) round
(*c*) upto (*d*) round to

27. The modern club is simply a more refined substitute .... the old fashioned tavern. **(B.Ed. 1994)**
(*a*) of (*b*) to (*c*) for (*d*) with

28. I prefer this book .... that.
(*a*) for (*b*) to (*c*) than (*d*) with

29. He sat .... the table to have food.
(*a*) at (*b*) upon (*c*) on (*d*) over

30. I have been working hard .... last year.
(*a*) in (*b*) from (*c*) for (*d*) since
(Stenographers' Exam, 1991)

31. She has been given a topic to write ....
(*a*) about (*b*) on (*c*) over (*d*) upon

32. His supporters began to .... and he was left alone.
(*a*) fall off (*b*) fall up
(*c*) fall out (*d*) fall away

33. She says she knows painting, but I don't think she .... **(Railways, 1995)**
(*a*) can (*b*) knew
(*c*) does (*d*) had known

34. No .... than twenty boys failed in a class of fifty.
(*a*) less (*b*) few
(*c*) fewer (*d*) little

35. I shall not do the work unless you .... me more money..
(*a*) pay (*b*) do not pay
(*c*) shall pay (*d*) won't pay

36. His parents are anxious .... his health.
(*a*) after (*b*) about (*c*) for (*d*) of

37. The minister flew .... the flooded areas in a helicopter. **(B.S.R.B. 1992)**
(*a*) about (*b*) in (*c*) over (*d*) along

38. He .... of his promise.
(*a*) backed down (*b*) backed up
(*c*) backed away (*d*) backed out

39. It has been their custom to shelter a stranger .... time immemorial.
(*a*) for (*b*) from (*c*) since (*d*) till

40. His name has become a synonym .... evil. **(M.B.A. 1990)**
(*a*) of (*b*) for (*c*) to (*d*) with

41. Mrs. Roy is a silly woman who books .... anyone who doesn't own a car.
(*a*) on (*b*) down
(*c*) down on (*d*) down off

42. If the evidence bears .... the charge, the man will be convicted.
(*a*) off (*b*) up (*c*) away (*d*) out

43. Hardly .... left the railway station when the train arrived. **(B.S.R.B. 1991)**
(*a*) he (*b*) did he
(*c*) he had (*d*) had he

44. Most of the youth in the present times are addicted .... drugs.
(*a*) for (*b*) to (*c*) in (*d*) about

45. Do not trouble yourself .... the worries and anxieties of life. **(S.S.C. 1994)**
(*a*) about (*b*) of (*c*) for (*d*) with

46. Can I entrust this task .... you?
(*a*) with (*b*) for (*c*) to (*d*) in

47. The queen was highly vain .... her beauty.
(*a*) of (*b*) from (*c*) over (*d*) for

48. Women can't .... a secret.
(*a*) keep under (*b*) keep up
(*c*) keep back (*d*) keep on

49. We should always stick to our decisions otherwise the people will mock .... us.
(*a*) over (*b*) at
(*c*) on (*d*) upon

50. Would you mind .... on the light?
(*a*) to switch (*b*) switching
(*c*) to switching (*d*) to be switching

ANSWERS

1. (*a*)	**2.** (*d*)	**3.** (*d*)	**4.** (*a*)	**5.** (*b*)	**6.** (*d*)	**7.** (*a*)	**8.** (*b*)	**9.** (*a*)	**10.** (*c*)
11. (*b*)	**12.** (*d*)	**13.** (*c*)	**14.** (*d*)	**15.** (*a*)	**16.** (*b*)	**17.** (*c*)	**18.** (*d*)	**19.** (*c*)	**20.** (*b*)
21. (*c*)	**22.** (*d*)	**23.** (*b*)	**24.** (*a*)	**25.** (*c*)	**26.** (*d*)	**27.** (*c*)	**28.** (*b*)	**29.** (*a*)	**30.** (*d*)
31. (*b*)	**32.** (*d*)	**33.** (*c*)	**34.** (*c*)	**35.** (*a*)	**36.** (*b*)	**37.** (*c*)	**38.** (*d*)	**39.** (*b*)	**40.** (*b*)
41. (*c*)	**42.** (*d*)	**43.** (*d*)	**44.** (*b*)	**45.** (*a*)	**46.** (*c*)	**47.** (*a*)	**48.** (*c*)	**49.** (*b*)	**50.** (*b*)

PRACTICE SET 24

1. He is willing to make a concession .... the demands of his employees.
(*a*) for (*b*) on (*c*) with (*d*) to
(B.S.R.B. 1996)

2. The teacher is angry .... Ravi.
(*a*) of (*b*) upon (*c*) with (*d*) on

3. I did .... I could which wasn't much.
(*a*) that (*b*) what
(*c*) how much (*d*) which
(Hotel Management, 1996)

4. They can't agree with each other .... anything.
(*a*) for (*b*) to (*c*) in
(*d*) on (*e*) about

5. The price situation continues to be worrisome .... strong growth in production.
(*a*) despite (*b*) instead of
(*c*) inspite (*d*) although

6. The new government took .... last year.
(*a*) after (*b*) over (*c*) out (*d*) up
(U.D.C. 1993)

7. All his decisions duly testify .... his truthfulness and honesty.
(*a*) to (*b*) about (*c*) of (*d*) for

8. You will have to catch the morning flight, so you .... better get ready. **(C.B.I. 1990)**
(*a*) would (*b*) may
(*c*) should (*d*) had

9. Please write me .... this address.
(*a*) to (*b*) at (*c*) on (*d*) upon

10. .... large city Bangalore has become in twenty years?
(*a*) What (*b*) What a
(*c*) How (*d*) How a

11. If I .... you I would not stand this humiliation. **(C.B.I. 1993)**
(*a*) be (*b*) were (*c*) am (*d*) was

12. The shopkeeper does not have the toys, I was looking ....
(*a*) at (*b*) for (*c*) about (*d*) to

13. The meeting was presided .... by the Prime Minister. **(S.S.C. 1992)**
(*a*) on (*b*) upon (*c*) up (*d*) over

14. My clothes are finer than ....
(*a*) my friend (*b*) a friend of mine
(*c*) my friend's (*d*) friend of mine

15. His master .... an explanation of his conduct.
(*a*) called off (*b*) called up
(*c*) called on (*d*) called for

16. The teacher warned him .... that type of lapse. **(Railways, 1993)**
(*a*) towards (*b*) of
(*c*) in (*d*) against

17. Put your signature .... blue ink.
(*a*) in (*b*) through
(*c*) by (*d*) with

18. I devote much of my time .... writing.
(*a*) in (*b*) to (*c*) on (*d*) at
(Stenographers' Exam. 1995)

19. The boss is unnecessarily insisting .... this point.
(*a*) for (*b*) at (*c*) in (*d*) on

20. He .... his camera on the railing.
(*a*) laid (*b*) lay (*c*) lain
(N.D.A. 1992)

21. The chief guest's wife gave .... the prizes.
(*a*) off (*b*) up (*c*) away (*d*) out

22 Arun reached home .... did not find his mother there.
(*a*) and (*b*) but
(*c*) yet (*d*) although

23. .... is the way to the public library?
(*a*) How (*b*) What
(*c*) Which (*d*) Where
(M.B.A. 1989)

24. He is hard .... these days.
(*a*) up (*b*) off (*c*) with (*d*) on

25. A poor man .... I knew nursed the orphan. **(I.Tax, 1994)**
(*a*) who (*b*) whom
(*c*) that (*d*) which

26. He decided to .... his affairs before leaving the country.
(*a*) call off (*b*) break up
(*c*) wind up (*d*) switch off

27. The sun is shining brightly, please .... the light. **(Hotel Management, 1993)**
(*a*) put on (*b*) put off
(*c*) put out (*d*) take off

28. The teacher advised Ritu to give more attention .... her studies.
(*a*) for (*b*) of (*c*) at (*d*) in

29. Everyone wants to .... for one's achievements. **(S.S.C. 1993)**
(*a*) be admired (*b*) admire
(*c*) being admired (*d*) be admiring

30. The employees demanded pay parity .... their counterparts in the Central Government.
(*a*) towards (*b*) as
(*c*) with (*d*) like

31. Everything he told me, I .... before.
(*a*) had heard (*b*) heard
(*c*) have heard **(N.D.A. 1993)**

32. A storm suddenly blew ....
(*a*) over (*b*) out (*c*) off (*d*) up

33. I shall take revenge .... you.
(*a*) at (*b*) on (*c*) with (*d*) from
(Stenographers' Exam, 1995)

34. After much inquiries, we found that the ship was bound .... Singapore.
(*a*) to (*b*) for
(*c*) towards (*d*) into

35. I cannot deprive him .... his rights.
(*a*) of (*b*) off (*c*) with (*d*) from

36. A new shop .... opened in the building, since last week. **(B.S.R.B. 1995)**
(*a*) will be (*b*) has been
(*c*) is (*d*) would be

37. She was compensated .... the loss of her belongings.
(*a*) over (*b*) for (*c*) against (*d*) at

38. The thief ran away .... he should be caught.
(*a*) unless (*b*) but
(*c*) lest (*d*) otherwise

39. Boys are usually dependent on their parents .... they earn enough money to support themselves.
(*a*) till (*b*) provided
(*c*) so (*d*) lest
(Stenographers' Exam, 1993)

40. He must .... his bad habits, if he wants to join us.
(*a*) give in (*b*) give off
(*c*) give away (*d*) give up

41. Just now I heard the news, it is so strange that you .... not believe it.
(*a*) will (*b*) could (*c*) might
(*d*) did (*e*) should **(B.S.R.B. 1994)**

42. I have absolutely no doubt .... the innocence of the accused.
(*a*) about (*b*) on (*c*) over (*d*) with

43. I took that person .... a thief.
(Railways, 1993)
(*a*) after (*b*) for (*c*) to (*d*) as

44. I will talk to him when ....
(*a*) he comes (*b*) he would come
(*c*) he has come (*d*) he will come

45. My first lesson .... forgiveness came from my father. **(C.D.S. 1993)**
(*a*) on (*b*) in
(*c*) about (*d*) upon

46. Do not put .... till tomorrow what you can do today.
(*a*) on (*b*) out (*c*) off (*d*) over

47. There was a understanding .... the two.
(*a*) in (*b*) between
(*c*) within (*d*) among

48. I have lived in Delhi ....
(*a*) since five years (*b*) for five years
(*c*) five years ago (*d*) for five years ago
(Hotel Management, 1996)

49. The pilot had been warned about the storm before he .... **(C.B.I. 1995)**
(*a*) took up (*b*) took away
(*c*) took off (*d*) took over

50. He has been entrusted .... this work.
(*a*) by (*b*) to (*c*) on (*d*) with

ANSWERS

1. (*d*)	**2.** (*c*)	**3.** (*b*)	**4.** (*d*)	**5.** (*a*)	**6.** (*b*)	**7.** (*a*)	**8.** (*d*)	**9.** (*c*)	**10.** (*b*)
11. (*b*)	**12.** (*b*)	**13.** (*d*)	**14.** (*c*)	**15.** (*d*)	**16.** (*d*)	**17.** (*a*)	**18.** (*b*)	**19** (*d*)	**20.** (*a*)
21. (*c*)	**22.** (*b*)	**23.** (*c*)	**24.** (*a*)	**25.** (*b*)	**26.** (*c*)	**27.** (*c*)	**28.** (*b*)	**29.** (*a*)	**30.** (*c*)
31. (*a*)	**32.** (*a*)	**33.** (*b*)	**34.** (*b*)	**35.** (*a*)	**36.** (*b*)	**37.** (*b*)	**38.** (*c*)	**39.** (*a*)	**40.** (*d*)
41. (*c*)	**42.** (*a*)	**43.** (*b*)	**44.** (*a*)	**45.** (*a*)	**46.** (*c*)	**47.** (*b*)	**48.** (*b*)	**49.** (*c*)	**50.** (*d*)

PRACTICE SET 25

1. While strolling on Janpath, I chanced to meet .... European.
(*a*) one (*b*) a (*c*) an (*d*) the
(Stenographers' Exam, 1995)

2. Her decent attitude compensates .... her short temper.
(*a*) for (*b*) with (*c*) off (*d*) to

3. He worked hard .... he should fail.
(*a*) else (*b*) except
(*c*) lest (*d*) if not

4. I am convinced .... his innocence.
(*a*) of (*b*) by (*c*) with (*d*) at
(S.S.C. 1995)

5. Ravi's father was annoyed with him as he could not .... his examination.
(*a*) get upon (*b*) get away
(*c*) get through (*d*) get on

6. I was informed on phone but no written confirmation .... so far.
(*a*) has received (*b*) has been received
(*c*) had received (*d*) had been received
(Hotel Management, 1995)

7. He often .... to Delhi on business trips.
(*a*) goes (*b*) has gone
(*c*) is going (*d*) has been going

8. Washing machines .... popular in India in the last ten years or so. **(C.B.I. 1994)**
(*a*) became (*b*) are become
(*c*) have become (*d*) are becoming

9. Finding fault .... others is a bad habit.
(*a*) in (*b*) with (*c*) of (*d*) about

10. I arrived at the decision in consultation .... my colleagues.
(*a*) to (*b*) by (*c*) with (*d*) about

11. In the fierce attack, the enemies were completely wiped ....
(*a*) out (*b*) off (*c*) away (*d*) over
(Stenographer's Exam, 1994)

12. Any successful manager should establish a feeling of confidence .... his clients.
(*a*) in (*b*) among
(*c*) with (*d*) to

13. True happiness consists .... giving pleasure to others. **(U.D.C. 1994)**
(*a*) for (*b*) by (*c*) in (*d*) of

14. The meeting was presided .... by the Prime Minister.
(*a*) on (*b*) over (*c*) at (*d*) upon

15. He is definitely ....
(*a*) wrongly (*b*) in wrong
(*c*) in a wrong (*d*) in the wrong

16. She came .... with me to see the circus.
(*a*) along (*b*) off
(*c*) after (*d*) across
(B.S.R.B. 1991)

17. I saw a .... of wolves roaming around the forest.
(*a*) flock (*b*) group
(*c*) herd (*d*) pack

18. You will have to work very hard to make .... the time you wasted yesterday.
(*a*) for (*b*) up for
(*c*) up (*d*) up with

19. The police has been looking for him .... four weeks. **(S.S.C. 1993)**
(*a*) since (*b*) till
(*c*) during (*d*) for

20. We should always side .... those who are true.
(*a*) together (*b*) to
(*c*) for (*d*) with

21. The passengers are cautioned .... pickpockets.
(*a*) to (*b*) against (*c*) for (*d*) about

22. .... knowledge is a dangerous thing.
(*a*) Less (*b*) Little
(*c*) A little (*d*) The little

23. Do not hanker .... worldly pleasures.
(*a*) after (*b*) about
(*c*) for (*d*) towards
(Assistant Grade, 1995)

24. She died because they did not immediately .... a doctor.
(*a*) call up (*b*) call for
(*c*) call in (*d*) call at

25. Do not take leave .... me; I will be left alone.
(*a*) by (*b*) of (*c*) off (*d*) from

26. The city was kept .... night curfew for for several days. **(B.S.R.B. 1993)**
(*a*) on (*b*) at (*c*) under (*d*) over

27. Give .... answer to this question.
(*a*) an (*b*) a
(*c*) the (*d*) None of these

28. Always attend .... what your teachers say.
(*a*) on (*b*) to (*c*) over (*d*) for

29. He is too dull .... the problem
(*a*) solves (*b*) to solve
(*c*) solving (*d*) to solving
(Stenographers' Exam, 1994)

30. The speaker drew the attention of the audience .... the burning issue.
(*a*) to (*b*) towards
(*c*) on (*d*) into

31. It's nine o'clock .... and I'm still at breakfast.
(*a*) till (*b*) yet (*c*) so (*d*) already

32. Although he is blind, he is very fast .... calculations. **(B.S.R.B. 1992)**
(*a*) in (*b*) with (*c*) at (*d*) about

33. Only about 50 percent of the children have been covered .... the immunisation programme.
(*a*) by (*b*) through
(*c*) in (*d*) against

34. He confided his troubles .... his friend.
(*a*) in (*b*) to (*c*) with (*d*) by

35. The lights .... just as we sat down to watch the movie on television.
(*a*) put out (*b*) gave off (*c*) went off
(*d*) shut out (*e*) blew down

36. The officer is quite popular .... his juniors.
(*a*) between (*b*) with
(*c*) among (*d*) in

37. He did not go .... the whole book before giving his opinion about it.
(*a*) through (*b*) into
(*c*) over (*d*) with
(B.S.R.B. 1995)

38. Sometimes it is difficult to deal .... a problem child.
(*a*) with (*b*) in (*c*) at (*d*) out

39. He has aptitude .... such a work.
(*a*) of (*b*) in (*c*) for
(*d*) to (*e*) at

40. She .... the two candles in one breath.
(*a*) put down (*b*) put up
(*c*) put away (*d*) put out
(C.B.I. 1994)

41. More often than not the programmes of family fail to take ....
(*a*) off (*b*) over (*c*) up (*d*) upon

42. The CRPF men swung into action and cordoned .... the area.
(*a*) over (*b*) off (*c*) out (*d*) of
(Stenographers' Exam, 1991)

43. The idea of a balanced diet is very difficult to .... to anyone who knows nothing about food values.
(*a*) make over (*b*) put across
(*c*) take in (*d*) put through

44. The celebrations went .... very well.
(*a*) on (*b*) over (*c*) off (*d*) up

45. All these years I .... him to keep away from such people, but he did not listen to me.
(*a*) warned (*b*) have been warning
(*c*) had warned (*d*) had been warning
(Hotel Management, 1995)

46. Ajeet was annoyed .... his wife.
(*a*) upon (*b*) on (*c*) with (*d*) at

47. He was so badly wounded that there was .... hope of his recovery.
(*a*) little (*b*) a little
(*c*) the little (*d*) less

48. When my uncle entered the house, I .... writing a letter. **(M.B.A. 1990)**
(*a*) was (*b*) would be
(*c*) had been (*d*) should be

49. A student who perseveres .... his studies is certain to get good marks.
(*a*) with (*b*) at (*c*) in (*d*) into

50. This sort of situation will not be allowed to last .... long.
(*a*) till (*b*) for (*c*) up (*d*) until

ANSWERS

1. (*b*)	**2.** (*a*)	**3.** (*c*)	**4.** (*a*)	**5.** (*c*)	**6.** (*b*)	**7.** (*a*)	**8.** (*c*)	**9.** (*b*)	**10.** (*c*)
11. (*a*)	**12.** (*a*)	**13.** (*c*)	**14.** (*b*)	**15.** (*d*)	**16.** (*a*)	**17.** (*d*)	**18.** (*b*)	**19.** (*d*)	**20.** (*d*)
21. (*b*)	**22.** (*c*)	**23.** (*a*)	**24.** (*c*)	**25.** (*b*)	**26.** (*c*)	**27.** (*a*)	**28.** (*b*)	**29.** (*b*)	**30.** (*a*)
31. (*d*)	**32.** (*c*)	**33.** (*a*)	**34.** (*b*)	**35.** (*c*)	**36.** (*b*)	**37.** (*a*)	**38.** (*a*)	**39.** (*c*)	**40.** (*d*)
41. (*a*)	**42.** (*b*)	**43.** (*b*)	**44.** (*c*)	**45.** (*d*)	**46.** (*c*)	**47.** (*a*)	**48.** (*a*)	**49.** (*b*)	**50.** (*b*)

PRACTICE SET 26

1. The jailer saw .... the prisoner's scheme. **(Central Excise, 1994)**
(*a*) to (*b*) through
(*c*) about (*d*) into

2. His company is greatly sought ....
(*a*) for (*b*) at (*c*) after (*d*) out

3. It .... since early morning.
(*a*) will rain (*b*) is raining
(*c*) rained (*d*) has been raining
(Stenographers' Exam, 1993)

4. We built the raft .... to hold us.
(*a*) very strong (*b*) too strong
(*c*) strong enough

5. We must wait until the invigilator .... the question papers.
(*a*) would give (*b*) given
(*c*) will give (*d*) gives
(Hotel Management, 1991)

6. Because of his rude behaviour, nobody can get .... with him.
(*a*) across (*b*) along

(*c*) about (*d*) over

7. The ruling party will have to put its own house .... order.
(*a*) into (*b*) to (*c*) in (*d*) on
(Stenographers' Exam, 1995)

8. The new education policy provides a useful .... for the planners to remove illiteracy. **(C.B.I. 1995)**
(*a*) break-in (*b*) breakaway
(*c*) break up (*d*) breakthrough

9. He is definitely elder .... me.
(*a*) to (*b*) than (*c*) of (*d*) by

10. After the advice of his father, he was reconciled .... his wife. **(C.B.I. 1993)**
(*a*) into (*b*) by (*c*) with (*d*) to

11. He had to wait until his sister's train arrived .... to take her to his house.
(*a*) as much as (*b*) as if
(*c*) so much so (*d*) so as

12. The doctor tried both penicillin and sulphanilamide; the penicillin proved to be the .... effective drug. **(N.D.A. 1992)**
(*a*) very (*b*) more (*c*) most

13. It will take five minutes to walk .... the bridge.
(*a*) across (*b*) through
(*c*) about (*d*) along

14. However honest he ...., I do not trust him. **(S.S.C. 1995)**
(*a*) is (*b*) may be
(*c*) might be (*d*) could be

15. He doesn't know how to look .... a word in the dictionary.
(*a*) on (*b*) up (*c*) to (*d*) for

16. Sometimes we have to put .... with something irksome or unpleasant.
(*a*) on (*b*) in (*c*) up (*d*) off

17. He became the Governor of a Province .... **(Stenographers' Exam, 1995)**
(*a*) little by little (*b*) by and large
(*c*) in course of time (*d*) at times

18. The performance passed .... peacefully.
(*a*) off (*b*) over (*c*) out (*d*) away

19. We are now confident .... winning the match.
(*a*) to (*b*) in (*c*) of
(*d*) into (*e*) towards

20. .... the rain stopped, the play had to be suspended. **(Central Excise, 1993)**
(*a*) While (*b*) Until
(*c*) When (*d*) Since

21. Italy has a lot to offer India in her efforts to leap .... the 21st century.
(*a*) to (*b*) in (*c*) into (*d*) over

22. Apparently he was feeling .... about his bad luck. **(N.D.A. 1993)**
(*a*) anger (*b*) angry (*c*) angrily

23. This sort of situation will not be allowed to last .... long.
(*a*) until (*b*) up (*c*) till (*d*) for

24. She .... her grandfather; she has blue eyes. **(Hotel Management, 1996)**
(*a*) takes in (*b*) takes to
(*c*) takes after (*d*) takes on

25. Let me acquaint him .... the topic
(*a*) about (*b*) with
(*c*) to (*d*) of

26. Everyone in this universe is accountable to God .... his action.
(*a*) for (*b*) of (*c*) about (*d*) against

27. The inspector of excise has to conduct regular checks and .... to visit the unit at least once a day. **(S.S.C. 1993)**
(*a*) is required (*b*) requires
(*c*) is requiring (*d*) required

28. There was nothing he could do .... wait.
(*a*) than (*b*) except
(*c*) and (*d*) otherwise

29. He has been recently discharged .... the army. **(Stenographers' Exam, 1992)**
(*a*) off (*b*) by (*c*) to (*d*) from

30. A burglar broke .... his house last night.
(*a*) up (*b*) out (*c*) into (*d*) down

31. The British enjoyed monopoly .... textiles.
(*a*) in (*b*) with (*c*) of (*d*) over

32. I wish I .... taller. **(Railways, 1993)**
(*a*) would be (*b*) could be
(*c*) had been (*d*) were

33. He prayed that his brother .... safely.
(*a*) arrived (*b*) may arrive
(*c*) might arrive (*d*) would arrive

34. When I pay him tomorrow, he .... received everything I owe him.
(*a*) might have (*b*) may have
(*c*) will have (*d*) might had
(*e*) must have **(B.S.R.B. 1996)**

35. The judge ordered that the criminal be put .... death.
(*a*) under (*b*) at
(*c*) through (*d*) to

36. By this time next year, Shashi .... her final examination.
(*a*) shall take (*b*) will have taken
(*c*) will take (*d*) would take

37. He .... for this company since 1972.
(*a*) is working (*b*) had worked
(*c*) worked (*d*) has been working
(S.S.C. 1994)

38. He is a postmaster .... a cock and bull story whenever his boss tries to pull him up for his negligence. **(N.D.A. 1993)**
(*a*) pulling out (*b*) hitting upon
(*c*) dishing out (*d*) cooking up

39. Deepak is negligent .... attending his classes.
(*a*) in (*b*) to
(*c*) about (*d*) towards

40. I have booked my ticket through the agent .... I know is very efficient.
(*a*) whom (*b*) which
(*c*) who (*d*) that

41. The police .... on duty.
(*a*) are (*b*) is (*c*) was (*d*) have
(Stenographers' Exam, 1993)

42. We are looking forward .... your cooperation.
(*a*) for (*b*) after (*c*) to (*d*) about

43. The committee has to submit its report .... two months.
(*a*) during (*b*) within
(*c*) until (*d*) till

44. He stands .... what he has done.
(*a*) upon (*b*) for (*c*) on (*d*) at

45. Savita kept talking loudly oblivious .... the fact that it was the college library and not the students' common room.
(*a*) regarding (*b*) of
(*c*) about (*d*) for **(C.B.I. 1993)**

46. Modern science began .... the influence of Copernicus.
(*a*) from (*b*) with (*c*) by (*d*) under

47. Make haste .... we shall miss the train.
(*a*) either (*b*) or (*c*) else **(M.B.A. 1989)**

48. If he .... hard, he would have passed the examination.
(*a*) worked (*b*) could work
(*c*) had worked (*d*) should work

49. The doctor advised him to take care .... his health.
(*a*) of (*b*) for (*c*) about (*d*) with

50. The dispute can be easily settled between you and .... **(M.B.A. 1990)**
(*a*) we (*b*) I (*c*) me (*d*) myself

ANSWERS

1. (*b*)	**2.** (*c*)	**3.** (*d*)	**4.** (*c*)	**5.** (*d*)	**6.** (*b*)	**7.** (*c*)	**8.** (*d*)	**9.** (*a*)	**10.** (*d*)
11. (*d*)	**12.** (*b*)	**13.** (*a*)	**14.** (*b*)	**15.** (*d*)	**16.** (*c*)	**17.** (*c*)	**18.** (*a*)	**19.** (*c*)	**20.** (*b*)
21. (*c*)	**22.** (*b*)	**23.** (*d*)	**24.** (*c*)	**25.** (*b*)	**26.** (*a*)	**27.** (*a*)	**28.** (*b*)	**29.** (*d*)	**30.** (*c*)
31. (*a*)	**32.** (*d*)	**33.** (*c*)	**34.** (*c*)	**35.** (*d*)	**36.** (*b*)	**37.** (*d*)	**38.** (*d*)	**39.** (*a*)	**40.** (*c*)
41. (*a*)	**42.** (*c*)	**43.** (*b*)	**44.** (*b*)	**45.** (*b*)	**46.** (*d*)	**47.** (*b*)	**48.** (*c*)	**49.** (*a*)	**50.** (*b*)

PRACTICE SET 27

1. More than twenty years have now passed .... I had my first flight.
(*a*) after (*b*) while
(*c*) since (*d*) when
(Stenographers' Exam, 1995)

2. These days everybody complains .... corruption in public life.
(*a*) for (*b*) of
(*c*) about (*d*) against

3. How long will our supplies .... ?
(*a*) hold out (*b*) hold on
(*c*) hold up (*d*) hold in

4. I hate sitting .... him as he always smells of garlic.
(*a*) along (*b*) beside
(*c*) besides (*d*) at
(Hotel Management, 1993)

5. It is better to send .... the doctor.
(*a*) upon (*b*) in (*c*) for (*d*) to

6. The spirit of morality pervades .... all the poems of Wordsworth.
(*a*) from (*b*) of (*c*) off (*d*) through

7. This work ought to have .... long ago.
(*a*) done (*b*) had done
(*c*) been done (*d*) being done
(Stenographers' Exam, 1991)

8. He is trying his best to keep .... the reputation of his family.
(*a*) up (*b*) to (*c*) on (*d*) over

9. Ever since his parents died, his uncle has .... all his needs. **(I. Tax, 1993)**
(*a*) seen to (*b*) seen off
(*c*) seen by (*d*) seen through

10. A meeting of opposition leaders was held recently to sort .... differences on policy matters.
(*a*) off (*b*) up (*c*) out (*d*) about

11. It should be the aim of every educated Indian to see that as .... as possible people become literate. **(U.D.C. 1994)**
(*a*) few (*b*) most
(*c*) many (*d*) much

12. They found him well qualified .... the post.
(*a*) for (*b*) to (*c*) about (*d*) of

13. The old man could not remember where he .... his money. **(Railways, 1995)**
(*a*) deposits (*b*) is depositing

(*c*) will deposit (*d*) had deposited

14. The title of 'Bharat Ratna' was conferred .... him at a colourful ceremony.
(*a*) at (*b*) over (*c*) to (*d*) on

15. The robbers were arrested and .... prison yesterday.
(*a*) taken to (*b*) taken into
(*c*) brought in (*d*) brought into
(Stenographers' Exam, 1994)

16. The blind man bumped .... my brother.
(*a*) into (*b*) at (*c*) with (*d*) by

17. She sings .... her mother does.
(*a*) like (*b*) as (*c*) as if (*d*) so as

18. By trying to take revenge, a man tries to get .... his enemy. **(C.B.I. 1994)**
(*a*) stronger than (*b*) even with
(*c*) equal with (*d*) better than

19. He was leaning .... the wall.
(*a*) on (*b*) towards
(*c*) with (*d*) against

20. I absolve you .... all blames.
(*a*) with (*b*) for (*c*) of (*d*) from

21. .... adequate pre-emptive action to avert this tragedy?
(*a*) Would you not be taking
(*b*) Would you have not taken
(*c*) Shall you not have taken
(*d*) Should you not have taken
(Hotel Management, 1995)

22. The leaders hoped that the two countries could profit .... each other's experience.
(*a*) from (*b*) by (*c*) on (*d*) through

23. He is given .... bad habits.
(*a*) for (*b*) in (*c*) up (*d*) to

24. Do not quarrel .... your neighbours.
(*a*) from (*b*) by (*c*) with (*d*) against
(B.S.R.B. 1992)

25. Had she known about it, she .... have stayed longer.
(*a*) would (*b*) might
(*c*) may (*d*) should

26. The people, who depend .... others, can never prosper in life.
(*a*) on (*b*) over (*c*) at (*d*) upon

27. They put his success .... to sheer hard work. **(S.S.C. 1993)**
(*a*) down (*b*) up (*c*) upon (*d*) on

28. .... what I know of him, I barely trust him.
(*a*) After (*b*) About
(*c*) From (*d*) Beyond

29. When I pay him tomorrow, he .... every thing I owe him.
(*a*) has received (*b*) will have received
(*c*) would receive (*d*) would have received

30. I told him not to be afraid .... his father. **(B.S.R.B. 1993)**
(*a*) to (*b*) of (*c*) with (*d*) from

31. The opposite forces went on fighting .... the night.
(*a*) in (*b*) during
(*c*) about (*d*) through

32. The opposition to re-marriage of widows blew .... in due course of time.
(*a*) off (*b*) out (*c*) up (*d*) over

33. The young politician .... with his party and decided to contest the election as an independent candidate.
(*a*) fell down (*b*) fell out
(*c*) fell through (*d*) fell in
(Stenographers' Exam, 1991)

34. When is the wedding coming .... ?
(*a*) on (*b*) up (*c*) of (*d*) off

35. While travelling to Bombay, I ran .... a very old friend of mine.
(*a*) into (*b*) against
(*c*) up (*d*) across

36. It .... too cold to go out last night, so we stayed at home. **(C.B.I. 1987)**
(*a*) had been (*b*) has been
(*c*) was (*d*) used to be

37. You should never laugh .... the poor.
(*a*) on (*b*) at (*c*) over (*d*) for

38. I cannot bear ....
(*a*) your separation (*b*) separation of you
(*c*) your's separation
(*d*) separation from you

39. We will be late if we .... not leave now.
(*a*) do (*b*) will (*c*) shall (*d*) did
(B.S.R.B. 1991)

40. The lady takes pride .... her beauty.
(*a*) over (*b*) of (*c*) in (*d*) at

41. You .... better wait for your turn.
(*a*) could (*b*) had
(*c*) should (*d*) may

42. .... work hard, you won't succeed.
(*a*) Unless you don't (*b*) Unless you
(*c*) Unless you do not (*d*) Lest you
(Railways, 1995)

43. The weather was .... than any she had ever experienced.
(*a*) worse (*b*) the worse
(*c*) worst (*d*) the worst

44. If only he .... told us the truth in the first place, things wouldn't have gone wrong. **(C.B.I. 1994)**
(*a*) has (*b*) would have
(*c*) had (*d*) should have

45. You will leave India before two months ....
(*a*) would pass (*b*) have passed
(*c*) will pass (*d*) would have passed

46. There were not more than .... supporters of this proposal in the Parliament. **(M.B.A. 1990)**
(*a*) a little (*b*) few

(c) a few (d) the few

47. He was not looking .... the blackboard when the teacher was writing on it.
(a) at (b) to (c) on (d) upto

48. After the Mahabharata war, the Pandavas renounced worldly life and made .... the Himalayas.
(a) for (b) to
(c) towards (d) into

49. The more things a man is ashamed .... the more respectable he is considered.
(a) with (b) by (c) of (d) for

50. Don't interfere .... her in this work.
(a) in (b) with (c) by (d) to

ANSWERS

1. (c)	**2.** (b)	**3.** (a)	**4.** (b)	**5.** (c)	**6.** (d)	**7.** (c)	**8.** (a)	**9.** (a)	**10.** (c)
11. (c)	**12.** (a)	**13.** (d)	**14.** (d)	**15.** (a)	**16.** (a)	**17.** (b)	**18.** (b)	**19.** (d)	**20.** (c)
21. (d)	**22.** (a)	**23.** (d)	**24.** (c)	**25.** (a)	**26.** (d)	**27.** (d)	**28.** (c)	**29.** (b)	**30.** (b)
31. (d)	**32.** (d)	**33.** (b)	**34.** (d)	**35.** (a)	**36.** (c)	**37.** (b)	**38.** (d)	**39.** (a)	**40.** (c)
41. (b)	**42.** (b)	**43.** (a)	**44.** (c)	**45.** (b)	**46.** (c)	**47.** (a)	**48.** (a)	**49.** (c)	**50.** (b)

PRACTICE SET 28

1. History records seventeen incursions of Sultan Mahmood .... India.
(a) against (b) into (c) upon (d) on
(Translator's Exam, 1994)

2. Your statement is replete .... contradictions.
(a) by (b) of (c) in (d) with

3. The man is blind .... one eye.
(a) of (b) by (c) in (d) from

4. One is struck by the realisation of being one with nature ; a union of mind .... body. **(Stenographers' Exam, 1993)**
(a) for (b) in (c) and (d) or

5. He was surprised .... the news.
(a) over (b) at (c) by (d) with

6. She smiled .... my words. **(M.B.A. 1989)**
(a) at (b) upon (c) on (d) over

7. The President will be provided .... all the facilities he is entitled to.
(a) of (b) to (c) by (d) with

8. The thief .... all the money. **(C.B.I. 1995)**
(a) made good (b) made do with
(c) made up (d) made off with

9. It is difficult for me to part .... my belongings.
(a) from (b) of (c) with (d) off

10. If you had informed me, I .... cautious.
(a) would be (b) had been
(c) would have been (d) could have been

11. The dacoits set the locality .... fire.
(a) on (b) upon (c) to (d) at

12. I congratulate you .... your success.
(a) in (b) at (c) on (d) for
(S.S.C. 1993)

13. .... I in your place, I would keep quiet.
(a) Would (b) Am (c) Was (d) Were

14. .... you do not work you cannot succeed. **(Railways, 1993)**
(a) If (b) Unless
(c) Till (d) Until

15. He ran as quickly as he ....
(a) can (b) could have
(c) could (d) would

16. The father advised his son to give .... bad company.
(a) away (b) up (c) out (d) off

17. The sun .... at six this morning.
(a) rose (b) raised
(c) arose (d) aroused
(Stenographers' Exam, 1994)

18. He was sorry .... what he had done.
(a) over (b) for (c) at (d) of

19. You're coming to the movie, ... ?
(a) can't you (b) aren't you
(c) won't you (d) isn't it
(Stenographers' Exam, 1995)

20. He was charged .... murder and brought to trial.
(a) by (b) for (c) of (d) with

21. He has put .... the meeting.
(a) up (b) off (c) away (d) out

22. He is being considered .... senior managerial position. **(B.S.R.B. 1994)**
(a) of (b) to (c) for
(d) towards (e) by

23. This is .... book I was looking for.
(a) a (b) an
(c) the (d) None of these

24. The High Court .... the death sentence of the prisoner. **(C.D.S. 1990)**
(a) set down (b) set upon
(c) set about (d) set aside

25. .... he invited me, I would have gone to the party.
(*a*) Unless (*b*) Had (*c*) If (*d*) Although

26. I object .... waiting. You are always late for appointments.
(*a*) to (*b*) to being kept
(*c*) to keep (*d*) to keeping
(Hotel Management, 1996)

27. He died .... inches repenting his crimes.
(*a*) for (*b*) by (*c*) in (*d*) to

28. Have you finished reading the book? No I'm .... in the middle of it.
(*a*) already (*b*) yet
(*c*) still (*d*) till

29. Baggage can be covered .... loss or accident during travel. **(C.B.I. 1993)**
(*a*) against (*b*) for
(*c*) along (*d*) with

30. His father was 45 when he ....
(*a*) has died (*b*) had died
(*c*) died (*d*) was dying

31. I suggest that the meeting .... postponed. **(N.D.A. 1993)**
(*a*) is (*b*) would be (*c*) be

32. An exhibition .... the new trends in lighting opened here today.
(*a*) to (*b*) on (*c*) of (*d*) for

33. The wood always .... on water.
(*a*) float (*b*) was floating
(*c*) floats (*d*) floated
(Stenographers' Exam, 1995)

34. Have complete trust .... God.
(*a*) upon (*b*) in (*c*) on (*d*) for

35. He does not like .... better.
(*a*) me doing (*b*) mine doing
(*c*) my doing (*d*) myself doing

36. By this time next year Rajesh will .... his University Degree in Marketing Management. **(B.S.R.B. 1996)**
(*a*) has taken (*b*) had taken
(*c*) have took (*d*) have taken

37. On my return from holiday, I had to .... with a lot of work.
(*a*) make do (*b*) catch up
(*c*) make up (*d*) catch on

38. There being no evidence against him, he was acquitted .... the charge.
(*a*) off (*b*) with (*c*) of (*d*) from
(S.S.C. 1995)

39. No buses are playing .... the road as the transport workers are on strike.
(*a*) on (*b*) upon (*c*) over (*d*) off

40. Hardly had he arrived .... it started raining. **(U.D.C. 1995)**
(*a*) after (*b*) than
(*c*) when (*d*) before

41. He was told not to worry .... the matter.
(*a*) with (*b*) for
(*c*) about (*d*) of

42. My friend has a strange habit of turning .... at odd hours. **(Railways, 1993)**
(*a*) over (*b*) up (*c*) down (*d*) out

43. You should adhere .... your principles.
(*a*) upon (*b*) on (*c*) with (*d*) to

44. Portia compared Mercy .... the gentle rain from heaven.
(*a*) to (*b*) by (*c*) with (*d*) from

45. Man cannot live .... bread alone.
(*a*) except (*b*) by
(*c*) without (*d*) with
(Stenographers' Exam, 1993)

46. Two cars collided .... each other near the school.
(*a*) into (*b*) over
(*c*) with (*d*) of

47. She comes .... a noble family.
(a) of (b) from
(c) off (d) out of

48. By air you .... almost half the distance to Bombay before I reach back home by my car. **(Hotel Management, 1995)**
(*a*) will cover (*b*) shall have covered
(*c*) would cover (*d*) would have covered

49. Hearing of his mother's illness, he at once started .... Kanpur.
(*a*) to (*b*) towards
(*c*) for (*d*) upto

50. .... works of reference are so valuable as the Encyclopaedia Britannica.
(*a*) Few (*b*) A few
(*c*) The few (*d*) Fewer
(C.B.I. 1995)

ANSWERS

1. (*b*)	**2.** (*a*)	**3.** (*a*)	**4.** (*c*)	**5.** (*b*)	**6.** (*a*)	**7.** (*d*)	**8.** (*d*)	**9.** (*c*)	**10.** (*c*)
11. (*a*)	**12.** (*c*)	**13.** (*d*)	**14.** (*a*)	**15.** (*c*)	**16.** (*b*)	**17.** (*a*)	**18.** (*b*)	**19.** (*b*)	**20.** (*d*)
21. (*b*)	**22.** (*c*)	**23.** (*c*)	**24.** (*d*)	**25.** (*b*)	**26.** (*b*)	**27.** (*b*)	**28.** (*c*)	**29.** (*a*)	**30.** (*c*)
31. (*c*)	**32.** (*b*)	**33.** (*c*)	**34.** (*b*)	**35.** (*c*)	**36.** (*d*)	**37.** (*b*)	**38.** (*c*)	**39.** (*a*)	**40.** (*c*)
41. (*c*)	**42.** (*b*)	**43.** (*d*)	**44.** (*a*)	**45.** (*b*)	**46.** (*c*)	**47.** (*a*)	**48.** (*b*)	**49.** (*c*)	**50.** (*a*)

PRACTICE SET 29

1. Because of the heavy rain, the match was .... **(Stenographers' Exam, 1995)**
(*a*) broken off (*b*) fallen off
(*c*) called off (*d*) set aside

2. He takes pains to hide his feelings, but at very unguarded moment the mark drops .... and reveals him to the most superficial observation.
(*a*) off (*b*) down (*c*) out (*d*) away

3. Hundreds of people die .... malaria in villages.
(*a*) from (*b*) by (*c*) with (*d*) of

4. Joseph introduced me .... his mother as the best batsman. **(C.B.I. 1994)**
(*a*) to (*b*) by (*c*) for (*d*) with

5. The painter climbed .... the ladder to paint the high wall of the building.
(*a*) on (*b*) upon (*c*) up (*d*) with

6. It was indeed unreasonable .... him to resign from this job.
(*a*) for (*b*) from (*c*) of (*d*) with

7. Mr. Manmohan's property was divided .... his daughter and sons.
(*a*) amidst (*b*) among
(*c*) between (*d*) in
(Stenographers' Exam, 1994)

8. You should not be angry .... your son.
(*a*) with (*b*) to (*c*) on (*d*) at

9. Since we decided to fight to the last, we were sure to prevail .... the enemy.
(*a*) above (*b*) over (*c*) with (*d*) upon

10. As the festival approaches, the number of customers .... **(S.S.C. 1993)**
(*a*) will be increased (*b*) increases
(*c*) will have increased (*d*) is increasing

11. Ten scholarships were competed ....
(*a*) for (*b*) of (*c*) with (*d*) against

12. She .... from the crowd because of her height and flaming red hair.
(*a*) stood by (*b*) stood off
(*c*) stood up (*d*) stood out
(S.C.R.A. 1994)

13. If I take a state roadways bus, I'll get late, ... **(Section Officers' 1993)**
(*a*) is it? (*b*) isn't it?
(*c*) will I? (*d*) won't I?

14. Why did you tear .... a page from my notebook?
(*a*) up (*b*) off (*c*) out (*d*) outside

15. He grew tired of hard work and began to despair .... success.
(*a*) of (*b*) with (*c*) for (*d*) about

16. Ajit promised me that he would come .... did not turn up. **(B.S.R.B. 1991)**
(*a*) and (*b*) though
(*c*) but (*d*) still

17. Your pay is .... for your work.
(*a*) high enough (*b*) enough high
(*c*) too highly (*d*) much high

18. The celebrations went .... very well.
(*a*) up (*b*) over (*c*) of (*d*) off
(Stenographers' Exam, 1991)

19. Even after hearing him for a fairly long time, we were at a loss to know what he was driving ....
(*a*) on (*b*) to (*c*) at (*d*) after

20. You should try to .... your expenditure.
(*a*) cut out (*b*) cut down
(*c*) cut off (*d*) cut under

21. There was nobody to attend .... the complaints of the customers.
(*a*) at (*b*) over (*c*) to (*d*) with
(B.S.R.B. 1993)

22. It took him a lot of time to arrive .... the conclusion.
(*a*) to (*b*) at (*c*) on (*d*) upon

23. He .... in the middle of his speech.
(*a*) broke down (*b*) broke out
(*c*) broke up (*d*) broke into

24. I take interest .... film making.
(*a*) for (*b*) with (*c*) to (*d*) in
(Railways, 1991)

25. When I met her last year, she .... for five years.
(*a*) was married (*b*) had been married
(*c*) had married (*d*) would have married

26. Many developing countries are moving .... privatisation and economic liberation.
(*a*) into (*b*) beyond
(*c*) towards (*d*) against

27. It was indeed unreasonable .... him to leave this job and start business.
(*a*) of (*b*) with (*c*) in (*d*) upon
(B.S.R.B. 1992)

28. This is the road to go ....
(*a*) through (*b*) to
(*c*) by (*d*) with

29. A great writer adopts a style appropriate .... his subject.
(*a*) with (*b*) for (*c*) about (*d*) to

30. The English schemed to continue their rule in India by playing off one community .... the other.
(*a*) with (*b*) against
(*c*) upon (*d*) before
(Assistant Grade, 1994)

31. He .... the bird but he always missed.
(*a*) shot (*b*) shot down
(*c*) shot at (*d*) shot up

32. He has fallen .... with his partner.
(*a*) through (*b*) off
(*c*) over (*d*) out
(B.S.R.B. 1992)

33. If these youths trespass .... my land again I shall be ready for them with a big stick.
(*a*) upon (*b*) into (*c*) on (*d*) over

34. The Second World War broke .... in 1939.
(*a*) off (*b*) up (*c*) out (*d*) away

35. However, a large number of employees kept .... from their offices today.
(*a*) on (*b*) out (*c*) away (*d*) up
(Stenographers' Exam, 1991)

36. There are thirty teachers .... the staff of this school.
(*a*) under (*b*) in (*c*) at (*d*) on

37. You should knock .... the door before you enter somebody's room.
(*a*) upon (*b*) at (*c*) about (*d*) on

38. .... the room, the door suddenly swung shut and hit him in the face.
(*a*) On entering (*b*) While entering
(*c*) As he entered (*d*) On having entered
(Railways, 1995)

39. I asked him to look after my things because I can confide .... him.
(*a*) in (*b*) on (*c*) with (*d*) to

40. He tried to .... smoking, but did not succeed. **(B.S.R.B. 1995)**
(*a*) put out (*b*) give up
(*c*) do away (*d*) get away

41. If you are suffering from fever, the best remedy lies .... complete rest.
(*a*) with (*b*) on (*c*) in (*d*) upon

42. Genius does what it must, and talent does what it .... **(M.B.A. 1990)**
(*a*) can (*b*) would
(*c*) may (*d*) should

ANSWERS

1. (*c*)	**2.** (*b*)	**3.** (*d*)	**4.** (*a*)	**5.** (*c*)	**6.** (*c*)	**7.** (*c*)	**8.** (*a*)	**9.** (*b*)	**10.** (*b*)
11. (*a*)	**12.** (*d*)	**13.** (*d*)	**14.** (*b*)	**15.** (*a*)	**16.** (*c*)	**17.** (*a*)	**18.** (*d*)	**19.** (*c*)	**20.** (*b*)
21. (*c*)	**22.** (*b*)	**23.** (*a*)	**24.** (*d*)	**25.** (*b*)	**26.** (*c*)	**27.** (*a*)	**28.** (*c*)	**29.** (*d*)	**30.** (*b*)
31. (*c*)	**32.** (*d*)	**33.** (*c*)	**34.** (*c*)	**35.** (*c*)	**36.** (*d*)	**37.** (*b*)	**38.** (*c*)	**39.** (*a*)	**40.** (*b*)
41. (*c*)	**42.** (*a*)								

---

12. PASSAGE COMPLETION (Cloze Test)

This test is to judge a candidate's knowledge of grammar usage and vocabulary. In this, a passage is given, with some (usually 5, 10 or 15) blank spaces in it. For each of these blanks, some alternatives are given. The candidate is required to first read the passage, understand what it is about and then choose the most appropriate word in the context of the passage, from the given alternatives.

Example : Without water ...(1)... animal can survive. In desert regions the greatest ...(2)... to life is drying up. But many creatures are able to make use of ...(3)... little water that exists in arid areas. One of nature's masterpieces ...(4)... creatures equipped to ...(5)... with desert life is the hardy camels. Stories range the desert lands far and wide about ...(6)... endurance feats by camels. It is said that camels can ...(7)... a distance of about 800 miles in eight days through continuous travel ...(8)... an intake of a single drop of water. The popular ...(9)... that camels store water in their hump is ...(10)... in a way; water is indeed stored there but in the form of fat.

1.	(*a*) every	(*b*) no	(*c*) any	(*d*) desert	(*e*) exceptional
2.	(*a*) need	(*b*) worry	(*c*) threat	(*d*) requirement	(*e*) inadequacy
3.	(*a*) what	(*b*) the	(*c*) very	(*d*) that	(*e*) extremely
4.	(*a*) for	(*b*) about	(*c*) among	(*d*) with	(*e*) of
5.	(*a*) live	(*b*) resist	(*c*) bear	(*d*) cope	(*e*) mix
6.	(*a*) remarkable	(*b*) little	(*c*) tolerable	(*d*) popular	(*e*) obvious
7.	(*a*) measure	(*b*) reduce	(*c*) lead	(*d*) reach	(*e*) cover
8.	(*a*) for	(*b*) without	(*c*) accepting	(*d*) receiving	(*e*) except
9.	(*a*) proverb	(*b*) guess	(*c*) belief	(*d*) version	(*e*) statement
10.	(*a*) baseless	(*b*) wrong	(*c*) misleading	(*d*) correct	(*e*) untruthful

Solution :

1. (*b*) : It is an established fact that no animal can survive without water.

2. (*c*) : In deserts, drying up is not the 'need' or 'requirement'. It is a 'threat' to living creatures.

3. (*b*) : Article 'the' should be used.

4. (*c*) : According to the passage, camel is a masterpiece amidst all creatures. Another word for 'amidst' is 'among'.

5. (*d*) : 'Mix' is absolutely wrong. The word 'live', 'resist' or 'bear' could be used only if the camel could remain thirsty for long. But since it stores water for future use, it is an adaptation i.e. a way to 'cope' with adverse circumstances.

6. (*a*) : Stories are popular about a creature when it has something unusual or 'remarkable'.

7. (*e*) : The word 'distance' takes the verb 'cover'.

8. (*b*) : Camel moves continuously without intake of water.

9. (*c*) : 'Proverb' is an old saying. 'Version' and 'statement' are clearly wrong in this context. 'Guess' can never be popular. The correct word is 'belief'.

10. (*c*) : Clearly, the belief is not 'correct'. Also, it is not 'baseless', 'wrong' or 'untruthful' as camels do store water though in a different form.
So, the answer is 'misleading'.

Now attempt the following Practice Sets 1 to 15 as per the following instructions:

Directions : ***In each of the following passages, there are blanks each of which has been numbered. These numbers are printed below the passage and against each, some words are suggested, one of which fits the blank appropriately. Find out the appropriate words.***

PRACTICE SET 1

Passage 1 **(Assistant Grade, 1996)**

Many parents greet their children's teenage years with needless dread. While teens ...(1)... assault us with heavy-metal music, ...(2)... outlandish clothes and spend all ...(3)... time with friends, such behaviour ...(4)... adds up to full-scale revolt. Teenage ...(5)..., according to psychologist Laurence Steinberg, has been ......(6)...... exaggerated. Sociologist Sanford Dornbusch agrees. "The ...(7)... that teenagers inevitably rebel is a ...(8)... that has the potential for great family ...(9)...," says Dornbusch. He believes the notion can ...(10)... communication during this critical time for parents to influence youngsters.

1. (*a*) can (*b*) must (*c*) may (*d*) should

2. (*a*) show (*b*) dress (*c*) put (*d*) flaunt

3. (*a*) her (*b*) his (*c*) their (*d*) our

4. (*a*) sporadically (*b*) always (*c*) infrequently (*d*) scarcely

5. (*a*) rebellion (*b*) subversion (*c*) mania (*d*) revolution

6. (*a*) always (*b*) never (*c*) greatly (*d*) hardly

7. (*a*) complaint (*b*) surmise (*c*) accusation (*d*) idea

8. (*a*) myth (*b*) story (*c*) fact (*d*) reality

9. (*a*) ruin (*b*) downfall (*c*) harm (*d*) defeat

10 (*a*) destroy (*b*) suffocate (*c*) damage (*d*) injure

Passage 2

The appointed day has come, and India stands ...(11)... again, after long ...(12)... and struggle, awake, vital, free and independent. The past ...(13)... on to us still in some ...(14)... and we have to do much before we ...(15)... our pledges. ...(16)..., it is fateful moment for us in India, for all Asia and for the world. A new star ...(17)..., the star of freedom in the East and a vision long cherished ...(18)... . May the star never set and out hopes never be ...(19)...! To India, our motherland –the ancient, the eternal and the ever new, we pay our ...(20)... homage and we bind ourselves afresh to her service.

11. (*a*) here (*b*) free (*c*) forth (*d*) forward

12. (*a*) period (*b*) slumber (*c*) compulsion (*d*) exile

13. (*a*) sticks (*b*) faces (*c*) extends (*d*) clings

14. (*a*) measure (*b*) quantity (*c*) limits (*d*) ways

15. (*a*) take (*b*) redeem (*c*) rectify (*d*) comply

16. (*a*) Moreover (*b*) However (*c*) Now (*d*) Although

17. (*a*) rises (*b*) rose (*c*) arises (*d*) arose

18. (*a*) falsifies (*b*) fulfils (*c*) performs (*d*) materialises

19. (*a*) left (*b*) betrayed (*c*) expired (*d*) drained

20. (*a*) sincere (*b*) faithful (*c*) reverent (*d*) friendly

Passage 3 **(Hotel Management, 1995)**

All writers are vain, selfish and lazy, and at the very ...(21)... of their motives there lies a mystery. Writing a book is a horrible, exhausting struggle, like a long ...(22)... of some painful illness. One would never undertake such a thing if one were not ...(23)... by some demon whom one can neither ...(24)... nor understand. For all one knows that demon is simply the same ...(25)... that makes a baby ...(26)... for attention. And yet it is also true that one can write nothing readable unless one constantly struggles to ...(27)... one's own personality. Good prose is like a window pane. I cannot say with certainty which of my motives are the strongest, but I know which of them deserve to be followed. And ...(28)... through my work, I see that it is ...(29)... where I lacked a political purpose that I wrote lifeless books and was ...(30)... into purple passages, sentences without meaning, decorative adjectives and humbug generally.

21. (*a*) mention (*b*) bottom (*c*) idea (*d*) consideration

22. (*a*) bout (*b*) feeling (*c*) source (*d*) condition

23. (*a*) driven out (*b*) driven for
(*c*) driven on (*d*) driven at

24. (*a*) help (*b*) resist
(*c*) like (*d*) conquer

25. (*a*) feeling (*b*) sense
(*c*) desire (*d*) instinct

26. (*a*) squall (*b*) play
(*c*) desire (*d*) look

27. (*a*) overcome (*b*) change
(*c*) efface (*d*) deface

28. (*a*) looking in (*b*) looking for
(*c*) looking at (*d*) looking back

29. (*a*) interestingly (*b*) seldom
(*c*) constantly (*d*) invariably

30. (*a*) inspired (*b*) betrayed
(*c*) moved (*d*) introduced

Passage 4

The keeper, Lord Shiva himself, is known to be the greatest hunter of them all, as he sits on a tiger skin and covers his ...(31)... body with animal fur. But to ...(32)... in ...(33)... killing of animals is against the ...(34)... law, as one may kill only that which one can ...(35)... However, man being man is the only ...(36)... who kills for sport, knowing it to be sport, thereby ...(37)... all norms of ...(38)... behaviour. The Americans ...(39)... out the bison from the face of North America, as the Indian Maharajas and British Sahibs did the cheetah and almost the lion and tiger from India—animals which you don't eat, but ...(40)... the walls of your house with.

31. (*a*) beautiful (*b*) bare
(*c*) vacant (*d*) uncovered

32. (*a*) involve (*b*) include
(*c*) indulge (*d*) interfere

33. (*a*) wanton (*b*) unreasonable
(*c*) rash (*d*) disregarded

34. (*a*) spiritual (*b*) cosmic
(*c*) supernatural (*d*) manly

35. (*a*) consume (*b*) devour
(*c*) gobble (*d*) grab

36. (*a*) beast (*b*) brute
(*c*) creature (*d*) animal

37. (*a*) transferring (*b*) neglecting
(*c*) transgressing (*d*) desecrating

38. (*a*) contingent (*b*) civilised
(*c*) complementary (*d*) crude

39. (*a*) eradicated (*b*) erased
(*c*) wiped (*d*) removed

40. (*a*) garnish (*b*) tarnish
(*c*) decorate (*d*) grandeur

Passage 5 **(Bank P.O. 1992)**

Fundamentally, all human ...(41)... possess combinations of fixed inherited traits. All men possess the ...(42)... highly developed nervous system, backbones, erect posture, hair etc. Therefore, ...(43)... among men arise only in ...(44)... changes of this ...(45)... pattern. Racial ...(46)... represent one of the finest distinctions and are based on certain ...(47)... differences. Two races may be ...(48)... in hair colour, in eye colour but ...(49)... in stature while two others may be ...(50)... in stature but differ in the colour of eyes and hair.

41. (*a*) animal (*b*) beings (*c*) mind
(*d*) society (*e*) thinking

42. (*a*) same (*b*) large (*c*) natural
(*d*) different (*e*) biological

43. (*a*) growth (*b*) sameness (*c*) substance
(*d*) variations (*e*) naturalness

44. (*a*) no (*b*) large (*c*) minor
(*d*) artificial (*e*) fundamental

45. (*a*) mad (*b*) basic (*c*) maddening
(*d*) fluctuating (*e*) picturesque

46. (*a*) hatred (*b*) clashes (*c*) tolerance
(*d*) sameness (*e*) differences

47. (*a*) neat (*b*) minor (*c*) massive
(*d*) clearcut (*e*) unnoticeable

48. (*a*) alike (*b*) different (*c*) beautiful
(*d*) untouched (*e*) mismatched

49. (*a*) same (*b*) tall (*c*) close
(*d*) matched (*e*) different

50. (*a*) ugly (*b*) tall (*c*) same
(*d*) short (*e*) uncouth

ANSWERS

1. (*c*)	**2.** (*d*)	**3.** (*c*)	**4.** (*b*)	**5.** (*a*)	**6.** (*c*)	**7.** (*d*)	**8.** (*d*)	**9.** (*a*)	**10.** (*b*)
11. (*c*)	**12.** (*b*)	**13.** (*d*)	**14.** (*a*)	**15.** (*b*)	**16.** (*b*)	**17.** (*a*)	**18.** (*d*)	**19.** (*b*)	**20.** (*c*)
21. (*b*)	**22.** (*a*)	**23.** (*d*)	**24.** (*b*)	**25.** (*c*)	**26.** (*a*)	**27.** (*c*)	**28.** (*d*)	**29.** (*d*)	**30.** (*c*)
31. (*b*)	**32.** (*c*)	**33.** (*a*)	**34.** (*b*)	**35.** (*a*)	**36.** (*d*)	**37.** (*c*)	**38.** (*b*)	**39.** (*c*)	**40.** (*c*)
41. (*b*)	**42.** (*a*)	**43.** (*d*)	**44.** (*c*)	**45.** (*b*)	**46.** (*e*)	**47.** (*d*)	**48.** (*a*)	**49.** (*e*)	**50.** (*c*)

PRACTICE SET 2

Passage 1 **(Bank P.O. 1995)**

This ...(1)... balance of payment situation must be seen along with an equally ...(2)... problem of deficits in the government's own budget. A growing ...(3)... exists between the government's total ...(4)... and the sum of its current revenue and capital receipts. This gap, which has to be met through either external assistance or ...(5)... deficit finance, has grown over the years. The government ...(6)... cannot resort to indefinitely growing volumes of external assistance of deficit finance to meet the increasing gap between its total ...(7)... and total receipts.

...(8)... these conditions, there has been strong pressure on government to ...(9)... various development programmes, welfare schemes and subsidies. Even if outlay in money terms are not actually cut, the ...(10)... of these programmes may be reduced in real terms or their rate of expansion at least brought down.

1. (*a*) expanding (*b*) increasing (*c*) yawning (*d*) widening (*e*) deteriorating

2 (*a*) ignored (*b*) posed (*c*) understood (*d*) serious (*e*) significant

3. (*a*) disparity (*b*) bond (*c*) gap (*d*) awareness (*e*) realisation

4. (*a*) resources (*b*) budget (*c*) outlay (*d*) planning (*e*) receipts

5. (*a*) zero (*b*) planning (*c*) budget (*d*) domestic (*e*) international

6. (*a*) perhaps (*b*) probably (*c*) willingly (*d*) obviously (*e*) notwithstanding

7. (*a*) outlay (*b*) services (*c*) planning (*d*) resources (*e*) expenditure

8. (*a*) Taking (*b*) From (*c*) Under (*d*) Above (*e*) Beside

9. (*a*) curtail (*b*) stop (*c*) reject (*d*) promote (*e*) evaluate

10. (*a*) services (*b*) outlay (*c*) scope (*d*) effect (*e*) impact

Passage 2

Interviews are very important for all of us. We must face interviews with confidence. There is ...(11)... any person who at one time or the other has not ...(12)... an interview situation. While ...(13)... are a day to day ...(14)... for people who ...(15)... with others in their daily chores, we are here ...(16)... with interview situations when one is a ...(17)... aspiring for an ...(18)... Such situations, not very ...(19)... happen in one's life, are ...(20)... when the candidate likes to come on top of the situation. This calls for careful study and preparation.

11. (*a*) perhaps (*b*) hardly (*c*) probably (*d*) possibly

12. (*a*) known (*b*) faced (*c*) measured (*d*) seen

13. (*a*) interviews (*b*) discussions (*c*) meetings (*d*) seminars

14. (*a*) possibility (*b*) feeling (*c*) happening (*d*) experience

15. (*a*) interact (*b*) speak (*c*) react (*d*) concern

16. (*a*) meeting (*b*) concerned (*c*) involved (*d*) interested

17. (*a*) beggar (*b*) candidate (*c*) person (*d*) student

18. (*a*) employment (*b*) estimation (*c*) elevation (*d*) establishment

19. (*a*) frequent (*b*) happy (*c*) important (*d*) consequent

20. (*a*) minutes (*b*) times (*c*) hours (*d*) occasions

Passage 3 **(C.B.I. 1993)**

Broadly speaking letters may be said to ...(21)... into two classes: the formal and ...(22)... Formal letters ...(23)... of official or business matters and are ...(24)... to an employer, officials of a department or institutions. Letters to the ...(25)... of a newspaper also belong to this class. In fact all ...(26)... using formal pattern is of this category. The ...(27)... has to be precisely stated. It must be ...(28)... in style and quite ...(29).... No ...(30)... element has any place in it.

21. (*a*) describe (*b*) fall
(*c*) escape (*d*) rise

22. (*a*) affectionate (*b*) abusive
(*c*) personal (*d*) flattering

23. (*a*) consist (*b*) apprise
(*c*) contain (*d*) comprise

24. (*a*) addressed (*b*) prayed
(*c*) respected (*d*) typed

25. (*a*) printer (*b*) publisher
(*c*) salesman (*d*) editor

26. (*a*) writings (*b*) columns
(*c*) correspondence (*d*) letters

27. (*a*) language (*b*) content
(*c*) criticism (*d*) objection

28. (*a*) lucid (*b*) florid
(*c*) high (*d*) descriptive

29. (*a*) creative (*b*) objective
(*c*) critical (*d*) subjective

30. (*a*) unifying (*b*) divisive
(*c*) malicious (*d*) personal

Passage 4

Life is an ...(31)... series of challenges and opportunities to be seized. You have to plan for exercising the right career choices and ...(32)... the right opportunities. Planned ...(33)... rather than a hasty decision is ...(34)... as far as your career is concerned. You need to ...(35)... what occupational groups, ...(36)... and types of organizations seem ...(37)... to you. An individual today has many more degrees of freedom in determining his or her future. Few of us ...(38)... this or take full ...(39)... of this freedom. Most of us let the future be ...(40)... by what is going to happen rather by personal life goals and plans for the future.

31. (*a*) enticing (*b*) exciting
(*c*) encharming (*d*) enhancing

32. (*a*) catching (*b*) offsetting
(*c*) grabbing (*d*) conceiving

33. (*a*) delay (*b*) hindrance
(*c*) wait (*d*) procastination

34. (*a*) desirable (*b*) deciphered
(*c*) inevitable (*d*) acceptable

35. (*a*) check (*b*) classify
(*c*) divide (*d*) analyse

36. (*a*) specifications (*b*) limitations
(*c*) qualifications (*d*) identification

37. (*a*) worthy (*b*) needful
(*c*) suitable (*d*) necessary

38. (*a*) reprimand (*b*) realise
(*c*) recognise (*d*) remember

39. (*a*) advantage (*b*) enjoyment
(*c*) privileges (*d*) compensation

40. (*a*) determined (*b*) swayed
(*c*) deprived (*d*) led

Passage 5 **(S.S.C. 1995)**

Dhritrashtra, the elder brother of the Pandu, was blind by birth. When he grew young, he was married to Gandhari. She loved him so ...(41)... that she ...(42)... up her own eyes with a cloth. A hundred sons were born to Dhritrashtra and Gandhari. They were called Kauravas. Duryodhana was the ...(43)... son of Dhritrashtra, who was quite obstinate by nature. When Kunti ...(44)... to Hastinapur with her five sons, Duryodhana did not ...(45)... it. He wanted that the Pandavas should live in the forest with their mother, Kunti. In fact he wanted to rule ...(46)... Hastinapur without any interference in his affairs, although outwardly he made a ...(47) .. of happiness. His mother Gandhari consoled Kunti but her son Duryodhana did not like this at all. Pandavas were so good and ...(48).. that every one who saw them ...(49)... them. The people of Hastinapur began to give greater ...(50)... to the Pandavas than to the Kauravas.

41. (*a*) closely (*b*) deeply
(*c*) keenly (*d*) excessively

42. (*a*) closed (*b*) folded
(*c*) bound (*d*) blinded

43. (*a*) eldest (*b*) greatest
(*c*) dearest (*d*) loveliest

44. (*a*) refreated (*b*) retracted
(*c*) receded (*d*) returned

45. (*a*) concede (*b*) approve
(*c*) understand (*d*) like

46. (*a*) on (*b*) over (*c*) upon (*d*) from

47. (*a*) show (*b*) pretention
(*c*) face (*d*) pretext

48. (*a*) feeble (*b*) attractive
(*c*) innocent (*d*) noble

49. (*a*) glorified (*b*) praised
(*c*) respected (*d*) applauded

50. (*a*) importance (*b*) praise
(*c*) consideration (*d*) admiration

ANSWERS

1. (*b*)	**2.** (*d*)	**3.** (*a*)	**4.** (*c*)	**5.** (*c*)	**6.** (*d*)	**7.** (*e*)	**8.** (*c*)	**9.** (*a*)	**10.** (*b*)
11. (*b*)	**12.** (*b*)	**13.** (*a*)	**14.** (*d*)	**15.** (*a*)	**16.** (*b*)	**17.** (*b*)	**18.** (*a*)	**19.** (*a*)	**20.** (*d*)
21. (*b*)	**22.** (*c*)	**23.** (*a*)	**24.** (*a*)	**25.** (*d*)	**26.** (*c*)	**27.** (*a*)	**28.** (*a*)	**29.** (*b*)	**30.** (*d*)
31. (*b*)	**32.** (*c*)	**33.** (*d*)	**34.** (*a*)	**35.** (*d*)	**36.** (*a*)	**37.** (*c*)	**38.** (*b*)	**39.** (*a*)	**40.** (*a*)
41. (*b*)	**42.** (*c*)	**43.** (*a*)	**44.** (*d*)	**45.** (*d*)	**46.** (*b*)	**47.** (*a*)	**48.** (*d*)	**49.** (*b*)	**50.** (*a*)

PRACTICE SET 3

Passage 1 **(Stenographers' Exam, 1995)**

I want to avoid violence. Non-violence ...(1)... the first article of my faith. It is also the ...(2)... article of my creed. But I had to ...(3)... my choice. I had either to submit ...(4)... a system which I considered ...(5)... done irreparable harm to my country, ...(6)... incur the risk of the mad fury ..(7)... my people bursting forth, when they ...(8)... the truth from my lips. I ...(9)... that my people have sometimes ...(10)... mad. I am deeply sorry for it.

1. (*a*) was (*b*) be (*c*) is (*d*) being
2. (*a*) last (*b*) common (*c*) simple (*d*) unique
3. (*a*) make (*b*) select (*c*) prepare (*d*) do
4. (*a*) over (*b*) in (*c*) against (*d*) to
5. (*a*) is (*b*) was (*c*) had (*d*) has
6. (*a*) nor (*b*) but (*c*) or (*d*) and
7. (*a*) with (*b*) by (*c*) in (*d*) of
8. (*a*) listen (*b*) get (*c*) understood (*d*) understand
9. (*a*) know (*b*) knows (*c*) knew (*d*) known
10. (*a*) going (*b*) gone (*c*) goes (*d*) went

Passage 2

Books give us all the information ...(11)... a man. They show ...(12)... interest. They are the ...(13)... to his mind. All the riches of the world ...(14)... their importance in the face of books. A man with money and ...(15)... books is a poor man. Books have become so cheap that a library can ...(16)... be made. Money spent on good books is never ...(17)... It is a ...(18)... to read good books. Thus man gains both ...(19)... and wisdom. You can ...(20)... your library with the expenditure of only a few hundred rupees.

11. (*a*) for (*b*) from (*c*) about (*d*) of
12. (*a*) his (*b*) their (*c*) that (*d*) personal
13. (*a*) road (*b*) access (*c*) index (*d*) approach
14. (*a*) loose (*b*) fade (*c*) lose (*d*) vanish
15. (*a*) some (*b*) with (*c*) few (*d*) without
16. (*a*) hardly (*b*) easily (*c*) frequently (*d*) scarcely
17. (*a*) wasted (*b*) recovered (*c*) justified (*d*) withdrawn
18 (*a*) blessing (*b*) pleasure (*c*) obsession (*d*) addiction
19. (*a*) skill (*b*) aptitude (*c*) knowledge (*d*) efficiency
20. (*a*) form (*b*) gather (*c*) constitute (*d*) begin

Passage 3 **(Bank P.O. 1995)**

New industries supported by foreign interests ....(21)... offer ...(22)... salaries to their employees at all levels of responsibility than ...(23)... locally owned industries. They need ...(24)... people and are ...(25)... to pay high wages to ...(26)... them. Local industries often ...(27)... the high salaries offered by foreign supported industries, arguing that this will ...(28)... raise all wages to an excessive level. Workers in local industries, seeing the sharp ...(29)... in job- pay will agitate for an improvement in their salaries. This eventually will drain the resources and ...(30)... their profitability.

21. (*a*) seldom (*b*) hardly (*c*) never (*d*) usually

(*e*) reluctantly

22. (*a*) better (*b*) comparable (*c*) unreasonable (*d*) proportionate (*e*) disproportionate

23. (*a*) did (*b*) do (*c*) their (*d*) does (*e*) could

24. (*a*) less (*b*) local (*c*) more (*d*) several (*e*) talented

25. (*a*) bound (*b*) willing (*c*) forced (*d*) reluctant (*e*) authorised

26. (*a*) hire (*b*) bribe (*c*) retain (*d*) enrich (*e*) entertain

27. (*a*) accept (*b*) pay (*c*) protest (*d*) uphold (*e*) imitate

28. (*a*) not (*b*) hardly (*c*) artificially (*d*) considerably (*e*) unreasonably

29. (*a*) hike (*b*) cut (*c*) decrease (*d*) difference (*e*) injustice

30. (*a*) check (*b*) lower (*c*) fulfil (*d*) enhance (*e*) augment

Passage 4

In 1893, Lokmanya Tilak converted the Ganpati festival into a public ceremony. He campaigned ...(31)... the ...(32)... circulation of this public celebration throughout Maharashtra. It was ...(33)... this festival that he could ...(34)... public ...(35)... to the nationalist movement. The desired ...(36)... of this festival was further ...(37)... by Shivaji festival. It was inaugurated in honour of Chhatrapati Shivaji, the greatest Maratha king, in the ...(38)... of several thousand people. In the ...(39)... the Marathas were ...(40)... and this helped a lot in mounting an attack on the British rule.

31. (*a*) towards (*b*) for (*c*) with (*d*) withstanding (*e*) against

32. (*a*) early (*b*) slow (*c*) wide (*d*) sudden (*e*) limited

33. (*a*) through (*b*) from (*c*) before (*d*) indeed (*e*) exactly

34. (*a*) advise (*b*) control (*c*) mobilise (*d*) demand (*e*) enhance

35. (*a*) places (*b*) support (*c*) festivals (*d*) grievances (*e*) celebrations

36. (*a*) strategy (*b*) impact (*c*) publicity (*d*) importance (*e*) decoration

37. (*a*) decided (*b*) displayed (*c*) generated (*d*) manifested (*e*) reinforced

38. (*a*) protest (*b*) honour (*c*) service (*d*) memory (*e*) presence

39. (*a*) fight (*b*) activity (*c*) process (*d*) beginning (*e*) meantime

40. (*a*) absent (*b*) defeated (*c*) neglected (*d*) glorified (*e*) forbidden

Passage 5 **(Asstt. Grade, 1994)**

It is not proper to damn a system without understanding it. The Indian bureaucracy may be as bad after all, as it is made out to be. Times without number, it has been ...(41)... that our bureaucrat is a ...(42)... creature who has the habit of sitting ...(43)...the files and also happens to sleep ...(44)... the remainders. What is worse is ...(45)... his own word. He turns a ...(46)... ear to the visitor's request and binds his hands and feet with ...(47)... tape. However, in all fairness ...(48)... the bureaucracy, it is necessary to note that a major reason for its ...(49)... to discharge its functions ...(50)... throughout has been the concentration of power in the hands of the politicians. The bureaucrat may be a devil, but because he has his own share of difficulties, we would not deny him his due.

41. (*a*) declared (*b*) proclaimed (*c*) said (*d*) pronounced

42. (*a*) strange (*b*) sober (*c*) sophisticated (*d*) solid

43. (*a*) on (*b*) at (*c*) by (*d*) with

44. (*a*) off (*b*) by (*c*) away (*d*) over

45. (*a*) minces (*b*) eats
(*c*) minds (*d*) shuffles
46. (*a*) busy (*b*) cold
(*c*) deaf (*d*) callous
47. (*a*) brown (*b*) blue
(*c*) red (*d*) green
48. (*a*) for (*b*) to
(*c*) with (*d*) of
49. (*a*) adequacy (*b*) efficacy
(*c*) position (*d*) inability
50. (*a*) effectively (*b*) elegantly
(*c*) evenly (*d*) equitably

ANSWERS

1. (*c*)	2. (*a*)	3. (*a*)	4. (*d*)	5. (*c*)	6. (*c*)	7. (*d*)	8. (*b*)	9. (*a*)	10. (*b*)
11. (*c*)	12. (*a*)	13. (*c*)	14. (*c*)	15. (*d*)	16. (*b*)	17. (*a*)	18. (*b*)	19. (*d*)	20. (*a*)
21. (*d*)	22. (*a*)	23. (*c*)	24. (*e*)	25. (*b*)	26. (*c*)	27. (*c*)	28. (*e*)	29. (*d*)	30. (*b*)
31. (*b*)	32. (*c*)	33. (*a*)	34. (*c*)	35. (*b*)	36. (*b*)	37. (*e*)	38. (*e*)	39. (*d*)	40. (*c*)
41. (*c*)	42. (*a*)	43. (*a*)	44. (*d*)	45. (*b*)	46. (*c*)	47. (*c*)	48. (*b*)	49. (*d*)	50. (*a*)

PRACTICE SET 4

Passage 1 (Asstt. Grade, 1995)

Some people believe that marriages are made in heaven. One cannot say ...(1)... this is true or not. However, in America now many ...(2)... who get married seek to evolve a fool proof ...(3)... to ensure that the marriage survives. However, the idea of married persons ...(4)... the burden of domestic chores, instead of all the dirty work being dumped on the woman has...(5)...been propagated by the feminist ...(6)... and it has gradually, if grudgingly, been ...(7)... This arrangement may work on a temporary basis but taking ...(8)... of a particular domestic work on a permanent basis will pose problems of its own. For instance, taking out the rubbish may ...(9)... make a refreshing change from washing baby's nappies. However, a contract is a contract and must be ...(10)... You may not like it but this is what life is coming out to be in the most modern of the countries in the world.

1. (*a*) whether (*b*) still
(*c*) however (*d*) that
2. (*a*) pairs (*b*) men
(*c*) couples (*d*) women
3. (*a*) method (*b*) project
(*c*) plan (*d*) system
4. (*a*) executing (*b*) dividing
(*c*) undertaking (*d*) sharing
5. (*a*) long (*b*) sometimes
(*c*) always (*d*) occasionally
6. (*a*) group (*b*) lobby
(*c*) section (*d*) faction
7. (*a*) affirmed (*b*) approved
(*c*) accepted (*d*) favoured
8. (*a*) control (*b*) care
(*c*) charge (*d*) duty
9. (*a*) occasionally (*b*) often
(*c*) intermittently (*d*) rarely
10. (*a*) respected (*b*) executed
(*c*) maintained (*d*) obeyed

Passage 2

Begin with a strong, ...(11)..., keen desire to the object which you want to achieve. If your desire is weak, momentary or ...(12)..., your achievements will also be likewise and there may be no ...(13)... at all. But if you go after your ...(14)... with energy, determination, persistence and an ever-present, ...(15)..., burning, clear-cut, definite desire, nothing under the sun can keep you from success. Remember that only ...(16)... the depth of your desire depends the swiftness of your progress towards success. Persistence and dogged ...(17)... will guarantee success against all ...(18)... No matter what happens, keep cool and keep trying. Never give up. The hardest man to beat is the one who will not ...(19)... He will ...(20)... the seeming setbacks and ultimately crown himself with success.

11. (*a*) persistent (*b*) consistent
(*c*) resistant (*d*) continuous

12. (*a*) frugal (*b*) immediate (*c*) transient (*d*) uncertain
13. (*a*) requirements (*b*) achievements (*c*) consequences (*d*) repurcussions
14. (*a*) goal (*b*) destination (*c*) desire (*d*) incentive
15. (*a*) biting (*b*) diminishing (*c*) gnawing (*d*) decaying
16. (*a*) over (*b*) upon (*c*) at (*d*) on
17. (*a*) determination (*b*) end (*c*) destination (*d*) aim
18. (*a*) obstacles (*b*) odds (*c*) hindrances (*d*) impediments
19. (*a*) quit (*b*) forgo (*c*) leave (*d*) shirk
20. (*a*) occupy (*b*) conquer (*c*) invade (*d*) confiscate

Passage 3 **(N.D.A. 1995)**

It is regrettable that the press, radio and television still tend too often to present old age in an unhappily one sided way. I believe that they do this from the ...(21)... of motives. They are trying to ...(22)... the conscience of society to the ...(23)... of those elderly people who refuse help, who are lonely, destitute, ill, ...(24)..., institutionalised and so on. I am ...(25)... the media achieve ...(26)... response and some amelioration of the situation for some of these people.

21. (*a*) worst (*b*) best (*c*) wildest
22. (*a*) awaken (*b*) disturb (*c*) pinch
23. (*a*) crisis (*b*) plight (*c*) misery
24. (*a*) bed-ridden (*b*) forgotten (*c*) lost
25. (*a*) worried (*b*) sure (*c*) uncertain
26. (*a*) some (*b*) little (*c*) any

Passage 4

Sericulture is fast becoming a household industry in the hill state of Himachal Pradesh. Having ...(27)... economic significance, sericulture has become an employment ...(28)... for the poor and weaker sections of society ...(29)... widows. Being a pollution free industry with little energy ...(30)... and very little ...(31)... period, the industry quickly ...(32)... the income of those engaged in this. Sericulture has surely been a ...(33)... of new hope and aspiration to thousands of families ...(34)... in this profession who are looking for a bright future in the ...(35)... new cottage industry.

27. (*a*) tremendous (*b*) enormous (*c*) immense (*d*) extensive
28. (*a*) capacity (*b*) potential (*c*) contingency (*d*) consistency
29. (*a*) including (*b*) engaging (*c*) embibing (*d*) excluding
30. (*a*) necessity (*b*) essentiality (*c*) requirement (*d*) inevitability
31. (*a*) gestation (*b*) lactation (*c*) development (*d*) ripening
32. (*a*) compensates (*b*) increases (*c*) supplements (*d*) concentrates
33. (*a*) messenger (*b*) harbinger (*c*) carrier (*d*) vector
34. (*a*) engaged (*b*) entailed (*c*) inculcated (*d*) entangled
35. (*a*) relatively (*b*) comparatively (*c*) consecutively (*d*) temporarily

Passage 5 **(B.S.R.B. 1995)**

Scientific psychology recognises a ...(36)... truth that no two individuals are ...(37)... in this world ...(38)... equality is a fostered norm of civil society, the truth is that men ...(39)... unequals in ...(40)... hues or degrees.

36. (*a*) clear (*b*) real (*c*) simple (*d*) direct (*e*) broken
37. (*a*) alike (*b*) close (*c*) liked (*d*) equal (*e*) correct
38. (*a*) when (*b*) since (*c*) as (*d*) neither (*e*) even though
39 (*a*) will (*b*) are (*c*) is (*d*) was (*e*) *were*
40. (*a*) high (*b*) total (*c*) no (*d*) varying (*e*) almost

Passage 6 **(U.D.C. 1993)**

We will be crushed if civil ...(41)... is started. It will be a ...(42)... to the clock. The technique of ...(43)... against it has been ...(44)... We may have to wait ...(45)... a year or more, for a suitable ...(46)... to be created. Any hasty ...(47)... may result in complete ...(48)... Labour troubles will ...(49)... to violence and there will be ...(50)... discord.

41. (*a*) riot (*b*) disturbance (*c*) war (*d*) disobedience
42. (*a*) damage (*b*) reversal (*c*) setback (*d*) rewinding

43. (*a*) defence (*b*) protection
(*c*) fighting (*d*) guarding
44. (*a*) learnt (*b*) practised
(*c*) rehearsed (*d*) perfected
45. (*a*) at least (*b*) minimum
(*c*) for (*d*) approximately
46. (*a*) condition (*b*) climate
(*c*) atmosphere (*d*) weather
47. (*a*) decision (*b*) work
(*c*) deed (*d*) action
48. (*a*) demoralization (*b*) doom
(*c*) disobedience (*d*) disaster
49. (*a*) draw (*b*) take
(*c*) lead (*d*) grow
50. (*a*) labour (*b*) communal
(*c*) religious (*d*) community

ANSWERS

1. (*a*)	**2.** (*c*)	**3.** (*d*)	**4.** (*d*)	**5.** (*a*)	**6.** (*b*)	**7.** (*c*)	**8.** (*c*)	**9.** (*a*)	**10.** (*a*)
11. (*a*)	**12.** (*c*)	**13.** (*b*)	**14.** (*a*)	**15.** (*c*)	**16.** (*b*)	**17.** (*a*)	**18.** (*b*)	**19.** (*a*)	**20.** (*b*)
21. (*b*)	**22.** (*a*)	**23.** (*c*)	**24.** (*b*)	**25.** (*b*)	**26.** (*a*)	**27.** (*a*)	**28.** (*b*)	**29.** (*a*)	**30.** (*c*)
31. (*a*)	**32.** (*c*)	**33.** (*b*)	**34.** (*a*)	**35.** (*a*)	**36.** (*c*)	**37.** (*a*)	**38.** (*e*)	**39.** (*b*)	**40.** (*d*)
41. (*d*)	**42.** (*c*)	**43.** (*c*)	**44.** (*a*)	**45.** (*a*)	**46.** (*c*)	**47.** (*d*)	**48.** (*d*)	**49.** (*c*)	**50.** (*b*)

PRACTICE SET 5

Passage 1 **(C.B.I. 1995)**

It looks like the trail that leads to a magical land. The path climbs out of the forest ...(1)... white and yellow butterflies flutter ...(2)... the hanging creepers. It emerges on a ...(3)... meadow basking in the sun. ...(4)... this is no fairy-tale country. The ...(5)... inhabitants of the meadows ...(6)... barely living human skeletons, with sunken, fevered ...(7)... and clothed in filthy and ...(8)... rags. They are the refugees who have ...(9)... to flee deeper into Thailand, and have ...(10)... instead to stay close to their Cambodian homeland, inspite of all the dangers and hardships they face everyday.

1. (*a*) that (*b*) when
(*c*) where (*d*) which
2. (*a*) among (*b*) at
(*c*) on (*d*) in
3. (*a*) stony (*b*) beautiful
(*c*) gaudy (*d*) dry
4. (*a*) As (*b*) And
(*c*) But (*d*) So
5. (*a*) happy (*b*) only
(*c*) erstwhile (*d*) cheerful
6. (*a*) were (*b*) are
(*c*) have (*d*) being
7. (*a*) eyes (*b*) ears
(*c*) feet (*d*) hand
8. (*a*) fluttered (*b*) cluttered
(*c*) tattered (*d*) battered
9. (*a*) denied (*b*) asked
(*c*) wanted (*d*) refused
10. (*a*) wondered (*b*) refused
(*c*) chosen (*d*) needed

Passage 2

...(11)..., even in Delhi, however, takes place in small ...(12)... shanties, where workers wear no ...(13)... clothing, and the process can be as ...(14)... as chopping the material, making it into long strings, and then beads, which can be later ...(15)... One has never seen any ...(16)... of ventilation in any of these factories, and the air often has an acrid, ...(17)... odour which even the workers ...(18)... about, given a chance. In the 'vata' where plastic is melted, to put it simplistically, the workers often ...(19)... over and inhale freely. Yet, such shanties are not small operations, and many of them are fit to be called small industries. The unrecognised, even ...(20)... status given to them forces them to behind iron fences, for reasons financial as well as to carry on unhindered.

11. (*a*) Reviving (*b*) Recycling
(*c*) Restoring (*d*) Replenishing
12. (*a*) clandestine (*b*) concentrated
(*c*) closed (*d*) isolated
13. (*a*) conservative (*b*) sheathing
(*c*) protective (*d*) enclosing
14. (*a*) cumbersome (*b*) crude
(*c*) strong (*d*) difficult
15. (*a*) moulded (*b*) structured
(*c*) manufactured (*d*) differentiated
16. (*a*) privileges (*b*) resources
(*c*) emoluments (*d*) facilities

17. (*a*) sweet (*b*) penacious
(*c*) pungent (*d*) purverse
18. (*a*) complain (*b*) comply
(*c*) assert (*d*) criticise
19. (*a*) rely (*b*) rest
(*c*) lean (*d*) bend
20. (*a*) lawful (*b*) humble
(*c*) illegitimate (*d*) unestimated

Passage 3 **(Bank P.O. 1994)**

One fairly well knows that ...(21)... of technological ...(22)... has been a shortage of jobs. As a result of automation and computerisation, which made ...(23)... progress over the last decade, managements have ...(24)... employment levels.

With the ...(25)... of globalisation loosening government controls all over the world, competition and performance judged on bottom line results is sweeping across numerous jobs. These factors and ...(26)... of mere survival are making voluntary retirement schemes a permanent feature of organisation ...(27)... exercises. What is ...(28)... is on its way to ...(29)... compulsory. When a reasonable provision for alimony is made by the organisation, it ...(30)... a character of mutual consent.

21. (*a*) fall (*b*) area
(*c*) upshot (*d*) increase
(*e*) expansion
22. (*a*) parks (*b*) research
(*c*) education (*d*) innovation
(*e*) upgradation
23. (*a*) slow (*b*) rapid
(*c*) wider (*d*) steady
(*e*) insignificant
24. (*a*) frozen (*b*) trained
(*c*) increased (*d*) descended
(*e*) established
25. (*a*) forces (*b*) revival
(*c*) economics (*d*) competition
(*e*) advancement
26. (*a*) urge (*b*) desire
(*c*) difficulties (*d*) competitions
(*e*) compulsions
27. (*a*) slimming (*b*) building
(*c*) growing (*d*) reducing
(*e*) developing
28. (*a*) choice (*b*) offered
(*c*) selective (*d*) voluntary
(*e*) inevitable
29. (*a*) offering (*b*) becoming
(*c*) obtaining (*d*) graduating
(*e*) establishing
30. (*a*) needs (*b*) acquires
(*c*) signifies (*d*) misses
(*e*) envelopes

Passage 4 **(Assistant Grade, 1993)**

The fact is that democracy is the only ...(31)... system that can preserve the Indian entity, constitute its whole beyond the sum of the various fragments that go into its making and ...(32)... its invaluable genius of stumbling along ...(33)... a humane order. If democracy in India is done ...(34)... with, India itself will ...(35)... in the morass of the various particularities that ...(36)... it. Universal adult ...(37)... and a periodic ...(38)... of the popular mandate ...(39)... by the government is ...(40)... for democracy and hence India's integrity.

31. (*a*) viable (*b*) fundamental
(*c*) possible (*d*) acceptable
32. (*a*) suggest (*b*) promote
(*c*) encourage (*d*) inspire
33. (*a*) with (*b*) towards
(*c*) to (*d*) for
34. (*a*) off (*b*) up
(*c*) away (*d*) out
35. (*a*) vanish (*b*) sink
(*c*) surrender (*d*) finish
36. (*a*) form (*b*) define
(*c*) outline (*d*) constitute
37. (*a*) sensibility (*b*) education
(*c*) participation (*d*) franchise
38. (*a*) survey (*b*) appearance
(*c*) action (*d*) renewal
39. (*a*) obtained (*b*) gained
(*c*) secured (*d*) reserved
40. (*a*) dispensable (*b*) indispensable
(*c*) obvious (*d*) desirable

Passage 5

There is no ...(41)... about the fact that travelling broadens the mind. It is a ...(42)... of education. People who have not travelled may be ...(43)... to frogs living in a well. Just like the frogs, they begin to ...(44)... that their village, or town, or city is the ...(45)... world. This way of thinking makes them ...(46)... minded and parochial. Those people who read books, magazines and newspapers come to ...(47)... something about the world outside, but this is not the same thing as seeing the outside world with one's own eyes. To see the beautiful Taj Mahal ...(48)... moonlight is an experience and lesson in ...(49)... beauty that no ...(50)... book or magazine can provide.

41. (*a*) proof (*b*) hesitation (*c*) doubt (*d*) picture
42. (*a*) site (*b*) way (*c*) method (*d*) means
43. (*a*) similar (*b*) compared (*c*) matched (*d*) like
44. (*a*) believe (*b*) credulous (*c*) mean (*d*) rely
45. (*a*) complete (*b*) entire (*c*) whole (*d*) full
46. (*a*) narrow (*b*) constricted (*c*) restricted (*d*) intelligent
47. (*a*) believe (*b*) see (*c*) know (*d*) think
48. (*a*) from (*b*) with (*c*) of (*d*) by
49. (*a*) admirable (*b*) aesthetic (*c*) commendable (*d*) remarkable
50. (*a*) figured (*b*) coloured (*c*) illustrated (*d*) remarkable

ANSWERS

1. (*c*)	**2.** (*a*)	**3.** (*b*)	**4.** (*d*)	**5.** (*a*)	**6.** (*b*)	**7.** (*a*)	**8.** (*c*)	**9.** (*d*)	**10.** (*c*)
11. (*b*)	**12.** (*a*)	**13.** (*c*)	**14.** (*b*)	**15.** (*a*)	**16.** (*d*)	**17.** (*c*)	**18.** (*a*)	**19.** (*c*)	**20.** (*c*)
21. (*c*)	**22.** (*d*)	**23.** (*b*)	**24.** (*a*)	**25.** (*a*)	**26.** (*e*)	**27.** (*c*)	**28.** (*d*)	**29.** (*b*)	**30.** (*c*)
31. (*a*)	**32.** (*b*)	**33.** (*b*)	**34.** (*c*)	**35.** (*b*)	**36.** (*d*)	**37.** (*d*)	**38.** (*a*)	**39.** (*b*)	**40.** (*b*)
41. (*c*)	**42.** (*d*)	**43.** (*b*)	**44.** (*a*)	**45.** (*b*)	**46.** (*a*)	**47.** (*c*)	**48.** (*d*)	**49.** (*b*)	**50.** (*c*)

PRACTICE SET 6

Passage 1 **(S.B.I.P.O. 1995)**

The cities are ...(1)... up and urban unemployment steadily grows. Very probably there is an equal measure of ...(2)... in the countryside. The poorest quarter of the population in developing lands ...(3)... being left almost entirely behind in the vast ...(4)... of the modern technological society. The "marginal men", the ...(5)... strugglers for survival on the ...(6)... of farm and city, may ...(7)... more than two billion. Can we ...(8)... any human order surviving with so ...(9)... a mass of ...(10)... piling up at its base ?

1. (*a*) filling (*b*) piling (*c*) growing (*d*) enlarging (*e*) developing
2. (*a*) diversity (*b*) imbalance (*c*) shortage (*d*) employment (*e*) worklessness
3. (*a*) risks (*b*) suffers (*c*) believes (*d*) condemns (*e*) endeavours
4. (*a*) result (*b*) struggle (*c*) surface (*d*) abundance (*e*) transformation
5. (*a*) brave (*b*) honest (*c*) aged (*d*) ultimate (*e*) wretched
6. (*a*) surface (*b*) ground (*c*) fringes (*d*) environment (*e*) background
7. (*a*) mount (*b*) extent (*c*) project (*d*) number (*e*) account
8. (*a*) argue (*b*) hope (*c*) suspect (*d*) imagine (*e*) question
9. (*a*) far (*b*) long (*c*) little (*d*) many (*e*) gross
10. (*a*) misery (*b*) humility (*c*) generation (*d*) population (*e*) degradation

Passage 2

The ...(11)... of a survey by the National Institute of ...(12)... health give ...(13)... for ...(14)... According to the survey about 14 million people in India are affected by ....(15)... mental ...(16)... at any point of time. In the case of mentally ill, it is ...(17)... enough difficult to ...(18)... them, let alone ....(19)... them. The most ...(20)... are those in the ...(21)..., for whatever ...(22)... for the mentally sick exist are concentrated around major urban centres.

11. (*a*) verdicts (*b*) measures (*c*) findings (*d*) decisions (*e*) judgements
12. (*a*) social (*b*) mental (*c*) physical (*d*) psychical (*e*) spiritual

13. (*a*) cause (*b*) food
(*c*) support (*d*) purpose
(*e*) reinforcement

14. (*a*) fear (*b*) alarm
(*c*) vexation (*d*) discontent
(*e*) dissatisfaction

15. (*a*) fatal (*b*) serious
(*c*) strong (*d*) important
(*e*) dangerous

16. (*a*) disorder (*b*) confusion
(*c*) dislocation (*d*) involvement
(*e*) perturbation

17. (*a*) hardly (*b*) never
(*c*) seldom (*d*) often
(*e*) occasionally

18. (*a*) cure (*b*) identify
(*c*) select (*d*) recognise
(*e*) rehabilitate

19. (*a*) treat (*b*) cure
(*c*) guide (*d*) advise
(*e*) facilitate

20. (*a*) serious (*b*) careless
(*c*) abandoned (*d*) indifferent
(*e*) neglected

21. (*a*) poor (*b*) urban
(*c*) rural (*d*) forest
(*e*) suburban

22. (*a*) avenues (*b*) remedies
(*c*) facilities (*d*) advantages
(*e*) solicitations

Passage 3 **(Central Excise, 1993)**

After an absence of thirty years, I decided to visit my old school again. I had ...(23)... to find changes, but not a ...(24)... different building. As I walked up ...(25)... school drive, I wondered for a ...(26)... if I had come to the ....(27)... address. The grimy, red-brick fortress with ...(28)... tall windows that had looked down ...(29)... on the playground and playing fields ...(30)... been swept away. In its place ...(31)... a bright, modern block raised from ...(32)... ground on great concrete stilts.

23. (*a*) known (*b*) expected
(*c*) hoped (*d*) imagined

24. (*a*) entirely (*b*) barely
(*c*) completely (*d*) very

25. (*a*) our (*b*) my
(*c*) the (*d*) a

26. (*a*) moment (*b*) while
(*c*) instance (*d*) period

27. (*a*) school (*b*) actual
(*c*) right (*d*) exact

28. (*a*) her (*b*) its
(*c*) the (*d*) some

29. (*a*) pleasantly (*b*) seriously
(*c*) grimly (*d*) sorrowfully

30. (*a*) did (*b*) has
(*c*) have (*d*) had

31. (*a*) stood (*b*) was
(*c*) appeared (*d*) rose

32. (*a*) solid (*b*) a
(*c*) the (*d*) low

Passage 4

The ...(33)... of today is a huge financial undertaking with the same outlook as any other limited company. The ...(34)... staff have to make circulation, and if they do not they will soon be ...(35)... by those who can. Their independence therefore suffers a grave limitation. It is further ...(36)... by the fact that a newspaper is as much an advertising medium as a vehicle for ...(37)... It is said that the ...(38)... which the public pays for its newspaper covers no more than a third of the ...(39)... of production; the other two-thirds is accounted ...(40)... by advertisement revenue.

33. (*a*) hospital (*b*) newspaper
(*c*) theatre (*d*) library

34. (*a*) performing (*b*) editorial
(*c*) company (*d*) teaching

35. (*a*) sustained (*b*) treated
(*c*) supplanted (*d*) cured

36. (*a*) destroyed (*b*) deepened
(*c*) curtailed (*d*) aggravated

37. (*a*) training (*b*) news
(*c*) business (*d*) patients

38. (*a*) cost (*b*) tax
(*c*) fee (*d*) price

39. (*a*) expenses (*b*) cost
(*c*) sale (*d*) amount

40. (*a*) into (*b*) in
(*c*) from (*d*) for

Passage 5 **(Bank P.O. 1993)**

Most experts agree that even people who think they are sleeping enough would ...(41)... be better off with more ...(42)... As evidence of a general sleep deficit, they ...(43)... the use of the bedside alarm clock used by people to ...(44)... their waking hours. The most relentless robber of ...(45)... is the complexity of every day life. Whenever pressures from work, family and community ...(46)..., many people ...(47)... with sleep. Another ...(48)... of sleep is the shift work. The ...(49)... of round-the-clock entertainment, especially all-night television, also takes its ...(50)...

41. (*a*) mainly (*b*) probably
(*c*) suddenly (*d*) attentively
(*e*) meaningfully

42. (*a*) rest (*b*) work (*c*) time (*d*) energy (*e*) freedom
43. (*a*) prove (*b*) cite (*c*) ignore (*d*) explain (*e*) overlook
44. (*a*) widen (*b*) disturb (*c*) prolong (*d*) improve (*e*) minimise
45. (*a*) stress (*b*) sleep (*c*) leisure (*d*) pleasure (*e*) motivation
46. (*a*) mount (*b*) unite (*c*) happen (*d*) diminish (*e*) disappear
47. (*a*) depend (*b*) desist (*c*) detach (*d*) deprive (*e*) dispense
48. (*a*) study (*b*) product (*c*) thief (*d*) drawback (*e*) contributor
49. (*a*) telecast (*b*) viewing (*c*) deficiency (*d*) requirement (*e*) availability
50. (*a*) toll (*b*) credit (*c*) risk (*d*) pressure (*e*) enjoyment

ANSWERS

1. (*c*)	**2.** (*e*)	**3.** (*b*)	**4.** (*b*)	**5.** (*a*)	**6.** (*c*)	**7.** (*d*)	**8.** (*b*)	**9.** (*e*)	**10.** (*d*)
11. (*c*)	**12.** (*b*)	**13.** (*a*)	**14.** (*b*)	**15.** (*b*)	**16.** (*a*)	**17.** (*d*)	**18.** (*b*)	**19.** (*b*)	**20.** (*e*)
21. (*c*)	**22.** (*c*)	**23.** (*b*)	**24.** (*c*)	**25.** (*c*)	**26.** (*a*)	**27.** (*c*)	**28.** (*b*)	**29.** (*c*)	**30.** (*d*)
31. (*a*)	**32.** (*c*)	**33.** (*b*)	**34.** (*b*)	**35.** (*c*)	**36.** (*c*)	**37.** (*b*)	**38.** (*d*)	**39.** (*b*)	**40.** (*d*)
41. (*b*)	**42.** (*a*)	**43.** (*b*)	**44.** (*d*)	**45.** (*b*)	**46.** (*a*)	**47.** (*e*)	**48.** (*c*)	**49.** (*e*)	**50.** (*a*)

PRACTICE SET 7

Passage 1 **(Central Excise, 1992)**

The feeling of insecurity among the people has increased even though there is ...(1)... use of the para-military and the military. The excesses ...(2)... by the two forces, particularly by the first, do not ...(3)... the type of anger it should because they are seen ...(4)... those who are trying to disintegrate the country. Even a ...(5)... for more say in the administration is shouted down. Human rights organisations and Civil liberty activists are considered a ...(6)..., if not unpatriotic. Even the ...(7)... cases of cruelty are not pursued by the government ...(8)... the inquiry should ...(9)... the forces and ...(10)... the instrument on which it has come to depend.

1. (*a*) free (*b*) reduced (*c*) little (*d*) liberal
2. (*a*) cleared (*b*) committed (*c*) condoned (*d*) displayed
3. (*a*) resist (*b*) evoke (*c*) convey (*d*) suppress
4. (*a*) obeying (*b*) ignoring (*c*) supporting (*d*) fighting
5. (*a*) demand (*b*) desire (*c*) prayer (*d*) plea
6. (*a*) nuisance (*b*) help (*c*) threat (*d*) boon
7. (*a*) minor (*b*) blatant (*c*) new (*d*) concealed
8. (*a*) because (*b*) for (*c*) till (*d*) lest
9. (*a*) disperse (*b*) derail (*c*) demoralise (*d*) degrade
10. (*a*) blunt (*b*) raise (*c*) change (*d*) lose

Passage 2

Political parties have a right to ...(11).. the electorate but when wooing ...(12).. into bribing, the very ...(13)... of democracy is defeated. Although it is illegal to buy votes, parties in power often ...(14)... to unhealthy tactics to keep sections of the electorate happy. Not only do they make ...(15)... promises but they announce various ...(16)... and relief to ...(17)... sections on the eve of an election. The people still ...(18)... the way in which Prime Minister Indira Gandhi tried to ...(19)... votes for her party by laying ...(20)... for various projects just before a general election. Over the years, the ...(21)... of the ruling party towards the electorate has not changed.

11. (*a*) win (*b*) woo (*c*) obviate (*d*) conquer (*e*) overcome

12. (*a*) revives (*b*) dangles (*c*) regenerates (*d*) degenerates (*e*) reverberates

13. (*a*) reason (*b*) view (*c*) outcome (*d*) purpose (*e*) reverence

14. (*a*) resort (*b*) restore (*c*) revert (*d*) render (*e*) reciprocate

15. (*a*) furious (*b*) lavish (*c*) luxurious (*d*) affirmative (*e*) rejuvinating

16. (*a*) bribes (*b*) facilities (*c*) assurances (*d*) concessions (*d*) opportunities

17. (*a*) varying (*b*) every (*c*) hitherto (*d*) different (*e*) differentiating

18. (*a*) remember (*b*) commend (*c*) brandish (*d*) exonerate (*e*) commemorate

19. (*a*) gain (*b*) collect (*c*) secure (*d*) gather (*e*) manage

20. (*a*) stepping (*b*) beginning (*c*) basis (*d*) foundation (*e*) commensurate

21. (*a*) bent (*b*) shift (*c*) aspect (*d*) attitude (*e*) inclination

Passage 3 **(Bank P.O. 1996)**

To the curious and the ...(22).. the sea still presents the challenge of the unknown, for ignorance is still the ...(23)... characteristic of man's relation to the sea. But now, more than ever, necessity ...(24)... us onward in our exploration of the sea. We now have submarines capable of ...(25)... submergence for many months ...(26)... missiles capable of ...(27)... many times greater than that ...(28)... by World War II. For ...(29)... reasons, therefore, we need ...(30)... to learn more about the ...(31).. of ocean bottom, about deep ocean currents, temperature, density and so on.

Another necessity ...(32)... us to learn to master the sea. That necessity is food. The lives of two-third of the world's people are wholly ...(33)... by that basic necessity; they are ...(34)... by hunger and by the weakness and disease which hunger generates.

22. (*a*) outgoing (*b*) watchful (*c*) intelligent (*d*) courageous (*e*) formidable

23. (*a*) critical (*b*) valuable (*c*) remarkable (*d*) outstanding (*e*) distinguishing

24. (*a*) makes (*b*) goads (*c*) excites (*d*) propels (*e*) projects

25. (*a*) steady (*b*) deadly (*c*) durable (*d*) turbulent (*e*) provocative

26. (*a*) guiding (*b*) directing (*c*) holding (*d*) providing (*e*) subjecting

27. (*a*) expansion (*b*) projection (*c*) domination (*d*) aggression (*e*) destruction

28. (*a*) forced (*b*) witnessed (*c*) wrought (*d*) conceived (*e*) experienced

29. (*a*) strategic (*b*) historical (*c*) academic (*d*) deliberate (*e*) traditional

30. (*a*) wilfully (*b*) cautiously (*c*) urgently (*d*) judiciously (*e*) drastically

31. (*a*) velocity (*b*) tenacity (*c*) resources (*d*) topography (*e*) distribution

32. (*a*) wants (*b*) presses (*c*) involves (*d*) provides (*e*) threatens

33. (*a*) dictated (*b*) projected (*c*) developed (*d*) challenged (*e*) galvanised

34. (*a*) salvaged (*b*) governed (*c*) oppressed (*d*) perturbed (*e*) controlled

Passage 4 **(N.D.A. 1994)**

A university stands for humanism, reason and the adventure of ideas. It stands for the onward ...(35)... of the human race ...(36).. higher objectives. If the universities ...(37)... their duty adequately, then it ...(38)... well with the nation and ...(39)... people. But if the temple of learning itself becomes a home of narrow bigotry and petty objectives, ...(40)... will the nation prosper?

35. (a) motion (b) march (c) progress
36. (a) towards (b) on (c) for
37. (a) finish (b) obey (c) discharge
38. (a) was (b) will be (c) is
39. (a) the (b) her (c) their
40. (a) when (b) why (c) how

Passage 5

The joint family gave way to the ...(41)... family. Despite the ...(42)... that it offers, children feel ...(43)..., lonely and frustrated leading to psychiatrist problems, pressures and ...(44)... A cross-section of children were interviewed, and they matter-of-factly ...(45)... problems, at the same time ...(46)... showing the way to ...(47)... solutions. Tell your children about your work. Young as they are, they ...(48)... where you have been all day. Explain to them 'Mummy has a teaching job. She teaches little children to read and write' or 'Daddy works in a factory. The factory makes scooters'. At least now the child ...(49)... a mental picture of how you spend the day. There develops a certain ...(50)... in that knowledge.

41. (a) lonely (b) individual (c) nuclear (d) self-centred
42. (a) seclusion (b) privacy (c) isolation (d) separation
43. (a) neglected (b) avoided (c) disregarded (d) segregated
44. (a) burdens (b) complexities (c) complications (d) controversies
45. (a) marked (b) declared (c) pin-pointed (d) designated
46. (a) inadvertently (b) unknowingly (c) obviously (d) painstakingly
47. (a) reasonable (b) plausible (c) remarkable (d) referred
48. (a) wonder (b) amaze (c) feel (d) estimate
49. (a) constructs (b) inculcates (c) develops (d) establishes
50. (a) security (b) assurance (c) solace (d) restfulness

ANSWERS

1. (d)	2. (b)	3. (b)	4. (d)	5. (a)	6. (a)	7. (b)	8. (d)	9. (c)	10. (a)
11. (b)	12. (d)	13. (d)	14. (a)	15. (b)	16. (d)	17. (d)	18. (a)	19. (c)	20. (d)
21. (d)	22. (b)	23. (c)	24. (b)	25. (a)	26. (c)	27. (e)	28. (b)	29. (a)	30. (c)
31. (d)	32. (b)	33. (a)	34. (c)	35. (b)	36. (a)	37. (c)	38. (b)	39. (b)	40. (c)
41. (c)	42. (b)	43. (a)	44. (b)	45. (c)	46. (a)	47. (b)	48. (a)	49. (c)	50. (a)

PRACTICE SET 8

Passage 1 **(S.S.C. 1995)**

Children are loved by all human beings. But ...(1).. this world of human ...(2)... there is no ...(3)... nuisance than a boy ...(4)... the age of fourteen. He is neither ornamental ...(5)... useful. It is impossible to ...(6)... affection on him as on a ...(7)... boy and he is always getting ...(8)... the way. If he talks with a childish lisp he is called a baby, and if he answers in a grown up way he is called impertinent. Then he is ...(9)... the unattractive, growing age. He grows out ...(10)... his clothes, with indecent haste. His voice begins to break and loses its childish charm.

1. (a) of (b) on (c) for (d) in
2. (a) affairs (b) life (c) beings (d) world
3. (a) worst (b) bad (c) worse (d) better
4. (a) at (b) of (c) on (d) in
5. (a) and (b) or (c) nor (d) so
6. (a) show (b) shower (c) repose (d) showering
7. (a) tiny (b) big (c) small (d) little
8. (a) through (b) in (c) on (d) off
9. (a) with (b) on (c) of (d) at

10. (*a*) of (*b*) from
(*c*) beyond (*d*) through

Passage 2

We need never feel dull in the country. No matter how often we walk ...(11)... the same road, over the same ...(12)... or through the same woodland paths, ...(13)... is always something new, something fresh to ...(14)... . It may be a little plant that ...(15)... up since last we visited the ...(16)..., a hedge that was just a lot of ...(17)... sticks may now be ...(18)... with flowers. We may find a bird's ...(19)... deep in a bush, if we are ...(20)... not to frighten the birds, as the days pass, see first the little legs and then the baby birds.

11. (*a*) at (*b*) into
(*c*) down (*d*) off

12. (*a*) fields (*b*) lanes
(*c*) corner (*d*) regions

13. (*a*) there (*b*) here
(*c*) this, (*d*) it

14. (*a*) see (*b*) smell
(*c*) scan (*d*) spot

15. (*a*) did come (*b*) has come
(*c*) would come (*d*) comes

16. (*a*) site (*b*) spot
(*c*) village (*d*) place

17. (*a*) twisted (*b*) brown
(*c*) thick (*d*) tall

18. (*a*) protected (*b*) shrouded
(*c*) covered (*d*) surrounded

19. (*a*) cell (*b*) hole
(*c*) hive (*d*) nest

20. (*a*) anxious (*b*) attentive
(*c*) thoughtful (*d*) careful

Passage 3 **(Bank P.O. 1994)**

Decisions may be ...(21)... at either through initiative or through inertia. Many misfortunes in the world come across the bridge of indecision. Power corrupts but weakness also corrupts. The fruits of weakness like fear, bitterness and suspicion can ...(22)... in a paralysis of decision. Inner division can produce indecision, and indecision results by weakness of character.

An occasional wrong decision may be sometimes ...(23)... to indecision. The ...(24)... man is often self-centred. He fears making a ...(25)... and the fear paralyses him. When indecision grips a nation, free men feel the need for an ...(26)... ruler and they are prepared to ...(27)... democracy overboard. In certain large democracies, the governments rule with a ...(28)... majority. They often know what decisions would be beneficial in the long run, but they ...(29)... to take them lest they be unpopular. Their ...(30)... to carry the opposition and to rally people to a larger purpose, makes them ineffective rulers.

21. (*a*) aimed (*b*) looked
(*c*) arrived (*d*) deferred
(*e*) formulated

22. (*a*) drown (*b*) result
(*c*) exist (*d*) indulge
(*e*) entangle

23. (*a*) useful (*b*) preferable
(*c*) acceptable (*d*) susceptible
(*e*) questionable

24. (*a*) dishonest (*b*) common
(*c*) selfish (*d*) indecisive
(*e*) trustworthy

25. (*a*) decision (*b*) query
(*c*) mistake (*d*) presentation
(*e*) submission

26. (*a*) indecisive (*b*) energetic
(*c*) eccentric (*d*) optimistic
(*e*) autocratic

27. (*a*) regard (*b*) accept
(*c*) throw (*d*) cultivate
(*e*) sacrifice

28. (*a*) derisive (*b*) slender
(*c*) vast (*d*) winning
(*e*) substantial

29. (*a*) like (*b*) fail
(*c*) prefer (*d*) decide
(*e*) hesitate

30. (*a*) desire (*b*) skill
(*c*) apathy (*d*) inability
(*e*) indifference

Passage 4

The Universities in India must learn to ...(31)... individuality, variety and dissent ...(32)... a climate of tolerance. Dissent there is, even now, but usually of a sensational kind. The general tendency however, is, to produce the 'organisation man' who is ...(33)... to challenge the accepted pattern of social behaviour and social institutions at the intellectual level and who is ...(34)... often anxious to worm himself into the good ...(35)... of the people who count so that he may be able to 'get on' in life.

31. (*a*) ignore (*b*) create
(*c*) suppress (*d*) establish

(*e*) encourage

32. (*a*) within (*b*) from
(*c*) but (*d*) before
(*e*) without

33. (*a*) free (*b*) naive
(*c*) afraid (*d*) willing
(*e*) ignorant

34. (*a*) never (*b*) less
(*c*) too (*d*) rarely
(*e*) hardly

35. (*a*) graces (*b*) looks
(*c*) charm (*d*) influence
(*e*) connection

Passage 5 **(C.D.S. 1994)**

Many of us believe that science is something modern, ...(36)... the truth is that ...(37)... has been using science for ...(38)... very long time. However, it has ...(39)... a greater effect on human lives in the last 25 ...(40)... 30 years than in the hundreds of years ...(41)... the invention of the plough. The ...(42)... gifts of science have made modern life ...(43)... and comfortable. But science has ...(44)... the same time created new problems. One of these, which may become ...(45)... in the years to come, is ...(46)... of 'jet- lag'. With the coming of modern jets, flying at more than 900 kilometres an hour, the world ...(47)... very small indeed. Today if you ...(48)... New Delhi at 4.00 in the morning, you ...(49)... eat an early breakfast in the sky ...(50)... Kabul, and be in London by about 1.00 p.m.

36. (*a*) unless (*b*) if (*c*) though
37. (*a*) people (*b*) man (*c*) men
38. (*a*) the (*b*) a (*c*) that
39. (*a*) have (*b*) had (*c*) has
40. (*a*) and (*b*) or (*c*) either
41. (*a*) from (*b*) for (*c*) since
42. (*a*) marvellous (*b*) costly
(*c*) inexpensive
43. (*a*) dull (*b*) exciting (*c*) aimless
44. (*a*) at (*b*) in (*c*) within
45. (*a*) bad (*b*) worse (*c*) good
46. (*a*) those (*b*) this (*c*) that
47. (*a*) can become (*b*) became
(*c*) has become
48. (*a*) leave (*b*) will leave
(*c*) would leave
49. (*a*) will (*b*) can (*c*) must
50. (*a*) at (*b*) on (*c*) over

ANSWERS

1. (*d*)	**2.** (*c*)	**3.** (*c*)	**4.** (*b*)	**5.** (*c*)	**6.** (*b*)	**7.** (*d*)	**8.** (*b*)	**9.** (*d*)	**10.** (*a*)
11. (*c*)	**12.** (*b*)	**13.** (*a*)	**14.** (*a*)	**15.** (*b*)	**16.** (*c*)	**17.** (*b*)	**18.** (*c*)	**19.** (*d*)	**20.** (*d*)
21. (*c*)	**22.** (*b*)	**23.** (*b*)	**24.** (*d*)	**25.** (*a*)	**26.** (*e*)	**27.** (*c*)	**28.** (*c*)	**29.** (*e*)	**30.** (*d*)
31. (*e*)	**32.** (*a*)	**33.** (*c*)	**34.** (*c*)	**35.** (*a*)	**36.** (*c*)	**37.** (*b*)	**38.** (*b*)	**39.** (*b*)	**40.** (*b*)
41. (*c*)	**42.** (*a*)	**43.** (*b*)	**44.** (*a*)	**45.** (*b*)	**46.** (*c*)	**47.** (*c*)	**48.** (*a*)	**49.** (*b*)	**50.** (*c*)

PRACTICE SET 9

Passage 1 **(S.B.I.P.O. 1994)**

'Quit India' came not from the lips but the aching heart of millions. In this open rebellion, the Indian ....(1)... reached its climax. The British were not only ...(2)... by it, but also were obliged to quit unilaterally. The importance of Quit India can be ...(3)... from Lord Linlithgow's statement, "I am engaged here, in meeting by far the most ...(4)... rebellion since that of 1857, the gravity and extent of which we have so far ...(5)... from the world for reasons of military security". Still more significant was Churchill's gloomy disclosure to the King Emperor that, "the idea of ...(6)... of power had become an admitted ...(7)... in the minds of British party leaders", although his public statements were diametrically opposite. The ...(8)... created by Quit India made the British ...(9)... that they could no longer keep India in ...(10)...

1. (*a*) patriotism (*b*) freedom
(*c*) liberation (*d*) revolution

(*e*) leadership

2. (*a*) attacked (*b*) inspired (*c*) enfeebled (*d*) threatened (*e*) impressed

3. (*a*) established (*b*) diffused (*c*) gauged (*d*) determined (*e*) invigorated

4. (*a*) trivial (*b*) serious (*c*) auspicious (*d*) praiseworthy (*e*) magnificent

5. (*a*) elicited (*b*) excluded (*c*) abstained (*d*) concealed (*e*) prevented

6. (*a*) transfer (*b*) seizure (*c*) grabbing (*d*) retainment (*e*) enhancement

7. (*a*) fantasy (*b*) tactics (*c*) occurrence (*d*) inevitability (*e*) disillusionment

8. (*a*) anarchy (*b*) violence (*c*) taboos (*d*) exigencies (*e*) vengeance

9. (*a*) anxious (*b*) realise (*c*) imagine (*d*) pretend (*e*) apprehend

10. (*a*) exile (*b*) power (*c*) bondage (*d*) suspense (*e*) abeyance

Passage 2

I am not writing this in praise of police, or to ...(11)... police, nor to hold them up as paragons of ...(12)... I ...(13)... want people to put the problem in proper ...(14)... and not be carried away by individual or ...(15)... incidents, for ...(16).. the entire police force, to ...(17)... that they are all callous brutes and tortures. There is increasingly a ...(18)... in the media to outrageously highlight individual ...(19)... in a manner which gives an impression about the entire police force having become thoroughly cruel ...(20)... of the people.

11. (*a*) eulogise (*b*) repent (*c*) raise (*d*) regard

12. (*a*) beauty (*b*) esteem (*c*) virtue (*d*) goodness

13. (*a*) rarely (*b*) merely (*c*) hardly (*d*) usually

14. (*a*) perspective (*b*) idea (*c*) form (*d*) ideal

15. (*a*) rare (*b*) stray (*c*) misleading (*d*) unusual

16. (*a*) humbling (*b*) degrading (*c*) condemning (*d*) disregarding

17. (*a*) impress (*b*) assert (*c*) establish (*d*) instil

18. (*a*) tendency (*b*) habit (*c*) nature (*d*) occupation

19. (*a*) occurrences (*b*) incidents (*c*) accidents (*d*) instances

20. (*a*) tyrants (*b*) brutes (*c*) oppressors (*d*) torturers

Passage 3 **(Section Officer's Exam, 1993)**

Why is it that the CRP, BSF and the Army give a better account of themselves than the state police? It is the structure of the state police that needs to be looked ...(21)... In a district or city, where there is a separate police force, a majority of the policemen are ...(22)... in police stations. The police station staff is often over-extended and no ...(23)... is available at that level. It is the state force that has to be called ...(24)... But it takes time to ...(25)... forces. If the law and order situation ...(26)... simultaneously at many places, there is manpower ...(27)... Thus once rioting breaks ...(28)..., it takes time to bring it under control so that there is a time ...(29).. between the first incident and the appearance of the adequate force to ...(30)... the situation. The public hue and cry about the delayed arrival of the police force is not unjustified.

21. (*a*) through (*b*) on (*c*) into (*d*) at

22. (*a*) detained (*b*) deployed (*c*) deputed (*d*) employed

23. (*a*) reserve (*b*) force (*c*) company (*d*) squad

24. (*a*) upon (*b*) up (*c*) at (*d*) on

25. (*a*) move (*b*) arrange (*c*) mobilise (*d*) prepare

26. (*a*) worsens (*b*) proliferates (*c*) degenerates (*d*) aggravates

27. (*a*) default (*b*) shortage (*c*) shortcoming (*d*) failure

28. (*a*) away (*b*) in (*c*) off (*d*) out

29. (*a*) lag (*b*) interval (*c*) delay (*d*) difference

30. (*a*) control (*b*) restrain (*c*) step (*d*) prevent

Passage 4

In earlier days, a handicraftsman, the typical labourer, received a certain ...(31)... from the work he did. His efforts were mostly to his own ...(32)... He saw the fruits of his own work in the ...(33)... object he produced. More-over, the ...(34)... of this object ...(35)... demanded his adaptability or inventiveness to overcome the ...(36)... which arose. In a real sense one can speak of his being educated by his ...(37)... Today all is ...(38).. A standardised job is done in a standardised ...(39)... and a standardised job for a standardised ...(40)...

31. (*a*) satisfaction (*b*) reward (*c*) remuneration (*d*) consolation
32. (*a*) advantage (*b*) profit (*c*) benefit (*d*) betterment
33. (*a*) complete (*b*) full (*c*) perfect (*d*) whole
34. (*a*) making (*b*) creating (*c*) attempting (*d*) discovering
35. (*a*) often (*b*) generally (*c*) mostly (*d*) invariably
36. (*a*) doubts (*b*) obstructions (*c*) riddles (*d*) difficulties
37. (*a*) trade (*b*) labour (*c*) talent (*d*) attempt
38. (*a*) changed (*b*) disappeared (*c*) reversed (*d*) revolutionised
39. (*a*) method (*b*) mode (*c*) manner (*d*) fashion
40. (*a*) pay (*b*) salary (*c*) wage (*d*) remuneration

Passage 5 **(U.D.C. 1994)**

To change the hearts of the ...(41)... in such a way as to make it ...(42)... for them to indulge in these ...(43)... without changing the ...(44)... of the governments that rule over ...(45)... is an impossibility. When ...(46)... reaches that point it will ...(47)... to be human; it will become a ...(48)... of supermen of gods and it will no ...(49)... need the guidance of ...(50)... of the type of Mahatma Gandhi.

41. (*a*) crowd (*b*) groups (*c*) men (*d*) mobs
42. (*a*) impossible (*b*) likely (*c*) unlikely (*d*) possible
43. (*a*) cruelties (*b*) misdeeds (*c*) brutalities (*d*) actions
44. (*a*) stands (*b*) hearts (*c*) minds (*d*) decisions
45. (*a*) you (*b*) us (*c*) them (*d*) people
46. (*a*) life (*b*) nature (*c*) humanity (*d*) behaviour
47. (*a*) continue (*b*) cease (*c*) start (*d*) begin
48. (*a*) committee (*b*) government (*c*) organisation (*d*) body
49. (*a*) less (*b*) further (*c*) more (*d*) longer
50. (*a*) men (*b*) man (*c*) god (*d*) gods

ANSWERS

1. (*d*)	**2.** (*c*)	**3.** (*a*)	**4.** (*e*)	**5.** (*d*)	**6.** (*a*)	**7.** (*d*)	**8.** (*d*)	**9.** (*b*)	**10.** (*c*)
11. (*a*)	**12.** (*c*)	**13.** (*b*)	**14.** (*a*)	**15.** (*b*)	**16.** (*c*)	**17.** (*b*)	**18.** (*a*)	**19.** (*d*)	**20.** (*c*)
21. (*c*)	**22.** (*d*)	**23.** (*b*)	**24.** (*a*)	**25.** (*c*)	**26.** (*a*)	**27.** (*b*)	**28.** (*d*)	**29.** (*a*)	**30.** (*a*)
31. (*a*)	**32.** (*d*)	**33.** (*c*)	**34.** (*b*)	**35.** (*a*)	**36.** (*d*)	**37.** (*b*)	**38.** (*c*)	**39.** (*c*)	**40.** (*c*)
41. (*c*)	**42.** (*a*)	**43.** (*c*)	**44.** (*b*)	**45.** (*c*)	**46.** (*c*)	**47.** (*b*)	**48.** (*d*)	**49.** (*d*)	**50.** (*a*)

PRACTICE SET 10

Passage 1 **(NABARD, 1994)**

Do women ...(1)... leadership differently than men do? And if so, will feminine leadership ...(2)... where ...(3)... leadership does not? A recent study suggests somewhat paradoxically that female managers ...(4)... their male ...(5)... even when the personal characteristics of both are very ...(6)... Of the two schools of thought, the structuralist theory argues that men and women do not receive the same treatment in the workplace and that stamping out ...(7)... bias would stamp out the observed ...(8)... In contrast, the socialisation theory contends that men and women experience work differently because men see work as more ...(9)... to their lives. These ...(10)... explanations apart, today business appears to be undergoing a feminisation of leadership.

1. (*a*) exercise (*b*) tolerate (*c*) empower (*d*) authorise (*e*) undertake
2. (*a*) compete (*b*) affect (*c*) succeed (*d*) progress (*e*) dominate
3. (*a*) masculine (*b*) benevolent (*c*) traditional (*d*) charismatic (*e*) authoritarian
4. (*a*) out-cast (*b*) out-do (*c*) out-live (*d*) out-work (*e*) out-stand
5. (*a*) superiors (*b*) employees (*c*) managers (*d*) subordinates (*e*) counterparts
6. (*a*) similar (*b*) unique (*c*) minimal (*d*) distinct (*e*) constant
7. (*a*) class (*b*) culture (*c*) gender (*d*) category (*e*) employment
8. (*a*) equalities (*b*) variations (*c*) distortions (*d*) resemblances (*e*) discriminations
9. (*a*) trivial (*b*) central (*c*) needy (*d*) desperate (*e*) preliminary
10. (*a*) identical (*b*) analogical (*c*) discriminating (*d*) contradictory (*e*) corresponding

Passage 2

U.S. policy ...(11)... human rights has been a major irritant in Asia. A case can be successfully made out that ...(12)... in the history of the world have the human ...(13)... of so many people improved so ...(14)... over so short a period of time as has happened in China in the last decade. Over a billion people now enjoy two ...(15)... meals a day and a standard of living they could hardly have imagined a few years ago. Most have access to basic ...(16)... Life expectancy at birth is longer in Shanghai today than it is in New York. At the same time ...(17)... conditions prevail in many areas as it always has in pre-industrial ...(18)... Over time, with the spread of prosperity and political pluralism will surely come ...(19)... in these conditions. Meanwhile identifying human rights as a major issue for confrontation further ...(20)... the problem instead of alleviating it.

11. (*a*) regarding (*b*) about (*c*) involving (*d*) after
12. (*a*) ever (*b*) seldom (*c*) never (*d*) often
13. (*a*) situation (*b*) condition (*c*) state (*d*) concept
14. (*a*) dramatically (*b*) theatrically (*c*) exhaustively (*d*) drastically
15. (*a*) rare (*b*) square (*c*) full (*d*) standard
16. (*a*) facilities (*b*) privileges (*c*) amenities (*d*) accessories
17. (*a*) tough (*b*) harsh (*c*) strong (*d*) rough
18. (*a*) societies (*b*) traditions (*c*) customs (*d*) festivities
19. (*a*) improvements (*b*) reshuffling (*c*) attainment (*d*) settlement
20. (*a*) accentuates (*b*) alleviates (*c*) endangers (*d*) diminishes

Passage 3 **(B.S.R.B. 1995)**

During the World War I, penicillin was ...(21)... on six patients. The ...(22)... were very much ...(23)..., but unfortunately due to the ...(24)... of penicillin two patients died. This tragic incident proved that it ...(25)... essential to ...(26)... the medicine ...(27)... large quantities. After many months of tireless efforts, a flawless ...(28)... of extracting penicillin in large quantities was evolved. ...(29)... the manufacture and use of it became ...(30)...

21. (*a*) invented (*b*) given (*c*) tested (*d*) suggested (*e*) recommended
22. (*a*) impact (*b*) results (*c*) actions (*d*) dangers (*e*) conditions
23. (*a*) bright (*b*) improving (*c*) deteriorating (*d*) encouraging (*e*) discouraging
24. (*a*) abundance (*b*) shortage (*c*) inefficiency (*d*) weaknesses (*e*) over-supply
25. (*a*) was (*b*) is (*c*) were (*d*) must (*e*) have been
26. (*a*) test (*b*) prove (*c*) give (*d*) inject

(*e*) produce

27. (*a*) in (*b*) by
(*c*) with (*d*) over
(*e*) into

28. (*a*) term (*b*) quality
(*c*) utensil (*d*) technique
(*e*) experiment

29. (*a*) While (*b*) As
(*c*) Soon (*d*) Early
(*e*) Before

30. (*a*) safe (*b*) risky
(*c*) famous (*d*) recognised
(*e*) widespread

Passage 4

Many large business ...(31)... undergo a ...(32)... ritual of ...(33)... young engineers and management trainees from ...(34)... institutions. Once the selection gets over, the corporate managers are faced with the problem of ...(35)... the new ...(36)... into the cultural set-up of their company. These are several psychological and sociological problems involved in passing from one social system to ...(37)... For the new recruits, as some of you would be, it is a transition from the world of books, academics and exams to an environment where you have to learn from your ...(38)... and understand how to ...(39)... to people and be successful in carrying out the ...(40)... given to you.

31. (*a*) centres (*b*) agreements
(*c*) deals (*d*) organizations

32. (*a*) timely (*b*) early
(*c*) traditional (*d*) regular

33. (*a*) recruiting (*b*) selecting
(*c*) managing (*d*) choosing

34. (*a*) famous (*b*) large
(*c*) prestigious (*d*) various

35. (*a*) assimilating (*b*) suiting
(*c*) fixing (*d*) appointing

36. (*a*) incomers (*b*) entrants
(*c*) selections (*d*) newcomers

37. (*a*) other (*b*) rest
(*c*) another (*d*) next

38. (*a*) activities (*b*) habits
(*c*) mistakes (*d*) experiences

39. (*a*) attach (*b*) endear
(*c*) relate (*d*) manage

40. (*a*) errands (*b*) responsibilities
(*c*) trifles (*d*) assignments

Passage 5 **(Transmission Executives' 1994)**

The Ganga all through its route is filled with innumerable points of interest. Its inspiring beauty, its spiritual value, its purity has no ...(41)... But what distinguishes it so much is the ...(42)... help it has been in bringing ...(43)... a sense of unity among the ...(44)... and thousands of people who live ...(45)... it. For, from ancient times, the river has been a bond ...(46)... the provinces that ...(47)... on its banks. The people who lived in these ...(48)... spoke different, ...(49)... different customs and ate different ...(50)... of food. All this should have made them strangers to one another. But it did not.

41. (*a*) rivals (*b*) adversaries
(*c*) enemies (*d*) opponents

42. (*a*) copious (*b*) voluminous
(*c*) spacious (*d*) tremendous

43. (*a*) up (*b*) round
(*c*) in (*d*) about

44. (*a*) dozens (*b*) hundreds
(*c*) lakhs (*d*) millions

45. (*a*) at (*b*) amidst
(*c*) by (*d*) alongside

46. (*a*) merging (*b*) covering
(*c*) uniting (*d*) mixing

47. (*a*) lie (*b*) stretch
(*c*) rest (*d*) stand

48. (*a*) palaces (*b*) spots
(*c*) sites (*d*) lodgings

49. (*a*) followed (*b*) obeyed
(*c*) pursued (*d*) chased

50. (*a*) forms (*b*) types
(*c*) sets (*d*) categories

ANSWERS

1. (*a*)	**2.** (*c*)	**3.** (*a*)	**4.** (*b*)	**5.** (*e*)	**6.** (*a*)	**7.** (*c*)	**8.** (*e*)	**9.** (*b*)	**10.** (*d*)
11. (*a*)	**12.** (*c*)	**13.** (*b*)	**14.** (*a*)	**15.** (*b*)	**16.** (*c*)	**17.** (*b*)	**18.** (*a*)	**19.** (*a*)	**20.** (*a*)
21. (*c*)	**22.** (*b*)	**23.** (*d*)	**24.** (*b*)	**25.** (*a*)	**26.** (*e*)	**27.** (*a*)	**28.** (*d*)	**29.** (*c*)	**30.** (*e*)
31. (*d*)	**32.** (*d*)	**33.** (*a*)	**34.** (*c*)	**35.** (*a*)	**36.** (*b*)	**37.** (*c*)	**38.** (*d*)	**39.** (*c*)	**40.** (*d*)
41. (*a*)	**42.** (*d*)	**43.** (*d*)	**44.** (*b*)	**45.** (*d*)	**46.** (*c*)	**47.** (*b*)	**48.** (*c*)	**49.** (*a*)	**50.** (*b*)

PRACTICE SET 11

Passage 1 **(Assistant Grade, 1993)**

History is an interesting subject but that which ...(1)... history, properly so called, is in great part ...(2)... from works on the subject. Only of late years have historians ...(3)... giving us, in any considered quantity, the truly valuable information. As in the past ages the ...(4)... was everything and the people nothing. So, in past histories, the ...(5)... of the king fill the picture, to which the national life forms but an ...(6)... background. While only now, when the ...(7)... of nations rather than the rulers is becoming the ...(8)... idea, are historians beginning to ...(9)... themselves to the phenomenon of social progress. What we are ...(10)... about, is the natural history of society. We want all facts which help us to understand how a nation has grown.

1. (*a*) creates (*b*) constitutes
(*c*) assumes (*d*) regards

2. (*a*) refuted (*b*) concealed
(*c*) withdrawn (*d*) omitted

3. (*a*) launched (*b*) started
(*c*) instituted (*d*) introduced

4. (*a*) king (*b*) leader
(*c*) queen (*d*) representative

5. (*a*) autobiographies (*b*) sayings
(*c*) doings (*d*) thoughts

6. (*a*) entire (*b*) obscure
(*c*) interesting (*d*) active

7. (*a*) goodwill (*b*) relevance
(*c*) concern (*d*) welfare

8. (*a*) rampant (*b*) dominant
(*c*) potent (*d*) impressive

9. (*a*) occupy (*b*) avail
(*c*) address (*d*) dwell

10. (*a*) involved (*b*) worried
(*c*) interested (*d*) concerned

Passage 2

To spoil a heritage is not difficult but to maintain it in its ...(11)... form is becoming ...(12)... difficult. While it was in tune with the times to hold the Republic Day parades marking the ...(13)... of India as the new Republic, and while it is lovely to see families and children gathering around the ...(14)... of India Gate during summer evenings, none of these things have ...(15)... the formal design of the place or its ...(16)... and atmosphere.

One must ...(17)... the carefully crafted geometry of the hexagon that served as the basic ...(18)... on which Edwin Lutyens designed New Delhi. It is sad that ...(19)... the entire area north of the Central Vista has been destroyed by development, so that the surroundings of Connaught Place look like a jungle of ill-conceived, fire prone multi-storeyed buildings of ...(20)... character reflecting the lust and greed of the new predators who have arrived on the Indian urban scene.

11. (*a*) true (*b*) real
(*c*) original (*d*) actual

12. (*a*) infinitely (*b*) increasingly
(*c*) incessantly (*d*) introvertly

13. (*a*) incoming (*b*) entrance
(*c*) emergence (*d*) appearance

14. (*a*) proximity (*b*) premises
(*c*) pavalion (*d*) precincts

15. (*a*) suffocated (*b*) mutilated
(*c*) mentioned (*d*) differentiated

16. (*a*) ambience (*b*) sanctity
(*c*) beauty (*d*) splendour

17. (*a*) appreciate (*b*) praise
(*c*) eulogise (*d*) affirm

18. (*a*) magnificence (*b*) foundation
(*c*) base (*d*) module

19. (*a*) virtually (*b*) overtly
(*c*) obviously (*d*) distinctly

20. (*a*) ominous (*b*) dubious
(*c*) prejudicial (*d*) foreboding

Passage 3 **(B.S.R.B. 1996)**

"One thing scientists have discovered", notes Thomas Dreier, is ...(21)... often-praised children become more ...(22)... than often-blamed ones. There's a creative element in praise".

Good leaders know that. Fundamentally, their job is to ...(23)... others make the most of themselves. Viewed in strictly ...(24)... terms, that is their greatest ...(25)... to their companies. People, employees, are a great untapped ...(26)... of energy. Leaders who can tap this source are ...(27)... to any organisation.

It doesn't elaborate ...(28)... to bring, out the best in people. If you ...(29)... their work, they'll ...(30)... give you the best that's in them.

21. (*a*) when (*b*) since
(*c*) that (*d*) quite
(*e*) because

22. (*a*) adamant (*b*) notorious
(*c*) rebellious (*d*) whimsical

(*e*) intelligent

23. (*a*) help (*b*) tell
(*c*) order (*d*) provide
(*e*) prevent

24. (*a*) casual (*b*) useful
(*c*) narrow (*d*) sensible
(*e*) commercial

25. (*a*) plight (*b*) right
(*c*) handicap (*d*) privilege
(*e*) contribution

26. (*a*) wastage (*b*) reservoir
(*c*) utilization (*d*) conservation
(*e*) consumption

27. (*a*) available (*b*) tolerable
(*c*) valuable (*d*) disastrous
(*e*) troublesome

28. (*a*) baits (*b*) pains
(*c*) troubles (*d*) benefits
(*e*) incentives

29. (*a*) share (*b*) ignore
(*c*) perform (*d*) recognize
(*e*) advertise

30. (*a*) seldom (*b*) usually
(*c*) probably (*d*) reluctant
(*e*) occasionally

Passage 4

The magic is ...(31)... all over again. India, the land ...(32)... legendary diamonds, precious stones, gold and silver, will once again become the treasury of the world. ...(33)... exports of gems and jewellery reach an all time high value of U.S. $5000 million in the year 1996. ...(34)... next year, seven out of every ten diamonds sold in the world's gem market, will be ...(35)... in India. Six thousand jewellery export companies will ...(36)... from the scores of seepz areas-export promotion zones set up by the government – to ...(37)... with the world's best designers to ...(38)... masterpieces of jewellery for connoisseurs and collectors. To ...(39)... this, the jewellery trade will ...(40)... an annual domestic sale figure of $7 million.

31. (*a*) coming (*b*) happening
(*c*) appearing (*d*) revoking

32. (*a*) for (*b*) with
(*c*) of (*d*) along

33. (*a*) as (*b*) when
(*c*) though (*d*) instead

34. (*a*) Till (*b*) Until
(*c*) By (*d*) Upto

35. (*a*) made (*b*) crafted
(*c*) created (*d*) formed

36. (*a*) function (*b*) form
(*c*) start (*d*) initiate

37. (*a*) fight (*b*) drive
(*c*) compete (*d*) comply

38. (*a*) create (*b*) form
(*c*) shape (*d*) cut

39. (*a*) rank (*b*) top
(*c*) supercede (*d*) mastermind

40. (*a*) gain (*b*) receive
(*c*) beckon (*d*) achieve

Passage 5 **(Bank P.O. 1993)**

First ...(41)... in all human relationships are crucially important. If ...(42)... well, they can ...(43)... the process of ...(44)... social relationships between ...(45)... and, at the same time, lay the foundation for future productive and ...(46)... beneficial ...(47)... Equally important is the business of closing an encounter. The ...(48)... of social relationships, even if only temporary, can ...(49)... trong emotions, since participants have usually ...(50)... some of their most inner feelings and thoughts to each other.

41. (*a*) encounter (*b*) knowledge
(*c*) appearance (*d*) association
(*e*) friendship

42. (*a*) treated (*b*) handled
(*c*) enacted (*d*) performed
(*e*) functioned

43. (*a*) begin (*b*) exhibit
(*c*) project (*d*) execute
(*e*) manage

44. (*a*) retarding (*b*) augmenting
(*c*) maintaining (*d*) exhilarating
(*e*) strengthening

45. (*a*) nations (*b*) spouses
(*c*) persons (*d*) friends
(*e*) organisations

46. (*a*) mutually (*b*) latently
(*c*) qualitatively (*d*) intellectually
(*e*) temperamentally

47. (*a*) rewards (*b*) positions
(*c*) advantages (*d*) applications
(*e*) transactions

48. (*a*) duration (*b*) quality
(*c*) association (*d*) termination
(*e*) advantages

49. (*a*) evoke (*b*) display
(*c*) suppress (*d*) manifest
(*e*) establish

50. (*a*) projected (*b*) revealed
(*c*) repressed (*d*) appreciated
(*e*) approached

ANSWERS

1. (*b*)	**2.** (*d*)	**3.** (*b*)	**4.** (*a*)	**5.** (*c*)	**6.** (*b*)	**7.** (*b*)	**8.** (*b*)	**9.** (*c*)	**10.** (*d*)
11. (*c*)	**12.** (*b*)	**13.** (*c*)	**14.** (*d*)	**15.** (*b*)	**16.** (*a*)	**17.** (*a*)	**18.** (*d*)	**19.** (*a*)	**20.** (*b*)
21. (*c*)	**22.** (*e*)	**23.** (*a*)	**24.** (*e*)	**25.** (*e*)	**26.** (*b*)	**27.** (*c*)	**28.** (*e*)	**29.** (*d*)	**30.** (*b*)
31. (*b*)	**32.** (*c*)	**33.** (*b*)	**34.** (*c*)	**35.** (*b*)	**36.** (*a*)	**37.** (*c*)	**38.** (*a*)	**39.** (*b*)	**40.** (*d*)
41. (*d*)	**42.** (*b*)	**43.** (*a*)	**44.** (*e*)	**45.** (*c*)	**46.** (*a*)	**47.** (*c*)	**48.** (*d*)	**49.** (*a*)	**50.** (*b*)

PRACTICE SET 12

Passage 1 **(I. Tax, 1995)**

Leadership is one element, probably the most important element, of the overall managerial job. For managerial effectiveness, leadership quality is ...(1)... Leadership is not status or ...(2)... but rather it is having ...(3)... over others. Managers are required to ...(4)... the objectives; leadership is exercised to ...(5)... them. Leadership is an individual ...(6)... and is proportional to individual's own personal ...(7)... to get people to do as he ...(8)... Thus leadership can stimulate and ...(9)... people to get their willingness and ...(10)... for achieving the proposed objectives of the organisation.

1. (*a*) fitting (*b*) desirable (*c*) suitable (*d*) preferable

2. (*a*) power (*b*) superiority (*c*) energy (*d*) command

3. (*a*) influence (*b*) authority (*c*) control (*d*) dominance

4. (*a*) achieve (*b*) complete (*c*) acclaim (*d*) discharge

5. (*a*) fetch (*b*) retain (*c*) attain (*d*) meet

6. (*a*) tactic (*b*) technique (*c*) power (*d*) ability

7. (*a*) resources (*b*) plans (*c*) sources (*d*) devices

8. (*a*) demands (*b*) wishes (*c*) thinks (*d*) slots

9. (*a*) compel (*b*) motivate (*c*) incite (*d*) instigate

10. (*a*) sympathy (*b*) commitment (*c*) conviction (*d*) endorsement

Passage 2

The ...(11)... citizen who has to get everyday jobs done by various municipal and government departments is ...(12)... driven up a tree first ...(13)... them, second explaining to them what is ...(14)... and lastly, getting the job done.

If this week I ...(15)... some personal experience in this column, it is because I can document them. It is not to ask for any special ...(16)... or voice personal ...(17)..., but to bring into public view the experiences of hundreds, if not thousands of citizens everyday of the year and express the collective ...(18)... of all of them. Because one's usual experience is that when such complaints are ...(19)... in such columns, the departments rush to ...(20)...

11. (*a*) average (*b*) ordinary (*c*) usual (*d*) normal

12. (*a*) seldom (*b*) often (*c*) usually (*d*) always

13. (*a*) meeting (*b*) informing (*c*) contacting (*d*) conniving

14. (*a*) essential (*b*) demanded (*c*) desired (*d*) required

15. (*a*) revive (*b*) recount (*c*) remember (*d*) revaluate

16. (*a*) facilities (*b*) luxuries (*c*) comforts (*d*) privileges

17. (*a*) enemities (*b*) grievances (*c*) follies (*d*) mistakes

18. (*a*) woes (*b*) misdeeds (*c*) misfortunes (*d*) disasters

19. (*a*) said (*b*) debated (*c*) voiced (*d*) given

20. (*a*) repair (*b*) restroke (*c*) manage (*d*) mend

Passage 3 **(S.B.I.P.O. 1995)**

Nations which have ...(21)... upon programmes of economic development often run into unsuspected barriers which threaten, and often ...(22)... the ...(23)... needed growth of the economy. Industrialisation ...(24)..., productivity fails to respond and the nations' goals of a rising standard of living for its people are ...(25)...

21. (*a*) initiated (*b*) insisted (*c*) decided (*d*) embarked (*e*) progressed
22. (*a*) cut (*b*) halt (*c*) activate (*d*) enlighten (*e*) deteriorate
23. (*a*) hopefully (*b*) alarmingly (*c*) positively (*d*) deceptively (*e*) desperately
24 (*a*) lowers (*b*) falters (*c*) deviates (*d*) dissolves (*e*) fluctuates
25. (*a*) fulfilled (*b*) suspended (*c*) criticised (*d*) frustrated (*e*) postponed

Passage 4

The Constitution of Independent India and the various laws ...(26)... to meet the Constitutional obligations have fortified the position of woman vis-a-vis the man. But it is ...(27)... on paper only. The myth that more and more women are getting higher education and are occupying position of responsibility in all walks of life is falsified by the ...(28)... of dowry deaths and divorce cases filed in the ...(29)... courts. One look at the national dailies will tell the ...(30)... tale of the Indian women, woman-who ...(31)... a child is bargained for a bridal price or when she grows up serves as a supplier of dowry for her husband's family or who, as a widow immolates herself on her husband's ...(32)... to be ...(33)... as sati.

Our study about woman's place in Indian society is mainly based on urban, professional and educated Indian women. Deep in the rural heartland of the country, the rapidly changing world has not even touched the ...(34)... of the life of a woman. Most men of orthodox families take ...(35)... in revealing that their ...(36)... folk stay in '*purdah*', a shield that ...(37)... a woman of the joys of free Nature. Still more alarming are the ...(38)... of atrocities of women ...(39)... incidents at Bantala, Singur and Birati are ...(40)...

26. (*a*) drawn (*b*) enacted (*c*) created
27. (*a*) just (*b*) all (*c*) something
28. (*a*) many (*b*) rise (*c*) number
29. (*a*) civil (*b*) social (*c*) criminal
30. (*a*) horrifying (*b*) sordid (*c*) painful
31. (*a*) since (*b*) as (*c*) being
32. (*a*) corpse (*b*) woods (*c*) pyre
33. (*a*) appreciated (*b*) marked (*c*) acclaimed
34. (*a*) end (*b*) edge (*c*) fringe
35. (*a*) fame (*b*) pride (*c*) boast
36. (*a*) women (*b*) woman (*c*) woman's
37. (*a*) prohibits (*b*) checks (*c*) deprives
38. (*a*) events (*b*) incidents (*c*) accidents
39. (*a*) Fresh (*b*) New (*c*) Recent
40. (*a*) intensifying (*b*) fearful (*c*) shocking

Passage 5 **(Stenographers' Exam, 1994)**

It is difficult to find a person who would put in a good word for the kind of bureaucracy we have in India. Incidentally, things may now be seen as coming to a head. ...(41)... the attainment of Independence, India ...(42)... from time to time several ...(43)... power Committees or Commissions to ...(44)... administration. Inspite of all this, the impression ...(45).. that the Indian variety of bureaucracy has been slow and slothful. Fact is that the ...(46)... of bureaucracy happens to be ...(47)... the same all over the world. Even in the U.S.A. Presidents have ...(48)... a great deal of concern. ...(49).. the manner in which bureaucracy has been functioning at various levels. Inspite of all this, not much change can be ...(50)... in the near future. One may feel like hanging one's head in despair unless one believes in some super-human power that looks after our universe.

41. (*a*) Till (*b*) Since (*c*) With (*d*) From
42. (*a*) appointed (*b*) arranged (*c*) selected (*d*) framed
43. (*a*) super (*b*) great (*c*) multiple (*d*) high
44. (*a*) revive (*b*) reform (*c*) transform (*d*) perform
45. (*a*) subsists (*b*) insists (*c*) persists (*d*) consists
46. (*a*) function (*b*) growth (*c*) structure (*d*) behaviour
47. (*a*) structurally (*b*) practically (*c*) strictly (*d*) precisely
48. (*a*) declared (*b*) asserted (*c*) voiced (*d*) waged

49. (*a*) at (*b*) on (*c*) with (*d*) from

50. (*a*) accepted (*b*) expected (*c*) affected (*d*) admitted

ANSWERS

1. (*d*)	**2.** (*b*)	**3.** (*a*)	**4.** (*a*)	**5.** (*c*)	**6.** (*d*)	**7.** (*a*)	**8.** (*b*)	**9.** (*b*)	**10.** (*b*)
11. (*a*)	**12.** (*c*)	**13.** (*c*)	**14.** (*d*)	**15.** (*b*)	**16.** (*d*)	**17.** (*b*)	**18.** (*a*)	**19.** (*c*)	**20.** (*d*)
21. (*d*)	**22.** (*a*)	**23.** (*e*)	**24.** (*b*)	**25.** (*d*)	**26.** (*b*)	**27.** (*b*)	**28.** (*c*)	**29.** (*a*)	**30.** (*b*)
31. (*b*)	**32.** (*c*)	**33.** (*c*)	**34.** (*c*)	**35.** (*b*)	**36.** (*a*)	**37.** (*c*)	**38.** (*b*)	**39.** (*c*)	**40.** (*c*)
41. (*b*)	**42.** (*a*)	**43.** (*d*)	**44.** (*b*)	**45.** (*c*)	**46.** (*c*)	**47.** (*b*)	**48.** (*c*)	**49.** (*c*)	**50.** (*b*)

PRACTICE SET 13

Passage 1 **(C.B.I. 1990)**

Something has happened in the last twenty years that surely must ...(1)... anything that has happened before. Some historians are already saying that thrust ...(2)... space represents a vital turning point in history. Moon flights are considered ...(3)... less than steps in human evolution ...(4)... to the time when life on earth emerged from the sea and established itself on land. Of course, not everyone ...(5)... enraptured by space. Critics have often said that space flight has been an ...(6)... use of resources that should have ...(7)... to feeding, clothing and housing people. There is, however, no proof that if we had ...(8)... been working on space we would have done anything of great human value. In fact, research and exploration have a ...(9)... spin-offs, quite apart from the fact that they demonstrate that ...(10)... is alive and insatiably curious.

1. (*a*) recede (*b*) precede (*c*) transcend (*d*) terminate

2. (*a*) into (*b*) in (*c*) upon (*d*) on

3. (*a*) probably (*b*) sufficiently (*c*) certainly (*d*) nothing

4. (*a*) matching (*b*) comparable (*c*) contrasting (*d*) exceeding

5. (*a*) being (*b*) had been (*c*) was (*d*) has been

6. (*a*) benevolent (*b*) appropriate (*c*) extravagant (*d*) economical

7. (*a*) gone (*b*) reserved (*c*) allotted (*d*) devoted

8. (*a*) possibly (*b*) seldom (*c*) occasionally (*d*) not

9. (*a*) relevant (*b*) remarkable (*c*) renounced (*d*) renowned

10. (*a*) individual (*b*) one (*c*) human (*d*) man

Passage 2

Politicians must ...(11)... that today's young generation will step into their shoes tomorrow. They must ...(12)... fanaticism and should ...(13)... communal or casteist ...(14)... which leads to rioting ...(15)... change, though a necessity, is not practically ...(16)... but at least a gradual ...(17)... of the violent trend has to be brought about. Hatred has to be shed at all costs as soon as possible before it's too late to turn back ...(18)... from drawing board or debating stage to ...(19)... is the only hope for the Indian child today. Only if this transition is made can the Indian child live in a place 'where the mind is ...(20)... fear and the head is held high,

11. (*a*) realise (*b*) recognise (*c*) relish (*d*) refer

12. (*a*) leave (*b*) reject (*c*) dispose (*d*) denounce

13. (*a*) incite (*b*) provoke (*c*) kindle (*d*) inspire

14. (*a*) creations (*b*) passions (*c*) views (*d*) thoughts

15. (*a*) Great (*b*) Dominant (*c*) Overpowering (*d*) Radical

16. (*a*) possible (*b*) feasible (*c*) realisable (*d*) accomplished

17. (*a*) reversal (*b*) transformation (*c*) aversion (*d*) retreat

18. (*a*) Change (*b*) Transition (*c*) Retrace (*d*) Demarcation

19. (*a*) incorporation (*b*) application (*c*) implementation (*d*) inculcation

20. (*a*) without (*b*) bereft (*c*) beside (*d*) over

Passage 3 **(Bank P.O. 1995)**

The world economy is in recession – the deepest and the most widespread ...(21)...

the 1930s. There are ...(22)... of ...(23)... in the industrial countries, but most serious economic ...(24)... anticipate that rates of growth and levels of economic activity will remain low.

In all that has been written about world ...(25)..., the ...(26)... have been overwhelmingly and narrowly economic. Few have ...(27)... the human consequences in more than a superficial manner. Not a single international study has ...(28)... the session's ...(29)... on the most vulnerable half of the world's population-the children.

The need for ...(30)... clearly the ...(31)... between world economic conditions and child welfare has thus become even more urgent in the last few years. The world scale of current child distress also makes it artificial to restrict the analysis of causes to the ...(32)... level.

21. (*a*) by (*b*) for (*c*) in (*d*) since (*e*) before

22. (*a*) tips (*b*) risks (*c*) studies (*d*) glimmers (*e*) histories

23. (*a*) impact (*b*) recovery (*c*) downfall (*d*) slackness (*e*) development

24. (*a*) surveys (*b*) findings (*c*) analysts (*d*) students (*e*) journalists

25. (*a*) wars (*b*) conflicts (*c*) economy (*d*) recession (*e*) development

26. (*a*) aims (*b*) glimpses (*c*) emphasis (*d*) suppositions (*e*) preoccupations

27. (*a*) taught (*b*) delved (*c*) manifested (*d*) propagated (*e*) investigated

28. (*a*) planned (*b*) analysed (*c*) prepared (*d*) understood (*e*) highlighted

29. (*a*) impact (*b*) study (*c*) analysis (*d*) overtures (*e*) undercurrents

30. (*a*) curbing (*b*) chalking out (*c*) propagating (*d*) implementing (*e*) bringing out

31. (*a*) linkages (*b*) fallouts (*c*) contrasts (*d*) similarities (*e*) dependence

32. (*a*) highest (*b*) low (*c*) political (*d*) international (*e*) national

Passage 4

Tea prices in the domestic ...(33)... continue to rule high in the ...(34)... year despite the expectation of a ...(35)... production as compared to the previous year. According to a preliminary assessment ...(36)... on the weather ...(37)... in recent months, tea output in the next year may reach 740 million kg as ...(38)... 700 million kg last year. During the past three months, tea prices have generally shown an ...(39)... Unlike last year, when tea prices rose dramatically, this year, prices seem to have ...(40)... at a rather high level. In the subsequent four months, the ...(41)... average price showed a downtrend but in September, the prices have ...(42)... hardened to a considerable extent.

33. (*a*) market (*b*) area (*c*) sector (*d*) profit (*e*) production

34. (*a*) last (*b*) first (*c*) current (*d*) second (*e*) earlier

35. (*a*) lower (*b*) large (*c*) higher (*d*) maximum (*e*) optimum

36. (*a*) shared (*b*) based (*c*) carried (*d*) strategy (*e*) conducted

37. (*a*) pattern (*b*) forecast (*c*) conditions (*d*) outbreak (*e*) outbursts

38. (*a*) to (*b*) per (*c*) above (*d*) against (*e*) compared

39. (*a*) upgrade (*b*) uptrend (*c*) reduction (*d*) increment (*e*) downtrend

40. (*a*) stabilised (*b*) surfaced (*c*) increased (*d*) moderated (*e*) synchronised

41. (*a*) annual (*b*) weekly (*c*) daily (*d*) quarterly (*e*) monthly

42. (*a*) now (*b*) then (*c*) since (*d*) never (*e*) again

Passage 5 **(Bank P.O. 1995)**

The year 1973 ...(43)... a watershed in the economic ...(44)... of young male high school graduates in the United States. In the twenty four years ...(45)... to this date, the medium income of 25 to 34 year old males ...(46)... highest level of educational attainment was a high school diploma ...(47)... from $14,483 to $24,482 (in constant 1987 dollars). This increase was the ...(48)... of the rapid growth of the U.S. economy ...(49)... this period. As the expression goes, the rapidly growing economy was like a rising tide that ...(50)... all boats. This rapid ...(51)... in income permitted several generations of young high-school educated men to enjoy a higher standard of living ...(52)... their fathers had.

43. (*a*) took (*b*) began (*c*) marked (*d*) arranged (*e*) substituted

44. (*a*) prospects (*b*) outcome (*c*) history (*d*) thinking (*e*) preparation

45. (*a*) as (*b*) ahead (*c*) hence (*d*) prior (*e*) subsequent

46. (*a*) since (*b*) where (*c*) when (*d*) whose (*e*) though

47. (*a*) started (*b*) increased (*c*) demanded (*d*) continued (*e*) reduced

48. (*a*) result (*b*) strength (*c*) reason (*d*) demand (*e*) expectation

49. (*a*) from (*b*) after (*c*) during (*d*) outside (*e*) between

50. (*a*) cracked (*b*) lifted (*c*) sunk (*d*) boasted (*e*) threatened

51. (*a*) outcome (*b*) increase (*c*) decrease (*d*) exchanged (*e*) deterioration

52. (*a*) when (*b*) from (*c*) to (*d*) before (*e*) than

ANSWERS

1. (*c*)	**2.** (*a*)	**3.** (*d*)	**4.** (*b*)	**5.** (*d*)	**6.** (*c*)	**7.** (*d*)	**8.** (*d*)	**9.** (*b*)	**10.** (*d*)
11. (*a*)	**12.** (*d*)	**13.** (*a*)	**14.** (*b*)	**15.** (*d*)	**16.** (*a*)	**17.** (*a*)	**18.** (*b*)	**19.** (*c*)	**20.** (*a*)
21. (*d*)	**22.** (*b*)	**23.** (*d*)	**24.** (*c*)	**25.** (*c*)	**26.** (*a*)	**27.** (*b*)	**28.** (*b*)	**29.** (*a*)	**30.** (*e*)
31. (*c*)	**32.** (*e*)	**33.** (*a*)	**34.** (*c*)	**35.** (*c*)	**36.** (*b*)	**37.** (*c*)	**38.** (*d*)	**39.** (*b*)	**40.** (*a*)
41. (*e*)	**42.** (*e*)	**43.** (*c*)	**44.** (*a*)	**45.** (*d*)	**46.** (*d*)	**47.** (*b*)	**48.** (*a*)	**49.** (*c*)	**50.** (*b*)
51. (*b*)	**52.** (*e*)								

PRACTICE SET 14

Passage 1 **(C.B.I. 1994)**

The first problem to be tackled was that of feeding the huge population of the country after Independence. It became ...(1)... to adopt ...(2)... for agricultural development. The ...(3)... of multipurpose ...(4)... with the development of ...(5)... as one of its ...(6)... components was the ...(7)... step towards the provision of ...(8)... infrastructure. It was realised that ...(9)... is the basic ...(10)... in developing agriculture. The total irrigation potential was, therefore, increased.

1. (*a*) essential (*b*) desirable (*c*) notional (*d*) optional

2. (*a*) crops (*b*) families (*c*) regions (*d*) strategies

3. (*a*) relocation (*b*) renovation (*c*) construction (*d*) visualisation

4. (*a*) offices (*b*) organisations (*c*) agencies (*d*) projects

5. (*a*) markets (*b*) irrigation (*c*) villages (*d*) fields

6. (*a*) major (*b*) financial (*c*) minor (*d*) subsidiary

7. (*a*) last (*b*) least (*c*) first (*d*) intermediate

8. (*a*) modern (*b*) agricultural
(*c*) productive (*d*) industrial
9. (*a*) electricity (*b*) rain
(*c*) fertiliser (*d*) water
10. (*a*) input (*b*) indicator
(*c*) ingredient (*d*) obstacle

Passage 2

Ancestors and dead relations were believed to punish ...(11)... for sins, both of commission and ...(12)... The ancestors were the guardians of ...(13)... society's morality, and they chastised those ...(14)... failed in their duty. The explanation ...(15)... heard was: 'He told lies about the ...(16)... and the ancestors killed him', or ...(17)... uncle's ghost killed him because he ...(18)... to look after his children or his ...(19)... felt disgraced by his conduct, ...(20)... killed him.

11. (*a*) friends (*b*) acquaintances
(*c*) people (*d*) descendants
12. (*a*) mission (*b*) omission
(*c*) permission (*d*) remission
13. (*a*) some (*b*) any
(*c*) the (*d*) a
14. (*a*) who (*b*) have
(*c*) what (*d*) which
15. (*a*) seldom (*b*) inevitably
(*c*) always (*d*) often
16. (*a*) land (*b*) wealth
(*c*) property (*d*) riches
17. (*a*) 'their (*b*) 'his
(*c*) 'that (*d*) 'the
18. (*a*) objected (*b*) tried
(*c*) rejected (*d*) failed
19. (*a*) 'spirits (*b*) 'tribesmen
(*c*) 'friends (*d*) 'ancestors
20. (*a*) they (*b*) ghosts
(*c*) someone (*d*) enemies

Passage 3 **(R.B.I. 1995)**

Motivating employees with traditional authority and financial ...(21)... has become increasingly ...(22)... as employees become economically secure and their dependency on any one particular organisation ...(23)... According to expectancy theorists, the motivation to ...(24)... increases when an employee feels his ...(25)... in an instrument for obtaining desired rewards. Nevertheless, in many organisations today employees are ...(26)... to organisational rewards just by being employed. Unions, governmental regulations, and the nature of the job itself in some cases ...(27)... management from ...(28)... financial rewards to performance. People may be attracted to join and remain in organisations to receive organisational rewards, but ...(29)... motivated to join an organisation is ...(30)... the same as being motivated to exert effort in an organisation.

21. (*a*) matters (*b*) curbs
(*c*) incentives (*d*) guidelines
(*e*) restrictions
22. (*a*) expensive (*b*) simple
(*c*) difficult (*d*) unrealistic
(*e*) illegitimate
23. (*a*) lasts (*b*) perishes
(*c*) endangers (*d*) increases
(*e*) decreases
24. (*a*) earn (*b*) work
(*c*) learn (*d*) expect
(*e*) depend
25. (*a*) training (*b*) strength
(*c*) behaviour (*d*) performance
(*d*) reliability
26. (*a*) entitled (*b*) exposed
(*c*) entrusted (*d*) subjected
(*e*) empowered
27. (*a*) compels (*b*) vitiates
(*c*) leaves (*d*) prevents
(*e*) encourages
28. (*a*) relating (*b*) donating
(*c*) attaching (*d*) establishing
(*e*) announcing
29. (*a*) having (*b*) being
(*c*) posing (*d*) getting
(*e*) finding
30. (*a*) only (*b*) just
(*c*) not (*d*) absolutely
(*d*) undoubtedly

Passage 4

Civilisation means outward ...(31)... whereas culture means inward perfection. We may be ...(32)... today, but we are not cultured. We have trains, aeroplanes and all the modern modes and ...(33)... This is ...(34)... on the road of materialism but we have lost our finer emotions. Civilisation has ...(35)... mystery and romance out of the heart of nature and ...(36)... her beauty and magic. It has placed ...(37)... power in the hands of man, making him a ...(38)... With a single atom or hydrogen bomb, he can rain death and ...(39)... on millions of innocent creatures. Thus, he is out to ...(40)... himself with his own hands.

31. (*a*) success (*b*) capability
(*c*) progress (*d*) enhancement

32. (*a*) perfect (*b*) educated
(*c*) decent (*d*) civilised
33. (*a*) means (*b*) resources
(*c*) equipments (*d*) gadgets
34. (*a*) advancement (*b*) heading
(*c*) movement (*d*) progress
35. (*a*) dug (*b*) destroyed
(*c*) plucked (*d*) marred
36. (*a*) damaged (*b*) destroyed
(*c*) disreputed (*d*) soiled
37. (*a*) immaterial (*b*) boundless
(*c*) infinite (*d*) unlimited
38. (*a*) ruthless (*b*) wild
(*c*) animal (*d*) brute
39. (*a*) destruction (*b*) dearth
(*c*) gloom (*d*) sadness
40. (*a*) stab (*b*) murder
(*c*) kill (*d*) strangle

Passage 5 **(Stenographer's Exam,1995)**

Each species has its special place or habitat. An ...(41)... bird watcher can look at ...(42)... forest, meadow, lake, swamp or field and ...(43)... almost exactly what birds he ...(44)... find there ...(45)... birds are found all over the world; others ...(46)... themselves to certain areas. Still ...(47)... migrate from one country to another in ...(48)... in search of warmth and ...(49)..., and then return in spring, ...(50)... the season is more favourable.

41. (*a*) active (*b*) advanced
(*c*) expert (*d*) experienced
42. (*a*) certain (*b*) a
(*c*) some (*d*) the
43. (*a*) calculate (*b*) prophesy
(*c*) suggest (*d*) predict
44. (*a*) will (*b*) might
(*c*) must (*d*) should
45. (*a*) All (*b*) Most
(*c*) Some (*d*) More
46. (*a*) involve (*b*) confine
(*c*) entrust (*d*) keep
47. (*a*) some (*b*) others
(*c*) few (*d*) they
48. (*a*) autumn (*b*) spring
(*c*) summer (*d*) winter
49. (*a*) food (*b*) fruit
(*c*) crops (*d*) seeds
50. (*a*) when (*b*) after
(*c*) until (*d*) while

ANSWERS

1. (*a*)	**2.** (*d*)	**3.** (*c*)	**4.** (*d*)	**5.** (*b*)	**6.** (*a*)	**7.** (*c*)	**8.** (*b*)	**9.** (*d*)	**10.** (*c*)
11. (*d*)	**12.** (*b*)	**13.** (*c*)	**14.** (*a*)	**15.** (*d*)	**16.** (*a*)	**17.** (*b*)	**18.** (*d*)	**19.** (*d*)	**20.** (*a*)
21. (*c*)	**22.** (*c*)	**23.** (*e*)	**24.** (*b*)	**25.** (*d*)	**26.** (*a*)	**27.** (*d*)	**28.** (*a*)	**29.** (*b*)	**30.** (*b*)
31. (*c*)	**32.** (*d*)	**33.** (*c*)	**34.** (*a*)	**35.** (*c*)	**36.** (*b*)	**37.** (*d*)	**38.** (*d*)	**39.** (*b*)	**40.** (*c*)
41. (*c*)	**42.** (*b*)	**43.** (*a*)	**44.** (*c*)	**45.** (*c*)	**46.** (*b*)	**47.** (*a*)	**48.** (*d*)	**49.** (*a*)	**50.** (*a*)

PRACTICE SET 15

Passage 1 **(S.S.C. 1992)**

People talk of ...(1)... to him in statues of bronze or marble or pillars and thus they ...(2)... him and ...(3)... his message. What tributes shall we ...(4)... to him that he would have appreciated? He has shown us the way to live and the way to die and if we have not ...(5)... that lesson, it would be better that we ...(6)... no memorial to him, for the only fit memorial is to follow ...(7)... in the path he showed us. To him India was dear because she had ...(8)... throughout the ...(9)... certain ...(10)... truths.

1. (*a*) epitaphs (*b*) tributes
(*c*) memorials (*d*) praises
2. (*a*) depreciate (*b*) ridicule
(*c*) overthrow (*d*) mock
3. (*a*) belie (*b*) refute
(*c*) berate (*d*) decry
4. (*a*) extend (*b*) pay
(*c*) offer (*d*) give
5. (*a*) accepted (*b*) understood
(*c*) realised (*d*) followed
6. (*a*) constructed (*b*) built
(*c*) erected (*d*) raised
7. (*a*) strictly (*b*) willingly
(*c*) readily (*d*) reverently
8. (*a*) adhered (*b*) represented
(*c*) offered (*d*) followed
9. (*a*) period (*b*) world
(*c*) ages (*d*) country
10. (*a*) durable (*b*) immortal
(*c*) higher (*d*) immutable

Passage 2

A man-eating tiger is a tiger that has been ...(11)..., through stress of circumstances ...(12)... its control to adopt a diet alien to it. The stress of ...(13)... is, in nine cases out of ten, wounds, and in the tenth case old age. The wound that has caused a ...(14)... tiger to take to man-eating might be the result of a carelessly fired shot and ...(15)... to follow up. Human beings are not the ...(16)... prey of tiger, and it is only when the tigers have been ...(17)... through wounds or old age that, in order to live, they are compelled to take to a ...(18)... of human flesh. A tiger when ...(19)... its natural prey, which it does either by stalking or lying in wait for it, depends for the success of its attack on its speed and to a lesser ...(20)..., on the condition of its teeth and claws.

11. (*a*) compelled (*b*) incited (*c*) encouraged (*d*) perpetuated
12. (*a*) behind (*b*) before (*c*) beyond (*d*) after
13. (*a*) environment (*b*) conditions (*c*) circumstances (*d*) situations
14. (*a*) special (*b*) particular (*c*) singular (*d*) definite
15. (*a*) failure (*b*) hinderance (*c*) lack (*d*) remainder
16. (*a*) superficial (*b*) eternal (*c*) ephemeral (*d*) natural
17. (*a*) incapacitated (*b*) inactivated (*c*) enfeebled (*d*) indefinite
18. (*a*) food (*b*) diet (*c*) meal (*d*) breakfast
19. (*a*) murdering (*b*) stabbing (*c*) killing (*d*) devouring
20. (*a*) extent (*b*) amount (*c*) quantity (*d*) degree

Passage 3 **(S.B.I. P.O. 1993)**

Conventional medical wisdom does not advise taking ...(21)... vitamins as pills and capsules. On the contrary, there was a strong lobby which ...(22)... the supplementary intake of vitamins. This used to leave the ...(23)... person confused. However, modern research is ...(24)... a surprise. More and more scientists are beginning to ...(25)... that ...(26)... medical view on vitamins has been ...(27)... Evidence shows that ...(28)... extra vitamins plays a role in assuring vitality and ...(29)... health than was ...(30)... thought.

21. (*a*) all (*b*) some (*c*) extra (*d*) strong (*e*) insoluble
22. (*a*) criticised (*b*) projected (*c*) advocated (*d*) facilitated (*e*) communicated
23. (*a*) sick (*b*) medical (*c*) average (*d*) educated (*e*) scientific
24. (*a*) trying (*b*) holding (*c*) inventing (*d*) practising (*e*) manufacturing
25. (*a*) trust (*b*) forget (*c*) refute (*d*) forget (*e*) suspect
26. (*a*) all (*b*) modern (*c*) indigent (*d*) allopathic (*e*) traditional
27. (*a*) limited (*b*) feasible (*c*) practical (*d*) correct (*e*) confusing
28. (*a*) taking (*b*) buying (*c*) marketing (*d*) swallowing (*e*) manufacturing
29. (*a*) useful (*b*) manly (*c*) optimal (*d*) stronger (*e*) pleasurable
30. (*a*) now (*b*) even (*c*) seriously (*d*) occasionally (*e*) previously

Passage 4

With Jeans becoming a household ...(31)... with whom all sections of the population ...(32)..., the Indian jeans market has become a happy hunting ground for the dukes of denimwear. Hitherto a product that was ...(33)... to the basic Indian ...(34)..., with changing lifestyles a large section of the population has ...(35)... to wearing jeans. With the jeans revolution gripping India, the ...(36)... jeans juggernauts have arrived in the country to launch a battle with the Indian manufacturers. Like the 'cola war' India is now ...(37)... for another 'mother of all battles' to be fought between the kings of denim - Lee, Levi Strauss, Lee Cooper, Pepe, Wrangler who have ...(38)... their brands in a ...(39)... to wrest a share of the 2000 crore jeans market. These international invaders have camped in India with an aggressive marketing and advertising ...(40)... they have launched an advertising blitzkrieg of a kind India has never seen before.

31. (*a*) errand (*b*) commodity

(*c*) fashion (*d*) craze

32. (*a*) affiliate (*b*) adjoin
(*c*) enjoin (*d*) intimidate

33. (*a*) alien (*b*) stranger
(*c*) new (*d*) unaccustomed

34. (*a*) attire (*b*) ethics
(*c*) designing (*d*) scheme

35. (*a*) reverted (*b*) graduated
(*c*) rivetted (*d*) enshrined

36. (*a*) whereabout (*b*) roundabout
(*c*) underworld (*d*) global

37. (*a*) bracing (*b*) enjoining
(*c*) embracing (*d*) acquiring

38. (*a*) loosened (*b*) unleashed
(*c*) disclosed (*d*) commenced

39. (*a*) bid (*b*) competition
(*c*) try (*d*) jest

40. (*a*) manipulations (*b*) plans
(*c*) manouevres (*d*) enticements

Passage 5 **(Assistant Grade, 1994)**

The Earth is one of the known planets that circle the sun. In ...(41)... times, the men who studied the ...(42)... noticed that while certain heavenly ...(43)... seemed fixed in the sky, others seemed to ...(44)... about. The latter they named planets or wanderers. ...(45)... astronomers have discovered that the four planets, Jupiter, Saturn, Uranus ...(46)... Neptune, are surrounded by poisonous gases and are so ...(47)... that any living thing attempting to ...(48)... on them would instantly be frozen to death. Of the five remaining ...(49)..., Venus most closely ...(50)... the Earth in size.

41. (*a*) past (*b*) antique
(*c*) ancient (*d*) modern

42. (*a*) light (*b*) stars
(*c*) earth (*d*) sun

43. (*a*) bodies (*b*) objects
(*c*) things (*d*) entities

44. (*a*) jump (*b*) roam
(*c*) run (*d*) move

45. (*a*) Upstart (*b*) Future
(*c*) Modern (*d*) New

46. (*a*) or (*b*) and
(*c*) nor (*d*) etc.

47. (*a*) cold (*b*) lukewarm
(*c*) dull (*d*) frigid

48. (*a*) squat (*b*) land
(*c*) walk (*d*) stay

49. (*a*) constellations (*b*) stars
(*c*) planets (*d*) meteors

50. (*a*) imitates (*b*) negates
(*c*) resembles (*d*) identifies

ANSWERS

1. (*c*)	**2.** (*a*)	**3.** (*a*)	**4.** (*b*)	**5.** (*b*)	**6.** (*c*)	**7.** (*a*)	**8.** (*c*)	**9.** (*c*)	**10.** (*d*)
11. (*a*)	**12.** (*c*)	**13.** (*c*)	**14.** (*b*)	**15.** (*a*)	**16.** (*d*)	**17.** (*a*)	**18.** (*b*)	**19.** (*c*)	**20.** (*a*)
21. (*c*)	**22.** (*c*)	**23.** (*a*)	**24.** (*b*)	**25.** (*a*)	**26.** (*b*)	**27.** (*d*)	**28.** (*a*)	**29.** (*c*)	**30.** (*e*)
31. (*b*)	**32.** (*a*)	**33.** (*a*)	**34.** (*a*)	**35.** (*b*)	**36.** (*d*)	**37.** (*a*)	**38.** (*b*)	**39.** (*a*)	**40.** (*c*)
41. (*c*)	**42.** (*b*)	**43.** (*a*)	**44.** (*d*)	**45.** (*c*)	**46.** (*b*)	**47.** (*a*)	**48.** (*b*)	**49.** (*c*)	**50.** (*c*)

Now, work out Practice Sets 16 to 22 as per the following instructions.

Directions : ***In each of the given passages at certain points, a choice of some words marked (a), (b), (c) and / or (d) is given. Choose the best word from these and indicate your choice.***

PRACTICE SET 16

Passage 1 **(C.D.S. 1993)**

Some scholars were exploring the forests of Middle America. They discovered, during their exploration some buildings which were in ruins. These buildings were ...(1)... (*a*) *surely* / (*b*) *reasonably* / (*c*) *apparently* ruined by the encroaching forest. It was also clear that these buildings were no ordinary structures. They were remnants of a ...(2)... (*a*) *great* / (*b*) *new* / (*c*) *ordinary* civilisation. The scholars got interested. They excavated more and discovered ...(3)... (*a*) *for* / (*b*) *at* / (*c*) *to* their utmost surprise, the remains of a fluorishing civilisation— the Maya's ...(4)... (*a*) *while* / (*b*) *as* / (*c*) *when* they named it. Thus, it was as late as in ...(5)... (*a*) *the* / (*b*) *then* / (*c*) *at* 19th century that the secrets of a new civilisation were ...(6)... (*a*) *unmatched*

/ (*b*) *unearthed* / (*c*) *unparalleled.* For sometime the scholars believed that the Mayans must have ...(7)... (*a*) *being* / (*b*) *become* / (*c*) *been* the descendants of the ancient Egyptians or one of the lost tribes of Israel; or perhaps a brand of the South East Asia's immigrants. However they could not come to an unanimous decision. Nevertheless, the fact remains that even today the Mayan culture is one of ...(8)... (*a*) *the* / (*b*) *a* / (*c*) *an* most fascinating ancient civilisations. The civilisation was situated in the ...(9)... (*a*) *tail* / (*b*) *heart* / (*c*) *head* of Middle America. It covered an area equivalent to France, ...(10)... (*a*) *but* / (*a*) *yet* / (*c*) *and* spread across Guatemala, Belize and some parts of Mexico Honduras. It started in 2500 B.C. and continued its progress till 34 ...(11)... (*a*) *decades* / (*b*) *centuries* / (*c*) *years* later. Throughout its period of progress, the people struggled against the invading ...(12)... (*a*) *civilisation* / (*b*) *forests* / (*c*) *enemies.* They used to burn the plants and make the land ...(13)... (*a*) *good* / (*b*) *fertile* / (*c*) *properly* for cultivation. Their staple food was maize. But even while ...(14)... (*a*) *doing* / (*b*) *fighting* / (*c*) *struggling* for existence, they found time to build remarkable buildings for ...(15)... (*a*) *it* / (*b*) *which* / (*c*) *that* they used mortar, sandstone and volcanic rock. The buildings do tell us about the technological advances they had attained.

Passage 2

Taj Mahal, a breath taking embodiment of humanity, love and creativity, a unique exercise in architectural excellence and a constant source of inspiration and exuberance for the world. Countless men and women the world over travel miles to ...(16)... (*a*) *appreciate* / (*b*) *adore* / (*c*) *analyse* the medieval masterpiece and ...(17)... (*a*) *revere* / (*b*) *repeat* / (*c*) *rehabilitate* its mesmeric ambiance. Soon, all this is set to change. Taj is dying a slow, ...(18)... (*a*) *frightening* / (*b*) *cursing* / (*c*) *choking* death. Rising air pollution is slowly ...(19)... (*a*) *clinching* / (*b*) *enhancing* / (*c*) *flinching* its pristine splendour. At ...(20)... (*a*) *stake* / (*b*) *fire* / (*c*) *verge* is the tourism industry, officially claimed as the largest bread earner for the town's eight lakh populace.

...(21)... (*a*) *Since* / (*b*) *For* / (*c*) *From* many years, the town is fast being pulled downwards in a relentless ...(22)... (*a*) *circle* / (*b*) *sphere* / (*c*) *spiral* of environmental decay and human misery. The alarming ...(23)... (*a*) *downfall* / (*b*) *decline* / (*c*) *depopularisation* in tourism has activated an insipid bureaucracy. Pushed by the hoteliers, it has been trying to work ...(24)... (*a*) *up* / (*b*) *over* / (*c*) *out* intelligent plans for boosting tourism. Besides unemployment in Agra has created an army of touts. There are lumpen youth who ...(25)... (*a*) *draw* / (*b*) *squeeze* / (*c*) *notch* out hefty commissions by ...(26)... (*a*) *leading* / (*b*) *fetching* / (*c*) *summoning* unsuspecting tourists to selected hotels.

Like unemployment, pollution is ...(27)... (*a*) *epidemic* / (*b*) *endemic* / (*c*) *geographic* in Agra. The Supreme Court ...(28)... (*a*) *summoned* / (*b*) *demanded* / (*c*) *ordered* the closure of polluting industrial units in Agra until they ...(29).. (*a*) *agreed* / (*b*) *abided* / (*c*) *complied* with the environmental standard. But this hasn't ended Agra's ...(30)... (*a*) *threats* / (*b*) *ravages* / (*c*) *woes.*

Passage 3 **(Translators' Exam, 1994)**

Apart from the great pleasure the cinema gives us as a means of entertainment, it is in many ways an ...(31)... (*a*) *engagement* / (*b*) *enjoyment* / (*c*) *education* / (*d*) *entertainment* in itself. The film companies from time to time produce historical pictures and these pictures are of great ...(32)... (*a*) *assistance* / (*b*) *enjoyment* / (*c*) *diversion* / (*d*) *entertainment* to the teacher of history. A couple of hours ...(33)... (*a*) *wasted* / (*b*) *given* / (*c*) *stayed* / (*d*) *spent* in the company of historical ...(34)... (*a*) *heroes* / (*b*) *characters* / (*c*) *models* / (*d*) *personages* dressed in the proper ...(35)... (*a*) *livery* / (*b*) *manner* / (*c*) *attire* / (*d*) *wardrobe* of the period can ...(36)... (*a*) *give* / (*b*) *relate* / (*c*) *grant* / (*d*) *teach* us far more than we can ...(37)... (*a*) *learn* / (*b*) *deduce* / (*c*) *draw* / (*d*) *beget* from a whole week's reading of a historical text-book. Some educational film companies ...(38)... (*a*) *squander* / (*b*) *devote* / (*c*) *spend* / (*d*) *deploy* their time to the filming of the habits and customs of animals and many other branches of scientific life. We can see the ...(39)... (*a*) *dropping* / (*b*) *hatching* / (*c*) *falling* / (*d*) *rolling* of the eggs of the fish and their ...(40)... (*a*) *formation* / (*b*) *increment* / (*c*) *development* / (*d*) *enlargement* into large fishes.

Passage 4

Democracy has its dangers, the greatest of which is that it may be the rule of ignorance. Citizens who are not ...(41)... (*a*) *barely* / (*b*) *sufficiently* / (*c*) *highly* / (*d*) *perfectly* intelligent and educated are ...(42)... (*a*) *sure* / (*b*) *deliberately* / (*c*) *unlikely* / (*d*) *likely* to commit errors of judgement in the casting of votes. The best men may thus ...(43)... (*a*) *fail* / (*b*) *succeed* / (*c*) *try* / (*d*) *desire* to get elected. Elections are usually a ...(44)... (*a*) *kind* / (*b*) *process* / (*c*) *matter* / (*d*) *result* of propaganda. Another criticism of democracy is that it is wanting ...(45)... (*a*) *of* / (*b*) *for* / (*c*) *at* / (*d*) *in* efficiency. For prompt and effective action, unity of action is ...(46)... (*a*) *enough* / (*b*) *dispensable* / (*c*) *essential* / (*d*) *superfluous*. In a multitude of minds, much ...(47)... (*a*) *profitable* / (*b*) *unprofitable* / (*c*) *detailed* / (*d*) *exhaustive* discussion takes place, whereas unity of control is needed for vigorous national life. This criticism, however, is not very ...(48)... (*a*) *unfair* / (*b*) *absurd* / (*c*) *strong* / (*d*) *convincing* because in times of war the British Prime Minister usually ...(49)... (*a*) *gains* / (*b*) *wields* / (*c*) *demands* / (*d*) *misuses* the powers of a dictator. Another criticism of democracy in times of war is that secrecy in military affairs becomes difficult, if not ...(50)... (*a*) *easy* / (*b*) *probable* / (*c*) *impossible* / (*d*) *obscure*, and that the Opposition usually lowers the morale of the people by its condemnation of the actions of the Cabinet.

ANSWERS

1. (*c*)	**2.** (*a*)	**3.** (*c*)	**4.** (*b*)	**5.** (*a*)	**6.** (*b*)	**7.** (*c*)	**8.** (*a*)	**9.** (*b*)	**10.** (*c*)
11. (*b*)	**12.** (*b*)	**13.** (*b*)	**14.** (*c*)	**15.** (*b*)	**16.** (*b*)	**17.** (*a*)	**18.** (*c*)	**19.** (*c*)	**20.** (*a*)
21. (*b*)	**22.** (*c*)	**23.** (*b*)	**24.** (*c*)	**25.** (*c*)	**26.** (*a*)	**27.** (*b*)	**28.** (*c*)	**29.** (*c*)	**30.** (*c*)
31. (*c*)	**32.** (*a*)	**33.** (*d*)	**34.** (*d*)	**35.** (*c*)	**36.** (*d*)	**37.** (*a*)	**38.** (*b*)	**39.** (*b*)	**40.** (*c*)
41. (*b*)	**42.** (*d*)	**43.** (*a*)	**44.** (*a*)	**45.** (*d*)	**46.** (*c*)	**47.** (*b*)	**48.** (*d*)	**49.** (*b*)	**50.** (*c*)

PRACTICE SET 17

Passage 1 **(B.S.R.B.1994)**

The story of Helen Keller is so much the history of her teacher ...(1)... [(*a*) who (*b*) when (*c*) that (*d*) how (*e*) where] one must lightly sketch Annie's background. She was the child ...(2)...[(*a*) to (*b*) of (*c*) from (*d*) about (*e*) with] poor Irish immigrants, her mother ...(3)... [(*a*) had (*b*) would (*c*) were (*d*) was (*e*) has] died ...(4)... [(*a*) when (*b*) hence (*c*) as (*d*) when (*e*) since] she was eight. Her father had ...(5)... [(*a*) given (*b*) left (*c*) reared (*d*) deserted (*e*) developed] the three children. ...(6)... [(*a*) Neatly (*b*) Plainly (*c*) Luckily (*d*) Sadly (*e*) Hardly] Annie, born nearly blind, had been ...(7)... [(*a*) send (*b*) sent (*c*) sending (*d*) handed (*e*) come] to state Infirmary.

Passage 2

The year was 1913. The Wright brothers had just ...(8)... (*a*) *failed* / (*b*) *involved* / (*c*) *succeeded* in making an aeroplane which ..(9)... (*a*) *hardly* / (*b*) *highly* / (*c*) *really* flew. I was deeply interested in ... (10)... (*a*) *flying* / (*b*) *science* / (*c*) *history* and was making my own ...(11)... (*a*) *toys* / (*b*) *experiments* / (*c*) *judgements* with flying machines. I really ...(12)... (*a*) *relied* / (*b*) *believed* / (*c*) *disbelieved* in that little machine I had ...(13)... (*a*) *hatched* / (*b*) *strapped* / (*c*) *patched* together and I decided it was time to prove its merits.

Passage 3 **(N.D.A. 1991)**

Three-fourth of the surface of our planet is covered by the sea. It both separates and unites the various races of mankind. The sea is the great highway ...(14)... [(*a*) at (*b*) along (*c*) in] which man may journey ...(15)... [(*a*) for (*b*) at (*c*) on] his will. The sea appeals to man's ...(16)... [(*a*) love (*b*) dislike (*c*) fear] of the unknown and knowledge. There is, said to be far ...(17)... [(*a*) most (*b*) much (*c*) more] living matter in the sea than there is in all the ...(18)... [(*a*) places (*b*) rest (*c*) sections] of the world. Sea water is full of millions of ...(19)... [(*a*) tiny (*b*) new (*c*) huge] plants.

Passage 4

The need today is for a will for ...(20)... [(*a*) hope (*b*) optimism (*c*) pessimism (*d*) tolerance], expressing life and creativity. Reason here does not ...(21)... [(*a*) match (*b*) go (*c*) rhyme (*d*) connect] with morosity and optimism is not an escape from reality. Today the need is for true meaning and the ...(22).. [(*a*) overlying (*b*) underlying (*c*) intimate (*d*) overbearing] influence of the ecological ...(23)... [(*a*) method (*b*) technique (*c*) trend (*d*) pathway] takes us back to unadulterated colours ...(24)... [(*a*) enabling (*b*) allowing (*c*) offering (*d*) reincarnating] us to rediscover a fusion with nature.

Passage 5 **(C.D.S. 1994)**

Be very wary of opinions that flatter your self-esteem. Both men and women, nine times out of ten, are firmly convinced ...(25)... (*a*) *at* / (*b*) *on* / (*c*) *of* the superior excellence of their own sex. That is abundant on ...(26)... (*a*) *few sides* / (*b*) *all* / (*c*) *both*. If you are a man, you can ...(27)... (*a*) *work* / (*b*) *point* / (*c*) *say* out that most posts are men, and many eminent scientists are male; if you are a woman you can retort that ...(28)... (*a*) *so* / (*b*) *they* / (*c*) *also* are most criminals. The question is inherently insoluble but self-esteem conceals this from most ...(29)... (*a*) *men* / (*b*) *women* / (*c*) *people*. We are all, whatever part of the world we come from, persuaded that ...(30)... (*a*) *his* / (*b*) *her* / (*c*) *our* nation is ...(31)... (*a*) *superior* / (*b*) *better* / (*c*) *inferior* to all others. Seeing that each nation has its characteristic ...(32)... (*a*) *values* / (*b*) *points* / (*c*) *merits* and demerits, we adjust our standard of values so as to make out that the merits possessed ...(33)... (*a*) *by* / (*b*) *for* / (*c*) *in* our nation are the really important ones while its demerits are ...(34)... (*a*) *commonly* / (*b*) *rarely* / (*c*) *comparatively* trivial. Here again the rational man ...(35)... (*a*) *should* / (*b*) *will* / (*c*) *could* admit that the question is one to which there is no demonstrably right ...(36)... (*a*) *answer* / (*b*) *angle* / (*c*) *reply*. It is more difficult to deal with ...(37)... (*a*) *an* / (*b*) *the* / (*c*) *a* self-esteem man as man, because we cannot argue out the matter with some non-human mind. The only way ...(38)... (*a*) *to* / (*b*) *of* / (*c*) *from* dealing with his general human conceit is to remind man of his unimportance in the universe, that man is a brief episode in the life of a small ...(39)... (*a*) *orbit* / (*b*) *star* / (*c*) *planet* in a little corner of the universe.

Passage 6

Embroidery is the ...(40)... (*a*) *embellishment* / (*b*) *craft* / (*c*) *emblaze* / (*d*) *threading* of any material with patterns or ...(41)... (*a*) *sketches* / (*b*) *pictures* / (*c*) *practices* / (*d*) *designs* done with a needle. No ...(42)... (*a*) *matter* / (*b*) *wonder* / (*c*) *doubt* / (*d*) *sooner* the Romans called it 'needle painting'. In India, each region developed a ...(43)... (*a*) *design* / (*b*) *plan* / (*c*) *style* / (*d*) *system* of its own. In the state of Himachal Pradesh the embroidery has a distinctive charm and is deeply rooted in the 'Pahari' culture, from which it has ...(44)... (*a*) *devised* / (*b*) *derived* / (*c*) *cultivated* / (*d*) *originated* its designs, colour combinations and techniques. Embroidery is essentially a child of the landscape and is, therefore, as ...(45)... (*a*) *varied* / (*b*) *cultured* / (*c*) *strong* / (*d*) *huge* in its richness and beauty as ...(46)... (*a*) *culture* / (*b*) *heritage* / (*c*) *beauty* / (*d*) *nature* is in her manifold representations. It is difficult to ...(47)... (*a*) *trace* / (*b*) *represent* / (*c*) *follow* / (*d*) *study* the history of 'Pahari' embroidery because cloth is a ...(48)... (*a*) *mortal* / (*b*) *perishable* / (*c*) *knitted* / (*d*) *delicate* material. From the available specimens it can be ...(49)... (*a*) *opined* / (*b*) *surmised* / (*c*) *found* / (*d*) *summarised* that the inhabitants of picturesque Himachal Pradesh practised this ...(50)... (*a*) *skill* / (*b*) *tradition* / (*c*) *craft* / (*d*) *style* till the first decade of the 20th century.

ANSWERS

1. (*c*)	**2.** (*b*)	**3.** (*a*)	**4.** (*a*)	**5.** (*d*)	**6.** (*c*)	**7.** (*b*)	**8.** (*c*)	**9.** (*c*)	**10.** (*a*)
11. (*b*)	**12.** (*b*)	**13.** (*c*)	**14.** (*b*)	**15.** (*b*)	**16.** (*a*)	**17.** (*c*)	**18.** (*b*)	**19.** (*a*)	**20.** (*b*)
21. (*c*)	**22.** (*b*)	**23.** (*c*)	**24.** (*a*)	**25.** (*c*)	**26.** (*c*)	**27.** (*b*)	**28.** (*a*)	**29.** (*c*)	**30.** (*c*)
31. (*a*)	**32.** (*c*)	**33.** (*a*)	**34.** (*c*)	**35.** (*a*)	**36.** (*a*)	**37.** (*c*)	**38.** (*b*)	**39.** (*c*)	**40.** (*d*)
41. (*d*)	**42.** (*b*)	**43.** (*c*)	**44.** (*b*)	**45.** (*a*)	**46.** (*d*)	**47.** (*a*)	**48.** (*b*)	**49.** (*b*)	**50.** (*c*)

PRACTICE SET 18

Passage 1 **(C.D.S.1995)**

Though attacks on hospital staff must be deplored, there seems to be no limit to negligence in public hospitals. The recent death of a patient ...(1)... (a) *within* / (b) *in* /(c) *inside* a public hospital, allegedly as a ...(2)... (a) *result* / (b) *follow up* / (c) *reason* of being administered kerosene ...(3)... (a) *inspite of* / (b) *instead of* / (c) *along with* a saline glucose solution, has alarmed health ...(4)... (a)*protectors* / (b) *supervisors* / (c) *officials.* Despite its free mandate, the inquiry committee has ...(5)... (a) *refused* / (b) *failed* / (c) *decided* to fix responsibility and it is doubtful ...(6)... (a) *when* / (b) *how* / (c) *whether* the police inquiry will discover anything ...(7)... (a) *spectacular* / (b) *new* / (c) *strange*. This kerosene incident and the removal ...(8)... (a) *from* / (b) *of* / (c) *off* the wrong eye of a young girl ...(9)... (a) *at* / (b) *on* / (c) *in* another hospital are not the only ...(10)... (a) *symbols* / (b) *instances* / (c) *illustrations* of quasi-criminal callousness. Often it is ...(11)... (a) *almost* / (b) *undoubtedly* / (c) *certainly* as unsafe to enter public hospitals ...(12)... (a) *as* / (b) *instead* / (c) *so as* to go untreated. The basic requirement of ...(13)... (a) *orderliness* / (b) *calmness* / (c) *cleanliness* is the first casualty in the wards. ...(14)... (a) *On* / (b) *In* / (c) *At* a renowned hospital, bacteria contamination was so ...(15)... (a) *intense* / (b) *deep* / (c) *acute* that 96 percent of the patients suffered from post-hospitalisation infection.

Passage 2

There is a reader who displays the utmost enthusiasm on meeting you. He appears so warm amd gratified that you think that here, after all, you have met your ideal reader. It has always been your ...(16)... (a) *idea* / (b) *hope* / (c) *feeling* that you would come across this ...(17)... (a) *good* / (b) *wonderful* / (c) *ideal* person some day, a man who by his very ...(18)... (a) *enthusiasm* / (b) *warmth* / (c) *contact* would make you feel that you ...(19)... (a) *did* / (b) *were doing* / (c) *have been doing* some important work, vital ...(20)... (a) *to* / (b) *for* / (c) *on* human welfare, that it ...(21)... (a) *turns out* / (b) *turns over* / (c) *turns on* to be a very short - lived ...(22)... (a) *experience* / (b) *gratification* / (c) *satisfaction*. Disillusionment is actually round ...(23)... (a) *this* / (b) *the* / (c) *a* corner. While you are hoping ...(24)... (a) *because* / (b) *for* / (c) *that* you are about to have the ...(25)... (a) *pleasure* / (b) *joy* / (c) *happiness* of listening to his ...(26)... (a) *reaction* / (b) *behaviour* / (c) *view* to your latest weekly effort he ...(27)... (a) *says* / (b) *tells* / (c) *asks* suddenly, 'I am proud to meet you ...(28)... (a) *yet* / (b) *still* / (c) *but* may I know what you ...(29)... (a) *usually* / (b) *invariably* / (c) *generally* write about? This is an unanswerable ...(30)... (a) *statement* / (b) *pronouncement* / (c) *question*.

Passage 3 **(N.D.A. 1995)**

Gandhiji's epithet is not just horrific; it tells the truth about him. He was indeed a 'great soul'. He may have been the ...(31)... (a) *greatest* / (b) *man* / (c) *smallest* of any that have made ...(32)... (a) *their* / (b) *sudden* / (c) *our* appearance in our time. He ...(33)... (a) *had* / (b) *was* / (c) *bore* undoubtedly the peer of the ...(34)... (a) *known* / (b) *available* / (c) *greatest* souls of previous ages from ...(35)... (a) *which* / (b) *those* / (c) *whom* we have surviving records of ...(36)... (a) *outstanding* / (b) *poor* / (c) *ordinary* personalities.

Passage 4

With increased ...(37)... (a) *faith* / (b) *confidence* / (c) *trust* / (d) *zeal* I took another step. Next moment I was ...(38)... (a) *hardly* / (b) *utmost* / (c) *surely* / (d) *almost* thrown off balance as the wind-crust suddenly gave ...(39)... (a) *way* / (b) *away* / (c) *up* / (d) *in* and I sank through it upto my ...(40)... (a) *waist* / (b) *knee* / (c) *head* / (d) *foot*. It took me a little ...(41)... (a) *effort* / (b) *time* / (c) *while* / (d) *rest* to get my breath back. Then I gradually pulled my leg out of the ...(42)... (a) *depression* / (b) *hole* / (c) *ditch* / (d) *pit*. I was almost upright ...(43)... (a) *then* / (b) *again* / (c) *after* / (d) *soon* when the wind-crust under the ...(44)... (a) *second* / (b) *upper* / (c) *other* / (d) *lower* foot gave way.

Passage 5 **(N.D.A. 1990)**

It is not true to say that stress and anxiety are experiences of recent origin for mankind. Every era has been an age of anxiety. A few hundred years ago, for example ...(45)... (a) *here* / (b) *then* / (c) *there* was no threat of nuclear war ...(46)...

(*a*) *but* / (*b*) *yet* / (*c*) *still* there was the terrible danger of ... 47)... (*a*) *a* / (*b*) *the* / (*c*) *that* plague, which quite literally destroyed whole ...(48)... (*a*) *continents* / (*b*) *populations* / (*c*) *departments*. And everything in human life is ...(49)... (*a*) *impossible* / (*b*) *uncertain* / (*c*) *unbearable* and contingent - you may be rich ...(50)... (*a*) *always* / (*b*) *now* / (*c*) *today* and poor tomorrow, or healthy or sick; this has been true throughout history.

ANSWERS

1. (*b*)	**2.** (*a*)	**3.** (*b*)	**4.** (*b*)	**5.** (*b*)	**6.** (*c*)	**7.** (*a*)	**8.** (*b*)	**9.** (*c*)	**10.** (*b*)
11. (*a*)	**12.** (*a*)	**13.** (*a*)	**14.** (*b*)	**15.** (*c*)	**16.** (*b*)	**17.** (*b*)	**18.** (*b*)	**19.** (*c*)	**20.** (*b*)
21. (*a*)	**22.** (*c*)	**23.** (*b*)	**24.** (*c*)	**25.** (*a*)	**26.** (*a*)	**27.** (*a*)	**28.** (*b*)	**29.** (*c*)	**30.** (*c*)
31. (*a*)	**32.** (*a*)	**33.** (*b*)	**34.** (*c*)	**35.** (*a*)	**36.** (*a*)	**37.** (*b*)	**38.** (*d*)	**39.** (*a*)	**40.** (*b*)
41. (*c*)	**42.** (*b*)	**43.** (*b*)	**44.** (*c*)	**45.** (*c*)	**46.** (*a*)	**47.** (*b*)	**48.** (*b*)	**49.** (*b*)	**50.** (*c*)

PRACTICE SET 19

Passage 1 (I.E.S. 1994)

Every bird has feathers, and nothing that is not a bird can show any trace of them. The whole body of the birds is fitted to the habit of flying. We have long envied the bird and its power to fly. In fact, it was the birds that **1.** [(*a*) trained (*b*) taught (*c*) demonstrated] us to build our aeroplanes after the **2.** [(*a*) strength (*b*) structure (*c*) shape] of their wings and bodies. The bird's wings **3.** [(*a*) have served (*b*) serve (*c*) can serve] as propellers, for they have both lifting and **4.** [(*a*) driving (*b*) soaring (*c*) flying] power. The tail is the rudder and helps to **5.** [(*a*) soar (*b*) dive (*c*) steer]. It also serves the important function of **6.** [(*a*) support (*b*) brake (*c*) anchor] when the bird alights. Some birds, like the birds of **7.** [(*a*) prey (*b*) passage (*c*) paradise], soar and remain in the air a long time **8.** [(*a*) with (*b*) at (*c*) on] motionless wings. They can sail in or **9.** [(*a*) spiral (*b*) circle (*c*) tangent] to a great height. Others dart like **10.** [(*a*) herons (*b*) swallows (*c*) swans].

Passage 2

During my service I have dealt with problems of **11.** [(*a*) serious (*b*) intentional (*c*) assertive (*d*) evasive] lawlessness. I have had to order arrests, **12.** [(*a*) spread (*b*) split (*c*) disperse (*d*) acquit] unruly crowds, deal with dangerous criminals, even of a nature where a hand grenade was thrown at me. I can **13.** [(*a*) vow (*b*) vouch (*c*) confess (*d*) observe] without fear of **14.** [(*a*) dispute (*b*) contradiction (*c*) counteraction (*d*) contention] from any reasonable quarter that when one is **15.** [(*a*) dealing (*b*) indulging (*c*) involved (*d*) entangled] with blatant lawlessness, **16.** [(*a*) fright (*b*) terror (*c*) threat (*d*) anticipation] of serious crime, it is **17.** [(*a*) awkward (*b*) unexpected (*c*) absurd (*d*) incredible] to expect that the situation can be tackled by **18.** [(*a*) pleading (*b*) begging (*c*) beckoning (*d*) pestering] to the law breakers and criminals to be **19.** [(*a*) confiscated (*b*) contained (*c*) arrested (*d*) capsized] without use of force, by not handcuffing where the criminal is a dangerous outlaw and can be **20.** [(*a*) expected (*b*) anticipated (*c*) believed (*d*) emancipated] to play with his life in assaulting to free himself.

Passage 3 (Railways, 1994)

I noticed George Ramsay at the restaurant. He was staring into space. He looked as though the burden of the whole world sat on his shoulders.

I **21.** [(*a*) agreed (*b*) suspected (*c*) believed] at once that his unfortunate brother **22.** [(*a*) will cause (*b*) was causing (*c*) had been causing] trouble again. I suppose every family has a black **23.** [(*a*) wolf (*b*) sheep (*c*) goat]. Tom had been a **24.** [(*a*) sweet (*b*) bitter (*c*) sore] trial to his family **25.** [(*a*) in (*b*) for (*c*) since] twenty years. He had begun life decently enough; he went **26.** [(*a*) to (*b*) for (*c*) into] business, married and had two children. The Ramsays were **27.** [(*a*) wholly (*b*) perfectly (*c*) utterly] respectable people, and there was every **28.** [(*a*) point (*b*) cause (*c*) reason] to suppose that Tom Ramsay would have a successful and **29.** [(*a*) honourable (*b*) bad (*c*) profitable] career. But one day without warning, he **30.** [(*a*) wrote (*b*) announced (*c*) said] that he did not like to work, and that he was not suited **31.** [(*a*) with (*b*) for (*c*) to] marriage. He wanted to enjoy **32.** [(*a*) others (*b*) idleness (*c*) himself]. He would listen **33.** [(*a*) with (*b*) in (*c*) to] no advice. He left his wife and his **34.** [(*a*) relatives (*b*) house (*c*) job]. He had **35.** [(*a*) no (*b*) little (*c*) a little] money and he spent two happy years in the various capitals of Europe. Rumours of his **36.** [(*a*) whereabouts (*b*) doings (*c*) habits] reached his relations from time to time and they were **37.** [(*a*) disappointed (*b*) shocked (*c*) deeply]. He certainly **38.** [(*a*) will have (*b*) had (*c*) has] a very good time. They shook their heads and asked what **39.** [(*a*) will happen (*b*) happened (*c*) would happen] when his money was spent They soon found out that he was broke and wanted to **40.** [(*a*) settle (*b*) go (*c*) come back] home.

Passage 4

The human mind seems to have built in **41.** [(*a*) ideas (*b*) prejudices (*c*) safeguards (*d*) interests] against original thought, for instance, we **42.** [(*a*) having been (*b*) may have (*c*) had (*d*) have] equipped with a wonderful **43.** [(*a*) capacity (*b*) capability (*c*) sense (*d*) sensibility] for accepting evidence which agrees with our **44.** [(*a*) thoughts (*b*) conceptions (*c*) preconceptions (*d*) views]. Almost unconsciously we allow our thinking to be **45.** [(*a*) rooted (*b*) biased (*c*) fixed (*d*) based] on what we first thought, or were **46.** [(*a*) said (*b*) spoke (*c*) told (*d*) expressed] when we approached the subject. If **47.** [(*a*) when (*b*) sometimes (*c*) only (*d*) frequently] man could be freed from the yoke **48.** [(*a*) on (*b*) in (*c*) under (*d*) of] his age-old assumptions, prejudices, traditional imagery and **49.** [(*a*) negation (*b*) certainty (*c*) negativeness (*d*) positiveness] about what is right and what is wrong **50.** [(*a*) they (*b*) he (*c*) man (*d*) men].

ANSWERS

1. (*b*)	**2.** (*c*)	**3.** (*b*)	**4.** (*a*)	**5.** (*c*)	**6.** (*b*)	**7.** (*a*)	**8.** (*a*)	**9.** (*a*)	**10.** (*b*)
11. (*a*)	**12.** (*c*)	**13.** (*b*)	**14.** (*b*)	**15.** (*a*)	**16.** (*c*)	**17.** (*c*)	**18.** (*a*)	**19.** (*c*)	**20.** (*a*)
21. (*b*)	**22.** (*b*)	**23.** (*b*)	**24.** (*b*)	**25.** (*b*)	**26.** (*c*)	**27.** (*b*)	**28.** (*c*)	**29.** (*c*)	**30.** (*b*)
31. (*b*)	**32.** (*c*)	**33.** (*c*)	**34.** (*c*)	**35.** (*c*)	**36.** (*b*)	**37.** (*b*)	**38.** (*b*)	**39.** (*c*)	**40.** (*c*)
41. (*c*)	**42.** (*a*)	**43.** (*a*)	**44.** (*d*)	**45.** (*b*)	**46.** (*c*)	**47.** (*c*)	**48.** (*d*)	**49.** (*b*)	**50.** (*b*)

PRACTICE SET 20

Passage 1 **(C.D.S. 1995)**

India will find herself again when freedom opens out new horizons. Future will then fascinate her far more than the immediate past of frustration and humiliation. She will go **1.** [(*a*) in (*b*) forward (*c*) up] with confidence, rooted in herself and yet eager to learn from others and cooperate with them. Today she swings **2.** [(*a*) amidst (*b*) among (*c*) between] a blind adherence to her old customs and a slavish imitation of foreign ways. In **3.** [(*a*) both (*b*) neither (*c*) either] of these can she find relief or life or growth. It is obvious that she has come out of her **4.** [(*a*) shell (*b*) groove (*c*) cell] and take full part **5.** [(*a*) in (*b*) between (*c*) of] the life and activities of the modern age. It should be equally **6.** [(*a*) patent (*b*) obvious (*c*) important] that there can be no real cultural or spiritual growth based on imitation. Such imitation can only be **7.** [(*a*) linked (*b*) confined (*c*) ascribed] to a small number which cuts itself **8.** [(*a*) down (*b*) out (*c*) off] from the masses and the **9.** [(*a*) springs (*b*) lakes (*c*) wells] of national life. True culture derives its **10.** [(*a*) inspiration (*b*) ideal (*c*) force] from every corner of the world, but it is **11.** [(*a*) original (*b*) indigenous (*c*) home-grown] and has to be **12.** [(*a*) identified (*b*) based (*c*) dependent] on the wide mass of the people. Art and literature remain **13.** [(*a*) inert (*b*) static (*c*) lifeless] if they are **14.** [(*a*) continually (*b*) blindly (*c*) rapidly] thinking of foreign models. The day of a **15.** [(*a*) communal (*b*) tribal (*c*) narrow] culture confined to a small fastidious group is past.

We have to think in terms of the people generally, and their culture must be a continuation and development of past trends and also represent their new urges and creative tendencies.

Passage 2

When in 1939, Trinity College offered me the Newton Mathematics Prize Scholarship I thought Dad was going to burst, he was so **16.** [(*a*) arrogant (*b*) vainglorious (*c*) proud]. We all drove up to the University city **17.** [(*a*) from (*b*) across (*c*) for] the weekend to check my future digs, before **18.** [(*a*) running (*b*) prancing (*c*) strolling] round the colleges' cloisters and through Great Court. The **19.** [(*a*) dark (*b*) only (*c*) peculiar] cloud on this otherwise **20.** [(*a*) tarnished (*b*) unilluminated (*c*) unblemished] horizon was the thunderous one of Nazi Germany. **21.** [(*a*) Prescription (*b*) Conscription (*c*) Subscription] for all those over twenty was being **22.** [(*a*) debated (*b*) nominated (*c*) amended] in Parliament, and I couldn't wait to play my **23.** [(*a*) part (*b*) battle (*c*) life] if Hitler dared to plant **24.** [(*a*) as much as (*b*) as much so (*c*) as long as] a toe on Polish soil. My first year at Cambridge **25.** [(*a*) disappeared (*b*) spent (*c*) went] well, mainly because I was being **26.** [(*a*) mastered (*b*) tutored (*c*) brought up] by Horace Badford who, along with his wife Victoria, were **27.** [(*a*) considered (*b*) admired (*c*) counted] to be the pick of the bunch **28.** [(*a*) at (*b*) among (*c*) of] a highly talented group of mathematicians who **29.** [(*a*) liked (*b*) are (*c*) were] teaching at the University at that time. Although Mrs. Badford was rumoured to have won the Wrangler's prize for coming out in flying colours, her husband explained that she was not given the **30.** [(*a*) costly (*b*) prestigious (*c*) respectable] award, simply because she was a woman.

Passage 3 **(Stenographers' Exam, 1994)**

Kunti was a worshipper of the Sun-god. One day she **31.** [(*a*) summoned (*b*) invited (*c*) invoked (*d*) attracted] the Sun-god with the help of a prayer-charm. This prayer-charm has been given to her by a sage. As a result the Sun-god **32.** [(*a*) appeared (*b*) stood (*c*) flashed (*d*) came] before her. Seeing the Sun-god before her she got **33.** [(*a*) amused (*b*) frightened (*c*) unconscious (*d*) demoralised] as she had never expected so. Consequently she began to **34.** [(*a*) wave (*b*) stammer (*c*) tremble (*d*) faint] with fear. She did not know what to do. Hence, she prayed to the Sun-god to go back to his kingdom in the sky, but the Sun-god **35.** [(*a*) warned (*b*) fondled (*c*) loved (*d*) chided] Kunti passionately. When he left for his kingdom in the sky, he **36.** [(*a*) gave (*b*) left (*c*) deserted (*d*) discarded] Kunti with a son in her womb. In due course of time Kunti became the mother of a very beautiful and **37.** [(*a*) ugly (*b*) freak (*c*) strange (*d*) promising] child. He was born with an armour as shining as **38.** [(*a*) silver (*b*) glass (*c*) gold (*d*) steel] itself. Besides he had strange, shining ear rings in his ears. This, as a result of the **39.** [(*a*) promise (*b*) wish (*c*) donation (*d*) compliment] granted to her by the Sun-god. Thus, Karna was born to Kunti even while she was unmarried. It was but natural, but she was extremely **40.** [(*a*) sorry (*b*) disturbed (*c*) annoyed (*d*) amused] in her mind.

Passage 4

The problem of adult literacy is **41.** [(*a*) making (*b*) giving (*c*) causing (*d*) compelling] rise to considerable **42.** [(*a*) anger (*b*) annoyance (*d*) anxiety (*d*) disappointment]. The number of young people who leave school without the **43.** [(*a*) power (*b*) skill (*c*) cleverness (*d*) ability] to read is rapidly **44.** [(*a*) increasing (*b*) collecting (*c*) crowding (*d*) widening]. It would seem that if urgent **45.** [(*a*) actions (*b*) cures (*c*) solutions (*d*) steps] are not taken to **46.** [(*a*) increase (*b*) accelerate (*c*) improve (*d*) stop] this situation, we shall soon be living **47.** [(*a*) in (*b*) with (*c*) by (*d*) for] a population **48.** [(*a*) equal (*b*) similar (*c*) like (*d*) resembling] to that of the middle **49.** [(*a*) years (*b*) centuries (*c*) ages (*d*) periods] when only a small number of people were **50.** [(*a*) literate (*b*) literacy (*c*) literal (*d*) littoral].

ANSWERS

1. (*b*)	**2.** (*c*)	**3.** (*b*)	**4.** (*a*)	**5.** (*a*)	**6.** (*b*)	**7.** (*b*)	**8.** (*c*)	**9.** (*a*)	**10.** (*a*)
11. (*c*)	**12.** (*b*)	**13.** (*b*)	**14.** (*b*)	**15.** (*c*)	**16.** (*c*)	**17.** (*c*)	**18.** (*c*)	**19.** (*a*)	**20.** (*c*)
21. (*b*)	**22.** (*a*)	**23.** (*a*)	**24.** (*a*)	**25.** (*c*)	**26.** (*b*)	**27.** (*a*)	**28.** (*c*)	**29.** (*c*)	**30.** (*b*)
31. (*c*)	**32.** (*a*)	**33.** (*b*)	**34.** (*c*)	**35.** (*d*)	**36.** (*b*)	**37.** (*c*)	**38.** (*c*)	**39.** (*b*)	**40.** (*b*)
41. (*b*)	**42.** (*c*)	**43.** (*b*)	**44.** (*a*)	**45.** (*d*)	**46.** (*c*)	**47.** (*a*)	**48.** (*b*)	**49.** (*c*)	**50.** (*a*)

PRACTICE SET 21

Passage 1 **(N.D.A.1996)**

When I got off the plane at Heathrow airport, I had the first taste of English hospitality. For I was immediately bounded off to a hospital. No, not because I was **1.** [(*a*) senseless (*b*) ill (*c*) wicked] but to find out whether I was. And truth to say, it wasn't **2.** [(*a*) actually (*b*) factually (*c*) materially] a hospital, but only the sick bay at the airport. Someone at the immigration counter had taken it into his **3.** [(*a*) judgement (*b*) head (*c*) mind] that I was too thin and an instant X-ray would be in order. Needless to say, I much **4.** [(*a*) resented (*b*) liked (*c*) respected] this extra attention. I would much rather have walked away like the other passengers. The X-ray **5.** [(*a*) extracted (*b*) demanded (*c*) took] an extra half-hour of my time. This did not **6.** [(*a*) please (*b*) annoy (*c*) excite] me as much as the discovery that the famous British sense of humour was by no means ubiquitous.

Passage 2

Operation Flood Scheme was **7.** [(*a*) devoted (*b*) launched (*c*) created (*d*) visualised] with the primary objective to **8.** [(*a*) locating (*b*) bringing (*c*) linking (*d*) joining] rural milk producers with urban milk consumers, by **9.** [(a) creating (*b*) providing (*c*) generating (d) exposing] viable producers' cooperatives in the milk sheds, and thus **10.** [(a) providing (*b*) enabling (*c*) activating (*d*) offering] rural milk producers earn higher income from milk. The programme **11.** [(*a*) leads (*b*) motivates (*c*) relates (*d*) covers] some 72 lakh members in nearly 61,600 village societies **12.** [(*a*) dispersed (*b*) spread (*c*) distributed (*d*) situated] over diverse ecologies in 174 milk sheds. These cooperatives procure an average of 90 lakh litres of milk a day to **13.** [(*a*) attend (*b*) satisfy (*c*) meet (*d*) control] the evergrowing urban demand for fresh milk of the country.

Passage 3 **(Assistant Grade, 1991)**

Our scientific spirit must be shocked not only by the **14.** [(*a*) comparison (*b*) existence (*c*) contrasts (*d*) phenomenon] of fabulous **15.** [(*a*) wealth (*b*) resources (*c*) prosperity (*d*) property] and **16.** [(*a*) growing (*b*) grovelling (*c*) rampant (*d*) common] poverty, but also by those of intense holiness and **17.** [(*a*) prevailing (*b*) popular (*c*) blind (*d*) religious] superstition. In our relations with one another, we have **18.** [(*a*) failed (*b*) succeeded (*c*) refused (*d*) attempted] to apply scientific and social wisdom. The failure is **19.** [(*a*) wrapped (*b*) wrought (*c*) written (*d*) writ] large **20.** [(*a*) for (*b*) among (*c*) on (*d*) in] our society. Some social **21.** [(*a*) obligations (*b*) functions (*c*) ceremonies (*d*) abuses] like untouchability are **22.** [(*a*) resisted (*b*) tolerated (*c*) approved (*d*) allowed] simply because the spirit in us is oppressed by the force of **23.** [(*a*) custom (*b*) society (*c*) habit (*d*) opinion]. These are practised by **24.** [(*a*) somewhat (*b*) otherwise (*c*) very (*d*) fairly] kindly persons who have ceased to feel and whose understanding is **25.** [(*a*) substantiated (*b*) subsidized (*c*) sanctified (*d*) stupefied] by tradition. There are millions in our country today who use scientific **26.** [(*a*) machines (*b*) apparatus (*c*) devices (*d*) discoveries] and yet **27.** [(*a*) revere (*b*) declare (*c*) decry (*d*) consider] superstition as mystical revelation and adhere to absurd social customs **28.** [(*a*) with (*b*) in (*c*) for (*d*) on] the name of tradition.

Passage 4

For freshers stepping out from the **29.** [(*a*) cloistered (*b*) populated (*c*) crowded] world of Archie and Tintin into hurly burly of university, there is this undiluted **30.** [(*a*) anticipation (*b*) excitement (*c*) demarcation] and thrill about seeking the new and the **31.** [(*a*) finding (*b*) search (*c*) probe] for one's destiny. Much like a toddler taking his first **32.** [(*a*) tentative (*b*) new (*c*) uncertain] steps. But then there is also this sense of **33.** [(*a*) ominous (*b*) illusion (*c*) foreboding], fear and nervousness about the unexpected. Fed on horror stories about ragging and the like, it is with a fair bit of **34.** [(*a*) trepidation (*b*) hesitation (*c*) fluster] that many a youngster set foot on the campus.

Passage 5 **(N.D.A. 1992)**

What is an earthquake and how is it caused? In the early history of the earth, when it was cooling down the rocks deep in the earth's crust created huge 'islands' which floated on the softer and hotter rocks below just as wood floats on water. Slowly these islands began to **35.** [(*a*) move (*b*) drift (*c*) float] apart to make the land masses we call **36.** [(*a*) countries (*b*) continents (*c*) mountains]. But even now these 'islands' are not stable. Their continued but imperceptibly slow movements create stress in the rocks many miles below the **37.** [(*a*) surface (*b*) covering (*c*) exterior]. Whenever a rock splits below, it sends a **38.** [(*a*) tremor (*b*) shock (*c*) stir] above, i.e., causes an earthquake. There are several zones in the world where earthquakes are more likely to occur. The recent earthquake in Garhwal was **39.** [(*a*) produced (*b*) caused (*c*) created] in such a zone or fault-line. Scientists believe that there are three other causes which lead to occurrences of earthquakes. At intervals the gravitational **40.** [(*a*) energy (*b*) pulls (*c*) powers] of the sun and the moon in certain situations combine to exert a stronger-than-normal influence on the earth.

Passage 6

There is a special need today for **41.** [(*a*) evolving (*b*) generating (*c*) producing (*d*) emerging] a new system of education in India which is in tune with the major values of natural tradition and **42.** [(*a*) loyalty (*b*) unity (*c*) integration (*d*) brotherhood]. Feeling of the Indian mind from **43.** [(*a*) outside (*b*) foreign (*c*) alien (*d*) strange] cultural subjugation is very urgent. So long as a foreign language **44.** [(*a*) left (*b*) remained (*c*) stayed (*d*) kept] the medium of higher **45.** [(*a*) learning (*b*) knowledge (*c*) effort (*d*) literature] in the country, it would be **46.** [(*a*) impossible (*b*) difficult (*c*) tough (*d*) competent] to conceive of the rise of national consciousness. After 26th January, 1965 when Hindi was **47.** [(*a*) declared (*b*) announced (*c*) stated (*d*) established] by the Constitution to be the official language of the Indian Union, it met with wide **48.** [(*a*) agreement (*b*) approval (*c*) acceptance (*d*) endorsement] and was **49.** [(*a*) endorsed (*b*) signified (*c*) described (*d*) identified] by all the members. It is **50.** [(*a*) important (*b*) necessary (*c*) inevitable (*d*) significant] that among the members there was a majority of those whose mother tongue was not Hindi.

ANSWERS

1. (*b*)	**2.** (*a*)	**3.** (*b*)	**4.** (*a*)	**5.** (*c*)	**6.** (*c*)	**7.** (*b*)	**8.** (*c*)	**9.** (*a*)	**10.** (*b*)
11. (*d*)	**12.** (*b*)	**13.** (*c*)	**14.** (*b*)	**15.** (*c*)	**16.** (*c*)	**17.** (*c*)	**18.** (*a*)	**19.** (*d*)	**20.** (*d*)
21. (*d*)	**22.** (*b*)	**23.** (*a*)	**24.** (*b*)	**25.** (*c*)	**26.** (*c*)	**27.** (*d*)	**28.** (*b*)	**29.** (*a*)	**30.** (*b*)
31. (*b*)	**32.** (*a*)	**33.** (*c*)	**34.** (*a*)	**35.** (*a*)	**36.** (*b*)	**37.** (*a*)	**38.** (*a*)	**39.** (*b*)	**40.** (*b*)
41. (*a*)	**42.** (*c*)	**43.** (*b*)	**44.** (*b*)	**45.** (*a*)	**46.** (*b*)	**47.** (*a*)	**48.** (*b*)	**49.** (*a*)	**50.** (*d*)

PRACTICE SET 22

Passage 1 **(S.S.C. 1994)**

Belief systems are the framework upon which cultures and societies function. It is the bond that **1.** [(*a*) holds (*b*) makes (*c*) compels (*d*) breaks] civilisations together, and it is the small voice **2.** [(*a*) around (*b*) inside (*c*) outside (*d*) about] each of us that urges us to be **3.** [(*a*) accurate (*b*) habitual (*c*) graceful (*d*) true] to what we have been taught. We cannot **4.** [(*a*) see (*b*) upset (*c*) separate (*d*) distinguish] our spiritual teachings from our learning, nor can we separate our beliefs about who and what we are **5.** [(*a*) on (*b*) from (*c*) about (*d*) near] our values and our behaviour. We ask that educational systems **6.** [(*a*) diminish (*b*) destroy (*c*) recognise (*d*) reach] our right to religious freedom and our right to live in harmony. Tribal beliefs vary, as does the **7.** [(*a*) practice (*b*) extent (*c*) capacity (*d*) nearness] to which a tribe embraces **8.** [(*a*) its (*b*) their (*c*) itself (*d*) about] traditional cultural beliefs. **9.** [(*a*) One (*b*) All (*c*) Several (*d*) Each] tribal group has distinct and unique beliefs that are basic to that tribe's culture. Most tribe's cling to the Old Teachings because they know that once gone, it would mean the **10.** [(*a*) regeneration (*b*) death (*c*) tradition (*d*) march] of their culture.

Passage 2

A modern welfare state cannot adopt a 'hands off' attitude in regard to the requirements of physical and mental well-being of its citizens. This is more so in the case of prisoners who are in **11.** [(*a*) captivation (*b*) custody (*c*) seizure (*d*) sentence] of the state and compelled to live, because of **12.** [(*a*) incarceration (*b*) compulsion (*c*) neglect (*d*) seclusion], under very difficult conditions– **13.** [(*a*) physically (*b*) bodily (*c*) structurally (*d*) literally] crowded and uncomfortable mentally **14.** [(*a*) debarred (*b*) devoured (*c*) isolated (*d*) flustered] and frustrated. **15.** [(*a*) Adequate (*b*) Required (*c*) Essential (*d*) Needy] care of prisoner's health is needed not merely on humanitarian **16.** [(*a*) basis (*b*) foundation (*c*) stage (*d*) grounds] but for jail discipline and **17.** [(*a*) acquiring (*b*) attaining (*c*) gaining (*d*) securing] positive **18.** [(*a*) response (*b*) attitude (*c*) support (*d*) reply] from the inmates to all. Such measures **19.** [(*a*) intended (*b*) introduced (*c*) induced (*d*) instigated] to ensure their moral **20.** [(*a*) construction (*b*) regeneration (*c*) revival (*d*) restoration] and social rehabilitation.

Passage 3 **(Central Excise 1992)**

His talk used to be full of wit and humour. He liked reading. He was a **21.** [(*a*) fervent (*b*) voracious (*c*) anxious (*d*) enthusiastic] reader and would pore over books **22.** [(*a*) barring (*b*) including (*c*) containing (*d*) covering] a wide range of interests as **23.** [(*a*) soon (*b*) quickly (*c*) firmly (*d*) urgently] as he got them. He had **24.** [(*a*) intimated (*b*) given (*c*) proclaimed (*d*) offered] a standing order to two book shops **25.** [(*a*) at (*b*) in (*c*) within (*d*) inside] Bombay to mail him catalogues **26.** [(*a*) of (*b*) about (*c*) for (*d*) to] all the latest titles. Books would **27.** [(*a*) sometimes (*b*) rarely (*c*) occasionally (*d*) often] come to him in crates, **28.** [(*a*) most (*b*) much (*c*) least (*d*) more] to the amazement of his friends. He **29.** [(*a*) liked (*b*) wanted (*c*) tried (*d*) used] to set apart a portion **30.** [(*a*) of (*b*) from (*c*) by (*d*) in] his salary every month for meeting the cost of these books.

Passage 4

If more people could travel-both inside and outside the country, there would be a **31.** [(*a*) immense (*b*) tremendous (*c*) enormous] increase in knowledge and understanding of their neighbours. Because people remain **32.** [(*a*) stationary (*b*) mobile (*c*) static] in their areas in which they are born, they **33.** [(*a*) resort (*b*) need (*c*) tend] to look upon those from other states as **34.** [(*a*) intruders (*b*) foreigners (*c*) enemies] and obstruct the **35.** [(*a*) promotion (*b*) propagation (*c*) increase] of national integration. If there was a greater volume of international travel, there would **36.** [(*a*) therefore (*b*) then (*c*) obviously] be a corresponding growth of international integration. This sort of understanding can grow only when we see how others live and think and become **37.** [(*a*) known (*b*) aware (*c*) concerned] of their problems and aspirations.

38. [(*a*) Boastfully (*b*) Since (*c*) Manifestly] this planet has infinite variety and indescribable beauty. But we have **39.** [(*a*) now (*b*) yet (*c*) soon] to **40.** [(*a*) discover (*b*) search (*c*) invent] this hidden variety and beauty. Tourism thus **41.** [(*a*) worth (*b*) leads (*c*) deserves] to be encouraged on a massive scale. One major disadvantage of immovable property is that it tends to keep us chained to one spot. How wonderful life **42.** [(*a*) would (*b*) will (*c*) shall] be if we were a little more mobile!

Passage 5 **(Stenographers' Exam, 1995)**

Well, it was done and the debt was paid. But I began to feel **43.** [(*a*) too (*b*) very (*c*) as (*d*) so] sorry for myself that I could not **44.** [(*a*) understand (*b*) bear (*c*) like (*d*) accept] it. I made up my mind never to steal **45.** [(*a*) ever (*b*) still (*c*) again (*d*) also]. I also made up my mind to tell **46.** [(*a*) everything (*b*) nothing (*c*) something (*d*) anything] to my father. But I did not have the **47.** [(*a*) gallantry (*b*) fortitude (*c*) courage (*d*) bravery] to speak to him. It was not that **48.** [(*a*) me (*b*) she (*c*) he (*d*) I] was afraid that my father would beat me. I **49.** [(*a*) did (*b*) do (*c*) should (*d*) would] not remember any time when he beat **50.** [(*a*) none (*b*) any (*c*) some (*d*) all] of us. I was afraid that my confession **51.** [(*a*) would (*b*) will (*c*) can (*d*) shall] cause him great pain. But I **52.** [(*a*) since (*b*) once (*c*) again (*d*) soon] felt that I had to take this risk. I would never be happy again unless I told everything to my father.

ANSWERS

1. (*a*)	**2.** (*b*)	**3.** (*d*)	**4.** (*c*)	**5.** (*b*)	**6.** (*c*)	**7.** (*b*)	**8.** (*a*)	**9.** (*d*)	**10.** (*b*)
11. (*b*)	**12.** (*a*)	**13.** (*a*)	**14.** (*c*)	**15.** (*a*)	**16.** (*d*)	**17.** (*d*)	**18.** (*a*)	**19.** (*a*)	**20.** (*b*)
21. (*b*)	**22.** (*d*)	**23.** (*a*)	**24.** (*b*)	**25.** (*b*)	**26.** (*a*)	**27.** (*d*)	**28.** (*b*)	**29.** (*d*)	**30.** (*a*)
31. (*b*)	**32.** (*c*)	**33.** (*c*)	**34.** (*b*)	**35.** (*a*)	**36.** (*c*)	**37.** (*b*)	**38.** (*c*)	**39.** (*b*)	**40.** (*a*)
41. (*c*)	**42.** (*a*)	**43.** (*d*)	**44.** (*b*)	**45.** (*c*)	**46.** (*a*)	**47.** (*c*)	**48.** (*d*)	**49.** (*a*)	**50.** (*b*)
51. (*a*)	**52.** (*d*)								

13. CHOOSING THE APPROPRIATE FILLER

This section deals with two types of questions :

TYPE I : ***Choosing the most appropriate phrase to complete a sentence***

Example 1. ***Pick out the best filler which can complete the given sentence correctly.***

He passed the examination in the first class because he...... **(Section Officer' 1993)**

(*a*) was working hard for it (*b*) had worked hard for it

(*c*) worked hardly for it (*d*) was hard working for it

Solution : Clearly, the correct sentence would be 'He passed the examination in the first class because he had worked hard for it'.

Hence, the answer is (*b*).

Example 2. ***Choose the correct alternative so as to fill in the blank and make the sentence meaningfully complete.***

He has no money now .... **(Bank P.O. 1995)**

(*a*) because he always spends money with utmost care.

(*b*) because he had received huge donations once.

(*c*) because he was very rich once.

(*d*) as he has given up all his wealth.

(*e*) although he was very poor once.

Solution. Clearly, the statements (*a*), (*b*), (*c*) contradict the given part of the sentence, and statement (*e*) also does not suit well. Thus, the correct sentence would be 'He has no money now although he was very poor once.'

Hence, the answer is (*d*).

TYPE 2 : ***Choosing the most appropriate sentences to complete a paragraph***

Example 3 : ***Find out which of the sentences A, B and C can fill up the gap between the given sentences in order to make the theme complete.***

The proposal was summarily rejected (..........).

Therefore, the public have the only option of resorting to guessing. **(S.B.I.P.O. 1995)**

(A) The authorities were convinced that there were some malpractices involved in bringing out the project.

(B) It was an outcome of unholy nexus between the traders and decision makers.

(C) However, they did not give any reason for rejection.

(*a*) Only A and B (*b*) Only B and A (*c*) Only A and C

(*d*) Only C and A (*e*) A or B and C

Solution. The first sentence talks about rejection of the proposal. Clearly, sentence (A) provides continuity by giving the reason for rejection. However, the last sentence given still does not come in continuity with the first two. Now, sentence (C) provides the reason for why people have to resort to guessing.

Hence, the most appropriate fillers in the correct order are A and C.So, the answer is (*c*).

PRACTICE SET

Directions : ***In each of the following questions, an incomplete statement followed by some fillers is given. Pick out the best one which can complete the incomplete statement correctly and meaningfully.***

1. He tames animals because he ....
(*a*) seldom loves them
(*b*) is afraid of them
(*c*) is fond of them
(*d*) hates them
(*e*) wants to set them free
(Bank P.O. 1995)

2. My mother is so poor .... **(S.S.C. 1993)**
(*a*) to send me to school
(*b*) because she will not work
(*c*) to get medical help for my father
(*d*) that she cannot buy food for us

3. 'Can you lend me a pencil, please?'
'..........'
(*a*) Yes, you can (*b*) Yes, here you!
(*c*) Yes, here (*d*) Yes, here it is!

4. Johnny, where are you? ...., up this tree. **(Section Officers' 1993)**

(*a*) Here I am (*b*) Here am I
(*c*) There I am (*d*) There am I

5. I don't know the time ....
(*a*) at which the accident happened
(*b*) the accident happened
(*c*) when the accident happened
(*d*) when the accident had happened

6. How much a man earns is as important as .... **(B.S.R.B. 1996)**
(*a*) when does he do so
(*b*) how does he do it
(*c*) where does he earn
(*d*) why does he earn of all
(*e*) how well he spends it

7. One of you must help me, ...
(*a*) Shan't you? (*b*) wouldn't you?
(*c*) won't you? (*d*) mustn't you?

8. He is so lazy that he ....
(*a*) always extends help to others to complete their work
(*b*) dislikes to postpone the work that he undertakes to do
(*c*) can seldom complete his work on time
(*d*) can't delay the schedule of completing the work
(*e*) can't depend on others for getting his work done **(Bank P.O. 1995)**

9. Whichever way you approach the problem, ... **(S.S.C. 1993)**
(*a*) no one will not solve it
(*b*) it will not be solve
(*c*) it will not solve
(*d*) it will not be solved

10. When I met her last year, ...
(*a*) she had married since five years
(*b*) she had been married for five years
(*c*) she was married five years ago
(*d*) she had been married since five years

11. The doctor warns him that unless he gives up smoking .... **(B.S.R.B. 1996)**
(*a*) will he be able to recover
(*b*) he will not suffer
(*c*) his health will soon be recovered
(*d*) he will not recover

12. I shall see him ....
(*a*) before I shall leave for England
(*b*) before I leave for England
(*c*) before I have left for England
(*d*) before I would be leaving for England

13. He seized control of the country ....
(*a*) by being a diplomat and forceful
(*b*) not only because of diplomacy but force
(*c*) by using diplomacy and force
(*d*) by diplomacy and being forceful **(C.B.I. 1995)**

14. In order to raise the company's profit, the employees .... **(Bank P.O. 1995)**
(*a*) demanded two additional increments
(*b*) decided to go on paid holidays
(*c*) decided to raise the cost of raw material
(*d*) requested the management to implement new welfare schemes
(*e*) offered to work over time without any compensation

15. Wait here ....
(*a*) while I come back
(*b*) unless I return back
(*c*) until I have come back
(*d*) till I come back

16. The more we looked at the piece of modern art, ... **(Bank P.O. 1995)**
(*a*) it looked better
(*b*) the more we like it
(*c*) we liked it less
(*d*) the less we liked it
(*e*) better we liked it

17. Unless you work very hard, ...
(*a*) you ought to be successful
(*b*) you be not successful
(*c*) you are not being successful
(*d*) you will not be successful **(S.S.C. 1993)**

18. Anything in this shop can be bought, ...
(*a*) can't we? (*b*) can't it?
(*c*) can't all? (*d*) can't anything?

19. .... I would not have helped such an ungrateful man. **(B.S.R.B. 1996)**
(*a*) Had I asked him for his help
(*b*) Though he did not deserve any help at all
(*c*) Had I been in your place
(*d*) Even after knowing that he was ungrateful
(*e*) If he had shown due respect to me

20. I shall not be late for dinner..........
(*a*) if the train is late
(*b*) unless the train is late
(*c*) unless the train will be late
(*d*) unless the train will not be late **(Stenographers' Exam, 1994)**

21. To succeed in a difficult task, ...
(*a*) one needs to be persistence
(*b*) persistent is needed
(*c*) you need a person of persistent
(*d*) one needs to be persistent
(*e*) persistent is what one needs **(Bank P.O. 1995)**

22. It is unfortunate that..........
(*a*) you lost your purse
(*b*) you have lost your purse

(c) you lose your purse
(d) your purse was lost

23. Seeing that the child was ill, the ....
(a) windows of the room were closed
(b) doctor was sent for
(c) mother sent for the doctor
(d) bottle of medicine was found empty

24. The Chairman rejected the proposal of increasing employee's salary because .... **(B.S.R.B. 1996)**
(a) the number of employees in the company was very small.
(b) the employees had been demanding it for a long time.
(c) the company had already gained three thousand crore profit.
(d) the company did not have sufficient funds to afford the rise.
(e) it was not difficult for the company to bear additional burden.

25. He always stammers in public meetings, but his today's speech......... **(Bank P.O. 1995)**
(a) was surprisingly fluent
(b) was fairly audible to everyone present in the hall
(c) was not liked by the audience
(d) was not received satisfactorily
(e) could not be understood properly

26. If you are unable to pay the amount by the specified date.........
(a) your name strike off our registers
(b) however your name will be strike off our registers
(c) and your name will be struck off our register
(d) your name will be struck off our register

27. With great difficulty, ... **(B.S.R.B. 1996)**
(a) he could not tolerate his nonsense.
(b) he could lose his temper.
(c) he could keep his cool.
(d) he could get annoyed.
(e) he could perform his usual functions easily.

28. 'Where are my spectacles?' ....
(a) Here are they, on your nose!
(b) Here they are, on your nose!
(c) There are they, on your nose!
(d) There they are, on your nose!
(I. Tax, 1993)

29. .... at all is doubtful.
(a) He will come (b) His coming
(c) Will he come (d) If he will come
(e) Whether he will come

30. The notice at the petrol pump should be .... **(Central Excise, 1993)**
(a) All engines need to be switched off.
(b) All engines have to be switched off.
(c) All engines must have to be switched off.
(d) All engines must be switched off.

31. Many people have law degrees, ...
(a) and some of them do have practice also
(b) but some of them do not practice it
(c) but not all of them practice law
(d) however it isn't practised by all
(e) yet some are not undergoing practices **(Bank P.O. 1995)**

32. The income tax raid was too sudden .... **(S.S.C. 1993)**
(a) then the man escaped
(b) for the man to escape
(c) so that the man escaped
(d) for the man escaping

33. Get me a glass of cold water, ...
(a) will you? (b) would you?
(c) shall you? (d) won't you?

34. Every person must learn.........
(a) to make wise use of his time
(b) to using his time in a wisely manner
(c) that his time needs a wise use
(d) wise ways in his time's use
(e) that how wisely his time can be used **(Bank P.O. 1995)**

35. When I saw him through the window .... **(S.S.C. 1993)**
(a) I should run out to open the door
(b) I am running out to open the door
(c) I ran out to open the door
(d) I have run out to open the door

36. This book is quite similar ....
(a) than a story told by our teacher
(b) to the one I read last week
(c) of that film we saw at school
(d) with the 'Treasure Island'

37. If they share burden alternately, they ....
(a) can't feel tiring (b) will get tired soon
(c) won't get tired (d) will get fatigued
(e) don't get tired **(B.S.R.B. 1995)**

Directions : In each question below, a theme is partially presented in two or three sentences. The complete theme comprises three, four or five logically arranged sentences. Out of these, the middle one or two sentences are not given. Three possible fillers denoted by A, B and C are given below the partially provided theme. You have to find out which one or two or either or none can fill up the gap between the given sentences in order to make the theme complete. Study the five alternatives (a), (b), (c), (d) and (e) carefully and select the best out of them.

38. In cultivating team spirit, one should not forget the importance of discipline. (..........). It is the duty of all the members of the team to observe discipline in its proper perspective. **(Bank P.O.1994)**

(A) A proper team spirit can seldom be based on discipline.

(B) It is a well-known fact that team spirit and discipline can never go hand in hand.

(C) Discipline in its right perspective would mean sacrificing 'self to some extent.'

(*a*) A and B only (*b*) B and C only
(*c*) C only (*d*) Either A or B only
(*e*) None of these

39. By reading books even our natural talents are also developed because they get inspiration from these (..........). Bacon has rightly said that some books are to be tasted, others to be swallowed and some few to be chewed and digested.

(A) Reading is an intellectual food for mind.

(B) There is no doubt that different persons choose different books according to their taste.

(C) Good and inspiring books can lead us to a noble and successful career in life.

(*a*) A and B only (*b*) B and C only
(*c*) A and C only (*d*) A or B and C
(*e*) None of these

40. Mr. Raman is undoubtedly a competent professional. (..........). So did the other professionals in the company.

(A) Still he contributed significantly to the growth of the company.

(B) At times he has had serious differences with the Chairman regarding the corporate policies.

(C) He was not considered for the post of the Chairman. **(S.B.I.P.O. 1995)**

(*a*) Only A and B (*b*) Only A and C
(*c*) Only B and C (*d*) B or C and A
(*e*) A and B or C

41. One of the major concerns of many European physicians today is the alarming increase in the incidence of suicides across the continent (..........). Among some age groups in Ireland, the increase is of the order of 700 percent.

(A) In many parts of Europe, suicide has long been common among older people.

(B) Recent studies indicate that more Europeans take their own lives than they die on the highways.

(C) While the traditionally high suicide rates in Austria, Hungary, Switzerland and Scandinavia have remained relatively stable, the low rates in Latin and Catholic countries have begun to grow dramatically in the last 20 years.

(*a*) A and B (*b*) B and C (*c*) A and C
(*d*) A, B and C (*e*) None of these

42. There has been pressure on employees for increasing profits. (..........). Of these two, the latter seems to be more appropriate and keeps in well with social objective also. **(S.B.I.P.O. 1995)**

(A) Profits can be increased by raising the selling price of the products.

(B) Reducing cost of raw materials is another strategy.

(C) It can also be achieved by augmenting labour productivity through employee motivation.

(*a*) Only A and B (*b*) Only B and C
(*c*) Only A and C (*d*) A and B or C
(*e*) B and C or A

43. It is pointed out that stable, matured companies generally distribute high dividends. (..........). It is suggested that matured firms, instead of distributing their earnings should put them to strategic uses for the long term vitality and survival. **(Bank P.O. 1994)**

(A) This displeases the shareholders of the company

(B) This is not a sound policy in the long run.

(C) The company should retain some portion of its earnings

(*a*) A and B only (*b*) B and C only
(*c*) A and C only
(*d*) Either A or B and C together
(*e*) Either C or A and B together

44. Ironically enough, the very 'success' of Operation Flood which is to make the cities flush with milk, has proved its undoing. (..........). Does this mean that the needs of consumers at home are met?

(A) Farmers in Maharashtra, Gujarat, Karnataka and Kerala are now faced with a surplus of supplies for which there are no takers.

(B) Operation Flood requires genetically superior cattle which in turn have to be provided with fodder, now in short supply all over the country.

(C) Indeed, some experts in the Union Agriculture Ministry are even going so far as to suggest that the country should export to neighbouring countries like Bangladesh.

(*a*) A and B (*b*) A and C

(*c*) A or B and C (*d*) B and C
(*e*) A, B and C

45. It is good to remember that we won our struggle for freedom in a unique manner (..........). But it is not good for diplomats to talk about this always. **(Bank P.O. 1994)**
(A) It is also good that our diplomats repeatedly make this known to the people world over.
(B) It is also good to remember that in some ways our foreign policy is unique.
(C) This is intensely exasperating and in the end becomes just boring.
(*a*) Only A (*b*) Only B (*c*) Only C
(*d*) Either A or B (*e*) None of these

46. Forests are gifts of nature. (..........). Yet with the spread of civilisation man has not only spurned the forests but has been ruthlessly destroying them.
(A) It is on historical record record that the vast Sahara desert of today once used to be full of thick forests.
(B) A large part of humanity still lives deep inside forests, particularly in the tropical regions of the earth.
(C) Human evolution itself has taken place in the foresıs.
(*a*) Only A and B (*b*) Only C and A
(*c*) Only C and B (*d*) C and A or B
(*e*) A, B and C

47. Agriculture has been commanding a pivotal position in the Indian economy. (..........) (..........). As a result of reforms, India's potential for export of agro-products is now being seriously explored. **(S.B.I.P.O. 1995)**
(A) India has been an agricultural exporter, for a fairly long time.
(B) Besides, any suggestion for producing just for export was seen unpatriotic.
(C) So far, it was strongly felt that we are just self-sufficient on the agro-products front.
(*a*) Only A and B (*b*) Only A and C
(*c*) Only B and C (*d*) Only C and A
(*e*) Only C and B

48. The function was presided over by a wealthy industrialist who was alleged to be a tax evader. He had agreed to donate a huge sum. (..........). They were of the opinion that both means and ends should be pure. **(Bank P.O. 1994)**
(A) He was invited not because he was genuinely interested in the activity, but he had agreed to donate a huge sum.
(B) Many organisers had reluctantly taken this decision because they felt that so long as they are doing a good cause, it does not matter where the money comes from.
(C) Some of the organisers were opposed to this strategy of the other section of organisers.
(*a*) Either A or B (*b*) B and C only
(*c*) Either A or B or C
(*d*) Either A and B together or B and C together
(*e*) Either A and C together or B and C together

49. Commuting was not the only problem for the city dwellers. (..........). Telephone exchange officials claimed that no complaints were received.
(A) A number of 'down' trains were cancelled and 'up' trains were running behind schedule.
(B) Callers to some exchanges were told that all lines were busy.
(C) Even the phone lines played truant.
(*a*) Only A and B (*b*) Only B and A
(*c*) Only A and C (*d*) Only B and C
(*e*) Only C and B **(S.B.I.P.O. 1995)**

50. In advanced countries, true professionals speak out against irrational and subjective decisions and actions (..........). We are servile when we confront our superiors **(Bank P.O. 1994)**
(A) In our country we do not disagree with our superiors.
(B) This is a terrible combination and makes us totally ineffective.
(C) We are feudalistic when we deal with our subordinates.
(*a*) A and B only (*b*) B and C only
(*c*) A and C only (*d*) Either A or B
(*e*) A, B and C

ANSWERS

1. (*c*)	**2.** (*d*)	**3.** (*d*)	**4.** (*a*)	**5.** (*b*)	**6.** (*b*)	**7.** (*d*)	**8.** (*c*)	**9.** (*d*)	**10.** (*b*)
11. (*d*)	**12.** (*b*)	**13.** (*c*)	**14.** (*e*)	**15.** (*d*)	**16.** (*d*)	**17.** (*d*)	**18.** (*b*)	**19.** (*c*)	**20.** (*b*)
21. (*d*)	**22.** (*a*)	**23.** (*c*)	**24.** (*d*)	**25.** (*a*)	**26.** (*d*)	**27.** (*c*)	**28.** (*d*)	**29.** (*e*)	**30.** (*d*)
31. (*c*)	**32.** (*b*)	**33.** (*a*)	**34.** (*a*)	**35.** (*c*)	**36.** (*b*)	**37.** (*c*)	**38.** (*c*)	**39.** (*c*)	**40.** (*d*)
41. (*b*)	**42.** (*a*)	**43.** (*b*)	**44.** (*b*)	**45.** (*a*)	**46.** (*c*)	**47.** (*e*)	**48.** (*e*)	**49.** (*c*)	**50.** (*c*)

UNIT IV

ERROR DETECTION

14. COMMON ERRORS – HOW TO AVOID THEM ?

ERRORS IN USE OF ARTICLES

ARTICLES

Indefinite	Definite
(a, an)	**(The)**

Use of 'An' :

1. Before words beginning with vowel sounds [a, e, i, o, u are called vowels. Others are consonants]
an apple, **an** egg, **an** owl.

2. Before words beginning with silent 'h'.
an hour, **an** honourable man, **an** heir, **an** honest man.

3. F, H, L, M, N, R, S, X are letters that are not vowels but begin with vowel sound e.g. 'M' has the sound of 'em'. So, **'an'** is used before abbreviations beginning with vowels or these letters.
eg. **an** M.L.A., **an** R.A.F., an N.C.C. officer, **an** F.I.R., **an** X-ray, **an** H.E. school**, an** S.P., **an** LEA school.

Use of 'A' :

1. (i) In the sense of one
e.g. He couldn't speak **a** word to save himself.
(ii) With 'one' (∵ 'one' begins with sound of 'w')
a one-man show, **a** one- rupee note.

2. Before words beginning with consonant sound *e.g.* **a** boy, **a** box, **a** dog.

3. With vowel letters having consonant value :
e.g. **a** university, **a** unique article, **a** euphenism, **a** unit, **a** European language.
(all these begin with consonant sound of 'yu')

4. With units and rate (per) :
e.g. He earns rupees five hundred **a** month.
Rice sells ten rupees **a** kilo.
Give me a metre length of the cloth.

5. In exclamatory expressions before singular countable nouns :
What **a** pretty girl !
How sunny **a** day !

6. When two subjects, or articles are thought of as a single unit.
He was ready with **a** cup and saucer.
A cigarette is made of **a** paper and tobacco.

7. With certain expressions of quantity :
a lot of, **a** dozen, **a** great deal of, **a** couple.

8. With a person's name to indicate that the person is perhaps unknown to the person addressed :
A Mr. Roy is at the door.

9. With a special meal (to celebrate something or in someone's honour)
I called my friends to **a** lunch to celebrate my success.
A dinner was arranged to welcome the Principal.

10. To make a common noun of a proper noun.
This man is '**a** second Newton'.
(This phrase means 'a philosopher as great as Newton')
'A Daniel' came to judgement.
(The phrase means 'a wise man')

Use of 'The'

1. When we speak of a particular person or thing already referred to :
I dislike **the** follow.
The boy near the taps is my brother.

I. ***When a singular noun represents a whole class :***

Ex. (*i*) The mango is considered the king among fruits.
(*ii*) The ass is used as a beast of burden.

Remark. *The nouns 'man' and 'woman' do not take 'the' before them.*

Ex. Man is the greatest of God's creations.

II. ***With names of :***

(a) *gulfs, rivers, oceans, islands and mountains e.g. the Himalayas, the Indian ocean, the Persian Gulf, the Red sea, the Andaman islands, the Brahmaputra river.*

III. ***Certain books :***
e.g. the Vedas, the Puranas, the Bible, the Ramacharitmanas.

IV. ***Musical instruments :***
e.g. the flute, the violin, the tabla, the trumpet.

V. ***The inventions :***

Ex. (*i*) I hate **the** telephone for its constant ringing.
(*ii*) **The** television is a gift of science.

VI. ***Parts of body :***

Ex. (*i*) He was wounded in **the** leg.
(*ii*) They hit him on **the** hands.

VII. ***Religious groups :***
the Sikhs, the Hindus, the Parsees.

VIII. ***Names enforcing law :***
the Police, the Navy, the Air Force.

IX. *Political parties :*
The Congress, the Janata Pary, the B.J.P.

X. *Aeroplanes, ships, trains etc.*
The Makalu' (aeroplane), the Vikrant Ship), the Rajdhani express (train).

XI. *Before names of an empire, dynasty or historical event.*
e.g. the Gupta dynastry, the Old Stone Age, the First World War, the American Revolution.

XII. *Clubs, foundations etc. :*
the Lion's Club, the Ford Foundation.

XIII. *Before common nouns denoting unique things :*
the sun, the sky, the earth, the world, the stars.

XIV. *With superlatives :*
Ex. (*i*) He is **the** best boy in the class.
(*ii*) Prizes would be given for **the** most outstanding performances.

XV. *With ordinals :*
Ex. (*i*) He took **the** first taxi that came his way.
(*ii*) He lives in **the** tenth block.
(*iii*) Our class is on **the** second floor.

XVI. *Before the comparative degree :*
Ex. (*i*) **The more** they get, **the** more they want.
(*ii*) He is **the** cleverer of **the** two.

XVII. *Before an adjective when the noun is understood :*
Ex. (*i*) **The** poor would favour him.
(*ii*) We must not shun **the** disabled.

ERRORS IN USE OF NOUNS

1. Nouns which are used in singular form :–

(i) Scenery, information, furniture, advice, machinery, stationery, news, poetry, business, mischief, fuel, issue, repair, bedding.
The **scenery** of this place is worth seeing.
He has received no **information** so far.

(ii) Physics, Mathematics, Economics, Classics, Ethics, Athletics, innings, gallows.
e.g. **Economics** is a very interesting subject.
The Indian team defeated the Australian by an **innings.**

(iii) Brick, bread, fruit, word (as 'promise')
e.g. Let me buy some **fruit.**
He is true to his **word.**

(iv) Words like dozen, score, hundred, thousand, million when preceded by a numeral.
e.g. He bought ten **dozen** oranges.
I have four **pair** of shoes.

(v) Expressions as a ten-rupee note, a two-hour journey, a four-mile walk, a Five-year plan, a six-man committe etc.
e.g. A ten-rupee note is lying there.

2. Nouns used only in plural form

(i) Cattle, police, poultry, people, gentry, peasantry, artillery.
e.g. The **police have** caught the thief.
Cattle are grazing in the field.

(ii) Scissors, trousers, stockings, spectacles, shorts, alms, remains, riches, goods, measles.
e.g. My **scissors** are very sharp.
My **spectacles** are missing.

3. Nouns used both as singular and plural in the same form.

(i) Deer, sheep, fish, apparatus, wages.
e.g. The **wages** of sin **is** death.
The **wages** of the workers **have** been raised.
I saw **a sheep** grazing in the field.
Sheep are sold cheaper than goat.

(ii) Collective nouns as jury, public, team, audience, committee, government, audience, congregation, orchestra.
e.g. The **team are** looking quite fit.
The **team has** not turned up yet.

4. Use of Collective Nouns

crowd of people
mob of angry people
herd of cattle/cows
fleet of ships/cruisers
team of players
pack of wolves
flight of birds
pack of cards
bouquet of flowers
loaf of bread
shoal/school of fish
heap of corn
bundle of sticks
stock of grain
army of soldiers
class of pupils
flock of sheep
bunch of grapes
crew of sailors
herd of lions
swarm of bees
pile of books

garland of beads
hoarde of nomads
gang of thieves
block of flats
library of books
file of papers

5. **One of** or **any of** is followed by plural words.
e.g. I want **one of** the **books** kept on the table.
Any of these **tools** may serve the purpose.

6. Plural nouns are used with fractions and decimal over 1.
e.g. It took us one and a half **hours.**

ERRORS IN USE OF PRONOUNS

Pronouns are words used to replace nouns or noun groups already mentioned.

Nominative / Vocative case (comes before verb)	Accurative/ Objective case (comes after verb)	Possessive case	Reflexive Pronoun
I	Me	My	Myself
We	Us	Our	Ourselves
He	Him	His	Himself
She	Her	Her	Herself
They	Them	Their	Themselves
Who	Whom	Whose	–

1. The pronoun *'One'* must be followed by *'One's'*.
e.g. One must do *one's* duty to one's country.

2. When 'one' means 'one in number', the pronoun for it is third person singular pronoun (he, she, it).
One of them has given up *one's* studies. (×)
One of them has given up *his* studies. (√)

3. 'Everyone' or 'Everybody' must be followed by 'his'.
e.g. Everyone should love *his* country.

4. Each, every, anyone, anybody must be followed by the singular pronoun of their person.
e.g. Anyone can do this if *he* tries.

5. 'Let' is followed by pronoun in the objective case.
e.g. Let *him* go.
Let you and *me* solve this puzzle.

6. 'But' and 'except' are followed by pronoun in the objective case.
e.g. Everyone attended the party except *him*.
'such as' is followed by pronoun in the subjective case.
e.g. I have no liking for such a man as *he*.

7. Verbs like 'enjoy', 'avail', 'pride', 'resign', 'apply', 'acquit', 'assert', 'absent' are followed by reflexive pronouns.
He absented *himself* from the class.
We enjoyed *ourselves* at the party.
I availed *myself* of the opportunity.
She prides *herself* on her wealth and beauty.
He resigned *himself* to fate.

8. Reflexive pronouns are never used with verbs 'keep', 'conceal', 'qualify', 'spread', 'rest', 'stay'.
e.g. I stayed away from my class.
He qualified in the test.
She kept away from the show.

9. When first, second and third person singular pronouns (I, you and He) are used together, they are placed in the order : You, he and I.
e.g. You, he and I are neighbous.
In case of plural pronouns, 'we' comes first, then 'you' and then 'they'.
e.g. We, you and they must work together.
But if we have only two persons including first, then first person pronoun is written first.
e.g. I and Sanjeev have done this job.

10. 'Who' denotes subject and 'whom' denotes object.
e.g. Who do you think did the job ?
Whom did you abuse ?

11. 'Whose' is used for persons and 'which' for lifeless objects.
e.g. This is the table which I was talking about.
He married Sunita *who* is the daughter of Mr. Roy.

12. 'Which' conveys additional information and 'that' explains a certain thing.
I will tell you the first thing *which* I remember.
I am talking about traffic management *that* forms a part of his duties.

13. The following expressions usually take 'that' in place of 'who' or 'which'.
Only, Any, It is, All, Superlatives
e.g. He is the only man *that* can do it.
Any man *that* listens to you is a fool.
It is the same watch *that* was stolen by him.
All *that* glitters is not gold.
This is the best *that* we can do.

14. *'Each other'* is used for two; *'one another'* for more than two.
Rahul and Renu love *each other.*
They help *one another.*

15. The complement of the verb *to be*, when it is expressed by a pronoun, should be in Nominative case.
e.g. It was *he* who did it.
If I were *he,* I would not go there.

16. When the same person is the subject and object, it is necessary to use reflexive pronouns.
e.g. I cut *me* shaving this morning. (×)
I cut *myself* shaving this morning. (√)

17. When a pronoun is the object of a verb or preposition it should be in objective case.
e.g. These books are for you and *I.* (×)
These books are for you and *me.* (√)
Between *him* and *me* there is an understanding.

18. The Relative Pronoun should be placed as near as possible to the antecedent.
e.g. Here is the book *that* you lent me.
I have read *Shakespeare's works who* was a great dramatist. (×)
I have read *the works of Shakespeare who* was a great dramatist.

19. The case of the pronoun following 'than' and 'as' is decided by mentally supplying the verb and completing the sentence.
e.g. She is taller than *I.* (am)
I love you more than *he.* (loves you)
I love more than (I love) *him.*

ERRORS IN USE OF PREPOSITIONS

A Preposition is a word used with a noun or pronoun to show its relation to some other word in a sentence.

Prepositions of Time

1. At is used :
(*a*) with a definite point of time—
e.g. I usually get up at 5 o'clock.
She leaves her house every day at 9 a.m.
(*b*) with festivals—
e.g. He will come at Holi.

2. In is used :
(*a*) with the parts of the day, (with **noon**, use **at**), months, seasons and years—
e.g. He takes a walk in the afternoon.
In summer the weather is warm.
(*b*) with the future tense referring to the period in which action may take place—
e.g. You must be careful in future.

3. On is used with days and dates :
e.g. My brother will arrive on Monday.
My birthday is on the first of June.

4. By refers to the latest time at which an action will be over :
e.g. The examination will be over by 5 p.m.

5. For is used with perfect continuous tense showing the duration of action :
I have been here for three years.

6. Since is used with the point of time when action begins and continues :
e.g. He has been ill since last Tuesday.
Since 1980, Shalini has lived in Delhi.

7. From refers to the starting point of action :
e.g. This water came from a spring.
She came from USA.

Prepositions of Position

1. At refers to an exact point :
e.g. The tourist stayed at the Tourist Hotel.
He studied at Oxford.
He is waiting at the door.

2. In refers to larger areas :
e.g. He lives in Bombay.

3. Between is used for two persons or two things :
e.g. Share these sweets between him and me.
It is a secret between you and me.

4. Among is used with more than two persons or things but before the word which starts with a consonant letter :
Divide the sweets among the three boys.

5. Amongst is also used with more than two persons or things but before the word which starts with a vowel letter :
e.g. Divide the sweets amongst us.

6. Above is used for **higher than :**
e.g. The sun rose above the horizon.
We were flying above the clouds.

7. Under is used for **vertically below :**
e.g. It is shady under the trees.

8. Below is used for **lower than :**
e.g. When the sun sets it goes below the horizon.
Your work is below average.

9. Over is used for **vertically above :**
e.g. There is an aircraft coming over.
The bathroom is over the kitchen.

10. Beneath means a lower position :
e.g. The ground was slippery beneath her.

Prepositions of Direction

1. To is used to express motion from one place to another :
e.g. We walked to the river and back.

2. Towards refers to direction :
e.g. He saw me running towards him.

She glanced towards the mirror.

3. **Into** denotes motion towards the inside of something :
e.g. She fell into a ditch.

4. **At** refers to aim :
e.g. He aimed at the bird.

5. **For** denotes direction :
e.g. I will leave for Pune today.
The Minister left for the U. K.

6. **Against** shows pressure :
e.g. She cleaned the edge of her knife against the plate.
He leaned against a tree.

7. **Off** refers to separation :
He was wiping sweat off his face.
Kim fell off his chair in a swoon.

8. **From** refers to the point of departure :
e.g. The man parted from his friends.
We scrambled from our trucks and ran after them.

Other Uses of Preposition

1. **About** shows nearness :
e.g. I was about to go to bed when there was a knock at the door.
His father is about to retire.

2. **Along** stands for **in the same line :**
e.g. She led them along the corridor.
The current passes along the wire here.

3. **After** refers to sequence :
e.g. She came after me.
Soon after, Faraday began his researches into electricity.

4. **Across** means from one side :
e.g. He blew a cloud of smoke across the table.
She ran across the field.

5. **Before** stands for **in front of :**
e.g. A thief was brought before the judge.
The garage is before the road.

6. **Behind** means **at the back of :**
e.g. She sat down behind the hedge.
The sun went behind a cloud.

7. **Beyond** means **on the farther side of :**
e.g. This is beyond his power.
Love is beyond all human control.

8. *e.g.* **Beside** means **by the side of :**
I sat down beside my wife.

9. **Besides** menas **in addition to :**
e.g. He is guilty of five killings and more besides.
Besides being a teacher, he is a skilled craftsman.

WORDS FOLLOWED BY PREPOSITIONS

abound with — abstain from
according to — accordance with
accuse of — accustomed to
acquaint with — acquit of
adverse to — affiliate to/with
afflict with — afraid of
agree to/on — aim at
allegation — about
allude to — alternate with
alternative to — angry with
apply to (body) — appreciation of
apprise of — approximate to
arraign against — arrest in
arrive at/in — ashamed of
aspire to/after/at — associate with
assure of — attribute to
averse from/to
belief in — bereft of
beset with — beware of
blink at — boast of
break off — bungle over
busy with
call on (somebody) — canvass for
careful of — cause of
centre on — charge with
clamour for — clamp on
coerce into — collide with
comment on — compatible with
complain of — comply with
compliment on — composed of
concur in — condole with
conducive to — confer on
confirmation of — conform to
congratulate on — conscious of
contiguity with — converge on
convict of — co-opt to
cope with — correspond with
converge on — convict of
co-opt to — cope with
correspond with — cost of
credit with — criticism of
cure of
debar from — decide on
deliberate on — delight in
denude of — depart to
departure for — depend on/upon
deprive of — derive from
derogate from — derogatory to
desist from — despair of
detrimental to — devoid of
difficulty in — diffident of
disabuse of — disagree with
disgusted with — dispose of
dissociate from — divest of

divide into
effort in (—ing)
embroil in
employ in
encroach on
enlarge on
essential to
extend to
focus on
fraught with
full of
grapple with
gratitude for
hanker after
identical with
incur on
indifferent to
infatuate with
infest with
insensible to
interest in
intoxicate with
intrude on
invest with (power)/ in (bank)
investigation of
jealous of
jump at
knock at
lay siege to
live on (income)
lure into
meddle with
oblivious of
opinion on
pay a call on
persist in
plead for
prefer to
present with
priority to
prohibit from
provide with
reconcile to
remonstrate with
replete with
research on
responsibility of (—ing)
sail for
satisfied with
sick of
sparing of

dressed in
election to
emphasis on
enamoured of
endow with
engage in
expostulate with
fed up with
forbid to
fritter in
give to
good at
guilty of
impose on
indict for
indulge in
infect with
information on
insist on
intimate to
intrigue with
involve in
jeer at
just to
lash at
leave for
long for
married to
operate on
overcome with
persevere in
plan for
pleased with
preference for
prevent from
probe into
proud of
recoil from
remand to
repent of
reply to
resolve on/to
satiate with
sentence to
side with
square with

stickler for
subsist on
succeed in
superior to
sure of
susceptible to
sympathise with
tamper with
testify to
throw at
tire of
trample on
try to (do)
vie with
wait for (or await)
wide of

stricture on
subversive of
sue for
supply with
surprised at
suspect of
sympathy for
thank for
tinker at
trace to
translate into
unequal to (the task)
vote for (a candidate)
ways of
wish for

SOME SPECIAL CASES

absolve from (blame) / of (sin)
admit to (hospital, place, class)
appear for (examination) / at
begin on (not from sunday)
blow down (the roof) / off (steam) / over (pass off)
buy in (market, store) / at (shop)
come / go by (bus, train)
come into (conflicit with)
compare with (one man height with another's) / to (one man's height to a building)
consist of (to denote the substance) / in (define the subject)
deal with (somebody) / in (goods)
die of (disease) / from (other causes)
differ from (to be different from) / with (to disagree)
due to (used after a noun, not after a verb)
entrust to (somebody a job)
entrust (somebody) with a job)
fill with (enthusiasm) / in (a form)
fire at (when not hit) / on (when injured to killed)
glad of (the news) / at (having arrivd safe)
hostility to / in hand (being attended to) / on hand (in possession of)
ingratiate (oneself) with
inquire into (matter) / of (person) / about, often (thing)
invest with (power) / in (bank)
key of (the door) / to (a problem)
level (charge) against

look at (consider evidence) / to (somebody for aid)
meeting (called) for (sunday)
motive in (doing) / for (an act)
neglect of (duty) / in (doing a thing)
nominated to (board)
noted for (good things)
owing to (used after a verb, not after a noun)
part from (people) / with (things)
preventive for priority
put out (light) / off (trip)
shoot at (when injured) / in (leg, head)
take up (job) / to (a hobby)
taste of (sensation) / for (liking)
tear off (remove) / up (to pieces)
vest with (The P.M. is vested with power to...) / in (Powers are vested in the P.M. to...)

ERRORS IN USE OF CONJUNCTIONS

1. **Scarcely** or **hardly** is followed by **when**.
   e.g. Scarcely had I entered the room when I heard a shriek.
   Hardly had I slept when the telephone rang.
2. **Though** is followed by **yet**.
   e.g. Though he worked hard yet he failed.
3. **No sooner** is followed by **than**.
   e.g. No sooner did we reach there than it began to rain.
4. **Not only** is followed by **but also**.
   e.g. Not only did he help her, but also dropped her home safely.
5. **Lest** is negative and so should not be followed by **not** ; it is followed by **should**.
   e.g. Work hard lest you should fail.
   If **would** or **may** is used in place of **should**, then **else** should be used in place of **lest**.
   e.g. Give him water, else he may die.
   Leave on time, else you would miss the train.
6. **Both** is complemented by **and**, not by **as well as**.
   e.g. Both Amit and Satish are good at Science.
7. **So.........as** is used in negative sentences, whereas **as ...... as** is used in affirmative sentences.
   e.g. He is not so tall as his brother.
   He is as tall as his brother.
8. **Other** is followed by **than**.
   e.g. He has no other claim than his wealth.
9. The word **reason** is not followed by **because**, but by **that**.
   e.g. The reason why he didn't go was that his mother was ill.
10. **because** denotes reason.
    in order that denotes purpose.
    e.g. He went to the doctor because he was ill.
    He went to Delhi in order that he might see Mr. Roy.
11. Words such as regard, describe, define, treat, mention, depict, portray are followed by **as.**
    e.g. I regard her as my sister.
    He was treated as a slave.
12. **As** and **since** are also used to express reason.
    e.g. As he was not there, I spoke to his brother.
    Since he did not come to the party, his gift was sent to him.
13. **Neither** is followed by **nor** and both are followed by same auxiliary verb.
    e.g. Neither Ravi nor Raju was seen.
    Neither did I read nor did I write.
14. **Either** is followed by **or.**
    e.g. Either you are or he is to blame.
15. **Unless, until, if not, so that** should not be followed by **not.**
    e.g. Wait here until I come.
    Do not go unless I return.
16. **If** is used in conditional sense ;
    Whether is used in uncertainty.
    e.g. If he does not return the books, he will not be awarded the certificate.
    I don't know whether he was present.
17. To express **time before** use **until** or **till** and to express **how long** use **as long as.**
    e.g. He continued to be lazy, **until** he was ten years old.
    Work **as long as** you live.
18. **Such** is followed by **as**.
    e.g. We talked about such subjects as the weather.
    Such is followed by **that** if we emphasize degree of something by mentioning the result.
    e.g. The extent of the disaster was such that not a single man could survive.
19. **Like** is followed by pronoun; **as** is followed by a clause.
    e.g. He runs like me.
    He runs as I do.

ERRORS IN SUBJECT-VERB AGREEMENT

1. Singular subject must have singular verb
   e.g. He writes. I write.
2. Plural subject must have plural verb :
   e.g. They write. We write.

3. Two subjects joined by **and** will always take a plural verb :
e.g. The doctor and nurse work together.
The doctor and nurses work together.
The doctors and nurse work together.

4. Two singular subjects joined by **or** or **nor** will take a singular verb :
e.g. A doctor or a nurse is working in the hospital.

5. A singular subject and a plural subject joined by **or** or **nor** will take a singular or plural verb depending on which subject is nearer the verb :
e.g. Neither Deepak nor his friends are joining the tour.
Neither his friends nor Deepak is joining the tour.

6. If the subject is singular and the predicate is plural, the verb must agree with its subject and not its predicate :
e.g. Physical conditioning and mental attitude are winning combination.
The winning combination is physical conditioning and mental attitude.

7. Indefinite pronouns such as someone, somebody, each, nobody, anyone, anybody, one, no one, everyone, everybody, either, neither etc. always take a singular verb :
e.g. Each of my friends calls me once a month.

8. Indefinite pronouns which indicate more than one (several, few, both, many) always take plural verbs :
e.g. Both of the books require careful reading.
Several of the fielders regularly run four or five kilometers a day.

9. Collective nouns (fleet, army, committee, crowd) are singular when the group works togehter as a unit and hence take singular verbs :
e.g. The jury has reached its verdict.
The team runs in a smooth way.

10. Collective nouns are plural when the members of the group are acting individually and hence take plural verbs :
e.g. The jury have argued for five hours.
The team are putting on their uniforms.

11 Some words (such as news, measles, mumps etc.) end in —s but represent a single thing. These words need singular verbs :
e.g. The 7'o clock news is about to begin.
Measles sometimes has rather serious side effects.

12. Some words (such as scissors, trousers, spectacles, shorts etc.) end in—s and seem to represent a single thing, but they are two parts to that single thing. These words take plural verbs :
e.g. The scissors are on the table.
His trousers are very costly.

13. Words (such as politics, ethics, athletics etc.) that end in —ics are usually singular and hence take singular verbs :
e.g. Mathematics is his favourite subject.
Politics is itself a dirty game.
But these words are singular when they refer to a study, science or practice. If these words have modifiers with them, they become plural and hence take plural verbs :
e.g. His politics are somewhat divided.
The mathematics of the tax-return are flawless.
The school's athletics are all for both boys and girls.

14. Title of the books need singular verbs :
e.g. Great Expectations is a good book.
Tom Jones is a book of Fielding.

15. Some nouns in the plural form represent an amount, a fraction, or an element of time. These nouns are considered singular and hence take singular verbs :
e.g. Sixty minutes is enough to finish this work.
Three-fourths of the land is barren.

16. If two subjects are joined together by **as well as** the verb will act according to the first subject :
e.g. Students as well as the teacher are playing.
He as well as his brothers is sitting there.
I as well as he am going out of station for a week.

17. The subject **Many a ...** is always followed by the singular verb :
e.g. Many a man was drowned in the sea.

18. If two subjects are joined together by **with** the verb will act according to the subject :
e.g. The Principal together with his students was seeing the final match.
The students together with the Principal were seeing the final match.

19. If the subject is **The number of**... use a singular verb :
e.g. The number of books is very small.
The number of boys in this team is ten.

20. If the subject begins with **A number of** ... (= many), use a plural verb :
e.g. A number of books are missing.

21. If two subjects express one idea, use a singular verb :

e.g. Bread and butter is wholesome food.
Soup and salad is too light a lunch.

22. When adjectives such as **much, less, little** and **more** are used as nouns, they must have a singular verb :
e.g. A little of good habits makes our life happy.
Less than a million of rupees is required.

ERRORS IN THE USE OF TENSES

The changed forms of a verb that indicate time of the action are called **tenses** of the verb.

1. When the verb in the Principal Clause is in the Past tense, the verbs of the Subordinate Clauses should be in the Past tense :
e.g. He said that he had finished his work.
I was infomed that her mother was ill.

2. But a Past tense in the Principal Clause may or may not be followed by the Past tense in the sub-ordinate clause if the latter expresses universal or habitual truth :
e.g. The teacher said that the earth revolves round the sun.
My brother told me that smoking is injurious to health.

3. Any tense may be used in the sub-ordinate clause if it gives a comparison by using the word **than :**
e.g. He respected you more than he respects his uncle.
The teacher liked Anil better than he liked me.

4. Any tense can be used when the sub-ordinate clause is in a quotation :
e.g. She said, "He will go to Madras tomorrow."
I said, "I am going to Delhi today."

5. The Present Perfect Tense (subject + has/have + V_3) cannot be used when an expression of Past time (yesterday, last night, ago etc.) is used :
e.g. We wrote to you yesterday about his mother.
I finished my letter last night.

6. In conditional sentences the subordinate clause, beginning with if, is generally is Present or Past tense but not in future tense :
e.g. If I go to Delhi, I shall see the Red Fort.
If he had worked hard, he would have passed.

7. With the phrases **as if** and **as though,** Past tense and plural form of the verb should be used :
e.g. He behaves as if he were a millionaire.

8. Past Perfect tense (subject + had + V_3) is used when a sentence refers to two past actions and one of them occurs earlier than the other :
e.g. When my uncle came to India I had passed M.A.

9. Words like **usually, generally, often, whenever** etc. are used in Present Indefinite tense :
I usually go to play cricket.
I often laugh at him.

10. If the action began in the past and is still continuing in the present, use Present Perfect tense (Subject + has/have + been V_1 + ing) :
e.g. I have been reading in this class for two months.

11. Do not use the Future or the Present tense after such expressions as **suppose that, it is high time, it is time, as if** etc. :
e.g. It is high time that you went home.
It is time that we played football.

GERUND & INFINITIVE

USE OF GERUND (V_1 + ing)

1. When an action is being considered in general sense, gerund is used as subject :
e.g. Swimming is his favourite pastime.
Walking is a good exercise.

2. Gerund is used as subject in short prohibitions :
e.g. Smoking is prohibited.

3. Verbs such as help, stop, detest, avoid, finish, dread, mind, prevent, dislike, risk, deny, recollect, no good, no use, resent, delay, postpone, defer, enjoy, forgive, pardon, excuse, suggest etc. are followed by the gerund :
e.g. It is no use saying.
It is no good repenting.
I avoid calling out loudly.

4. A gerund is placed after a preposition :
e.g. She is tired of walking.
He is fond of riding.
But the prepositions **except** and **but** are followed by an infinitive.

5. A gerund, showing physical activity, is put after **come** or **go :**
e.g. He is to go shooting.
Come fishing with us.

6. Nouns, followed by a gerund, are put in the possessive case.
e.g. He hates his brother's drinking everyday.
She dislikes her child's playing all the time.

7. If there is a sense of dislike, hesitation, risk etc. in a sentence, use gerund :
e.g. I dislike reading cheap novels.
She hesitates singing in the company of her friends.
8. Adjective before gerund are put in the possessive case :
e.g. I do not mind your going away.
What is the good of his trying to do that?
9. **With a view to** is always followed by a gerund and not an adjective.
e.g. We go to school with a view to studying.

INFINITIVE (To + V_1)—

1. Verbs such as learn, remember, promise, swear, consent, neglect, refuse, purpose, try, endeavour, attempt, fail, care, hope, decide, hesitate, prepare, determine, undertake, manage, arrange, seem, forget, agree, regret etc. are followed by infinitive :
e.g. We endeavour to invite such persons.
We promise to do this work soon.
2. Verbs such as order, tell, invite, oblige, allow, permit, compel, teach, instruct, advise, tempt, encourage, urge, request, show, remind, forbid, warm etc. are followed by object and infinitive :
e.g. The teacher instructed the students to go.
She told me to come there.
3. Verbs or expressions like—will, can, do, must, may, let are followed by infinitive without **to :**
e.g. Let him do this work.
Let it be done.
4. Expressions like would rather, would sooner, rather than, sooner than, had better are followed by infinitive without **to** :
e.g. You had better tell him.
I would do rather than suffer.
5. **See** can be used with infinitive or without it :
e.g. Go to see him.
Go and see him.
6. The infinitive is used after adjectives like delight, angry, glad, astonished, surprised, horrified, disappointed etc. :
e.g. I was astonished to find him.
I was horrified to see the scene.
7. The verb know is never directly followed by the infinitive. It is followed by a conjunction and then the infinitive :
Do you know to play the harmonium ? (×)
Do you know how to play the harmonium?(√)
8. **...had better** is always followed by the infinitive without to :
You had better to stop taking the medicine which has harmful side-effects. (×)
You had better stop taking the medicine which has harmful side-effects. (√)
9. Infinitive is not used with **to** after verbs of perception like-to see, to hear, to feel, to watch etc. :
e.g. I saw him cross the street.
She heard her come downstairs.
10. Avoid using split-infinitive :
He planned to not go on a vacation this year, (×)
He planned not to go on a vacation this year. (√)

AUXILIARY VERBS

These are helping verbs.

1. **May** implies permission, doubt or possibility :
e.g. It may rain tonight.
May I use your pen ?
2. **Might** is the past form of **may** but it does not necessarily represent past time. Often it implies more doubt than **may :**
e.g. If the clouds are salted, the rains might come.
3. **Can** is used to express ability :
e.g. He can do this work.
4. **Could** is the past form of **can** but it does not necessarily represent past time. Often it implies a more uncertain condition than **can.**
e.g. She could refuse, but she never does.
5. **Should** is the past form of **shall.** It is used in sub-ordinate clauses after **in case** and sometimes after **if :**
e.g. I shall get some money in case brother comes.
If you should see Raj, give him my regards.
It is also used in past sentences with **so that** and, **in order that :**
e.g. He turned the stereo down very low so that he should not disturb him.
Should can also be used in sub-ordinate clauses when we are expressing the idea that something must be done or is important. The fact is that this happens after verbs like command, order, request, insist, suggest, advise etc. & after adjectives like important, vital, essential, necessary, eager, anxious, concerned etc.
e.g. She insisted that the contract should be read aloud.
I am anxious that nobody should be hurt.

Should is also used in sub-ordinate clauses in sentences where we express personal reactions to events. We express our reactions with words like—amazing, interesting, shocked, sorry, normal, natural, it's a shame etc.

e.g. I am sorry you should think I did it on purpose.

I was shocked that she should not have invited Mr. Kapoor.

6. **Must** is followed by the infinitive without **to** :

e.g. I must get up at five tomorrow.

Must is used to give strong advice or orders :

e.g. I really must stop drinking.

You must be here by 8 o'clock.

Must is used to say that we are sure about something :

e.g. I am in love—that must be nice.

Must is used after a past reporting verb.

e.g. I felt there must be something wrong.

7. **Should** and **Ought** have similar meanings, but **ought** is followed by **to.** **Ought to** has a more objective force and is used when we are talking about laws, duties and regulations :

e.g. We ought to see her tomorrow.

Should and **ought to** can also be used to talk about strong probability :

e.g. He has bought thirty pints of whisky—that ought to be enough.

To talk about things which did not happen, although they were supposed to, we use **should** and **ought to** with the perfect infinitive :

e.g. The taxi should have arrived at 8.30.

8. **Do** is used to make question and negative forms of ordinary verbs :

e.g. Do you know Rajat ?

I don't like trout.

Do is used in question-tags and short answers :

e.g. You know painting, do you ?

Does he know I amd here ?—Yes, he does.

Do is used before an imperative to make the request more persuasive :

e.g. Do accompany us!

Do is not used in questions which have **who, what or which** as their subject :

e.g. Who said that ?

What happened ?

Which one's that ?

But if **who, what** or **which** is the object of the sentence, **do** is used :

e.g. Who did you see ?

Which department do you want ?

Do is also used with an **—ing** form when we want to talk of activity that takes a certain time or that is repeated. In this case we find determiners like—the, my, some, much, etc. :

I usually do most of my washing on Sundays.

Can you do the shopping for her ?

ERRORS IN USE OF ADJECTIVES

Word qualifying a noun or pronoun is called an **adjective.**

1. The adjectives ending in —ior (prior, junior, senior, superior, inferior, posterior) take 'to' and not 'than' after them.

e.g. He is senior to me.

This book is superior to that book.

2. Some adjectives like unique, ideal, perfect, extreme, complete, universal, infinite, perpetual, chief, entire, round, impossible are not compared.

e.g. It is the most unique book. (×)

It is a unique book (√)

3. Comparative degree is used in comparing two things or persons.

e.g. It is *the better* of the two books.

Superlative degree is used in comparing more than two things or persons.

e.g. He is *the best* of the three boys.

4. Double comparatives and double superlatives must not be used.

He is *more wiser* than his brother. (×)

He is *wiser* than his brother. (√)

5. When we compare two qualities in the same person or thing, the comparative ending —er is not used.

You are *wiser* than old. (×)

You are *more wise* than old. (√)

6. When two adjectives in superlative or comparative degree are used together, the one formed by adding 'more' or 'most' must follow the other adjective.

He is *more intelligent* and *wiser* than his brother. (×)

He is *wiser* and *more intelligent* than his brother. (√)

7. When two adjectives with differing degrees of comparison are used they should be complete in themselves.

He is as wise, if not wiser than his brother. (×)

He is as wise as, if not wiser than his brother. (√)

8. When two changes happen together, comparative degree is used in both.

e.g. *The higher* you go, *the cooler* you feel.

9. When comparative degree is used in superlative sense, it is followed by *'any other'*.
Kapil is better than *any* bowler. (×)
Kapil is better than *any other* bowler. (√)

10. Compound adjective formed by adding 'worth' is placed after the noun it qualifies.
This is a worth seeing sight. (×)
This is a sight worth seeing. (√)

11. When two or more comparatives are joined by **'and'**, they must be in the same degree.
e.g. Russel was one of the *wisest* and *most learned* men of the world.

12. When there are two objects of comparison, then to avoid repetition of noun, 'that' is used for singular noun and 'those' for plural noun.
e.g. The climate of Ranchi is better than Gaya. (×)
The climate of Ranchi is better than that of Gaya. (√)

13. If comparison is made by using 'other', 'than' is used instead of 'but'.
e.g. He turned out to be no other than my old friend.

14. **Likely, certain** and **sure** are followed by **'to'**.
e.g. He is likely to win.
We are sure to need help.

Confused Adjectives :

1. **Beautiful** is used for woman ; **handsome** for man.
e.g. He is a handsome youth.
She is a beautiful girl.

2. **Less** refers to quantity, **fewer** denotes number.
e.g. He takes no less than a litre of milk.
They have fewer books than I have.

3. **Last** is the final one ; **Latest** is last upto the present.
e.g. Z is the last letter of the alphabet.
This is the latest edition of the book.

4. **Each** is used for one of two or more things ; **every** is used for more than two things, taken as a group.
e.g. Each of the two boys was wrong.
He read every book I gave him.

5. **Older** refers to persons or things.
e.g. This tree is older than that.
Elder refers to persons only.
e.g. He is my elder brother.

6. **Little** means 'not much'.
A little means 'at least some'.
e.g. He slept little.
He slept a little.

7. **Farther** means 'more distant'.
Further means 'additional'
e.g. Bombay is farther than Delhi.
I shall get further information.

8. **Latter** means the second of two things.
Keats and Byron are romantic poets, but I prefer the latter.
Later refers to time.
She came to school later than I.

ERRORS IN USE OF ADVERBS :

Adverbs are words that add information about the verb.

Adverbs of manner, place and time are usually placed after the verb or object.
e.g. He was running *slowly.*
Reena does her work *carefully.*
I met him *yesterday.*
They followed Rachna *everywhere.*

2. Adverbs of frequency (e.g. never, often, usually, always, rarely, etc.) and other adverbs (like already, almost, just, quite, nearly, hardly) are normally put between subject and verb. If there is more than one word in the verb, they are put after first word.
e.g. He *often* goes to Delhi.
I *quite* agree with you.
But if verb is 'am', 'is' and 'are', adverb is placed after the verb.
e.g. I am *never* late for school.

3. The adverb *enough* is placed after the adjective.
e.g. She is *cunning* enough to tackle him.

4. 'Ever' is sometimes incorrectly used for 'never'.
He seldom or *ever* tells a lie. (×)
He seldom or *never* tells a lie. (√)

5. Adverb 'not' shouldn't be used with words having negative meaning.
The teacher forbade me not to go. (×)
The teacher forbade me to go. (√)

6. The word 'only' should be placed immediately before the word it modifies.
e.g. Hari answered *only* two questions.

7. An adverb should not be used before an infinitive.
He quickly did the job. (×)
He did the job quickly. (√)

8. The auxiliaries *have to* and *used to* come after the adverb.
He often *used to* go to cinema.

Some More Tips of Usage :

1. Avoid the use of **lots, a lot** and **a whole lot** in the sense of **much** or **a great deal** :
He expects to earn a lot of money on his sale of farm products. (×)

He expects to earn a great deal of money on his sale of farm products. (√)

2. **Plenty** is a noun and is always followed by **of:** *e.g.* He has plenty of room in his old house.

3. **Due to** always modifies a noun and not a verb. Hence, no sentence should begin with **due to,** it must be used only after some form of the verb **to be :** *e.g.* His death was due to natural causes.

4. **Alright** is incorrect, use **all right :**
I think it is quite alright if you stay. (×)
I think it is quite all right if you stay. (√)

5. If the gender is not determined, use the pronoun of the masculine gender :
If anybody has got the book let her return it. (×)
If anybody has got the book let him return it. (√)

6. When two nouns are closely connected, apostrophe —'s will be written after second only :
Ravi's and Shikha's mother is ill. (×)
Ravi and Shikha's mother is ill. (√)

7. **Both** and **as well as** cannot be used together in the same sentence because both convey the same sense :
Both Pinki as well as Pooja are beautiful. (×)
Both Pinki and Pooja are beautiful. (√)

8. **Supposing** and **if** cannot be used together in the same sentence :
Supposing if he fails, what will he do? (×)
If he fails, what will he do ? (√)

9. **Endure** sugests **suffering,** usually in silence and **tolerate,** means to allow it with some degree of approval :
e.g He endured the pain without complaint.
He will not tolerate laziness.

10. Avoid the use of **had** with **ought :**
You had not ought to do it. (×)
You ought not do it. (√)

11. **As** is used when one compares things or persons of equal or about equal size or quality, **so** is used when one compares things or persons which are unequal :
e.g. He weighs as much as his father.
He does not weigh so much as his father.

12. Avoid using the double comparative and double superlative :
The weather is more hotter than it was yesterday. (×)
The weather is hotter than it was yesterday. (√)
This pen is the most costliest in this store. (×)
This pen is the costliest in this store. (√)

13. **Cent per cent** and **word by word** are wrong uses. The real terms are **hundred percent** and **word for word.**

14. When two comparatives are used in a sentence for proportion, **the** is used before both of them :
e.g. The higher we go, the cooler it is.

15. **Do the needful** is incorrect, write **do what is necessary.**

16. Never say **family members,** say **members of the family :**
e.g. His family members have gone to Bombay. (×)
The members of his family have gone to Bombay. (√)

17. **Else** is always followed by **but** and never by **than :-**
It is nothing else but your pride which makes you say such a thing.

18. **All of** is used in conversation, not in standard written English :
She gave all of her antiques to the museum. (×)
She gave all her antiques to the museum. (√)

19. **Talking terms** is wrong, use **speaking terms :**
He is not on talking terms with his brother. (×)
He is not on speaking terms with his brother. (√)

20. Verbs like resemble, recommend, comprise, order, accompany, reach, join, shirk, attack, emphasise, discuss, fear, succeed, resist, request, assist, benefit, afford etc. are not followed by any preposition when used in the active voice.
He emphasised on the need for discipline. (×)
He emphasised the need for discipline. (√)
She will accompany with you to Madras. (×)
She will accompany you to Madras. (√)

21. The phrase **type of, sort of** and **kind of** do not follow **a** or **an :**
What kind of a friend are you ? ((×)
What kind of friend are you ? (√)

22. A full hour number follows **o'clock,** but in fraction it does not follow :
He left this place by 10.40 o'clock. (×)
He left this place by 10.40 (√)

23. **Yet** means up to the present time something that has not happened :
His brothers are not married even yet.

I hope the end is not yet.

Still means that a situation, state, or action which began at an earlier time has continued right up to the present :

I still do not understand.

24. **And** joins two clauses of the same nature, **but** joins two antithetical clauses of quite opposite meaning :

e.g. It was lovely and warm outside.

It was a long walk but it was worth it.

25. **Hardly** refers to degree, while **scarcely** refers to quantity :

e.g. I hardly see how I can finish this work.

I have scarcely enough money for my own needs.

26. Words like **divide** and **share** are followed by **between** when we use several singular nouns :

e.g. I divided my time between teaching, writing and delivering lecture.

I shared his property between his wife, his son and his daughter.

27. In relative sentences **any** is usually followed by **that,** not by **which** or **who** :

e.g. Borrow any book that interests you.

28. **Since** is used as an adverb, as a preposition and also as a conjunction :

I met Raj last Tuesday but have not seen him since. (Adverb)

Ajay has eaten nothing since yesterday. (Preposition)

What have you done since we last met ? (Conjunction)

15. Spotting Errors

PRACTICE SET 1

Directions : *In each of the following questions, find out which part of the sentence has an error. If there is no mistake, the answer is 'No error'.*

1. The road (*a*) / to famous monument (*b*) / passes through a forest (*c*) / No error (*d*) **(Stenographer's Exam, 1995)**
2. Our Housing Society comprises of (*a*) / six blocks and (*b*) / thirty three flats in an (*c*) / area of about thousand sq. metres. (*d*) / No error (*e*)
3. Now that she is living in her own flat, (*a*) / she cleans the windows, (*b*) / twice a week in the summer and once a week in the winter. (*c*) / No error (*d*) **(C.D.S. 1993)**
4. With little imagination and enterprise, (*a*) / the tournament could have been transformed (*b*) / into a major attraction (*c*) / No error (*d*)
5. These display (*a*) / the (*b*) / remarkable variety. (*c*) / No error (*d*) **(N.D.A. 1992)**
6. If you have faith in Almighty (*a*) / everything will turn out (*b*) / to be all right. (*c*) / No error (*d*)
7. According to the Bible (*a*) / it is meek and humble (*b*) / who shall inherit the earth. (*c*) / No error (*d*) **(C.B.I. 1995)**
8. I am not wealthy, (*a*) / so I cannot afford (*b*) / to buy a expensive car. (*c*) / No error (*d*)
9. Sunita opened a almirah (*a*) / full of books (*b*) / and took one of them (*c*) / for reading. (*d*) / No error (*e*) **(B.S.R.B. 1992)**
10. Most people would have (*a*) / attended the union meeting (*b*) / if they had (*c*) / had longer notice of it. (*d*) / No error (*e*)
11. My father is (*a*) / in bad mood (*b*) / today. (*c*) / No error (*d*) **(Stenographers' Exam, 1994)**
12. The need to set up (*a*) / a good library in the locality (*b*) / has been in the minds of people (*c*) / for some time now (*d*) / No error (*e*)
13. On my request (*a*) / Lalit introduced me (*b*) / to his friend (*c*) / who is singer and a scientist. (*d*) / No error (*e*) **(S.B.I.P.O. 1991)**
14. This town isn't very well known (*a*) / and there isn't much to see, (*b*) / so a few tourists come here. (*c*) / No error (*d*) **(M.B.A. 1993)**
15. He took to (*a*) / reading Times (*b*) / for better knowledge (*c*) / of the facts. (*d*) / No error (*e*)
16. The accelerating pace of life in our metropolitan city (*a*) / has had the tremendous effect (*b*) / on the culture and life-style of the people. (*c*) / No error (*d*) **(I. Tax, 1992)**
17. Both the civilians (*a*) / and armymen (*b*) / joined the First World War. (*c*) / No error (*d*)
18. The school is (*a*) / within hundred yards (*b*) / from my house. (*c*) / No error (*d*)
19. The majority of the (*a*) / computer professionals recommends (*b*) / that effective measures (*c*) / should be taken against software piracy. (*d*) / No error (*e*) **(Bank P.O. 1994)**
20. He obtained good marks (*a*) / not only in English essay (*b*) / but also in arithmetic which was (*c*) / full of complicated calculations. (*d*) / No error (*e*)
21. The famous Dr. Chandra (*a*) / is only dentist (*b*) / in our village. (*c*) / No error (*d*) **(Stenographers' Exam, 1995)**
22. This candidate lacks (*a*) / an experience (*b*) / otherwise he is well qualified. (*c*) / No error (*d*)
23. A person I met (*a*) / in the theatre (*b*) / was the playwright himself. (*c*) / No error (*d*) **(U.D.C. 1994)**
24. The war of Mahabharata (*a*) / is the full length illustration (*b*) / of a righteous war. (*c*) / No error (*d*)
25. The interviewer asked me (*a*) / if I knew that (*b*) / Kalidas was the greater (*c*) / than any other poet. (*d*) / No error (*e*)
26. The reason we have not been able to pay income tax (*a*) / is due to fact (*b*) / that we did not receive pay on time. (*c*) / No error (*d*) **(S.S.C. 1993)**
27. Even now when I see the spot (*a*) / I am reminded of an unique incident (*b*) / that took place several yeras ago. (*c*) / No error (*d*)
28. As soon as the teacher entered, (*a*) / everyone fell (*b*) / in a silence. (*c*) / No error (*d*)
29. As he had taken only a few sips (*a*) / there was still little water (*b*) / left in the glass. (*c*) / No error (*d*) **(Central Excise, 1994)**
30. As I was to reach (*a*) / early I left in aeroplane (*b*) / instead of (*c*) / going by train. (*d*) / No error (*e*)

31. To perform this experiment, (*a*) / drop little sugar (*b*) / into a glass of water. (*c*) / No error (*d*) **(S.S.C. 1994)**

32. It is written in Gita (*a*) / that God incarnates (*b*) / Himself (*c*) / in times of trouble. (*d*) / No error (*e*)

33. Troy was taken by Greeks ; (*a*) / this formed the basis of a story (*b*) / which has become famous. (*c*) / No error (*d*) **(Central Excise, 1995)**

34. These facts make it very clear (*a*) / that he had hand in the murder, (*b*) / though he still (*c*) / pleads innocence. (*d*) / No error (*e*)

35. A nationwide survey (*a*) / has brought up an (*b*) / interesting finding (*c*) / regarding infant mortality rate in India. (*d*) / No error **(Bank P.O. 1991)**

36. The man (*a*) / cannot live (*b*) / by bread alone. (*c*) / No error (*d*)

37. I go to the bed (*a*) / at eight (*b*) / every night. (*c*) / No error (*d*) **(Stenographers' Exam, 1995)**

38. If a man diligently seeks to come into the contact (*a*) / with the best that has been thought and said in this world (*b*) / he will become simple and selfish. (*c*) / No error (*d*) **(U.D.C. 1995)**

39. Gangotri has special significance (*a*) / for the devout (*b*) / as it is considered as (*c*) / the abode of King Bhagirath who brought the Ganga down to the earth. (*d*) / No error (*e*)

40. The recent study has (*a*) / indicated that there (*b*) / is perceptible change in (*c*) / the attitudes of the people. (*d*) / No error (*e*) **(Bank P.O. 1994)**

41. The disclosure of (*a*) / the synopsis of Thakkar Commission report (*b*) / on the assassination of Mrs. Indira Gandhi (*c*) / has raised several vital questions. (*d*) / No error (*e*)

42. He was fascinated by insects (*a*) / and the more he studied their habits (*b*) / greater was his fascination. (*c*) / No error (*d*) **(Clerks' Grade, 1995)**

43. We all (*a*) / must respect (*b*) / a honest person. (*c*) / No error (*d*)

44. With little patience (*a*) / you will be able to (*b*) / cross this hurdle. (*c*) / No error (*d*) **(Stenographer's Exam, 1994)**

45. He did not go (*a*) / to the city on foot, (*b*) / he went there (*c*) / by the train. (*d*) / No error (*e*)

46. My friends insisted (*a*) / that I should see the movie (*b*) / from beginning to the end. (*c*) / No error (*d*) **(U.D.C. 1994)**

47. Both optimists and pessimists contribute to society ; (*a*) / the optimist invents the aeroplane, (*b*) / the pessimist parachute. (*c*) / No error (*d*)

48. It being rainy day, (*a*) / we decided not to go out (*b*) / but to stay at home (*c*) / and watch a movie. (*d*) / No error (*e*)

49. By all standards (*a*) / he is a best soldier (*b*) / our military school (*c*) / has produced so far. (*d*) / No error (*e*) **(B.S.R.B. 1992)**

50. No stronger (*a*) / a figure than his (*b*) / is prescribed in the history. (*c*) / No error (*d*)

ANSWERS

1. (*b*) : Add 'the' before 'famous' 'the' is used before particular objects.
2. (*d*) : Add 'a' before 'thousand'. Here, 'a' is before 'thousand'
3. (*c*) : Remove 'the' before 'winter' and 'summer'
4. (*a*) : Add 'a' before 'little'.
5. (*b*) : Replace 'the' by 'a'
6. (*a*) : Add 'the' before 'Almighty'.
7. (*b*) : Add 'the' before 'meek'
8. (*c*) : Replace 'a' by 'an' because expensive' begins with a vowel — e.
9. (*a*) : Replace 'a' by 'an'.
10. (*d*) : Add 'a' before 'longer'
11. (*b*) : Add 'a' before 'bad mood'.
12. (*c*) : Add 'the' before 'people'
13. (*d*) : Add 'a' before 'singer'.
14. (*c*) : Remove 'a'
15. (*b*) : Add 'the' before 'Times'.
16. (*b*) : Replace 'the' by 'a'
17. (*b*) : Add 'the' before 'armymen'.
18. (*b*) : Add 'a' before 'hundred'. Here, 'a' is used for 'one'
19. (*a*) : The correct form is 'A majority of the ...'
20. (*b*) : Add 'the' before 'English essay'.
21. (*b*) : Add 'the' before 'only'
22. (*b*) : Remove 'an'.
23. (*a*) : Replace 'A' by 'The' The' is used before specified objects.
24. (*a*) : Add 'the' before 'Mahabharata'

25. (*c*) : Remove 'the'.
'the' is used before superlative degree i.e. 'greatest'
26. (*b*) : Add 'the' before 'fact'
27. (*b*) : Replace 'an' by 'a' because unique begins with the sound 'yu' and 'y' is a consonant
28. (*c*) : Remove 'a'.
29. (*b*) : Add 'a' before 'little'
30. (*b*) : Add 'an' before 'aeroplane'
31. (*b*) : Add 'a' before 'little'
32. (*a*) : Add 'the' before 'Gita'.
33. (*a*) : Add 'the' before 'Greeks'
34. (*b*) : Add 'a' before 'hand'.
35. (*d*) : Add 'the' before 'infant'
36. (*a*) : Remove 'the'.
37. (*a*) : Remove 'the'
38. (*a*) : Remove 'the'.
39. (*a*) : Add 'a' before 'special'
40. (*c*) : Add 'a' before 'perceptible'.
41. (*b*) : Add 'the' before 'Thakkar Commission report'
42. (*c*) : Add 'the' before 'greater'
43. (*c*) : Replace 'a' by 'an' because in 'honest',
'h' is silent so that it begins with vowel sound 'o'
44. (*a*) : Add 'a' before 'little'
45. (*d*) : Remove 'the'
46. (*c*) : Add 'the' before 'beginning'.
47. (*c*) : Add 'the' before 'parachute'
48. (*a*) : Add 'a' before 'rainy day'.
49. (*b*) : Replace 'a' by 'the'
50. (*c*) : Remove 'the'

PRACTICE SET 2

Directions : ***In the questions given below, some of the sentences have errors and some have none. Find out which part of a sentence has an error. If there is no mistake, the anser is 'No error'.***

1. One of the most (*a*) / widely spread (*b*) / bad habit (*c*) / is the use of tobacco. (*d*) / No error (*e*) **(S.B.I.P.O. 1991)**

2. Recently I visited Kashmir (*a*) / and found the sceneries (*b*) / to be marvellous. (*c*) / No error (*d*)

3. All the furnitures have been (*a*) / sent to the new house (*b*) / located in a village. (*c*) / No error (*d*) **(Section Officers', 1993)**

4. The crowd of angry students (*a*) / ordered the (*b*) / closing of shops. (*c*) / No error (*d*)

5. They left (*a*) / their luggages (*b*) / at the railway station. (*c*) / No error (*d*)

6. The bus could not (*a*) / ascend the steep hill (*b*) / because it was in the wrong gears. (*c*) / No error (*d*) **(I.E.S. 1994)**

7. The Indian force (*a*) / drove away (*b*) / the chinese. (*c*) / No error (*d*)

8. The polling was marred (*a*) / at many a place (*b*) / by attempts at nigging. (*c*) / No error (*d*) **(C.B.I. 1995)**

9. His mouth watered (*a*) / when he saw (*b*) / a bouquet of grapes. (*c*) / No error (*d*)

10. My brother-in-laws (*a*) / who live in Bombay (*b*) / have come to stay with us. (*c*) / No error (*d*) **(N.D.A. 1993)**

11. The customer handed over (*a*) / a hundred-rupees note (*b*) / to the shopkeeper. (*c*) / No error (*d*) **(Stenographers' Exam, 1994)**

12. These kind (*a*) / of shirts (*b*) / are rather expensive (*c*) / for him to buy. (*d*) / No error (*e*)

13. Yo can get (*a*) / all the informations you want (*b*) / in this book. (*c*) / No error (*d*) **(C.D.S. 1993)**

14. This article (*a*) / is not available in (*b*) / any of the shop (*c*) / in the market. (*d*) / No error (*e*)

15. The blinds (*a*) / deserve (*b*) / our sympathy. (*c*) / No error (*d*)

16. They have (*a*) / placed order (*b*) / for books. (*c*) / No error (*d*)

17. Students should not take part (*a*) / in party politics and political demonstrations (*b*) / as they interfere in serious study. (*c*) / No error (*d*) **(C.B.I. 1995)**

18. The flock of lions (*a*) / roamed about (*b*) / fearlessly inthe jungle. (*c*) / No error (*d*)

19. I hav done my best ; (*a*) / the whole thing is now (*b*) / in the laps of the Gods. (*c*) / No error (*d*) **(C.D.S. 1989)**

20. Satyajit Ray, who conceived, co-authored (*a*) / and directed a number of good films, was (*b*) / one of India's most talented film maker. (*c*) / No error (*d*) **(Stenographers' Exam, 1993)**

21. A trained gang of sailors (*a*) / was employed (*b*) / on the ship. (*c*) / No error (*d*)

22. The sound of (*a*) / a gun shot (*b*) / scattered the flock of birds. (*c*) / No error (*d*)

23. I saw (*a*) / a few children (*b*) / playing on sand. (*c*) / No error (*d*)

24. Interviews for (*a*) / the posts of lecturers (*b*) / will begin from Monday. (*c*) / No error (*d*) **(N.D.A. 1993)**

25. The rate of growing (*a*) / may be different for different people, (*b*) / but old age spares none. (*c*) / No error (*d*)

ANSWERS

1. (*c*) : Replace 'habit' by 'habits'.
2. (*b*) : Replace 'sceneries' by 'scenery'
3. (*a*) : Replace 'furnitures' by 'furniture'.
4. (*a*) : Replace 'crowd' by 'mob'
5. (*b*) : Replace 'luggages' by 'luggage'.
6. (*c*) : Replace 'gears' by 'gear'
7. (*a*) : Replace 'force' by 'forces'.
8. (*b*) : Replace 'a place' by 'places'
9. (*c*) : Replace 'bouquet' by 'bunch'.
10. (*a*) : Replace 'brother-in-laws' by 'brothers-in-law'
11. (*b*) : Replace 'rupees' by 'rupee'
12. (*a*) : Replace 'kind' by 'kinds'
13. (*b*) : Replace 'informations' by 'information'
14. (*c*) : Replace 'shop' by 'shops'.
15. (*a*) : Replace 'blinds' by 'blind'
16. (*b*) : Replace 'order' by 'orders'.
17. (*c*) : Replace 'study' by 'studies'
18. (*a*) : Replace 'flock' by 'herd'.
19. (*c*) : Replace 'laps' by 'lap'
20. (*c*) : Replace 'maker' by 'makers'.
21. (*a*) : Replace 'gang' by 'crew'
22. (*c*) : Replace 'flock' by 'flight'.
23. (*c*) : Replace 'sand' by 'sands'
24. (*b*) : Replace 'posts' by 'post'.
25. (*a*) : Replace 'growing' by 'growth'

PRACTICE SET 3

Directions : ***In the following questions, some of the sentences have errors and some have none. Find out which part of a sentence has an error. If there is no error, mark your answ. er as 'No error'.***

1. The interviewer asked the candidate (*a*) / to what district (*b*) / he came from. (*c*) / No error (*d*) **(S.S.C. 1991)**

2. The master did not know (*a*) / who of the servants (*b*) / broke the glass. (*c*) / No error (*d*)

3. The ruling party stood (*a*) / for implementation of the Bill (*b*) / and was ready to stake their political existence. (*c*) / No error (*d*) **(Asstt. Grade, 1991)**

4. This is the boy (*a*) / whom I think had won (*b*) / the gold medal in the Dance competition. (*c*) / No error (*d*)

5. Wherever they go, (*a*) / Indians easily adapt to (*b*) / local circumstances. (*c*) / No error (*d*) **(C.B.I. 1995)**

6. He is (*a*) / taller (*b*) / than me. (*c*) /No error (*d*)

7. It is not easy for anyone to command (*a*) / respect from both one's friends as well as critics (*b*) / as Dr. Johnson did for his integrity and honesty. (*c*) / No error (*d*)

8. Mahatma Gandhi taught us (*a*) / that one should respect (*b*) / the religions of others (*c*) / as much as his own. (*d*) / No error (*e*)

9. He, you and I (*a*) / will manage (*b*) / this problem together. (*c*) / No error (*d*)

10. Was it him (*a*) / who got injured (*b*) / in an accident this morning. (*c*) / No error (*d*)

11. I suppose (*a*) / you have heard the latest news (*b*) / John has married that girl. (*e*) / No error (*d*) **(C.D.S. 1994)**

12. As soon as he (*a*) / saw his mother (*b*) / he ran to her (*c*) / and embraced. (*d*) / No error (*e*)

13. Due to me being a newcomer (*a*) / I was unable to get a house (*b*) / suitable for my wife and me. (*c*) / No error (*d*) **(Assistant Grade, 1996)**

14. The audience (*a*) / are requested (*b*) / to be in its seats. (*c*) / No error (*d*)

15. The scientist must follow (*a*) / his hunches and his data (*b*) / wherever it may lead. (*c*) / No error (*d*) **(Assistant Grade, 1996)**

16. He is the general (*a*) / whom the reporters agree (*b*) / was most popular with the troops. (*c*) / No error (*d*)

17. There is no question (*a*) / of my failing (*b*) / in the examination. (*c*) / No error (*d*) **(I.E.S. 1994)**

18. The number of vehicles (*a*) / plying on this road (*b*) / is more than on the main road. (*c*) / No error (*d*)

19. Being a destitute, (*a*) / I admitted him (*b*) / to an old people's home. (*c*) / No error (*d*) **(Clerks' Grade, 1991)**

20. This is not the (*a*) / sense which (*b*) / concerns us here. (*c*) / No error (*d*)

21. One should make (*a*) / his best efforts (*b*) / if one wishes to achieve (*c*) / success in this organisation. (*d*) / No error (*e*)

22. May I (*a*) / know who you want (*b*) / to see please. (*c*) / No error (*d*) **(Hotel Management, 1996)**

23. Our is the only (*a*) / country in the world (*b*) / than can boast of (*c*) / unity in diversity. (*d*) / No error (*e*)

24. Last summer he went (*a*) / to his uncle's village, (*b*) / and enjoyed very much. (*c*) / No error (*d*) **(C.D.S. 1994)**

25. If I were him, (*a*) / I would have taught (*b*) / those cheats a lesson. (*c*) / No error (*d*) **(Stenographers Exam, 1994)**

26. Those sort of people (*a*) / usually do not (*b*) / earn fame in society. (*c*) / No error (*d*)

27. He could not plan his strategy (*a*) /until he knew (*b*) / whom his opponents could be. (*c*) / No error (*d*) **(Railways, 1993)**

28. Being a very (*a*) / hot day I (*b*) / remained indoors. (*c*) / No error (*d*) **(Asstt. Grade, 1995)**

29. Concurrent with this programme, (*a*) / educational institutions may be urged (*b*) / to inculcate patriotism (*c*) / in each and every one of its pupils. (*d*) / No error (*e*)

30. Inspite of the doctor's stern warning, (*a*) / he continued taking (*b*) / sugar in his tea. (*c*) / No error (*d*) **(Stenographers' Exam, 1995)**

31. Had I come (*a*) / to know about (*b*) / his difficulties (*c*) / I would have certainly helped. (*d*) / No error (*e*) **(Bank P.O. 1994)**

32. One of them (*a*) / forget to take their bag (*b*) / from the school. (*c*) / No error (*d*)

33. Mr. Sunil Pawar, our representative, (*a*) / he will attend the meeting (*b*) / on our behalf. (*c*) / No error (*d*) **(N.D.A. 1995)**

34. Being a destitute, (*a*) / I admitted him (*b*) / to an old peoples' home. (*c*) / No error (*d*)

35. If the teacher is good (*a*) / the students (*b*) / will respond (*c*) / positively to them. (*d*) / No error (*e*) **(B.S.R.B. 1995)**

36. Just before the race (*a*) / I asked him (*b*) / whom he thought (*c*) / was going to win. (*d*) / No error (*e*)

37. It is not difficult to believe that a man (*a*) / who has lived in this city for a long time (*b*) / he will never feel at home anywhere else in the world. (*c*) / No error (*d*) **(N.D.A. 1996)**

38. Each girl was (*a*) / given a bunch of flowers, (*b*) / which pleased her very much. (*c*) / No error (*d*)

39. The party chief made it a point to state that (*a*) / the Prime Minister and the Union Home Minister should also come (*b*) / and they see what his party men had seen. (*c*) / No error (*d*) **(Assistant Grade, 1996)**

40. I going there (*a*) / will not solve (*b*) / this complicated problem. (*c*) / No error (*d*)

41. As it was Rajan's (*a*) / first interview he dressed him (*b*) / in his most (*c*) / formal suit. (*d*) / No error (*e*) **(Bank P.O. 1994)**

42. Whatever work (*a*) / that which you undertake (*b*) / put your best efforts (*c*) / in it. (*d*) / No error (*e*) **(B.SR.B. 1995)**

43. The superintendent of police has announced that those who are found guilty of breach of peace (*a*) / or of taking the law into their own hands (*b*) / they will be taken to task. (*c*) / No error (*d*)

44. Myself and Gopalan (*a*) / will take care of (*b*) / the function on Sunday. (*c*) / No error (*d*) **(Hotel Management, 1996)**

ANSWERS

1. (*b*) : Replace 'to what' by 'which'
2. (*b*) : Replace 'who' by 'which'
3. (*c*) : Replace 'their' by 'its'
4. (*b*) : Replace 'whom' by 'who'
5. (*b*) : Add 'themselves' after 'adapt'
6. (*c*) : Replace 'me' by 'I'
7. (*b*) : Add 'one's' before 'critics'
8. (*d*) : Replace 'his' by 'one's'
9. (*a*) : The correct form is 'You, he and I'
10. (*a*) : Replace 'him' by 'he'
11. (*a*) : Add 'that' after 'suppose'
12. (*d*) : Add 'her' after 'embraced'
13. (*a*) : Replace 'me' by 'my'
14. (*c*) : Replace 'its' by 'their'
15. (*c*) : Replace 'it' by 'they'
16. (*b*) : Replace 'whom' by 'who'
17. (*b*) : Replace 'my' by 'me'
18. (*c*) : Add 'that' after 'than'

19. (a) :Add 'He' before 'being'
20. (b) : Replace 'which' by 'that'
21. (b) : Replace 'his' by 'one's'
22. (b) : Replace 'who' by 'whom'
23. (b) : Replace 'our' by 'ours'
24. (c) : Add 'himself' after 'enjoyed'
25. (a) : Replace 'him' by 'he'
26. (a) :Replace 'Those' by 'That'
27. (c) : Replace 'whom' by 'who'
28. (a) : Add 'It' before 'being'
29. (d) :Replace 'its' by 'their'
30. (c) : Remove 'his'
31. (d) :Add 'him' after 'helped'
32. (b) :Replace 'their' by 'his'
33. (b) :Remove 'he'
34. (a) :Add 'He' before 'being'
35. (d) :Replace 'them' by 'him'
36. (c) : Replace 'whom' by 'who'
37. (c) : Remove 'he'
38. (c) : Replace 'her' by 'them'
39. (c) : Remove 'they'
40. (a) :Replace 'I' by 'My'
41. (b) :Replace 'him' by 'himself'
42. (b) :Remove 'that which'
43. (c) : Remove 'they'.
44. (a) :Replace 'Myself and Gopalan' by 'Gopalan and I'

PRACTICE SET 4

Directions : ***In each of the following questions, find out which part of the sentence has an error. The error may be idiomatic or grammatical. If the sentence is correct, the answer is 'No error'.***

1. The widely publicised manifesto (a) / of the new party (b) / is not much different than ours. (c) / No error (d) **(C.D.S. 1994)**
2. I was taken with surprise (a) / when I saw (b) / the glamorous Appu Ghar. (c) / No error (d)
3. Man needs (a) / security and leisure (b) / of free thinking. (c) / No error (d)
4. This watch (a) / is superior and (b) / more expensive than that. (c) / No error (d) **(Stenographers' Exam, 1993)**
5. It was apparent for everyone present (a) / that if the patient did not receive (b) / medical attention fast (c) / he would die. (d) / No error (e)
6. He knows very well (a) / what is expected from him (b) / but he is not able to fulfil all the expectations. (c) / No error (d)
7. My brother (a) / has ordered (b) / for a new book. (c) / No error (d) **(S.S.C. 1994)**
8. That Brutus, who was his trusted friend (a) / had attacked on him (b) / and caused heartbreak to Julius Caesar. (c) / No error (d)
9. Rāna Pratap was (a) /blind with (b) / one eye. (c) / No error (d)
10. The doctor (a) / attended to the patient (b) / very quietly. (c) / No error (d) **(N.D.A. 1992)**
11. I was shocked to hear (a) / that his father (b) / died of an accident. (c) / No error (d)
12. I must start (a) / at dawn (b) / to reach the station in time. (c) / No error (d)
13. I will put on (a) / a note in this regard (b) / for your consideration (c) / and necessary decision. (d) / No error (e) **(B.S.R.B. 1995)**
14. None could (a) / dare to encroach (b) / on his rights. (c) / No error (d)
15. The father brought the sweets (a) / and distributed them (b) / between his five children. (c) / No error (d)
16. Raman developed the (a) / habit for sleeping late (b) / when he was (c) / staying in the hostel. (d) / No error (e)
17. It is the duty of every right thinking citizen (a) / to try to make the whole world (b) / a happier place to live. (c) / No error (d) **(Assistant Grade, 1995)**
18. The top-ranking candidates (a) / will be appointed in (b) / senior jobs in good companies. (c) / No error (d)
19. My niece has been (a) / married with (b) / the richest man of the town. (c) / No error (d)
20. The venue of examination (a) / is one mile further up (b) / the hill. (c) / No error (d) **(C.B.I. 1993)**
21. The doctor referred (a) / the patient for the O.P.D. (b) / without examining him. (c) / No error (d)
22. A man who always (a) / connives on the faults (b) / of his children (c) / is their worst enemy. (d) / No error (e)
23. I do not understand (a) / why he is. (b) / So angry at me. (c) / No error (d) **(N.D.A. 1989)**

24. I am hearing (a) / a lot about (b) / the problem of AIDS these days. (c) / No error (d)

25. Because of his innocence (a) / he cannot (b) / distinguish a cheat (c) / for an honest person. (d) / No error (e)

26. After opening the door (a) / we entered into the room (b) / next to the kitchen. (c) / No error (d) **(C.D.S. 1995)**

27. As the meeting was about to end (a) / he insisted to ask (b) / several questions. (c) / No error (d)

28. The watchman was kind enough (a) / to inform us about the conspiracy (b) / but declined to name (c) / the person behind it. (d) / No error (e)

29. The captain and his wife (a) / were invited (b) / for the cultural function (c) / at my home. (d) / No error (e)

30. The engineer came out (a) / to a novel solution (b) / which may even reduce (c) / daily energy consumption. (d) / No error (e)

31. On a holiday (a) / Madhu prefers reading (b) / than going out visiting friends. (c) / No error (d) **(Hotel Management, 1996)**

32. People who are averse with (a) / hard work (b) / generally do not (c) / succeed in life. (d) / No error (e)

33. Vishal is (a) / one year junior (b) / than Madan (c) / in our office. (d) / No error. (e)

34. They walked (a) / besides each other (b) / in silence. (c) / No error (d) **(Assistant Grade, 1995)**

35. Our Mathematics teacher (a) / often emphasises on (b) / the ned for a lot of practice. (c) / No error (d)

36. Please put away (a) / the candle (b) / before you leave. (c) / No error (d)

37. All the doctors were (a) / puzzled on the (b) / strange symptoms (c) / reported by the patient. (d) / No error (e) **(Bank P.O. 1991)**

38. Most of the Uttar Pradesh (a) / is an extremely fertile plain (b) / between which the river Ganga flows. (c) / No error (d)

39. He has been working on (a) / the problem from a long time (b) / but is still not (c) / able to solve it. (d) / No error (e) **(B.S.R.B. 1992)**

40. At the last day (a) / of your holidays (b) / you have started thinking about (c) / how to finish your work. (d) / No error (e)

41. India is in no way (a) / inferior than the U.S.A. (b) / in the fertility of soil (c) / and in the richness of mineral resources. (d) / No error (e)

42. The students were (a) / awaiting for (b) / the arrival of the chief guest. (c) / No error (d) **(C.D.S. 1995)**

43. I could not convince them (a) / because they persisted to suggest (b) / that I was lying. (c) / No error (d)

44. It was apparent for everyone present (a) / that if the patient (b) / did not receive medical attention fast (c) / he would die. (d) / No error (e)

45. The detective says that (a) / there is no chance for (b) / finding the person (c) / who wrote these letters. (d) / No error (e) **(S.B.I.P.O. 1991)**

46. In urban society (a) / the social circle is limited with the family (b) / but in the villages (c) / it encompasses the entire village. (d) / No error (e)

47. Being most loquacious (a) / among her brothers and sisters (b) / she related a good many tales (c) / in each breath (d) / No error (e)

48. The committee appointed to investigate into (a) / the said murder (b) / will convene next week (c) / to further discuss their strategy. (d) / No error (e)

49. Kamal's habit of (a) / delaying his work (b) / put his colleagues (c) / to lot of trobule. (d) / No error (e)

50. No effort has been made at all (a) / to cash on (b) / the refurbished image of Indian tennis. (c) / No error (d)

ANSWERS

1. (c) : The correct usage is 'different from ....'

2. (a) : Replace 'with' by 'by'

3. (c) : Replace 'of' by 'for'

4. (b) : Add 'to' after 'superior'. Adjectives ending in —ior take 'to' after them.

5. (a) : Replace 'for' by 'to'

6. (b) : Replace 'from' by 'of'

7. (c) : Remove 'for'

8. (b) : Remove 'on'. The verb 'attack' does not take a preposition

9. (b) : Replace 'with' by 'in'

10. (*b*) : Replace 'to' by 'upon'
11. (*c*) : The correct usage is 'died in an accident' and 'died of malaria'
12. (*b*) : Replace 'at' by 'by'
13. (*a*) : Replace 'on' by 'up'
14. (*c*) : Replace 'on' by 'upon'. The verb 'encroach' takes 'upon' after it
15. (*c*) : Replace 'between' by 'among'. 'Between' is used for two persons and 'among' for more than two persons.
16. (*b*) : Replace 'for' by 'of'
17. (*c*) : Add 'in' after 'live'
18. (*b*) : Replace 'in' by 'to'
19. (*b*) : Replace 'with' by 'to'. The verb 'marry' takes preposition 'to'
20. (*a*) : Replace 'of' by 'for'
21. (*b*) : Replace 'for' by 'to'. The verb 'refer' takes preposition 'to'
22. (*b*) : Replace 'on' by 'at'. 'Connive' takes the preposition 'at'
23. (*c*) : The correct form is 'angry with ...'
24. (*b*) : Replace 'about' by 'of'
25. (*d*) : Replace 'for' by 'from'
26. (*b*) : Remove 'into'. 'Enter' does not take any preposition.
27. (*b*) : The correct form is 'he insisted on asking'
28. (*b*) : Replace 'about' by 'of'.
29. (*c*) : Replace 'for' by 'to'
30. (*b*) : Replace 'to' by 'with'
31. (*c*) : Replace 'than' by 'to'. The verb 'prefer' takes preposition 'to'.
32. (*a*) : Replace 'with' by 'to'.
33. (*c*) : Replace 'than' by 'to'. Adjectives ending in —ior take 'to'.
34. (*b*) : Replace 'besides' by 'beside'
35. (*b*) : Remove 'on'.
36. (*a*) : The correct usage is 'put out the candle'
37. (*b*) : Replace 'on' by 'at'.
38. (*c*) : Replace 'between' by 'through'
39. (*e*) : No error.
40. (*a*) : Replace 'at' by 'on'
41. (*b*) : Replace 'than' by 'to'.
42. (*b*) : Remove 'for'
43. (*b*) : Replace 'to suggest' by 'in suggesting'
44. (*a*) : Replace 'for' by 'to'.
45. (*b*) : Replace 'for' by 'of'
46. (*b*) : Replace 'with' by 'to'
47. (*b*) : Replace 'among' by 'of'
48. (*a*) : Remove 'into'.
49. (*d*) : Replace 'to' by 'into'
50. (*b*) : The correct form is 'to cash in on'

PRACTICE SET 5

Directions : ***In each of the following questions, find out which part of the sentence has an error. If there is no mistake, the answer is 'No error'.***

1. He says that (*a*) / he has a car (*b*) / beside a scooter. (*c*) / No error (*d*)
(S.S.C. 1994)
2. Mahatma Gandhi laboured (*a*) / to the good (*b*) / of humanity. (*c*) / No error (*d*)
3. The blind old man was (*a*) / knocked down by a car (*b*) / upon crossing the road. (*c*) / No error (*d*)
4. In a report issued by Indian Statistical Institute, (*a*) / the Iron and Steel Industry is investing more than any other (*b*) / Indian industry in fighting pollution. (*c*) / No error (*d*)
(Central Excise, 1995)
5. I found it dificult (*a*) / to remove (*b*) / the chewing gum that (*c*) / stuck with my cap. (*d*) / No error (*e*)
6. My answer (*a*) / is different (*b*) / than yours. (*c*) / No error (*d*)
7. Of all the men (*a*) / known to me none is (*b*) / less inclined that he is (*c*) / to think ill to others. (*d*) / No error (*e*)
(Bank P.O. 1995)
8. Dr. Addison has been trying (*a*) / to develop a medicine for diabetes (*b*) / for the last ten years. (*c*) / No error (*d*)
9. As the party was going (*a*) / we noticed Mr. Roy fall back (*b*) / in his chair, gasping for breath. (*c*) / No error (*d*)
(Assistant Grade, 1991)
10. In this age of despair and despondency, (*a*) / only our rich cultural heritage (*b*) / can help us (*c*) / escape to the menacing doom. (*d*) / No error (*e*)
11. Rekha was trying for admission (*a*) / in the Engineering College (*b*) / even though her parents wanted (*c*) / her to take up medicine. (*d*) / No error (*e*)
(S.B.I.P.O. 1992)
12. All the players (*a*) except sam (*b*) / were present (*c*) / on the playground. (*d*) / No error (*e*)
13. It proves (*a*) / year after year (*b*) / that when it comes into judging new writing

(*c*) / we are on slippery ground. (*d*) / No error (*e*)

14. This kind of behaviour (*a*) / has not been seen here (*b*) / since the last four years. (*c*) / No error (*d*) **(C.D.S. 1994)**

15. He is in the habit (*a*) / of going out (*b*) / on a morning walk (*c*) / regularly. (*d*) / No error (*e*)

16. The management did not (*a*) / select him as he was (*b*) / not eligible to the post. (*c*) / No error (*d*)

17. Both the form and substance (*a*) / of what he says (*b*) / about his life and work (*c*) / testify for a great reserve of inner energy. (*d*) / No error (*e*)

18. I am vexed (*a*) / at him about what (*b*) / he has done. (*c*) / No error (*d*) **(C.B.I. 1993)**

19. Beside chocolates, (*a*) / they also bought (*b*) / many toys for the child. (*c*) / No error (*d*)

20. Young children should not sit close (*a*) / to the TV set (*b*) / as it affects on their eyes. (*c*) / No error (*d*) **(S.S.C. 1991)**

21. The child freed himself (*a*) / from his father's hold (*b*) / and ran on the road. (*c*) / No error (*d*)

22. Without a moment's hesitation (*a*) / the Principal agreed to write (*b*) / a foreword to my book. (*c*) / No error (*d*)

23. When the teachers are on strike (*a*) / and a notice to this effect is pasted on the college gate (*b*) / there is no sense to go there. (*c*) / No error (*d*) **(N.D.A. 1995)**

24. To gain reputation among your clients, (*a*) / you ought to finish (*b*) / every assignment you undertake (*c*) / within the stipulated deadline. (*d*) / No error (*e*)

25. Children often (*a*) / quarrel on (*b*) / petty issues. (*c*) / No error (*d*) **(Clerks' Grade, 1995)**

26. Rahul was in need (*a*) / of money and (*b*) / sold out his gold medal for hundred rupees (*c*) / to one of his friends. (*d*) / No error (*e*)

27. Our Mathematics teacher (*a*) / often emphasises on (*b*) / the need for a lot of practice. (*c*) / No error (*d*) **(I. Tax, 1992)**

28. Many a time (*a*) / the Minister had hinted on (*b*) / the destruction caused by floods. (*c*) / No error (*d*)

29. Having come to Calcutta (*a*) / he had found the people (*b*) / were warm and friendly (*c*) / and there was nothing pessimistic in them. (*d*) / No error (*e*)

30. Our laxity in duty (*a*) / increases with our (*b*) / aversion for work. (*c*) / No error (*d*) **(I. Tax, 1994)**

31. The teacher (*a*) / was pleased (*b*) / at Sanjay. (*c*) / No error (*d*)

32. None saw him (*a*) / worthy for the reward (*b*) / he received. (*c*) / No error (*d*)

33. My uncle frequently goes to abroad (*a*) / on business (*b*) / by air. (*c*) / No error (*d*) **(N.D.A. 1995)**

34. Yesterday, Sohan came across with (*a*) / one of his (*b*) / old friends. (*c*) / No error (*d*)

35. The Minister and some of his colleagues (*a*) / were invited (*b*) / for the charity show (*c*) / staged by the Dhawan College (*d*) / No error (*e*)

36. He fixed a metal ladder (*a*) / for the wall below his window (*b*) / so as to be able to (*c*) / escape if there was a fire. (*d*) / No error (*e*) **(Bank P.O. 1995)**

37. For nearly half a century he lived in that village, (*a*) / sharing the joys and sorrows of the people there, (*b*) / but later he left the village and has not been heard of since. (*c*) / No error (*d*)

38. A large scale exchange of nuclear weapons (*a*) / will produce unprecedented amounts of radiation (*b*) / that can penetrate into the biological tissue. (*c*) / No error (*d*) **(Assistant Grade, 1996)**

39. He did not complain, (*a*) / although the pain (*b*) / was behind his capacity (*c*) / to bear. (*d*) / No error (*e*)

40. On his attitude (*a*) / it seems that what he wants (*b*) / is that the decision making power (*c*) / should rest with him. (*d*) / No error (*e*) **(Bank P.O. 1994)**

41. The boy stood (*a*) / by me (*b*) / panting for breath. (*c*) / No error (*d*)

42. The plan is to go for (*a*) / the cinema and then have dinner (*b*) / but Ajay's late arrival (*c*) upset the whole thing. (*d*) / No error (*e*)

43. It is not possible for me (*a*) / to exchange the goods (*b*) / once the sale has been completed. (*c*) / No error (*d*) **(Stenographers' Exam, 1995)**

44. The teacher taught (*a*) / to the students (*b*) / like his own children. (*c*) / No error (*d*)

45. Mr. Smith was accused for murder (*a*) / but the court found him not guilty (*b*) / and acquitted him. (*c*) / No error (*d*) **(C.D.S. 1995)**

46. In my opinion (*a*) / this boy is very honest (*b*) / and can be depended. (*c*) / No error (*d*)

47. The earth we live in (*a*) / is enveloped (*b*) / on all sides by air. (*c*) / No error (*d*)

8. Several prominent figures (*a*) / involved in the scandal (*b*) / are required to appear (*c*) / to the investigation committee. (*d*) / No error (*e*) **(S.B.I.P.O. 1991)**

49. If I were the Principal of the college (*a*) / I would have never accepted (*b*) / such demands of the students. (*c*) / No error (*d*)

50. She had shifted her residence (*a*) / to this city to be (*b*) / close with the child (*c*) / she had wanted to adopt. (*d*) / No error (*e*)

ANSWERS

1. (*c*) : Replace 'beside' by 'besides'
'Beside' means 'by the side of', 'besides' means 'apart from'
2. (*b*) : Replace 'to' by 'for'
3. (*c*) : Replace 'upon' by 'while'
4. (*d*) : Replace 'in' by 'on'
5. (*d*) : 'Stuck' takes the preposition 'to', not 'with'.
6. (*c*) : The correct usage is 'different from'
7. (*d*) : The correct form is 'to think ill of others'
8. (*c*) : Replace 'for' by 'since'
9. (*a*) : Add 'on' after 'going'
10. (*d*) : Replace 'to' by 'from'
11. (*b*) : Replace 'in' by 'to'
12. (*d*) : Replace 'on' by 'in'
13. (*c*) : Replace 'into' by 'to'
14. (*c*) : Replace 'since' by 'for'
15. (*c*) : Replace 'on' by 'for'
16. (*c*) : The correct form is 'eligible for ...'
17. (*d*) : Replace 'for' by 'to'
18. (*b*) : Replace 'at' by 'with'
19. (*a*) : Replace 'beside' by 'besides'
20. (*c*) : Remove 'on'
21. (*c*) : Replace 'on' by 'across'
22. (*c*) : Replace 'to' by 'for'
23. (*c*) : Replace 'to go' by 'in going'
24. (*d*) : Replace 'within' by 'by'
25. (*b*) : Replace 'on' by 'over'
26. (*c*) : Remove 'out'
27. (*b*) : Replace 'on' by 'upon'
28. (*b*) : The correct form is 'hinted at ...'
29. (*d*) : Replace 'in' by 'about'
30. (*c*) : The correct form is 'aversion to'
31. (*c*) : The correct form is 'pleased with ...'
32. (*b*) : The correct form is 'worthy of ...'
33. (*a*) : Remove 'to'
34. (*b*) : Remove 'with'
35. (*c*) : The correct form is 'invited to ...'
36. (*b*) : Replace 'for' by 'to'
37. (*c*) : Add 'then' after 'since'
38. (*c*) : Remove 'into' The verb 'penetrate' doesn't take any preposition.
39. (*c*) : Replace 'behing' by 'beyond'
40. (*a*) : Replace 'on' by 'from'
41. (*b*) : Replace 'by' by 'before'
42. (*a*) : Replace 'for' by 'to'
43. (*c*) : Replace 'once' by 'after'
44. (*b*) : Remove 'to'
45. (*a*) : The correct form is 'accused of ...'
46. (*c*) : The correct form is 'depended upon'
47. (*b*) : Replace 'on' by 'from'
48. (*c*) : Replace 'to' by 'before'
49. (*c*) : Replace 'of' by 'from'
50. (*c*) : Replace 'with' by 'to'

PRACTICE SET 6

Directions : ***In each of the following questions, find out which part of the sentence has an error. If the sentence is correct, the answer is 'No error'***

1. He was honourably (*a*) / acquitted from (*b*) / the charge. (*c*) / No error (*d*) **(Stenographers' Exam, 1994)**

2. Ajay was suffering (*a*) / from cholera (*b*) / and ultimately he died by it. (*c*) / No error (*d*)

3. We returned to the guest house (*a*) / impressed by (*b*) / what we had seen. (*c*) / No error (*d*)

4. I am pleased to sanction (*a*) / one special increment (*b*) / to all the employees (*c*) / with this month. (*d*) / No error (*e*) **(B.S.R.B. 1995)**

5. It must be said (*a*) / to his credit that (*b*) / he stood towards his friend (*c*) / through thick and thin. (*d*) / No error (*e*)

6. To transport goods (*a*) / by sea is cheaper (*b*) / than land. (*c*) / No error (*d*) **(Clerks' Grade, 1995)**

7. Ritu was conscious to (*a*) / all that was going (*b*) / on around her place. (*c*) / No error (*d*)

8. I want this document (*a*) / to be detached off (*b*) / the main file and sent to me. (*c*) / No error (*d*)

9. It is easy to see that (*a*) / a lawyer's demeanour in court (*b*) / may be prejudicial against the interests of his client. (*c*) / No error (*d*) **(C.D.S. 1993)**

10. Of what I know (*a*) / of him, (*b*) / I hesitate to (*c*) / trust him. (*d*) / No error (*e*)

11. The Prince (*a*) / came on the throne (*b*) / at a very early age. (*c*) / No error (*d*)

12. Considering about these facts (*a*) / the principal has offered (*b*) / him a seat. (*c*) / No error (*d*) **(N.D.A. 1996)**

13. Two women were between (*a*) / those killed in the fire (*b*) / that broke out at the hotel. (*c*) / No error (*d*)

14. The angry boatsman threw (*a*) / the cracked oar (*b*) / in the river (*c*) / and returned home. (*d*) / No error (*e*)

15. The Third World countries must adopt (*a*) / a radically different approach for (*b*) / the dissemination of scientific information (*c*) / in view of the nature and magnitude of their problems. (*d*) / No error (*e*)

16. Yet the writers (*a*) / have no qualms in (*b*) / depicting the gory (*c*) / details of the violence. (*d*) / No error (*e*)

17. The director prefers (*a*) / your plan than (*b*) / that given by (*c*) / the other members of the committee. (*d*) / No error (*e*) **(B.S.R.B. 1992)**

18. I always prefer (*a*) / working in a relaxed atmosphere (*b*) / than one full of (*c*) / tension and anxiety. (*d*) / No error (*e*)

19. You should not discuss (*a*) / about a matter (*b*) / with friends who are likely (*c*) / to find it offensive (*d*) / No error (*e*)

20. When you have (*a*) / read these books, (*b*) / please return them to me. (*c*) / No error (*d*) **(S.S.C. 1994)**

21. Will you please buy (*a*) / some jaggery for me (*b*) / if you go to the market ?(*c*) / No error (*d*)

22. In my opinion (*a*) / Rajeev is very honest (*b*) / and can be depended. (*c*) / No error (*d*)

23. There are several ways (*a*) / of investing money prudently (*b*) / and making substantial profit (*c*) / from the investments. (*d*) / No error (*e*)

(S.B.I.P.O. 1991)

24. Rana Pratap was (*a*) / blind with (*b*) one eye. (*c*) / No error (*d*)

25. Having to stay (*a*) / in the jungle that night, (*b*) / they had nothing (*c*) / to feed at. (*d*) / No error (*e*)

26. The student (*a*) / answered to (*b*) / the question (*c*) / asked by the inspector of school (*d*) / No error (*e*) **(Railways, 1996)**

27. The plane took on (*a*) / as soon as (*b*) / the passengers boarded it. (*c*) / No error (*d*)

28. The boy attempted the questions (*a*) / so well (*b*) / that his teacher was exceedingly (*c*) / pleased at him. (*d*) / No error (*e*)

29. The Trust plans (*a*) / to set on (*b*) / a special school for (*c*) / dumb and deaf children. (*d*) / No error (*e*) **(B.S.R.B 1994)**

30. Amar's habit of (*a*) / delaying his work (*b*) / put his colleagues (*c*) / to lot of trouble. (*d*) / No error (*e*)

31. The wife is not (*a*) / yet acquainted with (*b*) / her husband's likings. (*c*) / No error (*d*)

32. The beauty of her autobiography (*a*) / lies in coming (*b*) / to terms with life (*c*) / facing its many challenges through a rare courage. (*d*) / No error (*e*)

33. We never buy any jam in the shops, (*a*) / because my wife makes all our jam from the fruit in our garden, (*b*) / and it tastes much better than the jam from the shops, we think. (*c*) / No error (*d*)

(C.D.S. 1994)

34. A shiver ran to Sachin's spine (*a*) / when he recalled the accident (*b*) / in which he (*c*) / was luckily saved. (*d*) / No error (*e*)

35. On the time when the house collapsed (*a*) / all the people in the house (*b*) / were fast asleep. (*c*) / No error (*d*)

36. I offered him part-time work (*a*) / but he turned it over (*b*) / saying that he would (*c*) / rather wait for a full-time job. (*d*) / No error (*e*) **(Bank P.O. 1995)**

37. These days very few people (*a*) / bother to do the work (*b*) / entrusted upon them. (*c*) / No error (*d*)

38. You will be tired of writing (*a*) / at the time you (*b*) / finish your research. (*c*) / No error (*d*) **(Clerks Grade, 1995)**

39. Young children should not sit (*a*) / close to the TV set (*b*) / as it affects on their eyes. (*c*) / No error (*d*)

40. He (*a*) / came across (*b*) / with a beggar. (*c*) / No error (*d*)

(Hotel Management, 1991)

41. If on doing so (*a*) / the critic arrives at (*b*) / embarrassingly adverse conclusions (*c*) / he does not shy at declaring them. (*d*) / No error (*e*)

42. The law is a sleeping giant (*a*) / and until someone affected by it (*b*) / makes it wake up (*c*) / it will continue to sleep. (*d*) / No error (*e*)

43. The visitors complained at (*a*) / the poor accommodation (*b*) / they were given. (*c*) / No error (*d*)

44. In the meeting, (*a*) / Mr. Mehta's suggestions with regard for (*b*) / certain administrative reforms (*c*) / were hailed by all the members. (*d*) / No error (*e*) **(S.B.I.P.O. 1992)**

45. Please do not forget (*a*) / to send me an express telegram (*b*) / on my address (*c*) / when yo reach Canada airport. (*d*) / No error (*e*)

46. Such natural imagery suggests that (*a*) / the killings were akin with (*b*) / a natural disaster and (*c*) / not a matter of individual responsibility, (*d*) / No error (*e*)

47. Emphasis on quality of life ensures (*a*) / for the health and happiness (*b*) / of every individual. (*c*) / No error (*d*) **(C.D.S. 1995)**

48. Some animals are much more capable (*a*) / than humans for perceiving (*b*) / certain kinds of stimuli (*c*) / which may precede earthquakes. (*d*) / No error (*e*)

49. The author's vision, (*a*) / suffused by an innocence and warmth, (*b*) / may not correspond (*c*) / to the country as it is today. (*d*) / No error (*e*)

50. On entering the room (*a*) / she was found hanging (*b*) / from the ceiling. (*c*) / No error (*d*) **(C.B.I. 1993)**

ANSWERS

1. (*b*) : Replace 'from' by 'of'
The verb 'acquitted' takes preposition 'of'
2. (*c*) : Replace 'by' by 'of'
3. (*b*) : Replace 'by' by 'with'
4. (*d*) : Replace 'with' by 'from'
5. (*c*) : Replace 'towards' by 'by'
6. (*c*) : Add 'by' before 'land'
7. (*a*) : Replace 'to' by 'of'
8. (*b*) : The correct usage is 'detached from'
9. (*d*) : No error
10. (*a*) : Replace 'of' by 'from'
11. (*b*) : Replace 'on' by 'to'
12. (*a*) : Remove 'about'
13. (*a*) : Replace 'between' by 'among'
14. (*c*) : Replace 'in' by 'into'
15. (*b*) : Replace 'for' by 'to'
16. (*b*) : Replace 'in' by 'about'
17. (*b*) : Replace 'than' by 'to'
18. (*c*) : Add 'in' before 'one'
19. (*b*) : Remove 'about'
20. (*a*) : Replace 'when' by 'After'
21. (*c*) : Replace 'if' by 'when'
22. (*c*) : The correct form is '... can be depended upon'
23. (*e*) : No error
24. (*b*) : Replace 'with' by 'in'
25. (*d*) : The correct usage is 'feed on'
26. (*b*) : Remove 'to'
27. (*a*) : The correct usage is 'The plane took off ...'
28. (*d*) : Replace 'at' by 'with'
29. (*b*) : Replace 'on' by 'up'
30. (*d*) : Replace 'to' by 'into'
31. (*d*) : No error
32. (*d*) : Replace 'through' by 'with'
33. (*a*) : Replace 'in' by 'from'
34. (*c*) : Replace 'in' by 'from'
35. (*a*) : Replace 'on' by 'At'
36. (*b*) : Replace 'over' by 'down'
37. (*c*) : Replace 'upon' by 'to'
38. (*b*) : Replace 'at' by 'by'
39. (*c*) : Remove 'on'
40. (*c*) : Remove 'with'
41. (*a*) : Replace 'on' by 'in'
42. (*b*) : Replace 'until' by 'unless'
43. (*a*) : Replace 'at' by 'about'
44. (*b*) : Replace 'for' by 'to'
45. (*c*) : Replace 'on' by 'to'
46. (*b*) : The correct usage is 'akin to ...'
47. (*b*) : Remove 'for'
48. (*b*) : Replace 'for' by 'of'
'capable' is followed by 'of'
49. (*b*) : Replace 'by' by 'with'
50. (*d*) : No error

PRACTICE SET 7

Directions : *In each of the following questions, find out which part of the sentence has an error. If the sentence is correct, the answer is 'No error'.*

1. The teacher called Ravi (*a*) / and asked him (*b*) / to describe about the incident. (*c*) / No error (*d*)
2. They shouted (*a*) / on the top (*b*) / of their voice. (*c*) / No error (*d*)
3. You should not (*a*) / violate against the rules (*b*) / laid down by the institution. (*c*) / No error (*d*)
4. His grandmother (*a*) / has taught him (*b*) / to pray God daily. (*c*) / No error (*d*)
5. I promptly (*a*) / answered to (*b*) / his questions. (*c*) / No error (*d*)
6. The warrior (*a*) / fell from (*b*) / his horse. (*c*) / No error (*d*)
7. He reminded (*a*) /me my (*b*) / childhood days. (*c*) / No error (*d*)
8. You cannot (*a*) / prevent me (*b*) / to go there. (*c*) / No error (*d*)
9. At the gate (*a*) / was hung a wooden board (*b*) / on which was written : (*c*) / 'Beware the danger'. (*d*) / No error (*e*)
10. This article was (*a*) / prepared by (*b*) / their own expense. (*c*) / No error (*d*)
11. He is (*a*) / angry and (*b*) / indifferent to me. (*c*) / No error (*d*)
12. He signed (*a*) / upon (*b*) / the application form. (*c*) / No error (*d*)
13. I was going to school (*a*) / when in the way (*b*) / I met an old man. (*c*) / No error (*d*)
14. I don't think (*a*) / I have any use (*b*) / of this book. (*c*) / No error (*d*)
15. They went (*a*) / on one side (*b*) / of the road. (*c*) / No error (*d*)
16. He ascended (*a*) / to the throne (*b*) / at the early age of ten. (*c*) / No error (*d*)
17. I advised (*a*) / to him (*b*) / to do this work. (*c*) / No error (*d*)
18. He is a loveable person (*a*) / but what makes most people dislike him (*b*) / is that he boasts his wealth. (*c*) / No error (*d*)
19. The teacher ordered (*a*) / the sutdents to (*b*) / open page 10. (*c*) / No error (*d*)
20. I am angry (*a*) / with your (*b*) / rude behaviour. (*c*) / No error (*d*)
21. He left to Bombay (*a*) / this morning (*b*) / for some official work. (*c*) / No error (*d*)
22. I gave him (*a*) / a gun to shoot. (*b*) /No error (*c*)
23. The police investigated (*a*) / into the case (*b*) / but could find no useful clues. (*c*) / No error (*d*)
24. Children must (*a*) / obey to the orders (*b*) / of their elders. (*c*) / No error (*d*)
25. Having resigned (*a*) / from his job, (*b*) / Mr. Kalkarni left the town. (*c*) / No error (*d*)
26. I requested him (*a*) / to listen what I said (*b*) / and work accordingly. (*c*) / No error (*d*)
27. I am content (*a*) / for what (*b*) / I have. (*c*) / No error (*d*)
28. Under such circumstances, (*a*) / you should (*b*) / guard from danger. (*c*) / No error (*d*)
29. Will you (*a*) / do to me (*b*) / a favour ? (*c*) / No error (*d*)
30. As soon as the curtain rose (*a*) / the spectators got up (*b*) / on their seats (*c*) / to have a better view of their beloved leader. (*d*) / No error (*e*)
31. The economic policy of the government (*a*) / is not quite in variance (*b*) / with the idea of (*c*) / the socialist pattern of society. (*d*) / No error (*e*)
32. All day long we saw the trees (*a*) / tossing in the wind (*b*) / and heard the waves (*c*) / crashing with the rocks (*d*) / No error (*e*)
33. It is not possible (*a*) / for one to overhaul a system (*b*) / so rotten into the core. (*c*) / No error (*d*)
34. Atul's habit of (*a*) / delaying his work (*b*) / put his colleagues (*c*) / to a lot of trouble. (*d*) / No error (*e*) **(S.B.I.P.O. 1991)**
35. Despite of a good monsoon this year, (*a*) / the production of foodgrains in the country (*b*) / did not go up. (*c*) / No error (*d*)
36. Supposing if the bridegroom (*a*) / doesn't arrive in time for the wedding, (*b*) / what will you do ?(*c*) / No error (*d*)
37. There is nothing that does (*a*) / irritate me more than seeing (*b*) / other people sitting about (*c*) / doing nothing when I am working. (*d*) / No error (*e*)
38. It is every one's duty (*a*) / to wipe out (*b*) / the tears from the eyes (*c*) / of people in distress. (*d*) / No error (*e*)
39. One of the world's smaller coins (*a*) / is found in the museum (*b*) /which is quite near from the old fort. (*c*) / No error (*d*)

40. There has not been any rainfall (*a*) / in this part of the country (*b*) / since the last two years. (*c*) / No error (*d*)

41. We may have to (*a*) / await for a new political order (*b*) / to restructure our economy by adopting (*c*) / a model of development closer to our needs. (*d*) / No error (*e*)

42. Even the imperial might of the British (*a*) / could not suppress (*b*) / our desire of freedom. (*c*) / No error (*d*)

43. Work hard (*a*) / in Christmas holidays (*b*) / so that you may (*c*) / catch up with the class. (*d*) / No error (*e*)

44. The religious argument (*a*) / is not the only basis (*b*) / over which the case for animal rights rests. (*c*) / No error (*d*)

45. She could not yet (*a*) / acclimatize herself in the (*b*) / strange conditions of this house. (*c*) / No error (*d*)

46. And though one did not (*a*) / quite believe his claim, (*b*) / one saw no harm (*c*) / in granting him permission. (*d*) / No error (*e*)

47. The article (*a*) / should not exceed (*b*) / more than five hundred words. (*c*) / No error (*d*) **(Stenographers' Exam, 1995)**

48. All the boys (*a*) / returned back home (*b*) / well in time for lunch. (*c*) / No error (*d*) **(N.D.A. 1996)**

49. Arun's parents died when he was young and (*a*) / he looked after his aunt (*b*) / who had no children. (*c*) / No error (*d*) **(U.D.C. 1995)**

50. Because of the emergency help (*a*) / that the patient received, (*b*) / he would have died. (*c*) / No error (*d*) **(C.B.I. 1995)**

ANSWERS

1. (*c*) : Remove 'about'
2. (*b*) : Replace 'on' by 'at'
3. (*b*) : Remove 'against'
4. (*c*) : Add 'to' after 'pray'
5. (*b*) : Remove 'to'
6. (*b*) : Replace 'from' by 'off'
7. (*b*) : The correct form is '... reminded me of ...
8. (*c*) : Replace 'to go' by 'from going'
9. (*d*) : The correct form is 'Beware of the danger'
10. (*b*) : Replace 'by' by 'at'
11. (*b*) : Add 'with' after 'angry'
12. (*b*) : Remove 'upon'
13. (*b*) : Replace 'in' by 'on'
14. (*c*) : Replace 'of' by 'for'
15. (*b*) : Replace 'on' by 'to'
16. (*b*) : Remove 'to'
17. (*b*) : Remove 'to'
18. (*c*) : Add 'of' after 'boasts'
19. (*c*) : Add 'at' after 'open'
20. (*b*) : Replace 'with' by 'at'
21. (*a*) : Replace 'to' by 'for'
22. (*b*) : Add 'with' after 'shoot'
23. (*b*) : Remove 'into'
24. (*b*) : Remove 'to'
25. (*b*) : Remove 'from'
26. (*b*) : Add 'to' after 'listen'
27. (*b*) : Replace 'for' by 'with'
28. (*c*) : Replace 'from' by 'against'
29. (*b*) : Remove 'to'
30. (*c*) : Replace 'on' by 'in'
31. (*b*) : Replace 'in' by 'at'
32. (*d*) : Replace 'with' by 'against'
33. (*c*) : Replace 'into' by 'to'
34. (*d*) : Replace 'to' by 'into'
35. (*a*) : Remove 'of'
36. (*a*) : Remove 'if'
37. (*c*) : Replace 'about' by 'around'
38. (*b*) : Replace 'out' by away'
39. (*c*) : Remove 'from'
40. (*d*) : No error
41. (*b*) : Remove 'for'
42. (*c*) : Replace 'of' by 'for'
43. (*b*) : Replace 'in' by 'during'
44. (*c*) : Replace 'over' by 'on'
45. (*b*) : Replace 'in' by 'to'
46. (*e*) : No error
47. (*c*) : Reove 'more than'
48. (*b*) : Remove 'back'
49. (*b*) : The correct form is 'he was looked after by his aunt'
50. (*a*) : Replace 'Because of' by 'But for'

PRACTICE SET 8

Directions : *In each of the following questions, find out which part of the sentence has an error. The error may be grammatical or idiomatic. If there is no mistake, the answer is 'No error'*

1. No sooner did I open the door (*a*) / when the rain, heavy and stormy, rushed in (*b*) / making us shiver from head to foot. (*c*) / No error (*d*) **(C.D.S. 1995)**

2. Be smart (*a*) / not only in dress (*b*) / and also in action. (*c*) / No error (*d*)

3. Hardly had I reached the airport (*a*) / where I learnt (*b*) / about the powerful bomb explosion. (*c*) / No error (*d*)

4. It is not (*a*) / such a good book (*b*) / that I expected. (*c*) / No error (*d*)

5. The downfall of this kind (*a*) / is to be attributed to (*b*) / nothing else than pride. (*c*) / No error (*d*) **(C.B.I. 1993)**

6. Unless he does not return (*a*) / all the library books (*b*) / he will not be (*c*) / relieved from the service. (*d*) / No error (*e*)

7. You must either tell me (*a*) / the whole story or, at least, (*b*) / the first half of it. (*c*) / No error (*d*)

8. The old woman has had the best medical facilities available (*a*) / but she will not be cured (*b*) / unless she does not have a strong desire to live. (*c*) / No error (*d*) **(Central Excise, 1992)**

9. My book has been (*a*) / missing from my room (*b*) / till yesterday. (*c*) / No error (*d*)

10. The manager of the bank was busy ; (*a*) / so he asked them to come and (*b*) / see him between two to three in the afternoon. (*c*) / No error (*d*) **(N.D.A. 1995)**

11. He is as clever if (*a*) / not cleverer (*b*) / than his brother. (*c*) / No error (*d*)

12. No sooner did the sun rise (*a*) / when we took a hasty breakfast (*b*) / and resumed the journey. (*c*) / No error (*d*) **(C.D.S. 1994)**

13. Hardly had the children (*a*) / left the school (*b*) / than it began to rain. (*c*) / No error (*d*)

14. Because he is physically strong, (*a*) / therefore he was selected (*b*) / for the school boxing team. (*c*) / No error (*d*)

15. The reason for (*a*) / his failure is because (*b*) / he did not work hard. (*c*) / No error (*d*) **(C.D.S. 1994)**

16. Bharat asked him (*a*) / that which was the way (*b*) / to the post office. (*c*) / No error (*d*)

17. Unless you do not listen to his advice (*a*) / I am not going (*b*) / to help you. (*c*) / No error (*d*)

18. How do you say (*a*) / that neither he or (*b*) / Ravi has qualified (*c*) / in the examination ? (*d*) / No error (*e*)

19. Being a strict vegetarian (*a*) / he depended on milk and fruit (*b*) / and had to cook for himself. (*c*) No error (*d*)

20. Even though the shirt is rather expensive (*a*) / but I wish to (*b*) / purchase it with my own money. (*c*) / No error (*d*) **(I.E.S. 1994)**

21. Unless Ashish does not (*a*) / return all the library books, (*b*) / he will not be (*c*) / awarded the pass certificate. (*d*) / No error (*e*)

22. Mohan could not (*a*) / go to the picnic (*b*) / for his mother (*c*) / was not well. (*d*) / No error (*e*) **(R.R.B. 1993)**

23. Ranjeet is as (*a*) / fast as or (*b*) / perhaps faster (*c*) / than Rohit. (*d*) / No error (*e*)

24. Though she was sick (*a*) / but (*b*) / she went to work. (*c*) / No error (*d*) **(I. Tax & Central Excise, 1993)**

25. Hardly had I (*a*) / reached the station where (*b*) / I learnt about (*c*) / the powerful bomb explosion. (*d*) / No error (*e*)

26. No sooner did (*a*) / the Chairman begin speaking, some (*b*) / participants started (*c*) / shouting slogans. (*d*) / No error (*e*) **(Bank P.O. 1994)**

27. The Management Committee has requested me (*a*) / not to take any action (*b*) / unless and until (*c*) / I don't see all the documents. (*d*) / No error (*e*)

28. As he is rich, (*a*) / so he spends (*b*) / lavishly. (*c*) / No error (*d*)

29. I am but (*a*) / a humble seeker after truth (*b*) / and bent upon finding it. (*c*) / No error (*d*)

30. Hardly he had arrived (*a*) / when the house caught fire (*b*) / and everything was reduced to ashes. (*c*) / No error (*d*) **(N.D.A. 1993)**

31. Neither the famine (*a*) / or the subsequent fire (*b*) / was able to destroy the spirit of the people. (*c*) / No error (*d*) **(Stenographers' Exam, 1993)**

32. Neither did he (*a*) / accept the punishment (*b*) / or apologised (*c*) / for his mistake. (*d*) / No error (*e*)

33. No sooner did the jeep arrive (*a*) / at the station (*b*) / than a young police officer (*c*) / jumped out of it. (*d*) / No error (*e*) **(Bank P.O. 1995)**

34. If you hate me, (*a*) / then you should (*b*) / leave my house. (*c*) / No error (*d*)

35. The managing director well as the Board members (*a*) / was in favour of taking strict action (*b*) / against the striking workers. (*c*) / No error (*d*) **(Asstt. Grade, 1991)**

36. We are not sure (*a*) / if he is coming (*b*) / to the party. (*c*) / No error (*d*)

37. Sooner than he had arrived (*a*) / his friends arranged a reception (*b*) / in his honour in (*c*) / the best hotel in town. (*d*) / No error (*e*) **(S.B.I.P.O. 1992)**

38. Mrs. Drakmanton went to Dublin (*a*) / because she might (*b*) / see Mrs. Roy. (*c*) / No error (*d*)

39. As much as I admire him for his sterling qualities, (*a*) / I cannot excuse him (*b*) / for being unfair to his friends. (*c*) / No error (*d*) **(C.B.I. 1995)**

40. He gave them no money (*a*) / nor he did help them (*b*) / in any way. (*c*) / No error (*d*)

41. He took out the spare tyre (*a*) / and was very disappointed (*b*) / when he was discovered (*c*) / that this tyre was also punctured. (*d*) / No error (*e*)

42. Since it was his first election campaign, the candidate was confused ; (*a*) / none could clearly understand (*b*) / either the principles he stood for or the benefits he promised. (*c*) / No error (*d*) **(C.D.S. 1995)]**

ANSWERS

1. (*b*) : Replace 'when' by 'than'
2. (*c*) : Replace 'and' by 'but'
3. (*b*) : Replace 'where' by 'when'
4. (*c*) : Replace 'that' by 'as'
5. (*c*) : Replace 'than' by 'but'
6. (*a*) : Replace 'does not return' by 'returns'
7. (*d*) : No error
8. (*c*) : Replace 'does not have' by 'has'
9. (*c*) : Replace 'till' by 'since'
10. (*c*) : Replace 'to' by 'and'
11. (*a*) : Add 'as' after 'clever'
12. (*b*) : Replace 'when' by 'than'
13. (*c*) : Replace 'than' by 'when'
14. (*b*) : Remove 'therefore'
15. (*b*) : Replace 'because' by 'that'
16. (*b*) : Remove 'that'
17. (*a*) : Remove 'do not'
18. (*b*) : Replace 'or' by 'nor'
19. (*c*) : Replace 'and' by 'or'
20. (*b*) : Remove 'but'
21. (*a*) : Replace 'Unless' by 'If'
22. (*e*) : No error
23. (*b*) : Remove 'as'
24. (*b*) : Replace 'but' by 'yet'
25. (*b*) : Replace 'where' by 'when'
26. (*b*) : Add 'than' before 'some'
27. (*d*) : Remove 'don't'
28. (*b*) : Remove 'so'
29. (*c*) : Remove 'and'
30. (*d*) : No error
31. (*b*) : Replace 'or' by 'nor'
32. (*c*) : Replace 'or' by 'nor'
33. (*e*) : No error
34. (*b*) : Remove 'then'
35. (*a*) : Add 'as' before 'well'
36. (*b*) : Replace 'if' by 'that'
37. (*a*) : The correct form is 'As soon as he arrived'
38. (*b*) : Replace 'becasue' by 'in order that'
39. (*a*) : Replace 'As much as' by 'Howsoever much'
40. (*b*) : The correct form is '... and also he did not help them'
41. (*b*) : Replace 'and' by 'but'
42. (*d*) : No error

PRACTICE SET 9

Directions : ***In the following questions, some of the sentences have errors and somes have none. Find out which part of a sentence has error. if there is no mistake, the answer is 'No error'***

1. Many a student (*a*) / are frustrated (*b*) / because of unemployment. (*c*) / No error. (*d*) **(Asstt. Grade, 1995)**

2. It is true (*a*) / that the poor is unable (*b*) / to get nourishing food even today. (*c*) / No error (*d*)

3. People have a right to ctiticise (*a*) / but at the same time (*b*) / each of them (*c*) / have to remember his duty also. (*d*) / No error (*e*)
4. The child (*a*) / picked up a burned paper (*b*) / from the street. (*c*) / No error (*d*)
(Section Officers, 1993)
5. Never did this exhibition of contempt and anger ceased (*a*) / so long as British rule remained (*b*) / a live thing in India. (*c*) / No error (*d*)
6. The teacher was angry (*a*) / when he found that (*b*) / you are not there. (*c*) / No error (*d*)
7. I would like you to (*a*) / complete this assignment (*b*) / before you will leave for Bombay. (*c*) / No error (*d*)
8. Ordinarily, when in difficulty (*a*) / Ruchi prefers keeping her counsel (*b*) / than running about (*c*) / taking advice. (*d*) / No error (*e*)
9. One of the drawbacks (*a*) / of modern education are (*b*) / that it does not encourage original thinking. (*c*) No error (*d*) **(Stenographers Exam, 1993)**
10. I enquired of him (*a*) / whe he is so negligent (*b*) / in his studies. (*c*) / No error (*d*)
11. There is no doubt (*a*) / that the majority of workers (*b*) / is in favour of the proposal. (*c*) / No error (*d*)
12. He laid unconscious for half an hour (*a*) / until he was seen (*b*) / by a passing motorist. (*c*) / No error (*d*)
13. None of my friends (*a*) / are applying (*b*) / for this job. (*c*) / No error (*d*)
14. Rohan was leading (*a*) / a happy and leisurely (*b*) / life after his retirement (*c*) / from service. (*d*) / No error (*e*)
(Railways, 1993)
15. When I went (*a*) / to Maniram's house, (*b*) / his mother told me (*c*) / that he was gone out of the country. (*d*) / No error (*e*)
16. One of his many (*a*) / good traits that (*b*) / come to my mind (*c*) / was his modesty. (*d*) / No error (*e*)
17. When the dentist came in (*a*) / my tooth was stopped aching (*b*) / out of fear that I might lose my tooth. (*c*) / No error (*d*)
(C.D.S. 1995)
18. The parents scolded the child (*a*) / for having broke the window (*b*) / but their words fell (*c*) / on deaf ears. (*d*) / No error (*e*)
19. Two-thirds of the book (*a*) / were (*b*) / rubbish. (*c*) / No error (*d*)
20. The chief idea of (*a*) / very common type of traveller (*b*) / is to see as many (*c*) / objects of interest as he possibly could. (*d*) / No error (*e*) **(S.B.I.P.O. 1991)**
21. The demand of the workers' union (*a*) / that the dismissed employee (*b*) / to be reinstated, has (*c*) / been accepted by the management, (*d*) / No error (*e*)
22. When he went out (*a*) / he left the radio on (*b*) / so that his parents shall think (*c*) / that he was still in the house. (*d*) / No error (*e*)
23. The foremost criterion of selection we adopted (*a*) / were the number of years of training (*b*) / a dancer had received (*c*) / under a particular guru. (*d*) / No error (*e*) **(Bank P.O. 1995)**
24. I can't understand why (*a*) / he did not told me (*b*) / the reason for his absence. (*c*) / No error (*d*)
25. He very promptly (*a*) / withdraw the remarks (*b*) / made by him (*c*) / on my office note. (*d*) / No error (*e*)
26. He won't return the money (*a*) / that he borrowed, (*b*) / will he ? (*c*) / No error (*d*) **(I. Tax, 1994)**
27. None of my friends (*a*) / are applying (*b*) / for this job. (*c*) / No error (*d*)
28. Bread and butter (*a*) / is (*b*) / wholesome food. (*c*) / No error (*d*)
29. The future is (*a*) / yet to come (*b*) / but you have a (*c*) / right to shape it. (*d*) / No error (*e*) **(B.S.R.B. 1995)**
30. I finished my work (*a*) / before we reached his place (*b*) / with great difficulty because of heavy traffic. (*c*) / No error (*d*)
31. If I knew (*a*) / that my friend had planned to visit the town today, (*b*) / I would have made his stay comfortable. (*c*) / No error (*d*) **(S.C.R.A. 1993)**
32. More widely popular (*a*) / than the hunting of deer or fox (*b*) / were the pursuit of the hare. (*c*) / No error (*d*)
(C.D.S. 1994)
33. The Committee Chief warned the party members (*a*) / that if they persist (*b*) / in their obstructionist attitude (*c*) / they would be suspended. (*d*) / No e rror (*e*)
(C.D.S. 1994)
34. If the Manager acted in time, (*a*) / the strike would (*b*) / not have lasted long. (*c*) / No error (*d*)
35. On hearing the news over the radio that (*a*) / India has won the hockey match, (*b*) / I jumped with joy. (*c*) / No error (*d*)
36. Cricket has become so popular (*a*) / that even elderly people (*b*) / are discussing

(c) / the game when they meet. (d) / No error (e)

37. The United States of America have (a) / a huge budget deficit (b) / despite the people's fabulous prosperity. (c) / No error (d)

38. The Hindi and the Marathi are (a) / different forms of the Sanskrit language, (b) / which were once spoken (c) / in almost every part of India. (d) / No error (e) **(Bank P.O. 1995)**

39. Developmental activities of the government (a) / come to a standstill (b) / due to paucity of funds. (c) / No error (d)

40. I am sure that (a) / neither the house nor its contents (b) / is for sale. (c) / No error (d) **(Asstt. Grade, 1991)**

41. The majority of labourers (a) / is demanding (b) / and increase in wages. (c) / No error (d)

42. Some of the devotees (a) / prostrate on the steps (b) / or the floor in front of the idol (c) / before leaving. (d) / No error (e)

43. The man told to her (a) / that he had not brought his dog (b) / out for a walk as he was afraid that it would rain. (c) / No error (d) **(I.E.S. 1994)**

44. Inspite of several reminders, (a) / he did not so far send (b) / any reply to my letters. (c) / No error (d)

45. Children visiting the (a) / park are amused (b) / by the monkeys (c) / play in the cages. (d) / No error (e) **(S.B.I.P.O. 1992)**

46. There goes Old Mrs. Roy (a) / and her meek (b) / little husband (c) / No error (d)

47. Not one of the hundreds (a) / of striking workers (b) / were allowed to go near the factory. (c) / No error (d) **(C.D.S. 1995)**

48. "I can't hear you. (a) / Please speak distinctly. (b) / Which telephone number you want ?" (c) / No error (d)

49. The news of his marriage to another girl (a) / was a shock to her (b) / but she bore up bravely (c) / and went on as if nothing has happened. (d) / No error (e)

50. If I was you (a) / I would not have (b) / committed this blunder. (c) / No error (d) **(N.D.A. 1992)**

ANSWERS

1. (b) : Replace 'are' by 'is'
   'Many a' takes singular subject and singular verb.
2. (b) : Replace 'is' by 'are'
   Here, 'poor' stands for 'poor people'
3. (d) : Replace 'have' by 'has'
4. (b) : Replace 'burned' by 'burnt'
5. (a) : Replace 'ceased' by 'cease'
6. (c) : Replace 'are' by 'were'
7. (c) : Remove 'will'
8. (c) : Replace 'running' by 'run'
9. (b) : Replace 'are' by 'is'
10. (b) : Replace 'is' by 'was'
11. (c) : Replace 'is' by 'are'
12. (a) : Replace 'laid' by 'lay'
13. (b) : Replace 'are' by 'is'
14. (a) : Replace 'was leading' by 'led'
15. (d) : Replace 'was' by 'had'
16. (d) : Replace 'was' by 'is'
17. (b) : Remove 'was'
18. (b) : Replace 'broke' by 'broken'
19. (b) : Replace 'were' by 'was'
20. (d) : Replace 'could' by 'can'
21. (c) : Remove 'to'
22. (e) : No error
23. (b) : Replace 'were' by 'was'
24. (b) : Replace 'told' by 'tell'
25. (b) : Replace 'withdraw' by 'withdrew'
26. (c) : Replace 'will' by 'would'
27. (b) : Replace 'are' by 'is'
28. (d) : No error
29. (a) : Replace 'is' by 'has'
30. (a) : Replace 'finished' by 'had finished'
31. (d) : No error
32. (c) : Replace 'were' by 'was'
33. (b) : Replace 'persist' by 'persisted'
34. (a) : Replace 'acted' by 'had' acted'
35. (b) : Replace 'has' by 'had'
36. (c) : Replace 'are discussiing' by 'discuss'
37. (a) : Replace 'have' by 'has'
38. (c) : Replace 'were' by 'was'
39. (b) : Replace 'come' by 'have come'
40. (c) : Replace 'is' by 'are'
41. (b) : Replace 'is' by 'are'
42. (b) : Add 'themselves' after 'prostrate'
43. (a) : Remove 'to'
44. (b) : The correct form is
    'he has not so far sent'
45. (d) : Replace 'play' by 'playing'
46. (a) : Replace 'goes' by 'go'
47. (c) : Replace 'were' by 'was'
48. (c) : The correct form is 'which telephone number do you want ?'
49. (d) : Replace 'has' by 'had'
50. (a) : Replace 'was' by 'were'

PRACTICE SET 10

Directions : *In each of the following questions, find out which part of the sentence has an error. If there is no mistake, the answer is 'No error'.*

1. Unless you stop to make noise at once, (*a*) / I will have no option but to (*b*) / bring the matter to the attention of the police. (*c*) / No error (*d*) **(C.D.S. 1995)**

2. The Minister along with his (*a*) / party colleagues have (*b*) / been invited to the party. (*c*) / No error (*d*)

3. A group of friends (*a*) / want to visit (*b*) / the new plant as early as possible. (*c*) / No error (*d*) **(Hotel Management, 1996)**

4. It is rude (*a*) / for the young (*b*) / making fun of their elders. (*c*) / No error (*d*)

5. Meerabai was sent away from her home (*a*) / because she spend most of the time (*b*) / in the company of holy men (*c*) / No error (*d*) **(N.D.A. 1995)**

6. If I was you (*a*) / I would have (*b*) / terminated his services then and there. (*c*) / No error (*d*)

7. As soon as I will reach Bombay (*a*) / I will send (*b*) / you the books (*c*) / you have asked for. (*d*) / No error (*e*)

8. The job is much worse than I expected. (*a*) / If I would have realised (*b*) / how awful it was going to be (*c*) / I would not have accepted it. (*d*) / No error (*e*) **(Bank P.O. 1995)**

9. Neither of the plans (*a*) / suits him and therefore (*b*) / he decided not to (*c*) / go out yesterday.(*d*) / No error (*e*)

10. The Cabinet Ministers and the Prime Minister (*a*) / was at the airport (*b*) / to receive the foreign dignitary. (*c*) / No error (*d*) **(S.S.C. 1991)**

11. While proceeding on leave (*a*) / he had orally committed that (*b*) / he will resume after two days. (*c*) / No error (*d*)

12. The number of people (*a*) / applying were so large (*b*) / that the college had to (*c*) / stop issuing application forms (*d*) / No error (*e*) **(S.B.I.P.O. 1992)**

13. A series of lectures (*a*) / of Indian philosophy (*b*) / are arranged by the University. (*c*) / No error (*d*)

14. The house with all its (*a*) / furniture and exotic plants (*b*) / were sold for Rs. 50,000. (*c*) / No error (*d*) **(Asstt. Grade, 1995)**

15. The teacher asked the students (*a*) / if everyone of them were interested in (*b*) / going on an excursion. (*c*) / No error (*d*)

16. Twice twelve (*a*) / makes (*b*) / twenty four. (*c*) / No error (*d*)

17. A physiologist in the last century demonstrated (*a*) / that puppies will die (*b*) / if kept awake for more than five days. (*c*) / No error (*d*)

18. It is unfortunate that (*a*) / many youngsters get (*b*) / addicted to gamble. (*c*) / No error (*d*) **(Section Officers, 1993)**

19. I have seen (*a*) / that film last year, (*b*) / but I do not remember its story. (*c*) / No error (*d*)

20. The flight purser took control (*a*) / of the plane after (*b*) / the pilot had had (*c*) / a heart attack. (*d*) / No error (*e*)

21. Our conception of (*a*) / what should a science of mental life be (*b*) / has changed considerably since James' time. (*c*) / No error (*d*)

22. We grieve our loss and cry helplessly (*a*) / while we should be fighting for our rights (*b*) / and die a noble death. (*c*) / No error (*d*)

23. Sharad was entrusted with (*a*) / the task of coordinating yesterday's programme, (*b*) / but due to certain difficulties (*c*) / he does not do it. (*d*) / No error (*e*) **(Bank P.O. 1993)**

24. Work hard (*a*) / lest you will (*b*) / fail. (*c*) / No error (*d*)

25. My friend did not see me (*a*) / for many years (*b*) / when I met him last week. (*c*) / No error (*d*).

26. Vipul was unhappy (*a*) / because he would (*b*) / not attend the marriage (*c*) / of his friend yesterday. (*d*) / No error (*e*) **(Railways, 1993)**

27. Until he has confessed his fault (*a*) / he will be kept (*b*) / in prison. (*c*) / No error (*d*)

28. Slow and steady (*a*) / win (*b*) / the race. (*c*) / No error (*d*)

29. After the allotted (*a*) / time was over (*b*) / they torn off all (*c*) / the papers which they had used. (*d*) / No error (*e*) **(B.S.R.B. 1992)**

30. Deep snow laid on the track (*a*) / as the Little Red Riding Hood struggled slowly (*b*) / against a biting wind (*c*) / for the lonely farm house. (*d*) / No error (*e*)

31. When I telephoned him (*a*) / the line was so bad (*b*) / that I cannot hear (*c*) / what he said. (*d*) / No error (*e*)

(B.S.R.B. 1992)

32. If any of the founding fathers of our constitution (*a*) / was to return to life for a day (*b*) / his opinion of our amendments (*c*) / would be interesting. (*d*) / No error (*e*)

33. The new facts he (*a*) / has discovered and the new (*b*) / arguments he has advanced (*c*) / has not changed my opinion. (*d*) / No error (*e*)

(Bank P.O. 1995)

34. Hardly had he went (*a*) / out of the class (*b*) / when a mob of angry students (*c*) / attacked him. (*d*) / No error (*e*)

35. He is going everyday (*a*) / for a morning walk (*b*) / with his friends and neighbours. (*c*) / No error (*d*)

(I.E.S. 1994)

36. When the thief (*a*) / entered the house, (*b*) / the watchman on duty (*c*) / was fast aslept. (*d*) / No error (*e*)

37. How long (*a*) / were you (*b*) / learning English for ? (*c*) / No error (*d*)

(Central Excise, 1993)

38. Knowledge of regional language (*a*) / is necessary for bank officers because (*b*) / they are to understand (*c*) / what their customers say. (*d*) / No error (*e*)

39. I have not (*a*) / played cricket (*b*) / since I have left college. (*c*) / No error (*d*)

(N.D.A. 1994)

40. Having deprived from (*a*) / their homes in the recent earthquake, (*b*) / they had no other option but (*c*) / to take shelter in a temple. (*d*) / No error (*e*)

41. I shall write (*a*) / to you (*b*) / when I shall reach Bangalore. (*c*) / No error (*d*)

(N.D.A. 1995)

42. This pen is (*a*) / very good but (*b*) / it costed me ten rupees. (*c*) / No error (*d*)

43. Good people will make good laws (*a*) / but good laws passed by a few (*b*) / does not necessarily make (*c*) / a good society, (*d*) / No error (*e*)

44. Every since the government (*a*) / announced its new policy, (*b*) / the private institutions had (*c*) / run into bad weather. (*d*) / No error (*e*)

(Bank P.O. 1994)

45. It cannot be forecasted (*a*) / how society will emerge (*b*) / a generation hence. (*c*) / No error (*d*) **(C.D.S. 1994)**

46. The Prime Minister has said that India would not have spent so much on defence (*a*) / if some of the neighbouring countries (*b*) / adopted the policy of restricting defence expenditure. (*c*) / No error (*d*)

47. I've been to a few of his lectures, (*a*) / but understood little of (*b*) / what he has said. (*c*) / No error (*d*)

(I. Tax & Central Excise, 1992)

48. More leisure, as well as an abundance of goods, (*a*) / are attainable (*b*) / through automation. (*c*) / No error (*d*)

49. Several visitors (*a*) / have been expected (*b*) / to visit (*c*) / the place tomorrow. (*d*) / No error (*e*)

50. Looking forward (*a*) / to (*b*) / meet you here. (*c*) / No error (*d*) **(Railways, 1996)**

ANSWERS

1. (*a*) : Replace 'to make' by 'making'
2. (*b*) : Replace 'have' by 'has'
3. (*b*) : Replace 'want' by 'wants' ('A group' is singular)
4. (*c*) : Replace 'making' by 'to make'
5. (*b*) : Replae 'spend' by 'spent' because it is being talked about the past
6. (*a*) : Replace 'was' by 'were' when a wish or an imagination is expressed, 'were' is used.
7. (*a*) : Remove 'will'
8. (*b*) : Replace 'would have' by 'had'
9 (*b*) : Replace 'suits' by 'suited'
10. (*b*) : Replace 'was' by 'were'
11. (*c*) : Replace 'will' by 'would'
12. (*b*) : Replae 'were' by 'was' ('The number ...' is singular)
13. (*c*) : Replace 'are' by 'is' ('A series' is singular)
14. (*c*) : Replace 'were' by 'was' ('The house' is singular)
15. (*b*) : Replace 'were' by 'was'
16. (*b*) : Replace 'makes' by 'is'
17. (*b*) : Replace 'will' by 'would'
18. (*c*) : Replace 'gamble' by 'gambling'
19. (*a*) : Replace 'have' by 'had'
20. (*c*) : Replace 'had had' by 'had'
21. (*b*) : The correct form is 'what a science of mental life should be'
22. (*b*) : Replace 'be figthing' by 'fight'
23. (*d*) : Replace 'does' by 'could'
24. (*b*) : Replace 'will' by 'should' 'lest' is followed by 'should'

25. (*a*) : Replace 'did not see' by 'had not seen'
26. (*b*) : Replace 'would' by 'could'
27. (*a*) : Replace 'has confessed' by 'confesses'
28. (*b*) : Replace 'win' by 'wins'
29. (*c*) : Replace 'torn' by 'tore'
30. (*a*) : Replace 'laid' by 'lay'
31. (*c*) : Replace 'cannot' by 'could not'
32. (*b*) : Replace 'was' by 'were'
33. (*d*) : Replace 'has' by 'have'
34. (*a*) : Replace 'went' by 'gone'
35. (*a*) : Replace 'is going' by 'goes'
Habitual actions are indicated by Simple Present Tense
36. (*d*) : Replace 'aslept' by 'asleep'
37. (*c*) : Replace 'were you' by 'have you been'
38. (*c*) : Replace 'are' by 'have'
39. (*c*) : Remove 'have'
40. (*a*) : The correct form is 'Having been deprived from ...'
41. (*c*) : Remove 'shall'
42. (*c*) : Replace 'costed' by 'cost'
43. (*c*) : Replace 'does' by 'do' ('laws' is plural)
44. (*c*) : Replace 'had' by 'have'
45. (*a*) : Replace 'forecasted' by 'forecast'
46. (*c*) : Add 'had' before 'adopted'
47. (*c*) : Remove 'has'
48. (*b*) : Replace 'are' by 'is'
49. (*b*) : Replace 'have been' by 'are'
50. (*c*) : Replace 'meet' by 'meeting'
'Looking forward to' is followed by 'ing' form of the verb.

PRACTICE SET 11

Directions : ***In each of the following sentences, find out which part of the sentence has an error. The error may be idiomatic or grammatical. If there is no mistake, the answer is 'No error'.***

1. The duties of a policeman are regulating the traffic, (*a*) / investigating crime (*b*) / and to contain anti-social elements. (*c*) / No error (*d*) **(C.D.S. 1994)**
2. If I was you (*a*) / I would not have (*b*) / committed this blunder. (*c*) / No error (*d*)
3. It is not surprising (*a*) / that her death cast (*b*) / a pall of gloom over all those (*c*) / who came in contact with her. (*d*) / No error (*e*)
4. Well, I spend six or seven years (*a*) / after high school (*b*) / trying to find a job for me (*c*) / but could not succeed in it. (*d*) / No error (*e*) **(Bank P.O. 1995)**
5. Hardly did she finish (*a*) / the typing when (*b*) / the Manager entered the room (*c*) / with some more work. (*d*) / No error (*e*)
6. You will get (*a*) / all the information (*b*) / if you read this booklet carefully. (*c*) / No error (*d*) **(I.E.S. 1994)**
7. Neither her husband (*a*) / nor her brother were able (*b*) / to help her in her work. (*c*) / No error (*d*)
8. As soon as the Principal (*a*) / entered the school (*b*) / all the students approached him (*c*) / and report the matter. (*d*) / No error (*e*) **(B.S.R.B. 1992)**
9. He is writing novels (*a*) / ever since (*b*) / he became a graduate. (*c*) / No error (*d*)
10. If my father (*a*) / will approve (*b*) / I will go to Bombay. (*c*) / No error (*d*)
11. Not only the bandits robbed (*a*) / the traveller of his purse (*b*) / but they also wounded him grievously. (*c*) / No error (*d*) **(Central Excise, 1992)**
12. Bacteria is probably (*a*) / the most common form (*b*) / of life on earth. (*c*) / No error (*d*)
13. Twenty miles are (*a*) / a long way (*b*) / to walk. (*c*) / No error (*d*) **(Clerk's Grade, 1995)**
14. Will you please (*a*) / remind him to (*b*) / switch off the fans (*c*) / when he left ? (*d*) / No error (*e*)
15. I pleaded with him with (*a*) / a view to convincing him (*b*) / of my innocence in the matter. (*c*) / No error (*d*) **(Asstt. Grade, 1995)**
16. He drank once again (*a*) / as he was (*b*) / feeling thirsty. (*c*) / No error (*d*)
17. With a view to help the Third World countries, (*a*) / the I.M.F. and the World Bank keep sending (*b*) / their experts to different regions of the world. (*c*) / No error (*d*)
18. One of these days (*a*) / I will be going to (*b*) / confront you with incontrovertible evidence. (*c*) / No error (*d*) **(N.D.A. 1992)**
19. It is necessary (*a*) / that everybody (*b*) / must have a house. (*c*) / No error (*d*)

20. This small table (*a*) / will collapse (*b*) / if you will stand on it. (*c*) / No error (*d*) **(S.S.C. 1995)**

21. Shobha asked the dealer (*a*) / what was the price (*b*) / of that bicycle and whether (*c*) / it is really made in Germany ? (*d*) / No error (*e*) **(Bank P.O. 1995)**

22. He refused to answer the question (*a*) / despite the fact (*b*) / that his silence will be interpreted as guilt. (*c*) / No error (*d*)

23. Sadhana was the one person (*a*) / who could somehow manage (*b*) / to working in that section (*c*) / for a long time. (*d*) / No error (*e*) **(S.B.I.P.O. 1992)**

24. When we consider all the factors, which are many, (*a*) / the number of school dropouts (*b*) / are quite disturbing. (*c*) / No error (*d*)

25. The lecture to be held (*a*) / in the auditorium tomorrow (*b*) / was open to the public (*c*) / and free of charge, (*d*) No error (*e*)

26. While proceeding on leave (*a*) / he had committed (*b*) / that he would be resumed after two days. (*c*) / No error (*d*)

27. Coffee seeds (*a*) / is dried and roasted (*b*) / before they are ground into powder. (*c*) / No error (*d*) **(I. Tax, 1993)**

28. If there had been (*a*) / no new thinking, (*b*) / life would follow the beaten track. (*c*) / No error (*d*)

29. My father did not (*a*) / heard from my younger brother (*b*) / who is abroad for over a month. (*c*) / No error (*d*)

30. While going (*a*) / through the report (*b*) / yesterday I find (*c*) / several factual mistakes. (*d*) / No error (*e*) **(Bank P.O. 1994)**

31. The meeting adjourned abruptly (*a*) / by the Chairman after (*b*) / about three hours of deliberation. (*c*) / No error (*d*) **(C.D.S. 1995)**

32. If the streets would have been (*a*) / clearly marked (*b*) / it would not have taken us (*c*) / so long to find his house. (*d*) / No errro (*e*)

33. I and you (*a*) / know each other (*b*) / for the last six years. (*c*) / No error (*d*)

34. The eminent speaker's speech (*a*) / was broadcasted over (*b*) / all the major radio stations. (*c*) / No error (*d*) **(Section Officers, 1993)**

35. Somewhere along the line (*a*) / I lost track of (*b*) / what Ashish said (*c*) / about heart ailments. (*d*) / No error (*e*)

36. When your father inquired (*a*) / about your marks (*b*) / you lied to him. (*c*) / Have you not ? (*d*) / No error (*e*) **(Bank P.O. 1991)**

37. I am sure that (*a*) / neither the flat nor its contents (*b*) / is for sale. (*c*) / No error (*d*)

38. It's time (*a*) / you started (*b*) / working. (*c*) / No error (*d*) **(Stenographers' Exam, 1995)**

39. You are learning Tamil (*a*) / for the last one year (*b*) / but you show (*c*) / no improvement whatsoever. (*d*) No error (*e*)

40. Many a profound thinker believe (*a*) / that the march of civilisation (*b*) / has not coincided with real human progress. (*c*) / No error (*d*) **(Central Excise, 1994)**

41. The last of the Mughal emperors of India (*a*) / was imprisoned (*b*) / and was later (*c*) / sent into exile by the British. (*d*) / No error (*e*)

42. The programme which (*a*) / came on television (*b*) / these days in the evenings (*c*) / is very interesting. (*d*) / No error (*e*) **(Railways, 1993)**

43. On reaching the railway station (*a*) / he was disappointed to learn (*b*) / that the train left. (*c*) / No error (*d*)

44. Neither India nor Pakistan (*a*) / have yet acquired (*b*) / the capability to produce nuclear weapons. (*c*) / No error (*d*) **(N.D.A. 1995)**

45. When I shall see him (*a*) / I shall tell him (*b*) / that you had called. (*c*) / No error (*d*)

46. I courteously asked him (*a*) / where was he going (*b*) / but he did not reply. (*c*) / No error (*d*) **(C.D.S. 1994)**

47. No body believed him (*a*) / when he said that (*b*) / his son was gone out of the country. (*c*) / No error (*d*)

48. It is high time (*a*) / that we send (*b*) / the answer. (*c*) / No error (*d*)

49. I have had to work (*a*) / at the fountain for almost (*b*) / ten hours before it could (*c*) / start functioning well. (*d*) / No error (*e*) **(Bank P.O. 1995)**

50. My body has long since exhausted all its energy, (*a*) / but it went on running (*b*) / just the same. (*c*) / No error (*d*)

ANSWERS

1. (*c*) : Replace 'to contain' by 'containing'
2. (*a*) : Replace 'was' by 'wee'
3. (*d*) : Replace 'came' by 'had come'
4. (*a*) : Replace 'spend' by 'spent'
5. (*a*) : Replace 'did she finish' by 'had she finished'
6. (*a*) : Replace 'will' by 'can'
7. (*b*) : Replace 'were' by 'was'
8. (*d*) : Replace 'report' by 'reported'
9. (*a*) : Replace 'is' by 'has been'
10. (*b*) : Replace 'will approve' by 'approves'
11. (*a*) : The correct form is 'Not only did the bandits rob'
12. (*a*) : Replace 'is' by 'are'. ('Bacteria' is plural)
13. (*a*) : Replace 'are' by 'is'
14. (*d*) : Replace 'left' by 'leaves'
15. (*b*) : Replace 'convincing' by 'convince'
16. (*d*) : No error
17. (*a*) : Replace 'help' by 'helping'
18. (*b*) : Replace 'will be' by 'am'
19. (*c*) : Replace 'must' by 'should'
20. (*c*) : Remove 'will'
21. (*d*) : Replace 'is' by 'was'
22. (*c*) : Replace 'will' by 'could'
23. (*c*) : Replace 'working' by 'work'
24. (*c*) : Replace 'are' by 'is'
25. (*c*) : Replace 'was' by 'is'
26. (*c*) : Replace 'be resumed' by 'resume'
27. (*b*) : Replace 'is' by 'are' ('seeds' is plural)
28. (*a*) : Replace 'had been' by 'was'
29. (*a*) : Replace 'did' by 'has'
30. (*c*) : Replace 'find' by 'found'
31. (*a*) : The correct form is : 'The meeting was abruptly adjourned ...'
32. (*a*) : Replace 'would have' by 'had'
33. (*b*) : Replace 'know' by 'have known'
34. (*b*) : Replace 'broadcasted' by 'broadcast'
35. (*c*) : Replace 'said' by 'was saying'
36. (*d*) : Replace 'Have' by 'Did'
37. (*c*) : Replace 'is' by 'are'
38. (*b*) :
39. (*a*) : Replace 'are' by 'have been'
40. (*a*) : Replace 'believe' by 'believes'
41. (*c*) : Remove 'was'
42. (*b*) : Replace 'came' by 'comes'
43. (*c*) : Add 'had' before 'left'
44. (*b*) : Replace 'have' by 'has'
45. (*a*) : Remove 'shall'
46. (*b*) : The correct form is 'where he was going'
47. (*c*) : Replace 'was' by 'had'
48. (*b*) : Replace 'send' by 'sent'
49. (*e*) : No error
50. (*b*) : Replace 'went' by 'goes'

PRACTICE SET 12

Directions : ***In the following questions, some of the sentences have errors and some have none. Find out which part of a sentence has an error. The letter corresponding to that part is your answer. If there is no mistake, the answer is 'No error'.***

1. Firstly you should (*a*) / think over the meaning of the words (*b*) / and then use them. (*c*) / No error (*d*) **(Assistant Grade, 1996)**
2. The driver tried his best (*a*) / to avert the accident by (*b*) / bringing the car (*c*) / to a suddenly stop .(*d*) / No error (*e*)
3. The Sunrise Hotel was (*a*) / fully equipped to offer (*b*) / leisure stay (*c*) / to its clients. (*d*) / No error (*e*)
4. The technician reminded (*a*) / them to have a (*b*) / thoroughly cleaning of the (*c*) / machine after each use. (*d*) / No error (*e*) **(Bank P.O. 1993)**
5. I am much glad (*a*) / that you have (*b*) / won the prize. (*c*) / No errror (*d*)
6. My observation is that (*a*) / between Vivek and Shashi, (*b*) / Vivek is the most intelligent. (*c*) / No error (*d*) **(Bank P.O. 1991)**
7. It very often (*a*) / happens that (*b*) / a man who talks most (*c*) / does little (*d*) / No error (*e*)
8. From all accounts (*a*) / I learn that (*b*) / he is the best and honest member (*c*) / of the new Cabinet. (*d*) / No error (*e*)
9. He is (*a*) / too intelligent (*b*) / to make a mistake. (*c*) / No error (*d*) **(U.D.C. 1995)**
10. The flood situation this year (*a*) / is worst than (*b*) / that prevailed in the last year. (*c*) / No error (*d*)
11. People invent new machines (*a*) / when they (*b*) / think independent. (*c*) / No error (*d*)

12. Geometry and Drawing (*a*) / are more easier than (*b*) / Geography and Social Studies. (*c*) / No error (*d*) **(N.D.A. 1989)**

13. Some people get (*a*) / used to changes (*b*) / very easily than (*c*) / others do. (*d*) / No error (*e*)

14. My uncle forbade me (*a*) / not to go through (*b*) / the contents of his letter. (*c*) / No error (*d*)

15. This road is the worst (*a*) / than any other road in Delhi (*b*) / but remains unrepaired. (*c*) / No error (*d*)

16. Of all the friends (*a*) / I have had, he is the most helpful (*b*) / and less arrogant. (*c*) / No error (*d*)

(Stenographers' Exam, 1993)

17. A man entered the tavern (*a*) / and asked for some bread and cheese (*b*) / with a decided foreign accent. (*c*) / No error (*d*)

18. Our new playground (*a*) / is big and cleaner (*b*) / than theirs. (*c*) / No error (*d*)

19. Watch how careful (*a*) / the sparrow knits the (*b*) / straws into one another (*c*) / to form a nest. (*d*) / No error (*e*)

(Bank P.O. 1991)

20. It is rather ironically (*a*) / that so much is being spent (*b*) / on the statue of the one who had dedicated (*c*) / his life to the uplift of the poor. (*d*) / No error (*e*)

21. The car flew off the road (*a*) / and fell ito the valley (*b*) / because Ashish (*c*) / was driving faster. (*d*) / No error (*e*)

(S.B.I.P.O. 1992)

22. He is very blind (*a*) / to read (*b*) / smallest of prints. (*c*) / No error (*d*)

23. What is worst, (*a*) / this distortion cannot be corrected (*b*) / by either contact lens or glasses. (*c*) / No error (*d*)

24. Inspite of working (*a*) / very neat and careful (*b*) / he could not win (*c*) / even the third prize. (*d*) / No error (*e*)

(B.S.R.B. 1992)

25. Sohanlal is (*a*) / richest (*b*) / of the two. (*c*) / No error (*d*)

26. On hearing the news, (*a*) / he went directly (*b*) / to the Manager's room. (*c*) / No error (*d*)

27. Even though it was (*a*) / raining bad (*b*) / I went out (*c*) / to get some medicines. (*d*) / No error (*e*)

(Bank P.O. 1993)

28. The Headmaster said that (*a*) / Sachin was capable of doing (*b*) / more better work. (*c*) / No error (*d*)

29. The night was bright, (*a*) / the clouds dispersed, (*b*) / and the stars were shining brightly in the sky. (*c*) / No error (*d*)

30. It is the duty of every citizen to do his utmost (*a*) / to defend the hardly-won (*b*) / freedom of the country. (*c*) / No error (*d*) **(C.D.S. 1994)**

31. Of the two (*a*) / he was trying the hardest (*b*) / to attain the highest percentage. (*c*) / No error (*d*)

32. Early rising (*a*) / brings out the better (*b*) / in a story writer. (*c*) / No error (*d*)

33. At the end of the Second World War (*a*) / the USA was stronger (*b*) / than any country in the world. (*c*) / No error (*d*)

34. Being the only people there (*a*) / their presence was (*b*) / most important. (*c*) / No error (*d*) **(C.B.I. 1993)**

35. He can play (*a*) / as good as (*b*) / he can write (*c*) / with his left hand. (*d*) / No error (*e*)

36. This is the more difficult (*a*) / piece of work (*b*) / I have every undertaken. (*c*) / No error (*d*)

37. He ultimately decided (*a*) / to willingly and cheerfully accept (*b*) / the responsibility entrusted to him. (*c*) / No error (*d*) **(Assistant Grade, 1991)**

38. The Principal was (*a*) / enough kind (*b*) / to grant me (*c*) / free studentship. (*d*) / No error (*e*)

39. He is now making matters (*a*) / a lot more worse (*b*) / by his almost daily apologies (*c*) / for having done so. (*d*) / No error (*e*)

40. I tried on both the dresses (*a*) / and finally decided (*b*) / to buy the expensive one. (*c*) / No error (*d*) **(C.D.S. 1993)**

41. It is (*a*) / nothing else (*b*) / than foolishness. (*c*) / No error (*d*)

42. The angry man walked hurriedly (*a*) / into the crowded room (*b*) / and shouted loud at the guest. (*c*) / No error (*d*)

(N.D.A. 1993)

43. It very often happens (*a*) / that a man who talks most (*b*) / does little. (*c*) / No error (*d*)

44. I will give you (*a*) / a reward if you (*b*) / do your work (*c*) / satisfactory. (*d*) / No error (*e*)

45. The recent census tells us (*a*) / that the population of Calcutta (*b*) / is greater than any other town in India. (*c*) / No error (*d*)

46. After toiling very hardly (*a*) / over a long period of time (*b*) / he found that people recognised him as a successful person. (*c*) / No error (*d*) **(M.B.A. 1995)**

47. The tried travellers were bundled off (*a*) / to the nearby cop house (*b*) / till anyone could come (*c*) / and vouch for their credentials. (*d*) / No error (*e*)

48. I advised my son (*a*) / to engage two coolies instead of one (*b*) / because the luggage was too much heavy for a single coolie. (*c*) / No error (*d*) **(N.D.A. 1993)**

49. Everyone felt that (*a*) / the big glittering diamond (*b*) / was most unique. (*c*) / No error (*d*) **(S.S.C. 1991)**

50. There is no one (*a*) / whom I esteem highly (*b*) / than your father. (*c*) / No error (*d*)

ANSWERS

1. (*a*) : Replace 'Firstly' by 'First'
2. (*d*) : Replace 'suddenly' by 'sudden'
3. (*c*) : Replace 'leisure' by 'leisurely'
4. (*c*) : Replace 'thoroughly' by 'thorough'
5. (*a*) : Replace 'much' by 'very'
6. (*c*) : Replace 'the most' by 'more'
7. (*c*) : Replace 'most' by 'much'
8. (*c*) : The correct form is 'he is the best and most honest member ...'
9. (*d*) : No error
10. (*b*) : Replace 'worst' by 'worse'
11. (*c*) : Replace 'independent' by 'independently'
12. (*b*) : Remove 'more'
    Double comparatives are not used
13. (*c*) : Replace 'very' by 'more'
14. (*b*) : Remove 'not'.
    'Forbade' has a negative meaning and double negatives are not used.
15. (*a*) : Replace 'the worst' by 'worse'
16. (*c*) : Replace 'less' by 'least'
17. (*c*) : Replace 'decided' by 'decidedly'
18. (*b*) : Replace 'big' by 'bigger'
    When two qualities are compared, the two adjectives should be of the same degree.
19. (*a*) : Replace 'careful' by 'carefully'
20. (*a*) : Replace 'ironically' by 'ironical'
21. (*d*) : Replace 'faster' by 'fast'
    No comparison has been made here and so Positive degree should be used.
22. (*a*) : Replace 'very' by 'too'
23. (*a*) : Replace 'worst' by 'worse'
24. (*b*) : The correct form is 'very neatly and carefully'
25. (*b*) : Replace 'richest' by 'richer'
    When a comparison is made between two, comparative degree is used.
26. (*b*) : Replace 'directly' by 'direct'
27. (*b*) : Replace 'bad' by 'badly'
28. (*c*) : Replace 'more' by 'much'
    Avoid using double comparatives
29. (*c*) : Replace 'brightly' by 'bright'
30. (*b*) : Replace 'hardly' by 'hard'
31. (*b*) : Replace 'the hardest' by 'harder'
32. (*b*) : Replace 'better' by 'best'
33. (*c*) : Replace 'any country' by 'any other country'
34. (*c*) : Remove 'most'
35. (*b*) : Replace 'good' by 'well'
36. (*a*) : Replace 'more' by 'most'
37. (*d*) : No error
38. (*b*) : The correct form is 'kind enough ...'
39. (*b*) : Remove 'more'
40. (*c*) : Add 'more' before 'expensive'
41. (*c*) : Replace 'than' by 'but'
42. (*c*) : Replace 'loud' by 'loudly'
43. (*c*) : Replace 'most' by 'much'
44. (*d*) : Replace 'satisfactory' by 'satistactorily'
45. (*c*) : The correct form is '... greater than that of any other town'
46. (*a*) : Replace 'hardly' by 'hard'
47. (*c*) : Replace 'anyone' by 'someone'
48. (*c*) : Remove 'much'
49. (*c*) : Remove 'most'
50. (*b*) : Add 'more' before 'highly'

PRACTICE SET 13

Directions : *In the questions given below, some of the sentences have errors and some have none. Find out which part of a sentence has an error. If there is no mistake, mark your answer as 'No error'.*

1. The signpost at the gate (*a*) / of the garden read : (*b*) / 'Trespassers will be persecuted'. (*c*) / No error (*d*) **(Stenographers' Exam, 1993)**

2. If you lose your passport (*a*) / in a foreign country (*b*) / it will effect you hardly. (*c*) / No error (*d*)

3. The verbal statement of the witness (*a*) / differed greatly (*b*) / from his written statement. (*c*) / No error (*d*)
4. Mahesh is a disciplined boy (*a*) / and does (*b*) / as he is told. (*c*) / No error (*d*)
5. A lot of travel delay is caused (*a*) / due to the inefficiency and lack of good management (*b*) / on behalf of the railways. (*c*) / No error (*d*) **(Section Officers, 1993)**
6. You should (*a*) / never carry tales or (*b*) / tell ill of others. (*c*) / No error (*d*)
7. Having written my papers (*a*) / in the examination to my satisfaction, (*b*) / it was not unreasonable on my part (*c*) / to expect a good position in the university. (*d*) / No error (*e*)
8. The manager called the clerk and said whether (*a*) / he was in the habit of (*b*) / sleeping at home as well. (*c*) / No error (*d*) **(N.D.A. 1995)**
9. It being a holiday (*a*) / all the hostel inmates (*b*) / decided to celebrate (*c*) / by going out to a movie. (*d*) / No error (*e*)
10. The crew were on board (*a*) / and they soon busied themselves (*b*) / in preparing to meet the storm. (*c*) / No error (*d*) **(Assistant Grade, 1996)**
11. I and my friends performed the task (*a*) / as good as we could, (*b*) / however it did not turn out to be satisfactory. (*c*) / No error (*d*)
12. The statement made by the writer (*a*) / appears to be incorrect (*b*) / as Gandhiji was never born in Ahmedabad. (*c*) / No error (*d*) **(N.D.A. 1994)**
13. The Minister said that (*a*) / such statements would definitely (*b*) / lower the moral of our soldiers. (*c*) / No error (*d*)
14. With the advancement of winter, (*a*) / the days grow shorter (*b*) / while the nights grow longer. (*c*) / No error (*d*) **(U.D.C. 1994)**
15. Such candidates who have not (*a*) / cleared the written test (*b*) / will not be called (*c*) / for the interview. (*d*) / No error (*e*)
16. My brother has been (*a*) / living in America (*b*) / with his family (*c*) / for the past ten years. (*d*) / No error (*e*) **(S.B.I.P.O. 1991)**
17. The house owners forget that even (*a*) / so simple a matter (*b*) / as cleaning and maintaining (*c*) / a lawn affects ecology and should not be neglected. (*d*) / No error (*e*)
18. The book is making (*a*) / waves and the sale (*b*) / is quite brisk in (*c*) / all major cities. (*d*) / No error (*e*) **(B.S.R.B. 1995)**
19. Amar introduced me (*a*) / to his friend (*b*) / who is a scientist and an engineer. (*c*) / No error (*d*)
20. When the college was established (*a*) / he was (*b*) / yet practising law. (*c*) / No error (*d*)
21. Like the Commission (*a*) / has recommended in its report, (*b*) / the rules need to be (*c*) / enforced more strictly. (*d*) / No error (*e*) **(Bank P.O. 1991)**
22. The book on sociology (*a*) / brought in the market recently (*b*) / is really an asset (*c*) / for all college students. (*d*) / No error (*e*)
23. Students should work (*a*) / hard in order to (*b*) / build their carrier. (*c*) / No error (*d*) **(Clerks' Grade, 1991)**
24. He is liable (*a*) / to be scolded (*b*) / for his misbehaviour (*c*) / before the guests. (*d*) / No error (*e*)
25. Each cigarette which (*a*) / a person smokes (*b*) / does some (*c*) / harm to him. (*d*) / No error (*e*) **(Bank P.O. 1992)**
26. There is still (*a*) / little tea (*b*) / left in the cup. (*c*) / No error (*d*)
27. The weather (*a*) / of the new place (*b*) / did not suit Ravi. (*c*) / No error (*d*)
28. The angry father threatened his son (*a*) / that he would be (*b*) / hanged from the roof. (*c*) / No error (*d*)
29. I will spend (*a*) / my remaining life (*b*) / in the village. (*c*) / No error (*d*) **(C.B.I. 1993)**
30. Mrs. Kulkarni's husband (*a*) / is a very good (*b*) / cooker. (*c*) / No error (*d*)
31. Good night, (*a*) / sir, (*b*) / have a seat. (*c*) / No error (*d*)
32. Some artists have taken a clue (*a*) / from medieval miniatures ; our epics and mythology (*b*) / and created works which please (*c*) / with their acute colour sense and skilful handling (*d*) / No error (*e*)
33. While luminaries of the dance world (*a*) / have no dearth of opportunities to display their art, (*b*) / upcoming dancers suffer from (*c*) / an unfortunate lack of exposure (*d*) / No error (*e*) **(Bank P.O. 1995)**
34. My father is (*a*) / appreciated by his friends (*b*) / for his honestness. (*c*) / No error (*d*)
35. The higher we climb (*a*) / up the mountain peak, (*b*) / the cooler (*c*) / we feel. (*d*) / No error (*e*) **(B.S.R.B. 1992)**

36. Any of these (*a*) / two girls is (*b*) / your sister. (*c*) / No error (*d*)

37. Even many people (*a*) / carry an infection (*b*) / without showing its symptoms. (*c*) / No error (*d*) **(S.S.C. 1993)**

38. Every one of the students (*a*) / has brought (*b*) / his identity card. (*c*) / No error (*d*)

39. Experience has taught me (*a*) / not to ignore any man, high or low (*b*) / not to ignore anything, great or small. (*c*) / No error (*d*) **(N.D.A. 1994)**

40. Michael and Johnson always help (*a*) / one another (*b*) / in times of need. (*c*) / No error (*d*)

41. You are the man (*a*) / who is held (*b*) / in high esteem by everybody. (*c*) / No error (*d*) **(Stenographers' Exam, 1995)**

42. The television (*a*) / was discovered (*b*) / by John Baird. (*c*) / No error (*d*)

43. Can I lend (*a*) / your pencil (*b*) / for a minute, please ? (*c*) / No error (*d*) **(Section Officers, 1993)**

44. The Chief Guest made (*a*) / an impressive speech (*b*) / after the Annual Function. (*c*) / No error (*d*)

45. One of the members (*a*) / expressed doubt if (*b*) / the Minister was an atheist. (*c*) / No error (*d*) **(Asstt. Grade, 1996)**

46. He is known in the office (*a*) / only by his first name (*b*) / and no one knows (*c*) / his family name. (*d*) / No error (*e*)

47. We did the job (*a*) / as good as we could ; (*b*) / however it did not turn out to be satisfactory. (*c*) / No error (*d*) **(S.S.C. 1991)**

48. Though the first portion (*a*) / of the book was dull (*b*) / the later part (*c*) / was quite interesting. (*d*) / No error (*e*)

49. Women are now working (*a*) / in every fields (*b*) / Like teaching, medicine, law, business, etc. (*c*) / No error (*d*) **(Clerks' Grade, 1991)**

50. My host suffered (*a*) / from the illusion (*b*) / that I was a political leader. (*c*) / No error (*d*)

ANSWERS

1. (*c*) : Replace 'persecuted' by 'prosecuted'
2. (*c*) : Replace 'effect' by 'affect' ('effect' is a noun)
3. (*a*) : Replace 'verbal' by 'oral' or 'vocal'
4. (*c*) : Replace 'as' by 'what'
5. (*c*) : Replace 'on behalf' by 'on the part of' 'behalf' means 'in place of someone'
6. (*c*) : Replace 'tell' by 'speak'
7. (*a*) : Replace 'written' by 'answered'
8. (*a*) : Replace 'said' by 'asked' 'whether' is not preceded by 'said'
9. (*d*) : Add 'see' before 'a movie'
10. (*c*) : Replace 'meet' by 'face'
11. (*b*) : Replace 'good' by 'well'
12. (*c*) : Replace 'never' by 'not'
13. (*c*) : Replace 'moral' by 'morale' 'moral' means 'lesson taught by a story' 'morale' means 'spirit'
14. (*a*) : Replace 'advancement' by 'advent'
15. (*a*) : Replace 'Such' by 'Those'
16. (*d*) : Replace 'past' by 'last'
17. (*d*) : Replace 'ecology' by 'environment' 'Ecology' is the science of environment.
18. (*c*) : Replace 'quite' by 'very'
19. (*c*) : The correct form is 'who is both a scientist and an engineer' or 'who is a scientist as well as an engineer'
20. (*c*) : Replace 'yet' by 'still'
21. (*a*) : Replace 'Like' by 'As'
22. (*b*) : Replace 'brought' by 'introduced'
23. (*c*) : Replace 'carrier' by 'career' 'Carries' is something that carries
24. (*e*) : No error
25. (*a*) : Replace 'each' by 'every'
26. (*b*) : Replace 'little' by 'some'
27. (*a*) : Replace 'weather' by 'climate' 'Climate' means 'general environmental conditions' 'Weather' denotes 'climatic conditions on a particular day'
28. (*c*) : Replace 'roof' by 'ceiling'
29. (*b*) : Replace 'my remaining life' by 'the rest of my life'
30. (*c*) : Replace 'cooker' by 'cook' 'cook' is 'one who cooks' 'cooker' is 'a vessel for cooking'
31. (*a*) : Replace 'Good night' by 'Good evening' When we meet someone, we say 'Good evening', not 'Good night'
32. (*a*) : Replace 'clue' by 'cue'
33. (*b*) : Add 'no' before 'dearth'
34. (*c*) : Replace 'honestness' by 'honesty'
35. (*b*) : Remove 'peak' 'peak' is the highest point of a mountain. So, it is correct to say that we climbed up the mountain, not mountain peak.

36. (*b*) : Replace 'any' by 'either'
'Either' is used to express 'one of the two'

37. (*a*) : Replace 'Even' by 'Often'.

38. (*a*) : Replace 'every' by 'each'

39. (*c*) : Replace 'great' by 'big'

40. (*b*) : Replace 'one another' by 'each other'
'Each other' is used for two persons, while 'one another' is used for more than two

41. (*c*) : Replace 'everybody' by 'all'

42. (*b*) : Replace 'discovered' by 'invented'
'discover' means 'tracing out something pre-existing but unknown'
'invent' means 'finding out something new'

43. (*a*) : Replace 'lend' by 'borrow'
'borrow' means 'taking something from someone'
'lend' means 'giving something to someone'

44. (*a*) : Replace 'made' by 'delivered.
A speech is always 'delivered'

45. (*b*) : Replace 'if' by 'that'

46. (*d*) : Replace 'family name' by 'surname'

47. (*b*) : Replace 'good' by 'well'

48. (*c*) : Replace 'later' by 'latter'
'Latter' means 'Second', 'Later' denotes 'coming after'

49. (*b*) : Replace 'every' by 'all'

50. (*b*) : Replace 'illusion' by 'delusion'
'illusion' means 'a defect in vision'; 'delusion' means 'a false opinion'

PRACTICE SET 14

Directions : ***In each of the following questions, find out which part of the sentence has an error, idiomatic or grammatical. If there is no mistake, the anser is 'No error'***

1. He was not only involved (*a*) in her kidnapping (*b*) / but also in her murder. (*c*) / No error (*d*) **(Assistant Grade, 1995)**

2. The presumption that the average investor did not understand (*a*) / or take interest in the affairs of the company (*b*) / is not correct. (*c*) / No error (*d*)

3. I can't (*a*) / afford to pay (*b*) / that much for it. (*c*) / No error (*d*) **(U.D.C. 1994)**

4. The two last (*a*) / chapters of the book (*b*) / are very interesting. (*c*) / No error (*d*)

5. Even though he found the subject (*a*) / rather interesting Rajesh could not (*b*) / manage good marks (*c*) / in the examination. (*d*) / No error (*e*)

6. You will come (*a*) / to my party tomorrow, (*b*) / isn't it ?(*c*) / No error (*d*) **(C.D.S. 1995)**

7. With the introduction of new syllabus (*a*) / the number of colleges reporting high result (*b*) / is decreasing year after year. (*c*) / No error (*d*)

8. What sort of a drug this is (*a*) / that no one seems to be able to predict its long-terms effects (*b*) / with any certainty? (*c*) / No error (*d*) **(N.D.A. 1995)**

9. Never before in the history of the world (*a*) / such a thing has happened, (*b*) / I don't think that it will ever happen again. (*c*) / No error (*d*)

10. The serial which appeared quite interesting initially (*a*) / turned out to be boring (*b*) / in its latter parts. (*c*) / No error (*d*) **(Section Officers, 1993)**

11. Books which would have been unintelligible to us at fourteen (*a*) / delight and interest us (*b*) / in our twenty. (*c*) / No error (*d*)

12. The Church Father emphasised (*a*) / that it is the duty (*b*) / laid on all Christians (*c*) / to love each other. (*d*) / No error (*e*)

13. Her fascinating stories are so captivating (*a*) / that even after finishing the book, (*b*) / one is tempted to start over again. (*c*) / No error (*d*)

14. Never I have listened to such beautiful music (*a*) / as the piece we heard (*b*) / on the radio last night. (*c*) / No error (*d*) **(C.D.S. 1994)**

15. Foolishly, Sarita opened (*a*) / the cooker when (*b*) / it was full steam (*c*) / and burnt her hands. (*d*) / No error (*e*)

16. He said that he was not afraid of thieves, (*a*) / for he had nothing (*b*) / that he could call as his own. (*c*) / No error (*d*)

17. The lawyer told his client (*a*) / that he would represent him (*b*) / only if he pays up his fee. (*c*) / No error (*d*) **(Stenographers' Exam, 1993)**

18. No one in the class (*a*) / is an intelligent (*b*) / as Ajay is. (*c*) / No error (*d*)

19. The world (*a*) / comprises (*b*) / good and bad people. (*c*) / No error (*d*)

20. The Manager asked the worker (*a*) / why was he (*b*) / again disturbing (*c*) / the schedule of production. (*d*) / No error (*e*)

21. If I were (*a*) / in his shoes (*b*) / I would die with shame. (*c*) / No error (*d*)
(C.B.I. 1993)

22. He was loyal (*a*) / and did good service (*b*) / in the war. (*c*) / No error (*d*)

23. Passengers should be prohibited (*a*) / to smoke in (*b*) / the trains and buses. (*c*) / No error (*d*)

24. Being a well known physicist (*a*) / he was invited (*b*) / to deliver (*c*) / a lecture on Laser technology. (*d*) / No error (*e*)
(S.B.I.P.O. 1991)

25. For young Donald, (*a*) / peace in Vietnam (*b*) / was almost terrible as war. (*c*) / No error (*d*)

26. The teacher asked the students (*a*) / if were they ready (*b*) / to attend extra classes (*c*) / in late evening hours. (*d*) / No error (*e*)

27. He speaks (*a*) / not only Tamil (*b*) / but Teluge as well. (*c*) / No error (*d*)
(Central Excise, 1995)

28. All the candidates (*a*) / felt that this year's (*b*) / question paper was very easy. (*c*) / No error (*d*)

29. A hypothesis is a supposition (*a*) / put forward in explanation of (*b*) / observed facts. (*c*) / No error (*d*)

30. The teacher insisted (*a*) / on me to participate (*b*) / in the debate. (*c*) / No error (*d*)

31. When Anil was not (*a*) / able to show his ticket (*b*) / the conductor made him (*c*) / buying ticket. (*d*) / No error (*e*)
(B.S.R.B. 1992)

32. Monika is going (*a*) / to her grandmother for a fortnight (*b*) / and after to Delhi. (*c*) / No error (*d*)

33. Her fascinating stories are so captivating (*a*) / that even after finishing the book, (*b*) / one is tempted (*c*) / to start over again. (*d*) / No error (*e*)

34. We all (*a*) / take vegetable (*b*) / and fruit. (*c*) / No error (*d*)

35. As a rule (*a*) / each of the boy (*b*) / cleans up the hostel (*c*) / thrice a month. (*d*) / No error (*e*)

36. The reason why (*a*) / he was rejected (*b*) / was because he was too young. (*c*) / No error (*d*) **(Assistant Grade, 1996)**

37. The demand of the workers' union (*a*) / that the dismissed (*b*) / employee to be reinstated, (*c*) / has been accepted by the management. (*d*) / No error (*e*)

38. She sang (*a*) / very well (*b*) / isn't it ? (*c*) / No error (*d*) **(I.E.S. 1994)**

39. I have hardly some money (*a*) / but I think I wil be able (*b*) / to get a loan tomorrow. (*c*) / No error (*d*)

40. People should decide (*a*) / to not give (*b*) / or take dowry. (*c*) / No error (*d*)
(Clerks' Grade, 1991)

41. Most of the people (*a*) / are afraid (*b*) / of snakes. (*c*) / No error (*d*)

42. Sunita was popular (*a*) / with her classmates that (*b*) / she always had someone or (*c*) / the other coming to her house. (*d*) / No error (*e*) **(Railways, 1993)**

43. He participated (*a*) / in many a stage dramas (*b*) / during his college. (*c*) / No error (*d*)

44. When learning to swim (*a*) / one of the most important things (*b*) / is to relax. (*c*) / No error (*d*) **(Clerks' Grade, 1992)**

45. The doctor had scarcely (*a*) / stepped out of his clinic (*b*) / when he met with an accident. (*c*) / No error (*d*)

46. Children who have had (*a*) / good pre-school education (*b*) / are most likely to out do (*c*) / other children at school. (*d*) / No error (*e*) **(S.B.I.P.O. 1992)**

47. Mine may not be (*a*) / a story of success (*b*) / but failures keep a person live. (*c*) / No error (*d*)

48. He couldn't but help (*a*) / shedding tears at the plight of the villagers (*b*) / rendered homeless by a devastating cyclone. (*c*) / No error (*d*) **(C.D.S. 1995)**

49. He has not only built (*a*) / this big theatre (*b*) / but he also built a few (*c*) / bungalows in this city. (*d*) / No error (*e*)

50. We wanted to purchase (*a*) / something but all the three stores (*b*) / in that area (*c*) / were closed on that day. (*d*) / No error (*e*) **(Bank P.O. 1995)**

ANSWERS

1. (*a*) : The correct form is 'He was involved not only in ...'

2. (*d*) : No error

3. (*d*) : No error

4. (*a*) : The correct form is 'The Last two ...'

5. (*c*) : The correct form is '... manage to get good marks'

6. (*c*) : Replace 'isn't it' by 'won't you ?

In a question tag, the negative of the same verb is used, which is used in the beginning of the sentence.

7. (*d*) : No error

8. (*a*) : Replace 'this is' by 'is this'

9. (*b*) : The correct form is '... has such a thing happened ...'

10. (*c*) : The correct form is '... towards the end'.

11. (*c*) : Replace 'twenty' by 'twenties'

12. (*d*) : Replace 'each other' by 'one another'

13. (*c*) : The correct form is '... one is tempted to start all over again'

14. (*a*) : The correct form is 'I have never listened such ...'

15. (*c*) : Replace 'full steam' by 'still steaming'

16. (*c*) : Remove 'as'

17. (*c*) : Remove 'up'

18. (*c*) : Remove 'is'

19. (*d*) : No error

20. (*b*) : The correct form is '... asked ... why he was ...'

21. (*c*) : The correct form is '... I would have died of shame'

22. (*d*) : No error

23. (*b*) : The correct form is '... prohibited from smoking ...'

24. (*e*) : No error

25. (*c*) : The correct form is '... almost as terrible as 'war'

26. (*b*) : The correct form is '... asked .. if they were ready ...'

27. (*c*) : Replace 'as well' by 'also'

28. (*b*) : The correct form is 'felt that this year the ...

29. (*b*) : The correct form is 'put forward to explain' or 'put forward as an explanation of'

30. (*b*) : The correct form is '... on my participating'

31. (*d*) : Replace 'buying ticket' by 'buy one'

32. (*c*) : Replace 'after' by 'afterwards'.

33. (*d*) : The correct form is 'to start all over again'

34. (*a*) : Replace 'we all' by 'All of us'

35. (*b*) : Replace 'each of the boy' by 'each boy'

36. (*c*) : Replace 'because' by 'that'

37. (*c*) : Remove 'to'

38. (*c*) : The correct form is 'didn't she?'

39. (*a*) : Replace 'some' by 'any'

40. (*b*) : The correct form is ... not to give ...'

41. (*d*) : No error

42. (*a*) : Add 'so' before 'popular'

43. (*d*) : No error

44. (*b*) : Add 'to remember' after 'things'

45. (*d*) : No error

46. (*e*) : No error

47. (*c*) : Replace 'live' by 'alive'

48. (*a*) : Remove 'but'

49. (*c*) : Remove 'he'

50. (*c*) : Replace 'that' by 'the'

PRACTICE SET 15

Directions : ***In the following questions, some of the sentences have errors and some have none. Find out which part of a sentence has an error. If there is no mistake, the answer is 'No error'.***

1. The Ahujas (*a*) / are living in this colongy (*b*) / for the last eight years. (*c*) / No error (*d*) **(Section Officers, 1993)**

2. Will that (*a*) / I were (*b*) / a millionaire. (*c*) / No error (*d*)

3. Although we reached his house on time (*a*) / he was left (*b*) / for the airport. (*c*) / No error (*d*) **(N.D.A. 1996)**

4. We should spend good part of the day (*a*) / in out of door activities and games (*b*) / because staying indoors all the time (*c*) / is bad for health. (*d*) / No error (*e*)

5. I am trying to finish (*a*) / this letter for the last one hour. (*b*) / I wish you would (*c*) / go away or stop disturbing me. (*d*) / No error (*e*) **(Bank P.O.1995)**

6. The factory which has been (*a*) / closed for the last (*b*) / six months has been (*c*) / guarded by the police. (*d*) / No errror (*e*)

7. The little care (*a*) / could have prevented (*b*) / this terrible accident. (*c*) / No error (*d*)

8. I am waiting (*a*) / for you (*b*) / at this spot (*c*) / for the last two hours. (*d*) / No error (*e*)

9. He has seen (*a*) / the picture (*b*) / yesterday. (*c*) / No error (*d*) **(Railways, 1996)**

10. She is wealthy (*a*) / and can afford (*b*) / all the pleasures of life (*c*) / without care. (*d*) / No error (*e*)

11. He is working in (*a*) / a bank in New Delhi (*b*) / for the past several months. (*c*) / No error (*d*) **(I.E.S. 1994)**

12. The remedy lies (*a*) / in promoting values of humanism (*b*) / and democracy so as to combat (*c*) / the oncoming brand of fascism. (*d*) / No error (*e*)

13. After yoou will return (*a*) / from Shimla (*b*) / I will come and see you. (*c*) / No error (*d*)

14. I was there (*a*) / many a times (*b*) / in the past. (*c*) / No error (*d*) **(C.B.I. 1995)**

15. I was standing (*a*) / at the bus stop (*b*) / waiting for him (*c*) / since eight O'clock. (*d*) / No error (*e*) **(Bank P.O. 1994)**

16. The man is the only creature (*a*) / that has developed (*b*) / the power of speech. (*c*) / No error (*d*)

17. This pond is flooded (*a*) / with water because it is raining (*b*) / continuously for the (*c*) / last three days. (*d*) / No error (*e*)

18. In the course of time (*a*) / the winged reptiles growing bigger and bigger (*b*) / and better and better at flying. (*c*) / No error (*d*) **(C.D.S. 1994)**

19. All the problems are been (*a*) / written clearly (*b*) / on the board. (*c*) / No error (*d*)

20. 'The Arabian Nights' (*a*) / have lots of interesting stories (*b*) / for young readers. (*c*) / No error (*d*)

(Stenographers' Exam, 1995)

21. Rich can get away (*a*) / with money and contacts (*b*) / but the poor have neither. (*c*) / No error (*d*)

22. Having deprived from their homes (*a*) / in the recent earthquake, (*b*) / they had no other option but (*c*) / to take shelter in a school. (*d*) / No error (*e*)

(Bank P.O. 1993)

23. When will we know (*a*) / who has won (*b*) / the competition ? (*c*) / No error (*d*)

24. If a thing (*a*) / is worth doing at all (*b*) / it is worth done well. (*c*) / No error (*d*)

(N.D.A. 1996)

25. My brother has (*a*) / and is still doing (*b*) / excellent work for his organisation. (*c*) / No error (*d*)

26. Few months after the assassination, (*a*) / Vinoba walked over to the village of Sevagram (*b*) / for a meeting with Gandhiji's closest followers. (*c*) / No error (*d*)

27. It was apparent to everyone present (*a*) / that he would die (*b*) / if he doesn't receive (*c*) / timely help. (*d*) / No error (*e*)

(Bank P.O. 1992)

28. It was a year of series of (*a*) / boundary situations forcing a thinking individual (*b*) / to face the absurdities and ambiguities (*c*) / of the human condition. (*d*) / No error (*e*).

29. If I will have enough (*a*) / time tomorrow (*b*) / I'll come and see you. (*c*) / No error (*d*) **(I. Tax, 1993)**

30. The remark made (*a*) / in the review is on (*b*) / the other chapter (*c*) / and having little relevance. (*d*) / No error (*e*)

31. We threw out some old furniture (*a*) / so that the new television set (*b*) / has enough space. (*c*) / No error (*d*)

32. At present both (*a*) / the civil and criminal powers (*b*) / are vested in the Head of the District. (*c*) / No error (*d*)

33. If I had known (*a*) / this yesterday (*b*) / I will have helped him. (*c*) / No error (*d*)

(C.D.S. 1995)

34. Every man, woman and child (*a*) / is now aware of (*b*) / the terrible consequences (*c*) / of habit of smoking. (*d*) / No error (*e*)

35. The mission provides (*a*) / able service to all (*b*) / the needy people in this area (*c*) / during last few years. (*d*) / No error (*e*) **(B.S.R.B. 1995)**

36. She was filled with peculiar joy (*a*) / when she met her lost husband (*b*) / after a gap of five years. (*c*) / No error (*d*)

37. Frozen foods are so popular today (*a*) / that many people wonder (*b*) / how they ever lived without them. (*c*) / No error (*d*) **(I. Tax, 1992)**

38. The fact that (*a*) / the compact car is better than conventional cars (*b*) / has been proved by its sales. (*c*) / No error (*d*)

39. He makes it clear in the very first novel (*a*) / of this period that (*b*) / he sees his life and work on dramatic terms. (*c*) / No error (*d*) **(N.D.A. 1994)**

40. Today onwards we have been (*a*) / looking forward (*b*) / to your satisfactory progress. (*c*) / No error (*d*)

41. She was told (*a*) / to give the award to whosoever (*b*) / she thought has done the most for the downtrodden. (*c*) / No error (*d*)

43. I wonder (*a*) / what he has done with the book (*b*) / I lend him. (*c*) / No error (*d*)

(Stenographer's Exam, 1995)

44. This is one of two types (*a*) / of communication receivers (*b*) / that is available for general use. (*c*) / No error (*d*)

45. Although we are free (*a*) / for the last forty five years or so, (*b*) / yet we continue to be economically backward. (*c*) / No error (*d*)

(Stenographers' Exam, 1993)

46. This room would look much better (*a*) / if you put a furniture (*b*) / in that corner. (*c*) / No error (*d*)

47. The teacher promised (*a*) / that he will explain it (*b*) / if they come (*c*) / before school the following day. (*d*) / No error (*e*)

(Bank P.O. 1995)

48. Mahabharata contains veritable wealth (*a*) / of material for deep study and research (*b*) / but all mankind in today's strife-torn world. (*c*) / No error (*d*)

49. I will discuss the matter with him (*a*) / when I will see him (*b*) / in the next few days. (*c*) / No error (*d*)

(Assistant Grade, 1991)

50. He fell from a running train (*a*) / and would have died (*b*) / if the villagers did not get him admitted in the nearby hospital immediately. (*c*) / No error (*d*)

(I.E.S. 1994)

ANSWERS

1. (*b*) : Replace 'are' by 'have been'
2. (*a*) : Replace 'will' by 'would'
3. (*b*) : Replace 'was' by 'had'
4. (*a*) : Add 'a' before 'good'
5. (*a*) : Replace 'am' by 'have been'
6. (*c*) : Replace 'has been' by 'is being'
7. (*a*) : Replace 'The' by 'A'
8. (*a*) : Replace 'am' by 'have been'
9. (*a*) : Replace 'has seen' by 'saw'
10. (*d*) : Add 'a' before 'care'
11. (*a*) : Replace 'is' by 'has been'
12. (*b*) : Add 'the' before 'values'
13. (*a*) : Remove 'will'
14. (*a*) : Replace 'was' by 'have been'
15. (*a*) : Replace 'was' by 'had been'
16. (*b*) : Remove 'the' before 'man'
17. (*b*) : Replace 'is' by 'has been'
18. (*b*) : Replace 'growing' by 'have grown'
19. (*a*) : Remove 'been'
20. (*b*) : Replace 'have' by 'has'
21. (*a*) : Add 'The' before 'rich'
22. (*a*) : Replace 'Having' by 'Having been'
23. (*a*) : Replace 'will' by 'shall'
24. (*c*) : Replace 'done' by 'being done'
25. (*a*) : Replace 'has' by 'has been'
26. (*d*) : No error
27. (*c*) : Replace 'doesn't' by 'didn't'
28. (*a*) : Add 'a' before 'series'
29. (*a*) : Remove 'will'
30. (*d*) : Replace 'having' by 'has'
31. (*c*) : Replace 'has' by 'might have'
32. (*b*) : Add 'the' before 'criminal'
33. (*c*) : Replace 'will' by 'would'
34. (*d*) : Add 'the' before 'habit'
35. (*a*) : Replace 'provides' by 'has provided'
36. (*a*) : Add 'a' before 'peculiar'
37. (*c*) : Add 'had' before 'ever'
38. (*b*) : Add 'the' before 'conventional'
39. (*a*) : Replace 'makes' by 'has made'
40. (*a*) : Replace 'have been' by 'shall be'
41. (*c*) : Replace 'has' by 'had'
42. (*c*) : Replace 'was' by 'is'
43. (*c*) : Replace 'lend' by 'lent'
44. (*a*) : Add 'the' before 'two'
45. (*a*) : Replace 'are' by 'have been'
46. (*b*) : Remove 'a'
47. (*b*) : Replace 'will' by 'would'
48. (*a*) : Add 'a' before 'veritable'
49. (*b*) : Remove 'will'
50. (*c*) : Replace 'did not get' by 'had not got'

PRACTICE SET 16

Directions : ***In the following questions, some of the sentences have errors and some have none. Find out which part of a sentence has an error. If there is no mistake, the answer is 'No error'.***

1. There are much inconveniences (*a*) / that have to be put up with (*b*) / when you are camping. (*c*) / No error (*d*)

(Assistant Grade, 1995)

2. It is out duty (*a*) / to put off our shoes (*b*) / before entering the sanctum sanctorum of any temple or mosque. (*c*) / No error (*d*)

3. Supposing if you (*a*) / are arrested, (*b*) / what will you do ? (*c*) / No error (*d*)

(Stenographers' Exam, 1993)

4. The child is very precocious (*a*) / and not only speaks English (*b*) / but also German and French. (*c*) / No error (*d*)

5. When I called at him (*a*) / yesterday, he was busy (*b*) / writing a book (*c*) / No error (*d*)

6. We have helped them not only (*a*) / with money but also (*b*) / with new machinery (*c*) / and raw material. (*d*) / No error (*e*) **(Bank P.O. 1995)**

7. He was advised (*a*) / to be more cautious (*b*) / lest he is robbed again. (*c*) / No error (*d*) **(Asstt. Grade, 1991)**

8. Rural women congregated the mud roofs (*a*) / when the colourful procession (*b*) / passed through the street. (*c*) / No error (*d*)

9. None of the students attending your class (*a*) / answered your questions (*b*) / did they ? (*c*) / No error (*d*) **(I.E.S. 1994)**

10. Everyone expected (*a*) / the bold officer will face (*b*) / the situation with courage. (*c*) / No error (*d*)

11. Jack has a far more expensive (*a*) / and luxurious apartment (*b*) / than John's. (*c*) / No error (*d*) **(S.C.R.A.1993)**

12. She is going (*a*) / to her aunt (*b*) / for the weekend (*c*) / and after to Bombay. (*d*) / No error (*e*)

13. Some leader feels (*a*) / that the use of English language (*b*) / will hamper (*c*) / the progress of the nation. (*d*) / No error (*e*) **(B.S.R.B. 1992)**

14. Some ruling party members (*a*) / objected to the opposition (*b*) / raising the Bofors issue. (*c*) / No error (*d*)

15. These Acts were (*a*) / pushed through Parliament (*b*) / inspite of opposition (*c*) / but for little modification. (*d*) / No error (*e*)

16. Wearing extremely fashionable clothes (*a*) / and surrounded by photographers and pressmen, (*b*) / she swept up to the microphone. (*c*) / No error (*d*) **(U.D.C. 1994)**

17. As though this were not bad enough (*a*) / nuclear power in India is vastly (*b*) / more expensive than it was (*c*) / assumed to be. (*d*) / No error (*e*)

18. It is an established fact that the transcendental American poets and philosophers, (*a*) / who lived in the latter half of the nineteenth century, (*b*) / were more influenced by Indian philosophy, in particular by Upanishadic philosophy. (*c*) / No error (*d*) **(C.D.S. 1995)**

19. Shalini and I (*a*) / are good friends (*b*) / and we meet (*c*) / each other often. (*d*) / No error (*e*)

20. Sheela has scored a first class (*a*) / in her final exams, (*b*) / isn't it ? (*c*) / No error (*d*) **(Section Officers, 1993)**

21. Our is the only country (*a*) / in the world (*b*) / that can boast of (*c*) / unity in diversity. (*d*) / No error (*e*)

22. The long-awaited moment at last came, (*a*) / and we set out for the station, (*b*) / as merry a band of children as I have ever seen before or since. (*c*) / No error (*d*) **(I. Tax, 1995)**

23. What this company needs (*a*) / is not only qualified (*b*) / manpower but also (*c*) / dedicated workers. (*d*) / No error (*e*)

24. The cause of earth quakes (*a*) / is the heat in the (*b*) / earth interior. (*c*) / No error (*d*) **(Stenographers' Exam, 1995)**

25. Had she not gone (*a*) / on writing the truth (*b*) / which she saw it (*c*) / these changes might have taken longer. (*d*) / No error(*e*)

26. As poor as they are (*a*) / they never refuse to donate, they have (*b*) / for any noble cause. (*c*) / No error (*d*) **(Central Excise, 1993)**

27. It is better (*a*) / to do not calculate (*b*) / your gains before (*c*) / they are realized. (*d*) / No error (*e*)

28. The wheat (*a*) / on this land is (*b*) / finer than last year. (*c*) / No error (*d*) **(S.S.C. 1995)**

29. The students asked the teacher (*a*) / what should they do (*b*) / after they had finished the text. (*c*) / No error (*d*)

30. Tell me the name of (*a*) / a country where every citizen is law-abiding (*b*) / and no trouble is there. (*c*) / No error (*d*) **(N.D.A. 1996)**

31. Rahul thought that (*a*) / he would pass in the examination (*b*) / although he did not answer (*c*) / most of the questions correctly. (*d*) / No error (*e*)

32. As there was only one taxi available (*a*) / I had no other alternative (*b*) / but to pay the fare demanded by the driver. (*c*) / No error (*d*)

33. My friend is the kind of person (*a*) / who will face up (*b*) / to the most demanding tasks. (*c*) / No error (*d*) **(C.B.I. 1993)**

34. He says he is (*a*) / going to (*b*) / Delhi tonight. (*c*) / No error (*d*)

35. I have (*a*) / to usually reach (*b*) / the office by 9.30 A.M. (*c*) / No error (*d*) **(Assistant Grade, 1995)**

36. Thinking that death is imminent (*a*) / one must perform (*b*) / noble deeds for virtue and goodness. (*c*) / No error (*d*)

37. The little boy knows (*a*) / how to start the engine (*b*) / but does not know to stop it. (*c*) / No error (*d*) **(U.D.C. 1995)**

38. Long ago, when I was yet a student (*a*) / I once went to Darjeeling, (*b*) / where I was charmed by the beautiful mountain sceneries (*c*) / that greeted me on all sides. (*d*) / No error (*e*)

39. Neither he (*a*) / nor his father is interested (*b*) / in joining the party (*c*) / No error (*d*)

40. No sooner the teacher entered the class (*a*) / than the pupils (*b*) / stopped talking. (*c*) / No error (*d*)

41. The fact that (*a*) / the compact car is better than conventional cars (*b*) / has been proved by its sales. (*c*) / No error (*d*)

42. This room would look much better (*a*) / if you put a furniture (*b*) / in that corner. (*c*) / No error (*d*) **(Railways, 1993)**

43. Several people (*a*) / saw the thief (*b*) / to snatch the jewellery. (*c*) / No error (*d*)

44. A high level meeting (*a*) / of officials is reporting (*b*) / to have discussed (*c*) / the issue in great detail. (*d*) / No error (*e*) **(Bank P.O. 1994)**

45. Swift's ***Gulliver's Travels*** (*a*) / have been read by me (*b*) / several times. (*c*) / No error (*d*) **(U.D.C. 1994)**

46. The difficult situation in which I found myself (*a*) / is not made easy (*b*) / by her constant nagging and grumbling. (*c*) / No error (*d*) **(C.B.I. 1995)**

47. Ever since the government (*a*) / announced its new policy, (*b*) / the private institutions had (*c*) / run into heavy weather. (*d*) / No error (*e*)

48. "Meatless Days" (*a*) / have been made (*b*) / into a film. (*c*) / No error (*d*) **(S.S.C. 1995)**

ANSWERS

1. (*a*) : Replace 'much' by 'many'
2. (*b*) : Replace 'put' by 'take'
3. (*a*) : Replace 'Supposing if' by 'In case'
4. (*b*) : Replace 'not only speaks' by 'speaks not only'
5. (*a*) : Replace 'at' by 'on'
6. (*e*) : No error
7. (*c*) : Replace 'is' by 'be'
8. (*a*) : Add 'on' after 'congregated'
9. (*c*) : Replace 'did they ?' by 'did any?'
10. (*b*) : Replace 'will' by 'to'
11. (*c*) : Replace 'John's' by 'John'
12. (*d*) : Replace 'after' by 'afterwards'
13. (*a*) : The correct form is 'some leaders feel'
14. (*b*) : Replace 'opposition' by 'opposition's'
15. (*d*) : Replace 'for' by 'with a'
16. (*d*) : No error
17. (*a*) : Replace 'though' by 'if'
18. (*c*) : Replace 'more' by 'much'
19. (*e*) : No error
20. (*c*) : Replace 'isn't it?' by 'hasn't she ?'
21. (*a*) : Replace 'our' by 'ours'
22. (*c*) : Replace 'before or since' by 'since or before'
23. (*e*) : No error
24. (*c*) : Replace 'earth' by 'earth's'
25. (*c*) : Replace 'which' by 'as'
26. (*a*) : The correct form is 'Poor as they are ...'
27. (*b*) : The correct form is 'not to calculate'
28. (*c*) : Replace 'year' by 'year's'
29. (*b*) : The correct form is '... what they should do'.
30. (*d*) : No error
31. (*b*) : Remove 'in'
32. (*d*) : No error
33. (*a*) : Replace 'the kind of person' by 'that kind of a person'
34. (*a*) : Add 'that' after 'says'
35. (*d*) : No error
36. (*c*) : Replace 'for' by 'of'
37. (*c*) : Add 'how' after 'know'
38. (*a*) : Replace 'yet' by 'still'
39. (*d*) : No error
40. (*a*) : The correct form is 'No sooner did the teacher eneter the class'
41. (*b*) : Add 'the' before 'conventional'
42. (*b*) : Remove 'a'
43. (*c*) : Remove 'to'
44. (*b*) : Replace 'reporting' by 'reported'
45. (*b*) : Replace 'have' by 'has'
46. (*b*) : Replace 'is' by 'was'
47. (*c*) : Replace 'had' by 'have'
48. (*b*) : Replace 'have' by 'has'

PRACTICE SET 17

Directions : ***The following sentences may contain errors in grammar, usage, diction (choice of words) or idiom. No sentence contains more than one error. You will find that the error, if there is none, is italicised and numbered. Assume that all other elements of the sentences are correct and cannot be changed. If there is an error, select the italicised part that must be changed to make the sentence correct. The number of that italicised part is your answer. If there is no mistake, the answer is 'No error'.***

1. The brand proposition now therefore had to be (1) / that Keokarpin Antiseptic Cream *is more effective* (2) / because it penetrates deep down (being light and non-sticky) and *works from within* (3) / (because of its ayurvedic ingredients) to keep skin blemish, free and helps cope with cuts, nicks, burns and nappy rash. *No error* (4) **(M.B.A. 1994)**

2. It is argued that if the income of capitalists is *taxed sufficiently* (1) / by putting a *ceiling to* (2) / the maximum income of capitalists and by introducing legislation for the welfare of laboureres and by freezing prices, the aims of socialism *will be realised* (3) / *No error* (4)

3. The average student, *devoid of* (1) / good accommodation or atmosphere for study at home, *utilises public libraries* for (2) / a great *advantage to himself.* (3) / No error (4)

4. Whereas Gandhi *appealed to* (1) / the good sense of the human nature and *sought after bringing out* (2) / the kinder elements in the capitalists and other selfish individuals, Nehru believed in a legally regulated *way of disciplining* (3) / the selfish elements in society. *No error* (4)

5. India has also become *quite conversant with* (1) / advancement *made by* (2) / the western civilization, science and culture *through the teaching of* (3) / the English language only. *No error* (4)

6. The *ability of plan,* (1) / organise and coordinate work is all *fundamental* (2) / to working within *deadline.* (3) / *No error* (4) **(M.B.A. 1994)**

7. In the legend of *churning the ocean* (1) / of the universe *we are told* (2) / that one of the objects *which came to* (3) / the surface was poison. *No error* (4)

8. Though today India is a free country, *yet that spirit* (1) / of unity appears *to have evaporated* (2) / which had made people think that they are *a one family* (3) / and one nation. *No error* (4)

9. Those suffering from *financial hardship,* (1) / should be *rendered* (2) / all possible help for the *prosecution of* (3) their studies . *No error* (4)

10. Another reason for pharmaceutical companies *beefing up their* (1) / OTC (Over the Counter) divisions is that prescription drugs with proven safety records which *have been reached* (2) / the end of their patent *protection period are* (3) / allowed to be sold without a prescription. *No error* (4) **(M.B.A. 1994)**

11. Although widow remarriage *is legalised* (1) / for nearly a century, the majority of *so-called high caste* (2) / Hindus still *observe the custom* (3) / of enforced widowhood. *No error* (4)

12. The foreigners *had robbed India of* (1) / many things, but the greatest *loss for the country* (2) / has been the *seeds of dissension* (3) / which were sown in society by them. *No error* (4)

13. Remember that you are *part of* (1) / the team and your success depends *on the support* (2) / you are able to give and get from your other team *members.* (3) / *No error* (4) **(M.B.A. 1994)**

14. Although the object of the Britishers *to introduce* (1) / English as the medium of instruction in India may have been quite selfish, yet there is no doubt that the western system of education *did introduce* (2) / in India the liberalism of the western philosophers and *widened the outlook* (3) / of the Indians. *No error* (4)

15. The single biggest *gainer in this process* (1) / was ITC' s Gold Flake Kings *sales are estimated* (2) / to have moved up from 50 million to 200 million sticks per month *during 1987 and last year.* (3) / No error (4) **(M.B.A. 1994)**

16. But if science is allowed to cause suffering and destruction, if it is *let off* (1) / without the control *dictated by* (2) / moral and human considerations, then science *becomes* (3) / a bad master. *No error* (4)

17. Although agriculture is practically the only national industry in India, it is conducted *in the unsatisfactory conditions* (1) / and the average yield per acre of the different crops is consequently *very much lower than in* (2) / countries where agriculture *is better organised.* (3) / *No error* (4).

18. The whole thing *moves* (1)/ around the concept of building a small *dynamic* (2) / organisation into a *larger one.* (3) / No error (4) **(M.B.A. 1994)**

19. When India *had got freedom,* (1) / she was *faced with* (2)/ the gigantic task of *ameliorating* (3) / the economic condition of her masses. *No error* (4)

20. While initial reports indicate that the brand *has been* (1) / well received *at the capital,* (2) / it is still too early to say how much *of an impact* (3) / it will have in the long run. *No error* (4) **(M.B.A. 1994)**

21. The most important *condition of* (1) / a happy home is that the income of the family *should be enough* (2) / *to meet the* (3) / expenses of the family. *No error* (4).

22. It is one of the greatest responsibilities of modern scientists *to see* (1) / that their discoveries and inventions are *utilised for* (2) / the progress and welfare of humanity *rather for its destruction.* (3) / *No error* (4)

23. If you are great at ideas but not very *good at getting into* (1) / the *nitty gritty* (2) / of things and implementing them, then you *work on a team* (3) / that has someone who can implement. *No error* (4) **(M.B.A. 1994)**

24. A role of great importance that *India played* (1) / in international field is that of *bringing about* (2) / a happy synthesis of *conflicting ideology.* (3) / *No error* (4)

25. Our ancestors would find themselves in a world *quite unlike* (1) / what they saw in their life-time if they *were to wake up* (2) / after their *sleep for centuries.* (3) / No error (4)

26. In management, *as you rise higher,* (1) / the problems you face become more and more unstructured and you can't just *fall back on* (2) / the tools you *had been* (3) / taught. *No error* (4) **(M.B.A. 1994)**

27. All writers *on the subject* (1) / of democracy have *dwelt* with (2) / the difficulty *against which* (3) / the aims and ideals of democracy have to contest. *No error* (4)

28. It was *in pursuance of* (1) / this policy of *divide and rule* (2) / that the Britishers got India *parted into* (3) / two countries. / *No error* (4)

ANSWERS

1. (1) :is
2. (2) :ceiling on
3. (2) :utilises public libraries to
4. (2) :sought to bring out
5. (4) :No error
6. (3) :the deadline
7. (1) :the churning of the ocean
8. (3) :one family
9. (4) :No error
10. (2) :have reached
11. (1) :has been legalised
12. (2) :loss to the country
13. (1) :a part of
14. (1) :in introducing
15. (2) sales of which are estimated
16. (1) :let loose
17. (1) :under the unsatisfactory conditions
18. (3) :large dynamic one
19. (1) :got freedom
20. (4) :No error
21. (1) :Condition for
22. (2) :utilised to
23. (3) :work in a team
24. (1) :India has played
25. (3) :sleep of centuries
26. (2) :fall back upon
27. (2) :dwelt on
28. (3) :partitioned into

TYPE 2: DETECTING ERRORS IN SPECIFIC WORDS IN A SENTENCE

In this type of questions, generally a sentence is given in which some words are marked and labelled (*a*), (*b*), (*c*) and (*d*). The candidate is required to choose out the erroneous part. The error may be in the spelling of the word, or in its usage in context of the sentence. If, however, all the four words are appropriate and correctly spelt, then option (*e*) i.e. 'All correct' is the answer.

Ex. 1. : The **distribution** (*a*) / of fuel and power resources is **irregular,** (*b*) / so that few **countries** (*c*) / have all sources **avalable** (*d*) / to them. All correct (*e*)

Sol. Clearly, in the given sentence, the word 'avalable' is wrongly spelt. The correct spelling is 'available'. Hence, the answer is (*d*).

Ex. 2. According (*a*) / to me he is the **ideal** (*b*) / choice for **performing** (*c*) / this **roll.** (*d*) / All correct (*e*)

Sol. Clearly, in the above sentence, the word 'roll' has been wrongly used. The correct word is 'role'. Hence, the answer is (*d*).

PRACTICE SET 18

Directions : ***In each sentence below, four words/group of words which are labelled (a), (b), (c) and (d) have been printed in bold type, one of which may be either inappropriate in the context of the sentence or wrongly spelt. If all the four are appropriate and also correctly spelt, mark 'All correct' as the answer.***

1. The **exhistence** (*a*) / and **attitudes** (*b*) / of the **colonial** (*c*) / army were **decisive** (*d*) / to the outbreak of the Civil War. All correct (*e*)
2. The **success** of a man (*a*) / in **business** (*b*) / depends **over** (*c*) / his **attention** to small things (*d*) / All correct (*e*)
3. No **contry** (*a*) / can **isolate** (*b*) / itself from **international** (*c*) / **politics** (*d*) / All correct (*e*) **(B.S.R.B. 1992)**
4. He **appears** (*a*) / to be **unreasonably** (*b*) / **anxious** (*c*) / about solving his **nighbour's** (*d*) / problem. All correct (*e*)
5. A very **important** secret of (*a*) / the art of **writing** (*b*) / **biographies** (*c*) / is that the secondary characters must be **deleneated** (*d*) / with the same care as the central figure. All correct (*e*)
6. The **peculiar** (*a*) / dress he **wear** (*b*) / gave him a **comical** (*c*) / **appearance** (*d*) / All correct (*e*) **(Bank P.O. 1992)**
7. If a country is to **prosper,** (*a*) / it must produce goods both for **domestic** (*b*) / **consumption** (*c*) / and for **imports** abroad (*d*) / All correct (*e*)
8. **Religious** people are (*a*) / **afraid** of (*b*) / **sinful** (*c*) / **actions** (*d*) / All correct (*e*) **(B.S.R.B. 1996)**
9. The **terrorists** (*a*) / **kidnaped** (*b*) / the son of a **wealthy** (*c*) / **businessman** (*d*) / All correct (*e*)
10. To **strengthen** (*a*) / his **arguments** (*b*) / the lawyer showed to the judge some of the **experts** (*c*) / from a **magazine** (*d*) / All correct (*e*) **(Bank P.O. 1992)**
11. In olden days' **contiguous** diseases (*a*) / like **cholera** (*b*) / took a heavy **toll** (*c*) / owing to the lack of medical **facilities** (*d*) / All correct (*e*)
12. Trees give **shed** for the benefit of others, (*a*) / and while they themselves **endure** (*b*) / the **scorching** heat (*c*) / they produce the fruit by which others **profit** (*d*) / All correct (*e*)
13. The **committee** (*a*) / **underestimates** (*b*) / the efforts **involved** (*c*) / and hence falls short of suggesting **majors** (*d*) / to solve the problem. All correct (*e*) **(S.B.I.P.O. 1991)**
14. The **enemy** (*a*) / **attacked** (*b*) / our **outpost** (*c*) / and **injured** five soldiers (*d*) / All correct (*e*)
15. The other half is the **spirite** (*a*) / in which the **organisation** (*b*) / functions and the **attitude** (*c*) / towards it of **successive** (*d*) / governments. All correct (*e*)
16. The **defendent** (*a*) / presented written **evidence** (*b*) / to **prove** (*c*) / that he was not present at the **scene.** (*d*) / All correct (*e*) **(Bank P.O. 1992)**
17. He is composing **articles** (*a*) / delivering **oraition** (*b*) / and **conducting** (*c*) / the most **impassioned** (*d*) / interviews. All correct (*e*)
18. In **search** (*a*) / of **food** (*b*) / the dog **left** (*c*) / the **village.** (*d*) / All correct (*e*)
19. **Jems** (*a*) / and **jewellery** (*b*) / have very low **export** (*c*) / **value.** (*d*) / All correct (*e*) **(B.S.R.B. 1996)**
20. The new **lecturer** (*a*) / has **devised** (*b*) / a **novel** method (*c*) / of solving this **problem.** (*d*) / All correct (*e*)

21. Every **human** (*a*) / being has a **responsibility** (*b*) / for **justise** (*c*) / anywhere in the **community** (*d*) / All correct (*e*)

22. **Multiple** (*a*) / choice papers, which set a large number of **questions** (*b*) / on the details of a **passage** (*c*) / to be read, **impose** (*d*) / a problem. All correct (*e*)

23. Through his **inspiring** (*a*) / speech, the officer **maintained** (*b*) / the **morale** (*c*) / of the **personal** (*d*) / in his division. All correct (*e*) **(Bank P.O. 1992)**

24. The **debtors** (*a*) / and the **recepients** (*b*) / of aid must also **acknowledge** (*c*) / their need to accept **reasonable** (*d*) / terms of aid. All correct (*e*)

25. The storm **soon** (*a*) / **disappeared** (*b*) / and the sun **started** (*c*) / **to shine.** (*d*) / All correct (*e*) **(C.B.I. 1991)**

26. The **lieutenant** (*a*) / **declared** that (*b*) / all boy scouts were **required** (*c*) / to put on khaki **half-pants** (*d*) / on the day of the function. All correct (*e*)

27. Language is a powerful tool and **skillful** (*a*) / writers and speakers can **manipulate** (*b*) / their audiences in many ways, often **harmlessly**, (*c*) / but sometimes to quite **devastating** effect (*d*) / All correct (*e*)

28. **Eradication** (*a*) / of **illeteracy** (*b*) / cannot be **attained** (*c*) / fully unless people cooperate **whole-heartedly.** (*d*) / All correct (*e*)

29. As **impressive** (*a*) / as the **quality** (*b*) / of his work is the fact that he did not use any highly **sofisticated** (*c*) / photographic **equipment** (*d*) / for the job. All correct (*e*)

30. No sooner **we entered** (*a*) / ***than*** (*b*) / he **got up** (*c*) / and **left** (*d*) / the room. All correct (*e*) **(C.B.I. 1991)**

31. A **religion** (*a*) / which takes no note of this **world** (*b*) / and only **harpes** (*c*) / on the one beyond, does not **deserve** (*d*) / the name. All correct (*e*)

32. **Scents** (*a*) / have **utter** (*b*) / **disregard** for wealth and (*c*) / **worldly** matters. (*d*) / All correct (*e*) **(B.S.R.B. 1996)**

33. The President has issued an **ordnance** (*a*) / to **confiscate** (*b*) / the property of the **accused** (*c*) / in the **misappropriation** (*d*) / case. All correct (*e*) **(Bank P.O. 1992)**

34. Whenever we are **attacked** (*a*) / by an ailment or disease, we **call in** (*b*) / a doctor who examines us, diagnoses our **malady** (*c*) / and **proscribes** a curative medicine. (*d*) / All correct (*e*)

35. Kashmir **valley** (*a*) / is **full** (*b*) / of wild **yallow** (*c*) / **flowers.** (*d*) / All correct (*e*) **(B.S.R.B. 1992)**

36. **Subtel** (*a*) / **nuances** (*b*) / and hues of the Indian **languages** (*c*) / as spoken in all these places settle down in his **psyche.** (*d*) / All correct (*e*)

37. Through **persistent** (*a*) / **exercises** (*b*) / and nourishing diet, he has **maintained** (*c*) / a fine **physic.** (*d*) / All correct (*e*) **(S.B.I.P.O. 1991)**

38. **Language** (*a*) / is based on man's deepest **emotions** (*b*) / and **enreached** (*c*) / by his **conceptual** (*d*) / grasp of the world. All correct (*e*)

39. They made **substantial** (*a*) / **investment** (*b*) / in production of **fertilizers** (*c*) / and **insecticides.** (*d*) / All correct (*e*) **(Bank P.O. 1992)**

40. The **advent** (*a*) / of the electricity has **definitely** (*b*) / **improved** (*c*) / the **quality** (*d*) / of life in villages. All correct (*e*)

41. Being very **docile** (*a*) / all **lenient,** (*b*) / he doesn't have **excess** (*c*) / to the higher **authorities.** (*d*) / All correct (*e*) **(Bank P.O. 1992)**

42. A **Seperate** (*a*) / bill will be **submitted** (*b*) / for discussion and **sympathetic** (*c*) / **reconsideration.** (*d*) / All correct (*e*)

43. **This is** (*a*) / the time **of** (*b*) / the year **where** (*c*) / the birds **came** (*d*) / to eat the crops. All correct (*e*) **(C.B.I. 1991)**

44. We are **expected** (*a*) / to **excel** (*b*) / in all **walks** (*c*) / of life during our **formative** (*d*) / years. All correct (*e*) **(B.S.R.B. 1991)**

45. He who is indeed of the **brotherhood** (*a*) / does not **voyage** (*b*) / in quest of the **picturisque,** (*c*) / but of certain jolly **humours.** (*d*) / All correct (*e*)

46. During India's freedom **struggle** (*a*) / the national leaders **ensured** (*b*) / the **masses** (*c*) / that in free India the Panchayats would get back their **lost** (*d*) / power and glory. All correct (*e*)

47. The **masterkey** (*a*) / to **success** (*b*) / is to work hard and not **west** (*c*) / time in **gossips.** (*d*) / All correct (*e*) **(B.S.R.B. 1996)**

48. You are **entitled** (*a*) / to **obtein** (*b*) / two **additional** (*c*) / **gifts.** (*d*) / All correct (*e*) **(B.S.R.B. 1992)**

49. Examiners of English language papers **coment** (*a*) / **frequently** (*b*) / and bitterly on the general inability of

candidates (*c*) / to use the **apostrophe** (*d*) / correctly. All correct (*e*)

50. If you know you become nervous on these **occassions** (*a*) / it's worth starting well in advance **practising** (*b*) / **techniques** (*c*) / for dealing with your **nervousness.** (*d*) / All correct (*e*)

ANSWERS

1. (*a*) : The correct spelling is 'existence'.
2. (*c*) : The word 'depend' takes preposition 'upon'.
3. (*a*) : The correct spelling is 'country'.
4. (*d*) : The correct spelling is 'neighbour's.'
5. (*d*) : The correct spelling is 'delineated'.
6. (*b*) : Replace 'wear' by 'wore'
7. (*d*) : Replace 'imports' by 'exports'. 'Export' refers to the act of sending out goods from a country. 'Import' means 'bringing goods into the country.'
8. (*e*) : All correct.
9. (*b*) : The correct spelling is 'kidnapped'.
10. (*c*) : Replace 'experts' by 'excerpts'. 'Excerpts' means 'extracts'.
11. (*a*) : The correct spelling is 'contagious'.
12. (*a*) : Replace 'shed' by 'shade'. 'Shed' is an enclosure for cattle. 'Shade' means 'shadow'.
13. (*d*) : Replace 'majors' by 'measures'. 'measures' means 'ways'.
14. (*d*) : Replace 'injured' by 'wounded'.
15. (*a*) : The correct spelling is 'spirit'.
16. (*a*) : The correct spelling is 'defendant'.
17. (*b*) : The correct spelling is 'oration'.
18. (*e*) : All correct.
19. (*a*) : The correct spelling is 'Gems'.
20. (*d*) : All correct
21. (*c*) : The correct spelling is 'justice'.
22. (*d*) : Replace 'impose' by 'pose'.
23. (*d*) : Replace 'personal' by 'personnel'. 'Personal' means 'private' and 'personnel' means 'working men'.
24. (*b*) : The correct spelling is 'recipients'.
25. (*d*) : Replace 'to shine' by 'shining'.
26. (*d*) : Replace 'half-pants' by 'shorts'.
27. (*a*) : The correct spelling is 'skilful'.
28. (*b*) : The correct spelling is 'illiteracy'.
29. (*c*) : The correct spelling is 'sophisticated'.
30. (*c*) : The correct form is 'No sooner did we enter...'
31. (*c*) : The correct spelling is 'harps'.
32. (*a*) : Replace 'Scents' by 'Saints'.
33. (*a*) : Replace 'ordnance' by 'ordinance.'
34. (*d*) : Replace 'proscribes' by 'prescribes'. 'prescribe' means 'recommend', 'proscribe' means 'disallow'
35. (*c*) : The correct spelling is 'yellow'.
36. (*a*) : The correct spelling is 'Subtle'.
37. (*a*) : Replace 'persistent' by 'regular'.
38. (*c*) : The correct spelling is 'enriched'.
39. (*e*) : All correct.
40. (*e*) : All correct.
41. (*c*) : Replace 'excess' by 'access'.
42. (*a*) : The correct spelling is 'separate'.
43. (*c*) : Replace 'where' by 'when'.
44. (*e*) : All correct.
45. (*c*) : The correct spelling is 'picturesque'.
46. (*b*) : Replace 'ensured' by 'assured'.
47. (*c*) : Replace 'west' by 'waste'.
48. (*b*) : The correct spelling is 'obtain'.
49. (*a*) : The correct spelling is 'comment'.
50. (*a*) : The correct spelling is 'occasions'.

PRACTICE SET 19

Directions : ***In each sentence below, four words which are printed in bold have been labelled (a), (b), (c) and (d). One of them may be either wrongly spelt or inappropriate in the context of the sentence. Find out the word which is wrongly spelt or inappropriate, if there is any. The letter corresponding to that word is the answer. If all the words printed in bold are spelt correctly and are appropriate in the context, mark 'All correct' as the answer.***

(B.S.R.B. 1992)

1. Every member of a **community** (*a*) / should **fulfill** (*b*) / his **moral** (*c*) / **obligations** (*d*) / towards the other fellow members. All correct (*e*). **(B.S.R.B. 1992)**

2. The **travel** (*a*) / **across** the sandy desert (*b*) / was an **exhausting** one (*c*) / for the **caravan.** (*d*) / All correct (*e*)

3. A **snake** (*a*) / **leaved** (*b*) / in the **hole** (*c*) / of a **giant** (*d*) / tree. All correct (*e*)

4. To keep **injuries** (*a*) / away from **interferring** (*b*) / with the progress of the game the player was advised to take **treatment** (*c*) / **off** (*d*) / the field. All correct (*e*).

5. People take **undue** (*a*) / **advantage** of his (*b*) / **simplicity** and (*c*) / **chit** him (*d*) / All correct (*e*) **(B.S.R.B. 1996)**

6. **Outside** (*a*) / the house there was a **heap** (*b*) / of **roten** (*c*) / egg **shells.** (*d*) / All correct (*e*) **(B.S.R.B. 1991)**
7. Our decisions **emanate** (*a*) / from our objective **evailuation** (*b*) / of the **realities** (*c*) / of the situation in any given **context.** (*d*) / All correct (*e*)
8. The purpose **of** (*a*) / the United Nations, **broad speaking,** (*b*) / **is** (*c*) / to maintain peace and security and **to encourage** (*d*) / respect for human rights. All correct (*e*) **(C.B.I. 1991)**
9. In these **Cirkumstances** (*a*) / the search for a **definable** (*b*) / Indian **culture** (*c*) / seems to be more or less an act of **folly** (*d*) / All correct (*e*)
10. **Whosoever** (*a*) / that **practises** (*b*) / religion is **endowed** (*c*) / with more merits and less **demerits.** (*d*) / All correct (*e*) **(B.S.R.B. 1992)**
11. When the world is **normally** (*a*) / cheerful and **comfortable,** (*b*) / we hold the **parodoxical** (*c*) / belief that **philosophers** (*d*) / were wise men. All correct (*e*)
12. The **ties** (*a*) / of love and **affection** (*b*) / are more important than **religious** (*c*) / **dogmas.** (*d*) / All correct (*e*) **(Bank P.O. 1992)**
13. Quite a **sizeable** majority of people (*a*) / are under the **impression** (*b*) / that happiness **consists** in getting (*c*) / as many physical comforts and **sensual** pleasures as possible. (*d*) / All correct (*e*)
14. The report **envisages** (*a*) / **crucial** (*b*) / **guidlines** (*c*) / on **extra-ordinary** (*d*) / research methods. All correct (*e*)
15. My uncle **has** (*a*) / **brought up** (*b*) / a book **which** (*c*) / is based **on** (*d*) / his research work. All correct (*e*) **(C.B.I. 1991)**
16. Had they been **true** (*a*) / to their **calling,** (*b*) / they should have been **vigorously** (*c*) / **combatting** (*d*) / it. All correct (*e*)
17. The **listeners** (*a*) / **responded** (*b*) / **favourable** (*c*) / to the leader's **appeal.** (*d*) / All correct (*e*) **(B.S.R.B. 1992)**
18. Painting and **sculpture** (*a*) / are the common **means** (*b*) / of emotional **aesthetic** (*c*) / **impression** (*d*) / of the artist with the help of pen and colour. All correct (*e*)
19. We seem to want the **advantages** (*a*) / of the **technological** (*b*) / advances of the **scientific** (*c*) / age but we try hard to keep our unscientific **tempre** (*d*) / intact. All correct (*e*)
20. The **casher** (*a*) / at the **counter** (*b*) / was busy **distributing** (*c*) / the **cheque.** (*d*) / No error (*e*) **(B.S.R.B. 1991)**
21. **Hardheaded** (*a*) / politicians are often **aiccused** (*b*) / by their rational **opponents** (*c*) / of consulting **astrologers.** (*d*) / All correct (*e*)
22. His **decision** was based on (*a*) / **adequate** and (*b*) / **acurate** (*c*) / **information.** (*d*) / All correct (*e*)
23. They **appreciated** (*a*) / his **wholehurted** (*b*) / **contribution** (*c*) / to the social **cause** (*d*) / All correct (*e*) **(B.S.R.B. 1996)**
24. He **mate** (*a*) / with a **fatal** (*b*) / **accident** (*c*) / last **Wednesday.** (*d*) / All correct (*e*) **(B.S.R.B. 1992)**
25. **Whatever** (*a*) / may be the difficulties or **inconviniences** (*b*) / in the **operation** (*c*) / of strict **bilingualism** (*d*) / it is the only safe course possible at present. All correct (*e*)
26. The **descriptions** (*a*) / in the **autobiography** (*b*) / range **wide** (*c*) / from **fanciful** (*d*) / to matter of fact. All correct (*e*) **(Bank P.O. 1992)**
27. Hundreds of jet aircraft **knifing** (*a*) / through the stratosphere at **supersonic** speeds (*b*) / inject large amounts of water vapour that cause **cloudiness** (*c*) / and hence a change of **reflection** of earth. (*d*) / All correct (*e*)
28. Sorry for the **inconvenience** (*a*) / caused due to our delayed **delivery** (*b*) / but the dispatcher is already **reprimanded** (*c*) / for this **elapse.** (*d*) / All correct (*e*)
29. The **terrorists** (*a*) / **kidnaped** (*b*) / the son of a **wealthy** (*c*) / **businessman.** (*d*) / All correct (*e*) **(B.S.R.B. 1991)**
30. The ideas **conceived** (*a*) / by the **scholar** (*b*) / were warmly **applauded** (*c*) / by the **audiance.** (*d*) / All correct (*e*)
31. If (*a*) / you **will buy** (*b*) / one box at the regular price, you would receive **another one** (*c*) / at **no** (*d*) / extra cost. All correct (*e*) **(C.B.I. 1991)**
32. All the **guests** (*a*) / **spontaneously** (*b*) / **remarked** (*c*) / that the dish was very **testy.** (*d*) / All correct (*e*) **(B.S.R.B. 1992)**
33. My relations would become more **perturbed** (*a*) / if I became a **succesfull** (*b*) / company **promoter**

(*c*) / with the most **materialistic** (*d*) / philosophy. No error (*e*)

34. Our country is ctitically **affected** (*a*) / by **widespread** (*b*) / **deforestation** (*c*) / and **steady** (*d*) / destruction of natural watersheds. All correct (*e*)

35. He was the only **influential** (*a*) / person to be **impressed** (*b*) / by his **scholarly** (*c*) / **deliberations.** (*d*) / All correct (*e*) **(Bank P.O. 1992)**

36. Nor is the **truaint** (*a*) / always in the streets, for if he **prefers,** (*b*) / he may go out by the gardened **suburbs** (*c*) / into the **country.** (*d*) / All correct (*e*)

37. He thought of a **cruel** (*a*) / plan to **taste** (*b*) / his **skill** (*c*) / in **archery.** (*d*) / All correct (*e*) **(B.S.R.B. 1996)**

38. Two world wars within a **generation** (*a*) / and the **potentialities** (*b*) / of nuclear warfare have made the **establishment** of international order (*c*) / the **paramount** (*d*) / concern of Western civilisation. All correct (*e*)

39. The old man **cut** (*a*) / the huge Ashoka tree **with** (*b*) / **hardly** (*c*) / **no effort** (*d*) / at all. All correct (*e*) **(C.B.I. 1991)**

40. **Whatever** (*a*) / the cause of the worry the best way to break out of this **viscous** (*b*) / circle is to seek help by talking to someone **whom** (*c*) / you can trust to take out **Seriously** (*d*) / and who might advise you. No error (*e*)

ANSWERS

1. (*b*) : The correct spelling is 'fulfil'.
2. (*a*) : Replace 'travel' by 'journey'.
3. (*b*) : The correct spelling is 'lived'.
4. (*b*) : The correct spelling is 'interfering'.
5. (*d*) : Replace 'chit' by 'cheat'.
6. (*c*) : The correct spelling is 'rotten'.
7. (*b*) : The correct spelling is 'evaluation'.
8. (*b*) : Replace 'broad' by 'broadly'.
9. (*a*) : The correct spelling is 'circumstances'.
10. (*e*) : All correct.
11. (*c*) : The correct spelling is 'paradoxical'.
12. (*e*) : All correct
13. (*a*) : The correct spelling is 'sizable'.
14. (*c*) : The correct spelling is 'guidelines'.
15. (*b*) : Replace 'brought up' by 'brought out'.
16. (*d*) : The correct spelling is 'combating'.
17. (*c*) : Replace 'favourable' by 'favourably'.
18. (*d*) : Replace 'impression' by 'expression'.
19. (*d*) : The correct spelling is 'temper'.
20. (*a*) : The correct spelling is 'cashier'.
21. (*b*) : The correct spelling is 'accused'.
22. (*c*) : The correct spelling is 'accurate'.
23. (*b*) : The correct spelling is 'whole hearted'.
24. (*a*) : Replace 'mate' by 'met'.
25. (*b*) : The correct spelling is 'inconveniences'.
26. (*c*) : Replace 'wide' by 'widely'.
27. (*d*) : Replace 'reflection' by 'reflectivity'.
28. (*d*) : Replace 'elapse' by 'lapse'.
29. (*b*) : The correct spelling is 'kidnapped'.
30. (*d*) : The correct spelling is 'audience'.
31. (*b*) : Remove 'will'.
32. (*d*) : The correct spelling is 'tasty'.
33. (*b*) : The correct spelling is 'successful'.
34. (*e*) : All correct.
35. (*e*) : All correct.
36. (*a*) : The correct spelling is 'truant'.
37. (*b*) : Replace 'taste' by 'test'.
38. (*b*) : The correct spelling is 'potentialities.'
39. (*d*) : Replace 'no' by 'any'.
40. (*b*) : Replace 'viscous' by 'vicious'.

16. SENTENCE IMPROVEMENT

This chapter is analogous to 'Spotting Errors'. In this type of questions, a sentence is given with a word or phrase italicised. The candidate is required to examine this italicised part in accordance with the rules of grammar usage and vocabulary and decide upon its correctness. Some substitutes to the italicised part are given below the sentence. The candidate is required to choose the alternative which when substitutes the italicised part, the sentence becomes grammatically correct. If the italicised part is correct as it is, then the correct option is 'No improvement' or 'No correction required'.

Here are a few examples.

Example 1 : This project would encourage development and enable every villager *to govern their* own destiny. **(Bank P.O. 1994)**

(*a*) to govern his (*b*) to governing his (*c*) have governed his
(*d*) may govern their (*e*) No correction required

Solution : Clearly, the usage 'to govern' is correct. But since 'villager' is singular, so 'his' should be used instead of 'their'.
Hence, the answer is (*a*).

Example 2 : He told his friends that he *drank* tea every morning.

(*a*) will drink (*b*) drinks (*c*) would drink
(*d*) drunk (*e*) No correction required

Solution : Since a habitual action is denoted by Simple Present Tense, so here 'drinks' should be used instead of 'drank'.
Hence, the answer is (*b*).

Example 3 : My school is *in a stone's throw* from my house.

(*a*) at a stone's throw (*b*) to a stone's throw (*c*) on a stone's throw
(*d*) within a stone's throw (*e*) No correction required

Solution : The correct idiom is 'within a stone's throw'. So, the answer is (*d*).

For Rules of Grammar & Vocabulary Usage, refer to the Section 'Tips for Correct Usage'.

PRACTICE SET 1

Directions : ***In each question, a part of sentence is printed in italics. Below each sentence, some phrases are given which can substitute the italicised part of the sentence. Find out the phrase which can correctly substitute that part of the sentence. If the sentence is correct as it is, the answer is 'No correction required' or 'No improvement'.***

1. All the allegations *levelled against* him were found to be baseless.
(*a*) levelled for (*b*) level with
(*c*) level against (*d*) levelling with
(*e*) No correction required
(S.B.I.P.O. 1994)

2. Rohit is *as fast as* or perhaps faster than Manish.
(*a*) equally fast (*b*) almost as fast
(*c*) as fast
(*d*) No correction required

3. I shall be grateful to you if you *are of help to* me now.
(*a*) would help (*b*) help
(*c*) shall help (*d*) No improvement

4. He cannot succeed in business because he works *by fits and starts*.
(*a*) with fits and starts
(*b*) fits and starts
(*c*) into fits and starts
(*d*) No improvement

5. He *did many mischiefs*. **(U.D.C. 1994)**
(*a*) made many a mischiefs
(*b*) made much mischief
(*c*) committed many mischiefs
(*d*) No improvement

6. You may appoint *whoever you think* can do the job most efficiently.
(*a*) anybody you think
(*b*) someone you think
(*c*) whomever you think

(*d*) whomsoever you think
(*e*) No correction required

7. This carpenter is the most skilled *of all the other carpenters* in our workshop.
(*a*) carpenter
(*b*) of all other carpenters
(*c*) of all carpenters (*d*) No improvement

8. He has said so out of affection, do not take *it to heart*. **(C.B.I. 1993)**
(*a*) in heart (*b*) it in the heart
(*c*) by the heart (*d*) No improvement

9. I love *the literature, the music, the art.*
(*a*) literature, music and art
(*b*) the literature, music and art
(*c*) literature, music and the art
(*d*) the literature, the music and the art
(*e*) No improvement

10. Before I met Rajeev, I *had had* a poor opinion of him.
(*a*) had (*b*) have had
(*c*) did have (*d*) No improvement

11. I *would gladly accompany* your sister if you had asked him. **(C.D.S. 1994)**
(*a*) would have gladly accompanied
(*b*) was to have gladly accompanied
(*c*) will gladly accompany
(*d*) No improvement

12. She was too clever to *see through his tricks*.
(*a*) see into his tricks (*b*) see his tricks
(*c*) see at his tricks (*d*) No improvement

13. The boy *told his teacher* to explain the passage.
(*a*) called his teacher
(*b*) said to his teacher
(*c*) asked his teacher
(*d*) No improvement

14. What *are* needed are not large houses but small cottages. **(N.D.A. 1995)**
(*a*) were (*b*) was
(*c*) is (*d*) No improvement

15. The police *broke away* the meeting as it turned violent.
(*a*) broke up (*b*) broke off
(*c*) broke through (*d*) No improvement

16. I wish my bus *did not arrive* so late; then I could have reached home before breakfast.
(*a*) has not arrived (*b*) does not arrive
(*c*) had not arrived (*d*) No improvement

17. Sumit *would have been looked* smart in traditional clothes. **(Bank P.O. 1993)**
(*a*) was looked (*b*) would be looked
(*c*) had looking (*d*) would have looked
(*e*) No correction required

18. If *you will pray* sincerely, God will listen to your prayers.
(*a*) you pray (*b*) you are praying
(*c*) you will be praying
(*d*) No improvement

19. Hardly had I finished writing the letter *before* Anil arrived.
(*a*) then (*b*) while (*c*) when
(*d*) as (*e*) No improvement

20. The main point *of his speech* was well understood. **(Bank P.O. 1992)**
(*a*) that he spoke
(*b*) in the speech of his
(*c*) made when he spoke
(*d*) made by his speech
(*e*) No correction required

21. I met the two girls, *whom I believe, are* twin- sisters.
(*a*) who I believe, are
(*b*) who I believe to be
(*c*) who, to my belief, are
(*d*) No improvement

22. *In* her views, they are going to present a report soon.
(*a*) As (*b*) On (*c*) With
(*d*) For (*e*) No improvement

23. His father won't be able to leave for Varanasi *until they have arrived.*
(*a*) until they arrive
(*b*) until they will arrive
(*c*) until they will have arrived
(*d*) No improvement **(C.D.S. 1994)**

24. They *cooked* a conspiracy to overthrow the monarch.
(*a*) created (*b*) fabricated
(*c*) hatched (*d*) No improvement

25. He returned with two *burning* mugs of coffee and set them down on her desk.
(*a*) heating (*b*) steaming
(*c*) blazing (*d*) No improvement

26. People are *tiring* very soon in an activity which they don't like. **(B.S.R.B. 1992)**
(*a*) tried (*b*) trying
(*c*) tired (*d*) tyring
(*e*) No improvement

27. *All his family members* are in Kanpur.
(*a*) All of his family members
(*b*) All the family members of his
(*c*) All the members of his family
(*d*) No correction required

28. On hearing the loud noise, he stopped and *got down from* his bicycle.
(*a*) got from (*b*) got down
(*c*) got off (*d*) No improvement

29. They felt humiliated because they realised that they *had cheated*.
(*a*) had been cheating
(*b*) had been cheated
(*c*) have been cheated
(*d*) were to be cheated
(*e*) No correction required

(Bank P.O. 1993)

30. They are working for the *upliftment of* their village.
(a) uplift of (b) uplifting of
(c) uplifting (d) No improvement

31. He never *tells* the truth.
(a) says (b) utters
(c) speaks (d) No improvement

32. Is there any *place* for me to sit?
(a) space (b) room
(c) area (d) No improvement
(C.B.I. 1994)

33. The plan *broke open* for want of funds.
(a) broke up (b) broke down
(c) broke out (d) No improvement

34. The plane touched down at Heathrow at six p.m., *on* schedule.
(a) at (b) with
(c) by (d) No improvement

35. The summer has *set out*, and the days are getting warm. (N.D.A. 1994)
(a) set up (b) set in
(c) set off (d) No improvement

36. I cannot *put forth* with this nasty fellow.
(a) put up (b) put in
(c) put out (d) No improvement

37. He grabbed the man *from* the overcoat and pulled him away from Ritu.
(a) off (b) by
(c) in (d) No improvement

38. She could not help *but laugh*. (C.D.S. 1995)
(a) laughing (b) but laughing
(c) laugh (d) No improvement

39. Brinjals are *dead cheap* these days.
(a) deadly cheap (b) dirt cheap
(c) dust cheap (d) No improvement

40. The child jumped with delight on seeing the *joker* at the circus.
(a) ruffian (b) clown
(c) dud (d) No improvement

41. I am sorry, but *I don't believe* what you say. (N.D.A. 1993)
(a) I will not believe
(b) I am not believing
(c) I will not be believing
(d) No improvement

42. The members attending the meeting were men *on* powerful positions, high in the councils of their respective governments.
(a) of (b) with (c) in
(d) No correction required

43. I often see him *dancing* the top.
(a) rotating (b) encircling
(c) dodging (d) spinning

44. Let's buy a new sari with the annual bonus, *can we*? (I.E.S. 1993)
(a) can't we (b) don't we
(c) shall we (d) No improvement

45. His voice was rough and gravelly, as though his throat *has had* suffered an injury.
(a) had (b) had had
(c) would have (d) No improvement

46. What is the time *in* your watch?
(a) on (b) by
(c) from (d) No improvement

47. Since 1986, there *is* no earthquakes here.
(a) have been (b) are
(c) were being (d) No improvement
(Stenographers' Exam, 1992)

48. They probably *would have caught* up the truck by now.
(a) will catch (b) shall have caught
(c) must have caught
(d) No improvement

49. One of their freighters, the Neptune, *will leave* in two weeks.
(a) would leave (b) will be leaving
(c) would have left
(d) No improvement

50. It is time the six year old *is learning* how to read and write. (C.D.S. 1991)
(a) has learned (b) learnt
(c) was learning (d) No improvement

ANSWERS

1. (e)	2. (c)	3. (b)	4. (d)	5. (c)	6. (e)	7. (a)	8. (d)	9. (a)	10. (d)
11. (a)	12. (d)	13. (c)	14. (c)	15. (a)	16. (c)	17. (d)	18. (a)	19. (c)	20. (e)
21. (a)	22. (d)	23. (a)	24. (c)	25. (b)	26. (c)	27. (c)	28. (c)	29. (b)	30. (a)
31. (c)	32. (a)	33. (b)	34. (d)	35. (b)	36. (a)	37. (c)	38. (a)	39. (b)	40. (b)
41. (d)	42. (c)	43. (d)	44. (a)	45. (a)	46. (b)	47. (a)	48. (d)	49. (b)	50. (b)

PRACTICE SET 2

Directions : *In each of the following questions, a part of the sentence is italicised. Below each sentence are given some possible substitutions for the italicised part. If one of them is better than the italicised part, indicate your response against the corresponding letter. If none of the substitutions improve the sentence, indicate 'No correction required' or 'No improvement' as your answer.*

1. He plays cricket and tennis *also*.
(*a*) both (*b*) besides
(*c*) too (*d*) No improvement
(N.D.A. 1992)

2. Shivani was really happy *while* I accepted her invitation for her birthday party.
(*a*) when (*b*) after
(*c*) as (*d*) No improvement

3. The constable was *a so big man* that he could not run fast enough to catch the thief.
(*a*) a such big man (*b*) so big man
(*c*) so big a man (*d*) such a big man
(*e*) No correction required

4. I am used to *hard work*. **(I.E.S. 1994)**
(*a*) hard working (*b*) work hard
(*c*) work hardly (*d*) No improvement

5. He *has eaten* his food.
(*a*) has had (*b*) has taken
(*c*) has swallowed (*d*) No improvement

6. Please *blow up* the candle.
(*a*) turn off (*b*) blow out
(*c*) put off (*d*) No improvement

7. Practically *every part* of the banana tree is used by man. **(C.D.S. 1994)**
(*a*) most part (*b*) any part
(*c*) each part (*d*) No improvement

8. Let *he and I* work together.
(*a*) him and I
(*b*) him and me (*c*) he and me
(*d*) No improvement

9. The customer said. 'Please give *me the another one*".
(*a*) me other one (*b*) me the other one
(*c*) the another one to me
(*d*) No improvement

10. *No sooner I saw* the tiger than I ran away. **(N.D.A. 1995)**
(*a*) No sooner I had seen
(*b*) No sooner did I see
(*c*) As soon as I saw (*d*) No improvement

11. The teacher has instructed all of us to finish the work by tomorrow, *isn't it?*
(*a*) has she? (*b*) didn't she?
(*c*) hasn't she? (*d*) No correction required

12. If you come across my umbrella anywhere, bring it to me, *can you?*
(*a*) don't you? (*b*) will you?
(*c*) isn't it? (*d*) No improvement

13. Try to be diplomatic when you refuse any invitation, *so far not* to cause bad feelings. **(Bank P.O. 1994)**
(*a*) as far not (*b*) so as not
(*c*) if as far not (*d*) since then not
(*e*) No correction required

14. You *will have to* return my book whenever I ask for it.
(*a*) will have (*b*) would have to
(*c*) will be (*d*) should have to
(*e*) No improvement

15. The reason *why he could not do the work was because* he had to attend to his mother who was ill.
(*a*) why he could not do the work was since
(*b*) for which he could not do the work was because
(*c*) why he could not do the work was that
(*d*) No improvement

16. The *need* of the hour was some fast action on the part of the leaders.
(*a*) needed (*b*) needing
(*c*) needs (*d*) No correction required
(I. Tax, 1993)

17. *The child* is father of *the man*.
(*a*) A child, man (*b*) Child, a man
(*c*) Child, man (*d*) No improvement

18. My mother asked me when *would I* have a glass of milk.
(*a*) I will (*b*) I would
(*c*) I shall (*d*) No improvement

19. The indecisive man *was readily persuaded* to change his mind again.
(*a*) was persuaded ready
(*b*) was ready to persuade
(*c*) was ready persuaded
(*d*) could readily persuade
(*e*) No improvement **(S.B.I.P.O. 1991)**

20. The burglars *broke in* Mr. Roy's house last night.
(*a*) broke through (*b*) broke into
(*c*) broke open (*d*) No improvement

21. The doctor *examined* my pulse.
(*a*) observed (*b*) saw
(*c*) felt (*d*) No improvement

22. Shakespeare lived *for* the reigns of Elizabeth I and James I. **(C.D.S. 1992)**
(*a*) in (*b*) since

(c) during (d) No improvement

23. *On attempting* to stage a drama, a new meaning to the story was discovered.
(a) When attempted
(b) On our attempting
(c) Attempting
(d) No correction required

24. The police *are* trying to solve the mystery.
(a) was (b) has been
(c) is (d) No improvement

25. He doesn't hesitate to do whatever his brother *does*. **(B.S.R.B. 1996)**
(a) will do (b) would do
(c) shall do (d) would done
(e) No correction required

26. We spent an hour discussing *about his character*.
(a) his character (b) on his character
(c) of his character (d) No improvement

27. The teacher asked the intruder *who was he and why was he* occupying his chair.
(a) who he was and why he was
(b) who he was and why was he
(c) who he had been and why he had been
(d) No improvement **(C.B.I. 1993)**

28. 'Hard Days' was his *last* novel.
(a) latter (b) recent
(c) latest (d) No improvement

29. Bad habits must be *nipped at the bud*.
(a) nipped off the bud
(b) nipped in the bud
(c) nipped on the bud
(d) No improvement **(C.D.S. 1995)**

30. *It is no good to cry* over spilt milk.
(a) It is no good crying
(b) It is of no good to cry
(c) It is of no good crying
(d) No improvement

31. Old habits *die hardly*. **(N.D.A. 1994)**
(a) die much hardly (b) die hard
(c) die too hard (d) No improvement

32. The teacher asked, *"Why you are late?"*
(a) Why you were late
(b) Why late you are
(c) Why are you late
(d) No correction required

33. It is ten years since I *have begun* living here.
(a) begun (b) had begun
(c) began (d) No improvement

34. The various practices and norms for bank's transactions *are laid down* by the Reserve Bank of India. **(Bank P.O. 1995)**
(a) are laid up (b) are led down
(c) are lead up (d) have been lay down
(e) No correction required

35. She *is having a lot of* money.
(a) is having lot of (b) has lot of
(c) has a lot of (d) No correction required

36. They all loved *each other*.
(a) among each other
(b) one another
(c) for each other (d) No improvement

37. No one *needs to worry* about me.
(a) will worry (b) need worry
(c) shall worry (d) No improvement
(Railways, 1993)

38. It is *most unique* piece of art.
(a) a unique (b) the most unique
(c) an unique (d) No improvement

39. When the soldiers realised that they had been fooled, they *rush* back.
(a) had rush (b) have rush
(c) had rushed (d) rushed
(e) No correction required **(B.S.R.B. 1992)**

40. The officer *looked on* my complaint.
(a) looked of (b) looked into
(c) looked to (d) No improvement

41. No sooner *he had returned home then* his mother felt happy. **(Section Officers, 1993)**
(a) he had returned home than
(b) had he returned home when
(c) did he return home than
(d) No improvement

42. Each boy and each girl *was busy in her work*.
(a) were busy in their work
(b) was busy in his work
(c) was busy in one's work
(d) No improvement

43. The actress said that it sometimes took her two hours to *put* her make-up.
(a) put over (b) put up
(c) put on (d) No improvement
(Stenographers' Exam, 1994)

44. The matter must be considered *in* every point of view. **(U.D.C. 1995)**
(a) with (b) from
(c) at (d) No improvement

45. Place a ladder *on* the wall.
(a) along (b) with
(c) against (d) No improvement

46. He enjoys *to tell stories* to children.
(a) how to tell stories (b) telling stories
(c) to narrate stories (d) No improvement
(N.D.A. 1993)

47. Galileo said that the earth *revolved* around the sun.
(a) has revolved (b) has been revolving
(c) revolves (d) is revolving
(e) No improvement

48. Manisha purchased *the very good* of all the saris kept in the shop. **(S.B.I.P.O. 1992)**
(a) the better (b) the very better

(*c*) the most good (*d*) the best
(*e*) No correction required

49. He was born *to* rich parents.
(*a*) from (*b*) with
(*c*) by (*d*) of

(*e*) No improvement

50. On seeing the lion she felt *too much* afraid. **(C.B.I. 1995)**
(*a*) very much (*b*) excessively
(*c*) much (*d*) No improvement

ANSWERS

1. (*c*)	**2.** (*a*)	**3.** (*c*)	**4.** (*d*)	**5.** (*b*)	**6.** (*c*)	**7.** (*d*)	**8.** (*d*)	**9.** (*b*)	**10.** (*b*)
11. (*c*)	**12.** (*b*)	**13.** (*b*)	**14.** (*d*)	**15.** (*c*)	**16.** (*d*)	**17.** (*d*)	**18.** (*c*)	**19.** (*e*)	**20.** (*b*)
21. (*c*)	**22.** (*c*)	**23.** (*b*)	**24.** (*d*)	**25.** (*e*)	**26.** (*a*)	**27.** (*b*)	**28.** (*c*)	**29.** (*b*)	**30.** (*a*)
31. (*b*)	**32.** (*c*)	**33.** (*c*)	**34.** (*e*)	**35.** (*c*)	**36.** (*b*)	**37.** (*b*)	**38.** (*a*)	**39.** (*d*)	**40.** (*b*)
41. (*c*)	**42.** (*d*)	**43.** (*c*)	**44.** (*b*)	**45.** (*d*)	**46.** (*b*)	**47.** (*c*)	**48.** (*d*)	**49.** (*d*)	**50.** (*a*)

PRACTICE SET 3

Directions : ***Look at the italicised part of each sentence. Below each sentence are given some possible substitutions for the italicised part. If one of them is better than the italicised part, indicate your response against the corresponding letter. If none of these substitutions improve the sentence, indicate 'No improvement' or 'No correction required' as your response.***

1. Last evening I went to the optician and bought *spectacles*. **(C.D.S. 1994)**
(*a*) a spectacle (*b*) two spectacles
(*c*) a pair of spectacles
(*d*) No improvement

2. The train *left* before we reached the station.
(*a*) had left (*b*) would have left
(*c*) has had left (*d*) No improvement

3. The teacher was angry *with* Hemant as he had not done the homework.
(*a*) on (*b*) from
(*c*) at (*d*) No correction required

4. Education is a *strong* instrument for moulding the character of the young.
(*a*) striking (*b*) powerful
(*c*) potent (*d*) No improvement **(C.D.S. 1992)**

5. My opinion *for* the film is that it will bag the national award.
(*a*) on (*b*) to
(*c*) about (*d*) No improvement

6. One of the men gave first aid to Hitesh *who is injured* in a road accident.
(*a*) who had injured
(*b*) who was injured
(*c*) which was injured
(*d*) as he was to injure
(*e*) No correction required **(Bank P.O. 1994)**

7. In the party she spoke to me *very friendly*.
(*a*) in very friendly manner
(*b*) with very friendly manner
(*c*) in a very friendly manner
(*d*) with a very friendly manner
(*e*) No correction required

8. Mrs. Johnson *had staying* here since 1954 and has made India her home.
(*a*) will stay (*b*) was to stay
(*c*) is staying (*d*) has been staying
(*e*) No correction required **(S.B.I.P.O. 1992)**

9. The problems of translation *are still remain*. **(N.D.A. 1996)**
(*a*) are remain (b) will remained
(*c*) will still remain (*d*) No improvement

10. Columbus *invented* America.
(*a*) searched (*b*) traced
(*c*) discovered (*d*) No improvement

11. They have stopped *from constructing* new buildings. **(Assistant Grade, 1995)**
(*a*) to contruct (*b*) at constructing
(*c*) constructing (*d*) No improvement

12. You *could be able to* work out these problems easily.
(*a*) can be able to (*b*) should be able to
(*c*) must be able to (*d*) No improvement

13. All over Russia, Indian films are more popular than *those in* any other country.
(*a*) in (*b*) that in
(*c*) that of (*d*) those of
(*e*) No improvement

14. Wise men *catch* time by the forelock.
(*a*) hold (*b*) seize
(*c*) take (*d*) No improvement

(C.B.I. 1993)

15. Seeing the injustice done to them by the Britishers, the sepoys *broke into* open revolt.
(*a*) broke to (*b*) broke upto
(*c*) resorted to (*d*) No improvement

16. The cloud of misfortunes appears to have blown *out*. **(Stenographers' Exam, 1995)**
(*a*) away (*b*) over
(*c*) up (*d*) No improvement

17. He has his meal at two, *when he has it*, he goes off to sleep.
(*a*) when he has had it
(*b*) when he will have it
(*c*) when he will have had it
(*d*) No improvement

18. Anand has the guts *to rise from* the occasion and come out successful.
(*a*) to rise against (*b*) in rising from
(*c*) to rise to (*d*) to raise with
(*e*) No correction required

(Bank P.O. 1994)

19. He is *too kind* man to refuse to help in such a case.
(*a*) a too kind (*b*) a too kindly
(*c*) too kind a (*d*) too kindly a
(*e*) No correction required

20. A bird in hand is worth *two in bush*.
(*a*) two in the bush (*b*) two at a bush
(*c*) two on bush (*d*) No improvement

21. Scarcely had he entered the room *than* the phone rang. **(C.D.S. 1994)**
(*a*) when (*b*) while
(*c*) as (*d*) No improvement

22. Let *he and I* do the work today itself.
(*a*) he with I (*b*) he and me
(*c*) him and me (*d*) him and myself
(*e*) No correction required

23. Kindly let us know the time of your arrival *by return of post*.
(*a*) by the return of post
(*b*) on return of post
(*c*) in return post (*d*) No improvement

24. Five years ago today, I *am sitting* in a small Japanese car, driving across Poland towards Berlin. **(C.D.S. 1995)**
(*a*) was sitting (*b*) have been sitting
(*c*) sat (*d*) No improvement

25. *On arriving at the station* my uncle was there to greet us.
(*a*) As we arrived at the station
(*b*) As soon as we arrived at the station
(*c*) When we arrived at the station
(*d*) No improvement

26. The man who is perpetually hesitating which of the two things he will do first, will ultimately do *either*.
(*a*) none (*b*) neither
(*c*) nothing (*d*) No improvement

27. Mother always *finds faults* with the maid servant. **(N.D.A. 1995)**
(*a*) find faults (*b*) is finding faults
(*c*) finds fault (*d*) No improvement

28. To make him succeed, the correct thing to do is to punish him *until he does not try*.
(*a*) until he tries (*b*) until he does try
(*c*) until he will not try
(*d*) until he did not try
(*e*) No improvement

29. The custom *of many centuries ago origin* is slowly disappearing. **(S.B.I.P.O. 1991)**
(*a*) which was originated ago many centuries
(*b*) originating for many centuries
(*c*) which originated many centuries ago
(*d*) with many centuries of origin
(*e*) No correction required

30. Hundreds of people were killed *by* the earthquake.
(*a*) from (*b*) in
(*c*) of (*d*) No improvement

31. He is not used *to walk* long distance.
(*a*) to walking
(*b*) to have walked
(*c*) to be walking
(*d*) to have been walking
(*e*) No improvement

32. If you had told your problem yesterday, we *might had* helped you. **(B.S.R.B. 1990)**
(*a*) would have (*b*) might have been
(*c*) would have been
(*d*) No correction required

33. He has no *knowledge and interest in music*.
(*a*) knowledge and interest of music
(*b*) knowledge for and interest of music
(*c*) knowledge of and interest in music
(*d*) No correction required

34. He stayed back so that it *can look* as if he was unaware of the entire incident.
(*a*) may look (*b*) would look
(*c*) will look (*d*) No improvement

(S.C.R.A. 1993)

35. *Day before yesterday* I saw her in the market.
(*a*) Day before the yesterday
(*b*) The day before yesterday
(*c*) The day before the yesterday
(*d*) No improvement

36. When he heard the rhetorical speech of the leader, he *was carried along* by his enthusiasm. **(C.D.S. 1994)**
(*a*) was carried away
(*b*) was carried down
(*c*) was carried aloft
(*d*) No improvement

37. The beautiful is not always the same *like the good.*
(*a*) as good (*b*) like good
(*c*) as the good (*d*) as like the good
(*e*) No improvement

38. The members of his family are coming *in* this train. **(Railways, 1994)**
(*a*) with (*b*) by
(*c*) on (*d*) No improvement

39. We are supposed *to take out* our shoes when we enter a place of worship.
(*a*) to put off (*b*) to put away
(*c*) to take off (*d*) No improvement

40. If he *had* time he will call you.
(*a*) would have (*b*) would have had
(*c*) has (*d*) No improvement
(I.E.S. 1994)

41. The houses in our street are more beautiful *than on the main road.*
(*a*) than that on the main road
(*b*) than those on the main road
(*c*) than there on the main road
(*d*) No correction required

42. The intruder stood quietly *for few moments.* **(Bank P.O. 1994)**
(*a*) for few time (*b*) for a few moments
(*c*) for the few moments
(*d*) No correction required

43. He *gave* the I.A.S. examination in all seriousness,
(*a*) appeared (*b*) took
(*c*) undertook (*d*) No improvement

44. A lot depends on your early *brought up* in the family. **(C.B.I. 1994)**
(*a*) bringing up (*b*) bringing on
(*c*) upbringing (*d*) No improvement

45. The dentist *pulled up* one of my teeth yesterday.
(*a*) pulled (*b*) pulled out
(*c*) pulled off (*d*) No improvement

46. The 'Three Musketeers' *have been written* by Dumas. **(N.D.A. 1993)**
(*a*) are written (*b*) are being written
(*c*) has been written (*d*) No improvement

47. The weather was not good; it was *a bit* pleasant.
(*a*) rather (*b*) to some extent
(*c*) fairly (*d*) a little
(*e*) No correction required

48. Many believed that girls who *received* western education would make slaves of their husbands. **(C.D.S. 1995)**
(*a*) could receive (*b*) had received
(*c*) have received (*d*) No improvement

49. My mother *is ill since* two months.
(*a*) has been ill since
(*b*) has been ailing since
(*c*) has been ailing for
(*d*) No correction required

50. I have not written any letter to him since my father *had died*. **(C.D.S. 1990)**
(*a*) died (*b*) was dead
(*c*) has died (*d*) No improvement

ANSWERS

1. (*c*)	**2.** (*a*)	**3.** (*d*)	**4.** (*b*)	**5.** (*c*)	**6.** (*b*)	**7.** (*c*)	**8.** (*d*)	**9.** (*c*)	**10.** (*c*)
11. (*c*)	**12.** (*b*)	**13.** (*d*)	**14.** (*b*)	**15.** (*d*)	**16.** (*b*)	**17.** (*a*)	**18.** (*c*)	**19.** (*c*)	**20.** (*a*)
21. (*d*)	**22.** (*c*)	**23.** (*d*)	**24.** (*a*)	**25.** (*c*)	**26.** (*b*)	**27.** (*c*)	**28.** (*a*)	**29.** (*c*)	**30.** (*b*)
31. (*a*)	**32.** (*a*)	**33.** (*c*)	**34.** (*b*)	**35.** (*b*)	**36.** (*a*)	**37.** (*c*)	**38.** (*b*)	**39.** (*c*)	**40.** (*c*)
41. (*b*)	**42.** (*b*)	**43.** (*b*)	**44.** (*c*)	**45.** (*b*)	**46.** (*c*)	**47.** (*c*)	**48.** (*b*)	**49.** (*c*)	**50.** (*a*)

PRACTICE SET 4

Directions : *In the following questions, a part of the sentences is italicised. Alternatives to the italicised part, which may improve the sentence, are given. Choose the appropriate alternative. In case, no improvement is needed, choose 'No Improvement' or 'No correction required' as your answer.*

1. He is very active and will finish the work *within no time.* **(C.B.I. 1993)**
(*a*) at no time (*b*) without taking time
(*c*) in no time (*d*) No improvement

2. Sensing that the contest would be very tough, she decided to *stand* down.
(*a*) lie (*b*) play
(*c*) sit (*d*) No improvement

3. *Would* you find me absent, please don't forget to leave a message behind.
(*a*) As (*b*) Should
(*c*) Unless (*d*) No improvement
(N.D.A. 1995)

4. No sooner did the Chief Guest climb up to the dias *then* the bomb exploded.
(*a*) than (*b*) before
(*c*) when (*d*) No improvement

5. The Manager *was unhappy at* Gaurav because he did not complete the work in time. **(Central Excise, 1993)**
(*a*) is unhappy at (*b*) is to be unhappy at
(*c*) was unhappy with
(*d*) No correction required

6. He has done nothing *from* yesterday.
(*a*) after (*b*) since
(*c*) through (*d*) No improvement

7. In the modern world it is difficult *to live through* one's ideals. **(I.E.S. 1993)**
(*a*) to live up to (*b*) to live by
(*c*) to live for (*d*) No improvement

8. It is *long since* I last saw you.
(*a*) long time (*b*) long before
(*c*) long ago (*d*) No improvement

9. It is unreasonable to *distort* the statement of a man simply because he does not agree with your opinions.
(*a*) discourage (*b*) denounce
(*c*) bend (*d*) No improvement
(C.D.S. 1994)

10. Kalidas is the greatest of *all other* dramatists.
(*a*) most other (*b*) the other
(*c*) any other (*d*) all the
(*e*) No correction required

11. The secret information was held *away* from me.
(*a*) off (*b*) back
(*c*) out (*d*) No improvement

12. She *gave* most of her time to music.
(*a*) devoted (*b*) spent
(*c*) lent (*d*) No improvement
(U.D.C. 1995)

13. James sat there in stunned silence, *to try* to absorb what Reeta was saying.
(*a*) so as to try (*b*) trying
(*c*) as if trying (*d*) No improvement

14. When I was fourteen, I *sat* the entrance examination for senior secondary school.
(*a*) sat for (*b*) sat in
(*c*) sat at (*d*) No improvement
(C.D.S. 1995)

15. When I lived in Allahabad, I *was going* to the cinema once a week.
(*a*) went (*b*) had been going
(*c*) had gone (*d*) used to be going
(*e*) No correction required

16. He has been working *off and on* for several years to compile a dictionary.
(*a*) on or off (*b*) on and off
(*c*) regularly (*d*) No correction required
(S.B.I.P.O. 1991)

17. A great deal of human invention *since the last 300 years* has been directed to taming the power hidden in nature, and to chanelling it into steady sources of energy that can drive machines.
(*a*) since the past 300 years
(*b*) in the last 300 years
(*c*) during the past 300 years
(*d*) No improvement

18. Rajni unnecessarily *picked up* a quarrel with Kashish and left the party hurriedly. **(Bank P.O. 1994)**
(*a*) picking up (*b*) picked on
(*c*) picked (*d*) has picked up
(*e*) No correction required

19. He spent much time and energy over it, and lost a sum *in the bargain*.
(*a*) off the bargain (*b*) for the bargain
(*c*) into the bargain (*d*) with the bargain
(*e*) No correction required

20. He complained that he had too much work *to cope up with*. **(C.D.S. 1992)**
(*a*) to cope with (*b*) for coping up with
(*c*) to cope (*d*) No improvement

21. We *have heard* her lecture yesterday.
(*a*) were hearing (*b*) would have heard
(*c*) heard (*d*) had been hearing
(*e*) No correction required

22. I noticed that *the opposite man* was staring at me.
(*a*) the opposed man (*b*) the man opposite
(*c*) the men opposite (*d*) No improvement

23. She did not like the movie, *nor I did*.
(*a*) nor did I (*b*) nor I like it
(*c*) nor I liked it (*d*) No improvement
(N.D.A. 1994)

24. It will take two hours to walk *across* the forest.
(*a*) over (*b*) between
(*c*) away (*d*) through
(*e*) No correction required

25. It shall depend on *they finishing* on time.
(*a*) they finish (*b*) them finishing
(*c*) their finishing (*d*) their's finishing
(*e*) No correction required

26. The unemployment rate has dropped sharply this month, *though it may only be temporary*. **(R.B.I. 1990)**
(*a*) but it may be only temporary
(*b*) but the drop may only be temporary
(*c*) even though the drop may only be temporary
(*d*) but such a drop may only be a temporary one
(*e*) No correction required

27. The contractor did not keep his promise that the work *will* be finished before the end of the week.

(*a*) could (*b*) shall
(*c*) would (*d*) No improvement

28. In accordance *to* your instructions, we have remitted the amount in the bank.
(*a*) by (*b*) with
(*c*) for (*d*) No improvement **(Section Officers, 1993)**

29. It is high time that we *did* something about it. **(C.D.S. 1995)**
(*a*) had done (*b*) would do
(*c*) have done (*d*) No improvement

30. The huge Negro *would have been* a comic figure if he had not been terrific, for he was dressed in a very loud grey check suit with a flowing salmon coloured tie.
(*a*) must have been (*b*) may have been
(*c*) should have been (*d*) No improvement

31. Not a word *they spoke* to the unfortunate wife about it. **(I.E.S. 1994)**
(*a*) they had spoken (*b*) did they speak
(*c*) they will speak (*d*) No improvement

32. There is sufficient fund to meet the requirement of *the entire schools* in our zone.
(*a*) schools (*b*) all the schools
(*c*) all of the schools
(*d*) No correction required

33. I am definitely late; the train *will have left* the station by the time I reach there.
(*a*) will be leaving (*b*) will leave
(*c*) would have left (*d*) No improvement

34. Shilpa was going to the temple *then Parul came on* meet her.
(*a*) after Parul was coming to
(*b*) when Parul was coming to
(*c*) when Parul came to
(*d*) before Parul was coming to
(*e*) No correction required

35. There is nothing *quite miserable* than handicap at such a tender age.
(*a*) as miserable (*b*) more miserable
(*c*) so miserable (*d*) very miserable
(*e*) No correction required

36. Young men and women should get *habituated* to reading and writing about current affairs. **(C.D.S. 1993)**
(*a*) prepared (*b*) trained
(*c*) used (*d*) No improvement

37. The bill will be paid *at sight or on demand*.
(*a*) at a sight or on a demand
(*b*) on sight or at demand
(*c*) at sight or demand
(*d*) No correction required

38. It is difficult for a simple person to see through her *artificial* schemes.
(*a*) artistic (*b*) artful
(*c*) aesthetic (*d*) No improvement **(C.B.I. 1995)**

39. Photographs from the satellites launched by NASA *at* the early 1970's have proved invaluable to the mapping of remote areas.
(*a*) towards (*b*) from
(*c*) since (*d*) No improvement

40. You ought not to *have gone* there, but you did. **(N.D.A. 1995)**
(*a*) be going (*b*) have been
(*c*) go (*d*) No improvement

41. Never has the inadequacy of police been in *clearer* focus than in the communal violence that flared up recently.
(*a*) higher (*b*) stronger
(*c*) better (*d*) sharper **(Translators' Exam, 1994)**

42. The main business of the Parliament is to deal with matters *pertained to* the Legislature.
(*a*) pertaining with (*b*) pertained with
(*c*) pertaining to (*d*) No improvement

43. *Being worked for* the whole day, you should have taken some rest and started the work tomorrow. **(Bank P.O. 1995)**
(*a*) After having work
(*b*) Having worked for
(*c*) Working for
(*d*) After being worked for
(*e*) No correction required

44. I wish *I have* all those luxuries my friend has.
(*a*) I will have (*b*) I am having
(*c*) I had (*d*) I had been having
(*e*) No correction required

45. Ravi has got many friends because he has got *much money*. **(C.D.S. 1992)**
(*a*) enough money (*b*) a lot of money
(*c*) bags of money (*d*) No improvement

46. You must try *making him to understand.*
(*a*) make him understand
(*b*) to making him understand
(*c*) to make him understand
(*d*) No improvement

47. He has cooked that meal so often he can do it with his *eyes closed*. **(N.D.A. 1993)**
(*a*) mind blank (*b*) eyes covered
(*c*) hands full (*d*) No improvemen

48. The enthusiastic voters were *queuing up* outside the polling station since morning.
(*a*) queued up (*b*) had queued up
(*c*) had been queuing up
(*d*) No improvement

49. Many a man *have died of cancer*.
(*a*) have died from cancer

(b) has died of cancer
(c) have been dying of cancer
(d) No improvement **(Railways, 1993)**

50. If you are living near a market place you should be ready *to bear* the disturbances caused by traffic.
(a) to bear with (b) to bear away
(c) to bear upon (d) No improvement

ANSWERS

1. (c)	**2.** (d)	**3.** (b)	**4.** (a)	**5.** (c)	**6.** (b)	**7.** (d)	**8.** (d)	**9.** (b)	**10.** (d)
11. (b)	**12.** (a)	**13.** (b)	**14.** (b)	**15.** (a)	**16.** (b)	**17.** (c)	**18.** (c)	**19.** (c)	**20.** (a)
21. (c)	**22.** (b)	**23.** (a)	**24.** (d)	**25.** (c)	**26.** (e)	**27.** (c)	**28.** (b)	**29.** (d)	**30.** (d)
31. (b)	**32.** (b)	**33.** (c)	**34.** (c)	**35.** (b)	**36.** (c)	**37.** (d)	**38.** (b)	**39.** (c)	**40.** (d)
41. (d)	**42.** (c)	**43.** (b)	**44.** (c)	**45.** (b)	**46.** (c)	**47.** (d)	**48.** (b)	**49.** (b)	**50.** (a)

PRACTICE SET 5

Directions : ***In each of the following questions, choose the alternative which can best improve the given sentence by substituting the italicised portion. If the sentence is correct as it is, choose 'No improvement' or 'No correction required' as your answer.***

1. Because of his mastery in this field, his suggestions *are wide accepted*.
(a) are widely accepted
(b) are wide acceptance
(c) have widely accepted
(d) have been wide accepted
(e) No correction required
(Bank P.O. 1993)

2. I hope, you vividly remember the premiere of the film when *I, my wife and you* were present in the hall.
(a) you, I and my wife
(b) my wife, I and you
(c) my wife, you and I
(d) No improvement

3. The fact finding committee has so far not made any *advancement*.
(a) progress (b) improvement
(c) stride (d) No improvement
(Translator's Exam, 1994)

4. *Having had* in the Foreign Service for a long time, Mr. Verma has met many prominent personalities.
(a) Having (b) He has been
(c) Having been (d) Had he been
(e) No correction required

5. Who does not know that this *was broadcasted* ten days ago? **(N.D.A. 1993)**
(a) had broadcast (b) was broadcast
(c) was broadcasting (d) No improvement

6. Since 1986, there *is* no earthquakes here.
(a) were being (b) have been
(c) are (d) No improvement

7. You are warned *against committing* the same mistake again. **(C.D.S. 1995)**
(a) for committing (b) against to commit
(c) to commit (d) No improvement

8. The teacher gave the students some *advice*. **(N.D.A. 1991)**
(a) advise (b) advises
(c) advices (d) No improvement

9. I shall *ring him* tomorrow in the afternoon.
(a) ring to him (b) ring up to him
(c) ring him up (d) No improvement

10. Older people *often* stay at home and watch TV because it is cold and dark in winter.
(a) seldom (b) frequently
(c) sometimes (d) No improvement

11. You must find *someone* to accompany you to Bombay. **(Stenographers' Exam, 1992)**
(a) no one (b) everyone
(c) anyone (d) No improvement

12. No sooner *he reached* home than all the villagers gathered at his home to listen to his story.
(a) would he reach (b) did he reach
(c) had he reached (d) No improvement

13. I wish I *was* with him. **(C.D.S. 1995)**
(a) have been (b) were
(c) am (d) No improvement

14. *Upto* the time the last vote was recorded it was difficult to decide whether victory lay with the ruling party or the opposition.
(a) To (b) Until

(*c*) Till (*d*) No improvement

15. He is the kindest and *generous of all my friends.* **(C.B.I. 1994)**
(*a*) more generous among all my friends
(*b*) more generous of all my friends
(*c*) the most generous of all my friends
(*d*) No improvement

16. I do not think I should tell you over and over again that *my family are early risers.*
(*a*) my family members are early risers
(*b*) my family is an early riser
(*c*) my family are an early riser
(*d*) No correction required

17. None of the guests *were introduced* to the bride. **(I.E.S. 1993)**
(*a*) introduced (*b*) was introduced
(*c*) have been introduced
(*d*) No improvement

18. Your brother has a great passion *to study*.
(*a*) for study (*b*) for studying
(*c*) to studying (*d*) No improvement

19. One should exercise *their* right to vote.
(*a*) his (*b*) our
(*c*) one's (*d*) No improvement
(N.D.A. 1996)

20. Putting in hard work to help others is what he likes *from* his heart.
(*a*) in (*b*) by
(*c*) at (*d*) No improvement

21. He stopped *to work* an hour ago.
(*a*) to working (*b*) to have worked
(*c*) working (*d*) No improvement
(N.D.A. 1994)

22. *Little* that I knew of the English language, was not sufficient to make me a teacher of English.
(*a*) Very little (*b*) The little
(*c*) A little (*d*) No improvement

23. Your results depend not only on how much you have studied *but how long* you have read. **(C.B.I. 1995)**
(*a*) but also how long
(*b*) but also on how long
(*c*) but also on how much long
(*d*) No improvement

24. As a gesture of goodwill India agreed to *write off* a huge amount of loan taken by some of her neighbours.
(*a*) do away with (*b*) put off
(*c*) give up (*d*) No improvement

25. She *cut a sad figure* in her first performance on the stage. **(C.D.S. 1994)**
(*a*) made a sorry figure
(*b*) cut a sorry face
(*c*) cut a sorry figure
(*d*) No improvement

26. Mr. Kulkarni is planning to settle in Kanpur as soon as he *will retire* in June next year.
(*a*) retires (*b*) is retired
(*c*) would retire (*d*) No improvement

27. When the professor fell off the stool, the students could not *avoid to laugh*.
(*a*) avoid laughing (*b*) refrain to laugh
(*c*) avoid laughter (*d*) stop laughter
(*e*) No correction required
(Bank P.O. 1992)

28. What *does agonise me most* is not this criticism, but the trivial reason behind it.
(*a*) I most agonised
(*b*) most agonising me
(*c*) agonises me most
(*d*) agonising me most
(*e*) No correction required
(S.B.I.P.O. 1994)

29. Ravi's father did not want him *to have spent* all his money at the fair.
(*a*) to be spending (*b*) to spend
(*c*) to have been spending
(*d*) No improvement

30. *All his answers* were correct. **(N.D.A. 1995)**
(*a*) His every answers
(*b*) His all answers
(*c*) All of his answers (*d*) No improvement

31. The young hikers went *as far as* they finally got lost in the valley.
(*a*) so far that (*b*) too far that
(*c*) so far as that (*d*) very far therefore
(*e*) No correction required

32. He gave me *an old scissor*.
(*a*) old scissor (*b*) an old scissors
(*c*) a pair of old scissors
(*d*) No improvement **(Railways, 1993)**

33. I shall finish up the work by the end of *this present month*.
(*a*) this month (*b*) this very month
(*c*) this same month
(*d*) this current month
(*e*) No correction required

34. He has been absent *for the past few months.*
(*a*) since the last (*b*) for last
(*c*) since the past
(*d*) No correction required

35. His trousers are *three sizes* large.
(*a*) three sizes too (*b*) three size
(*c*) three sizes over (*d*) No improvement
(Asstt. Grade, 1994)

36. He offered me tea but I *denied* it.
(*a*) refuted (*b*) neglected
(*c*) declined (*d*) No improvement

37. There is a shortage of well qualified teachers of most subjects, *specially of* English and Economics. **(U.D.C. 1994)**

(*a*) especially of (*b*) especially in
(*c*) in special of (*d*) No improvement

38. Desertification, *condition of the desert spreading into previously arable land,* is threatening the planet.
(*a*) spread of desert conditions into previously arable land
(*b*) condition where the desert spreads into previously arable land
(*c*) spread of conditions of desert where land was previously arable
(*d*) the situation when desert conditions spread into previously arable land
(*e*) No correction required

39. *The more they earn, more they spend.*
(*a*) More they earn, more they spend
(*b*) More they earn, the more they spend
(*c*) The more they earn, the more they spend
(*d*) No improvement
(C.D.S. 1995)

40. Those who study *at sixes and sevens* seldom succeed.
(*a*) by fits and starts
(*b*) by leaps and bounds
(*c*) from pillar to post
(*d*) No improvement

41. It is *easier walking than run.*
(*a*) easier walking to running
(*b*) easier to walk than to run
(*c*) easier walking than running
(*d*) No improvement **(S.C.R.A. 1994)**

42. Whenever my students come across new words, I ask them *to look for them* in the dictionary. **(C.D.S. 1994)**
(*a*) to look at them (*b*) to look it up
(*c*) to look them up (*d*) No improvement

43. They appointed him *as a manager* as he is efficient.
(*a*) as manager (*b*) manager
(*c*) a manager (*d*) No improvement

44. He dislikes the word dislike, *isn't he*?
(*a*) does he (*b*) doesn't he
(*c*) didn't he (*d*) hasn't he
(*e*) No correction required
(Bank P.O. 1994)

45. The prisoners walked slowly for they knew that as soon as they *cross* the gate the jailor would ask them to jog.
(*a*) crossed (*b*) would cross
(*c*) had crossed (*d*) shall cross
(*e*) No improvement

46. I asked him *that why he is* so lazy.
(*a*) why is he (*b*) why he was
(*c*) that why is he (*d*) No improvement
(U.D.C. 1993)

47. The brochure, which is being enclosed with the application form, will give you *information* that you need.
(*a*) informations (*b*) the information
(*c*) an information (*d*) No improvement
(C.D.S. 1991)

48. The film show *began* when we arrived in the hall.
(*a*) had began (*b*) had begun
(*c*) would begin (*d*) No improvement

49. We heard of *them having discovered* another stream.
(*a*) them discovering (*b*) their discovering
(*c*) their having discovered
(*d*) No improvement

50. You must *accustom yourself with* new ideas. **(N.D.A. 1996)**
(*a*) accustomed with (*b*) accustom to
(*c*) accustom yourself to
(*d*) No improvement

ANSWERS

1. (*a*)	**2.** (*d*)	**3.** (*a*)	**4.** (*c*)	**5.** (*b*)	**6.** (*b*)	**7.** (*d*)	**8.** (*d*)	**9.** (*c*)	**10.** (*d*)
11. (*d*)	**12.** (*b*)	**13.** (*b*)	**14.** (*c*)	**15.** (*c*)	**16.** (*d*)	**17.** (*b*)	**18.** (*b*)	**19.** (*c*)	**20.** (*a*)
21. (*c*)	**22.** (*b*)	**23.** (*b*)	**24.** (*d*)	**25.** (*c*)	**26.** (*a*)	**27.** (*a*)	**28.** (*c*)	**29.** (*b*)	**30.** (*d*)
31. (*a*)	**32.** (*c*)	**33.** (*a*)	**34.** (*d*)	**35.** (*a*)	**36.** (*c*)	**37.** (*b*)	**38.** (*d*)	**39.** (*c*)	**40.** (*a*)
41. (*b*)	**42.** (*c*)	**43.** (*b*)	**44.** (*b*)	**45.** (*a*)	**46.** (*b*)	**47.** (*b*)	**48.** (*b*)	**49.** (*c*)	**50.** (*c*)

PRACTICE SET 6

Directions : *In each of the following questions, a part of the sentence is italicised. Below are given alternatives to the italicised part which may improve the sentence. Choose the correct alternative. If no improvement is needed, mark your answer as 'No improvement' or 'No correction required'*

1. Can you tell me *why did you not speak* the truth? **(B.S.R.B. 1996)**
(*a*) why did not you speak
(*b*) that why did you not speak
(*c*) why you did not speak
(*d*) why did you not spoke
(*e*) No improvement

2. The function of education is to create such human beings *which* are integrated and therefore intelligent.
(*a*) who (*b*) that
(*c*) as (*d*) No improvement

3. The boy *which* came to see me this morning had come from Agra.
(*a*) that (*b*) whom
(*c*) who (*d*) No improvement
(C.D.S. 1992)

4. The partners swore *from fighting again*.
(*a*) not fighting again
(*b*) by not to fight again
(*c*) that they wouldn't fight again
(*d*) No improvement

5. Not till he got home *he did realise* that he had lost his keys in the theatre.
(*a*) did he realise (*b*) he did not realise
(*c*) he realised (*d*) No improvement
(Railways, 1994)

6. He has a house *for letting*.
(*a*) for letting out (*b*) to let
(*c*) to rent out (*d*) No improvement

7. Please remind me *of posting* these letters of my relatives. **(C.D.S. 1994)**
(*a*) for posting (*b*) to post
(*c*) by posting (*d*) No improvement

8. A boy has been *sunk* in this river.
(*a*) drowned (*b*) immersed
(*c*) submerged (*d*) No improvement

9. His manners indicate that he has no other intention *than* to steal his money.
(*a*) rather (*b*) except
(*c*) but (*d*) No improvement

10. Had we been on time, we *would not have* missed the train. **(S.B.I.P.O. 1992)**
(*a*) will not have (*b*) might have
(*c*) would have been (*d*) had not
(*e*) No correction required

11. *No king* in that period was so intensely involved in the welfare of his people as king Ashoka.
(*a*) Neither king (*b*) No other king
(*c*) None of the kings
(*d*) No improvement

12. When we saw him last, he *ran* to catch a bus. **(C.D.S. 1994)**
(*a*) was running (*b*) has run
(*c*) had run (*d*) No improvement

13. He enjoys nothing more than *drawing* swords with others.
(*a*) crossing (*b*) playing
(*c*) clashing (*d*) No improvement

14. *No* hill station is as beautiful as Darjeeling with its scenic beauty.
(*a*) Neither (*b*) No other
(*c*) Not other (*d*) No improvement

15. If you get confused while performing the act, just *don't stop to try*. **(S.B.I.P.O. 1991)**
(*a*) keep your try on
(*b*) continue your tries
(*c*) not give up trying (*d*) keep on trying
(*e*) No correction required

16. He *insisted on* he was innocent
(*a*) insisted that (*b*) insisted on that
(*c*) insists that (*d*) No improvement

17. It was indeed a shock for her, but she has *later* recovered from it. **(I.E.S. 1994)**
(*a*) afterwards (*b*) since
(*c*) then (*d*) No improvement

18. The doctor said that there was no *cause of* anxiety.
(*a*) cause to (*b*) cause for
(*c*) cause with (*d*) No improvement

19. I must study my books today *as I have to give* an examination tomorrow.
(*a*) for I have to give
(*b*) since I have to give
(*c*) as I have to take
(*d*) No improvement **(U.D.C. 1993)**

20. If you *call to him* and explain your problem he will help you.
(*a*) call at him (*b*) call upon him
(*c*) call in him (*d*) No improvement

21. Anybody would *like assist you* for improvement in the work. **(Bank P.O. 1992)**
(*a*) you like to assist
(*b*) like assist to you
(*c*) like to assist you
(*d*) No correction required

22. Two hours have elapsed since he *had fallen* asleep.
(*a*) fell (*b*) has fallen
(*c*) was fallen (*d*) No improvement

23. *Due to these reasons* we are all in favour of universal compulsory education.
(*a*) By these reasons
(*b*) For these reasons
(*c*) Out of these reasons
(*d*) No improvement **(C.D.S. 1995)**

24. When it was dark they decided to *put at* an inn.
(*a*) put up at (*b*) put in at
(*c*) put off with (*d*) put out in
(*e*) No improvement

25. He has very good command *on* English.
(*a*) of (*b*) over
(*c*) in (*d*) No improvement
(C.D.S. 1991)

26. Many a *young man have served his* country nobly.
(*a*) young men have served their
(*b*) young men have served his
(*c*) young man has served his
(*d*) No correction required

27. I am *looking forward to see* you soon.
(*a*) looking forward towards seeing
(*b*) looking forward for seeing
(*c*) looking forward to seeing
(*d*) No improvement **(Asstt. Grade, 1995)**

28. She would not go to his house unless I *go* with her.
(*a*) would go (*b*) went
(*c*) shall go (*d*) No improvement

29. His colleagues could not tell me *why did he not come* to office yesterday.
(*a*) why not had he come
(*b*) why he did not come
(*c*) why had he not come
(*d*) No improvement **(N.D.A. 1992)**

30. Bad movies affect people living in today's society more than *they did* in previous years.
(*a*) they had been done
(*b*) they had been doing
(*c*) they had done
(*d*) they were doing
(*e*) No correction required

31. I waited for half an hour for my friend, but he didn't *turn in*. **(S.C.R.A. 1993)**
(*a*) turn about (*b*) turn around
(*c*) turn up (*d*) No improvement

32. I will now deal with him in a manner different from the one *I have adopted* so far.
(*a*) I adopted (*b*) I was adopting
(*c*) I have been adopting
(*d*) No improvement

33. I shall not go *until I am invited*.
(*a*) if not I am invited
(*b*) till I am invited
(*c*) unless I am invited
(*d*) No improvement
(Stenographers' Exam, 1995)

34. He may have aged *when I last saw him*.
(*a*) from when I last saw him
(*b*) since I last saw him
(*c*) before I last saw him
(*d*) No correction required

35. Our departure from this place now depends on *their coming* here.
(*a*) they come (*b*) them coming
(*c*) they coming (*d*) their's coming
(*e*) No correction required
(Bank P.O. 1993)

36. Don't forget to telephone me after you *reach* Delhi.
(*a*) shall reach (*b*) you have reached
(*c*) would reach (*d*) will have reached
(*e*) No correction required

37. He *should not had* done it.
(*a*) should had not (*b*) should not have
(*c*) should have (*d*) had not
(*e*) No correction required
(Bank P.O. 1994)

38. Ramakrishna *availed himself of* all the leave to his credit.
(*a*) availed of (*b*) availed to
(*c*) availed (*d*) No improvement

39. The assistant was asked *that why he was* generally late. **(B.S.R.B. 1996)**
(*a*) why was he (*b*) why that he was
(*c*) why he was (*d*) that why he had been
(*e*) No correction required

40. After the heavy rains last week, the water in the lake *raised another two feet*.
(*a*) would raise another two feet.
(*b*) rised another two feet
(*c*) rose another two feet
(*d*) No improvement **(C.D.S. 1994)**

41. A true soldier is always *prepared to lie* down his life for the sake of the nation.
(*a*) prepared to lay (*b*) preparing to lie
(*c*) preparing to be laid
(*d*) prepared to be laying
(*e*) No correction required

42. It was quite clear that the runner *could be able* to improve upon his own record.
(*a*) will be able (*b*) should be able
(*c*) would be able (*d*) No improvement
(N.D.A. 1995)

43. They were all charmed by the *sweet and soothing* music.
(*a*) sweet and soothingly
(*b*) sweetly but soothing
(*c*) sweetened and soothing
(*d*) sweetly and soothing
(*e*) No correction required

44. With a thundering roar the huge rocket *soared up* from the launching pad.
(*a*) took off (*b*) went upwards
(*c*) flew up (*d*) No improvement
(C.D.S. 1993)

45. My elder sister and her daughter *helps me in* my domestic work. **(B.S.R.B. 1990)**
(*a*) helps me for (*b*) help me in
(*c*) help me about (*d*) helped me about
(*e*) No correction required

46. The good fortune *of being your student* in my younger days has helped me greatly in my life.
(*a*) of my being your student
(*b*) of myself being your student
(*c*) of my having been your student
(*d*) No correction required

47. I complimented him *for* his success in the examination. **(S.C.R.A. 1994)**
(*a*) about (*b*) on
(*c*) at (*d*) No improvement

48. Books for the used-book sales should be in good condition *and should have no writing in them or be underlined.*
(*a*) without having any writing or no underlining in them
(*b*) and contain no writing or underlining
(*c*) without containing writing or be underlined
(*d*) and should not have writings written or not be underlined
(*e*) No correction required **(R.B.I. 1990)**

49. We must *fight shy from* wicked company.
(*a*) fight shy with (*b*) fight shy off
(*c*) fight shy of (*d*) shy from
(*e*) No improvement

50. The orphans have been clamouring for nutritious food *from the past* two weeks.
(*a*) for past (*b*) since the past
(*c*) for the past (*d*) No improvement
(C.D.S. 1995)

ANSWERS

1. (*c*)	**2.** (*c*)	**3.** (*c*)	**4.** (*c*)	**5.** (*a*)	**6.** (*b*)	**7.** (*b*)	**8.** (*a*)	**9.** (*c*)	**10.** (*e*)
11. (*b*)	**12.** (*a*)	**13.** (*c*)	**14.** (*b*)	**15.** (*d*)	**16.** (*a*)	**17.** (*b*)	**18.** (*b*)	**19.** (*c*)	**20.** (*b*)
21. (*c*)	**22.** (*a*)	**23.** (*b*)	**24.** (*a*)	**25.** (*a*)	**26.** (*c*)	**27.** (*c*)	**28.** (*b*)	**29.** (*b*)	**30.** (*c*)
31. (*a*)	**32.** (*c*)	**33.** (*c*)	**34.** (*b*)	**35.** (*b*)	**36.** (*e*)	**37.** (*b*)	**38.** (*d*)	**39.** (*c*)	**40.** (*c*)
41. (*a*)	**42.** (*c*)	**43.** (*e*)	**44.** (*b*)	**45.** (*b*)	**46.** (*c*)	**47.** (*b*)	**48.** (*b*)	**49.** (*c*)	**50.** (*c*)

PRACTICE SET 7

Directions : ***In the following questions, a sentence has been given wherein a word/group of words has been italicised. Some alternatives are suggested for the italicised words/group of words which improves the sentence. In case no improvement is needed in the sentence, your answer is 'No improvement' or 'No correction required'.***

1. Will you *lend me few rupees* in this hour of need? **(Section Officers, 1993)**
(*a*) borrow me a few rupees
(*b*) lend me any rupees
(*c*) lend me a few rupees
(*d*) No improvement

2. I *made* him good-bye.
(*a*) wished (*b*) complimented
(*c*) bade (*d*) No improvement

3. We *must make for* our foreign policy on the basis of guarding national interest alone. **(Bank P.O. 1994)**
(*a*) must make to (*b*) have made for
(*c*) must make (*d*) must be making to
(*e*) No correction required

4. She wondered *if* the children were as lonely as she was.
(*a*) that if (*b*) whether
(*c*) that (*d*) No improvement

5. The man *who will score the maximum points,* will carry the trophy. **(C.D.S. 1992)**
(*a*) who scores the maximum points
(*b*) who the maximum points scores
(*c*) who would score the maximum points
(*d*) No improvement

6. The farmers *are working* in the field from sunrise and will continue to do so until sunset.
(*a*) have worked (*b*) have been working
(*c*) were working (*d*) No improvement

7. His father wrote to him, "It is high time you *start* preparing for the forthcoming examination". **(N.D.A. 1994)**
(*a*) would start (*b*) started
(*c*) had started (*d*) No improvement

8. Many of the boys in our class *were of kind who would be a nuisance* everywhere.
(*a*) were of the kind who would be a nuisance
(*b*) were of the kind who would be nuisance
(*c*) were of a kind who would be nuisance
(*d*) were to be nuisance

9. The standard of living of the working class is higher *than was the case thirty years ago*. **(Translator's Exam, 1994)**
(*a*) than it was before thirty years
(*b*) than that of thirty years ago
(*c*) than what it was thirty years ago
(*d*) No improvement

10. The child has been in the sick bed *for the last* one week. **(N.D.A. 1992)**
(*a*) for the past (*b*) for past
(*c*) since the past (*d*) No improvement

11. One of my colleagues *is an expert* in homoeopathy.
(*a*) is expert
(*b*) has expertised
(*c*) has been expertised
(*d*) No improvement

12. They are social insects, *living in communities*, regulated by definite laws, each member of society bearing a well-defined and separate part in the work of a colony. **(C.D.S. 1994)**
(*a*) living among a community
(*b*) who are living in communities
(*c*) who lives with a community
(*d*) No improvement

13. The roads are wet; it *must had* rained last night.
(*a*) might had (*b*) must have been
(*c*) must have (*d*) would have
(*e*) No correction required

14. He has been growing weaker and his life now *hangs like a thread*. **(C.B.I. 1995)**
(*a*) hangs with threads
(*b*) hangs by a thread
(*c*) hung on a thread
(*d*) No improvement

15. I advise you to *call at* the doctor for consultation.
(*a*) call in (*b*) call to
(*c*) call upon (*d*) No improvement

16. To get one's name in the Rowland Ward's book of hunting records was the *hot* ambition of every serious hunter.
(*a*) burning (*b*) extreme
(*c*) high (*d*) No improvement
(Assistant Grade, 1996)

17. She does not know *to sing and dance*.
(*a*) how to sing and how to dance
(*b*) how to sing and dance
(*c*) to sing and also dance
(*d*) No improvement

18. She did not ask *any question to him*.
(*a*) any question from him
(*b*) him any question
(*c*) to him any question
(*d*) No improvement **(U.D.C. 1995)**

19. I would like *that you finish the project on time*.
(*a*) you to finish the project on time
(*b*) you finishing the project on time
(*c*) that you should finish the project on time
(*d*) No improvement

20. *On some evenings* I leave office as late as seven o'clock. **(C.D.S. 1995)**
(*a*) In some evenings
(*b*) Some evenings
(*c*) On some of the evenings
(*d*) No improvement

21. The robber *entered into* the old man's room very quietly.
(*a*) entered inside (*b*) entered
(*c*) entered in (*d*) No improvement

22. Hold *hands of your child* while crossing the road. **(C.B.I. 1994)**
(*a*) your child's hands
(*b*) your child's hand
(*c*) hand of your child
(*d*) No improvement

23. It is *all and one* to me whether he lives in Bombay or Calcutta.
(*a*) all one (*b*) all but one
(*c*) all or one
(*d*) No correction required

24. I am tired as *I am working* since 8 o'clock in the morning.
(*a*) I was working
(*b*) I have been working
(*c*) I had been working
(*d*) No improvement

25. Had we been alone, we would have contended ourselves with any plain food that *give* us strength.
(*a*) should give (*b*) would give
(*c*) gives (*d*) would have given
(*e*) No improvement

26. There is a dearth of *woman doctor* in our state. We shall have to recruit some from the other states. **(I.E.S. 1994)**
(*a*) women doctor (*b*) woman doctors
(*c*) women doctors (*d*) No improvement

27. He was likely to win the elections *by the sweeping majority*.
(*a*) by a sweeping majority
(*b*) with sweeping a majority
(*c*) with the sweeping majority
(*d*) No improvement

28. There is plenty of time to *catch* the train.
(*a*) reach (*b*) get
(*c*) hold (*d*) No improvement

29. The policeman stopped him for jumping the red light but *let him out*.
(*a*) let him off (*b*) let him through
(*c*) let him by (*d*) No improvement

30. You will be late if you *do not leave* now.
(*a*) will not leave (*b*) did not leave
(*c*) left (*d*) did not happen to leave
(*e*) No correction required
(Bank P.O.1994)

31. They invited *I and my friend* to tea.
(*a*) my friend and I (*b*) my friend and me
(*c*) to me and my friend
(*d*) No improvement

32. Every time I *go in a lift* to my sixth floor apartment, I remember the calm and serenity of my ancestral home in the village. **(C.D.S. 1993)**
(*a*) move in a lift (*b*) take a lift
(*c*) ascend in a lift (*d*) No improvement

33. The shopkeeper said graciously, "I'll quote no price; the article is yours *for asking*."
(*a*) for the asking (*b*) if you ask
(*c*) for only asking (*d*) No improvement

34. Rohit assured Sunita that he *would look at* her work while she was on leave.
(*a*) would overlook (*b*) would look after
(*c*) would look down upon (*d*) will look
(*e*) No improvement **(B.S.R.B. 1996)**

35. He told us the story *in a nutshell*.
(*a*) in nutshell (*b*) in the nutshell
(*c*) putting it in a nut
(*d*) No improvement

36. It was hard to believe that he *was dead* for two years. **(N.D.A. 1995)**
(*a*) is dead (*b*) has been dead
(*c*) had been dead (*d*) No improvement

37. He prefers *to walk than to ride*.
(*a*) walking than riding
(*b*) to walk over riding
(*c*) walking to riding
(*d*) No improvement

38. The accused now flatly denies *have admitted* his guilt in this first statement.
(*a*) has admitted (*b*) having admitted
(*c*) had admitted
(*d*) have been admitting
(*e*) No correction required
(S.B.I.P.O. 1994)

39. The whole town *was being decorated* for the tourist week.
(*a*) is to be decorated
(*b*) will be decorated
(*c*) was to be decorated
(*d*) No correction required

40. The little child was knocked *out* by a car.
(*a*) up (*b*) away
(*c*) down (*d*) No improvement

41. He asked me if I *can* help him to lift the box. **(C.D.S. 1992)**
(*a*) may (*b*) would
(*c*) will (*d*) No improvement

42. She tried to eat another leaf of lettuce but she could no longer *fight* the stench.
(*a*) face (*b*) keep
(*c*) stand (*d*) No improvement

43. *Have you not reached* in time, we would have lost our lives. **(Bank P.O. 1995)**
(*a*) Had you not reach
(*b*) If you have not reached
(*c*) Had you not reached
(*d*) If you would not have reached
(*e*) No correction required

44. I wish that I *read* this book before the seminar.
(*a*) had read (*b*) can read
(*c*) was reading (*d*) No improvement

45. The rules of chess require that one *made* only one move at a time. **(I.E.S. 1993)**
(*a*) makes (*b*) will make
(*c*) make (*d*) No improvement

46. Let us *partake* a meal before we start.
(*a*) partake of (*b*) partake off
(*c*) partake in (*d*) No improvement

47. Do take an umbrella with you *lest you do not get wet*.
(*a*) lest you might not get wet
(*b*) lest you should not get wet
(*c*) lest you should get wet
(*d*) No improvement **(N.D.A. 1993)**

48. They will be coming to attend the farewell party, *isn't it*?
(*a*) aren't they? (*b*) wouldn't they ?
(*c*) won't they? (*d*) No improvement

49. Taxpayers *are to* be conscious of their privileges. **(C.D.S. 1995)**
(*a*) need (*b*) have to
(*c*) ought to (*d*) No improvement

50. You can't go that way, I'm afraid, as the road is *in repairs*. **(Railways, 1993)**
(*a*) under repairs (*b*) under repair
(*c*) on repairs (*d*) No improvement

ANSWERS

1. (*c*)	**2.** (*c*)	**3.** (*c*)	**4.** (*b*)	**5.** (*a*)	**6.** (*b*)	**7.** (*b*)	**8.** (*a*)	**9.** (*c*)	**10.** (*a*)
11. (*d*)	**12.** (*d*)	**13.** (*c*)	**14.** (*b*)	**15.** (*c*)	**16.** (*c*)	**17.** (*b*)	**18.** (*b*)	**19.** (*a*)	**20.** (*d*)
21. (*b*)	**22.** (*b*)	**23.** (*a*)	**24.** (*b*)	**25.** (*c*)	**26.** (*c*)	**27.** (*a*)	**28.** (*d*)	**29.** (*a*)	**30.** (*e*)
31. (*b*)	**32.** (*b*)	**33.** (*a*)	**34.** (*b*)	**35.** (*d*)	**36.** (*c*)	**37.** (*c*)	**38.** (*b*)	**39.** (*d*)	**40.** (*c*)
41. (*b*)	**42.** (*c*)	**43.** (*c*)	**44.** (*a*)	**45.** (*b*)	**46.** (*a*)	**47.** (*c*)	**48.** (*c*)	**49.** (*b*)	**50.** (*b*)

PRACTICE SET 8

Directions : ***In each of the following questions, a part of the sentence is italicised. Below are given alternatives to the italicised part which may improve the sentence. Choose the correct alternative. If no improvement is needed, mark your answer as 'No improvement' or 'No correction required'.***

1. I would have waited for you at the station if I *knew* that you would come.
(*a*) had known (*b*) have known
(*c*) was knowing (*d*) No improvement
(C.D.S. 1995)

2. I will not go *till he arrives*.
(*a*) till he has arrived
(*b*) until he arrives
(*c*) unless he has arrived
(*d*) No improvement

3. You *ought not behave* like that.
(*a*) ought to not behave
(*b*) ought not to behave
(*c*) ought not to have behaved
(*d*) No improvement

4. He is not *in the good books* of his master.
(*a*) in the good book
(*b*) into the good books
(*c*) in the better books
(*d*) in the best book
(*e*) No correction required
(S.B.I.P.O. 1991)

5. I have *done good at* the examination.
(*a*) attempted well at
(*b*) gone well over
(*c*) fared well in
(*d*) No correction required

6. I need not offer any explanation regarding this incident- my behaviour *is speaking itself*.
(*a*) speaks about itself
(*b*) speaks for itself
(*c*) has been speaking
(*d*) will speak to itself **(Bank P.O. 1994)**

7. As soon *did* the Manager came, the clerks started typing.
(*a*) was (*b*) had
(*c*) as (*d*) No improvement

8. There is an endless *running* of traffic on the Delhi- Ghaziabad road.
(*a*) heaviness (*b*) river
(*c*) stream (*d*) No improvement
(Stenographers' Exam, 1994)

9. The Chinese *are said to have* invented ice-cream almost three thousand years ago. **(B.S.R.B. 1992)**
(*a*) are said that they
(*b*) are saying to have
(*c*) have been said to have
(*d*) had said to have
(*e*) No correction required

10. This work is worse *by all that you did*.
(*a*) all of you did
(*b*) to what you did before
(*c*) than what you did before
(*d*) No improvement

11. He may have aged *when I last saw him*.
(*a*) since I saw him
(*b*) since I last saw him
(*c*) before I last saw him
(*d*) No correction required

12. I would like *to avail* a fifteen days' holiday this summer. **(C.D.S. 1994)**
(*a*) to avail myself (*b*) to avail of
(*c*) to avail myself of (*d*) No improvement

13. Work hard *lest you will fail* in the examinations.
(*a*) lest you would fail
(*b*) lest you should fail
(*c*) lest you shall fail (*d*) No improvement

14. The *weather* of Shimla does not suit me.
(*a*) climate (*b*) atmosphere
(*c*) environment (*d*) No improvement

15. *I think in my opinion* that all those who claim to be honest are not really so.
(*a*) In my opinion, I believe
(*b*) It seems to me

(*c*) It is my believing
(*d*) My believing is
(*e*) No correction required
(Bank P.O. 1992)

16. It *was a week* since he came home to his mother.
(*a*) is a week (*b*) shall be a week
(*c*) has been a week (*d*) had been a week
(*e*) No improvement

17. This project would encourage development and enable every villager *to govern their* own destiny.
(*a*) to govern his (*b*) to governing his
(*c*) may govern their
(*d*) have governed their
(*e*) No correction required
(Bank P.O. 1994)

18. The workers *protested* the Management's decision of not giving bonus that year.
(*a*) protested to (*b*) protested against
(*c*) protested at (*d*) protested for
(*e*) No improvement

19. *All along the journey* she remained silent.
(*a*) All along in the journey
(*b*) All during the journey
(*c*) All through the journey
(*d*) Throughout all journey
(*e*) No correction required

20. He is ill *from* typhoid.
(*a*) with (*b*) of
(*c*) off (*d*) No improvement

21. The officer *whom I went* reported that my case was pending. **(C.B.I. 1993)**
(*a*) whom I went to (*b*) who I went
(*c*) that I went to (*d*) No improvement

22. He killed the enemy *by his sword*.
(*a*) by sword (*b*) by a sword
(*c*) through his sword
(*d*) with his sword
(*e*) No improvement

23. He *enthusiastically* stated that his suggestions should be accepted without delay.
(*a*) eagerly (*b*) emphatically
(*c*) promptly (*d*) No improvement

24. She had no difficulty *to settle down* to her new life in the city. **(S.C.R.A. 1994)**
(*a*) in settling down (*b*) for settling down
(*c*) to settling down (*d*) No improvement

25. Do inform me of your well being after you *reach* Bombay.
(*a*) will reach (*b*) will have reached
(*c*) shall reach (*d*) No improvement

26. If I were a millionaire, *I would have helped* the poor. **(C.D.S. 1995)**
(*a*) can help (*b*) could have helped
(*c*) would help (*d*) No improvement

27. Right there she decided that she *too would become* part of that world.
(*a*) also will become (*b*) too will become
(*c*) too might become (*d*) too could become
(*e*) No correction required

28. They continued to work in the field *despite of the heavy rains*.
(*a*) inspite the heavy rains
(*b*) although heavily rains
(*c*) even though it rained heavily
(*d*) even though there is heavy rain
(*e*) No improvement **(Bank P.O. 1993)**

29. The walls of this house *need to be painted* again as soon as possible.
(*a*) need to have been painted
(*b*) should be painted
(*c*) ought to have been painted
(*d*) No improvement

30. They watched the sea lions *being fed* with fish. **(N.D.A. 1992)**
(*a*) had been fed (*b*) are being fed
(*c*) have been fed (*d*) No improvement

31. Nelson Mandela struggled hard to get equality *from* the whites in South Africa.
(*a*) for (*b*) with
(*c*) at (*d*) No improvement
(C.B.I. 1994)

32. He will try to succeed in business *by fair means or foul*.
(*a*) by fair means or by foul
(*b*) by fair or foul means
(*c*) by any means (*d*) No improvement

33. Despite his old age, his movements were as spirited as *a young man*.
(*a*) a young man's (*b*) if a young man
(*c*) those of a young man
(*d*) of a young man
(*e*) No correction required **(S.B.I.P.O. 1991)**

34. For me, journey by air is *preferable than* that by train.
(*a*) much more preferable than
(*b*) preferable to
(*c*) more preferable to
(*d*) No correction required

35. The floor of the hall was *covered by* a carpet. **(N.D.A. 1991)**
(*a*) covered with (*b*) covered upon
(*c*) covered in (*d*) No improvement

36. Michael, seated in the visitors' gallery, glanced at his watch for the third time *in* the past five minutes.
(*a*) within (*b*) during
(*c*) since (*d*) No improvement

37. Taxes are high in this country, *aren't they*?
(Bank P.O. 1990)
(*a*) aren't taxes? (*b*) don't they?
(*c*) do they? (*d*) isn't it?
(*e*) No correction required

38. Every human advance carries with it not only automatic benefits but also a new responsibility, and we must remain constantly *aware for* the dangers that lie in the possible misuse of our enormous skills. **(I.E.S. 1993)**
(*a*) aware about (*b*) aware of
(*c*) aware to (*d*) No improvement

39. You have no idea what would happen if *word of this leaked out*.
(*a*) a word of this leaks out
(*b*) word of this leaks out
(*c*) a word of this will leak out
(*d*) No improvement

40. After the successful performance of the great actor was over, there was *thunder-struck* applause for a few minutes. **(Bank P.O. 1994)**
(*a*) fearful (*b*) cheerful
(*c*) decisive (*d*) thunderous
(*e*) No correction required

41. *What struck me most* was their kindness.
(*a*) What struck one more
(*b*) What stroke one more
(*c*) What stroke one most
(*d*) No improvement

42. My brother as well as my sister *are staying* with me. **(N.D.A. 1994)**
(*a*) have stayed (*b*) were staying
(*c*) is staying (*d*) No improvement

43. She insisted *for accompanying* her husband on the tour.
(*a*) on accompanying (*b*) in accompanying
(*c*) to accompany (*d*) No improvement

44. He is *so handsome* man that people turn round to look at him.
(*a*) very handsome (*b*) such a handsome
(*c*) too handsome (*d*) No improvement
(Stenographers' Exam, 1992)

45. This time she is coming in holidays for an *extending* stay here.
(*a*) extensive (*b*) extension
(*c*) extended (*d*) No improvement

46. Any order which *curbs* a police officer from doing his duty is itself unlawful and should not be obeyed.
(*a*) restricts (*b*) prevents
(*c*) stops (*d*) obstructs
(Translators' Exam, 1994)

47. When Vinod came home from the party, he found his wife *had slept*.
(*a*) sleeping (*b*) was sleeping
(*c*) has been sleeping
(*d*) No correction required

48. With the Hubble Space Telescope, astronomers expect to learn the age and size of the universe and to *probe* its origin, evolution, and ultimate fate.
(*a*) probe after (*b*) probe for
(*c*) probe in (*d*) No improvement
(C.D.S. 1991)

49. I shall try to finish reading this novel by the end of *this present month*.
(*a*) this current month
(*b*) this month
(*c*) this very month (*d*) No improvement

50. He found it difficult to *adapt to* the changed circumstances.
(*a*) adapt himself to (*b*) adapt with
(*c*) adapt according to
(*d*) No improvement
(Assistant Grade, 1994)

ANSWERS

1. (*a*)	**2.** (*b*)	**3.** (*c*)	**4.** (*e*)	**5.** (*c*)	**6.** (*b*)	**7.** (*c*)	**8.** (*c*)	**9.** (*e*)	**10.** (*c*)
11. (*b*)	**12.** (*c*)	**13.** (*b*)	**14.** (*a*)	**15.** (*a*)	**16.** (*c*)	**17.** (*a*)	**18.** (*b*)	**19.** (*c*)	**20.** (*a*)
21. (*a*)	**22.** (*d*)	**23.** (*b*)	**24.** (*a*)	**25.** (*d*)	**26.** (*c*)	**27.** (*e*)	**28.** (*c*)	**29.** (*d*)	**30.** (*d*)
31. (*b*)	**32.** (*d*)	**33.** (*c*)	**34.** (*b*)	**35.** (*a*)	**36.** (*c*)	**37.** (*e*)	**38.** (*b*)	**39.** (*d*)	**40.** (*d*)
41. (*d*)	**42.** (*c*)	**43.** (*a*)	**44.** (*b*)	**45.** (*c*)	**46.** (*b*)	**47.** (*a*)	**48.** (*b*)	**49.** (*c*)	**50.** (*a*)

PRACTICE SET 9

Directions : *In each of the following questions, a part of the sentence is italicised. Below are given alternatives to the italicised part which may improve the sentence. Choose the correct alternative. If no improvement is needed, the answer is 'No improvement' or 'No correction required'.*

1. He was bitten by a snake, *walking in the garden*.
(*a*) as he walked in the garden
(*b*) while he walked in the garden
(*c*) while he was walking in the garden
(*d*) No improvement

2. No one could explain how a calm and balanced person like him could *penetrate* such a mindless act on his friends.
(*a*) perpetuate (*b*) perpetrate
(*c*) precipitate (*d*) No improvement **(C.D.S. 1995)**

3. He kept us all in *suspension* regarding his future plans.
(*a*) surprise (*b*) suspense
(*c*) suspicion (*d*) No improvement

4. I gave him *the little* money that I could spare then. **(C.D.S. 1992)**
(*a*) very little (*b*) some little
(*c*) a little (*d*) No improvement

5. Mahatma Gandhi was by far *a great man* of India.
(*a*) a very great man (*b*) too great a man
(*c*) the greatest man (*d*) No improvement

6. No sooner had the umpire given the batsman out *than the crowd* rushed into the field. **(S.C.R.A. 1994)**
(*a*) but the people (*b*) when the crowds
(*c*) and the crowd (*d*) No improvement

7. Eve-teasing is not only a moral offence *but* a crime punishable under law.
(*a*) as well as (*b*) as also
(*c*) but also (*d*) No correction required

8. Within a few years most of the fertile land *had underwent* forcible indigo cultivation. **(N.D.A. 1995)**
(*a*) has underwent (*b*) had undergone
(*c*) was undergone (*d*) No improvement

9. Reema didn't pay the subscription, and Nisha *didn't either*.
(*a*) did not (*b*) didn't neither
(*c*) did either (*d*) No improvement

10. If you have paid only twenty rupees for this purse, it *has really cheap*.
(*a*) has really cheapest
(*b*) is really cheap
(*c*) has been really cheapest
(*d*) is real cheap
(*e*) No correction required **(B.S.R.B. 1996)**

11. If the pain *is returning*, you would better take another pill. **(Asstt. Grade, 1995)**
(*a*) has returned (*b*) should return
(*c*) returned (*d*) No improvement

12. *From where did he obtain the money* is a mystery.
(*a*) Where from did he obtain the money
(*b*) Where did he obtain the money from
(*c*) Where he obtained the money from
(*d*) No improvement

13. Do you *remember to meet her* at my house last year? **(U.D.C. 1993)**
(*a*) remember of meeting her
(*b*) remember about meeting her
(*c*) remember having met her
(*d*) No improvement

14. *If you have been* careful, you could have avoided the accident.
(*a*) Have you had been
(*b*) If you are
(*c*) Had you have been
(*d*) Had you been
(*e*) No correction required

15. The monograph which was published 3 years ago, *would suggest* that by 2001 there will be 73 million T.V. sets in India.
(*a*) has been suggesting
(*b*) had suggested
(*c*) would have suggested
(*d*) will suggest **(Bank P.O. 1994)**

16. Vishal, who *studies* medicine at present, hopes to go abroad after graduation.
(*a*) has been studying (*b*) is studying
(*c*) will study (*d*) No improvement

17. The greatest thing in style is to have a *use* of metaphor. **(Assistant Grade, 1996)**
(*a*) command (*b*) knowledge
(*c*) need (*d*) No improvement

18. I *differ by you in this matter*.
(*a*) differ with you on this matter
(*b*) differ from you about this matter
(*c*) differ off you over this matter
(*d*) No correction required

19. Newton wanted to *know why did the apple fall* to the ground. **(C.B.I. 1993)**
(*a*) know that why did the apple fall
(*b*) know why the apple fell
(*c*) know that why the apple fell
(*d*) No improvement

20. You are *a most* unusual person.
(*a*) most (*b*) a mostly (*c*) mostly
(*d*) the mostly (*e*) No correction required

21. A good house has been *alloted* to him.
(*a*) aloted (*b*) alotted
(*c*) allotted (*d*) No improvement
(C.D.S. 1988)

22. Robert listened to the phone *ring* again and again.
(*a*) ringing (*b*) that rang
(*c*) as it rang (*d*) No improvement

23. Ashutosh *had occupying* this house for over 25 years and has no intention of vacating it now. **(Bank P.O. 1993)**
(*a*) is occupying (*b*) will occupy
(*c*) was to occupy
(*d*) has been occupying
(*e*) No correction required

24. One can live and work in a town without being aware of the daily march of the sun across the sky without *never* seeing the moon and stars. **(C.D.S. 1994)**
(*a*) seldom (*b*) hardly
(*c*) ever (*d*) No improvement

25. Unless the population growth *stabilised* environmentalists predict a worldwide starvation by 2000 A.D.
(*a*) will stabilise (*b*) stabilises
(*c*) must stabilise (*d*) No improvement

26. From next term we will *go all out* for sports. **(C.B.I. 1994)**
(*a*) all go out (*b*) all be out
(*c*) be all out (*d*) No improvement

27. Can this apparatus be adopted *in* this job?
(*a*) to (*b*) for
(*c*) by (*d*) No improvement

28. If you had attended the meeting, you *would have benefited* a great deal.
(*a*) would benefit (*b*) could benefit
(*c*) benefited (*d*) No improvement
(Stenographers' Exam, 1995)

29. My neighbours are extremely noisy but *even more are they quarrelsome.*
(*a*) they are even more quarrelsome
(*b*) even more they are quarrelsome
(*c*) they are quarrelsome even more
(*d*) No improvement

30. *Not only did he criticise* the party's policies but also the leader's personal matters. **(S.B.I.P.O. 1991)**
(*a*) He criticised not only
(*b*) He not only criticised
(*c*) Neither did he criticise
(*d*) He did not criticise
(*e*) No correction required

31. The article should not *exceed more than* hundred words.
(*a*) exceed beyond (*b*) exceed
(*c*) exceed than (*d*) No improvement

32. Though courageous, he could not *hold up* against the heavy odds.
(*a*) hold fast (*b*) hold out
(*c*) hold in (*d*) No improvement
(Translators' Exam, 1994)

33. The meeting was postponed *owing to* lack of quorum.
(*a*) due to (*b*) because of
(*c*) for (*d*) No improvement

34. Hoping not to be disturbed, I sat down in my easy chair to read the book *I won as a prize*. **(C.D.S. 1994)**
(*a*) I have won as prize
(*b*) I had won as a prize
(*c*) I had to win as a prize
(*d*) No improvement

35. He copied the details *word by word*.
(*a*) word to word (*b*) word for word
(*c*) word on word (*d*) No improvement

36. In India today many of our intellectuals still talk in terms of the French revolution and the Rights of Man, not appreciating that *much has happened* since then.
(*a*) much might happen
(*b*) much had happened
(*c*) much has been happening
(*d*) No improvement **(C.D.S. 1995)**

37. The Principal was angry on seeing a *wooden broken chair* lying in the corridor.
(*a*) broken wooden chair
(*b*) wooden and broken chair
(*c*) broken and wooden chair
(*d*) No improvement

38. He has been receiving no other message than an urgent telegram *asking him to rush his village* immediately.
(*a*) asking him rushing at his village
(*b*) asked him to rush his village
(*c*) asking him to have rush his village
(*d*) asking him to rush to his village
(*e*) No correction required
(Bank P.O. 1994)

39. He has been living in Delhi *since* the last two years.
(*a*) from (*b*) ever since
(*c*) for (*d*) since about
(*e*) No correction required

40. How one earned money is more important than how much *he earned*?
(*a*) he earns (*b*) he has earned
(*c*) one earns (*d*) one earned
(*e*) No correction required
(Bank P.O. 1992)

41. About a thousand sportsmen from all the colleges have arrived, the *highest* contingent being from Delhi.

(*a*) biggest (*b*) largest
(*c*) greatest (*d*) No improvement

42. The man *to who I sold* my house was a cheat. **(Rural Banks, 1994)**
(*a*) to whom I sell (*b*) to who I sell
(*c*) who was sold to (*d*) to whom I sold
(*e*) No correction required

43. He hasn't yet applied for the job *we told him*.
(*a*) we told him of (*b*) we told him about
(*c*) of which we told him
(*d*) No improvement

44. He has *fallen out* with the girl he wanted to marry. **(N.D.A. 1991)**
(*a*) fallen off (*b*) fallen in love
(*c*) fallen for (*d*) No improvement

45. The greater the demand, *higher* the price.
(*a*) the higher (*b*) high
(*c*) the high (*d*) No improvement

46. I *have been working* on this job for the last ten days. **(B.S.R.B. 1990)**
(*a*) am working (*b*) would be working
(*c*) have been worked
(*d*) No improvement

47. We had to stop for petrol because we had hardly *much* left.
(*a*) more (*b*) some
(*c*) any (*d*) No improvement

48. The Managing Director said that the firm had ordered the goods and *will* have to pay for them. **(Assistant Grade, 1994)**
(*a*) may (*b*) would
(*c*) shall (*d*) No improvement

49. He never recollected his grand father *to say* that his job was odd.
(*a*) say (*b*) to have said
(*c*) saying (*d*) while saying
(*e*) No correction required

50. Modern industrialized communities have lost touch with the soil and do not experience that joy which nature gives and the rich glow of health *that which comes from contact with* mother earth.
(*a*) which comes from contact with
(*b*) which comes out from contact with
(*c*) which flows how from contact with
(*d*) No improvement **(C.B.I. 1995)**

ANSWERS

1. (*c*)	**2.** (*b*)	**3.** (*b*)	**4.** (*c*)	**5.** (*c*)	**6.** (*d*)	**7.** (*c*)	**8.** (*b*)	**9.** (*d*)	**10.** (*b*)
11. (*c*)	**12.** (*c*)	**13.** (*c*)	**14.** (*d*)	**15.** (*b*)	**16.** (*b*)	**17.** (*b*)	**18.** (*a*)	**19.** (*b*)	**20.** (*e*)
21. (*c*)	**22.** (*d*)	**23.** (*d*)	**24.** (*c*)	**25.** (*b*)	**26.** (*a*)	**27.** (*b*)	**28.** (*d*)	**29.** (*a*)	**30.** (*a*)
31. (*b*)	**32.** (*b*)	**33.** (*c*)	**34.** (*b*)	**35.** (*b*)	**36.** (*d*)	**37.** (*a*)	**38.** (*d*)	**39.** (*c*)	**40.** (*c*)
41. (*a*)	**42.** (*d*)	**43.** (*b*)	**44.** (*b*)	**45.** (*a*)	**46.** (*d*)	**47.** (*c*)	**48.** (*d*)	**49.** (*c*)	**50.** (*a*)

PRACTICE SET 10

Directions : ***In each of the following questions, a part of sentence is printed in italics. Below each sentence some alternatives are given which can substitute the italicised part. Find out the choice which can correctly substitute that part of the sentence. If the sentence is correct as it is, give 'No improvement' or 'No correction required' as your answer.***

1. I *earnestly believe that* you will visit our relatives during your forthcoming trip to Bombay. **(Bank P.O. 1994)**
(*a*) certainly believing that
(*b*) could not believe
(*c*) had hardly believe
(*d*) sincerely would believe
(*e*) No correction required

2. The accused was ordered to be *hung to death*.
(*a*) hung till death (*b*) hanged to death
(*c*) hanged till death
(*d*) No correction required

3. It is sheer folly to believe that you can improve the situation by *doing away* people. **(C.D.S. 1994)**
(*a*) doing it to (*b*) doing away with
(*c*) doing with (*d*) No improvement

4. Would you mind *help* me with these questions?
(*a*) to help (*b*) of helping
(*c*) helping (*d*) No improvement

5. In fact, if it hadn't been for his *invaluable advice* on so many occasions I wouldn't have achieved anything in life.
(*a*) remarkable advice

(*b*) valuable advices
(*c*) priceless suggestions
(*d*) No improvement **(Asstt. Grade, 1996)**

6. He hesitated *to accept* the post as he did not think that the salary was enough for him to sustain his family.
(*a*) accepting (*b*) to accepting
(*c*) in accepting (*d*) while accepting
(*e*) No correction required

7. By temperament *the English* are reserved, so they prefer to live in solitary houses. **(N.D.A. 1993)**
(*a*) English (*b*) English people
(*c*) some English (*d*) No improvement

8. A basic step for career planning, and also for preparation for interviews is to give serious thought *to assess yourself* by taking stock of your needs, interests as well as your strengths and weaknesses.
(*a*) to have your assessment
(*b*) to assessing yourself
(*c*) to having assessed yourself
(*d*) No improvement

9. My father agreed *with my going alone* for the examination. **(S.C.R.A. 1994)**
(*a*) I go alone (*b*) to my going alone
(*c*) that I go alone (*d*) No improvement

10. As they met again at 9 p.m. he said, "*Good night*, very pleased to see you again".
(*a*) Good day (*b*) Good evening
(*c*) Good bye (*d*) No improvement

11. The question is, *how was* the motive of the robber in this particular case?
(*a*) what was (*b*) where was
(*c*) when was (*d*) who was
(*e*) No correction required
(Bank P.O. 1994)

12. I had never realised *that if an innocent act* like this could land a man into trouble.
(*a*) that an innocent act
(*b*) what an innocent act
(*c*) that even an innocent act
(*d*) No improvement

13. A bird in hand is worth *two in bush*.
(*a*) two on bush (*b*) two in the bush
(*c*) two at a bush (*d*) No improvement

14. Mala *was hurried* to reach the meeting when she slipped and fell down.
(*a*) is hurried (*b*) was being hurried
(*c*) was hurrying
(*d*) No correction required **(I. Tax, 1993)**

15. He is *so handsome* man that people turn round to look at him.
(*a*) very handsome (*b*) such a handsome
(*c*) too handsome (*d*) No improvement

16. Most donors would seriously *protest* any effort to extrapolate from such limited data.
(*a*) protest at (*b*) protest to
(*c*) protest against (*d*) No improvement

17. He should move on to the next point, and not *harp one string only*. **(C.D.S. 1994)**
(*a*) harp only one string
(*b*) harp on string only
(*c*) harp upon one string only
(*d*) No improvement

18. The dog eats its food *in* a plate.
(*a*) off (*b*) from
(*c*) with (*d*) No improvement

19. The artist continues to work *in* the medium he understands best, breathing his inborn individuality and vitality into newer forms.
(*a*) within (*b*) for (*c*) into
(*d*) with (*e*) No improvement

20. The parents became extremely *troubled* when their son did not return by midnight. **(U.D.C. 1995)**
(*a*) anxious (*b*) depressed
(*c*) sad (*d*) No improvement

21. I can't understand why he avoids *to speak to me*.
(*a*) to tell me (*b*) speaking to me
(*c*) saying to me (*d*) No improvement

22. Honestly and efficiently organised socialism is expected to make our economic structure work *accordingly with* the laws of business morality.
(*a*) according with (*b*) accordingly to
(*c*) in accordance with
(*d*) No improvement

23. He plans to *hurriedly complete this work.*
(*a*) to complete hurriedly this work
(*b*) to complete this work hurriedly
(*c*) to complete this work in a hurry
(*d*) No correction required

24. What *were you doing* ever since I last saw you? **(N.D.A. 1996)**
(*a*) did you do (*b*) are you doing
(*c*) have you been doing
(*d*) No improvement

25. Seeing them all at one place, we realised that something drastic *have to be done.*
(*a*) was to be done (*b*) had to be done
(*c*) will have to be done
(*d*) No improvement

26. I was waiting *until everybody will have left* the meeting place.
(*a*) until everybody had left
(*b*) until everybody left
(*c*) until everybody would leave
(*d*) No improvement

27. Are you *more cleverer than us* ?
(*a*) cleverer to us (*b*) more cleverer to us
(*c*) cleverer than us (*d*) No improvement
(Section Officers, 1993)

28. The forest is infested *of* snakes.
(*a*) with (*b*) by
(*c*) in (*d*) No improvement

29. Inspite of all those hurdles, the scheduled day *came of* in a few months.
(*a*) came up (*b*) came on
(*c*) came off (*d*) came over
(*e*) No correction required

30. When she *takes her exam* she will have a holiday. **(C.D.S. 1992)**
(*a*) has taken her exam
(*b*) took her exam
(*c*) had taken her exam
(*d*) No improvement

31. Millions of people in our country *are deprived* of two square meals since independence.
(*a*) are being deprived
(*b*) have been deprived
(*c*) has been deprived
(*d*) No improvement

32. *In quick time* he got attached to a renowned leader and politician.
(*a*) In enough time (*b*) In brief time
(*c*) In no time (*d*) On time only
(*e*) No correction required

33. Your statement that you were *thorough ignorant* of the consequences cannot be trusted. **(Bank P.O. 1995)**
(*a*) thoroughly in ignorance
(*b*) thoroughly ignorance
(*c*) thorough of ignorance
(*d*) thoroughly ignorant
(*e*) No correction required

34. *Not only did he invite* his relatives but also all his friends and colleagues.
(*a*) He did not invite only
(*b*) He invited not only
(*c*) Not only he invited
(*d*) He not only invited

35. There *is rumour* that a great leader has been assassinated.
(*a*) is the rumour (*b*) is rumours
(*c*) is a rumour (*d*) No improvement

36. Asking me *why was I absent, I was punished by the Headmaster.* **(C.B.I. 1993)**
(*a*) why was I absent, was I punished by the Headmaster
(*b*) why I was absent, was I punished by the Headmaster
(*c*) why I was absent, the Headmaster punished me
(*d*) No improvement

37. An educated man's way of life can be *contrasted to* that of an illiterate person.
(*a*) contrasted with (*b*) contrasted at
(*c*) contrasted against
(*d*) No improvement

38. Madan will not be *at home* until eight o'clock. **(N.D.A. 1994)**
(*a*) in home (*b*) to home
(*c*) home (*d*) No improvement

39. That is something *of which I'd rather not talk about.*
(*a*) I'd rather not talk about it
(*b*) I'd rather not talk about
(*c*) that I'd rather not talk about it
(*d*) No correction required

40. People are generally found *absorbing* in the activity which they like most.
(*a*) absorb (*b*) absorbed
(*c*) observe (*d*) observing
(*e*) No correction required **(B.S.R.B. 1990)**

41. *Had you been told* me about your problem, I would have helped you.
(*a*) Had you told
(*b*) Had you have told
(*c*) If you have told
(*d*) If you would have told
(*e*) No correction required

42. I am quite hopeful *of securing* very high marks in the examination.
(*a*) to secure (*b*) to having secured
(*c*) of having secured (*d*) No improvement
(Railways, 1993)

43. In the past, services of backward communities and weaker sections of society were used without *payment of some kind*.
(*a*) payment or kind
(*b*) payment of a kind
(*c*) payment of any kind
(*d*) No improvement

44. Nothing but books and magazines *pleases* her. **(N.D.A. 1996)**
(*a*) were pleasing (*b*) please
(*c*) are pleasing (*d*) No improvement

45. You *had better got* your reservation well in advance or you won't be able to go.
(*a*) had better get (*b*) had better to get
(*c*) had to better get (*d*) No improvement

46. Why *did you not spoken* to me earlier?
(*a*) did you not spoke
(*b*) you did not speak
(*c*) did you not speak
(*d*) were you not spoken
(*e*) No correction required **(B.S.R.B. 1996)**

47. The contractor did not keep his promise that the work *will* be finished before the end of the week.
(*a*) shall (*b*) would

(*c*) could (*d*) No improvement

48. The discovery of the radio and the television *have not been* without some effects.
(*a*) had not been (*b*) has not been
(*c*) could not be (*d*) No improvement

49. There is *no absolute worry* even if your son refuses to marry her.
(*a*) no absolutely worry
(*b*) absolutely no worry
(*c*) absolutely not worrying
(*d*) No improvement

50. He found it difficult *to cope along with his work*.
(*a*) to cope also with his work
(*b*) to cope with his work
(*c*) to cope up with his work
(*d*) to cope around his work **(C.B.I. 1995)**

ANSWERS

1. (*e*)	**2.** (*c*)	**3.** (*b*)	**4.** (*c*)	**5.** (*d*)	**6.** (*c*)	**7.** (*d*)	**8.** (*b*)	**9.** (*b*)	**10.** (*b*)
11. (*a*)	**12.** (*c*)	**13.** (*b*)	**14.** (*c*)	**15.** (*b*)	**16.** (*c*)	**17.** (*c*)	**18.** (*b*)	**19.** (*d*)	**20.** (*a*)
21. (*b*)	**22.** (*c*)	**23.** (*b*)	**24.** (*c*)	**25.** (*b*)	**26.** (*a*)	**27.** (*c*)	**28.** (*a*)	**29.** (*c*)	**30.** (*a*)
31. (*b*)	**32.** (*c*)	**33.** (*d*)	**34.** (*b*)	**35.** (*c*)	**36.** (*c*)	**37.** (*a*)	**38.** (*c*)	**39.** (*b*)	**40.** (*b*)
41. (*a*)	**42.** (*d*)	**43.** (*c*)	**44.** (*b*)	**45.** (*a*)	**46.** (*c*)	**47.** (*b*)	**48.** (*d*)	**49.** (*b*)	**50.** (*b*)

PRACTICE SET 11

Directions : Look at the italicised part of the sentence. Below each sentence are given some possible substitutions for the italicised part. If one of them is better than the italicised part, indicate your response against the corresponding letter. If none of the substitutions improve the sentence, indicate 'No improvement' or 'No correction required' as your response.

1. Each village adopted by the club was *provided by* electric supply. **(C.D.S. 1995)**
(*a*) provided (*b*) provided with
(*c*) provided for (*d*) No improvement

2. Kailash insisted *him to do this work*.
(*a*) insisted on him to do this work
(*b*) insisted him on doing this work
(*c*) insisted on his doing this work
(*d*) No correction required

3. Sports *is good to health*.
(*a*) is good for health
(*b*) are good to health
(*c*) are good for health
(*d*) No improvement

4. Even more than my father was she intolerant of demonstrativeness and the wearing of one's heart *on his sleeve*.
(*a*) on the sleeve (*b*) on one's sleeve
(*c*) on her sleeve (*d*) No improvement **(I.E.S. 1993)**

5. All work and no play *make* Jack a dull boy.
(*a*) made (*b*) would make
(*c*) makes (*d*) maketh
(*e*) No correction required

6. He is in the habit of purchasing the *very good* of all the things available.
(*a*) the most good (*b*) the better
(*c*) the very better (*d*) the best
(*e*) No improvement

7. I suggest that he *study* medicine.
(*a*) will study (*b*) studies
(*c*) studied (*d*) No improvement **(N.D.A. 1994)**

8. I was *attacked by* malaria.
(*a*) attacked with (*b*) afflicted by
(*c*) afflicted with (*d*) No improvement

9. Just watch out that your shirt's hanging out; *tuck it* at once.
(*a*) tuck it in (*b*) tuck it through
(*c*) tuck it into (*d*) No improvement

10. The baby was left *in charge of* a neighbour. **(Translators' Exam, 1994)**
(*a*) to care of (*b*) to care for
(*c*) in the charge of (*d*) No improvement

11. Holmes took up a second letter which *lay unnoticed* upon the table whilst he had been absorbed with the first.
(*a*) was lying unnoticed
(*b*) had been lying unnoticed
(*c*) had laid unnoticed
(*d*) No improvement

12. She asked me if I knew a person who could teach her French. I said I *wasn't*.
(*a*) do not know (*b*) didn't
(*c*) hadn't (*d*) No improvement

13. He found the gold coin *as he cleans* the floor. **(Bank P.O. 1993)**
(*a*) while he cleans
(*b*) as he had cleaning
(*c*) as he was cleaning
(*d*) while cleaning
(*e*) No correction required

14. His salary is not adequate for him to *make the both ends meet*.
(*a*) make both ends meet
(*b*) make both the ends meet
(*c*) make both his ends meet
(*d*) No correction required

15. An accident took place early *today morning*. **(C.B.I. 1994)**
(*a*) this morning (*b*) morning today
(*c*) at the morning (*d*) No improvement

16. The engagement ceremony *took place* in this very hotel last Sunday.
(*a*) was took place (*b*) did take place
(*c*) was taken place (*d*) No improvement

17. After a few minutes the unconscious boxer began to come *out*. **(N.D.A. 1993)**
(*a*) up (*b*) round
(*c*) on (*d*) No improvement

18. Had he turned down my offer, he *could not be* where he is today.
(*a*) may not be (*b*) should not be
(*c*) would not be (*d*) No improvement

19. He has frightened many a people *by his gun*.
(*a*) by gun (*b*) by a gun
(*c*) with his gun (*d*) No improvement

20. The farmer's way of life can be *contrasted to* that of the factory worker. **(C.D.S. 1991)**
(*a*) constrasted for (*b*) contrasted against
(*c*) contrasted with (*d*) No improvement

21. *But just how far* he will manage to run with those shoes remains to be seen.
(*a*) But just how farther
(*b*) But just how much far
(*c*) But just how further
(*d*) No improvement

22. The winter was *such severe* that even water in the taps was frozen.
(*a*) severe such (*b*) so severe
(*c*) severe so much (*d*) No improvement
(S.C.R.A. 1994)

23. I am unable to go on the excursion with my friends because I *broke* my leg.
(*a*) have broken (*b*) break
(*c*) had broken (*d*) No improvement

24. More than one person *was killed* in the accident. **(I.E.S. 1994)**
(*a*) have been killed (*b*) were killed
(*c*) are killed (*d*) No improvement

25. My employer *threatened me to dismiss* if I was late again.
(*a*) threatened of dismissing me
(*b*) threatened to dismiss me
(*c*) threatened dismiss me
(*d*) No improvement

26. To succeed in a difficult task, *persistent is needed*. **(Bank P.O. 1994)**
(*a*) persistence was needed
(*b*) persistence is what one needs
(*c*) one needs to be persistent
(*d*) persistence should have needed
(*e*) No correction required

27. The novelist stresses his opinion that *were it not for* the machinations of politicians, India would never have needed to be partitioned.
(*a*) was it not for (*b*) it were not for
(*c*) would it not for (*d*) No improvement

28. He didn't believe in God *but* he went to church regularly. **(C.D.S. 1992)**
(*a*) however (*b*) nevertheless
(*c*) yet (*d*) No improvement

29. I congratulated him on his *creditable* performance in the I.F.S. examination.
(*a*) credible (*b*) creditworthy
(*c*) credulous (*d*) No improvement

30. Is your *brother yet at* the university?
(*a*) brother still at
(*b*) brother continue at
(*c*) brother till at
(*d*) No improvement **(N.D.A. 1990)**

31. The farewell *took place* last Sunday.
(*a*) was took place (*b*) was taken place
(*c*) did take place
(*d*) No correction required

32. He is working hard *with a view to attain* good marks in the examination.
(*a*) with a view of attaining
(*b*) with a view to attaining
(*c*) with a view for attaining
(*d*) No improvement

33. *I, your brother and you* will be partners in the business. **(N.D.A. 1991)**
(*a*) I, you and your brother
(*b*) You, your brother and I
(*c*) You, I and your brother
(*d*) No improvement

34. The government is investing *more and more* money in developmental activities.
(*a*) more and most (*b*) much and more
(*c*) much more (*d*) No improvement

35. We demonstrated to them how we *were prepared* the artistic patterns.
(*a*) are prepared (*b*) have prepared
(*c*) are preparing (*d*) had prepared
(*e*) No correction required
(S.B.I.P.O. 1994)

36. I prefer football *for* cricket.
(*a*) to (*b*) than
(*c*) from (*d*) No improvement

37. Mr. Dewan has driven almost thrice *so far as* Mr. Gupta has.
(*a*) as far (*b*) as far as
(*c*) as much as (*d*) No improvement

38. Whenever the two sisters *go out for shopping*, they take their pet dog with them.
(*a*) go out shopping
(*b*) go out to shopping
(*c*) go out on shopping
(*d*) No improvement

39. While we would like *that all Indian children* to go to school, we need to ponder why they do not. **(C.D.S. 1995)**
(*a*) all Indian children
(*b*) that all the Indian children
(*c*) if all the children of India
(*d*) No improvement

40. *Scarcely had he left* when his friend came.
(*a*) He had scarcely left
(*b*) He had left scarcely
(*c*) He scarcely had left
(*d*) No improvement

41. A highly improved variety of seeds *is* available to the farmer these days.
(*a*) has been (*b*) are
(*c*) will be (*d*) No improvement

42. It is essential *to thoroughly clean* the machine after each use. **(S.B.I.P.O. 1991)**
(*a*) to thorough clean
(*b*) to clean thorough
(*c*) to thorough clean
(*d*) to thoroughly cleaning
(*e*) No correction required

43. He felt like a character in a story book *which had gazed out* for a moment in his brief, imagined life at the real world.
(*a*) that gazed out (*b*) who did gaze out
(*c*) who had gazed out
(*d*) No improvement

44. I have got some tea, but I do not have *a* sugar. **(Bank P.O. 1994)**
(*a*) some (*b*) any
(*c*) more (*d*) got
(*e*) No correction required

45. Tell your leader that I grant him permission *of stay* in my kingdom.
(*a*) for stay (*b*) about staying
(*c*) to stay (*d*) No improvement

46. I was delighted to see *him fully recover*.
(*a*) he full recovered
(*b*) him fully recovered
(*c*) his full recovery
(*d*) No correction required **(B.S.R.B. 1996)**

47. I told him what to do and how *he does it*.
(*a*) should he do it (*b*) to do it
(*c*) should it be done (*d*) he did it
(*e*) No correction required

48. *By definition, make a map* is to select certain features as relevant and ignore others. **(R.B.I. 1990)**
(*a*) To make a map by definition
(*b*) Map-making is defined as
(*c*) In making a map, the definition
(*d*) The map making process involves, by defining
(*e*) No correction required

49. The experience was as important to the artists as it was to the thousands *who comprise* the audience.
(*a*) who did comprise
(*b*) who comprised
(*c*) who would comprise
(*d*) who comprised of
(*e*) No correction required

50. Each of our *students pay their* tuition fee at the beginning of the month.
(*a*) student pay their
(*b*) student pays their
(*c*) students pays his
(*d*) No improvement
(Assistant Grade, 1994)

ANSWERS

1. (*b*)	**2.** (*c*)	**3.** (*a*)	**4.** (*b*)	**5.** (*c*)	**6.** (*d*)	**7.** (*b*)	**8.** (*c*)	**9.** (*a*)	**10.** (*c*)
11. (*c*)	**12.** (*b*)	**13.** (*d*)	**14.** (*a*)	**15.** (*a*)	**16.** (*d*)	**17.** (*b*)	**18.** (*c*)	**19.** (*c*)	**20.** (*c*)
21. (*d*)	**22.** (*b*)	**23.** (*a*)	**24.** (*b*)	**25.** (*b*)	**26.** (*c*)	**27.** (*d*)	**28.** (*c*)	**29.** (*d*)	**30.** (*a*)
31. (*d*)	**32.** (*b*)	**33.** (*b*)	**34.** (*d*)	**35.** (*d*)	**36.** (*a*)	**37.** (*b*)	**38.** (*a*)	**39.** (*a*)	**40.** (*d*)
41. (*d*)	**42.** (*e*)	**43.** (*c*)	**44.** (*b*)	**45.** (*c*)	**46.** (*b*)	**47.** (*b*)	**48.** (*c*)	**49.** (*b*)	**50.** (*c*)

PRACTICE SET 12

Directions : *In each question below, a part of sentence is printed in italics. Below each sentence, some phrases are given which can substitute the italicised part of the sentence. Find out the phrase which can correctly substitute that part of the sentence. If the sentence is correct as it is, the answer is 'No correction required' or 'No improvement'.*

1. Do not take another step, else your life *will face great* peril. **(C.D.S. 1994)**
(*a*) might be thrown into
(*b*) will be in
(*c*) would be placed in great
(*d*) No improvement

2. The political situation is *no better* and not even as good as it was last year.
(*a*) not better (*b*) not better than
(*c*) no better to (*d*) no better than
(*e*) No correction required

3. Mary met with an accident. She didn't just twist her leg, she *has broken it*.
(*a*) had broken it (*b*) breaks it
(*c*) broke it too (*d*) No improvement
(N.D.A. 1995)

4. The man *prides on* his wealth.
(*a*) is proud on (*b*) prides of
(*c*) prides himself on
(*d*) No improvement

5. The valley *lied quite and peaceful* in the sun.
(*a*) lied quietly and peacefully
(*b*) lay quite and peaceful
(*c*) lay quietly and peacefully
(*d*) No correction required

6. *If I was you*, I would not have joined the party. **(Bank P.O. 1994)**
(*a*) As you (*b*) If I am you
(*c*) Were I you (*d*) If I be you
(*e*) No correction required

7. *You, they and we* must go together.
(*a*) They, you and we
(*b*) You, we and they
(*c*) We, you and they
(*d*) No improvement

8. If you are absent for a week, you have to *catch with* the work when you return.
(*a*) catch up with (*b*) catch on with
(*c*) catch in with (*d*) No improvement
(Stenographers' Exam, 1994)

9. The Government has taken a number of steps with a view *to improving* the conditions of the backward classes.
(*a*) for improving (*b*) at improving
(*c*) to improve (*d*) No improvement

10. He was urgently in need *to get his eye operation*. **(C.B.I. 1994)**
(*a*) of an eye operation
(*b*) for operation on eye
(*c*) for eye to be operated
(*d*) No improvement

11. He *fled from* the country lest he should be arrested for his misdeeds.
(*a*) fled off (*b*) fled
(*c*) fled out of (*d*) No improvement

12. Having finished the book, *it was put away by him*. **(Assistant Grade, 1995)**
(*a*) he put it away
(*b*) it was being put away by him
(*c*) it was putting away by him
(*d*) No improvement

13. A well behaved boy is always obedient *towards his parents*.
(*a*) for his parents (*b*) of his parents
(*c*) to his parents (*d*) No improvement

14. When the thief heard the police siren, he showed *a pair of clean heels*.
(*a*) a clean pair of heels
(*b*) clean a pair of heels
(*c*) a pair of heels clean
(*d*) No improvement

15. When it was feared that the serfs might go too far and gain their freedom from serfdom, the Protestant leaders joined the princes *at crushing* them.
(*a*) into crushing (*b*) in crushing
(*c*) without crushing (*d*) No improvement
(C.D.S. 1995)

16. *Who do you think I was talking* over the phone when you came to see me.
(*a*) Whom do you think I was talking
(*b*) Whom do you think I was talking with
(*c*) Who do you think I was talking to
(*d*) No correction required

17. I told him clearly that he *hadn't ought to do* that to me. **(Bank P.O. 1993)**
(*a*) ought not have done
(*b*) ought not done
(*c*) ought not has done
(*d*) hasn't ought to do
(*e*) No correction required

18. He is the best and *popular* actor of Bollywood.
(*a*) the more popular
(*b*) the most popular
(*c*) popular most (*d*) No improvement

19. It is *easy for children than* for adults to learn a new language. **(Bank P.O. 1990)**
(*a*) as easy as children
(*b*) easy for children as
(*c*) very easy to children as
(*d*) easier for children than
(*e*) No correction required

20. The strangers were heading *into* a serious disaster.
(*a*) for (*b*) towards
(*c*) along (*d*) No improvement

21. The company goes to great length to ensure that employees *can be comfortable* in their work environment.
(*a*) will be comfortable
(*b*) should be comfortable
(*c*) are comfortable (*d*) No improvement
(C.D.S. 1994)

22. They could not complete the work; *neither could we.*
(*a*) neither we did (*b*) neither did we
(*c*) nor could we (*d*) nor did we
(*e*) No improvement

23. The quality of food served in this hotel is so poor that no respectable person *would want to eat* over here. **(Bank P.O. 1994)**
(*a*) will want to eat
(*b*) will want to have eaten
(*c*) will have wanted to eat
(*d*) will be wanting to eat
(*e*) No correction required

24. We should take up the first item, let *us begin this song*. **(U.D.C. 1994)**
(*a*) this song begin us
(*b*) us begin with this song
(*c*) us beginning this song
(*d*) No improvement

25. I do not give any cognizanee *on* what he says.
(*a*) to (*b*) about
(*c*) for (*d*) No improvement

26. *All, but her*, had made an attempt.
(*a*) All, but she (*b*) All, but herself
(*c*) All, but she herself
(*d*) No improvement **(I.E.S. 1994)**

27. He did not *obey to his orders*.
(*a*) obey his orders (*b*) obey him
(*c*) obey to him (*d*) No improvement

28. The notorious dacoit, with all his gangsters, *have been robbing* banks for the last few months. **(C.D.S. 1995)**
(*a*) is robbing (*b*) has been robbing
(*c*) are robbing (*d*) No improvement

29. He shouted *that he might attract attention*.
(*a*) for attracting attention
(*b*) to attract attention
(*c*) that he may attract attention
(*d*) No improvement

30. Our team is likely to lose unless all members learn to cooperate *with one other*. **(C.D.S. 1992)**
(*a*) with one and all (*b*) with one another
(*c*) one other with (*d*) No improvement

31. As he started to descend, someone lunged at him from above and *knocked his balance off*.
(*a*) knocked off his balance
(*b*) knocked him off balance
(*c*) knocked him off from his balance
(*d*) No correction required

32. *Any able bodied man is* eligible for the job.
(*a*) Any able-bodied men are
(*b*) Each able-bodied man is
(*c*) Any able-bodied men have been
(*d*) No improvement **(N.D.A. 1996)**

33. If *a person studied* this period of history, he would have wondered how such things had happened in India.
(*a*) a person had studied
(*b*) a person would study
(*c*) a person could have studied
(*d*) No improvement **(N.D.A. 1995)**

34. You will fail in the examination *if you will not* work hard.
(*a*) if you do not (*b*) if you did not
(*c*) if you shall not (*d*) No improvement

35. They succeeded *without hardly making* any effort. **(C.B.I. 1995)**
(*a*) hardly without making
(*b*) with hardly making
(*c*) without making hardly
(*d*) No improvement

36. He died *of a wound and not from malaria*.
(*a*) from a wound and not from malaria
(*b*) of a wound and not of malaria
(*c*) from a wound and not of malaria
(*d*) No improvement

37. Governments in developing countries are under increasing pressure *for the recruiting and training* teachers to meet the demands of their rapidly expanding systems of education. **(C.D.S. 1994)**
(*a*) so as to recruit and train
(*b*) to recruit and train
(*c*) in the recruiting and training of
(*d*) No improvement

38. Citizens should be prohibited *to smoke* in public places.
(*a*) for smoking (*b*) against smoking
(*c*) from smoking (*d*) No improvement

39. The workers are *hell bent at getting* what is due to them. **(C.D.S. 1995)**
(*a*) hell bent for getting

(*b*) hell bent on getting
(*c*) hell bent upon getting
(*d*) No improvement

40. You should not *discuss about* a matter with friends who are likely to find it offensive.
(*a*) discuss (*b*) discuss on
(*c*) discuss upon (*d*) No improvement

41. Miss Pillai teaches very well, *isn't it*?
(*a*) didn't she? (*b*) doesn't she?
(*c*) wasn't it? (*d*) No improvement
(N.D.A. 1991)

42. Indians invented the decimal system and the digit, algebra and geometry but the names of their inventors are buried *in* oblivion.
(*a*) to (*b*) into
(*c*) within (*d*) No improvement

43. *Leaving aside little room for* misinterpretation, the senior politician offered clarification about his role in the party elections. **(Bank P.O. 1994)**
(*a*) Leaving less room for
(*b*) Leaving little room for
(*c*) Having left less room for
(*d*) Leaving for little room to
(*e*) No correction required

44. It is high time he *starts to look* into his own flaws before speaking ill of others.
(*a*) started to look (*b*) starts looking
(*c*) started looking (*d*) No improvement
(Railways, 1993)

45. Students must give *ears* to what the teacher says.
(*a*) ear (*b*) the ears
(*c*) an ear (*d*) No improvement

46. *Neither* of the three boys came.
(*a*) No one (*b*) None
(*c*) Nil (*d*) No improvement

47. The fast train *came a halt to before* crossing the bridge. **(B.S.R.B. 1996)**
(*a*) came before to a halt
(*b*) came to a halt before
(*c*) came to halts before a
(*d*) came before a halt to
(*e*) No correction required

48. Mr. Hyon and the other dissident leaders *have taken shelter* at the church last month after the authorities ordered their arrest. **(C.D.S. 1991)**
(*a*) had taken shelter (*b*) took shelter
(*c*) are taking shelter
(*d*) No improvement

49. Our dwindling supplies were *replaced* when the new shipment arrived.
(*a*) restocked (*b*) replenished
(*c*) refilled (*d*) No improvement

50. When a man has to give evidence he must *have a clean breast* of the whole matter. **(Assistant Grade, 1994)**
(*a*) make a clean breast
(*b*) obtain a clean breast
(*c*) possess a clean breast
(*d*) No improvement

ANSWERS

1. (*c*)	**2.** (*d*)	**3.** (*a*)	**4.** (*c*)	**5.** (*b*)	**6.** (*c*)	**7.** (*c*)	**8.** (*a*)	**9.** (*d*)	**10.** (*a*)
11. (*b*)	**12.** (*a*)	**13.** (*c*)	**14.** (*a*)	**15.** (*b*)	**16.** (*c*)	**17.** (*a*)	**18.** (*b*)	**19.** (*d*)	**20.** (*a*)
21. (*c*)	**22.** (*e*)	**23.** (*d*)	**24.** (*b*)	**25.** (*a*)	**26.** (*a*)	**27.** (*b*)	**28.** (*b*)	**29.** (*b*)	**30.** (*b*)
31. (*b*)	**32.** (*b*)	**33.** (*a*)	**34.** (*a*)	**35.** (*a*)	**36.** (*c*)	**37.** (*b*)	**38.** (*c*)	**39.** (*c*)	**40.** (*a*)
41. (*b*)	**42.** (*d*)	**43.** (*b*)	**44.** (*c*)	**45.** (*a*)	**46.** (*b*)	**47.** (*b*)	**48.** (*b*)	**49.** (*b*)	**50.** (*a*)

PRACTICE SET 13

Directions : ***In each question, a part of sentence is printed in italics. Below each sentence some alternatives are given which can substitute the italicised part of the sentence. If the sentence is correct as it is, the answer is 'No improvement' or 'No correction required'.***

1. When the train finally *came into* the station the lonely traveller seemed relieved. **(Bank P.O. 1994)**
(*a*) pulled into (*b*) will pull into
(*c*) pulled to (*d*) have pulled into
(*e*) No correction required

2. When the clock strikes twelve, *I shall be waiting* here for four hours.
(*a*) I shall have been waiting
(*b*) I would have been waiting
(*c*) I shall have waited
(*d*) I would have waited

(*e*) No improvement

3. Just *in a hour's time*, he could complete the work to my satisfaction.
(*a*) in a hour (*b*) in an hour's time
(*c*) in the time of an hour
(*d*) in the duration of an hour
(*e*) No correction required **(S.B.I.P.O. 1991)**

4. If you ask nicely, your sister will probably *allow you have* a piece of cake.
(*a*) allow that you have
(*b*) let you have
(*c*) let you to have (*d*) No improvement

5. He was so rude that they were compelled *for asking him to leave.* **(U.D.C. 1993)**
(*a*) ask him to leave
(*b*) to ask him to leave
(*c*) him to ask to leave
(*d*) No improvement

6. Either the Chief Minister or his colleagues *have submitted his resignation.*
(*a*) has submitted his resignation
(*b*) has submitted their resignation
(*c*) have submitted their resignation
(*d*) No improvement

7. The poor villagers *have waited* in the bitter cold for more than four hours now.
(*a*) has been waiting (*b*) had waited
(*c*) have been waiting
(*d*) No improvement **(I.E.S. 1994)**

8. His idea of reducing the quality of the article to cope up with the increasing market prices was not *listened to.*
(*a*) welcomed (*b*) taken for granted
(*c*) agreed to (*d*) No improvement

9. A boy has been *sunk* in the river.
(*a*) capsized (*b*) immersed
(*c*) drowned (*d*) No improvement

10. May I know *who did accompany you* to the bus station? **(B.S.R.B. 1996)**
(*a*) whom did accompany you
(*b*) whom you accompanying
(*c*) whom did you accompany
(*d*) who accompanied you
(*e*) No correction required

11. As John dived off the spring board, he was horrified to see that the water *was drained from* the pool the night before.
(*a*) was drained away
(*b*) was drained
(*c*) had been drained off
(*d*) No improvement **(C.D.S. 1994)**

12. This is the same beggar *that* came yesterday.
(*a*) who (*b*) which
(*c*) whom (*d*) No improvement

13. The train will leave at 8.30 p.m., we *have been* ready by 7.30 p.m. so that we can reach the station in time.
(*a*) should have (*b*) must be
(*c*) were (*d*) are
(*e*) No correction required
(Bank P.O. 1994)

14. Can you tell me *what time is it*?
(*a*) what is time (*b*) what is the time
(*c*) what time it is (*d*) No improvement

15. Because of the patient's ill health, *losing weight was advised him by the doctor*.
(*a*) lose weight was what the doctor advised
(*b*) to lose weight was advised to him by the doctor
(*c*) he was advised by the doctor to lose weight
(*d*) No correction required
(Bank P.O. 1992)

16. Can I exchange *my book for yours*?
(*a*) my book (*b*) our book
(*c*) my book with yours
(*d*) No correction required

17. They *are waiting* for her since morning.
(*a*) were waiting (*b*) have been waiting
(*c*) wait (*d*) No improvement
(C.D.S. 1992)

18. They left the town *with bag and baggage.*
(*a*) with bags and baggages
(*b*) bags and baggages
(*c*) bag and baggage (*d*) No improvement

19. He *sent a word* to me that he would be coming late. **(C.D.S. 1993)**
(*a*) sent words (*b*) has sent a word
(*c*) sent word (*d*) No improvement

20. He has always been *very kind enough* to help me.
(*a*) kind enough (*b*) too kind enough
(*c*) enough kind (*d*) No improvement

21. Had you helped me, I *shall not be* miserable. **(C.B.I. 1993)**
(*a*) would not be (*b*) should not be
(*c*) would not have been
(*d*) No improvement

22. My mother *has been walking* in the park everyday since we moved into this area.
(*a*) walks (*b*) had been walking
(*c*) walked (*d*) No improvement

23. Tigers are *both found in Asia and in Africa.*
(*a*) found both in Asia and Africa
(*b*) found both in Asia and in Africa
(*c*) found in both Asia and Africa
(*d*) No improvement

24. When Shankar came home after a hard day in the office he found his wife *had slept.* **(N.D.A. 1993)**

(*a*) was sleeping (*b*) sleeping
(*c*) has been sleeping (*d*) No improvement

25. *None but the brave* deserves the fair.
(*a*) Only the brave
(*b*) None else but the brave
(*c*) Simply those who are brave
(*d*) No improvement

26. Certainly man must *look up* the future and find ways of providing for his needs.
(*a*) look for (*b*) look to
(*c*) look in (*d*) No improvement
(C.D.S. 1995)

27. It is so tough a competition that you just cannot get through it unless *you do not work hard.*
(*a*) you will work hard
(*b*) you work hard
(*c*) you do work hard (*d*) No improvement

28. It is a common belief that familiarity *dispenses with* the necessity of politeness.
(*a*) dispenses of (*b*) dispenses without
(*c*) dispenses from (*d*) No improvement
(I.E.S. 1993)

29. Frank was *bound* hand and foot and tightly blind- folded, but unharmed.
(*a*) bound by (*b*) bound in
(*c*) bound to (*d*) No improvement

30. *As he was much hated* by his contemporaries, posterity praises his statesmanship. **(C.B.I. 1995)**
(*a*) He was as much (*b*) So much he was
(*c*) Much as he was (*d*) No improvement

31. Would you like *other* piece of cake?
(*a*) another (*b*) more
(*c*) extra (*d*) No improvement

32. My mother asked me when *would I* have a glass of milk.
(*a*) I shall (*b*) I would
(*c*) I will (*d*) No improvement
(Stenographers' Exam, 1992)

33. Many accidents can be avoided if we *be careful*. **(R.R.B. 1994)**
(*a*) might be careful (*b*) are careful
(*c*) were careful (*d*) No improvement

34. The people in villages *are deprived* of essential commodities for the past two weeks. **(C.D.S. 1991)**
(*a*) has been deprived
(*b*) have been deprived
(*c*) are being deprived
(*d*) No improvement

35. If he had money, *he will buy a house*.
(*a*) he is buying a house
(*b*) he were buying a house
(*c*) he did buy a house
(*d*) No improvement

36. When he met her for the first time, he felt as if he *had been knowing* her all his life.
(*a*) knew (*b*) was knowing
(*c*) had known (*d*) No improvement

37. If I *would have seen* the book earlier, I would have recommended it to my students.
(*a*) could see (*b*) had seen
(*c*) saw (*d*) No correction required

38. Even if I had stood on a chair, I *would not have been able to reach* the light bulb.
(*a*) did not reach
(*b*) could not reach
(*c*) would not be reaching
(*d*) No improvement **(C.D.S. 1995)**

39. He did not even listen to me, *leaving aside* staying here.
(*a*) leave aside (*b*) leave beside
(*c*) leave besides (*d*) after leaving aside
(*e*) No correction required

40. The money is to be used *for the benefit of the poor.*
(*a*) for benefit of poor people
(*b*) for the benefit of the poors
(*c*) for the benefit of the poor people
(*d*) No improvement

41. *If we finish* our work in time, we'll go for a movie.
(*a*) If we finished (*b*) If we will finish
(*c*) If we would finish
(*d*) No improvement

42. Do you know who *she is going to marry*?
(*a*) who she is married?
(*b*) who is she going to marry?
(*c*) whom she is going to marry?
(*d*) No improvement **(N.D.A. 1994)**

43. She became conscientious when she realised that *the opposite man* was staring at her.
(*a*) the man opposite (*b*) the opposed man
(*c*) man opposite (*d*) No improvement

44. She told me that there was *more room* to accomodate all the guests.
(*a*) open space (*b*) sufficient room
(*c*) enough rooms (*d*) No improvement

45. After the communal frenzy, slogans now *occupy* the air, exhorting the people to promote peace, harmony and amity.
(*a*) thicken (*b*) fill
(*c*) infest (*d*) mark
(Translators' Exam, 1994)

46. The intellectual interest which is the mainspring of George Eliot's inspiration alters the angle from which she approaches *each aspect* of her subject matter.
(*a*) either aspect (*b*) every aspect

(*c*) any aspect (*d*) No improvement

47. *On basis* this information the Deputy Collector took strong action. **(N.D.A. 1996)**
(*a*) On basis of (*b*) On the basis
(*c*) On the basis of (*d*) No improvement

48. Mahatma Gandhi is *called as the Father of the Nation*. **(N.D.A. 1996)**
(*a*) Father of the Nation
(*b*) called Father of the Nation
(*c*) called the Father of the Nation
(*d*) No improvement

49. Don't be disturbed, *get with* your work.
(*a*) get up with (*b*) get over with
(*c*) get on with (*d*) No improvement

50. We *might have been* visited the sick man if we knew that he was in the hospital.
(*a*) would have been (*b*) will have
(*c*) would have (*d*) may have been
(*e*) No correction required

ANSWERS

1. (*a*)	**2.** (*c*)	**3.** (*b*)	**4.** (*b*)	**5.** (*b*)	**6.** (*c*)	**7.** (*c*)	**8.** (*a*)	**9.** (*c*)	**10.** (*d*)
11. (*c*)	**12.** (*d*)	**13.** (*b*)	**14.** (*c*)	**15.** (*d*)	**16.** (*c*)	**17.** (*b*)	**18.** (*c*)	**19.** (*d*)	**20.** (*a*)
21. (*c*)	**22.** (*d*)	**23.** (*b*)	**24.** (*b*)	**25.** (*d*)	**26.** (*b*)	**27.** (*b*)	**28.** (*d*)	**29.** (*d*)	**30.** (*c*)
31. (*a*)	**32.** (*b*)	**33.** (*b*)	**34.** (*b*)	**35.** (*c*)	**36.** (*c*)	**37.** (*b*)	**38.** (*d*)	**39.** (*a*)	**40.** (*c*)
41. (*d*)	**42.** (*b*)	**43.** (*a*)	**44.** (*b*)	**45.** (*b*)	**46.** (*b*)	**47.** (*c*)	**48.** (*c*)	**49.** (*c*)	**50.** (*c*)

PRACTICE SET 14

Directions : ***In each of the following questions, a part of the sentence is italicised. Alternatives to the portions italicised, which may improve the sentence, are given. Choose the appropriate alternative. In case no improvement is needed, choose 'No improvement' or 'No correction required' as your answer.***

1. I took the cycle *which he bought yesterday*. **(Stenographers' Exam, 1995)**
(*a*) that he bought yesterday
(*b*) that he had bought yesterday
(*c*) that which he had bought yesterday
(*d*) No improvement

2. Prices of pulses can go *as high to* Rs. 25 a kg.
(*a*) so high to (*b*) so high as
(*c*) as high as (*d*) No improvement

3. He came to the cave uphill and looked *up the valley*.
(*a*) into the valley (*b*) down the valley
(*c*) across the valley (*d*) No improvement

4. Sunita told me that she would mind *to stand and eating* the lunch.
(*a*) to stand and eat
(*b*) standing and eating
(*c*) standing and eat
(*d*) No correction required **(I. Tax, 1993)**

5. The good fortune *of being your student* in my younger days has helped me greatly in my life.
(*a*) of my having been your student
(*b*) of myself being your student
(*c*) of my being your student
(*d*) No correction required

6. Tell your leader that I grant him permission *of stay* in my kingdom.
(*a*) about stay (*b*) to stay
(*c*) with staying (*d*) for stay
(*e*) No correction required
(B.S.R.B. 1992)

7. The old man felled some trees with *hardly no effort* at all. **(C.D.S. 1995)**
(*a*) hard effort
(*b*) a hardly any effort
(*c*) hardly any effort (*d*) No improvement

8. He could not *cope up with* the heavy rush. **(N.D.A. 1994)**
(*a*) cope up to (*b*) cope by
(*c*) cope with (*d*) No improvement

9. We must *take it granted* that Shaloo will not come for today's function.
(*a*) have it granted (*b*) took it as granted
(*c*) take it for granted
(*d*) No correction required

10. We *might not be* able to change the situation quickly but we should continue our efforts in that direction.
(*a*) could not be (*b*) did not
(*c*) had not been (*d*) would not be
(*e*) No correction required
(Bank P.O. 1994)

11. The right to work implies the obligation on the part of the government to give a job to *all the unemployed*.
(*a*) any of the unemployed
(*b*) every unemployed
(*c*) each of the unemployed
(*d*) No improvement

12. Rakesh's wife *sung* a very sweet song in the party.
(*a*) singed the (*b*) singed
(*c*) sang a (*d*) No improvement

13. We *did not see* this movie yet.
(*a*) had seen (*b*) have not seen
(*c*) have seen (*d*) No improvement
(Stenographers' Exam, 1995)

14. He has formed a low opinion about him, so he *thinks little of him*. **(C.B.I. 1993)**
(*a*) thinks a little of him
(*b*) thinks the little of him
(*c*) little thinks about him
(*d*) No improvement

15. You can mix it *with some sugar* and eat it.
(*a*) any sugar (*b*) in some sugar
(*c*) into some sugar
(*d*) No correction required

16. Oliver was assigned the task of serving *a summons* on Mr. Higgins to appear in a court of law.
(*a*) a summon (*b*) the summons
(*c*) the summon (*d*) No improvement

17. I knew he could not be trusted; *he let off the cat from the bag*. **(C.D.S. 1994)**
(*a*) let the cat from the bag
(*b*) let the cat out of the bag
(*c*) let the cat jump out of the bag
(*d*) No improvement

18. They went *across* the forest into the deep valleys.
(*a*) into (*b*) between (*c*) over
(*d*) through (*e*) No improvement

19. The boys of our class have reported considerable progress *for the implementation of* their policies.
(*a*) in the implementation of
(*b*) by implementing
(*c*) by introducing implements
(*d*) towards implementing
(*e*) No correction required

20. The record for the biggest tiger hunt has not been *met* since 1911 when Lord Hardinge, then Viceroy of India, shot a tiger that measured eleven feet six and three-fourth inches.
(*a*) bettered (*b*) improved
(*c*) broken (*d*) No improvement
(Assistant Grade, 1996)

21. The teacher explained him politely that he *hadn't ought to do* that.
(*a*) hasn't ought to do
(*b*) ought not have done
(*c*) ought not done
(*d*) No correction required

22. It was so hot during the school parade that several of the weaker pupils passed *by*. **(N.D.A. 1992)**
(*a*) out (*b*) through
(*c*) over (*d*) No improvement

23. Having spent her childhood in Bombay, she has developed her ability to converse in Marathi *rather good*.
(*a*) rather well (*b*) rather better
(*c*) fairly well (*d*) good rather
(*e*) No correction required

24. As there was no time, the remaining items *were deferred into* the next meeting.
(*a*) were deferred to (*b*) were deferred till
(*c*) are deferred upto (*d*) No improvement

25. His *powerful desire* brought about his downfall. **(I.E.S. 1994)**
(*a*) His fatal desire
(*b*) His intense desire
(*c*) His desire for power
(*d*) No improvement

26. I *was living* in Dehradun for ten years when I was a child.
(*a*) had lived (*b*) had been living
(*c*) lived (*d*) No improvement

27. My friend and *me* study together during holidays.
(*a*) I (*b*) myself
(*c*) I myself (*d*) No improvement

28. He opened the letter without *caring* to read the address on the envelope.
(*a*) thinking (*b*) bothering
(*c*) worrying (*d*) No improvement
(U.D.C. 1995)

29. Even though viable alternatives exist, their use is yet to catch on *into a major way*.
(*a*) in a major way (*b*) under a major way
(*c*) upto a major way (*d*) No improvement

30. We were still standing in the queue when the *film was beginning*. **(Bank P.O. 1994)**
(*a*) film begins (*b*) film had begun
(*c*) film began
(*d*) beginning of the film was over
(*e*) No correction required

31. He *shook hand with me* after receiving the prize.
(*a*) shook my hand (*b*) shook my hands
(*c*) shook hands with me
(*d*) No improvement

32. Poor Tom *laid* in the shade of a tree before he could walk further. **(N.D.A. 1996)**
(*a*) lied (*b*) lain
(*c*) lay (*d*) No improvement

33. They asked me *that how I got* time to write all these books.
(*a*) how did I get (*b*) that how did I get
(*c*) how I got
(*d*) that how I was getting
(*e*) No correction required

34. He spent much time and energy over it, and lost a large sum *in the bargain*.
(*a*) into the bargain (*b*) with the bargain
(*c*) off the bargain (*d*) for the bargain
(*e*) No correction required
(S.B.I.P.O. 1991)

35. He was sure that given enough time, contentious issues *would be sort themselves out*.
(*a*) would sort themselves by
(*b*) would be sorted out
(*c*) would sort themselves out
(*d*) will sort themselves out
(*e*) No correction required

36. As soon as our plan is approved, I shall favour *its'* adoption. **(C.D.S. 1992)**
(*a*) our (*b*) it's
(*c*) its (*d*) No improvement

37. The blue jacket is the *least expensive* of the two apparels.
(*a*) the less expensive
(*b*) less expensive
(*c*) the lesser expensive
(*d*) No improvement

38. The Principal lamented that though a detailed report was submitted to the management a month ago *no action is being taken* so far. **(Bank P.O. 1994)**
(*a*) no action had taken
(*b*) no action has been taken
(*c*) no action was being taken
(*d*) any action had been taken
(*e*) No correction required

39. This is the very first criminal case in which the suspect's name has figured and no one *is quietly ready to hazard* a guess.
(*a*) is quite ready to hazard
(*b*) is quite readily to hazard
(*c*) was quite ready to hazard
(*d*) No correction required

40. The practical importance of the role of the industrialist in the establishment of the new order is greater than *the economist and the politician*.
(*a*) of the economist and the politicians
(*b*) that of the economist's and the politician's
(*c*) that of the economist and the politician
(*d*) No improvement **(Railways, 1993)**

41. Nanda *was hurried* to the station when she dashed against the car.
(*a*) was being hurried (*b*) is hurried
(*c*) was hurrying (*d*) was to hurry
(*e*) No correction required

42. I can always *count on him* in times of difficulty. **(B.S.R.B. 1996)**
(*a*) count at him (*b*) count on he
(*c*) count him on (*d*) count with him
(*e*) No correction required

43. Galileo escaped *burning* for heresy because he apologized and withdrew his previous statements. **(C.D.S. 1995)**
(*a*) being burnt (*b*) from being burnt
(*c*) from having been burnt
(*d*) No improvement

44. Whatever be our other problems, we have no *shortcoming* of cheap labour in India.
(*a*) deficit (*b*) scarcity
(*c*) default (*d*) No improvement

45. He *makes friends* with all kinds of people.
(*a*) makes friendship
(*b*) makes friend
(*c*) made friendship
(*d*) No improvement

46. The *car's doors are loose*. **(C.B.I. 1995)**
(*a*) car-doors are loose
(*b*) doors of car are loose
(*c*) doors of the car are loose
(*d*) No improvement

47. The country is in *as much disorder* that it will take years to set it right.
(*a*) much disorder (*b*) so disorder
(*c*) so much disorder (*d*) No improvement

48. When he arrived to attend the wedding of his brother, he *had been dressed* in a dark suit. **(N.D.A. 1996)**
(*a*) dressed (*b*) was dressed
(*c*) had dressed (*d*) No improvement

49. The detectives followed *on* several clues but failed to find the murderer.
(*a*) up (*b*) through
(*c*) by (*d*) No improvement

50. He gave *witness* at the sensational trial.
(*a*) evidence (*b*) proof
(*c*) advice (*d*) No improvement
(Stenographers' Exam, 1994)

ANSWERS

1. (*b*)	**2.** (*c*)	**3.** (*c*)	**4.** (*b*)	**5.** (*a*)	**6.** (*b*)	**7.** (*c*)	**8.** (*c*)	**9.** (*c*)	**10.** (*c*)
11. (*d*)	**12.** (*c*)	**13.** (*b*)	**14.** (*a*)	**15.** (*d*)	**16.** (*d*)	**17.** (*b*)	**18.** (*d*)	**19.** (*a*)	**20.** (*c*)
21. (*b*)	**22.** (*a*)	**23.** (*c*)	**24.** (*b*)	**25.** (*c*)	**26.** (*a*)	**27.** (*b*)	**28.** (*b*)	**29.** (*a*)	**30.** (*b*)
31. (*c*)	**32.** (*c*)	**33.** (*c*)	**34.** (*e*)	**35.** (*c*)	**36.** (*c*)	**37.** (*a*)	**38.** (*b*)	**39.** (*a*)	**40.** (*c*)
41. (*c*)	**42.** (*e*)	**43.** (*c*)	**44.** (*b*)	**45.** (*d*)	**46.** (*c*)	**47.** (*c*)	**48.** (*b*)	**49.** (*a*)	**50.** (*a*)

PRACTICE SET 15

Directions : *Look at the italicised part of the sentence. Below each sentence are given some possible substitutions for the italicised part. If one of them is better than the italicised part, indicate your response against the corresponding letter. If none of the substitutions improve the sentence, indicate 'No improvement' or 'No correction required' as your response.*

1. The situation remained the same, rather got worse, *all his efforts notwithstanding.* **(C.D.S. 1994)**
(*a*) for all his efforts notwithstanding
(*b*) with all his efforts notwithstanding
(*c*) inspite of all his efforts not withstanding
(*d*) No improvement

2. A thing of beauty *is joy* for ever.
(*a*) is joyous (*b*) is the joy
(*c*) is a joy (*d*) No improvement

3. By aligning with him, he was heading *into* a serious disaster.
(*a*) along (*b*) towards
(*c*) for (*d*) No improvement

4. *There is no more room* for you in this compartment. **(Section Officers, 1993)**
(*a*) There is no more accomodation
(*b*) There is no more space
(*c*) There is no more seat
(*d*) No improvement

5. We should be bound by a code of conduct, *isn't it ?*
(*a*) shouldn't we? (*b*) shouldn't we be?
(*c*) aren't we? (*d*) No improvement

6. The best of us are not without *faults or failings.*
(*a*) fault and failings
(*b*) faults and failures
(*c*) faults and failings
(*d*) No improvement

7. He drives as if the road *belongs* to him.
(*a*) has belonged (*b*) belonged
(*c*) is belonging (*d*) No improvement

8. Twenty kilometres *are not a great distance* in these days of fast moving vehicles. **(I.E.S. 1994)**
(*a*) is no distance
(*b*) is not a great distance
(*c*) aren't a great distance
(*d*) No improvement

9. As per my instructions he *sent a word* to me informing me of the sick man's condition.
(*a*) sent word (*b*) had sent a word
(*c*) sent words (*d*) No improvement

10. As far as good schooling is concerned, *none except few* privileged people can afford it for their children.
(*a*) none but few
(*b*) none more than a few
(*c*) none except a few
(*d*) No correction required

11. It is time *to immediately put the work in hand.* **(U.D.C. 1994)**
(*a*) to put the work immediately in hand
(*b*) to put the work in hand immediately
(*c*) immediately to put the work in hand
(*d*) No improvement

12. *I have already read this book twice.*
(*a*) I already twice have read this book.
(*b*) I twice have already read this book.
(*c*) I have twice already read this book.
(*d*) No improvement

13. Although India is still *by far* a poor country, it can become rich if its natural and human resources are fully utilised.
(*a*) by and by (*b*) by and large
(*c*) few and far between
(*d*) No improvement **(C.D.S. 1995)**

14. I don't understand *that how you think* of going to Kashmir in winter.
(*a*) that how do you think
(*b*) how you think
(*c*) that how you thought
(*d*) how do you think
(*e*) No improvement

15. He was selected for the job because he has very good command *on* English.
(*a*) over (*b*) of
(*c*) in (*d*) No improvement

16. He said firmly that he would *rather starve to stealing* to get what he needed.
(*a*) starve to rather stealing
(*b*) starve to rather steal
(*c*) rather starve than steal
(*d*) rather starving to stealing
(*e*) No correction required
(S.B.I.P.O. 1991)

17. By the end of this century, scientists surely *have discovered* a cure for cancer.
(*a*) are discovering
(*b*) will have discovered
(*c*) must discover
(*d*) will have been discovered
(*e*) No improvement

18. He is extraordinarily *clever at mimicking* his friends. **(C.D.S. 1992)**
(*a*) clever to mimick
(*b*) clever for mimicking
(*c*) clever in mimicking
(*d*) No improvement

19 The *less* chances you take, the greater your piece of mind will be but, then again, the high profits that you hope for may never eventuate.
(*a*) little (*b*) lesser
(*c*) fewer (*d*) No improvement

20. The popularity of the novels of Prem Chand, though they are full of sad and painful incidents, lies in the fact that they *end with happiness*.
(*a*) end happily
(*b*) are all ending with happiness
(*c*) have a happy ending
(*d*) No improvement

21. *As soon as* I stepped inside the hall, I could hear the sound of boys and girls singing aloud.
(*a*) No sooner had (*b*) Hardly
(*c*) Sooner than (*d*) No improvement

22. When the clock struck six I *was waiting* here for an hour. **(Asstt. Grade, 1995)**
(*a*) had waited (*b*) had been waiting
(*c*) shall have waited (*d*) No improvement

23. The gangsters *have taken shelter* at the old house last month after the police ordered their arrest.
(*a*) took shelter (*b*) are taking shelter
(*c*) had taken shelter (*d*) No improvement

24. *If the room had been brighter*, I would have been able to read for a while before bed time. **(C.D.S. 1993)**
(*a*) If the room was brighter
(*b*) If rooms are brighter
(*c*) Had the room been brighter
(*d*) No improvement

25. There is that special quality which makes him *who he is*.
(*a*) where he is (*b*) what he is
(*c*) why he is (*d*) whom he is
(*e*) No improvement

26. Most of the employees from Rajan's factory were not *inclination to* using the new technology. **(Bank P.O. 1994)**
(*a*) inclined to be (*b*) incline to
(*c*) inclined to (*d*) inclining to
(*e*) No correction required

27. Only a potter can shape *clay in a pot*.
(*a*) clay into a pot (*b*) clay as a pot
(*c*) the clay as a pot (*d*) No improvement

28. He did not respond to her inquiring, I *did not neither*.
(*a*) I did neither (*b*) nor did I
(*c*) I did either (*d*) No improvement

29. Evidently *very much people* are involved in the new scheme implementation.
(*a*) very many people
(*b*) very more people
(*c*) very such people
(*d*) No improvement

30. When the solider retunred home after the war was over, his wife received him *with open hands*. **(C.B.I. 1993)**
(*a*) with open arms
(*b*) with unfolded hands
(*c*) with an open heart
(*d*) No improvement

31. You ought to *stating the problem first* before proceeding to suggest the solution.
(*a*) state the problem at first
(*b*) state the problem first
(*c*) first stating the problem
(*d*) No improvement

32. Sri Pashupatinath is a *worth seeing temple* in Kathmandu.
(*a*) a temple worth seeing
(*b*) a temple to see its worth
(*c*) one of the worth seeing temples
(*d*) No improvement **(N.D.A. 1996)**

33. Even the people in authority agree that corruption has become *today's order*.
(*a*) the order of the day
(*b*) the order of today
(*c*) the day's order
(*d*) No improvement **(N.D.A. 1996)**

34. Being a handicapped youth, he *was put hard to* complete his military course.
(*a*) was hard put to
(*b*) was put to it hard
(*c*) was hardly put to
(*d*) No improvement **(C.D.S. 1994)**

35. When I get home, my children *would be* playing.
(*a*) would have been (*b*) will be
(*c*) have been
(*d*) No correction required

36. He didn't believe in God *but* he went to church regularly.
(*a*) yet (*b*) nevertheless
(*c*) however (*d*) No improvement

37. According to the Planning Commission estimates, by the year 2000, India *will have become* self-sufficient in petroleum products. **(N.D.A. 1995)**
(*a*) would have become
(*b*) shall have become
(*c*) should have become
(*d*) No improvement

38. *If he studied more*, Kamal would have been able to secure a good first division.
(*a*) If he would have studied more
(*b*) If he were studying more
(*c*) If he had studied more
(*d*) No improvement

39. He was extremely unhappy because of *the inordinately delay*. **(Bank P.O. 1995)**
(*a*) the inordinate delaying
(*b*) the inordinate delay
(*c*) the inordinately delaying
(*d*) inordinate delaying
(*e*) No correction required

40. She is not used *to work* for so long.
(*a*) to working (*b*) to have worked
(*c*) to be working (*d*) No improvement

41. She says she's already paid me back, but I can't remember, so I'll have *to take her word*. **(C.D.S. 1995)**
(*a*) to take her word true
(*b*) to take her at her word
(*c*) to take her word for it
(*d*) No improvement

42. As the poet ages, he naturally writes with sorrow of the process of decay *in the life and time*.
(*a*) in a life and a time
(*b*) in life and time
(*c*) in life and the time
(*d*) No improvement

43. After the discovery of the small pox vaccine, there *is* no cases of the disease in India.
(*a*) are (*b*) were being
(*c*) have been (*d*) No improvement

44. The mother has not seen the child for several months and now eagerly *looks forward* to seeing him. **(C.D.S. 1994)**
(*a*) looks for
(*b*) looks onto
(*c*) looks ahead to
(*d*) No improvement

45. Your father will *buy for you a new bag*.
(*a*) buy new bag for you
(*b*) buy you new bag
(*c*) buy you a new bag
(*d*) No correction required

46. *Although partially destroyed, the experts able to infer* from what remained that the treasure was buried in the cave.
(*a*) Although partially destroyed, the experts had inferred
(*b*) Partially destroyed though it had, the experts able to infer
(*c*) Destroyed partially, the experts were able to infer
(*d*) Although it had been partially destroyed, the experts were able to infer
(*e*) No correction required **(R.B.I. 1990)**

47. The expert *was very interesting* in this candidate.
(*a*) was having interest
(*b*) was very interested
(*c*) is having interest
(*d*) No improvement

48. I had a strange intrusion that *he will steal the watch*.
(*a*) he may steal the watch
(*b*) he would steal the watch
(*c*) he will be stealing the watch
(*d*) No correction required

49. To learn a language well, one must have patience and *readiness to work* hard.
(*a*) readiness to working
(*b*) be ready to working
(*c*) ready to working
(*d*) No improvement

50. You can't imagine *that she is rude and arrogant*.
(*a*) that she is rudely and arrogant
(*b*) how rude and arrogant she is
(*c*) what rudeness and arrogance she has
(*d*) No correction required

ANSWERS

1. (*b*)	**2.** (*c*)	**3.** (*c*)	**4.** (*b*)	**5.** (*a*)	**6.** (*c*)	**7.** (*b*)	**8.** (*b*)	**9.** (*a*)	**10.** (*c*)
11. (*b*)	**12.** (*d*)	**13.** (*b*)	**14.** (*b*)	**15.** (*b*)	**16.** (*c*)	**17.** (*b*)	**18.** (*c*)	**19.** (*c*)	**20.** (*c*)
21. (*d*)	**22.** (*b*)	**23.** (*d*)	**24.** (*c*)	**25.** (*b*)	**26.** (*c*)	**27.** (*a*)	**28.** (*b*)	**29.** (*a*)	**30.** (*a*)
31. (*b*)	**32.** (*a*)	**33.** (*a*)	**34.** (*a*)	**35.** (*b*)	**36.** (*a*)	**37.** (*d*)	**38.** (*c*)	**39.** (*b*)	**40.** (*a*)
41. (*b*)	**42.** (*b*)	**43.** (*c*)	**44.** (*d*)	**45.** (*c*)	**46.** (*d*)	**47.** (*b*)	**48.** (*b*)	**49.** (*d*)	**50.** (*b*)

17. PASSAGE CORRECTION

The questions under this section are very similar to those on sentence Correction, the only difference being that here a short passage is given in which certain words or phrases are italicised and are required to be improved by substituting them with one of the alternatives given.

PRACTICE SET

Directions : In the following passage, there are words/groups of words printed in italics, each of which was been numbered. These numbers are printed below the passage and against each, four words/group of words are suggested which can substitute the word printed in italics. Find out the choice which can correctly substitute that word. If the word/group of words is correct as it is and no correction is required, give 'No correction required' as your answer.

Passage 1 **(Bank P.O. 1994)**

What looks very much like genocide *has been* (1) taking place in Rwanda. People are pulled *on* (2) cars and buses, ordered to *defer* (3) their identity papers and then killed on the spot *until* (4) they belong to the wrong ethnic group. Thousands of bodies have already *given* (5) up, and the *peace* (6) continues despite the *present* (7) of 1700 United Nations peace keepers.

1. (*a*) would be (*b*) were not (*c*) has never been (*d*) will be (*e*) No correction required

2. (*a*) within (*b*) from (*c*) out (*d*) to (*e*) No correction required

3. (*a*) forget (*b*) dissolve (*c*) show (*d*) stand (*e*) No correction required

4. (*a*) why (*b*) then (*c*) again (*d*) if (*e*) No correction required

5. (*a*) piled (*b*) gone (*c*) stood (*d*) woken (*e*) No correction required

6. (*a*) future (*b*) understanding (*c*) life (*d*) killing (*e*) No correction required

7. (*a*) presence (*b*) followers (*c*) presenting (*d*) recurrance (*e*) No correction required

Passage 2

National integration is, therefore, the need of the hour. India *had already suffered*(8) centuries of servitude and enslavement. Perhaps India is the only country in the world, which has suffered foreign rule *of* (9) more than seven hundred and fifty years. The internal dissensions among the Rajput kings and princes allowed the Muslim *rulers* (10) to establish their foothold in India, which was *prolonged* (11) as long as five centuries. Then there was once again a time when destiny gave India a chance to be united. But the British ingenuously succeeded in creating a *rift* (12) between different kings and established their sway which was *discarded* (13) only when the different links of Indian nationhood were joined together again by Indian leaders of unparalleled political *skill* (14), who were not creations of history but creators of history. They had realised that India's sorrow had *risen* (15) from disunity. The mighty efforts of these leaders succeeded and India achieved independence, but India's heart *had been* (16) vivisected in the creation of Pakistan.

8. (*a*) has already suffered (*b*) has had already suffered (*c*) had already been suffering (*d*) suffered already (*e*) No correction required

9. (*a*) from (*b*) since (*c*) for (*d*) over (*e*) No correction required

10. (*a*) plunderers (*b*) intruders (*c*) invaders (*d*) attackers (*e*) No correction required

11. (*a*) prolonged to (*b*) prolonged for (*c*) prolonged over (*d*) prolonged upto (*e*) No correction required

12. (*a*) gap (*b*) differences (*c*) barrier (*d*) hindrance (*e*) No correction required

13. (*a*) abolished (*b*) overthrown (*c*) overruled (*d*) prohibited (*e*) No correction required

14. (*a*) aptitude (*b*) tact (*c*) acumen (*d*) attitude (*e*) No correction required

15. (*a*) developed (*b*) originated (*c*) arose (*d*) fructified (*e*) No correction required

16. (*a*) was being (*b*) had (*c*) has had (*d*) was (*e*) No correction required

Passage 3

Health is priceless wealth. It *is* (17) said so because ordinary lost wealth *may* (18) be regained but the health once lost cannot be *recouped* (19). A sound mind rests *in* (20) a healthy body.

17. (*a*) was (*b*) is being (*c*) has been (*d*) No correction required
18. (*a*) can (*b*) might (*c*) would (*d*) No correction required
19. (*a*) revived (*b*) replenished (*c*) compensated (*d*) No correction required
20. (*a*) with (*b*) within (*c*) inside (*d*) No correction required

Passage 4

Our body is a wondrous mechanism and when *revealed* (21) to unusual stress over a *spell* (22) of time, it adapts itself to deal more effectively with that stress. So, *if* (23) you exert your muscles *to* (24) resistance, they are forced to adapt and deal with this extraordinary workload. Strands of muscle fibres become thicker and stronger in response to the demands placed *over* (25) them.

21. (*a*) exposed (*b*) put (*c*) rendered (*d*) subjected (*e*) No correction required
22. (*a*) duration (*b*) period (*c*) lapse (*d*) interval (*e*) No correction required
23. (*a*) while (*b*) as (*c*) since (*d*) when (*e*) No correction required
24. (*a*) against (*b*) towards (*c*) upon (*d*) for (*e*) No correction required
25. (*a*) on (*b*) over (*c*) to (*d*) for (*e*) No correction required

Passage 5

If more people *could travel* (26)– both inside and outside the country - there would be a *splendid* (27) increase in knowledge and understanding of their neighbours. Because people remain *stationary* (28) in their areas, in which they are born, they tend to *look to* (29) those *in* (30) other states as foreigners and obstruct the *development* (31) of national integration.

26. (*a*) will travel (*b*) shall be travelling (*c*) travel (*d*) No change
27. (*a*) immense (*b*) tremendous (*c*) exciting (*d*) No change
28. (*a*) static (*b*) immobile (*c*) passive (*d*) No change
29. (*a*) look upon (*b*) look on (*c*) look down (*d*) No change
30. (*a*) of (*b*) from (*c*) on (*d*) No change
31. (*a*) advancement (*b*) progress (*c*) promotion (*d*) No change

Passage 6

Nehru was a humanist in the *way* (32) that he thought primarily *for* (33) human beings, their difficulties, worries and anxieties, *beyond* (34) Parliament, administration and all the trappings of civilisation. He had power, immense power, but that *would not* (35) diminish the interest he took in ordinary people, particularly children, and in human relationships.

32. (*a*) manner (*b*) sense (*c*) style (*d*) pretext (*e*) No correction required
33. (*a*) about (*b*) over (*c*) on (*d*) of (*e*) No correction required
34. (*a*) above (*b*) over (*c*) upon (*d*) beyond (*e*) No correction required
35. (*a*) did not (*b*) could not (*c*) won't (*d*) should not (*e*) No correction required

Passage 7

Since you have never had to *pester* (36) me for anything, perhaps you wouldn't be *averse to* (37) sticking to me now that I have *run under* (38) debt, and *realising* (39) these people, that it is *by* (40) no way a reflection on my character.

36. (*a*) assert (*b*) approach (*c*) reproach (*d*) No change
37. (*a*) desirous of (*b*) indifferent to (*c*) deprived of (*d*) No change
38. (*a*) run in (*b*) run on (*c*) run into (*d*) No change
39. (*a*) informing (*b*) convincing (*c*) alluding (*d*) No change
40. (*a*) in (*b*) to (*c*) for (*d*) No change

ANSWERS

1. (*e*)	**2.** (*b*)	**3.** (*c*)	**4.** (*d*)	**5.** (*a*)	**6.** (*d*)	**7.** (*a*)	**8.** (*a*)	**9.** (*c*)	**10.** (*c*)
11. (*e*)	**12.** (*e*)	**13.** (*b*)	**14.** (*c*)	**15.** (*b*)	**16.** (*e*)	**17.** (*c*)	**18.** (*a*)	**19.** (*d*)	**20.** (*b*)
21. (*d*)	**22.** (*b*)	**23.** (*d*)	**24.** (*a*)	**25.** (*a*)	**26.** (*d*)	**27.** (*b*)	**28.** (*a*)	**29.** (*a*)	**30.** (*b*)
31. (*c*)	**32.** (*b*)	**33.** (*d*)	**34.** (*a*)	**35.** (*a*)	**36.** (*c*)	**37.** (*d*)	**38.** (*c*)	**39.** (*b*)	**40.** (*a*)

18. CHOOSING THE CORRECT / INCORRECT SENTENCE

TYPE 1 : When different forms of the same sentence are given

Example : ***Below are given different forms of a sentence labelled as (a), (b), (c), (d) and (e). Choose the one which conveys the meaning of the sentence correctly.*** **(Bank P.O. 1996)**

(*a*) As the train which is my usual was missing I had to travel on the next.
(*b*) Having missed the train which I usually catch and had to travel on the next.
(*c*) The train which I usually catch being missed I had to travel on the next.
(*d*) I missed the train which I usually catch and had to travel by the next.
(*e*) I missed not only the train which I usually catch but had to travel on the next.

Solution : Clearly, sentence (*d*) is grammatically correct and it also conveys the exact meaning.

Hence, the answer is (*d*).

PRACTICE SET 1

Directions : ***In each of the following questions, some sentences are given which are on the same theme. Decide which sentence is the most preferable with respect to grammar, meaning and usage, suitable for a formal writing in English.***

1. (*a*) Our school had won the match if only we have concentrated.
(*b*) Our school would have won the match if only we would have concentrated.
(*c*) Our school would win the match only if we had concentrated.
(*d*) Our school had won the match if only we would have concentrated.
(*e*) Our school would have won the match if only we had concentrated. **(Bank P.O. 1996)**

2. (*a*) He will not pay unless he is not compelled.
(*b*) He will not pay unless he will be compelled.
(*c*) He will not pay unless he is compelled.
(*d*) He will not pay till he is compelled.

3. (*a*) The boy regretted that he had spend a greater part of his vacation in the chair with a plastered leg.
(*b*) With a plastered leg, the boy regretted that he had spent a greater part of his vacation in the chair.
(*c*) The boy regretted that with a plastered leg he had spent a greater part of his vacation in the chair.
(*d*) The boy with a plastered leg regretted that he had spent a greater part of his vacation in the chair. **(Assistant Grade, 1993)**

4. (*a*) If you will pay heed to the small details, the general plans will surely succeed.
(*b*) If you pay heed to the small details, the general plans will surely succeed.
(*c*) If you would heed the small details, the general plans would have succeeded.
(*d*) If you heeded to the small details, the general plans would surely succeed.

5. (*a*) It is a pleasure to see an alligator basking in the sunshine on a river bank as long as 90 feet.
(*b*) It is a pleasure to see an alligator as long as 90 feet basking in the sunshine on a river bnak.
(*c*) It is a pleasure to see an alligator basking in the sunshine as long as 90 feet on a river bank.
(*d*) It is a pleasure to see an alligator basking as long as 90 feet in the sunshine on a river bank. **(I. Tax & Central Excise, 1993)**

6. (*a*) Without your help I must try to carry out my task alone.
(*b*) Barring your help I should try to carry out my task alone.
(*c*) Besides help from you, I must try to carry out my task alone.
(*d*) Failing your help I must try to carry out my task alone.

7. (*a*) There will be a meeting in the long room at 4 o'clock of all the boys who play cricket and football.
(*b*) There will be a meeting of all the boys who play cricket and football in the long room at 4 o'clock.

(*c*) There will be in the long room at 4 o'clock a meeting of all the boys who play cricket and football.

(*d*) In the long room at 4 o'clock there will be a meeting of all the boys who play cricket and football.

(U.D.C. 1994)

8. (*a*) Since the dividend being declared than the notices were prepared for mailing.

(*b*) Scarcely had the dividend been declared than the notices were sent out.

(*c*) They had no sooner declared the dividend when they sent the notices to the stockholders.

(*d*) No sooner had the dividend been declared than the notices were prepared for mailing.

(*e*) The company had hardly declared the dividend till the notices were prepared for mailing.

(S.B.I.P.O. 1995)

9. (*a*) The dacoits being stopped to divide the booty, the police overtook them.

(*b*) Since the dacoits stopped to divide the booty, the police had overtaken them.

(*c*) The dacoits having stopped to divide the booty, the police overtook them.

(*d*) The dacoits having been stopped for dividing the botty, the police overtook them.

10. (*a*) Since he lacked needed money, he never turned down anyone who needed help.

(*b*) He wasn't rich by any means, although he never turned down anyone who needed help.

(*c*) Being not rich by any means, he never turned away anyone who needed help.

(*d*) He was't rich by any means, but he never turned away anyone who needed help.

(*e*) Since he wasn't rich by any means, he never turned away anyone who needed help. **(Bank P.O. 1996)**

11. (*a*) He came in too quickly to avoid waking his father.

(*b*) He entered in quickly, so as not to wake his father.

(*c*) Having not to wake his father, he came in quickly.

(*d*) He came in very quickly so that he might avoid waking his father.

12. (*a*) The harassed wife shot herself after bidding her husband the last good bye with a gun.

(*b*) The harassed wife with a gun shot herself ater bidding her husband the last goodbye.

(*c*) The harassed wife shot herself with a gun after bidding her husband the last goodbye.

(*d*) With a gun the harassed wife shot herself, ater bidding her husband the last goodbye.

(Assistant Grade, 1993)

13. (*a*) Many works must close owing to lack of fuel, if the strike lasts till the weekend.

(*b*) If the strike lasts for the weekend, owing to lack of fuel, many works must close.

(*c*) Owing to lack of fuel, many works must close if the strike lasts over the weekend.

(*d*) Having the strike lasting to the weekend, many works must close for lack of fuel.

14. (*a*) The receptionist must answer courteously the questions what are asked by the callers.

(*b*) The receptionist must answer courteously the questions of all the callers.

(*c*) The receptionist should answer courteously the questions of all callers.

(*d*) The receptionist courteously should answer the questions of all callers.

(*e*) There would have been no trouble if the receptionist had have always answered courteously.

(S.B.I.P.O. 1995)

15. (*a*) The teacher asked the student with a frown on his face, to leave the room.

(*b*) The teacher asked with a frown on his face the student to leave the room.

(*c*) With a frown on his face, the teacher asked the student to leave the room.

(*d*) The teacher asked the student to leave the room with a frown on his face. **(U.D.C. 1994)**

16. (*a*) He was shot without effect by a secretary under notice to quit, with whom he was finding fault, very fortunately.

(b) He was shot without effect very fortunately by a secretary, with whom he was finding fault, under notice to quit.
(c) By a secretary under notice to quit, with whom he was finding fault, he was very fortunately shot without effect.
(d) Very fortunately, he was shot without effect by a secretary under notice to quit, with whom he was finding fault.

17. (a) I was rather impressed by the manner of the speaker than by his matter.
(b) I was impressed by the manner of the speaker rather than by his matter.
(c) Rather I was impressed by the manner of the speaker than by his matter.
(d) I was impressed rather by the manner of the speaker than by his matter.
(I. Tax & Central Excise, 1993)

18. (a) We had in this village, some twenty years ago, an idiot boy, whom I well remember, who from a child showed strong propensity for bees.
(b) Some twenty years ago, we had an idiot boy in this village, who from a child showed strong propensity for bees, whom I well remember.
(c) We had an idiot boy, whom I well remember, who from a child showed strong propensity for bees, in this village some twenty years ago.
(d) In this village, we had an idiot boy some twenty years ago, who from a child showed strong propensity for bees, whom I well remember.

19. (a) Common people are rather impressed by the style of a speech than by its substance.
(b) Common people are impressed rather by the style of a speech than by its substance.
(c) Rather common people are impressed by the style of a speech than by its substance.
(d) Common people are impressed by the style of a speech than by its substance. **(Assistant Grade, 1993)**

20. (a) The committee was useless because there was no needed power to it.
(b) Since the committee lacked needed power it would not have delivered expected result.
(c) Since the committee lacked needed power it could not deliver the expected result.
(d) Since committee did not have needed power it has not delivered useful result.
(e) Being that the committee lacked needed power, it could not deliver expected result.

21. (a) Hoping to be hearing from you, I remain yours sincerely.
(b) Hoping to hear from you, I remain yours sincerely.
(c) Hoping to have heard from you, I sincerely remain yours.
(d) Sincerely I remain yours hoping to be hearing from you.

22. (a) The report was useless to them because there was no needed information.
(b) Since the report lacked needed information it would have not been useful to them.
(c) Since the report did not contain the needed information it ws not real useful to them.
(d) Bening that the report lacked the needed information, they could not use it.
(e) Since the report lacked needed information it was of no use to them. **(S.B.I.P.O. 1995)**

23. (a) In thirty seven bomb-blasts, fortunately only five lives were lost.
(b) In thirty seven bomb-blasts only five lives were fortunately lost.
(c) In fortunately thirty seven bomb-blasts, only five lives were lost.
(d) Fortunately, in thirty seven bomb-blasts, only five lives were lost.
(U.D.C. 1994)

24. (a) I have read such a lot about him that I am looking forward to seeing him very much.
(b) I am reading such a lot about him that I will be looking forward to seeing him very much.
(c) Having read such a lot about him that I am looking forward to seeing him very much.
(d) I had read such a lot about him that I am looking forward to seeing him very much.

(*e*) With regard to reading such a lot about him that I am looking forward to seeing him very much.

25. (*a*) As soon as holidays begin than this beach will become very crowded.
(*b*) Since the holidays being started this beach becomes very crowded.
(*c*) As soon as the holidays begin this beach will become very crowded.
(*d*) No sooner did the holidays begin than this beach will become very crowded.
(*e*) Scarcely had the holidays begin when this beach becomes very crowded. **(Bank P.O. 1996)**

26. (*a*) Anita was sitting with her husband on the steps of the temple with her lap full of newspapers, when Bunty and Bittoo came up.
(*b*) Anita, with her lap full of newspapers, was sitting with her husband on the steps of the temple when Bunty and Bittoo came up.
(*c*) With her lap full of newspapers, Anita was sitting with her husband on the steps of the temple when Bunty and Bittoo came up.
(*d*) Anita was sitting with her husband on the steps of the temple when Bunty and Bittoo came up with her lap full of newspapers. **(Central Excise, 1993)**

27. (*a*) It is far too hard an essay for me to attempt.
(*b*) It is too far hard an essay to attempt for me.
(*c*) Too far it is an essay hard for me to attempt.
(*d*) It is too hard an essay for me to far attempt.

28. (*a*) If you had told me that you were in Bombay I had certainly contacted by you instead of getting bored there.
(*b*) If you had told me that you were in Bombay I would have certainly contacted you despite getting bored there.
(*c*) If you had told me that you were in Bombay I would have certainly contacted you instead of getting bored there.
(*d*) If you would have told me that you were in Bombay I had certainly contacted you instead of getting bored there.
(*e*) If you would have told me that you were in Bombay I would have certainly contacted you instead of getting bored there. **(S.B.I.P.O. 1995)**

29. (*a*) The teaching staff must take their lectures regularly when are asked by the Principal.
(*b*) The teaching staff had taken the lectures regularly had they known that the Principal would come to know about it.
(*c*) The teaching staff would have taken lectures regularly had they known that the Principal would know about it.
(*d*) Many irregularities were found in their lectures by the Principal and he could not be disregarded them. **(Bank P.O. 1996)**

30. (*a*) As one travels from Karjat to Khandala, he finds the line most beautifully laid.
(*b*) Travelling from Karjat to Khandala, one finds the line most beautifully laid.
(*c*) While travelling from Karjat to Khandala, one would find the line most beautifully laid.
(*d*) If one travels from karjat to Khandala, he will find the line most beautifully laid.

31. (*a*) Nobody will want to play in his team if he does not treat people kindly.
(*b*) If he does not treat people kindly, nobody will play to want his team.
(*c*) Nobody will treat people kindly if he does not want to play in his team.
(*d*) Nobody will want to treat people if he does not play in his team kindly. **(I. Tax & Central Excise, 1993)**

32. (*a*) By June next year, Ajay will be twenty years working in the office.
(*b*) Being twenty years completed, Ajay will be working in this office till June next.
(*c*) Till June next year, Ajay will work in the office for twenty years.
(*d*) By June next year, Ajay will have been working in the office for twenty years.
(*e*) Ajay will be working in this office upon completing twenty years by next June. **(Bank P.O. 1996)**

33. (*a*) Our friends left in an imported car the hill station where they had been staying for quite some time.
(*b*) Our friends left the hill station in an imported car where they had been staying for quite some time.
(*c*) Our friends left the hill station where they had been staying for quite some time in an imported car.
(*d*) Our friends in an imported car left the hill station where they had been staying for quite some time.

34. (*a*) He blew out with a gun his brains, after bidding his wife goodbye.
(*b*) He blew out his brains, after bidding his wife goodbye with a gun.
(*c*) He blew out his brains with a gun, after bidding his wife goodbye.
(*d*) With a gun, he blew out his brains, after bidding his wife goodbye.
(I. Tax & Central Excise, 1993)

35. (*a*) Since managers can motivate people in the tasks that need to be done by getting them involved.
(*b*) The managers can motivate people in tasks by getting them involved that needs to be done.
(*c*) The managers not only do the tasks that need to be done by getting them involved but also can motivate people.
(*d*) People can be motivated by getting them involved in the tasks that need to be done by the managers.
(*e*) The managers can motivate people by getting them involved in the tasks that need to be done.

36. (*a*) I went yesterday to the bank to collect the pass-book.
(*b*) I went to the bank yesterday to collect the pass-book.
(*c*) Yesterday to collect the pass-book I went to the bank.
(*d*) To collect the pass-book yesterday, I went to the bank. **(U.D.C. 1994)**

37. (*a*) The typists had corrected the errors had they known that the supervisors would have seen the report.
(*b*) The supervisors reprimanded the typists whom they believed had made careless errors.
(*c*) The errors in the typed reports were so numerous that they could hardly be overlooked.
(*d*) The typists would have corrected the errors had they of known that the supervisors would see the report.
(*e*) Many errors were found in the report which they typed and could not disregarded them **(S.B.I.P.O. 1995)**

38. (*a*) The early age of three or four years, would begin our first recollection of the world, for many of us.
(*b*) Our first recollection of the world, for many of us, would be early age of three or four years.
(*c*) For many of us, our first recollection of the world being the early age of only three or four years.
(*d*) For many of us, our first recollection of the world has been the early age of only three or four years.
(*e*) For many of us, our first recollection of the world is from the early age of only three or four years. **(Bank P.O. 1996)**

ANSWERS

1. (*e*)	**2.** (*c*)	**3.** (*c*)	**4.** (*b*)	**5.** (*b*)	**6.** (*d*)	**7.** (*d*)	**8.** (*d*)	**9.** (*c*)	**10.** (*d*)
11. (*d*)	**12.** (*c*)	**13.** (*c*)	**14.** (*c*)	**15.** (*c*)	**16.** (*d*)	**17.** (*b*)	**18.** (*a*)	**19.** (*d*)	**20.** (*c*)
21. (*b*)	**22.** (*e*)	**23.** (*d*)	**24.** (*a*)	**25.** (*c*)	**26.** (*a*)	**27.** (*a*)	**28.** (*c*)	**29.** (*c*)	**30.** (*b*)
31. (*a*)	**32.** (*d*)	**33.** (*a*)	**34.** (*c*)	**35.** (*e*)	**36.** (*b*)	**37.** (*c*)	**38.** (*a*)		

TYPE 2 : When different sentences are given.

PRACTICE SET 2

Directions : *One of the four sentences given in each question is grammatically wrong. That alternatiave is your answer.*

1. (*a*) Our followers are but a handful.
(*b*) Neither he nor I was there.
(*c*) Many a glorious deeds were done.
(*d*) Everyone of the boys loves to ride.
(Hotel Management, 1995)

2. (*a*) Nothing but funny stories delights him.
(*b*) I cannot raise this lid.
(*c*) This is the book that I want.
(*d*) The thief divested the child from all her jewels.

3. (*a*) Eggs are sold by a dozen.
(*b*) The captain with his soldiers was killed.
(*c*) Why did you absent yourself from your classses ?
(*d*) He acquiesced in my proposal.

4. (*a*) She had finished her work when I met her.
(*b*) Do you believe in God ?
(*c*) He cut his hand with a knife.
(*d*) He challenged me for a duel.

5. (*a*) He feels bad about the defeat.
(*b*) All the boy scouts wear half-pants.
(*c*) He hopes to secure good marks.
(*d*) Gavaskar is the Bradman of India.

6. (*a*) Always write with ink.
(*b*) His tastes coincide with his wife's.
(*c*) Aurangzeb was bigoted in religion.
(*d*) There is no harm in doing this work.

7. (*a*) Copy it word by word.
(*b*) She is out of doors.
(*c*) She prides herself on her wealth and beauty.
(*d*) The dirty old man was repugnant to me.

8. (*a*) He was appointed to the post.
(*b*) Sunil cracks jokes with me.
(*c*) I am confident of securing victory.
(*d*) He has no house to live.

9. (*a*) He has wound up his watch.
(*b*) Children like rather to eat chocolates instead of sweets.
(*c*) He is senior to but less efficient than me.
(*d*) His employer often finds fault with him.

10. (*a*) I was taken ill yesterday.
(*b*) The teacher beat him black and blue.
(*c*) Mr. Roy died on the morning of 15th.
(*d*) He resisted from all temptation.

11. (*a*) He carried little Meenu and I on his shoulders.
(*b*) All that he said had no effect on me.
(*c*) Those who did this thing should be punished.
(*d*) It was I that gave away the prizes.
(Hotel Management,1995)

12. (*a*) Bread and butter is wholesome food.
(*b*) The committee is divided on this issue.
(*c*) It being a wet day, we kept indoors.
(*d*) The cattle are grazing in the fields.

13. (*a*) Neither you nor I am in a sound position.
(*b*) Laziness is detrimental for success.
(*c*) He begged the favour of my granting him leave.
(*d*) Your action is not in conformity with the law.

14. (*a*) She has an abhorrence of frogs.
(*b*) Starch is an antidote of iodine.
(*c*) This is the inference from his statement.
(*d*) I expostulated with Ravi abut his decision.

15. (*a*) It is time you went to bed.
(*b*) There is no end to troubles.
(*c*) We got out of the swimming pool and dried us.
(*d*) He gloried in his victory.

16. (*a*) The dacoits robbed my belongings.
(*b*) The first two pages of this book are torn.
(*c*) He came to us every third day.
(*d*) He atoned for the sin by giving alms to the poor.

17. (*a*) Sumit is my elder brother.
(*b*) He is two years younger to me.
(*c*) He is the eldest man of this village.
(*d*) Ravi is five years older than me.

18. (*a*) On entering the room I found the light quite dim.
(*b*) I don't remember to have met you before.
(*c*) We got into the train at last
(*d*) They fought to the last man.

19. (*a*) It is the most ideal place.
(*b*) The news is too good to be true.
(*c*) These flowers smell sweet.
(*d*) Your watch is better than mine.

20. (*a*) I shall inform them this.
(*b*) He boarded the train.

(*b*) He boarded the train.
(*c*) A bunch of keys has been lost.
(*d*) Ask him why he wastes his time.

21. (*a*) I ascribed his rudeness to his fatigue.
(*b*) He derives pleasure from teasing girls.
(*c*) I despaired for finding my lost watch.
(*d*) Don't trifle with the girl's affections.

22. (*a*) He has no desire for fame.
(*b*) I intend going to Calcutta.
(*c*) He is too miserly to part with his money.
(*d*) He has invited me for dinner.

(Hotel Management, 1995)

23. (*a*) There are not any books on the table.
(*b*) His trouser is very dirty.
(*c*) The roads of Delhi are wider than those of Calcutta.
(*d*) You walk faster than I.

24. (*a*) He was hung for murder.
(*b*) I offered him a chair to sit on.
(*c*) Let's not intrude on his privacy.
(*d*) You should comply with the rules.

25. (*a*) Politics is a dirty game.
(*b*) Twenty miles is a long distance.
(*c*) She did nothing but sang.
(*d*) His father is an S.D.O.

26. (*a*) He succumbed to his injuries.
(*b*) The headmaster testified the boy's ability.
(*c*) These plants are indigenous to India.
(*d*) Mr. Roy's statement was tantamount to a confession.

27. (*a*) The odds are against him.
(*b*) Let me thread the needle.
(*c*) A nurse is taking care of him.
(*d*) I don't know if snow is falling.

28. (*a*) He accompanied me to the park.
(*b*) Never have I heard of such a thing.
(*c*) He reached to his destination.
(*d*) He need not come to me.

29. (*a*) I prefer to read than to write.
(*b*) Each student must bring his pen and paper.
(*c*) Several years have passed since I saw you.
(*d*) I have purchased a pair of socks.

30. (*a*) The more I thought of it, the less I liked it.
(*b*) The teacher was angry with him.
(*c*) The climate of Ranchi is better than Patna.
(*d*) One should take care of one's health.

31. (*a*) Unless you do not work hard you cannot succeed.
(*b*) He was compelled to resign the post.
(*c*) Please pay me by cheque.
(*d*) I feel giddy.

32. (*a*) I found out that he was guilty.
(*b*) Much pains has been taken.
(*c*) The jury was divided in their opinions.
(*d*) Neither of the men was tall.

(Hotel Management, 1995)

33. (*a*) He does not know the English alphabet.
(*b*) We enjoyed during holidays.
(*c*) Have you ever been there ?
(*d*) Ashish gave me this news.

34. (*a*) If it had not been for your folly, you could have been a partner in the firm today.
(*b*) The storm having ceased, the sun came out.
(*c*) He stipulated for immediate supply of the articles.
(*d*) Why did you give false witness ?

35. (*a*) Let me put my sign here.
(*b*) These cattle are mine.
(*c*) He examined the book closely.
(*d*) He has no knowledge of and no interest in music.

36. (*a*) He is employed with a factory.
(*b*) Kashmir is celebrated for its scenery.
(*c*) I am convinced of my error.
(*d*) His betrayal was fatal to our plans.

37. (*a*) She is one of the best mothers that have ever lived.
(*b*) None of these words are now current.
(*c*) This is one of the best films that has been produced this year.
(*d*) Sachin, as well as Ashish and Jatin, likes milk.

(Hotel Management, 1995)

Directions : ***In each of the following questions, four sentences are given. Choose the one which is grammatically correct.***

38. (*a*) From which train did you come ?
(*b*) A series of incidents have taken place.
(*c*) It is a five--men committee.
(*d*) This pronunciation is peculiar to Bengalis.

39. (*a*) They have placed order for books
(*b*) He has applied for lecturership.

(*c*) The river has overflown its bank.
(*d*) Give me rupees two and a half.

40. (*a*) You have no excuse to be late.
(*b*) Tell me what is his name.
(*c*) He ordered my dismissal.
(*d*) The girl has given her examination.

41. (*a*) He is ill with fever.
(*b*) He as well as you are guilty.
(*c*) He insisted me to go there.
(*d*) I offered my thank to him.

42. (*a*) I wrote to him yesterday.
(*b*) This is the road to go.
(*c*) Let us aim to do good.
(*d*) Take down his address in your copy.

43. (*a*) He is wiser than brave.
(*b*) February has less days than January.
(*c*) He takes no less than two kilos of milk.
(*d*) It is the most unique piece.

44. (*a*) The Principal and Secretary are on leave.
(*b*) A number of students has failed in the examination.
(*c*) It is I who has committed this crime.
(*d*) Many a man runs after money.

45. (*a*) I was asked to stop writing.
(*b*) She denied to go with me.
(*c*) My hairs stood on end.
(*d*) I am reading this novel for four days.

46. (*a*) I forbid you not to meet him again.
(*b*) He is seeking for an employment.
(*c*) Being a wet day, we remained indoors.
(*d*) He is more learned but not as responsible as his father.

47. (*a*) I have not and shall not bear this trouble.
(*b*) Running down the street, the clock struck ten.
(*c*) He lost not only his ticket but also his luggage.
(*d*) I am very obliged to you.

48. (*a*) These three boys hate each other.
(*b*) Sanjeev lent Rs. 2,000 to Vineet.
(*c*) I, you and he belong to the same village.
(*d*) Anyone of the two students can solve this sum.

49. (*a*) He is a man whom I know is trustworthy.
(*b*) Until you remain idle you will make no progress.
(*c*) We talked about the weather.
(*d*) Half dozen books were burnt.

50. (*a*) The proceeds of the charity show are for riot victims.
(*b*) He asked Ajay and I to go.
(*c*) The weather of this place does not suit me.
(*d*) Either Rajesh or his friends has done it.

ANSWERS

1. (*c*) : Many a glorious deed was done.
2. (*d*) : The thief divested the child of all her jewels.
3. (*a*) : Eggs are sold by the dozen.
4. (*d*) : He challenged me to a duel.
5. (*b*) : All the boy scouts wear shorts.
6. (*a*) : Always write in ink.
7. (*a*) : Copy it word for word.
8. (*d*) : He has no house to live in.
9. (*b*) : Children like to eat chocolates rather than sweets.
10. (*d*) : He resisted all temptation.
11. (*a*) : He carried little Meenu and me on his shoulders.
12. (*b*) : The committee are divided on this issue.
13. (*b*) : Laziness is detrimental to success.
14. (*b*) : Starch is an antidote to iodine.
15. (*c*) : We got out of the swimming pool and dried ourselves.
16. (*a*) : The dacoits robbed me of my belongings.
17. (*c*) : He is the oldest man of this village.
18. (*b*) : I don't remember having met you before.
19. (*a*) : It is an ideal place.
20. (*a*) : I shall inform them of this.
21. (*c*) : I despaired of finding my lost watch.
22. (*d*) : He has invited me to dinner.
23. (*b*) : His trousers are very dirty.
24. (*a*) : He was hanged for murder.
25. (*c*) : She did nothing but sing.
26. (*b*) : The headmaster testified to the boy's ability.
27. (*d*) : I don't know whether snow is falling.
28. (*c*) : He reached his destination.
29. (*a*) : I prefer reading to writing.
30. (*c*) : The climate of Ranchi is better than that of Patna.
31. (*a*) : Unless you work hard, you cannot succeed.

32. (*c*) : The jury were divided in their opinions.

33.(*b*) : We enjoyed ourselves during holidays.

34. (*d*) : Why did you give false evidence ?

35. (*a*) : Let me put my signature here.

36. (*a*) : He is employed in a factory.

37. (*c*) : This is one of the best films that have been produced this year.

38. (*d*) : By which train did you come ?
A series of incidents has taken place.
It is a five-man committee.

39. (*d*) : They have placed orders for books.
He has applied for lecturership.
The river has overflowed its bank.

40.(*c*) : You have no excuse for being late.
Tell me his name.
The girl has taken her examination.

41 (*a*) : You as well as he is guilty.
He insisted on my going there.
I offered my thanks to him.

42. (*a*) : This is the road to go by.
Let us aim at doing good.
Take down his address in your notebook.

43. (*c*) : He is more wise than brave.
February has fewer days than January.
It is a unique piece.

44. (*d*) : The Principal as well as the Secretary is on leave. (or)
The principal and the Secretary are on leave.
A number of students have failed in the examination.
It is I who has committed this crime.

45. (*a*) : She refused to go with me.
My hair stood on end.
I have been reading this novel for four days.

46. (*d*) : I forbid you to meet him again.
He is seeking an employment.
It being a wet day, we reamaind, indoors.

47. (*c*) : I have not borne and shall not bear this trouble.
As I was running down the street, the clock struck ten.
I am much obliged to you.

48. (*b*) : These three boys hate one another.
You, he and I belong to the same village.
Either of the two students can solve this sum.

49. (*c*) : He is a man who I know is trustworthy.
As long as you remain idle, you will make no progress.
Half a dozen books were burnt.

50. (*a*) : He asked Ajay and me to go.
The climate of this place does not suit me.
Either Rajesh or his friends have done it.

UNIT V

REARRANGEMENT

19. RECONSTRUCTION OF SENTENCES

In this type of questions, you are provided with the first and last parts of a sentence. The remaining sentence is broken into four parts labelled (P), (Q), (R) and (S). You are required to arrange these parts so as to form a complete meaningful sentence and then choose the correct combination.

Example 1 :

(1) On being asked by the teacher
(P) and then picking up the bag
(Q) why he always came late
(R) to the class,
(S) the student first kept quiet
(6) left the class red with shame and anger.

The proper order is **(Stenographers' Exam, 1995)**

(*a*) RSPQ (*b*) QRSP (*c*) SPQR (*d*) PQRS

Solution : For solution, proceed by questioning.

On being asked by the teacher—what? — why he always came late—where?—to the class,—what did the student do?— the student first kept quiet and then? — and then picking up the bag - left the class red with shame and anger.

So, the correct combination is QRSP. Hence, the answer is (*b*).

Example 2 :

The Collector said that the
(P) supply of water for irrigation
(Q) dams should receive water
(R) upto a particular level
(S) to ensure uninterrupted

The proper sequence should be

(*a*) QRSP (*b*) RQSP (*c*) SPRQ (*d*) SRPQ

(N.D.A. 1996)

Solution : Clearly, the correct sentence which would be formed is : 'The Collector said that the dams should receive water upto a particular level to ensure uninterrupted supply of water for irrigation.'

Thus, the correct sequence is QRSP.

Hence, the answer is (*a*).

PRACTICE SET 1

1. When you
(P) which one is closest in meaning
(Q) read the four sentences in your text book and decide
(R) to the statement you have heard
(S) hear a statement **(C.D.S. 1994)**
(*a*) SRPQ (*b*) SQPR
(*c*) SPQR (*d*) QPSR

2. (1) Thick glass may
(P) which are available
(Q) of the home bottle-cuttlers
(R) in many large stores, but any fine
(S) be cut with one
(6) glass requires personal attention.
(*a*) PSRQ (*b*) QPSR
(*c*) RQSP (*d*) SQPR

3. (1) There is a fashion now-a-days
(P) as an evil
(Q) who is born with a silver spoon
(R) to bewail poverty
(S) and to pity the youngman
(6) in his mouth. **(S.S.C. 1992)**
(*a*) PSRQ (*b*) RPSQ
(*c*) RSQP (*d*) SPRQ

4. A typical Prakash Padukone day
(P) or even a game of tennis
(Q) starts off
(R) on some days
(S) with an early morning **(N.D.A. 1996)**
(*a*) QSPR (*b*) QSRP
(*c*) RPSQ (*d*) RSQP

5. (1) Long, long, time ago
(P) who lived with his virtuous wife
(Q) in a country called Chinchinchoo
(R) there ruled a noble king
(S) and seven daughters-
(6) pretty, graceful and well-versed in fine arts. **(Clerks' Grade, 1995)**
(*a*) PSQR (*b*) QRPS
(*c*) RPSQ (*d*) SQRP

6. (1) Those who
(P) expect others
(Q) cannot treat
(R) should not
(S) others well
(6) to treat them well.
(*a*) QPRS (*b*) QSRP
(*c*) RPQS (*d*) SRPQ
(Central Excise, 1993)

7. Alexander,
(P) was a disciple of Aristotle,
(Q) who was a great conqueror,
(R) whom the world acknowledges as the greatest philosopher
(S) the world has ever known
(*a*) PQSR (*b*) QPRS
(*c*) RPQS (*d*) SPQR

8. (1) When I reached my office
(P) to get home early
(Q) I phoned my mother
(R) that I wouldn't be able
(S) to tell her
(6) as I had promised.
(*a*) PQRS (*b*) QSRP
(*c*) RPQS (*d*) SQPR
(Stenographers' Exam, 1995)

9. (1) The department has initiated steps
(P) from the corporate sector
(Q) to evolve appropriate schemes
(R) and financial institutions for
(S) for mobilising investment
(6) the development of wastelands.
(*a*) PRSQ (*b*) QPSR
(*c*) QSPR (*d*) RPSQ

10. Jawaharlal Nehru
(P) under the Cabinet Mission Scheme
(Q) was the first to articulate
(R) long before such an assembly was set up
(S) the idea of a Constituent Assembly
(*a*) PQSR (*b*) QSRP
(*c*) RPQS (*d*) SRPQ
(C.D.S. 1993)

11. (P) when a chemical substance
(Q) the food poisoning occurred
(R) in the food preparations
(S) was mistaken for salt and used
(*a*) PSRQ (*b*) QPSR
(*c*) RQPS (*d*) SRQP

12. If
(P) a foreigner wishes to
(Q) learn standard English
(R) learn English
(S) he will, of course, **(N.D.A. 1993)**
(*a*) PQSR (*b*) PRQS
(*c*) PRSQ (*d*) SRQP

13. (1) According to reports
(P) were still trapped inside
(Q) bogies
(R) the wrecked
(S) some of the passengers
(6) of the express
(*a*) PRQS (*b*) PSQR
(*c*) RSQP (*d*) SPRQ

14. Only
(P) to make himself
(Q) by shouting at the top of his voice
(R) was he able
(S) heard **(N.D.A. 1995)**
(*a*) PSQR (*b*) PSRQ
(*c*) QPRS (*d*) QRPS

15. (P) One has no right in law
(Q) of a tenant's room
(R) to break open the lock
(S) and take its possession
(*a*) PQRS (*b*) PRQS
(*c*) PRSQ (*d*) SQRP

16. When he
(P) did not know
(Q) he was nervous and
(R) heard the hue and cry at midnight
(S) what to do **(Railways, 1994)**
(*a*) PQRS (*b*) QSPR
(*c*) RQPS (*d*) SQPR

17. (1) A number of measures
(P) the financial conditions
(Q) for mobilisation of resources
(R) in order to improve
(S) are being taken by the State Governments
(6) of the Municipal Corporations.
(*a*) PSQR (*b*) QRSP
(*c*) RSQP (*d*) SQRP

18. By this time
(P) at the railway station
(Q) reported mass looting
(R) reports of violence were flooding in
(S) while police dispatches **(C.D.S. 1995)**
(*a*) RSPQ (*b*) RSQP
(*c*) SPRQ (*d*) SQRP

19. (1) Paintings
(P) have been
(Q) which were submitted
(R) totally ruined by rain
(S) for the exhibition
(6) last night.
(*a*) PQRS (*b*) PRQS

(*c*) QRPS (*d*) QSPR

20. (1) A four-year study
(P) that babies feel more comfortable
(Q) conducted by the Infant Testing Centre
(R) around other babies
(S) clearly suggests
(6) than with strange adults.
(*a*) PRSQ (*b*) QPRS
(*c*) QSPR (*d*) SPRQ
(S.S.C. 1994)

21. (P) he told the journalists
(Q) that the government must take firm action
(R) that the meeting unanimously decided
(S) after coming out of the Conference Hall
(*a*) PRQS (*b*) PSQR
(*c*) SPQR (*d*) SPRQ

22. Work is the one thing
(P) and without it
(Q) that is necessary
(R) to keep the world going
(S) we all should die **(C.D.S. 1994)**
(*a*) QPSR (*b*) QRPS
(*c*) RPQS (*d*) SRPQ

23. The man
(P) is generally the one
(Q) who can work very hard
(R) when he must work
(S) who can play most heartily when he has the chance of playing
(*a*) PSQR (*b*) QRPS
(*c*) QRSP (*d*) SPQR

24. The natives of the Carribean
(P) regarded the papaya
(Q) because cf its ability
(R) as a magic tree
(S) to keep them healthy **(N.D.A. 1996)**
(*a*) PRQS (*b*) PRSQ
(*c*) RPQS (*d*) RPSQ

25. (1) The decomposers
(P) and hence help to clean the environment
(Q) help in decomposing the
(R) dead bodies of plants and animals
(S) and put back various useful elements
(6) into soil, air and water.
(*a*) PSQR (*b*) QPRS
(*c*) QRPS (*d*) SQRP

26. (P) while some people live
(Q) to eat and drink and wear
(R) many have not even enough
(S) in luxury **(N.D.A. 1993)**
(*a*) PQRS (*b*) PRQS
(*c*) PSRQ (*d*) RSQP

27. The claim is not
(P) of any kind
(Q) but
(R) that it is without morality
(S) that science is actively anti - moral
(*a*) PSQR (*b*) RPQS
(*c*) RQSP (*d*) SQRP
(S.C.R.A. 1993)

28. (1) Though Indian sportsmen
(P) who accompanied them
(Q) the large number of
(R) did not set many records in Seoul Asiad,
(S) officials and politicians
(6) did set a record of sorts.
(*a*) PRQS (*b*) QSRP
(*c*) PRQS (*d*) SPRQ

29. He reached his office at 10.00 a.m. and
(P) no sooner
(Q) than there was a huge explosion
(R) had he got out of the car
(S) and it went up in flames
(*a*) PQRS (*b*) PRQS
(*c*) RPQS (*d*) RPSQ
(C.D.S. 1995)

30. (1) At the end of the assignment,
(P) the field worker
(Q) submitted his papers
(R) for the work done by him
(S) and also bills
(6) to the office superintendent.
(*a*) PQSR (*b*) QPRS
(*c*) QSRP (*d*) RSQP
(B. Ed. 1994)

ANSWERS

1. (*b*)	**2.** (*d*)	**3.** (*b*)	**4.** (*a*)	**5.** (*b*)	**6.** (*b*)	**7.** (*b*)	**8.** (*b*)	**9.** (*c*)	**10.** (*b*)
11. (*b*)	**12.** (*c*)	**13.** (*d*)	**14.** (*d*)	**15.** (*b*)	**16.** (*c*)	**17.** (*d*)	**18.** (*d*)	**19.** (*d*)	**20.** (*c*)
21. (*d*)	**22.** (*b*)	**23.** (*b*)	**24.** (*a*)	**25.** (*c*)	**26.** (*c*)	**27.** (*d*)	**28.** (*c*)	**29.** (*b*)	**30.** (*a*)

PRACTICE SET 2

1. I was
(P) and stay for a few days in Delhi
(Q) when my father told me
(R) very excited
(S) that I could go with him
(*a*) PQRS (*b*) QRSP
(*c*) RQSP (*d*) SPQR
(Railways, 1994)

2. (1) They're mostly people
(P) and they find the club very convenient,
(Q) to get a reasonable meal
(R) who work in the neighbourhood,
(S) because it enables them
(6) without too much trouble
(*a*) PQRS (*b*) QPRS
(*c*) RPSQ (*d*) SQRP

3. The invasion of India
(P) is more interesting than any other episode of early Indian history
(Q) to most European readers
(R) by Alexander the Great of Macedonia
(S) which occurred during the rule of the Nandas **(C.D.S. 1993)**
(*a*) PQRS (*b*) QPRS
(*c*) RSPQ (*d*) SRPQ

4. (1) I have not come
(P) even if it means some humiliation
(Q) but the boy must learn
(R) to complain, he said,
(S) to be honest
(6) and admit he broke our window pane. **(S.S.C. 1993)**
(*a*) PRQS (*b*) QSPR
(*c*) RQSP (*d*) SPRQ

5. (1) If you are serious about
(P) vocabulary building not a hobby,
(Q) you will have to make
(R) an absorbing interest,
(S) increasing your vocabulary,
(6) or even an obsession.
(*a*) PQSR (*b*) PRQS
(*c*) RQPS (*d*) SQPR
(Stenographers' Exam, 1995)

6. Reading books
(P) is a habit
(Q) but also enlarges the mind
(R) because it not only increases knowledge
(S) which must be cultivated by everybody
(*a*) PQSR (*b*) PQRS
(*c*) PSRQ (*d*) SRPQ
(N.D.A. 1993)

7. (1) Every body
(P) attracts every other
(Q) whether big or small,
(R) body with the force
(S) in the universe
(6) of gravitation
(*a*) PRSQ (*b*) QPRS
(*c*) RSPQ (*d*) SQPR

8. (1) On reaching the station
(P) he first looked around
(Q) and when he could find none
(R) he just lifted his luggage
(S) for a coolie
(6) and walked down to the platform
(*a*) PSQR (*b*) QRPS
(*c*) RPSQ (*d*) SQRP
(Stenographers' Exam, 1993)

9. The boy
(P) with big blue eyes
(Q) watched him,
(R) and he never said a word
(S) that had an uncanny cold fire in them **(C.D.S. 1994)**
(*a*) PQRS (*b*) PQSR
(*c*) QPSR (*d*) QRPS

10. (1) The establishment of Delhi Sultanate
(P) new features in art and architecture
(Q) and their diffusion to all parts of the country
(R) saw the introduction of
(S) leading to the growth of
(6) India's composite culture.
(*a*) PRSQ (*b*) PSQR
(*c*) RPQS (*d*) SPQR

11. (1) If evil consisted
(P) men would be drawn to virtue
(Q) but, alas! how many know their duty
(R) merely in ignorance
(S) as soon as it was explained to them
(6) and yet do not do it **(C.B.I. 1995)**
(*a*) RPQS (*b*) RPSQ
(*c*) RSPQ (*d*) SPRQ

12. (1) There are people
(P) to be able to say
(Q) not because they enjoy the book,
(R) who read a book
(S) but because they want
(6) that they have read it.
(*a*) PSQR (*b*) RQSP
(*c*) RSPQ (*d*) SQPR

13. (1) Have never met
(P) a friendliness and hospitality
(Q) in your city,
(R) like the one
(S) I have met
(6) Calcutta **(S.S.C. 1995)**
(*a*) PQRS (*b*) PRSQ
(*c*) PSRQ (*d*) QPRS

14. (1) A sub-inspector of police,
(P) disturbing a public meeting
(Q) justice to his uniform,
(R) rounded up a group of 18 miscreants
(S) bent on doing
(6) and marched them to the local jail in Shimoga.
(*a*) PRSQ (*b*) QRPS
(*c*) RPSQ (*d*) SQRP

15. (1) What we would like to judge
(P) in this comprehension exercise,
(Q) the difficult words, phrases and sentence fragments
(R) and also the meanings of
(S) is your grasp of the content
(6) that constitute the paragraph
(*a*) PSRQ (*b*) QPSR
(*c*) RQPS (*d*) SRQP
(Stenographers' Exam, 1994)

16. (P) early today
(Q) at least five persons were killed and 32 injured
(R) when a passenger train rammed into
(S) a stationary goods train
(*a*) PQRS (*b*) QRSP
(*c*) RSPQ (*d*) RSQP

17. This is a letter
(P) from a young lady
(Q) who was lately wounded in a duel
(R) written in the most passionate terms
(S) wherein she laments the misfortune of a gentleman **(N.D.A. 1996)**
(*a*) PRQS (*b*) PRSQ
(*c*) RPQS (*d*) RPSQ

18. (1) The ravine was about ten yards wide
(P) and as I stepped down into it
(Q) and four or five feet deep
(R) on which I had
(S) a bird flew off a rock
(6) put my hand
(*a*) PSRQ (*b*) QPSR
(*c*) RSQP (*d*) SRQP

19. There was
(P) needed for its everyday life
(Q) a time when each family
(R) for itself most of the things it
(S) actually produced **(C.D.S. 1995)**
(*a*) QRSP (*b*) QSRP
(*c*) RQPS (*d*) RSPQ

20. (1) There is a continuous demand
(P) are formed to train humanity
(Q) for destructive purposes, and world organisations
(R) in the art of settling their disputes
(S) to ban the application of science
(6) by peaceful negotiations
(*a*) PRSQ (*b*) QSRP
(*c*) RPQS (*d*) SQPR

21. It was true that
(P) the pet dog
(Q) would never sleep anywhere
(R) we once had
(S) except on the sofa **(N.D.A. 1995)**
(*a*) PQSR (*b*) PRQS
(*c*) RPQS (*d*) SPQR

22. A policeman
(P) to abide
(Q) if he has to do well,
(R) by the strict letters of the law
(S) cannot afford
(*a*) PRQS (*b*) QSPR
(*c*) RQPS (*d*) SPRQ

23. (P) We must read
(Q) if we want to absorb the fruits of great literature
(R) but with concentration
(S) them not as we do cricket stories
(*a*) PRQS (*b*) PRSQ
(*c*) PSQR (*d*) QPSR
(C.D.S. 1994)

24. (P) I am planning to go
(Q) to the hill station
(R) to spend my vacation
(S) where an acquaintance of my father lives
(*a*) PQRS (*b*) PSQR
(*c*) RPQS (*d*) RQPS

25. (1) The little girl
(P) for the mother to leave
(Q) said to her friend
(R) little children on their own
(S) it was not quite right
(6) and go to work **(B.Ed. 1994)**
(*a*) PRQS (*b*) QSPR
(*c*) RPSQ (*d*) SQRP

26. (1) Western civilisation is
(P) in its character that
(Q) national culture by affecting
(R) it is bound to influence every
(S) so powerful and so uniform
(6) its external way of life
(*a*) PRSQ (*b*) QSRP
(*c*) RQSP (*d*) SPRQ

27. All religions are
(P) to advance the cause of peace
(Q) in a holy partnership
(R) justice and freedom
(S) bound together **(N.D.A. 1994)**
(*a*) PQRS (*b*) PRQS
(*c*) SPQR (*d*) SQPR

28. Milton said that
(P) those persons
(Q) would be damned
(R) who do not obey
(S) God's commands
(*a*) PQRS (*b*) PRSQ
(*c*) QPRS (*d*) RSPQ

29. (1) He dared
(P) the forty thieves
(Q) to fight
(R) who
(S) challenged him
(6) to a duel
(*a*) PQRS (*b*) QPRS
(*c*) RSQP (*d*) SPQR
(Stenographers' Exam, 1995)

30. The reporter of the newspaper informs us that
(P) Lala Lajpat Rai spent
(Q) lecturing widely and attracting many American leaders
(R) to sympathise with the Indian nationalist position
(S) almost five years in America
(*a*) PSQR (*b*) PSRQ
(*c*) RPSQ (*d*) SPQR

ANSWERS

1. (*c*)	**2.** (*c*)	**3.** (*c*)	**4.** (*c*)	**5.** (*d*)	**6.** (*c*)	**7.** (*d*)	**8.** (*a*)	**9.** (*c*)	**10.** (*c*)
11. (*b*)	**12.** (*b*)	**13.** (*b*)	**14.** (*d*)	**15.** (*a*)	**16.** (*b*)	**17.** (*b*)	**18.** (*b*)	**19.** (*b*)	**20,** (*d*)
21. (*b*)	**22.** (*b*)	**23.** (*d*)	**24.** (*c*)	**25.** (*b*)	**26.** (*d*)	**27.** (*d*)	**28.** (*a*)	**29.** (*b*)	**30.** (*a*)

PRACTICE SET 3

1. (1) The next stop
(P) lying in the centre
(Q) of a bay
(R) was a port
(S) that our ship halted at
(6) in South Wales
(*a*) PQRS (*b*) RSQP
(*c*) SRPQ (*d*) SRQP
(Stenographers' Exam, 1995)

2. (P) it becomes difficult
(Q) satisfying our desire
(R) but once we set about
(S) if not impossible to restrain them
(*a*) PQRS (*b*) QRPS
(*c*) RQPS (*d*) RQSP

3. The captain
(P) when engaged against the enemy
(Q) who was himself a brave man
(R) never to lose heart
(S) advised the soliders **(N.D.A. 1993)**
(*a*) PQSR (*b*) QPSR
(*c*) QSRP (*d*) SQRP

4. (1) Ashoka was successful
(P) by the cruelty and horrors of war
(Q) he was so disgusted
(R) in his military operations
(S) and alone among conquerors,
(6) that he renounced it
(*a*) PSQR (*b*) QPRS
(*c*) RSQP (*d*) SQPR

5. (1) Some remarks
(P) put the police on the right scent
(Q) by a woman
(R) and they discovered
(S) casually dropped
(6) the whole gang of brigands
(*a*) QSPR (*b*) RPSQ
(*c*) RQSP (*d*) SQPR
(Clerks' Grade, 1995)

6. (P) took place
(Q) when militants opened fire on BSF men
(R) the encounter lasting over two hours
(S) in the town around 8.30 a.m.
(*a*) QPRS (*b*) QSRP
(*c*) RPQS (*d*) RPSQ

7. They are plant eaters
(P) and various kinds of vegetation
(Q) browsing on grass
(R) and consume
(S) vast quantities of pasture
(*a*) QPRS (*b*) QSRP
(*c*) RSPQ (*d*) RSQP
(C.D.S. 1994)

8. Dermatologists tell us
(P) that the skin
(Q) is a finely laminated coating
(R) whose layered nature

(S) has inspired comparisons with onions
(*a*) PQRS (*b*) PRQS
(*c*) PRSQ (*d*) PSRQ

9. (P) when
(Q) a child develops best
(R) like a young plant
(S) he is left undisturbed in the same soil **(C.D.S. 1994)**
(*a*) PQRS (*b*) QPRS
(*c*) QPSR (*d*) PQSR

10. (1) The Arabs live in tents
(P) so that they can move from one oasis to another
(Q) and taken down very easily and quickly
(R) seeking grass and water
(S) than can be put up
(6) for their sheep, goats, camels and horses.
(*a*) PRSQ (*b*) QSPR
(*c*) SQPR (*d*) SRPQ

11. (1) At the end of the lecture
(P) for sparing their valuable time
(Q) the speaker thanked the audience
(R) and listening to him
(S) in coming to the meeting
(6) patiently
(*a*) PSRQ (*b*) QPSR
(*c*) RSPQ (*d*) SRQP
(Stenographers' Exam, 1993)

12. (1) Charles Goodyear once accidentally
(P) and found that the resulting rubber
(Q) dropped a mixture of natural rubber
(R) was harder, stronger, more elastic
(S) and sulphur over a hot stove
(6) and non-sticky.
(*a*) PSQR (*b*) QSPR
(*c*) RSQP (*d*) SQPR

13. It would
(P) appear from his statement
(Q) about the policy of the management
(R) in dealing with the strike
(S) that he was quite in the dark
(*a*) PRQS (*b*) PSQR
(*c*) RPSQ (*d*) RQPS
(C.D.S. 1995)

14. (1) The advantage of travelling
(P) customs and manners, is that
(Q) we learn to appreciate the good points of others
(R) in different places and having
(S) the opportunities of observing people's
(6) and our prejudice against them disappear
(*a*) PQRS (*b*) QRSP
(*c*) RSPQ (*d*) SPQR

15. Recently,
(P) containing memorable letters of Churchill
(Q) a book
(R) has been published
(S) by a reputed puslisher **(N.D.A. 1995)**
(*a*) PQRS (*b*) QPRS
(*c*) QRPS (*d*) RQPS

16. (P) the morning session lasting three hours, was spent
(Q) mainly on reviewing
(R) in the fourth round of talks
(S) the implementation of the decisions taken
(*a*) PQRS (*b*) PQSR
(*c*) PRQS (*d*) PRSQ

17. I enclose
(P) and the postage
(Q) a postal order
(R) the price of the books
(S) which will cover **(S.C.R.A. 1994)**
(*a*) QPSR (*b*) QSPR
(*c*) QSRP (*d*) RPSQ

18. (1) If the parachutes had failed to open
(P) the whole of his couch would
(Q) he could have pulled a liver to provide an emergency ejection
(R) and special parachutes would have unfolded
(S) then have been fired from the cabin
(6) to bring him down
(*a*) PSRQ (*b*) QPSR
(*c*) RSQP (*d*) SQPR

19. The practice of taking performance-boosting drugs among athletes
(P) but checking it is not going to be easy
(Q) is generally conceded to be unfair
(R) of the detection technology
(S) for the user is generally one jump ahead **(N.D.A. 1994)**
(*a*) QPRS (*b*) QPSR
(*c*) RQPS (*d*) RQSP

20. (P) we shall hardly expect to find life there
(Q) knowing that
(R) there is neither air nor water
(S) on the moon
(*a*) PQRS (*b*) QRSP
(*c*) RSPQ (*d*) SRQP

21. (1) Sugar
(P) and our average consumption of sugar

(Q) provides something like
(R) itself is rich in calories
(S) one-fifth of our
(6) total calorie intake
(*a*) PQRS (*b*) QRPS
(*c*) RPQS (*d*) RPSQ

(Stenographers' Exam, 1995)

22. Why do people
(P) despite a desire
(Q) to quit and despite
(R) continue smoking
(S) the known health hazards?
(*a*) PQRS (*b*) RPQS
(*c*) RQPS (*d*) RSPQ

23. As lightning accompanies thunder,
(P) was mingled with
(Q) so in my character
(R) the mutterings of my wrath
(S) a flash of humour **(Railways, 1993)**
(*a*) PRSQ (*b*) QPRS
(*c*) QRPS (*d*) QSPR

24. During hibernation
(P) they have lost a good deal of weight
(Q) of course the animals consume
(R) and when they awake again
(S) the fats accumulated in the summer **(C.D.S. 1993)**
(*a*) PQRS (*b*) QSRP
(*c*) RQSP (*d*) SQPR

25. (1) The district collector
(P) the next of kin
(Q) would be provided to
(R) announced that financial assistance
(S) of the deceased
(6) from the Chief Minister's Relief Fund
(*a*) PSRQ (*b*) QSPR
(*c*) RQPS (*d*) SQRP

26. (1) In the coming session,
(P) of our computer management services
(Q) to make them
(R) more useful, efficient and cost-effective
(S) we are undertaking a thorough review
(6) for your needs
(*a*) PQRS (*b*) QRSP
(*c*) RSPQ (*d*) SPQR

(Stenographers' Exam, 1994)

27. (1) Though the Govt. claims
(P) it has failed to arrest
(Q) the rate of inflation is down,
(R) or the decrease
(S) the rise in prices
(6) in the per capita income
(*a*) PQRS (*b*) PQSR
(*c*) PSQR (*d*) QPSR

(Assistant Grade, 1993)

28. (1) The greatest tragedy of Bhopal
(P) we in India
(Q) is that ever after the Bhopal disaster,
(R) have not realized
(S) the necessity
(6) of town planning
(*a*) PRQS (*b*) PRSQ
(*c*) QPRS (*d*) RSQP

29. The exhibition committee
(P) attractive and useful
(Q) to make the exhibition
(R) making efforts
(S) has been **(C.D.S. 1995)**
(*a*) QPRS (*b*) QPSR
(*c*) SRPQ (*d*) SRQP

30. The house,
(P) about half a mile distant
(Q) that stands in front of us,
(R) was built of stones
(S) which were dug out of its own site
(*a*) QPRS (*b*) QRPS
(*c*) QRSP (*d*) QSPR

ANSWERS

1. (*c*)	**2.** (*c*)	**3.** (*c*)	**4.** (*c*)	**5.** (*d*)	**6.** (*c*)	**7.** (*a*)	**8.** (*a*)	**9.** (*a*)	**10.** (*c*)
11. (*b*)	**12.** (*b*)	**13.** (*b*)	**14.** (*c*)	**15.** (*b*)	**16.** (*b*)	**17.** (*c*)	**18.** (*b*)	**19.** (*b*)	**20.** (*a*)
21. (*c*)	**22.** (*b*)	**23.** (*d*)	**24.** (*b*)	**25.** (*c*)	**26.** (*d*)	**27.** (*d*)	**28.** (*c*)	**29.** (*d*)	**30.** (*a*)

PRACTICE SET 4

1. We
(P) agreed with
(Q) the manner in which you said it
(R) but we objected to
(S) what you said **(N.D.A. 1996)**
(*a*) PSQR (*b*) PSRQ
(*c*) SPQR (*d*) SPRQ

2. (1) The Reserve Bank of India has taken the risk
(P) as measured by the Wholesale Price Index
(Q) by allowing a large flow of funds
(R) when the annual rate of inflation
(S) into the economy at a time
(6) is slowly moving up.
(*a*) PRQS (*b*) QSRP
(*c*) RSPQ (*d*) SQPR

3. (1) I reasoned with him
(P) but could not disabuse him
(Q) that the lawyer
(R) for an hour
(S) of the notion
(6) who had his case in hand was incompetent. **(Clerks' Grade, 1995)**
(*a*) PRSQ (*b*) QPSR
(*c*) RPSQ (*d*) SRPQ

4. (1) There are
(P) laid on school games
(Q) who support the emphasis
(R) still those devotees of sport
(S) and for whom sports is
(6) a kind of religion.
(*a*) PQRS (*b*) PSQR
(*c*) RPSQ (*d*) RQPS

5. (P) as environmental tools
(Q) for military purposes
(R) are finding various new uses
(S) the world's fastest computers initially conceived **(N.D.A. 1993)**
(*a*) PQRS (*b*) QPSR
(*c*) RPSQ (*d*) SQRP

6. (1) The fact that
(P) go to the police
(Q) did not let him
(R) to speak the truth
(S) he was a murderer
(6) about the theft.
(*a*) PRSQ (*b*) QSPR
(*c*) RQSP (*d*) SQPR

7. The U.S. soyabean
(P) in the developing world
(Q) and when famine strikes
(R) is America's singlemost lucrative export
(S) American soyabeans are a major source of high protein sustenance
(*a*) PRSQ (*b*) PSRQ
(*c*) RQPS (*d*) RQSP
(C.D.S. 1995)

8. (1) Yesterday, I chanced to meet
(P) where he lived
(Q) and asked him
(R) now in his seventies
(S) an old acquaintance,
(6) and what he did for his living.
(*a*) PSRQ (*b*) QPSR
(*c*) RQPS (*d*) SRQP
(Stenographers' Exam, 1995)

9. (1) Guru Nanak evolved
(P) on omnipresence of God
(Q) with his simple teachings
(R) a new religious outlook
(S) and removal of
(6) the evil religious practices.
(*a*) PQRS (*b*) QSPR
(*c*) PRSQ (*d*) RQPS

10. Women
(P) till the other day
(Q) who were content being housewives
(R) about spending their time cooking
(S) now sound apologetic
(*a*) PQRS (*b*) QPSR
(*c*) RQPS (*d*) RSPQ
(C.D.S. 1993)

11. (1) The Indians of coming generations
(P) and aware of the continuity of
(Q) will not be unconvincing and self conscious
(R) but will be men, rooted in their own traditions,
(S) copiers of European culture
(6) their own cultural heritage.
(*a*) QPSR (*b*) QRPS
(*c*) QSRP (*d*) SRQP

12. (1) If all the nations
(P) for the common good of mankind
(Q) then they will never fight with each other
(R) work together
(S) and agree to obey these laws,
(6) and there will be no war.
(*a*) PRQS (*b*) RPSQ
(*c*) RQPS (*d*) SQRP
(S.S.C. 1992)

13. (1) What handicapped people
(P) an opportunity to pull their weight
(Q) but what we are ready
(R) and do something useful
(S) want most of all is
(6) to offer is pity.
(*a*) PQSR (*b*) QSPR

(*c*) RPQS (*d*) SPRQ

14. Little
(P) that he had been let down
(Q) stood by all these years
(R) did he realise
(S) by a colleague whom he had
(*a*) QSPR (*b*) QSRP
(*c*) RPSQ (*d*) RSQP
(C.D.S. 1995)

15. It has been established that
(P) Einstein was
(Q) although a great scientist
(R) weak in arithmetic
(S) right from his school days
(*a*) QPRS (*b*) QPSR
(*c*) RQPS (*d*) SRPQ
(Railways, 1994)

16. (P) environmental and psychological stress and strain
(Q) He said that
(R) the development of positive attitudes to cope with
(S) what the world needed today was
(*a*) PQSR (*b*) QSRP
(*c*) RPQS (*d*) SRPQ

17. Without books
(P) no cultured society is possible
(Q) no fresh ideas are possible
(R) and
(S) without fresh ideas **(N.D.A. 1993)**
(*a*) PRSQ (*b*) QRSP
(*c*) RSPQ (*d*) RSQP

18. (1) The social groups in power
(P) especially when these happen to depend upon the state
(Q) have always manipulated the education systems
(R) for their very existence,
(S) to strengthen and perpetuate
(6) their own privileged position.
(*a*) QPRS (*b*) QRPS
(*c*) QSRP (*d*) SPQR

19. (1) No part of this publication may be
(P) without the written permission
(Q) reproduced, stored in or transmitted
(R) of the copyright owner and
(S) in any form or by any means
(6) the publisher of this book.
(*a*) PQRS (*b*) QSPR
(*c*) RPSQ (*d*) SRQP
(Stenographers' Exam, 1993)

20. (1) Fair play demands that
(P) which may tend to give a poor impression
(Q) before any comments are made
(R) the person concerned should be asked
(S) about a person,
(6) to give his side of the story.
(*a*) PSRQ (*b*) QPSR
(*c*) RQPS (*d*) SRQP

21. (1) The ongoing research
(P) to relax the vigil
(Q) for development of an AIDS vaccine
(R) is not reason enough
(S) due to enter laboratory-trials shortly
(6) against the killer - disease.
(*a*) PQSR (*b*) QSRP
(*c*) SQRP (*d*) SRQP
(Clerks' Grade, 1994)

22. (1) The unfortunate person,
(P) of social contempt
(Q) but he is also the victim
(R) who is unemployed, is
(S) not only the object of self-pity,
(6) and a danger to the society.
(*a*) PQSR (*b*) QPRS
(*c*) RSQP (*d*) SRPQ

23. The statement
(P) therefore you must listen carefully
(Q) what the speaker has said
(R) in order to understand
(S) will be made just once **(C.D.S. 1994)**
(*a*) RSPQ (*b*) SPQR
(*c*) SPRQ (*d*) SRQP

24. Towards midnight
(P) so that the sky was lighted with
(Q) and the clouds drifted away
(R) the rain ceased
(S) the incredible lamp of stars
(*a*) RPQS (*b*) RQPS
(*c*) SPQR (*d*) SQPR
(N.D.A. 1995)

25. The idea of the Yahoos
(P) too,
(Q) in all its devastating implications,
(R) is one to be explored
(S) but not taken as the last word about human nature
(*a*) PRQS (*b*) RQSP
(*c*) SPRQ (*d*) SRPQ

26. The administration will soon launch
(P) to educate the people about their rights
(Q) a consumer protection drive
(R) against using fraudulent means
(S) and to warn traders **(C.D.S. 1994)**
(*a*) PQSR (*b*) PSQR
(*c*) QPSR (*d*) SPQR

27. Some of our social sciences
(P) that cannot be attacked by modern society
(Q) such as psychology and sociology
(R) seem to have become
(S) sacred cows
(*a*) PQRS (*b*) QRSP
(*c*) RSPQ (*d*) RSQP

28. (1) Inaugurating the Bharat Bhawan
(P) the then Prime Minister, Mrs. Indira Gandhi said that
(Q) in all states so that the creative faculties of the people
(R) in Bhopal on February 13, 1982
(S) it had been her long cherished desire to see such bhavans come up
(6) could find their proper outlet
(*a*) PQRS (*b*) RPSQ
(*c*) SPQR (*d*) SRPQ
(Stenographers' Exam, 1994)

29. (1) I am aware of the exciting demands
(P) in the highest public office
(Q) these demands have to
(R) but I do not see that
(S) of security of those
(6) wildly inconsistent with the rights of a citizen.
(*a*) PRQS (*b*) RSPQ
(*c*) SPQR (*d*) SPRQ

30. Dear Lodger, I agree, the roof is leaking; but
(P) there would be no need
(Q) while it is raining
(R) and when the sun shines,
(S) I can't get it repaired **(N.D.A. 1992)**
(*a*) PRQS (*b*) QRSP
(*c*) RSPQ (*d*) SQRP

ANSWERS

1. (*b*)	**2.** (*b*)	**3.** (*c*)	**4.** (*d*)	**5.** (*d*)	**6.** (*d*)	**7.** (*d*)	**8.** (*d*)	**9.** (*d*)	**10.** (*b*)
11. (*c*)	**12.** (*b*)	**13.** (*d*)	**14.** (*c*)	**15.** (*a*)	**16.** (*b*)	**17.** (*b*)	**18.** (*a*)	**19.** (*b*)	**20.** (*b*)
21. (*c*)	**22.** (*c*)	**23.** (*c*)	**24.** (*b*)	**25.** (*a*)	**26.** (*c*)	**27.** (*b*)	**28.** (*b*)	**29.** (*d*)	**30.** (*d*)

PRACTICE SET 5

1. It was
(P) in keeping with my mood
(Q) a soft summer evening
(R) as I walked sedately
(S) in the direction of the new house
(*a*) QPRS (*b*) QRPS
(*c*) SQPR (*d*) SRPQ
(C.D.S. 1993)

2. (1) Freedom, which
(P) in the sense
(Q) that a wide gulf separates
(R) a modern woman enjoys.
(S) is the restricted kind,
(6) the rich and the poor women.
(*a*) PQRS (*b*) QPRS
(*c*) RSPQ (*d*) SRQP

3. Padukone's retirement
(P) as is obvious
(Q) his concern for the game
(R) has not diminished
(S) when he talks of the Badminton Association of India **(N.D.A. 1995)**
(*a*) PQRS (*b*) PSQR
(*c*) RPQS (*d*) RQPS

4. (1) After a laborious life
(P) to the quiet village where he was born
(Q) most of which he had spent in the metropolis,
(R) and where he intended to spend
(S) he retired in his old age
(6) his remaining years.
(*a*) QRPS (*b*) QSPR
(*c*) SPQR (*d*) SQPR
(Stenographers' Exam, 1994)

5. (P) The management having agreed
(Q) the workers called off the strike
(R) to increase their wages
(S) and returned to work
(*a*) PQRS (*b*) PRQS
(*c*) RSQP (*d*) SPQR

6. The Bible,
(P) has in many respects
(Q) the sacred book of all Christians
(R) among all the books of the world
(S) a unique character and position
(*a*) QPSR (*b*) QRPS
(*c*) RPQS (*d*) RQPS
(S.C.R.A. 1993)

7. The ultimate hope
(P) will force the nations
(Q) that the destructive nature of weapons
(R) to give up war
(S) has not been fulfilled
(*a*) PQRS (*b*) PRQS
(*c*) QPRS (*d*) RSQP

8. (P) deserve all honour in society
(Q) in doing their job well
(R) men of conscience who take pride
(S) whatever its nature **(N.D.A. 1993)**
(*a*) PRSQ (*b*) QRPS
(*c*) RQSP (*d*) SPQR

9. (P) I wonder
(Q) whenever I decide to go to the cinema
(R) with my moped
(S) why I always have trouble
(*a*) PRSQ (*b*) PSRQ
(*c*) QPSR (*d*) QRSP
(C.D.S. 1994)

10. (P) expresses itself in many diverse art forms
(Q) ancient in origin
(R) The essence of the spirit of Bulgaria
(S) of great creativity
(*a*) PQRS (*b*) PSRQ
(*c*) QPSR (*d*) RQPS

11. (1) He had started the book thinking
(P) he had decided to
(Q) that it would be an interesting work,
(R) but by the time
(S) he reached the middle,
(6) throw it into the bin.
(*a*) PSQR (*b*) QRSP
(*c*) RSPQ (*d*) SPRQ
(Stenographers' Exam, 1993)

12. (1) People read and recite the Ramayana,
(P) which refers to those high ideals of human conduct
(Q) with great devotion,
(R) that aspect of its greatness
(S) but they mostly fail to appreciate
(6) that this great epic places before us.
(*a*) PRQS (*b*) QSRP
(*c*) RSPQ (*d*) SRQP

13. This majestic mahogany table
(P) belongs to an old prince
(Q) which has one leg missing
(R) who is now impoverished
(S) but not without some pride
(*a*) PQSR (*b*) PRSQ
(*c*) QPRS (*d*) QRSP
(C.D.S. 1995)

14. If you have patience
(P) to become an interesting and enthusiastic listener
(Q) from the other person himself
(R) and if you train yourself
(S) you will get to know all the details, first hand
(*a*) PRSQ (*b*) PSRQ
(*c*) RPSQ (*d*) RSQP

15. (1) O why
(P) creator shatter
(Q) should the great
(R) one of
(S) his most adorable
(6) works! **(S.S.C. 1995)**
(*a*) PRQS (*b*) QPRS
(*c*) QPSR (*d*) RPQS

16. (P) a difficult construction job that calls for innovation
(Q) offer her
(R) in Mrs. Roy, a Bombay based business woman
(S) and you will find a willing taker
(*a*) PQRS (*b*) QPSR
(*c*) RQPS (*d*) SRPQ

17. (1) Even though he had prepared well
(P) in the examination hall
(Q) and could not do well
(R) for the examination,
(S) he got nervous
(6) as well as he had hoped to do
(*a*) PQRS (*b*) QRSP
(*c*) RSPQ (*d*) SPQR
(Stenographer's Exam, 1995)

18. As the whole human blood and its related blood products
(P) the collection and distribution is
(Q) are drugs,
(R) and rules there under
(S) regulated under Drugs and Cosmetics Act
(*a*) QSPR (*b*) PSRQ
(*c*) QPSR (*d*) SPRQ

19. Seventy-two people
(P) reports PTI
(Q) were affected by food poisoning
(R) including several women and children
(S) of the Tilak Vihar area of west Delhi
(*a*) RSPQ (*b*) RSQP
(*c*) SQRP (*d*) SRQP
(N.D.A. 1994)

20. (1) The main purpose
(P) how much
(Q) is to find out
(R) of this test
(S) of English
(6) he knows. **(Central Excise, 1993)**
(*a*) PQSR (*b*) PRQS
(*c*) RQPS (*d*) SPQR

21. (1) Excavators have discovered
(P) in Iraq's
(Q) and half animal figure
(R) a colossal half human
(S) dating back to the Ice Ages
(6) northern city of Mosul.
(*a*) PRQS (*b*) QSPR
(*c*) RQSP (*d*) SPRQ

22. You must leave a note
(P) otherwise she will be terribly worried
(Q) for your mother
(R) at the usual hour
(S) if you are not back home
(*a*) QPRS (*b*) QPSR

(*c*) SRPQ (*d*) SRQP

(C.D.S. 1995)

23. (1) The move to revert to a six-day week
(P) among the employees
(Q) while their leaders represented to the Chief Minister
(R) that they be taken into confidence
(S) led to an animated decision
(6) before any decision was taken.
(*a*) QPSR (*b*) RSPQ
(*c*) SPQR (*d*) SQPR

24. Some achievements
(P) have made
(Q) happier and more comfortable
(R) of science
(S) human life **(S.C.R.A. 1994)**
(*a*) PQRS (*b*) QRSP
(*c*) RPSQ (*d*) RSPQ

25. (1) The first component is
(P) and vocational training
(Q) so as to enable them
(R) the provision of further technical
(S) to both rural and urban youth
(6) to secure employment in industry and the services sector.
(*a*) PRSQ (*b*) RPSQ
(*c*) RSQP (*d*) SRPQ

26. As we all know
(1) a legislation
(Q) needs the assent of the President
(R) passed by the houses of Parliament
(S) to become law **(N.D.A. 1996)**
(*a*) PQSR (*b*) PRQS
(*c*) QPRS (*d*) SPQR

27. (1) It was obvious
(P) made by him
(Q) submitted at the meeting
(R) from the comments
(S) on the draft proposals
(6) that he was not satisfied with them.
(*a*) PSRQ (*b*) QRSP
(*c*) RPSQ (*d*) SQRP

(S.S.C. 1993)

28. (1) The Minister of State for power
(P) laying emphasis
(Q) in conservation of electricity in industries
(R) has written to his counterparts in State Governments
(S) on bringing about improvement
(6) by introduction of energy efficient equipment.
(*a*) QPSR (*b*) RPSQ
(*c*) SPQR (*d*) SQPR

29. As the situation has changed,
(P) since we last discussed this matter
(Q) it was best to contact you
(R) it appeared to me
(S) without losing time
(*a*) PQRS (*b*) PRQS
(*c*) PRSQ (*d*) SPRQ

(N.D.A. 1995)

30. (1) In reply to a question
(P) that securing extradition
(Q) operating from the U.K soil remained
(R) of anti-India elements
(S) the spokesman said
(6) New Delhi's 'first priority.'
(*a*) PRQS (*b*) QSPR
(*c*) RQSP (*d*) SPRQ

ANSWERS

1. (*a*)	**2.** (*c*)	**3.** (*d*)	**4.** (*b*)	**5.** (*b*)	**6.** (*a*)	**7.** (*c*)	**8.** (*c*)	**9.** (*b*)	**10.** (*d*)
11. (*b*)	**12.** (*b*)	**13.** (*c*)	**14.** (*c*)	**15.** (*b*)	**16.** (*b*)	**17.** (*c*)	**18.** (*c*)	**19.** (*b*)	**20.** (*c*)
21. (*c*)	**22.** (*b*)	**23.** (*c*)	**24.** (*c*)	**25.** (*b*)	**26.** (*b*)	**27.** (*c*)	**28.** (*b*)	**29.** (*b*)	**30.** (*d*)

PRACTICE SET 6

1. According to an engineer
(P) might hit the market next year
(Q) a newly developed air-cooler system
(R) that employed in conventional room coolers
(S) which is based on a principle radically different from **(C.D.S. 1994)**
(*a*) PQRS (*b*) QSRP
(*c*) RSQP (*d*) SQRP

2. (P) with an idea to reach the deprived child
(Q) by the United Nations Organisation
(R) the year 1979 has been declared as
(S) the International Year of the Child
(*a*) PQRS (*b*) PRSQ
(*c*) PSQR (*d*) RSPQ

3. (P) which is sold
(Q) for its horn
(R) the Rhinoceros is hunted by poachers
(S) at high prices **(N.D.A. 1993)**
(*a*) QPSR (*b*) QRSP

(*c*) RQPS (*d*) SQPR

4. It is
(P) the king and his four sons
(Q) believed that
(R) when they were riding in a royal procession
(S) were killed
(*a*) PQSR (*b*) PSQR
(*c*) QPRS (*d*) QPSR

5. When rescuers arrived
(P) they had to wait several hours
(Q) before the ground was
(R) at the ruins
(S) cool enough to stand on **(C.D.S. 1994)**
(*a*) PQRS (*b*) QSPR
(*c*) RPQS (*d*) SRPQ

6. (1) In the middle of the dark night,
(P) of a woman
(Q) by the shrill cry
(R) I was awakened
(S) who seemed to be wailing
(6) the death of someone close to her
(*a*) PSRQ (*b*) QPSR
(*c*) RQPS (*d*) SRQP

7. (1) A political decision or policy
(P) if judged by its immediate results,
(Q) in the light of its
(R) may seem to be very wise
(S) but may prove to be unsound
(6) ultimate consequences
(*a*) RPQS (*b*) RPSQ
(*c*) RQPS (*d*) SQPR
(Assistant Grade, 1993)

8. We can think of
(P) often confused in the public mind
(Q) which suggest the need for
(R) two factors
(S) an international language
(*a*) PRQS (*b*) RPQS
(*c*) RQSP (*d*) SQRP

9. (1) I am of the opinion that
(P) a terrible mistake
(Q) our Govt.
(R) is making
(S) by discontinuing the tram lines
(6) in Calcutta
(*a*) QRPS (*b*) PRQS
(*c*) SQRP (*d*) PQRS
(Stenographers' Exam, 1995)

10. (1) If we study the lives of great men
(P) achieve greatness and,
(Q) footmarks to guide others
(R) we are reminded that we too can
(S) when we die, leave behind us
(6) and infuse them with new life.
(*a*) PSRQ (*b*) RPSQ
(*c*) RQPS (*d*) SQPR

11. (1) Lakhs of students
(P) on all-India basis
(Q) from all over India
(R) which are held
(S) appear in the examinations
(6) by different recruiting organisations.
(*a*) PQSR (*b*) QSPR
(*c*) QSRP (*d*) SRQP
(S.S.C. 1992)

12. (P) four degrees below normal
(Q) icy winds lashed Srinagar
(R) with minimum temperature registering
(S) which was already in the grip of gruelling cold wave conditions
(*a*) PQSR (*b*) QSRP
(*c*) RPQS (*d*) SRPQ

13. (1) Almost every country in the world
(P) that it is of the chosen people
(Q) it has some special dispensation from Providence
(R) and that others are somewhat
(S) believes that
(6) inferior creatures **(C.B.I. 1995)**
(*a*) RPQS (*b*) RQPS
(*c*) SQPR (*d*) SQRP

14. The policeman
(P) to return the lady's purse
(Q) asked him
(R) who had caught a pick-pocket
(S) if he wished to avoid imprisonment
(*a*) PSQR (*b*) QRPS
(*c*) RQPS (*d*) SQRP

15. The world
(P) although it sometimes seems that way
(Q) is not a total chaos
(R) the newspaper headlines
(S) when we read **(C.D.S. 1991)**
(*a*) PQSR (*b*) QPSR
(*c*) QSRP (*d*) RSPQ

16. It is
(P) for a man
(Q) when he accompanies a lady
(R) an accepted custom
(S) to open the door **(N.D.A. 1996)**
(*a*) PSQR (*b*) PSRQ
(*c*) RPQS (*d*) RPSQ

17. (1) Haryana gets the credit
(P) for the first time
(Q) for training block level extension farmers
(R) for using INSAT-2
(S) in the country
(6) in various aspects of agriculture
(*a*) PSRQ (*b*) QPSR
(*c*) RPSQ (*d*) SQRP

18. The impact
(P) is to be seen
(Q) in the diverse changes in consumer habits
(R) of technological and industrial development
(S) in cities, towns and even in village conglomerates **(C.D.S. 1993)**
(*a*) PQRS (*b*) PSQR
(*c*) RPQS (*d*) RSPQ

19. The main cause of Industrial Revolution was
(P) owing to the geographical discoveries
(Q) in the 17th and 18th centuries
(R) the great increase in overseas trade
(S) of Columbus and Vasco - da - Gama
(*a*) RPQS (*b*) RQPS
(*c*) RSPQ (*d*) RSQP

20. (1) They would gather information
(P) and then report the findings
(Q) of the lands
(R) through which they travelled
(S) about the wealth and military strength
(6) to the king **(S.S.C. 1995)**
(*a*) PQSR (*b*) PSQR
(*c*) QRSP (*d*) SQRP

21. (1) Under the present system
(P) teaching
(Q) of mass education by classes
(R) and too little on
(S) too much stress is laid on
(6) active learning.
(*a*) QPRS (*b*) QPSR
(*c*) QRPS (*d*) QSPR

22. (1) Many people
(P) that the government can always pay out money quite easily,
(Q) that the government can only pay out money
(R) seem to think
(S) but they forget
(6) that it has received in taxes.
(*a*) PRQS (*b*) QPRS
(*c*) RPSQ (*d*) SQRP
(Clerks' Grade, 1994)

23. (P) accidents are still bound to happen
(Q) occasionally
(R) though
(S) despite everyone's best efforts
(*a*) PQRS (*b*) RSPQ
(*c*) SPRQ (*d*) SRPQ

24. All such students
(P) get success
(Q) who are honest and hardworking
(R) and recognition
(S) in every walk of life
(*a*) PRQS (*b*) PSRQ
(*c*) QPRS (*d*) SPRQ
(Railways, 1994)

25. (1) Above all,
(P) in the present age of light reading,
(Q) it is well if something heavier is cast now and then
(R) of reading hastily and thoughtlessly,
(S) that is,
(6) into the midst of the reading public.
(*a*) PQRS (*b*) PRQS
(*c*) PSRQ (*d*) QSRP

26. The Buddha
(P) who had
(Q) set views
(R) was opposed to all those
(S) or closed system of thought
(*a*) PQRS (*b*) PQSR
(*c*) RPQS (*d*) SRPQ
(N.D.A. 1995)

27. (1) Though the exact dimensions
(P) involved in the rocket
(Q) and the precise amounts
(R) it is clear that such a large scale operation
(S) are yet to be ascertained,
(6) could not have been possible without the connivance of officials at various levels.
(*a*) PSRQ (*b*) QPSR
(*c*) RQPS (*d*) SPRQ

28. We have to
(P) as we see it
(Q) speak the truth
(R) there is falsehood and darkness
(S) even if all around us **(C.D.S. 1995)**
(*a*) QPSR (*b*) QRPS
(*c*) RQSP (*d*) RSQP

29. (1) What the country needs
(P) and change tactics
(Q) who would encourage players
(R) are coaches and officials
(S) to read the game as it progresses
(6) accordingly.
(*a*) QSPR (*b*) RQPS
(*c*) RQSP (*d*) SPRQ

30. The ancient peoples of the Mediterranean
(P) like a horse with a long horn
(Q) elieved in the existence of the unicorn
(R) on its forehead
(S) a mythical animal supposed to look
(*a*) PRQS (*b*) QPSR
(*c*) QSPR (*d*) RSQP
(C.D.S. 1995)

ANSWERS

1. (b)	2. (b)	3. (c)	4. (d)	5. (c)	6. (c)	7. (b)	8. (b)	9. (a)	10. (b)
11. (c)	12. (b)	13. (c)	14. (c)	15. (b)	16. (d)	17. (c)	18. (c)	19. (b)	20. (d)
21. (d)	22. (c)	23. (c)	24. (c)	25. (b)	26. (c)	27. (b)	28. (a)	29. (c)	30. (c)

PRACTICE SET 7

1. He said that those who
(P) would miss a very interesting game
(Q) to be played
(R) between two famous teams
(S) would not accompany him
(*a*) QRPS (*b*) SPQR
(*c*) SQRP (*d*) SRPQ
(N.D.A. 1993)

2. (P) by the hard hitting cyclone
(Q) and bridges broken leaving the population marooned
(R) Fiji Islands presented the ghastly scene of an earthly paradise overrun by marauders
(S) after the tops of several houses were blown off **(C.D.S. 1993)**
(*a*) PQRS (*b*) PRQS
(*c*) RSQP (*d*) SRQP

3. Churchill observed that
(P) the impressive and inspiring spectacle
(Q) displayed the vigour and efficiency
(R) of the civil defence forces of London
(S) he had witnessed in Hyde park that morning
(*a*) PQRS (*b*) PSQR
(*c*) PSRQ (*d*) SPRQ

4. (P) Since they are swayed exclusively
(Q) the mental horizon of students
(R) has narrowed these days
(S) by considerations of career
(*a*) PQRS (*b*) PSQR
(*c*) QPRS (*d*) QRPS
(S.C.R.A. 1993)

5. (1) The candidate will be expected to have
(P) and will be responsible
(Q) a commitment to application-oriented research
(R) for development of methods/products
(S) in the emerging
(6) field of biotechnology
(*a*) PRSQ (*b*) QPRS
(*c*) QPSR (*d*) RSQP

6. Spiders
(P) build webs
(Q) in houses
(R) that many people fear
(S) those eight-legged bugs **(C.D.S. 1991)**
(*a*) PQRS (*b*) PQSR
(*c*) SPQR (*d*) SRPQ

7. (P) when the artist had started
(Q) singing a popular song
(R) in chorus
(S) everyone in the audience joined
(*a*) PQRS (*b*) PQSR
(*c*) RPQS (*d*) RQPS

8. He was so kind and generous that
(P) he not only
(Q) made others do so
(R) but also
(S) helped them himself **(C.D.S. 1995)**
(*a*) PRSQ (*b*) PSRQ
(*c*) QPRS (*d*) SPQR

9. A French woman
(P) committed suicide
(Q) where she had put up
(R) who had come to Calcutta
(S) by jumping from the first floor balcony of the hotel **(S.C.R.A. 1994)**
(*a*) PRQS (*b*) QSRP
(*c*) RPSQ (*d*) SRQP

10. (P) supported by soft term loans
(Q) to supply imported equipment worth Rs. 8 crore
(R) the Hungarian Government has offered
(S) with a very low rate of interest
(*a*) PSRQ (*b*) QPSR
(*c*) RQPS (*d*) SRQP

11. (1) Inspite of repeated attempts,
(P) in the dictionary
(Q) and finally had to ask his teacher
(R) he could not locate
(S) the strange - looking word
(6) what it meant. **(S.S.C. 1995)**
(*a*) PQRS (*b*) SPQR
(*c*) QRSP (*d*) RSPQ

12. (1) Believe it or not but
(P) to be a news reader
(Q) the Hindi film industry's leading actor
(R) was once dismissed
(S) for close to a decade

(6) on All India Radio
(*a*) PSQR (*b*) QSRP
(*c*) RPQS (*d*) SRPQ

13. (1) About a hundred Vintage beauties
(P) have been restored
(Q) over the years
(R) from the scrap
(S) many of which
(6) participate in the famous Vintage Car Rally every year.
(*a*) PQRS (*b*) SPQR
(*c*) SPRQ (*d*) SQPR

(Stenographers' Exam, 1994)

14. The workhouse authorities
(P) in the household
(Q) of a shopkeeper
(R) find her a job
(S) and she succeeds in placing Jackie with a kindly widow
(*a*) PRQS (*b*) QSRP
(*c*) RPQS (*d*) SQRP

15. (1) I wasn't sure
(P) to hear his voice
(Q) in my heart of hearts—
(E) through that window once more,
(S) what I really wished
(6) or never to see him there again.
(*a*) PRSQ (*b*) QSPR
(*c*) RSQP (*d*) SQPR

(Assistant Grade, 1994)

16. (1) The man whom I hit on the head
(P) says that when he meets me
(Q) on my way back home from school
(R) on the road
(S) he will beat me
(6) till I cry for mercy.
(*a*) PSRQ (*b*) QPRS
(*c*) RPSQ (*d*) RQSP

(Stenographers' Exam, 1995)

17. As his hunting skill increased,
(P) till at last it was as impossible for him
(Q) so did his love for the hunt
(R) as it is for the opium eater
(S) to pass a day without it
(6) to forgo his daily potion.
(*a*) PQRS (*b*) PSQR
(*c*) QPSR (*d*) RSQP

18. If you need help
(P) promptly and politely
(Q) ask for attendants
(R) to help our customers
(S) who have instructions **(C.D.S. 1995)**
(*a*) QPSR (*b*) QSRP
(*c*) SQPR (*d*) SQRP

19. (1) In every country, children
(P) in their proper development, because
(Q) a great care is taken
(R) are given good education and
(S) what they become depends
(6) upon this impressionable period of their lives.
(*a*) RSPQ (*b*) QSRP
(*c*) RQPS (*d*) PRSQ

20. After the awarding speeches
(P) the prize given
(Q) and
(R) had been made
(S) I got up to give my address in reply
(*a*) RQPS (*b*) RSQP
(*c*) SPQR (*d*) SRQP

(N.D.A. 1995)

21. (1) The two men who were following
(P) and who were separated from the tigress by the rock,
(Q) when they saw me stop
(R) a few yards behind me
(S) stood still
(6) and turn my head.
(*a*) PSQR (*b*) QSPR
(*c*) RPSQ (*d*) SQRP

(Assistant Grade, 1993)

22. The leader of the Opposition,
(P) in the manner he had planned to convince them,
(Q) on realising that he had failed to convince the assembly,
(R) who had a reputation for speech making,
(S) was very much disappointed
(*a*) PSRQ (*b*) QSRP
(*c*) RSQP (*d*) SPRQ

23. The professor
(P) who has explored many jungles
(Q) will lecture on the new expedition
(R) about which I have read
(S) which he is now planning
(*a*) PQRS (*b*) PRQS
(*c*) QRSP (*d*) RSPQ

(C.D.S. 1994)

24. The budget
(P) with high expectations
(Q) by all types of tax payers
(R) of tax relief
(S) is being awaited
(6) particularly the salaried middle-class.
(*a*) PRQS (*b*) QPRS
(*c*) RPSQ (*d*) SPRQ

25. During routine investigation
(P) other Harappan sites
(Q) archaeologists discovered artifacts
(R) that perfectly matched
(S) remains from **(N.D.A. 1996)**
(*a*) PQSR (*b*) PRQS
(*c*) QRSP (*d*) RSQP

ANSWERS

1. (b) 2. (c) 3. (b) 4. (b) 5. (b) 6. (d) 7. (b) 8. (b) 9. (c) 10. (c)
11. (d) 12. (b) 13. (c) 14. (c) 15. (d) 16. (b) 17. (c) 18. (b) 19. (c) 20. (a)
21. (c) 22. (c) 23. (b) 24. (d) 25. (c)

PRACTICE SET 8

1. (1) If the sovereignty
(P) of the people and their elected representatives,
(Q) and the unity
(R) in the hands
(S) of a country is not safe
(6) it cannot be safe in any other hands
(a) PQRS (b) QSRP
(c) RPQS (d) SRPQ
(Stenographers' Exam, 1993)

2. (1) Never
(P) that which
(Q) put off
(R) till tomorrow
(S) can be done
(6) today **(Central Excise, 1993)**
(a) QRPS (b) QRSP
(c) SQRP (d) SRQP

3. Political liberty
(P) is secured
(Q) whereby civil and religious liberty
(R) is no more
(S) than the instrument
(a) QPRS (b) QRPS
(c) QRSP (d) RSQP

4. Though he was only a child
(P) he often worked much harder
(Q) than was either necessary
(R) in order to please his parents
(S) or good for him **(C.D.S. 1995)**
(a) PRQS (b) PRSQ
(c) RPQS (d) RQSP

5. Be careful in choosing your companions, and
(P) never to be departed from, that
(Q) no youth ought to be called your friend
(R) lay this down as a rule
(S) who is addicted to indecent talk or who is fond of low society
(a) QPRS (b) QSPR
(c) RPQS (d) RPSQ

6. (1) There are many versions
(P) of a 15 ft. rope,
(Q) in which the magician
(R) of the Indian rope-trick
(S) firmly holds one end
(6) the other end of which he throws upwards
(a) PSQR (b) QRPS
(c) RQSP (d) SPQR
(S.S.C. 1995)

7. (P) to dispose off the waste matter
(Q) the modernisation would reduce
(R) provide better sanitary facilities
(S) manual labour considerably and would also
(a) PQSR (b) QSRP
(c) RPQS (d) SRPQ

8. (1) The leader's public meeting was disrupted
(P) by a section of the audience
(Q) any firm assurance
(R) he had not given them
(S) who felt that
(6) for the solution of their problems
(a) PSRQ (b) QPSR
(c) RQPS (d) SRQP
(Stenographers' Exam, 1995)

9. (1) China is clearly
(P) become a middle income nation
(Q) its economy and society, and
(R) and perhaps a super power
(S) determined to modernise
(6) in the next twenty five years
(a) PRSQ (b) QRPS
(c) RSQP (d) SQPR

10. People
(P) at his dispensary
(Q) went to him
(R) of all professions
(S) for medicine and treatment
(C.D.S. 1995)
(a) QPRS (b) QRPS
(c) RPQS (d) RQSP

11. Today
(P) we have the law
(Q) and 'might is right'
(R) to protect us all
(S) does not operate
(6) any more
(a) PRQS (b) QRPS
(c) RPSQ (d) SQRP

12. Athens
(P) it was also at its height
(Q) the first democracy in the world,
(R) was not only
(S) an almost perfect democracy
(*a*) QRPS (*b*) QRSP
(*c*) RQPS (*d*) PSRQ
(N.D.A. 1994)

13. (1) Kiran with a deep sigh
(P) as if she were the thief herself,
(Q) and at the top she placed
(R) replaced the inkstand in the box, and
(S) covered it with the linen
(6) the presents together with the bank note.
(*a*) PSQR (*b*) QSRP
(*c*) RPSQ (*d*) SQPR

14. It is a rule
(P) by anyone and admits
(Q) that must not
(R) of no variation
(S) be violated **(C.D.S. 1995)**
(*a*) PSQR (*b*) QPRS
(*c*) QSPR (*d*) RQPS

15. (1) The communique took note of
(P) facing the world and
(Q) support of terrorism and subversion
(R) the issues of peace and security
(S) called on all states to eschew any form of
(6) directed against other states.
(*a*) PSQR (*b*) RPSQ
(*c*) RQSP (*d*) SPQR

16. Education is
(P) of the proper sense of responsibilities
(Q) the first need
(R) in a citizen
(S) for the development **(Railways, 1994)**
(*a*) PQRS (*b*) QSPR
(*c*) QSRP (*d*) SQPR

17. (1) The Government has constituted
(P) keeping in mind the necessary
(Q) to ensure adequate inputs of science and technology
(R) environmental safeguards
(S) an expert group to incorporate strategies
(6) for ecologically sustainable production
(*a*) PRSQ (*b*) RQPS
(*c*) SPRQ (*d*) SQPR

18. (1) Nothing is more common than the idea
(P) of the twentieth century
(Q) in the western world
(R) the people living
(S) that we
(6) are eminently sane **(S.S.C. 1992)**
(*a*) PQRS (*b*) SPQR
(*c*) SRPQ (*d*) SRQP

19. (P) will normally be granted
(Q) candidates should note
(R) that no request for
(S) change of centre
(*a*) PSQR (*b*) QRSP
(*c*) RSPQ (*d*) SPQR

20. The doctor's offer
(P) not only saved Julie
(Q) but enabled her to blossom into a happy woman
(R) from the jaws of death
(S) of marriage **(N.D.A. 1995)**
(*a*) PQRS (*b*) PSQR
(*c*) SPRQ (*d*) SPQR

21. (1) Gandhiji wanted the Congress Party
(P) for he knew that
(Q) its usefulness and would merely be
(R) to be disbanded on Independence,
(S) after that the party had outlived
(6) used by some politicians for their own ends.
(*a*) PSQR (*b*) QSPR
(*c*) RPSQ (*d*) SQPR
(Assistant Grade, 1993)

22. I,
(P) one hand before me on the wall,
(Q) unlocked the door,
(R) to guide me in the heavy blackness
(S) and went softly down the stairs
(*a*) PQRS (*b*) QPRS
(*c*) QSPR (*d*) RQPS

23. He knew that
(P) and then to save himself
(Q) was to save all the lives
(R) entrusted to his care
(S) the duty of a captain **(S.C.R.A. 1994)**
(*a*) SQRP (*b*) SPRQ
(*c*) QSRP (*d*) PQRS

24. To much of the world.
(P) which produces radio and television
(Q) it is science
(R) by airplanes and satellites
(S) and which conquers space
(*a*) RSPQ (*b*) RQPS
(*c*) QRPS (*d*) QPSR
(C.D.S. 1994)

25. (1) In this stage of the world,
(P) that their gross ignorance of one another should be diminished
(Q) it is essential,
(R) when many nations are brought into close and vital contact for good and evil,
(S) as never before
(6) that they should begin to understand a little of one another's

historical experience and resulting mentality.
(*a*) PSRQ (*b*) PQRS
(*c*) PRSQ (*d*) RQSP

26. It is not, therefore
(P) that I pay a tribute
(Q) to conductors as a class
(R) with any feeling of unfriendliness
(S) to a particular member of that class
(*a*) PQRS (*b*) PSRQ
(*c*) RQPS (*d*) RSPQ
(C.D.S. 1993)

27. (1) The code
(P) is normally put onto cards
(Q) that the computer understands
(R) small holes are punched
(S) through which
(6) in specially arranged patterns
(*a*) PQSR (*b*) QPSR
(*c*) SRQP (*d*) SRPQ
(S.S.C. 1995)

28. I believed then
(P) that no matter
(Q) one should always find some time for exercise
(R) and I believe even now
(S) what amount of work one has
(*a*) PSRQ (*b*) PRQS
(*c*) RPSQ (*d*) RPQS

29. I know it is not nice to compromise but
(P) if placed in his situation
(Q) you can hardly blame him
(R) for doing what
(S) most people would do
(*a*) QRPS (*b*) QRSP
(*c*) SPQR (*d*) SPRQ
(C.D.S. 1995)

30. Village and small industries while requiring limited capital
(P) can provide
(Q) a variety of goods for consumption
(R) and produce
(S) employment to large numbers
(*a*) PQRS (*b*) PRQS
(*c*) PRSQ (*d*) PSRQ
(N.D.A. 1996)

ANSWERS

1. (*b*)	**2.** (*a*)	**3.** (*d*)	**4.** (*c*)	**5.** (*c*)	**6.** (*c*)	**7.** (*b*)	**8.** (*a*)	**9.** (*d*)	**10.** (*d*)
11. (*a*)	**12.** (*c*)	**13.** (*c*)	**14.** (*c*)	**15.** (*b*)	**16.** (*b*)	**17.** (*d*)	**18.** (*d*)	**19.** (*b*)	**20.** (*c*)
21. (*c*)	**22.** (*b*)	**23.** (*a*)	**24.** (*d*)	**25.** (*d*)	**26.** (*d*)	**27.** (*b*)	**28.** (*a*)	**29.** (*b*)	**30.** (*d*)

PRACTICE SET 9

1. I read an advertisement that said
(P) posh, airconditioned
(Q) gentlemen of taste
(R) are available for
(S) fully furnished rooms
(*a*) SRPQ (*b*) PSRQ
(*c*) PSQR (*d*) PQRS
(Railways, 1994)

2. (1) Nationalism in its extreme form
(P) that nations are not able to understand one another rightly
(Q) and good will, which are essential
(R) creates false notions with the result
(S) it stands in the way of mutual understanding
(6) for international peace and security.
(*a*) PRQS (*b*) QSRP
(*c*) RPSQ (*d*) SQPR
(S.S.C. 1994)

3. As a youth
(P) extravagant clothes and adopting
(Q) he was a dandy
(R) melodramatic Byronic poses
(S) who delighted in wearing
(*a*) PQRS (*b*) QPSR
(*c*) QRPS (*d*) QSPR

4. (1) The man
(P) to be changed
(Q) who resolves
(R) by the first counter suggestion of a friend
(S) but suffers his resolution
(6) can never accomplish anything great or useful.
(*a*) PRSQ (*b*) QPSR
(*c*) QRSP (*d*) RSQP
(Stenographer's Exam, 1995)

5. In the modern times
(P) certainly
(Q) hijackings are
(R) experienced by the air personnel
(S) the most cruel form of horror
(*a*) PRQS (*b*) QPSR
(*c*) RSQP (*d*) SQPR

6. They tell us
(P) in some places
(Q) there must have been

(R) that when the great glaciers of the Ice Age melted
(S) vast steppes or wide treeless plains
(*a*) QRPS (*b*) QRSP
(*c*) RQPS (*d*) RQSP

(C.D.S. 1995)

7. (P) after travelling in other countries,
(Q) he should not forget
(R) all about the countries he has travelled
(S) when a man returns home
(*a*) PRQS (*b*) RPQS
(*c*) SPQR (*d*) SRQP

(S.C.R.A. 1993)

8. The Indian woman wants
(P) in a male dominated society
(Q) as an equal partner
(R) and it is not too much to demand
(S) her rightful place **(N.D.A. 1996)**
(*a*) QPSR (*b*) RSQP
(*c*) SQPR (*d*) SRPQ

9. The national unity of a free people
(P) to make it impracticable
(Q) for there to be an arbitrary administration
(R) depends upon a sufficiently even balance of political power
(S) against a revolutionary opposition that is irreconcilably opposed to it
(*a*) QRPS (*b*) QRSP
(*c*) RPQS (*d*) RSPQ

(C.D.S. 1995)

10. (1) Variety, they say, is the spice of life,
(P) decided to take this adage to heart and
(Q) pieces of garlic
(R) serve sambar garnished with a few
(S) but a certain reputed hotel
(6) in its 'vegetarian food only' restaurant.
(*a*) PRQS (*b*) QSPR
(*c*) RQSP (*d*) SPRQ

11. (1) Strike
(P) when all the other methods
(Q) is a legitimate weapon of the worker
(R) to get better pay,
(S) shorter hours of work and better working conditions
(6) have failed.
(*a*) QRSP (*b*) QSPR
(*c*) RPSQ (*d*) SPRQ

(Stenographers' Exam, 1994)

12. The mother exclaimed that
(P) to have solved the puzzle
(Q) so quickly
(R) it was
(S) very clever of him
(*a*) PSQR (*b*) QRPS
(*c*) RSPQ (*d*) SPRQ

13. (1) If the sword fish really attacked
(P) it could have cut it
(Q) and that would have been
(R) to pieces very quickly
(S) the rubber raft with its vicious sword
(6) the end of the experiment.
(*a*) PRQS (*b*) QSPR
(*c*) RQSP (*d*) SPRQ

(Assistant Grade, 1993)

14. (1) India has been a land
(P) but in the sense that learning has always been very highly valued
(Q) not indeed in the sense that education has been universal,
(R) and the learned man has been held in higher esteem
(S) of learning throughout the ages
(6) than the warrior or the administrator.
(*a*) QPSR (*b*) RQPS
(*c*) SQRP (*d*) SRQP

15. The essay
(P) like that of the human face,
(Q) because the variety is infinite,
(R) is a literary form
(S) which is not easy to define
(*a*) PQRS (*b*) PQSR
(*c*) RSPQ (*d*) RSQP

(C.D.S. 1994)

16. (1) She had understood
(P) so she withdrew herself from the ordinary people,
(Q) like a curse to her father's house,
(R) that God had sent her,
(S) from her earliest childhood
(6) and tried to live apart.
(*a*) PRQS (*b*) QSPR
(*c*) SPQR (*d*) SRQP

17. (1) In this way, balancing his accounts
(P) would bring about
(Q) only extreme non-violence,
(R) with violence and non-violence,
(S) Gandhi concluded that
(6) the end of British rule. **(S.S.C. 1995)**
(*a*) RPQS (*b*) RQSP
(*c*) RSPQ (*d*) RSQP

18. (1) He said the agitation was launched
(P) after all other attempts
(Q) as a last resort
(R) the demands conceded
(S) to make the authorities implement
(6) nearly a decade ago failed
(*a*) PSRQ (*b*) QPSR
(*c*) QRSP (*d*) SRPQ

19. Almost thirty-five years ago
(P) seemed inconsequential compared to the benefits
(Q) scientists said, would flow from it

(R) the problems of dismantlement
(S) when nuclear power reactors first went on line **(C.D.S. 1995)**
(*a*) RSPQ (*b*) RSQP
(*c*) SRPQ (*d*) SRQP

20. Georgian loyalists and rebel forces
(P) after a week of fighting
(Q) agreed to
(R) a ceasefire today
(S) in which 51 people were killed
(*a*) PQRS (*b*) QPSR
(*c*) QRPS (*d*) QRSP

21. (1) If the question of record of human rights
(P) in the last fifty years or so,
(Q) it is difficult to see how most of the countries,
(R) had been raised in the past,
(S) that have staged the olympics
(6) would have been allowed to hold them. **(Stenographers' Exam, 1995)**
(*a*) PRQS (*b*) QPSR
(*c*) RPQS (*d*) RQSP

22. (1) The germanium metal
(P) should be so pure that
(Q) one part of copper impurity
(R) to be used in semi-conductor devices
(S) it should not contain more than
(6) in ten million parts of germanium.
(*a*) PSQR (*b*) PRQS
(*c*) RPSQ (*d*) SQRP

23. (1) Those that have seen the Hindus
(P) have naturally no more doubt
(Q) of the existence of other persons
(R) among them in their own country
(S) of their existence than they have
(6) whom they have met. **(S.S.C. 1992)**
(*a*) PSQR (*b*) PSRQ
(*c*) RPSQ (*d*) RQPS

24. (P) through the long, hot summer
(Q) if you plan to train hard
(R) continually
(S) you will need to acclimatise yourself
(*a*) PQRS (*b*) QRPS
(*c*) QRSP (*d*) SRPQ

25. The effectiveness of a film
(P) the needs of the audience
(Q) is judged by
(R) and its relation to
(S) its theme
(*a*) PQRS (*b*) PSQR
(*c*) QPRS (*d*) QSRP
(N.D.A. 1995)

ANSWERS

1. (*b*)	**2.** (*c*)	**3.** (*d*)	**4.** (*c*)	**5.** (*b*)	**6.** (*d*)	**7.** (*c*)	**8.** (*c*)	**9.** (*d*)	**10.** (*d*)
11. (*a*)	**12.** (*c*)	**13.** (*d*)	**14.** (*c*)	**15.** (*d*)	**16.** (*d*)	**17.** (*d*)	**18.** (*b*)	**19.** (*c*)	**20.** (*c*)
21. (*d*)	**22.** (*c*)	**23.** (*a*)	**24.** (*b*)	**25.** (*d*)					

20. REARRANGEMENT OF SENTENCES IN A PARAGRAPH

In this type of questions, six sentences are given and labelled S_1, P, Q, R, S and S_6. S_1 and S_6 are the first and the last sentences of a paragraph respectively. The middle four sentences viz. P, Q, R and S are given in a jumbled order. The candidate is required to arrange these four sentences in a meaningful sequence and then choose the correct order from among the alternatives provided.

Example : ***Considering the positions of S_1 and S_6 as fixed, rearrange the four sentences P, Q, R and S and choose one of the four alternatives which would be the most logical sequence of the sentences in the passage.***

S_1 : Speech was the first means of conveying information.

P : Thirdly printing helped in dissemination of knowledge in a permanent form.

Q : Then writing as a means introduced a capacity for storing information.

R : Computer is the only medium that can not only store but analyse information to make decision.

S : However, all these are passive media.

S_6 : Therefore, computer is hailed as the fourth information revolution.

(N.D.A. 1996)

The proper sequence should be

(*a*) PQSR (*b*) QPRS
(*c*) QPSR (*d*) QRPS

Solution : Clearly, the author speaks of 'passive media' of conveying information on the one hand and 'computer' on the other hand. In S_1, speech is talked of as the first means. Then comes sentence Q which talks of writing as the next means.

P follows Q because it discusses about printing as the third means.

The next sentence is S because the author conveys that all these three are passive media. Since S_6 (the last sentence) is concerned with computers, so the fifth sentence in the paragraph should be R.

Hence, the correct sequence is QPSR.

So, the answer is (*c*).

PRACTICE SET 1

Directions : ***In each of the following questions, there are six sentences marked S_1, S_6, P, Q, R, S. The positions of S_1 and S_6 are fixed. You are required to choose one of the four alternatives which would be the most logical sequence of the sentences in the passage.***

1. S_1. The Hound of Baskervilles was feared by the people of the area.

S_6. The Hound of Baskervilles remains an unsolved mystery.

P : Some people spoke of seeing a huge, shadowy form of a hound at midnight on the moor.

Q : But they spoke of it in tones of horror.

R : Nobody had actually seen the hound.

S : This shadowy form did not reveal any details about the animal.

(*a*) PQRS (*b*) PSRQ
(*c*) SPQR (*d*) SPRQ

(C.D.S. 1994)

2. S_1. Rammohan Roy was associated with several newspapers.

P : Many educationists protested vigorously against these measures.

Q : But this came to grief soon after the enactment in 1823, of new measures for the control of the press.

R : He brought out a bilingual, Bengali- English magazine.

S : Later, desiring an all - India circulation, he published a weekly in Persian, which was recognised then as the language of the cultured classes all over India.

S_6. Rammohan Roy even addressed a petition to the King - in - Council in England.

(*a*) QPRS (*b*) RQPS
(*c*) RSPQ (*d*) RSQP

3. S_1. Different countries show different patterns of growth.

P : Many others have a high birth rate with a low death rate.

Q: Some have a high birth rate and still have a high death rate.

R: The developing countries show the most rapid growth rate.

S: Some others like the European nations, have a low birth rate and a low death rate.

S6. Compared to this in Europe the growth rate is low. **(C.B.I. 1995)**

(*a*) PQSR (*b*) QSPR
(*c*) RSQP (*d*) SPQR

4. **S1.** There are examinations at school which a pupil can pass by cramming the texts.

P: But for spiritual knowledge mere memory of holy texts will be of no use in passing the texts.

Q: One can score in them by the power of memory.

R: A competent guru alone can provide the necessary guidance to an earnest disciple.

S: What the text says has to be reflected upon and experienced by the speaker.

S6. Thus, reading, reflection and experience are the three stages in gaining spiritual knowledge.

(*a*) QPSR (*b*) RSPQ
(*c*) RSQP (*d*) SRPQ

5. **S1.** The domestic cat is a contradiction in itself.

P: But the adult pet dog also sees its human family as the dominant members of the pack.

Q: Nursed in kittenhood it develops extraordinary intimacy with man-kind.

R: The dog, like the pet cat, sees its owners as pseudo - parents.

S: At the same time. however, the cat continues to retain its independence.

S6. Hence it has won such a reputation for obedience and loyalty.

(*a*) QSPR (*b*) QSRP
(*c*) SQPR (*d*) SQRP

(N.D.A. 1995)

6. **S1.** He could not rise.

S6. It was colder than usual.

P: All at once, in the distance, he heard an elephant trumpet.

Q: He tried again with all his might, but to no use.

R: The next moment he was on his feet.

S: He stepped into the river.

(*a*) PQSR (*b*) PRQS
(*c*) QPRS (*d*) QPSR

(N.D.A. 1996)

7. **S1.** An elderly lady suddenly became blind.

S6. The lady said that she had not been properly cured because she could not see all her furniture.

P: The doctor called daily and every time he took away some of her furniture he liked.

Q: At last, she was cured and the doctor demanded his fee.

R: She agreed to pay a large fee to the doctor who would cure her.

S: On being refused, the doctor wanted to know the reason.

(*a*) PQRS (*b*) RPQS
(*c*) RQPS (*d*) RSPQ

(Section Officers, 1993)

8. **S1.** Yawning or its absence has been related to various clinical conditions.

P: Interestingly, some clinicians claim that those with acute physical illness don't yawn until they are on the road to recovery.

Q: It can be a symptom of brain lesions, haemorrhage, motion sickness and encephalitis.

R: But what is currently known about yawning is essentially anecdotal, mostly because the yawn has not got the respect it deserves.

S: On the other hand, it has been reported that psychotics rarely yawn, except those suffering from brain damage.

S6. It is in reality a releasing stimulus.

(*a*) PSRQ (*b*) PSQR
(*c*) QSPR (*d*) QSRP

9. **S1.** Man has existed for about a million years.

P: Science, as a dominant factor in determining the beliefs of educated men, has existed for about 300 years; as a source of economic technique, for about 150 years.

Q: When we consider how recently it has risen to power, we find ourselves forced to believe that we are at the very beginning of its work in transforming human life.

R: In this brief period it has proved itself an incredibly powerful revolutionary force.

S: He has possessed writing for about 6,000 years, agriculture somewhat longer, but perhaps not much longer.

S6. What its future effects will be is a matter of conjecture, but possibly a study of its effects hitherto may make the conjecture a little less hazardous. **(Railways, 1994)**

(*a*) PQSR (*b*) PRSQ
(*c*) RQPS (*d*) SPRQ

10. **S1.** The path of Venus lies inside the path of the Earth.

S6. When at its brightest, it is easily seen with the naked eye in broad daylight.

P: When at its farthest from the Earth, Venus is 160 million miles away.

Q: With such a wide range between its greatest and least distances it is natural that at sometimes Venus appears much brighter than others.

R: No other body ever comes so near the Earth, with the exception of the Moon and an occasional comet or asteroid.

S: When Venus is at its nearest to the Earth, it is only 26 million miles away. **(C.D.S. 1993)**

(*a*) PSQR (*b*) QPRS
(*c*) SQRP (*d*) SRPQ

11. **S1.** Work with retarded children, in particular, involves superhuman patience and long-delayed rewards.

P: Another woman faithfully spent two hours a day, five days a week, with a bed-ridden retarded girl.

Q: It was three years before the girl made her first cut in a piece of paper.

R: The girl had never before responded to, or recognised anyone.

S: One woman decided to teach a young brain - damaged girl how to use scissors.

S6. After five years, the girl finally began to smile, when her foster grandparents entered the room.

(*a*) PSQR (*b*) QSPR
(*c*) RQSP (*d*) SQPR

12. **S1.** He tried the door.

P: The room was neat and clean.

Q: Then he stepped into the room.

R: He waited for a minute or two.

S: It opened easily and he peeped in.

S6. He was careful not to touch anything.

(*a*) PQRS (*b*) QSPR
(*c*) RPQS (*d*) SPRQ

(I. Tax & Central Excise, 1994)

13. **S1.** Frozen foods are so popular today that many people wonder how they ever lived without them.

S6. Now refrigerators and deep freezers preserve many foods that could not be kept any other way.

P: Near the North Pole, where the ground stays frozen all the year around, there is no problem of preserving foods.

Q: Actually, people who live in cool climates have had frozen foods for a long time.

R: Ice helped them when they could get it, but they couldn't get it very often.

S: But people who live in warm climates have not always been able to keep food fresh.

(*a*) PQRS (*b*) QPRS
(*c*) QPSR (*d*) SRQP

14. **S1.** Jawaharlal Nehru was born on November 14.

P: He loved children.

Q: On this day, children take part in many activities.

R: Sports, music, drama and debates are arranged in schools.

S: That is why his birthday is celebrated as Children's Day.

S6. Exhibitions of photographs of Pandit Nehru showing his life time are also arranged in some schools.

(*a*) PQRS (*b*) PSQR
(*c*) QPSR (*d*) SPQR

(B.Ed. Exam, 1994)

15. **S1.** For a conversation to be stimulating and sustained, the participants must be active talkers as well as active listeners.

S6. It's better to paint the big picture first, and if your partner wants to know more, you can always fill in with details.

P: This is usually unnecessary, confusing and even boring to your partner.

Q: Some people feel that they have to give long - winded explanations of their views.

R: Make a point of throwing the conversational ball to the other person after you have presented your ideas in an abridged form.

S: Be sure to do both in conversation.

(*a*) QPSR (*b*) SRQP
(*c*) PSRQ (*d*) RSPQ

16. **S_1.** But how does a new word get into the dictionary?

S_6. He sorts them according to their grammatical function, and carefully writes a definition.

P: When a new dictionary is being edited, a lexicographer collects all the alphabetically arranged citation slips for a particular word.

Q: The dictionary makers notice it and make a note of it on a citation slip.

R: The moment a new word is coined, it usually enters the spoken language.

S: The word then passes from the realm of hearing to the realm of writing. **(C.D.S. 1995)**

(*a*) PQRS (*b*) PRSQ
(*c*) RQPS (*d*) RSQP

17. **S_1.** Gandhi's first political fast was made soon after his return from Africa.

S_6. He did not fast against the mill owners, but in order to strengthen the determination of the strikers.

P: He had also received help from this man's sister.

Q: This was when the poor labourers of the cotton mills of Ahmedabad were on strike.

R: He was a friend of the largest mill-owner.

S: Gandhi had made the strikers promise to remain on strike until the owners agreed to accept the decision of an arbitrator.

(*a*) PQSR (*b*) QSRP
(*c*) RPQS (*d*) SRPQ

18. **S_1.** Kabir knew that Ramananda got up very early in the morning and went down on the steps of the 'ghat' to bathe in the waters of the sacred Ganges.

P: As Ramananda came down the steps before daybreak for his usual bath, he trod on the sleeping man.

Q: Kabir at once jumped up and threw himself at the feet of the preacher.

R: "Ram, Ram", he exclaimed in astonishment.

S: One dark night, Kabir went to the 'ghat' and lay down on one of the river steps.

S_6. He said, "You have given me the mantra, 'Ram, Ram,' I have become your disciple". **(N.D.A. 1993)**

(*a*) PQSR (*b*) PRQS
(*c*) RQPS (*d*) SPRQ

19. **S_1.** We must also understand that the fruits of labour are sweeter than the gifts of fortune.

S_6. The best life, therefore, is lived both in thought and deed.

P: Moreover, too much of thinking is also a disease.

Q: Indeed, thought and action can be separately analysed but can never be separated from each other.

R: Hence, thought to be complete demands action and action without thought also has no value.

S: It keeps us depressed and gloomy.

(*a*) PSRQ (*b*) QRSP
(*c*) RQPS (*d*) SPQR

20. **S_1.** Smoke oozed up between the planks.

P: Passengers were told to be ready to quit the ship.

Q: The rising gale fanned the smouldering fire.

R: Every one now knew there was a fire on board.

S: Flames broke out here and there.

S_6. Most people bore the shock bravely.

(*a*) QPSR (*b*) QSRP
(*c*) RSPQ (*d*) SRQP

(Assistant Grade, 1996)

21. **S_1.** The houses in the Indus Valley were built of baked bricks.

P: This staircase sometimes continued upwards on to the roof.

Q: Access to the upstairs rooms was by a narrow stone staircase at the back of the house.

R: The drains were incorporated in the walls.

S: The houses had bathrooms and water closets, rubbish chutes and excellent drainage systems.

S6. They led outside into covered sewers which ran down the side of the streets. **(N.D.A. 1994)**

(*a*) PSQR (*b*) QPSR
(*c*) QRPS (*d*) SPQR

22. S1. Most of the perishable foods are shipped by refrigerator ships.

S6. Ripe bananas are poor travellers and even one ripe banana at the start of the trip can spoil a whole ship load of fruit.

P: They are placed in the refrigerated hold of the ship.

Q: Some foods, such as bananas, are shipped before they get ripe.

R: As the green bananas are loaded, a man watches closely the signs of yellow on them.

S: The cool temperatures keep the bananas from getting ripe during the trip. **(S.S.C. 1993)**

(*a*) PQRS (*b*) PSQR
(*c*) QPSR (*d*) SRPQ

23. S1 A transformation of consciousness is now beginning to express itself in the field of theoretical architecture.

P: In the still theoretical structure, an attempt is being made to create a house that is "a domestication of an ecosystem."

Q: What is happening in the architecture is a shift from the international style of the post - industrial era to a symbolic structure.

R: Since architecture is the collective unconscious made visible, the architect does not himself always understand the full cultural implications of his own work.

S: The new form is not a celebration of power over new materials, but a celebration of cooperation with ecosystem.

S6. The relationship between culture and nature is changed, for the architect grows a house like a garden.

(*a*) PRSQ (*b*) QPSR
(*c*) RQSP (*d*) SQRP

24. S1. While on a fishing trip last summer, I watched an elderly man fishing off the edge of a dock.

P: "Why didn't you keep the other big ones?" I aksed.

Q: He caught an enormous trout, but apparently not satisfied with its size, he threw it back into the war.

R: He finally caught a small pike, threw it into his pail, and, smiling happily, prepared to live.

S: Amazed, I watched him repeat this performance.

S6. Cheerfully, the old man replied, "Small frying pan." **(N.D.A. 1995)**

(*a*) PSQR (*b*) QSRP
(*c*) RPQS (*d*) SQRP

25. S1. There was once a Persian king called Shahryar who had a beautiful wife.

P: When the King discovered this he killed her.

Q: He gave orders that he was to be provided with a new wife every day.

R: He loved her very much, but she was a wicked woman.

S: He decided that all women were wicked and that he would punish them.

S6. After one day's marriage he would cut off her head and marry again.

(*a*) PQRS (*b*) QSPR
(*c*) RPSQ (*d*) SPRQ
(C.B.I. 1995)

26. S1. We must never allow ourselves to lapse into the evil habit of borrowing money from others.

S6. We must not confuse money lending with generosity.

P: We must work hard and earn money, enough for our wants.

Q: Even if we are fortunate enough to possess surplus wealth, we should take care not to lend out money indiscriminately.

R: If borrowing is bad, lending is worse.

S: Borrowing of a habitual nature prevents us from being industrious.

(*a*) PSQR (*b*) QSRP
(*c*) RSQP (*d*) SPRQ

27. S1. There was a time Egypt faced economic crisis.

P: Cotton is the chief export commodity of Egypt.

Q: Foreign trade depends on cultivation of cotton on large scale.

R: It became necessary for Egypt to boost cotton crops.

S: Only by means of increasing foreign trade Egypt could survive.

S6. Egypt was able to sustain itself by its cotton produce.

(*a*) PQRS (*b*) QRPS
(*c*) RPSQ (*d*) SRQP

(I. Tax & Central Excise, 1993)

28. S1. While crossing a busy road we should obey the policeman on duty.

P: We should always cross the road at the zebra crossing.

Q: We must look to the signal lights and cross the road only when the road is clear.

R: If there are no signal lights at the crossing, we should look to the right, then to the left and again to the right before crossing the road.

S: If the road is not clear we should wait.

S6. We should never run while crossing a road. **(U.D.C. 1995)**

(*a*) PQRS (*b*) PSRQ
(*c*) QRPS (*d*) RQSP

29. S1. The commonest form of forgetfulness, I suppose, occurs in the matter of posting letters.

S6. Weary of holding it in my hand, I then put it for safety into one of my pockets and forget all about it.

P: So common is it that I am always reluctant to trust a departing visitor to post an important letter.

Q: As for myself, anyone who asks me to post a letter is a poor judge of character.

R: Even if I carry the letter in my hand I am always past the first pillar box before I remember that I ought to have posted it.

S: So little I rely on his memory that I put him on his oath before handing the letter to him.

(*a*) PRQS (*b*) PSQR
(*c*) QSPR (*d*) RQSP

(S.C.R.A. 1994)

30. S1. We must learn to depend on ourselves and not to look to others for help every time we are in trouble.

S6. A country's freedom can be preserved only by her own strength and self - reliance.

P: We should not forget that those who lean too much on others tend to become weak and helpless.

Q: Certainly we want to make friends with the rest of the world.

R: We welcome help and cooperation from every quarter, but we must depend primarily on our own resources.

S: We also seek the goodwill and cooperation of all those who reside in this country, whatever their race or nationality. **(I.E.S. 1994)**

(*a*) PQRS (*b*) QPRS
(*c*) QSRP (*d*) SRQP

31. S1. Anything you do that gives you some form of regular exercise will benefit your heart.

S6. But do not push too hard; tune into the warning signals from your body.

P: In fact, never choose an activity just because it is good for you.

Q: By all means work up a good sweat, and even a thirst perhaps.

R: If you can combine this with enjoyment, then so much the better.

S: You will soon get bored of it.

(*a*) PRSQ (*b*) PSRQ
(*c*) QRPS (*d*) RPSQ

32. S1. Proverbs contain homely but universal truths.

P: They point out the incongruities of situations in life.

Q: Naturally, therefore, they are translatable from one language to another.

R: Therefore, their appeal is direct.

S: Many of them had their birth in folk literature.

S6. They are everyman's philosophy.

(*a*) QPRS (*b*) QSPR
(*c*) RPSQ (*d*) SPQR

(C.B.I. 1993)

33. S1. Suddenly it began to climb swiftly, and I knew it was speeding eastward again till it became a speck in the blue morning.

S6. In that case there might be a chance on the moors to the right or left.

P : I didn't know what force they could command, but I was certain it would be sufficient.

Q : My enemies had located me, and the next thing would be a cordon round me.

R : That made me do some savage thinking.

S : The aeroplane had seen my bicycle, and would conclude that I would try to escape by the road.

(*a*) PSRQ (*b*) QPSR
(*c*) RQPS (*d*) SRQP

34. **S1.** Today the earth has many satellites besides the moon.

P : But the pull of the earth keeps them from doing so.

Q : The artificial satellites do not fall because they are going too fast to do so.

R : They are artificial satellites made by man and very much smaller than the man.

S : As they speed along, they tend to go straight off into space.

S6. As a result, they travel in an orbit round the earth. **(I.E.S. 1993)**

(*a*) PRQS (*b*) QPSR
(*c*) RQSP (*d*) SPRQ

35. **S1.** There have been many myths about women in world literature.

P : Odysseus found a way to save himself and his sailors from this evil fate.

Q : The sirens were beautiful maidens whose songs enchanted sailors on the seas.

R : Odysseus's encounter with the sirens during his return home after the fall of Troy is typical of this.

S : Their songs were so captivating that the sailors swam towards them and died miserable deaths.

S6. He filled his rower's ears with wax and had himself bound to the mast so that he could hear the sweet singing without diving overboard to his death. **(Railways, 1993)**

(*a*) PQRS (*b*) PQSR
(*c*) QSPR (*d*) RQSP

36. **S1.** The similarity between the human body and a machine is rather superficial.

S6. The points of difference far outweigh the points of resemblance.

P : Beyond that, comparison fails.

Q : No machine grows in size; no machine sees, hears or feels.

R: It can be summed up in the statement that both require fuel and oxygen and obtain energy.

S : No machine thinks. **(N.D.A. 1996)**

(*a*) QSPR (*b*) RPQS
(*c*) RPSQ (*d*) SQPR

ANSWERS

1. (*a*)	**2.** (*d*)	**3.** (*b*)	**4.** (*a*)	**5.** (*b*)	**6.** (*c*)	**7.** (*b*)	**8.** (*c*)	**9.** (*d*)	**10.** (*d*)
11. (*d*)	**12.** (*d*)	**13.** (*c*)	**14.** (*b*)	**15.** (*b*)	**16.** (*a*)	**17.** (*b*)	**18.** (*d*)	**19.** (*b*)	**20.** (*d*)
21. (*b*)	**22.** (*a*)	**23.** (*b*)	**24.** (*b*)	**25.** (*c*)	**26.** (*d*)	**27.** (*d*)	**28.** (*c*)	**29.** (*b*)	**30.** (*a*)
31. (*d*)	**32.** (*d*)	**33.** (*b*)	**34.** (*c*)	**35.** (*d*)	**36.** (*b*)				

PRACTICE SET 2

Directions : ***In each of the following questions, there are six sentences marked S1, S6, P, Q, R, S. The positions of S1 and S6 are fixed. You are required to choose one of the four alternatives which would be the most logical sequence of the sentences in the passage.***

1. **S1.** Jawaharlal Nehru was born in Allahabad on 14 Nov., 1889.

P : Nehru met Mahatma Gandhi in February, 1920.

Q : In 1905 he was sent to London to study at a school called Harrow.

R : He became the first Prime Minister of Independent India on 15 August, 1947.

S: He married Kamla Kaul in 1915.
S6. He died on 27 May, 1964.
(*a*) QRPS (*b*) QSPR
(*c*) RPQS (*d*) SQRP
(Section Officers, 1993)

2. **S1.** In other words, grammar grows and changes, and there is no such thing as correct use of English for the past, the present and the future.
S6. All the words that man has invented are divided into eight classes, which are called parts of speech.
P: "The door is broke."
Q: Yet this would have been correct in Shakespeare's time.
R: Today, only an uneducated person would say, "My arm is broke."
S: For example, in Shakespeare's play Hamlet, there is the line.
(*a*) PSQR (*b*) QPSR
(*c*) RSPQ (*d*) SPRQ

3. **S1.** The Bhagavadgita recognises the nature of man and the needs of man.
P: All these three aspects constitute the nature of man.
Q: It shows how the human being is a rational one, an ethical one and a spiritual one.
R: More than all, it must be a spiritual experience.
S. Nothing can give him fulfilment unless it satisfies his reason, his ethical conscience.
S6. A man who does not harmonise them, is not truly human.
(*a*) PSQR (*b*) PSRQ
(*c*) QPSR (*d*) RSPQ
(Assistant Grade, 1996)

4. **S1.** Silence is unnatural to man.
P: Even his conversation is in great measure a desperate attempt to prevent a dreadful silence.
Q: In the interval he does all he can to make a noise in the world.
R: There are few things of which he stands in more fear than of the absence of noise.
S: He begins life with a cry and ends it in stillness.
S6. He knows that ninety nine percent of human conversation means no more than the buzzing of a fly, but he longs to join in the buzz and to prove that he is a man and not a wax-work figure.
(*a*) PQRS (*b*) PRQS
(*c*) QPRS (*d*) SQRP

5. **S1.** During the Middle Ages the manufacture of cloth was divided amongst a number of associations of skilled workers who performed different operations required in its production.
S6. This was one of the reasons why the industry flourished in such rich countries as Flanders, Italy and Britain.
P: But the association of skilled workers lacked capital to buy it.
Q: Consequently, he began to assume the role of the employer.
R: With the mechanisation of these operations, complicated apparatus became necessary for economic production.
S: The banker, therefore, stepped in to finance the industrialisation of these operations. **(C.D.S. 1994)**
(*a*) PRQS (*b*) PRSQ
(*c*) RPQS (*d*) RPSQ

6. **S1.** I put the phone down and shook my head in bewilderment.
P: Then I am taken in tow by some moonlighting hare-brain with a passion for veteran aircraft, flying his own Mosquito through the night who happens to spot me.
Q: What a night, what an incredible night!
R: Then I get lost and short of fuel.
S: First I lose my radio and all my instruments.
S6. And finally a half-drunk ground-duty officer has the sense to put his runaway lights on in time to save me.
(*a*) QPSR (*b*) QSRP
(*c*) SPRQ (*d*) SRPQ

7. **S1.** It is very easy to acquire bad habits.
P: If we do not continue to do it, we feel unhappy.
Q: The more we do a thing, the more we tend to like doing it.
R: The force of habit should be fought against.
S: This is called the force of habit.
S6. Even good things should be done from time to time only. **(C.B.I. 1995)**

(*a*) PSQR (*b*) QPSR
(*c*) RPSQ (*d*) SQRP

8. **S_1.** Gandhiji had a vast amount of daily business to transact.

S_6. His practice on this point is something that is characteristic of the Indian tradition.

P : Yet Gandhiji was never too busy to withdraw temporarily from business affairs for recurrent periods of contemplation.

Q : Under present day conditions, that is the fate of any leader of any great movement.

R : In setting apart those times for contemplation Gandhiji was being true, not only to himself, but to India.

S : If he had not made this his practice, he would not, I suppose, have been able to go on doing his business, because his spells of contemplation were the source of his inexhaustible strength.

(*a*) PRSQ (*b*) QPSR
(*c*) RSPQ (*d*) SRPQ

9. **S_1.** A farmer was taking the grain to the mill in sacks.

S_6. But the farmer saw that he was none other than the nobleman.

P : It was too heavy for him to lift.

Q : On the way the horse stumbled, and one of the sacks fell to the ground.

R : Presently he saw a rider coming towards him.

S : He stood waiting till he found somebody to help him.

(*a*) PRQS (*b*) PSQR
(*c*) QPRS (*d*) QPSR

(N.D.A. 1996)

10. **S_1.** There is nothing strange in the fact that so many foreign students should wish to learn English.

S_6. This key will open to him whatever is valuable in the literature of the world.

P : If any valuable book is written in another language, an English translation of it is sure to be speedily published.

Q : Anyone who masters the English tongue acquires a key.

R : Most books found to be generally useful are written in English.

S : The English speaking people want no monopoly of knowledge.

(*a*) SQRP (*b*) SRPQ
(*c*) RSPQ (*d*) RPSQ

11. **S_1.** Once upon a time an ant lived on the bank of a river.

P : The dove saw the ant struggling in water in a helpless condition.

Q : All its efforts to come up failed.

R : One day it suddenly slipped into the water.

S : A dove lived in a tree on the bank not far from the spot.

S_6. She was touched. **(Railways, 1994)**

(*a*) PQRS (*b*) QRPS
(*c*) RQSP (*d*) SRPQ

12. **S_1.** The time has come for us to consider seriously the question of a Bharat brand of English.

P : I am not suggesting here a mongrelisation of the language.

Q : English must adopt the complexion of our life and assimilate its idiom.

R : Now the time is ripe for it to come to the dusty street, market place and under the banyan tree.

S : So far English has had a comparatively confined existence in our country, chiefly in the halls of learning, justice or administration.

S_6. Bharat English will respect the rule of law and maintain the dignity of grammar, but still have a swadeshi stamp about it.

(*a*) QPSR (*b*) RQSP
(*c*) SRPQ (*d*) SRQP

13. **S_1.** Some old people are oppressed by the fear of death.

S_6. Gradually the river grows wider, the banks recede, the waters flow more quietly, and in the end, without any visible break, they become merged in the sea and painlessly lose their individual being.

P : An individual human existence should be like a river-small at first, narrowly contained within its banks, and rushing passionately past boulders and over waterfalls.

Q : In the young there is a justification for this feeling.

R : Young men who have reason to fear that they will be killed in battle may justifiably feel bitter in the thought that they have been cheated of the best thing that life has to offer.

S : But in the old man who has known human joys and sorrows, the fear of death is somewhat object and ignoble, and the best way to overcome it is to make your interests gradually wider and more impersonal. **(C.D.S. 1993)**

(*a*) PQSR (*b*) QPSR
(*c*) QRSP (*d*) RSQP

14. **S_1.** It was early 1943 and the war in the East was going disastrously.

P : How this unlikely bunch of middle aged civilians accomplished their missions makes fascinating reading.

Q : To stop the sinkings a spy ring had to be broken, a German ship assaulted, and a secret radio transmitter silenced.

R : U-boats were torpedoing Allied ships in the Indian ocean faster than they could be replaced.

S : And the only people who could do the job were a handful of British businessmen in Calcutta-all men not called out for active service.

S_6. Boarding Party, James Leasor's latest best - seller is a record of this tale of heroics tinged with irony and humour. **(N.D.A. 1995)**

(*a*) PRSQ (*b*) QSRP
(*c*) RQSP (*d*) SQPR

15. **S_1.** The distinction between state or sovereign and government is developed by Rousseau with utmost exactness and accuracy.

P : While 'state' denotes the community as a whole, created by social pact and manifesting itself in supreme general will, 'government' denotes merely the individual or group of individuals that is designated by the community to carry into effect the sovereign will.

Q : Government, to Rousseau, means executive power.

R : The individuals, to whom this power is assigned are the officers or the agents of the sovereign.

S : The government is created not by any contract but by a decree of the sovereign, and its function is in no sense to make but only to administer law.

S_6. Collectively, they may be called 'prence' or 'magistracy'.

(*a*) PSQR (*b*) QSPR
(*c*) RPSQ (*d*) SQRP

16. **S_1.** Primitive man was helpless and weak.

S_6. Today the knowledge gained from science has armed him with superhuman strength.

P : He conceived of some divinity behing this.

Q : As ages passed, he began to think and to investigate nature's mysteries.

R : He bowed down before natural phenomena.

S : The flash of lightning, the clap of thunder struck him with awe.

(*a*) PSQR (*b*) RPSQ
(*c*) RSPQ (*d*) RSQP

(N.D.A. 1993)

17. **S_1.** We and all other animals breathe in and breathe out air all the time.

S_6. It is a part of the earth.

P : If we stop breathing, we die.

Q : It is because of this fact that we are able to live.

R : It is called the atmosphere.

S : All parts of the earth are surrounded by air.

(*a*) PQRS (*b*) PRQS
(*c*) QPSR (*d*) SRQP

18. **S_1.** Trucks, trains, planes and refrigerator ships are new ways of carrying food.

P : In many countries, women carry food to market on their heads.

Q : High in the Andes Mountains long lines of Illamas, each with a heavy bag of grain, pick their way along rocky trails.

R : But a great deal of food is still carried on the heads of women and the backs of animals.

S : Over the desert sands, camels carry loads of salt, dates and cheese from one oasis to another.

S_6. And in a lonely bay, a fisherman still rows home with the day's catch.

(*a*) PQRS (*b*) RPQS
(*c*) RPSQ (*d*) RSQP

(I. Tax & Central Excise, 1993)

19. **S_1.** This is the story of a tram that woke up at dead of night and went off on a trip all by itself to end in a disaster.

P : In the early morning of 19 January it suddenly started backing out of the depot on its own.

Q : Tramways sources explained that power supply to the overhead wires at the siding had been switched off for some repair work.

R : It went up a quarter mile away, crashed into state bus which caught fire when it smashed into an electric feeder box and a water tap.

S : There was presumably, some defect in the reversal handle of the tram and its main switch had not been put off.

S_6. As a result, when the power supply was restored in the early morning the tram began to move.

(*a*) PQRS (*b*) PRQS
(*c*) RPSQ (*d*) RSPQ

(N.D.A. 1994)

20. **S_1.** Growing up means not only getting larger, but also using our senses and our brains to become more aware of the things around us.

P : Not only does he have a memory but he is able to think and reason.

Q : In this, man differs from all other animals.

R : Before we spray our roadside plants or turn sewage into our rivers, we should pause to think what the results of our actions are likely to be.

S : That is to say, he is able to plan what he is going to do in the light of his experience before he does it.

S_6. In other words, we must develop and use our ability to reason, because the destruction or the preservation of the places in which we live depends on us. **(C.D.S. 1995)**

(*a*) QPSR (*b*) QRSP
(*c*) SPQR (*d*) SPRQ

21. **S_1.** But Mr. Ford was by no means the inventor of mass production.

P : It is difficult, indeed, to say who was.

Q : Brilliant men perfected cotton gins and looms.

R : The invention of the steam-engine gave manufacturers the cheap power they needed.

S : When the first large mills for the manufacture of cloth were built, mass production began.

S_6. When one huge machine began to perform rapidly due operations previously done slowly by hand, the age of mass production was born.

(*a*) PQRS (*b*) PSQR
(*c*) PSRQ (*d*) SPQR

22. **S_1.** For some time in his youth, Abraham Lincoln was manager of a shop.

S_6. Never before had Lincoln had so much time for reading as he had then.

P : Then a chance customer would come.

Q : Young Lincoln's way of keeping shop was entirely unlike anyone else's.

R : Lincoln would jump up and attend to his needs and then revert to his needs.

S : He used to lie full length on the counter of the shop eagerly reading a book. **(I.E.S. 1994)**

(*a*) QPSR (*b*) QSPR
(*c*) SQRP (*d*) SRQP

23. **S_1.** Obesity is a curse of modern times.

P : As a result, what is lost is the natural goodness of roughage and important nutrients.

Q : Invariably, fat and sugar which cause obesity are added to make food more palatable.

R : In these days, food gets more refined and cooking methods are more intricate.

S : Therefore, there are more obese people today than ever before.

S_6. This is because today's changed life styles often mean less physical exertion and an over indulgence in unhealthy food. **(N.D.A. 1993)**

(*a*) QPRS (*b*) RPQS
(*c*) RPSQ (*d*) RQPS

24. **S_1.** I was awakened in the night by a noise in the house.

P : I quickly put on my dressing gown and crept downstairs.

Q : In the living room I discovered two burglars breaking into my desk.

R : As I switched on the light I saw that it was 2 o'clock.

S : They were both tall, dark men.

S6. As soon as they saw me standing there, they rushed to the window and jumped out.

(*a*) PQRS (*b*) PQSR
(*c*) PSRQ (*d*) RPQS

(Central Excise, 1994)

25. S1. It is true that we cannot bring about social equality by law and that therefore there are still inequalities in Indian society.

P : In the United States of America, for instance, Negroes have equal rights under the Constitution but unfortunately these rights are not always given to them freely by the White majority.

Q : It takes time for people to change their way of thinking.

R : This is a problem common to many countries.

S : It is only when we realise that social equality means not only that men are equal before the law, but also equal in the eyes of God that we can begin to have a completely casteless society.

S6. The secular state as found in India, recognises the importance of religion to the individual by giving him freedom to practice it and tell others about it, within the limits of the Constitution.

(*a*) RPQS (*b*) RQPS
(*c*) SPQR (*d*) SRQP

26. S1. Ms. Subramaniam started a petrol pump in Madras.

P : A total of twelve girls now work at the pump.

Q : She advertised in newspapers for women staff.

R : They operate in two shifts.

S : The response was good.

S6. Thus she has shown the way for many others. **(U.D.C. 1995)**

(*a*) PQRS (*b*) PQSR
(*c*) QSPR (*d*) SQPR

27. S1. Science means finding out how things actually do happen.

S6. But Galileo proved his point experimentally by dropping weights from the Leaning Tower of Pisa.

P : He showed that a light object falls to the ground at the same rate as a heavy object.

Q : It does not mean laying down principles as to how they ought to happen.

R : This did not agree with the views of most learned men of that time.

S : The most famous example of this concerns Galileo's discovery about falling bodies.

(*a*) PSQR (*b*) QSPR
(*c*) RQPS (*d*) SQPR

28. S1. Moncure Conway devoted his life to two great objects : freedom of thought, and freedom of the individual.

P : They threaten both kinds of freedom.

Q : But something also has been lost.

R : There are now dangers, somewhat different in form from those of the past ages.

S : In regard to both these objects, something has been gained since his time.

S6. Unless a vigorous and vigilant public opinion can be aroused in defence of them, there will be much less of both a hundred years hence than there is now.

(*a*) PQRS (*b*) QSPR
(*c*) RSPQ (*d*) SQRP

(S.C.R.A. 1994)

29. S1. Human ways of life have steadily changed.

S6. During the last few years change has been even more rapid than usual.

P : From that time to this, civilisation has always been changing.

Q : About ten thousand years ago, man lived entirely by hunting.

R : Ancient Egypt -Greece - the Roman Empire - the Dark Ages and the Middle Ages - the Renaissance - the age of modern science and of modern nations one has succeeded the other; and history has never stood still.

S : A settled, civilised life began only when agriculture was discovered.

(*a*) QSPR (*b*) QSRP
(*c*) RSQP (*d*) SPRQ

(N.D.A. 1995)

30. S1. The city is almost a slum and stinks most of the time.

P : The slush on the road did not deter them.

Q : The occasional slips and falls were considered a small price to pay for the trip.

R : They were excited, fascinated by the sight of fresh snow on the road.

S : Even so, it looked beautiful to tourists of various categories.

S6. But some visitors came away with the unforgettable sight of young labourers scantily clad.

(*a*) QPRS (*b*) RQPS
(*c*) RSQP (*d*) SPQR

(Assistant Grade, 1995)

31. S1. When a boy grows into a young man, he finds himself in a new and strange world.

P : The relationship remains but its nature changes.

Q : The emotional ties that he had with them are now loosened.

R : The old pattern of his life in which his parents were the nucleus around which his life revolved now undergoes a change.

S : He finds in himself an emotional void which he must somehow fill.

S6. At this stage of his life he is like a body without a soul, an eye without light or a flower without fragrance.

(*a*) PRQS (*b*) RQPS
(*c*) RSQP (*d*) SRPQ

32. S1. Ingratitude stings strongest where relationship is closest.

P : Expectation turns innocent relationship into commerce.

Q : Human relationship is adulterated with sly commerce.

R : In commerce, of course, give and take is understood.

S : Most relationships are founded on mutual expectations.

S6. From any warm and healthy human relationship expectation of returns has to be weeded out.

(*a*) PQRS (*b*) QSPR
(*c*) RPSQ (*d*) SRQP

(C.B.I. 1993)

33. S1. If you want to do well in your examinations you need to be able to think for yourself which means not just following the guide - books but write what you think yourself.

P : That will not help much.

Q : Few if any students do this.

R : By discussing things with other students, with your teachers, and with any intelligent people you meet you will find you can pick up a lot of new ideas but it is no good first accepting these ideas, swallowing them undigested and then repeating them in the examination.

S : At first you will find it difficult but if you go on trying you will find clear independent thought becomes easier.

S6. If however you turn these ideas over in our mind accepting those which you agree with and fitting them into your stock of knowledge and rejecting the others you may get somewhere.

(*a*) PSQR (*b*) QSRP
(*c*) RSQP (*d*) SRQP

34. S1. We are living in an age in which technology has suddenly 'annihilated distance'.

P : Are we going to let this consciousness of our variety make us fear and hate each other?

Q : Physically we are now all neighbours, but psychologically we are still strangers to each other.

R : How are we going to react?

S : We have never been so conscious of our variety as we are now that we have come to such close quarters.

S6. In that event, we should be dooming ourselves to wipe each other out. **(I.E.S. 1993)**

(*a*) PQSR (*b*) PSQR
(*c*) QSRP (*d*) RQSP

35. S1. As a dramatist Rabindranath was not what might be called a success.

S6. Therefore, drama forms the essential part of the traditional Indian culture.

P : His dramas were moulded more on the lines of the traditional Indian village dramas than the dramas of the modern world.

Q : His plays were more a catalogue of ideas than a vehicle of the expression of action.

R : Actually drama has always been the life of the Indian people, as it deals with legends of gods and goddesses.

S: Although in his short stories and novels he was able to create living and well - defined characters, he did not seem to be able to do so in his dramas. **(Assistant Grade, 1994)**

(*a*) QPSR (*b*) QSPR
(*c*) RSQP (*d*) SRQP

36. **S_1.** One of the most dangerous insect pests is the locust.

S_6. At this stage, they gather in huge numbers and rise from the ground on their powerful wings in cloud.

P: At first they look just like ordinary grasshoppers, which are harmless and unable to fly very far.

Q: Until about thirty years ago, no one knew where locusts came from or why they appeared in the different countries they attacked.

R: Then they change in appearance and develop wings which enable them to fly long distances.

S: Then it was discovered that there are two stages in the life of locusts.

(*a*) PSQR (*b*) PSRQ
(*c*) QSPR (*d*) QSRP

(N.D.A. 1996)

ANSWERS

1. (*b*)	**2.** (*d*)	**3.** (*d*)	**4.** (*d*)	**5.** (*d*)	**6.** (*b*)	**7.** (*b*)	**8.** (*b*)	**9.** (*d*)	**10.** (*d*)
11. (*c*)	**12.** (*c*)	**13.** (*c*)	**14.** (*c*)	**15.** (*b*)	**16.** (*b*)	**17.** (*c*)	**18.** (*c*)	**19.** (*b*)	**20.** (*a*)
21. (*c*)	**22.** (*b*)	**23.** (*d*)	**24.** (*d*)	**25.** (*a*)	**26.** (*c*)	**27.** (*b*)	**28.** (*d*)	**29.** (*b*)	**30.** (*d*)
31. (*b*)	**32.** (*c*)	**33.** (*b*)	**34.** (*c*)	**35.** (*b*)	**36.** (*c*)				

PRACTICE SET 3

Directions : *In each of the following questions, there are six sentences marked S_1, S_6, P, Q, R, S. The positions of S_1 and S_6 are fixed. You are required to choose one of the four alternatives which would be the most logical sequence of the sentences in the passage.*

1. **S_1.** In 1857, fighting broke out all over the country.

P: Everywhere the people rose in rebellion.

Q: In March 1858 British troops attacked the fort at Jhansi.

R: Thousands of people were killed on both sides.

S: The British fought back.

S_6. The Rani's troops fought back bravely. **(C.B.I. 1995)**

(*a*) PSRQ (*b*) QSPR
(*c*) RPSQ (*d*) SQPR

2. **S_1.** Savita was lonely in the house.

S_6. It was the only thing she had learnt from the Convent School.

P: She was very good at that.

Q: She sat all day in a little room off the main drawing room.

R: She would sit on the rug and do needle work.

S: It was a little room with nothing in it but a few chairs and a rug.

(*a*) PQRS (*b*) QSRP
(*c*) RSPQ (*d*) SRPQ

3. **S_1.** We talk about democracy, but when it comes to any particular thing, we prefer a man belonging to our caste and community.

P: We must be in a position to respect a man as a man.

Q: It means our democracy is a phoney kind of democracy.

R: We must extend opportunities of development to those who deserve them.

S: Our weakness for our own caste and community should not influence our decision.

S_6. Favouritism and nepotism have been responsible for much discontent in our country.

(*a*) PQRS (*b*) QPRS
(*c*) RPQS (*d*) SRPQ

(Central Excise, 1993)

4. **S_1.** A man handed a pair of trousers to the departmental store-clerk and said, "I'd like these altered, please".

P: He said that free alteration is not possible without a receipt.

Q: The man said, "Okay, I'd like to return the trousers". The clerk took them back and returned his money.

R: The man pushed the money and said, "Now I want to buy them". The clerk put the trousers in a bag, issued a receipt and handed him both.

S: The clerk asked for the sales receipt but after searching his pockets the man replied that he had lost it.

S_6. Triumphantly he put the trousers and the receipt on the counter and said, "I'd like to have these altered, please." **(N.D.A. 1993)**

(*a*) PSQR (*b*) PSRQ
(*c*) QRPS (*d*) SPQR

5. S_1. Forecasting the weather has always been a difficult business.

S_6. He made his forecasts by watching flights of the birds or the way smoke rose from fire.

P: During a period of drought, streams and rivers dried up, the cattle died from thirst and the crops were ruined.

Q: Many different things affect the weather and we have to study them carefully to make an accurate forecast.

R: Ancient Egyptians had no need of this— weather in the Nile valley hardly ever changes.

S: In early times, when there were no instruments, such as thermometer or the barometer, man looked for tell-tale signs in the sky.

(*a*) PRQS (*b*) QPRS
(*c*) QRPS (*d*) SPQR

(C.D.S. 1993)

6. S_1. The motor car is one of the useful gifts of modern science.

P: One of these is the smoke and pollution that it creates.

Q: It has made short and medium distance journeys fast and comfortable.

R: The other is that it has made journey by road hazardous.

S: Yet we can't say that a motor car is a blessing without disadvantages.

S_6. Finally in this age of energy crisis a personal car is an expensive thing.

(*a*) PQRS (*b*) QSPR
(*c*) RSPQ (*d*) SPQR

7. S_1. The earliest reference to the playing card has been found in China, as long ago as the tenth century.

P: They appeared in Italy around 1320.

Q: Long before that the Chinese used paper money which was similar in design to the playing cards.

R: It is believed that perhaps travelling gypsies introduced them to Europe.

S: In olden days cards were used both for telling fortune and playing games.

S_6. The current pack of 52 cards was only regulated in the seventeenth century. **(N.D.A. 1995)**

(*a*) QRSP (*b*) QSRP
(*c*) RQSP (*d*) RSQP

8. S_1. Evolution is not progress.

S_6. For, like progress, evolution does, over the long run, imply betterment.

P: And yet, for all their differences, it is not wholly wrong to identify evolution with progress.

Q: As a noted scientist had said, "the tapeworm in its inglorious lot in man's intestine is an outcome of evolution as well as the lark at heaven's gate."

R: Three hundred million years after the first land creatures crawled out of the sea, the one-called amoeba is man himself.

S: The physical facts of evolution betray such advance.

(*a*) QPSR (*b*) RPSQ
(*c*) SPQR (*d*) SRQP

(I. Tax & Central Excise, 1992)

9. S_1. As I say, I was born and brought up in an atmosphere of the confluence of three movements, all of which were revolutionary.

S_6. He should not only have his own seeds but prepare his own soil.

P: I was born in a family which had to live its own life, which led me from my young days to seek guidance for my own self-expression in my own inner standard of judgement.

Q : No poet should borrow his medium ready-made from some shop of respectability.

R : But the language which belonged to the people had to be modulated according to the urging which I as an individual had.

S : The medium of expression, doubtless, was my mother tongue.

(*a*) PQRS (*b*) PQSR
(*c*) PSRQ (*d*) QSRP

(C.D.S. 1994)

10. **S₁.** Welcome to Madam Tussaud's.

P : Famous faces, notorious faces haunt these halls; royalty, and world leaders mingling with sports stars and murderers.

Q : But don't expect any responses to your smiles or greetings.

R : Don't be surprised at anything you see here.

S : See how many you can recognise.

S6. These life-like, casually posed figures are mere wax statues, though they may look alive.

(*a*) PSRQ (*b*) QRPS
(*c*) RPSQ (*d*) SQRP

11. **S₁.** A gentleman who lived alone always had two plates placed on the table at dinner time.

P : One day just as he sat down to dine, the cat rushed into the room.

Q : One plate was for himself and the other was for his cat.

R : She dropped a mouse into her own plate and another into her master's plate.

S : He used to give the cat a piece of meat from his own plate.

S6. In this way the cat showed her gratitude to her master.

(*a*) PSRQ (*b*) QRSP
(*c*) QSPR (*d*) RPQS

(Railways, 1994)

12. **S₁.** In the last few years, there has been increasing realisation of the importance of fibrous diet.

P : Its role in human nutrition was not fully understood.

Q : Plants contain indigestible substances in their cell-walls, and these contain fibre.

R : Later research has thrown light on many other ingredients that are not digested by man.

S : In the early days, people only knew that this fibre prevented constipation.

S6. This has resulted in a better appreciation of the role of fibrous food in human health.

(*a*) PQRS (*b*) QSRP
(*c*) SPRQ (*d*) SQPR

13. **S₁.** The 'age of computers' is considered to have begun in 1946.

S6. And now it is difficult to find a field where computers are not used.

P : Those early computers were huge and heavy affairs, with problems of speed and size.

Q : It was only with the introduction of electronics that the computers really came of age.

R : But computers were in use long before that.

S : They had several rotating shafts and gears which almost always doomed them to slow operation.

(*a*) PRQS (*b*) PRSQ
(*c*) RPQS (*d*) RPSQ

(N.D.A. 1996)

14. **S₁.** After the firing that evening the street that used to be full of people was completely deserted.

P : Nor were any windows open or lighted.

Q : Suddenly I detected a movement to my left.

R : There was no trace of any human being and all doors were firmly closed.

S : Surprisingly, even the stray dogs had disappeared.

S6. I was so frightened that I ran for my life.

(*a*) PQRS (*b*) PSQR
(*c*) RPSQ (*d*) RSPQ

15. **S₁.** Hungary, with a population of about ten million, lies between Czechoslovakia to the north and Yugoslavia to the south.

P : Here a great deal of grain is grown.

Q : In recent years, however, progress has been made also in the field of industrialisation.

R : Most of this country consists of an extremely fertile plain, through which the river Danube flows.

S : In addition to grain, the plain produces potatoes, sugar, wine and livestock.

S_6. The new industries derive mainly from agricultural production.

(*a*) PRSQ (*b*) QRSP
(*c*) RPSQ (*d*) RQSP

(C.D.S. 1995)

16. **S_1**. When Weiner was travelling in India, he visited a factory where he saw small frail children sitting on damp ground.

P : And the answer he got was that they were weaving carpets there.

Q : So he asked, "What are they doing there?"

R : And then he decided to study the problems of child labourers in India.

S : Weiner was shocked at the plight of the child workers.

S_6. Recently he has published this book and it is winning him acclaim all over the world. **(I.E.S. 1993)**

(*a*) PQRS (*b*) QPSR
(*c*) RPQS (*d*) RPSQ

17. **S_1**. There are divergent theories of education.

P : There is still another which holds that education has to be considered rather in relation to community than to the other.

Q : Yet again, some believe that a right proportion of all the theories should go into every system.

R : The other holds that the purpose of education is to impart culture.

S : The first considers that the sole purpose of education is to provide opportunities for growth.

S_6. No actual education proceeds wholly and completely on any one of the theories. **(N.D.A. 1993)**

(*a*) PQRS (*b*) PQSR
(*c*) SRPQ (*d*) SRQP

18. **S_1**. We don't see many banyan trees in our cities now-a- days.

S_6. And every village has at least one.

P : But in our overcrowded cities, where there is barely enough living space for people, banyan trees don't have much of a chance.

Q : These trees like to have plenty of space in which to spread themselves out.

R : Of course, many parks have banyan trees.

S : After all, a full grown banyan takes up as large an area as a three-storey apartment building.

(*a*) PQRS (*b*) QPSR
(*c*) RSQP (*d*) SRPQ

19. **S_1**. While talking to a group, one should feel self- confident and courageous.

P : Nor is it a gift bestowed by providence on only a few.

Q : One should also learn how to think calmly and clearly.

R : It is like the ability to play golf.

S : It is not as difficult as most men imagine.

S_6. Any man can develop his capacity if he has the desire to do so.

(*a*) QRSP (*b*) QSPR
(*c*) RSQP (*d*) SQPR

(Assistant Grade, 1996)

20. **S_1**. Nobody likes staying at home on a public holiday- especially if the weather is fine.

P : We had brought plenty of food with us and we got it out of the car.

Q : The only difficulty was that millions of other people had the same idea.

R : Now everything was ready so we sat down near a path at the foot of a hill.

S : We moved out of the city slowly behind a long line of cars, but at last we came to a quiet country road and, after sometime, stopped at a lonely farm.

S_6. It was very peaceful in the cool grass-until we heard bells ringing at the top of the hill. **(N.D.A. 1994)**

(*a*) PQRS (*b*) PSQR
(*c*) QSPR (*d*) SPQR

21. **S_1**. "You know my wife, Madhavi, always urged me to give up smoking".

P : I really gave it up.

Q : And so when I went to jail I said to myself I really must give it up, if for no other reason than of being self - reliant.

R: When I emerged from jail, I wanted to tell her of my great triumph.

S: But when I met her, there she was with a packet of cigarettes.

S6. "Poor girl!" **(Section Officers, 1993)**

(*a*) PSRQ (*b*) QPRS
(*c*) RSPQ (*d*) SPQR

22. **S1.** In hunting and gathering societies people live in what anthropologists call "the seasonal round."

P: When the salmon are running, it comes to the stream; when the wild grasses must be gathered, the band moves on again.

Q: The tribal band is delicately adjusted to nature.

R: It circulates through space in the rhythm of the seasons each year.

S. It moves through space with the flow of time.

S6. The circle is not broken into a line; the tribe does not stay in one place altering nature to suit the needs of the human settlement.

(*a*) PRQS (*b*) QPRS
(*c*) QSPR (*d*) RPQS

23. **S1.** Reena went shopping one morning.

P: Disappointed she turned around and returned to the parking lot.

Q: She got out and walked to the nearest shop.

R: She drove her car into the parking lot and stopped.

S: It was there that she realised that she'd forgotten her purse at home.

S6. She drove home with an empty shopping basket. **(U.D.C. 1995)**

(*a*) PQRS (*b*) QPRS
(*c*) RQSP (*d*) RSQP

24. **S1.** Those are fortunate people who have good, true and faithful friends.

S6. It must be borne in mind that prosperity breeds and multiplies friends and adversity tests them.

P: It is a sacred attachment or a bond of intimacy between two persons of a congenial mind.

Q: True friendship increases our happiness in prosperity and diminishes our misery in adversity.

R: Friendship often springs from similarity of taste, feelings and sentiments.

S: However, true friendship should be based on truth and such vices as selfishness, greed and falsehood should be kept out of it.

(*a*) PQRS (*b*) QRPS
(*c*) RPQS (*d*) SPRQ

25. **S1.** In the eighteenth century people expected most of their children to die before they were grown up.

P: Improvement began at the beginning of the nineteenth century, chiefly owing to vaccination.

Q: The general death rate in 1948 (10.8) was the lowest ever recorded upto that date.

R: In 1920 the infant mortality in England and Wales was 80 per thousand, in 1948 it was 34 per thousand.

S: It has continued ever since and is still continuing.

S6. There is no obvious limit to the improvement of health that can be brought about by medicine.

(*a*) PSRQ (*b*) QRPS
(*c*) RQPS (*d*) SPQR

(S.C.R.A. 1994)

26. **S1.** The exact cause of migraine is still not known.

P: Several factors like digestive disorders and psychological disturbances, have been said to be causative factors.

Q: Certain foods like cheese, chocolate or red wine have also been found to trigger off an attack.

R: The causative factors are numerous : psychologically, anxiety and frustration play an important part.

S: It seems to be hereditary and a majority of sufferers are women.

S6. On the other hand physical overexertion, fatigue, irregularities in dietary habits, prolonged eye strain are common precipitating factors. **(N.D.A. 1995)**

(*a*) QPRS (*b*) RQPS
(*c*) SPQR (*d*) SQPR

27. **S1.** The real cause for the rise and fall of the sea level was not known to men for a long time.

P: They found out that the Moon is a satellite and it travels a regular path around the Earth.

Q: As time passed and knowledge increased, men began to learn more about the heaven and the stars and the planets.

R: They noticed that the Moon rose each day about an hour later than it rose the day defore and the peak of the high tide also comes about an hour later each day.

S: Some imagined that the Earth itself was alive and the rising and falling of the tide was caused by the breathing of the Earth's big body.

S6. So they concluded that the Moon and the tide are connected in some way.

(*a*) PRQS (*b*) QPRS
(*c*) SQPR (*d*) SRQP

28. **S1.** The future beckons to us.

P: In fact we have hard work ahead.

Q: Where do we go and what shall be our endeavour?

R: We shall also have to fight and end poverty, ignorance and disease.

S: It will be to bring freedom and opportunity to the common man.

S6. There is no resting for anyone of us till we redeem our pledge in full. **(Assistant Grade, 1995)**

(*a*) PSRQ (*b*) QPSR
(*c*) QSRP (*d*) SRPQ

29. **S1.** Machines have parts made of iron.

P: They must be painted or chrome plated.

Q: Some parts rub against each other.

R: Iron gets rusted.

S: They must be lubricated with oil or grease.

S6. When the machine is not in use, it should be covered. **(C.B.I. 1995)**

(*a*) PRQS (*b*) QRPS
(*c*) QSRP (*d*) RPQS

30. **S1.** At the age of four, Jagdish Chandra Bose was sent to a village 'pathshala'.

P: This step proved beneficial to the boy, for he thus became familiar with his mother tongue and learnt to read and write it.

Q: This was very unusual because a man of his father's status was expected to send his son to an English school.

R: He also became acquainted with some of the rich treasures of Indian culture.

S: At the same time he mixed with children of all castes and lost the sense of class superiority.

S6. His mother, too, reinforced what he learnt and did at school.

(*a*) PSRQ (*b*) QPSR
(*c*) RSQP (*d*) SQRP

31. **S1.** I never took payment for speaking.

P: The Sunday Society would then assure me that on these terms I might lecture on anything I liked and how I liked.

Q: It often happened that provincial Sunday societies offered me the usual ten genuine fee to give the usual sort of lecture, avoiding controversial politics and religion.

R: Occasionally to avoid embarrassing other lecturers who lived by lecturing, the account was settled by a debit and credit entry, that is, I was credited with the usual fee and expenses and gave it back as a donation to the society.

S: I always replied that I never lectured on anything but very controversial politics and religion and that my fee was the price of my railway ticket third class if the place was farther off than I could afford to go at my own expense.

S6. In this way I secured perfect freedom of speech, and was warmed against the accusation of being a professional agitator.

(*a*) QSPR (*b*) QSRP
(*c*) SQPR (*d*) SQRP

(I.E.S. 1994)

32. **S1.** In ancient Indian history the city of Ujjain was quite famous.

S6. So one can see what a great love all who care for India must feel for the ancientry of Ujjain.

P: Here lived at one time the poet Kalidasa.

Q: He was a famous learned astronomer.

R: And here also worked and visited Rajah Jaysingh of Jaipur.

S: It was always renowned as a seat of learning. **(C.B.I. 1993)**

(*a*) PSRQ (*b*) QSRP
(*c*) SPRQ (*d*) SRPQ

33. **S_1.** Useful human beings are divided into two classes : those whose work is work and pleasure is pleasure; and those whose work and pleasure are one.

S_6. For them the working hours are never long enough.

P : The long hours in the office or factory give them keen appetite for pleasure even in its most modest forms.

Q : Their life is a natural harmony.

R : Of these the former are in majority.

S : But Fortune's favoured children belong to the second class.

(*a*) PSQR (*b*) QPRS
(*c*) RPSQ (*d*) SQPR

34. **S_1.** Governments are instituted among men to secure their certain inalienable rights.

S_6. Such was the necessity which constrained the united colonies of America to give up thier allegiance to the British Crown and declare themselves free and independent states.

P : Accordingly, men are more disposed to suffer than to right themselves by abolishing the forms of governments to which they are accustomed.

Q : But prudence will dictate that governments long established should not be changed for light and transient causes.

R : They derive their just powers from the consent of the governed, and therefore, can also be changed by them.

S: But whenever any form of government becomes destructive of these rights of the people, it is their duty to throw off such a government. **(C.D.S. 1994)**

(*a*) PRSQ (*b*) QRPS
(*c*) RQPS (*d*) SRQP

35. **S_1.** Just as some men like to play football or tennis, so some men like to climb mountains.

P : This is often very difficult to do, for mountains are not just big hills.

Q : Paths are usually very steep, and some mountain sides are straight up and down, so that it may take many hours to climb as little as one hundred feet.

R : There is always the danger that you may fall off and be killed or injured.

S : Men talk about conquering a mountain, and the wonderful feeling it is to reach the top of a mountain after climbing for hours and may be, even for days.

S_6. You look down and see the whole country below you.

(*a*) PQRS (*b*) QPSR
(*c*) RQPS (*d*) SRQP

(Assistant Grade, 1994)

ANSWERS

1. (*a*)	**2.** (*b*)	**3.** (*b*)	**4.** (*d*)	**5.** (*b*)	**6.** (*b*)	**7.** (*a*)	**8.** (*c*)	**9.** (*c*)	**10.** (*c*)
11. (*c*)	**12.** (*c*)	**13.** (*d*)	**14.** (*c*)	**15.** (*c*)	**16.** (*b*)	**17.** (*c*)	**18.** (*b*)	**19.** (*b*)	**20.** (*c*)
21. (*b*)	**22.** (*c*)	**23.** (*c*)	**24.** (*c*)	**25.** (*a*)	**26.** (*c*)	**27.** (*c*)	**28.** (*c*)	**29.** (*d*)	**30.** (*b*)
31. (*b*)	**32.** (*c*)	**33.** (*c*)	**34.** (*c*)	**35.** (*a*)					

PRACTICE SET 4

Directions : ***In each of the following questions, there are six sentences marked S_1, S_6, P, Q, R, S. The positions of S_1 and S_6 are fixed. You are required to choose one of the four alternatives which would be the most logical sequence of the sentences in the passage.***

1. **S_1.** The fifty seven storey Wool-worth Tower is in New York.

P : Soon it became one of the famous buildings in the world.

Q : It was completed in 1912.

R: Americans took pride in this tall skyscraper.

S: However, it was not long before five other buildings topped the Woolworth Tower.

S6. A new champion is the Empire State Building which rises 102 storeys into the sky.

(*a*) PQRS (*b*) QPRS
(*c*) QRSP (*d*) RPQS

(B.Ed. Exam, 1994)

2. S1. A certain young man was entrusted to the care of a teacher.

P: This dullard will come to grief if I send him away without a single lesson, thought the teacher.

Q: He was so dull of mind that he could not, even in three months, time, learn as much as a single lesson.

R: The young man came to ask the teacher's permission to go home.

S: It's my business to provide a good education to my pupils, to get on in life.

S6. The teacher asked him to wait.

(*a*) PSRQ (*b*) QPSR
(*c*) RQPS (*d*) SRQP

3. S1. American private lives may seem shallow.

P: Students would walk away with books they had not paid for.

Q: A Chinese journalist commented on a curious institution: the library.

R: Their public morality, however, impressed visitors.

S: But in general they returned them.

S6. This would not happen in China, he said. **(Assistant Grade, 1996)**

(*a*) PSQR (*b*) QPSR
(*c*) RPSQ (*d*) RQPS

4. S1. Widowhood in India used to be specially miserable.

P: There were widows even in ages ranging from five to ten.

Q: A widow was a widow always.

R: However, several communities began to rebel against the ill-treatment of widows.

S: She could not marry again however tender in age she might be.

S6. Today nobody looks upon remarriage of widows with disgust or disapproval. **(I.E.S. 1993)**

(*a*) PRSQ (*b*) QSPR
(*c*) RSQP (*d*) SPQR

5. S1. Production of coins starts with the buying of unmixed metals and their testing by the Assay Department.

P: These ingots are reheated until the temperature is hot enough for hot rolling.

Q: During this stage, the ingots pass through a series of rollers until they form long, thin sheets which are the thickness of a coin.

R: From these thin strips, blank discs are punched.

S: Then the metals are alloyed in oil-fired or electric arc furnaces, and cast into ingots 40 cm wide, 15 cm thick and 6 m long.

S6. The blanks are heated to soften them, then rolled so that the rim is raised and are stamped with the design of the coin. **(N.D.A. 1993)**

(*a*) PRSQ (*b*) PSQR
(*c*) SPQR (*d*) SQRP

6. S1. Much of our adult behaviour and our attitudes are determined by our upbringing.

P: But the process does not stop here.

Q: In particular by the effects of that small part of society which is our family.

R: As we grow we are constantly and increasingly affected by new forces such as the social pressure of our friends and the larger world of society.

S: The family and our early life have profound effect on our later life.

S6. Psychologists have studied these forces in depth.

(*a*) PRSQ (*b*) QSPR
(*c*) QPSR (*d*) SRPQ

7. S1. He took two cigarettes from my case.

P: But when the fit of coughing was over, he replaced it between his lips.

Q: He lit one of them and placed it between the lips.

R: Then with a feeble hand he removed the cigarette.

S: Slowly he took a pull at it and coughed violently.

S6. Then he continued to draw on it.

(*a*) PSQR (*b*) QPSR
(*c*) QSRP (*d*) SRPQ

(Railways, 1994)

8. **S_1.** Progress and success are attained in slow degrees.

S_6. However, we must realise the truth that perfection is attained in slow proportions to the amount of labour put in by us.

P: But slow progress makes us grow impatient, disheartened and discouraged.

Q: The general tendency is to find fault with the system.

R: It is for this reason that people condemn and criticise the government.

S: People expect miracles and nothing short of a magical transformation can convince them.

(*a*) PSQR (*b*) QPSR
(*c*) RSPQ (*d*) SQRP

9. **S_1.** Plastic containers are being used more and more to package soft drinks, milk, oil, fruit juices, ketchup, etc.

S_6. Yet as plastics do not decompose by bacteria or naturally in the air, they are a big threat to the environment.

P: Most people think that this is the right thing to do, as it is economical.

Q: Plastic containers are cheap and light.

R: It is easier to transport materials packaged in them than in glass bottles.

S: They also involve the least transport costs. **(N.D.A. 1996)**

(*a*) PQRS (*b*) PQSR
(*c*) QRSP (*d*) QSPR

10. **S_1.** Your letter was a big relief.

P: How did your exams go?

Q: After your result, you must come here for a week.

R: You hadn't written for over a month.

S: I am sure you will come out with flying colours.

S_6. But don't forget to bring chocolate for Geeta. **(U.D.C. 1995)**

(*a*) PSRQ (*b*) QRPS
(*c*) RPSQ (*d*) RSPQ

11. **S_1.** Ram Mohan Roy was a lover of his country.

S_6. Indians and Europeans met next year to put this idea into shape.

P: He said that it would be a good plan to build an English school or college.

Q: One evening he was talking with David and a few friends on the wisest way of uplifting the mind and character of the people of India.

R: But he thought of subjects beyond watches.

S: David was a watchmaker.

(*a*) PSQR (*b*) QSRP
(*c*) RSPQ (*d*) SPRQ

12. **S_1.** The role of the precious yellow metal is undergoing a dramatic change.

S_6. Again, it would not be an economic proposition to buy and sell gold ornaments as an instrument of investment as buying would be costlier and selling will be at a discount

P: In developing countries like India, where gold is used mainly for ornaments, a distinct change in attitude is in the offing.

Q: Slowly, the use of gold in the form of ornaments will be on the decline and even if gold prices shoot up, women folk would not like to sell off their ornaments.

R: The yellow metal will soon be treated as an investment instrument.

S: The maxim, "Larger the gold reserves, richer the country" will not hold good for a long time.

(*a*) PSQR (*b*) PSRQ
(*c*) SPQR (*d*) SPRQ

(I.E.S. 1994)

13. **S_1.** The December dance and music season in Madras is like the annual tropical cyclone.

S_6. Many a hastily planted shrub gets washed away in the storm.

P: A few among the new aspirants dazzle with the colour of youth, like fresh saplings.

Q: It rains an abundance of music for over a fortnight.

R: Thick clouds of expectation charge the atmosphere with voluminous advertisements.

S: At the end of it one is left with the feeling that the music of only those artists seasoned by careful nurturing, stands tall like well rooted trees. **(C.D.S. 1994)**

(*a*) QRPS (*b*) QRSP
(*c*) RQPS (*d*) RQSP

14. S1. The coming of the computer sparked the need for remotely operated controls.

P: It is silicon chip that is at the heart of the remote control.

Q: This produces an infra-red beam, which is made up of electromagnetic waves.

R: When you press the button on the remote control, the chip sets off an electronic vibration.

S: The beam carries a coded signal such as switch on, raise volume, etc.

S6. The code is based on binary digits.

(*a*) PQRS (*b*) PQSR
(*c*) PRQS (*d*) RPQS

15. S1. Go to the library and see the clerk.

P: When you have chosen the books you wish to take home, you take them to the clerk with the tickets.

Q: You will probably have to sign a form promising to take care of the books.

R: Then you are usually given two or three tickets with your name and address on them.

S: The clerk keeps the tickets until you return the books.

S6. He stamps the books with a date.

(*a*) PQRS (*b*) QRPS
(*c*) RQSP (*d*) SPRQ

(C.B.I. 1995)

16. S1. There were no finger prints anywhere.

P: First of all it was impossible even for a child to enter through the hole in the roof.

Q: When the investigators tried to reconstruct the crime, they came up against facts.

R: Moreover, when the detectives tried to push a silver vase, it was found to be double the size of the hole.

S: Again, the size of the hole was examined by the experts who said that nothing had been passed through it.

S6. These conclusions made the detectives think that it was a fake theft. **(N.D.A. 1994)**

(*a*) PQRS (*b*) PSRQ
(*c*) QPRS (*d*) SQPR

17. S1. In the middle of one side of the square sits the Chairman of the committee, the most important person in the room.

S6. From the moment its members meet, it begins to have a sort nebulous life of its own.

P: For a committee is not just a mere collection of individuals.

Q: On him rests much of the responsibility for the success or failure of the committee.

R: While this is happening we have an opportunity to get the 'feel' of this committee.

S: As the meeting opens, he runs briskly through a number of formalities. **(C.D.S. 1993)**

(*a*) PQRS (*b*) QSRP
(*c*) RSQP (*d*) SQPR

18. S1. Over the centuries the face of the earth has become crowded with monuments and memorials.

P: Films, pictures and even miniature models can be made of the relics for posterity interested in knowing about them.

Q: Some people however would contend that antiquity should be preserved for future generations.

R: If they were all to be preserved we will have very little space for other, more useful, things.

S: Personally, I do not agree with their contention.

S6. We must have more space for building new things and developing open countryside.

(*a*) PQRS (*b*) QRSP
(*c*) RQSP (*d*) SQRP

19. S1. Helen Keller has an ageless quality about her in keeping with her amazing life story.

P: Although warmed by this human reaction, she has no wish to be set aside from the rest of mankind.

Q: She is an inspiration to both blind and the seeing everywhere.

R: When she visited Japan after World War II, boys and girls from remote villages ran to her, crying "Helen Keller".

S: Blind, deaf and mute from early childhood, she rose above her triple handicap to become one of the best known characters in the modern world.

S6. She believes the blind should live and work with their fellows, with full responsibility. **(N.D.A. 1993)**

(*a*) RSPQ (*b*) RSQP
(*c*) SRQP (*d*) SQRP

20. S1. This year many States have been badly affected by the drought situation prevailing in the country.

P : No better is the situation elsewhere, where floods have ravaged the standing crop.

Q : Though some have been less affected, even these are facing an uphill task in managing the situation.

R : Especially pitiable is the plight of the poor farmer who cannot offord a tubewell to irrigate his land.

S : Here the predicament is more equitable, for everybody's land is similarly submerged under ten feet of water.

S6. Either way, it seems the lot of the Indian farmer to be at the mercy of the elements.

(*a*) RSPQ (*b*) QRPS
(*c*) PSRQ (*d*) PRQS

21. S1. There is a touching story of Professor Hardy visiting Ramanujan as he lay desperately ill in hospital at Putney.

S6. It is the lowest number that can be expressed in two different ways as the sum of two cubes."

P : "No Hardy, that is not a dull number in the very least.

Q : Hardy, who was a very shy man, could not find the words for his distress.

R : It was 1729.

S : The best he could do, as he got to the bedside was : "I say, Ramanujan, I thought the number of the taxi I came down in was a very dull number. **(C.D.S. 1995)**

(*a*) PRSQ (*b*) QSPR
(*c*) QSRP (*d*) SQRP

22. S1. I also demand adventure for myself.

P : As a physiologist I can try experiments on myself.

Q : Life without danger would be like life without mustard.

R : Love of adventure does not mean love of thrills.

S : I can also participate in wars and revolutions of which I approve.

S6. The satisfaction of adventure is something much more solid than a thrill. **(I. Tax & Central Excise, 1993)**

(*a*) PRQS (*b*) QPSR
(*c*) RPSQ (*d*) SQRP

23. S1. A small pool in the rocks outside my cottage in the Mussoorie hills provides me endless delight.

S6. It did and then, looking up, saw me and leapt across the ravine to disappear into the forest.

P : I stood very still, anxious that it should drink its fill.

Q : And once I saw a barking deer, head lowered at the edge of the pool.

R : Water beetles paddle the surface, while tiny fish lurk in the shallows.

S : Sometimes a spotted fork tail bird comes to drink, hopping delicately from rock to rock.

(*a*) PRSQ (*b*) PSQR
(*c*) RSQP (*d*) SQPR

24. S1. Always remember that regular and frequent practice is essential if you are to learn to write well.

S6. If you keep your eyes and ears open, you will find plenty of things to write about around you to be able to discipline yourself to write.

P : Even with the most famous writers, inspiration is rare.

Q : Writing is 99 percent hard work and one percent inspiration, so the sooner you get into the habit of writing, the better.

R : It is no good waiting until you have an inspiration before you write.

S : You learn to write by writing.

(*a*) QPSR (*b*) RPSQ
(*c*) SPRQ (*d*) SRPQ

(N.D.A. 1995)

25. S1. A father, having offered to take the baby out in a perambulator, was tempted by the sunny morning to slip into a pub for a glass of beer.

S6. She waited for him, anticipating the white face and quivering lips which would soon appear with the news that the baby had been stolen.

P: Indignant at her husband's behaviour, she decided to teach him a lesson.

Q: She wheeled away the pram.

R: A little later, his wife came by, where to her horror, she discovered her sleeping baby.

S: Leaving the pram outside, he disappeared inside the bar.

(*a*) PQSR (*b*) RQPS
(*c*) SPQR (*d*) SRPQ

(S.C.R.A. 1994)

26. **S1.** In the present day it is not necessary that generals or great officers should fight with their own hands, because it is their duty to direct the movements of their followers.

P: But in the ancient times, kings and great lords were obliged to put themselves into the very front.

Q: Therefore, it was of great consequence that they should be strong men and dexterous in the use of their arms.

R: The artillery and the soldiers shoot at the enemy, and men seldom mingle and fight hand to hand.

S: They fought like ordinary men with the lance and other weapons.

S6. Robert Bruce was so remarkably active and powerful that he came through many personal dangers.

(*a*) PQSR (*b*) QRSP
(*c*) RPSQ (*d*) SQRP

27. **S1.** And then Gandhi came.

P: Get off the backs of these peasants and workers, he told us, all you who live by their exploitation.

Q: He was like a powerful current of fresh air, like a beam of light, like a whirlwind that upset many things.

R: He spoke their language and constantly drew their attention to their appalling conditions.

S: He didn't descend from the top, he seemed to emerge from the masses of India.

S6. Political freedom took new shape then and acquired a new content then. **(Assistant Grade, 1995)**

(*a*) PRSQ (*b*) QSRP
(*c*) RSQP (*d*) SRQP

28. **S1.** Love for the country is a necessity.

S6. God created the globe, but man drew lines on it to demarcate countries and sow the seeds of hatred and enmity on it.

P: But it should in no way exceed the limits and take the shape of jingoism.

Q: Similarly nationalism has to be sacrificed at the altar of internationalism.

R: There is no reason why the nations of the world cannot treat one another as belonging to one family of nations.

S: Provincialism has to be sacrificed in the interest of the nation as a whole.

(*a*) PSQR (*b*) QRSP
(*c*) RQPS (*d*) SPRQ

29. **S1.** There has been an alarming increase in the number of vehicles on Delhi roads.

P: The pedestrian has, however, been the worst sufferer.

Q: There is no place where the pedestrian can move freely without the fear of traffic.

R: Zebra crossings like the pavements are no longer safe.

S: This has further aggravated the problem of pollution in the city.

S6. Should the pedestrians' case be allowed to go by default?

(*a*) PQRS (*b*) SPRQ
(*c*) SQRP (*d*) SRPQ

(I. Tax & Central Excise, 1994)

30. **S1.** Our own country is a little world in itself with an infinite variety and places for us to discover.

S6. I should like to go with them, not so much to the great cities of India as to the mountains and the forests and the great rivers and the old monuments, all of which tell us something of India's story.

P: I wish I had more time, so that I could visit the odd nooks and corners of India.

Q: I have travelled a great deal in this country and I have grown in years.

R: And yet I have not seen many parts of the country we love so much and seek to serve.

S : I would like to go there in the company of bright young children whose minds are opening out with wonder and curiosity as they make new discoveries.

(*a*) PQSR (*b*) QRPS
(*c*) RPQS (*d*) SPQR

31. **S_1.** The mail is first collected from different letter boxes.

S_6. Finally it is delivered to us.

P : From there it is sent to the head post office.

Q : It is then sorted out at the sorting office.

R : The mail is again sorted out at the head office by the concerned beat postman.

S : The sorted mail is sent to the zonal post office. **(C.B.I. 1993)**

(*a*) QPRS (*b*) QSPR
(*c*) RPQS (*d*) RSQP

32. **S_1.** Mr. Ford, it is commonly reported, once declared that history was "bunk".

P : Yet the American, generally speaking, is by no means ignorant of history or uninfluenced by his knowledge of it.

Q : This remarkable utterance of his, if indeed he made it, was in itself an outcome of history.

R : The Americans know more about our history than we know about theirs, though I hope that will soon be remedied.

S : Such contempt for all things past, and such engaging frankness in expressing it were themselves the outcome of the social history of the United States in the 19th century.

S_6. And the American's conception of his own country as the representative of freedom and of democracy is the product of history as popularly taught and conceived over there.

(*a*) QSPR (*b*) RPSQ
(*c*) SPRQ (*d*) SQRP

33. **S_1.** She used to work at the desk next to mine in the office several years ago.

P : But it must have been exasperating that a male sitting beside her was doing the same work as she was and being paid more.

Q : She is certain to be still there, in the same old brown suit and fur lined boots.

R : She was as kind as she was efficient.

S : Now she and all her friends have won their long campaign for the justice of equal pay to be recognised.

S_6. I am glad that their demands have been accepted. **(N.D.A. 1993)**

(*a*) QRPS (*b*) RQPS
(*c*) SPQR (*d*) SPRQ

34. **S_1.** Of the various kinds of insect defences that of the North American fungus - eating beetle is quite unusual.

P : Both ants as well as mammals such as deermice feed on this beetle.

Q : This little beetle is able to recognize the kind of predator coming towards it and accordingly adopts a suitable defence.

R : When facing a deermouse, the beetle secretes an irritant from certain glands in its abdomen.

S : While the beetle simply rolls itself into a compact ball in the face of an ant attack, it copes with the deer mouse differently.

S_6. The beetle's chemical secretion keeps the deer mouse at bay.

(*a*) PQSR (*b*) PRQS
(*c*) QPSR (*d*) QRPS

(Railways, 1993)

35. **S_1.** In a good many cases unnecessary timidity makes the trouble worse than it need be.

S_6. If you hold in Delhi the views that are conventional in Delhi, you much accept the consequences.

P : I am not, of course, thinking of extreme forms of defiance.

Q : If you show that you are afraid of them, you give promise of good hunting, whereas if you show indifference, they begin to doubt their own power and, therefore, tend to let you alone.

R : A dog will bark more loudly and bite more easily when people are afraid of him than when they treat him with contempt, and the human herd has something of this same characteristic.

S : Public opinion is always more tyrannical towards those who obviously fear it than towards those who feel indifferent to it.

(*a*) QPRS (*b*) RSPQ
(*c*) SRPQ (*d*) SRQP

(C.D.S. 1994)

ANSWERS

1. (*b*) **2.** (*b*) **3.** (*d*) **4.** (*b*) **5.** (*c*) **6.** (*b*) **7.** (*c*) **8.** (*a*) **9.** (*b*) **10.** (*c*)
11. (*b*) **12.** (*d*) **13.** (*a*) **14.** (*c*) **15.** (*b*) **16.** (*c*) **17.** (*b*) **18.** (*c*) **19.** (*d*) **20.** (*b*)
21. (*c*) **22.** (*d*) **23.** (*c*) **24.** (*d*) **25.** (*d*) **26.** (*c*) **27.** (*d*) **28.** (*a*) **29.** (*b*) **30.** (*b*)
31. (*a*) **32.** (*a*) **33.** (*a*) **34.** (*c*) **35.** (*b*)

PRACTICE SET 5

Directions : ***In each of the following questions, there are six sentences marked S_1, S_6, P, Q, R, S. The positions of S_1 and S_6 are fixed. You are required to choose one of the four alternatives which would be the most logical sequence of the sentences in the passage.***

1. **S_1.** You live either in a village or a town of India.
P : Many villages and towns form a tehsil or a taluka.
Q : There are also some areas in our country called Union Territories.
R : Many tehsils or talukas form a district and many districts form a State.
S : These, together with all the states of our country make India.
S_6. India is our motherland.

(*a*) PQRS (*b*) PRQS
(*c*) QPRS (*d*) RPQS

(S.S.C. 1993)

2. **S_1.** The tooth had abscessed and was causing considerable pain.
S_6. It has not returned to this day.
P : Finally, in desperation, she went inside a wooden pyramid model and sat down praying for miracles.
Q : Since it was Sunday morning, no dentist was available
R : What happened she is not sure, but after ten minutes the pain simply faded away.
S : Common pain killers had been of no avail.

(*a*) PSRQ (*b*) QSPR
(*c*) QRSP (*d*) SRQP

3. **S_1.** The Third Five - Year Plan ran into rough weather from the very start.
P : Large funds had to be diverted from development to defence.
Q : Food situation became critical and prices began to rise steep after the Indo - Pak conflict.
R : During this period, there was also the war with Pakistan in 1965.
S : There was the China War in 1962 which completely upset our economy.
S_6. The government had to resort to devaluation of the rupee.

(*a*) PSRQ (*b*) QPSR
(*c*) RPQS (*d*) SPRQ

(C.B.I. 1995)

4. **S_1.** The art of growing old is one which the passage of time has forced upon my attention.
P : One of these is undue absorption in the past.
Q : One's thoughts must be directed to the future and to things about which there is something to be done.
R : Psychologically, there are two dangers to be guarded against in old age.
S : It does not do to live in memories, in regrets for the good old days, or in sadness about friends who are dead.
S_6. This is not always easy; one's own past is a gradually increasing weight.

(I.E.S. 1994)

(*a*) QPRS (*b*) RPQS
(*c*) RPSQ (*d*) QSRP

5. **S_1.** Religion is not a matter of mere dogmatic conformity.

P : It is not merely going through the ritual prescribed to us.

Q : It is not a question of ceremonial piety.

R : Unless that kind of transformation occurs, you are not an authentically religious man.

S : It is the remaking of your own self, the transformation of your nature.

S_6. A man of that character is free from fear, free from hatred.

(*a*) PSRQ (*b*) QPSR
(*c*) SPQR (*d*) SPRQ

(Section Officers, 1993)

6. **S_1.** The right way to get people do things the way you want is not to compel them, drive them or for that matter even beg them or entreat them.

S_6. The secret of motivation, therefore, lies in your ability to arouse the right kind of want or thirst in the other people.

P : The sure way to antagonise an individual is to give him the impression that you are out to force or compel him to do something.

Q : The correct way is, therefore, to arouse a want in them and make them do, whatever you want them to do willingly, happily and eagerly.

R : It is the most difficult thing in the world to make an individual do anything against his will.

S : Even young, innocent children resent being made to do things.

(*a*) PRQS (*b*) QSPR
(*c*) RPSQ (*d*) SRQP

7. **S_1.** Urban problems differ from State to State and city to city.

S_6. There is no underground drainage system in most cities, and the narrow historical roads are already congested.

P : Most of the cities have neither water nor the required pipelines.

Q : The population in these cities has grown beyond the planners' imagination.

R : However, certain basic problems are common to all cities.

S : Only broad macro - planning was done for such cities, without envisaging the future growth, and this has failed to meet the requirements. **(Railways, 1994)**

(*a*) PQSR (*b*) QPSR
(*c*) RQPS (*d*) RSQP

8. **S_1.** Satyajit Ray made several films for children.

S_6. But today few think of Ray as a maker of children's films.

P : Later film - makers have followed his lead.

Q : Today other nations are making children's films in a big way.

R : This was at a time when no director considered children as potential audience.

S : Ray was, thus, a pioneer in the field.

(*a*) SQRP (*b*) RSQP
(*c*) RSPQ (*d*) PSRQ

9. **S_1.** Exercising daily is a must for good health.

P : Luckily, there is no link between the amount of money spent and beneficient exercise, else the poor would have creaking bodies for ever.

Q : While some cost you nothing, others may require the investment of some amount of money.

R : However, it is important to remember that exercises should not be overdone.

S : It can take any form from sedentary ones like walking to vigorous work - outs like a game of squash.

S_6. The key word, always, is moderation. **(N.D.A. 1993)**

(*a*) PQSR (*b*) QPRS
(*c*) RSQP (*d*) SQPR

10. **S_1.** There is no transportation system in any city that can compare in efficiency with the circulatory system of the body.

P : The larger one goes from the heart to the various other parts of the body.

Q : If you will imagine two systems of pipes, one large and one small, both meeting at a central pumping station, you'll have an idea of the circulatory system.

R: These pipes are called arteries, veins and capillaries.

S: The smaller system of pipes goes from the heart to the lungs and back.

S6. Arteries are blood vessels in which blood is going away from the heart.

(*a*) PQSR (*b*) QSPR
(*c*) RSQP (*d*) SPRQ

11. **S1.** It is regrettable that there is widespread corruption in the country at all levels.

P: So there is hardly anything that the government can do about it now.

Q: And there are graft and other malpractices too.

R: The impression that corruption is a universal phenomenon persists and the people do not cooperate in checking this evil.

S: Recently several offenders were brought to book, but they were not given deterrent punishment.

S6. This is indeed a tragedy of great magnitude.

(*a*) PQSR (*b*) QSRP
(*c*) RSQP (*d*) SQRP

(Assistant Grade, 1996)

12. **S1.** The press enables us to know about the world and happenings around us.

S6. While moulding it mends and mending it moulds the public opinion.

P: It governs the current ideas in the country and controls the course of events.

Q: There is no doubt that the newspaper is the only teacher of the common man.

R: It is indeed the mouthpiece of the people.

S: It is feared that in the absence of the press, government would be less responsible, the judge less honest and civil servant less efficient.

(*a*) PQRS (*b*) QPSR
(*c*) RSQP (*d*) SRPQ

13. **S1.** Of the scholars who compose a university, some may be expected to devote an unbroken leisure to learning, their fellows having the advantage of their knowledge from their conversation, and the world perhaps from their writings.

S6. There classes of persons, then, go to compose a university as we know it - the scholar, the scholar who is also a teacher, and those who come to be taught, the undergraduate.

P: Others, however, will engage themselves to teach as well as to learn.

Q: Those who come to be taught at a university have to provide evidence that they are not merely beginners and not only do they have displayed before them the learning of their teachers, but they are offered a curriculum of study, to be followed by a test and the award of a degree.

R: But here again, it is the special manner of the pedagogic enterprise which distinguishes a university.

S: A place of learning without this could scarcely be called a university. **(C.D.S. 1993)**

(*a*) QPSR (*b*) RQSP
(*c*) SPRQ (*d*) SRPQ

14. **S1.** Several sub-cities have been planned around the capital.

P: Dwarka is the first among them.

Q: They are expected to alleviate the problem of housing.

R It is coming up in the south-west of the capital.

S: It will cater to one million people when completed.

S6. Hopefully the housing problem will not be as acute as at present after these sub-cities are built.

(*a*) PQRS (*b*) PRSQ
(*c*) QPRS (*d*) QRSP

(U.D.C. 1995)

15. **S1.** India's non-alignment has not been an attitude of negative neutrality.

S6. This policy has been accepted, if not actually appreciated by the leading powers of the world.

P: In other words, it is not an aloofness from or indifference to other nations.

Q: Instead, it has been an attitude of constructive neutrality.

R: On the contrary, India has been taking a keen interest in all international developments.

S: India wants the goodwill of all nations and is hostile towards none.

(*a*) PSRQ (*b*) QPRS
(*c*) QRPS (*d*) SQRP

16. S_1. We speak today of self-determination in politics.

S_6. Cultural subjection is ordinarily of an unconscious character and it implies slavery from the very start.

P: So long as one is conscious of a restraint, it is possible to resist it or to bear it as a necessary evil and to keep free in spirit.

Q: Slavery begins when one ceases to feel the restraint and it depends on if the evil is accepted as good.

R: There is, however, a subtler domination exercised in the sphere of ideas by one culture on another.

S: Political subjection primarily means restraint on the outer life of people. **(C.D.S. 1994)**

(*a*) RSPQ (*b*) RSQP
(*c*) SPQR (*d*) SPRQ

17. S_1. Music, like literature, is an art that deals with sound.

P: Literature makes use of words which are sounds.

Q: They also have meanings.

R: And the writer must be concerned with the effect produced by the sounds he uses.

S: But words are not only sounds.

S_6. They refer to specific things other than themselves such as objects and ideas. **(Central Excise, 1993)**

(*a*) PRSQ (*b*) PSQR
(*c*) RPSQ (*d*) SRPQ

18. S_1. Why then, do sharks attack?

P: "The only way a shark can warn you is with its mouth and teeth," says Baldridge.

Q: In murky water it may simply be a case of mistaken identity.

R: Snork bumps and open - mouthed slashings are ways of trying to frighten you off.

S: But the most persuasive explanation is that they perceive their victim as a threat.

S_6. Attacks of this kind may be generated by a swimmer who unwittingly interrupts a courting procedure, trespasses in a shark's territory and cuts off its escape route.

(*a*) PRQS (*b*) PRSQ
(*c*) QPRS (*d*) QSPR

19. S_1. The essence of democracy is the active participation of the people in government affair.

P: When the people are active watchmen and participants, we have that fertile soil in which democracy fluorishes.

Q: This democracy of ours is founded upon a faith in the overall judgement of the people as a whole.

R: When the people do not participate, the spirit of democratic action dies.

S: When the people are honestly and clearly informed, their common sense can be relied upon to carry the nation safely through any crisis.

S_6. By and large it is the actual practice of our way of life.

(*a*) PRSQ (*b*) PSRQ
(*c*) RPSQ (*d*) SPQR

(N.D.A. 1995)

20. S_1. We do not know whether the machines are the masters or we are.

S_6. And if they don't get their meals when they expect them, they will just refuse to work.

P: They must be given or rather 'fed' with coal and given petrol to drink from time to time.

Q: Already man spends most of his time looking after and waiting upon them.

R: Yet he has grown so dependent on them that they have almost become the masters now.

S: It is very true that they were made for the sole purpose of being man's servants. **(N.D.A. 1996)**

(*a*) RSPQ (*b*) RSQP
(*c*) SPQR (*d*) SRQP

21. S_1. Instantly, the full load yanked Gordy towards the side of the bridge.

P: But the pull of the cable was too much.

Q: He could hardly feel the cable, slipping through his fingers, ripping off his gloves, and streaking over the railing like an escaping snake.

R: It smashed his hands hard against the top of the railing, causing a split - second feeling of fierce pain followed by numbness.

S: He held on to the cable; it had been hard work lifting it, and he did not want to have to start over again.

S6. Feeling a sharp burning sensation where the cable was speeding between his things, Gordy rose on tiptoe and as he did, the slithering coil of cable tightened around his left foot and yanked him over the railing.

(*a*) PRQS (*b*) QSRP
(*c*) RPQS (*d*) SPRQ

22. S1. Even the newsmen and spectators were not spared.

P: A homeguard in the gallery was hit on the face.

Q: They went only inches over the heads of newsmen in the press gallery.

R Three bludgeons which are hurled missed their mark.

S: This made the scribes run helter skelter.

S6. He fell down, his bleeding eye bulging. **(C.B.I. 1995)**

(*a*) PSRQ (*b*) QRPS
(*c*) RQSP (*d*) SRQP

23. S1. Politeness is not a quality possessed by only one nation or race.

P: One may observe that a man of one nation will remove his hat or fold his hands by way of greetings when he meets someone he knows.

Q: A man of another country will not do so.

R: It is a quality to be found among all peoples and nations in every corner of the earth.

S: Obviously, each person follows the custom of his particular country.

S6. In any case, we should not mock at other's habits.

(*a*) PRQS (*b*) QPRS
(*c*) RPQS (*d*) RPSQ

(Assistant Grade, 1995)

24. S1. You might say that all through history there have been wars and that mankind has survived inspite of them.

P: Now, if his purposes are those of destruction, each fresh advance in his mastery of nature only increases the danger from war, as men learn to destroy one another in ever great numbers, from ever great distances, and in ever more varied and ingenious ways.

Q: He has learned to tap the hidden forces of our planet and use them for his purposes.

R: It has even developed and become civilised inspite of them.

S: This is true, but unfortunately as part of his development man has enormously increased his power over nature.

S6. Man has now discovered how to release the colossal forces locked up in the atom. **(N.D.A. 1995)**

(*a*) PQSR (*b*) PRQS
(*c*) QPRS (*d*) RSQP

25. S1. Films developed from the silent stage to the talkie stage with a tremendous mass appeal.

P: Film makers of those days used film media to portray our struggle for freedom.

Q: The thirties and forties were decades of tremendous social, political and cultural upheavals.

R: That is what 'Alam Ara' did to the delirious delight of the audience and thus triggered off a revolution.

S: In the turbulent thirties, the silent Indian films began to talk, sing and dance.

S6. Extolling the virtues of bravery and making patriotic films was the order of the day.

(*a*) PSQR (*b*) QSRP
(*c*) SRQP (*d*) RPSQ

26. S1. Life is hazardous.

S6. Everything points to a special kind of arms race with elaborate strategies and counter-strategies for attack and defence. **(I. Tax, 1994)**

P: And prey have evolved adaptations that reduce the risk of being eaten.

Q: Many animals are killed and eaten by other animals.

R: And many predators die from starvation because they fail to secure prey.

S: Predators have continued to evolve adaptations that enable them to locate and kill prey.

(*a*) QPRS (*b*) QRPS
(*c*) QRSP (*d*) SQRP

27. S1. Of course, it is silly to try to overcome fears that keep us from destroying ourselves.

P: This is sensible.

Q: You wait until it is out of the way before crossing.

R: You need some fears to keep you from doing foolish things.

S: You are afraid of an automobile coming rapidly down the street you wish to cross.

S6. The only fears you need to avoid are silly fears which prevent you from doing what you should do.

(*a*) PQRS (*b*) PRSQ
(*c*) RPSQ (*d*) RSQP

(N.D.A. 1994)

28. S1. Most people know that economics deals with such items as population, natural resources, incomes, tariffs, money and prices.

P: Instead, it is how it organises and analyses its materials; it is the perspective from which it views the world that makes it a special field of study.

Q: However, it is not what economics deals with that makes it a distinctive science.

R: Indeed, the list of topics can be greatly extended.

S: Economics is a particular view of reality.

S6. From this view, human behaviour is seen as activity directed towards the achievement of various objectives through the use of various resources. **(S.C.R.A. 1994)**

(*a*) PQSR (*b*) QPSR
(*c*) RQPS (*d*) RSPQ

29. S1. When you meet someone and discover areas of common interest and experience, you gain building blocks to develop a deeper relationship.

S6. This creates a sense of familiarity and indicates your interest in discussing the topic further and sharing your ideas.

P: This gives you and your partner an opportunity to decide if you would like to get to know one another better.

Q: Remember, much of the point of conversation is to discuss different topics and experiences in order to find a common bond.

R: So, when you discover a connection, tell your partner right away.

S: If you have enough in common, then hopefully you will want to see each other again to share common interests.

(*a*) RPQS (*b*) PQRS
(*c*) QPSR (*d*) SRQP

30. S1. There is only one monkey we can thoroughly recommend as an idoor pet.

S6. Finally, let me say that no other monkey has a better temper or more winning ways.

P: They quickly die from colds and coughs after the first winter fogs.

Q: It is the beautiful and intelligent Capuchin monkey.

R: The lively little Capuchins, however, may be left for years in an English house without the least danger to their health.

S: The Marmosets, it is true, are more beautiful than the Capuchins and just as pleasing, but they are too delicate for the English climate. **(C.D.S. 1995)**

(*a*) PQRS (*b*) QRPS
(*c*) QSPR (*d*) RPSQ

31. S1. Egypt is located in north-east of Africa.

P: The land should be productive.

Q: It is on the coast of Mediterranean Sea.

R: The important thing is not just the area.

S: Its area is almost four times that of England.

S6. Egypt is mostly desert or semi-desert. **(C.B.I. 1993)**

(*a*) PQSR (*b*) QSRP
(*c*) RPQS (*d*) SRPQ

32. S1. The mother tongue is the true vehicle of mother wit.

S6. A man's native speech is almost like his shadow, inseparable from his personality.

P: Another medium of speech may bring with it a current of new ideas.

Q: It is through the vernacular (refined, though not weakened, by scholarship and taste) that the new conceptions of the mind should press their way to birth in speech.

R: But the mother tongue is one with the air in which a man is born.

S: This is almost universally true, except in cases so rare (like that of Joseph Conrad) as to emphasise the general rule. **(C.D.S. 1993)**

(*a*) PRQS (*b*) PRSQ
(*c*) PSQR (*d*) QRPS

33. S1. We may consider the political privileges of citizenship.

P: This gives the citizen the pleasant feeling that he has a share in the administration of his country.

Q: In addition, he may himself stand as a candidate for election to any office of the republic to which he belongs.

R: A citizen usually enjoys the right of voting of election to public bodies, and of holding public offices.

S: These advantages are of course only enjoyed by citizens under a democratic system of government.

S6. Under a dictatorship, people cannot choose their own representatives to run the government and the rights of voting and contesting are denied to them.

(*a*) PQRS (*b*) QSPR
(*c*) RPQS (*d*) SRQP

34. S1. The study of speech disorders due to brain injury suggests that patients can think without having adequate control over their language.

P: But they succeed in playing games of chess.

Q: Some patients, for example, fail to find the names of objects presented to them.

R: They can even use the concepts needed for chess playing, though they are unable to express many of the concepts in ordinary language.

S: They even find it difficult to interpret long written notices.

S6. How they manage to do this we do not know.

(*a*) PSQR (*b*) QSPR
(*c*) RPSQ (*d*) SRPQ

(C.D.S. 1994)

35. S1. Let me elaborate a little on what I mean by a properly channelled scientific approach.

P: There are planners deciding the strategy.

Q: In a major war, there are several different operations involved.

R: There are complex issues involving communications between different nerve centres.

S: There are factories producing the required armaments.

S6. And of course, there are soldiers, commandos, to say nothing of intelligence men, besides many others who do their bit to make a successful attack. **(N.D.A. 1993)**

(*a*) PSRQ (*b*) QPSR
(*c*) RSPQ (*d*) SRQP

ANSWERS

1. (*b*)	**2.** (*b*)	**3.** (*a*)	**4.** (*c*)	**5.** (*b*)	**6.** (*c*)	**7.** (*d*)	**8.** (*c*)	**9.** (*a*)	**10.** (*b*)
11. (*b*)	**12.** (*a*)	**13.** (*a*)	**14.** (*c*)	**15.** (*b*)	**16.** (*c*)	**17.** (*a*)	**18.** (*c*)	**19.** (*c*)	**20.** (*d*)
21. (*c*)	**22.** (*d*)	**23.** (*d*)	**24.** (*d*)	**25.** (*c*)	**26.** (*c*)	**27.** (*c*)	**28.** (*c*)	**29.** (*c*)	**30.** (*b*)
31. (*b*)	**32.** (*a*)	**33.** (*c*)	**34.** (*b*)	**35.** (*b*)					

21. RECONSTRUCTION OF PARAGRAPHS

In this section, the candidate is given a paragraph of five or six sentences, which are put in a jumbled order. The candidate is required to arrange the given sentences to form a meaningful paragraph and answer the questions based on the sequence so formed.

Example : ***Rearrange the following sentences into a meaningful sequence and then answer the questions that follow.*** **(Bank P.O. 1994)**

(A) But I think a better definition of happiness is 'the capacity for enjoyment'.

(B) Turning to adults, ask any adult what he means by happiness and you will find a puzzled face for a moment.

(C) In the teen age years the concept of happiness changes to enjoyment and pleasure.

(D) Because the more we can enjoy what we have, the happier we are.

(E) The meaning of the word happiness changes with growing years, for a child happiness has a magical quality.

(F) Leave the puzzled face and refer to a dictionary it defines happy as 'lucky' or 'fortunate'.

1. Which sentence should come first in the paragraph?
(*a*) B (*b*) C (*c*) D (*d*) E (*e*) F

2. Which sentence should come second in the paragraph?
(*a*) A (*b*) B (*c*) C (*d*) D (*e*) E

3. Which sentence should come third in the paragraph?
(*a*) B (*b*) C (*c*) D (*d*) E (*e*) F

4. Which sentence should come fourth in the paragraph?
(*a*) E (*b*) F (*c*) A (*d*) B (*e*) C

5. Which sentence should come last in the paragraph?
(*a*) C (*b*) D (*c*) E (*d*) F (*e*) A

Solution : Note that the sentence E gives a general comment on happiness and talks about what it means for *a child*. So, the correct answer of **1** is (*d*).

Next, we have sentence C because it deals with concept of happiness for *teenager*. So, the correct answer of **2** is (*c*). The third sentence should be B because it now moves on to the view of *adults*. So, the correct answer of **3** is (*a*) Since B ends with *'puzzled face'* and F begins with the same, so F should follow B as the fourth sentence. So, the correct answer of **4** is (*b*).

Next comes the author's view which is given in A. So, A is the fifth sentence.

Since sentence A talks about enjoyment & happiness and D gives the relation between these two, so D should follow A as the last sentence of the paragraph. So, the correct answer of **5** is (*b*).

PRACTICE SET 1

Directions : ***Rearrange the given five sentences A, B, C, D, and E in the proper sequence so as to form a meaningful paragraph and then answer the questions given below them.***

Questions 1 to 5 **(Bank P.O. 1994)**

(A) Would you steal a software program out of a retail shop?

(B) The industry on its part has formed an organisation to specially gather information, educate and drag the software pirates to courts.

(C) But more than the legality, there is always a different way of looking at piracy and that is in terms of morality.

(D) The Government on the other hand has initiated National Enforcement Committees.

(E) As far as the issue of tackling piracy is concerned, both the industry and the Government have already started initiating action.

1. Which of the following should be the third sentence?
(*a*) E (*b*) A (*c*) B (*d*) D (*e*) C

2. Which of the following should be the first sentence?
(*a*) B (*b*) C (*c*) A (*d*) E (*e*) D
3. Which of the following should be the second sentence?
(*a*) A (*b*) D (*c*) C (*d*) E (*e*) B
4. Which of the following should be the last sentence?
(*a*) C (*b*) B (*c*) E (*d*) A (*e*) D
5. Which of the following should be the fourth sentence?
(*a*) D (*b*) B (*c*) C (*d*) A (*e*) E

Questions 6 to 10

(A) As he got up, a frightened native told him about the man- eater.
(B) When he approached the thick bush, he saw the lion running towards him.
(C) Tom was awakened by the fearful screams of the villagers.
(D) In a stage of fright, a shot was fired accidentally by Tom, but it hit the lion.
(E) Tom decided to chase the lion and took out his gun.

6. Which of the following should be the first sentence ?
(*a*) A (*b*) B (*c*) C (*d*) D (*e*) E
7. Which of the following should be the second sentence?
(*a*) A (*b*) B (*c*) C (*d*) D (*e*) E
8. Which of the following should be the third sentence?
(*a*) A (*b*) B (*c*) C (*d*) D (*e*) E
9. Which of the following should be the fourth sentence?
(*a*) A (*b*) B (*c*) C (*d*) D (*e*) E
10. Which of the following should be the last sentence?
(*a*) A (*b*) B (*c*) C (*d*) D (*e*) E

Questions 11 to 17 **(Bank P.O. 1996)**

(A) Another important aspect of stress is that the human body reacts to stress in a stereotyped, physiological way.
(B) But as long as we are alive, we are experiencing stress.
(C) Besides the fact that stress is unavoidable, there are several aspects of stress that one should understand.
(D) Sometimes the stress is small and sometimes it is large.
(E) Stress cannot be avoided, and our stress level is never at zero.
(F) One is that both too high and too low a stress level is damaging.
(G) We are always under the stress as long as we are alive.

11. Which of the following would be the third sentence?
(*a*) A (*b*) B (*c*) D (*d*) E (*e*) G
12. Which of the following would be the sixth sentence?
(*a*) A (*b*) B (*c*) C (*d*) D (*e*) F
13. Which of the following would be the first sentence?
(*a*) B (*b*) D (*c*) E (*d*) F (*e*) G
14. Which of the following would be the fourth sentence?
(*a*) A (*b*) B (*c*) C (*d*) D (*e*) E
15. Which of the following would be the last (i.e. seventh) sentence?
(*a*) A (*b*) B (*c*) C (*d*) E (*e*) G
16. Which of the following would be the second sentence?
(*a*) A (*b*) B (*c*) C (*d*) D (*e*) G
17. Which of the following would be the fifth sentence?
(*a*) C (*b*) D (*c*) E (*d*) F (*e*) G

Questions 18 to 22

(A) Still seventy five percent of our countrymen live in villages.
(B) And on the hills were built summer capitals such as Simla, Nainital, Darjeeling, Ooty and other hill stations like Mussoorie, Shillong, Dalhousie etc.
(C) A thousand years ago the number of cities in India was much less than their number today.
(D) Later, the coming of the English resulted in the growth of such cities as Calcutta, Bombay, Madras, Karachi, Ahmedabad on the plains of India.
(E) With the coming of the Muslims the number of our cities began to multiply, because the Muslims brought with them many arts and crafts which could best fluorish in cities.

18. Which of the following should be the first sentence?
(*a*) A (*b*) B (*c*) C (*d*) D (*e*) E
19. Which of the following should be the last sentence?
(*a*) A (*b*) B (*c*) C (*d*) D (*e*) E
20. Which of the following should be the third sentence?
(*a*) A (*b*) B (*c*) C (*d*) D (*e*) E
21. Which of the following should be the second sentence?
(*a*) A (*b*) B (*c*) C (*d*) D (*e*) E

22. Which of the following should be the fourth sentence?
(*a*) A (*b*) B (*c*) C (*d*) D (*e*) E

Questions 23 to 27 **(Bank P.O. 1993)**

The recognition of task and relationship as two critical dimensions of a manager's behaviour has been an important part of management research over the last several decades.

(A) Therefore, it was also felt that it could be represented on a single continuum, moving from very authoritarian leader behaviour (task) at one end to very participative leader behaviour (relationship) at the other end.
(B) These two dimensions have been given various labels ranging from "autocratic" and "democratic" to "employee oriented" and "production oriented".
(C) In particular, extensive leadership studies at Ohio State University questioned this assumption and showed that other assumptions were more reasonable and would lead to more useful theories of leadership.
(D) For sometime, it was believed that task and relationship behaviours were either/or styles of leadership.
(E) In more recent years, the idea that task and relationship behaviours were either/or leadership styles has been dispelled.

23. Which one of the following should be the first sentence?
(*a*) A (*b*) D (*c*) B (*d*) E (*e*) C

24. Which one of the following should be the second sentence?
(*a*) A (*b*) D (*c*) B (*d*) E (*e*) C

25. Which one of the following should be the third sentence?
(*a*) A (*b*) D (*c*) B (*d*) E (*e*) C

26. Which one of the following should be the fourth sentence?
(*a*) A (*b*) D (*c*) B (*d*) E (*e*) C

27. Which one of the following should be the last sentence?
(*a*) A (*b*) D (*c*) B (*d*) E (*e*) C

Questions 28 to 32 **(Bank P.O. 1992)**

(A) Miss Sullivan arrived at the Keller home when Helen was seven.
(B) The deaf and blind Helen learned to communicate verbally.
(C) But eventually, Miss Sullivan's effort was rewarded.
(D) Before Helen Keller was two years old, she lost her sight and her hearing.
(E) Miss Sullivan worked closely with Helen, her new student.
(F) At times, the teacher became frustrated.

28. Which of the following should be the first sentence in the passage?
(*a*) A (*b*) B (*c*) C (*d*) D (*e*) E

29. Which of the following should be the last sentence in the passage?
(*a*) A (*b*) B (*c*) C (*d*) D (*e*) E

30. Which of the following should be the fourth sentence in the passage?
(*a*) B (*b*) C (*c*) D (*d*) E (*e*) F

31. Which of the following should be the third sentence in the passage?
(*a*) A (*b*) B (*c*) C (*d*) D (*e*) E

32. Which of the following should be the second sentence in the passage?
(*a*) A (*b*) C (*c*) D (*d*) E (*e*) F

Questions 33 to 37 **(B.S.R.B. 1996)**

(A) She decided to go to school and meet the principal.
(B) Suddenly she realised that she had no money with her.
(C) By the time she reached there, he had left the office.
(D) Therefore, she decided to go to the office of Ravi's father and get the money.
(E) Sudha wanted her son Ravi to get admission in a convent school.

33. Which sentence should come fourth in the paragraph?
(*a*) A (*b*) B (*c*) C (*d*) D (*e*) E

34. Which sentence should come second in the paragraph?
(*a*) A (*b*) B (*c*) C (*d*) D (*e*) E

35. Which sentence should come third in the paragraph?
(*a*) A (*b*) B (*c*) C (*d*) D (*e*) E

36. Which sentence should come first in the paragraph?
(*a*) A (*b*) B (*c*) C (*d*) D (*e*) E

37. Which sentence should come last in the paragraph?
(*a*) A (*b*) B (*c*) C (*d*) D (*e*) E

Questions 38 to 41 **(Bank P.O. 1993)**

(A) Absence of other parental figures in the family has worsened the situation.
(B) Drug abuse among youngsters seems to be on the increase.
(C) The need for many mothers to work has put an additional claim

on the time available for the children.

(D) Breakdown of the extended family has put a lot of burden on the parents.

(E) Psychologists attribute this to the growing alienation of the new generation from their parents.

38. Which sentence should come first in the paragraph?
(*a*) D (*b*) E (*c*) B (*d*) A (*e*) C

39. Which sentence should come last in the paragraph?
(*a*) C (*b*) B (*c*) D (*d*) A (*e*) E

40. Which sentence should come third in the paragraph?
(*a*) E (*b*) D (*c*) B (*d*) C (*e*) A

41. Which sentence should come second in the paragraph?
(*a*) B (*b*) E (*c*) D (*d*) A (*e*) C

Questions 42 to 46

(A) The subjugation or enslavement of people and countries is fast becoming a thing of the past.

(B) Since then the progress in science and technology and in other branches of knowledge has resulted in the betterment of the conditions of life in many countries of the world.

(C) The Industrial Revolution in England about the middle of the eighteenth century was history's great leap forward.

(D) All this is on the credit of modern civilisation.

(E) Society has been progressing and improving for thousands of years.

(F) The span of human life has been enlarged, the condition of the labouring classes in many countries has improved, knowledge and education have made great strides, the treatment of children has become more human, feats of engineering have done wonders, democracy and freedom have been granted to most countries of the world, and a very much larger percentage of people have become entitled to the good things of life.

42. Which sentence should come first in the paragraph?
(*a*) E (*b*) C (*c*) F (*d*) A (*e*) D

43. Which sentence should come second in the paragraph?
(*a*) B (*b*) C (*c*) D (*d*) E (*e*) F

44. Which sentence should come fourth in the paragraph?
(*a*) A (*b*) C (*c*) B (*d*) F (*e*) D

45. Which sentence should come fifth in the paragraph?
(*a*) F (*b*) D (*c*) B (*d*) A (*e*) C

46. Which sentence should come last in the paragraph?
(*a*) A (*b*) B (*c*) C (*d*) D (*e*) F

Questions 47 to 50 **(B.S.R.B. 1995)**

(A) But, we all helped in the first few days.

(B) Chandrapur is considered as a rural area.

(C) Pradeep was transferred to this office recently.

(D) Initially he was not getting adjusted to the city life.

(E) Now, Pradeep is very proud of his colleagues.

(F) Before that he was working in Chandrapur branch of our office.

47. Which sentence should come first in the paragraph?
(*a*) A (*b*) C (*c*) D (*d*) E (*e*) F

48. Which sentence should come second in the paragraph?
(*a*) B (*b*) C (*c*) D (*d*) E (*e*) F

49. Which sentence should come third in the paragraph?
(*a*) A (*b*) B (*c*) C (*d*) E (*e*) F

50. Which sentence should come last in the paragraph?
(*a*) A (*b*) C (*c*) D (*d*) E (*e*) F

ANSWERS

1. (*d*)	**2.** (*d*)	**3.** (*e*)	**4.** (*d*)	**5.** (*c*)	**6.** (*c*)	**7.** (*a*)	**8.** (*e*)	**9.** (*b*)	**10.** (*d*)
11. (*b*)	**12.** (*e*)	**13.** (*e*)	**14.** (*e*)	**15.** (*a*)	**16.** (*d*)	**17.** (*a*)	**18.** (*c*)	**19.** (*a*)	**20.** (*d*)
21. (*e*)	**22.** (*b*)	**23.** (*b*)	**24.** (*a*)	**25.** (*c*)	**26.** (*d*)	**27.** (*e*)	**28.** (*d*)	**29.** (*b*)	**30.** (*e*)
31. (*e*)	**32.** (*a*)	**33.** (*d*)	**34.** (*a*)	**35.** (*b*)	**36.** (*e*)	**37.** (*c*)	**38.** (*c*)	**39.** (*d*)	**40.** (*b*)
41. (*b*)	**42.** (*a*)	**43.** (*b*)	**44.** (*d*)	**45.** (*d*)	**46.** (*d*)	**47.** (*b*)	**48.** (*e*)	**49.** (*b*)	**50.** (*a*)

PRACTICE SET 2

Directions : *Read the following statements to decide their sequence to make a meaningful passage and then answer the questions given below them.*

Questions 1 to 4 **(Bank P.O. 1992)**

(A) The knowledge so far available about the endocrine glands is very limited.

(B) Nature has provided the body with proper regulators and protectors.

(C) These are our endocrine glands.

(D) And so the proper functioning of these controllers of our body is very important and most vital for health.

(E) However, all the medical sciences have accepted the fact that these endocrine glands secrete thousands of different types of hormones directly into our blood.

1. Which of the following should be the first sentence?
(*a*) A (*b*) B (*c*) C (*d*) D (*e*) E

2. Which of the following should be the second sentence?
(*a*) A (*b*) B (*c*) C (*d*) D (*e*) E

3. Which of the following should be the third sentence?
(*a*) A (*b*) B (*c*) C (*d*) D (*e*) E

4. Which of the following should be the fourth sentence?
(*a*) A (*b*) B (*c*) C (*d*) D (*e*) E

Questions 5 to 9 **(Bank P.O. 1993)**

(A) Seconds later, the glaring object swept past and he thought he had out manoeuvred it.

(B) While flying over enemy territory, Jones received the warning of an oncoming missile.

(C) He was proved wrong when he saw the vertical tail fins on fire.

(D) Without wasting time, he slammed the throttles forward and made the plane roll into a high-speed turn.

(E) Hardly had he responded to the message when he actually saw what every fighter pilot dreaded most.

5. Which sentence should come third in the paragraph?
(*a*) A (*b*) B (*c*) C (*d*) D (*e*) E

6. Which sentence should come last in the paragraph?
(*a*) A (*b*) B (*c*) C (*d*) D (*e*) E

7. Which sentence should come second in the paragraph?
(*a*) A (*b*) B (*c*) C (*d*) D (*e*) E

8. Which sentence should come fourth in the paragraph?
(*a*) A (*b*) B (*c*) C (*d*) D (*e*) E

9. Which sentence should come first in the paragraph?
(*a*) A (*b*) B (*c*) C (*d*) D (*e*) E

Questions 10 to 14 **(L.I.C. 1994)**

(A) A taxi was summoned and Satish was taken to Lifeline Hospital.

(B) While hurrying home from school, Satish was hit by a car.

(C) Since they did not succeed, they decided to take him to a hospital.

(D) When Satish opened his eyes, he found himself surrounded by doctors and nurses.

(E) Some people rushed towards him and tried to bring him to his senses.

(F) He was thrown a couple of feet away and lost consciousness.

10. Which sentence should come last (i.e. sixth) in the paragraph?
(*a*) B (*b*) C (*c*) A (*d*) D (*e*) E

11. Which sentence should come first in the paragraph?
(*a*) D (*b*) F (*c*) B (*d*) E (*e*) C

12. Which sentence should come second in the paragraph?
(*a*) E (*b*) A (*c*) D (*d*) C (*e*) F

13. Which sentence should come third in the paragraph?
(*a*) F (*b*) B (*c*) E (*d*) A (*e*) D

14. Which sentence should come fourth in the paragraph?
(*a*) C (*b*) E (*c*) F (*d*) B (*e*) A

Questions 15 to 18 **(S.B.I.P.O. 1992)**

(A) Many consider it wrong to blight youngsters by recruiting them into armed forces at a young age.

(B) It is very difficult to have an agreement on an issue when emotions run high.

(C) The debate has again come up whether this is right or wrong.

(D) In many countries military service is compulsory for all.

(E) Some of these detractors of compulsory draft are even very angry.

15. Which sentence should come fourth in the paragraph?
(*a*) A (*b*) B (*c*) C (*d*) D (*e*) E

16. Which sentence should come first in the paragraph?
(*a*) A (*b*) B (*c*) C (*d*) D (*e*) E

17. Which sentence should come last in the paragraph?
(*a*) A (*b*) B (*c*) C (*d*) D (*e*) E

18. Which sentence should come third in the paragraph?
(*a*) A (*b*) B (*c*) C (*d*) D (*e*) E

Questions 19 to 22

(A) The large crowd, these myriad activities and the bright lights combine to transform the beach into a photographers' delight.
(B) Sand and spray are all pervasive on a beach.
(C) They love to construct fragile sand castles and splash about in the shallow waters.
(D) Even the elderly seem to forget their ageing worries here.
(E) These make beaches a favourite haunt of children.

19. Which sentence should come first in the paragraph?
(*a*) A (*b*) B (*c*) C (*d*) D (*e*) E

20. Which sentence should come second in the paragraph?
(*a*) D (*b*) E (*c*) A (*d*) B (*e*) C

21. Which sentence should come last in the paragraph?
(*a*) D (*b*) A (*c*) E (*d*) C (*e*) B

22. Which sentence should come third in the paragraph?
(*a*) C (*b*) D (*c*) A (*d*) B (*e*) E

Questions 23 to 26 **(S.B.I.P.O. 1991)**

(A) I think our country is searching for an identity.
(B) Yet, I do not agree with the prophets of doom who see nothing but disaster ahead.
(C) And a new vision of the future will emerge of this.
(D) When I came to India after a stint in Northern Ireland, I felt I was trading a hotbed of intense religious and political violence for peace and quiet,
(E) However, the mayhem over the last few months is deeply shocking

23. Which sentence would come last in the paragraph?
(*a*) D (*b*) A (*c*) B (*d*) E (*e*) C

24. Which sentence would come third in the paragraph?
(*a*) D (*b*) A (*c*) B (*d*) E (*e*) C

25. Which sentence would come first in the paragraph?
(*a*) D (*b*) A (*c*) B (*d*) E (*e*) C

26. Which sentence would come second in the paragraph?
(*a*) D (*b*) A (*c*) B (*d*) E (*e*) C

Questions 27 to 30 **(S.B.I.P.O. 1995)**

(A) The following represents a condensed statement of what we think we now know about the relationship between education and employment.
(B) Although the linkages between education and employment are complex and, in the past, often analysed with simplistic notions of casuality, recent research results have yielded new insights about the nature of these linkages.
(C) In the interests of brevity, the argument is put forward as a series of major propositions and derivative strategies relating to the education employment nexus.
(D) Intensive research efforts are currently being supported throughout the developing world both by national governments and international donor agencies in the hope of improving understanding of the nature and causes of rising unemployment.
(E) The massive problems of widespread and chronic unemployment in less developed nations will remain among the most serious challenges to development policy during the next several decades

27. Which of the following would be the third sentence?
(*a*) A (*b*) B (*c*) C (*d*) D (*e*) E

28. Which of the following would be the first sentence?
(*a*) A (*b*) B (*c*) C (*d*) D (*e*) E

29. Which of the following would be the fifth sentence?
(*a*) A (*b*) B (*c*) C (*d*) D (*e*) E

30. Which of the following would be the second sentence?
(*a*) A (*b*) B (*c*) C (*d*) D (*e*) E

Questions 31 to 35

(A) Therefore large scale construction programme has to be launched.
(B) Construction has not kept with it and the shortage of accommodation has been accentuated.
(C) But high cost of materials and labour makes housing an unprofitable proposition.
(D) The census figures show that the population of our cities has increased immensely in the recent years.
(E) This shortage must be overcome in a reasonably short time.

31. Which of the following should be the first sentence?
(*a*) A (*b*) B (*c*) C (*d*) D (*e*) E

32. Which of the following should be the second sentence?
(*a*) A (*b*) B (*c*) C (*d*) D (*e*) E

33. Which of the following should be the last sentence?
(*a*) A (*b*) B (*c*) C (*d*) D (*e*) E

34. Which of the following should be the third sentence?
(*a*) A (*b*) B (*c*) C (*d*) D (*e*) E

35. Which of the following should be the fourth sentence?
(*a*) A (*b*) B (*c*) C (*d*) D (*e*) E

Questions 36 to 40 **(Bank P.O. 1995)**

(A) Indeed, the mutations that the family has undergone in this century have been more challenging than at any time of its evolution.
(B) Thus, we have nuclear families, single parent families, surrogate families and global families to name just a few.
(C) How these changes have redefined our world view is an interesting field of study in themselves.
(D) What we often forget is that the family as it exists today has expanded its orthodox definition to include several variations.
(E) Each of these has brought its own attitudes and priorities.

36. Which sentence should come first in the paragraph?
(*a*) A (*b*) B (*c*) C (*d*) D (*e*) E

37. Which sentence should come second in the paragraph?
(*a*) A (*b*) B (*c*) C (*d*) D (*e*) E

38. Which sentence should come third in the paragraph?
(*a*) A (*b*) B (*c*) C (*d*) D (*e*) E

39. Which sentence should come fourth in the paragraph?
(*a*) A (*b*) B (*c*) C (*d*) D (*e*) E

40. Which sentence should come last in the paragraph?
(*a*) A (*b*) B (*c*) C (*d*) D (*e*) E

Questions 41 to 45 **(Bank P.O. 1993)**

(A) But by then it was too late to correct things.
(B) It is impossible to steer such a large project to success without planning.
(C) He had to stand by and watch helplessly.
(D) The whole scheme was destined to fail from the beginning.
(E) Jack started realising this only towards the end.

41. Which sentence should come third in the paragraph?
(*a*) A (*b*) B (*c*) C (*d*) D (*e*) E

42. Which sentence should come last in the paragraph?
(*a*) A (*b*) B (*c*) C (*d*) D (*e*) E

43. Which sentence should come first in the paragraph?
(*a*) A (*b*) B (*c*) C (*d*) D (*e*) E

44. Which sentence should come fourth in the paragraph?
(*a*) A (*b*) B (*c*) C (*d*) D (*e*) E

45. Which sentence should come second in the paragraph?
(*a*) A (*b*) B (*c*) C (*d*) D (*e*) E

Questions 46 to 50

(A) The decision to end this agreement and begin a fresh one was taken at the meeting of the working group of the two countries.
(B) Indo-Polish trade will be conducted in convertible currency from January 1 next year.
(C) The two countries have decided to sign a new trade agreement, to be effected to convertible currency.
(D) A final agreement in this regard is expected to be signed soon.
(E) This follows the expiry of the existing rupee trade agreement from December 31, this year.

46. Which sentence should come third in the paragraph?
(*a*) E (*b*) A (*c*) D (*d*) C (*e*) B

47. Which sentence should come first in the paragraph?
(*a*) E (*b*) A (*c*) D (*d*) C (*e*) B

48. Which sentence should come last in the paragraph?
(*a*) E (*b*) A (*c*) D (*d*) C (*e*) B

49. Which sentence should come second in the paragraph?
(*a*) E (*b*) A (*c*) D (*d*) C (*e*) B

50. Which sentence should come fourth in the paragraph?
(*a*) E (*b*) A (*c*) D (*d*) C (*e*) B

Questions 51 to 55

(A) But we cannot consider the judgement of a single individual infallible.

(B) Any really great book, we want to read the second time even more than we wanted to read it the first time; and every additional time that we read it, we find new meanings and new beauties in it.

(C) The test of a great book is whether we want to read it only once or more than once.

(D) The opinion that makes a book great must be the opinion of many.

(E) A book that a person of education and good tastes does not care to read more than once is very probably not worth much.

51. Which sentence would be the fourth in the paragraph?
(*a*) A (*b*) B (*c*) C (*d*) D (*e*) E

52. Which sentence would be the second in the paragraph?
(*a*) A (*b*) B (*c*) C (*d*) D (*e*) E

53. Which sentence would be the last in the paragraph?
(*a*) A (*b*) B (*c*) C (*d*) D (*e*) E

54. Which sentence would be the first in the paragraph?
(*a*) A (*b*) B (*c*) C (*d*) D (*e*) E

55. Which sentence would be the third in the paragraph?
(*a*) A (*b*) B (*c*) C (*d*) D (*e*) E

ANSWERS

1. (*b*)	**2.** (*d*)	**3.** (*c*)	**4.** (*a*)	**5.** (*d*)	**6.** (*c*)	**7.** (*e*)	**8.** (*a*)	**9.** (*b*)	**10.** (*d*)
11. (*c*)	**12.** (*e*)	**13.** (*c*)	**14.** (*a*)	**15.** (*c*)	**16.** (*d*)	**17.** (*b*)	**18.** (*e*)	**19.** (*a*)	**20.** (*d*)
21. (*a*)	**22.** (*e*)	**23.** (*d*)	**24.** (*b*)	**25.** (*a*)	**26.** (*c*)	**27.** (*b*)	**28.** (*a*)	**29.** (*e*)	**30.** (*d*)
31. (*d*)	**32.** (*b*)	**33.** (*c*)	**34.** (*e*)	**35.** (*a*)	**36.** (*a*)	**37.** (*c*)	**38.** (*d*)	**39.** (*b*)	**40.** (*e*)
41. (*e*)	**42.** (*c*)	**43.** (*d*)	**44.** (*a*)	**45.** (*b*)	**46.** (*d*)	**47.** (*e*)	**48.** (*c*)	**49.** (*a*)	**50.** (*b*)
51. (*a*)	**52.** (*b*)	**53.** (*d*)	**54.** (*c*)	**55.** (*e*)					

PRACTICE SET 3

Questions 1 to 5 **(NABARD, 1994)**

(A) A case in point is the programme involving the Sardar Sarovar Dam which would displace about 2,00,000 people.

(B) Critics decry the fact that a major development institution appears to absorb more capital than it distributes to borrowers.

(C) For all its faults, critics, however concede that the bank remains a relatively efficient instrument for distribution of development-aid money.

(D) One of the key complaints focusses on this non-profit bank's recent "profitability".

(E) Although the lives of millions of people around the globe have been improved by the bank's activities, it is now under fire.

(F) The bank is also being blamed for large-scale involuntary resettlement to make way for dams and other construction projects.

1. Which sentence should come first in the paragraph?
(*a*) B (*b*) C (*c*) D (*d*) E (*e*) F

2. Which sentence should come second in the paragraph?
(*a*) A (*b*) C (*c*) D (*d*) E (*e*) F

3. Which sentence should come third in the paragraph?
(*a*) A (*b*) B (*c*) D (*d*) E (*e*) F

4. Which sentence should come fourth in the paragraph?
(*a*) A (*b*) B (*c*) C (*d*) E (*e*) F

5. Which sentence should come last (i.e. sixth) in the paragraph?
(*a*) A (*b*) B (*c*) C (*d*) D (*e*) E

Questions 6 to 10

(A) However, inspite of parental efforts kids are found to fall short of their potentiality.
(B) Bringing out the best of the child is a gradual process of support and encouragement on your part.
(C) Parents give natural ability of children as an explanation for this.
(D) These efforts pay off in peak performance-the stuff of every parent's dream.
(E) There are no short-cuts to bringing your child to do his best.

6. Which sentence should come first in the paragraph?
(*a*) D (*b*) E (*c*) B (*d*) A (*e*) C

7. Which sentence should come second in the paragraph?
(*a*) B (*b*) C (*c*) A (*d*) E (*e*) D

8. Which sentence should come third in the paragraph?
(*a*) E (*b*) C (*c*) B (*d*) A (*e*) D

9. Which sentence should come fourth in the paragraph?
(*a*) C (*b*) B (*c*) D (*d*) E (*e*) A

10. Which sentence should come last in the paragraph?
(*a*) A (*b*) B (*c*) C (*d*) D (*e*) E

Questions 11 to 15 **(R.B.I. 1991)**

(A) The alternative was a blitz by the health workers to popularise preventive measures.
(B) This information was considered inadequate.
(C) People have been reading about AIDS in the mass media.
(D) Nobody is sure as to how effective this would be.
(E) People were also not being influenced enough to take preventive measures

11. Which sentence should come first in the paragraph?
(*a*) C (*b*) D (*c*) B (*d*) E (*e*) A

12. Which sentence should come second in the paragraph?
(*a*) C (*b*) D (*c*) B (*d*) E (*e*) A

13. Which sentence should come third in the paragraph?
(*a*) C (*b*) D (*c*) B (*d*) E (*e*) A

14. Which sentence should come fourth in the paragraph?
(*a*) C (*b*) D (*c*) B (*d*) E (*e*) A

15. Which sentence should come last in the paragraph?
(*a*) C (*b*) D (*c*) B (*d*) E (*e*) A

Questions 16 to 20 **(Bank P.O. 1995)**

(A) A study to this effect suggests that the average white-collar worker demonstrates only about twenty-five percent listening efficiency.
(B) However, for trained and good listeners it is not unusual to see all the three approaches during a setting, thus improving listening efficiency.
(C) There are three approaches to listening : listening for comprehension, listening for empathy, and listening for evaluation.
(D) Although we spend nearly half of each communication interaction listening, we do not listen well.
(E) Each approach has a particular emphasis that may help us to receive and process information in different settings.

16. Which sentence should come fourth in the paragraph?
(*a*) B (*b*) C (*c*) E (*d*) A (*e*) D

17. Which sentence should come second in the paragraph?
(*a*) E (*b*) A (*c*) D (*d*) B (*e*) C

18. Which sentence should come first in the paragraph?
(*a*) D (*b*) A (*c*) C (*d*) E (*e*) B

19. Which sentence should come last in the paragraph?
(*a*) A (*b*) B (*c*) C (*d*) D (*e*) E

20. Which sentence should come third in the paragraph?
(*a*) C (*b*) A (*c*) D (*d*) B (*e*) E

Questions 21 to 25 **(Railways, 1991)**

(A) Modern science has produced some good drugs for these ailments.

(B) Heart ailments are very common these days.

(C) So I always prefer taking milk these days as it contains no fat.

(D) But this can also be prevented by taking fatless food.

(E) That is why people call this era as the age of heart troubles.

21. Which of the following should be the third sentence?
(*a*) B (*b*) D (*c*) A (*d*) E (*e*) C

22. Which of the following should be the first sentence?
(*a*) B (*b*) D (*c*) A (*d*) E (*e*) C

23. Which of the following should be the last sentence?
(*a*) B (*b*) D (*c*) A (*d*) E (*e*) C

24. Which of the following should be the second sentence?
(*a*) B (*b*) D (*c*) A (*d*) E (*e*) C

25. Which of the following should be the fourth sentence?
(*a*) B (*b*) D (*c*) A (*d*) E (*e*) C

Questions 26 to 30

(A) As soon as we realise this fact, we will understand that it is very important to choose a system of education which will really prepare children for life.

(B) But we can already see that free education for all is not enough.

(C) Education is not an end, but a means to an end.

(D) In many modern countries it has for sometime been fashionable to think that by free education for all, one can solve all the problems of society and build a perfect nation.

(E) In other words we do not educate children only for the purpose of educating them, the purpose is to fit them for life.

(F) We find in such countries a far larger number of people with university degrees than there are jobs for them to fill.

26. Which sentence should come first in the paragraph?
(*a*) A (*b*) B (*c*) C (*d*) D (*e*) E

27. Which sentence should come second in the paragraph?
(*a*) A (*b*) B (*c*) D (*d*) E (*e*) F

28. Which sentence should come third in the paragraph?
(*a*) A (*b*) B (*c*) C (*d*) E (*e*) F

29. Which sentence should come fifth in the paragraph?
(*a*) B (*b*) C (*c*) D (*d*) E (*e*) F

30. Which sentence should come last in the paragraph?
(*a*) A (*b*) B (*c*) C (*d*) E (*e*) F

Questions 31 to 35 **(Bank P.O. 1995)**

(A) What is clear is that no one has yet provided evidence for it to be conclusively rejected or validated.

(B) To some people such a notion seems perfectly reasonable; to others it seems quite ludicrous.

(C) Most of the people have curiosity and also possess some knowledge of astrology.

(D) Much of the evidence offering support for this fundamental notion is far from clear-cut.

(E) They appreciate that astrology attempts to relate human behaviour to the movements of stars and planets.

31. Which sentence should come second in the paragraph?
(*a*) A (*b*) B (*c*) C (*d*) D (*e*) E

32. Which sentence should come fourth in the paragraph?
(*a*) A (*b*) B (*c*) C (*d*) D (*e*) E

33. Which sentence should come first in the paragraph?
(*a*) A (*b*) B (*c*) C (*d*) D (*e*) E

34. Which sentence should come third in the paragraph?
(*a*) A (*b*) B (*c*) C (*d*) D (*e*) E

35. Which sentence should come last in the paragraph?
(*a*) A (*b*) B (*c*) C (*d*) D (*e*) E

Questions 36 to 40

(A) Further, he pretended to have a particular dislike for the lowest labouring classes declaring that they ought to be absolutely destroyed.

(B) One of his little eccentricities was violent disbelief in government by the people.

(C) He was a man who despised the aims and beliefs of his fellow- men, and a trifle eccentric.

(D) His closest friends, however, knew that these were all assumed attitudes, and that, secretly he was kindly disposed towards his fellow men, and the poor.

(E) It was contradiction in terms, he said, government by a single man was the only form of government that had ever been able to do things.

36. Which sentence should come second in the paragraph?
(a) C (b) D (c) E (d) A (e) B

37. Which sentence should come fourth in the paragraph?
(a) C (b) D (c) E (d) A (e) B

38. Which sentence should come first in the paragraph?
(a) C (b) D (c) E (d) A (e) B

39. Which sentence should come third in the paragraph?
(a) C (b) D (c) E (d) A (e) B

40. Which sentence should come last (i.e. fifth) in the paragraph?
(a) C (b) D (c) E (d) A (e) B

Questions 41 to 45 **(S.B.I.P.O. 1994)**

In the beginning of the last decade it looked as if an era of confrontation had given way to an era of negotiations.

(A) This policy helped in reducing the tensions among the great powers.

(B) India sincerely welcomed this development.

(C) Indeed, it saw in it a vindication and extension of its own policy of non-alignment.

(D) It was happy that it had contributed to the alleviation of tensions between the great powers.

(E) The resolution of conflicts between certain countries was an outcome of India's such policy.

41. Which of the following should be the first sentence?
(a) A (b) B (c) C (d) D (e) E

42. Which of the following should be the second sentence?
(a) A (b) B (c) C (d) D (e) E

43. Which of the following should be the third sentence?
(a) A (b) B (c) C (d) D (e) E

44. Which of the following should be the fourth sentence?
(a) A (b) B (c) C (d) D (e) E

45. Which of the following should be the last sentence?
(a) A (b) B (c) C (d) D (e) E

Questions 46 to 50 **(Bank P.O. 1993)**

(A) Marie Curie's discovery of radium led to much improved treatment for cancer.

(B) It has helped man to live a more comfortable life.

(C) However, it's how we use a thing that makes' it 'good' or 'bad'.

(D) The benefits conferred on the world in general by science have been manifold and varied.

(E) But the eventual discovery of the full properties of radium and uranium has brought great destruction in its train.

(F) No educated man would deny this but many would point out that it has brought evils as well as blessings.

46. Which of the following will be the last sentence?
(a) A (b) B (c) C (d) D (e) E

47. Which of the following will be the third sentence?
(a) B (b) C (c) D (d) E (e) F

48. Which of the following will be the first sentence?
(a) A (b) B (c) C (d) D (e) E

49. Which of the following will be the fifth sentence?
(a) A (b) B (c) C (d) D (e) E

50. Which of the following will be the second sentence?
(a) A (b) B (c) D (d) E (e) F

ANSWERS

1. (d)	2. (c)	3. (b)	4. (e)	5. (c)	6. (b)	7. (a)	8. (c)	9. (a)	10. (d)
11. (a)	12. (c)	13. (d)	14. (e)	15. (b)	16. (e)	17. (a)	18. (c)	19. (a)	20. (d)
21. (c)	22. (a)	23. (e)	24. (d)	25. (b)	26. (c)	27. (d)	28. (a)	29. (a)	30. (e)
31. (e)	32. (a)	33. (c)	34. (b)	35. (d)	36. (e)	37. (d)	38. (a)	39. (c)	40. (b)
41. (a)	42. (b)	43. (c)	44. (d)	45. (e)	46. (c)	47. (e)	48. (d)	49. (e)	50. (b)

22. REARRANGEMENT OF JUMBLED PARTS

In such type of questions, a sentence or a paragraph is broken into several parts which are then jumbled up and labelled (1), (2), (3), (4), (5), (6), ... The examinee is required to rearrange these parts into a meaningful format and then choose the correct order from among the alternatives provided.

Example :

(1) As they speed along
(2) artificial satellites do not fall
(3) the pull of the earth, or its gravity
(4) as a result
(5) keeps them from doing so
(6) because they are going too fast to do so
(7) they tend to go straight off into space
(8) they travel in an orbit round the earth

(G.I.C.A.A.O. 1990)

(*a*) 1, 3, 5, 7, 8, 6, 4, 2
(*b*) 2, 6,1, 7, 3, 5, 4, 8
(*c*) 2, 6, 7, 3, 1, 5, 8, 4
(*d*) 4, 2, 8, 6, 5, 7, 1, 3

Technique of Solving :

The first thing is what is being talked about.

In the above example, it is the 'artificial satellites'. Since all other parts except (2) contain 'they', so the introductory sentence should be (2).

After (2), a question arises : why they do not fall? The answer to this is (6). So, the next part is (6).

Now, we consider two alternatives (*b*) and (*d*).

On rearranging according to these, we find that a meaningful paragraph is formed with the order given in (*b*). Hence, the answer is (*b*).

PRACTICE SET

Directions : ***In each of the following questions, a paragraph or a sentence has been broken up into different parts. The parts have been scrambled and numbered as given below. Choose the correct order of these parts from the given alternatives.***

1. (1) is decidedly harmful
(2) disregarding other equally important aspects,
(3) to the total neglect of others
(4) in the life of a man or a woman
(5) is not wisdom but
(6) cultivating only one quality
(7) giving all attention and energy to one aspect of national life only,
(8) folly
(9) similarly in the life of a nation
(*a*) 4, 6, 2, 5, 8, 9, 7, 1, 3
(*b*) 4, 6, 3, 1, 9, 7, 2, 5, 8
(*c*) 6, 2, 4, 5, 1, 9, 7, 3, 8
(*d*) 6, 4, 2, 1, 9, 7, 3, 5, 8

2. (1) you can take
(2) you can't take
(3) the boy
(4) the village
(5) out of the village
(6) out of the boy
(7) but **(G.I.C.A.A.O. 1990)**
(*a*) 1, 3, 5, 7, 2, 4, 6 (*b*) 1, 5, 2, 6, 3, 7, 4
(*c*) 1, 6, 5, 3, 7, 2, 4 (*d*) 1, 7, 2, 4, 3 5, 6

3. (1) food supply
(2) storage, distribution and handling
(3) pastoral industry and fishing,
(4) besides increasing
(5) by preventing wastage in
(6) the productivity from agriculture
(7) can be increased
(*a*) 1, 7, 5, 2, 4, 3, 6 (*b*) 4, 1, 6, 7, 5, 3, 2
(*c*) 4, 6, 3, 1, 7, 5, 2 (*d*) 6, 3, 5, 7, 4, 1, 2

4. (1) in some of the developed countries
(2) in the developing countries
(3) mostly in the form of beef, pork etc.
(4) about 180 kilograms
(5) per capita consumption is
(6) of grain per capita annually
(7) the people
(8) five times that amount
(9) consume only
(*a*) 1, 7, 9, 4, 6, 2, 5, 8, 3
(*b*) 2, 5, 8, 2, 7, 9, 4, 6, 3
(*c*) 7, 2, 9, 4, 6, 1, 5, 8, 3
(*d*) 5, 8, 1, 2, 7, 9, 4, 6, 3

5. (1) The African elephant is usually larger
(2) being about three and a half metres in height
(3) than the Indian
(4) and 6000 kg in weight
(5) It has enormous ears
(6) which are valued for the ivory
(7) and very long tusks
(8) that they contain **(G.I.C.A.A.O. 1990)**
(*a*) 1, 3, 2, 4, 5, 7, 6, 8
(*b*) 1, 4, 2, 3, 6, 5, 8, 7
(*c*) 1, 5, 4, 2, 3, 8, 7, 6
(*d*) 5, 6, 2, 4, 1, 3, 7, 8

6. (1) not only for
(2) but also for
(3) lumbering
(4) construction purposes
(5) as an occupation
(6) on modern lines
(7) the manufacture of wood pulp, paper, resins etc.
(8) owing to the great demand for timber
(9) has developed
(*a*) 3, 9, 6, 5, 8, 1, 4, 2, 7
(*b*) 3, 8, 9, 5, 6, 1, 7, 2, 4
(*c*) 3, 5, 9, 6, 8, 1, 4, 2, 7
(*d*) 5, 3, 9, 6, 8, 1, 7, 2, 4

7. (1) keeper of the
(2) guardian of
(3) as well as
(4) The U.N.O. is supposed to be the
(5) the morally-conceived
(6) political conscience
(7) expressly defined rights and duties of sovereign states
(8) and
(*a*) 4, 1, 7, 3, 2, 5, 8, 6
(*b*) 4, 2, 6, 8, 1,3, 5, 7
(*c*) 4, 1, 6, 8, 2, 5, 3, 7
(*d*) 4, 2, 7, 3, 1, 5, 8, 6

8. (1) it is of vital importance
(2) if this can be prevented
(3) since man depends for his food
(4) upon articles
(5) that none of this soil should be wasted
(6) produced from the earth's layer of fertile soil **(G.I.C.A.A.O. 1990)**
(*a*) 3, 1, 2, 4, 6, 5 (*b*) 3, 1, 5, 4, 6, 2,
(*c*) 3, 4, 6, 1, 5, 2 (*d*) 3, 5, 1, 2, 6, 4

9. (1) are free from
(2) grow abundantly
(3) low plants
(4) Tundra regions
(5) during the short summer
(6) like mosses and lichens
(7) and
(8) ice
(*a*) 3, 6, 2, 5, 7, 4, 1, 8
(*b*) 4, 1, 8, 5, 7, 3, 6, 2
(*c*) 5, 3, 6, 2, 7, 4, 1, 8
(*d*) 5, 4, 1, 8, 7, 2, 3, 6

10. (1) Along the gutters it lingered,
(2) its tired breath a pale of chrysanthemum about the street lamps,
(3) sliding its warm tongue over silent pavements,
(4) The gentle fox curled softly down
(5) and rubbed its back against the huddled houses
(6) then it curled up and slept on corners
(7) Slowly it rose and fell,
(8) and pressing its blurred face against shop-windows
(9) It coiled its body around the black railings, **(G.I.C.A.A.O. 1990)**
(*a*) 1, 2, 3, 4, 5, 6, 7, 8, 9
(*b*) 2, 9, 6, 8, 5, 7, 4, 3, 1
(*c*) 4, 9, 5, 1, 3, 8, 7, 2, 6
(*d*) 9, 6, 8, 5, 7, 1, 4, 2, 3

ANSWERS

1. (*b*) **2.** (*a*) **3.** (*c*) **4.** (*c*) **5.** (*a*) **6.** (*c*) **7.** (*c*) **8.** (*c*) **9.** (*b*) **10.** (*c*)

23. WORD FORMATION

This is one of the recently added types of questions. In this, a word is given, whose alphabets are written in a jumbled order and numbered 1, 2, 3, 4, 5 and 6. The candidate is required to arrange these alphabets so as to form a meaningful word and then choose the correct order from the alternatives given.

Example : *Select the combination of numbers so that letters arranged accordingly will form a meaningful word.*

V A R S T E
1 2 3 4 5 6

(*a*) 2 3 1 6 4 5 (*b*) 4 5 2 3 1 6 (*c*) 6 3 4 5 2 1 (*d*) 3 2 4 5 6 1

Solution : The given letters, when rearranged in the order 452316, form the word 'STARVE'. Hence, the answer is (*b*).

PRACTICE SET

Directions : *Select the combination of numbers so that letters/words arranged accordingly will form a meaningful word.*

1. T R I F U **(Railways 1995)**
1 2 3 4 5
(*a*) 3 1 2 4 5 (*b*) 4 2 5 3 1
(*c*) 4 3 2 1 5 (*d*) 5 3 2 1 4

2. A C E S T H
1 2 3 4 5 6
(*a*) 6 1 4 5 3 2 (*b*) 2 6 1 4 5 3
(*c*) 4 3 5 6 1 2 (*d*) 6 3 2 1 4 5

3. G T A E N M
1 2 3 4 5 6
(*a*) 1 3 2 5 4 6 (*b*) 1 3 2 6 4 5
(*c*) 6 3 5 1 4 2 (*d*) 6 3 1 5 4 2

4. N R O C T A
1 2 3 4 5 6
(*a*) 1 6 2 4 3 5 (*b*) 2 3 5 4 6 1
(*c*) 4 6 2 5 3 1 (*d*) 6 5 2 3 1 4

5. G A N I M E
1 2 3 4 5 6
(*a*) 1 2 4 3 6 5 (*b*) 6 3 4 1 5 2
(*c*) 5 2 1 4 3 6 (*d*) 2 5 1 4 3 6

6. D I F E R N
1 2 3 4 5 6
(*a*) 1 4 3 6 2 5 (*b*) 6 4 3 5 2 1
(*c*) 3 5 2 4 6 1 (*d*) 5 4 3 2 6 1

7. K A T C E L
1 2 3 4 5 6
(*a*) 4 2 3 1 5 6 (*b*) 1 2 4 5 6 3
(*c*) 6 5 3 2 4 1 (*d*) 3 2 4 1 6 5

8. R U S G A
1 2 3 4 5
(*a*) 1 5 4 2 3 (*b*) 5 3 4 1 2
(*c*) 3 2 4 5 1 (*d*) 4 5 3 2 1

9. C E L S M U
1 2 3 4 5 6
(*a*) 4 6 3 5 2 1 (*b*) 5 6 4 1 3 2
(*c*) 4 6 5 2 3 1 (*d*) 5 2 3 1 6 4

10. H N R C A B
1 2 3 4 5 6
(*a*) 4 1 5 6 2 3 (*b*) 6 3 5 2 4 1
(*c*) 3 5 6 4 1 2 (*d*) 2 5 3 4 1 6

11. E L B M A G
1 2 3 4 5 6
(*a*) 6 5 4 3 2 1 (*b*) 3 1 6 4 5 2
(*c*) 4 5 6 3 1 2 (*d*) 2 1 6 3 5 4

12. R T A O U H
1 2 3 4 5 6
(*a*) 1 3 4 5 6 (*b*) 2 3 6 4 5 1
(*c*) 6 3 2 4 5 1 (*d*) 3 5 2 6 4 1

13. T L E M N A
1 2 3 4 5 6
(*a*) 2 6 4 5 3 1 (*b*) 3 2 4 6 5 1
(*c*) 4 3 5 1 6 2 (*d*) 5 3 2 4 6 1

14. A E H R K N
1 2 3 4 5 6
(*a*) 4 1 5 3 2 6 (*b*) 6 1 5 3 4 2
(*c*) 3 1 6 5 2 4 (*d*) 5 3 1 4 2 6

15. I N L A S G
1 2 3 4 5 6
(*a*) 6 1 3 5 4 2 (*b*) 5 1 6 2 4 3
(*c*) 3 4 6 1 2 5 (*d*) 2 4 3 6 1 5

16. T L P N A E
1 2 3 4 5 6
(*a*) 3 2 5 4 6 1 (*b*) 3 2 5 4 1 6
(*c*) 4 5 3 6 2 1 (*d*) 4 6 1 3 5 2

17. R P E D I
1 2 3 4 5
(*a*) 1 3 2 5 4 (*b*) 2 1 5 4 3
(*c*) 3 2 1 5 4 (*d*) 4 3 2 1 5

18. I P E L O C **(Railways, 1995)**
1 2 3 4 5 6
(*a*) 1 4 3 5 2 6 (*b*) 2 5 4 1 6 3
(*c*) 3 4 5 1 2 6 (*d*) 4 5 1 2 3 6

19. R M N B U E
1 2 3 4 5 6
(*a*) 2 6 3 4 1 5 (*b*) 4 6 3 2 1 5
(*c*) 3 5 2 4 6 1 (*d*) 1 5 4 2 6 3

20. T N D R A E
1 2 3 4 5 6

(*a*) 1 6 2 3 5 4 (*b*) 3 6 2 4 5 1
(*c*) 5 4 3 6 2 1 (*d*) 4 5 3 6 2 1

21. E H R A S P
1 2 3 4 5 6
(*a*) 5 2 4 6 1 3 (*b*) 6 2 3 4 5 1
(*c*) 2 4 6 1 3 5 (*d*) 3 4 2 1 6 5

22. T E L S C A
1 2 3 4 5 6
(*a*) 1 2 3 4 6 5 (*b*) 4 6 5 1 2 3
(*c*) 5 6 4 1 3 2 (*d*) 6 5 3 2 4 1

23. E O C D L I
1 2 3 4 5 6
(*a*) 3 2 5 4 6 1 (*b*) 4 2 3 5 6 1
(*c*) 3 2 4 5 6 1 (*d*) 4 2 3 6 5 1

24. A M D E N R
1 2 3 4 5 6
(*a*) 2 1 5 3 4 6 (*b*) 6 4 2 1 5 3
(*c*) 3 4 5 2 1 6 (*d*) 1 6 2 4 5 3

25. T I R B H G
1 2 3 4 5 6
(*a*) 1 3 2 4 6 5 (*b*) 4 3 2 6 5 1
(*c*) 4 5 2 3 6 1 (*d*) 3 2 6 5 4 1

26. R A C E T
1 2 3 4 5
(*a*) 1 2 3 4 5 (*b*) 3 2 1 4 5
(*c*) 5 2 3 4 1 (*d*) 5 1 2 3 4

27. L A E M V R
1 2 3 4 5 6
(*a*) 1 2 6 4 3 5 (*b*) 4 2 6 5 3 1
(*c*) 5 3 6 4 2 1 (*d*) 6 3 1 4 2 5

28. R T E O D P
1 2 3 4 5 6
(*a*) 1 3 5 6 4 2 (*b*) 2 3 1 6 4 5
(*c*) 5 3 6 4 1 2 (*d*) 6 3 5 1 4 2

29. E H N T O R
1 2 3 4 5 6
(*a*) 2 5 3 4 1 6 (*b*) 4 2 6 5 3 1
(*c*) 2 5 6 3 1 4 (*d*) 4 2 5 6 3 1

30. J C O P T E R
1 2 3 4 5 6 7
(*a*) 1 3 4 5 6 7 2 (*b*) 2 6 4 5 1 3 7
(*c*) 7 6 4 5 1 3 2 (*d*) 4 7 3 1 6 2 5

31. A C P E T S **(Railway 1995)**
1 2 3 4 5 6
(*a*) 1 6 3 4 2 5 (*b*) 2 3 4 1 5 6
(*c*) 5 6 3 4 1 2 (*d*) 6 5 3 4 2 1

32. R T A N U E
1 2 3 4 5 6
(*a*) 1 3 2 6 4 5 (*b*) 3 2 4 6 1 5
(*c*) 4 3 2 5 1 6 (*d*) 4 6 5 2 3 1

33. I N E T O C
1 2 3 4 5 6
(*a*) 2 5 4 1 6 3 (*b*) 3 6 4 1 2 5
(*c*) 4 3 6 5 2 1 (*d*) 6 5 2 3 4 1

34. T P S L O I
1 2 3 4 5 6
(*a*) 4 6 2 5 3 1 (*b*) 2 5 4 3 6 1
(*c*) 2 6 3 1 5 4 (*d*) 3 6 4 2 5 1

35. M F I A N E
1 2 3 4 5 6
(*a*) 1 6 2 3 4 5 (*b*) 2 4 1 3 5 6
(*c*) 5 6 2 3 1 4 (*d*) 4 2 3 1 6 5

36. N A E H L D
1 2 3 4 5 6
(*a*) 2 6 4 3 5 1 (*b*) 4 2 1 6 5 3
(*c*) 4 3 6 5 2 1 (*d*) 2 1 6 4 3 5

37. E T C K O P
1 2 3 4 5 6
(*a*) 3 1 4 5 6 2 (*b*) 6 5 3 4 1 2
(*c*) 2 1 6 5 3 4 (*d*) 4 1 2 3 5 6

38. E L G N I M
1 2 3 4 5 6
(*a*) 6 5 4 3 2 1 (*b*) 3 1 2 6 5 4
(*c*) 6 5 3 2 1 4 (*d*) 3 5 6 2 1 4

39. D A I M E N
1 2 3 4 5 6
(*a*) 1 5 4 2 3 6 (*b*) 4 5 1 2 3 6
(*c*) 4 2 3 1 5 6 (*d*) 1 2 5 6 3 4

40. R E S T L U **(Railways, 1995)**
1 2 3 4 5 6
(*a*) 3 4 6 1 2 5 (*b*) 4 5 3 2 6 1
(*c*) 5 6 3 4 1 2 (*d*) 6 5 2 1 4 3

ANSWERS

1. (*b*) FRUIT	**2.** (*b*) CHASTE	**3.** (*d*) MAGNET	**4.** (*c*) CARTON
5. (*b*) ENIGMA	**6.** (*c*) FRIEND	**7.** (*d*) TACKLE	**8.** (*c*) SUGAR
9. (*b*) MUSCLE	**10.** (*b*) BRANCH	**11.** (*a*) GAMBLE	**12.** (*d*) AUTHOR
13. (*c*) MENTAL	**14.** (*c*) HANKER	**15.** (*b*) SIGNAL	**16.** (*a*) PLANET
17. (*b*) PRIDE	**18.** (*b*) POLICE	**19.** (*c*) NUMBER	**20.** (*C*) ARDENT
21. (*b*) PHRASE	**22.** (*c*) CASTLE	**23.** (*d*) DOCILE	**24.** (*b*) REMAND
25. (*b*) BRIGHT	**26.** (*d*) TRACE	**27.** (*b*) MARVEL	**28.** (*c*) DEPORT
29. (*b*) THRONE	**30.** (*d*) PROJECT	**31.** (*a*) ASPECT	**32.** (*c*) NATURE
33. (*a*) NOTICE	**34.** (*c*) PISTOL	**35.** (*b*) FAMINE	**36.** (*b*) HANDLE
37. (*b*) POCKET	**38.** (*a*) MINGLE	**39.** (*c*) MAIDEn	**40.** (*c*) LUSTRE

UNIT VI

GENERAL USAGE

AN ADVANCED APPROACH TO DATA INTERPRETATION

R.S. Aggarwal

For Bank P.O., S.B.I.P.O., R.B.I., M.B.A., Hotel Management, Railways, I. Tax and Central Excise, I.A.S. (Prelims & Mains), C.B.I., Asstt. Grade, U.D.C., L.I.C., G.I.C.A.A.O. etc.

* A whole lot of questions on Bar Graphs, Line Graphs, Pie-Charts and Tabulation, fully solved.
* Illustrative examples with techniques to solve all types of problems.
* Previous years' questions included.

24. IDIOMS & PHRASES

TYPE 1 : CHOOSING THE CORRECT MEANING OF THE GIVEN IDIOM

In this type of questions, an idiom is given followed by four alternatives. The candidate is required to choose that alternative which correctly expresses the meaning of the given idiom.

Example : To meet one's Waterloo

(*a*) To die an ignoble death
(*b*) To meet a strong adversary
(*c*) To die fighting
(*d*) To meet one's final defeat

Solution : The idiom 'To meet one's Waterloo' means 'To meet one's final defeat'. Hence, the answer is (*d*).

PRACTICE SET 1

Directions : ***In each of the following questions, an idiomatic expression/a proverb has been given, followed by some alternatives. Choose the one which best expresses the meaning of the given idiom/proverb.***

1. **To turn over a new leaf**
(*a*) To change completely one's course of action
(*b*) To shift attention to new problems after having studied the old ones throughly
(*c*) To cover up one's faults by wearing new marks
(*d*) To change the old habits and adopt new ones **(Railways, 1995)**

2. **A fair crack of the whip**
(*a*) Severe punishment
(*b*) A good check
(*c*) A period of importance
(*d*) Failure of administration

3. **To talk one's head off**
(*a*) To talk loudly
(*b*) To talk in whispers
(*c*) To talk to oneself
(*d*) To talk excessively

4. **To hold something in leash**
(*a*) To restrain (*b*) To disappoint
(*c*) To dismiss (*d*) To discourage

5. **To play fast and loose**
(*a*) To trust others
(*b*) To be undependable
(*c*) To cheat people
(*d*) To hurt somebody's feelings

6. **To wrangle over an ass's shadow**
(*a*) To act in a foolish way
(*b*) To quarrel over trifles
(*c*) To waste time on petty things
(*d*) To do something funny **(S.B.I.P.O. 1984)**

7. **All Agog**
(*a*) Everybody (*b*) All ready
(*c*) Restless (*d*) Almighty

8. **To frame a person**
(*a*) To befool someone
(*b*) To make one appear guilty
(*c*) To praise someone
(*d*) A narrow escape

9. **A close shave**
(*a*) A lucky escape
(*b*) A clean shave
(*c*) A well guarded secret
(*d*) A narrow escape

10. **To take with a grain of salt**
(*a*) To take with some reservation
(*b*) To take with total disbelief
(*c*) To take whole heartedly
(*d*) To take seriously **(Asstt. Grade, 1984)**

11. **To keep one's head**
(*a*) To be agile and active
(*b*) To keep calm
(*c*) To think coherently
(*d*) None of these

12. **To cross swords**
(*a*) To fight (*b*) To defend
(*c*) To kill (*d*) To rob

13. **A snake in the grass**
(*a*) Secret or hidden enemy
(*b*) Unforeseen happening
(*c*) Unrecognisable danger
(*d*) Irreliable' person

14. **To give up the ghost**
(*a*) To suffer
(*b*) To fight evil forces
(*c*) To die
(*d*) To become rational

15. **Hobson's choice** **(Railways, 1991)**
(*a*) Feeling of insecurity
(*b*) Accept or leave the offer
(*c*) Feeling of strength
(*d*) Excellent choice

16. **To be at loggerheads**
(*a*) To have tough encounter
(*b*) To be at enmity or strife
(*c*) To face stiff opposition
(*d*) To tax one's mind and body

17. **To talk through one's hat**
(*a*) To speak fluently

(*b*) To talk nonsense
(*c*) To talk wisdom
(*d*) To speak at random

18. To snap one's fingers
(*a*) To speak abruptly
(*b*) To accept immediately
(*c*) To grasp eagerly
(*d*) To become contemptuous of
(*e*) To be anxious

19. A pipe dream
(*a*) A pleasant dream
(*b*) A bad dream
(*c*) An impracticable plan
(*d*) A foolish idea

20. To give up the ghost
(*a*) To die
(*b*) To make false appearance
(*c*) To terrify others by acting in suspicious manner
(*d*) To leave useless pursuits

21. To have an easy time of it
(*a*) To take the world lightly
(*b*) To indulge in frivolities
(*c*). To squander away resources
(*d*) To live in quiet and comfort

22. To stand to one's guns
(*a*) To keep the guns close to oneself even amid danger
(*b*) To persevere when hardships press
(*c*) To maintain dignified and unbending attitude
(*d*) To maintain one's position

23. To take the bull by the horns
(*a*) To punish a person severely for his arrogance
(*b*) To grapple courageously with a difficulty that lies in our way
(*c*) To handle it by fierce attack
(*d*) To bypass the legal process and take action according to one's own whims. **(Railways, 1995)**

24. To lose one's head
(*a*) To go mad
(*b*) To become nervous
(*c*) To become confused and over excited
(*d*) To lose the balance

25. By the skin of one's teeth
(*a*) Hardly (*b*) In time
(*c*) Hurriedly (*d*) Only just

26. To throw down the glove
(*a*) To resort to wrong tactics
(*b*) To give a challenge
(*c*) To accept defeat
(*d*) To reject the prize

27. To be in abeyance
(*a*) To be in trouble
(*b*) Dual minded
(*c*) In a fighting mood
(*d*) In suspense

28. To cast pearls before a swine
(*a*) To spend recklessly
(*b*) To spend a lot of money on the unkeep of domestic hogs
(*c*) To waste money over trifles
(*d*) To offer to a person a thing which he cannot appreciate
(C.I.C.A.A.O. 1990)

29. A chip off the old block
(*a*) A piece of wood
(*b*) An old friend
(*c*) Characteristics of one's ancestors
(*d*) A good bargain

30. To smell a rat
(*a*) To detect bad smell
(*b*) To misunderstand
(*c*) To suspect a trick or deceit
(*d*) To see hidden meaning

31. To take people by storm
(*a*) To put people in utter surprise
(*b*) To captivate them unexpectedly
(*c*) To exploit people's agitation
(*d*) To bring out something sensational attracting people's attention

32. To throw up the sponge
(*a*) To surrender or give up a contest
(*b*) To offer a challenge
(*c*) To become utterly disappointed
(*d*) To maintain grit and enthusiasm until the end

33. Harp on
(*a*) To comment (*b*) To criticise
(*c*) To keep on talking
(*d*) To keep on insulting

34. To catch somebody on the hop
(*a*) To give someone a surprise
(*b*) To catch somebody off guard
(*c*) To stand in the way of someone
(*d*) To catch somebody suddenly

35. To spill the beans
(*a*) To reveal secret information
(*b*) To misbehave
(*c*) To keep secrets
(*d*) To talk irrelevant

36. To bring one's eggs to a bad market
(*a*) To face a humiliating situation
(*b*) To bring one's commodities to a market where there is no demand for them
(*c*) To show one's talents before audience which is incapable of appreciating them
(*d*) To fail in one's plans because one goes to the wrong people for help
(S.B.I.P.O. 1984)

37. To hit below the belt
(*a*) To work confidentially

(*b*) To harm unfairly
(*c*) To strike at the exact position
(*d*) To hit the correct mark

38. To get cold feet
(*a*) To run for life (*b*) To be afraid
(*c*) To fall sick
(*d*) To become discourteous

39. To take a leap in the dark
(*a*) To take risk
(*b*) To hazard one self
(*c*) To do a task secretly
(*d*) To do a hazardous thing without any idea of the result

40. To give/get the bird **(M.B.A. 1993)**
(*a*) To get the awaited
(*b*) To have good luck
(*c*) To send away
(*d*) To get the impossible

41. To be at daggers drawn
(*a*) To be frightened
(*b*) To be ready to face danger
(*c*) To threaten one
(*d*) To be bitter enemy

42. To turn up one's nose at a thing
(*a*) To show eagerness to have something
(*b*) To show indifference
(*c*) To treat it with contemptuous dislike or disgust
(*d*) To start to grapple with it

43. To save one's face
(*a*) To hide oneself
(*b*) To oppose
(*c*) To evade disgrace
(*d*) To say plainly

44. To split hours
(*a*) To sidetrack the issue
(*b*) To quarrel over trifles
(*c*) To indulge in over-refined arguments
(*d*) To find faults with others

45. To wash one's dirty linen in public
(*a*) To criticise one's nature in public
(*b*) To quarrel in the open
(*c*) To do some ugly work in public
(*d*) To discuss dirty and scandalous matters of personal nature in the presence of strangers

46. A lady's man
(*a*) A woman-tailor
(*b*) A lover of woman company
(*c*) A man working as per a lady's directions
(*d*) A timid husband

47. To throw dust in one's eyes
(*a*) To show false things
(*b*) To make blind
(*c*) To harm someone (*d*) To deceive

48. To be rolling in money
(*a*) Wasting a lot of money
(*b*) Very rich
(*c*) Borrowing money liberally
(*d*) Spending more than his income

49. To get into hot waters
(*a*) To be impatient
(*b*) To suffer a huge financial loss
(*c*) To get into trouble
(*d*) To be in a confused state of mind

50. Will o' the wisp **(G.I.C.A.A.O. 1993)**
(*a*) Anything which eludes or deceives
(*b*) To act in a childish way
(*c*) To act in a foolish way
(*d*) To have desires unbacked by efforts

ANSWERS

1. (*d*)	2. (*c*)	3. (*d*)	4. (*a*)	5. (*b*)	6. (*b*)	7. (*c*)	8. (*b*)	9. (*d*)	10. (*a*)
11. (*b*)	12. (*a*)	13. (*c*)	14. (*c*)	15. (*b*)	16. (*b*)	17. (*b*)	18. (*d*)	19. (*c*)	20. (*a*)
21. (*d*)	22. (*b*)	23. (*b*)	24. (*c*)	25. (*d*)	26. (*b*)	27. (*d*)	28. (*d*)	29. (*c*)	30. (*c*)
31. (*b*)	32. (*a*)	33. (*c*)	34. (*b*)	35. (*a*)	36. (*d*)	37. (*b*)	38. (*b*)	39. (*d*)	40. (*c*)
41. (*d*)	42. (*c*)	43. (*c*)	44. (*c*)	45. (*d*)	46. (*b*)	47. (*d*)	48. (*b*)	49. (*c*)	50. (*a*)

PRACTICE SET 2

Directions : ***Each of the following idioms is followed by some alternatives. Choose the one which best expresses its meaning.***

1. To get into a scrape
(*a*) To get into a muddle
(*b*) To find oneself in an awkward predicament
(*c*) To get into irritating circumstances
(*d*) To be trapped in a conspiracy

2. To fly off the handle **(S.B.I.P.O. 1984)**
(*a*) To take off (*b*) To be indifferent
(*c*) To dislocate
(*d*) To lose one's temper

3. To read between the lines
(*a*) To concentrate (*b*) To read carefully
(*c*) To suspect
(*d*) To grasp the hidden meaning

4. To blaze trail
(*a*) To set on fire
(*b*) To be annoyed
(*c*) To vehemently oppose
(*d*) To inititate work in a movement

5. To be lost in the cloud
(*a*) To meet with one's death
(*b*) To be perplexed
(*c*) To be concealed from view
(*d*) To find oneself in a very uncomfortable position

6. To flog a dead horse
(*a*) To act in a foolish way
(*b*) To waste one's efforts
(*c*) To revive interest in an old subject
(*d*) To revive old memories

7. Hush money
(*a*) Money overdue
(*b*) Easy money
(*c*) Money earned by wrong means
(*d*) Bribe paid to secure silence

8. To pay one back in the same coin
(*a*) To provoke a person to quarrel
(*b*) To offer another polite attention
(*c*) To retaliate
(*d*) To give a word of encouragement or praise to another

9. A tall order
(*a*) A task difficult to perform
(*b*) A big problem
(*c*) A royal summon (*d*) A big demand

10. To draw a bead upon
(*a*) To make prayers
(*b*) To cause hindrance in work
(*c*) To count the benefits
(*d*) To take aim at

11. To turn the tables
(*a*) To defeat (*b*) To oppose
(*c*) To create chaos
(*d*) To change the sorry scheme
(*e*) To change completely the position of disadvantage

12. To keep the ball rolling
(*a*) To earn more and more
(*b*) To work constantly
(*c*) To keep the conversation going
(*d*) To make the best use of

(Bank P.O. 1988)

13. All and sundry
(*a*) Greater share (*b*) All of a sudden
(*c*) Completion of work
(*d*) Everyone without distinction

14. To worship the rising sun
(*a*) To honour a man who is coming into office
(*b*) To honour the promising people
(*c*) To indulge in flattery
(*d*) To welcome the coming events

15. To disabuse one's mind
(*a*) To conceal something
(*b*) To remove a misapprehension
(*c*) To banish from one's mind a thought
(*d*) To proceed cautiously so as to avoid risks and dangers

16. A storm in a teacup
(*a*) Unexpected event
(*b*) A danger signal
(*c*) Much excitement over something trivial
(*d*) A great noise

17. To play fast and loose
(*a*) To beguile others
(*b*) To be winning sometimes and losing at other times
(*c*) To play with someone's feelings
(*d*) To play tricks

18. To tempt providence
(*a*) To invite punishment
(*b*) To achieve a fortune
(*c*) To take reckless risks
(*d*) To have God's favour

19. To haul over the coals
(*a*) To put hand in a wrong task
(*b*) To throw into the fire
(*c*) To put to task
(*d*) To say the wrong words

20. To put the cart before the horse
(*a*) To offer a person what he cannot eat
(*b*) To force a person to do something
(*c*) To raise obstacles
(*d*) To reverse the natural order of things

21. To accept the Gauntlet
(*a*) To accept defeat
(*b*) To accept a challenge
(*c*) To suffer humiliation
(*d*) To accept an honour

22. To give currency
(*a*) To bestow importance
(*b*) To misinterpret
(*c*) To make publicly known
(*d*) To originate

23. French leave
(*a*) Long absence
(*b*) Leave on the pretext of illness
(*c*) Casual leave
(*d*) Absence without permission

24. Castles in the air
(*a*) Romantic designs
(*b*) Perfect plans

(c) Ideal projects
(d) Fanciful schemes
(e) Visionary projects

25. To have brush with **(Railways, 1995)**
(a) To start painting
(b) To have good and pleasing terms
(c) To be impressed
(d) To have a slight encounter

26. To lose face
(a) To look angry (b) To be humiliated
(c) To be helpless (d) To look vacant

27. To turn the other cheek
(a) To sulk and suffer
(b) To respond to violence with violence
(c) To respond to violence with non-violence
(d) To be indifferent to peace overtures

28. To pull one's socks up
(a) To prepare (b) To try hard
(c) To get ready (d) To depart

29. To bite one's lips
(a) To be angry (b) To feel sorry
(c) To have doubt
(d) To laugh at others

30. Within An Ace of
(a) Within one's reach
(b) Very near
(c) Within the hitting range
(d) Narrowly

31. Dog in the manger **(G.I.C.A.A.O. 1990)**
(a) An undersized bull almost the shape of a dog
(b) A dog that has no kennel of its own
(c) A person who puts himself in difficulties on account of other people
(d) A person who prevents others from enjoying something useless to himself

32. To blow hot and cold
(a) Changing weather
(b) To be untrustworthy
(c) To be inconsistent
(d) To be rich and poor frequently

33. To set the people by ears
(a) To box the people
(b) To insult and disgrace the people
(c) To punish heavily
(d) To excite people to a quarrel

34. To give chapter and verse for a thing
(a) To produce the proof of something
(b) To eulogize the qualities of a thing
(c) To make publicity of a thing
(d) To attach artificial value to a thing

35. To beggars' description
(a) A poor statement
(b) To describe things without care
(c) Beyond one's power to describe adequately
(d) None of these

36. To plough the sands
(a) To work hard to achieve one's aim
(b) To afford hope or ground for expecting a good result
(c) To busy oneself in a way which cannot lead to any profitable result
(d) To advance one's position in life

37. Foar in the mouth
(a) Bitten by a snake
(b) To reveal the secret
(c) To be furious
(d) To be in the exteme hatred

38. To take umbrage
(a) To feel depressed
(b) To be offended
(c) To be satisfied
(d) To be pleased

39. Something up one's sleeve
(a) A grand idea (b) A secret plan
(c) A profitable plan
(d) Something important
(Assistant Grade, 1994)

40. Adam's alc
(a) Grace (b) Pleasure
(c) Water (d) Wine

41. To draw the long bow
(a) To over-estimate oneself
(b) To put up high demands
(c) To demand a very high price
(d) To make an exaggerated statement

42. To hit the jackpot
(a) To gamble
(b) To make money unexpectedly
(c) To inherit money
(d) To become bankrupt

43. Tall order
(a) Simple (b) Difficult
(c) Customary (d) Too much

44. To drink like a fish
(a) To drink little (b) To drink alone
(c) To be a drunkard
(d) To drink in the company of others

45. To fight to the bitter end
(a) To fight with poison-tipped arrows
(b) To fight to the last point of enemy position
(c) To die fighting
(d) To carry on a contest regardless of consequences

46. To give a false colouring
(a) To misrepresent
(b) To submit the false report
(c) To be dishonest
(d) To conceal the facts

47. A red letter day
(*a*) An important day
(*b*) An auspicious day
(*c*) A dangerous day
(*d*) An unimportant day

48. Queer somebody's pitch
(*a*) Upset one's plan (*b*) Reprimand him
(*c*) Check him (*d*) Work him up

49. To make the grade
(*a*) To fail in a task
(*b*) To get good marks in an examination
(*c*) To come out successful
(*d*) To make good one's previous loss

50. To be up and doing
(*a*) To recover from illness
(*b*) To be actively engaged
(*c*) To progress satisfactorily
(*d*) To be expressive and explicit

ANSWERS

1. (*b*)	2. (*d*)	3. (*d*)	4. (*d*)	5. (*b*)	6. (*b*)	7. (*d*)	8. (*c*)	9. (*a*)	10. (*d*)
11. (*d*)	12. (*c*)	13. (*d*)	14. (*a*)	15. (*b*)	16. (*c*)	17. (*d*)	18. (*c*)	19. (*c*)	20. (*d*)
21. (*b*)	22. (*c*)	23. (*d*)	24. (*e*)	25. (*d*)	26. (*b*)	27. (*c*)	28. (*b*)	29. (*a*)	30. (*d*)
31. (*d*)	32. (*c*)	33. (*d*)	34. (*a*)	35. (*c*)	36. (*c*)	37. (*d*)	38. (*b*)	39. (*b*)	40. (*c*)
41. (*d*)	42. (*b*)	43. (*d*)	44. (*c*)	45. (*d*)	46. (*a*)	47. (*a*)	48. (*a*)	49. (*c*)	50. (*b*)

PRACTICE SET 3

Directions : *In each of the following questions, choose the alternative which best expresses the meaning of the idiom printed in bold.*

1. To see eye to eye with
(*a*) To agree (*b*) To stare fixedly
(*c*) To be angry (*d*) To take revenge

2. A jaundiced eye
(*a*) Jealousy (*b*) A generous view
(*c*) Angry (*d*) Prejudice

3. To see red
(*a*) To be very angry
(*b*) To victimise someone
(*c*) To find fault with
(*d*) To criticise others

4. To push somebody to the wall
(*a*) To defeat him
(*b*) To humiliate him
(*c*) To heckle him
(*d*) To knock him down

5. To be in two minds
(*a*) To be dominated by someone else
(*b*) To be uncertain
(*c*) To work on somebody else's advice
(*d*) To be in a critical state

6. Leave one to sink or swim
(*a*) To be in a dilemma
(*b*) To leave to one's fate
(*c*) To put one in difficulty
(*d*) Not to help one

7. To rip up old sores
(*a*) To revive a quarrel which was almost forgotten
(*b*) To censure someone in strong terms
(*c*) To strain one's thoughts to the most
(*d*) To preserve oneself from harm

8. A square peg in a round hole
(*a*) An impossible task
(*b*) A scheme that never works
(*c*) A person unsuited to the position he fills
(*d*) None of these

9. To carry off the bell
(*a*) To call others for help
(*b*) To bag the first position
(*c*) To steal all wealth and flee
(*d*) To trouble others

10. To live in clover
(*a*) To live in great comfort and luxury
(*b*) To live a carefree life
(*c*) To be surrounded by cares and worries
(*d*) To live in great difficulty

11. Pin-money
(*a*) Bribery
(*b*) Money paid for compensation
(*c*) Alimony
(*d*) Allowance made to a lady for her expenses

12. To keep the wolf away from the door
(*a*) To keep away from extreme poverty
(*b*) To keep off an unwanted and undesirable person
(*c*) To keep alive
(*d*) To hold the difficulties and dangers in check **(Railways, 1995)**

13. Get down to brass tacks
(*a*) Start unravelling the mystery

(*b*) Begin to discuss secret matters
(*c*) Begin to talk in plain, straight forward terms
(*d*) Get into the thick of a problem

14. To show the white feather
(*a*) To show signs of cowardice
(*b*) To seek peace
(*c*) To show arrogance
(*d*) To become polite

15. To leave no avenue unexplored
(*a*) To call in question
(*b*) To roam about
(*c*) To try every source
(*d*) To depend on

16. Spick and span
(*a*) Neat and clean (*b*) Outspoken
(*c*) A ready-made thing
(*d*) Garrulous

17. To take the wind out of another's sails **(I.E.S. 1985)**
(*a*) To manouevre to mislead another on the high seas
(*b*) To cause harm to another
(*c*) To defeat the motives of another
(*d*) To anticipate another and to gain advantage over him

18. To carry the coal to newcastle
(*a*) To work hard (*b*) To finish a job
(*c*) To do unnecessary things
(*d*) To do menial jobs

19. To turn the cover
(*a*) To take a new way of life
(*b*) To work hard
(*c*) To pass the crises
(*d*) To hide the reality

20. In double-quick time
(*a*) Steadily (*b*) Very quickly
(*c*) Gradually (*d*) Much time

21. The pros and cons **(Bank P.O. 1992)**
(*a*) For and aginst a thing
(*b*) Foul and fair
(*c*) Good and evil
(*d*) Former and latter

22. A sop to cerberus
(*a*) Bribery (*b*) Hush money
(*c*) Ransom to an enemy
(*d*) Money for compensation

23. To give one a long rope
(*a*) To speak ill of
(*b*) To get into trouble
(*c*) To dismiss
(*d*) To allow a man to continue his mistakes or crimes

24. To hit the nail on the head
(*a*) To hit the target
(*b*) To catch someone napping
(*c*) To guess right
(*d*) To settle the old score

25. A baker's dozen
(*a*) Twelve (*b*) Charity
(*c*) Thirteen (*d*) Allowance

26. To have full hands
(*a*) To be fully occupied
(*b*) To be rich
(*c*) To be in lot of troubles
(*d*) To lead an easy life

27. To run amuck
(*a*) To run a race
(*b*) To run about in frenzy
(*c*) To feel exhausted
(*d*) To run to somebody's help

28. A bull in a china shop
(*a*) A person who is very ugly but loves the beautiful things of life
(*b*) A person who takes a sadistic delight in harming innocent people
(*c*) A person who becomes too excited where no excitment is warranted
(*d*) A person who is rough and clumsy where skill and care are required
(G.I.C.A.A.O. 1990)

29. By fair means or foul
(*a*) Without using common sense
(*b*) Without difficulty
(*c*) In any way, honest or dishonest
(*d*) Having been instigated

30. To look down one's nose at
(*a*) To backbite (*b*) To show anger
(*c*) To insult in the presence of others
(*d*) To regard with half-hidden displeasure or contempt

31. Hard-pressed **(L.I.C.A.A.O. 1992)**
(*a*) Bewildered (*b*) Insulted
(*c*) Hard discipline (*d*) In difficulties

32. To be at one's finger's end
(*a*) To be hopeless
(*b*) To be highly perplexed
(*c*) To be completely conversant with
(*d*) To count things

33. To pull strings
(*a*) To exert hidden influence
(*b*) To tease someone
(*c*) To speed up
(*d*) To start something

34. A green horn
(*a*) An envious lady (*b*) A trainee
(*c*) An inexperienced man
(*d*) A soft-hearted man

35. To be old as the hills
(*a*) To be very ancient
(*b*) To be wise and learned
(*c*) To be old but foolish
(*d*) Not being worth the age

36. To look sharp
(*a*) To concentrate (*b*) To speak roughly
(*c*) To be attentive and active

(d) To be quick

37. To show one's teeth

(a) To ridicule (b) To face difficulties

(c) To adopt a threatening attitude

(d) To be humble

38. To pour oil in troubled water

(a) To foment trouble

(b) To add to the trouble

(c) To instigate

(d) To calm a quarrel with soothing words **(Railways, 1992)**

39. To play on a fiddle

(a) To play upon a musical instrument

(b) To play an important role

(c) To be busy over trifles

(d) To be busy over important matter

40. To mind one's P's and Q's

(a) To be cautious

(b) To be accurate and precise

(c) To be careful of one's accounts

(d) To be careful of one's personality

41. At one's beck and call

(a) Enjoying oneself without caring for others

(b) To be always at one's service

(c) To be under one's subjugation

(d) To be in an advantageous position

42. Swan-song

(a) Music as sweet as a song of birds

(b) A melodious song in praise of someone

(c) Praise of a woman by her lover

(d) Last work of a poet or musician before death

43. To play to the gallery

(a) To work hard to achieve the best

(b) Trying to get appreciation from least intelligent people

(c) Use wrong means to achieve success

(d) To be able to do a work easily

44. To break the ice

(a) To start quarreling

(b) To end the hostility

(c) To start a conversation

(d) To end up partnership

45. To oil the knocker

(a) To instigate a person to do a job

(b) To do a work with increased pace

(c) To tip the office-boy

(d) To revive old enmity

46. To cut the crackle

(a) To humiliate

(b) To annoy someone

(c) To act in a friendly way

(d) To stop talking and start

47. To take somebody for a ride

(a) To provide entertainment

(b) To keep company

(c) To deceive or humiliate him

(d) To exploit a person

48. To cool one's heels **(M.B.A. 1990)**

(a) To rest for sometime

(b) To give no importance to someone

(c) To remain in a comfortable position

(d) To be kept waiting for sometime

49. By the rule of thumb

(a) By the use of force

(b) By the use of trickery

(c) By cheating and deception

(d) By practical experience which is rather rough

50. A fool's errand

(a) A blunder

(b) An impossible task

(c) A useless undertaking

(d) None of these

ANSWERS

1. (a)	2. (d)	3. (c)	4. (a)	5. (b)	6. (d)	7. (a)	8. (c)	9. (b)	10. (a)
11. (d)	12. (a)	13. (c)	14. (a)	15. (c)	16. (a)	17. (d)	18. (c)	19. (c)	20. (b)
21. (a)	22. (c)	23. (d)	24. (c)	25. (c)	26. (a)	27. (b)	28. (d)	29. (c)	30. (d)
31. (d)	32. (c)	33. (a)	34. (c)	35. (a)	36. (d)	37. (c)	38. (d)	39. (c)	40. (b)
41. (b)	42. (d)	43. (b)	44. (c)	45. (c)	46. (d)	47. (c)	48. (d)	49. (d)	50. (c)

PRACTICE SET 4

Directions : *In each of the following questions, choose the alternative which best expresses the meaning of the idiom/phrase printed in bold type.*

1. **To put somebody in his place**
(*a*) To turn him out
(*b*) To honour him
(*c*) To give him due respect
(*d*) To make him humble

2. **To talk shop**
(*a*) To talk nonsense
(*b*) To talk reasonably
(*c*) To talk about business or professional affairs
(*d*) To abuse someone

3. **To keep one's head above water**
(*a*) To be cautious
(*b*) To keep out of debt
(*c*) To remain aloof
(*d*) None of these

4. **To go at each other hammer and tongs**
(*a*) To fight with weapons
(*b*) To argue noisly
(*c*) To hug each other
(*d*) To go crazy about meeting each other

5. **To live fast**
(*a*) To lead a life of dissipation
(*b*) To accomplish a purpose
(*c*) To do a task hurriedly
(*d*) To use up one's income as fast as it comes in

6. **Once in a blue moon**
(*a*) Once in a month
(*b*) Bi-weekly
(*c*) On rare occasions
(*d*) Every now and then

7. **To hold a brief for**
(*a*) To help someone
(*b*) To do someone a favour.
(*c*) To stay on for a brief period
(*d*) To defend someone

8. **To hold somebody to ransom**
(*a*) To keep captive and demand concession
(*b*) To humiliate somebody
(*c*) To offer bribe
(*d*) To blackmail and extract money

9. **To hit the jackpot**
(*a*) To gamble
(*b*) To get an unexpected victory
(*c*) To be wealthy
(*d*) To make money unexpectedly

10. **To let the cat out of the bag**
(*a*) To give latitude
(*b*) To show compassion
(*c*) To miss a golden opportunity
(*d*) To tell a secret without intending to do so

11. **To pay off old scores**
(*a*) To have one's revenge
(*b*) To settle a dispute
(*c*) To repay the old loan
(*d*) None of these

12. **A cock-and-bull story**
(*a*) A true story
(*b*) A children's story
(*c*) A story of animals
(*d*) A foolish and concocted story

13. **To beat the air**
(*a*) To make frantic efforts
(*b*) To act foolishly
(*c*) To make efforts that are useless or vain
(*d*) To make every possible effort

14. **To be a good Samaritan**
(*a*) To be law-abiding
(*b*) A wise person
(*c*) A religious person
(*d*) A genuinely charitable person

15. **To take a leaf out of somebody's book**
(*a*) To take him as a model
(*b*) To steal something valuable
(*c*) To follow the dictates of someone
(*d*) To conform to other's standard

16. **To set the thames on fire**
(*a*) To do something remarkable
(*b*) To try to do the impossible
(*c*) To burn something to ashes
(*d*) To fling ironical remarks

17. **To cast pearls before a swine**
(*a*) To offer someone a thing which he cannot appreciate
(*b*) To bring something good before the eyes of a greedy person

(c) To spend recklessly on a useless fellow
(d) To indulge in fruitless endeavours

18. To bear the palm
(a) To win
(b) To accept a challenge
(c) To accept defeat
(d) To endure something

19. To change colour
(a) To change appearance
(b) To shift allegiance to
(c) To favour the wrong person
(d) None of these

20. To cut the Gordian knot
(a) To solve a difficult problem
(b) To be victorious
(c) To break ties with someone
(d) To defeat a powerful person

21. To wrangle over an ass's shadow
(a) To act in a foolish way
(b) To do something funny
(c) To quarrel over trifles
(d) To quarrel over the possession of an ass

22. To have one's heart in one's boots
(a) To be deeply depressed
(b) To be frightened
(c) To get angry
(d) To keep a secret

23. To strike one's colours
(a) To fight vigorously
(b) To work hard
(c) To surrender
(d) To make a rude gesture

24. To cry wolf
(a) To grieve over something which cannot be recovered
(b) To cry from grief, inconsolably
(c) To raise a false alarm
(d) To announce to one and all

25. To give one's ears
(a) To make almost any sacrifice
(b) To listen carefully
(c) To refuse to listen
(d) To incite someone

26. To hang up one's hat
(a) To challenge
(b) To surrender
(c) To postpone
(d) To make oneself comfortable in another person's home

27. To get the hang of a thing
(a) To know a secret
(b) To understand the meaning of it
(c) To find the cause of something
(d) None of these

28. To make a shot
(a) To retaliate
(b) To hit someone
(c) To make a guess
(d) To achieve one's objective

29. A man of weight
(a) A fat person
(b) To truthful and trustworthy man
(c) A man of importance
(d) A notorious man

30. Pell-mell
(a) In hurried disorder
(b) Gaiety and excitement
(c) Extremely worried
(d) None of these

31. To put one on one's mettle
(a) To rouse one to do one's best
(b) To ruin somebody
(c) To discourage a person
(d) To incite a person to fight

32. To ride hell for Leather
(a) To ride with furious speed
(b) To adopt flase means to succeed
(c) To work hard for a small accomplishment
(d) To earn money by all means

33. To speak daggers
(a) To abuse someone
(b) To indulge in voracious talks
(c) To speak to a person with hostility
(d) None of these

34. Be in the mire
(a) Be under debt
(b) Be in love
(c) Be in difficulties
(d) Be uneasy

35. To give a rap on the knuckles
(a) To eulogise
(b) To chatise
(c) To condemn
(d) To rebuke

ANSWERS

1. (*d*)	**2.** (*c*)	**3.** (*b*)	**4.** (*b*)	**5.** (*a*)	**6.** (*c*)	**7.** (*d*)	**8.** (*a*)	**9.** (*b*)	**10.** (*d*)
11. (*b*)	**12.** (*d*)	**13.** (*c*)	**14.** (*d*)	**15.** (*a*)	**16.** (*b*)	**17.** (*a*)	**18.** (*a*)	**19.** (*b*)	**20.** (*a*)
21. (*c*)	**22.** (*a*)	**23.** (*c*)	**24.** (*c*)	**25.** (*a*)	**26.** (*d*)	**27.** (*b*)	**28.** (*c*)	**29.** (*c*)	**30.** (*a*)
31. (*a*)	**32.** (*a*)	**33.** (*c*)	**34.** (*c*)	**35.** (*d*)					

TYPE 2 : Choosing the correct meaning of an idiom as used in a sentence

In this type of questions, a sentence is given in which an idiom has been italicised. It is followed by four or five alternatives. The candidate is required to choose that alternative which best expresses the meaning of the italicised idiom.

Directions : ***Choose the correct meaning of the italicised idiom in the following sentences :***

Example 1 : Tell me the *sum and substance* of your pleadings.

(*a*) summary (*b*) explanation (*c*) result (*d*) effect

Solution : The idiom 'sum and substance' means 'the summary". Hence, the answer is (*a*).

Example 2 : In summer, woollen goods are *a drug in the market.*

(*a*) rarely available (*b*) worthless products
(*c*) commodities not in demand (*d*) available at cheap rates

Solution : The idiom 'a drug in the market' means something which is not in demand.

Hence, the answer is (*c*).

PRACTICE SET 5

Directions : ***In each of the following questions, some alternatives are suggested for the idiom/phrase in italic in the sentence. Choose the one which best expresses the meaning of the idiom/phrase in italics.***

1. The boy *turned a deaf ear* to the pleadings of all his well--wishers.
(*a*) listened carefully
(*b*) was deadly opposed
(*c*) posed indifference
(*d*) did not pay any attention
(Asstt. Grade, 1992)

2. The *mealy–mouthed* politician succeeded in influencing the voters
(*a*) ill--tempered (*b*) soft--tongued
(*c*) cunning (*d*) ambitious

3. It is a *moot point* whether we should stop work or struggle on.
(*a*) all too clear (*b*) a fixed belief
(*c*) a burning question
(*d*) a debatable point

4. We should *give a wide berth* to bad characters. **(Railways, 1995)**
(*a*) keep away from
(*b*) publicly condemn
(*c*) give publicly to
(*d*) not sympathise with

5. The parliamentary inquiry into the Bofors deal has not *brought to light* any startling facts.
(*a*) proved (*b*) highlighted
(*c*) disclosed (*d*) probed

6. He works *by fits and starts.*
(*a*) consistently (*b*) irregularly
(*c*) in high spirits (*d*) enthusiastically

7. Sumit had to look *high and low* before he could find his scooter key. **(C.B.I. 1993)**
(*a*) nowhere (*b*) always
(*c*) everywhere (*d*) somewhere

8. *To all intents and pruposes* he is a good man.
(*a*) Finally (*b*) Practically
(*c*) Above all (*d*) In practice
(*c*) To censure someone in strong terms

9. I am ambitious and never want to *rest on my laurels.*
(*a*) be dissatisfied (*b*) be satisfied
(*c*) be complacent (*d*) be good

(c) be complacent (d) be good

10. The casting vote of the chairman *clinched the issue.*
(a) closed (b) decided
(c) finished (d) started

11. It was such a messy affair but Manish somehow managed to *wash his hands of* the entire affair.
(a) subdue
(b) twist the facts of
(c) prove himself innocent in
(d) disclaim responsibility

12. He *threw cold water over* the project that the secretary had prepared.
(a) encouraged (b) discouraged
(c) cleared (d) rejected

13. He is a plain, simple and sincere man. He will always *call a spade a spade.*
(a) say something to be taken seriously
(b) desist from making controversial statement
(c) find meaning or purpose in your action
(d) avoid controversial situations
(e) be outspoken in language
(Bank P.O. 1993, 96)

14. He is *at loggerheads* with his assistants about the management of the concern.
(a) differing strongly
(b) in agreement
(c) in confusion (d) undecided

15. She rejected his proposal of marriage *point–blank.* **(Clerks' Grade, 1993)**
(a) directly (b) pointedly
(c) abruptly (d) briefly

16. Don't stick *your neck out.*
(a) interfere (b) look outside
(c) invite trouble unnecessarily
(d) move

17. The aroma from the kitchen *makes my mouth water.*
(a) makes me sick (b) makes me giddy
(c) makes me vomit
(d) stimulates my appetite

18. We should guard against our *green–eyed* friends. **(Translators' Exam, 1994)**
(a) rich (b) jealous
(c) handsome (d) enthusiastic

19. This place affords a *bird's eye view* of the green valley below.
(a) beautiful view (b) general view
(c) narrow view (d) ugly view

20. I won't mind even if he *goes to dogs.*
(a) goes mad (b) is insulted
(c) is ruined (d) becomes brutal

21. It is difficult to *keep a level head* in these days of mounting prices.
(a) remain cool and composed
(b) eke out existence
(c) make both ends meet
(d) maintain standard of living
(C.B.I. 1995)

22. The doctor says the patient has *turned the corner.*
(a) completely recovered
(b) become worse
(c) passed the crisis
(d) died

23. He is in the habit of *fishing in troubled waters.*
(a) putting others in trouble
(b) indulging in evil conspirancies
(c) aggravating the situation
(d) taking advantage of troubled conditions for personal profit

24. At a party, he is always *in high spirits.*
(a) talkative (b) cheerful
(c) drunk (d) uncontrollable
(N.D.A. 1991)

25. Things are progressing well–dont's do anything *to rock the boat.*
(a) create difficulties
(b) conspire against
(c) upset the balance
(d) agitate against

26. It *goes to his heart* to see so much misery.
(a) influences him
(b) touches him deeply
(c) makes him yield
(d) annoys him

27. Rahul fought *tooth and nail* to save his company. **(I. Tax & Central Excise, 1994)**
(a) with weapons
(b) as best as he could
(c) using unfair means
(d) with strength and fury

28. Mr. Roy is known as a *shop–lifter* in the city commercial centre.
(a) daily visitor
(b) buyer of all new things
(c) smuggler
(d) a thief in guise of customer

29. The robbery was committed *in the wee hours of the day.*
(a) after midnight (b) at dawn
(c) at noontime (d) in the evening

30. Harassed by repeated acts of injustice, he decided to *put his foot down.*
(a) resign (b) not to yield
(c) withdraw
(d) accept the proposal unconditionally
(S.B.I. P.O. 1994)

31. Mrs. Khanna has been *in the blues* for the last several weeks.
(a) unwell (b) lonely
(c) penniless (d) depressed

32. The popularity of the yesteryears' superstar is *on the wane.*
(*a*) growing more (*b*) at its peak
(*c*) growing less (*d*) at rock–bottom
(Section officers, 1993)

33. His father advised him to be *fair and square* in his dealings lest he should fall into trouble.
(*a*) considerate (*b*) upright
(*c*) careful (*d*) polite

34. Rajeev achieved success by resorting to a *hole and corner* method.
(*a*) obscure (*b*) usual
(*c*) underhand (*d*) clever

35. He has made his mark in politics.
(*a*) attained notoriety
(*b*) ruined his wealth
(*c*) acquired wealth
(*d*) distinguised himself
(Stenographers' Exam, 1993)

36. Shweta might *scream blue murder,* but I feel Ritu should get the promotion since she is better qualified for the job.
(*a*) suffer from persecution complex
(*b*) try to prove herself as more suited to the job
(*c*) regard it as an act of partiality
(*d*) make a great deal of noise and object vehemently

37. At christmas, even the elderly fathers *paint the town red.* **(Central Excise, 1993)**
(*a*) indulge in rioting
(*b*) paint the houses red
(*c*) spill red wine
(*d*) have a lively time

38. In almost every party, my friend tries to *rule the roost.*
(*a*) to make friends (*b*) to domineer
(*c*) to remain aloof (*d*) to become popular

39. We have to *keep our fingers crossed* till the final result is declared.
(*a*) keep praying (*b*) feel suspicious
(*c*) wait expectantly (*d*) feel scared

40. The members of the group were *at odds* over the selection procedure.
(*a*) acting foolishly (*b*) in dispute
(*c*) unanimous
(*d*) behaving childishly
(Asistant Grade, 1995)

41. The young heir to his father's huge estate *made ducks and drakes* of his patrimony.
(*a*) made best use of
(*b*) took stock of
(*c*) squandered lavishly
(*d*) invested wisely

42. There is *no love lost* between the two neighbours. **(C.B.I. 1995)**
(*a*) close friendship (*b*) intense dislike
(*c*) a love-hate relationship
(*d*) cool indifference

43. He *rides the high horse* becasue of his high connection.
(*a*) is famous (*b*) talks flatteringly
(*c*) puts on airs (*d*) is prosperous

44. Whenever I meet him he *pulls a long face.*
(*a*) looks angry (*b*) looks cheerful
(*c*) looks gloomy (*d*) looks indifferent

45. The speaker's observations on the subject were *beside the mark.*
(*a*) correct (*b*) exaggerated
(*c*) incorrect (*d*) irrelevant

46. In parliament, every member can *have the floor* with the permission of the speaker.
(*a*) leave the house (*b*) make a speech
(*c*) raise an issue
(*d*) speak against his own party

47. The Chief Minister had the Inspector General of Police to *fill him in* on the behaviour of the arrested terrorists.
(*a*) probe into the cases against the terrorists
(*b*) take action against the terrorists
(*c*) inform him about the terrorists
(*d*) None of these

48. I did not mind what he was saying, he was only *talking through his hat.*
(*a*) talking insultingly
(*b*) talking irresponsibly
(*c*) talking ignorantly
(*d*) talking nonsense
(Assistant Grade, 1996)

49. I *sent him about his business* as I could stand his insolence no longer.
(*a*) broke the partnership with him
(*b*) requested him to bother someone else
(*c*) dismissed him peremptorily
(*d*) abused him heartily

50. He is a *person after my own heart.*
(*a*) an object of mockery
(*b*) an emotional man
(*c*) a happy-go-lucky fellow
(*d*) exactly to one's own liking

ANSWERS

1. (*d*)	**2.** (*c*)	**3.** (*d*)	**4.** (*a*)	**5.** (*c*)	**6.** (*b*)	**7.** (*c*)	**8.** (*b*)	**9.** (*c*)	**10.** (*b*)
11. (*d*)	**12.** (*b*)	**13.** (*e*)	**14.** (*a*)	**15.** (*b*)	**16.** (*c*)	**17.** (*d*)	**18.** (*b*)	**19.** (*b*)	**20.** (*c*)
21. (*a*)	**22.** (*c*)	**23.** (*d*)	**24.** (*b*)	**25.** (*c*)	**26.** (*b*)	**27.** (*d*)	**28.** (*d*)	**29.** (*b*)	**30.** (*b*)
31. (*d*)	**32.** (*c*)	**33.** (*b*)	**34.** (*c*)	**35.** (*d*)	**36.** (*d*)	**37.** (*d*)	**38.** (*b*)	**39.** (*c*)	**40.** (*b*)
41. (*c*)	**42.** (*b*)	**43.** (*c*)	**44.** (*d*)	**45.** (*d*)	**46.** (*c*)	**47.** (*c*)	**48.** (*d*)	**49.** (*c*)	**50.** (*d*)

PRACTICE SET 6

Directions : ***In each of the following questions, out of the given alternatives, choose the one which best expresses the meaning of the idiom/phrase in italics in the sentence.***

1. If you pass this difficult examination, it will be a *feather in your cap.*
(*a*) you will get a very good job
(*b*) you will feel proud of it
(*c*) your parents will be very happy
(*d*) you will get a scholarship for higher studies **(Bank P.O. 1993)**

2. It is clear that the ideas of both reformers *ran in the same groove.*
(*a*) promoted each other
(*b*) clashed with each other
(*c*) advanced in harmony
(*d*) moved in different directions

3. He is *a wolf in sheep's clothing.*
(*a*) scoundrel (*b*) rogue
(*c*) hypocrite (*d*) crook

4. He is in the habit of *chewing the cuds.*
(*a*) accusing others
(*b*) crying over spilt milk
(*c*) forgetting things
(*d*) to muse on **(Hotel Management, 1992)**

5. He felt ill *at ease* after receiving the letter from his son.
(*a*) disturbed (*b*) relieved
(*c*) embarrassed (*d*) sick

6. With regard to licensing policy, it is advisable for every state to *cut corners.*
(*a*) become lenient
(*b*) amend the existing rules
(*c*) exercise strict control
(*d*) simplify the procedure

7. If you *rub him the wrong way,* he is bound to react. **(Railways, 1995)**
(*a*) annoy him (*b*) abuse him
(*c*) flatter him (*d*) encourage him

8. He is in the habit of responding *at the drop of a hat.*
(*a*) thoughtfully (*b*) wisely
(*c*) without delay (*d*) foolishly

9. You cannot *throw dust into my eyes.*
(*a*) hurt me (*b*) abuse me
(*c*) terrify me (*d*) cheat me

10. There was opposition to the new policy by *the rank and file* of the Government.
(*a*) the majority
(*b*) the ordinary members
(*c*) the cabinet members
(*d*) the official machinery
(Stenographers' Exam, 1995)

11. The company has been handed over to new masters *lock, stock and barrel.*
(*a*) financially (*b*) partially
(*c*) completely (*d*) administratively

12. Dowry is a *burning question* of the day.
(*a*) a relevant problem
(*b*) a dying issue
(*c*) an irrelevant problem
(*d*) a widely debated issue
(Assistant Grade, 1994)

13. You must not *mince matters*; tell the truth.
(*a*) cut short
(*b*) keep secret
(*c*) tell with frankness
(*d*) not to tell the whole truth

14. The sailor found himself *between the devil and the deep sea.*
(*a*) lost in the deep ocean
(*b*) facing two challenges
(*c*) facing two equally bad alternatives
(*d*) confronting two opportunities

15. The hero of Naipaul's novel 'A House for Biswas', like modern young men, wishes *to paddle his own canoe.* **(C.B.I. 1995)**
(*a*) lead an independent life
(*b*) depend on himself
(*c*) make the best of his life
(*d*) have his own means of livelihood

16. I am afraid the two brothers are *at cross purposes.*
(*a*) quarrel with each other
(*b*) dislike each other
(*c*) are working against each other
(*d*) are misunderstanding each other

17. Our school is *within a stone's throw* of the railway station. **(G.I.C.A.A.O. 1990)**
(*a*) within a certain radius
(*b*) at a short distance
(*c*) within a definite circumference
(*d*) very far off

18. My mother is *in raptures* over her new stove.
(*a*) very enthusiastic
(*b*) working vigorously
(*c*) completely dissatisfied with
(*d*) extremely angry

19. It was *out of place* for him to talk on politics when the seminar was arragned to discuss recent trends in literature.
(*a*) foolish (*b*) strange
(*c*) inappropriate (*d*) odd

20. His voice *gets on my nerves.*
(*a*) makes me sad
(*b*) irritates me
(*c*) makes me ill
(*d*) pierces my eardrums
(Central Excise, 1994)

21. The police are used to seeing the *seamy side of life.*
(*a*) an adventurous life
(*b*) a life full of risks
(*c*) immoral aspects of society
(*d*) criminal society

22. Do not *add fuel to the fire.*
(*a*) create problem
(*b*) harass
(*c*) aggravate trouble
(*d*) calm down

23. Some people have a habit of *wearing their heart on their sleeve.* **(Bank P.O. 1996)**
(*a*) avoiding being friendly with others
(*b*) saying something which is not to be taken seriously
(*c*) exposing their innermost feelings to others
(*d*) wasting their time on unnecessary details

24. When I saw him in the morning, he looked *like a duck in a thunderstorm.*
(*a*) timid (*b*) peaceful
(*c*) distressed (*d*) indomitable

25. It was a *Herculean task* for me.
(*a*) work requiring great effort
(*b*) impossible task
(*c*) easy work
(*d*) an entirely new task

26. In everything that he does he has *an eye to the main chance.*
(*a*) he organises it well.
(*b*) he evinces interest only in big things.
(*c*) he does not leave things to chance.
(*d*) his object is to make money.

27. The sight of the accident *made my flesh creep.* **(Section Officers, 1993)**
(*a*) worried me (*b*) frightened me
(*c*) confused me (*d*) drew my attention

28. Manoj always *keeps himself to himself.*
(*a*) is selfish
(*b*) does not take sides
(*c*) is unsociable
(*d*) is too busy

29. She was received by her friends *with open arms.*
(*a*) indifferently (*b*) warmly
(*c*) casually (*d*) coldly

30. Kamal was left *high and dry* by his friends when he lost all his money.
(*a*) isolated (*b*) rejected
(*c*) wounded (*d*) depressed
(C.B.I. 1994)

31. This report *calls in question* all previous research on the subject.
(*a*) recalls (*b*) criticises
(*c*) challenges (*d*) takes note of

32. I am sure he *means business.*
(*a*) is earnest (*b*) is inquisitive
(*c*) is a trader
(*d*) is anxious to make profit

33. I just paid him a *left-handed compliment.* **(Clerks' Grade, 1993)**
(*a*) an honest (*b*) a well deserved
(*c*) an insincere (*d*) a flattering

34. *Once in a while* he might gamble a little.
(*a*) frequently (*b*) continually
(*c*) seldom (*d*) occasionally

35. I *stood my ground* inspite of many pressures.
(*a*) remained firm (*b*) was obstinate
(*c*) was prejudiced (*d*) felt shaky

36. The train was late and we had to *kick our heels.*
(*a*) fun fast (*b*) wait eagerly
(*c*) waste time (*d*) play some game

37. The party stalwarts have advised the President to *take it lying down* for a while. **(Asstt. Grade, 1996)**
(*a*) to show no reaction
(*b*) to take rest
(*c*) to be on the defensive
(*d*) to be cautious

38. His hard-earned money has *gone down the drain.*
(*a*) has been wasted

(b) has been spent
(c) has been collected
(d) has been looted

39. A movement for the world unity is *in the offing.* **(C.D.S. 1994)**
(a) at the end (b) about to start
(c) on decline (d) in the air

40. He has *designs on* that young girl.
(a) wants to rape
(b) desires to be alone with
(c) wants to cheat
(d) wants to be intimate with

41. The captain played with determination because the honour of the team was *at stake.*
(a) inevitable (b) at the top
(c) necessary (d) in danger

42. He is a *queer fish*, I have failed to understand him.
(a) funny person (b) sensitive person
(c) strange person
(d) quarrelsome person
(Stenographers' Exam, 1993)

43. Childhood and innocence lie *cheek by jowl.*
(a) together (b) one after another
(c) side by side (d) proportionately

44. He is really a *broken reed.*
(a) a frustrated man
(b) an unsuccessful person
(c) undependable
(d) one who has lost in business

45. No caring for the family, Devender wanted *to gather roses only.*
(a) wanted to paint a rosy picture of the past
(b) wanted to start business of roses
(c) wanted to make safe investment
(d) wanted to seek all the enjoyments of life
(e) desired to attain fame by hard work
(Bank P.O. 1994)

46. He knew she was dead but was completely *at sea* about the cause of her death.
(a) anxious (b) confused
(c) ignorant (d) certain

47. His most trusted friend proved to be *a snake in the grass.* **(Asstt. Grade, 1993)**
(a) cowardly and brutal
(b) an unreliable and deceitful person
(c) a hidden enemy
(d) low and mean

48. It was after a long time that the police was able *to lay* the thief *by the heels.*
(a) run fast after (b) play tricks on
(c) chase and capture
(d) arrest

49. None of this *hanky-panky*; please talk straight.
(a) indifference (b) jugglery
(c) diversification (d) obsession

50. The new C.M. *stuck his neck out* today and promised 10 kgs. free wheat a month for all rural families.
(a) extended help (b) took an oath
(c) caused embarrassment
(d) took a risk **(Central Excise, 1995)**

ANSWERS

1. (b)	**2.** (c)	**3.** (c)	**4.** (d)	**5.** (c)	**6.** (d)	**7.** (a)	**8.** (c)	**9.** (d)	**10.** (b)
11. (c)	**12.** (d)	**13.** (b)	**14.** (c)	**15.** (b)	**16.** (d)	**17.** (b)	**18.** (a)	**19.** (c)	**20.** (b)
21. (c)	**22.** (c)	**23.** (c)	**24.** (c)	**25.** (a)	**26.** (d)	**27.** (b)	**28.** (c)	**29.** (b)	**30.** (b)
31. (c)	**32.** (a)	**33.** (c)	**34.** (d)	**35.** (a)	**36.** (c)	**37.** (a)	**38.** (a)	**39.** (b)	**40.** (a)
41. (d)	**42.** (c)	**43.** (c)	**44.** (a)	**45.** (d)	**46.** (b)	**47.** (c)	**48.** (c)	**49.** (b)	**50.** (d)

PRACTICE SET 7

Directions : ***In each of the following questions, choose the alternative which best expresses the meaning of the idiom in italics.***

1. The involvement of teachers in the scheme of education proves to be a *mare's nest.*
(a) a false invention (b) a noble thing
(c) a successful idea (d) a timely step
(R.R.B. 1995)

2. I want none of your *back-chat.*
(a) impertinent remarks
(b) complaints
(c) trenchant criticism
(d) pleasing remarks

3. We must always *bear in mind* that only hard work leads to success.
(a) understand (b) remember

(*c*) forget (*d*) think

4. Pt. Nehru was *born with a silver spoon in his mouth.* **(Asstt. Grade, 1994)**
(*a*) born in a royal family
(*b*) born in a middle class family
(*c*) born in a family of nationalists
(*d*) born in a wealthy family

5. There was a job for me *to cut my teeth on.*
(*a*) to try (*b*) to gain experience
(*c*) to sharpen my wits
(*d*) to earn a decent salary

6. Inspite of his poverty, Ravi believed in *keeping up appearances.*
(*a*) showing indifference
(*b*) maintaining outward show
(*c*) showing good manners
(*d*) revealing the truth

7. It is evident from the minister's statement that *heads will roll.*
(*a*) government will change
(*b*) transfers will take place
(*c*) dismissals will occur
(*d*) heads of department will have to repent

8. He has such a nature that he must *have a finger in every pie.*
(*a*) do things with his own hands
(*b*) help everyone in need
(*c*) meddle in every affair
(*d*) dominate everybody else.

9. He *burnt his fingers* by interfering in his neighbour's affairs. **(G.I.C.A.A.O. 1990)**
(*a*) got rebuked
(*b*) got himself insulted
(*c*) burnt himself
(*d*) got himself into trouble

10. The present syllabus leaves very *little elbowroom* for teachers to be innovative.
(*a*) cause (*b*) possibility
(*c*) freedom (*d*) necessity

11. Most of the present day politicians have *an axe to grind.*
(*a*) have promises to fulfil
(*b*) have obstacles to face
(*c*) have personal end to serve
(*d*) None of these

12. When the police came, the thieves *took to their heels.*
(*a*) were taken by surprise
(*b*) took to flight
(*c*) took shelter in a tall building
(*d*) unconditionally surrendered
(*e*) opened indiscriminate fire
(Bank P.O. 1993, S.B.I.P.O. 1995)

13. The sworn enemies have decided to *bury the hatchet.*
(*a*) to help each other
(*b*) to avoid each other
(*c*) to make peace
(*d*) to become partners

14. He is a strange fellow. It is very difficult to deal with him ; it seems that he has *a bee in his bonnet.* **(S.B.I.P.O. 1995)**
(*a*) an achievement to be proud of
(*b*) an obsession about something
(*c*) to face problems as a result of his senseless actions
(*d*) peculiar habit of confusing others
(*e*) unreliable and inconsistent way of behaving

15. The politician was able to sway the mob with his *gift of the gab.*
(*a*) fluency of speech
(*b*) flattering words
(*c*) abundance of promises
(*d*) political foresight
(Translator's Exam, 1994)

16. Honesty is *at a discount*, where corruption is the rule.
(*a*) discouraged (*b*) rare
(*c*) undervalued (*d*) unknown

17. Akshay can *turn his hand* to anything.
(*a*) refuse to do (*b*) adapt himself to
(*c*) take advantage of
(*d*) find fault with

18. The speaker gave a *bird's eye view* of the political conditions in the country.
(*a*) a detailed presentation
(*b*) a biased view
(*c*) a general view (*d*) a personal view
(Section officers, 1993)

19. His best jokes *fell flat.*
(*a*) were not paid attention to
(*b*) had no effect
(*c*) became completely unnerved
(*d*) faced total failure

20. The detective *left no stone unturned* to trace the culprit.
(*a*) did very irrelevant things
(*b*) used all available means
(*c*) took no pains
(*d*) resorted to illegitimate practices
(S.B.I.P.O. 1994)

21. Having sold off his factory, Mr. Roy is now a *gentleman at large.*
(*a*) held in high esteem
(*b*) respected by every body
(*c*) has no serious occupation
(*d*) living comfortably

22. They sold their house because it was a real *white elephant.* **(C.B.I. 1994)**
(*a*) an expensive one
(*b*) a big one
(*c*) a useless one
(*d*) a rare find

23. After a lot of arguments over losses in the partnership firm, Aditya *put his cards on the table* to show Rasheed his sincerity.
(*a*) withdrew his partnership
(*b*) reserved his right
(*c*) concealed nothing
(*d*) sought pardon

24. It will be wise on your part *to let the bygones be bygones.*
(*a*) resist the past (*b*) ignore the past
(*c*) recollect the past
(*d*) revive the past **(Assistant Grade, 1992)**

25. He always says that he will help, but when it *comes to the crunch,* he does nothing.
(*a*) decisive moment
(*b*) confused situation
(*c*) difficult time
(*d*) troublesome moment

26. The boy had a *hair-breadth escape* from a street accident.
(*a*) lucky (*b*) easy
(*c*) narrow (*d*) quick
(I. Tax and Central Excise, 1994)

27. Despite being under debt, Amit still *keeps a good table.*
(*a*) keeps up an outward show of prosperity
(*b*) entertains his guests sumptuously
(*c*) helps his friends with money
(*d*) is lively and gay when his friends call

28. When he tells stories about himself, he is inclined *to draw the long bone.*
(*a*) get excited (*b*) exaggerate
(*c*) get emotional (*d*) understate
(C.B.I. 1995)

29. I am afraid he is *burning the candle* at both ends.
(*a*) putting in sustained effort
(*b*) working at night also
(*c*) working hard
(*d*) overtaxing his energies

30. He always *leads others up the garden path.*
(*a*) befools others
(*b*) advises others to their advantage
(*c*) deceives others
(*d*) worries others

31. The great warrior, Baji-Prabhu, *held the enemy at bay* but was killed in the end.
(*a*) prevented the enemy from coming too near
(*b*) did not allow the enemy to attack his position
(*c*) launched a counter attack after initial success
(*d*) retreated initially but launched a heavy attack afterwards
(*e*) made the enemy to run away
(Bank P.O. 1994)

32. The recent film 'Secular India' has tried *to keep the pot* of Muslim Women's Bill *boiling.*
(*a*) to earn enough support for
(*b*) to force the authorities to reconsider
(*c*) keep the controversy alive
(*d*) none of these

33. Inspite of the efforts of all peace loving people, world peace is still *a far cry.*
(*a*) an abstract ideal
(*b*) a long way off
(*c*) an impracticable idea
(*d*) out of reach **(Asstt. Grade, 1994)**

34. One should be prepared to get *a bolt from the blue* in life, but should not get unnerved by them
(*a*) sad experience (*b*) unexpected loss
(*c*) sudden shock (*d*) depreciation

35. He has reached present position in his job through *elbow grease.*
(*a*) his persistent fighting
(*b*) his good connections
(*c*) flattering his superiors
(*d*) his hard work **(Central Excise, 1993)**

36. He will *win* this election *hands down.*
(*a*) win easily
(*b*) win with a big margin
(*c*) win with a narrow margin
(*d*) scrape through

37. He has been working *on and off* for several years on this research project.
(*a*) at intervals (*b*) continuously
(*c*) rarey (*d*) painstakingly

38. He was a king who ruled his subjects *with a high hand.* **(Bank P.O. 1996)**
(*a*) oppressively (*b*) kindly
(*c*) conveniently (*d*) sympathetically
(*e*) democratically

39. Those who *make no bones* about such actions face a tough opposition.
(*a*) invite no comments
(*b*) make no plan
(*c*) do without hesitation
(*d*) waste no time

40. He *got hold of the wrong end of the stick.*
(*a*) committed a blunder
(*b*) misjudged a situation
(*c*) fixed wrong priorities
(*d*) felt uneasy

41. Discipline is *on the wane* in schools and colleges these days.
(*a*) increasing (*b*) declining
(*c*) spreading (*d*) spiralling
(Slenographers' Exam, 1993)

42. He was *cool as a cucumber.*
(*a*) nervous (*b*) fainted
(*c*) dead (*d*) calm and composed

43. Some of us are really *in a Catch-22* situation.
(*a*) absurd (*b*) dangerous
(*c*) hopeful (*d*) depressive

44. Eloquent lamentations regarding the fate of the flora and fauna are certain to be rendered *a cry in the wilderness.*
(*a*) a cry in vain
(*b*) an unpleasant situation
(*c*) a cry with a laughter
(*d*) a laughter having no end
(Railways, 1995)

45. He *took to heart* the death of his wife as he was very much attached to her.
(*a*) was shocked by
(*b*) was ruined by
(*c*) was deeply affected by
(*d*) was condoled

46. As our army attacked, the enemy retreated *pell-mell.*
(*a*) hurriedly
(*b*) in a disorderly manner
(*c*) in a heap
(*d*) without the least thought

47. In the organised society of today no individual or nation can *plough a lonely furrow.* **(I. Tax, 1995)**
(*a*) remain unaffected
(*b*) do without the help of others
(*c*) survive in isolation
(*d*) remain non-aligned

48. He is *a great hand* at organising public meetings
(*a*) very fond of (*b*) expert at
(*c*) accustomed to (*d*) well qualified for

49. Let us admit that we could not *heap coals of fire on his head.*
(*a*) agitate him
(*b*) incite him to a fight
(*c*) put him to shame
(*d*) make him feel sorry

50. Kunika was *cocksure* that she was able to do the job as desired.
(*a*) doubtful
(*b*) not able to imagine
(*c*) least worried
(*d*) perfectly confident

ANSWERS

1. (*a*)	**2.** (*a*)	**3.** (*b*)	**4.** (*d*)	**5.** (*b*)	**6.** (*b*)	**7.** (*c*)	**8.** (*c*)	**9.** (*d*)	**10.** (*c*)
11. (*c*)	**12.** (*b*)	**13.** (*c*)	**14.** (*b*)	**15.** (*a*)	**16.** (*c*)	**17.** (*b*)	**18.** (*c*)	**19.** (*b*)	**20.** (*b*)
21. (*c*)	**22.** (*c*)	**23.** (*c*)	**24.** (*b*)	**25.** (*a*)	**26.** (*c*)	**27.** (*b*)	**28.** (*b*)	**29.** (*d*)	**30.** (*c*)
31. (*a*)	**32.** (*c*)	**33.** (*b*)	**34.** (*c*)	**35.** (*d*)	**36.** (*a*)	**37.** (*a*)	**38.** (*a*)	**39.** (*c*)	**40.** (*b*)
41. (*b*)	**42.** (*d*)	**43.** (*a*)	**44.** (*a*)	**45.** (*c*)	**46.** (*b*)	**47.** (*b*)	**48.** (*b*)	**49.** (*c*)	**50.** (*d*)

PRACTICE SET 8

Directions : *In each of the following questions, choose the alternative which best expresses the meaning of the idiom in italics.*

1. He always *cuts both ends.*
(*a*) works for both sides
(*b*) inflicts injuries on others
(*c*) argues in support of both sides of the issue
(*d*) behaves dishonestly
(*e*) creates discord among friends
(Bank P.O. 1993)

2. He is temporarily in charge of the company and is trying *to feather his nest.*
(Bank P.O. 1996)
(*a*) raise the image of the company
(*b*) bring order and discipline in the company
(*c*) act for his own future benefits
(*d*) practice his own brand of management philosophy
(*e*) diversify the products of the company

3. Chandu used very ugly words against his kind uncle; he *threw down the gauntlet* before him. **(S.B.I.P.O. 1995)**
(*a*) he abused and insulted him
(*b*) he threw the challenge
(*c*) he behaved as if he was very great and important person
(*d*) he put several conditions for negotiation
(*e*) he showed his readiness to leave the place

4. The captors of the kidnapped kept his family *on tenterhooks.*

(a) in excited wait (b) in seething anger
(c) on constant move
(d) in anxious suspense

5. Do not *ride rough shod over* the poor.
(a) give undue importance to
(b) hate (c) treat harshly
(d) pamper

6. He *did me a good turn* by recommending me for the post of Vice-Principal.
(a) became sudenly good
(b) improved my prospects
(c) did an act of kindness
(d) returned my kindness

(Section Officers, 1993)

7. Although both the partners are running the business for the last tweleve years but their business is now *on its last legs.*
(a) about to take off
(b) about to perish
(c) about to produce results
(d) about to fructify

8. It has been raining *cats and dogs.*
(a) incessantly (b) heavily
(c) endlessly (d) continuously

9. There is no *hard and fast rule* regarding this subject.
(a) rule that is difficult
(b) rule that is fast-changing
(c) rule that cannot be broken or modified
(d) rule that can be broken or modified

(Stenographer's Exam, 1995)

10. He *left* his friend *in lurch.*
(a) left forever (b) left temporarily
(c) left to his fate
(d) left when he was needing help

11. He has accomplished a *Herculean task.*
(a) allotted work
(b) work requiring great effort
(c) impossible job
(d) incomplete work

12. Being an introvert, he will only eat his *heart out.* **(I. Tax & Central Excise, 1993)**
(a) eat too much (b) keep brooding
(c) invite trouble (d) suffer silently

13. He can get the job if he has the mind.
(a) has the courtesy
(b) has the willingness
(c) has a good memory
(d) is intelligent

14. Since he already has *cushy job,* he can afford to be extravagant.
(a) luxurious job (b) job with no work
(c) everlasting job
(d) financially comfortable job

15. You will *get into hot water* if you commit the same mistake again.
(a) suffer (b) be in a fix
(c) incur loss (d) be in trouble

16. I have warned him *now and then* not to resort to violence.
(a) consistently (b) frequently
(c) occasionally (d) repeatedly

17. His phenomenal success shows that he has got the *midas touch.*
(a) fabulous wealth
(b) tremendous acquaintances and resources
(c) superhuman qualities
(d) ability to succeed in all projects

18. The new economic policy is likely *to run into rough weather.*
(a) make things difficult
(b) confuse matters
(c) encounter difficulties
(d) create problems

(Assistant Grade, 1994)

19 The story published in the newspaper is not true, but the journalist has *painted it in bright colours.*
(a) provided illustrations with it
(b) exaggerated it
(c) made it more comic
(d) added some emotional incident to it

20. It requires unparalleled courage *to set the Thames on fire*
(a) do a heroic deed
(b) destroy with fire
(c) do something extraordinary or brilliant
(d) wreak evil on something

21. The question of abolition of private property is still a *moot point.*
(a) unknown (b) undecided
(c) not clear (d) uncertain

(Central Excise, 1995)

22. He is *on the wrong side of fifty.*
(a) not yet fifty (b) over fifty years old
(c) a sinner (d) old and haggard

23. It is *out of the question* for only one to have a quiet meal with a set of ultras around him.
(a) unthinkable (b) undesirable
(c) impossible (d) unbecoming

24. Ladies fall vactim to *green eyed monster.*
(a) love (b) hatred
(c) jealousy (d) flattery

25. The boss *brought matters to a head* by forcing him to work more.
(a) made him unhappy
(b) created a lot of unhappiness
(c) created an atmosphere of confrontation
(d) brought matters to a decisive point

(Asstt. Grade, 1992)

26. Wait here, I shall be back *in a jiffy.*
(*a*) in a hurry (*b*) by some vehicle
(*c*) at once (*d*) after some time

27. Please do not indulge in *double dealing.*
(*a*) dealing improperly (*b*) deception
(*c*) two standards (*d*) two jobs

28. The M.P. from our constituency is fond of *blowing his own trumpet* whenever he gets a chance.
(*a*) parading his own good deeds
(*b*) speaking too loudly
(*c*) looking after his own interest
(*d*) making long speeches
(Stenographers' Exam, 1991)

29. When he met me at the street corner, he *cut me dead.*
(*a*) surprised me by his arrogance
(*b*) deliberately insulted me by ignoring me
(*c*) showered filthy abuses on me
(*d*) made an assault on me

30. He was undecided. He *let the grass grow under his feet.*
(*a*) moved away (*b*) loitered around
(*c*) stayed out (*d*) sat unmoving

31. He cannot *make both ends meet.*
(*a*) manage the business
(*b*) work hard
(*c*) earn enough (*d*) control affairs
(Hotel Management, 1992)

32. He *made light* of his father's advice.
(*a*) followed readily (*b*) disregarded
(*c*) treated lightly (*d*) rejected

33. It is Rashmi who *wears the trousers* in their house and he timidly allows it.
(*a*) dresses glamorously
(*b*) earns a living (*c*) is dominant
(*d*) makes all the decisions

34. I have come to know of your *hole and corner* method of dealing with people.
(*a*) strict (*b*) servile
(*c*) secret (*d*) suspicious
(Asstt. Grade, 1993)

35. By putting on the mime act, Deepak *stole some of the thunder* of Peter's speech.
(*a*) made unimpressive
(*b*) made a lot of noise
(*c*) filched something
(*d*) detracted the listeners from

36. The social worker rendered *yeoman service* to the victims
(*a*) excellent service
(*b*) paid service
(*c*) free, generous help
(*d*) needed aid

37. The soldiers *laid down their arms.*
(*a*) put their arms on the ground
(*b*) surrendered
(*c*) refused to obey orders
(*d*) put the arms in their place
(N.D.A. 1991)

38. His biographers discovered to their surprise that he was an atheist *to the backbone.*
(*a*) completely (*b*) by and large
(*c*) by birth (*d*) to some extent

39. In modern democratic societies *lynch law* seems to have become a common feature in almost all the spheres of life.
(*a*) law of the parliament
(*b*) law of the constitution
(*c*) law of the mob
(*d*) law of the underworld
(Section Officers, 1993)

40. Sachin *has bitten of more than he can chew.*
(*a*) is always hungry
(*b*) is trying to do too much
(*c*) is very greedy
(*d*) has little regard for others

41. Who will *carry the day* in this war ?
(*a*) win (*b*) attack first
(*c*) be defeated (*d*) withdraw first

42. The trade union's seemingly rightful demand is only a *stalking horse* to blackmail the management. **(C.B.I. 1994)**
(*a*) trick (*b*) proposal
(*c*) pretence (*d*) suggestion

43. Kamal told the audience *to hold their peace* until he had finished his address.
(*a*) remain peaceful
(*b*) keep silent
(*c*) remain seated
(*d*) become reconciled

44. Leaders should not only make speeches, they should also be prepared *to bell the cat.*
(*a*) to be alert of the enemy
(*b*) to take lead in danger
(*c*) to speak against a wrong policy
(*d*) to have enough say in the government

45. The teacher was *as good as his word.*
(*a*) incapable of action
(*b*) better than expected
(*c*) highly pretentious
(*d*) ready to fulfil his promise
(I. Tax, 1994)

46. One should not indulge in *tall talks.*
(*a*) flattering (*b*) boasting
(*c*) ideal talk (*d*) irrelevant talk

47. The lady was shedding *crocodile tears.*
(*a*) silent tears (*b*) profuse tears
(*c*) false tears (*d*) tears of happiness

48. He believes in the policy of *making hay while the sun shines.*
(*a*) giving bribes to get his work done
(*b*) making the best use of a favourable situation
(*c*) helping those who help him
(*d*) seeking advice from one and all
(Stenographers' Exam, 1995)

49. It is difficult for me to believe you, so please put down everything *in black and white.*
(*a*) in detail (*b*) in written form
(*c*) sequentially, as it happened
(*d*) what you saw

50. The number of *globetrotters* has increased after the Second World War.
(*a*) foreign countries
(*b*) great persons
(*c*) people of importance
(*d*) travellers around the world

ANSWERS

1. (*c*)	**2.** (*c*)	**3.** (*b*)	**4.** (*d*)	**5.** (*c*)	**6.** (*c*)	**7.** (*b*)	**8.** (*b*)	**9.** (*c*)	**10.** (*d*)
11. (*b*)	**12.** (*d*)	**13.** (*b*)	**14.** (*d*)	**15.** (*d*)	**16.** (*c*)	**17.** (*d*)	**18.** (*c*)	**19.** (*b*)	**20.** (*a*)
21. (*b*)	**22.** (*b*)	**23.** (*a*)	**24.** (*c*)	**25.** (*c*)	**26.** (*a*)	**27.** (*b*)	**28.** (*a*)	**29.** (*b*)	**30.** (*c*)
31. (*c*)	**32.** (*c*)	**33.** (*c*)	**34.** (*c*)	**35.** (*d*)	**36.** (*c*)	**37.** (*b*)	**38.** (*a*)	**39.** (*c*)	**40.** (*b*)
41. (*a*)	**42.** (*a*)	**43.** (*b*)	**44.** (*b*)	**45.** (*d*)	**46.** (*b*)	**47.** (*c*)	**48.** (*b*)	**49.** (*b*)	**50.** (*d*)

PRACTICE SET 9

Directions : ***In each of the following questions, some alternatives are suggested for the idiom/phrase in italics in the sentence. Choose the one which best expresses the meaning of the idiom/phrase in italics.***

1. It is a matter of gratification for me that he has *turned a new leaf.*
(*a*) begun a different mode of life
(*b*) started using his intelligence
(*c*) proved to be a worthy person on his job
(*d*) accepted the new job that was offered to him
(*e*) decided to use a different strategy to solve the problem **(Bank P.O. 1996)**

2. If we give them this concession, it will be *the thin end of the wedge.* **(I. Tax, 1994)**
(*a*) a compromise on principles
(*b*) the least we could do for them
(*c*) the beginning of further concessions
(*d*) inadequate for their needs

3. All the political parties are *tarred with the same brush.*
(*a*) work on the same principles
(*b*) have the same merits
(*c*) are treated equally
(*d*) possess the same defects

4. He was selected because he always manages to *steal a march* upon his opponents.
(*a*) resist (*b*) outshine
(*c*) defy (*d*) challenge

5. He is always *picking holes* in every project. **(Stenographers' Exam, 1993)**
(*a*) asking irrelevant questions on
(*b*) suggesting improvement in
(*c*) finding fault with
(*d*) creating problems in

6. Gambling makes a man *go broke.*
(*a*) lose temper (*b*) become rich
(*c*) become penniless
(*d*) sell all he has

7. Sanjay always *sets great store* by his father's advice.
(*a*) laughs at (*b*) values greatly
(*c*) ignores (*d*) neglects

8. If Gaurav does not complete the work allotted to him properly, we shall *send him packing.* **(Bank P.O. 1994)**
(*a*) put him in packing department
(*b*) give him our best wishes
(*c*) give him another work
(*d*) recall with honour
(*e*) terminate his services immediately

9. The operation was *touch and go* as new complications arose and were solved.
(*a*) safe (*b*) risky
(*c*) easy (*d*) quick

10. It is not easy to *strike gold* in this particular matter because the man who has implemented the scheme is very shrewd.

(*a*) make money
(*b*) find a line of argument
(*c*) benefit from
(*d*) get good results

11. Caesar was *done to death* by the conspirators. **(Clerks' Grade, 1993)**
(*a*) attacked (*b*) removed
(*c*) eliminated (*d*) murdered

12. Lord Clive *won his laurels* in the battle of Plassey.
(*a*) fought bravely
(*b*) defeated his enemies
(*c*) acquired distinction
(*d*) overpowered his enemies

13. He gave his erring son a *piece of his mind.*
(*a*) advised him (*b*) scolded him
(*c*) encouraged him (*d*) suggested anew

14. His boss was always *breathing down his neck.* **(Assistang Grade, 1995)**
(*a*) abusing and ill-treating him
(*b*) watching all his actions closely
(*c*) shouting loudly at him
(*d*) giving him strenuous work

15. The best policy is *to let sleeping dogs lie.*
(*a*) to be liberal (*b*) to be tolerant
(*c*) to be neutral
(*d*) to avoid discussing troublesome matters

16. Don't *thrust your nose into my affairs.*
(*a*) be in opposition to
(*b*) deal with
(*c*) advise me about
(*d*) meddle officiously in

17. He is *not worth his salt* if he fails at this juncture. **(G.I.C.A.A.O. 1990)**
(*a*) quite worthless
(*b*) very proud of himself
(*c*) quite depressed
(*d*) very strange

18. If he goes on drinking like that, *as sure as eggs is eggs,* he will have no liver left.
(*a*) in course of time (*b*) it is a fact
(*c*) quite certainly (*d*) unfortunately

19. Satish *kicked the bucket* last evening and his friends came to know about it very late.
(*a*) met with an accident
(*b*) was badly injured
(*c*) quarelled (*d*) died

20. He was *in a brown study* and did not seem to catch my point.
(*a*) in his study room
(*b*) absorbed in reading
(*c*) absent-minded
(*d*) in a state of shock

(Asstt. Grade, 1993)

21. It was clearly a case of *the pot calling the kettle black* when Dhruv said that Ravi was selfish.
(*a*) both being guilty of the same mistake
(*b*) a person accusing another of being black
(*c*) a person blaming another for something he has not done
(*d*) someone criticising another for a fault which he himself has

22. He *fights shy of* his young nephew, who is a crook.
(*a*) quarrels bitterly with
(*b*) is afraid of
(*c*) avoids from a feeling of mistrust
(*d*) is frightened by

23. He *threw cold water* over the project that the secretary had prepared.
(*a*) encouraged (*b*) cleared
(*c*) discouraged (*d*) rejected

24. He does not like to be friendly with Sarita; he always *gives her a cold shoulder.* **(Bank P.O. 1993)**
(*a*) pushes her with his shoulder whenever they meet
(*b*) creates all sorts of troubles for her
(*c*) insults her in the presence of others
(*d*) tries to be unfriendly by taking no notice of her
(*e*) argues with her on any issue

25. My friend *got the sack from* his first job.
(*a*) got tired of (*b*) was demoted from
(*c*) resigned (*d*) was dismissed from

26. With the existing management, the future of the company is *in doldrums.*
(*a*) dull (*b*) bright
(*c*) uncertain (*d*) secure
(Translators' Exam, 1994)

27. He *went out of his way* to support my candidature for the post of Manager.
(*a*) took special trouble
(*b*) was determined
(*c*) agreed whole-heartedly
(*d*) was hesitating

28. He has stolen a march on his rival.
(*a*) defeated (*b*) pushed back
(*c*) gained an advantage (*d*) deceived

29. His visit to France proved a *damp squib.*
(*a*) a great success (*b*) an utter failure
(*c*) a curtain raiser (*d*) a thaw

30. A man should, if possible, *steer clear* of money lenders.
(*a*) hate (*b*) dislike
(*c*) avoid (*d*) run after

31. Though he has a lot of money, yet all his plans are *built upon sand*.
(*a*) based on inexperience
(*b*) resting on immature ideas
(*c*) resting on cheap material
(*d*) established on insecure foundations
(Section officers, 1993)

32. The culprit was *brought to book*.
(*a*) made to swear (*b*) punished
(*c*) arrested (*d*) beaten

33. He *stuck to his guns* even in the face of stiff opposition
(*a*) clung to his weapon
(*b*) kept arguing
(*c*) followed the chosen path
(*d*) held on against attack or argument

34. It was such a strange affair that I could not *make head or tail of it*. **(Bank P.O. 1996)**
(*a*) face it (*b*) tolerate it
(*c*) remember it (*d*) understand it
(*e*) believe it

35. In these days of rising prices, we are *paying through our nose*.
(*a*) paying dearly
(*b*) reducing our purchases
(*c*) buying on credit
(*d*) paying in instalments

36. He came to meet me when I was *in the dumps*.
(*a*) in high spirits (*b*) in low spirits
(*c*) too busy
(*d*) engaged in official work

37. Sunil thought his skill would match up to Keshav's bulk, but in the fight he was *beaten neck and crop*.
(*a*) softly (*b*) completely
(*c*) swiftly (*d*) profoundly
(I. Tax & Central Excise, 1993)

38. It is better to have one friend who is *as true as steel* than to have fifty acquaintances who refuse to recognise you in your hour of need.
(*a*) is strong
(*b*) is physically and mentally fit
(*c*) is with you
(*d*) is very loyal and dependable
(*e*) always speaks the truth

39. She *thinks highly of you* but I doubt whether you would be able to prove youself to her expectations.
(*a*) gives you great regard
(*b*) wants you to rise high in life
(*c*) has a good opinion about you
(*d*) thinks that you pretend to be what you are not

40. His *oily tongue* has won him promotion.
(*a*) soft speech (*b*) word power
(*c*) flattery (*d*) fluency in speech
(Hotel Management, 1991)

41. The new boy always had a *hard nosed* attitude.
(*a*) inquisitive (*b*) abusive and rude
(*c*) liberal (*d*) tough and aggressive

42. We, being in a hurry, had *to cut off a corner* to reach in time.
(*a*) to go fast
(*b*) to take a short cut
(*c*) to take an alternative route
(*d*) None of these

43. Those persons who are ready *to sail close to the wind* can be successful in life.
(*a*) to take risk
(*b*) to manage the situation
(*c*) to work hard
(*d*) to be regular **(Railways, 1995)**

44. The lady was murdered *in cold blood*.
(*a*) coolly (*b*) deliberately
(*c*) unfeelingly (*d*) thoughtlessly

45. He put us *in a real fix* when he did not turn up to pick us up.
(*a*) feel awkward (*b*) bad mood
(*c*) made us feel bad
(*d*) difficult situation

46. A good teacher should have tne *gift of the gab*. **(Clerk's Grade, 1993)**
(*a*) a good personality
(*b*) a talent for acting
(*c*) a talent for speaking
(*d*) an interest in discipline

47. Suresh was truly *in his elements* and he easily impressed the audience with his erudition.
(*a*) in high spirits
(*b*) unusually confident
(*c*) at his best
(*d*) feeling relaxed and confident

48. Randhir will do anything *to rock the boat*, if he knows about your progress.
(*a*) agitate against
(*b*) conspire against
(*c*) create difficulties
(*d*) upset the balance

49. It was not long before the captain of the ship decided to *weigh anchor* that a sudden storm overtook the ship.
(*a*) estimate the load in the ship
(*b*) prepare to sail again
(*c*) unload the ship to keep balance
(*d*) drop the anchor

50. She exhibited remarkable *sang froid* during the crisis.
(*a*) temper (*b*) irritation
(*c*) composure (*d*) anger
(G.I.C.A.A.O. 1990)

ANSWERS

1. (*a*)	**2.** (*c*)	**3.** (*d*)	**4.** (*b*)	**5.** (*c*)	**6.** (*c*)	**7.** (*b*)	**8.** (*e*)	**9.** (*b*)	**10.** (*b*)
11. (*d*)	**12.** (*c*)	**13.** (*b*)	**14.** (*b*)	**15.** (*d*)	**16.** (*d*)	**17.** (*a*)	**18.** (*c*)	**19.** (*d*)	**20.** (*b*)
21. (*d*)	**22.** (*c*)	**23.** (*c*)	**24.** (*d*)	**25.** (*d*)	**26.** (*c*)	**27.** (*a*)	**28.** (*c*)	**29.** (*b*)	**30.** (*c*)
31. (*b*)	**32.** (*b*)	**33.** (*d*)	**34.** (*d*)	**35.** (*a*)	**36.** (*a*)	**37.** (*b*)	**38.** (*d*)	**39.** (*c*)	**40.** (*c*)
41. (*d*)	**42.** (*b*)	**43.** (*a*)	**44.** (*c*)	**45.** (*d*)	**46.** (*c*)	**47.** (*d*)	**48.** (*d*)	**49.** (*b*)	**50.** (*c*)

PRACTICE SET 10

Directions : ***In each of the following questions, some alternatives are suggested for the idiom/phrase in italics in the sentence. Choose the one which best expresses the meaning of the idiom/phrase in italics in the sentence.***

1. The meeting *ended in fiasco.*
(*a*) succeeded (*b*) in confusion
(*c*) in complete failure
(*d*) in acrimonious debate

2. If you *rub him the wrong way*, he is bound to react **(S.S.C. 1993)**
(*a*) flatter him (*b*) encourage him
(*c*) annoy him (*d*) abuse him.

3. He is *Argus-eyed.*
(*a*) far sighted (*b*) short sighted
(*c*) observant
(*d*) blind to the realities of life

4. I *raked my brains* to solve this difficult problem.
(*a*) I consulted several people
(*b*) I subjected my mind to hard thinking
(*c*) I read number of books
(*d*) I brainwashed several experts
(*e*) I used my common sense
(Bank P.O. 1996)

5. The cricket match proved to be *a big draw.*
(*a*) a game without any result
(*b*) a keen contest
(*c*) a lovely spectacle
(*d*) a huge attraction
(Assistant Grade, 1994)

6. I am *like a cog in the wheel* of this company.
(*a*) a technician
(*b*) the least paid employee
(*c*) an important person
(*d*) an unimportant person

7. It is time that government *seized the nettle* and stopped parleying with terrorists.
(*a*) seized properly
(*b*) overcame the difficulties
(*c*) got hold of
(*d*) dealt firmly

8. My father *strained every nerve* to enable me to get settled in life.
(*a*) worked very hard
(*b*) spent a huge amount
(*c*) tried all tricks
(*d*) bribed several persons
(Stenographer's Exam, 1995)

9. The two women are so jealous that *at the drop of a hat* they start insulting each other.
(*a*) on every occasion
(*b*) whenever they meet
(*c*) for no reason at all
(*d*) none of these

10. I must *take exception* to your remark.
(*a*) accept gladly (*b*) thank you for
(*c*) consider carefully (*d*) object to

11. The captain and the coach are trying *to pass the buck* on each other for the poor performance of their team.
(*a*) to repent (*b*) to shirk work
(*c*) to blame (*d*) to shift responsibility

12. The prices are going up *by leaps and bounds.*
(*a*) systematically (*b*) irregularly
(*c*) gradually (*d*) rapidly

13. He *bids fair* to be an excellent cricketer.
(*a*) seems likely (*b*) is ambitious
(*c*) is confident (*d*) is unlikely
(I. Tax, 1993)

14. To find real happiness in the world is *a wild goose chase.*
(*a*) ideal seeking (*b*) hunting
(*c*) futile search (*d*) real aim

15. The class could not *keep a straight face* on hearing the strange pronounciation of the new teacher. **(C.B.I. 1995)**

(a) remain serious
(b) remain unaffected
(c) remain silent
(d) remain indifferent

16. He had *to eat a humble pie* owing to his misdeeds.
(a) feel downtrodden
(b) apologise humbly
(c) be humiliated
(d) accept abuses

17. He managed to secure the job through *backstair influence.*
(a) sheer merit
(b) hard effort
(c) strong recommendation
(d) underhand means

18. The police fired *at random* at the violent crowd and several persons lost their lives. **(Stenographers' Exam, 1993)**
(a) pointedly (b) aimlessly
(c) unwillingly (d) intentionally

19. You cannot *have your cake and eat it too.*
(a) have it both ways
(b) fulfil all your wishes
(c) run away from responsibility
(d) always work according to your whims

20. He is really *worth his salt.*
(a) loyal (b) affectionate
(c) of value (d) untrustworthy

21. Some people now wonder whether we just pay lip service or genuinely subscribe to democracy.
(a) pay oral tribute
(b) attach no value
(c) remain indifferent
(d) show only outward respect
(Assistant Grade, 1994)

22. By foregoing your claim for damages done by Kanti, you have done the *handsome thing by him.*
(a) reduced his misery
(b) raised his morale
(c) behaved magnanimously
(d) changed his views

23. A hen pecked husband *plays second fiddle* to his wife.
(a) pleases (b) fondles with
(c) humours
(d) plays a subordinate role to

24. I saw him *make a wry face.*
(a) feel sick (b) cry with pain
(c) abuse (d) show disappointment

25. Before the actual interview, Manish was *truely in his elements.*
(a) flustered in nervousness
(b) feeling relaxed and confident
(c) at his best
(d) intuitive of failure

26. I have been betrayed by my own *flesh and blood.* **(Asstt. Grade, 1992)**
(a) relatives (b) friends
(c) children (d) acquaintances

27. He blew out all the candles *at one go.*
(a) suddenly (b) at once
(c) simultaneously (d) at one attempt

28. The people in North India are known for *keeping open house.*
(a) never locking it
(b) keeping house well-ventilated
(c) offering hospitality to every one
(d) not worrying about its security

29. Dishonesty is *at a premium* in almost all spheres of public life.
(a) prevalent (b) practised openly
(c) encouraged (d) valued highly
(Translator's Exam, 1994)

30. His letters to his ward *speak volumes* for his forbearance and good sense.
(a) speak ill of
(b) serve as strong testimony to
(c) show indications of
(d) are intended to impress

31. It was he who *put a spoke in my wheel.*
(a) tried to cause an accident
(b) helped in the execution of the plan
(c) thwarted the execution of the plan
(d) destroyed the plan
(Central Excise, 1995)

32. He finds no difficulty in *keeping the wolf away from the door.*
(a) guarding against wild animals
(b) keeping off starvation
(c) keeping aloof from disputed matters
(d) guarding himself against enemies

33. He is known to be the *right-hand man* of the minister.
(a) private secretary (b) trusted person
(c) bosom friend (d) bitter critic

34. The captain played with determination because the honour of the team was *at stake.* **(Asstt. Grade, 1993)**
(a) very low (b) at the top
(c) in danger (d) appropriate

35. He *knows what side his bread is buttered.*
(a) knows the art of cooking
(b) knows how to accomplish a task
(c) knows how to flatter
(d) knows where his advantage lies

36. Some kids *get a kick* smoking cigarettes as a guesture of revolt against adult domination.
(a) are kicked for (b) have fun
(c) are punished for (d) get a thrill

37. By doing these errands, he is merely trying to *curry favour* with his boss.
(*a*) earn goodwill (*b*) expect promotion
(*c*) gain favour (*d*) gain influence

38. His promotion is *on the cards.*
(*a*) due (*b*) evident
(*c*) certain (*d*) probable
(Railways, 1995)

39. As he does not listen to me, I do not *hold a brief* for him.
(*a*) admire (*b*) consult
(*c*) defend (*d*) finance

40. The two brothers have decided to go *hand in hand* in business.
(*a*) move in union
(*b*) make joint venture with others
(*c*) work in competition
(*d*) keep parallel accounts

41. He resigned the post of *his own accord.*
(*a*) according to his judgement
(*b*) which he liked
(*c*) voluntarily and willingly
(*d*) according to his convenience
(Section Officers, 1993)

42. It has been the first time in this office that a clerk *wiped the nose* of the boss.
(*a*) abused (*b*) slapped
(*c*) cheated (*d*) complained against

43. Kishen is a *chicken-hearted* fellow.
(*a*) weak (*b*) kind hearted
(*c*) bold (*d*) cowardly

44. The poor women do manual labour even when they are *in the family way.*
(*a*) in domestic routine
(*b*) doing household jobs
(*c*) unwell (*d*) pregnant

45. He *faced the music* for reaching home late. **(I. Tax, 1994)**
(*a*) faced punishment
(*b*) faced entertainment
(*c*) faced reprimand
(*d*) faced pleasure

46. He has *too many irons in the fire.*
(*a*) wants to grab everything
(*b*) is engaged in too many enterprises simultaneously
(*c*) pokes his nose in every affair
(*d*) is very selfish and greedy

47. David *has an eye* for detecting crime.
(*a*) is alert in
(*b*) is no good in
(*c*) has an extraordinary talent in
(*d*) none of these

48. I would advise you to *keep your nose clean.*
(*a*) be polite
(*b*) not to indulge in evil conspiracies
(*c*) keep out of trouble
(*d*) not to take to bad habits.

49. Though they knew that the defeat was inevitable, they *fought to the finish.*
(*a*) till the end
(*b*) till they died
(*c*) till peace was declared
(*d*) till they got good results

50. While the ladies continued their *small talk* in the drawing room, I felt bored.
(*a*) light conversation (*b*) gossip
(*c*) backbiting (*d*) whispering
(Asstt. Grade, 1996)

ANSWERS

1. (*c*)	**2.** (*c*)	**3.** (*c*)	**4.** (*b*)	**5.** (*d*)	**6.** (*d*)	**7.** (*d*)	**8.** (*a*)	**9.** (*c*)	**10.** (*d*)
11. (*d*)	**12.** (*d*)	**13.** (*a*)	**14.** (*c*)	**15.** (*a*)	**16.** (*b*)	**17.** (*d*)	**18.** (*b*)	**19.** (*a*)	**20.** (*c*)
21. (*d*)	**22.** (*c*)	**23.** (*d*)	**24.** (*d*)	**25.** (*b*)	**26.** (*c*)	**27.** (*d*)	**28.** (*c*)	**29.** (*d*)	**30.** (*b*)
31. (*c*)	**32.** (*b*)	**33.** (*b*)	**34.** (*c*)	**35.** (*d*)	**36.** (*d*)	**37.** (*c*)	**38.** (*c*)	**39.** (*c*)	**40.** (*a*)
41. (*c*)	**42.** (*c*)	**43.** (*d*)	**44.** (*d*)	**45.** (*c*)	**46.** (*b*)	**47.** (*c*)	**48.** (*c*)	**49.** (*a*)	**50.** (*a*)

PRACTICE SET 11

Directions : ***In each of the following questions, out of the given alternatives, choose the one which best expresses the meaning of the idiom/phrase in italics in the sentence.***

1. Tell me plainly who broke the mirror, *do not beat about the bush*. **(Bank P.O. 1993)**
(*a*) put any blame on others
(*b*) pretend to be unaware of the matter
(*c*) approach the matter in a round about way
(*d*) try to impress me with your arguments

2. He is disliked because of his habit of *making a mountain of a molehill.*
(a) exaggerating (b) boasting
(c) taking undue advantage of a favourable opportunity
(d) giving great importance to trifles

3. The point you have raised *has no bearing* on the issue we are discussing.
(a) has no relationship with
(b) is not affected by
(c) provides no evidence to
(d) has no impact on

4. In life, we have to *take the rough with the smooth.* **(I. Tax, 1994)**
(a) be tough in order to be successful
(b) use pleasant words to make things smooth
(c) accept unpleasant as well as pleasant things
(d) make unpleasant things better

5. The dispute regarding the granting of bonus to workers *came to a head* this week.
(a) reached a crisis
(b) settled amicably
(c) took a turn for the better
(d) resulted in senseless violence

6. It was discovered that the young man was *over head and ears* in love with her.
(a) secretly (b) openly
(c) completely (d) sufficiently

7. Nobody could *see through the design* of that wily fellow.
(a) learn the aim
(b) know the antecedents
(c) know the secret
(d) be aware of the trick

8. The reproduction of Mona Lisa portrait by the 8-year old child matches the original *to a hair.*
(a) not at all (b) vaguely
(c) to some extent (d) exactly

9. The trial was so important that the entire proceedings were *held in camera.*
(a) a secret (b) in strict vigilance
(c) not open to the public
(d) amidst great security

10. His *prodigal son* was a constant source of trouble to him.
(a) given into bad habits
(b) poor and miserly
(c) extravagant
(d) step-son

11. In the armed forces, it is considered a great privilege to *die in harness.*
(a) die with honour
(b) die on a horse back
(c) die while still working
(d) die in the battle field **(Asstt. Grade, 1994)**

12. He used his boyish, innocent looks to *take people in.*
(a) amuse people
(b) understand people
(c) cheat people
(d) accommodate guests

13. The arrival of the mother-in-law in the family proved *a rift in the lute.*
(a) brought about disharmony
(b) brought about a disciplined atmosphere
(c) caused unnecessary worries
(d) caused a pleasant atmosphere **(C.B.I. 1995)**

14. Pankaj had a *chequered career* since I first knew him as an assistant dealer in the transport company.
(a) indulged in odd jobs
(b) a career which helped him make lot of money
(c) a variety of jobs and experiences
(d) is jobless

15. He was *carried off his feet* when he was declared to have won the prize.
(a) became delirious
(b) danced on his toes
(c) was dizzy
(d) was wild with excitement **(G.I.C.A.A.O. 1990)**

16. My aunt was *in a flutter* last night.
(a) frightened (b) very angry
(c) in a jovial mood
(d) in a state of nervous excitement

17. All his schemes to murder the king *ended in smoke.*
(a) fructified gradually
(b) came to nothing
(c) were discarded
(d) were partially carried out

18. He has *turned the tables* on his enemy.
(a) behaved hospitably towards
(b) hit
(c) created obstacle for
(d) changed possible defeat into victory

19. He is the only civil servant I know who hates *red tape.*
(a) accepting bribes
(b) formal procedures
(c) corruption
(d) dishonesty

20. For the first week, the apprentice felt *like a fish out of water.*
(a) disappointed (b) frustrated
(c) uncomfortable (d) homeless

21. nflation is *running riot* and prices are out of control.
(*a*) becoming unbearable
(*b*) causing depression
(*c*) behaving wild
(*d*) moving upward

22. Do you know why I avoid this man? *He has a bee in bonnet.*
(*a*) is crazy (*b*) is ambitious
(*c*) is over confident (*d*) is frustrated
(*e*) is suspicious

23. Seema is a little *hard of hearing.*
(*a*) inaudible (*b*) disinterested
(*c*) deaf (*d*) insensitive
(Stenographers' Exam, 1994)

24. The recently won brand new Maruti car is *worth a jew's eye* for Rakesh.
(*a*) a costly item (*b*) unnecessary
(*c*) not a worthy possession
(*d*) a possession of high value

25. Sachin should do his own work instead of always *back-seat driving.*
(*a*) teasing others
(*b*) offering advice without responsibility
(*c*) interfering in others affairs
(*d*) being critical of the work being done by others

26. To tell you *in a nutshell,* lust for power and money has almost spoiled him.
(*a*) as objectively as possible
(*b*) in a simple and brief manner
(*c*) an actual experience deseribed vividly
(*d*) to take in confidence
(Bank P.O. 1994)

27. He did the mischief and I had to *carry the can.*
(*a*) get into trouble
(*b*) accept the blame
(*c*) face the repurcussions
(*d*) share the responsibility

28. It is *high time* that India did something about the population problem.
(*a*) auspicious moment
(*b*) desired occasion
(*c*) appropriate time (*d*) already late
(Asstt. Grade, 1994)

29. *At the eleventh hour,* Mridual arrived and saved him from the crisis.
(*a*) one hour before twelve
(*b*) right at the end
(*c*) at the last minute
(*d*) when in trouble

30. The servant had to confess his mistake when he was *caught red handed.*
(*a*) caught easily
(*b*) caught in the right time
(*c*) caught in the act of committing crime
(*d*) caught in a preplanned way

31. She was in a *brown study* and did not notice my entrance.
(*a*) reverie (*b*) fear
(*c*) sleep (*d*) dream
(Central Excise, 1995)

32. Since Peter can be boring, teaching his works is not *every lecturer's cup of tea.*
(*a*) refreshing drink
(*b*) what one likes and can do well
(*c*) routine work
(*d*) not liked by most people

33. By refusing to finance my industrial projects, the bank *threw a spanner* in them.
(*a*) defeated (*b*) disappointed
(*c*) sacked (*d*) sabotaged

34. The people of the town considered her a *scarlet woman* for her old habits.
(*a*) a whore
(*b*) a troublesome lady
(*c*) an ominous person
(*d*) a woman suffering from a mania

35. The authorities *took him to task* for this negligence. **(S.B.I.P.O. 1994)**
(*a*) forced him to resign
(*b*) suspended his assignment
(*c*) reprimanded him
(*d*) gave him additional work

36. I *rated* my assistant *soundly* for his slackness.
(*a*) suspended (*b*) censured strongly
(*c*) dismissed (*d*) criticised

37. Unless you *grease his palm* he will not do your work.
(*a*) talk to him (*b*) flatter him
(*c*) beat him (*d*) bribe him

38. If you give Ashish all your money, you are likely *to burn your fingers.*
(*a*) be ill (*b*) be happy
(*c*) suffer (*d*) be unhappy

39. Their attitude towards each other only tended to create *bad blood* between the brothers.
(*a*) jealousy (*b*) misunderstanding
(*c*) distrust (*d*) angry feeling

40. The *carrot and the stick policy* pays dividends in every organisation.
(*a*) fair and foul
(*b*) continuous vigilance
(*c*) democratic
(*d*) reward and punishment

41. Rejesh and Vikas have remained friends *through thick and thin.* **(C.B.I. 1994)**
(*a*) inspite of all difficulties

(*b*) always
(*c*) through days of struggle
(*d*) through happy days

42. Smuggling can get you *easy money.*
(*a*) tax-free income
(*b*) money to make one lazy
(*c*) money which can be spent easily
(*d*) money earned after very little work

43. The lawyer told Tajinder *straight from the shoulder* that his case was weak.
(*a*) standing very close to his shoulder
(*b*) discreetly
(*c*) without evasion
(*d*) in writing

44. I did not know that he was *pulling my leg* all the time. **(S.S.C. 1993)**
(*a*) befooling me (*b*) degrading me
(*c*) defaming me (*d*) complimenting me

45. He has had *second thoughts* about going to Delhi.
(*a*) decided to go elsewhere
(*b*) is reconsidering his decision
(*c*) planned very carefully
(*d*) is going to take somebody with him

46. In the times of the Mughal emperor Jahangir, Nur Jahan was the *power behind the throne.*
(*a*) who has real control and power
(*b*) an acknowledged leader
(*c*) who has control over the king
(*d*) who rules without others knowing it

47. If only teachers *come down from* their *ivory towers* and develop an intimacy with the students, can the student-teacher relationship improve ?
(*a*) feeling of superiority
(*b*) detachment and seclusion
(*c*) strict and uncomprising attitude
(*d*) false pride

48. The cause may be a trifle but he would not let you go without *splitting hairs.*
(*a*) making it a bit quarrel
(*b*) indulging in over-refind arguments
(*c*) reviving every small event
(*d*) annoying you

49. While going through the enquiry papers, the police inspector had *smelt a rat.*
(*a*) planned something evil
(*b*) changed his procedure
(*c*) smelt something suspicious
(*d*) perceived an obnoxious order

50. All his schemes *bite the dust* for lack of practicality.
(*a*) are humiliated (*b*) are stolen
(*c*) are looked down upon
(*d*) are killed

ANSWERS

1. (*c*)	**2.** (*d*)	**3.** (*a*)	**4.** (*c*)	**5.** (*a*)	**6.** (*c*)	**7.** (*d*)	**8.** (*d*)	**9.** (*c*)	**10.** (*c*)
11. (*c*)	**12.** (*c*)	**13.** (*a*)	**14.** (*c*)	**15.** (*d*)	**16.** (*d*)	**17.** (*b*)	**18.** (*d*)	**19.** (*b*)	**20.** (*d*)
21. (*c*)	**22.** (*a*)	**23.** (*c*)	**24.** (*d*)	**25.** (*b*)	**26.** (*b*)	**27.** (*b*)	**28.** (*d*)	**29.** (*c*)	**30.** (*c*)
31. (*a*)	**32.** (*b*)	**33.** (*d*)	**34.** (*a*)	**35.** (*c*)	**36.** (*b*)	**37.** (*d*)	**38.** (*c*)	**39.** (*d*)	**40.** (*d*)
41. (*c*)	**42.** (*d*)	**43.** (*c*)	**44.** (*a*)	**45.** (*b*)	**46.** (*a*)	**47.** (*b*)	**48.** (*b*)	**49.** (*c*)	**50.** (*a*)

SOME MORE IDIOMS

1. I am prepared *to meet you half-way* (come to a compromise with you).

2. This unexpected new difficulty *put me on my mettle.* (roused me to do my best)

3. From his attitude it is clear that he wants to *pay off old scores* (have his revenge)

4. He is *hand and glove* (very intimate) with my cousin.

5. He *turns* even his errors *to accont.* (profits by them)

6. In the manufacture of dyes the Germans *bear the palm* (are pre-eminent).

7. He was disappointed, but he *took heart* (cheered himself up) and tried again.

8. He is *falling foul of* (quarrelling with) everybody.

9. Just now *my hands are full.* (I am very busy)

10. That house is *put on the market.* (offered for sale)

11. He *took up the cudgels for* (defended vigorously) his friend.

12. *High words* (angry words) often come out in quarrels.

13. Some persons do not like to be under *petticoat government* (rule of women).

14. Every examinee is *on tiptoe* (anxious) to learn his result.

15. He *won his spurs* (gained reputation) by perseverance and knowledge.

16. This company has good *watch and ward.* (guard)

17. This officer seems to be quite *a green horn* (novice) in office work.

18. He lives from *hand to mouth*. (on daily earnings)

19. He will *ere long* (shortly) start for Shimla.

20. He narrated *chapter and verse* (full detail) on the subject.

21. If a leader *turns his coat,* (goes to opposite party) people suspect his intentions.

22. He is *playing ducks and drakes with* (squandering) his money.

23. She is a vain lady and *makes parade of* (speaks highly of) herself.

24. I will pay you in *monkey's money* (kind, not cash).

25. The *long and short* (main point) of it is that he won't come.

26. He *egged* Suresh *on* (instigated)to fight with Mohan.

27. He *looked blank* (seemed surprised) when he learnt that he was surprised.

28. All the documents were declared *null and void* (invalid)

29. His youngest son is the *apple of his eye.* (dearest thing)

30. 15th August is a *red-letter day* (auspicious day) in the history of our country.

31. Every man should have confidence in his *better half* (wife)

32. Our examination is *close at hand*. (very near)

33. He is *out of pocket*. (without money)

34. The pick-pocket is a *jail-bird*. (notorious offender).

35. Pt. Jawaharlal Nehru was *a man of parts.* (a man of ability).

36. Dr. Radha drishnan was *a man of letters.* (scholar)

37. Shivaji was *a man of spirit*. (courageous man)

38. She keeps all things in *apple-pie order* (perfect order)

39. His affairs are *at loose ends* (badly managed).

40. *Bad debts* (unrealisable debts) should not be included in the assets.

41. *Ever and anon* (frequently) we heard a cry from the other house.

42. We should not play *fast and loose* (unreliably) with anyone.

43. *Fast living* (luxurious living) is not appreciable.

44. *Flesh and blood* (Human nature) cannot bear it any larger.

45. He left the town *bag and baggage*. (with all belongings)

46. He was *born in the purple.* (born of royal parents).

47. He has managed to *butter his bread* (secure a comfortable living) pretty well.

48. He is bent on getting rich *by hook or crook* (by any means).

49. He earns his living *by the sweat of his brow* (by hard labour).

50. In this competition there is complete *fair play*. (no cheating)

51. James was timid *from the cradle*. (from childhood).

52. Many young men do their work *head over-heels* (hurriedly).

53. They all ran *helter skelter* (in a state of disorder) down the hill.

54. *In the long run* (ultimately) the honest man succeeds better than the dishonest.

55. He was no kinder to him than to his own *kith and kin* (relatives).

56. This is a hard *nut to crack*. (difficult problem to solve)

57. Whatever he earns, he earns *off his own bat* (by his own exertions)

58. These ladies now *put their heads together*. (consult together)

59. The carpenter *put* the broken tables *to rights* (put in good order).

60. The talk of two Hindi- speaking persons may *be Greek to* (unintelligible) American people.

61. The merchant *looked* rather *blue* (appeared disturbed) at having to pay Rs 3000 as income tax for the first time.

62. We should not *pick holes* (to find fault/ criticise) in other's reputation.

PHRASES

1. He *bore away* (won) the first prize.
The new king was able to *bear down* (overpower) all opposition
I cannot *bear with* (tolerate) her miserliness.
This new taxation will *bear hard upon* (press heavily) the farmers.
If the evidence *bears out* (confirms) the charge, he may be sentenced to death.

I bore up (kept up spirits) against my misfortunes.

2. A burglar *broke into* (entered forcibly) his house.
The thief *broke away* (freed from restraint) from the police custody.
The sun *broke forth* (came out suddenly) and all was bright.
The thief *broke open* (opened with force) the box.
An epidemic *broke out* (burst forth) in the village.
He *broke down* (failed) in the middle of his speech.
This man generally *breaks through* (fails to keep) an engagement.
The meeting *broke up* (came to an end) with shouts of applause.
He seems to have *broken with* (ceased to be friendly with) satish.

3. He *called at* (visited) her house yesterday.
Seeing my friend, I *called to* (addressed loudly) him.
Call in (send for) a doctor.
The Government *called in* (withdrew from circulation) all silver coins.
This job *calls for* (demands) extraordinary skill.
The old man could not *call up* (recollect) past events.
Names on a class roll are *called over* (recited in order).
Call upon (Pray to) me in the day of trouble.
He *called on* (paid a brief visit) me in my office.
He *called* his opponent *out* (challenged to fight).
Seeing my dog barking at the gentleman I *called* it off (diverted attention).

4. *Take away* (remove) these papers.
He *took* it *for* (misunderstood) a rope.
The dentist *took out* (extracted) his tooth.
He has *taken to* (resorted to) gambling.
She *takes after* (resembles) her mother.
He *took over* (accepted) the charge.
It was not proper for him to *take up with* (be friendly with) such a rude fellow.
I will *take down* (record) the speeches.
Satish was *taken in* (admitted).
The old man was *taken in* (deceived) by the sharpers.
We couldn't *take in* (comprehend) his meaning.
I'm quite *taken with* (pleased with) the style of this author.
He *took on* (undertook) the task.
He *took off* (removed) his hat.
He stopped and *took breath* (rested) for a while.
This should also be *taken into account* (considered).
He *took great pains* (attempted diligently) to do my work.

5. His head was *struck off* (cut ff) with a sword.
We were *struck dumb* (astonished) by the news.
The workers *struck work* (refused to work) to compel an increase in wages.
The last sentence should be *struck off* (erased).
Strike up (begin to play) the drums.

6. No one could *stand against* (withstand) Alexander.
He *stood up* (opposed) against caste system.
He will *stand for* (present as candidate) chairmanship in the election.
He *stood by* (assisted) me at all times.
He *stood up for* (fought for) his rights.
A contract *stands good* (remains true) when it is legally made.
He *stood out against* (refused to yield) all our efforts to persuade him.

7. The summer has *set in* (begun).
He *set out* (started on) on his journey.
The decision of the High Court was *set aside* (disregarded) by the Supreme Court.
He *set off* (departed) for Bombay.
This building has been *set up* (established) recently.
The dog *set upon* (attacked) the beggar.
You should *set about* (begin) your own business.
One day in a week is *set apart* (reserved) for a holiday.
The magistrate *set down* (recorded) the statement of the accused.
He *set forth* (explained) his views clearly.
He *set on* (incited) Mala to fight.

8. The date of examination is *drawing near* (approaching).
They *drew out* (prepared) a plan.
He will not *draw back* (withdraw) from his promise.
Wickedness will *draw down* (attract) punishment form a righteous God.
The snail *draws in* (pulls inside) its horns.
Draw off (Divert) your mind from exciting amusements.
Dr. Ambedkar *drew up* (drafted) the Constitution.

9. I *hold with* (agree with) you.
You should not *hold back* (conceal) anything.
This rule *holds good* (is applicable) here.
His application was *held over* (retained) for further consideration.
He fell down as there was nothing to *hold by* (catch hold of).
The troops *held on* (continued) their march for many days.
The supplies did not *hold out* (last, continue) for long.
He *holds to* (sticks to) what he says.
The horse was *held in* (restrained) to prevent damage to fields.
If the rain *holds off* (is away) for even an hour, our work shall be done.

10. He *kept up* (maintained) his spirits.
Keep off (ward off) the cattle from the fields.
Keep at (continue doing) your work.
He could not *keep to* (maintain) his word.
We should *keep our* passions under (control).
You should *keep from* (abstain from) smoking.
I will *keep nothing back* (conceal) from you.
He is an able man, but his large family *keeps him down*. (prevents from rising).

11. The dogs were *let loose* (set free).
He was *let in* (allowed to enter).
She *let down* (lowered) the bucket into the well.
He *let out* (to hire) his house on hire.
The bird in the cage was *let off* (released).
Businessmen will not *let you into* (allow to know) the secrets of trade.

12. You should *put away* (discard) bad habits.
He *put in* (presented) a claim for compensation.
Please *put out* (extinguish) the candle.
He has not *put by* (lay aside for future use) one shilling.
They managed to *put down* (supress) the rebellion.
Put on (wear) your shoes.
They *put up at* (stayed in) an inn.
I can't *put up with* (endure) such a nasty fellow.
The function was *put off* (postponed) till the 15th.
He *put forth* (exerted) all his strength.
Someone has *put this boy upto* (incited) being obstinate.

13. His folly has *brought about* (caused) his ruin.
I was *brought up* (reared) by my uncle.
An open enquiry will *bring out* (highlight) the truth.
The publishers have recently *brought out* (published) a new dictionary.
A life boat *brings off* (rescues) people from a sinking ship.
The rebels were *brought under* (subdued).
It will *bring* his pride *down* (humble).
A good tree *brings forth* (produces) good fruit.
The house *brings in* (yields) Rs. 1000 a month.
He managed to *bring* her *round* (convert her) to his views.
He *brought forward* (adduced) several arguments in support of his scheme.
The king tried to *bring over* (persuade to change sides) the rebels by offering a general pardon to all.

14. Diwali *comes off* (takes place) in November.
How did all this *come about* (happen)?
How did you *come by* (acquire) this bag?
Gold *came down* (descended) in the market yesterday.
The things you have bought will *come to* (amount to) a large sum of.
They have *come to* (arrived at) friendly terms.
The grapes were too high for the fox to *come at* (get within reach of).
Yesterday, I *came across* (met accidentally) an old friend of mine.
He *comes of* (issues from) a royal family.
At last the truth has *come out* (appeared)
A man on a bicycle may easily *come up with* (overtake) a man on foot.
He has *come round* (agreed) to our views.
He will *come round* (recover) within a view.

15. He *got off* (dismounted) the horse.
I hope he would *get off* (escape) with a fine.
I can't *get out* (remove) this stain.
It seems difficult for me to *get out of* (free from) debt.
The thief *got away* (escaped) with cash box.
He *got down* (came down) from the tree.
A rumour has *got abroad* (become public) that he is going to resign.
He managed to *get over* (overcome) all difficulties.

He is *getting on* (progressing) well at school.
He *gets up* (rises) early in the morning.
A collector *gets in* (receives) reports from all quarters of his district.
I tried hard, but could't *get in* (enter)
Intelligent students *get ahead* (advance) in the class.
He is *getting along* (prospering) well in business.
I won't let you *get before* (in forward position) me in learning.
The weather is so bad today that it is not advisable to *get about* (go about).
The dog tried to *get at* (reach) me

TYPE I : Choosing the meaning of a phrase as used in a sentence

In this type of questions, a sentence is given in which a phrase has been italicised, followed by some alternatives. The candidate is required to choose that alternative which best expresses the meaning of the italicised phrase.

Example : He has rejoined office after a week and looks *run down.*

(*a*) cheerful and bubbly (*b*) weak and tired
(*c*) active and energetic (*d*) busy and preoccupied **(Asstt. Grade, 1995)**

Solution : The phrase 'run down' means 'weak and tired'.
Hence, the answer is (*b*).

PRACTICE SET 12

Directions : In each of the following questions, four or five alternatives are given for the phrase in italics in the sentence. Choose the one which best expresses the meaning of the phrase in italics.

1. He has *come up* during the last five years. **(Stenographers' Exam, 1991)**
(*a*) fallen in rank (*b*) risen in status
(*c*) become proud (*d*) become humble

2. After tolerating a lot of exploitation at the hands of the authorities they finally decided to *stand up* for their rights.
(*a*) seize (*b*) enforce
(*c*) negotiate (*d*) vindicate

3. The boss should not have *called* Arun *names* in front of others.
(*a*) abused (*b*) summoned
(*c*) scolded (*d*) praised

4. Last evening I was *held up* at the meeting. **(N.D.A. 1995)**
(*a*) kept (*b*) detained
(*c*) stopped (*d*) delayed

5. I have a problem to *square up* with the manager.
(*a*) work out (*b*) consider
(*c*) discuss (*d*) settle

6. Sachin in not *cut out* for this kind of work.
(*a*) trained (*b*) acquainted
(*c*) suitable (*d*) considered

7. Have you *given up* the idea of accepting the new assignment? **(Clerk's Grade, 1993)**
(*a*) postponed (*b*) adopted
(*c*) amended (*d*) abandoned

8. The Committee could not *pare down* its report enough to suit the ruling party.
(*a*) cut down (*b*) make smaller
(*c*) reduce indictments (*d*) make austere

9. He *passed himself off* as a noble man.
(*a*) was thought to be
(*b*) was regarded as
(*c*) pretended to be
(*d*) No error

10. The promotions were granted *across the board.* **(Asstt. Grade, 1995)**
(*a*) to those sitting diagonally opposite
(*b*) to those working for the other board
(*c*) selectively with a few exceptions
(*d*) to all without exceptions

11. The child *bids fair to be* a great man.
(*a*) aims at becoming
(*b*) seems likely to be
(*c*) is trying hard to be
(*d*) keeps away from

12. Many people *called on* the minister when he was ill. **(Stenographer's Exam, 1994)**
(*a*) helped (*b*) surrounded
(*c*) visited (*d*) criticised

13. When it came to the turn of the press, the rumour was *blown* up and presented as if the incident actually occurred.
(*a*) exaggerated (*b*) wiped out
(*c*) advertised (*d*) made important

14. I was obliged to *set him down.*
(*a*) to oppose him (*b*) to ruin him
(*c*) to snub him (*d*) to humiliate him

15. The old man was *cut to the quick* when his rich son refused to recognise him.
(*a*) irritated (*b*) annoyed

(c) surprised (d) hurt intensely

(Asstt. Grade, 1996)

16. I had no alternative but to *set him down.*
(a) oppose him (b) snub him
(c) support him (d) pacify him

17. Only strict laws make the evil of dowry *die out.*
(a) drift (b) decrease
(c) decay (d) disappear

(Asstt. Grade, 1991)

18. Men of dissolute lives *cry down* religion because they would not be under its restraints.
(a) appreciate (b) follow
(c) emphasise (d) depreciate

19. *Over and above* the household work, she works in a factory on a part-time basis.
(a) beside (b) in addition to
(c) together with (d) in place of

(C.B.I., 1994)

20. He *worked upon* the ignorant villagers by his talent and worth.
(a) excited (b) influenced
(c) incited (d) tempted

21. Can't you *brush yourself up* a little ?
(a) improve your appearance
(b) rejuvenate yourself
(c) reconsider your views
(d) rest

22. We should abstain from *casting aspersions* on the character of our colleagues. **(C.D.S. 1994)**
(a) passing critical remarks
(b) cracking silly jokes
(c) paying left-handed compliments
(d) passing slanderous remarks

23. My friends promised to *look up* my sister whenever they went to London.
(a) survey (b) contact
(c) visit (d) greet

24. He has *fallen out* with his wife
(a) slipped away (b) had an accident
(c) had a quarrel (d) gone away together

25. *Over and above* the household work, she works in a factory on a part-time basis.
(a) together with (b) in place of
(c) in addition to (d) beside

(C.B.I. 1994)

26. He was *pulled up* by the President.
(a) rebuked (b) appreciated
(c) given a high rank (d) made fun of

27. They are going to *wrap up* the negotiations this week.
(a) terminate (b) argue out
(c) conduct (d) finalise

28. The staff have felt *on edge* ever since they heard the rumour about retrenchment. **(Asstt. Grade, 1995)**
(a) nervous (b) unhappy
(c) disheartened (d) scared

29. We shall be formidable if we *stand by* one another.
(a) support
(b) champion the cause of
(c) understand
(d) vindicate the rights of

30. He *worked upon* the ignorant villagers.
(a) befooled (b) influenced
(c) worked for the uplift of
(d) deceived

31. Half the people of the village were *carried off* by the epidemic.
(a) affected (b) forced to migrate
(c) killed (d) made homeless

32. He *tore up* the stairs of his house when he heard a cry.
(a) walked up (b) go up
(c) jumped up (d) ran up

33. He felt *at home* here in my house.
(a) happy (b) comfortable
(c) welcome (d) friendly

34. I *stood up for him* when everyone else was criticising him. **(C.D.S. 1994)**
(a) tolerated him (b) faced him boldly
(c) supported him energetically
(d) opposed him insistently

35. He was trying *to put across* his ideas to his audience. **(N.D.A. 1993)**
(a) to convey (b) to cross
(c) to influence (d) to convince

36. That young author is *cried up* by his friends.
(a) talked of (b) extolled
(c) disliked (d) condemned

37. The captain played with determination because the honour of the team was *at stake* **(Asstt. Grade, 1993)**
(a) very low (b) in danger
(c) at the top (d) appropriate

38. She feels very *put out* about the yesterday's incident.
(a) disturbed (b) pleased
(c) enraged (d) overjoyed

39. We shall be formidable if we *stand by* one another.
(a) champion the cause of (b) vindicate
(c) support (d) understand

40. No one would believe but before my eyes he *made away* with five thousand rupees from the bank.
(a) spent (b) stole
(c) withdrew (d) borrowed

41. The old father *brought home* the moral of unity by asking each of his sons to break the bundle of sticks.
(a) voiced (b) declared

(c) emphasised (d) suggested

(Stenographers' Exam, 1995)

42. I cannot *conceive* of a time when I was without a refrigerator.
(a) understand (b) imagine
(c) depend (d) wait for

43. The case was *held over* due to the great opposition to it.
(a) cancelled (b) dropped
(c) postponed (d) stopped

44. If he does not agree with your views, the best way is to *fall in* with him.
(a) agree (b) quarrel
(c) dissociate (d) agree

45. As is expected of him, Madhu is sure to *work up* the mob.
(a) excite (b) influence
(c) browbeat (d) tackle

46. At my friend's tea party I *fell in with* a strange fellow.
(a) had a quarrel with
(b) met accidentally
(c) had an argument with
(d) made friends with

47. I *ran out of* money on my European tour.

(Stenographers' Exam, 1993)

(a) carried a lot of (b) lost
(c) did not have enough
(d) exhausted my stock of

48. There is no need to *rake up* an old quarrel.
(a) end (b) forget
(c) revive (d) start

49. The rebels *held out* for about a month.
(a) bargained (b) resisted
(c) retreated (d) waited

(Section Officers, 1993)

50. He always *runs down* his brother only because the latter is poor.
(a) quarrels with (b) disagrees with
(c) influences adversely
(d) disparages

ANSWERS

1. (b)	**2.**(d)	**3.** (a)	**4.** (b)	**5.** (d)	**6.** (c)	**7.** (d)	**8.** (c)	**9.** (c)	**10.** (d)
11. (b)	**12.** (c)	**13.** (a)	**14.** (c)	**15.** (d)	**16.** (b)	**17.** (d)	**18.** (d)	**19.** (b)	**20.** (b)
21. (a)	**22.** (d)	**23.** (c)	**24.** (c)	**25.** (c)	**26.** (a)	**27.** (d)	**28.** (a)	**29.** (a)	**30.** (b)
31. (c)	**32.** (d)	**33.** (b)	**34.** (c)	**35.** (a)	**36.** (b)	**37.** (b)	**38.** (a)	**39.** (c)	**40.** (b)
41. (c)	**42.** (b)	**43.** (c)	**44.** (a)	**45.** (a)	**46.** (b)	**47.** (d)	**48.** (c)	**49.** (b)	**50.** (d)

PRACTICE SET 13

Directions : In each of the following questions, four or five alternatives are given for the phrase in italics in the sentence. Choose the one which best expresses the meaning of the phrase in italics.

1. I hope it will not *put you out* if I am late.
(a) worry out (b) please you
(c) irritate you (d) harm you

(Asstt. Grade, 1994)

2. His dealings are all *above board.*
(a) decent (b) friendly
(c) open (d) simple

3. My plan to have a new car *fell through* because of the price rise.
(a) was completed
(b) was completed with difficulty
(c) ws postponed
(d) failed to materialise

(Translators' Exam, 1994)

4. When I refused his request for a loan, he *was put out.*
(a) was annoyed
(b) threatened to use force
(c) started to cry
(d) collapsed

5. Rust has *eaten away* the plate
(a) consumed (b) corroded
(c) destroyed (d) swallowed

6. The father was *taken aback* by his son's rude behaviour.
(a) surprised (b) hurt
(c) annoyed (d) affected

7. After our steep climb, all of us were greatly *knocked out.*
(a) jubilant (b) depressed
(c) happy (d) exhausted

8. A large number of small-scale industries have been *set-up* in the rural areas.
(a) upgraded (b) opened
(c) demolished (d) encouraged

(Stenographer's Exam, 1994)

9. cannot *put up with* that nasty fellow.
(a) appreciate(b) endure

(*c*) control (*d*) forgive
(*e*) praise **(Bank P.O, 1993)**

10. My car *broke down* on way to college yesterday.
(*a*) dashed against another vehicle
(*b*) broke into pieces
(*c*) met with an accident
(*d*) stopped due to mechanical failure

11. He is *out and out* a reactionary.
(*a*) deadly against (*b*) in favour of
(*c*) no more (*d*) thoroughly
(Section Officers, 1993)

12. *Look sharp* if you wish to catch hold of this opportunity.
(*a*) Be quick (*b*) Be intelligent
(*c*) Be firm (*d*) Be careful

13. I was *hard up* last month because of heavy deductions from my salary.
(*a*) in acute tension
(*b*) in difficult circumstances
(*c*) in an unlucky phase
(*d*) not having enough money

14. It is *high time* that India did something about the population problem.
(*a*) desired occasion
(*b*) auspicious moment
(*c*) appropriate time
(*d*) already late **(Asstt. Grade, 1994)**

15. One cannot *get by* in a city without learning those sophisticated ways of dealing with the people.
(*a*) get a job (*b*) survive
(*c*) cope up
(*d*) continue your way of life

16. In his quest for knowledge, he has *knocked about* the world a great deal.
(*a*) gained experience (*b*) explored
(*c*) wandered about (*d*) exhausted

17. I expect he will *come round* within a week.
(*a*) arrive (*b*) visit us
(*c*) recover (*d*) call on us

18. The country's economy is beginning to *look up* now **(N.D.A. 1995)**
(*a*) remain static (*b*) improve
(*c*) look clear (*d*) go down

19. When I told him what I had done, he *went for* me like a wild beast.
(*a*) received (*b*) approached
(*c*) treated (*d*) attacked

20. Ramakant has *laid out* a large sum of money in the new factory.
(*a*) borrowed (*b*) invested
(*c*) collected (*d*) lost

21. Inspite of the immense pressure exerted by the militants, the Government has decided not to *give in*.
(*a*) conform (*b*) oblige
(*c*) accede (*d*) yield
(Assistant Grade, 1996)

22. Sher Singh could be easily arrested because the police were *tipped off* in advance.
(*a*) threatened (*b*) toppled over
(*c*) bribed
(*d*) given advance information

23. He is always *standing up for* the weak and oppressed.
(*a*) supporting
(*b*) boosting the claims of
(*c*) championing the cause of
(*d*) seeking help of others for

24. There are many things about behaviour that I can't *account for.*
(*a*) relate (*b*) pay for
(*c*) explain (*d*) enumerate

25. I am leaving India *for good.*
(*a*) permanently
(*b*) to do good for myself
(*c*) to do good for the country
(*d*) to do nobody good
(Clerk's Grade, 1994)

26. He has *drawn off* a major share of his profits from the company.
(*a*) to part with
(*b*) to transfer to some other name
(*c*) to write off (*d*) to withdraw

27. His views are *looked down upon* by his fellow workers.
(*a*) relied upon (*b*) regarded as inferior
(*c*) criticised (*d*) appreciated

28. The old beggar *ran amuck* and began to throw stones at the passerby.
(*a*) felt disgusted
(*b*) became annoyed
(*c*) ran about wildly
(*d*) became desperate **(C.B.I. 1995)**

29. There is no need to *go over* the second chapter of the book again.
(*a*) open up (*b*) overlook
(*c*) learn by heart (*d*) study carefully

30. I readily *closed with* his offer.
(*a*) turned down (*b*) accepted
(*c*) proclaimed (*d*) denied

31. You need rest; you look a bit *run down.*
(*a*) sad (*b*) in poor health
(*c*) ill (*d*) depressed
(Stenographer's Exam, 1994)

32. We were *bowled over* by the unexpected beauty of the landscape.
(*a*) shocked (*b*) overwhelmed
(*c*) confused (*d*) staggered

33. Enemy soldiers *fell upon* the platoon as soon as it crossed the border.
(*a*) warmly greeted
(*b*) accidentally met

(c) attacked (d) happened to see

34. They *fixed upon* him to do the work.
(a) relied upon (b) chose
(c) compelled (d) requested
(e) ordered

35. He generally *passed by* the faults of subordinates.
(a) succeeded in mending
(b) managed to make them realise
(c) tolerated (d) overlooked

36. The doctors have *given him up*.
(a) cured him
(b) convinced him
(c) have no hope of his recovery
(d) are fully hopeful of his recovery

37. I can't *put off* consulting the doctor any longer.
(a) decide (b) forget
(c) postpone (d) afford

38. In order to save himself from a thrashing, the boy *trumped up* a story.
(a) flung (b) fabricated
(c) followed (d) presented

39. We should *do away with* the present examination system. **(I. Tax, 1994)**
(a) prohibit (b) demolish
(c) extend (d) abolish

40. The merchants were *advised of* the risk.
(a) acquainted with (b) warned against
(c) told how to avoid
(d) advised not to take

41. Men generally get *broken down* in old age.
(a) helpless (b) frustrated
(c) fail in health
(d) have poor financial conditions

42. He *dashed off* three letters in ten minutes.
(a) wrote (b) went through
(c) packed up (d) dispatched

ANSWERS

1. (c)	**2.** (c)	**3.** (d)	**4.** (a)	**5.** (b)	**6.** (a)	**7.** (d)	**8.** (b)	**9.** (b)	**10.** (d)
11. (d)	**12.** (a)	**13.** (d)	**14.** (d)	**15.** (b)	**16.** (c)	**17.** (c)	**18.** (b)	**19.** (d)	**20.** (b)
21. (d)	**22.** (d)	**23.** (c)	**24.** (d)	**25.** (a)	**26.** (d)	**27.** (b)	**28.** (c)	**29.** (d)	**30.** (d)
31. (b)	**32.** (b)	**33.** (c)	**34.** (b)	**35.** (d)	**36.** (c)	**37.** (c)	**38.** (b)	**39.** (d)	**40.** (a)
41. (c)	**42.** (a)								

TYPE II ; USE OF PHRASES TO FILL IN THE BLANKS

In this type of questions, four phrases are suggested and labelled (a), (b), (c) and (d). These phrases serve as alternatives to fill in the blanks in some sentences that follow. The candidate is required to exmaine each phrase in context of the given sentence and then choose the most effective one as his answer. Here is an example.

Directions : Of the four alternatives given below find the one that best fits into the blank in each of the following sentences.

(a) call up (b) call for (c) call out (d) call to

1. The occasion .... prompt action.
2. The fire brigade was .... twice yesterday.
3. It is difficult for an old man to .... the events of his childhood.
4. Seeing my friend on the roadside in a car I .... him, but he could not hear me.
5. He .... his opponent ...., but the fellow was too great a coward to come.

Solution : '*call up*' means 'to bring to memory'. So, the blank in sentence **3** should be filled up with (a).

'*call for*' means 'to demand'. So, the blank in sentence **1** should be filled up with 'calls for'. Hence, answer is (b).

'call out' means 'to challenge' or 'to require'. So, (c) is the answer for sentences **2 & 5.**

'call to' means 'to address loudly'. So, (d) is the answer for sentence **4.**

PRACTICE SET 14

Directions : Of the alternatives given for each group of sentences, find the one that best fits into the blank in ecah of the following sentences :

Questions 1 to 5 (Hotel Management, 1995)

(*a*) carry away (*b*) carry out
(*c*) carry on (*d*) carry through

1. The soldier has no choice but to .... his officer's orders.
2. The audience was .... by his wit.
3. The troops have exhausted the ammunition.
They cannot .... any longer.
4. Our pooled resources will certainly .... us .... this crisis.
5. The South Koreans .... the 1995. Indira Gandhi Gold Cup in hockey

Questions 6 to 9

(*a*) put off (*b*) put by
(*c*) put up (*d*) put in
(*e*) put forward

6. He talked so fast that I could not .... a word.
7. While in Delhi, I always .... in a hotel.
8. When your salary is good, ... something against contingencies.
9. Never .... till tomorrow what you can do today.

Questions 10 to 14

(*a*) bring in (*b*) bring out
(*c*) bring up (*d*) bring forth

10. Idleness and luxury .... poverty and want.
11. The problem is who will .... this child.
12. The company intends to .... many books this year.
13. How much will this auction .... ?
14. Our teacher often tells us a story to .... the meaning of a lesson.

Questions 15 to 17

(*a*) blow out (*b*) blow up
(*c*) blow away

15. Please .... the candle.
16. When a man winnows grain, he lets the chaff ....
17. The army intends to .... the bridge with gunpowder.

Questions 18 to 22

(*a*) cut down (*b*) cut up
(*c*) cut off (*d*) cut out for

18. He is .... a sailor.
19. He was .... in the prime of his life.
20. You must .... your expenditure.
21. The news of his son's death .... him .... greatly.
22. They .... the old mango tree.

Questions 23 to 28

(*a*) deal with (*b*) deal by
(*c*) deal out (*d*) deal in

23. He .... the cards among the players.
24. This book .... questions on grammar.
25. My father .... sugar and allied products.
26. I shall not .... him again.
27. Some officers .... well .... their clerks.
28. A judge should .... equal justice to all

Questions 29 to 34

(*a*) do with (*b*) do up
(*c*) do for (*d*) do away with

29. Who will .... my room everyday in your absence ?
30. This cloth will .... you .... a wrapper.
31. Having walked twenty miles, he is quite ....
32. I am ....
33. We should .... with the dowry practice!
34. There is a pleasure in .... a debtor which none but a creditor can know.

Questions 35 to 41

(*a*) fall in (*b*) fall out
(*c*) fall back (*d*) fall off
(*e*) fall through

35. At last the rioters ....
36. The two brothers have .... with each other.
37. In the second school-term the attendance ....
38. As neither of us would give in, the bargain ....
39. At present many persons oppose my scheme, but by and by they will ....
40. Ripe mangoes have started ....
41. The standard of efficiency in public service has ....

Questions 42 to 45

(*a*) look over (*b*) look into
(*c*) look for (*d*) look out for

42. You should .... the matter.
43. I .... my accounts.
44. We are .... the lost keys.
45. The eagle is .... prey.

Questions 46 to 50

(*a*) lay out (*b*) lay by
(*c*) lay down (*d*) lay up

46. He resolved to .... a part of his income

47. Satish has .... a large sum in shares
48. The rebels .... their arms.
49. He is .... with fever.
50. People, who do not .... their money carefully, soon come to grief.

ANSWERS

1. (*b*) : carry out – execute
2. (*a*) : carried away – enamoured
3. (*c*) : carry on – continue
4. (*d*) : carry through – to get through
5. (*a*) : carried away – bore
6. (*d*) : put in – insert
7. (*c*) : put up – stay
8. (*b*) : put by – lay aside for future
9. (*a*) : put off – postpone
10. (*d*) : bring forth – cause
11. (*c*) : bring up – rear
12. (*b*) : bring out – publish
13. (*a*) : bring in – yield
14. (*b*) : bring out – show
15. (*a*) : blow out – extinguish by blowing
16. (*c*) : blow away – clear away by wind
17. (*b*) : blow up – destroy by explosion
18. (*d*) : cut out for – fitted to be
19. (*c*) : cut off – died
20. (*a*) : cut down – reduce
21. (*b*) : cut up – distressed
22. (*a*) : cut down
23. (*c*) : dealt out – distributed
24. (*a*) : deals with – treats
25. (*d*) : deals in – trades in
26. (*a*) : deal with
27. (*b*) : deal by – behave with
28. (*c*) : deal out – distribute
29. (*b*) : do up – make tidy
30. (*c*) : do for – serve the purpose of
31. (*b*) : done up – tired
32. (*c*) : done for – ruined
33. (*d*) : do away with – remove
34. (*b*) : doing up – making bankrupt
35. (*c*) : fell back – yielded
36. (*b*) : fallen out – quarrelled
37. (*d*) : fell off – diminished
38. (*e*) : fell through – came to nothing
39. (*a*) : fall in – agree
40. (*d*) : falling off – dropping
41. (*d*) : fallen off – deteriorated
42. (*b*) : look into – investigate
43. (*a*) : looked over – examined
44. (*c*) : looking for – searching for
45. (*d*) : looking out for – to be on watch for
46. (*b*) : lay by – save for future
47. (*a*) : laid out – invested
48. (*c*) : laid down – surrendered
49. (*d*) : laid up – confined to bed
50. (*a*) : lay out – spend

PRACTICE SET 15

Directions : of the alternatives given for each group of sentences, find the one that best fits into the blank in each of the given sentences :

Questions 1 to 5

(*a*) pass into (*b*) pass for
(*c*) pass off (*d*) pass away
(*e*) pass through

1. The old man .... without any trouble.
2. He .... a great dramatist.
3. His disease has .... a chronic state
4. The crew .... terrible sufferings.
5. He was caught while trying to .... a counterfeit rupee.
6. He .... himself .... as a nobleman.

Questions 7 to 11

(*a*) look to (*b*) look up
(*c*) look after (*d*) look on

7. The Indian economy is now ....
8. My uncle .... me.
9. .... the word in the dictionary.
10. .... your manners.
11. I .... him as my son.

Questions 12 to 18

(*a*) make up (*b*) make out
(*c*) make over (*d*) make of
(*e*) make for

12. I cannot .... his writing.
13. I cannot .... anything .... this telegram.
14. He .... his bungalow to an orphanage.
15. You have failed to .... your case.
16. The two brothers quarrelled some time ago, but they have now .... it ....
17. Contentment .... happiness.
18. I cannot .... the meaning of this verse.

Questions 19 to 23

(*a*) pull up (*b*) pull through
(*c*) pull down (*d*) pull together

19. The coach .... at a little roadside inn.
20. He managed to .... the examination.
21. Unless we .... we cannot succeed.
22. The building was ....
23. The doctor says the patient will ....

Questions 24 to 27

(*a*) cast away (*b*) cast down
(*c*) cast up (*d*) cast aside

24. The student who .... the instructions of his teacher cannot learn anything.
25. The ship was .... on the coast of Africa.
26. Please .... this column of figures.
27. He was much .... by his loss.

Questions 28 to 31

(*a*) throw up (*b*) throw out
(*c*) throw off (*d*) throw down

28. The Bill was ....
29. She .... all sense of shame.
30. The walls were ....
31. He .... his appointment.

Questions 32 to 35

(*a*) turn up (*b*) turn off
(*c*) turn out (*d*) turn away

32. This road .... to the right
33. The lost boy .... after two years.
34. Don't .... me .... of doors.
35. He .... his dishonest servant.

Questions 36 to 40

(*a*) give over (*b*) give out
(*c*) give in (*d*) give away

36. The Chief Guest .... the prizes.
37. The strikers seem determined, and are not likely to ....
38. The horses .... at the next milestone.
39. .... this foolish attempt.
40. It was .... that he was a bankrupt.

Questions 41 to 46

(*a*) go by (*b*) go through
(*c*) go down (*d*) go over

41. The auditor .... the balance-sheet.
42. You must .... this book again.
43. She has patiently .... the sufferings of life.
44. That story won't ....
45. He .... the directions of the officer.
46. Three months .... without the accused being traced out.

Questions 47 to 50

(*a*) give off (*b*) give way
(*c*) go into (*d*) go upon

47. He promised to .... the matter.
48. The fire .... a dense smoke.
49. The rope .... while the workmen were hauling up the iron pillar.
50. We have no data to ....

ANSWERS

1. (*d*) : passed away – died
2. (*b*) : passed for – is regarded as
3. (*a*) : passed into – changed into
4. (*e*) : passed through – underwent
5. (*c*) : pass off – impose fraudulently
6. (*c*) : passed himself over – pretended to be
7. (*b*) : looking up – improving
8. (*c*) : looks after – takes care of
9. (*b*) : look up – search for
10. (*a*) : look to – Be careful about
11. (*d*) : look on – regard
12. (*b*) : make out – decipher
13. (*d*) : make of – understand
14. (*c*) : made over – presented
15. (*b*) : make out – prove
16. (*a*) : made up – reconciled
17. (*e*) : makes for – results in
18. (*b*) : make out – discover
19. (*a*) : pulled up – came to halt
20. (*b*) : pull through – pass with difficulty
21. (*d*) : pull together – cooperate
22. (*c*) : pulled down – demolished
23. (*b*) : pull through – recover
24. (*c*) : casts aside – ignores as useless
25. (*a*) : cast away – wrecked
26. (*d*) : cast up – calculate
27. (*b*) : cast down – depressed
28. (*b*) : thrown out – rejected
29. (*c*) : threw off – discarded
30. (*b*) : thrown down – demolished
31. (*a*) : threw up – resigned
32. (*b*) : turns up – diverts
33. (*a*) : turned up – appeared
34. (*c*) : turn out – expel
35. (*d*) : turned away – dismissed
36. (*d*) : gave away – distributed
37. (*c*) : give in – yield
38. (*b*) : gave out – exhausted
39. (*a*) : give over – abandon
40. (*b*) : given out – proclaimed
41. (*d*) : went over – examined
42. (*b*) : go through – read
43. (*b*) : gone through – endured
44. (*c*) : go down – be believed
45. (*a*) : went by – followed
46. (*a*) : went by – elapsed
47. (*c*) : go into – investigate
48. (*a*) : gave off – emitted
49. (*b*) : gave way – broke
50. (*d*) : go upon – on which to base our conclusion

---

25. ACTIVE & PASSIVE VOICE

In a sentence, when the subject acts, the verb is said to be in **Active Voice,** but when the subject is passive and receives action, the verb is said to be in **Passive Voice.**

e.g. (i) Ajay writes a letter.

This sentence indicates that the subject 'Ajay' does something. So, it is in Active Voice.

(ii) A letter is written by Ajay.

In this sentence, the verb 'written' indicates that something is done by Ajay. So, the verb here is in Passive Voice.

The following are the different forms of sentences which are given to be transformed from one Voice to another :

Active Voice	**Passive Voice**
1. He *writes* a letter.	A letter *is written* by him.
2. He *wrote* a letter.	A letter *was written* by him.
3. He *will write* a letter.	A letter *will be written* by him.
4. He *is writing* a letter.	A letter *is being written* by him.
5. He *was writing* a letter.	A letter *was being written* by him.
6. He *has written* a letter.	A letter *has been written* by him.
7. He *had written* a letter.	A letter *had been written* by him.
8. He *will have written* a letter.	A letter *will have been written* by him.
9. Do not disturb the class.	Let the class not be disturbed.
10. Someone has stolen my pen.	My pen has been stolen.
11. People *speak* English all over the world.	English *is spoken* all over the world.
12. Who *did* this?	By whom *was* this done?
13. Why *did* your brother *write* such a letter?	Why *was* such a letter *written* by your brother?
14. Mr. Roy teaches us grammar?	We are taught grammar by Mr. Roy. Grammar is taught us by Mr. Roy.
15. Who taught you French?	By whom was French taught you? (or) By whom were you taught French?
16. One should keep one's promises.	Promises should be kept.
17. Your behaviour greatly astonishes me.	I am greatly astonished *at* your behaviour.
18. This box contains ice.	Ice is contained *in* this box.
19. I want to buy an umbrella.	I want an umbrella to be bought.
20. They objected to my proposal.	My proposal was objected to by them.
21. Since he had not done the preliminary work, we had to cancel the meeting.	Since the preliminary work had not been done by him, the meeting had to be cancelled (or) Since he had not done the preliminary work, the meeting had to be cancelled.

PRACTICE SET

Directions : ***In each of the following questions, a sentence has been given in Active (or Passive) Voice. Out of the four alternatives suggested select the one which best expresses the same sentence in Passive (or Active) voice.***

1. Mona was writing a letter to her father.
(*a*) A letter was written to her father by Mona.
(*b*) A letter has been written to her father by Mona.
(*c*) A letter was being written by Mona to her father.
(*d*) A letter was written by Mona to her father. **(Stenographers' Exam, 1994)**

2. He teaches us Grammar.
(*a*) Grammar is taught to us by him.
(*b*) We are being taught Grammar by him.
(*c*) Grammar is being taught us by him.
(*d*) We are taught Grammar by him.

3. Do you imitate others?
(*a*) Are others imitated by you?
(*b*) Are others being imitated by you?
(*c*) Were others being imitated by you?
(*d*) Have others been imitated by you?
(Stenographers' Exam, 1995)

4. I saw him conducting the rehearsal.
(*a*) He was seen conducting the rehearsal.
(*b*) I saw the rehearsal to be conducted by him.
(*c*) He was seen by me to conduct the rehearsal.
(*d*) I saw the rehearsal being conducted by him.

5. Have the box broken. **(Clerks' Grade, 1996)**
(*a*) Have the broken box.
(*b*) Break the box.
(*c*) Get someone to break the box.
(*d*) They have broken the box.

6. His pocket has been picked.
(*a*) They have his pocket picked.
(*b*) Picking has been done to his pocket.
(*c*) Picked has been his pocket.
(*d*) Someone has picked his pocket.
(Stenographers' Exam, 1992)

7. The French surrendered Quebec to the English in 1759.
(*a*) Quebec was surrendered by the French to the English in 1759.
(*b*) Quebec was surrendered to the English in 1759 by the French.
(*c*) The English were surrendered Quebec in 1759 by the French.
(*d*) Quebec was surrendered in 1759 by the French to the English.

8. Someone gave her a bull dog.
(*a*) She was given a bull dog.
(*b*) A bull dog was given to her.
(*c*) She has been given a bull dog.
(*d*) She is being given a bull dog by someone.
(Stenographers' Exam, 1991)

9. A stone struck me on the head.
(*a*) I was struck by a stone on the head.
(*b*) My head was struck by a stone.
(*c*) I had been struck by a stone on the head.
(*d*) I was struck on the head by a stone.

10. You must look into this matter.
(*a*) This matter has been looked into by you.
(*b*) This matter may be looked into by you.
(*c*) This matter should be looked into by you.
(*d*) This matter into looked by you.
(Hotel Management, 1991)

11. The Romans expected to conquer Carthage.
(*a*) Carthage was expected to be conquered by the Romans.
(*b*) The Romans were expected to conquer Carthage.
(*c*) It was expected by the Romans that they would conquer Carthage.
(*d*) The Romans expected to have conquered Carthage.

12. Rain disrupted the last day's play between India and Sri Lanka.
(*a*) The last day's play of India and Sri Lanka was disrupted by rain.
(*b*) India and Sri Lanka's play of the last day was disrupted by rain.
(*c*) The last day's play between India and Sri Lanka was disrupted by rain.
(*d*) The last day's play between India and Sri Lanka were disrupted by rain. **(Stenographers' Exam, 1994)**

13. My uncle promised me a present.
(*a*) A present was promised by my uncle to me.
(*b*) I was promised a present by my uncle.
(*c*) I had been promised a present by my uncle.
(*d*) I was promised by my uncle a present.

14. Darjeeling grows tea.
(*a*) Tea grows in Darjeeling.
(*b*) Tea is grown in Darjeeling.
(*c*) Let the tea be grown in Darjeeling.
(*d*) Tea is being grown in Darjeeling.
(Stenographers' Exam, 1995)

15. He was arrested on a charge of theft, but for lack of evidence he was released.
(*a*) He was arrested on a charge of theft, but was released for lack of evidence.
(*b*) The police arrested him on a charge of theft, but for lack of evidence he was released.
(*c*) The police arrested him on a charge of theft, but for lack of evidence released him.
(*d*) None of these

16. Please help me.
(*a*) You were requested to help me.
(*b*) You are being requested to help me.
(*c*) You are requested to help me.
(*d*) You have been requested to help me.
(Stenographers' Exam, 1991)

17. The residents celebrated the Independence Day.
(*a*) The Independence Day is celebrated by the residents.
(*b*) The Independence Day was celebrated by the residents.
(*c*) The Independence Day has been celebrated by the residents.
(*d*) Celebration of Independence Day was done by the residents.
(Stenographers' Exam, 1992)

18. I know him.
(*a*) He is known by me.
(*b*) He was known to me.
(*c*) He has been known by me.
(*d*) He is known to me.
(Stenographers' Exam, 1991)

19. They are building a house next door to our school.
(*a*) Next door to our school a house is being built by them.
(*b*) Next door to our school is being built a house by them.
(*c*) A house next door to our school is being built by them.
(*d*) A house is being built by them next door to our school.

20. One should keep one's promise.
(*a*) One's promise should be kept by us.
(*b*) One's promise has to be kept.
(*c*) A promise should be keeping
(*d*) A promise should be kept.

21. Who is creating this mess?
(*a*) Who has created this mess?
(*b*) By whom has this mess been created?
(*c*) By whom this mess is being created?
(*d*) By whom is this mess being created?

22. The clown was being laughed at by them.
(*a*) They were laughing at the clown.
(*b*) They were laughing on the clown.
(*c*) They laughed at the clown.
(*d*) The clown was laughed at by them.
(Stenographers' Exam, 1991)

23. I saw him leaving the house.
(*a*) He had been seen leaving the house.
(*b*) He was seen to be leaving the house.
(*c*) Leaving the house he was seen by me.
(*d*) He was seen leaving the house by me. **(Stenographers' Exam, 1992)**

24. A lion may be helped even by a little mouse.
(*a*) A little mouse may even help a lion.
(*b*) Even a little mouse may help a lion.
(*c*) A little mouse can even help a lion.
(*d*) Even a little mouse ought to help a lion. **(Stenographer's Exam, 1994)**

25. Who taught her such things?
(*a*) Who was she taught such things by?
(*b*) She was taught such things by who?
(*c*) By whom she was taught such things?
(*d*) By whom was she taught such things?

26. The noise of the traffic kept me awake.
(*a*) I remained awake by the noise of the traffic.
(*b*) I was kept waking by the noise of the traffic.
(*c*) I was kept awake by the noise of the traffic.
(*d*) The traffic kept me awake by the noise.

27. I remember my sister taking me to the museum.
(*a*) I remember taken to the museum by my sister.
(*b*) I remember myself being taken to the museum by my sister.
(*c*) I remember I was taken to the museum by my sister.
(*d*) I remember being taken to the museum by my sister.

28. Why do you waste time?
(*a*) Why is time wasted by you?
(*b*) Why is time been wasted by you?
(*c*) Why has time been wasted by you?
(*d*) Why is time being wasted by you?
(Hotel Management, 1991)

29. Who teaches you English?
(*a*) By whom were you taught English?

(*b*) By whom are you taught English?
(*c*) English is taught by whom?
(*d*) By whom will you be taught English?
(Stenographer's Exam, 1991)

30. We hope that we shall win the match.
(*a*) The match is hoped to be won.
(*b*) Match winning is our hope.
(*c*) It is hoped that the match will be won by us.
(*d*) Winning the match is hoped by us.
(Stenographers' Exam, 1992)

31. Somebody told me that there had been an explosion in the Town Hall.
(*a*) I was told by somebody about the explosion in the Town Hall.
(*b*) I was told about the explosion in the Town Hall.
(*c*) I was informed that there was an explosion in the Town Hall.
(*d*) I was told by somebody that there had been an explosion in the Town Hall. **(Stenographers' Exam, 1994)**

32. It is time to ring the bell.
(*a*) It is time the bell rings.
(*b*) It is being time to ring the bell.
(*c*) It is time for the bell to ring.
(*d*) It is time for the bell to be rung.

33. After driving Professor Kumar to the museum she dropped him at his hotel.
(*a*) After she was driving Professor Kumar to the museum she was dropping him at his hotel.
(*b*) After she had driven Professor Kumar to the museum she had dropped him at his hotel.
(*c*) Professor Kumar was being driven to the museum first, then he was being dropped at his hotel.
(*d*) After being driven to the museum, Professor Kumar was dropped at his hotel. **(Stenographers' Exam, 1995)**

34. You will have finished this work by tomorrow.
(*a*) This work will have been finished tomorrow.
(*b*) This work will be finished by tomorrow.
(*c*) This work will finished tomorrow.
(*d*) This work will have been finished by tomorrow.
(Stenographers' Exam, 1994)

35. People claim to have seen the suspect in several cities.
(*a*) The suspect is being seen in several cities.
(*b*) The suspect has been the people in several cities.
(*c*) The suspect is claimed to have been seen in several cities.
(*d*) The suspect was seen by people in several cities.
(Stenographers' Exam, 1992)

36. The teacher punished the boys who had not done their homework. **(Clerks' Grade, 1996)**
(*a*) The boys who had not done their homework had been punished by their teacher.
(*b*) The boys were punished by their teacher who had not done their homework.
(*c*) The boys who had not done their homework were punished by the teacher.
(*d*) The boys who had not done their homework were being punished by the teacher.

ANSWERS

1. (*c*)	**2.** (*d*)	**3.** (*a*)	**4.** (*d*)	**5.** (*c*)	**6.** (*d*)	**7.** (*a*)	**8.** (*b*)	**9.** (*d*)	**10.** (*c*)
11. (*c*)	**12.** (*c*)	**13.** (*b*)	**14.** (*b*)	**15.** (*c*)	**16.** (*c*)	**17.** (*b*)	**18.** (*d*)	**19.** (*d*)	**20.** (*d*)
21. (*d*)	**22.** (*a*)	**23.** (*d*)	**24.** (*b*)	**25.** (*d*)	**26.** (*c*)	**27.** (*d*)	**28.** (*a*)	**29.** (*b*)	**30.** (*c*)
31. (*d*)	**32.** (*d*)	**33.** (*d*)	**34.** (*d*)	**35.** (*c*)	**36.** (*c*)				

---

26. DIRECT AND INDIRECT SPEECH

Quoting the actual words of a speaker is termed as **Direct Speech.**
Reporting what a person said without quoting his exact words is termed as **Indirect (or Reported) Speech.**

Some Common Examples :

1. He says, "I am ready."
He says that he is ready."
2. He has said to me, "I did not do it."
He has told me that he did not do it.
3. He will say, "I am ready".
He will say that he is ready.
4. He said, "I write letters".
He said that he wrote letters.
5. He said, "I wrote a letter".
He said that he had written a letter.
6. He said, "I shall write letters."
He said that he would write letters.
7. He said, "I was writing letters."
He said that he had been writing letters.
8. He said, "I had gone to Bombay."
He said that he had gone to Bombay.
9. **Note :** There is no change in universal truths, general saying or habitual truths.
(i) The teacher said, "The sun rises in the east."
The teacher said that the sun rises in the east.
(ii) He said, "Honesty is the best policy."
He said that honesty is the best policy.
(iii) He said, "I take bath regularly."
He said that he takes bath regularly.
(iv) He said, "India became independent in 1947."
He said that India became independent in 1947.
10. He said, "I saw him here."
He said that he had seen him there.
11. He said, "Where is the book?"
He asked me where the book was.
12. "Where has she gone?" he asked me.
He asked me where she had gone.
13. She said to Meena, "Is it raining?"
She asked Meena if it was raining.
14. He said, "Hurry up !"
He asked me to hurry up.
15. He said, "Please let me go."
He requested them to let him go.
16. He said to Ravi, "Don't move."
He told Ravi not to move.
17. They said, "How silly of him!"
They exclaimed that it was very silly of him.
18. The boys said, "Hurrah! we've won the match".
The boys exclaimed with joy that they had won the match.
19. He said, "Alas! I am undone."
He exclaimed with sorrow that he was undone.
20. She said, "O that I were a boy."
She eagerly wished that she had been a boy.
21. The teacher said, "Well done ! my boys."
The teacher applauded the boys, saying that they had done well.
22. He said, "May you succeed."
He wished/prayed that I might succeed.
23. Harsh said, "Sir, may I go home?"
Harsh respectfully asked whether he could go home.
24. I said to him, "Do have a cup of tea."
I requested him to have a cup of tea.
25. He said, "I must go at once."
He said that he had to go at once.
26. I said to him, "Let us go out for a walk."
I proposed to him that we should go out for a walk.
27. They said to the teacher, "Let us go home."
They requested the teacher to allow them to go home.
28. 'Hello", he said to his sister. "How are you?"
He greeted his sister and asked her how she was.
29. "Oh dear! I have torn my shirt."
He sighed and said that he had torn his shirt.
30. "So help me Heaven!" he cried, "I will never steal again."
He called upon Heaven to witness his resolve never to steal again.

PRACTICE SET

Directions : ***In each of the following questions, a sentence has been given in Direct/Indirect Speech. Out of the four alternatives suggested select the one which best expresses the same sentence in Indirect/Direct Speech.***

1. He said to her, "Are you coming to the party?" **(Stenographers' Exam, 1991)**
(*a*) He asked her whether she was coming to the party.

(*b*) He told her if she was coming to the party.
(*c*) He asked her if she was coming to the party.
(*d*) He asked her if she will be coming to the party.

2. The sage said, "God helps those who help themselves."
(*a*) The sage said that God helps those who help themselves.
(*b*) The sage said that God helped those whose helped themselves.
(*c*) The sage said that God helps those who helped themselves.
(*d*) The sage said that God helped those who help themselves.

3. "Please don't go away", she said.
(*a*) She said to please her and not go away.
(*b*) She told me not to go away.
(*c*) She begged that I not go away.
(*d*) She begged me not to go away.
(Stenographer's Exam, 1995)

4. He said, "I clean my teeth twice a day."
(*a*) He said that he cleaned his teeth twice a day.
(*b*) He said that he cleans his teeth twice a day.
(*c*) He said that he used to clean his teeth twice a day.
(*d*) He said that he is used to cleaning his teeth twice a day.

5. He said to them, "Don't make a noise."
(*a*) He told them that don't make a noise.
(*b*) He told them not to make noise.
(*c*) He told them not to make a noise.
(*d*) He asked them not to make a noise.
(Stenographers' Exam, 1994)

6. The teacher said, "Be quiet, boys."
(*a*) The teacher said that they boys should be quiet.
(*b*) The teacher called the boys and ordered them to be quiet.
(*c*) The teacher urged the boys to be quiet.
(*d*) The teacher commanded the boys that they be quiet.

7. My friend said to me, "Has your father returned from Calcutta?"
(Stenographers' Exam, 1992)
(*a*) My friend said to me that my father has returned from Calcutta.
(*b*) My friend asked me if my father had returned from Calcutta.
(*c*) My friend told me that his father had returned from Calcutta.
(*d*) My friend enquired me if his father had returned from Calcutta.

8. He said, "Where shall I be this time next year!"
(*a*) He asked that where should he be that time next year.
(*b*) He wondered where he should be that time the next year.
(*c*) He contemplated where shall he be that time the following year.
(*d*) He wondered where he would be that time the following year.

9. Rajesh said, "I bought a car yesterday."
(*a*) Rajesh said that I have bought a car the previous day.
(*b*) Rajesh told that he had bought a car yesterday.
(*c*) Rajesh said that he bought a car the previous day.
(*d*) Rajesh said that he had bought a car the previous day.
(Stenographer's Exam, 1991)

10. The employer said to the workman, "I cannot pay you higher wages."
(*a*) The employer told the workman that he could not be paid higher wages.
(*b*) The employer told the workman that he could not pay him higher wages.
(*c*) The employer forbade the workman to pay higher wages.
(*d*) The employer warned the workman that he cannot pay him higher wages.

11. My cousin said, "My room-mate snored throughout the night."
(*a*) My cousin said that her room-mate had snored throughout the night.
(*b*) My cousin told me that her room-mate snored throughout the night.
(*c*) My cousin complained to me that her room-mate is snoring throughout the night.
(*d*) My cousin felt that her room-mate may be snoring throughout the night. **(Stenographer's Exam, 1995)**

12. He asked his teacher, "Need I read this chapter?"
(*a*) He asked his teacher whether there was a need to read that chapter.
(*b*) He asked his teacher whether he needed to read this chapter.
(*c*) He asked his teacher if it was necessary to read this chapter.
(*d*) He asked his teacher if he had to read that chapter.

13. He said, "What a beautiful scene !"

(*a*) He said that what a beautiful scene it was.

(*b*) He wondered that it was a beautiful scene.

(*c*) He exclaimed what a beautiful scene it was.

(*d*) He exclaimed that it was a very beautiful scene.

(Stenographer's Exam, 1994)

14. He said, "I saw a book here."

(*a*) He said that he saw a book here.

(*b*) He said that he saw a book there.

(*c*) He said that he had seen a book here.

(*d*) He said that he had seen a book there.

15. He said to me, "What time do the offices close?"

(*a*) He wanted to know what time the offices close.

(*b*) He asked me what time did the offices close.

(*c*) He asked me what time the offices closed.

(*d*) He asked me what time the offices did close.

16. Pinki said to Gaurav, "Will you help me in my work just now?"

(Stenographer's Exam, 1991)

(*a*) Pinki asked Gaurav if he would help her in her work just then.

(*b*) Pinki questioned to Gaurav that will you help me in my work just now.

(*c*) Pinki told Gaurav whether he will help her in her work just now.

(*d*) Pinki asked to Gaurav that will he help her in her work just now.

17. Sarita said to me, "I will do it now or never."

(*a*) Sarita told me that I would do it then or never.

(*b*) Sarita told me that she would do it now or never.

(*c*) Sarita told me that she will do that now or never.

(*d*) Sarita told me that she would do it then or never.

18. She said to him, "Why don't you go today?" **(Stenographer's Exam, 1995)**

(*a*) She said to him that why he don't go today.

(*b*) She asked him if he was going that day.

(*c*) She asked him why he did not go today.

(*d*) She asked him why he did not go that day.

19. Gavaskar said, "Bravo! Azhar, you have done well."

(*a*) Gavaskar exclaimed with joy that Azhar had done well.

(*b*) Gavaskar called Azhar and exclaimed that he had done well.

(*c*) Gavaskar congratulated Azhar, saying that he had done well.

(*d*) Gavaskar praised Azhar for his having done well.

20. He said to me, "Where is the post office?"

(*a*) He wanted to know where the post office was.

(*b*) He asked me that where the post office was.

(*c*) He asked me where the post office was.

(*d*) He asked me where was the post office. **(Stenographer's Exam, 1994)**

21. He said, "The mice will play, when the cat is away."

(*a*) He said that the mice will play when the cat is away.

(*b*) He said that the mice would play when the cat was away.

(*c*) He said that the mice would play when the cat would be away.

(*d*) He said that the mice shall play, when the cat is away.

22. He said to his servant, "Why are you so lazy today?" **(Stenographer's Exam, 1992)**

(*a*) He asked his servant why he was so lazy that day.

(*b*) He asked his servant why he had been so lazy that day.

(*c*) He asked his servant why he was being so lazy that day.

(*d*) He asked his servant why was he so lazy that day.

23. He said, "Can you sing?" And I said, "No".

(*a*) He asked me that could I sing and I refused.

(*b*) He asked me if I could sing and I said that I couldn't.

(*c*) I denied, when he asked me if I could sing.

(*d*) He asked me if I could sing and I said no.

24. He said to her, "May you succeed !"

(*a*) He told her that she might succeed.

(*b*) He prayed to God that she may succeed.

(*c* He wished her success.

(*a*) He said to her that she might succeed. **(Stenographer's Exam, 1991)**

25. He said, "May God grant peace to the departed soul!"
(*a*) He wished by God to grant peace to the departed soul.
(*b*) He wished that God may grant peace to the departed soul.
(*c*) He prayed that might God grant peace to the departed soul.
(*d*) He prayed that God would grant peace to the departed soul.

26. "Are you alone, my son?" asked a soft voice close behind me.
(*a*) A soft voice from my back asked if I was alone.
(*b*) A soft voice said to me are you alone son.
(*c*) A soft voice asked that what I was doing there alone.
(*d*) A soft voice behind me asked if I was alone. **(Stenographer's Exam, 1995)**

27. He said, "I must go next week".
(*a*) He said that he must go next week.
(*b*) He said that he must go the following week.
(*c*) He said that he would have to go the following week.
(*d*) He said that he was to go the following week.

28. He said to her, "Don't read so fast."
(*a*) He told her not to read so fast.
(*b*) He advised her don't read so fast.
(*c*) He requested her not to read so fast.
(*d*) He ordered her not to read so fast.
(Stenographer's Exam, 1994)

29. "I don't know the way. Do you?" he asked.
(*a*) He said that he didn't know the way and did I know it
(*b*) He told that he was not knowing the way, but wondered if I knew.
(*c*) He said that he didn't know the way and asked me if I did.
(*d*) He asked me if I knew the way which he didn't.

30. He said, "Will you listen to such a man?"
(*a*) He asked them will you listen to such a man.
(*b*) He asked them are you listening to such a man.
(*c*) He asked them whether they would listen to such a man.
(*d*) He asked them whether they will listen to such a man.
(Stenographer's Exam, 1992)

31. Mary said to Robert, "Let him come, then we shall see."
(*a*) Mary said to Robert that if he came, they would see him.
(*b*) Mary told Robert that they shall see him if he came.
(*c*) Mary told Robert that once he came, they would see him.
(*d*) Mary told Robert that they would see him if he might come.

32. He said, "I have often told you not to waste your time." **(Stenographer's Exam, 1994)**
(*a*) He said that he had often told not to waste your time.
(*b*) He said that he had often told him not to waste his time.
(*c*) He said that he had often suggested to him not to waste his time.
(*d*) He told that he had often told him not to waste his time.

33. Rajan said, "O that I were a child again !"
(*a*) Rajan exclaimed with wonder that he was a child again.
(*b*) Rajan wondered that were he a child again.
(*c*) Rajan strongly wished that he had been a child again.
(*d*) Rajan prayed that he were a child again.

34. I said to my brother, "Let us go to some hill station for a change."
(*a*) I asked my brother to go to some hill station for a change.
(*b*) I asked my brother if he would go to some hill station for a change.
(*c*) I permitted my brother to go to some hill station for a change.
(*d*) I suggested to my brother that we should go to some hill station for a change. **(Stenographer's Exam, 1992)**

35. The Manager said, "Well, what can I do for you?"
(*a*) The Manager asked what he could do for him.
(*b*) The Manager woundered what he could do for him.
(*c*) The Manager wanted to know what he could do for him.
(*d*) The Manager said that he couldn't do anything for him.

36. The traveller enquired of the farmer if he could tell him the way to the nearest inn.
(*a*) The traveller said to the farmer, "Where is the nearest inn?"
(*b*) The traveller said to the farmer, "Which is the way to the nearest inn?"
(*c*) The traveller said to the farmer, "Can you tell me the way to the nearest inn?"

(*d*) The traveller said to the farmer, "Can you tell me where is the nearest inn?"

(Stenographer's Exam, 1991)

37. The spectators said, "Bravo! well played, Ravi."

(*a*) The spectators called Ravi bravo because he had played well.

(*b*) The spectators said that Ravi played well and applauded him.

(*c*) The spectators encouraged Ravi saying that he played well.

(*d*) The spectators applauded Ravi, saying that he had played well.

38. "If you don't keep quiet I shall shoot you," he said to her in a calm voice.

(*a*) He warned her to shoot if she didn't keep quiet calmly.

(*b*) He said calmly that I shall shoot you if you don't be quiet.

(*c*) He warned her calmly that he would shoot her if she didn't keep quiet.

(*d*) Calmly he warned her that be quiet or else he will have to shoot her.

(Stenographer's Exam, 1995)

ANSWERS

1. (*c*)	**2.** (*a*)	**3.** (*d*)	**4.** (*b*)	**5.** (*d*)	**6.** (*c*)	**7.** (*b*)	**8.** (*d*)	**9.** (*d*)	**10.** (*b*)
11. (*a*)	**12.** (*d*)	**13.** (*d*)	**14.** (*d*)	**15.** (*c*)	**16.** (*a*)	**17.** (*d*)	**18.** (*d*)	**19.** (*c*)	**20.** (*c*)
21. (*a*)	**22.** (*a*)	**23.** (*b*)	**24.** (*c*)	**25.** (*d*)	**26.** (*d*)	**27.** (*c*)	**28.** (*a*)	**29.** (*c*)	**30.** (*c*)
31. (*d*)	**32.** (*b*)	**33.** (*c*)	**34.** (*d*)	**35.** (*c*)	**36.** (*c*)	**37.** (*d*)	**38.** (*c*)		

---

27. TRANSFORMATION

This section deals with questions related to different forms in which two sentences may be combined.

In this type of questions, generally two sentences are given followed by three proposed beginnings of a sentence, which are marked as (A), (B) and (C). The candidate is required to decide which of these three forms may be used to express the same meaning as that conveyed by the two given sentences in the form of single sentence.

Example. He was a good teacher. He was a successful administrator.

(A) Besides .... (B) He was not .... (C) Inspite of ....

(*a*) Only A (*b*) Only B (*c*) A & C (*d*) A & B (*e*) A, B & C

Solution. Clearly, the two given sentences may be combined as :

(A) Besides being a good teacher, he was a successful administrator.

(B) He was not only a good teahcer but also a successful administrator.

The beginning (C) cannot be used to express the above fact.

Hence, the answer is (*d*).

PRACTICE SET

Directions : ***In each question below, there are two sentences. These two sentences are to be combined into one sentence which should convey the same meaning as conveyed by the two sentences. It is possible to combine the pair of sentences in various different ways. Beginnings of three such sentences is given below each pair of sentences. You have to find out which one, two, three or none of them is the correct, appropriate and logical way to combine the pair of sentences into one sentence to convey the same meaning as conveyed by the two sentences.***

1. The boy got his leg badly injured. He was playing hockey. **(Bank P.O. 1995)**
(A) While the boy was ....
(B) While playing ....
(C) Since his leg was..........
(*a*) Only A (*b*) Only B
(*c*) Only C (*d*) A & B only

2. You are drunk. That aggravates your offence.
(A) As you are ....
(B) That you ....
(C) What aggravates ....
(*a*) Only A (*b*) Only B (*c*) Only C
(*d*) A & B (*e*) B & C

3. He worked hard. He did not succeed.
(A) Although he ....
(B) Notwithstanding ....
(C) Besides working ....
(*a*) Only A (*b*) A & B (*c*) B & C
(*d*) A & C (*e*) A, B & C

4. You run fast. You can win the race.
(A) Provided ....
(B) In case ....
(C) Supposing that ....
(*a*) Only A (*b*) Only B (*c*) A & B
(*d*) B & C (*e*) A, B & C

5. You will not recover fast. Refrain from smoking
(A) Unless you recover ....
(B) If you want to refrain from smoking ....
(C) Inspite of refraining from ....
(Bank P.O. 1995)
(*a*) Only A (*b*) Only B (*c*) Only C
(*d*) A and B only (*e*) None of these

6. He may be innocent. I do not know.
(A) I doubt .... (B) I do not ....
(C) That he is ....
(*a*) Only A (*b*) Only B (*c*) Only C
(*d*) A and B (*e*) B and C

7. He finished his exercise. He put away his books
(A) Having finished ....
(B) As he finished ....
(C) Finishing ....
(*a*) Only A (*b*) A & B (*c*) Only B
(*d*) A & C (*e*) Only C

8. He is poor. He is happy.
(A) Despite ....
(B) Admitting that ....
(C) He is poor indeed, ...
(*a*) Only A (*b*) A & B (*c*) A & C
(*d*) Only C (*e*) A, B & C

9. He has some weaknesses. He is the darling of everyone.
(A) Though ....
(B) Inspite of ....
(C) Besides ....
(*a*) Only A (*b*) Only B (*c*) A & B
(*d*) B & C (*e*) A & C

10. The Chief Guest arrived. The proceedings of the function began.

(A) Having ....
(B) Only when ....
(C) The arrival ....
(*a*) Only A (*b*) Only B (*c*) Only C
(*d*) A & B (*e*) B & C

11. He can walk fast. He is tall.
(A) He is tall because ....
(B) Because he is tall ....
(C) Since he can ....
(*a*) Only A (*b*) Only B (*c*) Only C
(*d*) A & B only (*e*) None of these
(Bank P.O. 1995)

12. He is short-sighted. Otherwise he is fit for the post.
(A) Except that he ....
(B) If he was not ....
(C) Despite being ....
(*a*) Only A (*b*) Only B (*c*) Only C
(*d*) A and B (*e*) B and C

13. The thief entered the room. He found it empty.
(A) Entering ....
(B) Although the thief ....
(C) As soon as ....
(*a*) Only A (*b*) A & B (*c*) Only C
(*d*) B & C (*e*) A & C

14. He saw me. He came to me.
(A) Since he ....
(B) As soon as ....
(C) No sooner did ....
(*a*) Only A (*b*) Only B (*c*) Only C
(*d*) B & C (*e*) A, B & C

15. The shopkeepers closed the shops. They feared arson and looting. **(Bank P.O. 1995)**
(A) With the apprehension of arson......
(B) Apprehending the closure of the .....
(C) Fearing the arson and looting by the shopkeeper ....
(*a*) Only A (*b*) Only B (*c*) Only C
(*d*) A, B & C (*e*) None of these

16. You are sincere. You can succeed.
(A) Unless you ....
(B) Be ....
(C) Should you ....
(*a*) Only A (*b*) Only B (*c*) A & B
(*d*) A & C (*e*) A, B & C

17. He made a promise. He kept it.
(A) Making ....
(B) He not only ....
(C) Besides making ....
(*a*) Only B (*b*) A & B (*c*) Only C
(*d*) B & C (*e*) A, B & C

18. He is in great troubles. He is cheerful.
(A) Besides being ....
(B) Since he ....
(C) For all ....
(*a*) Only A (*b*) Only B (*c*) Only C
(*d*) A & B (*e*) A & C

19. The watchman waved his cane. In the nick of time the barking dog ran away.
(A) As soon as the barking ....
(B) Hardly was the watchman ....
(C) No sooner does the watchman ....
(*a*) Only A (*b*) Only B (*c*) Only C
(*d*) A, B & C (*e*) None of these
(Bank P.O. 1995)

20. He is rich. He is kind.
(A) Although he ....
(B) Rich as ....
(C) Inspite of ....
(*a*) Only A (*b*) A & B (*c*) B & C
(*d*) Only C (*e*) A, B & C

21. The match was over. We left for home.
(A) Match .... (B) We left ....
(C) Besides the match ....
(*a*) Only B (*b*) A & B (*c*) B & C
(*d*) A & C (*e*) None of these

22. He could afford to lose something. He lost somewhat more.
(A) He lost ....
(B) What he could ....
(C) Despite ....
(*a*) Only A (*b*) A & B (*c*) Only B
(*d*) A & C (*e*) Only C

23. All his family members behave very cordially with one another. The home atmosphere is very conducive to all-round development. **(Bank P.O. 1995)**
(A) Because the home atmosphere is very conducive ....
(B) The cordial behaviour of all his family members ....
(C) Although all his family members ....
(*a*) Only A (*b*) Only B (*c*) Only C
(*d*) A & B only (*e*) None of these

24. She is very simple. She cannot see through his plans.
(A) She is too ....
(B) Being very ....
(C) She is so ....
(*a*) Only A (*b*) Only C (*c*) A & B
(*d*) A & C (*e*) A, B & C

ANSWERS

1. (*d*) : While the boy was playing hockey, he got his leg badly injured.
While playing hockey, the boy got his leg badly injured.

2. (*e*) : That you are drunk aggravates your offence.
What aggravates your offence is that you are drunk.

3. (*b*) : Although he worked hard, he did not succeed.
Notwithstanding his hard work, he did not succeed.

4. (*e*) : Provided you run fast, you can win the race.
In case you run fast, you can win the race.
Supposing that you run fast, you can win the race.

5. (*e*) : The correct forms are :
Unless you refrain from smoking, you cannot recover fast.
If you want to recover fast, you should refrain from smoking.

6. (*b*) : I do not know if he is innocent.

7. (*d*) : Having finished his exercise, he put away his books.
Finishing his exercise, he put away his books.

8. (*e*) : Despite his poverty, he is happy.
Admitting that he is poor, he is happy.
He is poor indeed, but he is happy.

9. (*c*) : Though he has some weaknesses, he is the darling of everyone.
Inspite of some weaknesses, he is the darling of everyone.

10. (*b*) : Only when the Chief Guest arrived did the proceedings of the function begin.

11. (*b*) : Because he is tall, he can walk fast.

12. (*a*) : Except that he is short-sighted, he is fit for the post.

13. (*a*) : Entering the room, the thief found it empty.

14. (*d*) : As soon as he saw me, he came to me.
No sooner did he see me than he came to me.

15. (*a*) : With the apprehension of arson and looting, the shopkeepers closed the shops.

16. (*e*) : Unless you are sincere, you cannot succeed.
Be sincere and you can succeed.
Should you be sincere, you can succeed.

17. (*d*) : He not only made a promise, but he also kept it.
Besides making a promise, he kept it.

18. (*c*) : For all his troubles, he is cheerful.

19. (*e*) : The correct forms are :
As soon as the watchman waved his cane, the barking dog ran away.
Hardly had the watchman waved his cane when the barking dog ran away.
No sooner did the watchman wave his cane than the barking dog ran away.

20. (*e*) : Although he is rich, he is kind.
Rich as he is, he is kind.
Inspite of being rich, he is kind.

21. (*b*) : Match over, we left for home.
We left for home after the match was over.

22. (*a*) : He lost more than he could afford.

23. (*b*) : The cordial behaviour of all his family members to one another makes the home atmosphere very conducive to all-round development.

24. (*e*) : She is too simple to see through his plans.
Being very simple, she cannot see through his plans.
She is so simple that she cannot see through his plans.

28. SPELLING TEST

Type 1 : Choosing the correct spelling

In this type of questions, four different spellings of a word are given as four alternatives (*a*), (*b*), (*c*) and (*d*). The candidate is required to choose the correct spelling of the given word.

Ex. 1 : ***Choose the correct spelling.*** :

(*a*) Comensurate (*b*) Commensurate (*c*) Comensurrate (*d*) Commensurrate

Sol. : Clearly, the correct spelling is 'Commensurate' Hence, the answer is (*b*).

Ex. 2 : ***Choose the correct spelling :***

(*a*) Manouvre (*b*) Manouevre (*c*) Manouver (*d*) Manoeuvre

Sol. : Clearly, the correct spelling is 'Manoeuvre'. Hence, the answer is (*d*).

PRACTICE SET 1

Directions : ***In each of the following questions, a word has been written in four different ways out of which only one is correctly spelt. Find the correctly spelt word.***

1. (*a*) Efflorascence (*b*) Efflorescence (*c*) Eflloresence (*d*) Eflorescence **(Asstt. Grade, 1996)**
2. (*a*) Aliennate (*b*) Allienate (*c*) Alienate (*d*) Alienatte
3. (*a*) Forefiet (*b*) Forefeit (*c*) Forfeit (*d*) Forfiet
4. (*a*) Comemorate (*b*) Commemmorate (*c*) Comemmorate (*d*) Commemorate
5. (*a*) Exemple (*b*) Exampel (*c*) Example (*d*) Exampal **(Clerks' Grade, 1994)**
6. (*a*) Psychology (*b*) Sycology (*c*) Psykology (*d*) Sychology
7. (*a*) Accesible (*b*) Accesibel (*c*) Accessible (*d*) Acessible
8. (*a*) Tresspass (*b*) Trespass (*c*) Tresspas (*d*) Trespas
9. (*a*) Argumant (*b*) Arguemant (*c*) Argument (*d*) Arguement **(Railways, 1995)**
10. (*a*) Mustach (*b*) Moustach (*c*) Mustache (*d*) Moustache
11. (*a*) Sedantry (*b*) Sedentery (*c*) Sedentary (*d*) Sedantary
12. (*a*) Aproched (*b*) Aprdached (*c*) Appraoched (*d*) Approached **(S.S.C. 1995)**
13. (*a*) Comentry (*b*) Commentry (*c*) Commentery (*d*) Commentary
14. (*a*) Commission (*b*) Comision (*c*) Comission (*d*) Commision
15. (*a*) Scriptur (*b*) Skripture (*c*) Scripture (*d*) Scripcher **(Stenographers' Exam, 1994)**
16. (*a*) Acquiescence (*b*) Aquicence (*c*) Acquisence (*d*) Acquissence
17. (*a*) Guerila (*b*) Gurilla (*c*) Gorila (*d*) Gorilla
18. (*a*) Desicate (*b*) Desiccate (*c*) Dessicate (*d*) Dessiccate
19. (*a*) Pasanger (*b*) Pessenger (*c*) Pesanger (*d*) Passenger **(Assistant Grade, 1994)**
20. (*a*) Tariff (*b*) Tarriff (*c*) Tarif (*d*) Tarrif
21. (*a*) Jewelery (*b*) Jewellry (*c*) Jwellry (*d*) Jewellery
22. (*a*) Grametic (*b*) Grammetic (*c*) Grammatic (*d*) Gramatic
23. (*a*) Blisfull (*b*) Blissful (*c*) Blisful (*d*) Blissfull
24. (*a*) Embarasment (*b*) Embarassment (*c*) Embarrasment (*d*) Embarrassment
25. (*a*) Sattellite (*b*) Satellite (*c*) Sattelite (*d*) Satelite **(Stenographers' Exam, 1995)**
26. (*a*) Distilry (*b*) Distillry (*c*) Distillery (*d*) Distilery
27. (*a*) Ocasion (*b*) Ocassion (*c*) Occasion (*d*) Occassion
28. (*a*) Commettee (*b*) Committe (*c*) Comittee (*d*) Committee **(C.B.I. 1994, M.B.A. 1989)**
29. (*a*) Posesion (*b*) Possession (*c*) Posession (*d*) Possesion
30. (*a*) Greivance (*b*) Grievance (*c*) Griveance (*d*) Grieveance
31. (*a*) Beligrent (*b*) Beligerent (*c*) Belligrent (*d*) Belligerent
32. (*a*) Inteligensia (*b*) Inteligentsia (*c*) Intelligensia (*d*) Intelligentsia
33. (*a*) Coruppt (*b*) Curropt (*c*) Corrupt (*d*) Currupt **(Railways, 1995)**
34. (*a*) Dielectic (*b*) Diallectic (*c*) Dilectic (*d*) Dialectic
35. (*a*) Variegated (*b*) Varegated

(*c*) Varigated (*d*) Variagated

36. (*a*) Sustinence (*b*) Sustenance
(*c*) Sustenence (*d*) Sustinance

37. (*a*) Achievment (*b*) Acheivment
(*c*) Achievement (*d*) Achevement
(Clerks' Grade, 1995)

38. (*a*) Coreander (*b*) Coriander
(*c*) Coriandar (*d*) Coreandor

39. (*a*) Kalidoscope (*b*) Kalaidoscope
(*c*) Kaleidoscope (*d*) Kaliedoscope

40. (*a*) Bouquete (*b*) Bouquet
(*c*) Boquet (*d*) Bouquette
(C.B.I. 1995)

41. (*a*) Translucent (*b*) Translusent
(*c*) Transluscent (*d*) Tranclucent

42. (*a*) Hetrogenous (*b*) Hetrogeneous
(*c*) Heterogenous (*d*) Heterogeneous

43. (*a*) Foreigner (*b*) Forienor
(*c*) Foriegnor (*d*) Foreiner
(Stenographers' Exam, 1991)

44. (*a*) Addultration (*b*) Adultration
(*c*) Addulteration (*d*) Adulteration

45. (*a*) Gorgette (*b*) Georgette
(*c*) Gorgete (*d*) Georget

46. (*a*) Examplary (*b*) Exemplary
(*c*) Examplery (*d*) Exemplery

47. (*a*) Sabotage (*b*) Sabbotage
(*c*) Sabotaze (*d*) Sabatage

48. (*a*) Brethoren (*b*) Brothren
(*c*) Brethren (*d*) Brethron

49. (*a*) Colaboration (*b*) Collaberation
(*c*) Colaberation (*d*) Collaboration

50. (*a*) Exagerate (*b*) Exadgerate
(*c*) Exaggerate (*d*) Exeggerate
(Stenographers' Exam, 1994)

ANSWERS

1. (*b*)	**2.** (*c*)	**3.** (*c*)	**4.** (*d*)	**5.** (*c*)	**6.** (*a*)	**7.** (*c*)	**8.** (*b*)	**9.** (*c*)	**10.** (*d*)
11. (*c*)	**12.** (*d*)	**13.** (*d*)	**14.** (*a*)	**15.** (*c*)	**16.** (*a*)	**17.** (*d*)	**18.** (*b*)	**19.** (*d*)	**20.** (*a*)
21. (*d*)	**22.** (*c*)	**23.** (*b*)	**24.** (*d*)	**25.** (*b*)	**26.** (*c*)	**27.** (*c*)	**28.** (*d*)	**29.** (*b*)	**30.** (*b*)
31. (*d*)	**32.** (*d*)	**33.** (*c*)	**34.** (*d*)	**35.** (*a*)	**36.** (*b*)	**37.** (*c*)	**38.** (*b*)	**39.** (*c*)	**40.** (*b*)
41. (*a*)	**42.** (*d*)	**43.** (*a*)	**44.** (*d*)	**45.** (*b*)	**46.** (*b*)	**47.** (*a*)	**48.** (*c*)	**49.** (*d*)	**50.** (*c*)

PRACTICE SET 2

Directions : *In each of the following questions, choose the correctly spelt word.*

1. (*a*) Acurrate (*b*) Accurate
(*c*) Acurate (*d*) Accuratte
(Clerks' Grade, 1995)

2. (*a*) Buisness (*b*) Bussiness
(*c*) Business (*d*) Buisiness

3. (*a*) Rapprochmant (*b*) Rapprochment
(*c*) Raproachment (*d*) Rapprochement

4. (*a*) Forecast (*b*) Forcaust
(*c*) Forcast (*d*) Forecaste
(Stenographers' Exam, 1994)

5. (*a*) Liesure (*b*) Leisure
(*c*) Leasure (*d*) Lesiure

6. (*a*) Calliberation (*b*) Caliberation
(*c*) Callibration (*d*) Calibration

7. (*a*) Adviceable (*b*) Advisable
(*c*) Advicable (*d*) Adviseable

8. (*a*) Puerille (*b*) Puerrile
(*c*) Puerile (*d*) Purrile
(C.B.I. 1995)

9. (*a*) Interegnum (*b*) Intregnum
(*c*) Interregnum (*d*) Interregnim

10. (*a*) Aforstation (*b*) Aforestation
(*c*) Afforstation (*d*) Afforestation

11. (*a*) Utrance (*b*) Utterance
(*c*) Uterance (*d*) Uttrance

12. (*a*) Entreprenuer (*b*) Entrepraneur
(*c*) Entrapreneur (*d*) Entrepreneur
(Assistant Grade, 1996)

13. (*a*) Superceed (*b*) Superseed
(*c*) Supercede (*d*) Supersede

14. (*a*) Inundated (*b*) Innundated
(*c*) Innandated (*d*) Inandated

15. (*a*) Commission (*b*) Commisson
(*c*) Commision (*d*) Comission
(M.B.A. 1989)

16. (*a*) Harasment (*b*) Harassment
(*c*) Harrassment (*d*) Harrasment

17. (*a*) Satellite (*b*) Satelite
(*c*) Sattelite (*d*) Sattellite

18. (*a*) Perseverance (*b*) Preservarance
(*c*) Perseverence (*d*) Preserverence
(C.B.I. 1994)

19. (*a*) Sovereignty (*b*) Soveriegnty
(*c*) Sovereignity (*d*) Soveriegnity

20. (*a*) Receding (*b*) Receeding (*c*) Reeceding (*d*) Recedeing
21. (*a*) Illusteous (*b*) Illistrious (*c*) Ilustrious (*d*) Illustrious

(Stenographers' Exam, 1991)

22. (*a*) Skillful (*b*) Skillfull (*c*) Skilful (*d*) Skilfull
23. (*a*) Septaganarian (*b*) Septagenarian (*c*) Septuaganarian (*d*) Septuagenarian
24. (*a*) Pitiaeble (*b*) Pitiable (*c*) Pitiaable (*d*) Pitiabale

(Railways, 1995)

25. (*a*) Incumbent (*b*) Incumbant (*c*) Incambant (*d*) Incambent
26. (*a*) Budgetary (*b*) Budgetry (*c*) Budgetery (*d*) Bugetary
27. (*a*) Paralelled (*b*) Parallelled (*c*) Paralleled (*d*) Parralleled

(Asstt. Grade, 1996)

28. (*a*) Arangemant (*b*) Arrangement (*c*) Arrangment (*d*) Arangement
29. (*a*) Cemetry (*b*) Cemetery (*c*) Cemetary (*d*) Cemmetery
30. (*a*) Vetniary (*b*) Vetarinary (*c*) Veteninary (*d*) Veterinary

(Stenographers' Exam, 1995)

31. (*a*) Lauriate (*b*) Laureat (*c*) Laureate (*d*) Lauriat
32. (*a*) Comander (*b*) Commander (*c*) Commandor (*d*) Comandar
33. (*a*) Tranquillity (*b*) Trenquillity (*c*) Trenquility (*d*) Tranquility

(Clerks' Grade, 1994)

34. (*a*) Alitration (*b*) Alliteration (*c*) Allitration (*d*) Aliteration
35. (*a*) Chaufer (*b*) Chauffer (*c*) Chaufeur (*d*) Chauffeur
36. (*a*) Remunaration (*b*) Remunration (*c*) Remeuneration (*d*) Remuneration
37. (*a*) Comitment (*b*) Comittment (*c*) Committment (*d*) Commitment
38. (*a*) Fullfil (*b*) Fulfil (*c*) Fulfill (*d*) Fullfill

(M.B.A. 1989)

39. (*a*) Genelogy (*b*) Genealogy (*c*) Geneology (*d*) Genalogy
40. (*a*) Defendant (*b*) Defendent (*c*) Defandent (*d*) Defandant
41. (*a*) Recommand (*b*) Recommend (*c*) Reccomend (*d*) Recomend

(C.B.I. 1994)

42. (*a*) Varstile (*b*) Verstile (*c*) Versatile (*d*) Vorstyle
43. (*a*) Correspondant (*b*) Corraspondent (*c*) Corraspondant (*d*) Correspondent
44. (*a*) Omenous (*b*) Ominous (*c*) Omineous (*d*) Ommineous

(Stenographers' Exam, 1994)

45. (*a*) Mathemetics (*b*) Mathamatics (*c*) Mathametics (*d*) Mathematics
46. (*a*) Finnancer (*b*) Financier (*c*) Financer (*d*) Financeir
47. (*a*) Comitee (*b*) Commitee (*c*) Comittee (*d*) Committee

(Asstt. Grade, 1994) (S.S.C. 1995)

48. (*a*) Dansuese (*b*) Danseus (*c*) Danseuse (*d*) Densuace
49. (*a*) Etiquete (*b*) Etiquette (*c*) Ettiquete (*d*) Ettiquette
50. (*a*) Overlapped (*b*) Overlaped (*c*) Overleped (*d*) Overelaped

(Railways, 1995)

ANSWERS

1. (*b*)	2. (*c*)	3. (*d*)	4. (*a*)	5. (*b*)	6. (*d*)	7. (*b*)	8. (*c*)	9. (*c*)	10. (*d*)
11. (*b*)	12. (*d*)	13. (*d*)	14. (*a*)	15. (*a*)	16. (*b*)	17. (*a*)	18. (*a*)	19. (*a*)	20. (*a*)
21. (*d*)	22. (*c*)	23. (*d*)	24. (*b*)	25. (*a*)	26. (*a*)	27. (*c*)	28. (*b*)	29. (*b*)	30. (*d*)
31. (*c*)	32. (*b*)	33. (*a*)	34. (*b*)	35. (*d*)	36. (*d*)	37. (*d*)	38. (*c*)	39. (*b*)	40. (*a*)
41. (*b*)	42. (*c*)	43. (*d*)	44. (*b*)	45. (*d*)	46. (*b*)	47. (*d*)	48. (*c*)	49. (*b*)	50. (*a*)

PRACTICE SET 3

Directions : ***In each of the questions below only one among the given alternatives is correctly spelt. Find out the word with correct spelling.***

1. (*a*) Necessary (*b*) Necesarry (*c*) Necesary (*d*) Neccessary

(Railways, 1995)

2. (*a*) Inocculate (*b*) Inoculate (*c*) Innoculate (*d*) Innocculate
3. (*a*) Comensurate (*b*) Commensurate (*c*) Commensurrate (*d*) Comensurate

4. (*a*) Benefeted (*b*) Benifited
(*c*) Benefitted (*d*) Benifitted

(Stenographers' Exam, 1994)

5. (*a*) Supreintendent (*b*) Superintendent
(*c*) Suprintendent (*d*) Supereintendent
6. (*a*) Temparament (*b*) Temprament
(*c*) Temperament (*d*) Temperamant
7. (*a*) Homeopathy (*b*) Homoepathy
(*c*) Homiopathy (*d*) Homoeopathy
8. (*a*) Numrator (*b*) Numerator
(*c*) Numerater (*d*) Numrater
9. (*a*) Sacrilegeous (*b*) Sacrilegious
(*c*) Sacriligious (*d*) Sacreligious

(C.B.I. 1994)

10. (*a*) Ommission (*b*) Omision
(*c*) Omission (*d*) Ommision
11. (*a*) Mountaineous (*b*) Mountaneous
(*c*) Mountainous (*d*) Mountanous
12. (*a*) Giraf (*b*) Gerraffe
(*c*) Geraff (*d*) Giraffe

(S.S.C. 1995)

13. (*a*) Legendary (*b*) Legendery
(*c*) Legendry (*d*) Legandery
14. (*a*) Aquaintence (*b*) Acquaintance
(*c*) Aquaintance (*d*) Acquaintence
15. (*a*) Arodrome (*b*) Airodrome
(*c*) Aerodrom (*d*) Aerodrome
16. (*a*) Forein (*b*) Fariegn
(*c*) Foriegn (*d*) Foreign

(Assistant Grade, 1994)

17. (*a*) Aprentice (*b*) Aperentice
(*c*) Apprentice (*d*) Apperentice
18. (*a*) Indigenous (*b*) Indigenuous
(*c*) Indiginous (*d*) Indeginuous
19. (*a*) Lackadaisical (*b*) Lackadisical
(*c*) Lackadaisicle (*d*) Lackdaisical

(C.B.I. 1995)

20. (*a*) Coleagu (*b*) Colleagu
(*c*) Coleague (*d*) Colleague
21. (*a*) Incandiery (*b*) Incendiary
(*c*) Incendiery (*d*) Incandiary
22. (*a*) Lieutinant (*b*) Lieutenant
(*c*) Leutenant (*d*) Liutenant
23. (*a*) Paralelogram (*b*) Paralellogram
(*c*) Parallelogram (*d*) Parallellogram
24. (*a*) Corigendum (*b*) Coridgendum
(*c*) Corrigendum (*d*) Corridgendum
25. (*a*) Sepulchral (*b*) Sepalchrle
(*c*) Sepalchral (*d*) Sepulchrle

(Assistant Grade, 1996)

26. (*a*) Repantance (*b*) Repantence
(*c*) Repentence (*d*) Repentance
27. (*a*) Prevalant (*b*) Prevalent
(*c*) Prevelant (*d*) Prevelent
28. (*a*) Milennium (*b*) Millenium
(*c*) Millennium (*d*) Milenium
29. (*a*) Acomodation (*b*) Accomodation
(*c*) Acommodation (*d*) Accommodation

(Stenographers' Exam, 1995)

30. (*a*) Efervescent (*b*) Efervesent
(*c*) Effervesent (*d*) Effervescent
31. (*a*) Countinence (*b*) Countenence
(*c*) Countenance (*d*) Countinance
32. (*a*) Inimitable (*b*) Innimatible
(*c*) Inimitible (*d*) Inimmitable

(S.S.C. 1994)

33. (*a*) Sachrine (*b*) Sacharine
(*c*) Saccharin (*d*) Saccharine
34. (*a*) Resplandance (*b*) Resplendance
(*c*) Resplendence (*d*) Resplandence
35. (*a*) Refrigerator (*b*) Refriderater
(*c*) Refridgerator (*d*) Referigerator

(M.B.A. 1989)

36. (*a*) Apallation (*b*) Appellation
(*c*) Appelation (*d*) Appallation
37. (*a*) Catlogg (*b*) Catlog
(*c*) Catlogue (*d*) Catalogue
38. (*a*) Quintessance (*b*) Quintessence
(*c*) Quintesance (*d*) Quintassence
39. (*a*) Obssession (*b*) Obssession
(*c*) Obsession (*d*) Obsessien

(Clerks' Grade, 1995)

40. (*a*) Alottee (*b*) Allotee
(*c*) Alotte (*d*) Allottee
41. (*a*) Seperable (*b*) Separable
(*c*) Saperable (*d*) Saparable
42. (*a*) Hindrence (*b*) Hindrance
(*c*) Hinderence (*d*) Hinderance

(Stenographers' Exam, 1994)

43. (*a*) Remambrance (*b*) Remembrance
(*c*) Remamberance (*d*) Rememberance
44. (*a*) Proprietry (*b*) Propriatory
(*c*) Proprietary (*d*) Proprietory
45. (*a*) Consceintious (*b*) Conscientous
(*c*) Conscintious (*d*) Conscientious

(C.B.I. 1994)

46. (*a*) Strategam (*b*) Strategem
(*c*) Stratagem (*d*) Stratagam
47. (*a*) Reharsal (*b*) Rehersal
(*c*) Rehearsal (*d*) Rehearsel
48. (*a*) Cancelation (*b*) Cancelletion
(*c*) Cancellation (*d*) Cancellasion

(Railways, 1995)

49. (*a*) Assasination (*b*) Asasination
(*c*) Assassination (*d*) Asassination
50. (*a*) Millonare (*b*) Millionaire
(*c*) Millionare (*d*) Millonaire

ANSWERS

1. (*a*)	**2.** (*b*)	**3.** (*b*)	**4.** (*c*)	**5.** (*b*)	**6.** (*c*)	**7.** (*d*)	**8.** (*b*)	**9.** (*b*)	**10.** (*c*)
11. (*c*)	**12.** (*d*)	**13.** (*a*)	**14.** (*b*)	**15.** (*d*)	**16.** (*d*)	**17.** (*c*)	**18.** (*a*)	**19.** (*a*)	**20.** (*d*)
21. (*b*)	**22.** (*b*)	**23.** (*c*)	**24.** (*c*)	**25.** (*a*)	**26.** (*d*)	**27.** (*b*)	**28.** (*c*)	**29.** (*d*)	**30.** (*d*)
31. (*c*)	**32.** (*a*)	**33.** (*d*)	**34.** (*c*)	**35.** (*a*)	**36.** (*b*)	**37.** (*d*)	**38.** (*a*)	**39.** (*c*)	**40.** (*d*)
41. (*b*)	**42.** (*b*)	**43.** (*b*)	**44.** (*c*)	**45.** (*d*)	**46.** (*c*)	**47.** (*c*)	**48.** (*c*)	**49.** (*c*)	**50.** (*b*)

PRACTICE SET 4

Directions : *In each of the following questions, choose the correctly spelt word out of the given alternatives.*

1. (*a*) Equannimity (*b*) Equinimity
(*c*) Equanimity (*d*) Equanimmity
(Stenographers' Exam, 1995)

2. (*a*) Draut (*b*) Drout
(*c*) Drougt (*d*) Drought

3. (*a*) Fabullous (*b*) Fablous
(*c*) Fabulous (*d*) Fabuleous

4. (*a*) Uttrance (*b*) Utterance
(*c*) Uterance (*d*) Utrance

5. (*a*) Accomplish (*b*) Ackmplesh
(*c*) Accompalish (*d*) Acomplush
(Asstt. Grade, 1994)

6. (*a*) Delinquescent (*b*) Deliquecent
(*c*) Deliquescent (*d*) Delinquesent

7. (*a*) Simaltanious (*b*) Simultaneous
(*c*) Simultanious (*d*) Simaltaneous

8. (*a*) Turnament (*b*) Tournamant
(*c*) Tournament (*d*) Turnamant

9. (*a*) Tomarow (*b*) Tomarrow
(*c*) Tomorrow (*d*) Tommorow

10. (*a*) Neihbour (*b*) Neighber
(*c*) Neighbour (*d*) Neibur

11. (*a*) Fasist (*b*) Facict
(*c*) Facist (*d*) Fascist

12. (*a*) Occurrance (*b*) Occurrence
(*c*) Occurance (*d*) Occurence
(C.B.I. 1994)

13. (*a*) Gaurantee (*b*) Guarantee
(*c*) Garuntee (*d*) Guaruntee
(Stenographers' Exam, 1995)

14. (*a*) Parlamentary (*b*) Parliamentary
(*c*) Parlimentary (*d*) Parliamentery
(S.S.C. 1995)

15. (*a*) Astrinjent (*b*) Estrinjent
(*c*) Astringent (*d*) Estringent

16. (*a*) Itinarary (*b*) Itenerary
(*c*) Itinerary (*d*) Itinarery
(C.B.I. 1995)

17. (*a*) Tentaitive (*b*) Tentative
(*c*) Tentitive (*d*) Tantitive
(Stenographers' Exam, 1991)

18. (*a*) Surveilance (*b*) Survellance
(*c*) Surveillance (*d*) Survaillance
(Assistant Grade, 1996)

19. (*a*) Efflorscence (*b*) Efflorescence
(*c*) Efflorsence (*d*) Efflorescence

20. (*a*) Careir (*b*) Career
(*c*) Caireer (*d*) Carreer
(Clerks' Grade, 1995)

21. (*a*) Rasteraunt (*b*) Restaurent
(*c*) Rastaurent (*d*) Restaurant

22. (*a*) Damage (*b*) Dammage
(*c*) Damaige (*d*) Dammege
(Stenographers' Exam, 1994)

23. (*a*) Agrandizment (*b*) Agrandizement
(*c*) Aggrandizment (*d*) Aggrandizement

24. (*a*) Sinchronize (*b*) Synchormise
(*c*) Syycronise (*d*) Synchronize
(M.B.A. 1989)

25. (*a*) Farenheit (*b*) Fahrenhiet
(*c*) Farenhiet (*d*) Fahrenheit

26. (*a*) Apparell (*b*) Aparrel
(*c*) Apparel (*d*) Apparrel

27. (*a*) Recommandation (*b*) Recomandation
(*c*) Recommendation (*d*) Recomendation
(S.S.C. 1994)

28. (*a*) Accessible (*b*) Accissible
(*a*) Acessible (*b*) Accesible

29. (*a*) Tempereture (*b*) Temparature
(*c*) Temperature (*d*) Tamperature
(Railways, 1995)

30. (*a*) Rennaisance (*b*) Rennaissance
(*c*) Renaissance (*d*) Renaisance

ANSWERS

1. (*c*)	**2.** (*d*)	**3.** (*c*)	**4.** (*b*)	**5.** (*a*)	**6.** (*c*)	**7.** (*d*)	**8.** (*b*)	**9.** (*c*)	**10.** (*c*)
11. (*d*)	**12.** (*b*)	**13.** (*b*)	**14.** (*b*)	**15.** (*c*)	**16.** (*c*)	**17.** (*b*)	**18.** (*c*)	**19.** (*d*)	**20.** (*b*)
21. (*d*)	**22.** (*a*)	**23.** (*d*)	**24.** (*d*)	**25.** (*d*)	**26.** (*c*)	**27.** (*c*)	**28.** (*a*)	**29.** (*c*)	**30.** (*c*)

TYPE 2 : Choosing the mis-spelt word

In this type of questions, four different words are given as four alternatives (a), (b), (c) and (d). The candidate is required to choose the word, the spelling of which is wrong. If all the given words are correctly spelt, the answer is (e) i.e. 'All correct'.

Ex. 1. ***Choose the mis-spelt words :***

(*a*) Originality (*b*) Gymnastics (*c*) Diagnosis (*d*) Salubrious

Sol. : ***Clearly, the correct spelling of (a) is 'Originality'.***

Hence, the answer is (a).

Ex. 2. ***From the following group of words, choose the mis-spelt word.***

(*a*) Opponent (*b*) Opportunity (*c*) Oppulence (*d*) Oppress

Sol. : Clearly, 'Oppulence' is the mis-spelt word. The correct spelling is 'Opulence'.

Hence, the answer is (c).

PRACTICE SET 5

Directions : In each question below, some words are given, one of which may be wrongly spelt. Find out that word, the spelling of which is wrong. If all the words are spelt correctly, your answer is (e) i.e. All correct.

1. (*a*) Designation (*b*) Amature (*c*) Controversy (*d*) Burglar **(B.S.R.B. 1995)**

2. (*a*) Deceive (*b*) Conceive (*c*) Perceive (*d*) Acheive

3. (a) Penance (*b*) Menace (*c*) Tendancy (*d*) Governance

4. (*a*) Prejudicial (*b*) Affectionate (*c*) Indispensible (*d*) Assiduous

5. (*a*) Kitten (*b*) Cumulative (*c*) Justified (*d*) Inediable **(B.S.R.B. 1994)**

6. (*a*) Hillock (*b*) Vilify (*c*) Mileage (*d*) Hillarious **(S.S.C. 1991)**

7. (*a*) Predilection (*b*) Discipline (*c*) Indigenous (*d*) Preferrable

8. (*a*) Suicide (*b*) Suiteable (*c*) Summarize (*d*) Superficial

9. (*a*) Neice (*b*) Neither (*c*) Neigh (*d*) Rein **(Asstt. Grade, 1991)**

10. (*a*) Light (*b*) Fight (*c*) Hight (*d*) Might

11. (*a*) Control (*b*) Confusion (*c*) Confrence (*d*) Committee

12. (*a*) Instantanious (*b*) Intermediate (*c*) Intermittent (*d*) Interference

13. (*a*) Breakage (*b*) Brevity (*c*) Breathless (*d*) Briliance **(Asstt. Grade, 1995)**

14. (*a*) Maline (*b*) Privacy (*c*) Cultured (*d*) Encourage

15. (*a*) Nuptial (*b*) Nickers (*c*) Nephew (*d*) Nuisance

16. (*a*) Explaination (*b*) Extermination (*c*) Exaggeration (*d*) Expectation **(C.B.I. 1993)**

17. (*a*) Covetous (*b*) Coherent (*c*) Consice (*d*) Consent

18. (*a*) Plateau (*b*) Plebian (*c*) Pledge (*d*) Pollinate

19. (*a*) Utility (*b*) Vitality (*c*) Speciality (*d*) Casualty **(Clerks' Grade, 1992)**

20. (*a*) Cruelly (*b*) Truly (*c*) Verbally (*d*) Rudely

21. (*a*) Oversear (*b*) Oscillate (*c*) Ossicle (*d*) Obscure

22. (*a*) Cruise (*b*) Deduse (*c*) Truce (*d*) Bruise **(Central Excise, 1991)**

23. (*a*) Democracy (*b*) Aristocracy (*c*) Advocacy (*d*) Courtecy

24. (*a*) Hyphen (*b*) Hygene (*c*) Hurdle (*d*) Haphazard

25. (*a*) Believe (*b*) Relieve (*c*) Grieve (*d*) Decieve

(Stenographers' Exam, 1993)

26. (*a*) Juice (*b*) Jersy (*c*) Jaggery (*d*) Japanese

27. (*a*) Envelop (*b*) Enthuse (*c*) Eratic (*d*) Emigrant

28. (*a*) Freshner (*b*) Forlorn (*c*) Foreign (*d*) Fruity

29. (*a*) Democracy (*b*) Beaureaucracy (*c*) Prophecy (*d*) Aristocracy

(Section Officers' 1993)

30. (*a*) Spurious (*b*) Studious (*c*) Subsidary (*d*) Sensible

31. (*a*) Charade (*b*) Colossus (*c*) Cartrige (*d*) Challenge

32. (*a*) Ballistic (*b*) Baloon (*c*) Bulletin (*d*) Bullock

(Assistant Grade, 1991)

33. (*a*) Winner (*b*) Winning (*c*) Writer (*d*) Writting

34. (*a*) Batalion (*b*) Believe (*c*) Bewilder (*d*) Bogie

35. (*a*) Asterisk (*b*) Audience (*c*) Acrue (*d*) Almighty

36. (*a*) Bearer (*b*) Governor (*c*) Conquerer (*d*) Admirer

(S.S.C. 1991)

37. (*a*) Ceremony (*b*) Agression (*c*) Schedule (*d*) Knowledge

38. (*a*) Phrasology (*b*) Possibility (*c*) Potassium (*d*) Preamble

39. (*a*) Careful (*b*) Untill (*c*) Fulfil (*d*) Final

(Stenographers' Exam, 1995)

40. (*a*) Essential (*b*) Rehabilitation (*c*) Appreciation (*d*) Concomitant

41. (*a*) Knack (*b*) Knee (*c*) Kneed (*d*) Kneel

(Translators' Exam, 1994)

42. (*a*) Amend (*b*) Commend (*c*) Assend (*d*) Comprehend

43. (*a*) Monotonous (*b*) Monastry (*c*) Monitor (*d*) Moraine

44. (*a*) Adultration (*b*) Adulation (*c*) Advancement (*d*) Admittance

(Stenographers' Exam, 1995)

45. (*a*) Soothe (*b*) Sponser (*c*) Stepney (*d*) Struggle

46. (*a*) Resembelance (*b*) Recuperate (*c*) Recommend (*d*) Resource

47. (*a*) Perpendicular (*b*) Boundry (*c*) Exaggerate (*d*) Flourish

(B.S.R.B. 1996)

48. (*a*) Rapport (*b*) Substance (*c*) Gravyard (*d*) Resistible

49. (*a*) Encompass (*b*) Encomium (*c*) Enimical (*d*) Encumber

50. (*a*) Hack (*b*) Hawl (*c*) Halve (*d*) Hark

(Stenographers' Exam, 1993)

ANSWERS

1. (*b*) Amateur	**2.** (*d*) Achieve	**3.** (*c*) Tendency	**4.** (*c*) Indispensable
5. (*d*) Inedible	**6.** (*d*) Hilarious	**7.** (*d*) Preferable	**8.** (*b*) Suitable
9. (*a*) Niece	**10.** (*c*) Height	**11.** (*c*) Conference	**12.** (*a*) Instantaneous
13. (*d*) Brilliance	**14.** (*a*) Malign	**15.** (*b*) Knickers	**16.** (*a*) Explanation
17. (*c*) Concise	**18.** (*b*) Plebeian	**19.** (*e*) All correct	**20.** (*b*) Truely
21. (*a*) Overseer	**22.** (*b*) Deduce	**23.** (*d*) Courtesy	**24.** (*b*) Hygiene
25. (*d*) Deceive	**26.** (*b*) Jersey	**27.** (*c*) Erratic	**28.** (*a*) Freshener
29. (*b*) Bureaucracy	**30.** (*c*) Subsidiary	**31.** (*c*) Cartridge	**32.** (*b*) Balloon
33. (*d*) Writing	**34.** (*a*) Battalion	**35.** (*c*) Accrue	**36.** (*c*) Conqueror
37. (*b*) Aggression	**38.** (*a*) Phraseology	**39.** (*b*) Until	**40.** (*d*) Concomiten.
41. (*c*) Knead	**42.** (*c*) Ascend	**43.** (*b*) Monastery	**44.** (*a*) Adulteration
45. (*b*) Sponsor	**46.** (*a*) Resemblance	**47.** (*b*) Boundary	**48.** (*c*) Graveyard
49. (*c*) Inimical	**50.** (*b*) Howl		

PRACTICE SET 6

Directions : *In each of the following questions, out of the given group of words, choose the mis-spelt one. If all the words are correctly spelt, your answer is (e) i.e. All correct.*

1. (*a*) Deficient (*b*) Efficient (*c*) Magnificient (*d*) Reticent
(Assistant Grade, 1991)
2. (*a*) Surender (*b*) Abbreviate (*c*) Qualification (*d*) Eccentric
3. (*a*) Sustenance (*b*) Maintainance (*c*) Movable (*d*) Manageable
4. (*a*) Intuition (*b*) Mischeivous (*c*) Vertebrate (*d*) Ascetic
5. (*a*) Deep (*b*) Heap (*c*) Sleep (*d*) Weap
(S.S.C. 1991)
6. (*a*) Address (*b*) Adiction (*c*) Advice (*d*) Adhere
7. (*a*) Memorendum (*b*) Quintessence (*c*) Ionisation (*d*) Spontaneous
8. (*a*) Overture (*b*) Affinity (*c*) Noteable (*d*) Prismatic
9. (*a*) Instructor (*b*) Grammer (*c*) Carrier (*d*) Organiser
(Stenographers' Exam, 1994)
10. (*a*) Impression (*b*) Competition (*c*) Miscelleneous (*d*) Reproach
11. (*a*) Spindle (*b*) Exorbitant (*c*) Tantalise (*d*) Parashute
12. (*a*) Intelligensia (*b*) Invigilator (*c*) Invertebrate (*d*) Impertinence
13. (*a*) Conquer (*b*) Passenger (*c*) Variety (*d*) Retalitate
(B.S.R.B. 1994)
14. (*a*) Controversial (*b*) Contemplate (*c*) Contemporery (*d*) Contingency
15. (*a*) Remarkable (*b*) Nervousness (*c*) Ambition (*d*) Difference
16. (*a*) Colliery (*b*) Colleague (*c*) Collaborate (*d*) Collony
17. (*a*) Homogenious (*b*) Honorarium (*c*) Honourable (*d*) Hooligan
(Stenographers' Exam, 1993)
18. (*a*) Mournful (*b*) Mucilaig (*c*) Mordant (*d*) Monocle
19. (*a*) Annex (*b*) Aniversary (*c*) Animate (*d*) Animosity
20. (*a*) Imperative (*b*) Ilicit (*c*) Imminent (*d*) Immature
(Section Officers' 1993)
21. (*a*) Semester (*b*) Senesent (*c*) Sensory (*d*) Salacious
22. (*a*) Feudal (*b*) Fumble (*c*) Fuel (*d*) Feugitive
23. (*a*) Teaser (*b*) Teething (*c*) Tedious (*d*) Teatotaller
(Asstt. Grade, 1995)
24. (*a*) Solution (*b*) Tuition (*c*) Circutous (*d*) Fruition
25. (*a*) Maiden (*b*) Widen (*c*) Rider (*d*) Foder
26. (*a*) Indefinite (*b*) Courteous (*c*) Advurtise (*d*) Periphery
(B.S.R.B. 1995)
27. (*a*) Bearer (*b*) Conquerer (*c*) Admirer (*d*) Governor
28. (*a*) Stolen (*b*) Eaten (*c*) Beaten (*d*) Writen
29. (*a*) Drummer (*b*) Slipper (*c*) Hammer (*d*) Rummor
30. (*a*) Device (*b*) Demice (*c*) Revise (*d*) Advice
31. (*a*) Loveable (*b*) Manageable (*c*) Usable (*d*) Soluble
(Asstt. Grade, 1991)
32. (*a*) Incidentally (*b*) Publiclly (*c*) Coolly (*d*) Really
33. (*a*) Garulous (*b*) Greedy (*c*) Grammar (*d*) Giraffe
34. (*a*) Illegal (*b*) Illitrate (*c*) Illegitimate (*d*) Illegible
(C.B.I. 1993)
35. (*a*) Secretry (*b*) Enunciate (*c*) Controversy (*d*) Campaign
36. (*a*) Kiln (*b*) Masculine (*c*) Muslin (*d*) Disciplin
(I. Tax & Central Excise, 1991)
37. (*a*) Conceit (*b*) Deceit (*c*) Receive (*d*) Percieve
(I. Tax & Central Excise, 1991)
38. (*a*) Appeal (*b*) Appetite (*c*) Appology (*d*) Approval
39. (*a*) Matrimony (*b*) Material (*c*) Mathamatics (*d*) Mattress
40. (*a*) Concession (*b*) Reconciliation (*c*) Humilliation (*d*) Palliation
41. (*a*) Exonerate (*b*) Quaternary (*c*) Hurricane (*d*) Surveillence
42. (*a*) Seige (*b*) Solemn (*c*) Syllable (*d*) Seize
(Stenographers' Exam, 1993)
43. (*a*) Governor (*b*) Stupor (*c*) Vendor (*d*) Invador
44. (*a*) Proprietor (*b*) Personel (*c*) Personal (*d*) Proposal
(Clerks' Grade, 1992)
45. (*a*) Terrace (*b*) Transmitter (*c*) Terorism (*d*) Tremor

46. (*a*) Kilometer (*b*) Knead (*c*) Knowledge (*d*) Kidnapper

47. (*a*) Slight (*b*) Shoot (*c*) Thrift (*d*) Subtle

(B.S.R.B. 1995)

48. (*a*) Immunity (*b*) Immaculate (*c*) Imminent (*d*) Immitate

49. (*a*) Sargeant (*b*) Shallot (*c*) Shackle (*d*) Shellac

50. (*a*) Beetle (*b*) Beautician (*c*) Bearable (*d*) Beautifull

(Stenographers' Exam, 1995)

ANSWERS

1. (*c*) Magnificent **2.** (*a*) Surrender **3.** (*b*) Maintenance **4.** (*b*) Mischievous
5. (*d*) Weep **6.** (*b*) Addiction **7.** (*a*) Memorandum **8.** (*c*) Notable
9. (*b*) Grammar **10.** (*c*) Miscellaneous **11.** (*d*) Parachute **12.** (*a*) Intelligentsia
13. (*d*) Retaliate **14.** (*c*) Contemporary **15.** (*e*) All correct **16.** (*d*) Colony
17. (*a*) Homogeneous **18.** (*b*) Mucilage **19.** (*b*) Anniversary **20.** (*b*) Illicit
21. (*b*) Senescent **22.** (*d*) Fugitive **23.** (*d*) Teetotaller **24.** (*c*) Circuitous
25. (*d*) Fodder **26.** (*c*) Advertise **27.** (*b*) Conqueror **28.** (*d*) Written
29. (*d*) Rumour **30.** (*b*) Demise **31.** (*a*) Lovable **32.** (*b*) Publicly
33. (*a*) Garrulous **34.** (*b*) Illiterate **35.** (*a*) Secretary **36.** (*d*) Discipline
37. (*d*) Perceive **38.** (*c*) Apology **39.** (*c*) Mathematics **40.** (*c*) Humiliation
41. (*d*) Surveillance **42.** (*a*) Siege **43.** (*d*) Invader **44.** (*b*) Personnel
45. (*c*) Terrorism **46.** (*a*) Kilometre **47.** (*e*) All correct **48.** (*d*) Imitate
49. (*a*) Sergeant **50.** (*d*) Beautiful

PRACTICE SET 7

Directions : ***In each of the following questions, out of the given group of words, choose the mis-spelt one. If all of them are spelt correctly, the answer is (e) i.e. All correct.***

1. (*a*) Anxiety (*b*) Ankel (*c*) Accommodation (*d*) Allergy

(Stenographers' Exam, 1993)

2. (*a*) Recuperate (*b*) Pasture (*c*) Populace (*d*) Penence

3. (*a*) Shutter (*b*) Silhoutte (*c*) Shepherd (*d*) Shield

4. (*a*) Marshall (*b*) Niece (*c*) Plaque (*d*) Surety

5. (*a*) Lonesome (*b*) Lovely (*c*) Ludicruous (*d*) Logical

(Section Officers' 1993)

6. (*a*) Parietal (*b*) Parole (*c*) Passtime (*d*) Pellagra

7. (*a*) Fortress (*b*) Forestry (*c*) Fiancee (*d*) Foresake

8. (*a*) Dairy (*b*) Dafodil (*c*) Dainty (*d*) Damage

(S.S.C. 1991)

9. (*a*) Reddress (*b*) Address (*c*) Embarrass (*d*) Harass

10. (*a*) Malefactor (*b*) Maestro (*c*) Malevolent (*d*) Malestorm

11. (*a*) Allottee (*b*) Almighty (*c*) Allright (*d*) Altogether

(Assistant Grade, 1991)

12. (*a*) Etiquete (*b*) Pattern (*c*) Privilege (*d*) Dialogue

13. (*a*) Anaemia (*b*) Attitude (*c*) Admiralty (*d*) Acquarium

14. (*a*) Coupious (*b*) Cautious (*c*) Captious (*d*) Capricious

(C.B.I. 1993)

15. (*a*) Nemesis (*b*) Necessary (*c*) Nectar (*d*) Nieghbour

16. (*a*) Occlude (*b*) Obsolesent (*c*) Oblique (*d*) Obedience

17. (*a*) Birth (*b*) Beginer (*c*) Benefit (*d*) Banana

(Clerk's Grade, 1992)

18. (*a*) Accustom (*b*) Accept (*c*) Accute (*d*) Accuse

19. (*a*) Assimilate (*b*) Afinity (*c*) Antagonise (*d*) Ameliorate

20. (*a*) Sattire (*b*) Scissors (*c*) Scullery (*d*) Spouse

21. (*a*) Weighty (*b*) Peity (*c*) Height (*d*) Gaeity

(Central Excise, 1991)

22. (*a*) Goverment (*b*) Professional (*c*) Grammar (*d*) Introduction

23. (*a*) Trachaea (*b*) Tragedy (*c*) Trajectory (*d*) Training

24. (*a*) Magnanimous (*b*) Magnetism (*c*) Magnificient (*d*) Magnify

(Translators' Exam, 1994)

25. (*a*) Chancellor (*b*) Trailor (*c*) Traitor (*d*) Inheritor

26. (*a*) Carpenter (*b*) Chauffeur (*c*) Callibre (*d*) Coalesce

27. (*a*) Foundary (*b*) Frontier (*c*) Fallacy (*d*) Flannel

28. (*a*) Municipality (*b*) Restaurant (*c*) Compartment (*d*) Approach

(B.S.R.B. 1995)

29. (*a*) Cureable (*b*) Currency (*c*) Campaign (*d*) Chronicle

30. (*a*) Glamorous (*b*) Granulate (*c*) Greatful (*d*) Gradient

31. (*a*) Dissect (*b*) Dispirit (*c*) Dossier (*d*) Deter

32. (*a*) Jewellry (*b*) Beneficiary (*c*) Military (*d*) Literary

(Stenographers' Exam, 1993)

33. (*a*) Carriage (*b*) Barriage (*c*) Garrage (*d*) Marriage

34. (*a*) Lantern (*b*) Labourer (*c*) Leakeage (*d*) Lather

35. (*a*) Miscellaneous (*b*) Precarious (*c*) Mischievious (*d*) Licentious

(Asstt. Grade, 1991)

36. (*a*) Ambasador (*b*) Atrocious (*c*) Aeronaut (*d*) Attribute

37. (*a*) Exuberant (*b*) Extraneous (*c*) Eroneous (*d*) Exemplify

38. (*a*) Handicapped (*b*) Hankerchief (*c*) Handiwork (*d*) Handicraft

39. (*a*) Repurcussion (*b*) Reference (*c*) Rebellion (*d*) Receptacle

40. (*a*) Gymnastics (*b*) Greediness (*c*) Guideance (*d*) Grandiose

41. (*a*) Exclaimation (*b*) Excellence (*c*) Exaggeration (*d*) Embroidery

42. (*a*) Referring (*b*) Openning (*c*) Beginning (*d*) Stopping

(Stenographers' Exam, 1994)

43. (*a*) Practice (*b*) Lice (*c*) Paradice (*d*) Advice

44. (*a*) Cumberous (*b*) Corruption (*c*) Crystalline (*d*) Contrive

45. (*a*) Auspicious (*b*) Available (*c*) Attainable (*d*) Auxilliary

46. (*a*) Handicraft (*b*) Handbar (*c*) Handkerchef (*d*) Handicap

(Stenographers' Exam, 1995)

47. (*a*) Tangible (*b*) Tantalize (*c*) Tantrum (*d*) Tecnique

48. (*a*) Impediment (*b*) Judgment (*c*) Merriment (*d*) Embarrassment

(Asstt. Grade, 1992)

49. (*a*) Butcher (*b*) Burrow (*c*) Buoyant (*d*) Buletin

50. (*a*) Suspicion (*b*) Superiority (*c*) Supercede (*d*) Supervise

---

ANSWERS

1. (*b*) Ankle	**2.** (*d*) Penance	**3.** (*b*) Silhouette	**4.** (*a*) Marshal
5. (*c*) Ludicrous	**6.** (*c*) Pastime	**7.** (*d*) Forsake	**8.** (*b*) Daffodil
9. (*a*) Redress	**10.** (*d*) Maelstorm	**11.** (*c*) Alright	**12.** (*a*) Etiquette
13. (*d*) Aquarium	**14.** (*a*) Copious	**15.** (*d*) Neighbour	**16.** (*b*) Obsolescent
17. (*b*) Beginner	**18.** (*c*) Acute	**19.** (*b*) Affinity	**20.** (*a*) Satire
21. (*d*) Gaiety	**22.** (*a*) Government	**23.** (*a*) Trachea	**24.** (*c*) Magnificent
25. (*b*) Trailer	**26.** (*c*) Calibre	**27.** (*a*) Foundry	**28.** (*e*) All correct
29. (*a*) Curable	**30.** (*c*) Grateful	**31.** (*e*) All correct	**32.** (*a*) Jewellery
33. (*b*) Barrage	**34.** (*c*) Leakage	**35.** (*c*) Mischievous	**36.** (*a*) Ambassador
37. (*c*) Erroneous	**38.** (*b*) Handkerchief	**39.** (*a*) Repercussion	**40.** (*c*) Guidance
41. (*a*) Exclamation	**42.** (*b*) Opening	**43.** (*c*) Paradise	**44.** (*a*) Cumbrous
45. (*d*) Auxiliary	**46.** (*c*) Handkerchief	**47.** (*d*) Technique	**48.** (*b*) Judgement
49. (*d*) Bulletin	**50.** (*c*) Supersede		

PRACTICE SET 8

Directions : ***In each of the following questions, out of the given group of words, choose the mis-spelt one. If all are spelt correctly, the answer is (e) i.e. All correct.***

1. (*a*) Familiar (*b*) Simmer (*c*) Hammer (*d*) Grammer **(Clerks' Grade, 1992)**

2. (*a*) Banquet (*b*) Benefector (*c*) Bestow (*d*) Behaviour

3. (*a*) Troup (*b*) Transcend (*c*) Treasure (*d*) Theatre

4. (*a*) Adhesive (*b*) Abusive (*c*) Applauce (*d*) Accomplice **(I. Tax & Central Excise, 1991)**

5. (*a*) Founder (*b*) Frajile (*c*) Introvert (*d*) Sanctity

6. (*a*) Anticipate (*b*) Antipathy (*c*) Antiseptic (*d*) Antonymn

7. (*a*) Superstitious (*b*) Accomodation (*c*) Commendable (*d*) Callous **(Stenographers' Exam, 1994)**

8. (*a*) Collar (*b*) Collaborate (*c*) Carporate (*d*) Corroborate

9. (*a*) Procession (*b*) Profession (*c*) Possession (*d*) Occassion

10. (*a*) Heritage (*b*) Ecstasy (*c*) Glimpse (*d*) Discription **(B.S.R.B. 1994)**

11. (*a*) Denunciation (*b*) Acceleration (*c*) Magnificient (*d*) Gravitation

12. (*a*) Focal (*b*) Vocal (*c*) Vehical (*d*) Mystical **(Asstt. Grade, 1991)**

13. (*a*) Heroin (*b*) Harmoniam (*c*) Herbaceous (*d*) Headquarters

14. (*a*) Committed (*b*) Submitted (*c*) Benifitted (*d*) Remitted **(Stenographers' Exam, 1993)**

15. (*a*) Narrator (*b*) Governor (*c*) Operator (*d*) Controller

16. (*a*) Excess (*b*) Ecsorbitant (*c*) Eczema (*d*) Ecstasy

17. (*a*) Ceramic (*b*) Ceribral (*c*) Ceremony (*d*) Cereal **(Clerks' Grade, 1991)**

18. (*a*) Inflammable (*b*) Inaugrate (*c*) Incandescent (*d*) Illustrate

19. (*a*) Pagent (*b*) Paroxysm (*c*) Pillory (*d*) Pipette

20. (*a*) Mischievious (*b*) Miscreant (*c*) Misdemeanour (*d*) Miserable **(Asstt. Grade, 1995)**

21. (*a*) Amorphous (*b*) Artilery (*c*) Attrition (*d*) Accessory

22. (*a*) Lieutenant (*b*) Laboratary (*c*) Lawlessness (*d*) Laudatory

23. (*a*) Projection (*b*) Educate (*c*) Curve (*d*) Headquaters **(B.S.R.B. 1995)**

24. (*a*) Enterance (*b*) Elementary (*c*) Endeavour (*d*) Eccentricity

25. (*a*) Behaviour (*b*) Mentenance (*c*) Commend (*d*) Appraise **(B.S.R.B. 1995)**

26. (*a*) Writting (*b*) Discrimination (*c*) Achievement (*d*) Humanitarian

27. (*a*) Besiege (*b*) Boundary (*c*) Bufoonery (*d*) Bifurcate

28. (*a*) Occupation (*b*) Occur (*c*) Occular (*d*) Occlude

29. (*a*) Numismatics (*b*) Nuisence (*c*) Nucleus (*d*) Numerous **(Section Officers' 1993)**

30. (*a*) Laudable (*b*) Honourable (*c*) Lovable (*d*) Honourary

31. (*a*) Audacity (*b*) Autumn (*c*) Aukward (*d*) Authority

32. (*a*) Device (*b*) Demice (*c*) Advice (*d*) Revise **(S.S.C. 1991)**

33. (*a*) Annualy (*b*) Alliance (*c*) Annihilate (*d*) Antiquity

34. (*a*) Counterfiet (*b*) Capsicum (*c*) Callous (*d*) Conference

35. (*a*) Repeatition (*b*) Renunciation (*c*) Recitation (*d*) Recapitulation **(C.B.I. 1993)**

36. (*a*) Mischeif (*b*) Belief (*c*) Thief (*d*) Grief

37. (*a*) Worried (*b*) Vegetable (*c*) Sacrifice (*d*) Temporary **(B.S.R.B. 1994)**

38. (*a*) Glistening (*b*) Genuine (*c*) Generater (*d*) Generosity

39. (*a*) Writing (*b*) Lightning (*c*) Leutenant (*d*) Lighten **(Stenographers' Exam, 1993)**

40. (*a*) Gynaecology (*b*) Bonafide (*c*) Aparthied (*d*) Aspersion

41. (*a*) Aerodrome (*b*) Airoplane (*c*) Aircraft (*d*) Aerial **(Asstt. Grade, 1991)**

42. (*a*) Juglery (*b*) Journalism (*c*) Jaundice (*d*) Jealousy

43. (*a*) Magistrial (*b*) Mausoleum (*c*) Miserable (*d*) Meticulous

44. (*a*) Rational (*b*) Release

(*c*) Demolish (*d*) Survival

(B.S.R.B. 1995)

45. (*a*) Supress (*b*) Surfeit
(*c*) Swallow (*d*) Symptom

46. (*a*) Trustee (*b*) Trienial
(*c*) Trolley (*d*) Torrent

47. (*a*) Frostbite (*b*) Fretricide
(*c*) Frenzy (*d*) Franchise

(Translators' Exam, 1994)

48. (*a*) Archeology (*b*) Adolescence
(*c*) Achievement (*d*) Affidavit

49. (*a*) Vacuum (*b*) Vaccinate
(*c*) Vacilate (*d*) Varnish

50. (*a*) Cieling (*b*) Celluloid
(*c*) Cease (*d*) Cemetery

(Stenographers' Exam, 1995)

ANSWERS

1. (*d*) Grammar	**2.** (*b*) Benefactor	**3.** (*a*) Troupe	**4.** (*c*) Applause
5. (*b*) Fragile	**6.** (*d*) Antonym	**7.** (*b*) Accommodation	**8.** (*c*) Corporate
9. (*d*) Occasion	**10.** (*d*) Description	**11.** (*c*) Magnificent	**12.** (*c*) Vehicle
13. (*b*) Harmonium	**14.** (*c*) Benefitted	**15.** (*d*) Controllor	**16.** (*b*) Exorbitant
17. (*b*) Cerebral	**18.** (*b*) Inaugurate	**19.** (*a*) Pageant	**20.** (*a*) Mischievous
21. (*b*) Artillery	**22.** (*b*) Laboratory	**23.** (*d*) Headquarters	**24.** (*a*) Entrance
25. (*b*) Maintenance	**26.** (*a*) Writing	**27.** (*c*) Buffoonery	**28.** (*c*) Ocular
29. (*b*) Nuisance	**30.** (*d*) Honorary	**31.** (*c*) Awkward	**32.** (*b*) Demise
33. (*a*) Annually	**34.** (*a*) Counterfeit	**35.** (*a*) Repetition	**36.** (*a*) Mischief
37. (*e*) All correct	**38.** (*c*) Generator	**39.** (*c*) Lieutenant	**40.** (*c*) Apartheid
41. (*b*) Aeroplane	**42.** (*a*) Jugglery	**43.** (*a*) Magisterial	**44.** (*e*) All correct
45. (*a*) Suppress	**46.** (*b*) Triennial	**47.** (*b*) Fratricide	**48.** (*a*) Archaeology
49. (*c*) Vacillate	**50.** (*a*) Ceiling		

PRACTICE SET 9

Directions : ***Each of the following questions consists of a group of words. In each group one word is mis-spelt. Find the mis-spelt word. If all are spelt correctly, the answer is (e) i.e. All correct.***

1. (*a*) Absess (*b*) Accessary
(*c*) Abrasive (*d*) Abstinence

(Clerks' Grade, 1991)

2. (*a*) Disjoint (*b*) Levy
(*c*) Primery (*d*) Enema

3. (*a*) Drapery (*b*) Dysentry
(*c*) Diffusion (*d*) Deceive

4. (*a*) Profligacy (*b*) Bureaucracy
(*c*) Hypocricy (*d*) Prophecy

(Asstt. Grade, 1991)

5. (*a*) Immature (*b*) Impasse
(*c*) Immacculate (*d*) Immpeccable

6. (*a*) Downtown (*b*) Downpore
(*c*) Downstairs (*d*) Downright

7. (*a*) Jeopardy (*b*) Jealosy
(*c*) Jaundice (*d*) Javelin

(C.B.I. 1993)

8. (*a*) Curiculum (*b*) Contingency
(*c*) Cauliflower (*d*) Cooperate

9. (*a*) Vengeance (*b*) Ventillation
(*c*) Veterinary (*d*) Villainy

10. (*a*) Allocation (*b*) Allotment
(*c*) Allmighty (*d*) Elocution

(Central Excise, 1991)

11. (*a*) Stupify (*b*) Subpoena
(*c*) Succumb (*d*) Sombre

12. (*a*) Permissible (*b*) Pneumatic
(*c*) Paladium (*d*) Peasantry

13. (*a*) Receive (*b*) Receipt
(*c*) Neighbour (*d*) Sieze

(Stenographers' Exam, 1994)

14. (*a*) Embellish (*b*) Capsised
(*c*) Exemplify (*d*) Drowned

15. (*a*) Bereavment (*b*) Beseech
(*c*) Bureaucracy (*d*) Billiards

16. (*a*) Nightmare (*b*) Unfruitfull
(*c*) Coarse (*d*) Unwavering
(B.S.R.B. 1994)

17. (*a*) Debater (*b*) Narrator
(*c*) Spectator (*d*) Orater

18. (*a*) Amunition (*b*) Analysable
(*c*) Annihilate (*d*) Asafoetida

19. (*a*) Etiquete (*b*) Ethnic
(*c*) Ethereal (*d*) Eulogize
(Translators' Exam, 1994)

20. (*a*) Instructor (*b*) Install
(*c*) Intution (*d*) Infantry

21. (*a*) Mislead (*b*) Obscure
(*c*) Cautious (*d*) Exihibit
(B.S.R.B. 1996)

22. (*a*) Tranquility (*b*) Tyranny
(*c*) Tendency (*d*) Temperature

23. (*a*) Admiror (*b*) Inspector
(*c*) Jailor (*d*) Proprietor
(Stenographers' Exam, 1993)

24. (*a*) Hybridize (*b*) Hosery
(*c*) Hierarchy (*d*) Hurriedly

25. (*a*) Nefarious (*b*) Nautical
(*c*) Nightmare (*d*) Napthalene

26. (*a*) Continuous (*b*) Valuable
(*c*) Criticize (*d*) Gentalman
(B.S.R.B. 1995)

27. (*a*) Prerequisite (*b*) Privelige
(*c*) Profession (*d*) Progression

28. (*a*) Loathesome (*b*) Logarithm
(*c*) Limerick (*d*) Legitimacy

29. (*a*) Precaution (*b*) Plebiscite
(*c*) Prarie (*d*) Penance

30. (*a*) Psychoanalyst (*b*) Physiologist
(*c*) Psychaitrist (*d*) Psychologist
(Section Officers' 1993)

31. (*a*) Restaurent (*b*) Retinue
(*c*) Rickshaw (*d*) Requirement

32. (*a*) Retreive (*b*) Rheumatism
(*c*) Reprieve (*d*) Reverberate

33. (*a*) Deference (*b*) Dence
(*c*) Pretence (*d*) Offence
(Assistant Grade, 1991)

34. (*a*) Sympozium (*b*) Sweater
(*c*) Syllable (*d*) Syringe

35. (*a*) Despair (*b*) Desperate
(*c*) Maintain (*d*) Maintainance

36. (*a*) Forehead (*b*) Feign
(*c*) Forfiet (*d*) Foreign

37. (*a*) Pretentious (*b*) Proclaimation
(*c*) Pronunciation (*d*) Promiscuous

38. (*a*) Abdominal (*b*) Clinical
(*c*) Machenical (*d*) Technical
(Clerks' Grade, 1992)

39. (*a*) Dilemma (*b*) Hinderance
(*c*) Disharmony (*d*) Algebra

40. (*a*) Confedration (*b*) Camaraderie
(*c*) Cataclysm (*d*) Carboniferous

41. (*a*) Impregnable (*b*) Imposter
(*c*) Improbable (*d*) Implausible
(Stenographers' Exam, 1995)

42. (*a*) Sanatorium (*b*) Scoundrel
(*c*) Salamandar (*d*) Sarcasm

43. (*a*) Madamoiselle (*b*) Manacle
(*c*) Mysterious (*d*) Metallurgy

44. (*a*) Clothing (*b*) Gathering
(*c*) Actualise (*d*) Reproach
(B.S.R.B. 1995)

45. (*a*) Loathsome (*b*) Livable
(*c*) Literature (*d*) Lizzard

46. (*a*) Photostate (*b*) Palmistry
(*c*) Posthumous (*d*) Polytechnic

47. (*a*) Allowance (*b*) Allusion
(*c*) Alltogether (*d*) Alternative
(Asstt. Grade, 1995)

48. (*a*) Stensil (*b*) Stubborn
(*c*) Spectre (*d*) Suffocate

49. (*a*) Naration (*b*) Neolithic
(*c*) Nostalgia (*d*) Nocturnal

50. (*a*) Termination (*b*) Culmination
(*c*) Determination (*d*) Defination
(Stenographers' Exam, 1993)

ANSWERS

1. (*a*) Abscess **2.** (*c*) Primary **3.** (*b*) Dysentery **4.** (*c*) Hypocrisy
5. (*d*) Impeccable **6.** (*b*) Downpour **7.** (*b*) Jealousy **8.** (*a*) Curriculum
9. (*b*) Ventilation **10.** (*c*) Almighty **11.** (*a*) Stupefy **12.** (*c*) Palladium
13. (*d*) Seize **14.** (*b*) Capsized **15.** (*a*) Bereavement **16.** (*b*) Unfruitful
17. (*d*) Orator **18.** (*a*) Ammunition **19.** (*a*) Etiquette **20.** (*c*) Intuition
21. (*d*) Exhibit **22.** (*a*) Tranquality **23.** (*a*) Admirer **24.** (*b*) Hosiery
25. (*d*) Naphthalene **26.** (*d*) Gentleman **27.** (*b*) Privilege **28.** (*a*) Loathsome
29. (*c*) Prairie **30.** (*c*) Psychiatrist **31.** (*a*) Restaurant **32.** (*a*) Retrieve
33. (*b*) Dense **34.** (*a*) Symposium **35.** (*d*) Maintenance **36.** (*c*) Forfeit

37. (*b*) Proclamation **38.** (*c*) Mechanical **39.** (*b*) Hindrance **40.** (*a*) Confederation
41. (*b*) Impostor **42.** (*c*) Salamander **43.** (*a*) Mademoiselle **44.** (*e*) All correct
45. (*d*) Lizard **46.** (*a*) Photostat **47.** (*c*) Altogether **48.** (*a*) Stencil
49. (*a*) Narration **50.** (*d*) Definition

PRACTICE SET 10

Directions : ***In each of the following questions, out of the given words, one word is mis-spelt. Find the mis-spelt word. If all words are spelt correctly, answer is 'All correct' i.e. (e).***

1. (*a*) Respite (*b*) Reciept (*c*) Reference (*d*) Recipe **(Stenographers' Exam, 1995)**

2. (*a*) Varnish (*b*) Viral (*c*) Various (*d*) Varity

3. (*a*) Debator (*b*) Declaration (*c*) Distress (*d*) Department

4. (*a*) Harmonise (*b*) Impression (*c*) Surrender (*d*) Enthusistic **(B.S.R.B. 1995)**

5. (*a*) Manoeuvre (*b*) Macabre (*c*) Millionare (*d*) Mediocre

6. (*a*) Boisterous (*b*) Baricade (*c*) Brochure (*d*) Brigadier

7. (*a*) Evasion (*b*) Ovation (*c*) Occassion (*d*) Erosion **(Assistant Grade, 1992)**

8. (*a*) Voluntary (*b*) Vomitting (*c*) Vocabulary (*d*) Vicisitude

9. (*a*) Installment (*b*) Innocence (*c*) Impetus (*d*) Incipient

10. (*a*) Assume (*b*) Presume (*c*) Cunsume (*d*) Subsume **(Railways, 1992)**

11. (*a*) Involuantary (*b*) Anxiety (*c*) Recuperate (*d*) Languish

12. (*a*) Agricultarist (*b*) Acclamation (*c*) Admirability (*d*) Archipelago

13. (*a*) Career (*b*) Furious (*c*) Territory (*d*) Objectionable **(B.S.R.B. 1994)**

14. (*a*) Acquisition (*b*) Acquaintence (*c*) Accompany (*d*) Accessible

15. (*a*) Submarine (*b*) Subsidize (*c*) Stamped (*d*) Stallion

16. (*a*) Adambrate (*b*) Calibrate (*c*) Celebrate (*d*) Proliferate **(Translators' Exam, 1994)**

17. (*a*) Confidence (*b*) Successfull (*c*) Quarrelsome (*d*) Antecedant

18. (*a*) Catastrophe (*b*) Centanarian (*c*) Commissioner (*d*) Confectionary

19. (*a*) Dwindle (*b*) Glorify (*c*) Exquisite (*d*) Gliter **(B.S.R.B. 1996)**

20. (*a*) Tenure (*b*) Trigonometry (*c*) Thalium (*d*) Turquoise

21. (*a*) Establish (*b*) Avoideable (*c*) Superior (*d*) Pleasant

22. (*a*) Squirrel (*b*) Spurious (*c*) Suffrage (*d*) Solstice

23. (*a*) Forebear (*b*) Gazette (*c*) League (*d*) Judiciary

24. (*a*) Apropriation (*b*) Oppose (*c*) Increment (*d*) Minute **(B.S.R.B. 1995)**

25. (*a*) Leguminous (*b*) Liquifiable (*c*) Loafer (*d*) Loquacious

26. (*a*) Overwhelm (*b*) Omlette (*c*) Offence (*d*) Opponent

27. (*a*) Beleive (*b*) Relieve (*c*) Receive (*d*) Deceive **(Stenographers' Exam, 1992)**

28. (*a*) Schedule (*b*) Scrutinise (*c*) Scavanger (*d*) Secede

29. (*a*) Mortgaze (*b*) Manicure (*c*) Miraculous (*d*) Mesmeric

30. (*a*) Governance (*b*) Essense (*c*) Penance (*d*) Finance **(Investigators' Exam, 1988)**

31. (*a*) Pellicle (*b*) Pilgrimage (*c*) Portrait (*d*) Parepet

32. (*a*) Flaccid (*b*) Earthernware (*c*) Zealot (*d*) Hilarious

33. (*a*) Omission (*b*) Muscular (*c*) Nineth (*d*) Roundish **(B.S.R.B 1994)**

34. (*a*) Spontanity (*b*) Secession (*c*) Sorcerer (*d*) Sinister

35. (*a*) Tenure (*b*) Utensil (*c*) Surender (*d*) Racquet

36. (*a*) Deficency (*b*) Disastrous (*c*) Discourteous (*d*) Decency

37. (*a*) Sceptic (*b*) Agnostic (*c*) Prolific (*d*) Assetic **(Assistant Grade, 1993)**

38. (*a*) Paleolithic (*b*) Porcelain
(*c*) Preliminary (*d*) Pedestrian

39. (*a*) Quadruple (*b*) Quarternary
(*c*) Quibble (*d*) Quiescent

40. (*a*) Harmony (*b*) Harmonius
(*c*) Harmful (*d*) Harmonium
(Stenographers' Exam, 1995)

41. (*a*) Luminiscent (*b*) Lusciousncess
(*c*) Laevatory (*d*) Localization

42. (*a*) Suculent (*b*) Spectacle
(*c*) Sonnet (*d*) Sentence

43. (*a*) Opulence (*b*) Offens
(*c*) Nonsense (*d*) Occurrence
(Asstt. Grade, 1992)

44. (*a*) Itching (*b*) Interview
(*c*) Interupt (*d*) Irrigate

45. (*a*) Perennial (*b*) Penitence
(*c*) Plaintiff (*d*) Pedastal

46. (*a*) Careful (*b*) Unlawful
(*c*) Harmful (*d*) Beautiful
(B.S.R.B. 1990)

47. (*a*) Oriental (*b*) Sargeant
(*c*) Zodiac (*d*) Prevailing

48. (*a*) Chrysanthemum (*b*) Chastisement
(*c*) Conflagration (*d*) Constelation

49. (*a*) Preparatory (*d*) Cursory
(*c*) Promisary (*d*) Emissary
(Translators' Exam, 1994)

50. (*a*) Merchandise (*b*) Missionary
(*c*) Municipality (*d*) Mediteranean

ANSWERS

1. (*b*) Receipt	**2.** (*d*) Variety	**3.** (*a*) Debater	**4.** (*d*) Enthusiastic
5. (*c*) Millionaire	**6.** (*b*) Barricade	**7.** (*c*) Occasion	**8.** (*d*) Vicissitude
9. (*a*) Instalment	**10.** (*c*) Consume	**11.** (*a*) Involuntary	**12.** (*a*) Agriculturist
13. (*e*) All correct	**14.** (*b*) Acquaintance	**15.** (*c*) Stampede	**16.** (*a*) Adambarate
17. (*b*) Successful	**18.** (*b*) Centenarian	**19.** (*d*) Glitter	**20.** (*c*) Thallium
21. (*b*) Avoidable	**22.** (*e*) All correct	**23.** (*a*) Forbear	**24.** (*a*) Appropriation
25. (*b*) Liquefiable	**26.** (*b*) Omelette	**27.** (*a*) Believe	**28.** (*c*) Scavenger
29. (*a*) Mortgage	**30.** (*c*) Essence	**31.** (*d*) Parapet	**32.** (*b*) Earthenware
33. (*c*) Ninth	**34.** (*a*) Spontaneity	**35.** (*c*) Surrender	**36.** (*a*) Deficiency
37. (*d*) Ascetic	**38.** (*a*) Palaeolithic	**39.** (*b*) Quaternary	**40.** (*b*) Harmonious
41. (*a*) Luminescent	**42.** (*a*) Succulent	**43.** (*b*) Offence	**44.** (*c*) Interrupt
45. (*d*) Pedestal	**46.** (*e*) All correct	**47.** (*b*) Sergeant	**48.** (*d*) Constellation
49. (*c*) Promissory	**50.** (*d*) Mediterranean		

PRACTICE SET 11

Directions : ***In each of the following questions, out of the given group of words, choose the mis-spelt one. If all the words are spelt correctly, the answer is (e) i.e. 'All correct'.***

1. (*a*) Legibel (*b*) Legislature
(*c*) Legalize (*d*) Legitimate
(Translators' Exam, 1994)

2. (*a*) Impression (*b*) Depression
(*c*) Supression (*d*) Oppression

3. (*a*) Corruption (*b*) Eruption
(*c*) Errudite (*d*) Erroneous

4. (*a*) Accurate (*b*) Accomodate
(*c*) Accrue (*d*) Accumulate
(Railways, 1992)

5. (*a*) Miscelleneous (*b*) Mathematics
(*c*) Cautiously (*d*) Competition

6. (*a*) Delactable (*b*) Dependent
(*c*) Diarrhoea (*d*) Detraction

7. (*a*) Surround (*b*) Surveillance
(*c*) Survey (*d*) Sureptitious
(S.S.C. 1988)

8. (*a*) Demonstration (*b*) Tution
(*c*) Mendacious (*d*) Audience

9. (*a*) Assailant (*b*) Appeasment
(*c*) Ancestry (*d*) Aerobatics

10. (*a*) Tuberculosis (*b*) Trachery
(*c*) Tincture (*d*) Thwart

11. (*a*) Inocuous (*b*) Intellectual (*c*) Invertebrate (*d*) Irruption

12. (*a*) Temparament (*b*) Spontaneous (*c*) Pilgrimage (*d*) Enormous

(B.S.R.B. 1994)

13. (*a*) Aberration (*b*) Abnormalty (*c*) Abscess (*d*) Accentuate

14. (*a*) Boast (*b*) Catalogue (*c*) Terrible (*d*) Heritage

(B.S.R.B. 1996)

15. (*a*) Concurence (*b*) Conscience (*c*) Commodore (*d*) Circumference

16. (*a*) Ocupation (*b*) Obvious (*c*) Occasion (*d*) Ocean

(Stenographers' Exam, 1992)

17. (*a*) Employee (*b*) Effeminate (*c*) Exclaimation (*d*) Ignorance

18. (*a*) Bourgeoise (*b*) Beverage (*c*) Blithsome (*d*) Behaviour

19. (*a*) Regular (*b*) Criminal (*c*) Couragous (*d*) Garbage

(B.S.R.B. 1995)

20. (*a*) Sapphire (*b*) Scurrilous (*c*) Secratariat (*d*) Seethe

21. (*a*) Melifluence (*b*) Margarine (*c*) Marionette (*d*) Marvellous

22. (*a*) Soldier (*b*) Beautiful (*c*) Infinite (*d*) Clearify

(B.S.R.B. 1994)

23. (*a*) Warrant (*b*) Wonderous (*c*) Woollen (*d*) Warrior

24. (*a*) Perpituity (*b*) Partiality (*c*) Preposterous (*d*) Penultimate

25. (*a*) Curiculum (*b*) Museum (*c*) Emporium (*d*) Medium

(Stenographers' Exam, 1995)

26. (*a*) Subservience (*b*) Souvenir (*c*) Succesor (*d*) Stirrup

27. (*a*) Redundant (*b*) Rejuvinate (*c*) Relieve (*d*) Robbery

28. (*a*) Barrister (*b*) Besiege (*c*) Borne (*d*) Begining

(Assistant Grade, 1992)

29. (*a*) Centenery (*b*) Cemetery (*c*) Century (*d*) Chemistry

30. (*a*) Percussive (*b*) Prefrential (*c*) Predicament (*d*) Predecessor

31. (*a*) Negligence (*b*) Affinity (*c*) Wisedom (*d*) Creativity

(B.S.R.B. 1990)

32. (*a*) Demarkation (*b*) Dandruff (*c*) Detonation (*d*) Deliquescence

33. (*a*) Ostracism (*b*) Obnoxious (*c*) Oblitrate (*d*) Obligatory

34. (*a*) Gorilla (*b*) Guarantee (*c*) Gaudy (*d*) Gauze

(Investigators' Exam, 1988)

35. (*a*) Architecture (*b*) Ceremoney (*c*) Believable (*d*) Conflict

36. (*a*) Shrubery (*b*) Senescent (*c*) Slaughter (*d*) Sneer

37. (*a*) Potassium (*b*) Pertinasious (*c*) Pisciculture (*d*) Pernicious

38. (*a*) Repudiate (*b*) Requisite (*c*) Rezemblance (*d*) Rescind

(Translators' Exam, 1994)

39. (*a*) Invigilator (*b*) Interstellar (*c*) Insectivorous (*d*) Inings

40. (*a*) Spinnerret (*b*) Stoppage (*c*) Strenous (*d*) Successive

41. (*a*) Kitchen (*b*) Obstakle (*c*) Perquisite (*d*) Permissible

(B.S.R.B. 1995)

42. (*a*) Sandwitch (*b*) Sculpture (*c*) Secrecy (*d*) Sovereign

43. (*a*) Renaissance (*b*) Revelation (*c*) Refrendum (*d*) Reverence

44. (*a*) Pudding (*b*) Pungent (*c*) Puncture (*d*) Puntuation

(Assistant Grade, 1993)

45. (*a*) Dependant (*b*) Detrimental (*c*) Describe (*d*) Deluge

46. (*a*) Anniversary (*b*) Anasthetic (*c*) Acknowledgement (*d*) Altogether

47. (*a*) Promising (*b*) Ancestry (*c*) Disterbance (*d*) Cardinal

(B.S.R.B. 1996)

48. (*a*) Leprosy (*b*) Licence (*c*) Lenient (*d*) Limerick

49. (*a*) Spoonfull (*b*) Subterranean (*c*) Stainless (*d*) Stupefaction

50. (*a*) Rumour (*b*) Reindeer (*c*) Rufian (*d*) Rogue

ANSWERS

1. (*a*) Legible	**2.** (*c*) Suppression	**3.** (*c*) Erudite	**4.** (*b*) Accommodate
5. (*a*) Miscellaneous	**6.** (*a*) Delectable	**7.** (*d*) Surreptitious	**8.** (*b*) Tuition
9. (*b*) Appeasement	**10.** (*b*) Treachery	**11.** (*a*) Innocuous	**12.** (*a*) Temperament
13. (*b*) Abnormality	**14.** (*e*) All correct	**15.** (*a*) Concurrence	**16.** (*a*) Occupation
17. (*c*) Exclamation	**18.** (*c*) Blithesome	**19.** (*c*) Courageous	**20.** (*c*) Secretariat
21. (*a*) Mellifluence	**22.** (*d*) Clarify	**23.** (*b*) Wondrous	**24.** (*a*) Perpetuity
25. (*a*) Curriculum	**26.** (*c*) Successor	**27.** (*b*) Rejuvenate	**28.** (*d*) Beginning
29. (*a*) Centenary	**30.** (*b*) Preferential	**31.** (*c*) Wisdom	**32.** (*a*) Demarcation
33. (*c*) Obliterate	**34.** (*d*) Gauge	**35.** (*b*) Ceremony	**36.** (*a*) Shrubbery
37. (*b*) Pertinacious	**38.** (*c*) Resemblance	**39.** (*d*) Innings	**40.** (*a*) Spinneret
41. (*b*) Obstacle	**42.** (*a*) Sandwich	**43.** (*c*) Referendum	**44.** (*d*) Punctuation
45. (*a*) Dependent	**46.** (*b*) Anaesthetic	**47.** (*c*) Disturbance	**48.** (*b*) License
49. (*a*) Spoonful	**50.** (*c*) Ruffian		

LATEST PAPER SCENARIO

BANK P.O. EXAMINATION, 1996

Directions : (*Questions 1 to 15*) : ***Read the following passage carefully and answer the questions given below it in the context of the passage. Certain words/phrases in the passage are printed in bold to help you to locate them while answering some of the questions.***

The strength of Indian democracy lies in its tradition, in the fusion of the ideas of democracy and national independence which was characteristic of the Indian nationalist movement long before independence. Although the British retained supreme authority in India until 1947, the provincial elections of 1937 provided real exercise in democratic practice before national independence; during the Pacific war India was not overrun or seriously invaded by the Japanese and after the war was over the transfer of power to a government of the Indian Congress Party was a peaceful one as far as Britain was concerned. By 1947 'Indianization' had already gone far in the Indian civil service and army, so that the new government could start with effective instruments of central control.

After independence, however, India was faced with two vast problems; the first, that of economic growth from a very low level of production and the second that of ethnic diversity and the aspirations of subnationalities. The Congress leadership was more aware of the former problem than of the second; as a new political elite which had rebelled not only against the British Raj but also against India's old social order, they were conscious of the need to initiate economic development and undertake social reforms, but as nationalists who had led a struggle against alien rule on behalf of all parts of India, they took the cohesion of the Indian nation too much for granted and underestimated the centrifugal forces of ethnic division, which were bound to be **accentuated** rather than diminished as the popular masses were more and more drawn into politics. The Congress Party was originally opposed to the idea of recognizing any divisions of India on a linguistic basis and preferred to retain the old provinces of British India which often cut across linguistic boundaries; it was only in response to strong pressures from below that the principle of linguistic states was **conceded** as the basis for a federal 'Indian Union'. The rights granted to the states created new problems for the central government. The idea of making Hindi the national language of a united India was **thwarted** by the **recalcitrance** of the speakers of other important Indian languages, and the autonomy of the states rendered central economic planning extremely difficult. Land reforms remained under the control of the states and many large-scale economic projects required a degree of co-operation between the central government and one or more of the states which it was found impossible to achieve.

Co-ordination of policies was difficult even when the Congress Party was in power both in the states and at the centre; when a congress Government in Delhi was confronted with non-Congress parties in office in the states, it became much harder.

1. The provincial elections of 1937 in India showed that the
   (*a*) British rule was not popular in India.
   (*b*) Supremacy of British in India was likely to be short-lived.
   (*c*) Indians were peace-loving people.
   (*d*) India was capable of bringing into practice the idea of democracy.
   (*e*) Indian Congress was the single largest party in India.

2. Why was India not overrun by the Japanese during the Pacific War?
   (*a*) Japan was sceptical about its success in the war.
   (*b*) Japan had friendly relations with Britain.
   (*c*) Japan was interested in India's freedom from the British rule.
   (*d*) It was not an advantageous proposition for Japan from the military perspective.
   (*e*) None of these

3. Which according to the passage, can be cited as exercise in democratic practice in India before independence?
(*a*) The Indianisation of the Indian civil service
(*b*) The handing over of power by British to India
(*c*) Several democratic institutions created by the Indian National Congress
(*d*) A neutral role played by the army
(*e*) None of these

4. Which of the following problems India was faced with after Independence?
(*a*) Improper co-ordination of various government policies
(*b*) Increasing the production from a very low level
(*c*) Military attack from a country across the border
(*d*) Lack of co-ordination between the central and state governments.
(*e*) None of these

5. Why was central economic planning found to be difficult?
(*a*) Ethnic diversity of the people
(*b*) Lack of will in implementing land reforms
(*c*) Autonomy given to the states in certain matters
(*d*) Lack of co-ordination in different government departments
(*e*) Multiplicity of states and union territories

6. The new government could start with effective instrument of central power after independence because the
(*a*) Indian army was organized on the pattern of British army
(*b*) transfer of power to the Indian Congress party was peaceful
(*c*) process of Indianization of the Indian Civil Service had already started
(*d*) people of India offered their whole hearted support to the government
(*e*) None of these

7. Which of the following issues was not appropriately realised by the central government?
(*a*) Centre-State relations
(*b*) A national language for the country
(*c*) Ethnic diversity of the people
(*d*) Implementation of the formulated policies
(*e*) None of these

8. Why was the linguistic reorganisation of the states accepted?
(*a*) No common national language could be emerged.
(*b*) The states were not co-operating with the central government
(*c*) Strong pressure from the states were exerted on the central government to create such states
(*d*) Non-Congress governments in the states demanded such a reorganisation of the states
(*e*) None of these

9. Which of the following statements is true in the context of the passage?
(*a*) During the Pacific war India was invaded by Japan
(*b*) After Independence India was faced with the problem of linguistic diversity of the people.
(*c*) Social reforms were neglected by the government.
(*d*) Congress leadership was not as much aware of the problem of ethnic diversity as much as of low production.
(*e*) Land reforms were under the control of the Central Government.

10. Which of the following statements is not true in the context of the passage?
(*a*) The political elite in India rebelled against the British Raj.
(*b*) By 1947, Indian army was fairly indianized.
(*c*) Economic development and social reforms were initiated soon after independence.
(*d*) The Congress party was originally opposed to the idea of division of states on lingustic basis.
(*e*) The Congress leadership was fully aware of the problem of ethnic diversity in India at the time of Independence.

11. Which word is most nearly the same in meaning as the word *'accentuated'* as used in the passage?
(*a*) exhibited (*b*) projected (*c*) sharpened (*d*) devalued (*e*) mitigated

12. Choose the word which is most opposite in meaning of the word *'conceded'* as used in the passage?
(*a*) accorded (*b*) criticised (*c*) rejected (*d*) denounced (*e*) withdrawn

13. Which word is most nearly the same in meaning as the word *'thwarted'* as used in the passage?

(a) diverted (b) opposed (c) accepted
(d) advocated (e) implemented

14. Choose the word which is most opposite in meaning of the word '*recalcitrance*' as used in the passage?
(a) provocation (b) opposition
(c) dedication (d) amenability
(e) vulnerability

15. Choose the word which is most opposite in meaning of the word '*harder*' as used in the passage.
(a) shorter (b) slower (c) easier
(d) larger (e) inferior

Directions (*Questions 16 to 25*) : ***Pick out the most effective word from the given words to fill in the blank to make the sentence meaningfully complete.***

16. As a general rule, politicians do not .... centre stage.
(a) foster (b) forbid (c) forgive
(d) forward (e) forsake

17. We cannot go on strike every year. Now that we have gone on strike we must .... this issue.
(a) canvass (b) cross (c) clinch
(d) culminate (e) co-ordinate

18. Indications are that the Government is .... to the prospect of granting bonus to the striking employees.
(a) relieved (b) aligned (c) obliged
(d) reconciled (e) authorised

19. I was totally .... by his line of thinking and could not put forth any argument.
(a) refuted (b) nonplussed
(c) degraded (d) exhausted
(e) demolished

20. The .... study on import of natural gas from Iran through pipeline would be completed shortly.
(a) natural (b) economic (c) feasibility
(d) calculated (e) reallocation

21. Man is .... , however, he is more in need of mental companionship than of physical companionship.
(a) biological (b) egoistic (c) gregarious
(d) democratic (e) emotional

22. Shivalal .... classical music. He always prefers Bhimsen Joshi to Asha Bhonsale and Pandit Jasraj to Kumar Sanu.
(a) adores (b) cares (c) cultivates
(d) apprehends (e) encompasses

23. He is the best man for this job. He has mental .... to carry it out.
(a) adroitness (b) durability
(c) persuasion (d) predilection
(e) assimilation

24. We still have not given our .... to conduct the survey of natural resources in our state.
(a) consent (b) request (c) provision
(d) projection (e) compliance

25. His party is solely to be blamed for the political .... in the country.
(a) revival (b) advocacy (c) stalemate
(d) devaluation (e) degradation

Directions ***(Questions 26 to 30) : In each of the questions below four sentences are given which are denoted by (A), (B), (C), (D). By using all the four sentences you have to frame a meaningful paragraph. The correct order of the sentences is your answer. Choose from the five alternatives and mark it as your answer.***

26. (A) Across the sky flashed scenes from his life.
(B) He dreamed, he was walking along the beach with the Lord.
(C) One night a man had a dream.
(D) For each scene, he noticed two sets of footprints in the sand; one belonging to him and the other to the Lord.
(a) CABD (b) CBAD (c) CBDA
(d) CDAB (e) CDBA

27. (A) You would be very surprised indeed to find it hot.
(B) Cold, of course.
(C) And yet that was what I found when I visited North Island, the northern part of New Zealand.
(D) When you go bathing in a river or a pond, do you expect the water to be hot or cold?
(a) ACBD (b) ACDB (c) CABD
(d) DABC (e) DBAC

28. (A) Because, if the manager's subordinates are inefficient and ineffective and are not helped to increase their efficiency and effectiveness, the task may not be achieved.
(B) This must be just as true as the responsibility for achieving his prescribed tasks.
(C) If it is achieved it is at too great a cost, or at the risk of other effects many of which are less obvious.
(D) It is often said that one of the prime responsibilities of a manager is the training and development of his staff.
(a) ADBC (b) BDAC (c) CABD

(d) CDBA (e) DBAC

29. (A) Modern research, however, has proved that there were invaders even before the Aryans poured into this land.
(B) It was thought that they came to a country which was uncivilised and barbarian.
(C) They had evolved a civilisation higher than that of the Aryan hordes who came in their wake.
(D) Till recently the Aryans were regarded as the earliest invaders of the land.
(a) ABCD (b) BDAC (c) BCAD
(d) DBAC (e) DCBA

30. (A) Organisations today are becoming increasingly populated by youthful, highly skilled, highly educated workers.
(B) Two of the most prevalent and provocative organisational dynamics of our time are the themes of participation and change
(C) These demands for participation are creating pressures for internal organisational change which are matched only by external environmental pressures for organisational change.
(D) These young, skilled and educated workers bring with them demands for a voice in the determination of their own organisational destiny—a change to participate in those decisions which affect their organisational lives.
(a) ABDC (b) ABCD (c) BADC
(d) BCDA (e) DCAB

Directions (*Questions 31 to 40*) : ***Read each sentence to find out whether there is any grammatical error in it. The error, if any, will be in one part of the sentence. The letter of that part is the answer. If there is no error, the answer is (e) i.e. 'No error'.***

31. By April next year (a) / I will have been (b) / working in this office (c) / for twenty years. (d) / No error (e)

32. Saroj is not only involved (a) / in organising conferences and seminars (b) / but also in conducting (c) / adult literacy programmes (d) / No error (e)

33. I have been travelling by local trains (a) /since last several years (b) / but have never experienced (c) / such a horrible situation as this. (d) / No error (e)

34. By the time he gets back (a) /from his holidays (b) / the milkman has left (c) / twenty one bottles of milk outside his door (d) / No error (e)

35. If I would have realised (a) / what a bad shape our library is in (b) /I would have done something (c) / to arrest the deterioration. (d) / No error (e)

36. He was having a bath (a) / when the phone rang. (b) / Very unwillingly he got out of the bath (c) / and went to answer it. (d) / No error (e)

37. I found this ring (a) / as I dig in the garden. (b) /It looks very old (c) / I wonder who it belonged to. (d) / No error (e)

38. When I heard his knock (a) / I went to the door (b) / and opened it (c) / but I was not recognise him. (d) / No error (e)

39. India today stands (a) / at crucial cross roads (b) / with its history (c) / as an independent nation. (d) / No error (e)

40. Have you heard the news? (a) / Mahesh and Mala are engaged. (b) / That is not new. (c) / I know it for ages. (d) / No error (e)

Directions (*Questions 41 to 50*) : ***In the following passage, there are blanks, each of which has been numbered. These numbers are again printed below the passage and against each five words are suggested, one of which fits the blank appropriately in the context of the whole passage. Find out the appropriate word.***

It is commonly expected that as science advances, superstition should ....(41)..... Certainly, science brings a new ....(42).... spirit of inquiry into a society where none existed and provides means of ....(43).... the so-called miracles. Thus claims of ash out of nothing, idols drinking milk or petrol created from herbs and water can be ....(44).... to rigorous tests and the findings ....(45).... with the known laws of science. ....(46)...., the greatest stumbling-block in this processs is the ....(47).... human desire to find or ....(48).... something extraordinary that ....(49).... one above the humdrum of daily living which is why people are ....(50).... to accept routine scientific explanations of unexpected events.

41. (a) recede (b) revive (c) dissolve
(d) abandon (e) depreciate

42. (*a*) volcanic (*b*) burning (*c*) critical (*d*) powerful (*e*) inflammatory
43. (*a*) diluting (*b*) diffusing (*c*) directing (*d*) disturbing (*e*) debunking
44. (*a*) attached (*b*) observed (*c*) subjected (*d*) projected (*e*) visualised
45. (*a*) cleared (*b*) exhibited (*c*) criticised (*d*) explained (*e*) projected
46. (*a*) yet (*b*) despite (*c*) instead (*d*) although (*e*) nevertheless
47. (*a*) innate (*b*) sober (*c*) wanted (*d*) critical (*e*) cultivated
48. (*a*) verify (*b*) express (*c*) witness (*d*) activate (*e*) propagate
49. (*a*) sharpens (*b*) replaces (*c*) lifts (*d*) enlightens (*e*) revitalises
50. (*a*) eager (*b*) curious (*c*) unworthy (*d*) reluctant (*e*) inquisitive

ANSWERS

1. (*d*)	**2.** (*e*)	**3.** (*e*)	**4.** (*d*)	**5.** (*c*)	**6.** (*c*)	**7.** (*c*)	**8.** (*c*)	**9.** (*d*)	**10.** (*e*)
11. (*c*)	**12.** (*c*)	**13.** (*b*)	**14.** (*d*)	**15.** (*b*)	**16.** (*e*)	**17.** (*d*)	**18.** (*d*)	**19.** (*b*)	**20.** (*c*)
21. (*c*)	**22.** (*a*)	**23.** (*d*)	**24.** (*a*)	**25.** (*e*)	**26.** (*b*)	**27.** (*e*)	**28.** (*e*)	**29.** (*d*)	**30.** (*c*)

31. (*a*) : Remove 'year'
32. (*a*) : Replace 'not only involved' by 'involved not only'
33. (*b*) : 'Since' by 'for'
34. (*c*) : Replace 'has' by 'will have'.
35. (*a*) : Replace 'would have' by 'had'
36. (*c*) : Replace 'got' by 'came'
37. (*b*) : Replace 'dig' by 'dug'
38. (*d*) : Replace 'was' by 'could'
39. (*c*) : Replace 'with' by 'of'
40. (*d*) : Replace 'know' by 'have known'.

41. (*a*)	**42.** (*c*)	**43.** (*e*)	**44.** (*c*)	**45.** (*b*)	**46.** (*e*)	**47.** (*a*)	**48.** (*e*)	**49.** (*c*)	**50.** (*d*)

Income Tax And Central Excise—1996

Directions : ***In Questions (1-15), you have three brief passages with questions following each passage. Read the passage carefully and choose the best answer to each question out of the four alternatives.***

Passage I (*Questions 1 to 5*) :

The object underlying the rules of natural justice 'is to prevent miscarriage of justice' and secure 'fair play in action.' As pointed out earlier the requirement about recording of reasons for its decision by an administrative authority exercising quasi-judicial functions achieves this object by excluding chances of arbitrariness and ensuring a degree of fairness in the process of decision-making. Keeping in view the expanding horizon of the principles of natural justice, we are of the opinion that the requirement to record reason can be regarded as one of the principles of natural justice which govern exercise of power by administrative authorities. The rules of natural justice are not embodied rules. The extent of their application depends upon the particular statutory framework where uner jurisdiction has been conferred on the administrative authority. With regard to the exercise of a particular power by an administrative authority including exercise of judicial or quasi-judicial functions the legislature, while coonferring the said power, may feel that it would not be in the larger public interest that the reasons for the order passed by the administrative authority be recorded in the order and be communicated to the aggrieved party and it may dispense with such a requirement.

1. According to the passage, there is always a gap between
   (*a*) demand for natural justice and its realisation.
   (*b*) intention and execution.
   (*c*) rules of natural justice and their application.

(*d*) conception of a rule and its concretisation.

2. According to the passage, natural justice can be brought about by :
(*a*) administrative authority framing rules suitably
(*b*) administrative authority observing the rules of fair play.
(*c*) administrative authority remaining vigilant.
(*d*) administrative authority upholding rules of natural justice.

3. 'To dispense with a requirement' means
(*a*) to drop the charge.
(*b*) to cancel all formal procedure.
(*c*) to alter the provisions of the case.
(*d*) to do without the demand.

4. 'The rules of the natural justice are not embodied rules' means that these rules :
(*a*) are flexible.
(*b*) can not be visualised.
(*c*) are left deliberately vague.
(*d*) can not be satisfactorily interpreted.

5. From the passage it is clear that it is the legislature that :
(*a*) invests the administrative authority with enormous powers.
(*b*) embodies rules.
(*c*) has the larger interests of public welfare.
(*d*) leaves administrative authority enough discretion to interpret rules.

Passage II (Questions 6 to 10) :

Many Sociologists have argued that there is a functional relationship between education and economic systems. They point to the fact that mass formal education began in industrial society and is an established part of all industrial societies. They note that the expansion of the economies of industrial societies is accompanied by a corresponding expansion of their educational systems. They explain this correspondence in terms of the needs of industry for skilled and trained man-power, needs which are met by the educational system. Thus, the provision of mass elementary education in Britain in 1870 can be seen as a response to the needs of industry for a literate and numerate work-force at a time when industrial processes were becoming more complex and the demand for technical skills was steadily growing.

6. The Sociologists referred to in the passage say that the relationship between industry and elementary education was one :
(*a*) based on mutual need.
(*b*) based entirely on the need of the industry.
(*c*) based entirely on economic need.
(*d*) based on some inexplicable historical forces.

7. The author agues that :
(*a*) formal education can be traced to industrial society.
(*b*) industrial society changed the pattern of education.
(*c*) industrial society is responsible for expansion of education at the mass level.
(*d*) industrial society changed the pattern of education.

8. By 'functional relationship' is meant :
(*a*) a short term relationship.
(*b*) temporary arrangement.
(*c*) practical and utilitarian relationship.
(*d*) close and unbreakable relationship.

9. The observations of the Sociologists are based on a study of :
(*a*) growth of industry in the 19th century.
(*b*) economic system of the 19th century.
(*c*) the statistical data available in a historical context.
(*d*) the correlation between industry and education in a historical context.

10. The industry needs a literate work-force because :
(*a*) it relies heavily on expertise.
(*b*) it promotes a competitive spirit.
(*c*) its expansion needs sound learning.
(*d*) its operations need intricate technical knowledge.

Passage III (Questions 11 to 15) :

Organizations are institutions in which members compete for status and power. They compete for the resources of the organization, for example, finance to expand their own departments, for career advancement and for power to control the activities of others. In pursuit of these aims, groups are formed and sectional interests emerge. As a result, policy decisions may serve the ends of the political and career systems rather than those of the concern. In this way, the goals of the organization may be displaced in favour of sectional interests and individual ambition. These preoccupations sometimes prevent the emergence of organic systems.

Many of the electronics firms in their study had recently created research and development departments employing highly qualified and well-paid scientists and technicians. Their high pay and expert knowledge were sometimes seen as a threat to the established order of rank, power and privilege. Many senior managers had little knowledge of the technicalities and possibilities of new developments and electronics. Some felt that close co-operation with the experts in an organic system would reveal their ignorance and show that their experience was now redundant.

11. The author makes out a case for :
(*a*) research and development in organizations.
(*b*) a refresher course for senior managers.
(*c*) an understanding between senior and middle level executives.
(*d*) organic system.

12. The author tends to see the senior managers as :
(*a*) ignorant and incompetent.
(*b*) jealous of their younger colleagues.
(*c*) a little out of step with their work environment.
(*d*) robbed of their rank, power and privilege.

13. 'Organic system', as related to the organization implies its :
(*a*) natural and unimpeded growth.
(*b*) growth with inputs from science and technology.
(*c*) growth with the help of expert knowledge.
(*d*) steady all-round development.

14. Policy decisions in organization would involve :
(*a*) modernization of the organization.
(*b*) co-operation at all levels in the organization.
(*c*) attracting highly qualified personnel.
(*d*) keeping in view the larger objectives of the organization.

15. The theme of the passage is :
(*a*) groupism in organizations.
(*b*) frustration of senior managers.
(*c*) individual ambitions in organizations.
(*d*) emergence of sectional interests in organizations.

Directions (***Questions 16 to 20***) **:** ***In each of these questions, out of the four given alternatives choose the one which best expresses the meaning of the given word.***

16. APLOMB
(*a*) adventure (*b*) assurance
(*c*) a powerful bomb (*d*) fear

17. RISQUE
(*a*) slightly humorous
(*b*) slightly improper
(*c*) slightly risky
(*d*) very risky

18. ILLICIT
(*a*) not sociable
(*b*) not legal
(*c*) not legible
(*d*) not attractive

19. COMPLEMENT
(*a*) to complete
(*b*) words of praise
(*c*) a grammatical category
(*d*) a geographical category

20. OCULIST
(*a*) One who makes optical instruments.
(*b*) One who possesses occult knowledge.
(*c*) A specialist in the treatment of ENT diseases.
(*d*) A specialist in the treatment of the diseases of the eye.

Directions (***Questions 21 to 25***) **:** ***In each of these questions, a group of words is given. Find the appropriate alternative which can best substitute the given words :***

21. ready to believe :
(*a*) credible (*b*) creditable
(*c*) credulous (*d*) incredible

22. a dramatic performance :
(*a*) Mask (*b*) Masque
(*c*) Mosque (*d*) Mascot

23. study of birds :
(*a*) ornithology (*b*) optology
(*c*) orology (*d*) ophthalmology

24. a cure for all diseases :
(*a*) Panax (*b*) Palliative
(*c*) Panache (*d*) Panacea

25. A drawing on transparent paper :
(*a*) blue print (*b*) red print
(*c*) transparency (*d*) negative

Directions (***Questions 26 to 30***) **:** ***In each of these questions, the first and the last sentences of the passage are numbered 1 and 6 respectively. The rest of the passage is split into four parts named P, Q, R, S. These four parts are not given in their proper order. Find out the correct combination from among the given alternatives.***

26. (1) : When a satellite is launched, the rocket begins by going slowly upwards through the air.
(*P*) : As a result there is less friction.
(*Q*) : For the atmosphere becomes thinner.
(*R*) : As the rocket goes higher, it travels faster.
(*S*) : However, the higher it goes, the less air it needs.
(6) : Consequently, the rocket still does not become so hot.
(*a*) RSQP (*b*) RQPS
(*c*) PQRS (*d*) PRSQ

27. (1) : A man can be physically confined within stone walls.
(*P*) : But his mind and spirit will still be free.
(*Q*) : His hopes and aspirations still remain with him.
(*R*) : Thus his freedom of action may be restricted.
(*S*) : Hence, he will be free spiritually if not physically.
(6) : No tyranny can intimidate a lover of liberty.
(*a*) QPRS (*b*) PRQS
(*c*) QPSR (*d*) PQRS

28. (1) : The dictionary is the best friend for your task.
(*P*) : That may not be possible always.
(*Q*) : It is wise to look it up immediately.
(*R*) : Then it must be firmly written on the memory and traced at the first opportunity.
(*S*) : Never allow a strange word to pass unchallenged.
(6) : Soon you will realize that this is an exciting task.
(*a*) SPQR (*b*) QRPS
(*c*) PQRS (*d*) SQPR

29. (1) : I had halted on the road,
(*P*) : As soon as I saw the elephant I knew I should not shoot him.
(*Q*) : I knew that his 'must' was already passing off.
(*R*) : It is a serious matter to shoot a working elephant.
(*S*) : The elephant was standing eighty yards from the road.
(6) : I decided to watch him for a while and then go home.
(*a*) SPQR (*b*) PQSR
(*c*) PRSQ (*d*) SRPQ

30. (1) : As he passed beneath her he heard the swish of her wings.
(*P*) : But it only lasted a minute.
(*Q*) : He could here nothing.
(*R*) : He was not falling head long now.
(*S*) : Then a monstrous terror seized him.
(6) : The next moment he felt his wings spread outwards.
(*a*) QSRP (*b*) SQPR
(*c*) PSRQ (*d*) PRQS

Directions (*Questions 31 to 35*) : *In the following passage some of the words have been left out. Fill in the blanks with the help of the given alternatives.*

As a rule of thumb, a manned mission costs from fifty to hundered times more than a comparable unmanned mission. Thus, for scientific exploration alone .....(31)..... missions, employing machine intelligence, are .....(32)...... However, there may well be .....(33)..... other than scientific for exploring .....(34)..... social, economic, political, cultural or .....(35).....

31. (*a*) manned (*b*) unmanned
(*c*) lunar (*d*) space

32. (*a*) preferred (*b*) liked
(*c*) used (*d*) wanted

33. (*a*) clues (*b*) causes
(*c*) reasons (*d*) objects

34. (*a*) sun (*b*) moon
(*c*) mission (*d*) space

35. (*a*) historic (*b*) historical
(*c*) histrionic (*d*) casual

Directions (*Questions 36 to 40*) : *In these questions, some of the sentences have errors and some are correct as they are. Find out which part of a sentence has an error. If a sentence is free from error, write (d) as the answer.*

36. A free press is not a privilege (*a*) / but the organic necessity (*b*) / in a free society. (*c*) / No error (*d*)

37. Were he (*a*) / to see you, (*b*) / he would have been surprised. (*c*) / No error. (*d*)

38. The number of marks carried by each question (*a*) / are indicated (*b*) / at the end of the question. (*c*) / No error (*d*)

39. It is time (*a*) / we did something (*b*) / to stop road accidents. (*c*) / No error. (*d*)

40. An animal (*a*) / can be just as unhappy in a vast area (*b*) / or in a small one. (*c*) / No error. (*d*)

Hints :

36. but an organic necessity
37. If he were
38. is indicated
40. as in a small one.

ANSWERS

1. (*c*)	**2.** (*b*)	**3.** (*d*)	**4.** (*a*)	**5.** (*a*)	**6.** (*b*)	**7.** (*a*)	**8.** (*c*)	**9.** (*a*)	**10.** (*d*)
11. (*d*)	**12.** (*a*)	**13.** (*b*)	**14.** (*c*)	**15.** (*d*)	**16.** (*b*)	**17.** (*b*)	**18.** (*b*)	**19.** (*a*)	**20.** (*d*)
21. (*c*)	**22.** (*b*)	**23.** (*a*)	**24.** (*d*)	**25.** (*c*)	**26.** (*a*)	**27.** (*b*)	**28.** (*d*)	**29.** (*c*)	**30.** (*b*)
31. (*b*)	**32.** (*a*)	**33.** (*c*)	**34.** (*d*)	**35.** (*b*)					

36. (*b*) : Replace 'the' by 'an'

37. (*a*) : The correct form is 'If he were to ......'

38. (*b*) : Replace 'are' by 'is'

39. (*d*) : No error

40. (*c*) : Replace 'or' by 'as'

S.S.C. CLERK'S GRADE EXAMINATION, 1996

Directions (*Questions 1 to 5*) : *Below is given a passage followed by five questions. Read the passage carefully and choose the best answer to each question out of the four alternatives.*

Language, they say, is the lens through which human beings perceive the world. If so, English is perhaps the most distorting lens through which to see animals. It has perpetuated a cross-eyed view of birds, beasts, fish and fowl. The very word 'animal' connotes the brutish and the sensual. Animal instinct implies baseness and vulgarity. The language transfers negative human traits to animals, making the former appear as characteristics of the latter. Thus, the chicken is cowardly, frightened, faint hearted ; the goat lustful and foolish ; the bear rough and ill-bred. Butterflies are flighty, seals slippery and foxes notorious for craftiness and cunning. Much the worst are the reptiles particularly the snake, creeping, base, malignant, abject, ungrateful and treacherous, always the snake in the grass.

Each species carries its denigration forever embedded in its English name giving the language as many unpleasant adjectives as it could possibly want. To be bull-headed is to be impetuous and obstinate ; the cattish woman is spiteful and back-biting. An elephant's walk is ungainly, bird-brains are to be ridiculed and the herd mentality draws only contempt. You can be as blind as a bat and batty, if you are crazy as well.

1. According to the passage, English language is the lens
(*a*) through which people see the beautiful animal world
(*b*) through which people see a distorted animal world
(*c*) through which people see a correct picture of the world
(*d*) that does not permit one to see a correct picture of the world

2. According to the passage, the chicken is
(*a*) faint-hearted, the goat lustful and ill-bred and the bear crafty
(*b*) simple, the goat foolish and the bear rough
(*c*) cowardly, the goat cunning and the bear ill-bred
(*d*) cowardly, the goat lustful and foolish and the bear rough and ill-bread

3. The phrase "Always the snake in the grass' implies
(*a*) a harmless person
(*b*) the snake hiding in the grass for its victims
(*c*) a dangerous person
(*d*) a person secretly working against you

4. According to the passage, elephant's walk is
(*a*) ugly, bird brains beautiful and herd mentality good
(*b*) ungainly, bird brains ridiculous and herd mentality contemptible
(*c*) ugly, bird brains ridiculous and herd mentality good
(*d*) beautiful, bird brains ridiculous and herd mentality contemptible

5. In the English language, the animals are
(*a*) not used for any comparisons
(*b*) used for pleasant comparisons
(*c*) used for unpleasant comparisons
(*d*) used for uninteresting comparisons

Directions (*Questions 6 to 10*) : ***In each of the following questions, out of the four alternatives, choose the one which best expresses the meaning of the given word.***

6. CHARGES
(*a*) Profit (*b*) Income
(*c*) Fee (*d*) Payment

7. SHREWD
(*a*) Clever (*b*) Cunning
(*c*) Smart (*d*) Intelligent

8. MALADY
(*a*) Ill-luck (*b*) Ill-will
(*c*) Ill-feeling (*d*) Illness

9. APPLAUD
(*a*) Praise (*b*) Flatter
(*c*) Congratulate (*d*) Adore

10. FANCIFUL
(*a*) Decorative (*b*) Extensive
(*c*) Imaginative (*d*) Elaborate

Directions (*Questions 11 to 15*) : ***In each of the following questions, choose the word opposite in meaning to the given word.***

11. REDUCE
(*a*) Broaden (*b*) Extend
(*c*) Increase (*d*) Exaggerate

12. IMPROPER
(*a*) Apt (*b*) Decent
(*c*) Clean (*d*) Orderly

13. IDENTICAL
(*a*) Different (*b*) Dissimilar
(*c*) Unlikely (*d*) Unfamiliar

14. DEPLORABLE
(*a*) Creditable (*b*) Memorable
(*c*) Laudable (*d*) Joyful

15. MONOGAMY
(*a*) Bigamy (*b*) Matrimony
(*c*) Polygamy (*d*) Polyandry

Directions (*Questions 16 to 20*) : ***In each of the following questions, a word has been written in four different ways out of which only one is correctly spelt. Find the correctly spelt word and indicate it.***

16. (*a*) Privelige (*b*) Privilege
(*c*) Previlige (*d*) Privelege

17. (*a*) Delima (*b*) Dellima
(*c*) Dilemna (*d*) Dilemma

18. (*a*) Campaine (*b*) Caimpagn
(*c*) Campaign (*d*) Compaign

19. (*a*) Canibal (*b*) Canebel
(*c*) Cannebol (*d*) Cannibal

20. (*a*) Fahrenheit (*b*) Farenhite
(*c*) Farenheit (*d*) Fahrinheit

Directions (*Questions 21 to 25*) : ***In the following questions, sentences are given with blanks to be filled in with appropriate word (s). Four alternatives are suggested for each question. Choose the correct alternative.***

21. The .... of wheat is increasing because of the Green Revolution.
(*a*) significance (*b*) variety
(*c*) production (*d*) crop

22. The terrorists were arrested for their .... activities.
(*a*) subversive (*b*) subordinate
(*c*) subsidiary (*d*) subservient

23. Sunita's face spoke .... for the happiness she was feeling.
(*a*) highly (*b*) wonders
(*c*) laurels (*d*) volumes

24. He is working hard so that he .... succeed.
(*a*) shall (*b*) might
(*c*) would (*d*) will

25. Our electricity was .... for about ten hours today.
(*a*) cut up (*b*) cut off
(*c*) cut out (*d*) cut down

Directions (***Questions 26 to 30***) : ***In the following questions, sentences have been given in Active/Passive Voice. From the given alternatives, choose the one which best expresses the sentence in Passive/Active Voice.***

26. Do you know her?
(*a*) Is she known by you?
(*b*) Has she been known by you?
(*c*) Are you known to her?
(*d*) Is she known to you?

27. People believe him to be innocent.
(*a*) He is believed to be innocent.
(*b*) He is believed innocent by the people.
(*c*) Him is believed to be innocent by the people.
(*d*) Him to be inocent is believed by the people.

28. They objected to my proposal.
(*a*) My proposal was objected by them.
(*b*) My proposal objected them.
(*c*) My proposal was objected to by them.
(*d*) Their proposal was objected by me.

29. The teacher punished the boys who had not done their homework.
(*a*) The boys who had not done their homework had been punished by their teacher.
(*b*) The boys were punished by their teacher who had not done their homework.
(*c*) The boys who had not done their homework were punished by the teacher.
(*d*) The boys who had not done their homework were being punished by the teacher.

30. Have the box broken.
(*a*) Have the broken box.
(*b*) Break the box.
(*c*) Get someone to break the box.
(*d*) They have broken the box.

Directions (*Questions 31 to 35*) : ***In the following questions, some of the sentences have errors and some have none. Find out which part of a sentence has an error—(a), (b) or (c). If there is no error, mark your answer as (d).***

31. This is an excellent site (*a*) / for a stadium (*b*) / and which we should like to acquire (*c*) / No error (*d*)

32. If you absent from (*a*) / college your name is likely (*b*) / to be struck off the rolls. (*c*) / No error (*d*)

33. When I lived in England (*a*) / it was natural for me (*b*) /to speak a lot of English. (*c*) / No error (*d*)

34. Neither he is (*a*) / nor his wife is (*b*) / coming. (*c*) / No error (*d*).

35. Can you (*a*) / repair my watch (*b*) / until Tuesday? (*c*) /No error (*d*)

Directions (*Questions 36 to 40*) : ***In each of the following questions, four alternatives are given for the idiom/phrase bold italicised in the sentence. Choose the alternative which best expresses the meaning of the idiom/phrase.***

36. My boss is, in fact, ***a livewire*** ; he works for twelve hours a day.
(*a*) lively and active
(*b*) sincere and efficient
(*c*) industrious and brilliant
(*d*) sincere and intelligent

37. Although he ***ran into*** debt, he did not stop gambling
(*a*) crashed into (*b*) incurred
(*c*) ran the risk of (*d*) met with

38. He ***toyed with*** the idea of joining the Labour Party
(*a*) considered calmly
(*b*) considered seriously
(*c*) rejected
(*d*) considered though not seriously

39. So far as hazards of pollution are concerned, the traffic policemen ***bear the brunt.***
(*a*) have to run the risk
(*b*) face the consequences
(*c*) are exposed to danger
(*d*) suffer the most

40. He went ahead and shot the elephant in order not to ***lose face*** in front of the natives.
(*a*) be criticised (*b*) be disfigured
(*c*) be balmed (*d*) be humiliated

Directions (*Questions 41 to 45*) : ***In each of the following questions, out of the four alternatives choose the one which can be substituted for the given words/sentence.***

41. An imaginary name assumed by an author for disguise
(*a*) Homonym (*b*) Nickname
(*c*) Pen-name (*d*) Pseudonym

42. A place for sick people who need long periods of treatment or rest
(*a*) Asylum (*b*) Sanatorium
(*c*) Clinic (*d*) Hospital

43. Likely to break apart easily
(*a*) Harsh (*b*) Brittle
(*c*) Thin (*d*) Breakable

44. A person who eats too much
(*a*) Omnivore (*b*) Sensualist
(*c*) Glutton (*d*) Reveller

45. Belonging to the same country and having same interests and feelings
(*a*) Native (*b*) Compatriot
(*c*) Patriot (*d*) Comrade

Directions (*Questions 46 to 50*) : ***In the following passage, some of the words have been left out. First read the passage over and try to understand what it is about. Then fill in the blanks with the help of the alternatives given.***

There are many kinds of hobbies with which one could entertain oneself. Railway modelling is one of the .....(46)..... popular of all hobbies, with an appeal that

.....(47)..... to all age groups and .....(48)....., to enthusiasts of both sexes. It is easy to .....(49)..... why it is so popular, for real railways are both .....(50)..... and romantic.

46. (*a*) greatly (*b*) most (*c*) expectedly (*d*) very

47. (*a*) catches (*b*) reaches (*c*) extends (*d*) touches

48. (*a*) indeed (*b*) really (*c*) probably (*d*) as

49. (*a*) feel (*b*) see (*c*) watch (*d*) look

50. (*a*) realistic (*b*) dramatic (*c*) futuristic (*d*) pragmatic

---

ANSWERS

1. (*b*) **2.** (*d*) **3.** (*d*) **4.** (*b*) **5.** (*c*) **6.** (*c*) **7.** (*b*) **8.** (*d*) **9.** (*a*) **10.**(*d*)
11. (*c*) **12.** (*a*) **13.** (*a*) **14.** (*c*) **15.** (*c*) **16.** (*b*) **17.** (*d*) **18.** (*c*) **19.** (*d*) **20.** (*a*)
21. (*c*) **22.** (*a*) **23.** (*d*) **24.** (*b*) **25.** (*b*) **26.** (*d*) **27.** (*a*) **28.** (*c*) **29.** (*c*) **30.** (*c*)
31. (*c*) : Replace 'should' by 'would'. **32.** (*a*) : Add 'yourself' after 'absent'
33. (*d*) : No error **34.** (*a*) : Remove 'is' **35.** (*c*) : Replace 'until' by 'by'
36. (*a*) **37.** (*b*) **38.** (*d*) **39.** (*b*) **40.** (*d*) **41.** (*d*) **42.** (*b*) **43.** (*b*) **44.** (*c*) **45.** (*b*)
46. (*b*) **47.** (*c*) **48.** (*c*) **49.** (*b*) **50.** (*a*)

Railway Recruitment Board Examination, 1996

Directions (*Questions 1 to 10*) : ***Some of the following sentences contain errors. No sentence has more than one error. The portions not underlined are correct. Select the underlined part containing the error. If there is no error, the answer is*** (*e*).

1. Six kilometers (*a*) / are (*b*) / a (*c*) / long (*d*) / distance. No error (*e*)

2. Either (*a*) / Ram or Shyam forgot (*b*) / to take (*c*) / their (*d*) / pen. No error (*e*)

3. The population of Calcutta (*a*) / is greater (*b*) / than Delhi (*c*) / although (*d*) / Delhi is the capital of India. No error (*e*)

4. An (*a*) / honest man is (*b*) / the noble (*c*) / work (*d*) / of God. No error (*e*)

5. To my (*a*) / surprise, this man whom (*b*) / I thought (*c*) / was (*d*) / crazy spoke quite sensibly. No error (*e*)

6 The dealer who had (*a*) / sent three orders and (*b*) / two requests for (*c*) / window display were (*d*) / visited by our representative. No error (*e*)

7. Of all (*a*) /the other students (*b*) /in the class, the teachers were unanimous (*c*) /that Rajesh was the most (*d*) /versatile. No error. (*e*)

8. We can't hardly (*a*) / believe that the situation is so serious as (*b*) / to justify (*c*) / such precautions as you have taken. (*d*) / No error. (*e*)

9. Nobody in their senses (*a*) / would have (*b*) / uttered (*c*) / such silly remarks. (*d*) / No error. (*e*)

10. He has requested to (*a*) / the manager once agian to (*b*) / mediate in (*c*) / the dispute and help settle (*d*) / it. No error. (*e*)

Directions (*Questions 11 to 15*) : ***In each of the following questions, select the word which is most similar in meaning to the given word.***

11. CHARITY
(*a*) philanthropy (*b*) forgiveness
(*c*) sympathy (*d*) kindness

12. LETHAL
(*a*) deadly (*b*) painful
(*c*) sharp (*d*) large

13. RUDE
(*a*) rough (*b*) impolite
(*c*) insulting (*d*) protected

14. INTEGRITY
(*a*) selflessness (*b*) selfishness
(*c*) honesty (*d*) durability

15. EXTRAVAGANT
(*a*) wasteful (*b*) excessive
(*c*) bankrupt (*d*) impecunious

Directions (*Questions 16 to 20*) : ***In each of the following questions select the word which is most nearly opposite in meaning to the given word.***

16. ANALYSIS
(*a*) synthesis (*b*) substitution
(*c*) emphasis (*d*) replacement

17. GENUINE
(*a*) innocent (*b*) spurious
(*c*) real (*d*) plutonic

18. DISSENT
(*a*) ascent (*b*) accent
(*c*) agreement (*d*) convergence

19. DEFICIT
(*a*) implicit (*b*) explicit
(*c*) surplus (*d*) superfluous

20. RETREAT
(*a*) advance (*b*) recede
(*c*) entice (*d*) caputre

Directions (*Questions 21 to 25*) : ***In each of the following questions, there are four different spellings of a common word. Choose the correct one.***

21. (*a*) servent (*b*) servant
(*c*) sarvant (*d*) sarvent

22. (*a*) Comittee (*b*) Commitee
(*c*) Committee (*d*) Committey

23. (*a*) Exempsion (*b*) Exemption
(*c*) Examption (*d*) Exumption

24. (*a*) Benefited (*b*) Benefitted
(*c*) Benifitted (*d*) Benifited

25. (*a*) Amateur (*b*) Amatuer
(*c*) Ameteur (*d*) Amature

Directions (*Questions 26 to 30*) : ***In each of these questions, each statement is followed by four words of which one expresses the statement correctly. Pick out the correct choice.***

26. *A school for infants and young children :*
(*a*) infantile (*b*) infirmary
(*c*) creche (*d*) nursery

27. *An assembly of listners :*
(*a*) spectators (*b*) audience
(*c*) mob (*d*) crowd

28. *Living for years and years :*
(*a*) perennial (*b*) permanent
(*c*) annual (*d*) continuous

29. *Agreed by all :*
(*a*) anonymous (*b*) unanimous
(*c*) ambiguous (*d*) majority

30. *The study of all heavenly bodies and the earth in relation to them :*
(*a*) astrology (*b*) cosmotics
(*c*) astronomy (*d*) palmistry

Directions (*Questions 31 to 35*) : ***In each of the following sentences, choose the proper substitution words.***

31. Copying in the examination is an .... act.
(*a*) mortal (*b*) immortal
(*c*) amoral (*d*) immoral

32. A horse rider has to adjust the saddle and .... before riding.
(*a*) maines (*b*) reins
(*c*) reigns (*d*) rains

33. His bright success was .... all expectations.
(*a*) beyond (*b*) above
(*c*) exceeded (*d*) over

34. The village was .... by the earthquake.
(*a*) dazed (*b*) raised
(*c*) razed (*d*) erased

35. He ....down on the sofa yesterday.
(*a*) lay (*b*) lays
(*c*) laid (*d*) layed

Directions (*Questions 36 to 40*) : ***Choose the correct word out of the given alternatives to fill in the blanks in each sentence :***

36. The problem must be studied .... all angles.
(*a*) from (*b*) with (*c*) for (*d*) in

37. Books were lying .... the curtain.
(*a*) after (*b*) under
(*c*) beyond (*d*) behind

38. We are justified in accusing him .... theft.
(*a*) for (*b*) with (*c*) due to (*d*) of

39. She takes delight .... teasing boys.
(*a*) on (*b*) by (*c*) in (*d*) at

40. He appealed .... the High Court .... the judgement of the district court.
(*a*) for-against (*b*) to-against
(*c*) against-for (*d*) with-for

Directions (*Questions 41 to 45*) : ***Each of the following questions consists of a short written conversation between two persons, a part of which has been omitted. Choose the alternative which correctly completes the conversation.***

41. "Do you know when the doctor arrived?"
"Yes, he came after the patient ...."
(*a*) died (*b*) has died
(*c*) dies (*d*) was dying

42. "Can we start our match?"
"No, we can't unless the referee ...."
(a) gives the signal
(b) does not give the signal
(c) will not give the signal
(d) did not give the signal

43. "Two of the boys are really very hardworking." "But ...., are idlers."
(a) other boys (b) the others
(c) the other boys (d) others

44. "I have a large family to provide for."
"Then you ...."
(a) must have been very economical in your habits
(b) must certainly be very extravagant in your habits
(c) might be very economical in your habits
(d) must certainly be very economical in your habits

45. "Ashok said that you have seen the movie three times."
"Yes, I found it very ...."
(a) amusing (b) amusement
(c) amuseful (d) amusingly

Directions (*Questions 46 to 50*) : ***Each of the idioms or phrases is followed by four meanings out of which only one is correct. Pick out the correct meaning.***

46. **To keep oneself to oneself :**
(a) To keep oneself alive
(b) To restrain oneself
(c) To hide things from others
(d) To live apart without company

47. **To bear the brunt of :**
(a) To offer to carry the heaviest weight
(b) To endure the main force of
(c) To share the lightest of responsibilities
(d) To give birth to some unsavoury matter

48. **To make hay while the sun shines :**
(a) To indulge in merry-making in good days
(b) To treat as of great importance
(c) To turn opportunity to the best advantage
(d) To turn a disappointment to the best possible count

49. **To turn over a new leaf :**
(a) To change completely one's course of action
(b) To shift attention to new problems
(c) To cover up one's faults
(d) To change the old habits and adopt new ones

50. **To carry one's point :**
(a) To explain one's opinion to others
(b) To exercise authority with crushing force
(c) To have one's aim always in mind
(d) To attain the goal aimed at

ANSWERS

1. (b) : Replace 'are' by 'is'
2. (d) : Replace 'their' by 'his'
3. (c) : The correct is 'than that of Delhi'
4. (e) : No error
5. (b) : Replace 'whom' by 'who'
6. (d) : Replace 'were' by 'was'
7. (b) : Remove 'other'
8. (a) : Replace 'can't' by 'can'
9. (a) : Replace 'their' by 'his'
10. (a) : Remove 'to'

11. (d)	12. (a)	13. (b)	14. (c)	15. (a)	16. (a)	17. (b)	18. (c)	19. (c)	20. (a)
21. (b)	22. (c)	23. (b)	24. (b)	25. (a)	26. (d)	27. (b)	28. (a)	29. (b)	30. (c)
31. (d)	32. (b)	33. (a)	34. (c)	35. (a)	36. (a)	37. (d)	38. (d)	39. (c)	40. (b)
41. (a)	42. (a)	43. (b)	44. (d)	45. (a)	46. (d)	47. (b)	48. (c)	49. (a)	50. (a)

R.B.I. EXAMINATION, 1996

Directions (*Questions 1 to 10*) : ***Which of the phrases (a), (b), (c) and (d) given below each sentence should replace the phrase printed in bold type to make the sentence grammatically correct ? If the sentence is correct as it is, mark (e) as the answer.***

1. The performance of our players was rather **worst than I had expected.**
(*a*) bad as I had expected
(*b*) worse than expectation
(*c*) worst than was expected
(*d*) worse than I had expected
(*e*) No correction required

2. It is always better to make people realise the importance of discipline than **to impose them on it.**
(*a*) impose it on them
(*b*) impose it with them
(*c*) impose them with it
(*d*) imposing them on it
(*e*) No correction required

3. He is too impatient **for tolerating** any delay
(*a*) at tolerating (*b*) with tolerating
(*c*) to tolerate (*d*) to toleratíng

4. For some days the new professor lectured **above the heads** of his pupils.
(*a*) on the heads of
(*b*) over the heads of
(*c*) through the heads of
(*d*) over the head of
(*e*) No correction required

5. The people generally try to **curry favour** with the corrupt but influential person.
(*a*) seek favour (*b*) display favour
(*c*) cook favour (*d*) extract favour
(*e*) No correction required

6. The crops are dying, it **must not had** rained.
(*a*) must not be
(*b*) must not have
(*c*) must not have been
(*d*) must had not
(*e*) No correction required

7. My hair **stood off ends** when I saw the horrible sight.
(*a*) stood at ends (*b*) stood to ends
(*c*) stood on ends (*d*) stands on ends
(*e*) No correction required

8. They **were all shocked at** his failure in the competition.
(*a*) were shocked at all
(*b*) had all shocked at
(*c*) had all shocked by
(*d*) had been all shocked on
(*e*) No correction required

9. Later he bacame unpopular because he tried to **lord it on** his followers.
(*a*) to lord it over (*b*) to lord it at
(*c*) to lord it for (*d*) to lord over
(*e*) No correction required.

10. **The long or short of it** is that I do not want to deal with that new firm.
(*a*) The long or short for it
(*b*) The long and short for it
(*c*) the long and short of it
(*d*) The short or long of it
(*e*) No correction required

Directions (*Questions 11 to 15*) : ***Read each sentence to find out whether there is any grammatical or idiomatic error in it. The error, if any, will be in one part of the sentence. Find which part of the sentence contains error. If there is no error, the answer is (e).***

11. Do not trouble (*a*) / yourself about writing to me (*b*) / unless you are quite (*c*) / in the humour for it. (*d*) / No error. (*e*)

12. He has a scheme (*a*) / of his own which he thinks (*b*) / more preferable to (*c*) / that of any other person. (*d*) / No error. (*e*)

13. The photograph will give (*a*) / the reader a far better (*b*) / notion of the structure (*c*) / than any verbal description. (*d*) / No error. (*e*)

14. Scarcely had (*a*) / he gone (*b*) / when a policeman (*c*) / knocked at the door. (*d*) / No error. (*e*)

15. The results of the recognition (*a*) / of this fact are seen (*b*) / in the gradual improvement (*c*) / of the diet of the poor. (*d*) / No error. (*e*)

Directions (*Questions 16 to 20*) : ***In each of the following sentences find out which one of the given pairs of words can be filled up in the blanks to make it meaningfully complete.***

16. Shyness is .... through abnormal behaviour in various ....
(*a*) shown, kinds
(*b*) developed, things
(*c*) removed, people
(*d*) manifested, ways
(*e*) enhanced, aspects

17. ...., there is a widespread .... among the educated youth which makes them increasingly alienated.
(*a*) Luckily, dedication
(*b*) Unfortunately, frustration
(*c*) Nevertheless, optimism
(*d*) Obviously, enthusiasm
(*e*) Co-incidentally, feeling

18. Right from the earliest ages, India's .... developed a sense of unity and .... among its people.
(*a*) culture, commonness
(*b*) population, diversification
(*c*) heritage, disparity
(*d*) rulers, commitment
(*e*) people, diversity

19. In many countries .... development arising out of fast technological .... has led to some problems.
(*a*) cultural, practices
(*b*) agricultural, development
(*c*) meagre, inventions
(*d*) excessive, progress
(*e*) optimum, intervention

20. The problem of .... another war has assumed great urgency because of the .... of nuclear weapons
(*a*) winning, growth
(*b*) preventing, invention
(*c*) stopping, need
(*d*) fighting, destruction
(*e*) precipitating, disarmament

Directions (*Questions 21 to 29*) : *Read the following passage carefully and answer the questions given below it.*

The Indian economy rests on agricultural base and for decades and generations the picture that India presented to the world was one of the famine and of an unchanging peasantry reluctant to depart from the cultural practices handed down to them by their forefathers. Indian agriculture, it was said, was a gamble on the rains. Some visionaries, and civil servants had sought to change all this. Their experiments at rural transformation were watched with amused interest and if their efforts, did not meet with more than temporary and isolated success, it was because they were operating individuals and in very limited areas within what was basically an inhospitable and unresponsive administrative environment. The scale of effort was enlarged during the Second World War with the launching of the 'grow more food compaign'. But, the administrative structure remained largely unaltered.

It was to change all this, that the Community Development Programme was introduced. There were three problems that had to be tackled. First, if the farmer was to change methods, he had to be educated to see the possibility to change through actual demonstration in his field at no cost to himself. If the farmer tilled the land in the same manner as his father before him, it was because tradition had not optimised risks and the farmer had no margin on the basis of which to gamble on strange new practices and risk no merely a financial loss but his very survival. Second, there was no one agency to whom the farmer could turn for assistance or advice. If he wanted better seeds, he had to go to the Agriculture Department. For irrigation he had to knock at the doors of the Irrigation Department. Roads were the responsibility of the Public Works Department. Land problems had to be taken up with the revenue authorities and so on. In short, the administration was totally fragmented at the point which touched the life of the farmer. Co-ordination was difficult and the totality of the farmer's problem could never be adequately comprehended, let alone ameliorated, by the administration. Third, even if the administration sought to promote rural transformation, and the farmers were willing, how was the new knowledge to be transmitted not merely to every village but to each cultivator ?

The Community Development Programme sought to provide answers to these three problems. Something in the nature of the single-line administration was established under a chain of command running through the District Development officer and Block Development officer to the multipurpose village-level worker. Instead of having to go to several departments to get anything done, the farmer could now deal with a single community development authority with which all the executive agencies involved in rural development were associated. The many thousands of field demonstrations laid out under the Community Development Programme demonstrated the possibility of change in a manner that carried conviction and at no risk to the peasant. Once the farmer was persuaded, his alleged age-old conservatism vanished and the next problem was to satisfy his evergrowing demands. Meanwhile, the establishment of a National Extension Service first time created a permanent transmission system for the propogation and demonstration of new ideas and methods, not just in isolated pockets, but over very wide areas.

21. For the people in the world, the image of Indian village is that of :
(*a*) an opponent of traditionalism and conservatism
(*b*) a rule-bound, conservative and culture-groomed person
(*c*) an inhospitable and unresponsive person
(*d*) a visionary and a perfect gambler
(*e*) None of these

22. Which of the following was the objective of launching Community Development Programme ?
(*a*) To minimise farmer's financial losses and risks.
(*b*) To eradicate illiteracy of the rural folk.
(*c*) To solve the diverse problems of farmers on a single platform.
(*d*) To switch over to mechanisation in agro-sector.
(*e*) None of these

23. The success of the efforts put in for rural transformation was limited because :
(*a*) these efforts were not whole-hearted
(*b*) their experiments were watched with amusement
(*c*) their focus was on temporary achievements
(*d*) of their limited field of operation in an advanced environment
(*e*) None of these

24. The experiments undertaken by some visionaries were aimed at :
(*a*) temporary and isolated success
(*b*) upliftment of peasants and rural development
(*c*) evolution of new operational strategies
(*d*) changes in administrative environment
(*e*) None of these

25. What was the probable disadvantage of the fragmented administration to the farmers ?
(*a*) Uncertainty of rains during the crop season
(*b*) Loss of time, money and energy
(*c*) Availability of manures, fertilisers and seeds
(*d*) Exposure to novel techniques and strategies
(*e*) None of these

26. The apparent plus-point of the Community Development Programme demonstrations was that :
(*a*) they were free from any cost or risk to the farmers
(*b*) they were conducted by single community development authority
(*c*) they were conducted by multipurpose workers
(*d*) they were not against the farmers' traditional practices.
(*e*) the changes as demonstrated were all familiar to the farmers.

27. What was the impact of these demonstrations on the farmers ?
(*a*) Their standard of living remained unaltered.
(*b*) Their tendency to cling to past traditions vanished.
(*c*) Their unreasonable demands increased disproportionately.
(*d*) National Extension Service was established by them.
(*e*) None of these

28. If the administration and also the farmers were willing to promote rural transformation, which was the main hindering factor in their way ?
(*a*) Lack of co-ordination among diferent agencies
(*b*) Lack of availability of facilities for cultivation
(*c*) Want of irrigation facilities
(*d*) Comprehension of the farmers' problems
(*e*) None of these

29. Which of the following was/were the advantage (s) of the Community Development Programmes ?
(A) Diverse problems of the farmers could be solved by a single authority.
(B) There was no danger of deviating from the past practices.
(C) These programmes didn't involve any risk to farmers.
(*a*) All the three (*b*) Only A and B
(*c*) Only A and C (*d*) Only B and C
(*e*) None of these

Directions (*Questions 30 to 34*) : *Pick out the most effective word from the given words to fill in the blank to make the sentence meaningfully complete.*

30. The earth is at present in great danger of becoming uninhabitable because of .... environmental pollution which is going on at an incredibly rapid pace.
(*a*) splendid (*b*) gigantic
(*c*) colossal (*d*) inhuman
(*e*) stupendous

31. The main purpose of having a .... of ration depots throughout the country is to arrange a regular supply of essential items to the common man at fixed reasonable rates.
(*a*) network (*b*) choice
(*c*) variety (*d*) necessity
(*e*) multitude

32. Now, the management graduate can expect to have a prosperous life on a .... income without having to tend the paternal estates.
(*a*) regular (*b*) substantial
(*c*) dependable (*d*) meaningful
(*e*) professional

33. If the rate of inflation in India remains substantially higher than those of her trading partners, it will be impossible to check the .... in the country's balance of payments.
(*a*) failure (*b*) capacity
(*c*) inability (*d*) degradation
(*e*) deterioration

34. Nothing probably has more contributed to .... the poverty and backwardness of India than the want of good roads.
(*a*) accelerate (*b*) alleviate
(*c*) accentuate (*d*) perpetuate
(*e*) circumvent

Directions (*Questions 35 to 44*) : *In the following passage, there are blanks each of which has been numbered. These numbers are printed below the passage and against each, five words are suggested, one of which fits the blank appropriately. Find out the appropriate word.*

Studies of cognitive development have shown that the child's .....(35)..... to use generalised .....(36)..... develops more slowly in history than in any other school subjects. This .....(37)..... development of reasoning is historical .....(38)..... makes it necessary for the historian to .....(39)..... upon events that may be included in the text. In many cases, the historian may need to .....(40)..... with special effort a generalised understanding of key concepts to be used in a .....(41)..... This .....(42)..... may well mean that school history cannot cover as many events as it does at present. Also, school histories may have to provide for topic work or theme-based .....(43)..... rather than merely observe .....(44)..... conformity.

35. (*a*) ability (*b*) power
(*c*) alertness (*d*) intellect
(*e*) preparedness

36 (*a*) theories (*b*) tasks
(*c*) concepts (*d*) principles
(*e*) procedures

37. (*a*) rapid (*b*) slower
(*c*) typical (*d*) matured
(*e*) accelerated

38. (*a*) arena (*b*) contexts
(*c*) conformity (*d*) chronology
(*e*) perspective

39. (*a*) focus (*b*) plan
(*c*) dwell (*d*) build
(*e*) deliver

40. (*a*) trade (*b*) tackle
(*c*) deliver (*d*) grapple
(*e*) provide

41. (*a*) forum (*b*) text
(*c*) debate (*d*) reference
(*e*) discussion

42. (*a*) fact (*b*) rationale
(*c*) necessity (*d*) requirement
(*e*) understanding

43. (*a*) projects (*b*) work-outs
(*c*) description (*d*) analysis
(*e*) presentation

44. (*a*) eternal (*b*) internal
(*c*) chronological (*d*) metaphorical
(*e*) time bound

Directions (*Questions 45 to 50*) : *Rearrange the given five sentences (A), (B), (C), (D) and (E) in the proper sequence to form a meaningful paragraph ; then answer the questions that follow :*

Questions 45 to 47

(A) The history of mankind is full of such fightings between communities, nation and people.
(B) From the primitive weapons of warfare, man has advanced to the modern nuclear weapons.
(C) Ever since the dawn of civilisation, man has been fighting with man.
(D) A modern war is scientific in character, but the effect is the

same, wiping human existence out of the earth.

(E) The only difference now seems to be in the efficiency of the instruments used for killing each other.

45. Which of the following should be the first sentence ?

(*a*) A (*b*) B (*c*) C (*d*) D (*e*) E

46. Which of the following should be the third sentence ?

(*a*) A (*b*) B (*c*) C (*d*) D (*e*) E

47. Which of the following should be the last sentence ?

(*a*) A (*b*) B (*c*) C (*d*) D (*e*) E

Questions 48 to 50

(A) In fact, it prevents us from helping children to analyse conflict, to learn to cope with it and counter it.

(B) Children have always known that there is conflict in the adult world.

(C) However, the make-believe world that nineteenth century rationally imposed on childhood in Europe and which we impose in an institutionalisd manner through our modern education system can hardly be described as related in this regard.

(D) We may therefore conclude that conflict in an istitutionalised manner is not a matter of faith in children's capacities, rather, it is lack of faith in ourselves as adults.

(E) Further, psychologists tell us and story tellers have always known that the child's desire to search for order and coherence gathers strength from the knowledge of conflict.

48. Which of the following should be the second sentence ?

(*a*) A (*b*) B (*c*) C (*d*) D (*e*) E

49. Which of the following should be the fourth sentence ?

(*a*) A (*b*) B (*c*) C (*d*) D (*e*) E

50. Which of the following should be the last sentence ?

(*a*) A (*b*) B (*c*) C (*d*) D (*e*) E

ANSWERS

1. (*d*) **2.** (*a*) **3.** (*c*) **4.** (*b*) **5.** (*e*) **6.** (*b*) **7.** (*c*) **8.** (*e*) **9.** (*a*) **10.** (*c*)

11. (*d*) : Replace 'humour' by 'mood'

12. (*c*) : Remove 'more'

13. (*c*) : Replace 'notion' by 'impression'

14. (*e*) : No error

15. (*d*) : The correct form is 'in the diet of the poor'

16. (*c*) **17.** (*b*) **18.** (*a*) **19.** (*d*) **20.** (*b*) **21.** (*a*) **22.** (*c*) **23.** (*e*) **24.** (*c*) **25.** (*b*)

26. (*a*) **27.** (*b*) **28.** (*e*) **29.** (*b*) **30.** (*c*) **31.** (*a*) **32.** (*a*) **33.** (*e*) **34.** (*a*) **35.** (*a*)

36. (*c*) **37.** (*b*) **38.** (*b*) **39.** (*a*) **40.** (*e*) **41.** (*b*) **42.** (*c*) **43.** (*d*) **44.** (*c*)

45. (*c*) : The correct sequence is CABDE.

46. (*b*) **47.** (*e*)

48. (*e*) : The correct sequence is BEACD.

49. (*c*) **50.** (*d*)

C.D.S. EXAMINATION, 1996

USAGE

Spotting Errors

Directions ***(Questions 1 to 15) : In this section, a number of sentences are given. The sentences are divided into three parts labelled as (a), (b) and (c). Read each sentence to find out whether there is an error in any part. No sentence has more than one error. When you find an error in any one of the parts (a, b or c) indicate your response. You may feel that there is no error in a sentence. In that case letter 'd' will signify a 'No error' response.***

1. This picture (*a*) / is the best (b) / of the two (c) / No error (d)

2. The drawing room was a mess (*a*) / with all the furnitures (b) / scattered in total disarray (c) / No error (d)

3. No sooner did (*a*) / the doctor enter the house (b) / then the patient died. (c) / No error (d)

4. As I prefer coffee than tea (*a*) / my friends always take the trouble (b) / to get me a cup of coffee, whenever I visit them. (c) No error (d)

5. I did ask him (*a*) / where you were (b) / but he didn't tell me (c) / No error (d)

6. Those who are excessively careful (*a*) / for their health (b) / are not generally healthy. (c) No error (d)

7. There has been (*a*) / little change in the patient's condition (b) / since he was moved to a special ward in the hospital. (c) / No error (d)

8. Once we have agreed on (*a*) / the fundamentals, there will hardly be (b) / anything left to discuss about. (c) / No error (d)

9. They cook meals, (*a*) / lay the table and wash up, (b) / clean the house and mend the clothes. (c) / No error (d)

10. I will wait for you (a) / at the office (b) / till you will finish your work. (c) / No error (d)

11. The gap between what he preaches (a) / and what he practises is too wide (b) / to accept by any sensible person. (c) / No error (d)

12. The king was embarrassed (a) / to find evidences (b) / against his own queen. (c) / No error (d)

13. While flying over India (a) / we had glimpses of the two sources of her culture (b) / Ganges and Himalayas. (c) No error (d)

14. They begged him (a) / not to go (b) / yet he was determined. (c) / No error (d)

15. I don't remember having met him before, (a) / although the voice sounds (b) / rather familiar to me. (c) / No error (d)

Sentence Improvement

Directions ***(Questions 16 to 30) : Look at the italicised part of each sentence. Below each sentence are given three possible substitutions for the italicised part. If one of them (a), (b) or (c) is better than the italicised part, indicate your response against the corresponding letter. If none of the substitutions improves the sentence, indicate (d) as your response***

16. The train was late *for* fifty minutes.

(*a*) around (*b*) by
(c) behind (d) No improvement

17. My father *is suffering* from diabetes for the past three years.

(*a*) has suffered (b) was suffering
(b) has been suffering
(d) No improvement

18. If neither of them *are to be trusted*, it is not at all advisable to invest further.

(a) is to be trusted (b) has to be trusted
(c) have to be trusted
(d) No improvement

19. These days it is difficult *to make both ends meet.*

(a) to make the ends meet
(b) to make two ends meet
(c) to make all ends meet
(d) No improvement

20. She was more beautiful than *either of her three sisters.*

(a) all of her three sisters

(b) each of her three sisters
(c) any of her three sisters
(d) No improvement

21. Let's have a party *some time the next week.*
(a) some time next week
(b) sometimes next week
(c) some time in the next week
(d) No improvement

22. If I *shall pass* this examination, my mother will be very happy.
(a) would pass (b) pass
(c) will pass (d) No improvement

23. Don't touch the door as it *has just been painted*
(a) is just painted
(b) just has been painted
(c) have just been painted
(d) No improvement

24. *Call in* this evening, if you can, I have something important to discuss.
(a) Call for (b) Call on
(c) Call off (d) No improvement

25. However great you may be, you cannot *trifle on* a man's feelings.
(a) trifle with (b) trifle upon
(c) trifle in (d) No improvement

26. I have been telling her that she had better *consult* a good doctor.
(a) consulting (b) been consulting
(c) consulted (d) No improvement

27. Before I could stop him, the boy *was throwing* the box down the stairs.
(a) threw (b) had thrown
(c) did throw (d) No improvement

28. He would have lent me a pen, if he *was knowing* that I didn't have one.
(a) had known (b) had been knowing
(c) would know (d) No improvement

29. The District Collector *gave up* the prizes to the winners at the end of the function.
(a) gave back (b) gave out
(c) gave away (d) No improvement

30. One day you will repent *over* what you have done.
(a) about (b) for
(c) of (d) No improvement

SELECTING WORDS

Simple Sentences

Directions *(Questions 31 to 40) : Each of the following sentences has a blank space and four words given after the sentence. Select whichever word you consider most appropriate for the blank space.*

31. It's very kind of you to .... to speak at the meeting.
(a) comply (b) accept
(c) agree (d) concur

32. An employment advertisement should .... the number of vacancies.
(a) declare (b) specify
(c) contain (d) provide

33. .... of old paintings is a job for the experts.
(a) Restoration (b) Resurrection
(c) Resumption (d) Retrieval

34. The passengers were afraid but the captain .... them that there was no danger.
(a) counselled (b) advised
(c) assured (d) promised

35. The family gave father a gold watch on the .... of fiftieth birthday.
(a) occasion (b) event
(c) celebration (d) time

36. Once he has signed the agreement, he won't be able to ....
(a) back out (b) back at
(c) back in (d) back up

37. She .... a brief appearance at the end of the party.
(a) put in (b) put up
(c) put on (d) put across

38. The battalion operating from the mountain was able to .... three enemy divisions.
(a) tie with (b) tie on
(c) tie down (d) tie up

39. I haven't seen you .... a week.
(a) since (b) for
(c) within (d) from

40. Do you know .... ?
(a) where from she comes

(b) where she comes from
(c) from where does she come
(d) where does she come from

Passage

Directions (*Questions 41 to 55*) : *In the following passage, at certain points, you are given a choice of three words marked (a), (b) and (c). Choose the best word from these three choices.*

Parents spend too much time worrying about their adolescents wasting time. But for an adolescent, many activities, parents consider wasteful are, in fact worthwhile. Parents complain that teenagers spend too much time day dreaming. Yet **41.** [(a) fantasy (b) dream (c) imagination] has important functions in teenagers' development. **42.** [(a) From (b) In (c) By] daydreams, all adolescents try out various **43.** [(a) roles (b) rolls (c) rules] as they search for the direction **44.** [(a) they (b) parents (c) teenagers] want to take in their lives. Many daydreams are ways of **45.** [(a) temporary (b) temporarily (c) temperamentally] escaping the stresses of everyday life. **46.** [(a) For (b) And (c) But] even they have some immediate tension-reducing **47.** [(a) purpose (b) value (c) development]. Some parents also claim about the **48.** [(a) rambling (b) rampant (c) random] conversations the teenagers have with one **49.** [(a) each (b) other (c) another] over the telephone. In fact, these **50.** [(a) apparent (b) apparently (c) really] pointless conversations are often a means **51.** [(a) through (b) under (c) with] which adolescents check out their own **52.** [(a) presumptions (b) conceptions (c) perceptions] of the world with others, gaining **53.** [(a) an idealistic (b) a realistic (c) a religious] view of themselves and others. For parents, the issue is the **54.** [(a) recognition (b) requisition (c) appreciation] of the fact that any kind of significant achievement **55.** [(a) requires (b) reserves (c) resists] hard work which the adolescents do not fully appreciate.

COMPREHENSION

Directions (*Questions 56 to 85*) : *In this section, you have six short passages. After each passage, you will find five items based on the passage. First, read passage I and attempt the items based on it. Then go on to the next passage.*

Passage I

Though it may be inessential to the imagination, travelling is necessary to an understanding of men. Only with long experience and the opening of his wares on many a beach where his language is not spoken, will the merchant come to know the worth of what he carries, and what is parochial and what is universal in his choice. Such delicate goods as justice, love and honour, courtesy, and indeed all the things we care for, are valid everywhere but they are variously moulded and often differently handled, and sometimes nearly unrecognisable if you meet them in a foreign land, and the art of learning fundamental common values is perhaps the greatest gain of travelling to those who wish to leave at ease among their fellows.

56. According to the passage, travelling leads to
(a) exploiting foreign lands
(b) selling our wares to the others
(c) understanding human nature
(d) establishing our superiority over foreigners

57. When we meet other people while we travel, we learn to differentiate between
(a) friends and foes
(b) communities and nationalities
(c) local and universal values
(d) imagination and understanding

58. The author terms justice, love, honour and courtesy as delicate goods because they are
(a) important (b) desirable
(c) fragile (d) perishable

59. Travelling helps those who
(a) want to learn foreign languages
(b) wish to make money
(c) want to resolve differences amongst people

(d) wish to learn fundamental common values

60. The things we care for are available in foreign lands in

(a) plenty (b) unrecognisable forms

(c) some form or the other

(d) easily recognisable forms

Passage II

Soft-bodied animals like caterpillars often fall a prey to voracious hunters like birds or reptiles. Despite having no means to 'actively' defend themselves, with weapons like claws or jaws, they have nevertheless, evolved other equally effective deterrents. A particular species of the caterpillar lives at an altitude of over 2,500 metres in the Himalayas. It uses prominent colours to inform would-be predators of its inedibility. In the event that an inexperienced or adventurous bird did eat the caterpillar, it would probably vomit it out soon after, and subsequently desist from attacking similar species in the future. Though this would do the unfortunate victim no good, the species benefits. A rare example of the martyr among animals.

61. Caterpillars cannot defend themselves because they

(a) are lazy

(b) have no claws or jaws

(c) are passive animals

(d) cannot acquire weapons

62. The expression "other equally effective deterrants" means

(a) deterrents that are as powerful as those the caterpillars have

(b) preventive weapons which have equal effect of others

(c) preventive equipment which is as effective as something that has been already mentioned in the passage

(d) mechanism which scares everyone equally well

63. The Himalayan caterpillar uses prominent colours to

(a) defend itself (b) warn the predator

(c) reveal itself (d) attack the predator

64. Experienced birds do not attack the Himalayan caterpillars because they are

(a) diseased (b) inedible

(c) repulsive (d) very aggressive

65. In the context of this passage, a martyr is one who dies

(a) to save others

(b) while defending one's homeland

(c) without any gain to oneself

(d) without putting up resistance

Passage III

I do not suggest that the cultural side of education should be ignored. On the contrary, I think, it is essential to the production of the sort of adult who best fits the modern world. But I think that what is important in cultural education should be conveyed, at any rate in the early stages, by methods far more attractive than those now usual. History and Geography should be taught at first by means of the cinema. When taught this way, they will give pleasure; attention will be spontaneous and therefore the impression will be less temporary. Inspite of reforming movements, there is still among educators a feeling that what is enjoyed without effort cannot have much educational value. I would have children made aware of the manners and customs of tribes and nations utterly remote from their own. Education conducted on these lines would do more than many books to cure provincialism in space and time and to make children realise that actual human beings with actual feelings can be outwardly very different from the people among whom they live, but inwardly composed of the same human material. A Zulu would not appear strange, remote or savage but one like themselves.

66. The writer said that the cultural side of education is needed to make man

(a) admire his environment

(b) suitable for modern civilisation

(c) appreciate other civilisations

(d) appreciate one's heritage

67. The writer criticised traditional educators for not

(a) imparting information about various cultures
(b) imparting information about remote tribes
(c) making learning an enjoyable activity
(d) using cinema as a method of teahing

68. The response of the learners to teaching through cinema is
(a) superficial (b) enthusiastic
(c) long-lasting (d) absorbing

69. The expression "to cure provincialism in space and time" means to get rid of
(a) selfish opinion (b) narrow views
(c) obscure ideas (d) regional feelings

70. One of the goals of education should be to make children realise that
(a) there is a unified system of human values underneath cultural diversity
(b) they must respect values of alien culture
(c) regional cultures should not be ignored
(d) human culture is diverse

Passage IV

"The history of science is the real history of mankind." In this striking epigram a nineteenth century writer links science with its background. Like most epigrams, its power lies in emphasising by contrast an aspect of truth which may be easily overlooked. In this case it is easy to overlook the relations between science and mankind and to treat the former as some abstract third party, which can sometimes be praised for its beneficial influences, but frequently and conveniently blamed for the horrors of war. Science and mankind cannot be divorced from time to time at men's convenience. Yet we have seen that, inspite of countless opportunities of improvement, the opening years of the present period of civilisation have been dominated by international conflict.

Is this the inevitable result of the progress of science or does the fault lie elsewhere?

71. The science "The history of science is the real history of mankind" means
(a) science has given man countless opportunities for improvement
(b) science and mankind cannot always be divorced
(c) mankind has progressed as science has developed
(d) the good and bad uses of science reflect the character of man

72. The epigram given in the passage highlights
(a) the evolution of science
(b) the real history of man
(c) the contrast between science and civilisation
(d) an elusive truth about human nature

73. The aspect of truth likely to be overlooked is that science
(a) has made war horrible
(b) is beneficial to man
(c) is what man has made it
(d) has created international conflicts

74. The writer implies that international conflict is the result of
(a) faulty relations between nations
(b) human weaknesses
(c) invention of deadly weapons
(d) progress of science

75. The last sentence suggests that
(a) civilisation could prosper well without scientific inventions
(b) the trouble lies with human beings themselves
(c) people have missed opportunities to improve their lot
(d) the horrors of modern life are the inevitable result of the progress of science.

Passage V

There is more than a modicum of truth in the assertion that "a working knowledge of ancient history is necessary to the intelligent interpretation of current events". But the sage who uttered these words of wisdom might well have added something on the benefits of studying, particularly, the famous battles of history for the lessons they contain for those of us who lead or aspire to leadership. Such a study will reveal certain qualities and attributes which enabled the winners to win—and certain deficiencies which caused the losers to lose. And the student will see that the same pattern recures consistently, again and again, throughout the centuries.

76. The expression "more than a modicum of truth" means
(a) nothing but truth
(b) some truth
(c) much truth
(d) more than a small amount of truth

77. In this context, "intelligent interpretation of current events" means
(a) skilful interpretation of events
(b) intellectual outlook on events
(c) appropriate understanding of events
(d) rational explanation of events

78. According to the writer, a study of the famous battles of history would
(a) provide food to modern leaders for reflection
(b) be beneficial to wise men
(c) help us understand the art of human warfare
(d) be more useful than a general knowledge of ancient history

79. A person who aspires to lead could learn from the history of battles
(a) the qualities and deficiencies of commanders of these battles.
(b) what led the previous leaders win a battle
(c) what made them lose a battle
(d) the strategies they have evolved in course of these battles

80. A knowledge of history is necessary to interpret current problems because
(a) they may be repetitions of past events
(b) only then they can be put in a proper context
(c) they have roots in the past
(d) they can be contrasted with the past events

Passage VI

No one knows when or by whom rockets were invented. In all probability the rocket was not suddenly 'invented' but evolved gradually over a long period of time, perhaps in different parts of the world at the same time. Some historians of rocketry, notably willy Ley, trace the development of rockets to 13th century China, a land noted in ancient times for its fire work display. In the year 1232 A.D., when the Mongols laid siege to the city of Kai—Feng Fu, the capital of Honan province, the Chinese defenders used weapons that were described as "arrows of flying fire". There is no explicit statement that these arrows were rockets, but some students have concluded that they were because the record does not mentioned bows or other means of shooting the arrows. In the same battle, we read, the defenders dropped from the walls of the city a kind of bomb described as "heaven—shaking thunder". From these meagre references some students have concluded that the Chinese, by the year 1232, had discovered gunpowder and had learned to use it to make explosive bombs as well as propulsive charges for rockets.

81. The passage gives primarily a history of
(a) the bravery of the Chinese
(b) the invention of rockets
(c) the attack on China by the Mongols
(d) the battle against the Chinese wall

82. According to this passage, rockets were invented by
(a) Willy Ley
(b) unknown people
(c) the Mongols
(d) the ruler of Honan Province

83. According to this passage, rockets were
(a) a gift of God to the Chinese
(b) invented in the twentieth century
(c) invented in 1232 A.D.
(d) developed over many centuries

84. The phrase "arrows of flying fire"
(a) means some ancient phenomenon in the skies
(b) refers to lightning and thunder
(c) is another name for rockets
(d) is assumed to refer to rockets

85. The bombs have been referred to as "heaven shaking thunder" becuase they
(a) contain gunpowder
(b) make thunderous noise
(c) are propelled by rockets
(d) seem to fall from heaven

VOCABULARY

Synonyms

Directions ***(Questions 86 to 95)*** : ***In this section, you find a number of sentences, part of which is bold italicised. For each italicised part, four words / phrases are listed below. Choose the word nearest in meaning to the italicised part.***

86. There is ***abundant*** supply of water for the crops.
(a) sufficient (b) adequate
(c) plentiful (d) considerable

87. The ***perpetual*** noise made it impossible for them to concentrate on the problems.
(a) recurrent (b) unlimited
(c) constant (d) irritating

88. I wonder if his ***intervention*** in the dispute will be of any help.
(a) meddling (b) mediation
(c) interruption (d) interception

89. Inspite of his best efforts the officer could not ***redeem*** his prestige.
(a) fulfil (b) extend
(c) raise (d) recover

90. He spoke ***impromptu*** on the occasion.
(a) with great force (b) eloquently
(c) without preparation
(d) without enthusiasm

91. He treats with ***disdain*** anyone who goes to him for help.
(a) disgust (b) contempt
(c) displeasure (d) insolence

92. All his attempts to win the favour of his boss proved ***infructuous***.
(a) fruitless (b) meaningless
(c) redundant (d) unnecessary

93. A strange mental ***aberration*** often made her forget her own name.
(a) illusion (b) disorder
(c) insanity (d) eccentricity

94. As she had never been in such a situation before, her ***apprehension*** was understandable.
(a) excitement (b) hesitation
(c) eagerness (d) fear

95. You should not get ***paranoid about*** what others think of you.
(a) upset by (b) obsessed with
(c) flattered by (d) influenced by

Antonyms

Directions ***(Questions 96 to 105)*** ***In this section, each item consists of a word or a phrase which is bold italicised in the sentence given. It is followed by four words or phrases. Select the one which is closest to the opposite in meaning of the italicised word or phrase.***

96. The new boss is well-known for his ***rigid*** approach to all problems.
(a) sympathetic (b) swift
(c) flexible (d) logical

97. On the hillside, he could see the ***vague*** shapes of sheep coming through the mist.
(a) apparent (b) plain
(c) transparent (d) clear

98. His ***repulsive*** behaviour could not be ignored by the members of the jury.
(a) attractive (b) lovely
(c) admirable (d) mild

99. ***Adversity*** is the source of numerous vices.
(a) Money (b) Luxury
(c) Wealth (d) Prosperity

100. His ***casual*** remarks were taken note of by all members of the board.
(a) sincere (b) careful
(c) flawless (d) precise

101. He is an ***amateur*** photographer.
(a) skilled (b) professional
(c) average (d) experienced

102. The artist led a very ***austere*** life.
(a) eventful (b) exciting
(c) boisterous (d) luxurious

103. If you ***pamper*** the child you will regret it.
(a) neglect (b) scold
(c) discourage (d) scorn

104. The witness ***affirmed*** on oath that he was an eyewitness to the crime under study.
(a) denied (b) contradicted
(c) opposed (d) disputed

105. These rules are meant to ***prevent*** further appointments

(a) aggravate (b) expedite
(c) accelerate (d) facilitate

ORDERING OF WORDS IN A SENTENCE

Directions *(Questions 106 to 115)* : *In each of the following questions, there is a sentence of which some parts have been jumbled up. You are required to rearrange these parts which are labelled P, Q, R and S to produce the correct sentence. Choose the proper sequence.*

106. Though he dialled frequently
(**P**) on telephone
(Q) my brother could not contact me
(R) and had left no information
(S) as I had gone out of office
(a) QPRS (b) QPSR
(c) SPQR (d) SQRP

107. He has
(**P**) while he was in a reverie
(Q) found the book
(R) at the bus-stop
(S) he lost
(a) PQSR (b) PRQS
(c) QRSP (d) QSRP

108. We went
(**P**) along the railway line
(Q) and had a right to
(R) where other people were not allowed to go
(S) but daddy belonged to the railway
(a) PRQS (b) PRSQ
(c) RPQS (d) RSQP

109. The master
(P) who was very loyal to him
(Q) punished the servant
(R) without giving any valid reason
(S) when he left the work unfinished
(a) QPSR (b) QRPS
(c) RQPS (d) RQSP

110. He sat
(P) through the Town Hall Park
(Q) which flanked a path running
(R) under the boughs
(S) of a spreading tamarind tree
(a) PQSR (b) PRSQ
(c) RSPQ (d) RSQP

111. Then the women
(P) lamenting their evil desire
(Q) that had brought
(R) wept loudly
(S) this sorrow upon them
(a) PQSR (b) PRQS
(c) RPQS (d) RQPS

112. Walking along the road
(P) before their enchanted mates
(Q) he saw
(R) from the orchard to his residence
(S) peacocks dancing
(a) QSPR (b) QSRP
(c) RPQS (d) RQSP

113. When it began to rain suddenly on the first of January
(P) to celebrate the new year
(Q) we ran for shelter
(R) to the neighbouring house
(S) where many people had gathered
(a) PRSQ (b) PSQR
(c) QRPS (d) QRSP

114. In the darkness
(P) the long, narrow beard
(Q) was clearly visible with
(R) the tall stooping figure of the doctor
(S) and the aquiline nose
(a) PSQR (b) QPRS
(c) RQPS (d) RSQP

115. The gorcer
(P) did not listen to the protests of the customer
(Q) who was in the habit of weighing less
(R) whom he had cheated
(S) with great audacity
(a) PQSR (b) QPRS
(c) PRSQ (d) QSPR

ORDERING OF SENTENCES

Directions *(Questions 116 to 120)* : ***In the following questions, each passage consists of six sentences. The first and the sixth sentences are given in the beginning. The middle four sentences in each have been removed and jumbled up. These are labelled P, Q, R and S. You are required to find out the proper order for the four sentences.***

116. **S_1**. Metals are today being replaced by polymers in many applications.

S_6. Many Indian Institutes of Science and Technology run special programmes on polymer science.

P : Above all, they are cheaper and easier to process, making them a viable alternative to metals.

Q : Polymers are essentially long chains of hydrocarbon molecules.

R : Today polymers as strong as metals have been developed

S : These have replaced the traditional chromiumplated metallic bumpers in cars.

(a) QRPS (b) QRSP
(c) RQSP (d) RSQP

117. **S_1**. The cooperative system of doing business is good wasy of encouraging ordinary workers to work hard.

S_6 The main object is to maintain the interest of every member of the society and to ensure that the members participate actively in the projects of the society.

P : If the society is to be well run, it is necessary to prevent insincere officials being elected to the committee which is solely responsible for the running of the business.

Q : They get this from experienced and professional workers who are not only familiar with the cooperative system, but also with efficient means of doing business.

R : To a large extent, many cooperative societies need advice and guidance.

S : The capital necessary to start a business venture is obtained by the workers' contributions.

(a) SQPR (b) SRQP
(c) PSRQ (d) PQSR

118. **S_1**. Biological evolution has not fitted man to any specific environment.

S_6 That brilliant sequence of cultural peaks can most appropriately be termed the ascent of Man.

P : It is by means a biological evolution, but it is a cultural one.

Q : His imaginatioin, his reason, his emotional subtlety and toughness, make it possible for him not to accept the environment but to change it.

R : And that series of inventions by which man from age to age has reshaped his environment is a different kind of evolution.

S : Among the multitude of animals which scamper, fly, burrow and swim around us, he is the only one who is not locked into his own environment.

(a) QRSP (b) QPRS
(c) SQRP (d) SRQP

119. **S_6**. Since the sixties there has been an increasing interest in human neurophysiology, which deals with the neural bases of mental activity and behaviour.

S_6. So far the journal has published a mixture of articles including reports and investigations.

P : It has format which is very similar to that of *Brain and Language,* a sister journal.

Q : Since then, a number of journals devoted entirely to this area of research have appeared.

R : Before the 1960s when this field was the concern of a small number of investigators, research articles were scattered in various neurological journals.

S : *Brain and Cognition* is one such journal.

(a) QRSP (b) QSPR
(c) RQSP (d) RSPQ

120. **S_1.** For decades, Americal society has been called a melting pot.

S_6. In recent years, such differences—accentuated by the arrival of immigrants from Asia and other parts of the world in the United States—have become something to celebrate and to nurture.

P : Differences remained—in appearance, mannerisms, Customs, speech, religion and more.

Q : The term has long been a cliche, and a half—truth.

R : But homogenisation was never achieved.

S : Yes, immigrants from diverse cultures and traditions did cast off vestiges of their native lands and become almost imperceptibly woven into the American fabric.

(a) QRSP (b) QSRP
(c) SQPR (d) SQRP

ANSWERS

1. (b) : Replace 'best' by 'better'
2. (b) : Replace 'furnitures' by 'furniture'
3. (c) : Replace 'then' by 'than'
4. (a) : Replace 'than' by 'to'
5. (b) : Replace 'where you were' by 'where he was'
6. (b) : Replace 'for' by 'of'
7. (d) : No error
8. (c) : Remove 'discuss'
9. (d) : No error
10. (c) : Remove 'will'
11. (c) : Replace 'to accept' by 'to be accepted'
12. (b) : Replace 'evidences' by 'evidence'
13. (c) : Add 'the' before 'Ganges' and 'Himalayas'
14. (d) : No error
15. (b) : Replace 'although' by 'though'

16. (*b*)	**17.** (*c*)	**18.** (*a*)	**19.** (*d*)	**20.** (*c*)	**21.** (*a*)	**22.** (*b*)	**23.** (*d*)	**24.** (*d*)	**25.** (*a*)
26. (*d*)	**27.** (*b*)	**28.** (*a*)	**29.** (*c*)	**30.** (*b*)	**31.** (*c*)	**32.** (*b*)	**33.** (*a*)	**34.** (*c*)	**35.** (*a*)
36. (*a*)	**37.** (*a*)	**38.** (*c*)	**39.** (*b*)	**40.** (*b*)	**41.** (*a*)	**42.** (*c*)	**43.** (*a*)	**44.** (*a*)	**45.** (*b*)
46. (*b*)	**47.** (*b*)	**48.** (*a*)	**49.** (*c*)	**50.** (*b*)	**51.** (*c*)	**52.** (*c*)	**53.** (*b*)	**54.** (*a*)	**55.** (*a*)
56. (*c*)	**57.** (*d*)	**58.** (*a*)	**59.** (*d*)	**60.** (*b*)	**61.** (*b*)	**62.** (*d*)	**63.** (*b*)	**64.** (*b*)	**65.** (*a*)
66. (*d*)	**67.** (*c*)	**68.** (*c*)	**69.** (*b*)	**70.** (*a*)	**71.** (*b*)	**72.** (*a*)	**73.** (*c*)	**74.** (*b*)	**75.** (*b*)
76. (*d*)	**77.** (*d*)	**78.** (*a*)	**79.** (*a*)	**80.** (*a*)	**81.** (*b*)	**82.** (*b*)	**83.** (*d*)	**84.** (*d*)	**85.** (*a*)
86. (*c*)	**87.** (*c*)	**88.** (*b*)	**89.** (*a*)	**90.** (*c*)	**91.** (*b*)	**92.** (*a*)	**93.** (*b*)	**94.** (*d*)	**95.** (*a*)
96. (*c*)	**97.** (*d*)	**98.** (*a*)	**99.** (*d*)	**100.** (*b*)	**101.** (*b*)	**102.** (*d*)	**103.** (*a*)	**104.** (*a*)	**105.** (*d*)
106. (*b*)	**107.** (*d*)	**108.** (*b*)	**109.** (*a*)	**110.** (*d*)	**111.** (*c*)	**112.** (*d*)	**113.** (*d*)	**114.** (*c*)	**115.** (*b*)
116. (*b*)	**117.** (*a*)	**118.** (*a*)	**119.** (*c*)	**120.** (*d*)					

LATEST QUESTION BANK

Directions (Questions 1 to 32) : In each of the following questions, a word followed by four/five alternative words has been given. You are to select the word which is nearest in meaning to that of the word in question.

1. BIZARRE **(M.B.A. 1997)**
(*a*) Colourful (*b*) Strange
(*c*) Exotic (*d*) Comical

2. ZENITH
(*a*) Top (*b*) Bright
(*c*) Wonderful (*d*) Smart

3. CURSORY
(*a*) Penetrating (*b*) Informal
(*c*) Superficial (*d*) Angry

4. DISMAL **(Bank P.O. 1997)**
(*a*) Deformed (*b*) Impolite
(*c*) Bleak (*d*) Watery

5. NEMESIS **(L.I.C. 1997)**
(*a*) Punishment (*b*) Victory
(*c*) Adventure (*d*) Reward

6. CONNIVE
(*a*) Threaten (*b*) Shield
(*c*) Instigate (*d*) Disregard

7. ERSATZ
(*a*) Liveliness (*b*) Imitation
(*c*) Freshness (*d*) Pleasure

8. ANNOTATION
(*a*) Translation (*b*) Prologue
(*c*) Quip
(*d*) Explanatory note

9. EXACERBATE
(*a*) Irritate (*b*) Enlighten
(*c*) Aggravate (*d*) Exaggerate

10. THRIVE
(*a*) Hurt (*b*) Persuade
(*c*) Push (*d*) Flourish

11. VAPID
(*a*) Virtuous (*b*) Vital
(*c*) Priceless (*d*) Dull

12. FRANTIC **(Assistant Grade, 1998)**
(*a*) Urgent (*b*) Excited
(*c*) Novel (*d*) Painful

13. EGREGIOUS
(*a*) Social (*b*) Shocking
(*c*) Common (*d*) Plain

14. MAMMOTH **(L.I.C.A.A.O. 1997)**
(*a*) Greedy (*b*) Wild
(*c*) Straight (*d*) Huge

15. HUMDRUM
(*a*) Thoughtful (*b*) Musical
(*c*) Unnatural (*d*) commonplace
(I.Tax & Central Excise, 1997)

16. MANIA
(*a*) Fame (*b*) Greatness
(*c*) Fear (*d*) Illusion

17. COMPREHEND
(*a*) Grasp (*b*) Encompass
(*c*) Emphasise (*d*) condense

18. PROSPER **(Bank P.O.1997)**
(*a*) thrive (*b*) Advance
(*c*) Enlarge (*d*) Increase

19. OBLOQUY **(M.B.A. 1997)**
(*a*) Lethargy (*b*) Burial service
(*c*) Verbal abuse (*c*) Vulgar joke

20. ENTHRAL
(*a*) Inspire (*b*) Charm
(*c*) Glorify (*d*) Annoy

21. BAFFLE
(*a*) Insult (*b*) Frustrate
(*c*) Defame (*d*) Antagonise

22. DAUNT **(Assistant Grade, 1998)**
(*a*) Detain (*b*) Annoy
(*c*) Abuse (*d*) Intimidate

23. BEHOLDEN
(*a*) Upright (*b*) Lovable
(*c*) Grateful (*d*) Obliged

24. SOLICIT **(L.I.C.A. A.O. 1997)**
(*a*) Beseech (*b*) Require
(*c*) Claim (*d*) Demand

25. CLUMSY
(*a*) Adroit (*b*) Dexterous
(*c*) Rough (*d*) Ungraceful

26. FRICASSEE **(C.A.T. 1997)**
(*a*) Grill (*b*) Decorate
(*c*) Stew (*d*) To baste

27. HINDER **(I.TAX, 1997)**
(*a*) Create (*b*) Protect
(*c*) Vindicate (*d*) Impede

28. ABIDE
(*a*) Hold (*b*) Encourage

(c) Accept (d) Comment

29. MONOLITHIC **(M.B.A. 1997)**

(a) Short-sighted (b) Black & white

(c) Repetitive (d) Very large

30. SYMBIOSIS

(a) Transformation (b) Close association

(c) Cure - all (d) Similarity

31. EGRESSION

(a) Digression (b) Effusion

(c) Departure (d) Hostility

32. PERNICIOUS **(C.A.T. 1997)**

(a) Relevant (b) Vigilant

(c) destructive (d) Minute care

Directions (Questions 33 to 42) : In this section, you find a number of sentences, parts of which are printed in bold. For each bold part, four words/ phrases are listed below. Choose the word nearest in meaning to the bold part.

(C.D.S. 1997)

33. The report makes **oblique** references to his shady past

(a) underhand (b) indirect (c) critical (d) oblivious

34. There was **an impasse** during the Indo - Pak deliberations on checking the infiltration across the border.

(a) a deadlock (b) a discussion

(c) a doubt

(d) a memorandum passed

35. They have heaped **encomiums** on her.

(a) blames (b) excesse

(c) excuses (d) praises

36. The film deals with **decadent** feudalism

(a) declining (b) diminishing

(c) unless (d) prevalent

37. The rebels made **an abortive** attempt to overthrow the government

(a) an overt (b) a violent

(c) a secret (d) an unsuccessful

38. The meteorological department has announced that there is little prospect of rain in the near future.

(a) possibility (b) foresight

(c) progress (d) prediction

39. Inspite of a number of problems, he maintained his **equanimity**.

(a) presence of mind (b) calmness of mind

(c) self - confidence (d) sense of humour

40. Each year food production in underdeveloped countries falls a bit further behind **burgeoning** population growth.

(a) alarming (b) decreasing

(c) expanding (d) recurring

41. A **transition** is taking place in the Indian society.

(a) degradation (b) advancement

(c) change (d) improvement

42. The woman sat inside reading **the scriptures.**

(a) books containing pictures

(b) holy books

(c) books about different scripts

(d) books about great heroes

Directions (Questions 43 to 47) : In each of the following questions, out of the given alternatives, choose the one which is nearest in meaning to the italicised bold part of the sentence.

43. The old ***adage*** that 'honesty is the best policy' still impires a large number of people.

(a) assumption (b) belief

(c) saying (d) superstition

44. Rapid industrialisation has played havoc with the ***idyllic*** landscape of the 'countryside.

(a) beautiful (b) pleasant (c) clean (d) noisy

45. The tendency to ***wrest*** what belongs to others, is playing havoc with our social ethos/relations.

(a) get (b) demand

(c) snatch (d) envy

46. The young executives are fond of fast food and ***snazzy*** dresses.

(a) loose (b) colourful

(c) tightfit (d) stylish

47. Despite his pompous style and gestures , the audience failed to ***evince*** any interest in his lecture.

(a) develop (b) show

(c) arouse (d) gain

Directions (Questions 48 to 56) : In each of the following questions, a word followed by certain alternative words has

been given. Select the word which is opposite in meaning to that of the word in question.

48. MOROSE
(*a*) Docile (*b*) Boorish
(*c*) Diffuse (*d*) Moody

49. SALIENT
(*a*) Emphatic (*b*) Striking
(*c*) Important (*d*) Incline

50. PRECEPT
(*a*) Discernment (*b*) Instruction
(*c*) Direction (*d*) Maxim

51. PALPABLE **(M.B.A. 1997)**
(*a*) Innovative (*b*) Fresh
(*c*) Imaginary (*d*) Creative

52. MALIGNANT
(*a*) Swallow (*b*) Prune
(*c*) Benign (*d*) Virulent

53. POLEMIC
(*a*) Aggressive attack (*b*) Warlike
(*b*) Logically argued (*d*) Controversial

54. DELIRIOUS **(M.B.A. 1997)**
(*a*) Large (*b*) Calm
(*c*) Insane (*d*) Responsive

55. JUVENILE
(*a*) Mature (*b*) Youthful
(*c*) Blind (*d*) Control

56. MORIBUND
(*a*) Restored (*b*) Healthy
(*c*) Wholesome (*d*) Growing

Directions (Questions 57 to 66) : In each of the following questions, a sentence is given with a word or a phrase printed in italic bold. It is followed by four words or phrases. Select the alternative which is closest to the opposite in meaning of the marked word.

(C.D.S. 1996)

57. He is very ***optimistic*** about his examination result
(*a*) sombre (*b*) pessimistic
(*c*) gloomy (*d*) desolate

58. He showed his ***cowardliness*** while confronting the rogues.
(*a*) guts (*b*) gallantry
(*c*) bravery (*d*) aggressiveness

59. The proposal got the ***concurrence*** of all the officials.
(*a*) dissent (*b*) denunciation
(*c*) disapproval (*d*) opposition

60. The proctor is a very ***strict*** person.
(*a*) generous (*b*) kind
(*c*) lenient (*d*) noble

61. The essay will read better if you ***condense*** it a little.
(*a*) modify (*b*) increase
(*c*) improve (*d*) elaborate

62. He is very ***frugal*** by nature.
(*a*) liberal (*b*) generous
(*c*) extravagant (*d*) careless

63. This glass is ***transparent***.
(*a*) dark (*b*) murky
(*c*) opaque (*d*) shaded

64. he appears to be very ***sagacious***.
(*a*) disrespectful (*b*) flippant
(*c*) foolish (*d*) sage - like

65. They have made ***tentative*** plans for their marriage but have not told us anything.
(*a*) obvious (*b*) foolproof
(*b*) distinct (*d*) definite

66. There is abundance of wheat in the market.
(*a*) lack (*b*) non - availability
(*c*) rarity (*d*) scarcity

(Questions 67 to 76) **(C.D.S. 1997)**

67. He is a ***valiant*** young man.
(*a*) weak (*b*) cowardly
(*c*) shy (*d*) sluggish

68. ***An obscure*** traveller was found dead on the board.
(*a*) A famous (*b*) A respectable
(*c*) A decent (*d*) An affluent

69. The pleasures of life are ***eternal***.
(*a*) periodical (*b*) occasional
(*c*) transient (*d*) brief

70. We were curious as to why the young man was looking so ***morose***.
(*a*) cheerful (*b*) haggard
(*c*) gloomy (*d*) healthy

71. We have carefully studied your explanation and it sounds ***plausible***.
(*a*) Impertinent (*b*) undesirable
(*c*) unconvincing (*d*) incoherent

72. Cotton - seed oil is ***harmful*** to heart patients.
(*a*) useful (*b*) advantageous
(*c*) profitable (*d*) beneficial

73. My father is a very **stern** man.

(a) lenient (b) indulgent
(c) liberal (d) emotional

74. Only a pragmatic approach to these problems can solve them.
(a) Idealistic (b) theoretical
(c) diplomatic (d) practical

75. He was used to a ***humdrum*** life.
(a) a daring (b) a stormy
(c) an active (d) an exciting

76. In the olden days the prisoners were kept in dark, and dank cells.
(a) dingy (b) dry (c) old (d) small

Directions (Questions 77 to 91) : Read the following passage carefully and answer the questions given below it. Certain words in the passage are printed in bold to help you to locate them easily for answering some of the questions.

(Bank P.O. 1997)

It is time we looked at the latent causes. Where does the strength of India **lie** ? Not in numbers , not necessarily in our moral stands on international issues. In modern times , the strength of a nation lies in its achievement in science and technology. This is not to say that other fields do not count.

In the five decades after independence , we have yet to demonstrate our originality in applied science and technology. Though Japan also started like us, by cultivating the technology of the West, the Japanese adapted , improved and displayed originality in several areas of science and technology. The generation which is at the helm of affairs in science and technology in our country after independence , mostly consisted of self - seekers. By and large, with a few exceptions, the science and technology managers in India concentrated in gaining power and influence. They loved publicity. Most of them stopped doing science while they **managed** science. Things would have been better had they been humble enough to acknowledge the difference between doing and managing science. Instead, they claimed they were the foremost in science and technology simply because they were at the helm of affairs. As a result, they ceased to inspire the younger lot. India continues to be a borrower of science and technology , even though its potential for originality is **substantial**.

Our achievements in nuclear science and technology may be **dazzling** to our people. But, in worth and originality, they are ordinary and routine. While our own people remain ignorant, the people of other countries know all about the pretentions to knowledge of our nuclear science and technology managers. One **subtle** way of sabotaging our nuclear goals is to help hollow persons reach and remain at the helm of affairs. International bodies came in as handy tools in that subtle process. The veil of secrecy effectively protects the mismanagement in our nuclear establishments. The talk of national security comes as an easy weapon to prevent any probe into mismanagement. On nuclear matters , the media in our country, by and large, avoid the investigative approach. As a result , the mismatch between promise and performance in the nuclear field does not get exposed as much as the management in other fields.

77. The author of the passage has
(a) appreciated the Japanese scientists unduly and exorbitantly
(b) criticised the power - hungry Indian technocrats
(c) underestimated the Japanese and Chinese scientists and technologists
(d) hailed India's technological advancement in the past five decades.
(e) unreasonably criticised the Indian politicians for their apathy.

78. What according to the passage is the criterion to decide the strength of a country?
(a) International understanding cherished by the people
(b) Potential of people to achieve desired targets
(c) The country's population
(d) The moral values of the people
(e) None of these

79. The author of the passage thinks that
(a) India lacks the necessary potential to compete with other nations
(b) India's potential for originality is not put to optimum utilisation
(c) India should continue to borrow

technology from abroad.

(d) Our achievements in nuclear science and technology are dazzling

(e) Our scientists did all their best to inspire the younger lot

80. Which of the following is the commonality between the Indian and the Japanese scientists ? Both have displayed

(a) an advancement of substandard quality

(b) greed for influence and power

(c) originality in applied sciences

(d) remarkable lust for publicity

(e) None of these

81. 'Doing science' and 'managing science' as applied by the author is analogous to.

(a) fact and fantasy

(b) Inspiration and aspiration.

(c) originality and adaptability

(b) Scientific investigations and discovery of principles

(e) set target and achieving it

82. What does the author mean by 'doing' science ?

(a) Concentrating on such researches which have very low practical utility.

(b) Demonstrating exaggerated performance without achieving the desired level

(c) Displaying genuine acumen and performance in scientific studies

(d) Managing effectively the administrative functions involved in the power game

(e) None of these.

83. Which of the following is the correct assessment of India's post - independence nuclear and scientific advancements ?

(a) Our achievements are of a very ordinary quality and routine nature.

(b) Our achievements in nuclear science and technology are dazzling.

(c) Originality and adaptability is duly displayed in the field of applied science.

(d) Our scientists have given full justice to the developmental needs of nuclear science.

(e) None of these.

84. Which of the following factors help prevent the exposure of drawbacks in nuclear establishments ?

(A) The concept of secrecy

(B) The constraint of National Security

(C) The investigative approach of the Media

(a) only A (b) only A and B (c) only A and C (d) only B

(e) only C

85. It appears that the author of the passage is fully convinced that

(a) India's potential for originality in science and technology is over utilised

(b) India's strength lies in its moral stands on international issues

(c) Most of the managers of science and technology are not doing their work properly

(d) Our scientists though criticised in our country are recognised abroad

(e) People lacking the desired qualities are supported to get at the helm of affairs.

Directions* (Questions 86 to 88) :** ***Pick out the word that is most nearly the same in meaning as the word printed in bold type as used in the passage.

86. PRETENSIONS

(a) Shortcomings (b) Claims

(c) Apathy (d) Access

(e) Permissiveness

87. MANAGED

(a) Conducted (b) Organized

(c) Trained (d) Manoeuvred

(e) Performed

88. SUBTLE

(a) Devastating (b) Insidious

(c) Dangerous (d) Innocent

(e) Soft

Directions* (Questions 89 to 91) :** ***Pick out the word that is most opposite in meaning of the word printed in bold type as used in the passage.

89. DAZZLING

(a) Lustrous (b) Glaring

(c) Unnoticeable (d) Unexposable

(e) Unscrupulous

90. SUBSTANTIAL

(a) Insignificant (b) Extensive

(c) Independent (d) Noteworthy

(e) Uncompromising

91. LATENT

(a) Apparent (b)`Conoealed

(c) Dubious (d) Real

(e) untrustworthy

Directions (Questions 92 to 97) : Read the following passage carefully and answer the questions given below.

(M.B.A. 1997)

The second of what I have called the three methods of setting about the pursuit of knowledge is that of the natural sciences. We need not attempt a complete definition of natural science and if we were to try we should find that its margins tend to grow indistinct as we concentrate on them. A perfectly adequate practical definition is the statement that its central function is to acquire verifiable knowledge. A verifiable fact is one that has shown itself to have a relation to certain definable conditions such that wherever and whenever the conditions have been produced the fact in question has always accompanied them such verification is the characteristic and only sanction of science. Whether we like a given fact or not and whether it seems true or revolts our reason, are quite irrelevant on its scientific validity.

All knowledge comes from noticing resemblances and recurrences in the events that happen around us. Although some of us may be much quicker than other in the power of seeing and comparing, it is obvious that the greatest talent cannot carry us very far as long as observation and experiment are applied only to random experience. It is the discovery of natural science that experience can be simplified so that on the one hand resemblances and recurrences in events can be, more easily seen, and on the other hand the conditions in which they occur can be completely specified. Thus, using the term in the broadest sense, is the experimental method. In one aspect it may be regarded as a mere refinement of the rough and ready trial and error of the craftsman and the common man. In another aspect, however, the change is so great as to be virtually a qualitative one and to make the method distinct from all others. It is not necessary to dilate here on the power it has displayed in advancing knowledge or the huge acceleration it has imparted to that process. It is more relevant to note the limits to which its application is subject. The scientific method is unfitted to tackle directly the turbulent stream of everyday experience and common affairs, it must run off minute fractions of it into carefully specified and engineered channels before it can bring its power to bear. Thus, for example, the work of social government is not as such directly accessible to it on account of the jumbled missellaneity of the matters involved.

In saying this I must guard myself against being thought to pronounce on a wholly different question which might be supposed to be similar. It is of course, obvious that government now existing fail to make use of much knowledge already established by science and capable of immediate application. Even, however, if this deplorable lag could be abolished, the direct application of scientific method to government itself as a whole would, with our present powers, be impossible.

After what has been to some extent a digression we pick up the line of our argument again when we ask ourselves what part in the scientific method is taken by what I have called the extended reasoning process. The history of science is generally supposed to furnish a wonderful display of tuiumphs of human reason. I must confess that the reading of it does not induce me any such grandiose conception of the mind. The separate steps of progress have really been much prepared for by long flights of rational forecast. Great investigators seem mostly to have led from fact to fact , to have depended on a kind of intuitive flair for behaviour of their material, and to have used reasoning rather for the planning of their work and the design of experiments than for elaborate structures of argument. Although rational and imaginative speculation is of the greatest general value to science in keeping it from going dry and orthodox, as an actual implement of research it has not very much to its credit.

92. According to the author the triumph of human reason

(a) is observed only in political fields
(b) is supposed to be wonderfully displayed in the history of science
(c) is displayed wonderfully in the foreign policy of different governments.
(d) is observed in none of the above occasions

93. According to the author, a complete practical definitions of natural science.
(a) is that its main function is to collect bits of knowledge from natural phenomena which are not repeatable.
(b) is that its main function is to conduct accurate experiments
(c) is that its main function is to acquire verifiable knowledge
(d) cannot be formulated accurately

94. The scientific method.
(a) is not deliberately applied by some government to the fields when it can bring improvement
(b) is not always applicable to the situation where jumbled miscellaneity of the matters is involved
(c) is applicable when all the required conditions are roughly satisfied
(d) is applicable in every aspect of life and its effect is of immense value to the progress of society and social government

95. We acquire knowledge about anything in the world
(a) through the quick and accurate observation of talented persons
(b) from the observation of randomly Accurring natural phenomena
(c) from the unnatural events that occur in nature occasionally
(d) from the resemblances and recurrences in the events around us

96. The direct application of the scientific method to government itself
(a) would be impossible on account of the jumbled miscellaneity of the matter involved
(b) is not done by any government as it cannot bring improvement to the public
(c) is never done by any government which aims at people's welfare
(d) is usually done by all socialist governments

97. A fact may said to be verifiable when
(a) it seems to be true according to our reason
(b) it has shown to have a relation to certain definable conditions such that whenever the conditions are reproduced the fact would accompany.
(c) it is occasionally repeated though the time of occurrence cannot be forecasted
(d) none of the above

Direction (Question 98 to 102) : Read the following passage carefully and answer the questions given below

Aquisitive nature has become the hallmark of people in modern times.

It a neighbour posseses a kitchen gadget like a mixie or a grinder, we two have the desire to own the same. All efforts are geared to make this purchase, whether the item is essential or not.

Shopkeepers vie with each other to sell these things. It is as if the whole world has conspired to sell the mixie or grinder to me whether I want it or not. Of course, my wife wants it.

98. In this passage acquisition means :
(a) working regularly
(b) being lazy
(c) gaining things
(d) giving away things

99. According to the passage, the purchase is made :
(a) when the article is useful
(b) because the article is essential
(c) whether the article is needed or not
(d) only when the article is in demand

100. Possessing new things sets up a kind of.
(a) Competition among neighbours
(b) love among neighbours
(c) hatred among neighbours
(d) indifference among neighbours

101. The writer considers acquisitive nature to be :
(a) a depressing quality in people
(b) a bad quality in people.
(c) a good quality in people

(d) an encouraging quality in people

102. From the passage it is clear that the writer

(a) wants to buy a mixie

(b) is keen on buying a mixie

(c) does not want to buy a mixie

(d) is indifferent to buy a mixie.

Directions (Questions 103 to 110) : Read the following passage carefully and answer the questions given below it. Certain words / phrases are printed in bold to help you to locate them while answering some of the questions. **(B.S.R.B. 1997)**

There is a fairly universal sentiment that the use of nuclear weapon is clearly contrary to morality and that its production probably so , does not go for enough. These activities are not only opposed to morality but also to law and if the legal objection can be added to the moral, the argument against the use and the manufacture of these weapons will considerably be reinforced. Now the time is ripe to evaluate the responsibility of scientists who knowingly use their expertise for the construction of such weapons which have **deleterious** effect on mankind.

To this must be added the fact that more than 50 percent of the skilled scientific manpower in the world is now engaged in the armaments industry. How appropriate it is that all this valuable skill should be **devoted** to the manufacture of weapons of death in a world of poverty is a question that must touch the scientific conscience.

A meeting of biologists on the long - term world wide biological consequences of Nuclear War added frightening dimensions to those forecasts. Its report suggested that the long biological effects resulting from climatic changes may at least be as serious as the immediate ones.

Sub - freezing temperatures, low light levels and high dose of ionizing and ultraviolet radiation extending for many months after a large - scale nuclear war could destroy the biological support systems of civilization , at least in the Northern Hemisphere. Productivity in natural and agricultural ecosystems could be severely restricted for a year or more. Post - war survivors would face starvation as well as freezing conditions in the dark and be exposed to nearlethal dose of radiation. If, as now seems possible, the southern Hemisphere were affected also, global disruption of the biosphere would ensue. In any event, there would be severe consequences, even in the areas not affected directly, because of the interdependence of the world economy. In either case the extinction of a large fraction of the earth's animals, plant and micro - organism seems possible. The population size of Homospiens conceivably could be reduced to prehistoric levels or below, and extinction of the human species itself cannot be excluded.

103. The author of the passage seems to be of the view that.

(a) the evaluation of the scientists' expertise show their incompetence

(b) spending money on manufacture of weapons may be justifiable subject to the availability of funds

(c) utilization of scientific skills in manufacture of weapons is appropriate

(d) utilization of valuable knowledge for manufacture of lethal weapons is inhuman

(e) manufacture of weapons of death would help eradication of poverty

104. It appears from the passage that the use of nuclear weapons is considered against morality by

(a) almost all the nations of the world

(b) a minority group of scientists who have the necessary skill and competence

(c) only those nations which cannot afford to manufacture weapons

(d) most of the scientists who devote their valuable skills to manufacture nuclear weapons

(e) only the superpowers who can afford to manufacture and sell weapons

105. The author's most important objective of writing the above passage seems to

(a) explain scientifically the climatic changes resulting from use of nuclear weapons

(b) summarise the long biological effects of use of nuclear weapons

(c) highlight the use of nuclear weapons as an effective population control measure
(d) duly highlight the supremacy of the nations which possess nuclear weapons
(e) illustrate the devastating effects of use of nuclear weapons on mankind

106. Which of the following is one of the consequences of Nuclear War ?
(a) Post - war survivors being very few will have abundant food
(b) Fertility of land will last only for a year or so
(c) Southern hemisphere would remain quite safe in the post - war period
(d) Lights would be cooler and more comfortable
(e) None of these

107. Which of the following statements (1), (2) and/or (3) is/are definitely true in the context of the passage?
(1) Living organisms in the areas which are not directly affected by the consequences of nuclear war would also suffer.
(2) There is a likelihood of extinction of the human species as a consequence of nuclear war
(3) The post - war survivors would be exposed to the risk of near - lethal radiation
(a) only (1) (b) only (2)
(c) only (3) (d) only (1) and (2)
(e) All the three

108. According to the passage, the argument against the use and manufacture of nuclear weapons
(a) becomes stronger if legal and moral considerations are combined
(b) is acceptable only on moral grounds
(c) does not stand the test of legality
(d) possesses legal strength although it does not have moral standing
(e) None of these

109. Which of the following best explains the meaning of the word' devoted' as used in the passage ?
(a) overutilized (b) underutilized
(c) utilized for betterment
(d) abused for destruction
(e) dedicated for a good cause

110. Choose the word which is most opposite in meaning of the word ' deleterious' as used in the passage :
(a) harmful (b) non-cognizable
(c) beneficial (d) revolutionary
(e) irreparable

Directions (Question 111 to 119) : Read the following passage carefully and answer the questions given below it. Certain words / phrases in the passage are given in bold to help you to locate them while answering some of the questions :
(B.S.R.B. 1997)

Globalisation, liberalisation and free market are some of the most significant modern trends in economy. **Most economists** in our country seem **captivated** by the spell of the free market. Consequently, nothing seems good or normal that does not accord with the requirements of the free market. A price that is determined by the seller or, for that matter, established by anyone other than the aggregate of consumers seems **pernicious**. Accordingly, it requires a major act of will to think of price - fixing as both normal and having a valuable economic function. In fact, price - fixing is normal in all industrialised societies because the industrial system itself provides, as an effortless consequence of its own development, the price - fixing that it requires. Modern Industrial planning requires and rewards great size. Hence a comparatively small number of large firms will be competing for the same group of consumers. That each large firm will act with consideration of its own needs and thus avoid selling its products for more than its competitors charge is commonly recognised by **advocates** of free - market economic theories. But each large firm will also act with full consideration of the needs that it has in common with the other large firms competing for the same customers. Each large firm will thus avoid significant price - cutting, because price - cutting will be prejudicial to the common interest in a **stable** demand for products. Most economists do not see price - fixing when it occurs because they expect it to be brought about by a number of **explicit** agreements among large firms' it is not.

Moreover, those economists who argue that allowing the free - market to operate without interference is the most efficient method of establishing prices have not considered the economics of non - socialist countries. Most of these economies employ intentional price - fixing, usually in an **overt** fashion. Formal price - fixing by cartel and informal price - fixing by agreements covering the members of an industry are common place. Were there something peculiarly efficient about the free market and inefficient about price - fixing, the countries that have avoided the first and used the second would have suffered drastically in their economic development. There is no indication that they have.

Socialist industry also works within a framework of controlled prices. In the early 1970's the Soviet Union began to give firms and industries some flexibility in adjusting prices that a more informal evolution has accorded the capitalist system. Economists in the USA have hailed the change as a return to the free - market. But the then Soviet firms were not in favour of the prices established by a free - market over which they exercised little influence ; rather, Soviet firms acquired some power to fix prices.

111. Considering the literal meaning and connotations of the words used in the passage, the author's attitude towards "most economists" can best be described as
- *(a)* critical and condescending
- *(b)* derogatory and antagonistic
- *(c)* impartial and unbiased
- *(d)* indifferent
- *(e)* spiteful and envious

112. The author feels that price fixed by seller seems pernicious because
- *(a)* people don't have faith in large firms
- *(b)* people don't want the Government to fix prices
- *(c)* people do not want to decide prices
- *(d)* most economists believe that consumers should determine prices
- *(e)* most economists believe that no one group should determine prices

113. According to the passage, price - fixing in non - socialistic countries is generally
- *(a)* conservative and scarce
- *(b)* conservative and inflexible
- *(c)* illegitimate but beneficial
- *(d)* intentional and widespread
- *(e)* legitimate and innovative

114. The author's primary concern seems to
- *(a)* criticise a point of view
- *(b)* make people aware of recent discoveries
- *(c)* predict the probable results of a practice
- *(d)* prepare a research proposal
- *(e)* Summarise conflicting viewpoints

115. Which of the following statements (A), (B) and/or (C) is/are TRUE in the context of the information given in the passage? The information in the passage is helpful to

(A) know some of the ways in which prices can be fixed

(B) identify the products for which price - fixing can be more beneficial

(C) differentiate between the economies of various countries

- *(a)* Only (A)
- *(b)* Only (A) and (B)
- *(c)* Only (B)
- *(d)* only (C)
- *(e)* None of these

116. Which of the following statements is definitely TRUE in the context of the passage ? Price fixing is
- *(a)* an inevitable result of the industrial system
- *(b)* the joint result of a number of carefully organised decisions
- *(c)* a phenomenon uncommon to industrialised societies
- *(d)* a profitable result of economic development
- *(e)* a result of joint venture of the Government and industry

117. The author's primary objective of writing the passage seems to
- *(a)* advocate that price-fixing is unavoidable and it is beneficial to the economy of any industrialised Society
- *(b)* believe the popular belief that the free-market helps enhance development of industrial societies
- *(c)* create awareness among the general public regarding combating price-fixing by large firms.

(*d*) explain the methodology of fixing price to stabilise free - market.

(*e*) prove that price - fixing and free-market are compatible and mutually beneficial to industrialised societies.

118. Which of the following statements about the socialist industry is/are false?

(A) It works under certain price restrictions

(B) It has no authority to determine prices

(C) It hails the strategy to price fixing, as a major deviation.

(*a*) Only (A) is false

(*b*) (A) and (B) are false

(*c*) Only (B) is false

(*d*) (B) and (C) are false

(*e*) Only (C) is false

119. What was the result of the then Soviet Union's change in economic policy in the 1970's ?

(*a*) They acquired some authority to fix prices.

(*b*) They became more responsive to free - market.

(*c*) They had less control over the free - market.

(*d*) They showed greater profits.

(*e*) They were able to adjust to techno - advancement.

Directions (Questions 120 to 122) : Choose the word which is most opposite in meaning of the word given in capitals as used in the passage.

120. PERNICIOUS :

(*a*) extravagant (*b*) harmful
(*c*) deadly (*d*) promotive
(*e*) impracticable

121. OVERT :

(*a*) obvious (*b*) concealed
(*c*) unambiguous (*d*) manifest
(*e*) inexplicable

122. CAPTIVATED :

(*a*) seized (*b*) tamed
(*c*) repelled (*d*) unlocked
(*e*) enchanted

Directions (Questions 123 to 125) : Choose the word which is most nearly the same in meaning as the word or group of words given in capitals as used in the passage.

123. ADVOCATES :

(*a*) lawyers (*b*) supporters
(*c*) experts (*d*) loyalist
(*e*) recommends

124. STABLE :

(*a*) permanent (*b*) unvarying
(*c*) uniform (*d*) fluctuating
(*e*) restored

125. EXPLICIT :

(*a*) unambiguous (*b*) obvious
(*c*) clean (*d*) implied
(*e*) specifically

Directions (Questions 126 to 130) : Read the following passage carefully and answer the questions given below :

(MBA 1997)

Entrepreneurs innovate. Innovation is the specific instrument of entrepreneurship. It is the act that endows resources with a new capacity to create wealth. Innovation, indeed, creates a resource. There is no such thing as a "resource" until man finds a use for something in nature and thus endows it with economic value. Until then, every plant is a weed and every mineral just another rock. Not more than a century ago, neither mineral oil seeping out of the ground nor bauxite, the ore of aluminium, were resources. They were nuisances; both render the soil infertile. The penicillin mold was a pest, not a resource. Bacteriologists went to great lengths to protect their bacterial cultures against contamination by it. Then in the 1920s, a London doctor, Alexander Fleming, realized that this "pest" was exactly the bacterial killer bacteriologists had been looking for - and the penicillin mold became a valuable resource.

The same holds just as true in the social and economic spheres. There is no greater resource in an economy than "purchasing power". But purchasing power is the creation of the innovating entrepreneur. The American farmer had virtually no purchasing power in the early nineteenth century, he therefore could not buy farm machinery. There were dozens of harvesting machines on the market, but however much he might have wanted them, the farmer could not pay for them. Then one of the many harvesting - machine inventors, Cyrus Mc Cormick,invented installment buying. This enabled the farmer to pay for a harvesting machine out of his future earnings rather than out of his past savings and suddenly the farmer had "purchasing power " to buy farm equipment.

Equally, whatever changes the wealth producing potential of already existing resources constitutes innovation. There was not much new technology involved in the idea of moving a truck body off its wheels and onto a cargo vessel. This "innovation", the container did not grow out of technology at all but out of a new perception of the "Cargo vessel" as a materials - handling device rather than a "ship", which meant that what really mattered was to make the time in port as short as possible. But this humdrum innovation roughly quadrupled the productivity of the ocean- going freighter and probably saved shipping.

Without it, the tremendous expansion of world trade in the last forty years - the fastest growth in any major economic activity ever recorded - could not possibly have taken place.

What really made universal schooling possible more so than the popular commitment to the value of education, the systematic training of teachers in schools of education, or pedagogic theory - was that lowly innovation, the textbook, Without the textbook, even a very good teacher cannot teach more than one or two children at a time ; with it, even a pretty poor teacher can get a little learning into the heads of thirty or thirty - five students.

Innovation, as these examples show, does not have to be teachnical does not indeed have to be a "thing" altogether. Few technical innovations can compete in terms of impact with such social innovations as the newspaper or insurance installment buying literally transforms economies. Wherever introduced, it changes the economy from supply-driven to demand-driven, regardless almost of the productive level of the economy. The hospital, in its modern form a social innovation of the enlightenment of the eighteenth century, has had greater impact on health-care than many advances in medicine. Management, that is the "useful knowledge" that enables man for the first time to render productive people of different skills and knowledge working together in an "Organisation". It has converted modern society into something brand new, something, by the way, for which we have neither political nor social theory; a society of organisations.

Books on economic history mention August Borsig as the first man to build steam locomotives in Germany. But surely far more important was his innovation - against strenuous opposition from craft guilds, teachers, and government bureaucrats - of what to this day is the German system of factor organisation and the foundation of Germany's industrial strength. It was Borsig who devised the idea of the Master, the highly skilled and highly respected senior worker who runs the shop with considerable autonomy ; and the apprenticeship system, which combines practical training on the job with schooling in the classroom.

And the twin inventions of modern government by Machiavelli in The Prince and of the modern national state by his early follower, Jean Bodin, sixty years later, have surely had more lasting impacts than most technologies.

126. Which of the following could be the most suitable title for the passage?
 (*a*) Natural resources
 (*b*) Innovation and science
 (*c*) Innovation and society
 (*d*) None of these

127. For the American farmer, the innovation was
 (*a*) cooperative farming
 (*b*) installment plan
 (*c*) harvesting machine
 (*d*) None of these

128. Which of the following statement' could be termed to be true as per the author ?
 (*a*) every innovation has to be technical
 (*b*) management is purely a non - technical innovation
 (*c*) ship is different from a Cargo vessel
 (*d*) hospital is a technical imnovation

129. Natural resources are so called because
 (*a*) somebody has been creative enough to put these to use
 (*b*) these are found in nature.
 (*c*) somebody has been able to locate these

(*d*) None of these

130. The innovation of a text book has

(*a*) helped the students

(*b*) helped the teachers

(*c*) helped the publishers do a business

(*d*) helped the cause of universal education

Directions (Questions 131 to 135) :

Read the following passage carefully and answer the questions given below :

August 6, day Hiroshima was atom - bombed in 1945, symbolises at once man's nightmare and his greatest dream, the nightmare of a nuclear war, and the dream of genuine and lasting peace. Beginning with the survivors of Hiroshima and Nagasaki, the awareness of the danger and sentiment for disarmament and peace has become universal, transcending national and ideological barriers. And yet more deadly nuclear weapons are being piled on top of the heap, that is enough to wipe out all traces of life from this planet. Forty years after Hiroshima, there is no light at the end of the tunnel - only occasional flickers. The arms limitation talks between the superpowers, who hold the key to disarmament and peace, have yielded nothing so far.

The main serponsinbility for suppressing the nuclear threat is that of the superpowers. However, other powers also have nuclear weapons and they must share the responsibility. And not only they, but those nations which have or are developing nuclear capability must see the issues in a longer term and larger perspective.

Nuclear war like peace is not divisible. Agreement on disarmament at the superpower level is essential. But, it must be followed by similar agreements on the bilateral and regional level, for all of us are in a sense the citizens of Hiroshima.

131. August 6, 1945 is a significant date in history because it was on this day that :

(*a*) a peace treaty was signed.

(*b*) the second World War came to an end.

(*c*) a nuclear weapon was used for the first time

(*d*) Japan surrendered to the Allies.

132. The atom bomb has produced a nightmarish effect on nations because of :

(*a*) the possibility of destruction of a whole civilization.

(*b*) its potential for unabashed arms race.

(*c*) the threat to peace from the powers that could produce such weapons.

(*d*) their awareness of man's defencelessness against such weapons.

133. The super powers are trying to counter the dangers of a nuclear way by :

(*a*) discontinuing nuclear tests.

(*b*) withholding financial aid to nations trying to go nuclear.

(*c*) holding talks on peace and disarmament.

(*d*) trying to stop making nuclear weapons.

134. The author thinks that negotiations for the control of nuclear arms have made

(*a*) little progress

(*b*) tremendous progress

(*c*) constructive suggestions

(*d*) contingency plans to stop the disasters

135. According to the author :

(*a*) superpowers alone should shoulder the responsibility of controlling nuclear arms.

(*b*) developing nations should hold talks for disarmament.

(*c*) other powers that have nuclear capability should join hands with superpowers to restrain potential nuclear powers.

(*d*) a nuclear disarmament agreement at the superpower level should be followed by similar agreements at bilateral and regional levels.

Directions (Questions 136 to 145) :

Read the following passage carefully and answer the questions given below it. Certain words / phrases are printed in bold to help you to locate them while answering some of the questions. **(Bank P.O. 1997)**

In modern times Abraham Lincoln stands as the model of a **compassionate** statesman. He showed this quality not only in striving for the emancipation of the American blacks but in the dignity with which he conducted the American Civil War.

Lincoln did not fancy himself as a

liberator. He thought it would be better for all if emancipation was a **gradual** process spread over many years. He proposed compensation for slave- owners in US bonds and grants for the rehabilitaton of blacks- 'colonisation' as he called it. But fate was to deem otherwise. The haste with which the south wanted to break away from the Union with the North, compelled him to move faster than he expected. Perhaps more than most men of his time he had thought through the issue of slavery. ' We must free the slaves', he said,' or be ourselves **subdued** '. Before reading his first draft of the Proclamation of Emancipation, he told his colleagues, ' In giving freedom to the slaves, we assure freedom to the free'.

On September 22, 1862, Lincoln set his hand on the Proclamation of Emancipation declaring that on the first day of January 1863, all persons held as slaves within any state. ' shall be then, and forever free'.

Lincoln's revulsion for slavery left him without any moral indignation or passion against the slave - owners. The guilt of the slave - owners, he felt, should be shared by the whole country, the North and the South, for it seemed to him that everyone in the nation was an accomplice in **perpetuating** that system. To have whipped up any hatred a gainst slave - owners would, to him, have been an act of malice.

I shall do nothing in malice ; he wrote, 'what I deal' with is too vast for malicious dealing; As the Civil War was coming to a successful conclusion, a Northerner demanded of Lincoln :

' Mr President, how are you going to treat the southerners when the war is over ?'

Lincoln replied. ' As of they never went to war?'

When the news came of the victory of the Northern against the confederate forces, some one suggested that the head of the confederation Administration, Jefferson Davies, really ought to be hanged. 'Judge not, that ye be not judged', Lincoln replied. As to the demand for the prosecution of rebels, Lincoln replies. We must extinguish our resentments if we expect harmony and union. This was his last recorded utterance.

136. What came in Lincoln's way of carrying out emancipation as a gradual process?'

(*a*) His proposition to give grant for the rehabilitation of slaves .

(*b*) His own over - enthusiasm to complete the process fast .

(*c*) The inadequate compensation given to slave - owners.

(*d*) The haste of the south to break away from the union with the North.

(*e*) None of these.

137. The sentence ' In giving freedom .... to the free ' means :

(*a*) if we give freedom to the slaves, they will serve us better.

(*b*) if we do not give freedom to the slaves, they will free themselves.

(*c*) by freeing slaves, we are honouring the concept of freedom.

(*d*) by freeing slaves, we are safe - guarding our own interests.

(*e*) None of these

138. The term 'colonisation' as used in the passage means :

(*a*) handing over slaves to the slaveowners.

(*b*) efforts made by American blacks to free themselves.

(*c*) making separate dwelling arrangements for slave - owners.

(*d*) rehabilitation arrangements made for slave - owners.

(*c*) None of these.

139. Which of the following makes Abraham Lincoln a compassionate statesman ?

(*a*) His hesitation in striving for emancipation of American blacks.

(*b*) His efforts to force the American blacks from slavery.

(*c*) His indifference in conducting the American Civil War.

(*d*) His efforts to conclude the American Civil War without dignity .

(*e*) None of these.

140. The incidents in the passage prove that Lincoln was :

(*a*) not an administrator.

(*b*) sympathetic and kind - hearted statesman.

(*c*) afraid of the majority of slaves.

(*d*) unduly concerned for the safety of rebels.

(e) unreasonably in favour of slaves.

141. According to Lincoln, the culprits of the system of slavery were :

(a) the slave - owners alone.
(b) the slaves alone
(c) both the slaves and the slave - owners.
(d) all the people in the country.
(e) unreasonably in favour of slaves.

142. The author of the passage seems to be :

(a) impressed with Lincoln's good qualities.
(b) an advocate of the system of slavery.
(c) an opponent of the system of slavery.
(d) a staunch and biased critic of Abraham Lincoln.
(e) indifferent to Lincoln's remarkable achievements.

143. Lincoln did not have any hatred for the slave-owners because.

(a) they were in a vast majority.
(b) they were not quility at all.
(c) they all belonged to upper caste.
(d) they would bave treated him with malice.
(e) None of these.

144. which of the following statements is true in the context of the passage ?

(a) Lincoln turned down the demand of the prosecution of rebels.
(b) Lincoln wondered how mere compassion could lead to harmony.
(c) Lincoln hailed the demand of hanging Jefferson Davies.
(d) The Civil War was fought by the Northerners and Southerners against the enemies.
(e) None of these.

145. Lincoln's reply to the Northerner's question regarding the treatment to southerners proves that :

(a) The Northerners were in favour of the southerners.
(b) Lincoln did not like the southerner's act of breaking away from the Union with the North.
(c) Lincoln did not have revengeful attitude towards the southerners.
(d) the southerners were wicked in their dealings.
(e) Lincoln could control his anguish against the southerners while expressing himself.

Directions (Questions 146 to 148) : Choose the word which is most nearly the same in meaning as the word or group of words given in bold as used in the passage.

146. PERPETUATING :

(a) destroying (b) aggravating
(c) pioneering (d) criticising
(e) continuing

147. REVULSION :

(a) avenge (b) violence
(c) feelings (d) disgust
(e) apathy

148. SUBDUED :

(a) conquered (b) entangled
(c) submerged (d) overwhelmed
(e) drowned

Directions (Questions 149 to 150) : Choose the word which is most opposite in meaning of the word or group of words given in bold as used in the passage.

149. COMPASSIONATE :

(a) unlawful (b) indecisive
(c) untrustworthy (d) unsympathetic
(e) humanistic

150. GRADUAL :

(a) rapid (b) dynamic
(c) energetic (d) unscruplous
(e) enthusiastic

Directions (Questions 151 to 155) : Read the following passage carefully and answer the questions given below.

As a result of economic liberalization and entry of a large number of multinational companies into India, the life of most middle class and upper middle class people in the last two decades of the present century has been characterized by artificiality in dress, manners and conversation and elaborate surface of formality and grace covering a certain amount of vice and a great deal of plain silliness.

151. The period discussed in the sentence is

(a) from 1981 to 1990 A.D.
(b) from 1981 to 2000 A.D.
(c) from 1990 to 2000 A.D.
(d) from 1980 to 2000 A.D.
(e) from 1991 to 2000 A.D.

152. The sentence lays emphasis on the fact

that the economic liberalization has

(*a*) raised the standard of living of the middle and upper middle class people.

(*b*) made people more artificial outwardly, without change in attitude.

(*c*) helped the people dispense with their Vicious behaviour.

(*d*) removed their poverty and raised their quality of life.

(*e*) helped people imbibe good qualities and moral values.

153. It appears that the author of the sentence criticizes economic liberalization for the peoples'

(*a*) lack of formality (*b*) poor mannerism
(*c*) lack of naturalness (*d*) lack of grace
(*e*) articulate conversation.

154. Which of the following is not true about most of the middle and upper middle class people of the period mentioned in the sentence ?

(*a*) They are wicked (*b*) They are formal
(*c*) They are witty (*d*) They are silly
(*e*) They are hypocritical

155. It can be inferred from the sentence that the middle and upper midle class peopvvchhle of the period people lived ....

(*a*) wicked lives
(*b*) conventional lives
(*c*) affluent lives
(*d*) very simple lives (*e*) virtuous lives

Direction (Questions 156 to 200) : Pick out from the words, given below each sentence, the word which would complete the sentence correctly and meaningfully.

156. The ship waited till the storm .... before sailing out to sea.

(*a*) trivialised (*b*) normalised
(*c*) abated (*d*) consolidated
(*e*) evaporated **Bank P.O.1997)**

157. It has always been the .... of the company to prompt existing staff to senior positions.

(*a*) Prerogative (*b*) procedure
(*c*) policy (*d*) decision
(C.D.S 1996)

158. The manager is to help his subordinates .... their potential in their present as well as in their future assignment.

(*a*) dealise (*b*) judge
(*c*) delegate (*d*) train
(*e*) respect

159. It is .... that we should remember him on his birthday.

(*a*) appreciating (b) loving
(*c*) fitting (*d*) advantageous
(*e*) critical

160. Shoppers used to surly clerks behind retail counters elsewhere in china are in for a .... **(M.B.A. 1997)**

(*a*) treat (*b*) shock
(*c*) gift (*d*) none of these

161. The doctor said that a small daily .... of the new drug would soon cure him.

(*a*) quantity (*b*) dose
(*c*) pill (*d*) tablet
(C.D.S. 1997)

162. Lots of people had come to attend his lecture because he is a very .... scholar.

(*a*) imminent (*b*) engaging
(*c*) popular (*d*) eminent

163. All of us must endeavour to .... the miseries of poor.

(*a*) exhibit (*b*) mitigate
(*c*) augment (*d*) discourage
(*e*) elaborate **(Bank P.O.1997)**

164. The non-cooperative attitude of the members can only .... the image of the society.

(*a*) deteriorate (*b*) defame
(*c*) degrade (*d*) improve
(*e*) spoil.

165. He was very angry as usual. However, his angry words .... me.

(*a*) thwarted (*b*) obstructed
(*c*) jolted (*d*) criticised
(*e*) fluttered **(A.O. Exam. 1997)**

166. The spectre that is haunting Western Europe represents both an opportunity and a .... **(C.D.S. 1997)**

(*a*) chance (*b*) challenge
(*c*) scope (*d*) freedom

167. All the respondents should express their .... views in this questionnaire

(*a*) capable (*b*) favourable

(c) candid (d) confident
(e) convenient **(Bank P.O. 1997)**

168. Having .... his prayers the old man slowly lay down on his bed to sleep.
(a) done (b) said
(c) sung (d) told
(C.D.S 1996)

169. His ways of doing things are .... with my thinking and perceptions.
(a) inconsequent (b) inspired
(c) incompatible (d) infatuated
(e) incomprehensible

170. This was dangerous method of .... popular support.
(a) expecting (b) extracting
(c) soliciting (d) securing

171. The chief guest came into the room .... by the chairman of the company.
(a) preceded (b) coupled
(c) joined (d) allowed
(e) watched **(Bank P.O. 1997)**

172. All progress in technology depends on a scientific .... of the way in which nature works, in order that we may make her work for our ends. **(C.D.S. 1996)**
(a) awareness (b) understanding
(c) education (d) consciousness

173. Anatomy and physiology were studied in ancient India and the principle of the .... of blood was suggested long before Harvey. **(C.D.S. 1997)**
(a) flow (c) circulation
(c) progression (d) movement

174. Nobody can .... me to do anything which I do not want to do.
(a) delegate (b) encourage
(c) oppose (d) compel
(e) request

175. I kept on .... at him till I remembered who he was. **(A.O. Exam, 1997)**
(a) dashing (b) aiming
(c) winking (d) peeking
(e) gazing

176. I like to talk to him. He is .... to reason. **(Bank P.O. 1997)**
(a) accountable (b) congenial
(c) accessible (d) conducive
(e) amenable

177. When Mahatma Gandhi visited the Buckingham Palace dressed in his loincloth, there were people who considered him .... **(C.D.S. 1996)**
(a) audacious (b) auspicious
(c) atrocious (d) suspicious

178. When we send a rocket above the ...., we follow the line begun by the invention of the wheel. **(C.D.S 1997)**
(a) atmosphere (b) ether
(c) earth (d) sky

179. What you say may be true but I hold exactly the. .... view of it.
(a) positive (b) analytical
(c) concerned (d) obverse
(e) logical

180. Small company funds have beaten their large company .... every year since 1991. **(M.B.A. 1997)**
(a) sisters (b) brethren
(c) managers (d) friends

181. "Listen to others patiently, even if you do not agree with them": That is a .... piece of advice. **(C.D.S. 1996)**
(a) sensuous (b) sensual
(c) sensitive (d) sensible

182. Lack of money .... me badly in my pursuit of higher education.
(a) directed (b) handicapped
(c) damaged (d) ventured
(e) diverted

183. The two teams were equally matched and appeared to be heading for a draw, and a/an .... was inevitable.
(a) replay (b) abandonment
(c) tie (d) showdown
(C.D.S. 1997)

184. I was filled with .... while hearing my old favourite songs.
(a) credibility (b) creativity
(c) commotion (d) nostalgia
(e) empathy

185. After hearing the .... news I was stunned and terror - stricken.
(a) unpleasant (b) alarming
(c) tragic (d) surprising
(C.D.S 1996)

186. It is .... in pursuit of these very objectives that our Government has made some basic changes in our economic policies.

(a) precisely (b) largely
(c) clearly (d) constantly
(e) greatly

187. .... liquids like juices and butter-milk, cold drinks have no nutritive value.

(a) Like (b) like
(c) unlike (d) Unlike

(M.B.A. 1997)

188. The autocratic boss .... even the few who genuinely supported his policy.

(a) identified (b) scolded
(c) alienated (d) differed from

(C.D.S. 1997)

189. It is sad that I could not .... the situation to my advantage.

(a) manipulate (b) exhibit
(c) fluster (d) culminate
(e) encounter

190. The single largest party decided to .... its claim to form the government.

(a) advance (b) risk
(c) propose (d) stake

(C.D.S 1996)

191. .... of these measures in increasing the agricultural production will be known shortly.

(a) Vitality (b) efficacy
(c) Propensity (d) Sincerity
(e) Advocacy **(A.O.Exam, 1997)**

192. The priest addressed the .... for more than an hour and was listened to with rapt attention. **(C.D.S.1997)**

(a) crew (b) çongregation
(c) audience (d) staff

193. Savita has a taste .... poetry.

(a) for (b) in
(c) on (d) about

(C.D.S. 1996)

194. You could eat your break fast .... the floor. **(M.B.A. 1997)**

(a) from (b) at
(c) off (d) on

195. After the robbery the shop installed a sophisticated alarm system as an insurance .... further losses.

(a) towards (b) against
(c) from (d) for

(C.D.S. 1997)

196. All the employees in the company are entitled reimbursement of medical expenses.

(a) with (b) to (c) on
(d) for (e) of

197. We pondered deeply .... the best course of action to be taken.

(a) about (b) over
(c) upon (d) as to

(C.D.S. 1997)

198. She is................ to be a dancer.

(a) cut out (b) made out
(c) set out (d) carved out

(C.D.S. 1996)

199. The commandos took a long time to ________ the resistance of the rebels.

(a) break down (b) cut down
(c) pull down (d) tone down

(C.D.S. 1997)

200. Information overload in ads is a common problem ______ drug companies marketing their products.

(a) from (b) of
(c) for (d) at

(M.B.A. 1997)

Directions (Questions 201 to 221) : In each of the following sentences there are two blank spaces . Below each sentence there are certain pairs of words denoted by (a) , (b) , (c) , (d) and (e) Find out which pair of words can be filled up in the blanks in the sentence in the same sequence to make the sentence meaningfully complete

201. His .... speach has seriously .... the young minds.

(a) eccentric , questioned
(b) audacious , delighted
(c) irresponsible , misled
(d) maiden , flattered
(e) humarous , dainaged

(Bank P.O.1997)

202. If you do not .... all yur monthly

(a) realise , enhance
(b) economise , exceed
(c) save , outwit
(d) spend , gain

(e) think , swallow

203. After careful .... the thief ....that he has committed the crime . **(B.S.R.B. 1997)**

(a) finding , insisted
(b) action , agreed
(c) consideration , felt
(d) questioning , divulge
(e) investigation , refused

204. Our latest battle plan .... some projects .... at saving the earth's biological diversity.

(a) excludes , arriving
(b) enocompasses , looked
(c) finances , looking
(d) destroys, stirring
(e) covers, aimed **(Bank P.O. 1996)**

205. A meeting of power couples in Delhi made .... some lost ground preceding the visit

(a) up, for (b) up , by
(c) at , for (d) for , up

(M.B.A. 1997)

206. After the present tax holiday period .... , the power cost to users may become .... **(Bank P.O.1997)**

(a) ends, intolerable
(b) enhances , negligible
(c) sets, perishable
(d) starts , unreasonable

207. Workers in earlier days were .... because of which the industries .... a lot .

(a) rich , flourished
(b) inefficient , suffered
(c) honest , lost
(d) idle , praspered
(e) autocrats , developed

208. All the teachers .... that Sunita would stand at the top in the examination , but she .... short of their expectation. **(B.S.R.B. 1997)**

(a) started , reached
(b) dreamt , achieved
(c) presumed , failed
(d) expected , ran
(e) thought ,fell

209. Transforming ....bureaucracies into dynamic, customer - driven or garisations is .... under any circumstances.

(a) inefficient , challenging
(b) ideal ,essential
(c) civilised , ineffective
(d) lazy , undesirable
(e) lethargic ,insurmountable

(Bank P.O.1996)

210. On .... of the enquiry , if it is found that the .... are true , the enquiry officer will report the matter to the higher authority .

(a) withdrawal , inferences
(b) demand , findings
(c) establishment , results
(d) completion , allegations
(e) instituting , charges

(Bank P.O . 1997)

211. The other servants had to .... since Monu alone .... all the food.

(a) eat , cooked
(b) cook , wasted
(c) leave, prepared
(d) wait , spoiled
(e) starve , consumed

212. Sachin has .... some unfinished work to .... up before he can go home . **(B.S.R.B. 1997)**

(a) set , give (b) let , take
(c) still , clear (d) since , come
(e) yet , get .

213. Trying to .... a team without a good and simple ....system is like trying to drive a car without a steering wheel **(Bank P.O.1996)**

(a) run , guidance
(b) form , working
(c) organise , empowering
(d) achieve , developmental
(e) lead , exploratory

214. A good teacher - student relationship helps create a .... and peaceful atmosphere where there is no room for any .... of educational activity .

(a) congenial , development
(b) cordial , education
(c) harmonious , interruption
(d) quiet , confusion
(e) delightful , exaggeration

(Bank P.O.1997)

215. The judge .... him because he was found .... on the basis of the evidence .

(a) pardoned, innocent
(b) suspended , involved
(c) punished , guilty
(d) acquitted , criminal
(e) sentenced , innocent

216. The mining activity comes under the ....of the forest conservation act and we must .... that the law is followed strictly **(B.S.R.B. 1997)**

(a) limits , stipulate
(b) purview , ensure
(c) control , insist
(d) course, observe
(e) debate , see

217. unless the authorities adopt the principle .... the strategies cannot become .... **(Bank P.O.1996)**

(a) forcefully , trivial
(b) legitimately , noteworthy
(c) mechanically , obsolete
(d) fully , defunct
(e) whole - heartedly , successful

218. A close of the bill shows that the provisions are and there is a need to add certain crucial elements to them.

(a) observation , helpful
(b) account , excellent
(c) examination ,sufficient
(d) file , numerous
(e) scruting , inadequate

(Bank P.O. 1997)

219. The speaker's .... over his subject was seen through his .... discourse.

(a) skill , pleasant
(b) grip , boring
(c) lethargy , dull
(c) efficiency , thorough
(e) mastery ,fluent

220. As a .... of Kamal's rude behaviour he was .... a memo by his boss. **(B.S.R.B. 1997)**

(a) reaction , presented
(b) sequel, issued
(c) part , delivered
(d) consequence , given
(e) punishment , rewarded

221. .... members of a group of ten .... influence the outcome of a consensus forecast .

(a) dominant, unduly
(b) permanent , exert
(c) minority , Inadvertently
(d) majority , rightly
(e) vocal , legitimately

(Bank P.O.1996)

Directions : In each of the following passages, there are blanks each of which has been numbered. These numbers are printed below the passage and against each , some words are suggested, one of which fits the blank appropriately . Find out the appropriate words. Questions (222 to 236). **(C.D.S. 1997)**

The most attractive and unique feature of crossword puzzle is that it is a game one can paly alone . There are several kinds of crossword puzzles . One kind is the prize competition in which the 222 who finds the correcrt answer gets a big prize 223 the answers are very hard to find , since several 224 appear equally appropriate : bad , mad or sad , for 225 in the clue sentence, "people are seldom popular " Such 226 attract people who are fond of gambling , because by 227 a small entry fee , they can win big prizes. The 228 type of crossword puzzle is one in which 229 is only one possible answer to every clue. But 230 answer is elusive and calls for some detective work 231 our part. The clue gives only hints about the word . A 232 like ' mate changes to flesh for food ' 233 elude you till you realise that by changing the 234 of ' mate ' you getr ' meat ' your comprehension and your 235 knowledge are put to the test . The effort to 236 such crosswords is an intellectual exercise.

222. (a) persons (b) person (c) actor
223. (a) although (b) though (c) But
224. (a) words (b) letters (c) alphabets
225. (a) illustration (b) assumption , (c) example
226. (a) puzzles (b) competitions (c) races
227. (a) buying (b) paying (c) giving
228. (a) second (b) another (c) two
229. (a) their (b) this (c) there

230. (*a*) this (*b*) an (*c*) any
231. (*a*) in (*b*) on (*c*) upon
232. (*a*) word (*b*) clue (*c*) pazzle
233. (*a*) did (*b*) shall (*c*) will
234. (*a*) words (*b*) spelling (*c*) lettering
235. (*a*) overall (*b*) common sense (*c*) general
236. (*a*) solve (*b*) think of (*c*) dissolve

(Bank P.O. 1996)

Questions 237 to 246

Women have 237 made 238 in the corporate workplace but certainly not as much as they had 239 We have new laws , rules and 240 relating to women in the workplace , but what we have not changed much is the male 241 Women have fallen short in their goals because we 242 the potency of the male need to 243 their power . We can abide 244 by the laws and rules we create in order to 245 women an equal opportunity in the corporate workplace and still not 246 the problems that afflicted and efentually capsized the women's raft.

237. (*a*) perhaps (*b*) seldom (*c*) optimistically (*d*) not (*e*) undoubtedly
238. (*a*) progress (*b*) efforts (*c*) attempts (*d*) decisions (*b*) automation
239. (*a*) predisposed (*b*) prescribed (*c*) expected (*d*) informed (*e*) encompassed
240. (*a*) activities (*b*) cases (*c*) policies (*d*) problems (*e*) revolutions
241. (*a*) hatred (b) patterns (*c*) achievements (*d*) population (*e*) behaviour
242. (a) retaliate (*b*) respect (*c*) risk (*d*) minimisse (*e*) underestimate
243. (*a*) maintain (*b*) know (*c*) absolve (*d*) evolve (*e*) diminish
244. (*a*) partially (*b*) occasionally (*c*) them (*d*) excessively (*e*) scrupulously
245. (*a*) share (*b*) deny (*c*) assure (*d*) donate (*e*) deprive
246. (*a*) overcome (*b*) mentioned (*c*) judge (*d*) explore (*e*) emphasise

Questions 247 to 250 **(Bank P.O. 1997)**

Architecture is a unique 247 of art and science that has 248 out of man's primary need for shelter. It is concerned with the design and 249 of buildings in their sociological, technological and environmental context . This field is not only 250 but also rrovides the 251 of designing and building pleasing and 252 refined struclures to serve various needs. 253 the fairly large number of practising architects , the countrywide 254 in the initial earnings in the field are relatively 255 what you make thereafter will depend enterely on your 256. enterely on your 256.

247. (*a*) prooess (*b*) procedure (*c*) blend (*d*) subject (*e*) portion
248. (*a*) arisen (*b*) earned (*c*) contrived (*d*) fizzled (*e*) drifted
249. (*a*) appearance (*b*) repairing (*c*) decoration (*d*) construction (*e*) painting
250. (*a*) rewarding (*b*) vast (*c*) enocouraging (*d*) strenuous (*e*) fatiguing
251. (*a*) readily (*b*) amenities (*c*) infrastructure (*d*) facility (*e*) satisfaction
252. (*a*) readily (*b*) Principally (*c*) aesthetically (*d*) ideologically (*e*) practically
253. (*a*) Despite (*b*) Regarding (*c*) Assuming (*d*) Having (*e*) considering
254. (*a*) deterioration (*b*) spurt (*c*) lethargy (*d*) slack (*e*) variation
255. (*a*) exorbitant (*b*) negligible (*c*) unpredictable (*d*) modest (*e*) escalating
256. (*a*) need (*b*) experience (*c*) expectation (*d*) appearance (*e*) ambition

Questions 257 to 271 **(C.D.S . 1996)**

It was with pleasant surprise that Swaminathan stumbled into his own set , which he had thought was not at school .except Rajam and Mani all were there . Under the huge tamarind tree they were playing some game Swaminathan joined them with a low , ecstatic cry . The 257 disappointed him . They turned their 258 to him with a faint 259 and returned to their game. What 260 Swaminathatn most was that even the 261 Somu was grim . something seemed to be 262 somewhere . Swaminathan assumed an easy 263 and shouted , " Boys , what about 264 place for me in the 265 ? " Nobody answered this Swaminathan paused and 266 that he was waiting for a 267 in the game . " It is a 268 " There are people who can be very 270 as tails , " said Samuel The 271 laughed at this , " you said tail , didn't you ? " asked Sankar .

257. *(a)* response *(b)* answer *(c)* reply
258. *(a)* heads *(b)* faces *(c)* profiles
259. *(a)* expression *(b)* assessment *(c)* smile
260. *(a)* surprised *(b)* bewildered *(c)* astonished
261. *(a)* sympathetic *(b)* hearty *(c)* genial
262. *(a)* improper *(b)* wrong *(c)* unreasonable
263. *(a)* accent *(b)* modulation *(c)* tone
264. *(a)* a little *(b)* a small *(c)* some
265. *(a)* match *(b)* game *(c)* sport
266. *(a)* announced *(b)* reported *(c)* proclaimed
267. *(a)* situation *(b)* position *(c)* place
268. *(a)* fellow - feeling *(b)* disaster *(c)* pity
269. *(a)* Suddenly *(b)* curtly *(c)* briefly
270. *(a)* efficient *(b)* capable *(c)* skilful
271. *(a)* balance *(b)* remainder *(c)* rest

Questions 272 to 281 **(B.S . R.B.1997)**

Faced with an 272 number and variety of products on the market , managers are finding it more difficult to 273 demand and plan production and orders 274 As a result 275 forecasts are increasing and , along with them , the costs of those errors

Many managers today , 276 speed is the 277 , have turned to one or another popular production scheduling system . But these tools tackle only part of the problem 278 really needed is a way to 279 forecasts and simultaneously redesign planning processes to 280 the impact of 281 forecasts .

272. *(a)* equal *(b)* exact *(c)* eccentric *(d)* unprecedented *(e)* optimum
273. *(a)* register *(b)* accept *(c)* ignore *(d)* predict *(e)* meet
274. *(a)* spontaneously *(b)* positively *(c)* accordingly *(d)* quickly *(e)* immediately
275. *(a)* exorbitant *(b)* inadequate *(c)* frequent *(d)* buoyant *(e)* inaccurate
276. *(a)* notwithstanding *(b)* believing *(c)* visualizing *(d)* neglecting *(e)* consider
277. *(a)* lacuna *(b)* outcome *(c)* source *(d)* answer *(e)* problem
278. *(a)* what's *(b)* That's *(c)* One *(d)* Managers *(e)* companies
279. *(a)* improve *(b)* negate *(c)* Vitiate *(d)* obtain *(e)* ignore
280. *(a)* popular *(b)* counter *(c)* manimize *(d)* substantiate *(e)* dangerous
281. *(a)* popular *(b)* erroneous *(c)* unpredicted *(d)* absolute *(e)* dangerous

Questions 282 to 291 **(Bank P.O.1997)**

Now - a - days , under the 282 system of education , however good it may be , when a young man comes out of the university , there seems to be this 288 in him htat the higher the standard of living rises , the less should a man work . Thus , mathematically , higher the standard of living , according to this misconceived notion, the less the 284 ultimately , what ? should be the highest standard of living then ? 285 work ! This leads to an unhealthy 286 among the workers . A typist who types over twenty letters a day asks his 287 how many letters he had typed that day . The latter 288 " fifteen " . The former thinks , " Tomorrow I should type only fifteen or even 289 This tendency is quite 290 and may ultimately lead to 291 even one's family life may be affected adversely due to such tendency.

282. (a) Extinct (b) proposed (c) developed (d) modern (e) outdated

283. (a) apprehension (b) realisation (c) anxiety (d) worry (e) misconception

284. (a) work (b) time (c) salary (d) energy (e) comfort

285. (a) Ample (b) No (c) Minimum (d) Less (e) Maximum

286. (a) ambition (b) Jealousy (c) delay (d) dispute (e) competition

287. (a) colleague (b) client (c) boss (d) subordinate (e) employee

288. (a) remembers (b) types (c) suggests (d) replies (e) does

289. (a) more (b) all (c) less (d) some (e) few

290. (a) unnatural (b) unfortunates (c) healthy (d) heartening (e) discouraging

291. (a) retardation (b) denial (c) evil (d) complexity (e) progress

Questions 292 to 301

In view of the 292 demand for personnel with commerce background, in the post - liberalisation period, cousses in commerce have 293 the attention of students and parents. There is growing 294 for these courses not only in schools but also in colleges. But the 295 of commerce education in schools leaves 296 to be desired. Its po;ularity, importance and quality, to a large extent, depends much on the teaching methodology being 297 in schools. Of coourse, the 298 review and 299 of syllabi also 300. But this aspect is 301 taken care fo suitably, by the concerned organisations

292. (a) diminishing (b) exaggerated (c) increasing (d) teemendous (b) unreasonable

293. (a) attracted (b) ameliorated (c) distorted (d) encouraged (e) weighed

294. (a) commotion (b) contempt (c) demand (d) dissatisfaction (e) urgency

295. (a) awareness (b) quality (c) intricacy (d) necessity (e) status

296. (a) every thing (b) much (c) nothing (d) scope (e) short

297. (a) abandoned (b) assimilated (c) contemplated (d) practised (e) taught

298. (a) expert (b) general (c) partial (d) periodical (e) unserupulous

299. (a) formulation (b) discussions (c) perusal (d) reduction (e) updating

300. (a) desires (b) encompasses (c) flourishes (d) matter (e) needs

301. (a) being (b) duly (c) never (d) often (e) seldom

Directions : In each of the following questions, an incomplete stem of sentence is given. It is folowed by five parts of sentence labelled as (a), (b), (c), (d), and (e) to complete the incomplet stem. Pick out the most appropriate part to complete the sentence meaningfull. **(B.S.R.B. 1997)**

Questions 302 to 306 302 It is not easy to remain tranquil when those around you ....

(a) exhibit generous and magnanimous gestures
(b) agree to whatever you say
(c) are losing their heads
(d) exhibit pleasant mannerism
(e) hehave in a socially acceptable manner

303. The officer who had neglected to file his income tax returns had to ....
(a) give warning (b) play mischief
(c) be rewarded (d) pay a fine
(e) return the files

303. Although initial investigations pointed towards him ....
(a) he gave an open confession of his crime
(b) the subsequent events proved that he was innocent
(c) the subsequent events established that he was guilty
(d) the additional information confirmed his guilt

(e) the preceding events corroborated his involvement in the crime .

305. The employer appeared to be in such an affabel mood that Rahul ....

(a) was painted to press his demand for a new flat

(b) promised him that he would not commit mistake again

(c) felt very guilty for his inadverteent slip

(d) was scared to talk to him about his leave

(e) decided to ask for a raise in his salary

306. Since it is already midnight. we ....

(a) might as well as - leave

(b) ought to have leave

(c) must have been leave

(d) should take our leave

(e) had better leaving

Questions 307 to 311 (Bank P.O.1997)

307. Even though it is a very large house, ...

(a) the servants take long time to clean it

(b) there is a lot of space abailable in it for children

(c) the municipal taxes on it are very heavy

(d) there is hardly any space available for children

(e) there is no dearth of space for children

308. The weather outside was extremely pleasant and hence we decided to...........

(a) refrain from going out for a morning walk

(b) employ this rare opportunity for writing letters

(c) utilise our time in watching the television

(d) remain seated in our rooms in the bungalow

(e) enjoy a morning ride in the open

309. Despite his best efforts to conceal his anger ....

(a) people came to know that he was annoyed

(b) he could succeed in doing it easily

(c) we could detect that he was very happy

(d) he succeeded in camouflaging his emotions

(e) he failed to give us an impression of his agony

310. Practically , very little work could be completed in the last week as it was ....

(a) loaded with work

(b) a very busy week

(c) full of holidays

(d) a very hectic week

(e) full of working days

311. His appearance is unsmiling but ....

(a) he is uncompromising on matters of task performance

(b) his heart is full of compassion for others

(c) he is full of jealousy towards his colleagues

(d) people are abraid of him

(e) he looks very serious on most occasions

Questions 312 to 316 **(Bank P.O . 1996)**

312. His behaviour is so unpredictable that he ....

(a) seldom trusts others as far as the work scheduls is concerned

(b) always insists on getting the work completed on time

(c) always finds it difficult to keep his word

(d) is seldom trusted by others

(e) never depends upon others for getting his work done

313. Owing to the acute power shortage , the people of our locality have decided to ....

(a) resort to use of electrical only when it is enevitable

(b) explore other avenues for utilising the excess power

(c) off - switch the electrical appliamce wjem mpt om ise

(d) resort to abundant use of electricity for illumination

(e) dispense with other non conventional energyh sources

314. In order to help the company attain its goal of enhacing profit, all the employees ....

(a) decided to enhance production at the cost of quality of the product

(b) voluntarily offered to render additional services in lieu of nothing

(c) Voluntarily offered to work overtime with lucrative compensation

(d) appealed the management to implement new welfare schemes

(e) urged the management to grant paid leave

315. Because he believes in democratic principles , he always

(a) listens to others views and enforces his own

(b) imposes his own views on others

(c) decides all the matters himself

(d) reconciles with the majority's views and gives us his own

(e) shows respect to others opinions if they match his own

316. She never visits any zoo because she is a strong opponent of the idea of ....

(a) holding the animals in captivity for our joy

(b) going out of the house on a holiday

(c) watching the animals in their natural abode

(d) feeding the animals while others are watching

(e) setting the animals free into the forest

Direction (Question 317 to321) : In each question , a group of 3-4 sentences , which constitute a small paragraph to elaborate an idea, is given , with one / two of the middle sentences suppressed . Below it are given three pŏssible fillers A , B and C . One of them or more than one or none may meaningfull fill up the gap of the suppressed sentence (s) and thus completes the paragaph cogently . Find out which one , two or more of these sentence can fill up the gap to meaningfully complete the paragraph and choose your answer from (a) ,(b) , (c) , or (e) as per the description given . **(Bank P.O. 1997)**

317. As for airline maintenance procedures , they are . rigorous ( ) . Major overhauls are done every year.

(A) They involve daily checks of planes .

(B) All minor problems are immediately corrected .

(C) Due to urgency or want of spare aircraft , certain problems though detected are overlooked.

(a) Only (A) (b) and (B) (c) Only (B) (d) Only (C) Al l the three

318. Perception of people assumes great importance ( ) . Therefore, sometimes perception assumes even greater importance than reality itself.

(A) We should be fair and impartial in our dealings with others.

(B) Being fair and impartial in our dealings with others in necessary but not sufficient.

(C) But we should also be perceived so by others .

(a) only (A) & (B) or (B) & (C) (b) only (A) & (C)

(c) Only (A) & (C) or (B) & (C) (d) Only (B) & (C)

(e) All the three

319. Photography is a very expensive hobby . ( ) therefore. it is obvious that the satisfaction derived out of such a hobby is much more than anything else .

(A) People with low income cannot aafford to nurture this hobby .

(B) But hobbies are , after all hobbies and there can't be any compromise .

(C) I know some people who prefer even to starfe rather than giving up this hobby .

(a) only (A)& (B) only (A)& (C) (c)only (B) & (C) (d)only (C) (c) All the there

320. The admiration for those who fight against corruption in high places has always been very spontaneous amongst the ardinary people in India. ( ). It has been one of the bulwarks which has helped in a big way to save democracy.

(A) People who make sacrifices on principles and moral issues. are always held in high esteem.

(B) People recegnise their act in verbose speeches but , in spirit they condemn those who expose public servants.

(C) They unhsitantly appreciate such acts but are afraid of openly doing so for fear of the high - ups .

(a) Only *(A)* . *(b)* Both *(A)* & (B)
(c) Only *(B)* *(d)* Both *(B)* & *(C)*
(e) Only (C)

321. The interrogation lasted for about nine full days . ( ) The judge Observed that he was impressed with the outcome as the matter had become very clear.

(A) hardly anything worth the name came out of such a marathon interrogation.

(B) The prosucution lawyer had relentlessly applied all.

(C) The accused broke down and ultimately admitted that he had committed the crime

(a) Only *(A)* & *(B)* *(b)* only *(A)* & *(C)*
(c) only *(B)* & *(C)* *(d)* All the three
(e) Nane of these

Directions Qs 322 to 367 : Read each sentence to find out whether there is any error in it . The error , if any , will be in one part of the sentense . The letter indicating that part is the answer . If there is no error, the answer is (e)

322. Why come people don't get *(a)* / what they deserve *(b)* / and why others get what they don't deserve *(c)* / is a matter decided by luck. *(d)* / No error *(e)*

(Bank P.O. 1997)

323. The committee is thankful to Mr. Roy *(a)* / for preparing not only the main report *(b)* / but also for preparing *(c)* the agenda notes and minutes . *(d)* / No error *(e)*

324. By the time *(a)* / she finished typing *(b)* / it was not hardly ten . *(c)* / No error *(d)*

(C.D.S. 1997)

325. In order to save petrol , (a) / motorists must have to *(b)* / be very cautious (c) / while driving along the highways. *(d)* / No error *(e)*

326. No country can long endure *(a)* / if its foundations *(b)* / were not laid deep *(c)* / in the material prosperity . *(d)* / No error *(e)* **(Bank P.O.1997)**

327. Due to certain inevitable circumstances *(a)* / the scheduled programme had to be *(b)* / post poned indefinite *(c)* / but the members could not be informed . *(d)* / No error *(e)*

328. All three products help wean smokers *(a)* / from cigarettes by providing small doses *(b)* / of nicotine designed to replace the basic level *(c)* / of average smoker's day's nicotine consumption . *(d)* No error *(e)*

(M.B.A. 1997)

329. The main lesson is that *(a)* / the mosquito eradication campaigns *(b)* / such as the one the French conducted *(c)* / needs to be followed up . (d) / No error *(e)*

330. By arresting the local criminals *(a)* / and encouraging good people , *(b)* / we can end *(c)* / hostilities of that area *(d)* / No error *(e)*

(B.S.R.B.1997)

331. We admired thre way*(a)* / he had completed all his work *(b)* / and appreciation the method *(c)* / adopted by him . *(d)* / No error **(Bank P.O.1997)**

332. I was being astonished *(a)* / when I heard that *(b)* / he had left the country *(c)* / without informing anyone of us . *(d)* / No. error *(e)*

333. They decided to arrange a grand party on the eve of her retirement *(a)* / especially as she had been working for th firm *(b)* / since almost twenty years. *(c)* / No.error *(d)*

334. The Head of the Department , along with his colleagues *(a)* / are coming to attend *(b)* / the conference which is *(c)* / scheduled this afternoon. *(d)* / No error *(e)*

335. Govind loved his Guru immensely *(a)* / and gave him fullest loyalty , *(b)* / yet he had his own *(c)* / independent way of thinking *(d)* / No error *(e)*

(Bank P.O. 1997)

336. In a very harsh tone , *(a)* / he shouted at his servants *(b)* / and told them that *(c)* / he does not need their services *(d)* / No error *(e)*

337. This is an important difference in *(a)* / that it marks the first move towards *(b)* / an institution for money - earning

proposition . (d) / No error (e)
(M.B.A 1997)

338. Rahul is so rich that *(a)* / he is having four bungalows in Delhi *(b)* / and two in Bombay . *(c)* / No error *(d)*

339. The ultimate problem of physies (a) ./ is to reduce matter by analysis *(b)* / to its lowest condition of divisibility *(c)* / No.error *(d)* **(C.D.S. 1997)**

340. Inwas astonished *(a)* / to find that I scarcely had *(b)* / enough money *(c)* / to pay the bills . *(d)* / No error *(e)*

341. We can not handle *(a)* / this complicated case to day *(b)* / unless full details are not given *(c)* / to us by now . *(d)* / No error *(e)* **(Bank P.O. 1997)**

342. Even after worked in the office *(a)* / for as many as fifteen years, *(b)* / he still does not understand *(c)* / the basic objectives of the work . *(d)* / No error (e)
(Bank P.O. 1997)

243. He was the one student (a) / whom we all expected *(b)* /would get the national scholarship . *(c)* / No error *(d)*

344 . Earlier this year , *(a)* / constantine had entered the news via a video - taped interview *(b)* / telecasted by a commercial television channel *(c)* / No error (d)
(C.D.S. 1997)

345. Neither the earthquake *(a)* / nor the subsequent fire (b) / was able to dampen *(c)* / the spirit of the residents, (d) / No error *(e)* **(B.S.R.B. 1997)**

346. Our school is making *(a)* / every possible effort *(b)* / to provide best facilities *(c)* / land person attention for each child *(d)* / No error *(e)*

347. Our neighbours had repeated (a) / the same illogical sequence of activites (b) / if we had not brought the *(c)* /facts to their notice. (d) / No error *(e)*

348. This has forced them to focus at *(a)* / how to reach and serve their customers, *(b)* / rather than , say , pumping money *(c)* / into fancy graphics that look good in management meetings . *(d)* / No error *(e)*
(M.B.A. 1997)

349. The loss of forests thus entail *(a)* / large social and economic costs ; *(b)* the lives of more than one billion people *(c)* / are already affected by loss of this forest cover *(d)* / No error (e)

350. From the plane *(a)* / the houses looked like as if *(b)* / they were toy houses . *(c)* / No error *(d)* **(C.D.S 1997)**

351. Not one of the children *(a)* / has ever sang *(b)* / on any occasion *(c)* / in public before. *(d)* / No error *(e)* **(B.S.R.B. 1997)**

352. Reasonable ambition , if supported *(a)* / at persistent efforts , *(b)* / is likely to yield (c) / the desied results . *(d)* / No error *(e)* **(Bank P.O.1997)**

353. I would have lost *(a)* / my luggage and other belonging *(b)* / if I would have left the compartment *(c)* / and gone out to fetch drinking water. *(d)* / No errro *(e)*

354. Whether this happens , and whether the BIFR will *(a)* / once again reconsider the Sirmour package *(b)* / are questions those will be *(c)* / answered in the comming months . *(d)* / No error *(e)* **(M.B.A 1997)**

355. The extraordinary ability of the satellites to see , listen and communicate (a) / has made them integral with modern warfare (b)/ and nuclear war strategies in particular . *(c)* / No error *(d)*
(C.D.S. 1997)

356. We now look forward for *(a)* / some great achievements *(b)* / which to some extent *(c)* / can restore the country's prestige once again *(d)* / No error *(e)*

357. Honesty and integrity are *(a)* / the qualityes which cannot be *(b)* / done away with *(c)* / and hence assume a lot of importance *(d)* / No error *(e)*

358. The foreign funds are cheaper than those *(a)* / available the domestic market and *(b)* / the company is competent that *(c)* / it will soon touch its earlier annual turnover, *(d)* / No error *(e)*(**M.B.A. 1997)**

359. He asked me *(a)* / if I am ill *(b)* / and I answered that I was not *(c)* / No error *(d)*
(D.D.S . 1997)

360. Honesty , integrity and being intelligent *(a)* / are the qualities which *(b)* / we look for when *(c)* / we interview applicants *(d)* / No error *(e)*

361. Not only the judges acquitted *(a)* / him of all the charges *(b)* / levelled against him, but *(c)* / also commended all his actions . (d) / No error (e) **(Bank P.O. 1997)**

362. Thinking that he has finally found *(a)* / someone with similar interest, *(b)* / the scholar tried to strike up a conversation. *(c)*/ No error (d) **(C.D.S. 1997)**

363. One of the most effective *(a)* / solutions is that *(b)* / she should work on Sunday *(c)* / and complete the assignment . *(d)* / No error *(e)*

364. Our system of assigning *(a)* / different jobs to different people *(b)* / should be based on (c) / their strengths and weaknesses *(d)* / No error (e)

365. There he stood on the dais , *(a)* / debunked the manner in which the company was run (b) / by the former chairman and managing director , (c) / and promising higher growth and industry . *(d)* No error *(e)*

366. If you permit me to speak the truth , (a) / I shall say without hesitation *(b)* / that you have done a mistake *(c)* / No erroe *(d)*

367. If he by - stander had not been *(a)* / familiar with first - aid techniques , (b) / the driver which had met *(c)* / with the accident would have died *(d)* / No error *(e)*

Directions (Questions 368 to 416 : In each of the following questions , find out which of the phrases given below each sentence should replace the phrase printed in bold type to make the sentence grammatically correct ?If the sentence is correct as it is , mark ' No improvement ' or ' No correction required as the answer .

368. Earlier, I would not have accepted it.
(a) In case I would have
(b) Had I
(c) Had I been
(d) If I have had
(e) No correction required
(Bank P.O. 1996)

369. Can't you never understand what has been said ?
(a) ever understand
(b) rather understand
(c) at all understand
(d) No improvement **(C.D.S. 1997)**

370. By such time you finish that chapter, I will write a letter .
(a) By that time (b) The time
(c) By the time *(d)* The time when
(e) No correction required

371. The erime ahs growth repidly in Russia since the disintegration of the communist system. **(B.S.R.B 1997)**
(a) crime has grown rapid
(b) rapid crime has grown
(c) crimes have been rapidly grown
(d) crimes grow rapidly
(e) no correction required

372. His wife awoke him because he forgot to set his alarm before he went to bed
(a) had awakened ham because he forgot to set his alarm before he went .
(b) awoke him because he had forgotten to set his alarm before he went .
(c) awoke him because he forgot to set his alarm before he had gone
(d) had awakened him because he forgot to set his alarm before he had gone.
(e) nocorrection required

373. Be sure to contact with as many teachers as possible.
(a) contact to *(b)* contact on
(c) contact *(d)* No improvement

374. Though we have kept in mind to try and maintain most facilities , we would like to request you to kindly bear with us any inconvenience that may be caused.
(a) have kept in mind trying and maintain
(b) should bave kept in mind to try and to maintain
(c) must keep mind to try and maintain
(d) would keep in mind to try and maintain
(e) No correction required

375. They examined both the samples very carefully but failed to detect any difference in them . **(Bank P.O.1997)**
(a) any difference among
(b) some difference in
(c) any difference between
(d) some difference between *(e)* No correction required

376. It started to rain while we played tennis.
(a) had been playing
(b) were playing
(c) had played

(*c*) No improvement

377. Nearly everyone suffers when unemployment rises . **(C.D.S . 1997)**

(*a*) Nearly each one
(*b*) everyone nearly
(*c*) Nearly all
(*d*) No improvement

378. Their earnings are such that they find it difficult to make both ends to meet.

(*a*) to make both ends for meeting
(*b*) for making both the ends meet
(*c*) to making both the ends meet
(*d*) to make both ends meet
(*e*) No correction required

379. He confidently asked the crowd if they thought he was right and the crowd shouted that they did. **(Bank P.O. 1996)**

(*a*) htat he didn't
(*b*) that he is
(*c*) that he did
(*d*) that they had
(*e*) No correction required

380. He asked me where was my book.

(*a*) is my book
(*b*) my book is
(*c*) my book was
(*d*) No improvement

381. He admired the speed with which he completed the work and appreciating the method adopted by him .

(*a*) appreciated the adopting method
(*b*) appreciate the method of adoption
(*c*) appreciated the method adopted
(*d*) appreciate the method being adopted
(*e*) No correction required

(Bank P. O. 1997)

382. We can't have a fire here until we have swept the chimney.

(*a*) sweep
(*b*) shall sweep
(*c*) shall have swept
(*d*) No improvement

383. after a six - hour marathon session , the two political parties are united together.

(*a*) joined (*b*) together
(*c*) united (*d*) No improvement

(C.D.S . 1997)

384. The moment the manager came to know of the fraudulent action of his assistant, he order immediately dismissed him. **(Bank P.O. 1996)**

(*a*) ordered for immediately dismissal him
(*b*) immediately order dismissal of his
(*c*) ordered his immediately dismissal
(*d*) immediately ordered his dismissed
(*e*) No correction required

385. Anyone interested in the use of computers can learn much if you have access to a personal computer.

(*a*) access can be available
(*b*) they have access
(*c*) one of them have access
(*d*) he or she has access
(*e*) No correction required

386. Technology must use to feed the forces of change . **(B.S.R.B. 1997)**

(*a*) they be using to feed
(*b*) must use having fed
(*c*) must have been using to feed
(*d*) must be used to feed
(*e*) No correction requied

387. Despite of their difference on matters of priciples, they all agree on the demand of hiks in salary .

(*a*) Despite of the
(*b*) Despite their
(*c*) Despite off their
(*d*) Despitte for their
(*e*) No correction required

388. The limestone formations suggest that in the distant past . the area was a vast sea filled with creatures that absorb calcium compounds from the water.

(*a*) had absorbed
(*b*) absorbs
(*c*) absorbed
(*d*) No improvement **(C .D.S. 1997)**

389. The man who has committed such a serious crime must get the mostly severe punishment . **(Bank P.O. 1996)**

(*a*) hae been getting the severemost
(*b*) have got the most severely
(*c*) get the most severe
(*d*) be be getting the mostly severely
(*e*) No correction required

390. This is the first time in my memory tha the river has overflown the banks.

(*a*) overflowed
(*b*) overflew
(*c*) has overflowed
(*d*) No improvement

391. He never has and ever will take such strong measures **(Bank P.O. 1997)**
(*a*) had and ever will take
(*b*) has and never will take
(*c*) had taken and will ever take
(*d*) had taken nor wil ever take
(*e*) No correction required

392. By this time ext year Rohit will take his university degree.
(*a*) would take
(*b*) will heve taken
(*c*) will have been taking
(*d*) No improvement

393. If you wrote to me earlier, I would have easily solved your problem
(*a*) had written
(*b*) were writing
(*c*) have written
(*d*) No improvement **(C.D.S 1997)**

394. The tea - estate adiministration is in such mess there is no leader to set the things right. **(Bank P.O.1996)**
(*a*) with such a mess that there
(*b*) in such a mess that there
(*c*) in a such mess that here
(*d*) in such a mess here
(*e*) no correction required

395. My doctor knew that I would eventually recover and do the kind of work I would be doing before.
(*a*) had been done
(*b*) would have been doing
(*c*) had been doing
(*d*) would have done
(*e*) No correction required

396. They should have calmly thought of, the advantages that would accrue to them.
(*a*) should have calmly think of
(*b*) should have to calmly thought of
(*c*) should have to calmly thought of
(*d*) should have been calm in thinking about
(*e*) No correction required

397. Being given to understand that there is a vacancy of an assistant in the firm, an application was submitted by me
(*a*) I submitted an application
(*b*) an application has been submitted by myself
(*c*) an application by me was submitted
(*d*) No improvement **(C.D.S 1997)**

398. Acquisition of certain specific skills can be facilitated from general awareness, education and exposure to novel situations.
(*a*) can be facilitated by
(*b*) may facilitete through
(*c*) can be felicitated with
(*d*) may be felicitated with
(*e*) No correction required

399. Sheela is waiting for her since morning
(*a*) was waiting
(*b*) would be waiting
(*c*) has been waiting
(*d*) No emprovement

400. The population of Tokyo is greater than that of any other town in the world.
(*a*) greater than all other
(*b*) greatest among any other
(*c*) greater than any other
(*d*) greater than those of any other
(*e*) No correction required
(Bank P.O. 1997)

401. The chemist hadn't hardly any of those kind of medicines
(*a*) had hardly any of those kind
(*b*) had scarcely any of those kind
(*c*) had hardly not any of those kinds
(*d*) had hardly any of those kinds
(*e*) No correction required

402. If you are thinking about investigation overseas, inn't it makes sense to find an experienced guide? **(B.S.R.B. 1997)**
(*a*) is it making
(*b*) does it make
(*c*) is it not making
(*d*) doesn't it make
(*e*) No correction required

403. The judge asked the miser if the bag he Lost contained one hundred and ten pounds.
(*a*) the bag he has lost was containing
(*b*) the bag he lost was containing
(*c*) the bag he had lost contains

(d) the gag he had lost contained
(e) No correction required

404. She drives her car at eighty miles each hour. **(C.D.S 1997)**
(a) an hour (b) hourly
(c) every hour (d) No improvement

405. We met him immediately after the session in which he had been given a nice speech . **(Bank P.O.1996)**
(a) had given
(b) will have given
(c) has been given
(d) would be giving
(e) No correction required

406. The courts are actively to saveguard the interests and the rights of the poor .
(a) are actively in safeguarding
(b) have to active in safeguarding
(c) have been actively safeguarding
(d) are actively to safeguarding
(e) No correction required

407. I gave my niece a children's very colourfully illustrated encyclopaedia .
(a) an issustrated child's very colourful encyclopaedia
(b) a very colourfully illustrated children's encyclopaedia
(c) a child's very colourfully illustrated encyclopaedia
(d) No improvement **(C.D.S. 1997)**

408. The research study is an eye - opener and attempts to acquaint us with the problems of the poor nations .
(a) attempt to acquaint
(b) attempting to acquaint
(c) attempted to acquaint
(d) attempts at acquainting
(e) (No correction required
(Bank P.O. 1996)

409. Suddenly she became conscious regarding the presence of a stranger in the room .
(a) over (b) of
(c) about (d) No improvement

410. Tax evaders should heavily fined as they do it intentionally .
(a) should have heavily fined
(b) should be heavy fined
(c) should be heavily fined
(d) should have heavy fine
(e) No correction required
(Bank P.O. 1997)

411. What I learned is that freedom is really the result of how you will remove abstacles. **(C.D.S 1997)**
(a) you remove
(b) you would remove
(c) you can remove
(d) No improvement

412. The drama had many scenes which were so humorous that it was hardly possible to keep a straight face. **(Bank P.O. 1996)**
(a) hardly possible keeping
(b) hardly impossible to keep
(c) hardly impossible keeping
(d) hardly possible for keeping
(e) No correction required

413. Had I realised how close I was to the edge of the valley , I would not have carried the bags there.
(a) Had I had realised
(b) when realised
(c) If I would have realised
(d) Had I been realised
(e) No correction required

414. In addition to enhanced their reputations through strategic use of philanthropy, companies are sponsoring social initiatives to open new markets.
(a) to have their reputation enhancing
(b) to enhancing their reputation
(c) to having enhance their reputation
(d) of enhancing their reputations
(e) No correction required
(B.S.R.B. 1997)

415. He is a singer of repute , but his yesterday's
(a) yesterday performance was
(b) yesterday performance were
(c) performances for yesterday were
(d) performances about yesterday were
(e) No correction required

416. I hope it will not rain when they have started their journey .
(a) they will start their journey
(b) they start their journey
(c) they will have started their journey
(d) No improvement **(C.D.S. 1997)**

Diredtions (Questions 417 to 425) : Some proverbs / idioms are given below together with their meanings choose the correct meaning of the proverb / idiom If there is no correct meaning given, then the answer ' None o fthese",

417. A black sheep **(Bank P.O. 1997)**
(*a*) An ugly person
(*b*) An unlucky person
(*b*) A negro
(*c*) A partner who takes no share of the profits
(*e*) None of these

418. To drive home
(*a*) To emphasise
(*b*) To find one's roots
(*c*) Back to original position(*d*) To return to place of rest
(*e*) None of these

419. To above board **(Bank P.O. 1997)**
(*a*) To have no debts
(*b*) To have a good height
(*c*) To be honest
(*d*) To be honest in any business deal
(*e*) None of these

420. To pick holes
(*a*) To cut some part of an item
(*b*) To criticise Someone
(*c*) To destroy something
(*d*) To find some reason to quarrel
(*e*) None of these

421. To smell a rat **(Bank P.O. 1997)**
(*a*) To be in a bad mood
(*b*) To suspect foul dealings
(*c*) To get bad smell of a dead rat
(*d*) To see signs of plague epidemic
(*e*) None of these

422. To beg the question
(*a*) To be discussed
(*b*) To raise objections
(*c*) To take for granted
(*d*) To refer to
(*e*) None of these

423. To have an axe to grind
(*a*) To work for both sides
(*b*) To have no result
(*c*) A private end to serve
(*d*) To fail to arouse interest
(*e*) None of these **(Bank P.O.1997)**

424. To keep one's temper
(*a*) To be aloof from
(*b*) To preserve one's energy
(*c*) To be in good mood
(*d*) To become angry
(*e*) None of these

425. To catch a tarter **(Bank P.O.1997)**
(*a*) To catch a dangerous person
(*b*) To trap a wanted criminal with great difficulty
(*c*) To dal with a person who is more than one's watch
(*d*) To meet with disaster
(*e*) None of these

Directions (Questions 426 to 431) : In each of the following questions , a sentence followed by four alternative meanings has been given . Every sentence contains an idiom/ phrase . You are to select the alternative meaning which best expresses the meaning of the idiom/ phrase of each of the questions. **(M.B.A. 1997)**

426. Why can't he see the wood for the trees ?
(*a*) to encourage
(*b*) silly person
(*c*) a fool
(*d*) unable to see the main point

427. Ever since I met her , I have been on the horns of a dilemma . .
(*a*) to be very confused
(*b*) of the first quality
(*c*) to have a choice between two equal evils
(*d*) to be very busy

428. I am sure you are not taking a fancy to her charms.
(*a*) becoming fond of
(*b*) falling in a trop
(*c*) dreaming of
(*d*) refusing to see

429. You alone can afford to play ducks and drakes with your family .
(*a*) to save money
(*b*) to squander money
(*c*) to fight back
(*d*) to be on the sky

430. Management schools must keep abreast of the negative developments in management education

(*a*) to be informed about
(*b*) welcome
(*c*) become defensive
(*d*) become hostile

431. Please do not act as a turn - coat , we don't appreciate it
(*a*) a wet coat
(*b*) a multi - purpose person
(*c*) a useful person
(*d*) none of these

Directions : Read each sentence carefully . Four choices are given as (a) , (b) , (c) and (d) for each sentence , You have to choose the one that is closest in meaning to the original sentence.

(B.S.R.B. 19997)

432. You would have won the "Best Paper Award" if you had used transparencies and black board in your presentation.
(*a*) "Best Paper Award is the prestigious one and presentator should ensure to use trans parencies during presentation .
(*b*) Without using transparencies and black board in the presentation it is very difficult to win the award.
(*c*) Using transparencies and black board during presentation is very important .
(*d*) You did not win the award only because you did not use trans-parencies in your presentation
(*e*) None of these .

433. The minister told his secretary that at present , he is not interested in making any announcement which he can't fulfil .
(*a*) The minister told his secretary that he will not make any announcement, at present .
(*b*) At present , making announcement only , is not attracting the minister abserved by secretary .
(*c*) The secretary advised the minister that better avoid making any announcement at present. .
(*d*) The minister told his secretary that at present if he makes announcement he will fulfil it also .
(*e*) None of these

434. Had all the call letters been sent earlier, more candidates would have appeared in the examination.
(*a*) Not many candidates could appear in the examination because call letters were delayed.
(*b*) Call letters were sent earlier , with the hope that all the candidates would appear in the examination .
(*c*) More number of candidates appeared in the examination because call letters were despatched to them .
(*d*) Sincd the call letters were not sent earlier , fewer candidates appeared in the examination .
(*e*) None of these

Directions (Questions 435 to 440) : In each question below , there are two statements which can be combined into a single statement in a number of different ways without changing their meaning. Below them are given three possible starters of such combined sentence . One , two , three or none of them may be correct. Decide upon which is / are eorrect, if any , and answer the questions .

435. Sushil learned all the tricks of the trade. He never could succed in the trade.
(*a*) Sushil's learning all the tricks
(*b*) Having learned all the tricks
(*c*) learning all the tricks
(*d*) only A
(*b*) only B
(*c*) only C
(*d*) only B and C
(*e*) None of these

436. Jagdish studies regularly every day .He has performed well in all the examinations.
(*a*) Doing regularly his study
(*b*) By studying regularly
(*c*) Everyday studying
(*e*) Only A and B
(*b*) Only A and C
(*c*) Only B and C
(*d*) All the three
(*e*) None of these

437. Neeta was very much imppressed with the beauty of the brassware. she purchased 7 good pieces.

(*a*) Impressing with the
(*b*) The brassiware being impressed
(*c*) Impressed with the
(*d*) Only A
(*e*) None of these

438. Dhanraj was ill for last six months . He could not attend to his business.

(a) on account of his illness
(*b*) Attending to his illness
(*c*) Because of his illness
(*d*) only A and B
(*a*) only A and B
(*b*) only A and B
(*c*) All the three
(*d*) only A
(*e*) None of these

439. Dina made all efforts to catch the train He could not catch it.

(*a*) Inspite Dina's train all efforts
(*b*) Despite his all efforts
(*c*) Although to catch train
(*a*) only A
(*b*) only B
(*c*) only A and B
(*a*) only A
(*b*) only B
(*c*) only A and B
(*d*) only A and C
(*e*) All the three

440. The election day passed peacefully. There were few problems at some places

(*a*) Bearing few problems
(*b*) Despite few problems
(*c*) Besides few problems
(*a*) only A
(*b*) only B
(*c*) only C
(*d*) only A and B
(*e*) All the three

ANSWERS

1. (*b*)	2. (*a*)	3. (*c*)	4. (*c*)	5. (*a*)
6. (*d*)	7. (*b*)	8. (*d*)	9. (*a*)	10. (*d*)
11. (*d*)	12. (b)	13. (*b*)	14. (*d*)	15. (*d*)
16. (*d*)	17. (*a*)	18. (*a*)	19. (*c*)	20. (*b*)
21. (*b*)	22. (*d*)	23. (*d*)	24. (*a*)	25. (*d*)
26. (*c*)	27. (*d*)	28. (*c*)	29. (*c*)	30. (*b*)
31. (*c*)	32. (*c*)	33. (*b*)	34. (*a*)	35. (*d*)
36. (*a*)	37 (*d*)	38 (*a*)	39 (*b*)	40 (*c*)
41 (*c*)	42 (*b*)	50 (*a*)	51 (*c*)	52 (*c*)
53 (*b*)	54 (*b*)	55 (*a*)	56 (*d*)	57 (*b*)
58 (*c*)	59 (*c*)	60 (*c*)	61 (*d*)	62 (*c*)
63 (*c*)	64 (*c*)	65 (*d*)	66 (*d*)	67 (*b*)
68 (*a*)	69 (*c*)	70 (*a*)	71 (*c*)	72 (*d*)
73 (*a*)	74 (b)	75 (*d*)	76 (*b*)	77 (*b*)
78 (*e*)	79 (*b*)	80 (*e*)	81 (*c*)	82 (*c*)
83 (*a*)	84 (*b*)	85 (*c*)	86 (*b*)	87 (*d*)
88 (*b*)	89 (*c*)	90 (*a*)	91 (*a*)	92 (*b*)
93 (*d*)	94 (*b*)	95 (*d*)	96 (*a*)	97 (*b*)
98 (*c*)	99 (*c*)	100 (*a*)	101 (*b*)	102 (*d*)
103 (*d*)	104 (*a*)	105 (*e*)	106 (*b*)	107 (*e*)
108 (*a*)	109 (d)	110 (c)	111 (*c*)	112 (*d*)
113 (*d*)	114 (*e*)	115 (a)	116 (*a*)	117 (*a*)
118 (*e*)	119 (*b*)	120 (*d*)	121 (*b*)	122 (*c*)
123 (*b*)	124 (*a*)	125 (*b*)	126 (*c*)	127 (*b*)
128 (*b*)	129 (*a*)	130 (*d*)	131 (*c*)	132 (*a*)
133 (*c*)	134 (*a*)	135 (*d*)	136 (*d*)	137 (*c*)
138 (e)	139 (e)	140 (*b*)	141 (*d*)	142 (*a*)
143 (*e*)	144 (*a*)	145 (*c*)	146 (*e*)	147 (*d*)
148 (*a*)	149 (*e*)	150 (*a*)	151 (*b*)	152 (*b*)
153 (*d*)	154 (*a*)	155 (*c*)	156 (*c*)	157 (*c*)
158 (*a*)	159 (*b*)	160 (*a*)	161 (*b*)	162 (*d*)
163 (*b*)	164 (*e*)	165 (*e*)	166 (*b*)	167 (*c*)
168 (*b*)	169 (*c*)	170 (*c*)	171 (*a*)	172 (*b*)
173 (*b*)	174 (*d*)	175 (*e*)	176 (*e*)	177 (*c*)
178 (*a*)	179 (*d*)	180 (*c*)	181 (*d*)	182 (*d*)
183 (*a*)	184 (*e*)	185 (*c*)	186 (*a*)	187 (*c*)
188 (*b*)	189 (*a*)	190 (*b*)	191 (*b*)	192 (*b*)
193 (*a*)	194 (*d*)	195 (*b*)	196 (*b*)	197 (*b*)
198 (*a*)	199 (*a*)	200 (*b*)	201 (*d*)	202 (*b*)
203 (*d*)	204 (*e*)	205 (*a*)	206 (*e*)	207 (*b*)
208 (*e*)	209 (*a*)	210 (*b*)	211 (*e*)	212 (*c*)
213 (*b*)	214 (a)	215 (*a*)	216 ( )	217 (*e*)
218 (*e*)	219 (e)	220 (*b*)	221 (*a*)	222 (*b*)
223 (*c*)	224 (*a*)	225 (*c*)	226 (*b*)	227 (*b*)
228 (a)	229 (*c*)	230 (*b*)	231 (*b*)	232 (*c*)
233 (*b*)	234 (*b*)	235 (*c*)	236 (*a*)	237 (e)
238 (*a*)	239 (*c*)	240 (*c*)	241 (*e*)	242 (*b*)
243 (*a*)	244 (*d*)	245 (*c*)	246 (*a*)	247 (c)
248 (*a*)	249 (*d*)	250 (*b*)	251 (*c*)	252 (*c*)
253 (*a*)	254 (*b*)	255 (*d*)	256 (*b*)	257 (*a*)
258 (*a*)	259 (*c*)	260 (*a*)	261 (*c*)	262 (*b*)
263 (*c*)	264 (*a*)	265 (*d*)	266 (*c*)	267 (*c*)
268 (*c*)	269 (*b*)	270 (*c*)	271 (*c*)	272 (*d*)
273 (*d*)	274 (c)	275 (*e*)	276 (*b*)	277 (*d*)
278 (*a*)	279 (*a*)	280 (*c*)	281 (*b*)	282 (*d*)

283 (e) 284 (a) 285 (b) 286 (a) 287 (c)
288 (d) 289 (c) 290 (e) 291 (a) 292 (c)
293 (a) 294 (c) 295 (b) 296. (b) 297 (d)
298 (d) 299 (c) 300(d) 301 (e) 302 (c)
303 (d) 304 (b) 305 (c) 306 (a) 307 (d)
308 (e) 309 (a) 310 (c) 311 (d) 312(d)
313(a) 314 (b) 315 (d) 316 (a) 317 (b)
318 (e) 319 (e) 320 (a) 321 (c)

322 (d) Remove ' a matter '
323 (c) : Remove ' for preparing '
324 (c) : Remove ' not'
325 (b) : Either must ' or ' 'have to' alone should be used
326 (c) : Raplace ' were ' by ' are ' .
327 (c) : Replace ' indefinite ' by ' indefinitely '
328 (d) : Replace ' days ' by daily ' .
329 (d) : Replace ' needs ' by ' need
330 (d) : Replace ' of ' by in '
331 (c) : Replace ' appreciating ' by ' appreciated
332 (a) : Remove' being'
333 (c) : Replace 'since' by 'for'
334 (b) : Replace 'are' by 'is'
335 (d) : Remove 'independent'
336 (d) : Replace 'does' by 'did'
337 (d) : Replace 'for' by 'of'
338 (b) : Replace 'is having' by 'has'
339 (e) : no error
340 (c) : Replace 'enough' by 'any'
341 (c) : Remove 'not'
342 (a) : Add 'having' after 'after'
343 (b) : Replace 'whom' by'who'
344 (c) : Replace 'telecasted' by 'telecast'
345 (c) : Replace 'was able to 'by 'could'
346 (d) : Replace 'for' by 'to'
347 (a) : Replace 'had' by 'would have'
348 (c) : Replace 'pumping' by 'pump'
349 (a) : Replace 'ential' by 'entails'
350 (b) : Remove 'like'
351 (b) : Replace 'sang' by 'sung'
352 (b) : Replace 'at' by 'with'
353 (c) : Replace 'would have' by 'had'
354 (c) : Replace 'those' by 'which'
355 (b) : Replace 'with' by 'to'
356 (a) : Replace 'for' by 'two'
357 (d) : Add 'they' before 'assume'
358 (b) : Add 'which are' before 'available'
359 (b) : Replace 'am' by 'was'
360 (a) : Replace 'being intelligent' by 'intelligence'
361 (a) : The correct form is 'The judges not onlyacquitted........'
362 (d) : no error
362 (e) : no error
364 (b) : The correct form is '............. different people diferent jobs..............'
365 (d): Replace 'promising' by 'promissed'.
366 (c): Replace 'done' by 'made'
367 (c): Replace 'which' by 'go'

368 (b) 369 (a) 370 (c) 371 (a) 372 (b)
373 (c) 374 (e) 375 (c) 376 (b) 377 (d)
378 (d) 379 (e) 380 (c) 381 (c) 382 (a)
383 (c) 384 (c) 385 (d) 386 (d) 387 (b)
388 (c) 389 (c) 390 (a) 391 (d) 392 (b)
393 (a) 394 (b) 395 (c) 396 (d) 397 (a)
398 (a) 399 (c) 400 (e) 401 (d) 402 (d)
403 (d) 404 (a) 405 (a) 406 (c) 407 (b)
408 (d) 409 (b) 410 (c) 411 (a) 412 (e)
413 (e) 414 (b) 415 (c) 416 (b) 417 (e)
418 (a) 419 (d) 420 (b) 421 (b) 422 (c)
423 (c) 424 (c) 425 (a) 426 (d) 427 (a)
428 (a) 429 (b) 430 (d) 431 (d) 432 (b)
433 (d) 434 (a) 435 (d) 436 (a) 437 (c)
438 (d) 439 (b) 440 (d)

GUIDES FOR MEDICAL AND ENGINEERING EXAMINATIONS

S. CHAND'S OBJECTIVE BOTANY FOR MEDICAL ENTRANCE EXAMINATIONS

S.R. Singh

The book has been specifically prepared for the students appearing in various medical entrance examinations – AIIMS, CPMT, BHU PMT, DPMT, etc. Problems are mainly based on the points previously asked in various medical entrance examinations. So it is a good Question Bank for the students preparing for medical entrance examinations. For convenient study the questions have been arranged topic-wise.

06 092

ISBN:81-219-1628-3 **pp. 500**

S. CHAND'S OBJECTIVE CHEMISTRY FOR MEDICAL AND ENGINEERING ENTRANCE EXAMINATIONS

H.Kaur

The subject matter in this book has been tailored especially to meet the requirements of aspirants who wish to compete for medical intrance examinations such as AIIMS, CPMT, CBSE, PMT, PMDT, AFMC, BHU, AMU and EAMCET of Andhra Pradesh. This book is also indispensable for engineering competitions like NNR, IIT(JEE), BIT (Ranchi) and NISE etc. The book comprises of five sections. The sections are devoted to Physical Chemistry, Inorganic Chemistry, Organic, Biochemistry and General Chemistry.

06 090

ISBN:81-219-1657-7 **pp. 1152**

BIOLOGY FOR PRE-MEDICAL/ PRE-DENTAL ENTRANCE EXAMINATION

Vinay Kumar

This book has been written keeping in view the needs of students preparing for C.B.S.E., Pre-Medical/ Pre-Dental Entrance Examination. A special feature of this book is that it covers to the entire spectrum of theoretical discussions followed by the wide-ranging solved questions with explanatory notes of leading medical colleges in the country. This book is expected to equip the students with confidence and necessary background which is essential for Pre-Medical Entrance Examination.

06 088

ISBN:81-219-1768-9 **pp. 1088**

PHYSICS FOR IIT AND OTHER ENGINEERING ENTRANCE EXAMINATIONS

Mahesh Jain

This book is written for the students preparing for the Engineering entrance examinations, specially for the IIT-Jee. It is also useful for Civil Services (Prelim), JRF (U.G.C) and other similar competitive examinations. It consists of necessary theoretical concepts and formulas followed by various types of solved questions; objective questions; and advanced numericals problems.

06 102

ISBN:81-219-1798-0

NUMERICAL CHEMISTRY

J.J. Gurtu, R. Kapoor , V.B. Rana & A. Kapoor

This book caters to the needs of students appearing for IIT (JEE), Roorkee, MLNREC, Aligarh, Dhanbad, Ranchi, BHU, CPMT, AFMC, AIIMS, and other engineering and medical entrance examinations. It is intended primanily for self-study by students who wish to develop their skills in chemical calculation to match their mastery of fundamental principles. Various types of questions asked in different engineering examinations and various Boards have been solved with analytical approach which will definitely lead the students to test their basic concepts.

04 169

ISBN:81-219-0409-9 **pp. 864**

EAMCET MATHEMATICS

V. Venkateswara Rao, N. Krishna Murty, B.V.S.S. Sarma, S. Anjaneya Sastry

This is a completely revised book, strictly prepared in accordance with the latest syllabus. It is assumed that the student has already studied and has good grasp of the concept of the syllabus prescribed by the Board of Intermediate Education A.P. Some objective type questions are solved by short-cut methods wherever possible and some by condensing steps. More number of Analytical type questions have been added in every exercise.

ISBN 81-219-1498-1 **PP. 1180**

06 086

S. CHAND'S OBJECTIVE PHYSICS FOR MEDICAL & ENGINEERING ENTRANCE EXAMINATIONS

Mahesh Jain

This book is written for the students preparing for the Medical and Engineering Entrance Examinations of all Indian Universities and institutes. It is also useful for Civil Services (Prelim), J.R.F. (U.G.C.) and other similar competitive examinations. The book has been written in a style which makes it extremely useful for self-study. In the beginning of each chapter all the necessary theoritical concepts and formulas are given and discussed. The book consists of 34 chapters. In addition there is a zero-chapter which gives advice to students on how to study Physics for competitions. In the end, there is an appendix giving useful mathematical formulas.

ISBN 81-219-1530 **pp. 1172**

06 083

OBJECTIVE ZOOLOGY

P.S. Verma & P.C. Srivastava

This book has been specifically prepared for the students apppreaing in various medical entrance examinations–AIIMS, CPMT, BHU PMT, DPMT, etc. Problems are mainly based on the points previously asked in various medical entrance examinations. So it is a good Question Bank for the students preparing for medical entrance examinations. For convenient study the questions have been arranged topic-wise.

ISBN:81-219-1799-9 **In press**

06 087

BOOKS FOR COMPETITIVE EXAMINATIONS

OBJECTIVE GENERAL ENGLISH

R.S. Aggarwal
Monika Aggarwal

The book is meant for candidates appearing for various competitive examinations. The subject matter in this book is comprehensive, rigorous, yet very simple. Even an average student will find no difficulty in understanding the various concepts. The book has been divided into six units, namely Vocabulary Usage, Comprehension Ability, Selecting Phrases/Words, Error Detection, Rearrangement, General Usage. This book surely will lead the readers to success.

06 082 **ISBN 81-219-1531-7** **PP. 664**

S. CHAND'S GENERAL STUDIES

C.S. Bedi & R.S. Aggarwal

This second updated edition of the book presents the subject of General Studies in a clear style that meets the most exacting standards of readability. One of the unique features of the book is that it **discusses** problems, issues, movements, etc., in such a way that it provide intellectual exercise to the reader. It is a valuable book for Central Services (Preliminary) Examination and all other High Grade Competitive examinations.

FEATURES: Part I - General Science • Part II — Indian History and Culture • Part III — Indian Polity and Economy • Part IV - World Geography • Part V - Miscellaneous Information • Part VI - Current Affairs.

06 081 **ISBN:81-219-1496-5** **pp. 1880**

S. CHAND'S GENERAL ENGLISH FOR COMPETITIONS

A.N. Kapoor

This book is meant to equip students preparing for various competitive examinations. The aim of the book is to help students to master the correct use of English words and phrases on one hand and to develop in him/her a sense of belongingness for the English language.

06 093 **ISBN:-81-219-1762-0** **pp. 480**

YOUR INTERVIEW

K.L. Kumar

The book will enable the young job seekers to discover his strengths and weaknesses and inspire him to prepare and face the interview board with courage and confidence. Sample interviews, caricatures and quick-review inset sheets have increased the utility of the book. It is a valuable book for the young job seekers.

06 091 **ISBN:81-219-1618-6** **pp. 144**

ADVANCED OBJECTIVE GENERAL KNOWLEDGE

R.S. Aggarwal

The book comprises of subjective type questions based on Science, History, Indian Polity, Economics, Geography and General Awareness. The salient features of the book are that more than 10,000 multiple choice questions give a vast coverage of all the above subjects; references of the questions asked in various competitive examina-tions, given on memory basis, help to know the type of questions asked in a particular examination; and separate Model Set for rarely available Matching Type questions, the questions on Assertion - Reason and those based on diagrams.

06 068 **ISBN:81-219-1227-X** **pp. 512**

MANI RAM AGGARWAL'S

GENERAL KNOWLEDGE DIGEST AND GENERAL STUDIES

K. Mohan

This book is for the candidates who are appearing for Union and State Public Service Commissions' Competitive Examinations, L.I.C., G.I.C., A.A.O's, RBI Grade A and B, Bank PO's, CDS/NDA/OTA, Delhi Police S.I., Income Tax, Central Excise Inspectors, SSC's Asstt. Grade, L.D.C., Accounts & Auditors, M.BA, Hotel Management, etc., Entrance Examinations. The book is no doubt an appropriate and relevant guide.

06 001 **ISBN:81-219-0798-5** **pp. 788**

R.S. Aggarwal

A MODERN APPROACH TO VERBAL AND NON-VERBAL REASONING

R.S. Aggarwal

This book contains all types of questions asked in various competitive examinations; fully solved examples with explanatory answers; and a huge collection of practisable questions. It is a unique book of Reasoning which is meant for competitive examinations like Bank Clerical, Bank P.O., LIC., GIC, M.B.A., Assistant Grade, Excise and Income Tax, IAS, IFS, AAO, Railways, Hotel Management and others. Question papers and references given on memory basis will lead the students to success.

06 055 **ISBN:81-219-0551-6** **pp. 912**

ARITHMETIC

Subjective & Objective for Competitive Examinations

R.S. Aggarwal

This book is an asset to those who plan to appear in a competitive examination conducted by Banks, LIC, GIC, Excise & Income Tax, Railways, U.P.S.C and other departments for Clerical Grade, Assistant Grade, A.A.O., Inspectors, Probationary Officers, N.D.A. C.D.S., MBA, C.A.T. and other executive posts. The book carries both subjective and objective type of questions.

14 101 **ISBN:81-219-0742-X** **pp. 610**

QUANTITATIVE APTITUDE

(Fully Solved)

R.S. Aggarwal

This revised edition of the book will be an asset to the candidates appearing for Bank P.O., Insurance A.A.O., Assistant Grade; Excise & Income Tax Inspectors; C.B.I. Sub-Inspectors; Teachers' Exam.; C.D.S; Railways; Hotel Management; M.B.A. and all other competitive examinations. It contains a huge accumulation of objective type questions with their solutions by short cut methods. Latest questions asked in various examinations have been added. It is hoped that the book will help the students to get through their competitive exams in flying colours.

06 008 **ISBN:81-219-0632-6** **pp. 592**

A MODERN APPROACH TO VERBAL REASONING

R.S. Aggarwal

The book is unique for its coverage of all types of questions asked including those in logical deduction and all the study material available around. It contains a huge collection of practisable questions with fully solved examplyes and explanatory answers. This book is meant for competitive examinations like Bank Clerical, Bank P.O., LIC, GIC, M.B.A., Assistant Grade, Excise & Income Tax, IAS, IFS, AAO, Railways and others. It is assured that the book will do its deal in making students the masters in this competitive field.

06 053 **ISBN:81-219-0552-4** **pp. 496**

A MODERN APPROACH TO NON-VERBAL REASONING

R.S. Aggarwal

The requirements of the candidates have been a major factor kept in mind during the compilation of this book and with this end in view all types of solved questions with a huge collection of practisable questions have been provided. This book also consists of well illustrated examples and fully solved exercises with explanatory answers and clues. This book is highly meant for the competitive examinations like Bank Clerical, Bank P.O., SBI P.O., R.B.I., L.I.C., G.I.C., A.A.O., M.B.A., I.A.S., I.F.S., Railways, V.D.C., Sub-inspectors of Police, Asstt. Grade, income Tax and Central Excise, etc.

06 054 **ISBN:81-219-0553-2** **pp. 440**

MATHEMATICS FOR C.D.S.
(Fully Solved)

R.S. Aggarwal

Salient features of this book are: (a) Solutions by short-cut methods (b) Large number of challenging problems, fully solved (c) whole lot of solved examples to clarity the facts (d) Latest questions included on memory basis. This book on mathematics is really an asset to those who plan to appear in competitive examination for C.D.S.

06 066 **ISBN:81-219-1019-6** **pp. 700**

MATHEMATICS FOR M.B.A. (Fully Solved)

R.S. Aggarwal

This book is an efficient Guide for the candidates preparing for the M.B.A. entrance examination. The book contains a huge accumulation of objective type questions fully solved by short-cut methods and it is hoped that the subject matter will lead candidates to success.

06 056 **ISBN:81-219-0845-0** **pp. 744**

MATHEMATICS FOR N.D.A. (Fully Solved)

R.S. Aggarwal

This book provides a comprehensive study of all topics included in N.D.A. syllabus. It contains a large number of challenging problems with solutions; a lot of solved examples to clarify the facts; and latest questions included on memory basis. The subject matter of this book is according to the needs of the students and it is hoped that it will creat a confidence among students to successfully clear N.D.A. examination.

06 065 **ISBN:81-219-1018-8** **pp. 712**

A MODERN APPROACH TO LOGIC REASONING

R.S. Aggarwal

This book contains all types of questions asked in various competitive examinations; fully solved examples with explanatory answers; and a huge collection of practisable questions. It is a unique book of Reasoning which is meant for competitive examinations like Bank Clerical, Bank P.O., LIC., GIC, M.B.A., Assistant Grade, Excise and Income Tax, IAS, IFS AAO, Railways, Hotel Management and others. Question papers and references given on memory basis will lead the students to success.

06 104 **ISBN:81-219-1905-3** **pp. 162**

MATHEMATICS FOR M.C.A.

R.S. Aggarwal
Deepak Aggarwal

The salient features of the book are: (i) Strictly according to the syllabi prescribed by various universities for M.C.A. entrance examinations (ii) Separate exercises for objective and descriptive type questions, fully solved (iii) previous year's questions included. The book is expected to prove a sune shot to success in Mathematics for all aspiring candidates for M.C.A. entrance examination.

06 084 **2nd Edn. Rep. 1998** **ISBN:81-219-1482-5** **pp. 320**

अंकगणित (वस्तुनिष्ठ प्रश्नों सहित)

आर.एस. अग्रवाल

हिन्दी भाषी राज्यों की सिविल सेवा परीक्षा, रेलवे सेवा, जीवन बीमा निगम, साधारण बीमा निगम, पुलिस, आयकर, आबकारी, बैंकिंग सेवा, फारेस्ट रेंजर्स, क्लर्कस ग्रेड परीर्क्षा, असिस्टेंट ग्रेड तथा दूसरी प्रतियोगी परीक्षाओं के लिए यह सर्वोत्तम पुस्तक है। सभी परीक्षाओं की आपूर्ति हेतु विषयात्मक तथा वस्तुनिष्ठ प्रश्नों का अपार भंडार इस पुस्तक में निहित है। विभिन्न परीक्षाओं में पूछे गए प्रश्नों के विवरण परीक्षार्थियों से पूछ कर उनकी स्मृति के आधार पर एवं विभिन्न प्रकार की बाज़ार में उपलब्ध मैगजीन आदि से दिए गए हैं।

14 200 **ISBN:81-219-0835-3** **pp. 608**

वस्तुनिष्ठ सामान्य हिन्दी
(Objective General Hindi)

आर.एस. अग्रवाल, मोनिका अग्रवाल

यह पुस्तक उ.प्र. सी.पी.एम.टी., बी.एड. प्रवेश परीक्षा, यू.जी.सी. परीक्षा, असिस्टेंट ग्रेड स्टेनोग्राफर, लेखा-परीक्षक, हिन्दी अनुवादक, पुलिस सब-इन्सपैक्टर, डिप्टी जेलर, सी.बी.आई., बैंक पी.ओ., ग्रामीण बैंक, जीवन बीमा निगम, पी.सी. एस., रेलवे भर्ती बोर्ड परीक्षा, तथा अन्य प्रतियोगी परीक्षाओं के लिए अति-उपयोगी है। इस पुस्तक में विभिन्न प्रतियोगी परीक्षाओं में पूछे गए प्रश्नों के आधार पर पूर्ण सामाग्री समाहित की गई है। आशा है कि इस पुस्तक के अध्ययन से सभी प्रतियोगी परीक्षाओं में सामान्य हिन्दी में सफलता प्राप्त करने में प्रतियोगीयों को कोई कठिनाई नहीं होगी।

06 095 **ISBN:81-219-1753-0** **pp. 392**

संख्यात्मक अभिरुची
(Quantitative Aptitude)

आर.एस. अग्रवाल

यह पुस्तक सिविल सेवा परीक्षा, रेलवे निगम, पुलिस, आयकर, वन्य सेवा, बैकिंग सेवा, क्लर्कस ग्रेड परीक्षा, असिस्टैंट ग्रेड तथा दूसरी प्रतियोगी परीक्षाओं के लिए यह पुस्तक अति-उपयोगी है। सभी परीक्षाओं की आपूर्ति हेतु वास्तुनिष्ठ प्रश्नों का अपार भंडार इस पुस्तक में निहित है। विभिन्न परीक्षाओं में पूछे गए प्रश्नों के विवरण परीक्षार्थियों से पूछ कर उनकी स्मृति के आधार पर एवं विभिन्न प्रकार की बाजार में उपलब्ध मैगजीन आदि से दिए गए हैं।

06 070 **ISBN:81-219-1228-8** **pp. 488**

वस्तुनिष्ट अंकगणित
(पूर्ण हल सहित)

आर.एस. अग्रवाल

प्रस्तुत पुस्तक प्रतियोगी परीक्षाओं के लिए अंकगणित पर आधारित वस्तुनिष्ट प्रश्नों से विहित है। सभी प्रश्नों को संक्षिप्त विधि से हल किया गया है। विभिन्न परीक्षाओं में पूछे गए प्रश्नों का विवरण परीक्षार्थियों से पूछ कर उनकी स्मृति के आधार पर दिया गया है। बाजार में उपलब्ध विभिन्न मैगजीनों के प्रश्न भी दिए गए है

06 033 **ISBN:81-219-0426-9** **pp. 528**

S. CHAND'S OBJECTIVE BOTANY FOR MEDICAL ENTRANCE EXAMINATIONS

S.R. Singh

The book has been specifically prepared for the students appearing in various medical entrance examinations – AIIMS, CPMT, BHU PMT, DPMT, etc. Problems are mainly based on the points previously asked in various medical entrance examinations. So it is a good Question Bank for the students preparing for medical entrance examinations. For convenient study the questions have been arranged topic-wise.

06 092 **ISBN:81-219-1628-3** **pp. 500**

S. CHAND'S OBJECTIVE CHEMISTRY FOR MEDICAL AND ENGINEERING ENTRANCE EXAMINATIONS

H.Kaur

The subject matter in this book has been tailored especially to meet the requirements of aspirants who wish to compete for medical intrance examinations such as AIIMS, CPMT, CBSE, PMT, PMDT, AFMC, BHU, AMU and EAMCET of Andhra Pradesh. This book is also indispensable for engineering competitions like NNR, IIT(JEE), BIT (Ranchi) and NISE etc. The book comprises of five sections. The sections are devoted to Physical Chemistry, Inorganic Chemistry, Organic, Biochemistry and General Chemistry.

06 090 **ISBN:81-219-1657-7** **pp. 1152**

BIOLOGY FOR PRE-MEDICAL/ PRE-DENTAL ENTRANCE EXAMINATION

Vinay Kumar

This book has been written keeping in view the needs of students preparing for C.B.S.E., Pre-Medical/Pre-Dental Entrance Examination. A special feature of this book is that it covers to the entire spectrum of theoretical discussions followed by the wide-ranging solved questions with explanatory notes of leading medical colleges in the country. This book is expected to equip the students with confidence and necessary background which is essential for Pre-Medical Entrance Examination.

06 088 **ISBN:81-219-1768-9** **pp. 1088**

PHYSICS FOR IIT AND OTHER ENGINEERING ENTRANCE EXAMINATIONS

Mahesh Jain

This book is written for the students preparing for the Engineering entrance examinations, specially for the IIT-Jee. It is also useful for Civil Services (Prelim), JRF (U.G.C) and other similar competitive examinations. It consists of necessary theoretical concepts and formulas followed by various types of solved questions; objective questions; and advanced numericals problems.

06 102 **ISBN:81-219-1798-0**

NUMERICAL CHEMISTRY

J.J. Gurtu, R. Kapoor , V.B. Rana & A. Kapoor

This book caters to the needs of students appearing for IIT (JEE), Roorkee, MLNREC, Aligarh, Dhanbad, Ranchi, BHU, CPMT, AFMC, AIIMS, and other engineering and medical entrance examinations. It is intended primanily for self-study by students who wish to develop their skills in chemical calculation to match their mastery of fundamental principles. Various types of questions asked in different engineering examinations and various Boards have been solved with analytical approach which will definitely lead the students to test their basic concepts.

04 169 **ISBN:81-219-0409-9** **pp. 864**

EAMCET MATHEMATICS

V. Venkateswara Rao, N. Krishna Murty, B.V.S.S. Sarma, S. Anjaneya Sastry

This is a completely revised book, strictly prepared in accordance with the latest syllabus. It is assumed that the student has already studied and has good grasp of the concept of the syllabus prescribed by the Board of Intermediate Education A.P. Some objective type questions are solved by short-cut methods wherever possible and some by condensing steps. More number of Analytical type questions have been added in every exercise.

06 086 ISBN 81-219-1498-1 PP. 1180

S. CHAND'S OBJECTIVE PHYSICS FOR MEDICAL & ENGINEERING ENTRANCE EXAMINATIONS

Mahesh Jain

This book is written for the students preparing for the Medical and Engineering Entrance Examinations of all Indian Universities and Institutes. It is also useful for Civil Services (Prelim), J.R.F. (U.G.C.) and other similar competitive examinations. The book has been written in a style which makes it extremely useful for self-study. In the beginning of each chapter all the necessary theoritical concepts and formulas are given and discussed. The book consists of 34 chapters. In addition there is a zero-chapter which gives advice to students on how to study Physics for competitions. In the end, there is an appendix giving useful mathematical formulas.

06 083 ISBN 81-219-1530 pp. 1172

OBJECTIVE ZOOLOGY

P.S. Verma & P.C. Srivastava

This book has been specifically prepared for the students apppreaing in various medical entrance examinations–AIIMS, CPMT, BHU PMT, DPMT, etc. Problems are mainly based on the points previously asked in various medical entrance examinations. So it is a good Question Bank for the students preparing for medical entrance examinations. For convenient study the questions have been arranged topic-wise.

06 087 ISBN:81-219-1799-9 In press